MILLER

SUMMARIZED-CASE EDITION

# BUSINESS LAW:

## THE FIRST COURSE—

### SUMMARIZED-CASE EDITION

**Roger LeRoy Miller**

*Institute for University Studies*
*Arlington, Texas*

CENGAGE
Learning

Australia • Brazil • Japan • Mexico • Singapore • United Kingdom • United States

**CENGAGE**
Learning™

# Business Law:
# The First Course—
## SUMMARIZED-CASE EDITION

## Roger LeRoy Miller

Senior Vice President,
Global Product Management
Higher Education:
Jack W. Calhoun

Vice President and
General Manager,
Social Sciences
& Qualitative Business:
Erin Joyner

Product Director:
Michael Worls

Senior Product Manager:
Vicky True-Baker

Senior Content Developer:
Jan Lamar

Product Assistant:
Tristann Jones

Marketing Director:
Kristen Hurd

Senior Marketing Manager:
Robin LeFevre

Marketing Coordinator:
Chris Walz

Senior Art Director:
Michelle Kunkler

Senior Content Project Manager:
Ann Borman

Senior Media Developer:
Kristen Meere

Manufacturing Planner:
Kevin Kluck

Compositor:
Parkwood Composition Service

Cover and Internal Designer:
Red Hangar Design

Design Elements:
linen texture: Lisa-Blue/iStockphoto; justice scales:
imagedb.com/Shutterstock; gavel: koosen/Shutterstock;
media network: solarseven/Shutterstock; building
windows: Nneirda/Shutterstock; puzzle icon: Shebeko/
Shutterstock; spotlight: Ivan Lord/Shutterstock; ethics
scale: Lightspring/Shutterstock; magnifying glass icon:
sergign/Shutterstock; globe: mj007/Shutterstock;
compass: TADDEUS/Shutterstock; Insight Global globe:
evantravels/Shutterstock

For product information and technology assistance, contact us at
**Cengage Learning Customer & Sales Support**
**1-800-354-9706**

For permission to use material from this text or product,
submit all requests online at
**www.cengage.com/permissions**.

Further permissions questions can be e-mailed to
**permissionrequest@cengage.com**.

Library of Congress Control Number: 2013953769

ISBN-13: 978-1-305-08785-9

Cengage Learning
200 First Stamford Place, 4th Floor
Stamford, CT 06902
USA

Cengage Learning is a leading provider of customized learning solutions with office locations around the globe, including Singapore, the United Kingdom, Australia, Mexico, Brazil, and Japan. Locate your local office at: **www.cengage.com/global.**

Cengage Learning products are represented in Canada by Nelson Education, Ltd.

To learn more about Cengage Learning, visit **www.cengage.com.**

Purchase any of our products at your local college store or at our preferred online store **www.cengagebrain.com.**

Printed in Canada
1 2 3 4 5 6 7 17 16 15 14 13

# BRIEF CONTENTS

# CONTENTS

v

## UNIT FIVE
## AGENCY AND EMPLOYMENT  435

## CHAPTER 25
## Agency Formation and Duties  436

## CHAPTER 26
## Agency Liability to Third Parties and Termination  450

## CHAPTER 27
## Employment, Immigration, and Labor Law  468

## CHAPTER 28
## Employment Discrimination and Diversity  490

## UNIT SIX
## BUSINESS ORGANIZATIONS  511

## CHAPTER 29
## Sole Proprietorships and Franchises  512

# CONCEPT SUMMARIES

# EXHIBITS

*Business Law: The First Course—Summarized-Case Edition* is an exciting, new textbook that has been tailor-made for those instructors who teach a one-semester course of business law and prefer summarized cases. This text is the result of repeated requests and recommendations from a wide variety of users of my best-selling textbook, *Business Law: Text and Cases,* for a smaller, more focused text on the basics of business law. After extensive research and study, I created this thirty-two-chapter text with emphasis on those topics—the legal environment, torts and crimes, contracts, agency and employment, and business organizations—which most instructors cover in their introduction to business law courses.

I have spent a great deal of effort making *Business Law: The First Course—Summarized-Case Edition* contemporary, exciting, and visually appealing. Many features and special pedagogical devices focus on the legal, ethical, global, and e-commerce environments, while addressing core curriculum requirements.

# DIGITAL LEARNING SYSTEMS

Before discussing the many aspects of this text, I wish to point out the exciting digital products offered in conjunction with *Business Law: The First Course—Summarized-Case Edition.*

## *CengageNOW for Business Law: The First Course: Interactive Assignment System*

**CengageNOW**™ is a powerful course management tool that provides control and customization to optimize the student learning experience and produce desired outcomes. The application features a variety of question types to test simple reading comprehension, complex critical thinking, legal reasoning, and case analysis skills.

*CengageNOW* includes:

- **An Interactive book.**
- **Auto-Graded Homework** with the following consistent question types:
  - *Worksheets*—Interactive worksheets prepare students for class by ensuring reading and comprehension.
  - *Video Activities*—Real-world video exercises make business law engaging and relevant.
  - *Brief Hypotheticals*—These applications provide students practice in spotting the issue and applying the law in the context of a short, factual scenario.
  - *Case Problem Blueprints*—These case problems promote deeper critical thinking and legal reasoning by building on acquired knowledge to truly assess their understanding of legal principles.
- **A Personalized Student Plan** with multimedia study tools and videos.
- **A *Test Bank*.**
- **Reporting and Assessment Options.**

By using the optional *CengageNOW* system, students can complete the assignments online and can receive instant feedback on their answers. Instructors can utilize *CengageNOW* to upload their course syllabi, create and customize homework assignments, and keep track of their students' progress. Instructors can also communicate with their students about assignments and due dates, and create reports summarizing the data for an individual student or for the whole class.

## *CourseMate*

*CourseMate* for *Business Law: The First Course—Summarized-Case Edition* brings business law concepts to life with interactive learning, study, and exam-preparation tools that support the printed textbook. Built-in engagement tracking tools allow instructors to assess the study activities of their students.

Additionally, *CourseMate* includes an interactive online textbook, which contains the complete content of the print textbook enhanced by the many advantages of a digital environment.

## Cengage Learning Testing Powered by Cognero

*Cengage Learning Testing Powered by Cognero* is a flexible, online system that allows instructors to do the following:

- Author, edit, and manage *Test Bank* content from multiple Cengage Learning solutions.
- Create multiple test versions in an instant.
- Deliver tests from a Learning Management System (LMS), the classroom, or wherever an instructor wants.

**START RIGHT AWAY!** *Cengage Learning Testing Powered by Cognero* works on any operating system or browser.

- No special installs or downloads are needed.
- Create tests from school, home, the coffee shop—anywhere with Internet access.

**WHAT YOU WILL FIND:**

- *Simplicity at every step.* A desktop-inspired interface features drop-down menus and familiar intuitive tools that take you through content creation and management with ease.
- *Full-featured test generator.* Create ideal assessments with your choice of fifteen question types—including true/false, multiple choice, opinion scale/Likert, and essay. Multi-language support, an equation editor, and unlimited metadata help ensure your tests are complete and compliant.
- *Cross-compatible capability.* Import and export content into other systems.

## A COMPLETE SUPPLEMENTS PACKAGE

*Business Law: The First Course—Summarized-Case Edition* is accompanied by a vast number of teaching and learning supplements, which are available on the password-protected portion of the Instructor's Companion Web Site. In addition, the complete teaching/learning package offers numerous other supplements, including those listed below.

For further information on the *Business Law: The First Course—Summarized-Case Edition* teaching/

learning package, contact a local sales representative or visit the text's Web site by going to www.cengage.com and entering ISBN 9781305087859.

## Instructor's Companion Web Site

The Instructor's Companion Web Site includes the following supplements:

- **Instructor's Manual.** Includes sections entitled "Additional Cases Addressing This Issue" at the end of selected case synopses.
- **Solutions Manual.** Provides answers to all questions presented in the text, including the questions in each case, feature, and unit-ending pedagogy.
- **Test Bank.** A comprehensive test bank that contains multiple choice, true-false, and short essay questions.
- **PowerPoint slides.**

## Software, Video, and Multimedia Supplements

- **Business Law Digital Video Library**— Provides access to ninety videos, including the *Drama of the Law* videos and video clips from actual Hollywood movies. Access to the digital library is available in an optional package with each new text at no additional cost. Instructors can access the *Business Law Digital Video Library*—along with corresponding *Video Questions* that are related to specific chapters in the text—at www.cengagebrain.com.
- **CengageNOW**
- **CourseMate**
- **Westlaw®**—Ten free hours for qualified adopters.

## SPECIAL FEATURES AND PEDAGOGY

To make sure that *Business Law: The First Course—Summarized-Case Edition* engages students, solidifies their understanding of legal concepts, and provides the best teaching tools available, the following items in this section are offered either in the text or in conjunction with the text.

Suggested answers to all of these questions and problems are included in both the *Instructor's Manual* and the *Solutions Manual* for this text.

## *Managerial Strategy* Features

*Managerial Strategy* features focus on the management aspects of business law. Special emphasis is given to sustainability, ethical trends, and changing managerial responsibilities.

Each feature includes a short section entitled *Managerial Implications* that provides concrete information for managers and connects the topic under discussion to operating a business. Each feature also concludes with two *Business Questions* that prompt students to further examine the issues discussed.

Topics examined in these features include:

- Budget Cuts for State Courts Can Affect Businesses (Chapter 2)
- Facing Breach of Contract Issues (Chapter 22)
- Many Companies Have to Revise Their Social Media Policies (Chapter 27)
- Small Business Owners Now Have Recourse When Cyber Thieves Empty Their Bank Accounts (Chapter 31)

## *Examples* and *Case in Point* Illustrations

Many instructors use cases and examples to illustrate how the law applies to business. The highlighted numbered *Examples* and *Cases in Point* features in every chapter are uniquely designed and consecutively numbered throughout each chapter for easy reference. *Examples* illustrate how the law applies in a specific situation. *Cases in Point* present the facts and issues of an actual case and then describe the court's decision and rationale.

The numbered *Examples* and *Cases in Point* features are integrated throughout the text to help students better understand how courts apply the principles in the real world.

## *Spotlight Cases* and *Spotlight Case Problems*

For *Business Law: The First Course—Summarized-Case Edition,* certain cases and case problems have been carefully chosen as exceptionally good teaching cases. *Spotlight Cases* and *Spotlight Case*

*Problems* are labeled either by the name of one of the parties or by the subject involved. Some examples include a *Spotlight Case* on Amazon.com, Nike, the Seattle Mariners, beer labels, and Internet porn.

Instructors will find these *Spotlight Cases* useful to illustrate the legal concepts under discussion. Students will enjoy studying these cases because the parties are often familiar and the cases involve interesting and memorable facts.

## *Issue Spotters*

A section called *Issue Spotters* is included at the conclusion of each chapter. The section includes two questions that are related to the chapter's topics. The *Issue Spotters* facilitate student learning and provide a review of the materials. (Suggested answers to the *Issue Spotters* in every chapter are provided in Appendix B at the end of the text.)

## *Legal Reasoning Group Activities*

For instructors who want their students to engage in group projects, each chapter includes a special *Legal Reasoning Group Activity.* Each activity begins by describing a business scenario and then requires each group of students to answer a specific question pertaining to the scenario based on the information that they learned in the chapter. These projects may be used in class to spur discussion or as homework assignments.

## *Insight into . . .* Features

*Insight into [E-Commerce, Ethics, the Global Environment, or Social Media]* features appear in selected chapters. These features provide valuable insights into how the courts and the law are dealing with specific issues. Each of these features ends with a *Legal Critical Thinking* question that explores some cultural, environmental, or technological aspect of the issue.

The following are some of the topics explored in these features:

- *Insight into E-Commerce*—Do Computers Have Free Speech Rights? (Chapter 4)
- *Insight into Ethics*—Warning Labels for Video Games (Chapter 7)
- *Insight into the Global Environment*— Is It Legal to Resell Textbooks Purchased Abroad? (Chapter 8)

- *Insight into Social Media*—"Catfishing": Is That Online "Friend" Who You Think It Is? (Chapter 15)

## Emphasis on Business and Critical Thinking

*Business Law: The First Course—Summarized-Case Edition* focuses on making the text more business related. To that end, I have carefully chosen cases, features, and problems that are relevant to operating a business.

In addition, I recognize that today's business leaders must often think "outside the box" when making business decisions. For this reason, I have included numerous critical thinking and legal reasoning elements in this text. Almost all of the features and cases presented in the text conclude with some type of critical thinking question.

Cases may include one or more of the following critical thinking questions:

- *What If the Facts Were Different?*
- *The Ethical Dimension*
- *The E-Commerce Dimension*
- *The Global Dimension*
- *The Legal Environment Dimension*

In addition to the critical thinking questions, I have also included special case pedagogy at the end of selected cases that have particular importance for business managers. This section, called **Managerial Implications,** points out the significance of the court's ruling in the case for business owners and managers.

## Reviewing . . . Features

I offer a *Reviewing* . . . feature at the end of every chapter to help solidify students' understanding of the chapter materials. Each *Reviewing* . . . feature presents a hypothetical scenario and then asks a series of questions that require students to identify the issues and apply the legal concepts discussed in the chapter.

These features are designed to help students review the chapter topics in a simple and interesting way and see how the legal principles discussed in the chapter affect the world in which they live. An instructor can use these features as the basis for in-class discussion or encourage students to use them for self-study before completing homework assignments.

## Concept Summaries and Exhibits

When key areas of the law need additional emphasis, *Concept Summaries* are a popular pedagogical tool. This text includes more than thirty of these summaries.

When appropriate, I also illustrate important aspects of the law in graphic form in exhibits. In all, more than thirty exhibits are featured in *Business Law: The First Course—Summarized-Case Edition.*

## Case Problems

Every chapter includes a 2012 or 2013 case problem in its *Business Case Problems* section. These problems are designed to clarify how modern courts deal with the business issues discussed in the chapter.

Every business scenario and case problem features a label that identifies the chapter topic to which the question relates. These labels make it easier for instructors who wish to assign only certain questions to their students. In addition, page references to the text where the problem's answer can be found are also included.

I have also included two special problems—the *Spotlight Case Problems* (mentioned earlier), which are based on good teaching cases with interesting facts, and the *Business Case Problem with Sample Answer.* The *Business Case Problem with Sample Answer* is based on an actual case, and students can access a sample answer in Appendix C.

## BUSINESS LAW: THE FIRST COURSE—SUMMARIZED-CASE EDITION ON THE WEB

The Web site for *Business Law: The First Course—Summarized-Case Edition* can be found by going to www.cengagebrain.com and entering ISBN 9781305087859. The Web site offers a broad array of teaching/learning resources, including flashcards, a glossary, legal reference materials, and links to *CourseMate* and other digital products.

## ACKNOWLEDGMENTS

I owe a debt of extreme gratitude to the numerous individuals who worked directly with me or at

Cengage Learning. In particular, I wish to thank Vicky True-Baker, Rob Dewey, and Michael Worls for their helpful advice and guidance during all of the stages of this new textbook. I extend my thanks to Jan Lamar, my longtime senior content developer, for her many useful suggestions and for her efforts in coordinating the text and ensuring the timely and accurate publication of all supplemental materials. I am also indebted to Kristen Hurd for her excellent marketing advice.

My senior project manager, Ann Borman, made sure that we came out with an error-free, visually attractive edition. I appreciate her efforts. I am also indebted to the staff at Parkwood Composition, the compositor. Their ability to generate the pages for this text quickly and accurately made it possible to meet an ambitious printing schedule.

I especially wish to thank Katherine Marie Silsbee for her management of the entire project, as well as for the application of her superb research and editorial skills. I also wish to thank William Eric Hollowell, who co-authored the *Instructor's Manual* and the *Test Bank,* for his excellent research efforts. I was fortunate enough to have the copy-editing of Pat Lewis and the proofreading services of Beverly Peavler. I am also grateful for the efforts of Vickie Reierson and Roxanna Lee for their proofreading and other assistance, which helped to ensure an error-free text. Finally, thank you to Suzanne Jasin of K & M Consulting for her many special efforts on this project.

Lastly, I am indebted to those many instructors who participated in the surveys, which were vital to the creation and completion of *Business Law: The First Course—Summarized-Case Edition.* I welcome all comments about this new textbook and promise to respond promptly. By incorporating other ideas and suggestions, I can continue to write a business law text that is best for instructors and students.

Roger LeRoy Miller

## Dedication

To Julie and Stéphane,

Great people,
Great family,
Great values,
Great to be your neighbors,

R. L. M.

MILLER

SUMMARIZED-CASE EDITION

# Unit One

# The Legal Environment of Business

## Contents

## CHAPTER 1

# LAW AND LEGAL REASONING

One of the important functions of law in any society is to provide stability, predictability, and continuity so that people can know how to order their affairs. If any society is to survive, its citizens must be able to determine what is legally right and legally wrong. They must know what sanctions will be imposed on them if they commit wrongful acts. If they suffer harm as a result of others' wrongful acts, they must know how they can seek compensation. By setting forth the rights, obligations, and privileges of citizens, the law enables individuals to go about their business with confidence and a certain degree of predictability.

Although law has various definitions, they are all based on the general observation that **law** consists of *enforceable rules governing relationships among individuals and between individuals and their society*. These "enforceable rules" may consist of unwritten principles of behavior established by a nomadic tribe. They may be set forth in a law code, such as the Code of Hammurabi in ancient Babylon (c. 1780 B.C.E.) or the law code of one of today's European nations. They may consist of written laws and court decisions created by modern legislative and judicial bodies, as in the United States. Regardless of how such rules are created, they all have one thing in common: they establish rights, duties, and

privileges that are consistent with the values and beliefs of their society or its ruling group.

In this introductory chapter, we first look at an important question for any student reading this text: How does the legal environment affect business decision making? We next describe the major sources of American law, the common law tradition, and some basic schools of legal thought. We conclude the chapter with sections offering practical guidance on several topics, including how to find the sources of law discussed in this chapter (and referred to throughout the text) and how to read and understand court opinions.

## BUSINESS ACTIVITIES AND THE LEGAL ENVIRONMENT

Laws and government regulations affect almost all business activities—from hiring and firing decisions to workplace safety, the manufacturing and marketing of products, business financing, and more. To make good business decisions, a basic knowledge of the laws and regulations governing these activities is beneficial—if not essential.

Realize also that in today's business world, a knowledge of "black-letter" law is not enough. Businesspersons are also pressured to make ethical decisions. Thus, the study of business law necessarily involves an ethical dimension.

## Many Different Laws May Affect a Single Business Decision

As you will note, each chapter in this text covers specific areas of the law and shows how the legal rules in each area affect business activities. Though compartmentalizing the law in this fashion promotes conceptual clarity, it does not indicate the extent to which a number of different laws may apply to just one decision.

**LESSONS FROM FACEBOOK** When Mark Zuckerberg started Facebook as a Harvard student, he probably did not imagine all the legal challenges his company would face as a result of his business decisions.

• As you may know from the movie, *The Social Network,* shortly after Facebook was launched, others claimed that Zuckerberg had stolen their ideas for a social networking site. Their claims involved alleged theft of intellectual property (see Chapter 8), fraudulent misrepresentation (see Chapter 15), partnership law and securities law. Facebook ultimately paid a significant amount ($65 million) to settle those claims out of court (see Chapter 2).

- Facebook has also been sued repeatedly for violating users' privacy (such as by disseminating private information to third parties for commercial purposes—see Chapters 4 and 9).
- In 2012, a *class-action* lawsuit was filed against Facebook that seeks damages of $15 billion for violating users' privacy (and federal wiretapping law) by tracking their Web site usage.
- Facebook's business decisions have also come under scrutiny by federal regulators, such as the Federal Trade Commission (FTC) and the Securities and Exchange Commission (SEC).
- In 2011, the company settled a complaint filed by the FTC alleging that Facebook failed to keep "friends" lists and other user information private.
- In 2012, Facebook conducted a much-anticipated initial public offering (IPO) of its stock. The IPO did not go well, however, and many investors suffered losses. Facebook is facing dozens of lawsuits (including class actions) related to business decisions made with regard to the IPO and alleged violations of securities laws.
- The SEC is also investigating whether Facebook engaged in any wrongdoing with regard to its IPO and trading of stock.

**POINTS TO CONSIDER** A key to avoiding business disputes is to think ahead when starting or running a business or entering a contract. Learn what you can about the laws pertaining to that specific enterprise or transaction. Have some idea of the legal ramifications of your business decisions and seek the advice of counsel when in doubt. Exhibit 1–1 on the following page illustrates the various areas of law that may influence business decision making.

## Ethics and Business Decision Making

Merely knowing the areas of law that may affect a business decision is not sufficient in today's business world. Businesspersons must also take ethics into account. As you will learn in Chapter 5, *ethics* generally is defined as the principles governing what constitutes right or wrong behavior.

Today, business decision makers need to consider not just whether a decision is legal, but also whether it is ethical. Often, as in several of the claims against Facebook discussed above, disputes arise in business because one party feels that he or she has been treated unfairly. Thus, the underlying reason for bringing some lawsuits is a breach of ethical duties (such as when a partner or employee attempts to secretly take advantage of a business opportunity).

Throughout this text, you will learn about the relationship between the law and ethics, as well as about some of the types of ethical questions that often arise in business. For example, the unit-ending *Focus on Ethics* features are devoted solely to the exploration of ethical questions pertaining to topics treated within the unit. We have also included *Ethical Dimension* questions for selected cases that focus on ethical considerations in today's business climate and *Insight into Ethics* features that appear in selected chapters. A *Question of Ethics* case problem is included at the conclusion of every chapter to introduce you to the ethical aspects of specific cases involving real-life situations. Additionally, Chapter 5 offers a detailed look at the importance of business ethics.

### SECTION 2
# SOURCES OF AMERICAN LAW

There are numerous sources of American law. *Primary sources of law,* or sources that establish the law, include the following:

1. The U.S. Constitution and the constitutions of the various states.
2. Statutory law—including laws passed by Congress, state legislatures, or local governing bodies.
3. Regulations created by administrative agencies, such as the Food and Drug Administration.
4. Case law and common law doctrines.

We describe each of these important sources of law in the following pages.

*Secondary sources of law* are books and articles that summarize and clarify the primary sources of law. Examples include legal encyclopedias, treatises, articles in law reviews, and compilations of law, such as the *Restatements of the Law* (which will be discussed shortly). Courts often refer to secondary sources of law for guidance in interpreting and applying the primary sources of law discussed here.

**EXHIBIT 1-1 Areas of the Law That May Affect Business Decision Making**

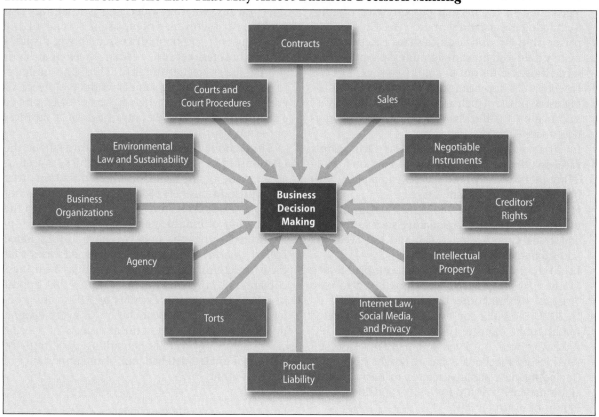

## Constitutional Law

The federal government and the states have separate written constitutions that set forth the general organization, powers, and limits of their respective governments. **Constitutional law** is the law as expressed in these constitutions.

According to Article VI of the U.S. Constitution, the Constitution is the supreme law of the land. As such, it is the basis of all law in the United States. A law in violation of the Constitution, if challenged, will be declared unconstitutional and will not be enforced, no matter what its source. Because of its importance in the American legal system, we present the complete text of the U.S. Constitution in Appendix B and discuss it in depth in Chapter 4.

The Tenth Amendment to the U.S. Constitution reserves to the states all powers not granted to the federal government. Each state in the union has its own constitution. Unless it conflicts with the U.S. Constitution or a federal law, a state constitution is supreme within the state's borders.

## Statutory Law

Laws enacted by legislative bodies at any level of government, such as statutes passed by Congress or by state legislatures, make up the body of law known as **statutory law.** When a legislature passes a statute, that statute ultimately is included in the federal code of laws or the relevant state code of laws (discussed later in this chapter).

Statutory law also includes local **ordinances**— statutes (laws, rules, or orders) passed by municipal or county governing units to govern matters not covered by federal or state law. Ordinances commonly have to do with city or county land use (zoning ordinances), building and safety codes, and other matters affecting the local community.

A federal statute, of course, applies to all states. A state statute, in contrast, applies only within the state's borders. State laws thus may vary from state to state. No federal statute may violate the U.S. Constitution, and no state statute or local ordinance may violate the U.S. Constitution or the relevant state constitution.

**UNIFORM LAWS** During the 1800s, the differences among state laws frequently created difficulties for businesspersons conducting trade and commerce among the states. To counter these problems, a group of legal scholars and lawyers formed the National Conference of Commissioners on Uniform State Laws (NCCUSL, **www.uniformlaws.org**) in 1892 to draft **uniform laws** (model statutes) for the states to consider adopting. The NCCUSL still exists today and continues to issue uniform laws.

Each state has the option of adopting or rejecting a uniform law. *Only if a state legislature adopts a uniform law does that law become part of the statutory law of that state.* Note that a state legislature may adopt all or part of a uniform law as it is written, or the legislature may rewrite the law however the legislature wishes. Hence, even though many states may have adopted a uniform law, those states' laws may not be entirely "uniform."

The earliest uniform law, the Uniform Negotiable Instruments Law, was completed by 1896 and adopted in every state by the 1920s (although not all states used exactly the same wording). Over the following decades, other acts were drawn up in a similar manner. In all, more than two hundred uniform acts have been issued by the NCCUSL since its inception. The most ambitious uniform act of all, however, is the Uniform Commercial Code.

**THE UNIFORM COMMERCIAL CODE** One of the most important uniform acts is the Uniform Commercial Code (UCC), which was created through the joint efforts of the NCCUSL and the American Law Institute.[1] The UCC was first issued in 1952 and has been adopted in all fifty states,[2] the District of Columbia, and the Virgin Islands.

The UCC facilitates commerce among the states by providing a uniform, yet flexible, set of rules governing commercial transactions. Because of its importance in the area of commercial law, we cite the UCC frequently in this text. We also present the full UCC in Appendix C. From time to time, the NCCUSL revises the articles contained in the UCC and submits the revised versions to the states for adoption.

## Administrative Law

Another important source of American law is **administrative law,** which consists of the rules,

orders, and decisions of administrative agencies. An **administrative agency** is a federal, state, or local government agency established to perform a specific function. Administrative law and procedures constitute a dominant element in the regulatory environment of business.

Rules issued by various administrative agencies now affect almost every aspect of a business's operations. Regulations govern a business's capital structure and financing, its hiring and firing procedures, its relations with employees and unions, and the way it manufactures and markets its products. Regulations enacted to protect the environment also often play a significant role in business operations.

**FEDERAL AGENCIES** At the national level, the cabinet departments of the executive branch include numerous **executive agencies.** The U.S. Food and Drug Administration, for example, is an agency within the U.S. Department of Health and Human Services. Executive agencies are subject to the authority of the president, who has the power to appoint and remove their officers.

There are also major **independent regulatory agencies** at the federal level, such as the Federal Trade Commission, the Securities and Exchange Commission, and the Federal Communications Commission. The president's power is less pronounced in regard to independent agencies, whose officers serve for fixed terms and cannot be removed without just cause.

**STATE AND LOCAL AGENCIES** There are administrative agencies at the state and local levels as well. Commonly, a state agency (such as a state pollution-control agency) is created as a parallel to a federal agency (such as the Environmental Protection Agency). Just as federal statutes take precedence over conflicting state statutes, federal agency regulations take precedence over conflicting state regulations.

## Case Law and Common Law Doctrines

The rules of law announced in court decisions constitute another basic source of American law. These rules include interpretations of constitutional provisions, of statutes enacted by legislatures, and of regulations created by administrative agencies.

Today, this body of judge-made law is referred to as **case law.** Case law—the doctrines and principles announced in cases—governs all areas not covered by

---

1. This institute was formed in the 1920s and consists of practicing attorneys, legal scholars, and judges.
2. Louisiana has not adopted Articles 2 and 2A (covering contracts for the sale and lease of goods), however.

statutory law or administrative law and is part of our common law tradition. We look at the origins and characteristics of the common law tradition in some detail in the pages that follow.

See *Concept Summary 1.1* below for a review of the sources of American law.

## SECTION 3
# THE COMMON LAW TRADITION

Because of our colonial heritage, much of American law is based on the English legal system, which originated in medieval England and continued to evolve in the following centuries. Knowledge of this system is necessary to understanding the American legal system today.

## Early English Courts

The origins of the English legal system—and thus the U.S. legal system as well—date back to 1066, when the Normans conquered England. William the Conqueror and his successors began the process of unifying the country under their rule. One of the means they used to do this was the establishment of the king's courts, or *curiae regis*.

Before the Norman Conquest, disputes had been settled according to the local legal customs and traditions in various regions of the country. The king's courts sought to establish a uniform set of customs for the country as a whole. What evolved in these courts was the beginning of the **common law**—a body of general rules that applied throughout the entire English realm. Eventually, the common law tradition became part of the heritage of all nations that were once British colonies, including the United States.

**COURTS OF LAW AND REMEDIES AT LAW** The early English king's courts could grant only very limited kinds of **remedies** (the legal means to enforce a right or redress a wrong). If one person wronged another in some way, the king's courts could award as compensation one or more of the following: (1) land, (2) items of value, or (3) money.

The courts that awarded this compensation became known as **courts of law,** and the three remedies were called **remedies at law.** (Today, the remedy at law normally takes the form of monetary **damages**— an amount given to a party whose legal interests have been injured.) This system made the procedure for settling disputes more uniform. When a complaining party wanted a remedy other than economic compensation, however, the courts of law could do nothing, so "no remedy, no right."

**COURTS OF EQUITY** *Equity* is a branch of law— founded on notions of justice and fair dealing—that seeks to supply a remedy when no adequate remedy at law is available. When individuals could not obtain an adequate remedy in a court of law, they petitioned the king for relief. Most of these petitions were decided by an adviser to the king, called a **chancellor,** who had the power to grant new and unique remedies. Eventually, formal chancery courts, or **courts of equity,** were established.

---

## CONCEPT SUMMARY 1.1
### Sources of American Law

| SOURCE | DESCRIPTION |
| --- | --- |
| **Constitutional Law** | The law as expressed in the U.S. Constitution and the state constitutions. The U.S. Constitution is the supreme law of the land. State constitutions are supreme within state borders to the extent that they do not violate a clause of the U.S. Constitution or a federal law. |
| **Statutory Law** | Laws (statutes and ordinances) enacted by federal, state, and local legislatures and governing bodies. None of these laws can violate the U.S. Constitution or the relevant state constitution. Uniform laws, when adopted by a state, become statutory law in that state. |
| **Administrative Law** | The rules, orders, and decisions of federal, state, and local government administrative agencies. |
| **Case Law and Common Law Doctrines** | Judge-made law, including interpretations of constitutional provisions, of statutes enacted by legislatures, and of regulations created by administrative agencies. |

**REMEDIES IN EQUITY** The remedies granted by the equity courts became known as **remedies in equity,** or equitable remedies. These remedies include specific performance, an injunction, and rescission. *Specific performance* involves ordering a party to perform an agreement as promised. An *injunction* is an order to a party to cease engaging in a specific activity or to undo some wrong or injury. *Rescission* is the cancellation of a contractual obligation. We will discuss these and other equitable remedies in more detail at appropriate points in the chapters that follow, particularly in Chapter 19.

As a general rule, today's courts, like the early English courts, will not grant equitable remedies unless the remedy at law—monetary damages—is inadequate. ▶ **Example 1.1** Ted forms a contract (a legally binding agreement—see Chapter 11) to purchase a parcel of land that he thinks will be perfect for his future home. The seller **breaches,** or fails to fulfill, this agreement. Ted could sue the seller for the return of any deposits or down payment he might have made on the land, but this is not the remedy he really seeks. What Ted wants is to have the court order the seller to perform the contract. In other words, Ted wants the court to grant the equitable remedy of specific performance because monetary damages are inadequate in this situation. ◀

**EQUITABLE MAXIMS** In fashioning appropriate remedies, judges often were (and continue to be) guided by so-called **equitable maxims**—propositions or general statements of equitable rules. Exhibit 1–2 below lists some important equitable maxims.

The last maxim listed in that exhibit—"Equity aids the vigilant, not those who rest on their rights"—merits special attention. It has become known as the equitable doctrine of **laches** (a term derived from the Latin *laxus,* meaning "lax" or "negligent"), and it can be used as a defense. A **defense** is an argument raised by the **defendant** (the party being sued) indicating why the **plaintiff** (the suing party) should not obtain the remedy sought. (Note that in equity proceedings, the party bringing a lawsuit is called the **petitioner,** and the party being sued is referred to as the **respondent.**)

The doctrine of laches arose to encourage people to bring lawsuits while the evidence was fresh. What constitutes a reasonable time, of course, varies according to the circumstances of the case. Time periods for different types of cases are now usually fixed by **statutes of limitations.** After the time allowed under a statute of limitations has expired, no action (lawsuit) can be brought, no matter how strong the case was originally.

# Legal and Equitable Remedies Today

The establishment of courts of equity in medieval England resulted in two distinct court systems: courts of law and courts of equity. The courts had different sets of judges and granted different types of remedies. During the nineteenth century, however, most states in the United States adopted rules of procedure that resulted in the combining of courts of law and equity. A party now may request both legal and equitable remedies in the same action, and the trial court judge may grant either or both forms of relief.

The distinction between legal and equitable remedies remains relevant to students of business law, however, because these remedies differ. To seek the proper remedy for a wrong, one must know what

---

## EXHIBIT 1–2 Equitable Maxims

1. *Whoever seeks equity must do equity.* (Anyone who wishes to be treated fairly must treat others fairly.)

2. *Where there is equal equity, the law must prevail.* (The law will determine the outcome of a controversy in which the merits of both sides are equal.)

3. *One seeking the aid of an equity court must come to the court with clean hands.* (The plaintiff must have acted fairly and honestly.)

4. *Equity will not suffer a wrong to be without a remedy.* (Equitable relief will be awarded when there is a right to relief and there is no adequate remedy at law.)

5. *Equity regards substance rather than form.* (Equity is more concerned with fairness and justice than with legal technicalities.)

6. *Equity aids the vigilant, not those who rest on their rights.* (Equity will not help those who neglect their rights for an unreasonable period of time.)

remedies are available. Additionally, certain vestiges of the procedures used when there were separate courts of law and equity still exist. For example, a party has the right to demand a jury trial in an action at law, but not in an action in equity. Exhibit 1–3 below summarizes the procedural differences (applicable in most states) between an action at law and an action in equity.

## The Doctrine of *Stare Decisis*

One of the unique features of the common law is that it is *judge-made* law. The body of principles and doctrines that form the common law emerged over time as judges decided legal controversies.

**CASE PRECEDENTS AND CASE REPORTERS** When possible, judges attempted to be consistent and to base their decisions on the principles suggested by earlier cases. They sought to decide similar cases in a similar way and considered new cases with care because they knew that their decisions would make new law. Each interpretation became part of the law on the subject and thus served as a legal **precedent.** A precedent is a decision that furnishes an example or authority for deciding subsequent cases involving identical or similar legal principles or facts.

In the early years of the common law, there was no single place or publication where court opinions, or written decisions, could be found. By the fourteenth century, portions of the most important decisions from each year were being gathered together and recorded in *Year Books,* which became useful references for lawyers and judges. In the sixteenth century, the *Year Books* were discontinued, and other forms of case publication became available. Today, cases are published, or "reported," in volumes called **reporters,** or *reports.* We describe today's case reporting system in detail later in this chapter.

***STARE DECISIS* AND THE COMMON LAW TRADITION**
The practice of deciding new cases with reference to former decisions, or precedents, became a cornerstone of the English and American judicial systems. The practice formed a doctrine known as *stare decisis*[3] (a Latin phrase meaning "to stand on decided cases"). Under this doctrine, judges are obligated to follow the precedents established within their jurisdictions. The term *jurisdiction* refers to a geographic area in which a court or courts have the power to apply the law—see Chapter 2.

Once a court has set forth a principle of law as being applicable to a certain set of facts, that court must apply the principle in future cases involving similar facts. Courts of lower rank (within the same jurisdiction) must do likewise. Thus, *stare decisis* has two aspects:

1. A court should not overturn its own precedents unless there is a compelling reason to do so.
2. Decisions made by a higher court are binding on lower courts.

**CONTROLLING PRECEDENTS** Controlling precedents in a jurisdiction are referred to as binding authorities. A **binding authority** is any source of law that a court must follow when deciding a case. Binding authorities include constitutions, statutes, and regulations that govern the issue being decided, as well as court decisions that are controlling precedents within the jurisdiction. United States Supreme Court case decisions, no matter how old, remain controlling until they are overruled by a subsequent decision of the Supreme Court or changed by further legislation or a constitutional amendment.

***STARE DECISIS* AND LEGAL STABILITY** The doctrine of *stare decisis* helps the courts to be more efficient because, if other courts have analyzed a similar case,

---

3. Pronounced *ster*-ay dih-*si*-ses.

## EXHIBIT 1–3 Procedural Differences between an Action at Law and an Action in Equity

| Procedure | Action at Law | Action in Equity |
|---|---|---|
| **Initiation of lawsuit** | By filing a complaint | By filing a petition |
| **Parties** | Plaintiff and defendant | Petitioner and respondent |
| **Decision** | By jury or judge | By judge (no jury) |
| **Result** | Judgment | Decree |
| **Remedy** | Monetary damages | Injunction, specific performance, or rescission |

their legal reasoning and opinions can serve as guides. *Stare decisis* also makes the law more stable and predictable. If the law on a subject is well settled, someone bringing a case can usually rely on the court to rule based on what the law has been in the past.

**DEPARTURES FROM PRECEDENT** Although courts are obligated to follow precedents, sometimes a court will depart from the rule of precedent if it decides that the precedent should no longer be followed. If a court decides that a ruling precedent is simply incorrect or that technological or social changes have rendered the precedent inapplicable, the court might rule contrary to the precedent. Cases that overturn precedent often receive a great deal of publicity.

▶ **Case in Point 1.2** The United States Supreme Court expressly overturned precedent in the case of *Brown v. Board of Education of Topeka.*[4] The Court concluded that separate educational facilities for whites and blacks, which it had previously upheld as constitutional,[5] were inherently unequal. The Court's departure from precedent in this case received a tremendous amount of publicity as people began to realize the ramifications of this change in the law. ◀

Note that judges do have some flexibility in applying precedents. For instance, a lower court may avoid applying a precedent set by a higher court in its jurisdiction by distinguishing the two cases based on their facts. When this happens, the lower court's ruling stands unless it is appealed to a higher court and that court overturns the decision.

**WHEN THERE IS NO PRECEDENT** Occasionally, courts must decide cases for which no precedents exist, called cases of *first impression.* For instance, as you will read throughout this text, the extensive use of the Internet has presented many new and challenging issues for the courts to decide.

In deciding cases of first impression, courts often look at **persuasive authorities** (precedents from other jurisdictions) for guidance. A court may also consider legal principles and policies underlying previous court decisions or existing statutes. Other factors that courts look at include fairness, social values and customs, and **public policy** (governmental policy based on widely held societal values).

## *Stare Decisis* and Legal Reasoning

In deciding what law applies to a given dispute and then applying that law to the facts or circumstances of the case, judges rely on the process of **legal reasoning.** Through the use of legal reasoning, judges harmonize their decisions with those that have been made before, as the doctrine of *stare decisis* requires.

Students of business law and the legal environment also engage in legal reasoning. For example, you may be asked to provide answers for some of the case problems that appear at the end of every chapter in this text. Each problem describes the facts of a particular dispute and the legal question at issue. If you are assigned a case problem, you will be asked to determine how a court would answer that question, and why. In other words, you will need to give legal reasons for whatever conclusion you reach.[6] We look here at the basic steps involved in legal reasoning and then describe some forms of reasoning commonly used by the courts in making their decisions.

**BASIC STEPS IN LEGAL REASONING** At times, the legal arguments set forth in court opinions are relatively simple and brief. At other times, the arguments are complex and lengthy. Regardless of the length of a legal argument, however, the basic steps of the legal reasoning process remain the same. These steps, which you can also follow when analyzing cases and case problems, form what is commonly referred to as the *IRAC method* of legal reasoning. IRAC is an acronym formed from the first letters of the following words: *Issue, Rule, Application,* and *Conclusion.* To apply the IRAC method, you would ask the following questions:

1. **Issue**—*What are the key facts and issues?* Suppose that a plaintiff comes before the court claiming *assault* (words or acts that wrongfully and intentionally make another person fearful of immediate physical harm—see Chapter 6). The plaintiff claims that the defendant threatened her while she was sleeping. Although the plaintiff was unaware that she was being threatened, her roommate heard the defendant make the threat. The legal issue is whether the defendant's action constitutes the tort (civil wrong) of assault, given that the plaintiff was unaware of that action at the time it occurred.

---

**4.** 347 U.S. 483, 74 S.Ct. 686, 98 L.Ed. 873 (1954). A later section in this chapter explains how to read legal citations.
**5.** See *Plessy v. Ferguson,* 163 U.S. 537, 16 S.Ct. 1138, 41 L.Ed. 256 (1896).

---

**6.** See Appendix A for further instructions on how to analyze case problems.

2. **Rule**—*What rules of law apply to the case?* A rule of law may be a rule stated by the courts in previous decisions, a state or federal statute, or a state or federal administrative agency regulation. In our hypothetical case, the plaintiff **alleges** (claims) that the defendant committed a tort. Therefore, the applicable law is the common law of torts—specifically, tort law governing assault (see Chapter 6). Case precedents involving similar facts and issues thus would be relevant. Often, more than one rule of law will be applicable to a case.

3. **Application**—*How do the rules of law apply to the particular facts and circumstances of this case?* This step is often the most difficult because each case presents a unique set of facts, circumstances, and parties. Although cases may be similar, no two cases are ever identical in all respects. Normally, judges (and lawyers and law students) try to find **cases on point**—previously decided cases that are as similar as possible to the one under consideration. (Because of the difficulty—and importance—of this step in the legal reasoning process, we discuss it in more detail in the next subsection.)

4. **Conclusion**—*What conclusion should be drawn?* This step normally presents few problems. Usually, the conclusion is evident if the previous three steps have been followed carefully.

## There Is No One "Right" Answer

Many people believe that there is one "right" answer to every legal question. In most legal controversies, however, there is no single correct result. Good arguments can usually be made to support either side of a legal controversy. Quite often, a case does not involve a "good" person suing a "bad" person. In many cases, both parties have acted in good faith in some measure or in bad faith to some degree.

Additionally, each judge has her or his own personal beliefs and philosophy (see the discussion in the next section), which shape the legal reasoning process, at least to some extent. This means that the outcome of a particular lawsuit before a court cannot be predicted with absolute certainty. Sometimes, even though the law would seem to favor one party's position, judges, through creative legal reasoning, have found ways to rule for the other party to prevent injustice.

Legal reasoning and other aspects of the common law tradition are reviewed in *Concept Summary 1.2* below.

## The Common Law Today

Today, the common law derived from judicial decisions continues to be applied throughout the United States. Common law doctrines and principles, how-

---

### CONCEPT SUMMARY 1.2
### The Common Law Tradition

| ASPECT | DESCRIPTION |
|---|---|
| **Origins of the Common Law** | The American legal system is based on the common law tradition, which originated in medieval England. Following the conquest of England in 1066 by William the Conqueror, king's courts were established throughout England, and the common law was developed in these courts. |
| **Legal and Equitable Remedies** | Remedies at law (money or items of value, such as land) and remedies in equity (including specific performance, injunction, and rescission of a contractual obligation) originated in the early English courts of law and courts of equity, respectively. |
| **Case Precedents and the Doctrine of *Stare Decisis*** | In the king's courts, judges attempted to make their decisions consistent with previous decisions, called precedents. This practice gave rise to the doctrine of *stare decisis*. This doctrine, which became a cornerstone of the common law tradition, obligates judges to abide by precedents established in their jurisdictions. |
| ***Stare Decisis* and Legal Reasoning** | Legal reasoning is the reasoning process used by judges in applying the law to the facts and issues of specific cases. Legal reasoning involves becoming familiar with the key facts of a case, identifying the relevant legal rules, applying those rules to the facts, and drawing a conclusion. |

ever, govern only areas *not* covered by statutory or administrative law. In a dispute concerning a particular employment practice, for instance, if a statute regulates that practice, the statute will apply rather than the common law doctrine that applied before the statute was enacted.

**COURTS INTERPRET STATUTES**  Even in areas governed by statutory law, though, judge-made law continues to be important because there is a significant interplay between statutory law and the common law. For instance, many statutes essentially codify existing common law rules, and regulations issued by various administrative agencies usually are based, at least in part, on common law principles. Additionally, the courts, in interpreting statutory law, often rely on the common law as a guide to what the legislators intended.

Furthermore, how the courts interpret a particular statute determines how that statute will be applied. If you wanted to learn about the coverage and applicability of a particular statute, for example, you would necessarily have to locate the statute and study it. You would also need to see how the courts in your jurisdiction have interpreted and applied the statute. In other words, you would have to learn what precedents have been established in your jurisdiction with respect to that statute. Often, the applicability of a newly enacted statute does not become clear until a body of case law develops to clarify how, when, and to whom the statute applies.

**RESTATEMENTS OF THE LAW CLARIFY AND ILLUSTRATE THE COMMON LAW**  The American Law Institute (ALI) has published compilations of the common law called *Restatements of the Law,* which generally summarize the common law rules followed by most states. There are *Restatements of the Law* in the areas of contracts, torts, agency, trusts, property, restitution, security, judgments, and conflict of laws. The *Restatements,* like other secondary sources of law, do not in themselves have the force of law, but they are an important source of legal analysis and opinion. Hence, judges often rely on them in making decisions.

Many of the *Restatements* are now in their second, third, or fourth editions. We refer to the *Restatements* frequently in subsequent chapters of this text, indicating in parentheses the edition to which we are referring. For example, we refer to the third edition of the *Restatement of the Law of Contracts* as simply the *Restatement (Third) of Contracts.*

## SECTION 4
# SCHOOLS OF LEGAL THOUGHT

How judges apply the law to specific cases, including disputes relating to the business world, depends in part on their philosophical approaches to law. Thus, the study of law, or **jurisprudence,** involves learning about different schools of legal thought and how the approaches to law characteristic of each school can affect judicial decision making.

Clearly, a judge's function is not to *make* the laws—that is the function of the legislative branch of government—but to interpret and apply them. From a practical point of view, however, the courts play a significant role in defining the laws enacted by legislative bodies, which tend to be expressed in general terms. Judges thus have some flexibility in interpreting and applying the law. It is because of this flexibility that different courts can, and often do, arrive at different conclusions in cases that involve nearly identical issues, facts, and applicable laws.

## The Natural Law School

An age-old question about the nature of law has to do with the finality of a nation's laws at a given point in time. What if a particular law is deemed to be a "bad" law by a substantial number of that nation's citizens? According to the **natural law** theory, a higher or universal law exists that applies to all human beings, and written laws should imitate these inherent principles. If a written law is unjust, then it is not a true (natural) law and need not be obeyed.

The natural law tradition is one of the oldest and most significant schools of jurisprudence. It dates back to the days of the Greek philosopher Aristotle (384–322 B.C.E.), who distinguished between natural law and the laws governing a particular nation. According to Aristotle, natural law applies universally to all humankind.

The notion that people have "natural rights" stems from the natural law tradition. Those who claim that a specific foreign government is depriving certain citizens of their human rights are implicitly appealing to a higher law that has universal applicability. The question of the universality of basic human rights also comes into play in the context of international business operations. ▶ **Example 1.3**  U.S. companies that have operations abroad often hire foreign workers as employees. Should the same laws that protect

U.S. employees apply to these foreign employees? This question is rooted implicitly in a concept of universal rights that has its origins in the natural law tradition. ◄

## The Positivist School

In contrast to natural law, *positive,* or national, law (the written law of a given society at a particular time) applies only to the citizens of that nation or society. Those who adhere to **legal positivism** believe that there can be no higher law than a nation's positive law.

According to the positivist school, there are no "natural rights." Rather, human rights exist solely because of laws. If the laws are not enforced, anarchy will result. Thus, whether a law is "bad" or "good" is irrelevant. The law is the law and must be obeyed until it is changed—in an orderly manner through a legitimate lawmaking process.

A judge with positivist leanings probably would be more inclined to defer to an existing law than would a judge who adheres to the natural law tradition.

## The Historical School

The **historical school** of legal thought emphasizes the evolutionary process of law by concentrating on the origin and history of the legal system. This school looks to the past to discover what the principles of contemporary law should be. The legal doctrines that have withstood the passage of time—those that have worked in the past—are deemed best suited for shaping present laws. Hence, law derives its legitimacy and authority from adhering to the standards that historical development has shown to be workable.

Adherents of the historical school are more likely than those of other schools to strictly follow decisions made in past cases.

## Legal Realism

In the 1920s and 1930s, a number of jurists and scholars, known as *legal realists,* rebelled against the historical approach to law. **Legal realism** is based on the idea that law is just one of many institutions in society and that it is shaped by social forces and needs. The law is a human enterprise, and judges should take social and economic realities into account when deciding cases.

Legal realists also believe that the law can never be applied with total uniformity. Given that judges are human beings with unique personalities, value systems, and intellects, different judges will obviously bring different reasoning processes to the same case. Female judges, for instance, might be more inclined than male judges to consider whether a decision might have a negative impact on the employment of women or minorities.

Legal realism strongly influenced the growth of what is sometimes called the **sociological school,** which views law as a tool for promoting justice in society. In the 1960s, for example, the justices of the United States Supreme Court helped advance the civil rights movement by upholding long-neglected laws calling for equal treatment for all Americans, including African Americans and other minorities. Generally, jurists who adhere to this philosophy of law are more likely to depart from past decisions than are jurists who adhere to other schools of legal thought.

*Concept Summary 1.3* on the following page reviews the schools of jurisprudential thought.

**SECTION 5**

# CLASSIFICATIONS OF LAW

The law may be broken down according to several classification systems. For example, one classification system divides law into substantive law and procedural law. **Substantive law** consists of all laws that define, describe, regulate, and create legal rights and obligations. **Procedural law** consists of all laws that outline the methods of enforcing the rights established by substantive law.

Note that many statutes contain both substantive and procedural provisions. ▶ **Example 1.4** A state law that provides employees with the right to *workers' compensation benefits* for on-the-job injuries is a substantive law because it creates legal rights. Procedural laws establish the method by which an employee must notify the employer about an on-the-job injury, prove the injury, and periodically submit additional proof to continue receiving workers' compensation benefits. ◄

Other classification systems divide law into federal law and state law, private law (dealing with relationships between private entities) and public law (addressing the relationship between persons and their governments), and national law and international law. Here we look at still another classification

---

## CONCEPT SUMMARY 1.3
### Schools of Jurisprudential Thought

| SCHOOL OF THOUGHT | DESCRIPTION |
|---|---|
| **Natural Law School** | One of the oldest and most significant schools of legal thought. Those who believe in natural law hold that there is a universal law applicable to all human beings. |
| **Positivist School** | A school of legal thought centered on the assumption that there is no law higher than the laws created by the government. |
| **Historical School** | A school of legal thought that stresses the evolutionary nature of law and looks to doctrines that have withstood the passage of time for guidance in shaping present laws. |
| **Legal Realism** | A school of legal thought that advocates a less abstract and more realistic and pragmatic approach to the law and takes into account customary practices and the circumstances surrounding the particular transaction. |

---

system, which divides law into civil law and criminal law, as well as at what is meant by the term *cyberlaw.*

## Civil Law and Criminal Law

**Civil law** spells out the rights and duties that exist between persons and between persons and their governments, as well as the relief available when a person's rights are violated. Typically, in a civil case, a private party sues another private party who has failed to comply with a duty (note that the government can also sue a party for a civil law violation). Much of the law that we discuss in this text is civil law. Contract law, for example, covered in Chapters 11 through 19, is civil law. The whole body of tort law (see Chapters 6 and 7) is also civil law.

**Criminal law,** in contrast, is concerned with wrongs committed *against the public as a whole.* Criminal acts are defined and prohibited by local, state, or federal government statutes. Criminal defendants are thus prosecuted by public officials, such as a district attorney (D.A.), on behalf of the state, not by their victims or other private parties. (See Chapter 10 for a further discussion of the distinction between civil law and criminal law.)

## Cyberlaw

As mentioned, the use of the Internet to conduct business transactions has led to new types of legal issues. In response, courts have had to adapt traditional laws to situations that are unique to our age.

Additionally, legislatures at both the federal and the state levels have created laws to deal specifically with such issues.

Frequently, people use the term **cyberlaw** to refer to the emerging body of law that governs transactions conducted via the Internet. Cyberlaw is not really a classification of law, nor is it a new *type* of law. Rather, it is an informal term used to refer to both new laws and modifications of traditional laws that relate to the online environment. Throughout this book, you will read how the law in a given area is evolving to govern specific legal issues that arise in the online context. We have also devoted Chapter 9 entirely to Internet law, social media, and privacy.

### SECTION 6
# HOW TO FIND PRIMARY SOURCES OF LAW

This text includes numerous references, or *citations,* to primary sources of law—federal and state statutes, the U.S. Constitution and state constitutions, regulations issued by administrative agencies, and court cases.

A **citation** identifies the publication in which a legal authority—such as a statute or a court decision or other source—can be found. In this section, we explain how you can use citations to find primary sources of law. Note that in addition to being published in sets of books, as described next, most federal and state laws and case decisions are available online.

# Finding Statutory and Administrative Law

When Congress passes laws, they are collected in a publication titled *United States Statutes at Large.* When state legislatures pass laws, they are collected in similar state publications. Most frequently, however, laws are referred to in their codified form—that is, the form in which they appear in the federal and state codes. In these codes, laws are compiled by subject.

**UNITED STATES CODE** The *United States Code* (U.S.C.) arranges all existing federal laws by broad subject. Each of the fifty subjects is given a title and a title number. For instance, laws relating to commerce and trade are collected in Title 15, "Commerce and Trade." Titles are subdivided by sections.

A citation to the U.S.C. includes both title and section numbers. Thus, a reference to "15 U.S.C. Section 1" means that the statute can be found in Section 1 of Title 15. ("Section" may be designated by the symbol §, and "Sections," by §§.) In addition to the print publication, the federal government provides a searchable online database of the *United States Code* at **www.gpo.gov** (click on "Libraries" and then "Core Documents of Our Democracy" to find the U.S.C.).

Commercial publications of federal laws and regulations are also available. For instance, Legal Solutions from Thomson Reuters (formerly West Group) publishes the *United States Code Annotated* (U.S.C.A.). The U.S.C.A. contains the official text of the U.S.C., plus notes (annotations) on court decisions that interpret and apply specific sections of the statutes. The U.S.C.A. also includes additional research aids, such as cross-references to related statutes, historical notes, and library references. A citation to the U.S.C.A. is similar to a citation to the U.S.C.: "15 U.S.C.A. Section 1."

**STATE CODES** State codes follow the U.S.C. pattern of arranging law by subject. They may be called codes, revisions, compilations, consolidations, general statutes, or statutes, depending on the preferences of the states.

In some codes, subjects are designated by number. In others, they are designated by name. ▶ **Example 1.5** "13 Pennsylvania Consolidated Statutes Section 1101" means that the statute can be found in Title 13, Section 1101, of the Pennsylvania code. "California Commercial Code Section 1101" means that the statute can be found under the subject heading "Commercial Code" of the California code in Section 1101. Abbreviations are often used. For example, "13 Pennsylvania Consolidated Statutes Section 1101" is abbreviated "13 Pa. C.S. § 1101," and "California Commercial Code Section 1101" is abbreviated "Cal. Com. Code § 1101." ◀

**ADMINISTRATIVE RULES** Rules and regulations adopted by federal administrative agencies are initially published in the *Federal Register,* a daily publication of the U.S. government. Later, they are incorporated into the *Code of Federal Regulations* (C.F.R.).

Like the U.S.C., the C.F.R. is divided into fifty titles. Rules within each title are assigned section numbers. A full citation to the C.F.R. includes title and section numbers. ▶ **Example 1.6** A reference to "17 C.F.R. Section 230.504" means that the rule can be found in Section 230.504 of Title 17. ◀

# Finding Case Law

Before discussing the case reporting system, we need to look briefly at the court system (which will be discussed in detail in Chapter 2). There are two types of courts in the United States, federal courts and state courts.

Both the federal and the state court systems consist of several levels, or tiers, of courts. *Trial courts,* in which evidence is presented and testimony given, are on the bottom tier (which also includes lower courts that handle specialized issues). Decisions from a trial court can be appealed to a higher court, which commonly is an intermediate *court of appeals,* or *appellate court.* Decisions from these intermediate courts of appeals may be appealed to an even higher court, such as a state supreme court or the United States Supreme Court.

**STATE COURT DECISIONS** Most state trial court decisions are not published in books (except in New York and a few other states, which publish selected trial court opinions). Decisions from state trial courts are typically filed in the office of the clerk of the court, where the decisions are available for public inspection. (Increasingly, they can be found online as well.)

Written decisions of the appellate, or reviewing, courts, however, are published and distributed (in print and online). As you will note, most of the state court cases presented in this textbook are from state appellate courts. The reported appellate decisions are published in volumes called *reports* or *reporters,* which are numbered consecutively. State appellate court decisions are found in the state reporters of that particular state. Official reports are published by the state, whereas unofficial reports are published by non-government entities.

***Regional Reporters.*** State court opinions appear in regional units of the National Reporter System, published by West Group (now Thomson Reuters). Most lawyers and libraries have these reporters because they report cases more quickly and are distributed more widely than the state-published reporters. In fact, many states have eliminated their own reporters in favor of the National Reporter System.

The National Reporter System divides the states into the following geographic areas: *Atlantic* (A., A.2d, or A.3d), *North Eastern* (N.E. or N.E.2d), *North Western* (N.W. or N.W.2d), *Pacific* (P., P.2d, or P.3d), *South Eastern* (S.E. or S.E.2d), *South Western* (S.W., S.W.2d, or S.W.3d), and *Southern* (So., So.2d, or So.3d). (The *2d* and *3d* in the preceding abbreviations refer to *Second Series* and *Third Series,* respectively.) The states included in each of these regional divisions are indicated in Exhibit 1–4 on the following page, which illustrates the National Reporter System.

***Case Citations.*** After appellate decisions have been published, they are normally referred to (cited) by the name of the case; the volume, name, and page number of the state's official reporter (if different from the National Reporter System); the volume, name, and page number of the National Reporter; and the volume, name, and page number of any other selected reporter. (Citing a reporter by volume number, name, and page number, in that order, is common to all citations. The year that the decision was issued is often included at the end in parentheses.) When more than one reporter is cited for the same case, each reference is called a *parallel citation.*

Note that some states have adopted a "public domain citation system" that uses a somewhat different format for the citation. For example, in Wisconsin, a Wisconsin Supreme Court decision might be designated "2013 WI 40," meaning that the case was decided in the year 2013 by the Wisconsin Supreme Court and was the fortieth decision issued by that court during that year. Parallel citations to the *Wisconsin Reports* and the *North Western Reporter* are still included after the public domain citation.

▶ **Example 1.7** Consider the following case citation: *Colbert v. Carr,* 140 Conn.App. 229, 57 A.3d. 878 (2013). We see that the opinion in this case can be found in Volume 140 of the official *Connecticut Appellate Court Reports,* on page 229. The parallel citation is to Volume 57 of the *Atlantic Reporter, Third Series,* page 878. ◀

When we present opinions in this text (starting in Chapter 2), in addition to the reporter, we give the name of the court hearing the case and the year of the court's decision. Sample citations to state court decisions are explained in Exhibit 1–5 on page 17.

**FEDERAL COURT DECISIONS** Federal district (trial) court decisions are published unofficially in the *Federal Supplement* (F.Supp. or F.Supp.2d), and opinions from the circuit courts of appeals (reviewing courts) are reported unofficially in the *Federal Reporter* (F., F.2d, or F.3d). Cases concerning federal bankruptcy law are published unofficially in the *Bankruptcy Reporter* (Bankr. or B.R.).

The official edition of the United States Supreme Court decisions is the *United States Reports* (U.S.), which is published by the federal government. Unofficial editions of Supreme Court cases include the *Supreme Court Reporter* (S.Ct.) and the *Lawyers' Edition of the Supreme Court Reports* (L.Ed. or L.Ed.2d). Sample citations for federal court decisions are also listed and explained in Exhibit 1–5 on pages 17–18.

**UNPUBLISHED OPINIONS** Many court opinions that are not yet published or that are not intended for publication can be accessed through Westlaw® (abbreviated in citations as "WL"), an online legal database maintained by Thomson Reuters (formerly West Group). When no citation to a published reporter is available for cases cited in this text, we give the WL citation (see Exhibit 1–5 on page 19 for an example).

**OLD CASE LAW** On a few occasions, this text cites opinions from old, classic cases dating to the nineteenth century or earlier. Some of these are from the English courts. The citations to these cases may not conform to the descriptions just presented because the reporters in which they were originally published were often known by the names of the persons who compiled the reporters.

**SECTION 7**
# HOW TO READ AND UNDERSTAND CASE LAW

The decisions made by the courts establish the boundaries of the law as it applies to almost all business relationships. It thus is essential that businesspersons know how to read and understand case law.

**EXHIBIT 1-4 National Reporter System—Regional/Federal**

| Regional Reporters | Coverage Beginning | Coverage |
|---|---|---|
| Atlantic Reporter (A., A.2d, or A.3d) | 1885 | Connecticut, Delaware, District of Columbia, Maine, Maryland, New Hampshire, New Jersey, Pennsylvania, Rhode Island, and Vermont. |
| North Eastern Reporter (N.E. or N.E.2d) | 1885 | Illinois, Indiana, Massachusetts, New York, and Ohio. |
| North Western Reporter (N.W. or N.W.2d) | 1879 | Iowa, Michigan, Minnesota, Nebraska, North Dakota, South Dakota, and Wisconsin. |
| Pacific Reporter (P., P.2d, or P.3d) | 1883 | Alaska, Arizona, California, Colorado, Hawaii, Idaho, Kansas, Montana, Nevada, New Mexico, Oklahoma, Oregon, Utah, Washington, and Wyoming. |
| South Eastern Reporter (S.E. or S.E.2d) | 1887 | Georgia, North Carolina, South Carolina, Virginia, and West Virginia. |
| South Western Reporter (S.W., S.W.2d, or S.W.3d) | 1886 | Arkansas, Kentucky, Missouri, Tennessee, and Texas. |
| Southern Reporter (So., So.2d, or So.3d) | 1887 | Alabama, Florida, Louisiana, and Mississippi. |
| **Federal Reporters** | | |
| Federal Reporter (F., F.2d, or F.3d) | 1880 | U.S. Circuit Courts from 1880 to 1912; U.S. Commerce Court from 1911 to 1913; U.S. District Courts from 1880 to 1932; U.S. Court of Claims (now called U.S. Court of Federal Claims) from 1929 to 1932 and since 1960; U.S. Courts of Appeals since 1891; U.S. Court of Customs and Patent Appeals since 1929; U.S. Emergency Court of Appeals since 1943. |
| Federal Supplement (F.Supp. or F.Supp.2d) | 1932 | U.S. Court of Claims from 1932 to 1960; U.S. District Courts since 1932; U.S. Customs Court since 1956. |
| Federal Rules Decisions (F.R.D.) | 1939 | U.S. District Courts involving the Federal Rules of Civil Procedure since 1939 and Federal Rules of Criminal Procedure since 1946. |
| Supreme Court Reporter (S.Ct.) | 1882 | United States Supreme Court since the October term of 1882. |
| Bankruptcy Reporter (Bankr.) | 1980 | Bankruptcy decisions of U.S. Bankruptcy Courts, U.S. District Courts, U.S. Courts of Appeals, and the United States Supreme Court. |
| Military Justice Reporter (M.J.) | 1978 | U.S. Court of Military Appeals and Courts of Military Review for the Army, Navy, Air Force, and Coast Guard. |

**NATIONAL REPORTER SYSTEM MAP**

- □ Pacific
- □ North Western
- □ South Western
- ■ North Eastern
- ■ Atlantic
- ■ South Eastern
- ■ Southern

**EXHIBIT 1–5  How to Read Citations**

## STATE COURTS

285 Neb. 88, 825 N.W.2d 429 (2013)[a]

> *N.W.* is the abbreviation for Thomson Reuters's publication of state court decisions rendered in the *North Western Reporter* of the National Reporter System. *2d* indicates that this case was included in the *Second Series* of that reporter. The number 825 refers to the volume number of the reporter; the number 429 refers to the page in that volume on which this case begins.

> *Neb.* is an abbreviation for *Nebraska Reports,* Nebraska's official reports of the decisions of its highest court, the Nebraska Supreme Court.

213 Cal.App.4th 1, 152 Cal.Rptr.3d 30 (2013)

> *Cal.Rptr.* is the abbreviation for the unofficial reports—titled *California Reporter—* of the decisions of California courts.

102 A.D.3d 774, 958 N.Y.S.2d 440 (2013)

> *N.Y.S.* is the abbreviation for the unofficial reports—titled *New York Supplement*—of the decisions of New York courts.

> *A.D.* is the abbreviation for *Appellate Division,* which hears appeals from the New York Supreme Court—the state's general trial court. The New York Court of Appeals is the state's highest court, analogous to other states' supreme courts.

___ Ga.App. ___, 736 S.E.2d 480 (2013)

> *Ga.App.* is the abbreviation for *Georgia Appeals Reports,* Georgia's official reports of the decisions of its court of appeals.

## FEDERAL COURTS

___ U.S. ___, 133 S.Ct. 721, 184 L.Ed.2d 553 (2013)

> *L.Ed.* is an abbreviation for *Lawyers' Edition of the Supreme Court Reports,* an unofficial edition of decisions of the United States Supreme Court.

> *S.Ct.* is the abbreviation for Thomson Reuters's unofficial reports—titled *Supreme Court Reporter*—of decisions of the United States Supreme Court.

> *U.S.* is the abbreviation for *United States Reports,* the official edition of the decisions of the United States Supreme Court. The blank lines in this citation (or any other citation) indicate that the appropriate volume of the case reporter has not yet been published and no page number is available.

**a.** The case names have been deleted from these citations to emphasize the publications. It should be kept in mind, however, that the name of a case is as important as the specific page numbers in the volumes in which it is found. If a citation is incorrect, the correct citation may be found in a publication's index of case names. In addition to providing a check on errors in citations, the date of a case is important because the value of a recent case as an authority is likely to be greater than that of older cases from the same court.

*Continued*

**EXHIBIT 1–5 How to Read Citations—Continued**

### FEDERAL COURTS (Continued)

**705 F.3d 315 (8th Cir. 2013)**

> *8th Cir.* is an abbreviation denoting that this case was decided in the U.S. Court of Appeals for the Eighth Circuit.

**___ F.Supp.2d ___ (D.D.C. 2013)**

> *D.D.C.* is an abbreviation indicating that the U.S. District Court for the District of Columbia decided this case.

### ENGLISH COURTS

**9 Exch. 341, 156 Eng.Rep. 145 (1854)**

> *Eng.Rep.* is an abbreviation for *English Reports, Full Reprint,* a series of reports containing selected decisions made in English courts between 1378 and 1865.

> *Exch.* is an abbreviation for *English Exchequer Reports*, which includes the original reports of cases decided in England's Court of Exchequer.

### STATUTORY AND OTHER CITATIONS

**18 U.S.C. Section 1961(1)(A)**

> *U.S.C.* denotes *United States Code*, the codification of *United States Statutes at Large*. The number 18 refers to the statute's U.S.C. title number and 1961 to its section number within that title. The number 1 in parentheses refers to a subsection within the section, and the letter A in parentheses to a subsection within the subsection.

**UCC 2–206(1)(b)**

> *UCC* is an abbreviation for *Uniform Commercial Code*. The first number 2 is a reference to an article of the UCC, and 206 to a section within that article. The number 1 in parentheses refers to a subsection within the section, and the letter b in parentheses to a subsection within the subsection.

***Restatement (Third) of Torts,* Section 6**

> *Restatement (Third) of Torts* refers to the third edition of the American Law Institute's *Restatement of the Law of Torts*. The number 6 refers to a specific section.

**17 C.F.R. Section 230.505**

> *C.F.R.* is an abbreviation for *Code of Federal Regulations*, a compilation of federal administrative regulations. The number 17 designates the regulation's title number, and 230.505 designates a specific section within that title.

**EXHIBIT 1-5  How to Read Citations—Continued**

## WESTLAW® CITATIONS[b]

**2013 WL 285688**

*WL* is an abbreviation for Westlaw. The number 2013 is the year of the document that can be found with this citation in the Westlaw database. The number 285688 is a number assigned to a specific document. A higher number indicates that a document was added to the Westlaw database later in the year.

## UNIFORM RESOURCE LOCATORS (URLs)

**web2.westlaw.com[c]**

The suffix *com* is the top-level domain (TLD) for this Web site. The TLD *com* is an abbreviation for "commercial," which usually means that a for-profit entity hosts (maintains or supports) this Web site.

*westlaw* is the host name—the part of the domain name selected by the organization that registered the name. In this case, West Group (now Thomson Reuters) registered the name. This Internet site is the Westlaw database on the Web.

*web2* describes Web sites that use software allowing users to interact and collaborate with each other in a social media dialogue, rather than limiting users to the passive viewing of static content.

**http://www.uscourts.gov**

This is "The Federal Judiciary Home Page." The host is the Administrative Office of the U.S. Courts. The TLD *gov* is an abbreviation for "government." This Web site includes information and links from, and about, the federal courts.

*www* is an abbreviation for "World Wide Web." The Web is a system of Internet servers that support documents formatted in *HTML* (hypertext markup language) and other formats as well.

**http://www.law.cornell.edu/index.html**

This part of a URL points to a Web page or file at a specific location within the host's domain. This page is a menu with links to documents within the domain and to other Internet resources.

This is the host name for a Web site that contains the Internet publications of the Legal Information Institute (LII), which is a part of Cornell Law School. The LII site includes a variety of legal materials and links to other legal resources on the Internet. The TLD *edu* is an abbreviation for "educational institution" (a school or a university).

**http://www.ipl.org/div/news**

This part of the Web site points to a static *news* page at this Web site, which provides links to online newspapers from around the world.

*ipl* is an abbreviation for "Internet Public Library," which is an online service that provides reference resources and links to other information services on the Web. The IPL is supported chiefly by the School of Information at the University of Michigan. The TLD *org* is an abbreviation for "organization" (normally nonprofit).

*div* is an abbreviation for "division," which is the way that the Internet Public Library tags the content on its Web site as relating to a specific topic.

**b.** Many court decisions that are not yet published or that are not intended for publication can be accessed through Westlaw, an online legal database.

**c.** The basic form for a URL is "service://hostname/path." The Internet service for all of the URLs in this text is *http* (hypertext transfer protocol). Because most Web browsers add this prefix automatically when a user enters a host name or a hostname/path, we have generally omitted the *http://* from the URLs listed in this text.

The cases that we present in this text have been condensed from the full text of the courts' opinions and are presented in a special format. In all of the cases (including the cases designated as Classic and Spotlight), we have summarized the background and facts, as well as the court's decision and remedy, in our own words. In the decision and remedy section of each case, we indicate how the court ruled and explain the reasoning underlying the decision. We also often include selected quotes from the court's opinion that help to clarify how the court applied the law to the facts and arrived at its particular conclusion in the case.

The following sections will provide useful insights into how to read and understand case law.

## Case Titles and Terminology

The title of a case, such as *Adams v. Jones,* indicates the names of the parties to the lawsuit. The *v.* in the case title stands for *versus,* which means "against." In the trial court, Adams was the plaintiff—the person who filed the suit. Jones was the defendant. If the case is appealed, however, the appellate court will sometimes place the name of the party appealing the decision first, so the case may be called *Jones v. Adams* if Jones is appealing.

Because some appellate courts retain the trial court order of names, it is often impossible to distinguish the plaintiff from the defendant in the title of a reported appellate court decision. You must carefully read the facts of each case to identify the parties. Otherwise, the discussion by the appellate court may be difficult to understand.

The following terms, phrases, and abbreviations are frequently encountered in court opinions and legal publications.

**PARTIES TO LAWSUITS** As mentioned previously, the party initiating a lawsuit is referred to as the *plaintiff* or *petitioner,* depending on the nature of the action. The party against whom a lawsuit is brought is the *defendant* or *respondent.* Lawsuits frequently involve more than one plaintiff and/or defendant.

When a case is appealed from the original court or jurisdiction to another court or jurisdiction, the party appealing the case is called the **appellant.** The **appellee** is the party against whom the appeal is taken. (In some appellate courts, the party appealing a case is referred to as the petitioner, and the party against whom the suit is brought or appealed is called the respondent.)

**JUDGES AND JUSTICES** The terms *judge* and *justice* are usually synonymous and represent two designations given to judges in various courts. All members of the United States Supreme Court, for instance, are referred to as justices, and justice is the formal title often given to judges of appellate courts, although this is not always the case. In New York, a *justice* is a judge of the trial court (called the Supreme Court), and a member of the Court of Appeals (the state's highest court) is called a *judge.*

The term *justice* is commonly abbreviated to J., and *justices,* to JJ. A United States Supreme Court case might refer to Justice Sotomayor as  Sotomayor, J., or to Chief Justice Roberts as Roberts, C.J.

**DECISIONS AND OPINIONS** Most decisions reached by reviewing, or appellate, courts are explained in written **opinions.** The opinion contains the court's reasons for its decision, the rules of law that apply, and the judgment. You may encounter several types of opinions as you read appellate cases, including the following:

- When all the judges (or justices) agree, a *unanimous opinion* is written for the entire court.
- When there is not unanimous agreement, a **majority opinion** is generally written. It outlines the views of the majority of the judges deciding the case.
- A judge who agrees (concurs) with the majority opinion as to the result but not as to the legal reasoning often writes a **concurring opinion.** In it, the judge sets out the reasoning that he or she considers correct.
- A **dissenting opinion** presents the views of one or more judges who disagree with the majority view.
- Sometimes, no single position is fully supported by a majority of the judges deciding a case. In this situation, we may have a **plurality opinion.** This is the opinion that has the support of the largest number of judges, but the group in agreement is less than a majority.
- Finally, a court occasionally issues a ***per curiam*** **opinion** (*per curiam* is Latin for "of the court"), which does not indicate which judge wrote the opinion.

## A Sample Court Case

Knowing how to read and understand court opinions and the legal reasoning used by the courts is an essential step in undertaking accurate legal research. A further step is "briefing," or summarizing, the case. Legal researchers routinely brief cases by reducing the texts of the opinions to their essential elements. Instructions on how to brief a case are given in Appendix A.

The cases within the chapters of this text have already been analyzed and briefed by the authors, and the essential aspects of each case are presented in a convenient format consisting of two sections: *Background and Facts* and *Decision and Rationale*. This format is illustrated in the sample court case in Exhibit 1–6 on page 22, which has been annotated to explain the kind of information that commonly appears in cases. Throughout the text, we continue to explain any terms that may be unfamiliar to students in brackets.

The case we present and annotate in Exhibit 1–6 is an actual case decided by a federal trial court located in California.

**THE SAMPLE COURT CASE STARTS ON THE FOLLOWING PAGE.**

**EXHIBIT 1-6 A Sample Court Case**

| | |
|---|---|
| This section contains the citation—the name of the case, the name of the court that heard the case, the year of the decision, and reporters in which the court's opinion can be found. | **APPLE, INC. v. AMAZON.COM, INC.**<br><br>United States District Court, Northern District of California,<br><br>__ F.Supp.2d __ , 2013 WL 11896 (2013). |

**BACKGROUND AND FACTS** Apple, Inc., has sold applications ("apps") for its mobile devices (iPads, iPhones, iPods) through its APP STORE service since July of 2008. In 2011, Amazon.com launched an Appstore for viewing and downloading applications to Android devices, such as the Kindle Fire. Apple (the plaintiff) filed a lawsuit **alleging** that Amazon's use of the name "Appstore" constitutes false advertising

> To *allege* is to assert to be true as described.

and trademark infringement (see Chapter 8). Apple argued that because Amazon's "Appstore" did not possess the characteristics and qualities that the public has come to expect from Apple's APP STORE, it misled the public. Amazon requested a **summary judgment** on the false advertising cause of action. The issue before the

> A *summary judgment* is a judgment that a court enters without beginning or continuing a trial. This judgment can be entered only if no facts are in dispute and the only question is how the law applies to the facts.

court is whether Amazon's use of "Appstore" might mislead the public into thinking that Amazon's Appstore is affiliated with Apple and offers the same content.

**DECISION AND RATIONALE** The United States District Court for the Northern District of California **granted** Amazon's motion for summary judgment as to the cause

> To *grant* is to approve, warrant, or order a motion or some other request.

of action for false advertising. The court reasoned that to establish a false advertising claim, the plaintiff must show that the defendant made a false statement of fact in a commercial advertisement about its own or another's product. Apple did not identify a single false statement that Amazon made about the nature, characteristics, or quality of the Amazon Appstore for Android (or the Amazon Appstore, which allows viewing and downloading of apps for the Kindle Fire). "The mere use of "Appstore" by Amazon to designate a site for viewing and downloading/purchasing apps cannot

> To *construe* is to interpret or explain the sense of something according to judicial standards.

be **construed** as a representation that the nature, characteristics, or quality of the Amazon Appstore is the same as that of the Apple APP STORE." Because Apple failed to show "that Amazon made any false statement (express or implied) that actually deceived or had the tendency to deceive a substantial segment of its audience," there was no **triable issue.**

> A *triable* issue is an issue that is subject to judicial examination and trial.

## Reviewing: Law and Legal Reasoning

Suppose that the California legislature passes a law that severely restricts carbon dioxide emissions from automobiles in that state. A group of automobile manufacturers files suit against the state of California to prevent the enforcement of the law. The automakers claim that a federal law already sets fuel economy standards nationwide and that fuel economy standards are essentially the same as carbon dioxide emission standards. According to the automobile manufacturers, it is unfair to allow California to impose more stringent regulations than those set by the federal law. Using the information presented in the chapter, answer the following questions.

1. Who are the parties (the plaintiffs and the defendant) in this lawsuit?
2. Are the plaintiffs seeking a legal remedy or an equitable remedy?
3. What is the primary source of the law that is at issue here?
4. Where would you look to find the relevant California and federal laws?

**DEBATE THIS ...** *Under the doctrine of* stare decisis, *courts are obligated to follow the precedents established in their jurisdiction unless there is a compelling reason not to. Should U.S. courts continue to adhere to this common law principle, given that our government now regulates so many areas by statute?*

## Terms and Concepts

administrative agency 5
administrative law 5
allege 10
appellant 20
appellee 20
binding authority 8
breach 7
case law 5
case on point 10
chancellor 6
citation 13
civil law 13
common law 6
concurring opinion 20
constitutional law 4
court of equity 6
court of law 6
criminal law 13
cyberlaw 13

damages 6
defendant 7
defense 7
dissenting opinion 20
equitable maxim 7
executive agency 5
historical school 12
independent regulatory agency 5
jurisprudence 11
laches 7
law 2
legal positivism 12
legal realism 12
legal reasoning 9
majority opinion 20
natural law 11
opinion 20
ordinance 4
persuasive authority 9

*per curiam* opinion 20
petitioner 7
plaintiff 7
plurality opinion 20
precedent 8
procedural law 12
public policy 9
remedy 6
remedy at law 6
remedy in equity 7
reporter 8
respondent 7
sociological school 12
*stare decisis* 8
statute of limitations 7
statutory law 4
substantive law 12
uniform law 5

## Issue Spotters

1. Under what circumstances might a judge rely on case law to determine the intent and purpose of a statute? **(See page 5.)**

2. After World War II, several Nazis were convicted of "crimes against humanity" by an international court. Assuming that these convicted war criminals had not disobeyed any law of their country and had merely been following their government's orders, what law had they violated? Explain. **(See page 11.)**

• **Check your answers to the Issue Spotters against the answers provided in Appendix E at the end of this text.**

## Business Scenarios

**1–1. Binding versus Persuasive Authority.** A county court in Illinois is deciding a case involving an issue that has never been addressed before in that state's courts. The Iowa Supreme Court, however, recently decided a case involving a very similar fact pattern. Is the Illinois court obligated to follow the Iowa Supreme Court's decision on the issue? If the United States Supreme Court had decided a similar case, would that decision be binding on the Illinois court? Explain. **(See page 8.)**

**1–2. Sources of Law.** This chapter discussed a number of sources of American law. Which source of law takes priority in the following situations, and why? **(See page 3.)**

(a) A federal statute conflicts with the U.S. Constitution.

(b) A federal statute conflicts with a state constitutional provision.

(c) A state statute conflicts with the common law of that state.

(d) A state constitutional amendment conflicts with the U.S. Constitution.

**1–3. *Stare Decisis.*** In the text of this chapter, we stated that the doctrine of *stare decisis* "became a cornerstone of the English and American judicial systems." What does *stare decisis* mean, and why has this doctrine been so funda-

mental to the development of our legal tradition? **(See page 8.)**

**1–4. Remedies.** Assume that Arthur Rabe is suing Xavier Sanchez for breaching a contract in which Sanchez promised to sell Rabe a painting by Vincent Van Gogh for $30 million. **(See page 7.)**

(a) In this lawsuit, who is the plaintiff and who is the defendant?

(b) Suppose that Rabe wants Sanchez to perform the contract as promised. What remedy would Rabe seek from the court?

(c) Now suppose that Rabe wants to cancel the contract because Sanchez fraudulently misrepresented the painting as an original Van Gogh when in fact it is a copy. What remedy would Rabe seek?

(d) Will the remedy Rabe seeks in either situation be a remedy at law or a remedy in equity? What is the difference between legal and equitable remedies?

(e) Suppose that the trial court finds in Rabe's favor and grants one of these remedies. Sanchez then appeals the decision to a higher court. On appeal, which party will be the appellant (or petitioner), and which party will be the appellee (or respondent)?

## Business Case Problems

**1–5. Spotlight on AOL—Common Law.**  AOL, LLC, mistakenly made public the personal information of 650,000 of its members. The members filed a suit, alleging violations of California law. AOL asked the court to dismiss the suit on the basis of a "forum-selection" clause in its member agreement that designates Virginia courts as the place where member disputes will be tried. Under a decision of the United States Supreme Court, a forum-selection clause is unenforceable "if enforcement would contravene a strong public policy of the forum in which suit is brought." California courts have declared in other cases that the AOL clause contravenes a strong public policy. If the court applies the doctrine of *stare decisis*, will it dismiss the suit?

Explain. [*Doe 1 v. AOL LLC*, 552 F.3d 1077 (9th Cir. 2009)] **(See page 8.)**

**1–6. BUSINESS CASE PROBLEM WITH SAMPLE ANSWER— Reading Citations.**  *Assume that you want to read the entire court opinion in the case of* United States v. Yi, *704 F.3d 800 (9th Cir. 2013). Refer to the subsection entitled "Finding Case Law" in this chapter, and then explain specifically where you would find the court's opinion.* **(See page 14.)**

• **For a sample answer to Problem 1–6, go to Appendix F at the end of this text.**

**1–7. A QUESTION OF ETHICS—The Common Law Tradition.**

 *On July 5, 1884, Dudley, Stephens, and Brooks— "all able-bodied English seamen"—and a teenage English boy were cast adrift in a lifeboat following a storm at sea. They had no water with them in the boat, and all they had for sustenance were two one-pound tins of turnips. On July 24, Dudley proposed that one of the four in the lifeboat be sacrificed to save the others. Stephens agreed with Dudley, but Brooks refused to consent—and the boy was never asked for his opinion. On July 25, Dudley killed the boy, and the three men then fed on the boy's body and blood. Four days later, a passing vessel rescued the men. They were taken to England and tried for the murder of the boy. If the men had not fed on the boy's body, they would probably have* died of starvation within the four-day period. The boy, who was in a much weaker condition, would likely have died before the rest. *[Regina v. Dudley and Stephens, 14 Q.B.D. (Queen's Bench Division, England) 273 (1884)]* **(See page 11.)**

(a) The basic question in this case is whether the survivors should be subject to penalties under English criminal law, given the men's unusual circumstances. Were the defendants' actions necessary but unethical? Explain your reasoning. What ethical issues might be involved here?

(b) Should judges ever have the power to look beyond the written "letter of the law" in making their decisions? Why or why not?

## Legal Reasoning Group Activity

**1–8. Court Opinions.** Read through the subsection in this chapter entitled "Decisions and Opinions." **(See page 20.)**

(a) One group will explain the difference between a concurring opinion and a majority opinion.

(b) Another group will outline the difference between a concurring opinion and a dissenting opinion.

(c) A third group will explain why judges and justices write concurring and dissenting opinions, given that these opinions will not affect the outcome of the case at hand, which has already been decided by majority vote.

# CHAPTER 2

# COURTS AND ALTERNATIVE DISPUTE RESOLUTION

The United States has fifty-two court systems—one for each of the fifty states, one for the District of Columbia, and a federal system. Keep in mind that the federal courts are not superior to the state courts. They are simply an independent system of courts, which derives its authority from Article III, Section 2, of the U.S. Constitution. By the power given to it under the U.S. Constitution, Congress has extended the federal court system to U.S. territories such as Guam, Puerto Rico, and the Virgin Islands.[1]

As we shall see, the United States Supreme Court is the final controlling voice over all of these fifty-two systems, at least when questions of federal law are involved. The Supreme Court's decisions—whether on affirmative action, health-care reform, immigration, or same-sex marriage—represent the last word in the most controversial legal debates in our society. Nevertheless, many of the legal issues that arise in our daily lives, such as the use of social media by courts, employers, and law enforcement, have not yet come before the nation's highest court. The lower courts usually resolve such pressing matters, making these courts equally important in our legal system.

Although an understanding of our nation's court systems is beneficial for anyone, it is particularly crucial for businesspersons, who will likely face a lawsuit at some time during their careers. Anyone involved in business should be familiar with the basic requirements that must be met before a party can bring a lawsuit before a particular court. We discuss these requirements in this chapter. It is also increasingly important for businesspersons to understand the various methods of alternative dispute resolution, which are discussed at the end of this chapter.

---

1. In Guam and the Virgin Islands, territorial courts serve as both federal courts and state courts. In Puerto Rico, they serve only as federal courts.

---

## THE JUDICIARY'S ROLE IN AMERICAN GOVERNMENT

As you learned in Chapter 1, the body of American law includes the federal and state constitutions, statutes passed by legislative bodies, administrative law, and the case decisions and legal principles that form the common law. These laws would be meaningless, however, without the courts to interpret and apply them. The essential role of the judiciary—the courts—in the American governmental system is to interpret the laws and apply them to specific situations.

### Judicial Review

As the branch of government entrusted with interpreting the laws, the judiciary can decide, among other things, whether the laws or actions of the other two branches are constitutional. The process for making such a determination is known as **judicial review.** The power of judicial review enables the judicial branch to act as a check on the other two branches of government, in line with the system of checks and balances established by the U.S. Constitution.[2]

### The Origins of Judicial Review in the United States

The power of judicial review is not mentioned in the U.S. Constitution (although many constitutional scholars believe that the founders intended the judi-

---

2. In a broad sense, judicial review occurs whenever a court "reviews" a case or legal proceeding—as when an appellate court reviews a lower court's decision. When discussing the judiciary's role in American government, however, the term *judicial review* refers to the power of the judiciary to decide whether the actions of the other two branches of government violate the U.S. Constitution.

ciary to have this power). The United States Supreme Court explicitly established this power in 1803 in the case *Marbury v. Madison.*[3] In that decision, the Court stated, "It is emphatically the province [authority] and duty of the Judicial Department to say what the law is. . . . If two laws conflict with each other, the courts must decide on the operation of each. . . . [I]f both [a] law and the Constitution apply to a particular case, . . . the Court must determine which of these conflicting rules governs the case. This is of the very essence of judicial duty." Since the *Marbury v. Madison* decision, the power of judicial review has remained unchallenged. Today, this power is exercised by both federal and state courts.

## SECTION 2
# BASIC JUDICIAL REQUIREMENTS

Before a lawsuit can be brought before a court, certain requirements must be met. These requirements relate to jurisdiction, venue, and standing to sue. We examine each of these important concepts here.

## Jurisdiction

In Latin, *juris* means "law," and *diction* means "to speak." Thus, "the power to speak the law" is the literal meaning of the term **jurisdiction.** Before any court can hear a case, it must have jurisdiction over the person (or company) against whom the suit is brought (the defendant) or over the property involved in the suit. The court must also have jurisdiction over the subject matter of the dispute.

### JURISDICTION OVER PERSONS OR PROPERTY
Generally, a particular court can exercise **in personam jurisdiction** (personal jurisdiction) over any person or business that resides in a certain geographic area. A state trial court, for example, normally has jurisdictional authority over residents (including businesses) of a particular area of the state, such as a county or district. A state's highest court (often called the state supreme court[4]) has jurisdictional authority over all residents within the state.

A court can also exercise jurisdiction over property that is located within its boundaries. This kind of jurisdiction is known as **in rem jurisdiction,** or "jurisdiction over the thing." ▶ **Example 2.1**  A dispute arises over the ownership of a boat in dry dock in Fort Lauderdale, Florida. The boat is owned by an Ohio resident, over whom a Florida court normally cannot exercise personal jurisdiction. The other party to the dispute is a resident of Nebraska. In this situation, a lawsuit concerning the boat could be brought in a Florida state court on the basis of the court's *in rem* jurisdiction. ◀

***Long Arm Statutes and Minimum Contacts.*** Under the authority of a state **long arm statute,** a court can exercise personal jurisdiction over certain out-of-state defendants based on activities that took place within the state. Before a court can exercise jurisdiction, though, it must be demonstrated that the defendant had sufficient contacts, or *minimum contacts,* with the state to justify the jurisdiction.[5]

Generally, the minimum-contacts requirement means that the defendant must have sufficient connection to the state for the judge to conclude that it is fair for the state to exercise power over the defendant. For instance, if an out-of-state defendant caused an automobile accident within the state or breached a contract formed there, a court will usually find that minimum contacts exist to exercise jurisdiction over that defendant. Similarly, a state may exercise personal jurisdiction over a nonresident defendant that is sued for selling defective goods within the state.

▶ **Case in Point 2.2**  An Xbox game system caught fire in Bonnie Broquet's home in Texas and caused substantial personal injuries. Broquet filed a lawsuit in a Texas court against Ji-Haw Industrial Company, a nonresident company that made the Xbox components. Broquet alleged that Ji-Haw's components were defective and had caused the fire. Ji-Haw argued that the Texas court lacked jurisdiction over it, but a state appellate court held that the Texas long arm statute authorized the exercise of jurisdiction over the out-of-state defendant.[6] ◀

***Corporate Contacts.*** Because corporations are considered legal persons, courts use the same principles to determine whether it is fair to exercise jurisdiction

**3.** 5 U.S. (1 Cranch) 137, 2 L.Ed. 60 (1803).
**4.** As will be discussed shortly, a state's highest court is often referred to as the state supreme court, but there are exceptions. For instance, in New York the supreme court is a trial court.
**5.** The minimum-contacts standard was first established in *International Shoe Co. v. State of Washington,* 326 U.S. 310, 66 S.Ct. 154, 90 L.Ed. 95 (1945).
**6.** *Ji-Haw Industrial Co. v. Broquet,* 2008 WL 441822 (Tex.App.—San Antonio 2008).

over a corporation.[7] A corporation normally is subject to personal jurisdiction in the state in which it is incorporated, has its principal office, and/or is doing business. Courts apply the minimum-contacts test to determine if they can exercise jurisdiction over out-of-state corporations.

The minimum-contacts requirement is usually met if the corporation advertises or sells its products within the state, or places its goods into the "stream of commerce" with the intent that the goods be sold in the state. ▶ **Example 2.3** A business is incorporated under the laws of Maine but has a branch office and manufacturing plant in Georgia. The corporation also advertises and sells its products in Georgia. These activities would likely constitute sufficient contacts with the state of Georgia to allow a Georgia court to exercise jurisdiction over the corporation. ◀

Some corporations do not sell or advertise products or place any goods in the stream of commerce. Determining what constitutes minimum contacts in these situations can be more difficult. ▶ **Case in Point 2.4** Independence Plating Corporation is a New Jersey corporation that provides metal-coating services. Its only office and all of its personnel are located in New Jersey, and it does not advertise out of state. Independence had a long-standing business relationship with Southern Prestige Industries, Inc., a North Carolina company. Eventually, Southern Prestige filed suit in North Carolina against Independence for defective workmanship. Independence argued that North Carolina did not have jurisdiction over it, but the court held that Independence had sufficient minimum contacts with the state to justify jurisdiction. The two parties had exchanged thirty-two separate purchase orders in a period of less than twelve months.[8] ◀

**JURISDICTION OVER SUBJECT MATTER** Subject-matter jurisdiction refers to the limitations on the types of cases a court can hear. Certain courts are empowered to hear certain kinds of disputes.

*General and Limited Jurisdiction.* In both the federal and the state court systems, there are courts of *general* (unlimited) *jurisdiction* and courts of *limited jurisdiction*. A court of general jurisdiction can decide cases involving a broad array of issues. An example of a court of general jurisdiction is a state trial court or a federal district court.

An example of a state court of limited jurisdiction is a probate court. **Probate courts** are state courts that handle only the disposition of a person's assets and obligations after that person's death, including issues relating to the custody and guardianship of children. An example of a federal court of limited subject-matter jurisdiction is a bankruptcy court. **Bankruptcy courts** handle only bankruptcy proceedings, which are governed by federal bankruptcy law.

A court's jurisdiction over subject matter is usually defined in the statute or constitution that created the court. In both the federal and the state court systems, a court's subject-matter jurisdiction can be limited by any of the following:

1. The subject of the lawsuit.
2. The sum in controversy.
3. Whether the case involves a felony (a more serious type of crime) or a misdemeanor (a less serious type of crime).
4. Whether the proceeding is a trial or an appeal.

*Original and Appellate Jurisdiction.* The distinction between courts of original jurisdiction and courts of appellate jurisdiction normally lies in whether the case is being heard for the first time. Courts having original jurisdiction are courts of the first instance, or trial courts. These are courts in which lawsuits begin, trials take place, and evidence is presented. In the federal court system, the *district courts* are trial courts. In the various state court systems, the trial courts are known by different names, as will be discussed shortly.

The key point here is that any court having original jurisdiction normally serves as a trial court. Courts having appellate jurisdiction act as reviewing, or appellate, courts. In general, cases can be brought before appellate courts only on appeal from an order or a judgment of a trial court or other lower courts.

**JURISDICTION OF THE FEDERAL COURTS** Because the federal government is a government of limited powers, the jurisdiction of the federal courts is limited. Federal courts have subject-matter jurisdiction in two situations: when a federal question is involved and when there is diversity of citizenship.

*Federal Questions.* Article III of the U.S. Constitution establishes the boundaries of federal judicial power. Section 2 of Article III states that "the judicial Power shall extend to all Cases, in Law and Equity, arising under this Constitution, the Laws of the United

---

7. In the eyes of the law, corporations are "legal persons"—entities that can sue and be sued.
8. *Southern Prestige Industries, Inc. v. Independence Plating Corp.*, 690 S.E.2d 768 (N.C. 2010).

States, and Treaties made, or which shall be made, under their Authority."

In effect, this clause means that whenever a plaintiff's cause of action is based, at least in part, on the U.S. Constitution, a treaty, or a federal law, a **federal question** arises. If a case involves a federal question, the case comes under the judicial power of the federal courts. A person who claims that her constitutional rights have been violated, for instance, can file the lawsuit in a federal court. Note that in a case based on a federal question, a federal court will apply federal law.

***Diversity of Citizenship.*** Federal district courts can also exercise original jurisdiction over cases involving **diversity of citizenship.** The most common type of diversity jurisdiction[9] requires *both* of the following:

1. The plaintiff and defendant must be residents of different states.
2. The dollar amount in controversy must exceed $75,000.

---

**9.** Diversity jurisdiction also exists in cases between (1) a foreign country and citizens of a state or of different states and (2) citizens of a state and citizens or subjects of a foreign country. Cases based on these types of diversity jurisdiction occur infrequently.

For purposes of diversity jurisdiction, a corporation is a citizen of both the state in which it is incorporated and the state in which its principal place of business is located. A case involving diversity of citizenship can be filed in the appropriate federal district court. If the case starts in a state court, it can sometimes be transferred, or "removed," to a federal court.

A large percentage of the cases filed in federal courts each year are based on diversity of citizenship. As noted before, a federal court will apply federal law in cases involving federal questions. In a case based on diversity of citizenship, in contrast, a federal court will apply the relevant state law (which is often the law of the state in which the court sits).

The following dispute focused on whether diversity jurisdiction existed. A boat owner was severely burned when his boat exploded after being filled with excessive fuel at a marina in the U.S. Virgin Islands. The owner filed a suit in a federal district court against the marina and sought a jury trial. The defendant argued that a plaintiff in an admiralty, or maritime (on the sea), case does not have a right to a jury trial unless the court has diversity jurisdiction. The defendant claimed that because it, like the plaintiff, was a citizen of the Virgin Islands, the court had no such jurisdiction.

---

## CASE 2.1

### Mala v. Crown Bay Marina, Inc.
United States Court of Appeals, Third Circuit, 704 F.3d 239 (2013).

**BACKGOUND AND FACTS**  Kelley Mala was severely burned when his boat exploded after being over-fueled at Crown Bay Marina, Inc., in the United States Virgin Islands. Mala filed a lawsuit in a federal district court against Crown Bay, alleging that the marina negligently maintained its gas pump. (*Negligence* is the failure to exercise the standard of care that a reasonable person would exercise in similar circumstances, as will be discussed in Chapter 6. Negligence is a *tort*—a breach of a legal duty that proximately causes harm or injury to another—that forms the basis for a claim subject to applicable state law.)

Mala sought a jury trial. Crown Bay, however, argued that a plaintiff in an admiralty, or maritime, case does not have a right to a jury trial unless the court has diversity jurisdiction. Crown Bay asserted that it, like Mala, was a citizen of the Virgin Islands. At trial, Mala did not provide evidence that Crown Bay was anything other than a citizen of the Virgin Islands. The district court struck down Mala's demand for a jury trial, but opted to empanel an advisory jury. The district court then rejected the jury's recommendation for a verdict in Mala's favor and entered a judgment for Crown Bay. Mala appealed.

**DECISION AND RATIONALE**  The U.S. Court of Appeals for the Third Circuit affirmed the U.S. District Court's decision. The defendant argued that the federal trial court had improperly refused to conduct a jury trial, but this claim ultimately depends on whether the district court had diversity jurisdiction. The appellate court pointed out that "District Courts have jurisdiction only if the parties are completely

CASE 2.1 CONTINUES ▶

**CASE 2.1 CONTINUED**

diverse. This means that no plaintiff may have the same state or territorial citizenship as any defendant. The parties agree that Mala was a citizen of the Virgin Islands." The defendant argued that the district court was incorrect when it concluded that Crown Bay was also a citizen of the Virgin Islands, but the defendant had the burden of proving that. Mala "failed to meet that burden because he did not offer evidence that Crown Bay was anything other than a citizen of the Virgin Islands."

The appeals court pointed out that "allegations are insufficient at trial. And they are especially insufficient on appeal, . . ." Mala presented no credible evidence that Crown Bay was anything other than a citizen of the Virgin Islands. "Accordingly, the parties were not diverse, and Mala does not have a jury-trial right."

**THE LEGAL ENVIRONMENT DIMENSION** *What specifically is "diversity of citizenship"?*

**THE SOCIAL DIMENSION** *How does the presence—or lack—of diversity of citizenship affect a lawsuit?*

---

**EXCLUSIVE VERSUS CONCURRENT JURISDICTION**
When cases can be tried only in federal courts or only in state courts, exclusive jurisdiction exists. Federal courts have **exclusive jurisdiction** in the following types of cases:

1. Federal crimes.
2. Bankruptcy.
3. Most patent and copyright claims.
4. Any lawsuits against the United States.
5. Some areas of admiralty law (law governing seaborne transportation and ocean waters).

State courts also have exclusive jurisdiction over certain subjects—for example, divorce and adoption.

When both federal and state courts have the power to hear a case, as is true in suits involving diversity of citizenship, **concurrent jurisdiction** exists. When concurrent jurisdiction exists, a party may choose to bring a suit in either a federal court or a state court. Many factors can affect a party's decision to litigate in a federal versus a state court. Examples include the availability of different remedies, the distance to the respective courthouses, or the experience or reputation of a particular judge. For instance, if the dispute involves a trade secret, a party might conclude that a federal court—which has exclusive jurisdiction over copyrights and patents—would have more expertise in the matter. A party might also choose a federal court over a state court if a state court has a reputation for bias against certain types of cases or plaintiffs.

In contrast, a plaintiff might choose to litigate in a state court if the court has a reputation for awarding substantial amounts of damages or if the judge is perceived as being pro-plaintiff. The concepts of exclusive and concurrent jurisdiction are illustrated in Exhibit 2–1 below.

**EXHIBIT 2–1 Exclusive and Concurrent Jurisdiction**

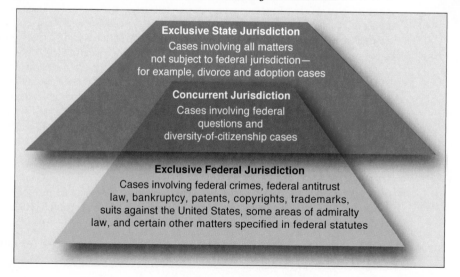

**Exclusive State Jurisdiction**
Cases involving all matters not subject to federal jurisdiction— for example, divorce and adoption cases

**Concurrent Jurisdiction**
Cases involving federal questions and diversity-of-citizenship cases

**Exclusive Federal Jurisdiction**
Cases involving federal crimes, federal antitrust law, bankruptcy, patents, copyrights, trademarks, suits against the United States, some areas of admiralty law, and certain other matters specified in federal statutes

# Jurisdiction in Cyberspace

The Internet's capacity to bypass political and geographic boundaries undercuts the traditional basis on which courts assert personal jurisdiction. This basis includes a party's contacts with a court's geographic jurisdiction.

As already discussed, for a court to compel a defendant to come before it, there must be at least minimum contacts—the presence of a salesperson within the state, for instance. When a defendant's only contacts with the state are through a Web site, however, it is more difficult to determine whether these contacts are sufficient for a court to exercise jurisdiction.

**THE "SLIDING-SCALE" STANDARD** The courts have developed a "sliding-scale" standard to determine when they can exercise personal jurisdiction over an out-of-state defendant based on the defendant's Web activities. The sliding-scale standard identifies three types of Internet business contacts and outlines the following rules for jurisdiction:

1.  When the defendant conducts substantial business over the Internet (such as contracts and sales), jurisdiction is proper.
2.  When there is some interactivity through a Web site, jurisdiction may be proper, depending on the circumstances. Even a single contact can satisfy the minimum-contacts requirement in certain situations.
3.  When a defendant merely engages in passive advertising on the Web, jurisdiction is never proper.[10] An Internet communication is typically considered passive if people have to voluntarily access it to read the message and active if it is sent to specific individuals.

▶ **Case in Point 2.5**   A Louisiana resident, Daniel Crummey, purchased a used recreational vehicle (RV) from sellers in Texas after viewing photos of it on eBay. The sellers' statements on eBay claimed that

"Everything works great on this RV and will provide comfort and dependability for years to come. This RV will go to Alaska and back without problems!"

Crummey picked up the RV in Texas, but on the drive back to Louisiana, the RV quit working. He filed a suit in Louisiana against the sellers, alleging that the vehicle was defective. The sellers claimed that the Louisiana court lacked jurisdiction. The court found that Louisiana had jurisdiction because the sellers had used eBay to market and sell the RV to a Louisiana buyer—and had regularly used eBay to sell vehicles to remote parties in the past.[11] ◀

*Concept Summary 2.1* on page 33 reviews the various types of jurisdiction, including jurisdiction in cyberspace.

**INTERNATIONAL JURISDICTIONAL ISSUES** Because the Internet is international in scope, it obviously raises international jurisdictional issues. The world's courts seem to be developing a standard that echoes the requirement of minimum contacts applied by the U.S. courts.

Most courts are indicating that minimum contacts—doing business within the jurisdiction, for example—are enough to compel a defendant to appear and that a physical presence in the country is not necessary. The effect of this standard is that a business firm has to comply with the laws in any jurisdiction in which it targets customers for its products. This situation is complicated by the fact that many countries' laws on particular issues—free speech, for instance—are very different from U.S. laws.

The following case illustrates how federal courts apply a sliding-scale standard to determine if they can exercise jurisdiction over a foreign defendant whose only contact with the United States is through a Web site.

---

10. For a leading case on this issue, see *Zippo Manufacturing Co. v. Zippo Dot Com, Inc.*, 952 F.Supp. 1119 (W.D.Pa. 1997).

11. *Crummey v. Morgan*, 965 So.2d 497 (La.App. 1 Cir. 2007). But note that a single sale on eBay does not necessarily confer jurisdiction. Jurisdiction depends on whether the seller regularly uses eBay as a means for doing business with remote buyers. See *Boschetto v. Hansing*, 539 F.3d 1011 (9th Cir. 2008).

## SP TLIGHT on Gucci

### Case 2.2   Gucci America, Inc. v. Wang Huoqing
United States District Court, Northern District of California, ___ F.Supp.2d ___ (2011).

**BACKGROUND AND FACTS** Gucci America, Inc., is a New York corporation headquartered in New York City. Gucci manufactures and distributes high-quality luxury goods, including footwear, belts, sunglasses, handbags, and wallets, which are sold worldwide. In connection with its products, Gucci uses

CASE 2.2 CONTINUES ▶

twenty-one federally registered trademarks (trademark law will be discussed in Chapter 8). Gucci also operates a number of boutiques, some of which are located in California.

Wang Huoqing, a resident of the People's Republic of China, operates numerous Web sites. When Gucci discovered that Wang Huoqing's Web sites offered for sale counterfeit goods—products bearing Gucci's trademarks but not genuine Gucci articles—it hired a private investigator in San Jose, California, to buy goods from the Web sites. The investigator purchased a wallet that was labeled Gucci but was counterfeit. Gucci filed a trademark infringement lawsuit against Wang Huoqing in a federal district court in California seeking damages and an injunction to prevent further infringement. Wang Huoqing was notified of the lawsuit via e-mail (see the discussion of *service of process* on page 00) but did not appear in court. Gucci asked the court to enter a default judgment—that is, a judgment entered when the defendant fails to appear. First, however, the court had to determine whether it had personal jurisdiction over Wang Huoqing based on the Internet sales.

**DECISION AND RATIONALE** The U.S. District Court for the Northern District of California held that it had personal jurisdiction over the foreign defendant, Huoqing. The court reasoned that the due process clause allows a federal court to exercise jurisdiction over a defendant who has had sufficient minimum contacts with the court's forum—the place where the court exercises jurisdiction. Specifically, jurisdiction exists when (1) the nonresident defendant engages in some act or transaction with the forum "by which he purposefully avails himself of the privilege of conducting activities in the forum, thereby invoking the benefits and protections of its laws; (2) the claim must be one which arises out of or results from the defendant's forum-related activities; and (3) exercise of jurisdiction must be reasonable."

To determine whether Huoqing had purposefully conducted business activities in Gucci's district, the court used a sliding-scale analysis. Under this analysis, passive Web sites do not create sufficient contacts for such a finding, but interactive sites may do so. Huoqing's Web sites were fully interactive. In addition, Gucci presented evidence that Huoqing had advertised and sold the counterfeited goods within the court's district, and that he had made one actual sale within the district—the sale to Gucci's private investigator. The court therefore entered a default judgment against Huoqing and granted Gucci an injunction.

**WHAT IF THE FACTS WERE DIFFERENT?** *Suppose that Gucci had not presented evidence that Wang Huoqing had made one actual sale through his Web site to a resident (the private investigator) of the court's district. Would the court still have found that it had personal jurisdiction over Wang Huoqing? Why or why not?*

**THE LEGAL ENVIRONMENT DIMENSION** *Is it relevant to the analysis of jurisdiction that Gucci America's principal place of business is in New York rather than California? Explain.*

# Venue

Jurisdiction has to do with whether a court has authority to hear a case involving specific persons, property, or subject matter. **Venue**[12] is concerned with the most appropriate location for a trial. For instance, two state courts (or two federal courts) may have the authority to exercise jurisdiction over a case. Nonetheless, it may be more appropriate or convenient to hear the case in one court than in the other.

The concept of venue reflects the policy that a court trying a case should be in the geographic neighborhood (usually the county) where the incident occurred or where the parties reside. Venue in a civil case typically is where the defendant resides, whereas venue in a criminal case normally is where the crime occurred. Pretrial publicity or other factors, though, may require a change of venue to another community, especially in criminal cases in which the defendant's right to a fair and impartial jury has been impaired.

▶ **Example 2.6** Police raid a compound of religious polygamists in Texas and remove many children from the ranch. Authorities suspect that some of the girls were being sexually and physically abused. The raid receives a great deal of media attention, and people living in the nearby towns would likely be influenced by this publicity. If the government files criminal charges against a member of the religious sect, that individual may request a change of venue to another location. ◀

---

12. Pronounced *ven-yoo*.

---

## CONCEPT SUMMARY 2.1
### Jurisdiction

| TYPE OF JURISDICTION | DESCRIPTION |
| --- | --- |
| Personal | Exists when a defendant is located in the territorial boundaries within which a court has the right and power to decide cases. Jurisdiction may be exercised over out-of-state defendants under state long arm statutes. Courts have jurisdiction over corporate defendants that do business within the state, as well as corporations that advertise, sell, or place goods into the stream of commerce in the state. |
| Property | Exists when the property that is subject to a lawsuit is located within the territorial boundaries within which a court has the right and power to decide cases. |
| Subject Matter | Limits the court's jurisdictional authority to particular types of cases.<br>1. *Limited jurisdiction*—Exists when a court is limited to a specific subject matter, such as probate or divorce.<br>2. *General jurisdiction*—Exists when a court can hear cases involving a broad array of issues. |
| Original | Exists with courts that have the authority to hear a case for the first time (trial courts). |
| Appellate | Exists with courts of appeal and review. Generally, appellate courts do not have original jurisdiction. |
| Federal | 1. *Federal questions*—A federal court can exercise jurisdiction when the plaintiff's cause of action is based at least in part on the U.S. Constitution, a treaty, or a federal law.<br>2. *Diversity of citizenship*—A federal court can exercise jurisdiction in cases between citizens of different states when the amount in controversy exceeds $75,000 (or in cases between a foreign country and citizens of a state or of different states and in cases between citizens of a state and citizens or subjects of a foreign country). |
| Concurrent | Exists when both federal and state courts have authority to hear the same case. |
| Exclusive | Exists when only state courts or only federal courts have authority to hear a case. |
| Jurisdiction in Cyberspace | The courts have developed a sliding-scale standard to use in determining when jurisdiction over a Web site owner or operator in another state is proper. |

---

Note, though, that venue has lost some significance in today's world because of the Internet and 24/7 news reporting. Courts now rarely grant requests for a change of venue. Because everyone has instant access to all information about a purported crime, courts reason that no community is more or less informed or prejudiced for or against a defendant.

## Standing to Sue

Before a party can bring a lawsuit to court, that party must have **standing to sue,** or a sufficient stake in a matter to justify seeking relief through the court system. Standing means that the party that filed the action in court has a legally protected interest at stake in the litigation. At times, a person can have standing to sue on behalf of another person, such as a minor (child) or a mentally incompetent person.

Standing can be broken down into three elements:

1. *Harm.* The party bringing the action must have suffered or will imminently suffer harm—an invasion of a legally protected interest. The controversy must be real and substantial rather than hypothetical.
2. *Causation.* There must be a causal connection between the conduct complained of and the injury.
3. *Remedy.* It must be likely, as opposed to merely speculative, that a favorable court decision will remedy, or make up for, the injury suffered.

▶ **Case in Point 2.7**  The federal government's Legal Services Corporation (LSC) subsidizes legal services for people who cannot afford them. LSC restricts the use of its funds to certain purposes. In an attempt to cut costs, the state of Oregon tried to consolidate some of its legal assistance programs with similar programs provided by other organizations, including LSC. LSC did not approve, however, because Oregon's plan would integrate programs receiving federal funds with programs that engaged in restricted activities.

Oregon filed a suit against LSC, alleging that the state's ability to provide legal services to its citizens was frustrated, but the court dismissed the suit. Oregon had not accepted any federal funds and was not injured by the federal government's decision to subsidize certain private activities. The state had no standing to sue the federal government over federal subsidies to private parties.[13] ◄

## SECTION 3
# THE STATE AND FEDERAL COURT SYSTEMS

As mentioned earlier in this chapter, each state has its own court system. Additionally, there is a system of federal courts. Although no two state court systems are exactly the same, the right-hand side of Exhibit 2–2 below illustrates the basic organizational framework characteristic of the court systems in many states. The exhibit also shows how the federal court system is structured. We turn now to an examination of these court systems, beginning with the state courts.

---

13. *Oregon v. Legal Services Corp.*, 552 F.3d 965 (9th Cir. 2009).

## The State Court Systems

Typically, a state court system includes several levels, or tiers, of courts, as shown in Exhibit 2–2. State courts may include (1) trial courts of limited jurisdiction, (2) trial courts of general jurisdiction, (3) appellate courts (intermediate appellate courts), and (4) the state's highest court (often called the state supreme court).

Generally, any person who is a party to a lawsuit has the opportunity to plead the case before a trial court and then, if he or she loses, before at least one level of appellate court. Finally, if the case involves a federal statute or federal constitutional issue, the decision of a state supreme court on that issue may be further appealed to the United States Supreme Court. (See this chapter's *Managerial Strategy* feature on the facing page for a discussion of how state budget cuts are making it more difficult to bring cases in some state courts.)

The states use various methods to select judges for their courts. Usually, voters elect judges, but in some states judges are appointed. For instance, in Iowa, the governor appoints judges, and then the general population decides whether to confirm their appointment in the next general election. The states usually specify the number of years that judges will serve. In contrast, as you will read shortly, judges in the federal court system are appointed by the president of the United States and, if they are confirmed by the Senate, hold office for life—unless they engage in blatantly illegal conduct.

**TRIAL COURTS** Trial courts are exactly what their name implies—courts in which trials are held and tes-

**EXHIBIT 2–2** **The State and Federal Court Systems**

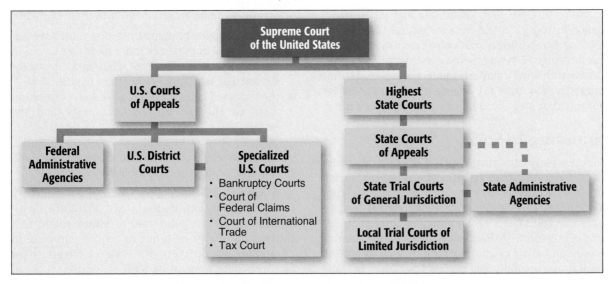

# MANAGERIAL STRATEGY

## Budget Cuts for State Courts Can Affect Businesses

In the United States, businesses use the courts far more than anyone else. Most civil court cases involve a business suing another business for breach of contract or fraud, for instance. Additionally, when one company fails to pay another company for products or services, the unpaid company will often turn to the court system. If that firm does not have ready access to the courts, its financial stability can be put at risk.

### Court Budgets Have Been Reduced

According to the National Center for State Courts, since 2008 forty-two state legislatures have reduced funding for their state courts. California's courts have experienced the steepest cuts—$844 million from their annual budget since 2011. Recently, the Alabama legislature cut its court funding by almost 9 percent. As a result, the state's chief justice ordered courthouses to close on Fridays. The number of weeks that jury trials are available to civil litigants in Alabama has been reduced by 50 percent.

### Intellectual Property Cases Take Longer to Resolve

Today, the value of a company's intellectual property, such as its copyrights and patents, often exceeds the value of its physical property. Not surprisingly, disputes over intellectual property have grown in number and importance. As a result of the court budget cuts, these disputes also take longer to resolve. In California, for example, a typical patent lawsuit used to last twelve months. Today, that same lawsuit might take three to five years.

Investors are reluctant to invest in a company that is the object of a patent or copyright lawsuit because they fear that if the company loses, it may lose the rights to its most valuable product. Consequently, when litigation drags on for years, some companies may suffer because investors abandon them even though the companies are otherwise healthy.

### Other Types of Litigation Take Longer, Too

Other types of lawsuits are also taking longer to conclude. Now attorneys must tell businesses to consider not only the cost of bringing a lawsuit, but also the length of time involved. The longer the litigation lasts, the larger the legal bills and the greater the drain on company employees' time. Roy Weinstein, managing director of Micronomics in California, argues that the economic impact of court delays on businesses is substantial. During the years that a lawsuit can take, some businesses find that they cannot expand or hire new employees, and they are reluctant to spend on additional marketing and advertising.

In fact, it is not unusual for a company to win its case but end up going out of business. As a result of putting its business on hold for years, the company becomes insolvent.

### Some Meritorious Cases Are Never Filed

Facing long delays in litigation with potential negative effects on their companies,  business managers are becoming reluctant to bring lawsuits, even when their cases clearly have merit. In Alabama, for instance, the number of civil cases filed has dropped by more than a third in the last few years. Judge J. Scott Vowell of Jefferson County attributes this decline to delays and higher court costs.

## MANAGERIAL IMPLICATIONS

Before bringing a lawsuit, a manager must now take into account the possibility of long delays before the case is resolved. A cost-benefit analysis for undertaking litigation must include the delays in the calculations. Managers can no longer just stand on principle because they know that they are right and that they will win a lawsuit. They have to look at the bigger picture, which includes substantial court delays.

## BUSINESS QUESTIONS

*1.* *What are some of the costs of increased litigation delays caused by court budget cuts?*

*2.* *In response to budget cuts, many states have increased their filing fees. Is this fair? Why or why not?*

---

timony is taken. State trial courts have either general or limited jurisdiction.

***General Jurisdiction.*** Trial courts that have general jurisdiction as to subject matter may be called county, district, superior, or circuit courts.[14] State trial courts of general jurisdiction have jurisdiction over a wide variety of subjects, including both civil disputes and

---

**14.** The name in Ohio and Pennsylvania is Court of Common Pleas. The name in New York is Supreme Court, Trial Division.

criminal prosecutions. In some states, trial courts of general jurisdiction may hear appeals from courts of limited jurisdiction.

*Limited Jurisdiction.* Courts of limited jurisdiction as to subject matter are generally inferior trial courts or minor judiciary courts. Limited jurisdiction courts might include local municipal courts (which could also have separate traffic courts and drug courts) and domestic relations courts (which handle divorce and child-custody disputes).

**Small claims courts** are inferior trial courts that hear only civil cases involving claims of less than a certain amount, such as $5,000 (the amount varies from state to state). Procedures in small claims courts are generally informal, and lawyers are not required (in a few states, lawyers are not even allowed). Decisions of small claims courts and municipal courts may sometimes be appealed to a state trial court of general jurisdiction.

A few states have also established Islamic law courts, which are courts of limited jurisdiction that serve the American Muslim community. These courts decide cases with reference to the *sharia,* a system of law used in most Islamic countries that is derived from the Qur'an and the sayings and doings of Muhammad and his followers.

*Appellate, or Reviewing, Courts.* Every state has at least one court of appeals (appellate court, or reviewing court), which may be an intermediate appellate court or the state's highest court. About three-fourths of the states have intermediate appellate courts.

Generally, courts of appeals do not conduct new trials, in which evidence is submitted to the court and witnesses are examined. Rather, an appellate court panel of three or more judges reviews the record of the case on appeal, which includes a transcript of the trial proceedings. The appellate court hears arguments from attorneys and determines whether the trial court committed an error.

Reviewing courts focus on questions of law, not questions of fact. A **question of fact** deals with what really happened in regard to the dispute being tried—such as whether a party actually burned a flag. A **question of law** concerns the application or interpretation of the law—such as whether flag-burning is a form of speech protected by the First Amendment to the U.S. Constitution. Only a judge, not a jury, can rule on questions of law.

Appellate courts normally defer (or give weight) to the trial court's findings on questions of fact because the trial court judge and jury were in a better position to evaluate testimony. The trial court judge and jury can directly observe witnesses' gestures, demeanor, and other nonverbal behavior during the trial. An appellate court cannot.

**HIGHEST STATE COURTS** The highest appellate court in a state is usually called the supreme court but may be designated by some other name. For instance, in both New York and Maryland, the highest state court is called the Court of Appeals. The highest state court in Maine and Massachusetts is the Supreme Judicial Court, and in West Virginia, it is the Supreme Court of Appeals.

The decisions of each state's highest court on all questions of state law are final. Only when issues of federal law are involved can the United States Supreme Court overrule a decision made by a state's highest court. ▶ **Example 2.8** A city enacts an ordinance that prohibits citizens from engaging in door-to-door advocacy without first registering with the mayor's office and receiving a permit. A religious group then sues the city, arguing that the law violates the freedoms of speech and religion guaranteed by the First Amendment. If the state supreme court upholds the law, the group could appeal the decision to the United States Supreme Court—because a constitutional (federal) issue is involved. ◀

## The Federal Court System

The federal court system is basically a three-tiered model consisting of (1) U.S. district courts (trial courts of general jurisdiction) and various courts of limited jurisdiction, (2) U.S. courts of appeals (intermediate courts of appeals), and (3) the United States Supreme Court.

Unlike state court judges, who are usually elected, federal court judges—including the justices of the Supreme Court—are appointed by the president of the United States, subject to confirmation by the U.S. Senate. All federal judges receive lifetime appointments under Article III of the U.S. Constitution, which states that federal judges "hold their offices during good Behaviour." In the entire history of the United States, only seven federal judges have been removed from office through impeachment proceedings.

**U.S. DISTRICT COURTS** At the federal level, the equivalent of a state trial court of general jurisdiction is the district court. U.S. district courts have original jurisdiction in matters involving a federal question and concurrent jurisdiction with state courts when diversity jurisdiction exists. Federal cases typically originate in district courts. There are other federal courts with original, but special (or limited), jurisdiction, such as the federal bankruptcy courts and others shown in Exhibit 2–2 on page 34.

There is at least one federal district court in every state. The number of judicial districts can vary over time, primarily owing to population changes and corresponding changes in caseloads. Today there are ninety-four federal judicial districts. Exhibit 2–3 below shows the boundaries of both the U.S. district courts and the U.S. courts of appeals (discussed next).

**U.S. COURTS OF APPEALS** In the federal court system, there are thirteen U.S. courts of appeals—referred to as U.S. circuit courts of appeals. Twelve of the federal courts of appeals (including the Court of Appeals for the D.C. Circuit) hear appeals from the federal district courts located within their respective judicial circuits,

or geographic boundaries (see Exhibit 2–3 below).[15] The Court of Appeals for the Thirteenth Circuit, called the Federal Circuit, has national appellate jurisdiction over certain types of cases, such as those involving patent law and those in which the U.S. government is a defendant.

The decisions of a circuit court of appeals are binding on all courts within the circuit court's jurisdiction and are final in most cases, but appeal to the United States Supreme Court is possible.

**THE UNITED STATES SUPREME COURT** The highest level of the three-tiered federal court system is the United States Supreme Court. According to the U.S. Constitution, there is only one national Supreme Court. All other courts in the federal system are considered "inferior." Congress is empowered to create other inferior courts as it deems necessary. The

---

**15.** Historically, judges were required to "ride the circuit" and hear appeals in different courts around the country, which is how the name "circuit court" came about.

## EXHIBIT 2-3   Geographic Boundaries of the U.S. Courts of Appeals and U.S. District Courts

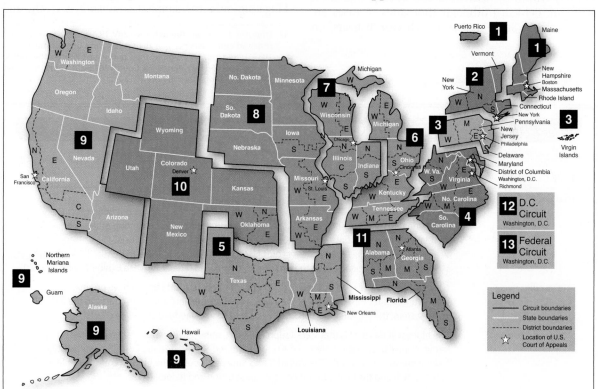

Source: Administrative Office of the United States Courts.

inferior courts that Congress has created include the second tier in our model—the U.S. circuit courts of appeals—as well as the district courts and the various federal courts of limited, or specialized, jurisdiction.

The United States Supreme Court consists of nine justices. Although the Supreme Court has original, or trial, jurisdiction in rare instances (set forth in Article III, Sections 1 and 2), most of its work is as an appeals court. The Supreme Court can review any case decided by any of the federal courts of appeals. It also has appellate authority over cases involving federal questions that have been decided in the state courts. The Supreme Court is the final authority on the Constitution and federal law.

***Appeals to the Supreme Court.*** To bring a case before the Supreme Court, a party requests the Court to issue a writ of *certiorari*.[16] A **writ of *certiorari*** is an order issued by the Supreme Court to a lower court requiring the latter to send it the record of the case for review. The Court will not issue a writ unless at least four of the nine justices approve of it. This is called the **rule of four.**

Whether the Court will issue a writ of *certiorari* is entirely within its discretion, and most petitions for writs are denied. (Although thousands of cases are filed with the Supreme Court each year, it hears, on average, fewer than one hundred of these cases.)[17] A denial of the request to issue a writ of *certiorari* is not a decision on the merits of the case, nor does it indicate agreement with the lower court's opinion. Also, denial of the writ has no value as a precedent. Denial simply means that the lower court's decision remains the law in that jurisdiction.

***Petitions Granted by the Court.*** Typically, the Court grants petitions in cases that raise important constitutional questions or when the lower courts have issued conflicting decisions on a significant issue. The justices, however, never explain their reasons for hearing certain cases and not others, so it is difficult to predict which type of case the Court might select.

See *Concept Summary 2.2* below to review the courts in the federal and state court systems.

### SECTION 4
# ALTERNATIVE DISPUTE RESOLUTION

**Litigation**—the process of resolving a dispute through the court system—is expensive and time consuming. Litigating even the simplest complaint is costly, and

---

16. Pronounced sur-shee-uh-*rah*-ree.

17. From the mid-1950s through the early 1990s, the Supreme Court reviewed more cases per year than it has since then. In the Court's 1982–1983 term, for example, the Court issued written opinions in 151 cases. In contrast, during the Court's 2012–2013 term, the Court issued written opinions in only 79 cases.

---

| **CONCEPT SUMMARY 2.2** | |
|---|---|
| **Types of Courts** | |
| **TYPE OF COURT** | **DESCRIPTION** |
| **Trial Courts** | Trial courts are courts of original jurisdiction in which actions are initiated.<br>1. *State courts*—Courts of general jurisdiction can hear any case that has not been specifically designated for another court. Courts of limited jurisdiction include, among others, domestic relations courts, probate courts, municipal courts, and small claims courts.<br>2. *Federal courts*—The federal district court is the equivalent of the state trial court. Federal courts of limited jurisdiction include the bankruptcy courts and others shown in Exhibit 2–2 on page 00. |
| **Intermediate Appellate Courts** | Courts of appeals are reviewing courts. Generally, appellate courts do not have original jurisdiction. About three-fourths of the states have intermediate appellate courts. In the federal court system, the U.S. circuit courts of appeals are the intermediate appellate courts. |
| **Supreme Courts** | The highest state court is that state's supreme court, although it may be called by some other name. Appeal from state supreme courts to the United States Supreme Court is possible only if a federal question is involved. The United States Supreme Court is the highest court in the federal court system and the final authority on the Constitution and federal law. |

because of the backlog of cases pending in many courts, several years may pass before a case is actually tried. For these and other reasons, more and more businesspersons are turning to **alternative dispute resolution (ADR)** as a means of settling their disputes.

The great advantage of ADR is its flexibility. Methods of ADR range from the parties sitting down together and attempting to work out their differences to multinational corporations agreeing to resolve a dispute through a formal hearing before a panel of experts. Normally, the parties themselves can control how they will attempt to settle their dispute. They can decide what procedures will be used, whether a neutral third party will be present or make a decision, and whether that decision will be legally binding or nonbinding. ADR also offers more privacy than court proceedings and allows disputes to be resolved relatively quickly.

Today, more than 90 percent of civil lawsuits are settled before trial using some form of ADR. Indeed, most states either require or encourage parties to undertake ADR prior to trial. Many federal courts have instituted ADR programs as well. In the following pages, we examine the basic forms of ADR.

## Negotiation

The simplest form of ADR is **negotiation,** a process in which the parties attempt to settle their dispute informally, with or without attorneys to represent them. Attorneys frequently advise their clients to negotiate a settlement voluntarily before they proceed to trial. Parties may even try to negotiate a settlement during a trial or after the trial but before an appeal.

Negotiation traditionally involves just the parties themselves and (typically) their attorneys. The attorneys, though, are advocates—they are obligated to put their clients' interests first.

## Mediation

In **mediation,** a neutral third party acts as a mediator and works with both sides in the dispute to facilitate a resolution. The mediator normally talks with the parties separately as well as jointly, emphasizes points of agreement, and helps the parties to evaluate their options.

Although the mediator may propose a solution (called a mediator's proposal), he or she does not make a decision resolving the matter. The mediator, who need not be a lawyer, usually charges a fee for his or her services (which can be split between the parties). States that require parties to undergo ADR before trial often offer mediation as one of the ADR options or (as in Florida) the only option.

One of the biggest advantages of mediation is that it is less adversarial than litigation. In mediation, the mediator takes an active role and attempts to bring the parties together so that they can come to a mutually satisfactory resolution. The mediation process tends to reduce the antagonism between the disputants, allowing them to resume their former relationship while minimizing hostility. For this reason, mediation is often the preferred form of ADR for disputes between business partners, employers and employees, or other parties involved in long-term relationships.

## Arbitration

A more formal method of ADR is **arbitration,** in which an arbitrator (a neutral third party or a panel of experts) hears a dispute and imposes a resolution on the parties. Arbitration differs from other forms of ADR in that the third party hearing the dispute makes a decision for the parties. Exhibit 2–4 on the following page outlines the basic differences among the three traditional forms of ADR.

Usually, the parties in arbitration agree that the third party's decision will be *legally binding,* although the parties can also agree to *nonbinding* arbitration. (Arbitration that is mandated by the courts often is not binding on the parties.) In nonbinding arbitration, the parties can go forward with a lawsuit if they do not agree with the arbitrator's decision.

In some respects, formal arbitration resembles a trial, although usually the procedural rules are much less restrictive than those governing litigation. In a typical arbitration, the parties present opening arguments and ask for specific remedies. Both sides present evidence and may call and examine witnesses. The arbitrator then renders a decision.

**THE ARBITRATOR'S DECISION** The arbitrator's decision is called an **award.** It is usually the final word on the matter. Although the parties may appeal an arbitrator's decision, a court's review of the decision will be much more restricted in scope than an appellate court's review of a trial court's decision. The general view is that because the parties were free to frame the issues and set the powers of the arbitrator at the outset, they cannot complain about the results. A court will set aside an award only in the event of one of the following:

1. The arbitrator's conduct or "bad faith" substantially prejudiced the rights of one of the parties.
2. The award violates an established public policy.

**EXHIBIT 2-4 Basic Differences in the Traditional Forms of ADR**

| Type of ADR | Description | Neutral Third Party Present | Who Decides the Resolution |
|---|---|---|---|
| **Negotiation** | Parties meet informally with or without their attorneys and attempt to agree on a resolution. This is the simplest and least expensive method of ADR. | No | The parties themselves reach a resolution. |
| **Mediation** | A neutral third party meets with the parties and emphasizes points of agreement to bring them toward resolution of their dispute.<br>1. This method of ADR reduces hostility between the parties.<br>2. Mediation is preferred for resolving disputes between business partners, employers and employees, or others involved in long-term relationships. | Yes | The parties, but the mediator may suggest or propose a resolution. |
| **Arbitration** | The parties present their arguments and evidence before an arbitrator at a hearing, and the arbitrator renders a decision resolving the parties' dispute.<br>1. This ADR method is the most formal and resembles a court proceeding because some rules of evidence apply.<br>2. The parties are free to frame the issues and set the powers of the arbitrator.<br>3. If the parties agree that the arbitration is binding, then the parties' right to appeal the decision is limited. | Yes | The arbitrator imposes a resolution on the parties that may be either binding or nonbinding. |

3. The arbitrator exceeded her or his powers—that is, arbitrated issues that the parties did not agree to submit to arbitration.

**ARBITRATION CLAUSES** Almost any commercial matter can be submitted to arbitration. Frequently, parties include an **arbitration clause** in a contract (a written agreement—see Chapter 11) specifying that any dispute arising under the contract will be resolved through arbitration rather than through the court system. Parties can also agree to arbitrate a dispute *after* it arises.

**ARBITRATION STATUTES** Most states have statutes (often based, in part, on the Uniform Arbitration Act of 1955) under which arbitration clauses will be enforced.

Some state statutes compel arbitration of certain types of disputes, such as those involving public employees.

At the federal level, the Federal Arbitration Act (FAA), enacted in 1925, enforces arbitration clauses in contracts involving maritime activity and interstate commerce. Because of the breadth of the commerce clause (see Chapter 4), arbitration agreements involving transactions only slightly connected to the flow of interstate commerce may fall under the FAA. The FAA established a national policy favoring arbitration.

In the following case, the parties had agreed to arbitrate disputes involving their contract, but a state law allowed one party to void a contractual provision that required arbitration outside the state. The court had to decide if the FAA *preempted* (took priority over, or blocked—see Chapter 4) the state law.

## CASE 2.3

### Cleveland Construction, Inc. v. Levco Construction, Inc.
Court of Appeals of Texas, First District, 359 S.W.3d 843 (2012).

**BACKGROUND AND FACTS** Cleveland Construction, Inc. (CCI), was the general contractor on a project to build a grocery store in Houston, Texas. CCI hired Levco Construction, Inc., as a subcontractor to perform excavation and grading. The contract included an arbitration provision stating that any disputes

CASE 2.3 CONTINUED       would be resolved by arbitration in Ohio. When a dispute arose between the parties, Levco filed a suit against CCI in a Texas state court. CCI sought to compel arbitration in Ohio under the Federal Arbitration Act (FAA), but a Texas statute allows a party to void a contractual provision that requires arbitration outside Texas. The Texas court granted an emergency motion preventing arbitration. CCI appealed.

**DECISION AND RATIONALE**  The Texas appellate court reversed the trial court, holding that the FAA preempts the Texas statute. The FAA requires courts to enforce valid arbitration agreements, and it "preempts . . . inconsistent state laws . . . under the Supremacy Clause of the United States Constitution." In this case, the Texas statute provided that an agreement to arbitrate was voidable if it required arbitration outside Texas. Thus, if the court applied the Texas statute, it would void the parties' agreement to arbitrate any disputes in Ohio. Voiding the agreement, the court found, "would undermine the declared federal policy of rigorous enforcement of arbitration agreements." The court held that the parties had a valid arbitration agreement because the FAA preempted the Texas statute.  Therefore, CCI could compel arbitration in Ohio.

**THE LEGAL ENVIRONMENT DIMENSION**  *How would business be affected if each state could pass a statute, like the one in Texas, allowing parties to void out-of-state arbitration?*

**THE SOCIAL DIMENSION**  *Considering the relative bargaining power of the parties, was it fair to enforce the arbitration clause in this contract? Why or why not?*

---

**THE ISSUE OF ARBITRABILITY**  The terms of an arbitration agreement can limit the types of disputes that the parties agree to arbitrate. Disputes can arise, however, when the parties do not specify limits or when the parties disagree on whether the particular matter is covered by their arbitration agreement.

When one party files a lawsuit to compel arbitration, it is up to the court to resolve the issue of *arbitrability*. That is, the court must decide whether the matter is one that must be resolved through arbitration.

If the court finds that the subject matter in controversy is covered by the agreement to arbitrate, then a party may be compelled to arbitrate the dispute. Usually, a court will allow the claim to be arbitrated if the court finds that the relevant statute (the state arbitration statute or the FAA) does not exclude such claims.

No party, however, will be ordered to submit a particular dispute to arbitration unless the court is convinced that the party has consented to do so. Additionally, the courts will not compel arbitration if it is clear that the arbitration rules and procedures are inherently unfair to one of the parties.

**MANDATORY ARBITRATION IN THE EMPLOYMENT CONTEXT**  A significant question for businesspersons has concerned mandatory arbitration clauses in employment contracts. Many employees claim they are at a disadvantage when they are forced, as a condition of being hired, to agree to arbitrate all disputes and thus waive their rights under statutes designed to protect employees. The United States

Supreme Court, however, has held that mandatory arbitration clauses in employment contracts are generally enforceable.

▶ **Case in Point 2.9**  In a landmark decision, *Gilmer v. Interstate Johnson Lane Corp.*,[18] the Supreme Court held that a claim brought under a federal statute prohibiting age discrimination could be subject to arbitration. The Court concluded that the employee had waived his right to sue when he agreed, as part of a required application to be a securities representative, to arbitrate "any dispute, claim, or controversy" relating to his employment. ◀

Compulsory arbitration agreements often spell out the rules for a mandatory proceeding. For example, an agreement may address in detail the amount and payment of filing fees and other expenses. Employment-related agreements often require the parties to split the costs, but some courts have overturned those provisions when an individual worker lacked the ability to pay.[19]

## Other Types of ADR

The three forms of ADR just discussed are the oldest and traditionally the most commonly used forms. In addition, a variety of new types of ADR have emerged in recent years, including those described here.

---

18. 500 U.S. 20, 111 S.Ct. 1647, 114 L.Ed.2d 26 (1991).
19. See, for example, *Davis v. O'Melveny & Myers, LLC*, 485 F.3d 1066 (9th Cir. 2007); and *Nagrampa v. MailCoups, Inc.*, 469 F.3d 1257 (9th Cir. 2006).

1. In **early neutral case evaluation,** the parties select a neutral third party (generally an expert in the subject matter of the dispute) and then explain their respective positions to that person. The case evaluator assesses the strengths and weaknesses of each party's claims.

2. In a **mini-trial,** each party's attorney briefly argues the party's case before the other party and a panel of representatives from each side who have the authority to settle the dispute. Typically, a neutral third party (usually an expert in the area being disputed) acts as an adviser. If the parties fail to reach an agreement, the adviser renders an opinion as to how a court would likely decide the issue.

3. Numerous federal courts now hold **summary jury trials,** in which the parties present their arguments and evidence and the jury renders a verdict. The jury's verdict is not binding, but it does act as a guide to both sides in reaching an agreement during the mandatory negotiations that immediately follow the trial.

4. Other alternatives being employed by the courts include summary procedures for commercial litigation and the appointment of special masters to assist judges in deciding complex issues.

## Providers of ADR Services

Both government agencies and private organizations provide ADR services. A major provider of ADR services is the **American Arbitration Association (AAA).** The AAA was founded in 1926 and now handles more than 200,000 claims a year in its numerous offices worldwide.

Cases brought before the AAA are heard by an expert or a panel of experts in the area relating to the dispute and are usually settled quickly. Generally, about half of the panel members are lawyers. To cover its costs, the AAA charges a fee, paid by the party filing the claim. In addition, each party to the dispute pays a specified amount for each hearing day, as well as a special additional fee in cases involving personal injuries or property loss.

Hundreds of for-profit firms around the country also provide dispute-resolution services. Typically, these firms hire retired judges to conduct arbitration hearings or otherwise assist parties in settling their disputes. The judges follow procedures similar to those of the federal courts and use similar rules. Usually, each party to the dispute pays a filing fee and a designated fee for a hearing session or conference.

## Online Dispute Resolution

An increasing number of companies and organizations are offering dispute-resolution services using the Internet. The settlement of disputes in these online forums is known as **online dispute resolution (ODR).** The disputes resolved in these forums have most commonly involved rights to domain names (Web site addresses—see Chapter 9) or the quality of goods sold via the Internet, including goods sold through Internet auction sites.

ODR may be best for resolving small- to medium-sized business liability claims, which may not be worth the expense of litigation or traditional ADR methods. Rules being developed in online forums may ultimately become a code of conduct for everyone who does business in cyberspace. Most online forums do not automatically apply the law of any specific jurisdiction. Instead, results are often based on general, more universal legal principles. As with offline methods of dispute resolution, any party may appeal to a court at any time if the ODR is nonbinding arbitration.

Some cities use ODR as a means of resolving claims against them. ▶ **Example 2.10**   New York City uses Cybersettle.com to resolve auto accident, sidewalk, and other personal-injury claims made against the city. Parties with complaints submit their demands, and the city submits its offers confidentially online. If an offer exceeds a demand, the claimant keeps half the difference as a bonus, plus the original claim. ◀

### SECTION 5
# INTERNATIONAL DISPUTE RESOLUTION

Businesspersons who engage in international business transactions normally take special precautions to protect themselves in the event that a party with whom they are dealing in another country breaches an agreement. Often, parties to international contracts include special clauses in their contracts providing for how disputes arising under the contracts will be resolved.

## Forum-Selection and Choice-of-Law Clauses

As you will read in Chapter 20, parties to international sales and lease transactions often include forum-selection and choice-of-law clauses in their contracts. These clauses designate the jurisdiction (court or country) where any dispute arising under the contract will be litigated and which nation's law will be applied.

When an international contract does not include such clauses, any legal proceedings arising under the contract will be more complex and attended by much more uncertainty. For instance, litigation may take place in two or more countries, with each country applying its own national law to the particular transactions.

Furthermore, even if a plaintiff wins a favorable judgment in a lawsuit litigated in the plaintiff's country, the defendant's country could refuse to enforce the court's judgment. As will be discussed in Chapter 24, the judgment may be enforced in the defendant's country for reasons of courtesy. The United States, for example, will generally enforce a foreign court's decision if it is consistent with U.S. national law and policy. Other nations, however, may not be as accommodating as the United States, and the plaintiff may be left empty-handed.

## Arbitration Clauses

International contracts also often include arbitration clauses that require a neutral third party to decide any contract disputes. In international arbitration proceedings, the third party may be a neutral entity (such as the International Chamber of Commerce), a panel of individuals representing both parties' interests, or some other group or organization.

The United Nations Convention on the Recognition and Enforcement of Foreign Arbitral Awards[20] has been implemented in more than 145 countries, including the United States. This convention assists in the

---

**20.** June 10, 1958, 21 U.S.T. 2517, T.I.A.S. No. 6997 (the "New York Convention").

enforcement of arbitration clauses, as do provisions in specific treaties among nations. The American Arbitration Association provides arbitration services for international as well as domestic disputes.

## International Treaties and Arbitration

International treaties (formal agreements among several nations—see Chapter 24) sometimes also stipulate arbitration for resolving disputes. This is a tactic that has been used in the past to increase foreign investment. ▶ **Example 2.11** In the 1990s, Argentina encouraged foreign investment by forming bilateral investment treaties with other nations, including the United States and France. The treaties required Argentina to protect investors' property rights and provided that any grievances would be settled by arbitration at the International Centre for the Settlement of Investment Disputes (ICSID), which is part of the World Bank. Foreign investment in Argentina skyrocketed, in part, because companies had the security of knowing that disputes would be settled by the ICSID rather than by Argentina's courts.

After Argentina's economy collapsed in 2001, companies that had suffered significant losses filed claims against Argentina with the ICSID. The ICSID, however, resolved most claims in Argentina's favor. The few companies that won awards from the ICSID, such as Philip Morris International, then had to ask courts in Argentina to enforce the judgments. These problems have caused some nations to withdraw from the ICSID. Others, including Australia, have indicated that they will not enter any future trade agreements that require their domestic investors who invest in other countries to submit to arbitration. ◀

## Reviewing: Courts and Alternative Dispute Resolution

Stan Garner resides in Illinois and promotes boxing matches for SuperSports, Inc., an Illinois corporation. Garner created the concept of "Ages" promotion—a three-fight series of boxing matches pitting an older fighter (George Foreman) against a younger fighter. The concept had titles for each of the three fights, including "Battle of the Ages." Garner contacted Foreman and his manager, who both reside in Texas, to sell the idea, and they arranged a meeting in Las Vegas, Nevada. During negotiations, Foreman's manager signed a nondisclosure agreement prohibiting him from disclosing Garner's promotional concepts unless the parties signed a contract. Nevertheless, after negotiations fell through, Foreman used Garner's "Battle of the Ages" concept to promote a subsequent fight. Garner filed

*Continued*

a suit against Foreman and his manager in a federal district court located in Illinois, alleging breach of contract. Using the information presented in the chapter, answer the following questions.

1. On what basis might the federal district court in Illinois exercise jurisdiction in this case?
2. Does the federal district court have original or appellate jurisdiction?
3. Suppose that Garner had filed his action in an Illinois state court. Could an Illinois state court exercise personal jurisdiction over Foreman or his manager? Why or why not?
4. Assume that Garner had filed his action in a Nevada state court. Would that court have had personal jurisdiction over Foreman or his manager? Explain.

**DEBATE THIS . . .** *In this age of the Internet, when people communicate via e-mail, texts, tweets, Facebook, and Skype, is the concept of jurisdiction losing its meaning?*

## Terms and Concepts

alternative dispute resolution (ADR) 39
American Arbitration Association (AAA) 42
arbitration 39
arbitration clause 40
award 39
bankruptcy court 28
concurrent jurisdiction 30
diversity of citizenship 29
early neutral case evaluation 42

exclusive jurisdiction 30
federal question 29
*in personam* jurisdiction 27
*in rem* jurisdiction 27
judicial review 26
jurisdiction 27
litigation 38
long arm statute 27
mediation 39
mini-trial 42
negotiation 39

online dispute resolution (ODR) 42
probate court 28
question of fact 36
question of law 36
rule of four 38
small claims court 36
standing to sue 33
summary jury trial 42
venue 32
writ of *certiorari* 38

## Issue Spotters

1. Sue uses her smartphone to purchase a video security system for her architectural firm from Tipton, Inc., a company that is located in a different state. The system arrives a month after the projected delivery date, is of poor quality, and does not function as advertised. Sue files a suit against Tipton in a state court. Does the court in Sue's state have jurisdiction over Tipton? What factors will the court consider? **(See page 27.)**

2. The state in which Sue resides requires that her dispute with Tipton be submitted to mediation or nonbinding arbitration. If the dispute is not resolved, or if either party disagrees with the decision of the mediator or arbitrator, will a court hear the case? Explain. **(See page 39.)**

• **Check your answers to the Issue Spotters against the answers provided in Appendix E at the end of this text.**

## Business Scenarios

**2–1. Standing.** Jack and Maggie Turton bought a house in Jefferson County, Idaho, located directly across the street from a gravel pit. A few years later, the county converted the pit to a landfill. The landfill accepted many kinds of trash that cause harm to the environment, including major appliances, animal carcasses, containers with hazardous content warnings, leaking car batteries, and waste oil. The Turtons complained to the county, but the county did nothing. The Turtons then filed a lawsuit against the county alleging violations of federal environmental laws pertaining to groundwater contamination and other pollution. Do the Turtons have standing to sue? Why or why not? **(See page 33.)**

**2–2. Jurisdiction.** Marya Callais, a citizen of Florida, was walking along a busy street in Tallahassee, Florida, when a large crate flew off a passing truck and hit her, causing numerous injuries. She experienced a great deal of pain and suffering, incurred significant medical expenses, and could not work for six months. She wants to sue the truck-ing firm for $300,000 in damages. The firm's headquarters are in Georgia, although the company does business in Florida. In what court might Callais bring suit—a Florida state court, a Georgia state court, or a federal court? What factors might influence her decision? **(See page 27.)**

## Business Case Problems

### 2–3. BUSINESS CASE PROBLEM
### WITH SAMPLE ANSWER: Arbitration Clause.

 *Kathleen Lowden sued cellular phone company T-Mobile USA, Inc., contending that its service agreements were not enforceable under Washington state law. Lowden requested that the court allow a class-action suit, in which her claims would extend to similarly affected customers. She contended that T-Mobile had improperly charged her fees beyond the advertised price of service and charged her for roaming calls that should not have been classified as roaming.*

*T-Mobile moved to force arbitration in accordance with the provisions that were clearly set forth in the service agreement. The agreement also specified that no class-action suit could be brought, so T-Mobile also asked the court to dismiss the request for a class-action suit. Was T-Mobile correct that Lowden's only course of action was to file for arbitration personally? Why or why not?* [Lowden v. T-Mobile USA, Inc., *512 F.3d 1213 (9th Cir. 2008)]* **(See page 41.)**

• **For a sample answer to Problem 2–3, go to Appendix F at the end of this text.**

**2–4. Venue.** Brandy Austin used powdered infant formula to feed her infant daughter shortly after her birth. Austin claimed that a can of Nestlé Good Start Supreme Powder Infant Formula was contaminated with *Enterobacter sakazakii* bacteria. The bacteria can cause infections of the bloodstream and central nervous system, in particular, meningitis (inflammation of the tissue surrounding the brain or spinal cord). Austin filed an action against Nestlé in Hennepin County District Court in Minnesota. Nestlé argued for a change of venue because the alleged tortious action on the part of Nestlé occurred in South Carolina. Austin is a South Carolina resident and gave birth to her daughter in that state. Should the case be transferred to a South Carolina venue? Why or why not? [*Austin v. Nestlé USA, Inc.,* 677 F.Supp.2d 1134 (D.Minn. 2009)] **(See page 32.)**

**2–5. Arbitration.** PRM Energy Systems owned patents licensed to Primenergy to use in the United States. Their contract stated that "all disputes" would be settled by arbitration. Kobe Steel of Japan was interested in using the technology represented by PRM's patents. Primenergy agreed to let Kobe use the technology in Japan without telling PRM. When PRM learned about the secret deal, the firm filed a suit against Primenergy for fraud and theft. Does this dispute go to arbitration or to trial? Why? [*PRM Energy Systems v. Primenergy,* 592 F.3d 830 (8th Cir. 2010)] **(See page 40.)**

**2–6. Spotlight on the National Football League—Arbitration.**

 Bruce Matthews played football for the Tennessee Titans. As part of his contract, he agreed to submit any dispute to arbitration. He also agreed that Tennessee law would determine all matters related to workers' compensation. After Matthews retired, he filed a workers' compensation claim in California. The arbitrator ruled that Matthews could pursue his claim in California but only under Tennessee law. Should this award be set aside? Explain. [*National Football League Players Association v. National Football League Management Council,* 2011 WL 1137334 (S.D.Cal. 2011)] **(See page 39.)**

**2–7. Minimum Contacts.** Seal Polymer Industries sold two freight containers of latex gloves to Med-Express, Inc., a company based in North Carolina. When Med-Express failed to pay the $104,000 owed for the gloves, Seal Polymer sued in an Illinois court and obtained a judgment against Med-Express. Med-Express argued that it did not have minimum contacts with Illinois and therefore the Illinois judgment based on personal jurisdiction was invalid. Med-Express stated that it was incorporated under North Carolina law, had its principal place of business in North Carolina, and therefore had no minimum contacts with Illinois. Was this statement alone sufficient to prevent the Illinois judgment from being collected against Med-Express in North Carolina? Why or why not? [*Seal Polymer Industries v. Med-Express, Inc.,* 725 S.E.2d 5 (N.C.App. 2012)] **(See page 27.)**

**2–8. Arbitration.** Horton Automatics and the Industrial Division of the Communications Workers of America, the union that represented Horton's workers, negotiated a collective bargaining agreement. If an employee's discharge for a workplace-rule violation was submitted to arbitration, the agreement limited the arbitrator to determining whether the rule was reasonable and whether the employee violated it. When Horton discharged employee Ruben de la Garza, the union appealed to arbitration. The arbitrator found that de la Garza had violated a reasonable safety rule, but "was not totally convinced" that Horton should have treated the violation more seriously than other rule violations. The arbitrator ordered de la Garza reinstated. Can a court set aside this order? Explain. *[Horton Automatics v. The Industrial Division of the Communications Workers of America, AFL-CIO,* 2013 WL 59204 (5th Cir. 2013)] **(See page 39.)**

**2–9. A QUESTION OF ETHICS: Agreement to Arbitrate.**

 *Nellie Lumpkin, who suffered from various illnesses, including dementia, was admitted to the Picayune Convalescent Center, a nursing home. Because of her mental condition, her daughter, Beverly McDaniel, filled out the admissions paperwork and signed the admissions agreement. It included a clause requiring parties to submit to arbitration any disputes that arose. After Lumpkin left the center two years later, she sued, through her husband, for negligent treatment and malpractice during her* stay. *The center moved to force the matter to arbitration. The trial court held that the arbitration agreement was not enforceable. The center appealed. [Covenant Health & Rehabilitation of Picayune, LP v. Lumpkin, 23 So.3d 1092 (Miss.App. 2009)]* **(See page 41.)**

(a) Should a dispute involving medical malpractice be forced into arbitration? This is a claim of negligent care, not a breach of a commercial contract. Is it ethical for medical facilities to impose such a requirement? Is there really any bargaining over such terms? Discuss fully.

(b) Should a person with limited mental capacity be held to the arbitration clause agreed to by the next-of-kin who signed on behalf of that person? Why or why not?

## Legal Reasoning Group Activity

**2–10. Access to Courts.** Assume that a statute in your state requires that all civil lawsuits involving damages of less than $50,000 be arbitrated. Such a case can be tried in court only if a party is dissatisfied with the arbitrator's decision. The statute also provides that if a trial does not result in an improvement of more than 10 percent in the position of the party who demanded the trial, that party must pay the entire costs of the arbitration proceeding. **(See page 41.)**

(a) One group will argue that the state statute violates litigants' rights of access to the courts and to trial by jury.

(b) Another group will argue that the statute does not violate litigants' rights of access to the courts.

(c) A third group will evaluate how the determination on rights of access would be changed if the statute was part of a pilot program and affected only a few judicial districts in the state.

# CHAPTER 3
# COURT PROCEDURES

Americal and English courts follow the *adversarial system of justice*. Although parties are allowed to represent themselves in court (called *pro se* representation),[1] most parties to lawsuits hire attorneys to repre-sent them. Each lawyer acts as his or her client's advocate, presenting the client's version of the facts in such a way as to convince the judge (or the judge and jury, in a jury trial) that this version is correct.

Most of the judicial procedures that you will read about in the following pages are rooted in the adversarial framework of the American legal sys-tem. In this chapter, after a brief over-view of judicial procedures, we illustrate the steps involved in a lawsuit with a hypothetical civil case (criminal proce-dures will be discussed in Chapter 10). We also discuss how judges are coping with courtroom tweeting in this chap-ter's *Insight into Social Media* feature on page 00.

---

**1.** This right was definitively established in *Faretta v. California*, 422 U.S. 806, 95 S.Ct. 2525, 45 L.Ed.2d 562 (1975).

---

## SECTION 1
## PROCEDURAL RULES

The parties to a lawsuit must comply with the proce-dural rules of the court in which the lawsuit is filed. Although people often think that substantive law determines the outcome of a case, procedural law can have a significant impact on a person's ability to pur-sue a legal claim. Procedural rules provide a frame-work for every dispute and specify what must be done at each stage of the litigation process.

Procedural rules are complex, and they vary from court to court and from state to state. There is a set of federal rules of procedure as well as various sets of rules for state courts. Additionally, the applicable procedures will depend on whether the case is a civil or criminal proceeding. All civil trials held in federal district courts are governed by the **Federal Rules of Civil Procedure (FRCP)**.[2]

## Stages of Litigation

Broadly speaking, the litigation process has three phases: pretrial, trial, and posttrial. Each phase involves specific procedures, as discussed in this chapter. Although civil lawsuits may vary greatly in terms of complexity, cost, and detail, they typically progress through the stages charted in Exhibit 3–1 on the next page.

To illustrate the procedures involved in a civil lawsuit, we will use a simple hypothetical case. The case arose from an automobile accident, which occurred when a car driven by Antonio Carvello, a resident of New Jersey, collided with a car driven by Jill Kirby, a resident of New York. The accident took place at an intersection in New York City. Kirby suffered personal injuries, which caused her to incur medical and hospital expenses as well as lost wages for four months. In all, she calculated that the cost to her of the accident was $100,000.[3] Carvello and Kirby have been unable to agree on a settlement, and Kirby now must decide whether to sue Carvello for the $100,000 compensation she feels she deserves.

## Consulting with an Attorney

As mentioned, rules of procedure often affect the outcome of a dispute—a fact that highlights the

---

**2.** The United States Supreme Court has authority to establish these rules, as spelled out in 28 U.S.C. Sections 2071–2077. Generally, though, the federal judiciary appoints committees that make recom-mendations to the Supreme Court. The Court then publishes any proposed changes in the rules and allows for public comment before finalizing the rules.

**3.** In this example, we are ignoring damages for pain and suffering and for permanent disabilities. Often, plaintiffs in personal-injury cases seek such damages.

**EXHIBIT 3-1   Stages in a Typical Lawsuit**

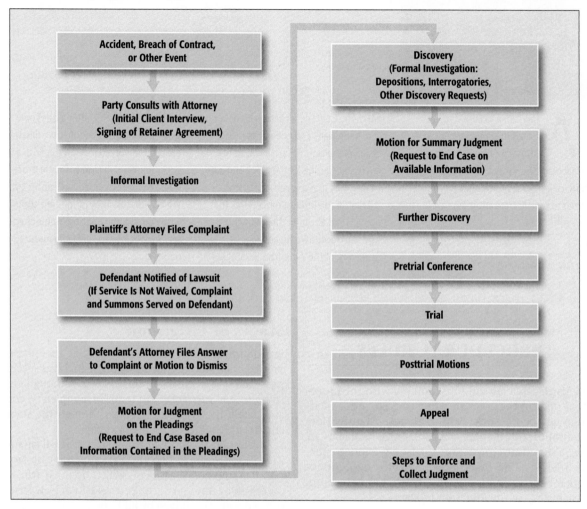

importance of obtaining the advice of counsel. The first step taken by almost anyone contemplating a lawsuit is to seek the guidance of a qualified attorney.[4]

In the hypothetical Kirby-Carvello case, assume that Kirby consults with a lawyer. The attorney will advise her regarding what she can expect in a lawsuit, her probability of success at trial, and the procedures that will be involved. If more than one court would have jurisdiction over the matter, the attorney will also discuss the advantages and disadvantages of filing in a particular court. In addition, the attorney will indicate how long it will take to resolve the dispute

through litigation in a particular court and provide an estimate of the costs involved.

The attorney will also inform Kirby of the legal fees that she will have to pay in an attempt to collect damages from the defendant, Carvello. Attorneys base their fees on such factors as the difficulty of a matter, the amount of time involved, the experience and skill of the attorney in the particular area of the law, and the cost of doing business. In the United States, legal fees range from $175 to $700 per hour or even higher (the average fee is between $200 and $425 per hour). In addition, the client must also pay various expenses related to the case (called "out-of-pocket" costs), such as court filing fees, travel expenses, and the cost of expert witnesses and investigators.

---

4. Normally, you will seek out an attorney who is licensed to practice in your state.

**TYPES OF ATTORNEYS' FEES** For a particular legal matter, an attorney may charge one type of fee or a combination of several types.

1. *Fixed fees* may be charged for the performance of such services as drafting a simple will.
2. *Hourly fees* may be charged for matters that will involve an indeterminate period of time. The amount of time required to bring a case to trial, for instance, probably cannot be precisely estimated in advance.
3. *Contingency fees* are fixed as a percentage (usually between 25 and 40 percent) of a client's recovery in certain types of lawsuits, such as a personal-injury lawsuit.[5] If the lawsuit is unsuccessful, the attorney receives no fee, but the client will have to reimburse the attorney for all out-of-pocket costs incurred.

Because Kirby's claim involves a personal injury, her lawyer will likely take the case on a contingency-fee basis, but she may have to pay an amount up front to cover the court costs. In some cases, the winning party may be able to recover at least some portion of her or his attorneys' fees from the losing party.

**SETTLEMENT CONSIDERATIONS** Once an attorney has been retained, the attorney is required to pursue a resolution of the matter on the client's behalf. Nevertheless, the amount of energy an attorney will spend on a given case is also determined by the time and funds the client wishes to devote to the process. If the client is willing to pay for a lengthy trial and one or more appeals, the attorney may pursue those actions. Often, however, after learning of the substantial costs that litigation entails, a client may decide to pursue a settlement of the claim. Attempts to settle the case may be ongoing throughout the litigation process.

Another important consideration in deciding whether to pursue litigation is the defendant's ability to pay the damages sought. Even if Kirby is awarded damages, it may be difficult to enforce the court's judgment if, for example, the amount exceeds the limits of Carvello's automobile insurance policy. (We will discuss the problems involved in enforcing a judgment later in this chapter.)

# SECTION 2
# PRETRIAL PROCEDURES

The pretrial litigation process involves the filing of the *pleadings,* the gathering of evidence (called *discovery*), and possibly other procedures, such as a pretrial conference and jury selection.

## The Pleadings

The *complaint* and *answer* (and other legal documents discussed below), taken together, are known as the **pleadings.** The pleadings inform each party of the other's claims and specify the issues (disputed questions) involved in the case. Because the rules of procedure vary depending on the jurisdiction of the court, the style and form of the pleadings may be different from those shown in this chapter.

**THE PLAINTIFF'S COMPLAINT** Kirby's action against Carvello commences when her lawyer files a **complaint**[6] with the clerk of the appropriate court. The complaint contains a statement alleging (1) the facts showing that the court has subject-matter and personal jurisdiction, (2) the facts establishing the plaintiff's basis for relief, and (3) the remedy the plaintiff is seeking. Complaints can be lengthy or brief, depending on the complexity of the case and the rules of the jurisdiction.

Exhibit 3–2 on the next page illustrates how a complaint in the Kirby-Carvello case might appear. The complaint asserts facts indicating that the federal district court has subject-matter jurisdiction because of diversity of citizenship. It then gives a brief statement of the facts of the accident and alleges that Carvello negligently drove his vehicle through a red light, striking Kirby's car and causing serious personal injury and property damage. The complaint goes on to state that Kirby is seeking $100,000 in damages, although in some state civil actions the plaintiff need not specify the amount of damages sought.

***Service of Process.*** Before the court can exercise personal jurisdiction over the defendant (Carvello)—in effect, before the lawsuit can begin—the court must

---

5. Note that attorneys may charge a contingency fee only in certain types of cases and are typically prohibited from entering into this type of fee arrangement in criminal cases, divorce cases, and cases involving the distribution of assets after death.

6. Sometimes, the document filed with the court is called a *petition* or a *declaration* instead of a complaint.

**EXHIBIT 3-2  A Typical Complaint**

IN THE UNITED STATES DISTRICT COURT
FOR THE SOUTHERN DISTRICT OF NEW YORK

JILL KIRBY                                                    CIVIL NO. 9-1047

                        Plaintiff,

v.                                                            COMPLAINT

ANTONIO CARVELLO

                        Defendant.

    The plaintiff brings this cause of action against the defendant, alleging as follows:

1. This action is between the plaintiff, who is a resident of the State of New York, and the defendant, who is a resident of the State of New Jersey. There is diversity of citizenship between the parties.
2. The amount in controversy, exclusive of interest and costs, exceeds the sum of $75,000.
3. On September 10th, 2014, the plaintiff, Jill Kirby, was exercising good driving habits and reasonable care in driving her car through the intersection of Boardwalk and Pennsylvania Avenue, New York City, New York, when the defendant, Antonio Carvello, negligently drove his vehicle through a red light at the intersection and collided with the plaintiff's vehicle.
4. As a result of the collision, the plaintiff suffered severe physical injury, which prevented her from working, and property damage to her car.

    WHEREFORE, the plaintiff demands judgment against the defendant for the sum of $100,000 plus interest at the maximum legal rate and the costs of this action.

By _Joseph Roe_

Joseph Roe
Attorney for Plaintiff
100 Main Street
1/3/15                                      New York, New York

have proof that the defendant was notified of the lawsuit. Formally notifying the defendant of a lawsuit is called **service of process.**

The plaintiff must deliver, or serve, a copy of the complaint and a **summons** (a notice requiring the defendant to appear in court and answer the complaint) to the defendant. The summons notifies Carvello that he must file an answer to the complaint within a specified time period (twenty days in the federal courts) or suffer a default judgment against him. A **default judgment** in Kirby's favor would mean that she would be awarded the damages alleged in her complaint because Carvello failed to respond to the allegations. A typical summons is shown in Exhibit 3–3 on the following page.

**Method of Service.** How service of process occurs depends on the rules of the court or jurisdiction in

**EXHIBIT 3-3  A Typical Summons**

```
                    UNITED STATES DISTRICT COURT
              FOR THE SOUTHERN DISTRICT OF NEW YORK

                                   CIVIL ACTION, FILE NO. 9-1047

   JILL KIRBY

                        Plaintiff,

   v.                                         SUMMONS

   ANTONIO CARVELLO

                        Defendant.


To the above-named Defendant:

You are hereby summoned and required to serve upon Joseph Roe,
plaintiff's attorney, whose address is 100 Main Street, New York, NY, an
answer to the complaint which is herewith served upon you, within 20 days
after service of this summons upon you, exclusive of the day of service.
If you fail to do so, judgment by default will be taken against you for
the relief demanded in the complaint.


C. H. Hynek                          January 3, 2015
_____               _____
CLERK                                DATE


John Dolan
_____
BY DEPUTY CLERK
```

which the lawsuit is brought. Under the Federal Rules of Civil Procedure, anyone who is at least eighteen years of age and is not a party to the lawsuit can serve process in federal court cases. In state courts, the process server is often a county sheriff or an employee of an independent company that provides process service in the local area.

Usually, the server hands the summons and complaint to the defendant personally or leaves it at the defendant's residence or place of business. In some states, process can be served by mail if the defendant consents (accepts service). When the defendant cannot be reached, special rules provide for alternative means of service, such as publishing a notice in the local newspaper. In some situations, courts have allowed service of process via e-mail, as long as it is reasonably calculated to provide notice and an opportunity to respond.

In cases involving corporate defendants, the summons and complaint may be served on an officer or on a *registered agent* (representative) of the corporation. The name of a corporation's registered agent can usually be obtained from the secretary of state's office in the state where the company incorporated its business (and, frequently, from the secretary of state's office in any state where the corporation does business).

***Waiver of Formal Service of Process.*** In many instances, the defendant is already aware that a lawsuit is being filed and is willing to waive (give up) her or his right to be served personally. The Federal Rules of Civil Procedure (FRCP) and many states' rules allow defendants to waive formal service of process, provided that certain procedures are followed. Kirby's attorney, for example, could mail to defendant Carvello a copy of the complaint, along with "Waiver of Service of Summons" forms for Carvello to sign. If Carvello signs and returns the forms within thirty days, formal service of process is waived.

Moreover, under the FRCP, defendants who agree to waive formal service of process receive additional time to respond to the complaint (sixty days, instead of twenty days). Some states provide similar incentives to encourage defendants to waive formal service of process and thereby reduce associated costs and foster cooperation between the parties.

**THE DEFENDANT'S RESPONSE** Typically, the defendant's response to the complaint takes the form of an **answer.** In an answer, the defendant either admits or denies each of the allegations in the plaintiff's complaint and may also set forth defenses to those allegations. Under the federal rules, any allegations that are not denied by the defendant will be deemed by the court to have been admitted. If Carvello admits to all of Kirby's allegations in his answer, a judgment will be entered for Kirby. If Carvello denies Kirby's allegations, the matter will proceed further.

***Affirmative Defenses.*** Carvello can also admit the truth of Kirby's complaint but raise new facts to show that he should not be held liable for Kirby's damages. This is called raising an **affirmative defense.** As will be discussed in subsequent chapters, defendants in both civil and criminal cases can raise affirmative defenses. For example, Carvello could assert Kirby's own negligence as a defense by alleging that Kirby was driving negligently at the time of the accident. In some states, a plaintiff's contributory negligence operates as a complete defense. In most states, however, the plaintiff's own negligence constitutes only a partial defense (see Chapter 6).

***Counterclaims.*** Carvello could also deny Kirby's allegations and set forth his own claim that the accident occurred as a result of Kirby's negligence and therefore she owes Carvello for damage to his car. This is appropriately called a counterclaim. If Carvello files a **counterclaim,** Kirby will have to submit an answer to the counterclaim.

## Dismissals and Judgments before Trial

Many actions for which pleadings have been filed never come to trial. The parties may, for example, negotiate a settlement of the dispute at any stage of the litigation process. There are also numerous procedural avenues for disposing of a case without a trial. Many of them involve one or the other party's attempts to get the case dismissed through the use of various motions.

A **motion** is a procedural request submitted to the court by an attorney on behalf of her or his client. When a motion is filed with the court, the filing party must also send to, or personally serve, the opposing party a *notice of motion*. The notice of motion informs the opposing party that the motion has been filed. **Pretrial motions** include the motion to dismiss, the motion for judgment on the pleadings, and the motion for summary judgment, as well as the other motions listed in Exhibit 3–4 on page 54.

**MOTION TO DISMISS** Either party can file a **motion to dismiss** asking the court to dismiss the case for the reasons stated in the motion. Normally, though, it is the defendant who requests dismissal.

A defendant can file a motion to dismiss if the plaintiff's complaint fails to state a claim for which relief (a remedy) can be granted. Such a motion asserts that even if the facts alleged in the complaint are true, they do not give rise to any legal claim against the defendant. For example, if the allegations in Kirby's complaint do not constitute negligence on Carvello's part, Carvello can move to dismiss the case for failure to state a claim. Defendant Carvello could also file a motion to dismiss on the grounds that he was not properly served, that the court lacked jurisdiction, or that the venue was improper.

If the judge grants the motion to dismiss, the plaintiff generally is given time to file an amended complaint. If the judge denies the motion, the suit will go forward, and the defendant must then file an answer. Note that if Carvello wishes to discontinue the suit because, for example, an out-of-court settlement has been reached, he can likewise move for dismissal. The court can also dismiss a case on its own motion.

In the following case, one party filed a complaint against two others, alleging a breach of contract. The defendants filed a motion to dismiss on the ground that the venue was improper. The court denied the motion, and the defendants appealed.

## CASE 3.1

### Espresso Disposition Corp. 1 v. Santana Sales & Marketing Group, Inc.

Florida Court of Appeal, Third District, 105 So.3d 592 (2013).

**BACKGROUND AND FACTS**  Espresso Disposition Corporation 1 and Santana Sales & Marketing Group, Inc., entered into an agreement that included a mandatory *forum-selection clause*—that is, a provision in a contract designating the court or jurisdiction that will decide any disputes arising under the contract. This clause stated that, "the venue with respect to any action pertaining to this Agreement shall be the State of Illinois." When Santana Sales filed a lawsuit against Espresso in a Florida state court, Espresso filed a motion to dismiss based on the agreement's forum-selection clause. Santana responded to the motion to dismiss by claiming that the forum-selection clause had been a mistake. Specifically, Santana said that when the agreement was drafted, another agreement between different parties had been copied, and by mistake, the venue provision had not been changed from Illinois to Florida. The court denied Espresso's motion to dismiss. Espresso appealed.

**DECISION AND RATIONALE**  The state intermediate appellate court reversed the trial court's denial of Espresso's motion to dismiss and remanded the case to the lower court for the entry of an order of dismissal. The appeals court pointed out that Florida had long recognized that forum-selection clauses are presumptively valid. This is because "forum selection clauses provide a degree of certainty to business contracts by obviating [avoiding] jurisdictional struggles and by allowing parties to tailor the dispute resolution mechanism to their particular situation. Moreover, forum selection clauses reduce litigation over venue, thereby conserving judicial resources, reducing business expenses, and lowering consumer prices." The parties seeking to avoid enforcement of a forum-selection clause must show that enforcement would be unjust or unreasonable. The only way to do that is to establish that enforcement "would result in no forum at all."

In this case, clearly Illinois state courts do exist. Here, "the agreement's plain language provides that the venue for any action relating to a controversy under the agreement . . . shall be the state of Illinois. The explicit language unequivocally renders the forum selection clause mandatory.

**THE LEGAL ENVIRONMENT DIMENSION**  *Why did the appellants in this case file a motion to dismiss?*

**THE SOCIAL DIMENSION**  *What impact will the court's decision most likely have on the parties to this dispute? Explain.*

---

**MOTION FOR JUDGMENT ON THE PLEADINGS**  At the close of the pleadings, either party may make a **motion for judgment on the pleadings.** This motion asks the court to decide the issue solely on the pleadings without proceeding to trial. The judge will grant the motion only when there is no dispute over the facts of the case and the sole issue to be resolved is a question of law. For example, in the Kirby-Carvello case, if Carvello had admitted to all of Kirby's allegations in his answer and had raised no affirmative defenses, Kirby could file a motion for judgment on the pleadings.

In deciding a motion for judgment on the pleadings, the judge may consider only the evidence con-

tained in the pleadings. In contrast, in a motion for summary judgment, discussed next, the court may consider evidence outside the pleadings, such as sworn statements and other materials that would be admissible as evidence at trial.

**MOTION FOR SUMMARY JUDGMENT**  Either party can file a **motion for summary judgment,** which asks the court to grant a judgment in that party's favor without a trial. The motion can be made before or during the trial. As with a motion for judgment on the pleadings, a court will grant a motion for summary judgment only if no facts are in dispute and the only question is how the law applies to the facts. In

**EXHIBIT 3-4 Pretrial Motions**

**MOTION TO DISMISS**

A motion normally filed by the defendant in which the defendant asks the court to dismiss the case for a specified reason, such as improper service, lack of personal jurisdiction, or the plaintiff's failure to state a claim for which relief can be granted.

**MOTION TO STRIKE**

A motion filed by the defendant in which the defendant asks the court to strike (delete) certain paragraphs from the complaint. Motions to strike help to clarify the underlying issues that form the basis for the complaint by removing paragraphs that are redundant or irrelevant to the action.

**MOTION TO MAKE MORE DEFINITE AND CERTAIN**

A motion filed by the defendant to compel the plaintiff to clarify the basis of the plaintiff's cause of action. The motion is filed when the defendant believes that the complaint is too vague or ambiguous for the defendant to respond to it in a meaningful way.

**MOTION FOR JUDGMENT ON THE PLEADINGS**

A motion that may be filed by either party in which the party asks the court to enter a judgment in his or her favor based on information contained in the pleadings. A judgment on the pleadings will be made only if there are no facts in dispute and the only question is how the law applies to a set of undisputed facts.

**MOTION TO COMPEL DISCOVERY**

A motion that may be filed by either party in which the party asks the court to compel the other party to comply with a discovery request. If a party refuses to allow the opponent to inspect and copy certain documents, for example, the party requesting the documents may make a motion to compel production of those documents.

**MOTION FOR SUMMARY JUDGMENT**

A motion that may be filed by either party in which the party asks the court to enter judgment in his or her favor without a trial. Unlike a motion for judgment on the pleadings, a motion for summary judgment can be supported by evidence outside the pleadings, such as witnesses' affidavits, answers to interrogatories, and other evidence obtained prior to or during discovery.

determining whether no facts are in contention, the court considers the evidence in the light most favorable to the other party.

To support a motion for summary judgment, a party can submit evidence obtained at any point before the trial that refutes the other party's factual claim. The evidence may consist of **affidavits** (sworn statements by parties or witnesses) or copies of documents, such as contracts, e-mails, and letters obtained through the course of discovery (discussed next). Of course, the evidence must be *admissible* evidence—that is, evidence that the court would allow to be presented during the trial. As mentioned, the use of additional evidence is one feature that distinguishes the motion for summary judgment from the motion to dismiss and the motion for judgment on the pleadings.

## Discovery

Before a trial begins, the parties can use a number of procedural devices to obtain information and gather

evidence about the case. Kirby, for example, will want to know how fast Carvello was driving. She will also want to learn whether he had been drinking, was under the influence of medication, and was wearing corrective lenses if required by law to do so while driving.

The process of obtaining information from the opposing party or from witnesses prior to trial is known as **discovery.** Discovery includes gaining access to witnesses, documents, records, and other types of evidence. In federal courts, the parties are required to make initial disclosures of relevant evidence to the opposing party.

Discovery prevents surprises at trial by giving both parties access to evidence that might otherwise be hidden. This allows the litigants to learn as much as they can about what to expect at a trial before they reach the courtroom. Discovery also serves to narrow the issues so that trial time is spent on the main questions in the case. A court can impose sanctions on a party who fails to respond to discovery requests.

The question in the following case was what a court could do when a plaintiff failed to disclose the names of expert witnesses during discovery, even though the court deemed that such witnesses were necessary to establish the plaintiff's claim.

## CASE 3.2

### Blankenship v. Collier
Supreme Court of Kentucky, 302 S.W.3d 665 (2010).

**BACKGROUND AND FACTS**  In February 2004, Horace Collier was admitted to Caritas Medical Center with abdominal pain. The following day, after undergoing tests and being diagnosed by Dr. Robert Blankenship as having appendicitis, Collier had an appendectomy. One year later, Collier sued Blankenship and Caritas Health Services in a Kentucky state court, contending that they had been negligent because they had failed to evaluate and treat him in a timely manner. Specifically, Collier claimed that he had been ignored for several hours while awaiting treatment and had suffered severe abdominal pain. He also claimed that the X-ray of his abdomen had not been stored properly, causing further delay in his diagnosis and treatment. Collier alleged that as a result of the defendants' medical negligence, he had sustained permanent physical and mental injuries, prolonged pain and mental anguish, impairment of his power to work and earn income, and significant medical expenses.

More than nine months later, Collier had not yet disclosed the identities of any expert witnesses who would testify on his behalf, and the court ordered him to do so by January 30, 2006. At Collier's request, this deadline was later extended—to February 28. Finally, on March 14, 2006, after Collier had still had not disclosed any names, the defendants filed motions for summary judgment, arguing that there could be no issue of material fact in this medical malpractice (negligence by professionals—see Chapter 6) case without expert testimony. The trial court granted the motions. Collier appealed, arguing that summary judgment was inappropriate because it was being used only as a sanctioning tool to punish him for failing to timely disclose his experts. He further asserted that there was a "serious question" as to whether he would even need experts to prove his medical malpractice claim. The intermediate appellate court agreed and reversed the trial court's decision. The defendants appealed the decision to the Supreme Court of Kentucky.

**DECISION AND RATIONALE**  The Supreme Court of Kentucky reversed the decision of the lower appellate court and reinstated the trial court's decision. The trial court had not abused its discretion by granting summary judgment for the defendants. After all, Collier had never disputed that a medical expert was necessary to prove his claim of medical negligence. He had continually told the trial court that he would obtain an expert witness, but had never done so. The trial court gave Collier ample opportunity "to respond and complete discovery before the court entered its ruling." The reviewing court concluded that "Collier had completely failed to identify any expert witnesses and could not sustain his burden of proof without expert testimony and, thus, no material issue of fact existed in the record and the defendants were entitled to summary judgment as a matter of law."

**THE ETHICAL DIMENSION**  *Collier contended that there was a "serious question" as to whether he would even need experts to prove his medical malpractice claim. Is it fair to Collier to prevent the trial from proceeding, even though the lack of expert testimony might have made it difficult—if not impossible—for him to win the case? Explain.*

**MANAGERIAL IMPLICATIONS**  *Business owners and managers should be aware that initiating discovery procedures and responding to discovery requests in a timely fashion are important in any litigation. Although the court in this case claimed that summary judgment was not a sanction imposed on the plaintiff for delays during discovery, one could argue (as a dissenting judge did) that it was indeed a sanction—and a very harsh one. Courts have also dismissed cases when the plaintiffs have caused undue delay by not meeting procedural deadlines.*

**DISCOVERY RULES** The FRCP and similar state rules set forth the guidelines for discovery activity. Generally, discovery is allowed regarding any matter that is relevant to the claim or defense of any party. Discovery rules also attempt to protect witnesses and parties from undue harassment, and to safeguard privileged or confidential material from being disclosed. Only information that is relevant to the case at hand—or likely to lead to the discovery of relevant information—is discoverable.

If a discovery request involves privileged or confidential business information, a court can deny the request and can limit the scope of discovery in a number of ways. For instance, a court can require the party to submit the materials to the judge in a sealed envelope so that the judge can decide if they should be disclosed to the opposing party.

**DEPOSITIONS** Discovery can involve the use of depositions. A **deposition** is sworn testimony by a party to the lawsuit or by any witness, recorded by an authorized court official. The person deposed gives testimony and answers questions asked by the attorneys from both sides. The questions and answers are recorded, sworn to, and signed. These answers, of course, will help the attorneys prepare their cases.

Depositions also give attorneys the opportunity to ask immediate follow-up questions and to evaluate how their witnesses will conduct themselves at trial. In addition, depositions can be employed in court to **impeach** (challenge the credibility of) a party or a witness who changes his or her testimony at the trial. A deposition can also be used as testimony if the witness is not available at trial.

**INTERROGATORIES** Discovery can also involve **interrogatories,** which are written questions for which written answers are prepared and then signed under oath. The main difference between interrogatories and written depositions is that interrogatories are directed to a party to the lawsuit (the plaintiff or the defendant), not to a witness. The party usually has thirty days to prepare answers.

The party's attorney often drafts the answers to interrogatories in a manner calculated to give away as little information as possible. Whereas depositions elicit candid answers not prepared in advance, interrogatories are designed to obtain accurate information about specific topics, such as how many contracts were signed and when. The scope of interrogatories is also broader because parties are obligated to answer questions, even if that means

disclosing information from their records and files. Note that, as with discovery requests, a court can impose sanctions on a party who fails to answer interrogatories.

▶ **Case in Point 3.1** Computer Task Group, Inc. (CTG), hired William Brotby as an information technology consultant. As a condition of his employment, Brotby signed an agreement that restricted his ability to work for CTG's customers if he left CTG. Less than two years later, Brotby left CTG and began working for Alyeska Pipeline Service Company, a CTG client, in breach of the agreement. CTG sued Brotby. During discovery, Brotby refused to respond fully to CTG's interrogatories. He gave contradictory answers, made frivolous objections, filed baseless motions, and never disclosed all the information that CTG sought. The court ordered Brotby to comply with discovery requests five times. Nevertheless, Brotby continued to make excuses and changed his story repeatedly, making it impossible for CTG to establish basic facts with any certainty. Eventually, CTG requested and the court granted a default judgment against Brotby based on his failure to cooperate.[7] ◀

**REQUESTS FOR ADMISSIONS** One party can serve the other party with a written request for an admission of the truth of matters relating to the trial. Any fact admitted under such a request is conclusively established as true for the trial. For example, Kirby can ask Carvello to admit that his driver's license was suspended at the time of the accident. A request for admission shortens the trial because the parties will not have to spend time proving facts on which they already agree.

**REQUESTS FOR DOCUMENTS, OBJECTS, AND ENTRY UPON LAND** A party can gain access to documents and other items not in her or his possession in order to inspect and examine them. Carvello, for example, can gain permission to inspect and copy Kirby's car repair bills. Likewise, a party can gain "entry upon land" to inspect the premises.

**REQUESTS FOR EXAMINATIONS** When the physical or mental condition of one party is in question, the opposing party can ask the court to order a physical or mental examination by an independent examiner. If the court agrees to make the order, the opposing party can obtain the results of the examination. Note

---

**7.** *Computer Task Group, Inc. v. Brotby,* 364 F.3d 1112 (9th Cir. 2004).

that the court will make such an order only when the need for the information outweighs the right to privacy of the person to be examined.

**ELECTRONIC DISCOVERY** Any relevant material, including information stored electronically, can be the object of a discovery request. The federal rules and most state rules (as well as court decisions) specifically allow individuals to obtain discovery of electronic "data compilations." Electronic evidence, or **e-evidence,** consists of all computer-generated or electronically recorded information, such as e-mail, voice mail, tweets, blogs, social media posts, spreadsheets, documents, and other data stored electronically.

E-evidence can reveal significant facts that are not discoverable by other means. Computers, smartphones, cameras, and other devices automatically record certain information about files—such as who created the file and when, and who accessed, modified, or transmitted it—on their hard drives. This information is called **metadata,** which can be thought of as "data about data." Metadata can be obtained only from the file in its electronic format—not from printed-out versions.

▶ **Example 3.2** In 2012, John McAfee, the programmer responsible for creating McAfee antivirus software, was wanted for questioning in the murder of his neighbor in Belize. McAfee left Belize and was on the run from police, but he allowed a journalist to come with him and photograph him. When the journalist posted photos of McAfee online, some metadata were attached to a photo. The police used the metadata to pinpoint the latitude and longitude of the image and subsequently arrested McAfee in Guatemala. ◀

*E-Discovery Procedures.* The Federal Rules of Civil Procedure deal specifically with the preservation, retrieval, and production of electronic data. Although traditional interrogatories and depositions are still used to find out whether e-evidence exists, a party usually must hire an expert to retrieve the evidence in its electronic format. The expert uses software to reconstruct e-mail, text, and other exchanges to establish who knew what and when they knew it. The expert can even recover computer files that the user thought had been deleted.

*Advantages and Disadvantages.* Electronic discovery has significant advantages over paper discovery. Electronic versions of documents, e-mail, and text

messages can provide useful—and often quite damaging—information about how a particular matter progressed over several weeks or months. E-discovery can uncover the proverbial smoking gun that will win the lawsuit, but it is also time consuming and expensive, especially when lawsuits involve large firms with multiple offices. Also, many firms are finding it difficult to fulfill their duty to preserve electronic evidence from a vast number of sources.

A party that fails to preserve e-evidence may even find itself at such a disadvantage that it will settle a dispute rather than continue litigation. ▶ **Case in Point 3.3** Advanced Micro Devices, Inc. (AMD), sued Intel Corporation, one of the world's largest microprocessor suppliers, for violating antitrust laws. Immediately after the lawsuit was filed, Intel began collecting and preserving the electronic evidence on its servers and instructed its employees to retain documents and e-mails related to competition with AMD. Nevertheless, many employees saved only copies of the e-mails that they had received and not e-mails that they had sent. In addition, Intel did not stop its automatic e-mail deletion system, causing other information to be lost. In the end, although Intel produced data equivalent to "somewhere in the neighborhood of a pile 137 miles high" in paper, its failure to preserve e-discovery led it to settle the dispute.[8] ◀

## Pretrial Conference

After discovery has taken place and before the trial begins, the attorneys may meet with the trial judge in a **pretrial conference,** or hearing. Usually, the conference consists of an informal discussion between the judge and the opposing attorneys after discovery has taken place. The purpose is to explore the possibility of a settlement without trial and, if this is not possible, to identify the matters in dispute and to plan the course of the trial. In particular, the parties may attempt to establish ground rules to restrict the number of expert witnesses or discuss the admissibility or costs of certain types of evidence.

## The Right to a Jury Trial

The Seventh Amendment to the U.S. Constitution guarantees the right to a jury trial for cases at law

---

**8.** *In re Intel Corp. Microprocessor Antitrust Litigation,* 2008 WL 2310288 (D.Del. 2008).

in *federal* courts when the amount in controversy exceeds $20. Most states have similar guarantees in their own constitutions (although the threshold dollar amount is higher than $20).

The right to a trial by jury need not be exercised, and many cases are tried without a jury. In most states and in federal courts, one of the parties must request a jury, or the judge presumes the parties waive this right. If there is no jury, the judge determines the truth of the facts alleged in the case.

## Jury Selection

Before a jury trial commences, a panel of jurors must be selected. Although some types of trials require twelve-person juries, most civil matters can be heard by six-person juries. The jury selection process is known as ***voir dire***.[9] In most jurisdictions, attorneys for the plaintiff and the defendant ask prospective jurors oral questions to determine whether they are biased or have any connection with a party to the action or with a prospective witness. In some jurisdictions, the judge may do all or part of the questioning based on written questions submitted by counsel for the parties.

During *voir dire*, a party may challenge a certain number of prospective jurors *peremptorily*—that is, ask that an individual not be sworn in as a juror without providing any reason. Alternatively, a party may challenge a prospective juror *for cause*—that is, provide a reason why an individual should not be sworn in as a juror. If the judge grants the challenge, the individual is asked to step down. A prospective juror, however, may not be excluded by the use of discriminatory challenges, such as those based on racial criteria or gender.

See *Concept Summary 3.1* on the facing page for a review of pretrial procedures.

## SECTION 3
# THE TRIAL

Various rules and procedures govern the trial phase of the litigation process. There are rules governing what kind of evidence will or will not be admitted during the trial, as well as specific procedures that the

participants in the lawsuit must follow. Today, some judges also have rules prohibiting or limiting the use of social media by jurors and others during trials, as discussed in this chapter's *Insight into Social Media* feature on page 60.

## Opening Statements

At the beginning of the trial, both attorneys are allowed to make **opening statements** setting forth the facts that they expect to prove during the trial. The opening statement provides an opportunity for each lawyer to give a brief version of the facts and the supporting evidence that will be used during the trial. Then the plaintiff's case is presented. In our hypothetical case, Kirby's lawyer would introduce evidence (relevant documents, exhibits, and the testimony of witnesses) to support Kirby's position.

## Rules of Evidence

Whether evidence will be admitted in court is determined by the **rules of evidence.** These are a series of rules that the courts have created to ensure that any evidence presented during a trial is fair and reliable. The Federal Rules of Evidence govern the admissibility of evidence in federal courts.

**EVIDENCE MUST BE RELEVANT TO THE ISSUES** Evidence will not be admitted in court unless it is relevant to the matter in question. **Relevant evidence** is evidence that tends to prove or disprove a fact in question or to establish the degree of probability of a fact or action. For example, evidence that the defendant was in another person's home when the victim was shot would be relevant—because it would tend to prove that the defendant was not the shooter.

**HEARSAY EVIDENCE NOT ADMISSIBLE** Generally, hearsay is not admissible as evidence. **Hearsay** is testimony someone gives in court about a statement made by someone else who was not under oath at the time of the statement. Literally, it is what someone heard someone else say. For example, if a witness in the Kirby-Carvello case testified in court concerning what he or she heard another observer say about the accident, that testimony would be hearsay, or secondhand knowledge. Admitting hearsay into evidence carries many risks because, even though it may be relevant, there is no way to test its reliability.

---

**9.** Pronounced *vwahr deehr*. These verbs based on Old French mean "to speak the truth." In legal language, the phrase refers to the process of questioning jurors to learn about their backgrounds, attitudes, and similar attributes.

## CONCEPT SUMMARY 3.1
### Pretrial Procedures

| PROCEDURE | DESCRIPTION |
|---|---|
| **The Pleadings** | 1. *The plaintiff's complaint*—The plaintiff's statement of the cause of action and the parties involved, filed with the court by the plaintiff's attorney. After the filing, the defendant is notified of the suit through service of process. |
| | 2. *The defendant's response*—The defendant's response to the plaintiff's complaint may take the form of an answer, in which the defendant admits or denies the plaintiff's allegations. The defendant may raise an affirmative defense and/or assert a counterclaim. |
| **Pretrial Motions** | 1. *Motion to dismiss*—May be made by either party to request that the judge dismiss the case for reasons stated in the motion (such as failure to state a claim for which relief can be granted). |
| | 2. *Motion for judgment* on the pleadings—May be made by either party and will be granted only if no facts are in dispute and only questions of law are at issue. |
| | 3. *Motion for summary judgment*—May be made by either party and will be granted only if no facts are in dispute and only questions of law are at issue. Unlike the motion for judgment on the pleadings, the motion for summary judgment may be supported by evidence outside the pleadings, such as testimony and other evidence obtained during discovery. |
| **Discovery** | The process of gathering evidence concerning the case, which may involve the following: |
| | 1. *Depositions* (sworn testimony by either party or any witness). |
| | 2. *Interrogatories* (in which parties to the action write answers to questions with the aid of their attorneys). |
| | 3. Requests for admissions, documents, examinations, or other information relating to the case. |
| | 4. Requests for electronically recorded information, such as e-mail, text messages, voice mail, and other data. |
| **Pretrial Conference** | A pretrial hearing, at the request of either party or the court, to identify the matters in dispute after discovery has taken place and to explore the possibility of settling the dispute without a trial. If no settlement is possible, the parties plan the course of the trial. |
| **Jury Selection** | In a jury trial, the selection of members of the jury from a pool of prospective jurors. During a process known as *voir dire,* the attorneys for both sides may challenge prospective jurors either for cause or peremptorily (for no cause). |

## Examination of Witnesses and Potential Motions

Because Kirby is the plaintiff, she has the burden of proving that her allegations are true. Her attorney begins the presentation of Kirby's case by calling the first witness for the plaintiff and examining, or questioning, the witness. (For both attorneys, the types of questions and the manner of asking them are governed by the rules of evidence.) This questioning is called **direct examination.** After Kirby's attorney is finished, the witness is subject to **cross-examination** by Carvello's attorney. Then Kirby's attorney has another opportunity to question the witness in *redirect examination,* and Carvello's attorney may follow the redirect examination with a *recross-examination.* When both attorneys have finished with the first witness, Kirby's attorney calls the succeeding witnesses in the plaintiff's case, each of whom is subject to examination by the attorneys in the manner just described.

**EXPERT WITNESSES** As part of their cases, both the plaintiff and the defendant may present testimony from one or more expert witnesses, such as forensic

# INSIGHT INTO SOCIAL MEDIA
## To Tweet or Not to Tweet Inside the Courtroom

About two-thirds of all adult Internet users access social networking sites such as Twitter and Facebook.[a] Ordinarily, this is not a problem, but what if the adult is a member of a jury hearing a case? Typically, a trial judge will instruct jurors not to communicate with anyone about the case they are hearing. Nevertheless, many jurors are apparently ignoring these instructions when it comes to social media. When former Baltimore mayor Sheila Dickson was being tried for corruption, for example, five members of the jury communicated with each other via Facebook. Their posts were detected by a newspaper reporter. (Before the judge could sanction the jurors, the case was settled.)

Many judges worry that what jury members say online could be construed as generating bias about the case. Furthermore, they might reveal information about a trial before the information was supposed to be released to the public. Another problem is that jurors may look for information about the case and learn details that are not admissible at trial. The use of social media by journalists in the courtroom raises similar concerns.

### How Can a Judge Know Who Is Tweeting?

A major difficulty with policing social media use by jurors and journalists is that a judge rarely knows who is tweeting. When the Federal Judicial Center asked judges if they would know if a juror violated a social media ban, almost 80 percent said no. About the only way a judge can learn that a juror has ignored the ban is if someone has access to the juror's postings and then informs the court, as happened in the Dickson trial mentioned above.

Some defense attorneys are asking judges to require jurors to disclose their Twitter "handles." Supposedly, the defense can then make sure that the jurors are not researching or tweeting about the case.

### What Should Be the Policy Concerning Reporters?

Despite judges' efforts to prohibit anyone in the courtroom from using social media during a trial, reporters argue that social media are useful for providing "play-by-play" commentary for the public as events unfold. Judges respond

that reporters "feverishly" tweeting on their smartphones distract jurors and witnesses.

The judge in the high-profile sexual abuse case of former Penn State assistant football coach Jerry Sandusky did allow reporters to tweet during pretrial hearings, but he prohibited photographs and verbatim transmittals via social media. During the trial itself, the judge banned live tweets. To ensure that reporters did not tweet, he required them to disclose their Twitter "handles" and asked a member of the sheriff's department to track their accounts.

Later, the same judge developed stricter guidelines. Now he places a digital clock in the front of the courtroom and requires reporters to synchronize their smartphones, tablet devices, and laptops with the clock. When court is adjourned, the time is noted. Any reporter who transmitted information earlier than that time may be fined or jailed.[b]

### A Different Approach from the United Kingdom

The United Kingdom has taken a different approach to social media in the courtroom. For the past several years, journalists have been able to use their Twitter accounts without even asking the judge's permission. The Lord Chief Justice—the most senior judge—issued *Practice Guidance Notes* that allow for the "use of live text-based forms of communications (including Twitter)."[c] The chief justice said that live communications would enable the media to produce fair and accurate reports of court proceedings.

Only text-based communications are permitted, however. Reporters are still prohibited from making sound recordings or taking photographs in the courtrooms.

### LEGAL CRITICAL THINKING

#### INSIGHT INTO THE TECHNOLOGICAL ENVIRONMENT

*Why is it so difficult for judges to effectively prohibit social media communications from the courtroom?*

---

**a.** Pew Research Center Survey, Summer 2012

**b.** *Decorum Order Governing the Sentencing Hearing,* in the Court of Common Pleas of Centre County, Pennsylvania, *Commonwealth of Pennsylvania v. Jerold A. Sandusky.* October 3, 2012. By the order of the court John M. Cleland, S.J.

**c.** Lord Chief Justice of England and Wales, December 14, 2011.

---

scientists, physicians, and psychologists. An *expert witness* is a person who, by virtue of education, training, skill, or experience, has scientific, technical, or other specialized knowledge in a particular area beyond that of an average person. In Kirby's case, her

attorney might hire an accident reconstruction specialist to establish Carvello's negligence or a physician to testify to the extent of Kirby's injuries.

Normally, witnesses can testify only about the facts of a case—that is, what they personally observed. When witnesses are qualified as experts in a particular field, however, they can offer their opinions and conclusions about the evidence in that field. Expert testimony is an important component of litigation today. Because numerous experts are available for hire and expert testimony is powerful and effective with juries, there is tremendous potential for abuse. Therefore, in federal courts and most state courts, judges act as gatekeepers to ensure that the experts are qualified and that their opinions are based on scientific knowledge.[10]

---

10. See Paul C. Giannelli and Edward J. Imwinkelried, *Scientific Evidence,* 4th ed. (Newark, N.J.: LexisNexis, 2007), Sections 1.06 and 1.16.

If a party believes that the opponent's expert witness is not a qualified expert in the relevant field, that party can make a motion to prevent the witness from testifying. In the following case, a court had refused to allow an expert to testify as to his opinion because the plaintiffs had failed to file a discovery report outlining the expert's testimony and credentials. The appellate court had to decide whether to reverse the trial court's decision regarding the expert's testimony.

## CASE 3.3

### Downey v. Bob's Discount Furniture Holdings, Inc.
United States Court of Appeals, First Circuit, 633 F.3d 1 (2011).

**BACKGROUND AND FACTS**  Yvette Downey bought a children's bedroom set from Bob's Discount Furniture Holdings, Inc., in 2004. Soon, Downey and her daughter, Ashley Celester, began to experience skin irritation. In July 2005, they discovered insects on Ashley's body and in their home. Downey immediately called Allegiance Pest Control and spoke to Edward Gordinier, a licensed and experienced exterminator. Gordinier inspected Downey's home that day. He found bedbugs throughout the house and identified Ashley's bedroom set as the main source of the infestation. Downey informed Bob's about the problem. Although Bob's retrieved the bedroom set and refunded the purchase price, it refused to pay for the costs of extermination or any other damages. Downey and her daughter filed a lawsuit in a federal district court seeking compensation for health problems, emotional distress, and economic loss.

Before the trial, the plaintiffs named Gordinier as a witness but did not submit a written report describing his anticipated testimony or specifying his qualifications. Rule 26 of the Federal Rules of Civil Procedure requires that a written report be filed for an expert witness who is retained or specially employed to provide expert testimony. The plaintiffs asserted that Gordinier had not been specially employed as an expert and, therefore, no such disclosures were required. The defendants argued that Gordinier could not testify as to his expert opinion because the plaintiffs had not filed a written report. The district court agreed with the defendants and allowed Gordinier to testify only about the facts, such as his inspection of the premises, not about his opinion of the source of the bedbug infestation. The court granted a judgment for the defendants based, in part, on their claim that the plaintiffs had not proved that the furniture was infested with bedbugs when it was delivered. The plaintiffs appealed.

**DECISION AND RATIONALE**  The United States Court of Appeals for the First Circuit decided that the trial court had abused its discretion by not allowing Gordinier's expert opinion testimony. The court reasoned that Rule 26 of the Federal Rules of Civil Procedure requires the filing of a written report only for an expert witness who is "retained or specially employed to provide expert testimony in the case." The circumstances of this case indicated that Gordinier was not the type of expert witness who needed to file such a report. "For one thing, there is no evidence that Gordinier was a person who held himself out for hire as a purveyor of expert testimony. For another thing, there is no evidence that he was charging a fee for his testimony." The court, therefore, reversed the district court's judgment and remanded the case for a new trial.

**THE LEGAL ENVIRONMENT DIMENSION**  *Why can only an expert testify about the source of a bedbug infestation?*

**THE ETHICAL DIMENSION**  *Is it fair to require plaintiffs who hire expert witnesses to pay for and submit written reports that specify what the experts will say at trial? Why or why not?*

**POTENTIAL MOTION AND JUDGMENT** At the conclusion of the plaintiff's case, the defendant's attorney may ask the judge to direct a verdict for the defendant on the ground that the plaintiff has presented no evidence to support her or his claim. This is called a **motion for a judgment as a matter of law** (or a **motion for a directed verdict** in state courts). In considering the motion, the judge looks at the evidence in the light most favorable to the plaintiff and grants the motion only if there is insufficient evidence to raise an issue of fact. (Motions for directed verdicts at this stage of a trial are seldom granted.)

**DEFENDANT'S EVIDENCE** The defendant's attorney then presents the evidence and witnesses for the defendant's case. Witnesses are called and examined by the defendant's attorney. The plaintiff's attorney has the right to cross-examine them, and there may be a redirect examination and possibly a recross-examination.

At the end of the defendant's case, either attorney can move for a directed verdict. Again, the test is whether the jury can, through any reasonable interpretation of the evidence, find for the party against whom the motion has been made. After the defendant's attorney has finished introducing evidence, the plaintiff's attorney can present a **rebuttal** by offering additional evidence that refutes the defendant's case. The defendant's attorney can, in turn, refute that evidence in a **rejoinder.**

## Closing Arguments, Jury Instructions, and Verdict

After both sides have rested their cases, each attorney presents a **closing argument.** In the closing argument, each attorney summarizes the facts and evidence presented during the trial and indicates why the facts and evidence support his or her client's claim. In addition to generally urging a verdict in favor of the client, the closing argument typically reveals the shortcomings of the points made by the opposing party during the trial.

**JURY INSTRUCTIONS** Attorneys usually present closing arguments whether or not the trial was heard by a jury. If it was a jury trial, the attorneys will have met with the judge before the closing arguments to determine how the jury will be instructed on the law. The attorneys can refer to these instructions in their closing arguments. After closing arguments are completed, the judge instructs the jury in the law that applies to the case (these instructions are often called

*charges*). The jury then retires to the jury room to deliberate a verdict.

Juries are instructed on the standard of proof they must apply to the case. In most civil cases, the standard of proof is a *preponderance of the evidence.*[11] In other words, the plaintiff (Kirby in our hypothetical case) need only show that her factual claim is more likely to be true than the defendant's. (As you will read in Chapter 10, in a criminal trial the prosecution has a higher standard of proof to meet—it must prove its case *beyond a reasonable doubt.*)

**VERDICT** Once the jury has reached a decision, it issues a **verdict** in favor of one party. The verdict specifies the jury's factual findings. In some cases, the jury also decides on the amount of the *award* (the compensation to be paid to the prevailing party). After the announcement of the verdict, which marks the end of the trial itself, the jurors are dismissed.

See *Concept Summary 3.2* on the following page for a review of trial procedures.

## SECTION 4
# POSTTRIAL MOTIONS

After the jury has rendered its verdict, either party may make a posttrial motion. The prevailing party usually requests that the court enter a judgment in accordance with the verdict. The nonprevailing party frequently files one of the motions discussed next.

## Motion for a New Trial

At the end of the trial, the losing party may make a motion to set aside the adverse verdict and any judgment and to hold a new trial. After looking at all the evidence, the judge will grant the **motion for a new trial** only if she or he believes that the jury was in error and that it is not appropriate to grant judgment for the other side.

Usually, a new trial is granted only when the jury verdict is obviously the result of a misapplication of the law or a misunderstanding of the evidence presented at trial. A new trial can also be granted on the grounds of newly discovered evidence, misconduct by the participants during the trial (such as when a juror

---

11. Note that some civil claims must be proved by "clear and convincing evidence," meaning that the evidence must show that the truth of the party's claim is *highly* probable. This standard is often applied in situations that present a particular danger of deception, such as allegations of fraud.

---

## CONCEPT SUMMARY 3.2
### Trial Procedures

| PROCEDURE | DESCRIPTION |
|---|---|
| **Opening Statements** | Each party's attorney is allowed to present an opening statement indicating what the attorney will attempt to prove during the course of the trial. |
| **Examination of Witnesses** | 1. Plaintiff's introduction and direct examination of witnesses, cross-examination by defendant's attorney, possible redirect examination by plaintiff's attorney, and possible recross-examination by defendant's attorney.<br>2. Both the plaintiff and the defendant may present testimony from one or more expert witnesses.<br>3. At the close of the plaintiff's case, the defendant may make a motion for a directed verdict (or for judgment as a matter of law), which, if granted by the court, will end the trial before the defendant presents witnesses.<br>4. Defendant's introduction and direct examination of witnesses, cross-examination by plaintiff's attorney, possible redirect examination by defendant's attorney, and possible recross-examination by plaintiff's attorney.<br>5. Possible rebuttal of defendant's argument by plaintiff's attorney, who presents more evidence.<br>6. Possible rejoinder by defendant's attorney to meet that evidence. |
| **Closing Arguments, Jury Instructions, and Verdict** | Each party's attorney argues in favor of a verdict for his or her client. The judge instructs (or charges) the jury as to how the law applies to the issue, and the jury retires to deliberate. When the jury renders its verdict, the trial comes to an end. |

---

has made prejudicial and inflammatory remarks), or an error by the judge.

## Motion for Judgment *N.O.V.*

If Kirby wins and if Carvello's attorney has previously moved for a judgment as a matter of law, then Carvello's attorney can make a second *motion for a judgment as a matter of law* (the terminology used in federal courts). State courts may use different terms for these motions. In many state courts, if the defendant's attorney moved earlier for a directed verdict, he or she may now make a **motion for judgment n.o.v.**—from the Latin *non obstante veredicto*, meaning "notwithstanding the verdict." Such a motion will be granted only if the jury's verdict was unreasonable and erroneous.

If the judge grants the motion, then the jury's verdict will be set aside, and a judgment will be entered in favor of the opposing party (Carvello). If the motion is denied, Carvello may then appeal the case. (Kirby may also appeal the case, even though she won at trial. She might appeal, for example, if she received a smaller monetary award than she had sought.)

## SECTION 5
## THE APPEAL

Either party may appeal not only the jury's verdict but also the judge's ruling on any pretrial or posttrial motion. Many of the appellate court cases that appear in this text involve appeals of motions for summary judgment or other motions that were denied by trial court judges.

Note that a party must have legitimate grounds to file an appeal (some legal error) and that few trial court decisions are reversed on appeal. Moreover, the expenses associated with an appeal can be considerable.[12]

### Filing the Appeal

If Carvello decides to appeal the verdict in Kirby's favor, then his attorney must file a *notice of appeal* with the clerk of the trial court within a prescribed period of time. Carvello then becomes the *appellant*

---

12. See, for example, *Phansalkar v. Andersen Weinroth & Co.*, 356 F.3d 188 (2d Cir. 2004).

or *petitioner*. The clerk of the trial court sends to the reviewing court (usually an intermediate court of appeals) the *record on appeal*. The record contains all the pleadings, motions, and other documents filed with the court and a complete written transcript of the proceedings, including testimony, arguments, jury instructions, and judicial rulings.

Carvello's attorney will file an appellate *brief* with the reviewing court. The **brief** is a formal legal document outlining the facts and issues of the case, the judge's rulings or jury's findings that should be reversed or modified, the applicable law, and arguments on Carvello's behalf (citing applicable statutes and relevant cases as precedents). The attorney for the *appellee* (Kirby, in our hypothetical case) usually files an answering brief. Carvello's attorney can file a reply, although it is not required. The reviewing court then considers the case.

## Appellate Review

As mentioned in Chapter 2, a court of appeals does not hear any evidence. Rather, it reviews the record for errors of law. Its decision concerning a case is based on the record on appeal and the briefs and arguments. The attorneys present oral arguments, after which the case is taken under advisement. The court then issues a written opinion. In general, appellate courts do not reverse findings of fact unless the findings are unsupported or contradicted by the evidence.

An appellate court has the following options after reviewing a case:

1. The court can *affirm* the trial court's decision. (Most decisions are affirmed.)
2. The court can *reverse* the trial court's judgment if it concludes that the trial court erred or that the jury did not receive proper instructions.
3. The appellate court can *remand* (send back) the case to the trial court for further proceedings consistent with its opinion on the matter.
4. The court might also affirm or reverse a decision *in part*. For example, the court might affirm the jury's finding that Carvello was negligent but remand the case for further proceedings on another issue (such as the extent of Kirby's damages).
5. An appellate court can also *modify* a lower court's decision. If the appellate court decides that the jury awarded an excessive amount in damages, for example, the court might reduce the award to a more appropriate, or fairer, amount.

## Higher Appellate Courts

If the reviewing court is an intermediate appellate court, the losing party may decide to appeal the decision to the state's highest court, usually called its supreme court. Although the losing party has a right to ask (petition) a higher court to review the case, the party does not have a right to have the case heard by the higher appellate court. Appellate courts normally have discretionary power and can accept or reject an appeal. Like the United States Supreme Court, state supreme courts generally deny most petitions for appeal.

If the petition for review is granted, new briefs must be filed before the state supreme court, and the attorneys may be allowed or requested to present oral arguments. Like the intermediate appellate courts, the supreme court can reverse or affirm the lower appellate court's decision or remand the case. At this point, the case typically has reached its end (unless a federal question is at issue and one of the parties has legitimate grounds to seek review by a federal appellate court).

*Concept Summary 3.3* on the next page reviews the options that the parties may pursue after the trial.

## SECTION 6
# ENFORCING THE JUDGMENT

The uncertainties of the litigation process are compounded by the lack of guarantees that any judgment will be enforceable. Even if the jury awards Kirby the full amount of damages requested ($100,000), for example, Carvello's auto insurance coverage might have lapsed. If so, the company would not pay any of the damages. Alternatively, Carvello's insurance policy might be limited to $50,000, meaning that Carvello personally would have to pay the remaining $50,000.

## Requesting Court Assistance in Collecting the Judgment

If the defendant does not have the funds available to pay the judgment, the plaintiff can go back to the court and request that the court issue a *writ of execution*. A **writ of execution** is an order directing the sheriff to seize and sell the defendant's nonexempt assets, or property (certain assets are exempted by law from creditors' actions). The proceeds of the sale are then used to pay the damages owed, and any excess proceeds are returned to the defendant. Alternatively, the nonexempt property itself could be transferred to the plaintiff in lieu of an outright payment. (There are creditors' remedies available, and there are issues of exempt and nonexempt property.)

## Availability of Assets

The problem of collecting a judgment is less pronounced, of course, when a party is seeking to satisfy a judgment against a defendant with substantial assets that can be easily located, such as a major corporation. Usually, one of the factors considered by the plaintiff and his or her attorney before a lawsuit is initiated is whether the defendant has sufficient assets to cover the amount of damages sought. In addition, during the discovery process, attorneys routinely seek information about the location of the defendant's assets that might potentially be used to satisfy a judgment.

---

### CONCEPT SUMMARY 3.3
### Posttrial Options

| PROCEDURE | DESCRIPTION |
|---|---|
| **Posttrial Motions** | 1. *Motion for a new trial*—If the judge believes that the jury was in error but is not convinced that the losing party should have won, the motion normally is granted. It can also be granted on the basis of newly discovered evidence, misconduct by the participants during the trial, or error by the judge. <br> 2. *Motion for judgment n.o.v. ("notwithstanding the verdict")*—The party making the motion must have filed a motion for a directed verdict at the close of the presentation of evidence during the trial. The motion will be granted if the judge is convinced that the jury was in error. |
| **Appeal** | Either party can appeal the trial court's judgment to an appropriate court of appeals. <br> 1. *Filing the appeal*—The appealing party must file a notice of appeal with the clerk of the trial court, who forwards the record on appeal to the appellate court. Attorneys file appellate briefs. <br> 2. *Appellate review*—The appellate court does not hear evidence but bases its opinion, which it issues in writing, on the record on appeal and the attorneys' briefs and oral arguments. The court may affirm or reverse all (or part) of the trial court's judgment and/or remand the case for further proceedings consistent with its opinion. Most decisions are affirmed on appeal. <br> 3. *Further review*—In some cases, further review may be sought from a higher appellate court, such as a state supreme court. If a federal question is involved, the case may ultimately be appealed to the United States Supreme Court. |

---

## Reviewing: Court Procedures

Ronald Metzgar placed his fifteen-month-old son, Matthew, awake and healthy, in his playpen. Ronald left the room for five minutes and on his return found Matthew lifeless. A toy block had lodged in the boy's throat, causing him to choke to death. Ronald called 911, but efforts to revive Matthew were to no avail. There was no warning of a choking hazard on the box containing the block. Matthew's parents hired an attorney and sued Playskool, Inc., the manufacturer of the block, alleging that the manufacturer had been negligent in failing to warn of the block's hazard. Playskool filed a motion for summary judgment, arguing that the danger of a young child choking on a small block was obvious. Using the information presented in the chapter, answer the following questions.

*Continued*

1. Suppose that the attorney the Metzgars hired agreed to represent them on a contingency-fee basis. What does that mean?
2. How would the Metzgars' attorney likely have served process (the summons and complaint) on Playskool, Inc.?
3. Should Playskool's request for summary judgment be granted? Why or why not?
4. Suppose that the judge denied Playskool's motion and the case proceeded to trial. After hearing all the evidence, the jury found in favor of the defendant. What options do the plaintiffs have at this point if they are not satisfied with the verdict?

**DEBATE THIS . . .** *Some consumer advocates argue that attorneys' high contingency fees—sometimes reaching 40 percent—unfairly deprive winning plaintiffs of too much of their awards. Should the government cap contingency fees at, say, 20 percent of the award? Why or why not?*

## Terms and Concepts

affidavit 54
affirmative defense 52
answer 52
brief 64
closing argument 62
complaint 49
counterclaim 52
cross-examination 59
default judgment 50
deposition 56
direct examination 59
discovery 54
e-evidence 57
Federal Rules of Civil Procedure (FRCP) 47

hearsay 58
impeach 56
interrogatories 56
metadata 57
motion 52
motion for a directed verdict 62
motion for a judgment as a matter of law 62
motion for a new trial 62
motion for judgment *n.o.v.* 63
motion for judgment on the pleadings 53
motion for summary judgment 53
motion to dismiss 52

opening statement 58
pleadings 49
pretrial conference 57
pretrial motion 52
rebuttal 62
rejoinder 62
relevant evidence 58
rules of evidence 58
service of process 50
summons 50
verdict 62
*voir dire* 58
writ of execution 64

## Issue Spotters

1. At the trial, after Sue calls her witnesses, offers her evidence, and otherwise presents her side of the case, Tom has at least two choices between courses of actions. Tom can call his first witness. What else might he do? **(See page 62.)**

2. After the trial, the judge issues a judgment that includes a grant of relief for Sue, but the relief is less than Sue wanted. Neither Sue nor Tom is satisfied with this result. Who can appeal to a higher court? **(See page 63.)**

• Check your answers to the Issue Spotters against the answers provided in Appendix E at the end of this text.

## Business Scenarios

**3–1. Discovery Rules.** In the past, the rules of discovery were very restrictive, and trials often turned on elements of surprise. For example, a plaintiff would not necessarily know until the trial what the defendant's defense was going to be. In the last several decades, however, new rules of discovery have substantially changed this situation. Now each attorney can access practically all of the evidence that the other side intends to present at trial, with the exception of certain information—namely, the opposing attorney's work product. Work product is not a precise concept. Basically, it includes all of the attorney's thoughts on the case. Can you see any reason why such information should not be made available to the opposing attorney? Discuss fully. **(See page 54.)**

**3–2. Motions.** When and for what purpose is each of the following motions made? Which of them would be appropriate if a defendant claimed that the only issue between the parties was a question of law and that the law was favorable to the defendant's position? **(See page 52.)**

(a) A motion for judgment on the pleadings.

(b) A motion for a directed verdict.

(c) A motion for summary judgment.

(d) A motion for judgment *n.o.v.*

**3–3. Motion for a New Trial.** Washoe Medical Center, Inc., admitted Shirley Swisher for the treatment of a fractured pelvis. During her stay, Swisher suffered a fatal fall from her hospital bed. Gerald Parodi, the administrator of her estate, and others filed an action against Washoe seeking damages for the alleged lack of care in treating Swisher. During *voir dire,* when the plaintiffs' attorney returned a few minutes late from a break, the trial judge led the prospective jurors in a standing ovation. The judge joked with one of the prospective jurors, whom he had known in college, about his fitness to serve as a judge and person-

ally endorsed another prospective juror's business. After the trial, the jury returned a verdict in favor of Washoe. The plaintiffs moved for a new trial, but the judge denied the motion. The plaintiffs then appealed, arguing that the tone set by the judge during *voir dire* prejudiced their right to a fair trial. Should the appellate court agree? Why or why not? **(See page 62.)**

**3–4. Discovery.** Advance Technology Consultants, Inc. (ATC), contracted with RoadTrac, LLC., to provide software and client software systems for the products of global positioning satellite (GPS) technology being developed by RoadTrac. RoadTrac agreed to provide ATC with hardware with which ATC's software would interface. Problems soon arose, however. ATC claimed that RoadTrac's hardware was defective, making it difficult to develop the software. RoadTrac contended that its hardware was fully functional and that ATC had simply failed to provide supporting software. ATC told RoadTrac that it considered their contract terminated. RoadTrac filed a suit in a Georgia state court against ATC alleging breach of contract. During discovery, RoadTrac requested ATC's customer lists and marketing procedures. ATC objected to providing this information because RoadTrac and ATC had become competitors in the GPS industry. Should a party to a lawsuit have to hand over its confidential business secrets as part of a discovery request? Why or why not? What limitations might a court consider imposing before requiring ATC to produce this material? **(See page 54.)**

## Business Case Problems

**3–5. Discovery.** Rita Peatie filed a suit in a Connecticut state court against Wal-Mart Stores, Inc., to recover for injuries to her head, neck, and shoulder. Peatie claimed that she had been struck two years earlier by a metal cylinder falling from a store ceiling. The parties agreed to nonbinding arbitration. Ten days before the hearing, the plaintiff asked for, and was granted, four more months to conduct discovery. On the morning of the rescheduled hearing, she asked for more time, but the court denied this request. The hearing was held, and the arbitrator ruled in Wal-Mart's favor. Peatie filed a motion for a new trial, which was granted. Five months later, she sought through discovery to acquire any photos, records, and reports held by Wal-Mart regarding her alleged injury. The court issued a "protective order" against the request, stating that the time for discovery had long been over. On the day of the trial—four years after the alleged injury—the plaintiff asked the court to lift the order. Should the court do so? Why or why not? [*Peatie v. Wal-Mart Stores, Inc.,* 112 Conn. App. 8, 961 A.2d 1016 (2009)] **(See page 54.)**

**3–6. Jury Misconduct.** Michelle Fleshner worked for Pepose Vision Institute (PVI), a surgical practice. She was fired

after she provided information to the U.S. Department of Labor about PVI's overtime pay policy. She sued for wrongful termination, and the jury awarded her $125,000. After the trial, a juror told PVI's attorneys that another juror had made anti-Semitic statements during jury deliberations. The comments concerned a witness who testified on PVI's behalf. According to the juror, the other juror said, about the witness: "She is a Jewish witch." "She is a penny-pinching Jew." "She was such a cheap Jew that she did not want to pay Plaintiff unemployment compensation." Another juror confirmed the remarks. PVI filed a motion for a new trial on the basis of juror misconduct. The trial judge held that the comments did not prevent a fair trial from occurring. PVI appealed. Do you think such comments are sufficient to require a new trial, or must a juror's bias be discovered during *voir dire* for it to matter? Explain. [*Fleshner v. Pepose Vision Institute,* 304 S.W.3d 81 (Mo. 2010)] **(See page 62.)**

**3–7. Service of Process.** Dr. Kevin Bardwell owns Northfield Urgent Care, LLC, a Minnesota medical clinic. Northfield ordered flu vaccine from Clint Pharmaceuticals, a licensed distributor of flu vaccine located in Tennessee. The parties signed a credit agreement that specified that any disputes would be litigated in the Tennessee state courts. When Northfield failed to pay what it owed for the vaccine, Clint Pharmaceuticals filed a lawsuit in Tennessee and served process on the clinic via registered mail to Dr. Bardwell, the registered agent of Northfield. Bardwell's wife, who worked as a receptionist at the clinic and handled inquiries on the clinic's Facebook site, signed for the letter. Bardwell did not appear on the trial date, however, and the Tennessee court entered a default judgment against Northfield. When Clint Pharmaceuticals attempted to collect on the judgment in Minnesota, Bardwell claimed that the judgment was unenforceable. He asserted that he had not been properly served because his wife was not a registered agent. Should the Minnesota court invalidate the Tennessee judgment? Was service of process proper when it was mailed to the defendant medical clinic and the wife of the physician who owned the clinic opened the letter? Explain. [*Clint Pharmaceuticals v. Northfield Urgent Care, LLC,* 2012 WL 3792546 (Minn.App. 2012).] **(See page 49.)**

### 3–8. BUSINESS CASE PROBLEM
### WITH SAMPLE ANSWER: Discovery.

*Jessica Lester died from injuries suffered in an auto accident caused by the driver of a truck owned by Allied Concrete Co. Jessica's widower, Isaiah, filed a suit against Allied for damages. The defendant requested copies of all of Isaiah's Facebook photos and other postings. Before responding, Isaiah "cleaned up" his Facebook page. Allied suspected that some items had been deleted, including a photo of Isaiah holding a beer can while wearing a T-shirt that declared "I [heart] hotmoms." Can this material be recovered? If so, how? What effect might Isaiah's "postings" have on the result in this case? Discuss. [Allied Concrete Co. v. Lester, 736 S.E.2d 699 (2013)]* **(See page 57.)**

- **For a sample answer to Problem 3–8, go to Appendix F at the end of this text.**

### 3–9. A QUESTION OF ETHICS: Service of Process.

*Narnia Investments, Ltd., filed a suit in a Texas state court against several defendants, including Harvestons Securities, Inc., a securities dealer. (Securities are documents evidencing the ownership of a corporation, in the form of stock, or debts owed by it, in the form of bonds.) Harvestons is registered with the state of Texas. Thus, a party may serve a summons and a copy of a complaint on Harvestons by serving the Texas Securities Commissioner. In this case, the return of service indicated that process was served on the commissioner "by delivering to JoAnn Kocerek defendant, in person, a true copy of this [summons] together with the accompanying copy(ies) of the [complaint]." Harvestons did not file an answer, and Narnia obtained a default judgment against the defendant for $365,000, plus attorneys' fees and interest. Five months after this judgment, Harvestons filed a motion for a new trial, which the court denied. Harvestons appealed to a state intermediate appellate court, claiming that it had not been served in strict compliance with the rules governing service of process. [Harvestons Securities, Inc. v. Narnia Investments, Ltd., 218 S.W.3d 126 (Tex.App.—Houston 2007)]* **(See page 49.)**

(a) Harvestons asserted that Narnia's service was invalid, in part, because "the return of service states that process was delivered to 'JoAnn Kocerek'" and did not show that she "had the authority to accept process on behalf of Harvestons or the Texas Securities Commissioner." Should such a detail, if it is required, be strictly construed and applied? Should it apply in this case? Explain.

(b) Who is responsible for ensuring that service of process is accomplished properly? Was it accomplished properly in this case? Why or why not?

## Legal Reasoning Group Activity

**3–10. Court Procedures.** Bento Cuisine is a lunch-cart business. It occupies a street corner in Texarkana, a city that straddles the border of Arkansas and Texas. Across the street—and across the state line, which runs down the middle of the street—is Rico's Tacos. The two businesses compete for customers. Recently, Bento has begun to suspect that Rico's is engaging in competitive behavior that is illegal. Bento's manager overheard several of Rico's employees discussing these competitive tactics while on a break at a nearby Starbucks. Bento files a lawsuit against Rico's in a federal court based on diversity jurisdiction. **(See page 52.)**

(a) The first group will discuss whether Rico's could file a motion claiming that the federal court lacks jurisdiction over this dispute.

(b) The second group will assume that the case goes to trial. Bento believes that it has both the law and the facts on its side. Nevertheless, at the end of the trial, the jury decides against Bento, and the judge issues a ruling in favor of Rico's. If Bento is unwilling to accept this result, what are its options?

(c) As discussed in this chapter, hearsay is literally what a witness says he or she heard another person say. A third group will decide whether Bento's manager can testify about what he heard some of Rico's employees say to one another while at a coffee shop. This group will also discuss what makes the admissibility of hearsay evidence potentially unethical.

# CHAPTER 4

# BUSINESS AND THE CONSTITUTION

Laws that govern business have their origin in the lawmaking authority granted by the U.S. Constitution, which is the supreme law in this country.[1] As mentioned in Chapter 1, neither Congress nor any state may pass a law that is in conflict with the Constitution.

Constitutional disputes frequently come before the courts. For instance, numerous states challenged the Obama administration's Affordable Care Act on constitutional grounds. The United States Supreme Court decided in 2012 that the provisions of this law, which require most Americans to have health insurance by 2014, did not exceed the constitutional authority of the federal government. The Court's decision in the matter continues to have a significant impact on the business environment.

In this chapter, we examine some basic constitutional concepts and clauses and their significance for businesspersons. We then look at certain freedoms guaranteed by the first ten amendments to the Constitution—the Bill of Rights—and discuss how these freedoms affect business activities.

---

**1.** See Appendix B for the full text of the U.S. Constitution.

---

## SECTION 1
## THE CONSTITUTIONAL POWERS OF GOVERNMENT

Following the Revolutionary War, the states adopted the Articles of Confederation. The Articles created a *confederal form of government* in which the states had the authority to govern themselves and the national government could exercise only limited powers. When problems arose because the nation was facing an economic crisis and state laws interfered with the free flow of commerce, a national convention was called, and the delegates drafted the U.S. Constitution. This document, after its ratification by the states in 1789, became the basis for an entirely new form of government.

### A Federal Form of Government

The new government created by the U.S. Constitution reflected a series of compromises made by the convention delegates on various issues. Some delegates wanted sovereign power to remain with the states. Others wanted the national government alone to exercise sovereign power. The end result was a compromise—a **federal form of government** in which the national government and the states *share* sovereign power.

**FEDERAL POWERS** The Constitution sets forth specific powers that can be exercised by the national government. It further provides that the national government has the implied power to undertake actions necessary to carry out its expressly designated powers (or *enumerated powers*). All other powers are expressly "reserved" to the states under the Tenth Amendment to the U.S. Constitution.

**REGULATORY POWERS OF THE STATES** As part of their inherent **sovereignty** (independence), state governments have the authority to regulate affairs within their borders. As mentioned, this authority stems, in part, from the Tenth Amendment, which reserves all powers not delegated to the national government to the states or to the people.

State regulatory powers are often referred to as **police powers.** The term encompasses more than just the enforcement of criminal laws. Police powers also give state governments broad rights to regulate private activities to protect or promote the public order, health, safety, morals, and general welfare. Fire and building codes, antidiscrimination laws, parking regulations, zoning restrictions, licensing requirements, and thousands of other state statutes have been enacted pursuant to states' police powers.

Local governments, including cities, also exercise police powers.[2] Generally, state laws enacted pursuant to a state's police powers carry a strong presumption of validity.

## Relations Among the States

The U.S. Constitution also includes provisions concerning relations among the states in our federal system. Particularly important are the *privileges and immunities clause* and the *full faith and credit clause*.

**THE PRIVILEGES AND IMMUNITIES CLAUSE** Article IV, Section 2, of the Constitution provides that the "Citizens of each State shall be entitled to all Privileges and Immunities of Citizens in the several States." This clause is often referred to as the interstate **privileges and immunities clause.**[3] It prevents a state from imposing unreasonable burdens on citizens of another state—particularly with regard to means of livelihood or doing business.

When a citizen of one state engages in basic and essential activities in another state (the "foreign state"), the foreign state must have a *substantial reason* for treating the nonresident differently from its own residents. Basic activities include transferring property, seeking employment, or accessing the court system. The foreign state must also establish that its reason for the discrimination is *substantially related* to the state's ultimate purpose in adopting the legislation or regulating the activity.[4]

**THE FULL FAITH AND CREDIT CLAUSE** Article IV, Section 1, of the U.S. Constitution provides that "Full Faith and Credit shall be given in each State to the public Acts, Records, and judicial Proceedings of every other State." This clause, which is referred to as the **full faith and credit clause,** applies only to civil matters. It ensures that rights established under deeds, wills, contracts, and similar instruments in one state will be honored by other states.

It also ensures that any judicial decision with respect to such property rights will be honored and enforced in all states.

▶ **Example 4.1** The legal issues raised by same-sex marriage involve, among other things, the full faith and credit clause because that clause requires each state to honor marriage decrees issued by another state. Therefore, if same-sex partners marry in Washington, which legalized same-sex marriage in 2012, and the couple later moves to another state, that state would be required to recognize the validity of their marriage. ◀

The full faith and credit clause has contributed to the unity of American citizens because it protects their legal rights as they move about from state to state. It also protects the rights of those to whom they owe obligations, such as a person who is awarded monetary damages by a court. The ability to enforce such rights is extremely important for the conduct of business in a country with a very mobile citizenry.

## The Separation of Powers

To make it difficult for the national government to use its power arbitrarily, the Constitution provided for three branches of government. The legislative branch makes the laws, the executive branch enforces the laws, and the judicial branch interprets the laws. Each branch performs a separate function, and no branch may exercise the authority of another branch.

Additionally, a system of **checks and balances** allows each branch to limit the actions of the other two branches, thus preventing any one branch from exercising too much power. Some examples of these checks and balances include the following:

1. The legislative branch (Congress) can enact a law, but the executive branch (the president) has the constitutional authority to veto that law.
2. The executive branch is responsible for foreign affairs, but treaties with foreign governments require the advice and consent of the Senate.
3. Congress determines the jurisdiction of the federal courts, and the president appoints federal judges, with the advice and consent of the Senate. The judicial branch has the power to hold actions of the other two branches unconstitutional.[5]

---

2. Local governments derive their authority to regulate their communities from the state, because they are creatures of the state. In other words, they cannot come into existence unless authorized by the state to do so.

3. Interpretations of this clause commonly use the terms *privilege* and *immunity* synonymously. Generally, the terms refer to certain rights, benefits, or advantages enjoyed by individuals.

4. This test was first announced in *Supreme Court of New Hampshire v. Piper,* 470 U.S. 274, 105 S.Ct. 1272, 84 L.Ed.2d 205 (1985). For another example, see *Lee v. Miner,* 369 F.Supp.2d 527 (D.Del. 2005).

5. As discussed in Chapter 2, the power of judicial review was established by the United States Supreme Court in *Marbury v. Madison,* 5 U.S. (1 Cranch) 137, 2 L.Ed. 60 (1803).

# The Commerce Clause

To prevent states from establishing laws and regulations that would interfere with trade and commerce among the states, the Constitution expressly delegated to the national government the power to regulate interstate commerce. Article I, Section 8, of the U.S. Constitution explicitly permits Congress "[t]o regulate Commerce with foreign Nations, and among the several States, and with the Indian Tribes." This clause, referred to as the **commerce clause,** has had a greater impact on business than any other provision in the Constitution. The commerce clause provides the basis for the national government's extensive regulation of state and even local affairs.

Initially, the courts interpreted the commerce clause to apply only to commerce between the states (*interstate* commerce) and not commerce within the states (*intrastate* commerce). In 1824, however, the United States Supreme Court decided the landmark case of *Gibbons v. Ogden.*[6] The Court held that commerce within the states could also be regulated by the national government as long as the commerce *substantially affected* commerce involving more than one state.

### THE EXPANSION OF NATIONAL POWERS UNDER THE COMMERCE CLAUSE

As the nation grew and faced new kinds of problems, the commerce clause became a vehicle for the additional expansion of the national government's regulatory powers. Even activities that seemed purely local in nature came under the regulatory reach of the national government if those activities were deemed to substantially affect interstate commerce. In 1942, the Supreme Court held that wheat production by an individual farmer intended wholly for consumption on his own farm was subject to federal regulation.[7]

▶ **Case in Point 4.2**  In *Heart of Atlanta Motel v. United States,*[8] a landmark case decided in 1964, the Supreme Court upheld the federal government's authority under the commerce clause to prohibit racial discrimination nationwide in public facilities. The case was brought by an Atlanta motel owner who refused to rent rooms to African Americans, in violation of the Civil Rights Act of 1964. The Court concluded that local motels and restaurants do affect interstate commerce. The Court stated that "if it is interstate commerce that feels the pinch, it does not matter how local the operation that applies the squeeze." ◀

### THE COMMERCE CLAUSE TODAY

Today, at least theoretically, the power over commerce authorizes the national government to regulate almost every commercial enterprise in the United States. The breadth of the commerce clause permits the national government to legislate in areas in which Congress has not explicitly been granted power.

In the last twenty years, the Supreme Court has on occasion curbed the national government's regulatory authority under the commerce clause. In 1995, the Court held—for the first time in sixty years—that Congress had exceeded its regulatory authority under the commerce clause. The Court struck down an act that banned the possession of guns within one thousand feet of any school because the act attempted to regulate an area that had "nothing to do with commerce."[9] Subsequently, the Court invalidated key portions of two other federal acts on the ground that they exceeded Congress's commerce clause authority.[10]

### MEDICAL MARIJUANA AND THE COMMERCE CLAUSE

In one notable case, however, the Supreme Court did allow the federal government to regulate noncommercial activities taking place wholly within a state's borders. ▶ **Case in Point 4.3**  More than a dozen states, including California, have adopted laws that legalize marijuana for medical purposes. Marijuana possession, however, is illegal under the federal Controlled Substances Act (CSA).[11] After the federal government seized the marijuana that two seriously ill California women were using on the advice of their physicians, the women filed a lawsuit. They argued that it was unconstitutional for the federal statute to prohibit them from using marijuana for medical purposes that were legal within the state.

The Supreme Court, though, held that Congress has the authority to prohibit the *intrastate* possession and noncommercial cultivation of marijuana as part of a larger regulatory scheme (the CSA).[12] In other

---

**6.** 22 U.S. (9 Wheat.) 1, 6 L.Ed. 23 (1824).

**7.** *Wickard v. Filburn,* 317 U.S. 111, 63 S.Ct. 82, 87 L.Ed. 122 (1942).

**8.** 379 U.S. 241, 85 S.Ct. 348, 13 L.Ed.2d 258 (1964).

**9.** The Court held the Gun-Free School Zones Act of 1990 to be unconstitutional in *United States v. Lopez,* 514 U.S. 549, 115 S.Ct. 1624, 131 L.Ed.2d 626 (1995).

**10.** *Printz v. United States,* 521 U.S. 898, 117 S.Ct. 2365, 138 L.Ed.2d 914 (1997), involving the Brady Handgun Violence Prevention Act of 1993; and *United States v. Morrison,* 529 U.S. 598, 120 S.Ct. 1740, 146 L.Ed.2d 658 (2000), concerning the federal Violence Against Women Act of 1994.

**11.** 21 U.S.C. Sections 801 *et seq.*

**12.** *Gonzales v. Raich,* 545 U.S. 1, 125 S.Ct. 2195, 162 L.Ed.2d 1 (2005).

words, state medical marijuana laws do not insulate the users from federal prosecution. ◄

**THE "DORMANT" COMMERCE CLAUSE** The Supreme Court has interpreted the commerce clause to mean that the national government has the *exclusive* authority to regulate commerce that substantially affects trade and commerce among the states. This express grant of authority to the national government is often referred to as the "positive" aspect of the commerce clause. But this positive aspect also implies a negative aspect—that the states do *not* have the authority to regulate interstate commerce. This negative aspect of the commerce clause is often referred to as the "dormant" (implied) commerce clause.

The dormant commerce clause comes into play when state regulations affect interstate commerce. In this situation, the courts weigh the state's interest in regulating a certain matter against the burden that the state's regulation places on interstate commerce. Because courts balance the interests involved, it is difficult to predict the outcome in a particular case.

In the following case, the plaintiffs—a group of California wineries and others—contended that a Massachusetts statute discriminated against out-of-state wineries in violation of the dormant commerce clause. A federal district court agreed and enjoined (prevented) the enforcement of the statute. The commonwealth of Massachusetts appealed the trial court's decision.

---

## CASE 4.1

### Family Winemakers of California v. Jenkins[a]
United States Court of Appeals, First Circuit, 592 F.3d 1 (2010).

**BACKGROUND AND FACTS** Since the 1930s, most states, including Massachusetts, have used a three-tier system to control the sale of alcoholic beverages within their territories. Producers can sell beverages only to licensed in-state wholesalers. Licensed wholesalers can sell only to licensed retailers, such as stores, taverns, restaurants, and bars. Nonetheless, many states allow for direct shipping of alcoholic beverages to consumers in their states. Direct shipping offers economic advantages to small wineries throughout the country. It also benefits consumers because it eliminates wholesaler and retailer price markups. In 2006, Massachusetts passed a law that bases wineries' eligibility for direct shipping licenses on whether they are *small* or *large*. Presumably, this system does not distinguish between in-state and out-of-state wineries. Large wineries are defined as those that produce more than 30,000 gallons per year. These wineries must choose between using the existing three-tier system or selling directly to consumers. Small wineries can simultaneously use both systems and therefore have a competitive advantage.

Family Winemakers of California argued that this law has a discriminatory effect. Family pointed out that 98 percent of all wine in the United States is produced by "large" wineries and that all of these wineries are outside of Massachusetts. Under the law, "small" wineries within Massachusetts can use multiple distribution methods not available to "large" out-of-state wineries. Family argued that the law's true purpose was "to ensure that Massachusetts wineries obtained advantages over their out-of-state counterparts." A federal district court agreed and prevented enforcement of the statute. Massachusetts appealed.

**DECISION AND RATIONALE** The United States Court of Appeals for the First Circuit affirmed the lower court's decision. "Here, the totality of the evidence introduced by plaintiffs demonstrates that [the law's] preferential treatment of 'small' wineries . . . is discriminatory." The reviewing court agreed with Family that the 2006 law confers a "clear competitive advantage to 'small' wineries," which includes all of the wineries located in the state of Massachusetts. All "large" wineries, "none of which are in Massachusetts," are at a competitive disadvantage because of the law.

**WHAT IF THE FACTS WERE DIFFERENT?** *Suppose that most "small" wineries, as defined by the 2006 Massachusetts law, were located out of state. How could the law be discriminatory in that situation?*

---

**a.** The case was brought against Eddie J. Jenkins, the chair of the Massachusetts Alcoholic Beverages Control Commission, in his official capacity.

**CASE 4.1 CONTINUED**  **THE ETHICAL DIMENSION** *People who favor laws that prohibit direct-to-consumer shipping of alcoholic beverages, particularly wine, claim that such laws prevent minors from having easy access to alcoholic beverages. Is this argument sufficiently strong to justify states' prohibiting such shipments within their borders? Why or why not?*

## The Supremacy Clause and Federal Preemption

Article VI of the U.S. Constitution, commonly referred to as the **supremacy clause,** provides that the Constitution, laws, and treaties of the United States are "the supreme Law of the Land." When there is a direct conflict between a federal law and a state law, the state law is rendered invalid. Because some powers are *concurrent* (shared by the federal government and the states), however, it is necessary to determine which law governs in a particular circumstance.

When Congress chooses to act (legislate) exclusively in an area in which the federal government and the states have concurrent powers, **preemption** occurs. A valid federal statute or regulation will take precedence over a conflicting state or local law or regulation on the same general subject.

**FEDERAL STATUTES MAY SPECIFY PREEMPTION** Sometimes, the federal statute will include a preemption provision to make it clear that Congress intends the legislation to preempt any state laws on the matter. ▶ **Case in Point 4.4**  A man who alleged that he had been injured by a faulty medical device (a balloon catheter that was inserted into his artery following a heart attack) sued the manufacturer.

The case ultimately came before the United States Supreme Court, which noted that the Medical Device Amendments of 1976 had included a preemption provision. The medical device had passed the U.S. Food and Drug Administration's rigorous premarket approval process. Therefore, the Court concluded that the federal regulation of medical devices preempted the injured party's state common law claims for negligence, strict liability, and implied warranty (see Chapters 6 and 7).[13] ◀

**WHEN THE STATUTE DOES NOT EXPRESSLY MENTION PREEMPTION** Often, it is not clear whether Congress, in passing a law, intended to preempt an entire subject area against state regulation. In those situations, the courts determine whether Congress intended to exercise exclusive power over a given area.

No single factor is decisive as to whether a court will find preemption. Generally, congressional intent to preempt will be found if a federal law regulating an activity is so pervasive, comprehensive, or detailed that the states have no room to regulate in that area. Also, when a federal statute creates an agency—such as the National Labor Relations Board—to enforce the law, matters that come within the agency's jurisdiction will likely preempt state laws.

## The Taxing and Spending Powers

Article I, Section 8, of the U.S. Constitution provides that Congress has the "Power to lay and collect Taxes, Duties, Imposts, and Excises." Section 8 further requires uniformity in taxation among the states, and thus Congress may not tax some states while exempting others.

In the distant past, if Congress attempted to regulate indirectly, by taxation, an area over which it had no authority, the courts would invalidate the tax. Today, however, if a tax measure is reasonable, it generally is held to be within the national taxing power. Moreover, the expansive interpretation of the commerce clause almost always provides a basis for sustaining a federal tax.

Article I, Section 8, also gives Congress its spending power—the power "to pay the Debts and provide for the common Defence and general Welfare of the United States." Congress can spend revenues not only to carry out its expressed powers but also to promote any objective it deems worthwhile, so long as it does not violate the Bill of Rights. The spending power necessarily involves policy choices, with which taxpayers (and politicians) may disagree.

### SECTION 2
# BUSINESS AND THE BILL OF RIGHTS

The importance of a written declaration of the rights of individuals caused the first Congress of the United States to submit twelve amendments to the U.S. Constitution to the states for approval. Ten of these

---

**13.** *Riegel v. Medtronic, Inc.,* 552 U.S. 312, 128 S.Ct. 999, 169 L.Ed.2d 892 (2008).

amendments, known as the **Bill of Rights,** were adopted in 1791 and embody a series of protections for the individual against various types of interference by the federal government.[14]

The protections guaranteed by these ten amendments are summarized in Exhibit 4–1 below.[15] Some of these constitutional protections apply to business entities as well. For example, corporations exist as separate legal entities, or *legal persons,* and enjoy many of the same rights and privileges as *natural persons* do.

## Limits on Federal and State Governmental Actions

As originally intended, the Bill of Rights limited only the powers of the national government. Over time, however, the United States Supreme Court "incorporated" most of these rights into the protections against state actions afforded by the Fourteenth Amendment to the Constitution.

**THE FOURTEENTH AMENDMENT** The Fourteenth Amendment, passed in 1868 after the Civil War, provides, in part, that "[n]o State shall . . . deprive any

person of life, liberty, or property, without due process of law." Starting in 1925, the Supreme Court began to define various rights and liberties guaranteed in the U.S. Constitution as constituting "due process of law," which was required of state governments under that amendment.

Today, most of the rights and liberties set forth in the Bill of Rights apply to state governments as well as the national government. In other words, neither the federal government nor state governments can deprive persons of those rights and liberties.

**JUDICIAL INTERPRETATION** The rights secured by the Bill of Rights are not absolute. Many of the rights guaranteed by the first ten amendments are set forth in very general terms. The Second Amendment states that people have a right to keep and bear arms, but it does not explain the extent of this right. As the Supreme Court noted in 2008, this does not mean that people can "keep and carry any weapon whatsoever in any manner whatsoever and for whatever purpose."[16] Legislatures can prohibit the carrying of concealed weapons or certain types of weapons, such as machine guns.

Ultimately, it is the United States Supreme Court, as the final interpreter of the Constitution, that gives meaning to these rights and determines their bound-

---

14. Another of these proposed amendments was ratified more than two hundred years later (in 1992) and became the Twenty-seventh Amendment to the Constitution. See Appendix B.
15. See the Constitution in Appendix B for the complete text of each amendment.

16. *District of Columbia v. Heller,* 554 U.S. 570, 128 S.Ct. 2783, 171 L.Ed.2d 637 (2008).

---

**EXHIBIT 4–1 Protections Guaranteed by the Bill of Rights**

**First Amendment:** Guarantees the freedoms of religion, speech, and the press and the rights to assemble peaceably and to petition the government.

**Second Amendment:** States that the right of the people to keep and bear arms shall not be infringed.

**Third Amendment:** Prohibits, in peacetime, the lodging of soldiers in any house without the owner's consent.

**Fourth Amendment:** Prohibits unreasonable searches and seizures of persons or property.

**Fifth Amendment:** Guarantees the rights to indictment by grand jury, to due process of law, and to fair payment when private property is taken for public use; prohibits compulsory self-incrimination and double jeopardy (being tried again for an alleged crime for which one has already stood trial).

**Sixth Amendment:** Guarantees the accused in a criminal case the right to a speedy and public trial by an impartial jury and with counsel. The accused has the right to cross-examine witnesses against him or her and to solicit testimony from witnesses in his or her favor.

**Seventh Amendment:** Guarantees the right to a trial by jury in a civil case involving at least twenty dollars.[a]

**Eighth Amendment:** Prohibits excessive bail and fines, as well as cruel and unusual punishment.

**Ninth Amendment:** Establishes that the people have rights in addition to those specified in the Constitution.

**Tenth Amendment:** Establishes that those powers neither delegated to the federal government nor denied to the states are reserved to the states and to the people.

a. Twenty dollars was forty days' pay for the average person when the Bill of Rights was written.

aries. Changing public views on controversial topics, such as privacy in an era of terrorist threats or the rights of gay men and lesbians, may affect the way the Supreme Court decides a case. On several occasions, justices on the Supreme Court have even mentioned that they have considered foreign laws in reaching a decision.

## Freedom of Speech

A democratic form of government cannot survive unless people can freely voice their political opinions and criticize government actions or policies. Freedom of speech, particularly political speech, is thus a prized right, and traditionally the courts have protected this right to the fullest extent possible.

**Symbolic speech**—gestures, movements, articles of clothing, and other forms of expressive conduct— is also given substantial protection by the courts. The Supreme Court has held that the burning of the American flag as part of a peaceful protest is a constitutionally protected form of expression.[17] Similarly, wearing a T-shirt with a photo of a presidential candidate is a constitutionally protected form of expression. ▶ **Example 4.5** As a form of expression, Nate has gang signs tattooed on his torso, arms, neck, and legs. If a reasonable person would interpret this conduct as conveying a message, then it might be a protected form of symbolic speech. ◀

An interesting topic in today's legal environment is whether computers should have free speech rights. For a discussion of this issue, see this chapter's *Insight into E-Commerce* feature on page 77.

**REASONABLE RESTRICTIONS** Expression—oral, written, or symbolized by conduct—is subject to reasonable restrictions. A balance must be struck between a government's obligation to protect its citizens and those citizens' exercise of their rights. Reasonableness is analyzed on a case-by-case basis.

***Content-Neutral Laws.*** Laws that regulate the time, manner, and place, but not the content, of speech receive less scrutiny by the courts than do laws that restrict the content of expression. If a restriction imposed by the government is content neutral, then a court may allow it. To be content neutral, the restriction must be aimed at combatting some societal problem, such as crime or drug abuse, and not be aimed

at suppressing the expressive conduct or its message. Courts have often protected nude dancing as a form of symbolic expression but typically allow content-neutral laws that ban all public nudity.

▶ **Case in Point 4.6** Ria Ora was charged with dancing nude at an annual "anti-Christmas" protest in Harvard Square in Cambridge, Massachusetts, under a statute banning public displays of open and gross lewdness. Ora argued that the statute was overbroad and unconstitutional, and a trial court agreed. On appeal, however, a state appellate court upheld the statute as constitutional in situations in which there was an unsuspecting or unwilling audience.[18] ◀

***Laws That Restrict the Content of Speech.*** If a law regulates the content of the expression, it must serve a compelling state interest and must be narrowly written to achieve that interest. Under the **compelling government interest** test, the government's interest is balanced against the individual's constitutional right to free expression. For the statute to be valid, there must be a compelling government interest that can be furthered only by the law in question.

The United States Supreme Court has held that schools may restrict students' speech at school events. ▶ **Case in Point 4.7** Some high school students held up a banner saying "Bong Hits 4 Jesus" at an off-campus but school-sanctioned event. The Supreme Court ruled that the school did not violate the students' free speech rights when school officials confiscated the banner and suspended the students for ten days. Because the banner could reasonably be interpreted as promoting drugs, the Court concluded that the school's actions were justified. Several justices disagreed, however, noting that the majority's holding creates an exception that will allow schools to censor any student speech that mentions drugs.[19] ◀

At issue in the following case was an Indiana state law that barred most sex offenders from using social networking sites such as Facebook, instant messaging services such as Twitter, and chat programs that the offenders knew were accessible to minors. Was this law unconstitutional under the First Amendment?

---

17. *Texas v. Johnson*, 491 U.S. 397, 109 S.Ct. 2533, 105 L.Ed.2d 342 (1989).

18. *Commonwealth v. Ora*, 451 Mass. 125, 883 N.E.2d 1217 (2008).
19. *Morse v. Frederick*, 551 U.S. 393, 127 S.Ct. 2618, 168 L.Ed.2d 290 (2007).

# CASE 4.2

## Doe[a] v. Prosecutor, Marion County, Indiana
United States Court of Appeals, Seventh Circuit, 705 F.3d 694 (2013).

**BACKGROUND AND FACTS**  John Doe was convicted of child exploitation in Marion County, Indiana. After his release from prison, he was not subject to court supervision, but was required to register as a sex offender with the state. Under an Indiana statute that covered child exploitation and other sex offenses, Doe could not use certain Web sites and programs. Doe filed a suit in a federal district court against the Marion County prosecutor, alleging that the statute violated his right to freedom of speech under the First Amendment. Doe asked the court to issue an injunction to block enforcement of the law. The court held that "the regulation is narrowly tailored to serve a significant state interest" and entered a judgment for the defendant. Doe appealed to the U.S. Court of Appeals for the Seventh Circuit.

**DECISION AND RATIONALE**  The U.S. Court of Appeals for the Seventh Circuit reversed the lower court's judgment in the defendant's favor and remanded the case for the entry of a judgment for Doe. An Indiana law prohibits sex offenders from knowingly or intentionally using a social networking Website or an instant messaging or chat room program that "the offender knows allows a person who is less than eighteen (18) years of age to access or use the Web site or program." The appellate court pointed out that this statute clearly implicated Doe's First Amendment rights. "It not only precludes [prohibits] expressions through the medium of social media, it also limits his rights to receive information and ideas."

The government of Indiana agreed that there is nothing dangerous about Doe's use of social media "as long as he does not improperly communicate with minors." But because illicit communication comprises a tiny part of the universe of social network activity, "the Indiana law targets substantially more activity than the evil it seeks to redress." The appellate court further pointed out that Indiana has other methods to fight inappropriate communications between minors and sex offenders. The Indiana statute was deemed over inclusive. A law that concerns rights under the First Amendment must be narrowly tailored to accomplish its objective. The blanket ban on Doe's social media access in this case did not pass this test.

**THE LEGAL ENVIRONMENT DIMENSION**  *What is an injunction? What did the plaintiff in this case hope to gain by seeking an injunction?*

**THE SOCIAL DIMENSION**  *Could a state effectively enforce a law that banned all communication between minors and sex offenders through social media sites? Why or why not?*

---

a.   The names *John Doe* and *Jane Doe* are used as placeholders in litigation to represent a party whose true identity is either unknown or being with held for some reason.

---

**CORPORATE POLITICAL SPEECH**  Political speech by corporations also falls within the protection of the First Amendment. Many years ago, the United States Supreme Court struck down as unconstitutional a Massachusetts statute that prohibited corporations from making political contributions or expenditures that individuals were permitted to make.[20] The Court has also held that a law forbidding a corporation from including inserts with its bills to express its views on controversial issues violates the First Amendment.[21]

Corporate political speech continues to be given significant protection under the First Amendment. ▶ **Case in Point 4.8**  In *Citizens United v. Federal Election Commission,*[22] the Supreme Court issued a landmark decision that overturned a twenty-year-old precedent on campaign financing. The case involved Citizens United, a nonprofit corporation that has a *political action committee* (an organization that registers with the government and campaigns for or against political candidates).

Citizens United had produced a film called *Hillary: The Movie* that was critical of Hillary Clinton, who was seeking the Democratic nomination for presidential

20.  *First National Bank of Boston v. Bellotti,* 435 U.S. 765, 98 S.Ct. 1407, 55 L.Ed.2d 707 (1978).
21.  *Consolidated Edison Co. v. Public Service Commission,* 447 U.S. 530, 100 S.Ct. 2326, 65 L.Ed.2d 319 (1980).
22.  558 U.S. 310, 130 S.Ct. 876, 175 L.Ed.2d 753 (2010).

# INSIGHT INTO E-COMMERCE
## Do Computers Have Free Speech Rights?

When you do a Web search using Bing, Google, or any other search engine, the program inherent in the engine gives you a list of results. When you use a document-creation program, such as Microsoft Word, it often guesses what you intend and corrects your misspellings automatically. Do computers that make such choices engage in "speech," and if so, do they enjoy First Amendment protection? This question is not as absurd as it may seem at first.

### Are Google's Search Results "Speech"?

More than a decade ago, a company dissatisfied with its rankings in Google's search results sued. Google argued that its search results were constitutionally protected speech. The plaintiff, Search King, Inc., sought an injunction against Google, but a federal district court decided in Google's favor. The court ruled that the ranking of results when a search is undertaken "constitutes opinions protected by the First Amendment. . . . *Page Ranks* are opinions—opinions are the significance of particular Web sites as they correspond to a search query." Therefore, the First Amendment applied to the search results.[a]

### Google versus the Federal Trade Commission

For the last few years, Google has been the dominant search engine. Yet in the 1990s, the federal government was worried that Microsoft's search engine was too dominant and was crushing the search engines of Yahoo!, AltaVista, and Lycos. Today, of course, AltaVista and Lycos no longer exist, and Microsoft's new search engine, Bing, is a relatively minor player in the field.

Fast-forward to 2011. The Federal Trade Commission (FTC) contemplated bringing charges against Google for favoring its own offerings, such as restaurant reviews, in its search results. Now it was Microsoft that was encouraging the FTC to proceed. After a nineteen-month investiga-

tion, in early 2013 the FTC announced that it would *not* prosecute Google. The FTC's decision was a blow to search engines that compete with Google, including Microsoft's Bing.

### The First Amendment Protection Argument

Google commissioned Eugene Volokh and Donald Falk, two legal experts in this field, to research the issue of whether search engine results are protected by the First Amendment.[b] The researchers concluded that search engine results are the same as the editorial judgments that a newspaper makes in deciding which wire service stories to run and which op-ed and business columnists to feature. The authors further claim that free speech applies to editorial choices no matter what their format. Search engines are protected even when they are "unfair" in ranking search results. Whether the search engine uses a computerized algorithm to compile its rankings is irrelevant.

Columbia Law professor Tim Wu disagrees. He argues that the First Amendment was intended to protect humans against the evils of state censorship and that protecting a computer's speech is not related to that purpose. At best, he says, search engine results are *commercial speech,* which has always received limited protection under the First Amendment. After all, computers make trillions of invisible decisions each day. Is each of those decisions protected speech?

### LEGAL CRITICAL THINKING
#### INSIGHT INTO SOCIAL MEDIA

*Facebook has numerous computers, all programmed by humans, of course. If Facebook's computers make decisions that allow your private information to be shared without your knowledge, should the First Amendment protect Facebook? Why or why not?*

---

a. *Search King, Inc. v. Google Technology, Inc.,* 2003 WL 21464568 (W.D.Okla. 2003). See also *Langdon v. Google, Inc.,* 474 F.Supp.2d 622 (D.Del. 2007).

b. Eugene Volokh and Donald Falk, "First Amendment Protection for Search Engine Search Results: White Paper Commissioned by Google" (UCLA School of Law Research Paper No. 12-22, April 20, 2012).

---

candidate. Campaign-finance law restricted Citizens United from broadcasting the movie, however. The Court ruled that the restrictions were unconstitutional and that the First Amendment, prevents limits from being placed on independent political expenditures by corporations. ◄

**COMMERCIAL SPEECH** The courts also give substantial protection to *commercial speech,* which consists of communications—primarily advertising and marketing—made by business firms that involve only their commercial interests. The protection given to commercial speech under the First Amendment is less extensive than that afforded to noncommercial speech, however.

A state may restrict certain kinds of advertising, for instance, in the interest of preventing consumers from being misled. States also have a legitimate interest in roadside beautification and therefore may impose restraints on billboard advertising. ▶ **Case in Point 4.9** Café Erotica, a nude dancing establishment, sued the state after being denied a permit to erect a billboard along an interstate highway in Florida. The state appellate court decided that because the law directly advanced a substantial government interest in highway beautification and safety, it was not an unconstitutional restraint on commercial speech.[23] ◀

---

23. *Café Erotica v. Florida Department of Transportation,* 830 So.2d 181 (Fla.App. 1 Dist. 2002); review denied by *Café Erotica We Dare to Bare v. Florida Department of Transportation,* 845 So.2d 888 (Fla. 2003).

Generally, a restriction on commercial speech will be considered valid as long as it meets three criteria:

1. It must seek to implement a substantial government interest.
2. It must directly advance that interest.
3. It must go no further than necessary to accomplish its objective.

At issue in the following case was whether a government agency had unconstitutionally restricted commercial speech when it prohibited the inclusion of a certain illustration on beer labels.

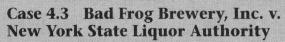

## SPOTLIGHT on Beer Labels

### Case 4.3   Bad Frog Brewery, Inc. v. New York State Liquor Authority
United States Court of Appeals, Second Circuit, 134 F.3d 87 (1998).

**BACKGROUND AND FACTS** Bad Frog Brewery, Inc., makes and sells alcoholic beverages. Some of the beverages feature labels that display a drawing of a frog making the gesture generally known as "giving the finger." Bad Frog's authorized New York distributor, Renaissance Beer Company, applied to the New York State Liquor Authority (NYSLA) for brand label approval, as required by state law before the beer could be sold in New York.

The NYSLA denied the application, in part, because "the label could appear in grocery and convenience stores, with obvious exposure on the shelf to children of tender age." Bad Frog filed a suit in a federal district court against the NYSLA, asking for, among other things, an injunction against the denial of the application. The court granted summary judgment in favor of the NYSLA. Bad Frog appealed to the U.S. Court of Appeals for the Second Circuit.

**DECISION AND RATIONALE** The U.S. Court of Appeals for the Second Circuit reversed the judgment of the district court and remanded the case for judgment to be entered in favor of Bad Frog. The appellate court held that the NYSLA's denial of Bad Frog's application violated the First Amendment. The ban on the use of the labels lacked a "reasonable fit" with the state's interest in shielding minors from vulgarity, and the NYSLA did not adequately consider alternatives to the ban.

The court acknowledged that the NYSLA's interest "in protecting children from vulgar and profane advertising" was "substantial." The question was whether banning Bad Frog's labels "directly advanced" that interest. "In view of the wide currency of vulgar displays throughout contemporary society, including comic books targeted directly at children, barring such displays from labels for alcoholic beverages cannot realistically be expected to reduce children's exposure to such displays to any significant degree." The court concluded that a "commercial speech limitation" must be "part of a substantial effort to advance a valid state interest, not merely the removal of a few grains of offensive sand from a beach of vulgarity."

Finally, as to whether the ban on the labels was more extensive than necessary to serve this interest, the court pointed out that there were "numerous less intrusive alternatives." For example, the NYSLA's "concern could be less intrusively dealt with by placing restrictions on the permissible locations where the appellant's products may be displayed within . . . stores."

**WHAT IF THE FACTS WERE DIFFERENT?** *If Bad Frog had sought to use the offensive label to market toys instead of beer, would the court's ruling likely have been the same? Why or why not?*

**THE LEGAL ENVIRONMENT DIMENSION** *Whose interests are advanced by the banning of certain types of advertising?*

**UNPROTECTED SPEECH** The United States Supreme Court has made it clear that certain types of speech will not be protected under the First Amendment. Speech that violates criminal laws (threatening speech and pornography, for example) is not constitutionally protected. Other unprotected speech includes fighting words, or words that are likely to incite others to respond violently. Speech that harms the good reputation of another, or defamatory speech (see Chapter 6), also is not protected under the First Amendment.

**Obscene Speech.** The First Amendment, as interpreted by the Supreme Court, also does not protect obscene speech. Establishing an objective definition of obscene speech has proved difficult, however, and the Court has grappled from time to time with this problem. In *Miller v. California,*[24] the Supreme Court created a test for legal obscenity, including a set of requirements that must be met for material to be legally obscene. Under this test, material is obscene if all of the following are true:

1. The average person finds that it violates contemporary community standards.
2. The work taken as a whole appeals to a prurient (arousing or obsessive) interest in sex.
3. The work shows patently offensive sexual conduct.
4. The work lacks serious redeeming literary, artistic, political, or scientific merit.

Because community standards vary widely, the *Miller* test has had inconsistent applications, and obscenity remains a constitutionally unsettled issue. Numerous state and federal statutes make it a crime to disseminate obscene materials, including child pornography.

**Online Obscenity.** Congress's first two attempts at protecting minors from pornographic materials on the Internet—the Communications Decency Act (CDA) of 1996[25] and the Child Online Protection Act (COPA) of 1998[26]—failed. Ultimately, the United States Supreme Court struck down both the CDA and COPA as unconstitutional restraints on speech, largely because the wording of these acts was overbroad and would restrict nonpornographic materials.

In 2000, Congress enacted the Children's Internet Protection Act (CIPA),[27] which requires public schools and libraries to install **filtering software** on computers to keep children from accessing adult content. Such software is designed to prevent persons from viewing certain Web sites based on a site's Internet address or its **meta tags,** or key words. The CIPA was challenged on constitutional grounds, but in 2003 the Supreme Court held that the act does not violate the First Amendment. The Court concluded that because libraries can disable the filters for any patrons who ask, the system is reasonably flexible and does not burden free speech to an unconstitutional extent.[28]

**Virtual Pornography.** In 2003, Congress enacted the Prosecutorial Remedies and Other Tools to end the Exploitation of Children Today Act (Protect Act).[29] The act makes it a crime to knowingly advertise, present, distribute, or solicit "any material or purported material in a manner that reflects the belief, or that is intended to cause another to believe, that the material or purported material" depicts actual child pornography.

Thus, it is a crime to intentionally distribute virtual child pornography—which uses computer-generated images, not actual people—without indicating that it is computer generated. In a case challenging the constitutionality of the Protect Act, the Supreme Court held that the statute was valid because it does not prohibit a substantial amount of protected speech.[30] Rather, the act generally prohibits offers to provide, and requests to obtain, child pornography—both of which are unprotected speech. Nevertheless, because of the difficulties of policing the Internet, as well as

---

**24.** 413 U.S. 15, 93 S.Ct. 2607, 37 L.Ed.2d 419 (1973).
**25.** 47 U.S.C. Section 223(a)(1)(B)(ii).
**26.** 47 U.S.C. Section 231.

**27.** 17 U.S.C. Sections 1701–1741.
**28.** *United States v. American Library Association,* 539 U.S. 194, 123 S.Ct. 2297, 156 L.Ed.2d 221 (2003).
**29.** 18 U.S.C. Section 2252A(a)(5)(B).
**30.** *United States v. Williams,* 553 U.S. 285, 128 S.Ct. 1830, 170 L.Ed.2d 650 (2008).

the constitutional complexities of prohibiting online obscenity through legislation, it remains a problem worldwide.

## Freedom of Religion

The First Amendment states that the government may neither establish any religion nor prohibit the free exercise of religious practices. The first part of this constitutional provision is referred to as the **establishment clause,** and the second part is known as the **free exercise clause.** Government action, both federal and state, must be consistent with this constitutional mandate.

**THE ESTABLISHMENT CLAUSE** The establishment clause prohibits the government from establishing a state-sponsored religion, as well as from passing laws that promote (aid or endorse) religion or show a preference for one religion over another. Although the establishment clause involves the separation of church and state, it does not require a complete separation.

*Applicable Standard.* Establishment clause cases often involve such issues as the legality of allowing or requiring school prayers, using state-issued vouchers to pay tuition at religious schools, and teaching creation theories versus evolution. Federal or state laws that do not promote or place a significant burden on religion are constitutional even if they have some impact on religion. For a government law or policy to be constitutional, it must not have the primary effect of promoting or inhibiting religion.

*Religious Displays.* Religious displays on public property have often been challenged as violating the establishment clause, and the United States Supreme Court has ruled on a number of such cases. Generally, the Court has focused on the proximity of the religious display to nonreligious symbols, such as reindeer and candy canes, or to symbols from different religions, such as a menorah (a nine-branched candelabrum used in celebrating Hanukkah). The Supreme Court took a slightly different approach when it held that public displays having historical, as well as religious, significance do not necessarily violate the establishment clause.[31]

▶ **Case in Point 4.10** Mount Soledad is a prominent hill near San Diego. There has been a forty-foot cross on top of Mount Soledad since 1913. In the 1990s, a war memorial with six walls listing the names of veterans was constructed next to the cross. The site was privately owned until 2006, when Congress authorized the property's transfer to the federal government "to preserve a historically significant war memorial."

Steve Trunk and the Jewish War Veterans filed lawsuits claiming that the cross violated the establishment clause because it endorsed the Christian religion. A federal appellate court agreed, finding that the primary effect of the memorial as a whole sent a strong message of endorsement of Christianity and exclusion (of non-Christian veterans). Although the inclusion of a cross in a war memorial does not always violate the establishment clause, the cross in this case physically dominated the site. Also, the cross was originally dedicated to religious purposes, had a long history of religious use, and was the only portion visible to drivers on the freeway below.[32] ◀

**THE FREE EXERCISE CLAUSE** The free exercise clause guarantees that a person can hold any religious belief that she or he wants, or a person can have no religious belief. The constitutional guarantee of personal freedom restricts only the actions of the government and not those of individuals or private businesses.

*Restrictions Must Be Necessary.* The government must have a compelling state interest for restricting the free exercise of religion, and the restriction must be the only way to further that interest. ▶ **Case in Point 4.11** Members of a particular Mennonite church must use horses and buggies for transportation, but they can use tractors to take their agricultural products to market. Their religion requires the tractors to have steel cleats on the tires, and they drove tractors with cleats on county roads for many years. Then the county passed an ordinance that prohibited the use of steel cleats because the cleats tend to damage newly surfaced roads.

When a member of the church received a citation for driving a tractor with cleats, he claimed that the ordinance violated the church's right to freely exercise its religion. Ultimately, the court ruled in his favor. The county had not met its burden of showing that the ordinance served a compelling state interest and was the least restrictive means of attaining that interest. There was no evidence of how much the cleats harmed the roads, other events also harmed

---

31. *Van Orden v. Perry,* 545 U.S. 677, 125 S.Ct. 2854, 162 L.Ed.2d 607 (2005).

32. *Trunk v. City of San Diego,* 629 F.3d 1099 (9th Cir. 2011).

the roads, and the county had allowed the cleats to be used for many years. Therefore, the ordinance was not carefully tailored to achieve the stated objective of road preservation.[33] ◀

***Public Welfare Exception.*** When religious *practices* work against public policy and the public welfare, though, the government can act. For instance, the government can require that a child receive certain types of vaccinations or medical treatment if his or her life is in danger—regardless of the child's or parent's religious beliefs. When public safety is an issue, an individual's religious beliefs often have to give way to the government's interest in protecting the public.

▶ **Example 4.12** In the Muslim faith, it is a religious violation for a woman to appear in public without a scarf over her head. Due to public safety concerns, many courts today do not allow any headgear to be worn in courtrooms. A courthouse in Georgia prevented a Muslim woman from entering because she refused to remove her scarf. As she left, she uttered an expletive at the court official and was arrested and brought before the judge, who ordered her to serve ten days in jail. ◀

## Searches and Seizures

The Fourth Amendment protects the "right of the people to be secure in their persons, houses, papers, and effects." Before searching or seizing private property, law enforcement officers must usually obtain a **search warrant**—an order from a judge or other public official authorizing the search or seizure.

**SEARCH WARRANTS AND PROBABLE CAUSE** To obtain a search warrant, law enforcement officers must convince a judge that they have reasonable grounds, or probable cause, to believe a search will reveal evidence of a specific illegality. To establish **probable cause,** the officers must have trustworthy evidence that would convince a reasonable person that the proposed search or seizure is more likely justified than not.

Furthermore, the Fourth Amendment prohibits *general* warrants. It requires warrants to include a particular description of whatever is to be searched or seized. General searches through a person's belongings are impermissible. The search cannot extend beyond what is described in the warrant. Although search warrants must be specific, if a warrant is issued

for a person's residence, officers may search items found in that residence even though they belong to other individuals.

▶ **Case in Point 4.13** Paycom Billing Services, Inc., an online payment service, stores vast amounts of customer credit-card information. Christopher Adjani, a former Paycom employee, threatened to sell Paycom's confidential client information if the company did not pay him $3 million. Pursuant to an investigation, the Federal Bureau of Investigation (FBI) obtained a search warrant to search Adjani's person, automobile, and residence, including computer equipment. When the FBI agents served the warrant, they discovered evidence of the criminal scheme in the e-mail communications on a computer in Adjani's residence that belonged to Adjani's live-in girlfriend. The court held that the search of the computer was proper given the involvement of computers in the alleged crime.[34] ◀

**SEARCHES AND SEIZURES IN THE BUSINESS CONTEXT** Because of the strong government interest in protecting the public, a warrant normally is not required for seizures of spoiled or contaminated food. Nor are warrants required for searches of businesses in such highly regulated industries as liquor, guns, and strip mining.

The standard used for highly regulated industries is sometimes applied in other contexts as well, such as screening for airline travel. ▶ **Case in Point 4.14** Christian Hartwell was attempting to board a flight from Philadelphia to Phoenix, Arizona. When he walked through the security checkpoint, he set off the alarm. Airport security took him aside and eventually discovered that he had two packages of crack cocaine in his pocket. When Hartwell was convicted of possession of drugs, he appealed, claiming that the airport search was suspicionless and violated his Fourth Amendment rights. A federal appellate court held that airports can be treated as highly regulated industries and that suspicionless checkpoint screening of airline passengers is constitutional.[35] ◀

Generally, however, government inspectors do not have the right to enter business premises without a warrant, although the standard of probable cause is not the same as that required in nonbusiness contexts. The existence of a general and neutral enforcement plan will normally justify issuance of the warrant. Lawyers and accountants frequently possess

---

**33.** *Mitchell County v. Zimmerman,* 810 N.W.2d 1 (Iowa Sup.Ct. 2012).

**34.** *United States v. Adjani,* 452 F.3d 1140 (9th Cir. 2006); *cert.* denied, 549 U.S. 1025, 127 S.Ct. 568, 166 L.Ed.2d 420 (2006).

**35.** *United States v. Hartwell,* 436 F.3d 174 (3d Cir. 2006).

the business records of their clients, and inspecting these documents while they are out of the hands of their true owners also requires a warrant.

## Self-Incrimination

The Fifth Amendment guarantees that no person "shall be compelled in any criminal case to be a witness against himself." Thus, in any court proceeding, an accused person cannot be forced to give testimony that might subject him or her to any criminal prosecution. The guarantee applies to both federal and state proceedings because the due process clause of the Fourteenth Amendment extends the protection to state courts.

The Fifth Amendment's guarantee against self-incrimination extends only to natural persons. Therefore, neither corporations nor partnerships receive Fifth Amendment protection. When a partnership is required to produce business records, it must do so even if the information provided incriminates the individual partners of the firm. In contrast, sole proprietors and sole practitioners (those who fully own their businesses) cannot be compelled to produce their business records. These individuals have full protection against self-incrimination because they function in only one capacity, and there is no separate business entity.

## SECTION 3
# DUE PROCESS AND EQUAL PROTECTION

Other constitutional guarantees of great significance to Americans are mandated by the *due process clauses* of the Fifth and Fourteenth Amendments and the *equal protection clause* of the Fourteenth Amendment.

## Due Process

Both the Fifth and Fourteenth Amendments provide that no person shall be deprived "of life, liberty, or property, without due process of law." The **due process clause** of these constitutional amendments has two aspects—procedural and substantive. Note that the due process clause applies to "legal persons" (that is, corporations), as well as to individuals.

**PROCEDURAL DUE PROCESS** *Procedural* due process requires that any government decision to take life,

liberty, or property must be made equitably. In other words, the government must give a person proper notice and an opportunity to be heard. Fair procedures must be used in determining whether a person will be subjected to punishment or have some burden imposed on her or him.

Fair procedure has been interpreted as requiring that the person have at least an opportunity to object to a proposed action before an impartial, neutral decision maker (which need not be a judge). ▶ **Example 4.15** Doyle Burns, a nursing student in Kansas, poses for a photograph standing next to a placenta used as a lab specimen. Although she quickly deletes the photo from her library, it ends up on Facebook. When the director of nursing sees the photo, Burns is expelled. She sues for reinstatement and wins. The school violated Burns's due process rights by expelling her from the nursing program for taking a photo without giving her an opportunity to present her side to school authorities. ◀

**SUBSTANTIVE DUE PROCESS** *Substantive* due process focuses on the content of legislation rather than the fairness of procedures. Substantive due process limits what the government may do in its legislative and executive capacities. Legislation must be fair and reasonable in content and must further a legitimate governmental objective. A city cannot, for instance, pass an ordinance that allows police officers to break up any group of two or more persons who are standing together if one of those persons is believed to be a gang member.

If a law or other governmental action limits a fundamental right, the state must have a legitimate and compelling interest to justify its action. Fundamental rights include interstate travel, privacy, voting, marriage and family, and all First Amendment rights. Thus, a state must have a substantial reason for taking any action that infringes on a person's free speech rights.

In situations not involving fundamental rights, a law or action does not violate substantive due process if it rationally relates to any legitimate government purpose. In these circumstances, only state conduct that is arbitrary or shocks the conscience will violate substantive due process. Under this test, almost any business regulation will be upheld as reasonable.

## Equal Protection

Under the Fourteenth Amendment, a state may not "deny to any person within its jurisdiction the equal protection of the laws." The United States Supreme Court has interpreted the due process clause of the Fifth

Amendment to make the **equal protection clause** applicable to the federal government as well. Equal protection means that the government cannot enact laws that treat similarly situated individuals differently.

Equal protection, like substantive due process, relates to the substance of a law or other governmental action. When a law or action limits the liberty of *all* persons, it may violate substantive due process. When a law or action limits the liberty of *some* persons but not others, it may violate the equal protection clause. ▶ **Example 4.16** If a law prohibits all persons from buying contraceptive devices, it raises a substantive due process question. If it prohibits only unmarried persons from buying the same devices, it raises an equal protection issue. ◀

In an equal protection inquiry, when a law or action distinguishes between or among individuals, the basis for the distinction—that is, its classification—is examined. Depending on the classification, the courts apply different levels of scrutiny, or "tests," to determine whether the law or action violates the equal protection clause. The courts use one of three standards: strict scrutiny, intermediate scrutiny, or the "rational basis" test.

**STRICT SCRUTINY** If a law or action prohibits or inhibits some persons from exercising a fundamental right, the law or action will be subject to "strict scrutiny" by the courts. Under this standard, the classification must be necessary to promote a *compelling state interest.* Also, if the classification is based on a *suspect trait*—such as race, national origin, or citizenship status—it must be necessary to promote a compelling government interest.[36]

Compelling state interests include remedying past unconstitutional or illegal discrimination but do not include correcting the general effects of "society's discrimination." ▶ **Example 4.17** For a city to give preference to minority applicants in awarding construction contracts, it normally must identify past unconstitutional or illegal discrimination against minority construction firms. Because the policy is based on suspect traits (race and national origin), it will violate the equal protection clause *unless* it is necessary to promote a compelling state interest. ◀ Generally, few laws or actions survive strict-scrutiny analysis by the courts.

**INTERMEDIATE SCRUTINY** A higher standard, that of *intermediate scrutiny,* is applied in cases involving

discrimination based on gender or discrimination against illegitimate children (children born out of wedlock). Laws using these classifications must be *substantially related to important government objectives.* For instance, an important government objective is preventing illegitimate teenage pregnancies. Because males and females are not similarly situated in this regard, a law that punishes men but not women for statutory rape will be upheld, even though it treats men and women unequally.

The state also has an important objective in establishing time limits (called *statutes of limitation*) for how long after an event a particular type of action can be brought. Nevertheless, the limitation period must be substantially related to the important objective of preventing fraudulent or outdated claims. ▶ **Example 4.18** A state law requires illegitimate children to bring paternity suits within six years of their births in order to seek support from their fathers. A court will strike down this law if legitimate children are allowed to seek support from their parents at any time. Distinguishing between support claims on the basis of legitimacy is not related to the important government objective of preventing fraudulent or outdated claims. ◀

**THE "RATIONAL BASIS" TEST** In matters of economic or social welfare, a classification will be considered valid if there is any conceivable *rational basis* on which the classification might relate to a legitimate government interest. It is almost impossible for a law or action to fail the rational basis test.

▶ **Example 4.19** A city ordinance prohibits all pushcart vendors, except a specific few, from operating in a particular area of the city. It will be upheld under the equal protection clause if the city provides a rational basis—such as reducing the traffic in the particular area—for the ordinance. ◀ In contrast, a law that provides unemployment benefits only to people over six feet tall would clearly fail the rational basis test because it could not further any legitimate government objective.

## SECTION 4
# PRIVACY RIGHTS

The U.S. Constitution does not explicitly mention a general right to privacy. In a 1928 Supreme Court case, *Olmstead v. United States,*[37] Justice Louis Brandeis

---

**36.** See *Johnson v. California,* 543 U.S. 499, 125 S.Ct. 1141, 160 L.Ed.2d 949 (2005).

**37.** 277 U.S. 438, 48 S.Ct. 564, 72 L.Ed. 944 (1928).

stated in his dissent that the right to privacy is "the most comprehensive of rights and the right most valued by civilized men." The majority of the justices at that time, however, did not agree with Brandeis.

It was not until the 1960s that the Supreme Court endorsed the view that the Constitution protects individual privacy rights. In a landmark 1965 case, *Griswold v. Connecticut,*[38] the Supreme Court held that a constitutional right to privacy was implied by the First, Third, Fourth, Fifth, and Ninth Amendments.

## Federal Statutes Affecting Privacy Rights

In the 1960s, Americans were sufficiently alarmed by the accumulation of personal information in government files that they pressured Congress to pass laws permitting individuals to access their files. Congress responded in 1966 with the Freedom of Information Act, which allows any person to request copies of any information on her or him contained in federal government files.

In 1974, Congress passed the Privacy Act, which also gives persons the right to access such information. Since then, Congress has passed numerous other laws protecting individuals' privacy rights with respect to financial transactions, electronic communications, and other activities in which personal information may be gathered and stored by organizations.

Since the 1990s, one of the major concerns of individuals has been how to protect privacy rights in cyberspace and to safeguard private information that may be revealed online. The increasing value of personal information for online marketers has exacerbated the situation. Chapter 9 discusses online privacy in more detail.

**PRETEXTING** A *pretext* is a false motive put forth to hide the real motive, and *pretexting* is the process of obtaining information by false means. Pretexters may try to obtain personal data by claiming that they are taking a survey for a research firm, a political party, or even a charity. The Gramm-Leach-Bliley Act[39] makes pretexting to obtain financial information illegal, but it does not mention lying to obtain *nonfinancial* information (for purposes other than identity theft).

▶ **Example 4.20**  To find out who had leaked confidential company information to the press, Patricia

C. Dunn, the chair of Hewlett-Packard, hired private investigators. They used false pretenses to access individuals' personal cell phone records. Dunn claimed that she had not been aware of the investigators' methods and had assumed that they had obtained the information from a public record. Criminal charges were filed but later dropped. Nevertheless, the scandal was highly publicized, and several civil lawsuits followed. Hewlett-Packard wound up paying millions to settle these lawsuits, including $14.5 million in fines to settle a claim filed by the California attorney general. ◀

To clarify the law on pretexting to gain access to phone records, Congress enacted the Telephone Records and Privacy Protection Act.[40] This act makes it a federal crime to pretend to be someone else or to make false representations for the purpose of obtaining another person's confidential phone records. The Federal Trade Commission investigates and prosecutes violators, who can be fined and sentenced to up to ten years in prison.

**MEDICAL INFORMATION** Responding to the growing need to protect the privacy of individuals' health records—particularly computerized records—Congress passed the Health Insurance Portability and Accountability Act (HIPAA).[41] This act defines and limits the circumstances in which an individual's "protected health information" may be used or disclosed.

HIPAA also requires health-care providers and health-care plans, including certain employers who sponsor health plans, to inform patients of their privacy rights and of how their personal medical information may be used. The act also states that a person's medical records generally may not be used for purposes unrelated to health care—such as marketing, for example—or disclosed to others without the individual's permission. Congress later expanded HIPAA's provisions to apply to vendors (those who maintain personal health records for health-care providers) and to electronic records shared by multiple medical providers. Congress also authorized the Federal Trade Commission to enforce HIPAA and pursue violators.

**THE USA PATRIOT ACT** The USA Patriot Act was passed by Congress in the wake of the terrorist attacks of September 11, 2001, and then reauthorized

---

**38.** 381 U.S. 479, 85 S.Ct. 1678, 14 L.Ed.2d 510 (1965).

**39.** Also known as the Financial Services Modernization Act, Pub. L. No. 106-102 (1999), 113 Stat. 1338, codified in numerous sections of 12 U.S.C.A.

**40.** 18 U.S.C. Section 1039.

**41.** HIPAA was enacted as Pub. L. No. 104-191 (1996) and is codified in 29 U.S.C.A. Sections 1181 *et seq.*

in 2006.[42] The Patriot Act has given government officials increased authority to monitor Internet activities (such as e-mail and Web site visits) and to gain access to personal financial information and student information. Law enforcement officials can now track the telephone and e-mail communications of one party to find out the identity of the other party or parties. Privacy advocates argue that this law adversely affects the constitutional rights of all Americans, and it has been widely criticized in the media.

To gain access to these communications, the government must certify that the information likely to be obtained by such monitoring is relevant to an ongoing criminal investigation. The government need not provide proof of any wrongdoing.[43]

---

42. The Uniting and Strengthening America by Providing Appropriate Tools Required to Intercept and Obstruct Terrorism Act of 2001, also known as the USA Patriot Act, was enacted as Pub. L. No. 107-56 (2001) and reauthorized by Pub. L. No. 109-173 (2006).
43. See, for example, *American Civil Liberties Union v. National Security Agency*, 493 F.3d 644 (6th Cir. 2007), in which a federal appellate court upheld the government's warrantless monitoring of electronic communications.

▶ **Example 4.21** In 2012, General David Petraeus, who ran the wars in Iraq and Afghanistan, resigned as director of the Central Intelligence Agency after his extramarital affair with Paula Broadwell, his biographer, became public. Apparently, after Petraeus broke off the affair with Broadwell, she sent harassing e-mails to another woman. When she reported the harassment, the FBI investigated, accessed Petraeus's e-mail accounts, and discovered that he had communicated with Broadwell via messages left in a draft folder on his e-mail account. Although there was no evidence that Petraeus did anything illegal, he was urged to resign and did so. ◀

## Other Laws Affecting Privacy

State constitutions and statutes also protect individuals' privacy rights, often to a significant degree. Privacy rights are also protected to some extent under tort law (see Chapter 6), Internet law (see Chapter 9), and employment law. Additionally, the Federal Trade Commission has played an active role in protecting the privacy rights of online consumers.

## Reviewing: Business and the Constitution

A state legislature enacted a statute that required any motorcycle operator or passenger on the state's highways to wear a protective helmet. Jim Alderman, a licensed motorcycle operator, sued the state to block enforcement of the law. Alderman asserted that the statute violated the equal protection clause because it placed requirements on motorcyclists that were not imposed on other motorists. Using the information presented in the chapter, answer the following questions.

1. Why does this statute raise equal protection issues instead of substantive due process concerns?
2. What are the three levels of scrutiny that the courts use in determining whether a law violates the equal protection clause?
3. Which standard of scrutiny, or test, would apply to this situation? Why?
4. Applying this standard, or test, is the helmet statute constitutional? Why or why not?

**DEBATE THIS . . .** *Legislation aimed at "protecting people from themselves" concerns the individual as well as the public in general. Protective helmet laws are just one example of such legislation. Should individuals be allowed to engage in unsafe activities if they choose to do so?*

## Terms and Concepts

| | | |
|---|---|---|
| Bill of Rights 74 | compelling government interest 75 | establishment clause 80 |
| checks and balances 70 | due process clause 82 | federal form of government 69 |
| commerce clause 71 | equal protection clause 83 | filtering software 79 |

## Issue Spotters

1. Can a state, in the interest of energy conservation, ban all advertising by power utilities if conservation could be accomplished by less restrictive means? Why or why not? **(See page 82.)**

2. Suppose that a state imposes a higher tax on out-of-state companies doing business in the state than it imposes on in-state companies. Is this a violation of equal protection if the only reason for the tax is to protect the local firms from out-of-state competition? Explain. **(See page 82.)**

• **Check your answers to the Issue Spotters against the answers provided in Appendix E at the end of this text.**

## Business Scenarios

**4–1. Commerce Clause.** A Georgia state law requires the use of contoured rear-fender mudguards on trucks and trailers operating within Georgia state lines. The statute further makes it illegal for trucks and trailers to use straight mudguards. In approximately thirty-five other states, straight mudguards are legal. Moreover, in Florida, straight mudguards are explicitly required by law. There is some evidence suggesting that contoured mudguards might be a little safer than straight mudguards. Discuss whether this Georgia statute violates any constitutional provisions. **(See page 71.)**

**4–2. Freedom of Religion.** Thomas worked in the nonmilitary operations of a large firm that produced both military and nonmilitary goods. When the company discontinued the production of nonmilitary goods, Thomas was transferred to a plant producing military equipment. Thomas left his job, claiming that it violated his religious principles to participate in the manufacture of goods to be used in destroying life. In effect, he argued, the transfer to the military equipment plant forced him to quit his job. He was denied unemployment compensation by the state because he had not been effectively "discharged" by the employer but had voluntarily terminated his employment. Did the state's denial of unemployment benefits to Thomas violate the free exercise clause of the First Amendment? Explain. **(See page 80.)**

**4–3. Equal Protection.** With the objectives of preventing crime, maintaining property values, and preserving the quality of urban life, New York City enacted an ordinance to regulate the locations of commercial establishments that featured adult entertainment. The ordinance expressly applied to female, but not male, topless entertainment. Adele Buzzetti owned the Cozy Cabin, a New York City cabaret that featured female topless dancers. Buzzetti and an anonymous dancer filed a suit in a federal district court against the city, asking the court to block the enforcement of the ordinance. The plaintiffs argued, in part, that the ordinance violated the equal protection clause. Under the equal protection clause, what standard applies to the court's consideration of this ordinance? Under this test, how should the court rule? Why? **(See page 82.)**

## Business Case Problems

**4–4. Spotlight on Plagiarism—Due Process.**  The Russ College of Engineering and Technology of Ohio University announced in a press conference that it had found "rampant and flagrant plagiarism" in the theses of mechanical engineering graduate students. Faculty singled out for "ignoring their ethical responsibilities" included Jay Gunasekera, chair of the department. Gunasekera was prohibited from advising students. He filed a suit against Dennis Irwin, the dean of Russ College, for violating his due process rights. What does due process require in these circumstances? Why? [*Gunasekera v. Irwin,* 551 F.3d 461 (6th Cir. 2009)] **(See page 82.)**

**4–5. Commerce Clause.** Under the federal Sex Offender Registration and Notification Act (SORNA), sex offenders must register and update their registration as sex offenders when they travel from one state to another. David Hall, a convicted sex offender in New York, moved to Virginia, where he did not update his registration. He was charged with violating SORNA. He claimed that the statute is unconstitutional, arguing that Congress cannot criminalize interstate travel if no commerce is involved. Is that reasonable? Why or why not? [*United States v. Guzman,* 591 F.3d 83 (2d Cir. 2010)] **(See page 71.)**

**4–6. BUSINESS CASE PROBLEM**
**WITH SAMPLE ANSWER: Establishment Clause.**

 *Judge James DeWeese hung a poster in his courtroom showing the Ten Commandments. The American Civil Liberties Union (ACLU) filed a suit, alleging that the poster violated the establishment clause. DeWeese responded that his purpose was not to promote religion but to express his view about "warring" legal philosophies—moral relativism and moral absolutism. "Our legal system is based on moral absolutes from divine law handed down by God through the Ten Commandments." Does this poster violate the establishment clause? Why or why not?* [American Civil Liberties Union of Ohio Foundation, Inc. v. DeWeese, *633 F.3d 424 (6th Cir. 2011)]* **(See page 80.)**

- **For a sample answer to Problem 4–6, go to Appendix F at the end of this text.**

**4–7. The Dormant Commerce Clause.** In 2001, Puerto Rico enacted a law that requires specific labels on cement sold in Puerto Rico and imposes fines for any violations of these requirements. The law prohibits the sale or distribution of cement manufactured outside Puerto Rico that does not carry a required label warning that the cement may not be used in government-financed construction projects. Antilles Cement Corp., a Puerto Rican firm that imports foreign cement, filed a complaint in federal court, claiming that this law violated the dormant commerce clause. (The dormant commerce clause doctrine applies not only to commerce among the states and U.S. territories, but also to international commerce.) Did the 2001 Puerto Rican law violate the dormant commerce clause? Why or why not? [*Antilles Cement Corp. v. Fortuno,* 670 F.3d 310 (1st Cir. 2012)] **(See page 72.)**

**4–8. Freedom of Speech.** Mark Wooden sent an e-mail to an alderwoman for the city of St. Louis. Attached was a nineteen-minute audio file that compared her to the biblical character Jezebel. The audio said she was a "bitch in the Sixth Ward," spending too much time with the rich and powerful and too little time with the poor. In a menacing, maniacal tone, Wooden said that he was "dusting off a sawed-off shotgun," called himself a "domestic terrorist," and referred to the assassination of President John Kennedy, the murder of federal judge John Roll, and the shooting of Representative Gabrielle Giffords. Feeling threatened, the alderwoman called the police. Wooden was convicted of harassment under a state criminal statute. Was this conviction unconstitutional under the First Amendment? Discuss. [*State v. Wooden,* 388 S.W.3d 522 (Mo. 2013)] **(See page 75.)**

**4–9. A QUESTION OF ETHICS: Defamation.**

 *Aric Toll owns and manages the Balboa Island Village Inn, a restaurant and bar in Newport Beach, California. Anne Lemen lives across from the inn. Lemen complained to the authorities about the inn's customers, whom she called "drunks" and "whores." She referred to Aric's wife as "Madam Whore" and told neighbors that the owners were involved in illegal drugs and prostitution. Lemen told the inn's bartender Ewa Cook that Cook "worked for Satan." She repeated her statements to potential customers, and the inn's sales dropped more than 20 percent. The inn filed a suit against Lemen.* [Balboa Island Village Inn, Inc. v. Lemen, *40 Cal.4th 1141, 156 P.3d 339 (2007)]* **(See page 79.)**

(a) Are Lemen's statements about the inn's owners, customers, and activities protected by the U.S. Constitution? Should such statements be protected? In whose favor should the court rule? Why?

(b) Did Lemen behave unethically in the circumstances of this case? Explain.

## Legal Reasoning Group Activity

**4–10. Free Speech and Equal Protection.** For many years, New York City has had to deal with the vandalism and defacement of public property caused by unauthorized graffiti. In an effort to stop the damage, the city banned the sale of aerosol spray-paint cans and broad-tipped indelible markers to persons under twenty-one years of age. The new rules also prohibited people from possessing these items on property other than their own. Within a year, five people under age twenty-one were cited for violations of these regulations, and 871 individuals were arrested for actually making graffiti.

Lindsey Vincenty and other artists wished to create graffiti on legal surfaces, such as canvas, wood, and clothing. Unable to buy her supplies in the city or to carry them in the city if she bought them elsewhere, Vincenty and others filed a lawsuit on behalf of themselves and other young artists against Michael Bloomberg, the city's mayor, and others. The plaintiffs claimed that, among other things, the new rules violated their right to freedom of speech. **(See page 75.)**

(a) One group will argue in favor of the plaintiffs and provide several reasons why the court should hold that the city's new rules violate the plaintiffs' freedom of speech.

(b) Another group will develop a counterargument that outlines the reasons why the new rules do not violate free speech rights.

(c) A third group will argue that the city's ban violates the equal protection clause because it applies only to persons under age twenty-one.

# CHAPTER 5

# BUSINESS ETHICS

One of the most complex issues businesspersons and corporations face is ethics. It is not as well defined as the law, and yet it can have tremendous impacts on a firm's finances and reputation. Consider, for instance, the experience of the Chick-fil-A restaurant chain in 2012 when its chief operating officer made several statements about the company's commitment to supporting traditional marriage.

After those comments were made, it became public knowledge that Chick-fil-A had made donations to Christian organizations perceived to be opposed to same-sex marriage. Opponents of same-sex marriage held support rallies and Chick-fil-A appreciation days. Supporters of same-sex marriage held "kiss-ins" at local Chick-fil-A restaurants. Some politicians denounced Chick-fil-A's position and said that they would block expansion of the company in their cities. Eventually, Chick-fil-A issued a statement saying that it had ceased donations to any organization that promotes discrimination in any way. Chick-fil-A no longer sponsors charities that discriminate against same-sex couples or those who identify as gay, lesbian, bisexual, or transgendered.

Chick-fil-A was not accused of violating any laws, but its actions raised questions about the role of corporations and the effect of corporate ethics on profit. This chapter addresses some of those same questions. First, we look at business ethics—its definitions, its importance, and its relationship to the law. Next, we examine the philosophical bases for making ethical decisions. Finally, we discuss the application of business ethics to global situations.

## SECTION 1
## BUSINESS ETHICS

At the most basic level, the study of **ethics** is the study of what constitutes right or wrong behavior. It is a branch of philosophy focusing on morality and the way moral principles are derived and implemented. Ethics has to do with the fairness, justness, rightness, or wrongness of an action.

The study of **business ethics** typically looks at the decisions businesses make or have to make and whether those decisions are right or wrong. It has to do with how businesspersons apply moral and ethical principles in making their decisions. Those who study business ethics also evaluate what duties and responsibilities exist or should exist for businesses.

At the end of every unit in this book, we present a series of ethical issues in features called *Focus on Ethics*. In each of these features, we expand on the concepts of business ethics discussed in this chapter.

## Why Is Studying
## Business Ethics Important?

Over the last two hundred years, the public perception of the corporation has changed from an entity that primarily generates revenues for its owners to an entity that participates in society as a corporate citizen. Originally, the only goal or duty of a corporation was to maximize profits. Although many people today may view this idea as greedy or inhumane, the rationale for the profit-maximization theory is still valid.

**PROFIT MAXIMIZATION** In theory, if all firms strictly adhere to the goal of profit maximization, resources flow to where they are most highly valued by society. Corporations can focus on their strengths, and other entities that are better suited to deal with social problems and perform charitable acts can specialize in those activities. The government, through taxes and other financial allocations, can shift resources to those other entities to perform public services. Thus, in an ideal world, profit maximization leads to the most efficient allocation of scarce resources.

**THE RISE OF CORPORATE CITIZENSHIP**  Over the years, as resources were not sufficiently reallocated to cover the costs of social needs, many people became dissatisfied with the profit-maximization theory. Investors and others began to look beyond profits and dividends and to consider the **triple bottom line**—a corporation's profits, its impact on people, and its impact on the planet. Magazines and Web sites began to rank companies based on their environmental impacts and their ethical decisions. The corporation came to be viewed as a "citizen" that was expected to participate in bettering communities and society.

Even so, many still believe that corporations are fundamentally money-making entities that should have no responsibility other than profit maximization.

## The Importance of Ethics in Making Business Decisions

Whether one believes in the profit-maximization theory or corporate citizenship, ethics is important in making business decisions. Corporations should strive to be "good citizens." When making decisions, a business should evaluate:

1. The legal implications of each decision.
2. The public relations impact.
3. The safety risks for consumers and employees.
4. The financial implications.

This analysis will assist the firm in making decisions that not only maximize profits but also reflect good corporate citizenship.

**LONG-RUN PROFIT MAXIMIZATION**  In attempting to maximize profits, however, corporate executives and employees have to distinguish between *short-run* and *long-run* profit maximization. In the short run, a company may increase its profits by continuing to sell a product, even though it knows that the product is defective. In the long run, though, because of lawsuits, large settlements, and bad publicity, such unethical conduct will cause profits to suffer. Thus, business ethics is consistent only with long-run profit maximization. An overemphasis on short-term profit maximization is the most common reason that ethical problems occur in business.

▶ **Case in Point 5.1**  When the powerful narcotic painkiller OxyContin was first marketed, its manufacturer, Purdue Pharma, claimed that it was unlikely to lead to drug addiction or abuse. Internal company documents later showed that the company's executives knew that OxyContin could be addictive, but kept this risk a secret to boost sales and maximize short-term profits.

Subsequently, Purdue Pharma and three former executives pleaded guilty to criminal charges that they misled regulators, patients, and physicians about OxyContin's risks of addiction. Purdue Pharma agreed to pay $600 million in fines and other payments. The three former executives agreed to pay $34.5 million in fines and were barred from federal health programs for a period of fifteen years. Thus, the company's focus on maximizing profits in the short run led to unethical conduct that hurt profits in the long run.[1] ◀

**THE INTERNET CAN RUIN REPUTATIONS**  In the past, negative information or opinions about a company might remain hidden. Now, however, cyberspace provides a forum where disgruntled employees, unhappy consumers, or special interest groups can post derogatory remarks. Thus, the Internet has increased the potential for a major corporation (or other business) to suffer damage to its reputation or loss of profits through negative publicity.

Wal-Mart and Nike in particular have been frequent targets for advocacy groups that believe that those corporations exploit their workers. Although some of these assertions may be unfounded or exaggerated, the courts generally have refused to consider them *defamatory* (the tort of defamation will be discussed in Chapter 6). Most courts regard online attacks as simply the expression of opinion and therefore a form of speech protected by the First Amendment. Even so, corporations often incur considerable expense in running marketing campaigns to thwart bad publicity and may even face legal costs (if the complaint leads to litigation).

**IMAGE IS EVERYTHING**  The study of business ethics is concerned with the purposes of a business and how that business achieves those purposes. Thus, business ethics is concerned with the image of the business and the impacts that the business has on the environment, customers, suppliers, employees, and the global economy.

Unethical corporate decision making can negatively affect suppliers, consumers, the community, and society as a whole. It can also have a negative impact on the reputation of the company and the

---

1. *United States v. Purdue Frederick Co.*, 495 F.Supp.2d 569 (W.D.Va. 2007).

individuals who run that company. Hence, an in-depth understanding of business ethics is important to the long-run viability of any corporation today.

## The Relationship of Law and Ethics

Because the law does not codify all ethical requirements of all persons, compliance with the law is not always sufficient to determine "right" behavior. Laws have to be general enough to apply in a variety of circumstances. Laws are broad in their purpose and their scope. They prohibit or require certain actions to avoid significant harm to society.

When two competing companies secretly agree to set prices on products, for instance, society suffers harm—typically, the companies will charge higher prices than they could if they continued to compete. This harm inflicted on consumers has negative consequences for the economy, and so colluding to set prices is an illegal activity. Similarly, when a company is preparing to issue stock, the law requires certain disclosures to potential investors. This requirement is meant to avoid harms that come with uninformed investing, such as occurred in the 1920s and contributed to the stock market crash and the Great Depression.

**MORAL MINIMUM** Compliance with the law is sometimes called the **moral minimum.** If people and entities merely comply with the law, they are acting at the lowest ethical level society will tolerate. The study of ethics goes beyond those legal requirements to evaluate what is right for society.

Businesspersons must remember that just because an action is legal does not mean it is ethical. For instance, no law specifies the salaries that publicly held corporations (companies that sell their shares to the public) can pay their officers (executive employees). Nevertheless, if a corporation pays its officers an excessive amount relative to other employees, or relative to what officers at other corporations are paid, the executives' compensation might be viewed as unethical.

In the following case, the court had to determine if a repair shop was entitled to receive full payment of an invoice or a lesser amount given its conduct in the matter.

---

## CASE 5.1

### Johnson Construction Co. v. Shaffer
Court of Appeal of Louisiana, Second Circuit, 87 So.3d 203 (2012).

**BACKGROUND AND FACTS** A truck owned by Johnson Construction Company needed repairs. John Robert Johnson, Jr., the company's president, took the truck with its attached fifteen-ton trailer to Bubba Shaffer, doing business as Shaffer's Auto and Diesel Repair. The truck was supposedly fixed, and Johnson paid the bill. The truck continued to leak oil and water. Johnson returned the truck to Shaffer, who again claimed to have fixed the problem. Johnson paid the second bill. The problems with the truck continued, however, so Johnson returned the truck and trailer a third time. Shaffer gave a verbal estimate of $1,000 for the repairs, but he ultimately sent an invoice for $5,863.49. Johnson offered to settle for $2,480, the amount of the initial estimate ($1,000), plus the costs of parts and shipping. Shaffer refused the offer and would not return Johnson's truck or trailer until full payment was made. Shaffer also charged Johnson a storage fee of $50 a day and 18 percent interest on the $5,863.49.

Johnson Construction filed a suit against Shaffer alleging unfair trade practices. The trial court determined that Shaffer had acted deceptively and wrongfully in maintaining possession of the trailer, on which no work had been performed. The trial court awarded Johnson $3,500 in general damages, plus $750 in attorneys' fees. Shaffer was awarded the initial estimate of $1,000 and appealed.

**DECISION AND RATIONALE** The state intermediate appellate court affirmed the trial court's judgment in favor of Johnson Construction, and also assessed Shaffer all costs of the appeal. The court examined the testimony with respect to the verbal estimate of $1,000 for the repairs of the truck. Johnson had testified that he agreed to the initial $1,000 estimate but did not authorize Shaffer to perform additional repairs or tear down the engine. A mechanic employed by Shaffer had testified that Johnson had not authorized additional repairs to the truck. Thus, the trial court had concluded that those repairs were

**CASE 5.1 CONTINUED**

not part of any agreement because they involved tearing down the engine, and that Shaffer's testimony on the issue was "disingenuous." The appellate court did not find any error in the trial court's reasoning.

"As for the amount that Shaffer contends is due for storage, had it invoiced Mr. Johnson the amount of the original estimate in the first place, there would have been no need to store the truck or trailer." Therefore, the appellate court rejected the request for storage fees. Finally, the court found that "the trial court did not err in its determination that Shaffer's retention of Johnson Contruction's trailer [for four years!] was a deceptive conversion of the trailer." The award of $3,500 in general damages to Johnson Construction seemed appropriate for such lengthy period of time unlawfully holding the trailer.

**WHAT IF THE FACTS WERE DIFFERENT?**  *Suppose that Shaffer had invoiced Johnson for only $1,500. Would the outcome have been different? Why or why not?*

**THE ETHICAL DIMENSION**  *Would it have been ethical for Shaffer's mechanic to lie to support his employer's case? Discuss.*

---

**ETHICS AND PRIVATE LAW** Most companies attempt to link ethics and law through the creation of internal codes of ethics. Company codes are not law. Instead, they are rules that the company sets forth that it can also enforce (by terminating an employee who does not follow them, for instance). Codes of conduct typically outline the company's policies on particular issues and indicate how employees are expected to act.

▶ **Example 5.2**  Google's code of conduct starts with the motto "Don't be evil." The code then makes general statements about how Google promotes integrity, mutual respect, and the highest standard of ethical business conduct. Google's code also provides specific rules on a number of issues, such as privacy, drugs and alcohol, conflicts of interest, co-worker relationships, and confidentiality—it even has a dog policy. The company takes a stand against employment discrimination that goes further than the law requires. It prohibits discrimination based on sexual orientation, gender identity or expression, and veteran status. ◀

Numerous industries have also developed their own codes of ethics. The American Institute of Certified Public Accountants (AICPA) has a comprehensive Code of Professional Conduct for the ethical practicing of accounting. The American Bar Association has model rules of professional conduct for attorneys, and the American Nurses Association has a code of ethics that applies to nurses. These codes can give guidance to decision makers facing ethical questions. Violation of a code may result in discipline of an employee or sanctions against a company from

the industry organization. Remember, though, that these internal codes are not laws, so their effectiveness is determined by the commitment of the industry or company leadership to enforcing the codes.

**ETHICAL UNCERTAINTY** Ethics can be a difficult subject for corporate officers to fully understand. Because it is often highly subjective and subject to change over time without any sort of formal process, ethics is less certain than law.

The law can also be uncertain, however, and contains numerous "gray areas" that make it difficult to predict with certainty how a court will apply a given law to a particular action. Uncertainty can make decision making difficult, especially when a law requires a court to determine what is "foreseeable" or "reasonable" in a particular situation. Because a business has no way of predicting how a specific court will decide these issues, decision makers need to proceed with caution and evaluate an action and its consequences from an ethical perspective.

Ethics is based more on judgment than research. A company that can show it acted ethically, responsibly, and in good faith (honestly) has a better chance of succeeding in a dispute than one that cannot make such a showing.

In the following case, the court concluded that the employer's response to complaints about a hostile work environment was so inadequate that it not only violated the employee's rights but was unethical enough to warrant a large penalty against the corporation. Notice the court's language about the company's behavior.

# CASE 5.2

## May v. Chrysler Group, LLC

United States Court of Appeals, Seventh Circuit, 692 F.3d 734 (2012).

**COMPANY PROFILE** Chrysler Group, LLC, is the parent company of Fiat, Chrysler, Dodge, Jeep, and several other automobile manufacturers. (An LLC is a limited liability company.) Chrysler Group was created in 2009 to manage the consolidation of the different automobile companies during the economic downturn of the late 2000s. The company employs more than 64,000 people at thirty-two manufacturing facilities. Its 2013 revenue was estimated to be $60 billion.

**BACKGROUND AND FACTS** Between 2002 and 2005, Otto May, Jr., a pipefitter at Chrysler's Belvedere Assembly Plant, was the target of more than fifty racist, homophobic, and anti-Semitic messages and graffiti. He found six death-threat notes in his toolbox, his bike and car tires were punctured, and someone poured sugar into the gas tank of his car twice. At one point, a dead bird wrapped in toilet paper to look like a member of the Ku Klux Klan (including the white pointed hat) was left at his work station. May complained to Chrysler. The director of human resources met with May, documented the complaints, and initiated an internal investigation. As part of that investigation, records were checked to determine who was in the building when the incidents occurred, and the handwriting on the notes and graffiti was analyzed.

The director held two meetings with about sixty employees (out of more than a thousand plant employees). At the meetings, the director reminded the workers that harassment was not acceptable. The harassers were never caught, and the harassment continued after the meetings. Chrysler's headquarters became involved only after the Anti-Defamation League wrote a letter on May's behalf. May sued Chrysler for hostile work environment harassment and was awarded $709,000 in compensatory damages and $3.5 million in punitive damages (or punishment). The judge overturned the punitive damages award, and May appealed.

**DECISION AND RATIONALE** The federal appellate court reinstated the punitive damages award based on the reprehensible and unethical nature of Chrysler's actions in failing to sufficiently address the workplace harassment. The court pointed out that to recover punitive damages, May had to present sufficient evidence for the jury to conclude that Chrysler acted with either malice or with reckless indifference. Chrysler's response to May's harassment was "shockingly thin as measured against the gravity" of that harassment. "We are convinced that the punitive damage award does not violate the Constitution and should therefore be reinstated in full." Chrysler's long-term recklessness in the face of repeated violence against May and his family was "sufficiently reprehensible [shameful] to support" such an award.

**THE ETHICAL DIMENSION** *Does an organization have an ethical obligation to secure a safe and harassment-free workplace for its employees? Why or why not? Discuss.*

**MANAGERIAL IMPLICATIONS** *It is clear from this opinion that employers have a significant duty to take complaints of harassment seriously. Even if Chrysler believed that May was harassing himself (perhaps in order to obtain compensation from the company), as the company implied at the trial, it had an obligation to do a serious investigation, to set up clear policies and procedures, and to follow those procedures when a complaint was made.*

---

## SECTION 2
# BUSINESS ETHICS AND SOCIAL MEDIA

Although most young people think of social media— Facebook, Twitter, Pinterest, Google+, MySpace, LinkedIn, and the like—as simply ways to communicate rapidly, businesses face ethical issues with respect to these same social media platforms.

## Hiring Procedures

In the past, to learn about a prospective employee, the employer would ask the candidate's former employers for references. Today, employers are likely to also conduct Internet searches to discover what job candidates have posted on their Facebook pages, blogs, and tweets. Nevertheless, many people believe that judging a job candidate based on what she or he does outside the work environment is unethical.

Sometimes, too, the opposite situation occurs, and job candidates are rejected because they *do not* participate in any social media. Given that the vast majority of younger people do use social media, some employers have decided that the failure to do so raises a red flag. Some consider this employer behavior to be unethical as well.

## The Use of Social Media to Discuss Work-Related Issues

Because so many Americans use social media many times a day, they often discuss work-related issues there. Numerous companies have provided strict guidelines about what is appropriate and inappropriate when making posts at one's own or others' social media accounts. A number of companies have fired employees for such activities as criticizing other employees or managers through social media outlets. Until recently, such disciplinary measures were considered ethical and legal.

Today, in contrast, a ruling by the National Labor Relations Board (NLRB—the federal agency that investigates unfair labor practices) has changed the legality of such actions. ▶ **Example 5.3** Costco's social media policy specified that its employees should not make statements that would damage the company, harm another person's reputation, or violate the company's policies. Employees who violated these rules were subject to discipline and could be fired.

In 2012, the NLRB ruled that Costco's social media policy violated federal labor law, which protects employees' right to engage in "concerted activities." Employees can freely associate with each other and have conversations about common workplace issues without employer interference. This right extends to social media posts. Therefore, Costco cannot broadly prohibit its employees from criticizing the company or co-workers, supervisors, or managers via social media. ◀

## Ethics in Reverse

While most of the discussion in this chapter involves business ethics, employee ethics is also an important issue. For instance, is it ethical for employees to make negative posts in social media about other employees or, more commonly, about managers? After all, negative comments about managers reflect badly on those managers, who often are reluctant to respond via social media to such criticism. Disgruntled employees may exaggerate the negative qualities of managers whom they do not like.

Some may consider the latest decision by the National Labor Relations Board outlined earlier in *Example 5.3* to be too lenient toward employees and too stringent toward management. There is likely to be an ongoing debate about how to balance employees' right to free expression against employers' right to prevent inaccurate negative statements being spread across the Internet.

SECTION 3

# ETHICAL PRINCIPLES AND PHILOSOPHIES

As Dean Krehmeyer, executive director of the Business Roundtable's Institute for Corporate Ethics, once said, "Evidence strongly suggests being ethical—doing the right thing—pays." Instilling ethical business decision making into the fabric of a business organization is no small task, even if ethics "pays." How do business decision makers decide whether a given action is the "right" one for their firms? What ethical standards should be applied?

Broadly speaking, **ethical reasoning**—the application of morals and ethics to a situation—applies to businesses just as it does to individuals. As businesses make decisions, they must analyze the alternatives in a variety of ways, one of which is the ethical implications.

Generally, the study of ethics is divided into two major categories—duty-based ethics and outcome-based ethics. **Duty-based ethics** is rooted in the idea that every person has certain duties to others, including both humans and the planet. Those duties may be derived from religious principles or from other philosophical reasoning. **Outcome-based ethics** focuses on the impacts of a decision on society or on key *stakeholders*.

## Duty-Based Ethics

Duty-based ethics focuses on the obligations of the corporation. It deals with standards for behavior that traditionally were derived from revealed truths, religious authorities, or philosophical reasoning. These standards involve concepts of right and wrong, and duties owed and rights to be protected.

Corporations today often describe these values or duties in their mission statements or strategic plans. Some companies base their statements on a nonreligious rationale, but others still derive their values from religious doctrine (such as the statements of Chick-fil-A, discussed in the introduction to this chapter).

**RELIGIOUS ETHICAL PRINCIPLES** Nearly every religion has principles or beliefs about how one should treat others. In the Judeo-Christian tradition, which is the dominant religious tradition in the United States, the Ten Commandments of the Old Testament establish these fundamental rules for moral action. The principles of the Muslim faith are set out in the Qur'an, and Hindus find their principles in the four Vedas.

Religious rules generally are absolute with respect to the behavior of their adherents. ▶ **Example 5.4** The commandment "Thou shalt not steal" is an absolute mandate for a person who believes that the Ten Commandments reflect revealed truth. Even a benevolent motive for stealing (such as Robin Hood's) cannot justify the act because the act itself is inherently immoral and thus wrong. ◀

For businesses, religious principles can be a unifying force for employees or a rallying point to increase employee motivation. They can also be problematic, however, because different owners, suppliers, employees, and customers may all have different religious backgrounds. As the introduction to this chapter illustrated, taking an action based on religious principles, especially when those principles address socially or politically controversial topics, can lead to negative publicity and even to protests or boycotts.

**PRINCIPLES OF RIGHTS** Another view of duty-based ethics focuses on basic rights. The principle that human beings have certain fundamental rights (to life, freedom, and the pursuit of happiness, for example) is deeply embedded in Western culture. As discussed in Chapter 1, the natural law tradition embraces the concept that certain actions (such as killing another person) are morally wrong because they are contrary to nature (the natural desire to continue living).

Those who adhere to this **principle of rights,** or "rights theory," believe that a key factor in determining whether a business decision is ethical is how

that decision affects the rights of others. These others include the firm's owners, its employees, the consumers of its products or services, its suppliers, the community in which it does business, and society as a whole.

***Conflicting Rights.*** A potential dilemma for those who support rights theory, however, is that they may disagree on which rights are most important. When considering all those affected by a business decision to downsize a firm, for example, how much weight should be given to employees relative to shareholders? Which employees should be laid off first—those with the highest salaries or those who have worked there for less time (and have less seniority)? How should the firm weigh the rights of customers relative to the community, or employees relative to society as a whole?

***Resolving Conflicts.*** In general, rights theorists believe that whichever right is stronger in a particular circumstance takes precedence. ▶ **Example 5.5** Murray Chemical Corporation has to decide whether to keep a chemical plant in Utah open, thereby saving the jobs of a hundred and fifty workers, or shut it down. Closing the plant will avoid contaminating a river with pollutants that would endanger the health of tens of thousands of people. In this situation, a rights theorist can easily choose which group to favor because the value of the right to health and well-being is obviously stronger than the basic right to work. (Not all choices are so clear-cut, however.) ◀

**KANTIAN ETHICAL PRINCIPLES** Duty-based ethical standards may also be derived solely from philosophical reasoning. The German philosopher Immanuel Kant (1724–1804) identified some general guiding principles for moral behavior based on what he thought to be the fundamental nature of human beings. Kant believed that human beings are qualitatively different from other physical objects and are endowed with moral integrity and the capacity to reason and conduct their affairs rationally.

***People Are Not a Means to an End.*** Based on this view of human beings, Kant said that when people are treated merely as a means to an end, they are being treated as the equivalent of objects and are being denied their basic humanity. For instance, a manager who treats subordinates as mere profit-making tools is less likely to retain motivated and loyal employees than a manager who respects his or her employees. Management research has shown that employees who feel empowered to share their thoughts, opinions, and solutions to problems are happier and more productive.

***Categorical Imperative.*** When a business makes unethical decisions, it often rationalizes its action by saying that the company is "just one small part" of the problem or that its decision would have "only a small impact." A central theme in Kantian ethics is that individuals should evaluate their actions in light of the consequences that would follow if everyone in society acted in the same way. This **categorical imperative** can be applied to any action.

▶ **Example 5.6** CHS Fertilizer is deciding whether to invest in expensive equipment that will decrease profits but will also reduce pollution from its factories. If CHS has adopted Kant's categorical imperative, the decision makers will consider the consequences if every company invested in the equipment (or if no company did so). If the result would make the world a better place (less polluted), CHS's decision would be clear. ◀

## Outcome-Based Ethics: Utilitarianism

In contrast to duty-based ethics, outcome-based ethics focuses on the consequences of an action, not on the nature of the action itself or on any set of preestablished moral values or religious beliefs. Outcome-based ethics looks at the impacts of a decision in an attempt to maximize benefits and minimize harms. The premier philosophical theory for outcome-based decision making is **utilitarianism,** a philosophical theory developed by Jeremy Bentham (1748–1832) and modified by John Stuart Mill (1806–1873)—both British philosophers.

"The greatest good for the greatest number" is a paraphrase of the major premise of the utilitarian approach to ethics.

**COST-BENEFIT ANALYSIS** Under a utilitarian model of ethics, an action is morally correct, or "right," when, among the people it affects, it produces the greatest amount of good for the greatest number or creates the least amount of harm for the fewest people. When an action affects the majority adversely, it is morally wrong. Applying the utilitarian theory thus requires the following steps:

1. A determination of which individuals will be affected by the action in question.
2. A **cost-benefit analysis,** which involves an assessment of the negative and positive effects of alternative actions on these individuals.
3. A choice among alternative actions that will produce maximum societal utility (the greatest positive net benefits for the greatest number of individuals).

Thus, if expanding a factory would provide hundreds of jobs but generate pollution that could endanger the lives of thousands of people, a utilitarian analysis would find that saving the lives of thousands creates greater good than providing jobs for hundreds.

**PROBLEMS WITH THE UTILITARIAN APPROACH**
There are problems with a strict utilitarian analysis. In some situations, an action that produces the greatest good for the most people may not seem to be the most ethical. ▶ **Example 5.7** Phazim Company is producing a drug that will cure a disease in 85 percent of patients, but the other 15 percent will experience agonizing side effects and a horrible, painful death. A quick utilitarian analysis would suggest that the drug should be produced and marketed because the majority of patients will benefit. Many people, however, have significant concerns about manufacturing a drug that will cause such harm to anyone. ◀

## Corporate Social Responsibility

In pairing duty-based concepts with outcome-based concepts, strategists and theorists developed the idea of the corporate citizen. **Corporate social responsibility (CSR)** combines a commitment to good citizenship with a commitment to making ethical decisions, improving society, and minimizing environmental impact.

CSR is a relatively new concept in the history of business, but a concept that becomes more important every year. Although CSR is not imposed on corporations by law, it does involve a commitment to self-regulation in a way that attends to the text and intent of the law, ethical norms, and global standards. A survey of U.S. executives undertaken by the Boston College Center for Corporate Citizenship found that more than 70 percent of those polled agreed that corporate citizenship must be treated as a priority. More than 60 percent said that good corporate citizenship added to their companies' profits.

CSR can be an incredibly successful strategy for companies, but corporate decision makers must not lose track of the two descriptors in the title: *corporate* and *social*. The company must link the responsibility of citizenship with the strategy and key principles of the business. Incorporating both the social and the corporate components of CSR and making ethical decisions can help companies grow and prosper.

**THE SOCIAL ASPECTS OF CSR** First, the social aspect requires that corporations demonstrate that they are promoting goals that society deems worthwhile and are moving toward solutions to social problems. Because business controls so much of the wealth and power of this country, business, in turn, has a responsibility to society to use that wealth and power in socially beneficial ways. Companies may be judged on how much they donate to social causes, as well as how they conduct their operations with respect to employment discrimination, human rights, environmental concerns, and similar issues.

Some corporations publish annual social responsibility reports, which may also be called corporate sustainability (referring to the capacity to endure) or citizenship reports. ▶ **Example 5.8** The Hitachi Group has Web pages dedicated to its CSR initiatives and includes reports outlining its environmental strategies, its human rights policies, and its commitment to diversity. The software company Symantec Corporation issues corporate responsibility reports to demonstrate its focus on critical environmental, social, and governance issues.

In its 2012 report, Symantec pointed out that 88 percent of facilities it owns or leases on a long-term basis are certified as environmentally friendly by the LEED program. LEED stands for Leadership in Energy and Environmental Design. Certification requires the achievement of high standards for energy efficiency, material usage in construction, and other environmental qualities. ◀

**THE CORPORATE ASPECTS OF CSR** Arguably, any socially responsible activity will benefit a corporation. The corporation may see an increase in goodwill from the local community for creating a park. Corporations may see increases in sales if they are viewed as good citizens.

At times, the benefit may not be immediate. Constructing a new plant that meets the high LEED standards may cost more initially. Nevertheless, over the life of the building, the savings in maintenance and utilities may more than make up for the extra cost of construction.

Surveys of college students about to enter the job market confirm that young people are looking for socially responsible employers. Socially responsible activities may cost a corporation now, but may lead to more impressive, and more committed employees. Corporations that engage in meaningful social activities retain workers longer, particularly younger ones.

Corporate responsibility is most successful when a company undertakes activities that are significant and related to its business operations. ▶ **Example 5.9** In 2012, the Walt Disney Company announced that in an effort to curb childhood obesity, it was issuing strict nutritional standards for all products advertised through its media outlets. In addition to focusing on a major social issue, the initiative was intended to clarify Disney's mission and values, as well as enhance its reputation as a trustworthy, family-friendly company. The initiative has been praised by commentators and politicians and is expected to increase Disney's revenue in the long term. ◀

**STAKEHOLDERS** One view of CSR stresses that corporations have a duty not just to shareholders, but also to other groups affected by corporate decisions—called **stakeholders.** The rationale for this "stakeholder view" is that, in some circumstances, one or more of these other groups may have a greater stake in company decisions than the shareholders do.

Under this approach, a corporation considers the impact of its decisions on its employees, customers, creditors, suppliers, and the community in which it operates. Stakeholders could also include advocacy groups such as environmental groups and animal rights groups. To avoid making a decision that may be perceived as unethical and result in negative publicity or protests, a corporation should consider the impact of its decision on the stakeholders. The most difficult aspect of the stakeholder analysis is determining which group's interests should receive greater weight if the interests conflict.

For instance, during the last few years, layoffs numbered in the millions. Nonetheless, some corporations succeeded in reducing labor costs without layoffs. To avoid slashing their workforces, these employers turned to alternatives such as (1) four-day workweeks, (2) unpaid vacations and voluntary furloughs, (3) wage freezes, (4) pension cuts, and (5) flexible work schedules. Some companies asked their workers to accept wage cuts to prevent layoffs, and the workers agreed. Companies finding alternatives to layoffs included Dell (extended unpaid holidays), Cisco Systems (four-day end-of-year shutdowns), Motorola (salary cuts), and Honda (voluntary unpaid vacation time).

## SECTION 4
# MAKING ETHICAL BUSINESS DECISIONS

Even if officers, directors, and others in a company want to make ethical decisions, it is not always clear what is ethical in a given situation. Thinking beyond things that are easily measured, such as profits, can be challenging. Although profit projections are not always accurate, they are more objective than considering the personal impacts of decisions on employees, shareholders, customers, and even the community. But this subjective component to decision making potentially has a great influence on a company's profits.

Companies once considered leaders in their industry, such as Enron and the worldwide accounting firm Arthur Andersen, were brought down by the unethical behavior of a few. A two-hundred-year-old British investment banking firm, Barings Bank, was destroyed by the actions of one employee and a few of his friends. Clearly, ensuring that all employees get on the ethical business decision-making "bandwagon" is crucial in today's fast-paced world.

Individuals entering the global corporate community, even in entry-level positions, must be prepared to make hard decisions. Sometimes, there is no "good" answer to the questions that arise. Therefore, it is important to have tools to help in the decision-making process and a framework for organizing those tools. Business decisions can be complex and may involve legal concerns, financial questions, possibly health and safety concerns, and ethical components.

## A Systematic Approach

Organizing the ethical concerns and issues and approaching them systematically can help a business-person eliminate various alternatives and identify the strengths and weaknesses of the remaining alternatives. Ethics consultant Leonard H. Bucklin of Corporate-Ethics.US™ has devised a procedure that he calls Business Process Pragmatism™. It involves five steps:

**Step 1: Inquiry.** First, the decision maker must understand the problem. To do this, one must identify the parties involved (the stakeholders) and collect the relevant facts. Once the ethical problem or problems are clarified, the decision maker lists any relevant legal and ethical principles that will guide the decision.

**Step 2: Discussion.** In this step, the decision maker lists possible actions. The ultimate goals for the decision are determined, and each option is evaluated using the laws and ethical principles listed in Step 1.

**Step 3: Decision.** In this step, those participating in the decision making work together to craft a consensus decision or consensus plan of action for the corporation.

**Step 4: Justification.** In this step, the decision maker articulates the reasons for the proposed action or series of actions. Generally these reasons should come from the analysis done in Step 3. This step essentially results in documentation to be shared with stakeholders explaining why the proposal is an ethical solution to the problem.

**Step 5: Evaluation.** This final step occurs once the decision has been made and implemented. The solution should be analyzed to determine if it was effective. The results of this evaluation may be used in making future decisions.

## The Importance of Ethical Leadership

Talking about ethical business decision making is meaningless if management does not set standards. Furthermore, managers must apply the same standards to themselves as they do to the company's employees.

**ATTITUDE OF TOP MANAGEMENT** One of the most important ways to create and maintain an ethical workplace is for top management to demonstrate its commitment to ethical decision making. A manager who is not totally committed to an ethical workplace rarely succeeds in creating one. Management's behavior, more than anything else, sets the ethical tone of a firm. Employees take their cues from management. ▶ **Example 5.10** Devon, a BioTek employee, observes his manager cheating on her expense account. Later, when Devon is promoted to a managerial position, he "pads" his expense account as well, knowing that he is unlikely to face sanctions for doing so. ◀

Managers who set unrealistic production or sales goals increase the probability that employees will act unethically. If a sales quota can be met only through high-pressure, unethical sales tactics, employees will try to act "in the best interest of the company" and will continue to behave unethically.

A manager who looks the other way when she or he knows about an employee's unethical behavior also sets an example—one indicating that ethical transgressions will be accepted. Managers have found that discharging even one employee for ethical reasons has a tremendous impact as a deterrent to unethical behavior in the workplace. This is true even if the company has a written code of ethics. If management does not enforce the company code, the code is essentially nonexistent.

The following case demonstrates the types of situations that can occur when management demonstrates a lack of concern about ethics.

---

## CASE 5.3

### Moseley v. Pepco Energy Services, Inc.
United States District Court, District of New Jersey, 2011 WL 1584166 (2011).

**BACKGROUND AND FACTS**   Eustace Lloyd Moseley was employed by Pepco Energy Services, Inc., or its predecessors for over twenty-five years. He was originally hired as an engineer, then promoted to lead engineer, then as a maintenance manager, a position he held until December 31, 2009.

In 1998, Thomas Herzog became a vice president and it was to Herzog that Moseley and others directly reported.  Starting in 2002, employees were required to complete and annual ethics survey. In 2007, Moseley and two co-workers determined that their superior, Herzog, had been improperly using company assets, had improperly hired immedmiate family members and friends, and had possibly been engaging in other unethical activities. They disclosed this information on the annual "ethics survey." Herzog had employed his daughter as his secretary without posting the position first, which was a violation of the company's anti-nepotism (favoritism to relatives) policies. Herzog also hired his girlfriend's daughter as a secretary without posting the position. Herzog hired his son as a project manager through a third-party independent contractor. Herzog leased a new car with company funds that were not approved by the company.

As a result of a subsequent investigation by the company, Herzog was fired. The next year, Moseley's performance review was negative, which he felt was an act of retaliation for his disclosure of Herzog's conduct. A few months later, Moseley was passed over for a plant-operations manager position, which he felt he should have received. Again, he believed this was a further act of retaliation for his disclosures.

Moseley filed an action for retaliatory firing. Defendant Pepco Energy Services made a motion for a summary judgment, arguing that Moseley could not make out a *prima facie* claim against the company.

**DECISION AND RATIONALE**   The United States District Court looked closely at the Conscientious Employee Protection Act (CEPA), which was enacted to protect and encourage employees to report illegal or unethical workplace activities. That New Jersey statute prohibits an employer from taking retaliatory action against an employee who objects to "any activity, policy or practice which the employee reasonably believes is in violation of applicable law." To be sheltered by the CEPA, Moseley reasonably had to have believed that the complained-of conduct "was violating a 'law, rule, or regulation promulgated pursuant to law, including any violation involving deception of, misrepresentation to, any shareholder, investor, client, patient, customer, employee, former employee, retiree or pensioner of the employer or any government entity.'"

Pepco Energy argued that Moseley merely disclosed a violation of company policy. The court believed, though, that "a plaintiff need not demonstrate that there was a violation of the law or fraud, but instead that he 'reasonably believed' that to be the case." The court found that the facts supported an objectively "reasonable belief that a violation of law or fraudulent contact was being committed by" Moseley's supervisor, Herzog. Because a jury could reasonably adopt an inference of retaliation, summary judgment was inappropriate and the court denied the motion.

**THE SOCIAL DIMENSION**   *Using duty-based ethical principles, what facts or circumstances in this case would lead Moseley to disclose Herzog's behavior?*

**THE ETHICAL DIMENSION**   *Using outcome-based ethical principles, what issues would Moseley have to analyze in making the decision to report Herzog's behavior? What would be the risks to Moseley? The benefits?*

**BEHAVIOR OF OWNERS AND MANAGERS** Business owners and managers sometimes take more active roles in fostering unethical and illegal conduct. This may indicate to their co-owners, co-managers, employees, and others that unethical business behavior will be tolerated. Business owners' misbehavior can have negative consequences for themselves and their business. Not only can a court sanction the owners and managers, but it can also issue an injunction that prevents them from engaging in similar patterns of conduct in the future.

▶ **Example 5.11** Lawyer Samir Zia Chowhan posted a help-wanted ad on Craigslist seeking an "energetic woman" for the position of legal secretary. The ad stated that the position included secretarial and paralegal work, as well as "additional duties" for two lawyers in the firm. Applicants were asked to send pictures and describe their physical features.

When a woman applied for the job, Chowhan sent her an e-mail saying that "in addition to the legal work, you would be required to have sexual interaction with me and my partner, sometimes together sometimes separate." He also explained that she would need to perform sexual acts at the job interview so that he and his partner could determine whether she would be able to handle these duties. The woman filed a complaint with the Illinois Bar Association, which suspended Chowhan's law license for a year for making false statements about the ad. Because the bar association's ethics rules prohibited attorneys from having sex with their clients, but not with potential employees, Chowhan could only be disciplined for lying. ◀

**THE SARBANES-OXLEY ACT** The Sarbanes-Oxley Act of 2002[2] requires companies to set up confidential systems so that employees and others can "raise red flags" about suspected illegal or unethical auditing and accounting practices. (The Sarbanes-Oxley Act covers additional issues, and excerpts from and explanatory comments on this important law appear in Appendix D of this text.)

Some companies have implemented online reporting systems to accomplish this goal. In one such system, employees can click on an icon on their computers that anonymously links them with NAVEX Global, an organization based in Oregon. Through NAVEX, employees can report suspicious accounting practices, sexual harassment, and other possibly unethical behavior. NAVEX, in turn, alerts management personnel or the audit committee at the designated company to the possible problem. Those who

have used the system say that it is less inhibiting than calling a company's toll-free number.

---

**SECTION 5**
# GLOBAL BUSINESS ETHICS

Just as different religions have different moral codes, different countries, regions and even states have different ethical expectations and priorities. Some of these differences are based in religious values, whereas others are cultural in nature. As a result of the various cultures and religions throughout the world, making ethical business decisions can be even more difficult.

For instance, in certain countries the consumption of alcohol and specific foods is forbidden for religious reasons. It would be considered unethical for a U.S. business to build a factory to produce alcohol and employ local workers in a culture in which alcohol is forbidden.

International transactions often involve issues related to employment and financing. Congress has addressed some of these issues, not eliminating the ethical components but clarifying some of the conflicts between the ethics of the United States and the ethics of other nations. For example, the Civil Rights Act of 1964 and the Foreign Corrupt Practices Act (discussed in more detail below) have clarified the U.S. ethical position on employment issues and bribery in foreign nations. (Other nations, including Mexico, have also enacted laws that prohibit bribery, as discussed in this chapter's *Insight into the Global Environment* feature on the following page.)

## The Monitoring of Employment Practices of Foreign Suppliers

Many businesses contract with companies in developing nations to produce goods, such as shoes and clothing, because the wage rates in those nations are significantly lower than those in the United States. Yet what if a foreign company hires women and children at below-minimum-wage rates, for example, or requires its employees to work long hours in a workplace full of health hazards? What if the company's supervisors routinely engage in workplace conduct that is offensive to women? What if plants located abroad routinely violate labor and environmental standards?

▶ **Example 5.12** Apple, Inc., owns Pegatron Corporation, a subsidiary company based in China,

---

**2.** 15 U.S.C. Sections 7201 *et seq.*

# INSIGHT INTO THE GLOBAL ENVIRONMENT
## Bribery and the Foreign Corrupt Practices Act

Many countries have followed in the footsteps of the United States by passing their own anticorruption laws, some of which are similar to our Foreign Corrupt Practices Act. Nevertheless, some countries are still not diligent in weeding out corruption—of government officials, for instance.

### Mexico Faces a Corruption Issue

Recently, Mexico passed an anticorruption law that prevents hospital administrators from approving contracts. Medical device supplier Orthofix International NV, based in Texas, faced a problem after passage of the new law. It wanted to continue providing bone-repair products to Mexico. It therefore bribed regional government officials instead of hospital administrators. Over several years, Orthofix paid more than $300,000 in bribes to Mexican officials to retain government health-care contracts. Employees at Orthofix called these bribes "chocolates." The contracts generated almost $8.7 million in revenues for the company.

### The Bribing Process

Before the anticorruption law was enacted, Orthofix's Mexican subsidiary, Promeca, regularly offered cash and gifts, such as vacation packages, televisions, and laptops, to hospital employees in order to secure sales contracts. These employees then submitted falsified receipts for imaginary expenses such as meals and new car tires. When the bribes became too large to hide in this manner, Promeca's employees falsely attributed the payments to promotional and training expenses. After the new law was passed, Mexico formed a special national committee to approve medical contracts. Promeca employees then sim-

ply bribed committee members to ensure that the company was awarded the contracts.

### No Compliance Policy or Training to Prevent Violations

As it turned out, Orthofix did not provide any training in how to prevent violations of the Foreign Corrupt Practices Act or have a compliance policy in place in Mexico. Orthofix did create a code of ethics and antibribery training materials, but they were only distributed in English. When Orthofix managers found out about Promeca's overbudget expenses, they questioned the amounts, but initially took no further steps.

### The U.S. Government Investigates

Sometime after Orthofix learned of the payments, it self-reported them to the U.S. Securities and Exchange Commission (SEC). After negotiations with the SEC, Orthofix agreed to terminate the Promeca executives who had engaged in the bribery and to end Promeca's operations. Orthofix required mandatory training for all employees and strengthened its auditing of company payments. In addition, the company paid more than $7 million in penalties.

### LEGAL CRITICAL THINKING
**INSIGHT INTO THE LEGAL ENVIRONMENT**

*Because managers are potentially responsible for all actions of their foreign subsidiaries whether or not they knew of the illegal conduct, what actions should Orthofix's upper management have taken before this corruption scandal came to light?*

which supplies parts for iPads and other Apple products. In December 2011, there was an explosion at a Pegatron factory in Shanghai. Dozens of employees were injured when aluminum dust from polishing cases for iPads caught fire and caused the explosion. Allegations surfaced that the conditions at the factory violated labor and environmental standards. California-based Apple did not comment on the issue. ◄

Given today's global communications network, few companies can assume that their actions in other nations will go unnoticed by "corporate watch" groups that discover and publicize unethical corporate behavior. As a result, U.S. businesses today usu-

ally take steps to avoid such adverse publicity—either by refusing to deal with certain suppliers or by arranging to monitor their suppliers' workplaces to make sure that the employees are not being mistreated.

## The Foreign Corrupt Practices Act

Another ethical problem in international business dealings has to do with the legitimacy of certain side payments to government officials. In the United States, the majority of contracts are formed within the private sector. In many foreign countries, however, government officials make the decisions on most major construction and manufacturing contracts because of extensive government regulation and control over trade and industry.

Side payments to government officials in exchange for favorable business contracts are not unusual in such countries, nor are they considered to be unethical. In the past, U.S. corporations doing business in these nations largely followed the dictum "When in Rome, do as the Romans do."

In the 1970s, however, the U.S. media uncovered a number of business scandals involving large side payments by U.S. corporations to foreign representatives for the purpose of securing advantageous international trade contracts. In response to this unethical behavior, in 1977 Congress passed the Foreign Corrupt Practices Act[3] (FCPA), which prohibits U.S. businesspersons from bribing foreign officials to secure beneficial contracts.

**PROHIBITION AGAINST THE BRIBERY OF FOREIGN OFFICIALS**  The first part of the FCPA applies to all U.S. companies and their directors, officers, shareholders, employees, and agents. This part prohibits the bribery of most officials of foreign governments if the purpose of the payment is to motivate the official to act in his or her official capacity to provide business opportunities.

The FCPA does not prohibit payment of substantial sums to minor officials whose duties are ministerial. A ministerial action is a routine activity such as the processing of paperwork with little or no discretion involved in the action. These payments are often referred to as "grease," or facilitating payments. They

are meant to accelerate the performance of administrative services that might otherwise be carried out at a slow pace. Thus, for instance, if a firm makes a payment to a minor official to speed up an import licensing process, the firm has not violated the FCPA.

Generally, the act, as amended, permits payments to foreign officials if such payments are lawful within the foreign country. Payments to private foreign companies or other third parties are permissible—unless the U.S. firm knows that the payments will be passed on to a foreign government in violation of the FCPA. The U.S. Department of Justice also uses the FCPA to prosecute foreign companies suspected of bribing officials outside the United States.

**ACCOUNTING REQUIREMENTS**  To prevent bribes from being concealed in the corporate financial records, the second part of the FCPA is directed toward accountants. All companies must keep detailed records that "accurately and fairly" reflect their financial activities. Their accounting systems must provide "reasonable assurance" that all transactions entered into by the companies are accounted for and legal. These requirements assist in detecting illegal bribes. The FCPA prohibits any person from making false statements to accountants or false entries in any record or account.

**PENALTIES FOR VIOLATIONS**  The FCPA provides that business firms that violate the act may be fined up to $2 million. Individual officers or directors who violate the FCPA may be fined up to $100,000 (the fine cannot be paid by the company) and may be imprisoned for up to five years.

---

**3.** 15 U.S.C. Sections 78dd-1 *et seq.*

## Reviewing: Business Ethics

James Stilton is the chief executive officer (CEO) of RightLiving, Inc., a company that buys life insurance policies at a discount from terminally ill persons and sells the policies to investors. RightLiving pays the terminally ill patients a percentage of the future death benefit (usually 65 percent) and then sells the policies to investors for 85 percent of the value of the future benefit. The patients receive the cash to use for medical and other expenses, the investors are "guaranteed" a positive return on their investment, and RightLiving profits on the difference between the purchase and sale prices. Stilton is aware that some sick patients might obtain insurance policies through fraud (by not revealing the illness on the insurance application). Insurance companies that discover this will cancel the policy and refuse to pay. Stilton believes that most of the policies he has purchased are legitimate, but he knows that some probably are not. Using the information presented in this chapter, answer the following questions.

1. Would a person who adheres to the principle of rights consider it ethical for Stilton not to disclose the potential risk of cancellation to investors? Why or why not?

*Continued*

2. Using Immanuel Kant's categorical imperative, are the actions of RightLiving, Inc., ethical? Why or why not?

3. Under utilitarianism, are Stilton's actions ethical? Why or why not? What difference does it make if most of the policies are legitimate and will be paid rather than being fraudulently procured and void?

4. Using the Business Process Pragmatism™ steps discussed in this chapter, discuss the decision process Stilton should use in deciding whether to disclose the risk of fraudulent policies to potential investors.

**DEBATE THIS . . .** *Executives in large corporations are ultimately rewarded if their companies do well, particularly as evidenced by rising stock prices. Consequently, should we let those who run corporations decide what level of negative side effects of their goods or services is "acceptable"?*

## Terms and Concepts

business ethics 88

categorical imperative 95

corporate social responsibility (CSR) 95

cost-benefit analysis 95

duty-based ethics 93

ethical reasoning 93

ethics 88

moral minimum 90

outcome-based ethics 93

principle of rights 94

stakeholders 96

triple bottom line 89

utilitarianism 95

## Issue Spotters

1. News, Inc., is always looking for ways to increase the number of its viewers. Recently, it was the first network to interview surviving witnesses on location after a tragic school shooting. Are there ethical concerns about putting traumatized children on the news immediately after an event like this? Why or why not? **(See page 89.)**

2. Johnny Sport is a world-famous athlete. He is careful to avoid using any performance-enhancing drugs that are banned by his sport's oversight organization. Is it ethical for Johnny to take a performance-enhancing drug that has not been banned? Why or why not? **(See page 97.)**

- Check your answers to the Issue Spotters against the answers provided in Appendix E at the end of this text.

## Business Scenarios

**5–1. Business Ethics.** Jason Trevor owns a commercial bakery in Blakely, Georgia, that produces a variety of goods sold in grocery stores. Trevor is required by law to perform internal tests on food produced at his plant to check for contamination. On three occasions, the tests of food products containing peanut butter were positive for salmonella contamination. Trevor was not required to report the results to U.S. Food and Drug Administration officials, however, so he did not. Instead, Trevor instructed his employees to simply repeat the tests until the results were negative. Meanwhile, the products that had originally tested positive for salmonella were eventually shipped out to retailers.

Five people who ate Trevor's baked goods that year became seriously ill, and one person died from a salmo-nella infection. Even though Trevor's conduct was legal, was it unethical for him to sell goods that had once tested positive for salmonella? Why or why not? **(See page 93.)**

**5–2. Ethical Conduct.** Internet giant Zoidle, a U.S. company, generated sales of £2.5 billion in the United Kingdom in 2013 (approximately $4 billion in U.S. dollars). Its net profits before taxes on these sales were £200 million, and it paid £6 million in corporate tax, resulting in a tax rate of 3 percent. The corporate tax rate in the United Kingdom is between 20 percent and 24 percent.

The CEO of Zoidle held a press conference stating that he was proud of his company for taking advantage of tax loopholes and for sheltering profits in other nations to avoid paying taxes. He called this practice "capitalism at its finest." He further stated that it would be unethical for Zoidle not to take advantage of loopholes and that it would be borderline illegal to tell shareholders that the company paid more taxes than it had to pay because it felt that it should. Zoidle receives significant benefits for doing business in the United Kingdom, including tremendous sales tax exemptions and some property tax breaks. The United Kingdom relies on the corporate income tax to provide services to the poor and to help run the agency that regulates corporations. Is it ethical for Zoidle to avoid paying taxes? Why or why not? **(See page 95.)**

## Business Case Problems

**5–3. Spotlight on Pfizer, Inc.—Corporate Social Responsibility.**

Methamphetamine (meth) is an addictive drug made chiefly in small toxic labs (STLs) in homes, tents, barns, or hotel rooms. The manufacturing process is dangerous and often results in explosions, burns, and toxic fumes. Government entities spend time and resources to find and destroy STLs, imprison meth dealers and users, treat addicts, and provide services for affected families. Meth cannot be made without ingredients that are also used in cold and allergy medications. Arkansas has one of the highest numbers of STLs in the United States. To recoup the costs of fighting the meth epidemic, twenty counties in Arkansas filed a suit against Pfizer, Inc., which makes cold and allergy medications. What is Pfizer's ethical responsibility here, and to whom is it owed? Why? [*Ashley County, Arkansas v. Pfizer, Inc.*, 552 F.3d. 659 (8th Cir. 2009)] **(See page 95.)**

**5–4. Ethical Leadership.** David Krasner, who worked for HSH Nordbank AG, complained that his supervisor, Roland Kiser, fostered an atmosphere of sexism that was demeaning to women. Among other things, Krasner claimed that career advancement was based on "sexual favoritism." He objected to Kiser's relationship with a female employee, Melissa Campfield, who was promoted before more qualified employees, including Krasner. How do a manager's attitudes and actions affect the workplace? [*Krasner v. HSH Nordbank AG*, 680 F.Supp.2d 502 (S.D.N.Y. 2010)] **(See page 97.)**

**5–5. BUSINESS CASE PROBLEM
WITH SAMPLE ANSWER: Online Privacy.**
*Facebook, Inc., launched a program called "Beacon" that automatically updated the profiles of users on Facebook's social networking site when those users had any activity on Beacon "partner" sites. For example, one partner site was Blockbuster.com. When a user rented or purchased a movie through Blockbuster.com, the user's Facebook profile would be updated to share the purchase. The Beacon program was set up as a default setting, so users never consented to the program, but they could opt out. What are the ethical implications of an opt-in program versus an opt-out program in social media?* [Lane v. Facebook, Inc., 696 F.3d 811 (9th Cir. 2011)] **(See page 92.)**

• **For a sample answer to Problem 5–5, go to Appendix F at the end of this text.**

**5–6. Business Ethics on a Global Scale.** After the fall of the Soviet Union, the new government of Azerbaijan began converting certain state-controlled industries to private ownership. Ownership in these companies could be purchased through a voucher program. Frederic Bourke, Jr., and Viktor Kozeny wanted to purchase the Azerbaijani oil company, SOCAR, but it was unclear whether the Azerbaijani president would allow SOCAR to be put up for sale. Kozeny met with one of the vice presidents of SOCAR (who was also the son of the president of Azerbaijan) and other Azerbaijani leaders to discuss the sale of SOCAR.

To obtain their cooperation, Kozeny set up a series of parent and subsidiary companies through which the Azerbaijani leaders would eventually receive two-thirds of the SOCAR profits without ever investing any of their own funds. In return, the Azerbaijani leaders would attempt to use their influence to convince the president to put SOCAR up for sale. Assume that Bourke and Kozeny are operating out of a U.S. company. Discuss the ethics of this scheme, both in terms of the Foreign Corrupt Practices Act (FCPA) and as a general ethical issue. What duties did Kozeny have under the FCPA? [*United States v. Kozeny*, 667 F.3d 122 (2d Cir. 2011)] **(See page 99.)**

**5–7. Business Ethics.** Mark Ramun worked as a manager for Allied Erecting and Dismantling Co., where he had a tense relationship with his father, who was Allied's president. After more than ten years, Mark left Allied, taking 15,000 pages of Allied's documents on DVDs and CDs, which constituted trade secrets. Later, he joined Allied's competitor, Genesis Equipment & Manufacturing, Inc. Genesis soon developed a piece of equipment that incorporated elements of Allied equipment. How might business ethics have been violated in these circumstances? Discuss. [*Allied Erecting and Dismantling Co. v. Genesis Equipment & Manufacturing, Inc.*, 2013 WL 85907 (6th Cir. 2013)] **(See page 97.)**

**5–8. A QUESTION OF ETHICS: Consumer Rights.**

*Best Buy, a national electronics retailer, offered a credit card that allowed users to earn "reward points" that could be redeemed for discounts on Best Buy goods. After reading a newspaper advertisement for the card, Gary Davis applied for, and was given, a credit card. As part of the application process, he visited a Web page containing Frequently Asked Questions as well as terms and conditions*

*for the card. He clicked on a button affirming that he understood the terms and conditions. When Davis received his card, it came with seven brochures about the card and the reward point program. As he read the brochures, he discovered that a $59 annual fee would be charged for the card. Davis went back to the Web pages he had visited and found a statement that the card "may" have an annual fee. Davis sued, claiming that the company did not adequately disclose the fee. [Davis v. HSBC Bank Nevada, N.A., 691 F.3d 1152 (9th Cir. 2012)]* **(See page 89.)**

(a) Online applications frequently have click-on buttons or boxes to check for consumers to acknowledge that they have read and understand the terms and conditions of applications or purchases. Often, the terms and conditions are so long that they cannot all be seen on one screen and users must scroll to view the entire document.

Is it unethical for companies to put terms and conditions, especially terms that may cost the consumer, in an electronic document that is too long to read on one screen? Why or why not? Does this differ from having a consumer sign a hard-copy document with terms and conditions printed on it? Why or why not?

(b) The Truth-in-Lending Act requires that credit terms be clearly and conspicuously disclosed in application materials. Assuming that the Best Buy credit-card materials had sufficient legal disclosures, discuss the ethical aspects of businesses strictly following the language of the law as compared to following the intent of the law.

## Legal Reasoning Group Activity

**5–9. Global Business Ethics.** Pfizer, Inc., developed a new antibiotic called Trovan (trovafloxacinmesylate). Tests showed that in animals Trovan had life-threatening side effects, including joint disease, abnormal cartilage growth, liver damage, and a degenerative bone condition. Several years later, an epidemic of bacterial meningitis swept across Nigeria. Pfizer sent three U.S. physicians to test Trovan on children who were patients in Nigeria's Infectious Disease Hospital. Pfizer did not obtain the patients' consent, alert them to the risks, or tell them that Médecins Sans Frontières (Doctors without Borders) was providing an effective conventional treatment at the same site. Eleven children died in the experiment, and others were left blind, deaf, paralyzed, or brain damaged. Rabi Abdullahi and other Nigerian children filed a suit in a U.S. federal court against Pfizer, alleging a violation of a customary international law norm prohibiting involuntary medical experimentation on humans. **(See page 93.)**

(a) One group should use the principles of ethical reasoning discussed in this chapter to develop three arguments that Pfizer's conduct was a violation of ethical standards.

(b) A second group should take a pro-Pfizer position and argue that the company did not violate any ethical standards (and counter the first group).

(c) A third group should come up with proposals for what Pfizer might have done differently to avert the consequences.

# UNIT ONE  Focus on Ethics

## Ethics and the Legal Environment of Business

In Chapter 5, we examined the importance of ethical standards in the business context. We also offered suggestions on how business decision makers can create an ethical workplace. Certainly, it is not wrong for a businessperson to try to increase his or her firm's profits. But there are limits, both ethical and legal, to how far businesspersons can go. In preparing for a career in business, you will find that a background in business ethics and a commitment to ethical behavior are just as important as a knowledge of the specific laws that are covered in this text. Of course, no textbook can give an answer to each and every ethical question that arises in the business environment. Nor can it anticipate the types of ethical questions that will arise in the future, as technology and globalization continue to transform the workplace and business relationships.

The most we can do is examine the types of ethical issues that businesspersons have faced in the past and that they are facing today. In the *Focus on Ethics* sections in this book, we provide examples of specific ethical issues that have arisen in various areas of business activity.

In this initial *Focus on Ethics* feature, we look first at the relationship between business ethics and business law. We then examine various obstacles to ethical behavior in the business context. We conclude the feature by exploring the parameters of corporate social responsibility through a discussion of whether corporations have an ethical duty to the community or society at large.

## Business Ethics and Business Law

Business ethics and business law are closely intertwined because ultimately the law rests on social beliefs about right and wrong behavior in the business world. Thus, businesspersons, by complying with the law, are acting ethically. Mere legal compliance (the "moral minimum" in terms of business ethics), however, is often not enough. This is because the law does not—and cannot—provide the answers for all ethical questions.

In the business world, numerous actions may be unethical but not necessarily illegal. Consider an example. Suppose that a pharmaceutical company is banned from marketing a particular drug in the United States because of the drug's possible adverse side effects. Yet no law prohibits the company from selling the drug in foreign markets—even though some consumers in those markets may suffer serious health problems as a result of using the drug. At issue here is not whether it would be legal to market the drug in other countries but whether it would be *ethical* to do so. In other words, the law has its limits—it cannot make all ethical decisions for us. Rather, the law assumes that those in business will behave ethically in their day-to-day dealings. If they do not, the courts will not come to their assistance.

### LEGAL REASONING

1. *Can you think of a situation in which a business firm may be acting ethically but not in a socially responsible manner? Explain.*

## Obstacles to Ethical Business Behavior

People sometimes behave unethically in the business context, just as they do in their private lives. Some businesspersons knowingly engage in unethical behavior because they think that they can "get away with it"—that is, no one will ever learn of their unethical actions.

Examples of this kind of unethical behavior include padding expense accounts, casting doubts on the integrity of a rival co-worker to gain a job promotion, and stealing company supplies or equipment. Obviously, these acts are unethical, and many of them are illegal as well. In some situations, however, businesspersons who would choose to act ethically may be deterred from doing so because of situational circumstances or external pressures.

**Ethics and the Corporate Environment**  Individuals in their personal lives normally are free to decide ethical issues as they wish and to follow through on those decisions. In the business world, and particularly in the corporate environment, rarely is such a decision made by *one* person. If you are an officer or a manager of a large company, for example, you will find that the decision as to what is right or wrong for the company is not totally yours to make. Your input may weigh in the decision, but ultimately a corporate decision is a collective undertaking.

Additionally, collective decision making, because it places emphasis on consensus and unity of opinion, tends to hinder individual ethical assertiveness. For example, suppose that a director has ethical misgivings about a planned corporate venture that promises to be highly profitable. If the other directors have no such misgivings, the director who does may be swayed by the others' enthusiasm for the project and downplay her or his own criticisms.

Furthermore, just as no one person makes a collective decision, so no one person (normally) is held accountable for the decision. The corporate enterprise thus tends to shield corporate personnel from both individual exposure to the consequences of their decisions (such as direct contact with someone who suffers harm from a corporate product) and personal accountability for those decisions.

**Ethics and Management**  Much unethical business behavior occurs simply because management does not always make clear what ethical standards and behaviors are expected of the firm's employees. Although most firms now issue ethical policies or codes of conduct, these policies and codes are not always effective in creating an ethical workplace. At times, this is because the firm's ethical policies are not communicated clearly to employees or do not bear on the real ethical issues confronting decision makers. Additionally, particularly in a large corporation, unethical behavior in one corporate

FOCUS ON ETHICS CONTINUES ▶

department may simply escape the attention of those in control of the corporation or the corporate officials responsible for implementing and monitoring the company's ethics program.

Unethical behavior may also occur when corporate management, by its own conduct, indicates that ethical considerations take a second seat. If management makes no attempt to deter unethical behavior—through reprimands or employment terminations, for example—it will be obvious to employees that management is not very serious about ethics. Likewise, if a company gives promotions or salary increases to those who clearly use unethical tactics to increase the firm's profits, then employees who do not resort to such tactics will be at a disadvantage. An employee in this situation may decide that because "everyone else does it," he or she might as well do it too.

Of course, an even stronger encouragement of unethical behavior occurs when employers engage in blatantly unethical or illegal conduct and expect their employees to do so as well. An employee in this situation faces two options, neither of which is satisfactory: participate in the conduct or "blow the whistle" on (inform authorities of) the employer's actions—and, of course, risk being fired. (Whistleblowing is a controversial issue because it is sometimes difficult to prove employers' motivations for dismissals.)

### LEGAL REASONING

2. *What might be some other deterrents to ethical behavior in the business context, besides those discussed in this* Focus on Ethics *feature?*

## Corporate Social Responsibility

As discussed in Chapter 5, just what constitutes corporate social responsibility has been debated for some time. In particular, questions arise concerning a corporation's ethical obligations to its community and to society as a whole.

**A Corporation's Duty to the Community**  In some circumstances, the community in which a business enterprise is located is greatly affected by corporate decisions and therefore may be considered a stakeholder. Assume, for example, that a company employs two thousand workers at one of its plants. If the company decides that it would be profitable to close the plant, the employees—and the community—would suffer as a result. To be considered ethical in that situation (and, in some circumstances, to comply with laws governing plant shutdowns), a corporation must take both the employees' needs and the community's needs into consideration when making its decision.

Another ethical question sometimes arises when a firm moves into a community. Does the company have an obligation to evaluate first how its presence will affect that community (even though the community is not a stakeholder yet)? This question has surfaced in regard to the expansion of Wal-Mart Stores, Inc., into smaller communities. Generally, most people in such communities welcome the lower prices and wider array of goods that Wal-Mart offers relative to other, smaller stores in the area. A vocal minority of people in some communities, however, claim that smaller stores often find it impossible to compete with Wal-Mart's prices and thus are forced to go out of business. Many of these smaller stores have existed for years and, according to Wal-Mart's critics, enhance the quality of community life. These critics claim that it is unethical of Wal-Mart to disregard a town's interest in the quality and character of its community life.

In addition to expanding, Wal-Mart has been consolidating some of its smaller stores into large "superstores." As it consolidates, Wal-Mart is closing stores in some of the very towns in which it drove its smaller competitors out of business. This development raises yet another ethical question: Does a store such as Wal-Mart have an obligation to continue operations in a community once it has driven its competitors out of business?

### LEGAL REASONING

3. *Why are consumers and the public generally more concerned with ethical and socially responsible business behavior today than they were, say, fifty years ago?*

**A Corporation's Duty to Society**  Perhaps the most disputed area of corporate social responsibility is the nature of a corporation's duty to society at large. Those who contend that corporations should first and foremost attend to the goal of profit maximization would argue that it is by generating profits that a firm can best contribute to society. Society benefits from profit-making activities because profits can only be realized when a firm markets products or services that are desired by society. These products and services enhance the standard of living, and the profits accumulated by successful business firms generate national wealth. Our laws and court decisions promoting trade and commerce reflect the public policy that the fruits of commerce (wealth) are desirable and good. Because our society values wealth as an ethical goal, corporations, by contributing to that wealth, automatically are acting ethically.

Those arguing for profit maximization as a corporate goal also point out that it would be inappropriate to use the power of the corporate business world to further society's goals by promoting social causes. Determinations as to what exactly is in society's best interest involve questions that are essentially political. Therefore the public, through the political process, should have a say in making those determinations. Thus, the legislature—not the corporate boardroom—is the appropriate forum for making such decisions.

Critics of the profit-maximization view believe that corporations should become actively engaged in seeking and furthering solutions to social problems. Because business controls so much of the wealth and power of this country, business has a responsibility to use its resources in socially beneficial ways. Corporations should therefore promote human rights, strive for equal treatment of minorities and women in the workplace, take steps to preserve the environment, and generally not profit from activities that society has deemed unethical. The critics also point out that it is ethically irresponsible to leave decisions concerning social welfare up to the government, because many social needs are not being met sufficiently through the political process.

### LEGAL REASONING

4. *Suppose that an automobile manufacturing company has to choose between two alternatives: contributing $1 million annually to the United Way or reinvesting the $1 million in the company. In terms of ethics and social responsibility, which is the better choice? Why?*

## It Pays to Be Ethical

Most corporations today have learned that it pays to be ethically responsible—even if this means less profit in the short run (and it often does). Today's corporations are subject to more intensive scrutiny—by both government agencies and the public—than corporations of the past. "Corporate watch"

groups monitor the activities of U.S. corporations, including activities conducted in foreign countries. Through the Internet, complaints about a corporation's practices can easily be disseminated to a worldwide audience. Similarly, dissatisfied customers and employees can voice their complaints about corporate policies, products, or services in Internet chat rooms and other online forums. Thus, if a corporation fails to conduct its operations ethically or to respond quickly to an ethical crisis, its goodwill and reputation (and future profits) will likely suffer as a result.

There are other reasons as well for a corporation to behave ethically. For example, companies that demonstrate a commitment to ethical behavior—by implementing ethical programs, complying with environmental regulations, and promptly investigating product complaints, for example—often receive more lenient treatment from government agencies and the courts. Additionally, investors may shy away from a corporation's stock if the corporation is perceived to be socially irresponsible. Finally, unethical (and/or illegal) corporate behavior may result in government action, such as new laws imposing further requirements on corporate entities.

### LEGAL REASONING

5. *Have Internet chat rooms and online forums affected corporate decision makers' willingness to consider the community and public interest when making choices? Are corporate decision makers more apt to make ethical choices in the cyber age?*

# MILLER
## SUMMARIZED-CASE EDITION

## Unit Two

# TORTS AND CRIMES

## CONTENTS

# CHAPTER 6

# TORTS

**P**art of doing business today—and, indeed, part of everyday life—is the risk of being involved in a lawsuit. The list of circumstances in which businesspersons can be sued is long and varied. A customer who is injured by a security guard at a business establishment, for instance, may sue the business owner, claiming that the security guard's conduct was intentionally wrongful. The parents of a young girl who is bitten while feeding a dolphin may file a suit against Sea World, alleging *negligence* (to be explained later in this chapter).

Any time that one party's allegedly wrongful conduct causes injury to another, an action may arise under the law of *torts* (the word *tort* is French for "wrong"). Through tort law, society compensates those who have suffered injuries as a result of the wrongful conduct of others.

Many of the lawsuits brought by or against business firms are based on the tort theories discussed in this chapter and the next chapter, which covers strict liability and product liability. In addition, Chapter 9 discusses how tort law applies to wrongful actions in the online environment.

---

## THE BASIS OF TORT LAW

Two notions serve as the basis of all **torts:** wrongs and compensation. Tort law is designed to compensate those who have suffered a loss or injury due to another person's wrongful act. In a tort action, one person or group brings a lawsuit against another person or group to obtain compensation (monetary damages) or other relief for the harm suffered.

### The Purpose of Tort Law

Generally, the purpose of tort law is to provide remedies for the violation of various *protected interests*. Society recognizes an interest in personal physical safety. Thus, tort law provides remedies for acts that cause physical injury or that interfere with physical security and freedom of movement. Society recognizes an interest in protecting property, and tort law provides remedies for acts that cause destruction of or damage to property.

### Damages Available in Tort Actions

Because the purpose of tort law is to compensate the injured party for the damage suffered, you need to have an understanding of the types of damages that plaintiffs seek in tort actions.

**COMPENSATORY DAMAGES** A plaintiff is awarded **compensatory damages** to compensate or reimburse the plaintiff for actual losses. Thus, the goal is to make the plaintiff whole and put her or him in the same position that she or he would have been in had the tort not occurred. Compensatory damages awards are often broken down into *special damages* and *general damages*.

*Special damages* compensate the plaintiff for quantifiable monetary losses. Such losses might include medical expenses, lost wages and benefits (now and in the future), extra costs, the loss of irreplaceable items, and the costs of repairing or replacing damaged property.

▶ **Case in Point 6.1** Seaway Marine Transport operates the *Enterprise,* a large cargo ship, which has twenty-two hatches for storing coal. When the *Enterprise* positioned itself to receive a load of coal on the shores of Lake Erie, in Ohio, it struck a land-based coal-loading machine operated by Bessemer & Lake Erie Railroad Company. A federal court found Seaway liable and awarded $522,000 in special damages to compensate Bessemer for the cost of repairing the damage to the loading boom.[1] ◀

*General damages* compensate individuals (not companies) for the nonmonetary aspects of the harm suffered, such as pain and suffering. A court might award general damages for physical or emotional pain and suffering, loss of companionship, loss of consortium (losing the emotional and physical benefits of a spousal relationship), disfigurement, loss of reputation, or loss or impairment of mental or physical capacity.

**PUNITIVE DAMAGES** Occasionally, the courts also award **punitive damages** in tort cases to punish the wrongdoer and deter others from similar wrongdoing. Punitive damages are appropriate only when the defendant's conduct was particularly egregious (reprehensible).

Usually, this means that punitive damages are available in *intentional* tort actions and only rarely in negligence lawsuits (negligence actions will be discussed later in this chapter). They may be awarded, however, in suits involving *gross negligence*. Gross negligence can be defined as an intentional failure to perform a manifest duty in reckless disregard of the consequences of such a failure for the life or property of another.

Courts exercise great restraint in granting punitive damages to plaintiffs in tort actions because punitive damages are subject to limitations under the due process clause of the U.S. Constitution (see Chapter 4). The United States Supreme Court has held that to the extent an award of punitive damages is grossly excessive, it furthers no legitimate purpose and violates due process requirements.[2] Consequently, an appellate court will sometimes reduce the amount of punitive damages awarded to a plaintiff on the ground that it is excessive and thereby violates the due process clause.[3]

## Tort Reform

Tort law performs a valuable function by enabling injured parties to obtain compensation. Nevertheless, critics contend that certain aspects of today's tort law encourage too many trivial and unfounded lawsuits, which clog the courts and add unnecessary costs. They say that damages awards are often excessive and bear little relationship to the actual damage suffered, which inspires more plaintiffs to file lawsuits. The result, in the critics' view, is a system that disproportionately rewards a few plaintiffs while imposing a "tort tax" on business and society as a whole. For instance, to avoid *medical malpractice* (see page 123) suits, physicians and hospitals often order more tests than necessary.

**TYPES OF REFORMS** The federal government and a number of states have begun to take some steps toward tort reform. Measures to reduce the number of tort cases can include any of the following:

1. Limiting the amount of both punitive damages and general damages that can be awarded.
2. Capping the amount that attorneys can collect in *contingency fees* (attorneys' fees that are based on a percentage of the damages awarded to the client—see Chapter 3).
3. Requiring the losing party to pay both the plaintiff's and the defendant's expenses.

**FEDERAL REFORM** At the federal level, the Class Action Fairness Act (CAFA) of 2005[4] shifted jurisdiction over large interstate tort and product liability class-action lawsuits from the state courts to the federal courts. (A *class action* is a lawsuit in which a large number of plaintiffs bring the suit as a group. *Product liability* suits involve the manufacture, sale, and distribution of dangerous and defective goods—see Chapter 7 for details.)

The CAFA prevents plaintiffs' attorneys from *forum shopping*—looking for a state court known to be sympathetic to their clients' cause. Previously, some state courts had been predisposed to award large damages in class-action suits, even when the case had only a weak connection to that jurisdiction. State courts no longer have jurisdiction over class actions under the CAFA.

**STATE REFORMS** At the state level, more than half of the states have placed caps ranging from $250,000 to $750,000 on noneconomic general damages (for example, pain and suffering), especially in medical malpractice suits. More than thirty states have limited punitive damages, with some imposing outright bans.

Note that the supreme courts in about half a dozen states have declared their state's damages caps to be unconstitutional. ▶ **Case in Point 6.2** Naython

---

**1.** *Bessemer & Lake Erie Railroad Co. v. Seaway Marine Transport,* 357 F.3d 596 (6th Cir. 2010).

**2.** *State Farm Mutual Automobile Insurance Co. v. Campbell,* 538 U.S. 408, 123 S.Ct. 1513, 155 L.Ed.2d 585 (2003).

**3.** See, for example, *Buell-Wilson v. Ford Motor Co.,* 160 Cal.App.4th 1107, 73 Cal.Rptr.3d 277 (2008).

**4.** 28 U.S.C. Sections 1711–1715, 1453.

Watts was born with disabling brain injuries because Cox Medical Centers, in Missouri, and its associated physicians were negligent in providing health-care services. At the age of six, Naython cannot walk, talk, or feed himself. He has the mental capacity of a two-year-old, suffers from seizures, and needs around-the-clock care. His mother, Deborah Watts, sued the medical center on his behalf. Watts won a $1.45 million jury award for noneconomic damages plus $3.37 million for future medical damages.

The trial court reduced the noneconomic damages award to $350,000—the statutory cap under Missouri's law. State law also required the trial court to split the future damages award into two parts, with half the amount payable in yearly installments for fifty years (Naython's life expectancy). Watts appealed. Missouri's highest court struck down the state's damages cap, holding that it violated the state constitution's right to trial by jury. The court reasoned that the amount of damages is a fact for the jury to determine, and the legislature cannot place caps on jury awards independent of the facts of a case.[5] ◄

## Classification of Torts

There are two broad classifications of torts: *intentional torts* and *unintentional torts* (torts involving negligence). The classification of a particular tort depends largely on how the tort occurs (intentionally or negligently) and the surrounding circumstances. Intentional torts result from the intentional violation of person or property (fault plus intent). Negligence results from the breach of a duty to act reasonably (fault without intent).

## Defenses

Even if a plaintiff proves all the elements of a tort, the defendant can raise a number of legally recognized *defenses* (reasons why the plaintiff should not obtain damages). The defenses available may vary depending on the specific tort involved. A common defense to intentional torts against persons, for instance, is *consent*. When a person consents to the act that damages her or him, there is generally no liability. The most widely used defense in negligence actions is *comparative negligence* (see page 127). A successful defense releases the defendant from partial or full liability for the tortious act.

---

5. *Watts v. Lester E. Cox Medical Centers*, 376 S.W.3d 633 (Mo. 2012).

# INTENTIONAL TORTS AGAINST PERSONS

An **intentional tort,** as the term implies, requires intent. The **tortfeasor** (the one committing the tort) must intend to commit an act, the consequences of which interfere with another's personal or business interests in a way not permitted by law. An evil or harmful motive is not required—in fact, the person committing the action may even have a beneficial motive for doing what turns out to be a tortious act.

In tort law, *intent* means only that the person intended the consequences of his or her act or knew with substantial certainty that specific consequences would result from the act. The law generally assumes that individuals intend the *normal* consequences of their actions. Thus, forcefully pushing another—even if done in jest—is an intentional tort (if injury results), because the object of a strong push can ordinarily be expected to fall down.

In addition, intent can be transferred when a defendant intends to harm one individual, but unintentionally harms a second person. This is called **transferred intent. ▶ Example 6.3** Alex swings a bat intending to hit Blake but misses and hits Carson instead. Carson can sue Alex for the tort of battery (discussed shortly) because Alex's intent to harm Blake can be transferred to Carson. ◄

## Assault

An **assault** is any intentional and unexcused threat of immediate harmful or offensive contact—words or acts that create a reasonably believable threat. An assault can occur even if there is no actual contact with the plaintiff, provided that the defendant's conduct creates a reasonable apprehension of imminent harm in the plaintiff. Tort law aims to protect individuals from having to expect harmful or offensive contact.

## Battery

If the act that created the apprehension is *completed* and results in harm to the plaintiff, it is a **battery**—an unexcused and harmful or offensive physical contact *intentionally* performed. **▶ Example 6.4** Ivan threatens Jean with a gun and then shoots her. The pointing of the gun at Jean is an assault. The firing of the gun (if the bullet hits Jean) is a battery. ◄

The contact can be harmful, or it can be merely offensive (such as an unwelcome kiss). Physical injury need not occur. The contact can involve any part of the body or anything attached to it—for instance, a hat, a purse, or a jacket. The contact can be made by the defendant or by some force set in motion by the defendant, such as by throwing a rock. Whether the contact is offensive is determined by the *reasonable person standard*.[6]

If the plaintiff shows that there was contact, and the jury (or judge, if there is no jury) agrees that the contact was offensive, then the plaintiff has a right to compensation. A plaintiff may be compensated for the emotional harm or loss of reputation resulting from a battery, as well as for physical harm. A defendant may assert self-defense or defense of others in an attempt to justify his or her conduct.

## False Imprisonment

*False imprisonment* is the intentional confinement or restraint of another person's activities without justification. False imprisonment interferes with the freedom to move without restraint. The confinement can be accomplished through the use of physical barriers, physical restraint, or threats of physical force. Moral pressure does not constitute false imprisonment. It is essential that the person being restrained does not wish to be restrained. (The plaintiff's consent to the restraint bars any liability.)

Businesspersons often face suits for false imprisonment after they have attempted to confine a suspected shoplifter for questioning. Under the "privilege to detain" granted to merchants in most states, a merchant can use *reasonable force* to detain or delay persons suspected of shoplifting and hold them for the police. Although laws pertaining to this privilege vary from state to state, generally any detention must be conducted in a *reasonable* manner and for only a *reasonable* length of time. Undue force or unreasonable detention can lead to liability for the business.

Cities and counties may also face lawsuits for false imprisonment if they detain individuals without reason. ▶ **Case in Point 6.5**  Police arrested Adetokunbo Shoyoye for an unpaid subway ticket and for a theft that had been committed by someone who had stolen his identity. A court ordered him to be released, but a county employee mistakenly confused Shoyoye's paperwork with that of another person—who was scheduled to be sent to state prison. As a result, instead of being released, Shoyoye was held in county jail for more than two weeks. Shoyoye later sued the county for false imprisonment and won.[7] ◀

## Intentional Infliction of Emotional Distress

The tort of *intentional infliction of emotional distress* involves an intentional act that amounts to extreme and outrageous conduct resulting in severe emotional distress to another. To be **actionable** (capable of serving as the ground for a lawsuit), the act must be extreme and outrageous to the point that it exceeds the bounds of decency accepted by society.

**OUTRAGEOUS CONDUCT**  Courts in most jurisdictions are wary of emotional distress claims and confine them to situations involving truly outrageous behavior. Generally, repeated annoyances (such as those experienced by a person who is being stalked), coupled with threats, are enough. Acts that cause indignity or annoyance alone usually are not sufficient.

▶ **Example 6.6**  A father attacks a man who has had consensual sexual relations with the father's nineteen-year-old daughter. The father handcuffs the man to a steel pole and threatens to kill him unless he leaves town immediately. The father's conduct may be sufficiently extreme and outrageous to be actionable as an intentional infliction of emotional distress. ◀

**LIMITED BY THE FIRST AMENDMENT**  When the outrageous conduct consists of speech about a public figure, the First Amendment's guarantee of freedom of speech also limits emotional distress claims.

▶ **Case in Point 6.7**  *Hustler* magazine once printed a false advertisement that showed a picture of the late Reverend Jerry Falwell and described him as having lost his virginity to his mother in an outhouse while he was drunk. Falwell sued the magazine for intentional infliction of emotional distress and won, but the United States Supreme Court overturned the decision. The Court held that creators of parodies of public figures are protected under the First Amendment from intentional infliction of emotional distress claims. (The Court used the same standards that apply to public figures in defamation lawsuits, discussed next.)[8] ◀

---

6. The *reasonable person standard* is an "objective" test of how a reasonable person would have acted under the same circumstances. See "The Duty of Care and Its Breach" later in this chapter.

7. *Shoyoye v. County of Los Angeles*, 203 Cal.App.4th 947, 137 Cal.Rptr.3d 839 (2012).

8. *Hustler Magazine, Inc. v. Falwell*, 485 U.S. 46, 108 S.Ct. 876, 99 L.Ed.2d 41 (1988). For another example of how the courts protect parody, see *Busch v. Viacom International, Inc.*, 477 F.Supp.2d 764 (N.D.Tex. 2007), involving a false endorsement of televangelist Pat Robertson's diet shake.

# Defamation

As discussed in Chapter 4, the freedom of speech guaranteed by the First Amendment is not absolute. The courts are required to balance the vital guarantee of free speech against other pervasive and strong social interests, including society's interest in preventing and redressing attacks on reputation.

**Defamation** of character involves wrongfully hurting a person's good reputation. The law imposes a general duty on all persons to refrain from making false, defamatory *statements of fact* about others. Breaching this duty in writing or other permanent form (such as a digital recording) involves the tort of **libel.** Breaching this duty orally involves the tort of **slander.** The tort of defamation also arises when a false statement of fact is made about a person's product, business, or legal ownership rights to property.

To establish defamation, a plaintiff normally must prove the following:

1. The defendant made a false statement of fact.
2. The statement was understood as being about the plaintiff and tended to harm the plaintiff's reputation.
3. The statement was published to at least one person other than the plaintiff.
4. If the plaintiff is a public figure, she or he must prove *actual malice* (discussed on page 116).

**STATEMENT-OF-FACT REQUIREMENT** Often at issue in defamation lawsuits (including online defamation, which will be discussed later in this chapter) is whether the defendant made a statement of fact or a *statement of opinion.* Statements of opinion normally are not actionable because they are protected under the First Amendment.

In other words, making a negative statement about another person is not defamation unless the statement is false and represents something as a fact rather than a personal opinion. ▶ **Example 6.8** The statement "Lane cheats on his taxes," if false, can lead to liability for defamation. The statement "Lane is a jerk," however, cannot constitute defamation because it is an opinion. ◀

**THE PUBLICATION REQUIREMENT** The basis of the tort of defamation is the publication of a statement or statements that hold an individual up to contempt, ridicule, or hatred. *Publication* here means that the defamatory statements are communicated (either intentionally or accidentally) to persons other than the defamed party. ▶ **Example 6.9** If Rodriques sends Andrews a private handwritten letter falsely accusing him of embezzling funds, the action does not constitute libel. If Peters falsely states that Gordon is dishonest and incompetent when no one else is around, the action does not constitute slander. In neither instance was the message communicated to a third party. ◀

The courts have generally held that even dictating a letter to a secretary constitutes publication, although the publication may be privileged (a concept that will be explained shortly). Moreover, if a third party merely overhears defamatory statements by chance, the courts usually hold that this also constitutes publication. Defamatory statements made via the Internet are actionable as well. Note also that any individual who repeats or republishes defamatory statements normally is liable even if that person reveals the source of the statements.

**DAMAGES FOR LIBEL** Once a defendant's liability for libel is established, general damages are presumed as a matter of law. General damages are designed to compensate the plaintiff for nonspecific harms such as disgrace or dishonor in the eyes of the community, humiliation, injured reputation, and emotional distress—harms that are difficult to measure. In other words, to recover damages, the plaintiff need not prove that he or she was actually harmed in any specific way as a result of the libelous statement.

**DAMAGES FOR SLANDER** In contrast to cases alleging libel, in a case alleging slander, the plaintiff must prove *special damages* to establish the defendant's liability. The plaintiff must show that the slanderous statement caused her or him to suffer actual economic or monetary losses.

Unless this initial hurdle of proving special damages is overcome, a plaintiff alleging slander normally cannot go forward with the suit and recover any damages. This requirement is imposed in slander cases because oral statements have a temporary quality. In contrast, a libelous (written) statement has the quality of permanence and can be circulated widely, especially through tweets and blogs. Also, libel usually results from some degree of deliberation by the author.

**SLANDER *PER SE*** Exceptions to the burden of proving special damages in cases alleging slander are made for certain types of slanderous statements. If a false statement constitutes "slander *per se*," it is actionable with no proof of special damages required. In most states, the following four types of declarations are considered to be slander *per se:*

1. A statement that another has a particular type of disease (such as a sexually transmitted disease or mental illness).
2. A statement that another has committed improprieties while engaging in a profession or trade.
3. A statement that another has committed or has been imprisoned for a serious crime.
4. A statement that a person (usually only unmarried persons and sometimes only women) is unchaste or has engaged in serious sexual misconduct.

**DEFENSES TO DEFAMATION** Truth is normally an absolute defense against a defamation charge. In other words, if a defendant in a defamation case can prove that the allegedly defamatory statements of fact were true, normally no tort has been committed.

Other defenses to defamation may exist if the speech is *privileged* or concerns a public figure. Note that the majority of defamation actions are filed in state courts, and state laws differ somewhat in the defenses they allow, such as privilege (discussed shortly).

At the heart of the following case were allegedly defamatory statements posted online that criticized a doctor for what the son of one of the doctor's patients perceived as rude and insensitive behavior.

## CASE 6.1

### McKee v. Laurion
Supreme Court of Minnesota, 825 N.W.2d 725 (2013).

**BACKGROUND AND FACTS** Kenneth Laurion was admitted to St. Luke's Hospital in Duluth, Minnesota, after suffering a hemorrhagic stroke. Two days later, he was transferred from the intensive care unit (ICU) of St. Luke's to a private room. The attending physician arranged for Dr. David McKee, a neurologist, to examine him. Kenneth's son, Dennis, and other Laurion family members were present during the examination.

After Kenneth was discharged from the hospital, Dennis posted the following statements on "rate-your-doctor" Web sites: [Dr. McKee] seemed upset that my father had been moved [into a private room]. Never having met my father or his family, Dr. McKee said, "When you weren't in ICU, I had to spend time finding out if you transferred or died." When we gaped at him, he said, "Well, 44 percent of hemorrhagic strokes die within 30 days. I guess this is the better option." When my father said his gown was just hanging from his neck without a back, Dr. McKee said, "That doesn't matter." My wife said, "It matters to us; let us go into the hall."

After learning of the posts, Dr. McKee filed a suit in a Minnesota state court against Dennis, asserting defamation. The court issued a summary judgment in Dennis's favor. A state intermediate appellate court reversed this judgment. Dennis appealed.

**DECISION AND RATIONALE** The Minnesota Supreme Court concluded that the lower court properly granted summary judgment in favor of Dennis and reversed the decision of the intermediate appellate court. The state's highest court pointed out that truth is a complete defense to a defamation action and that true statements, however disparaging, are not actionable. "If the statement is true in substance, minor inaccuracies of expression or detail are immaterial. Minor inaccuracies do not amount to falsities so long as the substance, the gist, the sting of the libelous charge is justified."

Dr. McKee acknowledged in his deposition that when he examined Kenneth, he did communicate to those present that some intensive-care-unit patients die, although he denied referencing a specific percentage. The court believed that even without an exact percentage in his statement, Dr. McKee's statement satisfied the test "for substantial truth because it would have the same effect on the reader regardless of whether a specific percentage reference [or whether the percentage is accurate]."

The statements by Laurion's son Dennis were not actionable as defamation. There was no genuine question as to the falsity of the statements—they were substantially true.

CASE 6.1 CONTINUES ➡

**CASE 6.1 CONTINUED**

**THE LEGAL ENVIRONMENT DIMENSION** *What are the required elements to establish a claim of defamation? Which party has to plead and prove these elements?*

**WHAT IF THE FACTS WERE DIFFERENT?** *Suppose that Laurion had posted online "When I mentioned Dr. McKee's name to a friend who is a nurse, she said, 'Dr. McKee is a real tool!'" Would this statement have been defamatory? Explain.*

---

*Privileged Communications.* In some circumstances, a person will not be liable for defamatory statements because she or he enjoys a **privilege,** or immunity. Privileged communications are of two types: absolute and qualified.[9] Only in judicial proceedings and certain government proceedings is an *absolute privilege* granted. Thus, statements made by attorneys and judges in the courtroom during a trial are absolutely privileged, as are statements made by government officials during legislative debate.

In other situations, a person will not be liable for defamatory statements because he or she has a *qualified,* or *conditional, privilege.* An employer's statements in written evaluations of employees, for instance, are protected by a qualified privilege. Generally, if the statements are made in good faith and the publication is limited to those who have a legitimate interest in the communication, the statements fall within the area of qualified privilege.

▶ **Example 6.10** Jorge has worked at Sony Corporation for five years and is being considered for a management position. His supervisor, Lydia, writes a memo about Jorge's performance to those evaluating him for the position. The memo contains certain negative statements, which Lydia honestly believes are true. If Lydia limits the disclosure of the memo to company representatives, her statements will likely be protected by a qualified privilege. ◀

*Public Figures.* Politicians, entertainers, professional athletes, and others in the public eye are considered **public figures.** In general, public figures are considered "fair game," and false and defamatory statements about them that are published in the media will not constitute defamation unless the statements are made with **actual malice.**

To be made with actual malice, a statement must be made *with either knowledge of its falsity or a reckless disregard of the truth.*[10] Statements made about public figures, especially when they are communicated via a public medium, usually are related to matters of general public interest. Public figures generally have some access to a public medium for answering belittling falsehoods about themselves. For these reasons, public figures have a greater burden of proof in defamation cases (to show actual malice) than do private individuals.

## Invasion of Privacy

A person has a right to solitude and freedom from prying public eyes—in other words, to privacy. As mentioned in Chapter 4, the courts have held that certain amendments to the U.S. Constitution imply a right to privacy. Some state constitutions explicitly provide for privacy rights, as do a number of federal and state statutes. Tort law also safeguards these rights through the tort of *invasion of privacy.* Generally, to sue successfully for an invasion of privacy, a person must have a reasonable expectation of privacy, and the invasion must be highly offensive.

**INVASION OF PRIVACY UNDER THE COMMON LAW**
The following four acts qualify as an invasion of privacy under the common law:

1. *Intrusion into an individual's affairs or seclusion.* Invading someone's home or searching someone's briefcase or laptop without authorization is an invasion of privacy. This tort has been held to extend to eavesdropping by wiretap, unauthorized scanning of a bank account, compulsory blood testing, and window peeping. ▶ **Example 6.11** A female sports reporter for ESPN is digitally videoed while naked through the peephole in the door of her hotel room. She will probably win a lawsuit

---

**9.** Note that the term *privileged communication* in this context is not the same as privileged communication between a professional, such as an attorney, and his or her client.

**10.** *New York Times Co. v. Sullivan,* 376 U.S. 254, 84 S.Ct. 710, 11 L.Ed.2d 686 (1964). As mentioned earlier, the First Amendment also protects the creator of a parody from liability for defamation of a public figure.

against the man who took the video and posted it on the Internet. ◄

2. *False light.* Publication of information that places a person in a false light is also an invasion of privacy. For instance, it is an invasions of privacy to write a story about a person that attributes ideas and opinions not held by that person. (Publishing such a story could involve the tort of defamation as well.) ▶ **Example 6.12**  An Arkansas newspaper prints an article with the headline "Special Delivery: World's oldest newspaper carrier, 101, quits because she's pregnant!" Next to the article is a picture of a ninety-six-year-old woman who is not the subject of the article (and not pregnant). She sues the paper for placing her in a false light and probably will prevail. ◄

3. *Public disclosure of private facts.* This type of invasion of privacy occurs when a person publicly discloses private facts about an individual that an ordinary person would find objectionable or embarrassing. A newspaper account of a private citizen's sex life or financial affairs could be an actionable invasion of privacy. This is so even if the information revealed is true, because it should not be a matter of public concern.

   Note, however, that news reports about public figures' personal lives are often not actionable because a public figure's behavior *is* a legitimate public concern. For instance, when U.S. Congressman Anthony Weiner posted partially nude photos of himself on Twitter, his action was a matter of legitimate public concern. In contrast, the same online communications by a neighbor would likely not be a matter of public concern.

4. *Appropriation of identity.* Using a person's name, picture, likeness, or other identifiable characteristic for commercial purposes without permission is also an invasion of privacy. An individual's right to privacy normally includes the right to the exclusive use of her or his identity. ▶ **Example 6.13**  An advertising agency asks a singer with a distinctive voice and stage presence to do a marketing campaign for a new automobile. The singer rejects the offer. If the agency then uses someone who imitates the singer's voice and dance moves in the ad, it would be actionable as an appropriation of identity. ◄

**APPROPRIATION STATUTES** Most states today have codified the common law tort of appropriation of identity in statutes that establish the distinct tort of appropriation or right of publicity. States differ as to the degree of likeness that is required to impose liability for appropriation, however.

Some courts have held that even when an animated character in a video or a video game is made to look like an actual person, there are not enough similarities to constitute appropriation. ▶ **Case in Point 6.14**  The Naked Cowboy, Robert Burck, is a street entertainer in New York City who performs for tourists wearing only a white cowboy hat, white cowboy boots, and white underwear. He carries a guitar strategically placed to give the illusion of nudity and has become famous. Burck sued Mars, Inc., the maker of M&Ms candy, over a video it showed on billboards in Times Square that depicted a blue M&M dressed exactly like The Naked Cowboy. The court, however, held that the use of Burck's signature costume did not amount to appropriation.[11] ◄

## Fraudulent Misrepresentation

A misrepresentation leads another to believe in a condition that is different from the condition that actually exists. Although persons sometimes make misrepresentations accidentally because they are unaware of the existing facts, the tort of **fraudulent misrepresentation,** or *fraud,* involves *intentional* deceit for personal gain. The tort includes several elements:

1. A misrepresentation of material facts or conditions with knowledge that they are false or with reckless disregard for the truth.
2. An intent to induce another party to rely on the misrepresentation.
3. A justifiable reliance on the misrepresentation by the deceived party.
4. Damages suffered as a result of that reliance.
5. A causal connection between the misrepresentation and the injury suffered.

For fraud to occur, more than mere **puffery,** or *seller's talk,* must be involved. Fraud exists only when a person represents as a fact something he or she knows is untrue. For instance, it is fraud to claim that the roof of a building does not leak when one knows that it does. Facts are objectively ascertainable, whereas seller's talk (such as "I am the best accountant in town") is not.

Normally, the tort of fraudulent misrepresentation occurs only when there is reliance on a *statement of fact.* Sometimes, however, reliance on a *statement of opinion* may involve the tort of fraudulent misrepresentation if the individual making the statement of opinion has

---

11. *Burck v. Mars, Inc.,* 571 F.Supp.2d 446 (S.D.N.Y. 2008).

superior knowledge of the subject matter. For instance, when a lawyer makes a statement of opinion about the law in a state in which the lawyer is licensed to practice, a court might treat it as a statement of fact.

## Abusive or Frivolous Litigation

Tort law recognizes that people have a right not to be sued without a legally just and proper reason. It therefore protects individuals from the misuse of litigation. If the party that initiated a lawsuit did so out of malice and without a legitimate legal reason, and ended up losing that suit, the party can be sued for *malicious prosecution.*

*Abuse of process* can apply to any person using a legal process against another in an improper manner or to accomplish a purpose for which the process was not designed. The key difference between the torts of abuse of process and malicious prosecution is the level of proof. Abuse of process is not limited to prior litigation and does not require the plaintiff to prove malice. It can be based on the wrongful use of subpoenas, court orders to attach or seize real property, or other types of formal legal process.

*Concept Summary 6.1* below reviews intentional torts against persons.

## SECTION 3
# BUSINESS TORTS

The torts known as *business torts* generally involve wrongful interference with another's business rights. Business torts involving wrongful interference generally fall into two categories: interference with a contractual relationship and interference with a business relationship.

## Wrongful Interference with a Contractual Relationship

Three elements are necessary for wrongful interference with a contractual relationship to occur:

1. A valid, enforceable contract must exist between two parties.
2. A third party must know that this contract exists.
3. This third party must *intentionally induce* a party to the contract to breach the contract.

▶ **Case in Point 6.15** A landmark case in this area involved an opera singer, Joanna Wagner, who was under contract to sing for a man named Lumley for a specified period of years. A man named Gye, who knew of this contract, nonetheless "enticed"

---

### CONCEPT SUMMARY 6.1
## Intentional Torts against Persons

| NAME OF TORT | DESCRIPTION |
|---|---|
| **Assault and Battery** | Any unexcused and intentional act that causes another person to be apprehensive of immediate harm is an assault. An assault resulting in physical contact is a battery. |
| **False Imprisonment** | An intentional confinement or restraint of another person's movement without justification. |
| **Intentional Infliction of Emotional Distress** | An intentional act that amounts to extreme and outrageous conduct resulting in severe emotional distress to another. |
| **Defamation (Libel or Slander)** | A false statement of fact, not made under privilege, that is communicated to a third person and that causes damage to a person's reputation. For public figures, the plaintiff must also prove that the statement was made with actual malice. |
| **Invasion of Privacy** | Publishing or otherwise making known or using information relating to a person's private life and affairs, with which the public has no legitimate concern, without that person's permission or approval. |
| **Fraudulent Misrepresentation (Fraud)** | A false representation made by one party, through misstatement of facts or through conduct, with the intention of deceiving another and on which the other reasonably relies to his or her detriment. |
| **Abusive or Frivolous Litigation** | The filing of a lawsuit without legitimate grounds and with malice. Alternatively, the use of a legal process in an improper manner. |

Wagner to refuse to carry out the agreement, and Wagner began to sing for Gye. Gye's action constituted a tort because it interfered with the contractual relationship between Wagner and Lumley. (Of course, Wagner's refusal to carry out the agreement also entitled Lumley to sue Wagner for breach of contract.)[12] ◄

The body of tort law relating to wrongful interference with a contractual relationship has increased greatly in recent years. In principle, any lawful contract can be the basis for an action of this type. The contract could be between a firm and its employees or a firm and its customers. Sometimes, a competitor of a firm draws away one of the firm's key employees. Only if the original employer can show that the competitor knew of the contract's existence, and intentionally induced the breach, can damages be recovered from the competitor.

## Wrongful Interference with a Business Relationship

Businesspersons devise countless schemes to attract customers. They are prohibited, however, from unreasonably interfering with another's business in their attempts to gain a greater share of the market.

There is a difference between *competitive practices* and *predatory behavior*—actions undertaken with the intention of unlawfully driving competitors completely out of the market. Attempting to attract customers in general is a legitimate business practice, whereas specifically targeting the customers of a competitor is more likely to be predatory.

▶ **Example 6.16**  A shopping mall contains two athletic shoe stores: Joe's and Zappato's. Joe's cannot station an employee at the entrance of Zappato's to divert customers to Joe's by telling them that Joe's will beat Zappato's prices. Doing this would constitute the tort of wrongful interference with a business relationship because it would interfere with a prospective economic advantage. Such behavior is commonly considered to be an unfair trade practice. If this type of activity were permitted, Joe's would reap the benefits of Zappato's advertising. ◄

Generally, a plaintiff must prove that the defendant used predatory methods to intentionally harm an established business relationship or prospective economic advantage. The plaintiff must also prove that the defendant's interference caused the plaintiff to suffer economic harm.

---

12. *Lumley v. Gye*, 118 Eng.Rep. 749 (1853).

## Defenses to Wrongful Interference

A person will not be liable for the tort of wrongful interference with a contractual or business relationship if it can be shown that the interference was justified, or permissible. Bona fide competitive behavior—through aggressive marketing and advertising strategies, for instance—is a permissible interference even if it results in the breaking of a contract.

▶ **Example 6.17**  Taylor Meats advertises so effectively that it induces Sam's Restaurant to break its contract with Burke's Meat Company. In that situation, Burke's Meat Company will be unable to recover against Taylor Meats on a wrongful interference theory. The public policy that favors free competition through advertising outweighs any possible instability that such competitive activity might cause in contractual relations. ◄

### SECTION 4

# INTENTIONAL TORTS AGAINST PROPERTY

Intentional torts against property include trespass to land, trespass to personal property, conversion, and disparagement of property. These torts are wrongful actions that interfere with individuals' legally recognized rights with regard to their land or personal property.

The law distinguishes real property from personal property. *Real property* is land and things permanently attached to the land, such as a house. *Personal property* consists of all other items, including cash and securities (stocks, bonds, and other ownership interests in companies).

## Trespass to Land

A **trespass to land** occurs when a person, without permission, does any of the following:

1. Enters onto, above, or below the surface of land that is owned by another.
2. Causes anything to enter onto land owned by another.
3. Remains on land owned by another or permits anything to remain on it.

Actual harm to the land is not an essential element of this tort because the tort is designed to protect the right of an owner to exclusive possession.

Common types of trespass to land include walking or driving on another's land, shooting a gun over another's land, and throwing rocks at a building that belongs to someone else. Another common form of trespass involves constructing a building so that part of it extends onto an adjoining landowner's property.

**ESTABLISHING TRESPASS** Before a person can be a trespasser, the real property owner (or another person in actual and exclusive possession of the property, such as a renter) must establish that person as a trespasser. For instance, "posted" trespass signs expressly establish as a trespasser a person who ignores these signs and enters onto the property. A guest in your home is not a trespasser—unless he or she has been asked to leave and refuses. Any person who enters onto another's property to commit an illegal act (such as a thief entering a lumberyard at night to steal lumber) is established impliedly as a trespasser, without posted signs.

**DAMAGES** At common law, a trespasser is liable for any damage caused to the property and generally cannot hold the owner liable for injuries that the trespasser sustains on the premises. This common law rule is being abandoned in many jurisdictions, however, in favor of a *reasonable duty of care* rule that varies depending on the status of the parties.

For instance, a landowner may have a duty to post a notice that guard dogs patrol the property. Also, if young children were attracted to the property by some object, such a swimming pool or a sand pile, and were injured, the landowner may be held liable for their injuries. This is the so-called *attractive nuisance doctrine*. An owner can normally use reasonable force, however, to remove a trespasser from the premises—or detain the trespasser for a reasonable time—without liability for damages.

**DEFENSES AGAINST TRESPASS TO LAND** One defense to a claim of trespass is to show that the trespass was warranted—such as when a trespasser enters a building to assist someone in danger. Another defense exists when the trespasser can show that she or he had a *license* to come onto the land.

A **licensee** is one who is invited (or allowed to enter) onto the property of another for the licensee's benefit. A person who enters another's property to read an electric meter, for example, is a licensee. When you purchase a ticket to attend a movie or sporting event, you are licensed to go onto the property of another to view that movie or event.

Note that licenses to enter onto another's property are *revocable* by the property owner. If a property owner asks an electric meter reader to leave and she or he refuses to do so, the meter reader at that point becomes a trespasser.

## Trespass to Personal Property

Whenever any individual wrongfully takes or harms the personal property of another or otherwise interferes with the lawful owner's possession and enjoyment of personal property, **trespass to personal property** occurs. This tort may also be called *trespass to chattels* or *trespass to personalty*.[13] In this context, harm means not only destruction of the property, but also anything that diminishes its value, condition, or quality.

Trespass to personal property involves intentional meddling with a possessory interest (one arising from possession), including barring an owner's access to personal property. ▶ **Example 6.18** Kelly takes Ryan's business law book as a practical joke and hides it so that Ryan is unable to find it for several days before the final examination. Here, Kelly has engaged in a trespass to personal property (and also *conversion*, the tort discussed next). ◀

If it can be shown that trespass to personal property was warranted, then a complete defense exists. Most states, for instance, allow automobile repair shops to hold a customer's car (under what is called an *artisan's lien*) when the customer refuses to pay for repairs already completed.

## Conversion

Any act that deprives an owner of personal property or of the use of that property without the owner's permission and without just cause can constitute **conversion.** Even the taking of electronic records and data may form the basis of a conversion claim. Often, when conversion occurs, a trespass to personal property also occurs because the original taking of the personal property from the owner was a trespass. Wrongfully retaining the property is conversion.

Conversion is the civil side of crimes related to theft, but it is not limited to theft. Even when the rightful owner consented to the initial taking of the property, so no theft or trespass occurred, a failure to return the property may still be conversion. ▶ **Example 6.19** Chen borrows Mark's iPad mini to

---

**13.** Pronounced *per-sun-ul-tee.*

use while traveling home from school for the holidays. When Chen returns to school, Mark asks for his iPad back, but Chen says that he gave it to his little brother for Christmas. In this situation, Mark can sue Chen for conversion, and Chen will have to either return the iPad or pay damages equal to its replacement value. ◄

Conversion can occur even when a person mistakenly believed that she or he was entitled to the goods. In other words, good intentions are not a defense against conversion. Someone who buys stolen goods, for instance, may be sued for conversion even if he or she did not know the goods were stolen. If the true owner brings a tort action against the buyer, the buyer must either return the property to the owner or pay the owner the full value of the property (despite having already paid the purchase price to the thief).

## Disparagement of Property

**Disparagement of property** occurs when economically injurious falsehoods are made about another's product or property rather than about another's reputation (as in the tort of defamation). *Disparagement of property* is a general term for torts that can be more specifically referred to as *slander of quality* or *slander of title.*

**SLANDER OF QUALITY** The publication of false information about another's product, alleging that it is not what its seller claims, constitutes the tort of **slander of quality,** or **trade libel.** To establish trade libel, the plaintiff must prove that the improper publication caused a third person to refrain from dealing with the plaintiff and that the plaintiff sustained economic damages (such as lost profits) as a result.

An improper publication may be both a slander of quality and a defamation of character. For instance, a statement that disparages the quality of a product may also, by implication, disparage the character of a person who would sell such a product.

**SLANDER OF TITLE** When a publication falsely denies or casts doubt on another's legal ownership of property, resulting in financial loss to the property's owner, the tort of **slander of title** occurs. Usually, this is an intentional tort in which someone knowingly publishes an untrue statement about another's ownership of certain property with the intent of discouraging a third person from dealing with the person slandered. For instance, it would be difficult for a car dealer to attract customers after competitors published a notice that the dealer's stock consisted of stolen automobiles.

See *Concept Summary 6.2* below for a review of intentional torts against property.

## SECTION 5
# UNINTENTIONAL TORTS (NEGLIGENCE)

The tort of **negligence** occurs when someone suffers injury because of another's failure to live up to a required *duty of care.* In contrast to intentional torts, in torts involving negligence, the tortfeasor neither wishes to bring about the consequences of the act nor believes that they will occur. The person's conduct merely creates a risk of such consequences. If no risk

---

### CONCEPT SUMMARY 6.2
## Intentional Torts against Property

| NAME OF TORT | DESCRIPTION |
| --- | --- |
| **Trespass to Land** | The invasion of another's real property without consent or privilege. Once a person is expressly or impliedly established as a trespasser, the property owner has specific rights, which may include the right to detain or remove the trespasser. |
| **Trespass to Personal Property** | The intentional interference with an owner's right to use, possess, or enjoy his or her personal property without the owner's consent. |
| **Conversion** | The wrongful possession or use of another person's personal property without just cause. |
| **Disparagement of Property** | Any economically injurious falsehood that is made about another's product or property; an inclusive term for the torts of *slander of quality* and *slander of title.* |

is created, there is no negligence. Moreover, the risk must be foreseeable. In other words, it must be such that a reasonable person engaging in the same activity would anticipate the risk and guard against it. In determining what is reasonable conduct, courts consider the nature of the possible harm.

Many of the actions giving rise to the intentional torts discussed earlier in the chapter constitute negligence if the element of intent is missing (or cannot be proved). ▶ **Example 6.20** Juan walks up to Maya and intentionally shoves her. Maya falls and breaks her arm as a result. In this situation, Juan is liable for the intentional tort of battery. If Juan carelessly bumps into Maya, however, and she falls and breaks her arm as a result, Juan's action constitutes negligence. In either situation, Juan has committed a tort. ◀

To succeed in a negligence action, the plaintiff must prove each of the following:

1. *Duty.* The defendant owed a duty of care to the plaintiff.
2. *Breach.* The defendant breached that duty.
3. *Causation.* The defendant's breach caused the plaintiff's injury.
4. *Damages.* The plaintiff suffered a legally recognizable injury.

## The Duty of Care and Its Breach

Central to the tort of negligence is the concept of a **duty of care.** The basic principle underlying the duty of care is that people are free to act as they please so long as their actions do not infringe on the interests of others. When someone fails to comply with the duty to exercise reasonable care, a potentially tortious act may have been committed.

Failure to live up to a standard of care may be an act (accidentally setting fire to a building) or an omission (neglecting to put out a campfire). It may be a careless act or a carefully performed but, nevertheless, dangerous act that results in injury. Courts consider the nature of the act (whether it is outrageous or commonplace) and the manner in which the act is performed (carelessly versus cautiously). In addition, courts look at the nature of the injury (whether it is serious or slight) in determining whether the duty of care has been breached. Creating a very slight risk of a dangerous explosion might be unreasonable, whereas creating a distinct possibility of someone's burning his or her fingers on a stove might be reasonable.

**THE REASONABLE PERSON STANDARD** Tort law measures duty by the **reasonable person standard.** In determining whether a duty of care has been breached, the courts ask how a reasonable person would have acted in the same circumstances. The reasonable person standard is said to be objective. It is not necessarily how a particular person *would* act. It is society's judgment of how an ordinarily prudent person *should* act. If the so-called reasonable person existed, he or she would be careful, conscientious, even tempered, and honest.

The courts frequently use the hypothetical reasonable person standard in other areas of law as well. That individuals are required to exercise a reasonable standard of care in their activities is a pervasive concept in business law. Many of the issues discussed in subsequent chapters of this text have to do with the duty of reasonable care.

In negligence cases, the degree of care to be exercised varies, depending on the defendant's occupation or profession, her or his relationship with the plaintiff, and other factors. Generally, whether an action constitutes a breach of the duty of care is determined on a case-by-case basis. The outcome depends on how the judge (or jury, if it is a jury trial) decides a reasonable person in the position of the defendant would have acted in the particular circumstances of the case.

**THE DUTY OF LANDOWNERS** Landowners are expected to exercise reasonable care to protect individuals coming onto their property from harm. In some jurisdictions, as mentioned earlier, landowners may even have a duty to protect trespassers against certain risks. Landowners who rent or lease premises to tenants are expected to exercise reasonable care to ensure that the tenants and their guests are not harmed in common areas, such as stairways, entryways, and laundry rooms.

*The Duty to Warn Business Invitees of Risks.* Retailers and other companies that explicitly or implicitly invite persons to come onto their premises have a duty to exercise reasonable care to protect these **business invitees.** The duty normally requires storeowners to warn business invitees of foreseeable risks, such as construction zones or wet floors, about which the owners knew or *should have known.*

▶ **Example 6.21** Liz enters a supermarket, slips on a wet floor, and sustains injuries as a result. If there was no sign or other warning that the floor was wet at the time Liz slipped, the supermarket owner would be liable for damages. A court would hold that the owner was negligent by failing to exercise a reasonable degree of care to protect customers against the foreseeable risk of injury from slipping on the wet floor. The owner should have taken care to avoid this risk or warn the customer of it (by posting a sign or setting out orange cones, for example). ◄

The landowner also has a duty to discover and remove any hidden dangers that might injure a customer or other invitee. Hidden dangers might include uneven surfaces or defects in the pavement of a parking lot or a walkway. Store owners also have a duty to protect customers from slipping and injuring themselves on merchandise that has fallen off the shelves, for example. Thus, the owners of business premises should evaluate and frequently reassess potential hazards on the property to ensure the safety of business invitees.

***Obvious Risks Provide an Exception.*** Some risks, of course, are so obvious that an owner need not warn of them. For example, a business owner does not need to warn customers to open a door before attempting to walk through it. Other risks, however, even though they may seem obvious to a business owner, may not be so in the eyes of another, such as a child. In addition, even if a risk is obvious, that does not necessarily excuse a business owner from the duty to protect its customers from foreseeable harm.

▶ **Case in Point 6.22** Giorgio's Grill is a restaurant in Florida that becomes a nightclub after hours. At those times, traditionally, as the manager of Giorgio's knew, the staff and customers throw paper napkins into the air as the music plays. The napkins land on the floor, but no one picks them up. One night, Jane Izquierdo went to Giorgio's. Although she had been to the club on prior occasions and knew about the napkin-throwing tradition, she slipped and fell, breaking her leg. She sued Giorgio's for negligence, but lost at trial because a jury found that the risk of slipping on the napkins was obvious. A state appellate court reversed, however, holding that the obviousness of a risk does not discharge a business owner's duty to its invitees to maintain the premises in a safe condition.[14] ◄

**THE DUTY OF PROFESSIONALS** If an individual has knowledge or skill superior to that of an ordinary person, the individual's conduct must be consistent with that status. Professionals—including physicians, dentists, architects, engineers, accountants, and lawyers,

among others—are required to have a standard minimum level of special knowledge and ability. Therefore, in determining what constitutes reasonable care in the case of professionals, the law takes their training and expertise into account. Thus, an accountant's conduct is judged not by the reasonable person standard, but by the reasonable accountant standard.

If a professional violates his or her duty of care toward a client, the client may bring a suit against the professional, alleging **malpractice,** which is essentially professional negligence. For instance, a patient might sue a physician for *medical malpractice.* A client might sue an attorney for *legal malpractice.*

## Causation

Another element necessary to a negligence action is *causation.* If a person breaches a duty of care and someone suffers injury, the person's act must have caused the harm for it to constitute the tort of negligence.

**COURTS ASK TWO QUESTIONS** In deciding whether the requirement of causation is met, the court must address two questions:

1. *Is there causation in fact?* Did the injury occur because of the defendant's act, or would it have occurred anyway? If the injury would not have occurred without the defendant's act, then there is causation in fact.

    **Causation in fact** usually can be determined by use of the *but for* test: "but for" the wrongful act, the injury would not have occurred. This test determines whether there was an actual cause-and-effect relationship between the act and the injury suffered. In theory, causation in fact is limitless. One could claim, for example, that "but for" the creation of the world, a particular injury would not have occurred. Thus, as a practical matter, the law has to establish limits, and it does so through the concept of proximate cause.

2. *Was the act the proximate, or legal, cause of the injury?* **Proximate cause,** or *legal cause,* exists when the connection between an act and an injury is strong enough to justify imposing liability. Proximate cause asks whether the injuries sustained were foreseeable or were too remotely connected to the incident to trigger liability. Judges use proximate cause to limit the scope of the defendant's liability to a subset of the total number of potential plaintiffs that might have been harmed by the defendant's actions.

    ▶ **Example 6.23** Ackerman carelessly leaves a campfire burning. The fire not only burns

---

**14.** *Izquierdo v. Gyroscope, Inc.,* 946 So.2d 115 (Fla.App. 2007).

down the forest but also sets off an explosion in a nearby chemical plant that spills chemicals into a river, killing all the fish for a hundred miles downstream and ruining the economy of a tourist resort. Should Ackerman be liable to the resort owners? To the tourists whose vacations were ruined? These are questions of proximate cause that a court must decide. ◄

Both of these causation questions must be answered in the affirmative for liability in tort to arise. If there is causation in fact but a court decides that the defendant's action is not the proximate cause of the plaintiff's injury, the causation requirement has not been met. Therefore, the defendant normally will not be liable to the plaintiff.

**FORESEEABILITY** Questions of proximate cause are linked to the concept of foreseeability because it would be unfair to impose liability on a defendant unless the defendant's actions created a foreseeable risk of injury.

Probably the most cited case on the concept of foreseeability and proximate cause is the *Palsgraf* case, which is presented next. In determining the issue of proximate cause, the court addressed the following question: Does a defendant's duty of care extend only to those who may be injured as a result of a foreseeable risk, or does it also extend to a person whose injury could not reasonably be foreseen?

## CLASSIC CASE 6.2

### Palsgraf v. Long Island Railroad Co.
Court of Appeals of New York, 248 N.Y. 339, 162 N.E. 99 (1928).

**BACKGROUND AND FACTS** The plaintiff, Helen Palsgraf, was waiting for a train on a station platform. A man carrying a package was rushing to catch a train that was moving away from a platform across the tracks from Palsgraf. As the man attempted to jump aboard the moving train, he seemed unsteady and about to fall. A railroad guard on the car reached forward to grab him, and another guard on the platform pushed him from behind to help him board the train.

In the process, the man's package, which (unknown to the railroad guards) contained fireworks, fell on the railroad tracks and exploded. There was nothing about the package to indicate its contents. The repercussions of the explosion caused scales at the other end of the train platform to fall on Palsgraf, causing injuries for which she sued the railroad company. At the trial, the jury found that the railroad guards had been negligent in their conduct. The railroad company appealed. The appellate court affirmed the trial court's judgment, and the railroad company appealed to New York's highest state court.

**DECISION AND RATIONALE** The New York Court of Appeals dismissed Palsgraf's complaint. The conduct of the railroad employees may have been negligent toward the man with the package, but it was not negligent in relation to Palsgraf, who was standing far away. The railroad was not negligent toward her because her injury had not been foreseeable. "Nothing in the situation gave notice . . . of peril to persons thus removed. . . . [No] hazard was apparent to the eye of ordinary vigilance . . . with reference to her." The court stated the principle as "the risk reasonably to be perceived defines the duty to be obeyed." To rule otherwise "would entail liability for any and all consequences, however novel or extraordinary."

**IMPACT OF THIS CASE ON TODAY'S LAW** *The Palsgraf case established foreseeability as the test for proximate cause. Today, the courts continue to apply this test in determining proximate cause—and thus tort liability for injuries. Generally, if the victim or the consequences of a harm done were unforeseeable, there is no proximate cause. Note, though, that in the online environment, distinctions based on physical proximity, such as that used by the court in this case, are largely inapplicable.*

**THE GLOBAL DIMENSION** *What would be the advantages and disadvantages of a universal principle of proximate cause applied everywhere by all courts in all relevant cases? Discuss.*

## The Injury Requirement and Damages

For a tort to have been committed, the plaintiff must have suffered a *legally recognizable* injury. To recover damages (receive compensation), the plaintiff must have suffered some loss, harm, wrong, or invasion of a protected interest. Essentially, the purpose of tort law is to compensate for legally recognized harms and injuries resulting from wrongful acts. If no harm or injury results from a given negligent action, there is nothing to compensate—and no tort exists.

For instance, if you carelessly bump into a passerby, who stumbles and falls as a result, you may be liable in tort if the passerby is injured in the fall. If the person is unharmed, however, there normally can be no suit for damages because no injury was suffered.

As mentioned at the start of this chapter, compensatory damages are the norm in negligence cases. Occasionally, though, a court will award punitive damages if the defendant's conduct was *grossly negligent*, meaning that the defendant intentionally failed to perform a duty with reckless disregard of the consequences to others.

## Negligence *Per Se*

Certain conduct, whether it consists of an action or a failure to act, may be treated as **negligence *per se*** ("in or of itself"). Negligence *per se* may occur if an individual violates a statute or an ordinance providing for a criminal penalty and that violation causes another to be injured. The statute must be designed to prevent the type of injury that the plaintiff suffered and must clearly set out what standard of conduct is expected. The statute must also indicate when, where, and of whom that conduct is expected. The standard of conduct required by the statute is the duty that the defendant owes to the plaintiff, and a violation of the statute is the breach of that duty.

▶ **Case in Point 6.24** A Delaware statute states that anyone "who operates a motor vehicle and who fails to give full time and attention to the operation of the vehicle" is guilty of inattentive driving. Michael Moore was cited for inattentive driving after he collided with Debra Wright's car when he backed a truck out of a parking space. Moore paid the ticket, which meant that he pleaded guilty to violating the statute. The day after the accident, Wright began having back pain, which eventually required surgery. She sued Moore for damages, alleging negligence *per se*. The court ruled that the inattentive driving statute sets forth a sufficiently specific standard of conduct to warrant application of negligence *per se*.[15] ◀

## Good Samaritan Statutes

Most states now have what are called **Good Samaritan statutes.**[16] Under these statutes, someone who is aided voluntarily by another cannot turn around and sue the "Good Samaritan" for negligence. These laws were passed largely to protect physicians and medical personnel who volunteer their services in emergency situations to those in need, such as individuals hurt in car accidents.[17] Indeed, the California Supreme Court has interpreted that state's Good Samaritan statute to mean that a person who renders nonmedical aid is not immune from liability.[18] Thus, only medical personnel and persons rendering medical aid in emergencies are protected in California.

## Dram Shop Acts

Many states have also passed **dram shop acts**,[19] under which a bar's owner or bartender may be held liable for injuries caused by a person who became intoxicated while drinking at the bar. The owner or bartender may also be held responsible for continuing to serve a person who was already intoxicated.

Some states' statutes also impose liability on *social hosts* (persons hosting parties) for injuries caused by guests who became intoxicated at the hosts' homes. Under these statutes, it is unnecessary to prove that the bar owner, bartender, or social host was negligent.

▶ **Example 6.25** Jane hosts a Super Bowl party at which Brett, a minor, sneaks alcoholic drinks. Jane is potentially liable for damages resulting from Brett's drunk driving after the party. ◀

---

15. *Wright v. Moore*, 931 A.2d 405 (Del.Supr. 2007).
16. These laws derive their name from the Good Samaritan story in the Bible. In the story, a traveler who had been robbed and beaten lay along the roadside, ignored by those passing by. Eventually, a man from the region of Samaria (the "Good Samaritan") stopped to render assistance to the injured person.
17. See, for example, the discussions of various state statutes in *Chamley v. Khokha*, 730 N.W.2d 864 (N.D. 2007), and *Mueller v. McMillian Warner Insurance Co.*, 2006 WI 54, 290 Wis.2d 571, 714 N.W.2d 183 (2006).
18. *Van Horn v. Watson*, 45 Cal.4th 322, 197 P.3d 164, 86 Cal.Rptr.3d 350 (2008).
19. Historically, a dram was a small unit of liquid, and distilled spirits (strong alcoholic liquor) were sold in drams. Thus, a dram shop was a place where liquor was sold in drams.

## SECTION 6
# DEFENSES TO NEGLIGENCE

Defendants often defend against negligence claims by asserting that the plaintiffs have failed to prove the existence of one or more of the required elements for negligence. Additionally, there are three basic *affirmative* defenses in negligence cases (defenses that a defendant can use to avoid liability even if the facts are as the plaintiff states): *assumption of risk, superseding cause,* and *contributory and comparative negligence.*

## Assumption of Risk

A plaintiff who voluntarily enters into a risky situation, knowing the risk involved, will not be allowed to recover. This is the defense of **assumption of risk,** which requires:

1. Knowledge of the risk.
2. Voluntary assumption of the risk.

The defense of assumption of risk is frequently asserted when the plaintiff was injured during recreational activities that involve known risk, such as skiing and skydiving. Courts do not apply the assumption of risk doctrine in emergency situations. Note that assumption of risk can apply not only to participants in sporting events, but also to spectators and bystanders who are injured while attending those events.

In the following *Spotlight Case,* the issue was whether a spectator at a baseball game voluntarily assumed the risk of being hit by an errant ball thrown while the players were warming up before the game.

## SP TLIGHT on the Seattle Mariners

### Case 6.3   Taylor v. Baseball Club of Seattle, LP
Court of Appeals of Washington, 132 Wash.App. 32, 130 P.3d 835 (2006).

**BACKGROUND AND FACTS** Delinda Taylor went to a Seattle Mariners baseball game at Safeco Field with her boyfriend and two minor sons. Their seats were four rows up from the field along the right field foul line. They arrived more than an hour before the game so that they could see the players warm up and get their autographs. When she walked in, Taylor saw that Mariners pitcher, Freddy Garcia, was throwing a ball back and forth with José Mesa right in front of their seats.

As Taylor stood in front of her seat, she looked away from the field, and a ball thrown by Mesa got past Garcia and struck her in the face, causing serious injuries. Taylor sued the Mariners for the allegedly negligent warm-up throw. The Mariners filed a motion for summary judgment in which they argued that Taylor, a longtime Mariners fan, was familiar with baseball and the inherent risk of balls entering the stands. Thus, the motion asserted, Taylor had assumed the risk of her injury. The trial court granted the motion and dismissed Taylor's case. Taylor appealed.

**DECISION AND RATIONALE** The state intermediate appellate court affirmed the lower court's judgment. Taylor, as a spectator in an unprotected area of seats, voluntarily undertook the risk associated with being hit by an errant baseball thrown during warm-ups before the start of the game. "The risk of injuries such as Taylor's are within the normal comprehension of a spectator who is familiar with the game."

The court observed that there was substantial evidence that Taylor was familiar with the game. She was a seasoned Mariners fan, and both of her sons had played baseball for at least six years. "She attended many of her sons' baseball games, she witnessed balls entering the stands, she had watched Mariners' games both at the Kingdome and on television, and she knew that there was no screen protecting her seats, which were close to the field."

It was not legally relevant that the injury occurred during the pregame warm-up because "it is the normal, every-day practice at all levels of baseball for pitchers to warm up in the manner that led to this incident." The Mariners had satisfied their duty to protect spectators from balls entering the stands by providing a protective screen behind home plate. Taylor chose not to sit in the protected area and thus knowingly put herself at risk.

CASE 6.3 CONTINUED **WHAT IF THE FACTS WERE DIFFERENT?** *Would the result in this case have been different if it had been Taylor's minor son, rather than Taylor herself, who had been struck by the ball? Should courts apply the doctrine of assumption of risk to children? Discuss.*

**THE LEGAL ENVIRONMENT DIMENSION** *What is the basis underlying the defense of assumption of risk? How does that basis support the court's decision in this case?*

## Superseding Cause

An unforeseeable intervening event may break the causal connection between a wrongful act and an injury to another. If so, the intervening event acts as a **superseding cause**—that is, it relieves the defendant of liability for injuries caused by the intervening event.

▶ **Example 6.26** While riding his bicycle, Derrick negligently hits Julie, who is walking on the sidewalk. As a result of the impact, Julie falls and fractures her hip. While she is waiting for help to arrive, a small aircraft crashes nearby and explodes, and some of the fiery debris hits her, causing her to sustain severe burns. Derrick will be liable for the damages related to Julie's fractured hip, because the risk of injuring her with his bicycle was foreseeable. Normally, Derrick will not be liable for the burns caused by the plane crash—because the risk of a plane crashing nearby and injuring Julie was not foreseeable. ◀

## Contributory Negligence

All individuals are expected to exercise a reasonable degree of care in looking out for themselves. In the past, under the common law doctrine of **contributory negligence,** a plaintiff who was also negligent (failed to exercise a reasonable degree of care) could not recover anything from the defendant. Under this rule, no mat-ter how insignificant the plaintiff's negligence was relative to the defendant's negligence, the plaintiff would be precluded from recovering any damages. Today, only a few jurisdictions still hold to this doctrine.

## Comparative Negligence

In most states, the doctrine of contributory negligence has been replaced by a **comparative negligence** standard. Under this standard, both the plaintiff's and the defendant's negligence are computed, and the liability for damages is distributed accordingly. Some jurisdictions have adopted a "pure" form of comparative negligence that allows the plaintiff to recover, even if the extent of his or her fault is greater than that of the defendant. Under pure comparative negligence, if the plaintiff was 80 percent at fault and the defendant 20 percent at fault, the plaintiff may recover 20 percent of his or her damages.

Many states' comparative negligence statutes, however, contain a "50 percent" rule that prevents the plaintiff from recovering any damages if she or he was more than 50 percent at fault. Under this rule, a plaintiff who is 35 percent at fault could recover 65 percent of his or her damages, but a plaintiff who is 65 percent (more than 50 percent) at fault could recover nothing.

## Reviewing: Torts

Elaine Sweeney went to Ragged Mountain Ski Resort in New Hampshire with a friend. Elaine went snow tubing down a snow-tube run designed exclusively for snow tubers. There were no Ragged Mountain employees present in the snow-tube area to instruct Elaine on the proper use of a snow tube. On her fourth run down the trail, Elaine crossed over the center line between snow-tube lanes, collided with another snow tuber, and was injured. Elaine filed a negligence action against Ragged Mountain seeking compensation for the injuries that she sustained. Two years earlier, the New Hampshire state legislature had enacted a statute that prohibited a person who participates in the sport of skiing from suing a ski-area operator for injuries caused by the risks inherent in skiing. Using the information presented in the chapter, answer the following questions.

1. What defense will Ragged Mountain probably assert?

*Continued*

2.  The central question in this case is whether the state statute establishing that skiers assume the risks inherent in the sport bars Elaine's suit. What would your decision be on this issue? Why?

3.  Suppose that the court concludes that the statute applies only to skiing and not to snow tubing. Will Elaine's lawsuit be successful? Explain.

4.  Now suppose that the jury concludes that Elaine was partly at fault for the accident. Under what theory might her damages be reduced in proportion to the degree to which her actions contributed to the accident and her resulting injuries?

**DEBATE THIS . . .** *Each time a state legislature enacts a law that applies the assumption of risk doctrine to a particular sport, participants in that sport suffer.*

## Terms and Concepts

| | | |
|---|---|---|
| actionable 113 | dram shop act 125 | puffery 117 |
| actual malice 116 | duty of care 122 | punitive damages 111 |
| assault 112 | fraudulent misrepresentation 117 | reasonable person standard 122 |
| assumption of risk 126 | Good Samaritan statute 125 | slander 114 |
| battery 112 | intentional tort 112 | slander of quality 121 |
| business invitee 122 | libel 114 | slander of title 121 |
| causation in fact 122 | licensee 120 | superseding cause 127 |
| comparative negligence 127 | malpractice 122 | tort 110 |
| compensatory damages 110 | negligence 121 | tortfeasor 112 |
| contributory negligence 127 | negligence *per se* 125 | trade libel 121 |
| conversion 120 | privilege 116 | transferred intent 112 |
| defamation 114 | proximate cause 122 | trespass to land 119 |
| disparagement of property 121 | public figure 116 | trespass to personal property 120 |

## Issue Spotters

1.  Jana leaves her truck's motor running while she enters a Kwik-Pik Store. The truck's transmission engages, and the vehicle crashes into a gas pump, starting a fire that spreads to a warehouse on the next block. The warehouse collapses, causing its billboard to fall and injure Lou, a bystander. Can Lou recover from Jana? Why or why not? **(See page 123.)**

2.  A water pipe bursts, flooding a Metal Fabrication Company utility room and tripping the circuit breakers on a panel in the room. Metal Fabrication contacts Nouri, a licensed electrician with five years' experience, to check the damage and turn the breakers back on. Without testing for short circuits, which Nouri knows that he should do, he tries to switch on a breaker. He is electrocuted, and his wife sues Metal Fabrication for damages, alleging negligence. What might the firm successfully claim in defense? **(See page 127.)**

• **Check your answers to the Issue Spotters against the answers provided in Appendix E at the end of this text.**

## Business Scenarios

**6–1. Defamation.** Richard is an employee of the Dun Construction Corp. While delivering materials to a construction site, he carelessly backs Dun's truck into a passenger vehicle driven by Green. This is Richard's second accident in six months. When the company owner, Dun, learns of this latest accident, a heated discussion ensues, and Dun fires Richard. Dun is so angry that he immediately writes a letter to the union of which Richard is a member and to all other construction companies in the community, stating that Richard is the "worst driver in the city" and that "anyone who hires him is asking for legal liability." Richard files a suit against Dun, alleging libel on the basis of the statements made in the letters. Discuss the results. **(See page 114.)**

**6–2. Wrongful Interference.** Lothar owns a bakery. He has been trying to obtain a long-term contract with the owner of Martha's Tea Salons for some time. Lothar starts a local advertising campaign on radio and television and in the newspaper. This advertising campaign is so persuasive that Martha decides to break the contract she has had with Harley's Bakery so that she can patronize Lothar's bakery.

Is Lothar liable to Harley's Bakery for the tort of wrongful interference with a contractual relationship? Is Martha liable for this tort? Why or why not? **(See page 118.)**

**6–3. Liability to Business Invitees.** Kim went to Ling's Market to pick up a few items for dinner. It was a stormy day, and the wind had blown water through the market's door each time it opened. As Kim entered through the door, she slipped and fell in the rainwater that had accumulated on the floor. The manager knew of the weather conditions but had not posted any sign to warn customers of the water hazard. Kim injured her back as a result of the fall and sued Ling's for damages. Can Ling's be held liable for negligence? Discuss. **(See page 122.)**

## Business Case Problems

**6–4. Spotlight on Intentional Torts—Defamation.** Sharon Yeagle was an assistant to the vice president of student affairs at Virginia Polytechnic Institute and State University (Virginia Tech). As part of her duties, Yeagle helped students participate in the Governor's Fellows Program. The *Collegiate Times*, Virginia Tech's student newspaper, published an article about the university's success in placing students in the program. The article's text surrounded a block quotation attributed to Yeagle with the phrase "Director of Butt Licking" under her name. Yeagle sued the *Collegiate Times* for defamation. She argued that the phrase implied the commission of sodomy and was therefore actionable. What is *Collegiate Times's* defense to this claim? [*Yeagle v. Collegiate Times*, 497 S.E.2d 136 (Va. 1998)] **(See page 115.)**

**6–5. Proximate Cause.** Galen Stoller was killed at a railroad crossing when an AMTRAK train hit his car. The crossing was marked with a stop sign and a railroad-crossing symbol, but there were no flashing lights. Galen's parents filed a suit against National Railroad Passenger Corp. (AMTRAK) and Burlington Northern & Santa Fe Railroad Corp., alleging negligence in the design and maintenance of the crossing. The defendants argued that Galen had not stopped at the stop sign. Was AMTRAK negligent? What was the proximate cause of the accident? Discuss. [*Henderson v. National Railroad Passenger Corp.*, __ F.3d __ (10th Cir. 2011)] **(See page 123.)**

**6–6. Business Torts.** Medtronic, Inc., is a medical technology company that competes for customers with St. Jude Medical S.C., Inc. James Hughes worked for Medtronic as a sales manager. His contract prohibited him from working for a competitor for one year after leaving Medtronic. Hughes sought a position as a sales director for St. Jude. St. Jude told Hughes that his contract with Medtronic was unenforceable and offered him a job. Hughes accepted. Medtronic filed a suit, alleging wrongful interference. Which type of interference was most likely the basis for

this suit? Did it occur here? Explain. [*Medtronic, Inc. v. Hughes*, __ N.W.2d __ (Minn.App. 2011)] **(See page 118.)**

**6–7. Intentional Infliction of Emotional Distress.** While living in her home country of Tanzania, Sophia Kiwanuka signed an employment contract with Anne Margareth Bakilana, a Tanzanian living in Washington, D.C. Kiwanuka traveled to the United States to work as a babysitter and maid in Bakilana's house. When Kiwanuka arrived, Bakilana confiscated her passport, held her in isolation, and forced her to work long hours under threat of having her deported. Kiwanuka worked seven days a week without breaks and was subjected to regular verbal and psychological abuse by Bakilana. Kiwanuka filed a complaint against Bakilana for intentional infliction of emotional distress, among other claims. Bakilana argued that Kiwanuka's complaint should be dismissed because the allegations were insufficient to show outrageous intentional conduct that resulted in severe emotional distress. If you were the judge, in whose favor would you rule? Why? [*Kiwanuka v. Bakilana*, 844 F.Supp.2d 107 (D.D.C. 2012)] **(See page 113.)**

**6–8. BUSINESS CASE PROBLEM WITH SAMPLE ANSWER: Negligence.**

*At the Weatherford Hotel in Flagstaff, Arizona, in Room 59, a balcony extends across thirty inches of the room's only window, leaving a twelve-inch gap with a three-story drop to the concrete below. A sign prohibits smoking in the room but invites guests to "step out onto the balcony" to smoke. Toni Lucario was a guest in Room 59 when she climbed out of the window and fell to her death. Patrick McMurtry, her estate's personal representative, filed a suit against the Weatherford. Did the hotel breach a duty of care to Locario? What might the Weatherford assert in its defense? Explain.* [*McMurtry v. Weatherford Hotel, Inc.*, 293 P.3d 520 (Ariz.App. 2013)] **(See page 126.)**

- **For a sample answer to Problem 6–8, go to Appendix F at the end of this text.**

**6–9. A QUESTION OF ETHICS: Wrongful Interference with a Contractual Relationship.**

 *White Plains Coat & Apron Co. is a New York–based linen rental business. Cintas Corp. is a competitor. White Plains had five-year exclusive contracts with some of its customers. As a result of Cintas's soliciting of business, dozens of White Plains' customers breached their contracts and entered into rental agreements with Cintas. White Plains filed a suit against Cintas, alleging wrongful interference. [White Plains Coat & Apron Co. v. Cintas Corp., 8 N.Y.3d 422, 867 N.E.2d 381 (2007)]* **(See page 118.)**

(a) What are the two important policy interests at odds in wrongful interference cases? Which of these interests should be accorded priority?

(b) The U.S. Court of Appeals for the Second Circuit asked the New York Court of Appeals to answer a question: Is a general interest in soliciting business for profit a sufficient defense to a claim of wrongful interference with a contractual relationship? What do you think? Why?

## Legal Reasoning Group Activity

**6–10. Negligence.** Donald and Gloria Bowden hosted a cookout at their home in South Carolina, inviting mostly business acquaintances. Justin Parks, who was nineteen years old, attended the party. Alcoholic beverages were available to all of the guests, even those like Parks, who were between the ages of eighteen and twenty-one. Parks consumed alcohol at the party and left with other guests. One of these guests detained Parks at the guest's home to give Parks time to "sober up." Parks then drove himself from this guest's home and was killed in a one-car accident. At the time of death, he had a blood alcohol content of 0.291 percent, which exceeded the state's limit for driving a motor vehicle. Linda Marcum, Parks's mother, filed a suit in a South Carolina state court against the Bowdens and others, alleging that they were negligent. **(See page 125.)**

(a) The first group will present arguments in favor of holding the social hosts liable in this situation.

(b) The second group will formulate arguments against holding the social hosts liable based on principles in this chapter.

(c) The states vary widely in assessing liability and imposing sanctions in the circumstances described in this problem. The third group will determine the reasons why courts do not treat social hosts the same as parents who serve alcoholic beverages to their underage children.

# CHAPTER 7

# STRICT LIABILITY AND PRODUCT LIABILITY

In this chapter, we look at a category of tort called **strict liability,** or *liability without fault*. Under the doctrine of strict liability, a person who engages in certain activities can be held responsible for any harm that results to others, even if the person used the utmost care.

We open this chapter with an examination of this doctrine and then look at an area of tort law of particular importance to businesspersons—product liability. The manufacturers and sellers of products may incur **product liability**

when product defects cause injury or property damage to consumers, users, or bystanders (people in the vicinity of the product when it fails).

Although multimillion-dollar product liability claims often involve big automakers, pharmaceutical companies, or tobacco companies, many businesses face potential liability. For instance, in the last few years, there have been numerous reports of energy drinks, such as Monster, Red Bull, Rockstar, and 5-hour Energy, having serious adverse effects—especially on young people.

Several individuals have been hospitalized, and some have even died after consuming energy drinks. In 2012, the federal government issued a report concerning the adverse effects of these products and launched an investigation into their safety. Parents of a teenage girl who died after consuming two Monster energy drinks then filed a lawsuit against Monster Beverage Corporation in California—perhaps the first case in a wave of lawsuits against makers of energy drinks.

SECTION 1
## STRICT LIABILITY

The modern concept of strict liability traces its origins, in part, to an English case decided in 1868. ▶ **Case in Point 7.1** In the coal-mining area of Lancashire, England, the Rylands, who were mill owners, had constructed a reservoir on their land. Water from the reservoir broke through a filled-in shaft of an abandoned coal mine nearby and flooded the connecting passageways in an active coal mine owned by Fletcher.

Fletcher sued the Rylands, and the court held that the defendants (the Rylands) were liable, even though the circumstances did not fit within existing tort liability theories. The court held that a "person who for his own purposes brings on his land and collects and keeps there anything likely to do mischief if it escapes . . . is *prima facie*[1] answerable for all the damage which

is the natural consequence of its escape."[2] ◀ British courts liberally applied the doctrine that emerged from the case.

Initially, few U.S. courts accepted this doctrine, presumably because the courts were worried about its effect on the expansion of American business. Today, however, the doctrine of strict liability is the norm rather than the exception.

### Abnormally Dangerous Activities

Strict liability for damages proximately caused by an abnormally dangerous, or ultrahazardous, activity is one application of strict liability. Courts apply the doctrine of strict liability in these situations because of the extreme risk of the activity. Abnormally dangerous activities are those that involve a high risk of serious harm to persons or property that cannot be completely guarded against by the exercise of reasonable care.

---

**1.** *Prima facie* is Latin for "at first sight." Legally, it refers to a fact that is presumed to be true unless contradicted by evidence.

**2.** *Rylands v. Fletcher,* 3 L.R.–E & I App. [Law Reports, English & Irish Appeal Cases] (H.L. [House of Lords] 1868).

Activities such as blasting or storing explosives qualify as abnormally dangerous. Even if blasting with dynamite is performed with all reasonable care, there is still a risk of injury. Considering the potential for harm, it seems reasonable to ask the person engaged in the activity to pay for injuries caused by that activity. Although there is no fault, there is still responsibility because of the dangerous nature of the undertaking.

## Other Applications of Strict Liability

Persons who keep wild animals are strictly liable for any harm inflicted by the animals. The basis for applying strict liability is that wild animals, should they escape from confinement, pose a serious risk of harm to people in the vicinity. An owner of domestic animals (such as dogs, cats, cows, or sheep) may be strictly liable for harm caused by those animals if the owner knew, or should have known, that the animals were dangerous or had a propensity to harm others.

A significant application of strict liability is in the area of product liability—liability of manufacturers and sellers for harmful or defective products. Liability here is a matter of social policy and is based on two factors:

1. The manufacturer can better bear the cost of injury because it can spread the cost throughout society by increasing the prices of its goods.
2. The manufacturer is making a profit from its activities and therefore should bear the cost of injury as an operating expense.

We will discuss product liability in greater detail next. Strict liability is also applied in certain types of *bailments* (a bailment exists when goods are transferred temporarily into the care of another).

## SECTION 2
# PRODUCT LIABILITY

Those who make, sell, or lease goods can be held liable for physical harm or property damage caused by those goods to a consumer, user, or bystander. This is called *product liability*. Product liability may be based on the theories of negligence, misrepresentation, strict liability, and warranties (see Chapter 23). Multiple theories of liability can be, and often are, asserted in the same case. We look here at product liability based on negligence and on misrepresentation.

## Based on Negligence

In Chapter 6, *negligence* was defined as the failure to exercise the degree of care that a reasonable, prudent person would have exercised under the circumstances. If a manufacturer fails to exercise "due care" to make a product safe, a person who is injured by the product may sue the manufacturer for negligence.

**DUE CARE MUST BE EXERCISED** Manufacturers must use due care in all of the following areas:

1. Designing the product.
2. Selecting the materials.
3. Using the appropriate production process.
4. Assembling and testing the product.
5. Placing adequate warnings on the label to inform the user of dangers of which an ordinary person might not be aware.
6. Inspecting and testing any purchased components used in the product.

**PRIVITY OF CONTRACT NOT REQUIRED** A product liability action based on negligence does not require *privity of contract* between the injured plaintiff and the defendant-manufacturer. As will be discussed in Chapter 17, *privity of contract* refers to the relationship that exists between the parties to a contract. Privity is the reason that normally only the parties to a contract can enforce that contract.

In the context of product liability law, privity is not required. A person who is injured by a defective product may bring a negligence suit even though he or she was not the one who actually purchased the product—and thus is not in privity. A manufacturer, seller, or lessor is liable for failure to exercise due care to *any person* who sustains an injury proximately caused by a negligently made (defective) product. Relative to the long history of the common law, this exception to the privity requirement is a fairly recent development—it dates to the early part of the twentieth century.[3]

## Based on Misrepresentation

When a user or consumer is injured as a result of a manufacturer's or seller's fraudulent misrepresentation, the basis of liability may be the tort of fraud. In

---

3. A landmark case in this respect is *MacPherson v. Buick Motor Co.*, 217 N.Y. 382, 111 N.E. 1050 (1916).

this situation, the misrepresentation must have been made knowingly or with reckless disregard for the facts. The intentional mislabeling of packaged cosmetics, for instance, or the intentional concealment of a product's defects would constitute fraudulent misrepresentation.

The misrepresentation must be of a material fact, and the seller must have intended to induce the buyer's reliance on the misrepresentation. Misrepresentation on a label or advertisement is enough to show an intent to induce the reliance of anyone who may use the product. In addition, the buyer must have relied on the misrepresentation.

## SECTION 3
# STRICT PRODUCT LIABILITY

As discussed at the beginning of this chapter, under the doctrine of strict liability, people may be liable for the results of their acts regardless of their intentions or their exercise of reasonable care. In addition, liability does not depend on privity of contract. Thus, the injured party does not have to be the buyer, as required under contract warranty theory (see Chapter 23). In the 1960s, courts applied the doctrine of strict liability in several landmark cases involving manufactured goods, and it has since become a common method of holding manufacturers liable.

## Strict Product Liability and Public Policy

The law imposes strict product liability as a matter of public policy. This public policy rests on the threefold assumption that:

1. Consumers should be protected against unsafe products.
2. Manufacturers and distributors should not escape liability for faulty products simply because they are not in privity of contract with the ultimate user of those products.
3. Manufacturers and distributors can better bear the costs associated with injuries caused by their products—because they can ultimately pass the costs on to all consumers in the form of higher prices.

**DEVELOPMENT OF THE DOCTRINE** California was the first state to impose strict product liability in tort on manufacturers. ▶ **Case in Point 7.2** William Greenman was injured when his Shopsmith combination power tool threw off a piece of wood that struck him in the head. He sued the manufacturer, claiming that he had followed the product's instructions and the product must be defective. In a landmark decision, *Greenman v. Yuba Power Products, Inc.,*[4] the California Supreme Court set out the reason for applying tort law rather than contract law (including laws governing warranties) in cases involving consumers who were injured by defective products.

According to the *Greenman* court, the "purpose of such liability is to [e]nsure that the costs of injuries resulting from defective products are borne by the manufacturers . . . rather than by the injured persons who are powerless to protect themselves." ◀ Today, the majority of states recognize strict product liability, although some state courts limit its application to situations involving personal injuries (rather than property damage).

**STATED PUBLIC POLICY** Public policy may be expressed in a statute or in the common law. Sometimes, public policy may be revealed in a court's interpretation of a statute, as in the following case.

---

**4.** 59 Cal.2d 57, 377 P.2d 897, 27 Cal.Rptr. 697 (1962).

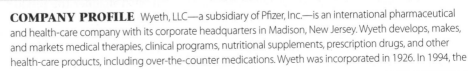

**SP✷TLIGHT on Injuries from Vaccines**

### Case 7.1 Bruesewitz v. Wyeth, LLC
Supreme Court of the United States, __ U.S. __, 131 S.Ct. 1068, 179 L.Ed.2d 1 (2011).

**COMPANY PROFILE** Wyeth, LLC—a subsidiary of Pfizer, Inc.—is an international pharmaceutical and health-care company with its corporate headquarters in Madison, New Jersey. Wyeth develops, makes, and markets medical therapies, clinical programs, nutritional supplements, prescription drugs, and other health-care products, including over-the-counter medications. Wyeth was incorporated in 1926. In 1994, the

CASE 7.1 CONTINUES ▶

**CASE 7.1 CONTINUED**

company bought Lederle Laboratories. Since 1948, Lederle had been making the diphtheria, tetanus, and pertussis (DTP) vaccine for children.

**BACKGROUND AND FACTS** When Hannah Bruesewitz was six months old, her pediatrician administered a dose of the DTP vaccine according to the Centers for Disease Control's recommended childhood immunization schedule. Within twenty-four hours, Hannah began to experience seizures. She suffered more than one hundred seizures during the next month. Her doctors diagnosed her with "residual seizure disorder" and "developmental delay." Hannah's parents, Russell and Robalee Bruesewitz, filed a claim for relief in the U.S. Court of Federal Claims under the National Childhood Vaccine Injury Act (NCVIA) of 1986, which set up a no-fault compensation program for persons injured by vaccines. The claim was denied. The Bruesewitzes then filed a suit in a state court against Wyeth, LLC, the maker of the vaccine, alleging strict product liability. The suit was moved to a federal district court, which held that the claim was preempted by the NCVIA, which includes provisions protecting manufacturers from liability for "a vaccine's unavoidable, adverse side effects." The U.S. Court of Appeals for the Third Circuit affirmed the district court's judgment. The Bruesewitzes appealed to the United States Supreme Court.

**DECISION AND RATIONALE** The United States Supreme Court affirmed the lower court's judgment in favor of the defendants. The NCVIA preempted the Bruesewitzes' claim against Wyeth for injury to their daughter caused by the DTP vaccine's side effects. The Court reasoned that Congress enacted the NCVIA as a matter of public policy to stabilize the vaccine market and facilitate compensation. In the no-fault compensation program set up by the NCVIA, a person with a vaccine-related claim files a petition with the U.S. Court of Federal Claims. The court may award compensation for legal, medical, rehabilitation, counseling, special education, and vocational training expenses, as well as for diminished earning capacity, pain and suffering, and death. The awards are funded by a tax on the vaccine. In exchange for the "informal, efficient" compensation program, vaccine manufacturers that comply with the regulatory requirements are "immunized" from liability. The Court found that the statute thus strikes a balance between paying victims harmed by vaccines and protecting the vaccine industry from collapsing under the costs of tort liability.

**THE ECONOMIC DIMENSION** *What is the public policy expressed by the provisions of the NCVIA?*

**THE POLITICAL DIMENSION** *If the public wants to change the policy outlined in this case, which branch of the government—and at what level—should be lobbied to make the change? Explain.*

---

# The Requirements for Strict Product Liability

After the *Restatement (Second) of Torts* was issued in 1964, Section 402A became a widely accepted statement of how the doctrine of strict liability should be applied to sellers of goods (including manufacturers, processors, assemblers, packagers, bottlers, wholesalers, distributors, retailers, and lessors).

The bases for an action in strict liability that are set forth in Section 402A of the *Restatement (Second) of Torts* can be summarized as a set of six requirements, which are listed here. Depending on the jurisdiction, if these requirements are met, a manufacturer's liability to an injured party can be almost unlimited.

1. The product must be in a *defective condition* when the defendant sells it.
2. The defendant must normally be engaged in the *business of selling* (or otherwise distributing) that product.
3. The product must be *unreasonably dangerous* to the user or consumer because of its defective condition (in most states).
4. The plaintiff must incur *physical harm* to self or property by use or consumption of the product.
5. The defective condition must be the *proximate cause* of the injury or damage.
6. The *goods must not have been substantially changed* from the time the product was sold to the time the injury was sustained.

**PROVING A DEFECTIVE CONDITION** Under these requirements, in any action against a manufacturer, seller, or lessor, the plaintiff need not show why or in what manner the product became defective. The plaintiff does, however, have to prove that the product was defective at the time it left the hands of the seller or lessor. The plaintiff must also show that this defective condition made the product "unreasonably dangerous" to the user or consumer.

Unless evidence can be presented to support the conclusion that the product was defective when it was sold or leased, the plaintiff will not succeed. If the product was delivered in a safe condition and subsequent mishandling made it harmful to the user, the seller or lessor normally is not strictly liable.

**UNREASONABLY DANGEROUS PRODUCTS** The *Restatement* recognizes that many products cannot be made entirely safe for all uses. Thus, sellers or lessors are liable only for products that are *unreasonably* dangerous. A court could consider a product so defective as to be an **unreasonably dangerous product** in either of the following situations:

1. The product was dangerous beyond the expectation of the ordinary consumer.
2. A less dangerous alternative was *economically* feasible for the manufacturer, but the manufacturer failed to produce it.

As will be discussed next, a product may be unreasonably dangerous due to a flaw in the manufacturing process, a design defect, or an inadequate warning.

## Product Defects

The *Restatement (Third) of Torts: Products Liability* defines the three types of product defects that have traditionally been recognized in product liability law—manufacturing defects, design defects, and inadequate warnings.

**MANUFACTURING DEFECTS** According to Section 2(a) of the *Restatement (Third) of Torts,* a product "contains a manufacturing defect when the product departs from its intended design even though all possible care was exercised in the preparation and marketing of the product." Basically, a manufacturing defect is a departure from a product unit's design specifications that results in products that are physically flawed, damaged, or incorrectly assembled. A glass bottle that is made too thin and explodes in a consumer's face is an example of a product with a manufacturing defect.

***Quality Control.*** Usually, such defects occur when a manufacturer fails to assemble, test, or adequately check the quality of a product. Liability is imposed on the manufacturer (and on the wholesaler and retailer) regardless of whether the manufacturer's quality control efforts were "reasonable." The idea behind holding defendants strictly liable for manufacturing defects is to encourage greater investment in product safety and stringent quality control standards.

***Expert Testimony.*** Cases involving allegations of a manufacturing defect are often decided based on the opinions and testimony of experts. ▶ **Case in Point 7.3** Kevin Schmude purchased an eight-foot stepladder and used it to install radio-frequency shielding in a hospital room. While Schmude was standing on the ladder, it collapsed, and he was seriously injured. He filed a lawsuit against the ladder's maker, Tricam Industries, Inc., based on a manufacturing defect.

Experts testified that the preexisting holes in the ladder's top cap did not properly line up with the holes in the rear right rail and backing plate. As a result of the misalignment, the rivet at the rear legs of the ladder was more likely to fail. A jury concluded that this manufacturing defect made the ladder unreasonably dangerous and awarded Schmude more than $677,000 in damages.[5] ◀

**DESIGN DEFECTS** Unlike a product with a manufacturing defect, a product with a design defect is made in conformity with the manufacturer's design specifications. Nevertheless, the product results in injury to the user because the design itself was faulty. A product "is defective in design when the foreseeable risks of harm posed by the product could have been reduced or avoided by the adoption of a reasonable alternative design by the seller or other distributor, or a predecessor in the commercial chain of distribution, and the omission of the alternative design renders the product not reasonably safe."[6]

To successfully assert a design defect, a plaintiff has to show that:

1. A reasonable alternative design was available.
2. The defendant's failure to adopt the alternative design rendered the product not reasonably safe.

In other words, a manufacturer or other defendant is liable only when the harm was reasonably preventable.

According to the *Restatement,* a court can consider a broad range of factors. These include the magnitude and probability of the foreseeable risks as well as the relative advantages and disadvantages of the product as it was designed and as it could have been designed.

***Risk-Utility Analysis.*** Most courts engage in a risk-utility analysis to determine whether the risk of harm from the product as designed outweighs its utility to the user and to the public. ▶ **Case in Point 7.4** Jodie Bullock smoked cigarettes manufactured by Philip Morris for forty-five years. When she was diagnosed with lung

---

5. *Schmude v. Tricam Industries, Inc.,* 550 F.Supp.2d 846 (E.D.Wis. 2008).
6. *Restatement (Third) of Torts: Products Liability,* Section 2(b).

cancer, Bullock brought a product liability suit against Philip Morris. She presented evidence that by the late 1950s, scientists had proved that smoking caused lung cancer. Nonetheless, Philip Morris had issued full-page announcements stating that there was no proof that cigarette smoking caused cancer and that "numerous scientists" questioned "the validity of the statistics." At trial, the judge instructed the jury to consider the gravity of the danger posed by the design, as well as the likelihood that the danger would cause injury.

The jury found that there was a defect in the design of the cigarettes and that they had been negligently designed. It awarded Bullock $850,000 in compensatory damages and $28 million in punitive damages. Philip Morris appealed, claiming that no evidence had been

offered to show that there was a safer design for cigarettes. Nonetheless, the reviewing court found that the jury had been properly instructed. The court affirmed the award but remanded the case for a reconsideration of the proper amount of punitive damages.[7] ◄

**Consumer-Expectation Test.** Other courts apply the consumer-expectation test to determine whether a product's design was defective. Under this test, a product is unreasonably dangerous when it fails to perform in the manner that would reasonably be expected by an ordinary consumer. The court applied this test in the following case.

7. *Bullock v. Philip Morris USA, Inc.,*159 Cal.App.4th 655, 71 Cal.Rptr.3d 775 (2008).

---

## CASE 7.2

### Wilson Sporting Goods Co. v. Hickox
District of Columbia Court of Appeals, 59 A.3d 1267 (2013).

**BACKGROUND AND FACTS** At a retreat for Major League Baseball umpires, a Wilson Sporting Goods Company representative gave Edwin Hickox an umpire's mask. The representative claimed this mask featured a new, safer design. The mask was a traditional umpire's mask, but had a newly designed throat guard that angled forward instead of extending straight down. Later, Hickox wore the mask while working behind home plate as an umpire during a game in Washington, D.C. In the top of the ninth inning, a foul-tipped ball struck the mask. The impact of the ball gave Hickox a concussion and damaged a joint between the bones in his inner ear. As a result, he suffered a permanent hearing loss. Hickox and his wife filed a suit in a District of Columbia court against Wilson, claiming product liability based on a design defect. A jury rendered a verdict for the plaintiffs, awarding $750,000 to Hickox and $25,000 to his wife. Wilson appealed, arguing that the evidence was insufficient to support the verdict.

**DECISION AND RATIONALE** The District of Columbia Court of Appeals affirmed the lower court's judgment. The appellate court determined that "Considering all the evidence, a reasonable juror could conclude that an ordinary consumer would have expected the mask to perform more safely than it did." The court went on to say "The evidence indicated that the mask at issue was more dangerous than comparable masks sold at the time, such as hockey-style masks, because the [new] masks could concentrate energy at the point of impact, rather than distribute energy evenly throughout the padded area of the mask." Such concentration of energy necessarily increased the risk of severe injury.

At the time that Edwin Hickox used the mask, alternative masks with detachable throat guards and no forward angle worked well and did not excessively restrict the umpire's movement. Had Mr. Hickox been wearing such an alternative mask, he would not have suffered injury to his ear. Further, a jury could have concluded that statements made by Wilson's representative to Mr. Hickox reflected Wilson's standard marketing approach. "An ordinary consumer therefore would have expected the mask to perform more safely than other models." Therefore, a reasonable juror "could infer that an ordinary consumer would have expected baseball masks to disperse, rather than concentrate energy."

**THE LEGAL DIMENSION** *Can a jury make "inferences" to arrive at a verdict? Explain.*

**WHAT IF THE FACTS WERE DIFFERENT?** *Suppose that Hickox suffered an injury in a second incident while wearing the type of mask that he claimed to be a safer, alternative design. Would this be enough to show that the mask was not a safer, alternative design? Explain.*

**INADEQUATE WARNINGS** A product may also be deemed defective because of inadequate instructions or warnings. A product will be considered defective "when the foreseeable risks of harm posed by the product could have been reduced or avoided by the provision of reasonable instructions or warnings by the seller or other distributor . . . and the omission of the instructions or warnings renders the product not reasonably safe."[8]

*Content of Warnings.* Important factors for a court to consider include the risks of a product, the "content and comprehensibility" and "intensity of expression" of warnings and instructions, and the "characteristics of expected user groups."[9] Courts apply a "reasonableness" test to determine if the warnings adequately alert consumers to the product's risks. For instance, children will likely respond readily to bright, bold, simple warning labels, whereas educated adults might need more detailed information.

An action alleging that a product is defective due to an inadequate label can be based on state law. (For a discussion of a case involving a state law that required warning labels on violent video games, see this chapter's *Insight into Ethics* feature on page 139.)

In the following case, the court had to decide whether the plaintiff could pursue a theory of recovery alleging both a design defect and inadequate warnings.

---

**8.** *Restatement (Third) of Torts: Products Liability,* Section 2(c).

**9.** *Restatement (Third) of Torts: Products Liability,* Section 2, Comment h.

---

## CASE 7.3

### Johnson v. Medtronic, Inc.
Missouri Court of Appeals, 365 S.W.3d 226 (2012).

**BACKGROUND AND FACTS** In 2005, Jeffrey Johnson was taken to the emergency room for an episode of atrial fibrillation, a heart rhythm disorder. Dr. David Hahn used a defibrillator manufactured by Medtronic, Inc., to deliver electric shocks to Johnson's heart. The defibrillator had synchronous and asynchronous modes, and it reverted to the asynchronous mode after each use. Dr. Hahn intended to deliver synchronized shocks, which required him to select the synchronous mode for each shock.

Unfortunately, Dr. Hahn did not read the device's instructions, which Medtronic provided both in a manual and on the device itself. As a result, he delivered a synchronized shock, followed by twelve asynchronous shocks that endangered Johnson's life. Johnson and his wife filed a product liability suit against Medtronic, asserting both that Medtronic had provided inadequate warnings about the defibrillator and that the device had a design defect. The trial court found for Medtronic under both product liability theories. The Johnsons appealed.

**DECISION AND RATIONALE** The Missouri appellate court held that Johnson could not pursue a claim based on the inadequacy of Medtronic's warnings, but that he could pursue a claim alleging a design defect. Thus, the trial court's decision was affirmed in part and reversed in part. The court first held that Johnson could not pursue a claim alleging that Medtronic provided inadequate warnings. Johnson had offered no evidence that he was harmed because the defibrillator was sold without an adequate warning. Instead, the record showed that Medtronic's instructions would have prevented Johnson's injuries, but Dr. Hahn failed to follow or even read them.

The court ruled that Johnson could pursue his design defect claim because Johnson had presented evidence that Hahn's misuse was reasonably foreseeable. Importantly, Medtronic had known that other users had inadvertently delivered asynchronous shocks after failing to reset the device. The court concluded that Johnson was not precluded from bringing a claim for design defect simply because he could not pursue a claim of inadequate warnings. In some cases, "a manufacturer may be held liable where it chooses to warn of the danger . . . rather than preclude [rule out] the danger by design."

**THE LEGAL ENVIRONMENT DIMENSION** *What could Medtronic have done to avoid possible liability to plaintiffs like the Johnsons? Was there a reasonable alternative design for the defibrillator?*

**THE ECONOMIC DIMENSION** *Could Hahn or the hospital be held liable for Johnson's injury on a product liability theory? Explain.*

***Obvious Risks.*** There is no duty to warn about risks that are obvious or commonly known. Warnings about such risks do not add to the safety of a product and could even detract from it by making other warnings seem less significant. As will be discussed later in the chapter, the obviousness of a risk and a user's decision to proceed in the face of that risk may be a defense in a product liability suit based on an inadequate warning.

▶ **Case in Point 7.5** Sixteen-year-old Gary Crosswhite failed in an attempt to do a back flip on a trampoline and was paralyzed as a result. There were nine warning labels affixed to the trampoline, an instruction manual with safety warnings, and a placard attached to the entrance that advised users not to do flips. Crosswhite sued the manufacturer for inadequate warnings. The court found that the warnings were sufficient to make the risks obvious and insulate the manufacturer from liability for Crosswhite's injuries.[10] ◀

Risks that may seem obvious to some users, though, will not be obvious to all users, especially when the users are likely to be children. A young child may not be able to read or understand warning labels or comprehend the risk of certain activities. To avoid liability, the manufacturer would have to prove that the warnings it provided were adequate to make the risk of injury obvious to a young child.[11]

***Foreseeable Misuses.*** Generally, a seller must warn those who purchase its product of the harm that can result from the foreseeable misuse of the product as well. The key is the foreseeability of the misuse. Sellers are not required to take precautions against every conceivable misuse of a product, just those that are foreseeable.

## Market-Share Liability

Ordinarily, in all product liability claims, a plaintiff must prove that the defective product that caused his or her injury was the product of a specific defendant. In a few situations, however, courts have dropped this requirement when plaintiffs could not prove which of many distributors of a harmful product supplied the particular product that caused the injuries. Under a theory of **market-share liability,** a court can hold each manufacturer responsible for a percentage of the plaintiff's damages that is equal to the percentage of its market share.

▶ **Case in Point 7.6** John Smith suffered from hemophilia (a blood-clotting disorder). Because of

his condition, Smith received injections of a blood protein known as antihemophiliac factor (AHF) concentrate. Smith later tested positive for the acquired immune deficiency syndrome (AIDS) virus. Because there was no way to determine which manufacturer was responsible for the particular AHF received by Smith, the court held that all of the manufacturers of AHF could be held liable.[12] ◀

Many jurisdictions do not recognize this theory of liability because they believe that it deviates too significantly from traditional legal principles. Jurisdictions that do recognize market-share liability apply it only when it is difficult to determine which company made a particular product. Cases usually involve drugs or chemicals.

## Other Applications of Strict Product Liability

Almost all courts extend the strict liability of manufacturers and other sellers to injured bystanders. Thus, if a defective forklift that will not go into reverse injures a passerby, that individual can sue the manufacturer for product liability (and possibly bring a negligence action against the forklift operator as well).

Strict product liability also applies to suppliers of component parts. ▶ **Example 7.7** Toyota buys brake pads from a subcontractor and puts them in Corollas without changing their composition. If those pads are defective, both the supplier of the brake pads and Toyota will be held strictly liable for the injuries caused by the defects. ◀

**SECTION 4**

# DEFENSES TO PRODUCT LIABILITY

Defendants in product liability suits can raise a number of defenses. One defense, of course, is to show that there is no basis for the plaintiff's claim. If a defendant can show that the plaintiff has *not* met the requirements (such as causation) for an action in negligence, for instance, generally the defendant will not be liable.

Similarly, in a case involving strict product liability, a defendant can claim that the plaintiff failed to meet one of the requirements. For instance, if the

---

**10.** *Crosswhite v. Jumpking, Inc.,* 411 F.Supp.2d 1228 (D.Or. 2006).

**11.** See, for example, *Bunch v. Hoffinger Industries, Inc.,*123 Cal.App.4th 1278, 20 Cal.Rptr.3d 780 (2004).

**12.** *Smith v. Cutter Biological, Inc.,* 72 Haw. 416, 823 P.2d 717 (1991). See also *Sutowski v. Eli Lilly & Co.,* 82 Ohio St.3d 347, 696 N.E.2d 187 (1998); and *In re Methyl Tertiary Butyl Ether ("MTBE") Products Liability Litigation,* 447 F.Supp.2d 289 (S.D.N.Y. 2006).

# INSIGHT INTO ETHICS
## Warning Labels for Video Games

Almost every product that you purchase in the physical world has one or more warning labels. Indeed, some critics argue that these labels have become so long and ubiquitous that consumers ignore them. In other words, putting warnings on just about everything defeats their original purpose.

Until recently, video games have largely escaped mandated warning labels, although the video game industry has instituted a voluntary rating system to provide information about a video game's content. Each video game is assigned one of six age-specific ratings, ranging from "Early Childhood" to "Adults Only."

Should video games, whether downloaded or bought on a CD-ROM or DVD, have additional warnings to advise potential users (or their parents) that the games might be overly violent? When the California legislature enacted a law imposing restrictions and a labeling requirement on the sale or rental of "violent video games" to minors, this issue became paramount.[a]

### Video Software Dealers Sue the State

The Video Software Dealers Association, along with the Entertainment Software Association, immediately brought a suit in federal district court seeking to invalidate the law. The court granted summary judgment in favor of the plaintiffs.

The act defined a violent video game as one in which "the range of options available to a player includes killing, maiming, dismembering, or sexually assaulting an image of a human being." While agreeing that some video games

are unquestionably violent by everyday standards, the trial court pointed out that many video games are based on popular novels or motion pictures and have extensive plot lines.

Accordingly, the court found that the definition of a violent video game was unconstitutionally vague and thus violated the First Amendment's guarantee of freedom of speech. The court also noted the existence of the voluntary rating system. The U.S. Court of Appeals for the Ninth Circuit affirmed the district court's decision.[b]

### The United States Supreme Court's Decision

The state of California appealed to the United States Supreme Court, but in 2011 the Court affirmed the decision in favor of the video game and software industries. The Court noted that video games are entitled to First Amendment protection. Because California had failed to show that the statute was justified by a compelling government interest and that the law was narrowly tailored to serve that interest, the Court ruled that the statute was unconstitutional.[c]

### LEGAL CRITICAL THINKING
**INSIGHT INTO THE SOCIAL ENVIRONMENT**

*Should victims of a mass shooting be able to sue the manufacturer of a violent video game for a design defect if the shooter had been a devoted player of that game? Discuss.*

---

a. California Civil Code Sections 1746–1746.5.

b. *Video Software Dealers Association v. Schwarzenegger,* 556 F.3d 950 (9th Cir. 2009).

c. *Brown v. Entertainment Merchants Association,* ___ U.S. ___, 131 S.Ct. 2729, 180 L.Ed.2d 708 (2011).

---

defendant shows that the goods were altered after they were sold, normally the defendant will not be held liable. Defendants may also assert the defenses discussed next.

## Preemption

A defense that has been successfully raised by defendants in recent years is preemption—that government regulations preempt claims for product liability (see *Spotlight Case* 7.1 on page 133, for example). An injured party may not be able to sue the manufacturer of defective products that are subject to comprehensive federal regulatory schemes. Medical devices, for instance,

are subject to extensive government regulation and undergo a rigorous premarket approval process.

## Assumption of Risk

Assumption of risk can sometimes be used as a defense in a product liability action. To establish assumption of risk, the defendant must show the following:

1. The plaintiff knew and appreciated the risk created by the product defect.
2. The plaintiff voluntarily assumed the risk—by express agreement or by words or conduct—even though it was unreasonable to do so.

For instance, if a buyer failed to heed a seller's product recall, the buyer may be deemed to have assumed the risk of the product defect that the seller had offered to repair. (See Chapter 6 for a more detailed discussion of assumption of risk.)

Some states do not allow the defense of assumption of risk in strict product liability claims, however. ▶ **Case in Point 7.8**  When Savannah Boles became a customer of Executive Tans, she signed a contract that included a clause stating that she was using a tanning booth at her own risk. The clause also stated that she released the manufacturer and others from any liability for any injuries.

Later, Boles's fingers were partially amputated when they came into contact with a tanning booth's fan. Boles sued the manufacturer for strict product liability. The Colorado Supreme Court held that assumption of risk was not applicable because strict product liability is driven by public-policy considerations. The theory focuses on the nature of the product rather than the conduct of either the manufacturer or the person injured.[13] ◀

## Product Misuse

Similar to the defense of voluntary assumption of risk is that of **product misuse,** which occurs when a product is used for a purpose for which it was not intended. The courts have severely limited this defense, however, and it is now recognized as a defense *only when the particular use was not foreseeable.* If the misuse is reasonably foreseeable, the seller must take measures to guard against it.

## Comparative Negligence (Fault)

Comparative negligence or fault (see Chapter 6) can also affect strict liability claims. Today, courts in many jurisdictions consider the negligent or intentional actions of both the plaintiff and the defendant when apportioning liability and damages. A defendant may be able to limit some of its liability if it can show that the plaintiff's misuse of the product contributed to his or her injuries.

When proved, comparative negligence differs from other defenses in that it does not completely absolve the defendant of liability, but it can reduce the total amount of damages that will be awarded to the plaintiff. Note that some jurisdictions allow only intentional conduct to affect a plaintiff's recovery, whereas other states allow ordinary negligence to be used as a defense to product liability. ▶ **Case in Point 7.9**  Dan Smith, a mechanic, was not wearing a hard hat at work when he was asked to start the diesel engine of an air compressor. Because the compressor was an older model, he had to prop open a door to start it. When the engine started, the door fell from its position and hit Smith's head. The injury caused him to suffer from seizures. Smith sued the manufacturer, claiming that the engine was defectively designed. The manufacturer contended that Smith had been negligent by failing to wear a hard hat and propping open the door in an unsafe manner. Smith argued that ordinary negligence could not be used as a defense in product liability cases. The court ruled that defendants can use the plaintiff's ordinary negligence to reduce their liability proportionately.[14] ◀

## Commonly Known Dangers

The dangers associated with certain products (such as matches and sharp knives) are so commonly known that, as mentioned, manufacturers need not warn users of those dangers. If a defendant succeeds in convincing the court that a plaintiff's injury resulted from a *commonly known danger,* the defendant will not be liable. ▶ **Case in Point 7.10**  In a classic example from 1957, Marguerite Jamieson was injured when an elastic exercise rope slipped off her foot and struck her in the eye, causing a detachment of the retina. Jamieson claimed that the manufacturer should be liable because it had failed to warn users that the exerciser might slip off a foot in such a manner.

The court stated that to hold the manufacturer liable in these circumstances "would go beyond the reasonable dictates of justice in fixing the liabilities of manufacturers." After all, stated the court, "almost every physical object can be inherently dangerous or potentially dangerous in a sense. . . . A manufacturer cannot manufacture a knife that will not cut or a hammer that will not mash a thumb or a stove that will not burn a finger. The law does not require [manufacturers] to warn of such common dangers."[15] ◀

## Knowledgeable User

A related defense is the *knowledgeable user* defense. If a particular danger (such as electrical shock) is or should be commonly known by particular users of a product (such as electricians), the manufacturer need not warn these users of the danger. ▶ **Case in Point 7.11**  The parents of teenagers who had become overweight and developed health problems filed a product liability suit against McDonald's. The teenagers claimed that the fast-food chain had

---

13. *Boles v. Sun Ergoline, Inc.,* 223 P.3d 724 (Col.Sup.Ct. 2010).

14. *Smith v. Ingersoll-Rand Co.,* 14 P.3d 990 (Alaska 2000).
15. *Jamieson v. Woodward & Lothrop,* 247 F.2d 23 (D.C.Cir. 1957).

failed to warn customers of the adverse health effects of eating its food. The court rejected this claim, however, based on the knowledgeable user defense.

The court found that it is well known that the food at McDonald's contains high levels of cholesterol, fat, salt, and sugar and is therefore unhealthful. The court's opinion, which thwarted future lawsuits against fast-food restaurants, stated: "If consumers know (or reasonably should know) the potential ill health effects of eating at McDonald's, they cannot blame McDonald's if they, nonetheless, choose to satiate their appetite with a surfeit [excess] of super-sized McDonald's products."[16] ◄

## Statutes of Limitations and Repose

As noted in Chapter 1, statutes of limitations restrict the time within which an action may be brought.

The statute of limitations for product liability cases varies according to state law. Usually, the injured party must bring a product liability claim within two to four years. Often, the running of the prescribed period is **tolled** (that is, suspended) until the party suffering an injury has discovered it or should have discovered it.

To ensure that sellers and manufacturers will not be left vulnerable to lawsuits indefinitely, many states have passed **statutes of repose,** which place *outer* time limits on product liability actions. For instance, a statute of repose may require that claims be brought within twelve years from the date of sale or manufacture of the defective product. If the plaintiff does not bring an action before the prescribed period expires, the seller cannot be held liable.

---

16. *Pelman v. McDonald's Corp.,* 237 F.Supp.2d 512 (S.D.N.Y. 2003).

## Reviewing: Strict Liability and Product Liability

Shalene Kolchek bought a Great Lakes Spa from Val Porter, a dealer who was selling spas at the state fair. Kolchek signed an installment contract. Porter then handed her the manufacturer's paperwork and arranged for the spa to be delivered and installed for her. Three months later, Kolchek left her six-year-old daughter, Litisha, alone in the spa. While exploring the spa's hydromassage jets, Litisha stuck her index finger into one of the jet holes and was unable to remove her finger from the jet.

Litisha yanked hard, injuring her finger, then panicked and screamed for help. Kolchek was unable to remove Litisha's finger, and the local police and rescue team were called to assist. After a three-hour operation that included draining the spa, sawing out a section of the spa's plastic molding, and slicing the jet casing, Litisha's finger was freed. Following this procedure, the spa was no longer functional. Litisha was taken to the local emergency room, where she was told that a bone in her finger was broken in two places. Using the information presented in the chapter, answer the following questions.

1. Under which theories of product liability can Kolchek sue Porter to recover for Litisha's injuries?
2. Would privity of contract be required for Kolchek to succeed in a product liability action against Great Lakes? Explain.
3. For an action in strict product liability against Great Lakes, what six requirements must Kolchek meet?
4. What defenses to product liability might Porter or Great Lakes be able to assert?

**DEBATE THIS . . .** *All liability suits against tobacco companies for lung cancer should be thrown out of court now and forever.*

## Terms and Concepts

market-share liability 138

product liability 131

product misuse 140

statute of repose 141

strict liability 131

tolling 141

unreasonably dangerous product 135

## Issue Spotters

1. Rim Corporation makes tire rims that it sells to Superior Vehicles, Inc., which installs them on cars. One set of rims is defective, which an inspection would reveal. Superior does not inspect the rims. The car with the defective rims is sold to Town Auto Sales, which sells the car to Uri. Soon, the car is in an accident caused by the defective rims, and Uri is injured. Is Superior Vehicles liable? Explain your answer. **(See page 132.)**

2. Real Chocolate Company makes a box of candy and sells it to Sweet Things, Inc., a distributor. Sweet sells the box to a Tasty Candy store, where Jill buys it. Jill gives it to Ken, who breaks a tooth on a stone the same size and color as a piece of the candy. If Real, Sweet, and Tasty were not negligent, can they be liable for the injury? Why or why not? **(See page 132.)**

• Check your answers to the Issue Spotters against the answers provided in Appendix E at the end of this text.

## Business Scenarios

**7–1. Strict Liability.** Danny and Marion Klein were injured when part of a fireworks display went astray and exploded near them. They sued Pyrodyne Corp., the pyrotechnic company that was hired to set up and discharge the fireworks. The Kleins alleged, among other things, that the company should be strictly liable for damages caused by the fireworks display. Will the court agree with the Kleins? What factors will the court consider in making its decision? Discuss fully. **(See page 131.)**

**7–2. Product Liability.** Jason Clark, an experienced hunter, bought a paintball gun. Clark practiced with the gun and knew how to screw in the carbon dioxide cartridge, pump the gun, and use its safety and trigger. Although Clark was aware that he could purchase protective eyewear, he chose not to buy it. Clark had taken gun safety courses and understood that it was "common sense" not to shoot anyone in the face. Clark's friend, Chris Wright, also owned a paintball gun and was similarly familiar with the gun's use and its risks.

Clark, Wright, and their friends played a game that involved shooting paintballs at cars whose occupants also had the guns. One night, while Clark and Wright were cruising with their guns, Wright shot at Clark's car, but

hit Clark in the eye. Clark filed a product liability lawsuit against the manufacturer of Wright's paintball gun to recover for the injury. Clark claimed that the gun was defectively designed. During the trial, Wright testified that his gun "never malfunctioned." In whose favor should the court rule? Why? **(See page 134.)**

**7–3. Defenses to Product Liability.** Baxter manufactures electric hair dryers. Julie purchases a Baxter dryer from her local Ace Drugstore. Cox, a friend and guest in Julie's home, has taken a shower and wants to dry her hair. Julie tells Cox to use the new Baxter hair dryer that she has just purchased. As Cox plugs in the dryer, sparks fly out from the motor, and sparks continue to fly as she operates it. Despite this, Cox begins drying her hair. Suddenly, the entire dryer ignites into flames, severely burning Cox's scalp.

Cox sues Baxter on the basis of negligence and strict liability in tort. Baxter admits that the dryer was defective but denies liability, particularly because Cox was not the person who purchased the dryer. In other words, Cox had no contractual relationship with Baxter. Discuss the validity of Baxter's defense. Are there any other defenses that Baxter might assert to avoid liability? Discuss fully. **(See page 138.)**

## Business Case Problems

**7–4. Defenses to Product Liability.** Brandon Stroud was driving a golf car made by Textron, Inc., to transport guests at Christmas party. The golf car did not have lights, but Textron did not warn against using it on public roads at night. When Stroud attempted to cross a road at 8:30 P.M., his golf car was struck by a vehicle driven by Joseph Thornley. Stroud was killed. His estate filed a suit against Textron, alleging strict product liability and product liability based on negligence. The charge was that the golf car was defective and unreasonably dangerous. What defense might Textron assert? Explain. [*Moore v. Barony House Restaurant, LLC*, 382 S.C. 35, 674 S.E.2d 500 (S.C.App. 2009)] **(See page 138.)**

**7–5. Product Misuse.** Five-year-old Cheyenne Stark was riding in the backseat of her parents' Ford Taurus. Cheyenne

was not sitting in a booster seat. Instead, she was using a seatbelt designed by Ford, but was wearing the shoulder belt behind her back. The car was involved in a collision. As a result, Cheyenne suffered a spinal cord injury and was paralyzed from the waist down. The family filed a suit against Ford Motor Co., alleging that the seatbelt was defectively designed. Could Ford successfully claim that Cheyenne had misused the seatbelt? Why or why not? [*Stark v. Ford Motor Co.*, 693 S.E.2d 253 (N.C.App. 2010)] **(See page 140.)**

**7–6. Design Defects.** Yun Tung Chow tried to unclog a floor drain in the kitchen of the restaurant where he worked. He used a drain cleaner called Lewis Red Devil Lye that contained crystalline sodium hydroxide. The product label said to wear eye protection, to put one tablespoon of lye directly into the drain, and to keep one's face away from the drain because there could be dangerous backsplash. Without eye protection, Chow mixed three tablespoons of lye in a can and poured that mixture down the drain while bending over it. Liquid splashed back into his face, causing injury. He brought a product liability suit based on inadequate warnings and design defect. The trial court granted summary judgment to the manufacturer, and Chow appealed. An expert for Chow stated that the product was defective because it had a tendency to backsplash. Is that a convincing argument? Why or why not? [*Yun Tung Chow v. Reckitt & Coleman, Inc.*, 69 A.D.3d 413, 891 N.Y.S.2d 402 (N.Y.A.D. 1 Dept. 2010)] **(See page 135.)**

**7–7. Strict Product Liability.** David Dobrovolny bought a new Ford F-350 pickup truck. A year later, the truck spontaneously caught fire in Dobrovolny's driveway. The truck was destroyed, but no other property was damaged, and no one was injured. Dobrovolny filed a suit in a Nebraska state court against Ford Motor Co. on a theory of strict product liability to recover the cost of the truck. Nebraska limits the application of strict product liability to situations involving personal injuries. Is Dobrovolny's claim likely to succeed? Why or why not? Is there another basis for liability on which he might recover? Explain. [*Dobrovolny v. Ford Motor Co.*, 281 Neb. 86, 793 N.W.2d 445 (2011)] **(See page 133.)**

**7–8. BUSINESS CASE PROBLEM WITH SAMPLE ANSWER: Product Liability.**

 *While driving on Interstate 40 in North Carolina, Carroll Jett became distracted by a texting system in the cab of his tractor-trailer truck. He smashed into several vehicles that were slowed or stopped in front of him, injuring Barbara and Michael Durkee and others. The injured motorists filed a suit in a federal district court against Geologic Solutions, Inc., the maker of the texting system, alleging product liability. Was the accident caused by Jett's inattention or the texting device? Should a manufacturer be required to design a product that is incapable of distracting*

*a driver? Discuss.* [Durkee v. Geologic Solutions, Inc., *2013 WL 14717 (4th Cir. 2013)*] **(See page 132.)**

• **For a sample answer to Problem 7–8, go to Appendix F at the end of this text.**

**7–9. A QUESTION OF ETHICS: Dangerous Products.**

 *Susan Calles lived with her four daughters—Amanda, age eleven; Victoria, age five; and Jenna and Jillian, age three. In March 1998, Calles bought an Aim N Flame utility lighter, which she stored on the top shelf of her kitchen cabinet. A trigger can ignite the Aim N Flame after an "ON/OFF" switch is slid to the "on" position. On the night of March 31, Calles and Victoria left to get videos. Jenna and Jillian were in bed, and Amanda was watching television. Calles returned to find fire trucks and emergency vehicles around her home. Robert Finn, a fire investigator, determined that Jenna had started a fire using the lighter. Jillian suffered smoke inhalation, was hospitalized, and died on April 21. Calles filed a suit in an Illinois state court against Scripto-Tokai Corp., which distributed the Aim N Flame, and others. In her suit, which was grounded, in part, in strict liability claims, Calles alleged that the lighter was an "unreasonably dangerous product." Scripto filed a motion for summary judgment.* [Calles v. Scripto-Tokai Corp., *224 Ill.2d 247, 864 N.E.2d 249, 309 Ill. Dec. 383 (2007)*] **(See page 135.)**

(a) A product is "unreasonably dangerous" when it is dangerous beyond the expectation of the ordinary consumer. Whose expectation—Calles's or Jenna's—applies? Does the lighter pass this test? Explain.

(b) Calles presented evidence as to the likelihood and seriousness of injury from lighters that do not have child-safety devices. Scripto argued that the Aim N Flame is an alternative source of fire and is safer than a match. Calles admitted that she knew the dangers presented by lighters in the hands of children. Scripto admitted that it had been a defendant in several suits for injuries under similar circumstances. How should the court rule? Why?

## Legal Reasoning Group Activity

**7–10. Product Liability.** Bret D'Auguste was an experienced skier when he rented equipment to ski at Hunter Mountain Ski Bowl in New York. When D'Auguste entered an extremely difficult trail, he noticed immediately that the surface consisted of ice with almost no snow. He tried to exit the steeply declining trail by making a sharp right turn, but in the attempt, his left ski snapped off. D'Auguste lost his balance, fell, and slid down the mountain, striking his face and head against a fence along the trail.

According to a report by a rental shop employee, one of the bindings on D'Auguste's skis had a "cracked heel housing." D'Auguste filed a lawsuit against the bindings'

manufacturer on a theory of strict product liability. The manufacturer filed a motion for summary judgment. **(See page 134.)**

(a) The first group will take the position of the manufacturer and develop an argument why the court should *grant* the summary judgment motion and dismiss the strict product liability claim.

(b) The second group will take the position of D'Auguste and formulate a basis for why the court should *deny* the motion and allow the strict product liability claim.

# CHAPTER 8

# INTELLECTUAL PROPERTY RIGHTS

**I**ntellectual property is any property that results from intellectual, creative processes—that is to say, the products of an individual's mind. Although it is an abstract term for an abstract concept, intellectual property is nonetheless familiar to almost everyone. The apps for your iPhone and iPad, the movies you see, and the music you listen to are all forms of intellectual property. More than two hundred years ago, the framers of the U.S. Constitution recognized the importance of protecting creative works in Article I, Section 8 (see Appendix B). Statutory protection of these rights began in the 1940s and continues to evolve to meet the needs of modern society.

Of significant concern to businesspersons is the need to protect their rights in intellectual property, which in today's world may exceed the value of physical property, such as machines and buildings. Consider, for instance, the importance of intellectual property rights to technology companies, such as Apple, Inc. Intellectual property rights can be a company's most valuable assets, which is why Apple sued rival Samsung Electronics Company. Apple claimed that Samsung's Galaxy line of mobile phones and tablets (those that run Google's Android software) copied the look, design, and user interface of Apple's iPhone and iPad. Although Apple is one of Samsung's biggest customers and buys many of its components from Samsung, Apple must also protect its iPhone and iPad revenues from competing Android products. You will read about the verdict in this case on page 151.

You will read about the verdict in this case on page 151.

## SECTION 1
## TRADEMARKS AND RELATED PROPERTY

A **trademark** is a distinctive mark, motto, device, or implement that a manufacturer stamps, prints, or otherwise affixes to the goods it produces so that they can be identified on the market and their origins made known. In other words, a trademark is a source indicator. At common law, the person who used a symbol or mark to identify a business or product was protected in the use of that trademark. Clearly, by using another's trademark, a business could lead consumers to believe that its goods were made by the other business. The law seeks to avoid this kind of confusion. In this section, we examine various aspects of the law governing trademarks.

In the following classic case concerning Coca-Cola, the defendants argued that the Coca-Cola trademark was entitled to no protection under the law because the term did not accurately represent the product.

## CLASSIC CASE 8.1

### The Coca-Cola Co. v. The Koke Co. of America
Supreme Court of the United States, 254 U.S. 143, 41 S.Ct. 113, 65 L.Ed.189 (1920).

**COMPANY PROFILE** John Pemberton, an Atlanta pharmacist, invented a caramel-colored, carbonated soft drink in 1886. His bookkeeper, Frank Robinson, named the beverage Coca-Cola after two of the ingredients, coca leaves and kola nuts. Asa Candler bought the Coca-Cola Company (**www.coca-colacompany.com**) in 1891, and within seven years, he had made the soft drink available throughout the United States, as well as in parts of Canada and Mexico. Candler continued to sell

CASE 8.1 CONTINUED  Coke aggressively and to open up new markets, reaching Europe before 1910. In doing so, however, he attracted numerous competitors, some of which tried to capitalize directly on the Coke name.

**BACKGROUND AND FACTS**  The Coca-Cola Company sought to enjoin (prevent) the Koke Company of America and other beverage companies from, among other things, using the word *Koke* for their products. The Koke Company of America and other beverage companies contended that the Coca-Cola trademark was a fraudulent representation and that Coca-Cola was therefore not entitled to any help from the courts. The Koke Company and the other defendants alleged that the Coca-Cola Company, by its use of the Coca-Cola name, represented that the beverage contained cocaine (from coca leaves), which it no longer did. The trial court granted the injunction against the Koke Company, but the appellate court reversed the lower court's ruling. Coca-Cola then appealed to the United States Supreme Court.

**DECISION AND RATIONALE**  The United States Supreme Court upheld the district court's decision and allowed the injunction to stand. Other beverage companies were not allowed to call their products Koke. The Court acknowledged that before 1900 Coca-Cola's goodwill was enhanced by the presence of a small amount of cocaine, but that the cocaine had long been eliminated from the drink.[a]

The Court underscored that Coca-Cola was not "a medicine" and that its attraction did not lie in producing "a toxic effect." Since 1900 sales had greatly increased. The name had come to characterize a well-known beverage to be had almost anywhere "rather than a compound of particular substances." The Court noted that before this suit was brought Coca-Cola had advertised that the public would not find cocaine in Coca-Cola. "It would be going too far to deny the plaintiff relief against a palpable fraud because possibly here and there an ignorant person might call for the drink with the hope for incipient cocaine intoxication."

**IMPACT OF THIS CASE ON TODAY'S LAW**  *In this early case, the United States Supreme Court made it clear that trademarks and trade names (and nicknames for those marks and names, such as the nickname "Coke" for "Coca-Cola") that are in common use receive protection under the common law. This holding is significant historically because it is the predecessor to the federal statute later passed to protect trademark rights—the Lanham Act of 1946, to be discussed next. In many ways, this act represented a codification of common law principles governing trademarks.*

**WHAT IF THE FACTS WERE DIFFERENT?**  *Suppose that Coca-Cola had been trying to make the public believe that its product contained cocaine. Would the result in this case likely have been different? Why or why not?*

---

**a.** In reality, until 1903 the amount of active cocaine in each bottle of Coke was equivalent to one "line" of cocaine.

# Statutory Protection of Trademarks

Statutory protection of trademarks and related property is provided at the federal level by the Lanham Act of 1946.[1] The Lanham Act was enacted, in part, to protect manufacturers from losing business to rival companies that used confusingly similar trademarks.

The Lanham Act incorporates the common law of trademarks and provides remedies for owners of trademarks who wish to enforce their claims in federal court. Many states also have trademark statutes.

**TRADEMARK DILUTION**  In 1995, Congress amended the Lanham Act by passing the Federal Trademark Dilution Act,[2] which allowed trademark owners to bring suits in federal court for trademark **dilution.** In 2006, Congress further amended the law on trademark dilution by passing the Trademark Dilution Revision Act (TDRA).[3]

Under the TDRA, to state a claim for trademark dilution, a plaintiff must prove the following:

1.  The plaintiff owns a famous mark that is distinctive.

---

**1.** 15 U.S.C. Sections 1051–1128.

**2.** 15 U.S.C. Section 1125.
**3.** Pub. L. No. 103-312, 120 Stat. 1730 (2006).

2. The defendant has begun using a mark in commerce that allegedly is diluting the famous mark.
3. The similarity between the defendant's mark and the famous mark gives rise to an *association* between the marks.
4. The association is likely to impair the distinctiveness of the famous mark or harm its reputation.

Trademark dilution laws protect "distinctive" or "famous" trademarks (such as Rolls Royce, McDonald's, and Apple) from certain unauthorized uses even when the use is on noncompeting goods or is unlikely to confuse. More than half of the states have also enacted trademark dilution laws.

**SIMILAR MARKS MAY CONSTITUTE TRADEMARK DILUTION** Note that a famous mark may be diluted by the use of an *identical* mark or by the use of a *similar* mark.[4] A similar mark is more likely to lessen the value of a famous mark when the companies using the marks provide related goods or compete against each other in the same market.

▶ **Case in Point 8.1** Samantha Lundberg opened "Sambuck's Coffeehouse," in Astoria, Oregon, even though she knew that "Starbucks" is one of the largest coffee chains in the nation. When Starbucks Corporation filed a dilution lawsuit, the federal court ruled that use of the "Sambuck's" mark constituted trademark dilution because it created confusion for consumers. Not only was there a "high degree" of similarity between the marks, but also both companies provided coffee-related services and marketed their services through "stand-alone" retail stores. Therefore, the use of the similar mark (Sambuck's) reduced the value of the famous mark (Starbucks).[5] ◀

## Trademark Registration

Trademarks may be registered with the state or with the federal government. To register for protection under federal trademark law, a person must file an application with the U.S. Patent and Trademark Office in Washington, D.C. Under current law, a mark can be registered (1) if it is currently in commerce or (2) if the applicant intends to put it into commerce within six months.

In special circumstances, the six-month period can be extended by thirty months. Thus, the applicant would have a total of three years from the date of notice of trademark approval to make use of the mark and file the required use statement. Registration is postponed until the mark is actually used.

During this waiting period, any applicant can legally protect his or her trademark against a third party who previously has neither used the mark nor filed an application for it. Registration is renewable between the fifth and sixth years after the initial registration and every ten years thereafter (every twenty years for those trademarks registered before 1990).

## Trademark Infringement

Registration of a trademark with the U.S. Patent and Trademark Office gives notice on a nationwide basis that the trademark belongs exclusively to the registrant. The registrant is also allowed to use the symbol ® to indicate that the mark has been registered. Whenever that trademark is copied to a substantial degree or used in its entirety by another, intentionally or unintentionally, the trademark has been *infringed* (used without authorization).

When a trademark has been infringed, the owner of the mark has a cause of action against the infringer. To succeed in a trademark infringement action, the owner must show that the defendant's use of the mark created a likelihood of confusion about the origin of the defendant's goods or services. The owner need not prove that the infringer acted intentionally or that the trademark was registered (although registration does provide proof of the date of inception of the trademark's use).

The most commonly granted remedy for trademark infringement is an *injunction* to prevent further infringement. Under the Lanham Act, a trademark owner that successfully proves infringement can recover actual damages, plus the profits that the infringer wrongfully received from the unauthorized use of the mark. A court can also order the destruction of any goods bearing the unauthorized trademark. In some situations, the trademark owner may also be able to recover attorneys' fees.

## Distinctiveness of the Mark

A trademark must be sufficiently distinctive to enable consumers to identify the manufacturer of the goods easily and to distinguish between those goods and competing products.

**STRONG MARKS** Fanciful, arbitrary, or suggestive trademarks are generally considered to be the most

---

4. See *Louis Vuitton Malletier S.A. v. Haute Diggity Dog, LLC*, 507 F.3d 252 (4th Cir. 2007); and *Moseley v. V Secret Catalogue, Inc.*, 537 U.S. 418, 123 S.Ct. 1115, 155 L.Ed.2d 1 (2003).
5. *Starbucks Corp. v. Lundberg*, 2005 WL 3183858 (D.Or. 2005).

distinctive (strongest) trademarks. Marks that are fanciful, arbitrary, or suggestive are protected as inherently distinctive without demonstrating secondary meaning. These marks receive automatic protection because they serve to identify a particular product's source, as opposed to describing the product itself.

***Fanciful and Arbitrary Trademarks.*** Fanciful trademarks are inherently distinctive and include invented words, such as "Xerox" for one manufacturer's copiers and "Google" for search engines. Arbitrary trademarks are those that use common words in an uncommon way that is nondescriptive, such as "Dutch Boy" as a name for paint.

Even a single letter used in a particular style can be an arbitrary trademark. ▶ **Case in Point 8.2** Sports entertainment company ESPN sued Quiksilver, Inc., a maker of youth-oriented clothing, alleging trademark infringement. ESPN claimed that Quiksilver's clothing had used the stylized "X" mark that ESPN uses in connection with the "X Games" (extreme action sports competitions). Quiksilver filed counterclaims for trademark infringement and dilution, arguing that it had a long history of using the stylized X on its products.

ESPN created the X Games in the mid-1990s, and Quiksilver has been using the X mark since 1994. ESPN asked the court to dismiss Quiksilver's counterclaims, but the court refused, holding that the X on Quiksilver's clothing is clearly an arbitrary mark. The court found that the two Xs are "similar enough that a consumer might well confuse them."[6] ◀

***Suggestive Trademarks.*** Suggestive trademarks indicate something about a product's nature, quality, or characteristics, without describing the product directly. These marks require imagination on the part of the consumer to identify the characteristic. For example, "Dairy Queen" suggests an association between its products and milk, but it does not directly describe ice cream.

"Blu-ray" is a suggestive mark that is associated with the high-quality, high-definition video contained on a particular optical data storage disc. Although blue-violet lasers are used to read *blu-ray* discs, the term *blu-ray* does not directly describe the disc.

**SECONDARY MEANING** Descriptive terms, geographic terms, and personal names are not inherently distinctive and do not receive protection under the law until they acquire a secondary meaning. A secondary meaning may arise when customers begin to associate a specific term or phrase (such as *London Fog*) with specific trademarked items (coats with "London Fog" labels) made by a particular company.

▶ **Case in Point 8.3** Frosty Treats, Inc., sells frozen desserts out of ice cream trucks. The video game series Twisted Metal depicts an ice cream truck with a clown character on it that is similar to the clowns on Frosty Treats' trucks. In the last game of the series, the truck bears the label "Frosty Treats." Frosty sued the video game maker for trademark infringement. The court, however, held that "Frosty Treats" is a descriptive term and is not protected by trademark law unless it has acquired a secondary meaning.

To establish secondary meaning, Frosty Treats would have had to show that the public recognized its trademark and associated it with a single source. Because Frosty Treats failed to do so, the court entered a judgment in favor of the video game producer.[7] ◀

Once a secondary meaning is attached to a term or name, a trademark is considered distinctive and is protected. Even a color can qualify for trademark protection, as did the color schemes used by some state university sports teams, including Ohio State University and Louisiana State University.[8]

**GENERIC TERMS** Generic terms that refer to an entire class of products, such as *bicycle* and *computer,* receive no protection, even if they acquire secondary meanings. A particularly thorny problem arises when a trademark acquires generic use. For instance, *aspirin* and *thermos* were originally the names of trademarked products, but today the words are used generically. Other trademarks that have acquired generic use are *escalator, trampoline, raisin bran, dry ice, lanolin, linoleum, nylon,* and *cornflakes.*

## Service, Certification, and Collective marks

A **service mark** is essentially a trademark that is used to distinguish the *services* (rather than the products) of one person or company from those of another. For example, each airline has a particular mark or symbol associated with its name. Titles and character names used in radio and television are frequently registered as service marks.

---

6. *ESPN, Inc. v. Quiksilver, Inc.,* 586 F.Supp.2d 219 (S.D.N.Y. 2008).

7. *Frosty Treats, Inc., v. Sony Computer Entertainment America, Inc.,* 426 F.3d 1001 (8th Cir. 2005).

8. *Board of Supervisors of Louisiana State University v. Smack Apparel Co.,* 438 F.Supp.2d 653 (E.D.La. 2006). See also *Abraham v. Alpha Chi Omega,* 781 F.Supp.2d 396 (N.D.Tex. 2011).

Other marks protected by law include certification marks and collective marks. A **certification mark** is used by one or more persons, other than the owner, to certify the region, materials, mode of manufacture, quality, or other characteristic of specific goods or services. Certification marks include "Good Housekeeping Seal of Approval" and "UL Tested."

When used by members of a cooperative, association, or other organization, a certification mark is referred to as a **collective mark.** Collective marks appear at the ends of motion picture credits to indicate the various associations and organizations that participated in the making of the films. The union marks found on the tags of certain products are also collective marks.

## Trade Dress

The term **trade dress** refers to the image and overall appearance of a product. Trade dress is a broad concept and can include either all or part of the total image or overall impression created by a product or its packaging.

▶ **Example 8.4** The distinctive decor, menu, layout, and style of service of a particular restaurant may be regarded as trade dress. Trade dress can also include the layout and appearance of a catalogue, the use of a lighthouse as part of the design of a golf hole, the fish shape of a cracker, or the G-shaped design of a Gucci watch. ◀

Basically, trade dress is subject to the same protection as trademarks. In cases involving trade dress infringement, as in trademark infringement cases, a major consideration is whether consumers are likely to be confused by the allegedly infringing use.

## Counterfeit Goods

Counterfeit goods copy or otherwise imitate trademarked goods, but they are not the genuine trademarked goods. The importation of goods that bear counterfeit (fake) trademarks poses a growing problem for U.S. businesses, consumers, and law enforcement. In addition to the negative financial effects on legitimate businesses, certain counterfeit goods, such as pharmaceuticals and nutritional supplements, can present serious public health risks.

Although Congress has enacted statutes against counterfeit goods (discussed next), the United States cannot prosecute foreign counterfeiters because our national laws do not apply to them. Instead, one effective tool that U.S. officials use to combat online

sales of counterfeit goods is to obtain a court order to close down the domain names of Web sites that sell such goods.

▶ **Example 8.5** In 2012, U.S. agents shut down 101 domain names on the Monday after Thanksgiving ("Cyber Monday," the online version of "Black Friday," the day after Thanksgiving when the holiday shopping season begins). Although the criminal enterprises may continue selling counterfeit versions of brand-name products under different domain names, shutting down the Web sites, particularly on key shopping days, prevents some counterfeit goods from entering the United States. ◀

**THE STOP COUNTERFEITING IN MANUFACTURED GOODS ACT** The Stop Counterfeiting in Manufactured Goods Act[9] (SCMGA) was enacted to combat counterfeit goods. The act makes it a crime to traffic intentionally in or attempt to traffic in counterfeit goods or services, or to knowingly use a counterfeit mark on or in connection with goods or services.

Before this act, the law did not prohibit the creation or shipment of counterfeit labels that were not attached to any product. Therefore, counterfeiters would make labels and packaging bearing another's trademark, ship the labels to another location, and then affix them to an inferior product to deceive buyers. The SCMGA closed this loophole by making it a crime to knowingly traffic in counterfeit labels, stickers, packaging, and the like, regardless of whether the items are attached to any goods.

**PENALTIES FOR COUNTERFEITING** Persons found guilty of violating the SCMGA may be fined up to $2 million or imprisoned for up to ten years (or more if they are repeat offenders). If a court finds that the statute was violated, it must order the defendant to forfeit the counterfeit products (which are then destroyed), as well as any property used in the commission of the crime. The defendant must also pay restitution to the trademark holder or victim in an amount equal to the victim's actual loss.

▶ **Case in Point 8.6** Wajdi Beydoun pleaded guilty to conspiring to import cigarette-rolling papers from Mexico that were falsely marked as "Zig-Zags" and selling them in the United States. The court sentenced Beydoun to prison and ordered him to pay $566,267 in restitution. On appeal, the court affirmed the prison sentence but reversed the restitution

---

9. Pub. L. No. 109-181 (2006), which amended 18 U.S.C. Sections 2318–2320.

because the amount exceeded the actual loss suffered by the legitimate sellers of Zig-Zag rolling papers.[10] ◀

The United States has also joined with other nations in a new international agreement aimed at combatting counterfeiting (see the discussion on page 159).

## Trade Names

Trademarks apply to *products*. A **trade name** indicates part or all of a business's name, whether the business is a sole proprietorship, a partnership, or a corporation. Generally, a trade name is directly related to a business and its goodwill.

A trade name may be protected as a trademark if the trade name is also the name of the company's trademarked product—for example, Coca-Cola. Unless it is also used as a trademark or service mark, a trade name cannot be registered with the federal government. Trade names are protected under the common law, but only if they are unusual or fancifully used. The word *Safeway,* for example, was sufficiently fanciful to obtain protection as a trade name for a grocery chain.

## Licensing

One way to avoid litigation and still make use of another's trademark or other form of intellectual property is to obtain a license to do so. A **license** in this context is an agreement, or contract, permitting the use of a trademark, copyright, patent, or trade secret for certain purposes. The party that owns the intellectual property rights and issues the license is the *licensor,* and the party obtaining the license is the *licensee.*

A license grants only the rights expressly described in the license agreement. A licensor might, for example, allow the licensee to use the trademark as part of its company or domain name, but not otherwise use the mark on any products or services. Disputes frequently arise over licensing agreements, particularly when the license involves Internet uses.

▶ **Case in Point 8.7**   George V Restauration S.A. and others owned and operated the Buddha Bar Paris, a restaurant with an Asian theme in Paris, France. One of the owners allowed Little Rest Twelve, Inc., to use the Buddha Bar trademark and its associated concept in New York City under the name *Buddha Bar NYC.* Little Rest paid royalties for its use of the Buddha Bar mark and advertised Buddha Bar NYC's affiliation

with Buddha Bar Paris, a connection also noted on its Web site and in the media.

When a dispute arose, the owners of Buddha Bar Paris withdrew their permission for Buddha Bar NYC's use of their mark, but Little Rest continued to use it. The owners of the mark filed a suit in a New York state court against Little Rest. The court granted an injunction to prevent Little Rest from using the mark.[11] ◀

# SECTION 2
# PATENTS

A **patent** is a grant from the government that gives an inventor the exclusive right to make, use, or sell his or her invention for a period of twenty years. Patents for designs, as opposed to those for inventions, are given for a fourteen-year period. The applicant must demonstrate to the satisfaction of the U.S. Patent and Trademark Office that the invention, discovery, process, or design is novel, useful, and not obvious in light of current technology.

Until recently, U.S. patent law differed from the laws of many other countries because the first person to invent a product obtained the patent rights rather than the first person to file for a patent. It was often difficult to prove who invented an item first, however, which prompted Congress to change the system in 2011 by passing the America Invents Act.[12] Now the first person to file an application for a patent on a product or process will receive patent protection. In addition, the new law established a nine-month limit for challenging a patent on any ground.

The period of patent protection begins on the date the patent application is filed, rather than when the patent is issued, which may sometimes be years later. After the patent period ends (either fourteen or twenty years later), the product or process enters the public domain, and anyone can make, sell, or use the invention without paying the patent holder.

## Searchable Patent Databases

A significant development relating to patents is the availability online of the world's patent databases.

---

**10.** *United States v. Beydoun,* 469 F.3d 102 (5th Cir. 2006).

**11.** *George V Restauration S.A. v. Little Rest Twelve, Inc.,* 58 A.D.3d 428, 871 N.Y.S.2d 65 (2009).

**12.** The full title of this law is the Leahy-Smith America Invents Act, Pub. L. No. 112-29 (2011), which amended 35 U.S.C. Sections 1, 41, and 321.

The Web site of the U.S. Patent and Trademark Office (**www.uspto.gov**) provides searchable databases covering U.S. patents granted since 1976. The Web site of the European Patent Office (**www.epo.org**) provides online access to 50 million patent documents in more than seventy nations through a searchable network of databases.

Businesses use these searchable databases in many ways. Because patents are valuable assets, businesses may need to perform patent searches to list or inventory their assets. Patent searches may also be conducted to study trends and patterns in a specific technology or to gather information about competitors in the industry.

## What Is Patentable?

Under federal law, "[w]hoever invents or discovers any new and useful process, machine, manufacture, or composition of matter, or any new and useful improvement thereof, may obtain a patent therefor, subject to the conditions and requirements of this title."[13] Thus, to be patentable, the applicant must prove that the invention, discovery, process, or design is *novel, useful,* and *not obvious* (in light of current technology).

In sum, almost anything is patentable, except the laws of nature, natural phenomena, and abstract ideas (including algorithms[14]). Even artistic methods and works of art, certain business processes, and the structures of storylines are patentable, provided that they are novel and not obvious.[15]

Plants that are reproduced asexually (by means other than from seed), such as hybrid or genetically engineered plants, are patentable in the United States, as are genetically engineered (or cloned) microorganisms and animals. ▶ **Case in Point 8.8** Monsanto, Inc., sells its patented genetically modified (GM) seeds to farmers as a way to achieve higher yields from crops using fewer pesticides. It requires farmers who buy GM seeds to sign licensing agreements promising to plant the seeds for only one crop and to pay a technology fee for each acre planted. To ensure compliance, Monsanto has many full-time

employees whose job is to investigate and prosecute farmers who use the GM seeds illegally. Monsanto has filed nearly 150 lawsuits against farmers in the United States and has been awarded more than $15 million in damages (not including out-of-court settlement amounts).[16] ◀

## Patent Infringement

If a firm makes, uses, or sells another's patented design, product, or process without the patent owner's permission, that firm commits the tort of patent infringement. Patent infringement may occur even though the patent owner has not put the patented product into commerce. Patent infringement may also occur even though not all features or parts of a product are copied. (To infringe the patent on a process, however, all steps or their equivalent must be copied.)

**PATENT INFRINGEMENT SUITS AND HIGH-TECH COMPANIES** Obviously, companies that specialize in developing new technology stand to lose significant profits if someone "makes, uses, or sells" devices that incorporate their patented inventions. Because these firms are the holders of numerous patents, they are frequently involved in patent infringement lawsuits (as well as other types of intellectual property disputes).

Many companies that make and sell electronics and computer software and hardware are based in foreign nations (for example, Samsung Electronics Company is a Korean firm). Foreign firms can apply for and obtain U.S. patent protection on items that they sell within the United States. Similarly, U.S. firms can obtain protection in foreign nations where they sell goods.

**LIMITATIONS ON EXPORTED SOFTWARE** The United States Supreme Court has narrowly construed patent infringement as it applies to exported software. As a general rule, under U.S. law, no patent infringement occurs when a patented product is made and sold in another country.

▶ **Case in Point 8.9** AT&T Corporation holds a patent on a device used to digitally encode, compress, and process recorded speech. AT&T brought an infringement case against Microsoft Corporation, which admit-

---

13. 35 U.S.C. Section 101.
14. An *algorithm* is a step-by-step procedure, formula, or set of instructions for accomplishing a specific task. An example is the set of rules used by a search engine to rank the listings contained within its index in response to a query.
15. For a United States Supreme Court case discussing the obviousness requirement, see *KSR International Co. v. Teleflex, Inc.,* 550 U.S. 398, 127 S.Ct. 1727, 167 L.Ed.2d 705 (2007).

16. See, for example, *Monsanto Co. v. Bowman,* 657 F.3d 1341 (Fed.Cir. 2011); and *Monsanto Co. v. Scruggs,* 2009 WL 1228318 (Fed.Cir. 2009).

ted that its Windows operating system incorporated software code that infringed on AT&T's patent.

The case reached the United States Supreme Court on the question of whether Microsoft's liability extended to computers made in another country. The Court held that it did not. Microsoft was liable only for infringement in the United States and not for the Windows-based computers produced in foreign locations. The Court reasoned that Microsoft had not "supplied" the software for the computers but had only electronically transmitted a master copy, which the foreign manufacturers copied and loaded onto the computers.[17] ◄

**APPLE, INC. V. SAMSUNG ELECTRONICS COMPANY** As mentioned in the chapter introduction, Apple sued Samsung alleging that Samsung's Galaxy mobile phones and tablets that use Google's HTC Android operating system infringe on Apple's patents. Apple has design patents that cover the graphical user interface (the display of icons on the home screen), the device's shell, and the screen and button design. Apple also has patents that cover the way information is displayed on iPhones and other devices, the way windows pop open, and the way information is scaled and rotated.

In 2012, a jury issued a verdict in favor of Apple and awarded more than $1 billion in damages—one of the largest awards ever made in a patent case (a judge later ruled that part of the damages had been incorrectly calculated, however).[18] The jury found that Samsung had willfully infringed five of Apple's patents. The case provides an important precedent for Apple in its legal battles against Android devices made by other companies worldwide. Nevertheless, litigation between the two companies has continued.

## Remedies for Patent Infringement

If a patent is infringed, the patent holder may sue for relief in federal court. The patent holder can seek an injunction against the infringer and can also request

damages for royalties and lost profits. In some cases, the court may grant the winning party reimbursement for attorneys' fees and costs. If the court determines that the infringement was willful, the court can triple the amount of damages awarded (treble damages).

In the past, permanent injunctions were routinely granted to prevent future infringement. In 2006, however, the United States Supreme Court ruled that patent holders are not automatically entitled to a permanent injunction against future infringing activities.The courts have discretion to decide whether equity requires it. According to the Court, a patent holder must prove that it has suffered irreparable injury and that the public interest would not be disserved by a permanent injunction.[19] This decision gives courts discretion to decide what is equitable in the circumstances and allows them to consider what is in the public interest rather than just the interests of the parties.

▶ **Case in Point 8.10** In the first case applying this rule, a court found that although Microsoft had infringed on the patent of a small software company, the latter was not entitled to an injunction. According to the court, the small company was not irreparably harmed and could be adequately compensated by monetary damages. Also, the public might suffer negative effects from an injunction because the infringement involved part of Microsoft's widely used Office Suite software.[20] ◄

**SECTION 3**
# COPYRIGHTS

A **copyright** is an intangible property right granted by federal statute to the author or originator of a literary or artistic production of a specified type. The Copyright Act of 1976,[21] as amended, governs copyrights. Works created after January 1, 1978, are automatically given statutory copyright protection for the life of the author plus 70 years. For copyrights owned by publishing houses, the copyright expires 95 years from the date of publication or 120 years from the date of creation, whichever comes first. For works by more than one author, the copyright

**17.** *Microsoft Corp. v. AT&T Corp.,* 550 U.S. 437, 127 S.Ct. 1746, 167 L.Ed.2d 737 (2007).
**18.** *Apple, Inc. v. Samsung Electronics Co.,* CV 11-1846 and CV 12-0630 (N.D.Cal. August 24, 2012). In 2013, a judge ruled that part of the damages awarded were incorrectly calculated and excessive, invalidating approximately $450.5 million of the jury's award. The judge ordered a new trial to determine the appropriate amount of damages. *Apple, Inc. v. Samsung Electronics Co.,* ___ F.Supp.2d ___, 2013 WL 772525 (N.D.Cal. 2013).

**19.** *eBay, Inc. v. MercExchange, LLC,* 547 U.S. 388, 126 S.Ct. 1837, 164 L.Ed.2d 641 (2006).
**20.** *Z4 Technologies, Inc. v. Microsoft Corp.,* 434 F.Supp.2d 437 (E.D.Tex. 2006).
**21.** 17 U.S.C. Sections 101 *et seq.*

expires 70 years after the death of the last surviving author.[22]

Copyrights can be registered with the U.S. Copyright Office (**www.copyright.gov**) in Washington, D.C. A copyright owner no longer needs to place the symbol © or the term *Copr.* or *Copyright* on the work to have the work protected against infringement. Chances are that if somebody created it, somebody owns it.

Generally, copyright owners are protected against the following:

1. Reproduction of the work.
2. Development of derivative works.
3. Distribution of the work.
4. Public display of the work.

## What Is Protected Expression?

Works that are copyrightable include books, records, films, artworks, architectural plans, menus, music videos, product packaging, and computer software. To be protected, a work must be "fixed in a durable medium" from which it can be perceived, reproduced, or communicated. Protection is automatic. Registration is not required.

Section 102 of the Copyright Act explicitly states that it protects original works that fall into one of the following categories:

1. Literary works (including newspaper and magazine articles, computer and training manuals, catalogues, brochures, and print advertisements).
2. Musical works and accompanying words (including advertising jingles).
3. Dramatic works and accompanying music.
4. Pantomimes and choreographic works (including ballets and other forms of dance).
5. Pictorial, graphic, and sculptural works (including cartoons, maps, posters, statues, and even stuffed animals).
6. Motion pictures and other audiovisual works (including multimedia works).
7. Sound recordings.
8. Architectural works.

**SECTION 102 EXCLUSIONS** It is not possible to copyright an *idea*. Section 102 of the Copyright Act specifically excludes copyright protection for any "idea, procedure, process, system, method of operation, concept, principle, or discovery, regardless of the form in which it is described, explained, illustrated, or embodied." Thus, anyone can freely use the underlying ideas or principles embodied in a work.

What is copyrightable is the particular way in which an idea is *expressed*. Whenever an idea and an expression are inseparable, the expression cannot be copyrighted. Generally, anything that is not an original expression will not qualify for copyright protection. Facts widely known to the public are not copyrightable. Page numbers are not copyrightable because they follow a sequence known to everyone. Mathematical calculations are not copyrightable.

**COMPILATIONS OF FACTS** Unlike ideas, *compilations* of facts are copyrightable. Under Section 103 of the Copyright Act, a compilation is "a work formed by the collection and assembling of preexisting materials or data that are selected, coordinated, or arranged in such a way that the resulting work as a whole constitutes an original work of authorship."

The key requirement in the copyrightability of a compilation is originality. If the facts are selected, coordinated, or arranged in an original way, they can qualify for copyright protection. Therefore, the White Pages of a telephone directory do not qualify for copyright protection because they simply list alphabetically names and telephone numbers. The Yellow Pages of a directory can be copyrightable, provided the information is selected, coordinated, or arranged in an original way. Similarly, a compilation of information about yachts listed for sale has qualified for copyright protection.[23]

## Copyright Infringement

Whenever the form or expression of an idea is copied, an infringement of copyright has occurred. The reproduction does not have to be exactly the same as the original, nor does it have to reproduce the original in its entirety. If a substantial part of the original is reproduced, the copyright has been infringed.

In the following case, rapper Curtis Jackson—better known as "50 Cent"—was the defendant in a suit that claimed his album *Before I Self–Destruct*, and the companion film of the same name, infringed the copyright of Shadrach Winstead's book, *The Preacher's Son—But the Streets Turned Me into a Gangster.*

---

**22.** These time periods reflect the extensions of the length of copyright protection enacted by Congress in the Copyright Term Extension Act of 1998, 17 U.S.C. Section 302. The United States Supreme Court upheld the constitutionality of the act in 2003. See *Eldred v. Ashcroft,* 537 U.S. 186, 123 S.Ct. 769, 154 L.Ed.2d 683 (2003).

**23.** *BUC International Corp. v. International Yacht Council, Ltd.,* 489 F.3d 1129 (11th Cir. 2007).

## CASE 8.2

### Winstead v. Jackson

United States Court of Appeals, Third Circuit, 2013 WL 139622 (2013).

**BACKGROUND AND FACTS** Shadrach Winstead dictated the text of his original work, *The Preacher's Son—But the Streets Turned Me into a Gangster,* and gave the audiotapes to another individual to transcribe. Before the publication of the book, this individual either gave a copy to Curtis Jackson or gave the copy to individuals who passed it on to Jackson. Later, Jackson released the CD, *Before I Self-Destruct,* featuring his original songs and lyrics, and a companion film of the same name. Jackson wrote, starred in, and directed the film. Winstead filed a lawsuit in a federal district court against Jackson, alleging that his CD and film infringed the copyright of Winstead's book. The court dismissed the complaint, concluding that Jackson did not improperly copy protected aspects of Winstead's book. Winstead appealed to the U.S. Court of Appeals for the Third Circuit.

**DECISION AND RATIONALE** The U.S. Court of Appeals for the Third Circuit affirmed the lower court's decision dismissing Winstead's complaint. A comparison of Winstead's book and Jackson's CD and film did not support a claim of copyright infringement. "Not all copying is copyright infringement, so even if actual copying is proven, the court must decide, by comparing the allegedly infringing work with the original work, whether the copy was unlawful. Copying may be proved inferentially [by inference] by showing that the allegedly infringing work is substantially similar to the copyrighted work." Therefore, a court must determine why the allegedly infringing work is similar to the original. Is it because the work appropriates "unique expressions of the original work," or merely because it contains elements that would be expected when two works examine the same idea?

The reviewing court went on to point out that Winstead's book and Jackson's works share similar themes and settings but that "the story of an angry and wronged protagonist who turns to a life of violence and crime has long been a part of the public domain." Any of the alleged "direct phrases" from Winstead's book that appear in Jackson's film are either common in general or common with respect to hip hop culture. They do not enjoy copyright protection.

**THE LEGAL ENVIRONMENT DIMENSION** *Is all copying copyright infringement? If not, what is the test for determining whether a creative work has been unlawfully copied?*

**THE SOCIAL DIMENSION** *Does it seem likely that most creative works are in the public domain— and available for anyone to use without charge? If not, should they be? Discuss.*

---

**REMEDIES FOR COPYRIGHT INFRINGEMENT** Those who infringe copyrights may be liable for damages or criminal penalties. These range from actual damages or statutory damages, imposed at the court's discretion, to criminal proceedings for willful violations.

Actual damages are based on the harm caused to the copyright holder by the infringement, while statutory damages, not to exceed $150,000, are provided for under the Copyright Act. Criminal proceedings may result in fines and/or imprisonment. A court can also issue a permanent injunction against a defendant when the court deems it necessary to prevent future copyright infringement.

▶ **Case in Point 8.11** Rusty Carroll operated an online term paper business, R2C2, Inc., that offered up to 300,000 research papers for sale at nine Web sites. Individuals whose work was posted on these Web sites without their permission filed a lawsuit against Carroll for copyright infringement. Because Carroll had repeatedly failed to comply with court orders regarding discovery, the court found that the copyright infringement was likely to continue unless an injunction was issued. The court therefore issued a permanent injunction prohibiting Carroll and R2C2 from selling any term paper without sworn documentary evidence that the paper's author had given permission.[24] ◀

---

24. *Weidner v. Carroll,* 2010 WL 310310 (S.D.Ill. 2010).

**THE "FAIR USE" EXCEPTION** An exception to liability for copyright infringement is made under the "fair use" doctrine. In certain circumstances, a person or organization can reproduce copyrighted material without paying royalties (fees paid to the copyright holder for the privilege of reproducing the copyrighted material). Section 107 of the Copyright Act provides as follows:

> [T]he fair use of a copyrighted work, including such use by reproduction in copies or phonorecords or by any other means specified by [Section 106 of the Copyright Act], for purposes such as criticism, comment, news reporting, teaching (including multiple copies for classroom use), scholarship, or research, is not an infringement of copyright. In determining whether the use made of a work in any particular case is a fair use the factors to be considered shall include—
>
> (1) the purpose and character of the use, including whether such use is of a commercial nature or is for nonprofit educational purposes;
> (2) the nature of the copyrighted work;
> (3) the amount and substantiality of the portion used in relation to the copyrighted work as a whole; and
> (4) the effect of the use upon the potential market for or value of the copyrighted work.

**WHAT IS FAIR USE?** Because these guidelines are very broad, the courts determine whether a particular use is fair on a case-by-case basis. Thus, anyone who reproduces copyrighted material may be committing a violation. In determining whether a use is fair, courts have often considered the fourth factor to be the most important.

▶ **Case in Point 8.12** BMG Music Publishing, an owner of copyrighted music, granted a license to Leadsinger, Inc., a manufacturer of karaoke devices. The license gave Leadsinger permission to reproduce the sound recordings, but not to reprint the song lyrics, which appeared at the bottom of a TV screen when the karaoke device was used.

BMG demanded that Leadsinger pay a "lyric reprint" fee and a "synchronization" fee. Leadsinger refused to pay, claiming that its use of the lyrics was educational and thus did not constitute copyright infringement under the fair use exception. A federal appellate court disagreed. The court held that Leadsinger's display of the lyrics was not a fair use because it would have a negative effect on the value of the copyrighted work.[25] ◀

## The First Sale Doctrine

Section 109(a) of the Copyright Act provides that "the owner of a particular copy or phonorecord lawfully made under [the Copyright Act], or any person authorized by such owner, is entitled, without the authority of the copyright owner, to sell or otherwise dispose of the possession of that copy or phonorecord." This rule is known as the first sale doctrine.

Under this doctrine, once a copyright owner sells or gives away a particular copy of a work, the copyright owner no longer has the right to control the distribution of that copy. Thus, for example, a person who buys a copyrighted book can sell it to someone else.

In 2011, a court held that the first sale doctrine also applies to a person who receives promotional CDs, such as a music critic or radio programmer. ▶ **Case in Point 8.13** Universal Music Group (UMG) regularly ships promotional CDs to people in the music industry. Troy Augusto obtained some of these promotional CDs from various sources and sold them through online auction sites. UMG filed a copyright infringement lawsuit. Augusto argued that the music company had given up its right to control further distribution of the CDs under the first sale doctrine. Ultimately, a federal appellate court held in favor of Augusto. The promotional CDs were dispatched to the recipients without any prior arrangement as to those particular copies. Therefore, the court concluded that UMG had conveyed title of the copyrighted promotional CDs to the recipients.[26] ◀

In 2012, the United States Supreme Court heard the appeal of a case involving the resale of textbooks on eBay. To read about the Court's decision in this important case, see this chapter's *Insight into the Global Environment* feature on the following page.

## Copyright Protection for Software

In 1980, Congress passed the Computer Software Copyright Act, which amended the Copyright Act of 1976 to include computer programs in the list of creative works protected by federal copyright law.[27] Generally, copyright protection extends to those parts of a computer program that can be read by humans, such as the "high-level" language of a source code. Protection also extends to the binary-language object code, which is readable only by the computer, and to

**25.** *Leadsinger, Inc. v. BMG Music Publishing*, 512 F.3d 522 (9th Cir. 2008).

**26.** *UMG Recordings, Inc. v. Augusto*, 628 F.3d 1175 (9th Cir. 2011).
**27.** Pub. L. No. 96-517 (1980), amending 17 U.S.C. Sections 101, 117.

---

# INSIGHT INTO THE GLOBAL ENVIRONMENT
## Is It Legal to Resell Textbooks Purchased Abroad?

Students and professors alike complain about the high price of college textbooks. Some enterprising students have found that if they purchase textbooks printed abroad, they can sometimes save enough to justify the shipping charges. Textbook prices are lower in other countries because (1) production costs are lower there and (2) average incomes are also lower, so students are unable to pay the higher prices that U.S. students face. (Also, neither students nor professors abroad have the full range of paper and digital supplements that are offered with most textbooks in the United States.)

### A Cornell University Student Starts a Side Business

Supap Kirtsaeng, a citizen of Thailand, started his studies at Cornell University in 1997 and then went on to a Ph.D. program at the University of Southern California. He enlisted friends and family in Thailand to buy copies of textbooks there and ship them to him in the United States. To pay for his education, Kirtsaeng resold the textbooks on eBay, where he eventually made about $100,000. John Wiley & Sons, Inc., which had printed eight of those textbooks in Asia, sued Kirtsaeng in federal district court for copyright infringement under Section 602(a)(1) of the Copyright Act. Wiley claimed that it is impermissible to import a work "without the authority of the owner." Kirtsaeng's defense was that Section 109(a) of the Copyright Act allows the first purchaser-owner of a book to sell or otherwise dispose of it without the copyright owner's permission. Kirtsaeng did not prevail.[a]

### Kirtsaeng Appeals the Verdict

Kirtsaeng appealed to the U.S. Court of Appeals for the Second Circuit, but the court upheld the lower court's judgment.[b] The majority held that the first sale doctrine of the Copyright Act refers specifically to works that are manufactured in the United States. Therefore, the doctrine does not apply to textbooks printed and sold abroad, and then resold in the United States. Kirtsaeng appealed to the United States Supreme Court.

### The Supreme Court Weighs In

The Supreme Court had to decide this question: Can any copy of a book or CD or DVD that was legally produced abroad, acquired abroad, and then imported into the United States be resold in the United States without the copyright owner's permission? The answer to this question has implications for discount sellers, such as Costco, and online businesses, such as eBay and Google, all of which offer "good" prices on many products that were made abroad.

The Supreme Court ruled that in Kirtsaeng's favor, reversing the appellate court's decision.[c] The majority of the Court ruled that the first sale doctrine applies, even when the good was purchased abroad: " [T]he common-law history of the 'first-sale' doctrine . . . favors a non-geographical interpretation. We . . . doubt that Congress would have intended to create the practical copyright-related harms with which a geographical interpretation would threaten ordinary scholarly, artistic, commercial activities." As it turned out, much of the Court's decision concerned the potential consequences of what might occur if the Court did not reverse the appellate court's decision. Allowing that decision to stand would have meant that one "could prevent a buyer from domestically selling or even giving away copies of a video game made in Japan, a film made in Germany or a dress (with a design copyright) made in China."

### LEGAL CRITICAL THINKING
#### INSIGHT INTO THE SOCIAL ENVIRONMENT

*What options do textbook publishers face given this Supreme Court decision?*

---

a. *John Wiley & Sons, Inc. v. Kirtsaeng,* 93 U.S.P.Q.2d 1432 (S.D.N.Y. 2009).
b. *John Wiley & Sons, Inc. v. Kirtsaeng,* 654 F.3d 210 (2d Cir. 2011).
c. *Kirtsaeng v. John Wiley & Sons, Inc.,* ___ U.S. ___, 133 S.Ct. 1351, ___ L.Ed.2d ___ (2013).

---

such elements as the overall structure, sequence, and organization of a program.

Not all aspects of software are protected, however. Courts typically have not extended copyright protection to the "look and feel"—the general appearance, command structure, video images, menus, windows, and other screen displays—of computer programs. ▶ **Example 8.14** MiTek develops a software program for laying out wood trusses (used in construction). Another company comes out with a different program that includes similar elements, such as the menu and submenu command tree-structures. MiTek cannot successfully sue for copyright infringement because the command structure of software is not protected. ◄ (Note that copying the "look and feel" of another's product may be a violation of trade dress or trademark laws, however.)

As will be explored in Chapter 9, technology has vastly increased the potential for copyright infringement via the Internet.

# SECTION 4
# TRADE SECRETS

The law of trade secrets protects some business processes and information that are not, or cannot be, patented, copyrighted, or trademarked against appropriation by competitors. A **trade secret** is basically information of commercial value, such as customer lists, plans, and research and development. Trade secrets may also include pricing information, marketing methods, production techniques, and generally anything that makes an individual company unique and that would have value to a competitor.

Unlike copyright and trademark protection, protection of trade secrets extends both to ideas and to their expression. (For this reason, and because there are no registration or filing requirements for trade secrets, trade secret protection may be well suited for software.) Of course, the secret formula, method, or other information must be disclosed to some persons, particularly to key employees. Businesses generally attempt to protect their trade secrets by having all employees who use a process or information agree in their contracts, or in confidentiality agreements, never to divulge it.

## State and Federal
## Law on Trade Secrets

Under Section 757 of the *Restatement of Torts*, those who disclose or use another's trade secret, without authorization, are liable to that other party if:

1. They discovered the secret by improper means, or
2. Their disclosure or use constitutes a breach of a duty owed to the other party.

Stealing confidential business data by industrial espionage, such as by tapping into a competitor's computer, is a theft of trade secrets without any contractual violation and is actionable in itself.

Although trade secrets have long been protected under the common law, today most states' laws are based on the Uniform Trade Secrets Act,[28] which has been adopted in forty-seven states. Additionally, the Economic Espionage Act[29] (to be discussed in Chapter 10) makes the theft of trade secrets a federal crime.

## Trade Secrets in Cyberspace

Computer technology is undercutting many business firms' ability to protect their confidential information, including trade secrets. For example, a dishonest employee could e-mail trade secrets in a company's computer to a competitor or a future employer. If e-mail is not an option, the employee might walk out with the information on a flash drive.

A former employee's continued use of a Twitter account after leaving the company may provide grounds for a suit alleging misappropriation of trade secrets. ▶ **Case in Point 8.15** Noah Kravitz worked for a company called PhoneDog for four years as a product reviewer and video blogger. PhoneDog provided him with the Twitter account "@PhoneDog_Noah." Kravitz's popularity grew, and he had approximately 17,000 followers by the time he quit. PhoneDog requested that Kravitz stop using the Twitter account.

Although Kravitz changed his handle to "@noah kravitz," he continued to use the account. PhoneDog subsequently sued Kravitz for misappropriation of trade secrets, among other things. Kravitz moved for a dismissal, but the court found that the complaint adequately stated a cause of action for misappropriation of trade secrets and allowed the suit to continue.[30] ◄

For a comprehensive summary of trade secrets and the other forms of intellectual property discussed in this chapter, see Exhibit 8–1 on the following page.

# SECTION 5
# INTERNATIONAL PROTECTION
# FOR INTELLECTUAL PROPERTY

For many years, the United States has been a party to various international agreements relating to intellectual property rights. For instance, the Paris Convention of 1883, to which about 173 countries are signatory, allows parties in one country to file for

---

**28.** The Uniform Trade Secrets Act, as drafted by the National Conference of Commissioners on Uniform State Laws (NCCUSL), can be found at **uniformlaws.org**.

**29.** 18 U.S.C. Sections 1831–1839.

**30.** *PhoneDog v. Kravitz,* 2011 WL 5415612 (N.D.Cal. 2011). See also *Mintel Learning Technology, Inc. v. Ambrow Education Holding Ltd.,* 2012 WL 762126 (N.D.Cal. 2012).

**EXHIBIT 8-1  Forms of Intellectual Property**

| Form | Definition | How Acquired | Duration | Remedy for Infringement |
|------|-----------|-------------|----------|------------------------|
| **Patent** | A grant from the government that gives an inventor exclusive rights to an invention. | By filing a patent application with the U.S. Patent and Trademark Office and receiving its approval. | Twenty years from the date of the application; for design patents, fourteen years. | Monetary damages, including royalties and lost profits, *plus* attorneys' fees. Damages may be tripled for intentional infringements. |
| **Copyright** | The right of an author or originator of a literary or artistic work, or other production that falls within a specified category, to have the exclusive use of that work for a given period of time. | Automatic (once the work or creation is put in tangible form). Only the *expression* of an idea (and not the idea itself) can be protected by copyright. | For authors: the life of the author, plus 70 years.<br><br>For publishers: 95 years after the date of publication or 120 years after creation. | Actual damages plus profits received by the party who infringed *or* statutory damages under the Copyright Act, *plus* costs and attorneys' fees in either situation. |
| **Trademark (service mark and trade dress)** | Any distinctive word, name, symbol, or device (image or appearance), or combination thereof, that an entity uses to distinguish its goods or services from those of others. The owner has the exclusive right to use that mark or trade dress. | 1. At common law, ownership created by use of the mark. 2. Registration with the appropriate federal or state office gives notice and is permitted if the mark is currently in use or will be within the next six months. | Unlimited, as long as it is in use. To continue notice by registration, the owner must renew by filing between the fifth and sixth years, and thereafter, every ten years. | 1. Injunction prohibiting the future use of the mark. 2. Actual damages plus profits received by the party who infringed (can be increased under the Lanham Act). 3. Destruction of articles that infringed. 4. *Plus* costs and attorneys' fees. |
| **Trade Secret** | Any information that a business possesses and that gives the business an advantage over competitors (including formulas, lists, patterns, plans, processes, and programs). | Through the originality and development of the information and processes that constitute the business secret and are unknown to others. | Unlimited, so long as not revealed to others. Once revealed to others, it is no longer a trade secret. | Monetary damages for misappropriation (the Uniform Trade Secrets Act also permits punitive damages if willful), *plus* costs and attorneys' fees. |

patent and trademark protection in any of the other member countries. Other international agreements in this area include the Berne Convention, the Trade-Related Aspects of Intellectual Property Rights (known as the TRIPS agreement), the Madrid Protocol, and the Anti-Counterfeiting Trade Agreement.

## The Berne Convention

Under the Berne Convention of 1886, if a U.S. citizen writes a book, every country that has signed the convention must recognize the U.S. author's copyright in the book. Also, if a citizen of a country that has not signed the convention first publishes a book in one of the 165 countries that have signed, all other countries that have signed the convention must recognize that author's copyright. Copyright notice is not needed to gain protection under the Berne Convention for works published after March 1, 1989.

This convention and other international agreements have given some protection to intellectual property on a worldwide level. None of them, however, has been as significant and far reaching in scope as the TRIPS agreement, discussed in the next subsection.

In 2011, the European Union agreed to extend the period of royalty protection for musicians from fifty years to seventy years. This decision aids major record labels as well as performers and musicians who previously faced losing royalties from sales of their older recordings. The profits of musicians and record companies have been shrinking in recent years because of the sharp decline in sales of compact discs and the rise in illegal downloads.

In the following case, the United States Supreme Court had to decide if Congress had exceeded its authority under the U.S. Constitution when it enacted a law that restored copyright protection to many foreign works that were already in the public domain. (*Public domain* means that rights to certain intellectual property, such as songs and other published works, belong to everyone and are not protected by copyright or patent laws.)

## CASE 8.3

### Golan v. Holder

Supreme Court of the United States, ___ U.S. ___, 132 S.Ct. 873, 181 L.Ed.2d 835 (2012).

**BACKGROUND AND FACTS** The United States joined the Berne Convention in 1989, but it failed to give foreign copyright holders the same protections enjoyed by U.S. authors. Contrary to the Berne Convention, the United States did not protect any foreign work that had already entered the public domain.

In 1994, Congress enacted the Uruguay Round Agreements Act (URAA), which "restored" copyright protection for many foreign works that were already in the public domain. The URAA put foreign and domestic works on the same footing, allowing their copyrights to extend for the same number of years. Lawrence Golan, along with a group of musicians, conductors, and publishers, filed a suit against Eric Holder, in his capacity as the U.S. attorney general. These individuals had enjoyed free access to foreign works in the public domain before the URAA's enactment. They claimed that the URAA violated the copyright clause of the U.S. Constitution and thus that Congress had exceeded its constitutional authority in passing the URAA.

A federal appellate court held that Congress did not violate the copyright clause by passing the URAA. The petitioners appealed. The United States Supreme Court granted *certiorari* to resolve the matter.

**DECISION AND RATIONALE** The United States Supreme Court affirmed the judgment of the federal appellate court. The copyright clause empowers Congress "to promote the Progress of Science . . . by securing for limited Times to Authors . . . the exclusive Right to their Writings." The Supreme Court concluded that Congress is not barred from protecting works in the public domain simply because a copyright must exist for only a "limited time." The Court relied heavily on the precedent set by its decision in an earlier case in which it held that Congress did not violate the copyright clause by extending existing copyrights by twenty years.[a] In that case, the Court declined to interpret the text of the copyright clause as requiring that a "time prescription, once set, becomes forever 'fixed' or 'inalterable.'"

The Court held that in passing the Uruguay Round Agreements Act (URAA), Congress did not create perpetual copyrights. Therefore, the URAA does not violate the copyright clause. Thus, Golan and others could no longer use, without permission, any of the foreign works that were previously in the public domain. In effect, the URAA took those works out of the public domain and extended copyright protection to them. U.S. copyright and patent laws now cover all such foreign intellectual property.

**THE GLOBAL DIMENSION** *What does the Court's decision in this case mean for copyright holders in the United States who want copyright protection in other countries? Will other nations be more or less inclined to protect U.S. authors? Explain.*

**THE ECONOMIC DIMENSION** *Why did a group of musicians, conductors, publishers, and others file this suit? What did they hope to gain by a decision in their favor?*

---

**a.** See *Eldred v. Ashcroft,* 537 U.S. 186, 123 S.Ct. 769, 154 L.Ed.2d 683 (2003).

# The TRIPS Agreement

Representatives from more than one hundred nations signed the TRIPS agreement in 1994. The agreement established, for the first time, standards for the international protection of intellectual property rights, including patents, trademarks, and copyrights for movies, computer programs, books, and music. The TRIPS agreement provides that each member country of the World Trade Organization must include in its domestic laws broad intellectual property rights and effective remedies (including civil and criminal penalties) for violations of those rights.

Generally, the TRIPS agreement forbids member nations from discriminating against foreign owners of intellectual property rights (in the administration, regulation, or adjudication of such rights). In other words, a member nation cannot give its own nationals (citizens) favorable treatment without offering the same treatment to nationals of all other member countries. ▶ **Example 8.16**  A U.S. software manufacturer brings a suit for the infringement of intellectual property rights under Germany's national laws. Because Germany is a member of the TRIPS agreement, the U.S. manufacturer is entitled to receive the same treatment as a German manufacturer. ◀

Each member nation must also ensure that legal procedures are available for parties who wish to bring actions for infringement of intellectual property rights. Additionally, a related document established a mechanism for settling disputes among member nations.

# The Madrid Protocol

In the past, one of the difficulties in protecting U.S. trademarks internationally was the time and expense required to apply for trademark registration in foreign countries. The filing fees and procedures for trademark registration vary significantly among individual countries. The Madrid Protocol, which was signed into law in 2003, may help to resolve these problems.

The Madrid Protocol is an international treaty that has been signed by eighty-six countries. Under its provisions, a U.S. company wishing to register its trademark abroad can submit a single application and designate other member countries in which the company would like to register its mark. The treaty was designed to reduce the costs of international trademark protection by more than 60 percent.

Although the Madrid Protocol may simplify and reduce the cost of trademark registration in foreign countries, it remains to be seen whether it will provide significant benefits to trademark owners. Even with an easier registration process, there are still questions as to whether all member countries will enforce the law and protect the mark.

# The Anti-Counterfeiting Trade Agreement

In 2011 Australia, Canada, Japan, Korea, Morocco, New Zealand, Singapore, and the United States signed the Anti-Counterfeiting Trade Agreement (ACTA), an international treaty to combat global counterfeiting and piracy. The members of the European Union, Mexico, Switzerland, and other nations that support ACTA are still developing domestic procedures to comply with its provisions. Once a nation has adopted appropriate procedures, it can ratify the treaty.

**PROVISIONS AND GOALS**  The goals of the treaty are to increase international cooperation, facilitate the best law enforcement practices, and provide a legal framework to combat counterfeiting. The treaty will have its own governing body.

ACTA applies not only to counterfeit physical goods, such as medications, but also to pirated copyrighted works being distributed via the Internet. The idea is to create a new standard of enforcement for intellectual property rights that goes beyond the TRIPS agreement and encourages international cooperation and information sharing among signatory countries.

**BORDER SEARCHES**  Under ACTA, member nations are required to establish border measures that allow officials, on their own initiative, to search commercial shipments of imports and exports for counterfeit goods. The treaty neither requires nor prohibits random border searches of electronic devices, such as laptops, tablet devices, and smartphones, for infringing content. If border authorities reasonably believe that any goods in transit are counterfeit, the treaty allows them to keep the suspect goods unless the owner proves that the items are authentic and noninfringing.

The treaty allows member nations, in accordance with their own laws, to order online service providers to furnish information about (including the identity of) suspected trademark and copyright infringers.

## Reviewing: Intellectual Property Rights

Two computer science majors, Trent and Xavier, have an idea for a new video game, which they propose to call "Hallowed." They form a business and begin developing their idea. Several months later, Trent and Xavier run into a problem with their design and consult a friend, Brad, who is an expert in designing computer source codes. After the software is completed but before Hallowed is marketed, a video game called Halo 2 is released for both the Xbox and the Playstation systems. Halo 2 uses source codes similar to those of Hallowed and imitates Hallowed's overall look and feel, although not all the features are alike. Using the information presented in the chapter, answer the following questions.

1. Would the name *Hallowed* receive protection as a trademark or as trade dress? Explain.
2. If Trent and Xavier had obtained a patent on Hallowed, would the release of Halo 2 have infringed on their patent? Why or why not?
3. Based only on the facts described above, could Trent and Xavier sue the makers of Halo 2 for copyright infringement? Why or why not?
4. Suppose that Trent and Xavier discover that Brad took the idea of Hallowed and sold it to the company that produced Halo 2. Which type of intellectual property issue does this raise?

**DEBATE THIS . . .** *Congress has amended copyright law several times so that copyright holders now have protection for many decades. Was Congress right in extending these copyright time periods?*

## Terms and Concepts

certification mark 148

collective mark 148

copyright 151

dilution 145

intellectual property 144

license 149

patent 149

service mark 147

trade dress 148

trade name 149

trade secret 156

trademark 144

## Issue Spotters

1. Roslyn is a food buyer for Organic Cornucopia Food Company when she decides to go into business for herself as Roslyn's Kitchen. She contacts Organic's suppliers, offering to buy their entire harvest for the next year, and Organic's customers, offering to sell her products for less than her ex-employer. Has Roslyn violated any of the intellectual property rights discussed in this chapter? Explain. **(See page 156.)**

2. Global Products develops, patents, and markets software. World Copies, Inc., sells Global's software without the maker's permission. Is this patent infringement? If so, how might Global save the cost of suing World for infringement and at the same time profit from World's sales? **(See page 150.)**

• **Check your answers to the Issue Spotters against the answers provided in Appendix E at the end of this text.**

## Business Scenarios

**8–1. Fair Use.** Professor Wise is teaching a summer seminar in business torts at State University. Several times during the course, he makes copies of relevant sections from business law texts and distributes them to his students. Wise does not realize that the daughter of one of the textbook authors is a member of his seminar. She tells her father about Wise's copying activities, which have taken place without her father's or his publisher's permission. Her father sues Wise for copyright infringement. Wise claims protection under the fair use doctrine. Who will prevail? Explain. **(See page 154.)**

**8–2. Patent Infringement.** John and Andrew Doney invented a hard-bearing device for balancing rotors. Although they obtained a patent for their invention from the U.S. Patent and Trademark Office, it was never used as

an automobile wheel balancer. Some time later, Exetron Corp. produced an automobile wheel balancer that used a hard-bearing device with a support plate similar to that of the Doneys' device. Given that the Doneys had not used their device for automobile wheel balancing, does Exetron's use of a similar device infringe on the Doneys' patent? Why or why not? **(See page 150.)**

## Business Case Problems

**8–3. Trade Secrets.** Briefing.com offers Internet-based analyses of investment opportunities to investors. Richard Green is the company's president. One of Briefing.com's competitors is StreetAccount, LLC (limited liability company), whose owners include Gregory Jones and Cynthia Dietzmann. Jones worked for Briefing.com for six years until he quit in March 2003 and was a member of its board of directors until April 2003. Dietzmann worked for Briefing.com for seven years until she quit in March 2003. As Briefing.com employees, Jones and Dietzmann had access to confidential business data. For instance, Dietzmann developed a list of contacts through which Briefing.com obtained market information to display online. When Dietzmann quit, she did not return all of the contact information to the company. Briefing.com and Green filed a suit in a federal district court against Jones, Dietzmann, and StreetAccount, alleging that they had appropriated these data and other "trade secrets" to form a competing business. What are trade secrets? Why are they protected? Under what circumstances is a party liable at common law for their appropriation? How should these principles apply in this case? [*Briefing.com v. Jones*, 2006 WY 16, 126 P.3d 928 (2006)] **(See page 156.)**

**8–4. Licensing.** Redwin Wilchcombe composed, performed, and recorded a song called *Tha Weedman* at the request of Lil Jon, a member of Lil Jon & the East Side Boyz (LJESB), for LJESB's album *Kings of Crunk*. Wilchcombe was not paid, but was given credit on the album as a producer. After the album had sold 2 million copies, Wilchcombe filed a suit against LJESB, alleging copyright infringement. The defendants claimed that they had a license to use the song. Do the facts support this claim? Explain. [*Wilchcombe v. TeeVee Toons, Inc.*, 555 F.3d 949 (11th Cir. 2009)] **(See page 149.)**

**8–5. BUSINESS CASE PROBLEM WITH SAMPLE ANSWER: Trade Secrets.**

 *Jesse Edwards, an employee of Carbon Processing and Reclamation, LLC (CPR), put unmarked boxes of company records in his car. Edwards's wife, Channon, who suspected him of hiding financial information from her, gained access to the documents. William Jones, the owner of CPR, filed a suit, contending that Channon's unauthorized access to the files was a theft of trade se-*

*crets. Could the information in the documents be trade secrets? Should liability be imposed? Why or why not?* [Jones v. Hamilton, 53 So.3d 134 (Ala.Civ.App. 2010)] **(See page 156.)**

• **For a sample answer to Problem 8–5, go to Appendix F at the end of this text.**

**8–6. Spotlight on Macy's—Copyright Infringement.** United  Fabrics International, Inc., bought a fabric design from an Italian designer and registered a copyright to it with the U.S. Copyright Office. When Macy's, Inc., began selling garments with a similar design, United filed a copyright infringement suit against Macy's. Macy's argued that United did not own a valid copyright to the design and so could not claim infringement. Does United have to prove that the copyright is valid to establish infringement? Explain. [*United Fabrics International, Inc. v. C&J Wear, Inc.*, 630 F.3d 1255 (9th Cir. 2011)] **(See page 152.)**

**8–7. Theft of Trade Secrets.** Hanjuan Jin, a citizen of the People's Republic of China, began working at Motorola in 1998. She worked as a software engineer in a division that created proprietary standards for cellular communications. In 2004 and 2005, contrary to Motorola's policies, Jin also began working as a consultant for Lemko Corp. Lemko introduced Jin to Sun Kaisens, a Chinese software company. During 2005, Jin returned to Beijing on several occasions and began working with Sun Kaisens and with the Chinese military. The following year, she started corresponding with Sun Kaisens's management about a possible full-time job in China. During this period, she took several medical leaves of absence from Motorola. In February 2007, after one of these medical leaves, she returned to Motorola.

During the next several days at Motorola, she accessed and downloaded thousands of documents on her personal laptop as well as on pen drives. On the following day, she attempted to board a flight to China but was randomly searched by U.S. Customs and Border Protection officials at Chicago's O'Hare International Airport. Ultimately, U.S. officials discovered the downloaded Motorola documents. Are there any circumstances under which Jin could avoid being prosecuted for theft of trade secrets? If so, what are these circumstances? Discuss fully. [*United States v. Hanjuan Jin*, 833 F.Supp.2d 977 (N.D.Ill. 2012)] **(See page 156.)**

**8–8. Copyright Infringement.** SilverEdge Systems Software hired Catherine Conrad to perform a singing telegram. SilverEdge arranged for James Bendewald to record Conrad's performance of her copyrighted song to post on its Web site. Conrad agreed to wear a microphone to assist in the recording, told Bendewald what to film, and asked for an additional fee only if SilverEdge used the video for a commercial purpose. Later, the company chose to post a video of a different performer's singing telegram instead. Conrad filed a suit in a federal district court against SilverEdge and Bendewald for copyright infringement. Are the defendants liable? Explain. [*Conrad v. Bendewald,* 2013 WL 310194 (7th Cir. 2013)] **(See page 152.)**

**8–9. A QUESTION OF ETHICS: Copyright Infringement.**

 *Custom Copies, Inc., prepares and sells course-packs, which contain compilations of readings for college courses. A teacher selects the readings and delivers a syllabus to the copy shop, which obtains the materials from a library, copies them, and binds the copies. Blackwell Publishing, Inc., which owns the copyright to some of the materials, filed a suit, alleging copyright infringement.* [Blackwell Publishing, Inc. v. Custom Copies, Inc., *2006 WL 1529503 (N.D.Fla. 2006)]* **(See page 152.)**

(a) Custom Copies argued, in part, that creating and selling did not "distribute" the coursepacks. Does a copy shop violate copyright law if it only copies materials for coursepacks? Does the copying fall under the "fair use" exception? Should the court grant the defendant's motion? Why or why not?

(b) What is the potential impact if copies of a book or journal are created and sold without the permission of, and the payment of royalties or a fee to, the copyright owner? Explain.

## Legal Reasoning Group Activity

**8–10. Patents.** After years of research, your company develops a product that might revolutionize the green (environmentally conscious) building industry. The product is made from relatively inexpensive and widely available materials combined in a unique way that can substantially lower the heating and cooling costs of residential and commercial buildings. The company has registered the trademark it intends to use on the product, and has filed a patent application with the U.S. Patent and Trademark Office. **(See page 149.)**

(a) One group should provide three reasons why this product does or does not qualify for patent protection.

(b) Another group should develop a four-step procedure for how your company can best protect its intellectual property rights (trademark, trade secret, and patent) and prevent domestic and foreign competitors from producing counterfeit goods or cheap knockoffs.

(c) Another group should list and explain three ways your company can utilize licensing.

# CHAPTER 9

# INTERNET LAW, SOCIAL MEDIA, AND PRIVACY

The Internet has changed our lives and our laws. Technology has put the world at our fingertips and now allows even the smallest business to reach customers around the globe. At the same time, the Internet presents a variety of challenges for the law. Courts are often in uncharted waters when deciding disputes that involve the Internet, social media, and online privacy. There may not be any common law precedents for judges to rely on when resolving a case. Long-standing principles of justice may be inapplicable. New rules are evolving, as we discuss in this chapter, but often not as quickly as technology.

## SECTION 1
## INTERNET LAW

A number of laws specifically address issues that arise only on the Internet. Three such issues are unsolicited e-mail, domain names, and cybersquatting, as we discuss here. We also discuss how the law is dealing with problems of trademark infringement and dilution online.

### Spam

Businesses and individuals alike are targets of **spam.**[1] Spam is the unsolicited "junk e-mail" that floods virtual mailboxes with advertisements, solicitations, and other messages. Considered relatively harmless in the early days of the Internet, by 2013 spam accounted for roughly 75 percent of all e-mails.

**STATE REGULATION OF SPAM** In an attempt to combat spam, thirty-six states have enacted laws that prohibit or regulate its use. Many state laws that regulate spam require the senders of e-mail ads to instruct the recipients on how they can "opt out" of further e-mail ads from the same sources. For instance, in some states, an unsolicited e-mail must include a toll-free phone number or return e-mail address that the recipient can use to ask the sender to send no more unsolicited e-mails.

**THE FEDERAL CAN-SPAM ACT** In 2003, Congress enacted the Controlling the Assault of Non-Solicited Pornography and Marketing (CAN-SPAM) Act.[2] The legislation applies to any "commercial electronic mail messages" that are sent to promote a commercial product or service. Significantly, the statute preempts state antispam laws except for those provisions in state laws that prohibit false and deceptive e-mailing practices.

Generally, the act permits the sending of unsolicited commercial e-mail but prohibits certain types of spamming activities. Prohibited activities include the use of a false return address and the use of false, misleading, or deceptive information when sending e-mail. The statute also prohibits the use of "dictionary attacks"—sending messages to randomly generated e-mail addresses—and the "harvesting" of e-mail addresses from Web sites through the use of specialized software.

▶ **Example 9.1** Federal officials arrested Robert Alan Soloway, considered to be one of the world's most prolific spammers. Soloway, known as the "Spam King," had been using *botnets* (automated spamming networks) to send out hundreds of millions of unwanted e-mails. In 2008, Soloway pleaded guilty to mail fraud, spam, and failure to pay taxes. ◀

Arresting prolific spammers, however, has done little to curb spam, which continues to flow at a rate of 70 billion messages per day.

**THE U.S. SAFE WEB ACT** After the CAN-SPAM Act of 2003 prohibited false and deceptive e-mails originating in the United States, spamming from servers

---

**1.** The term *spam* is said to come from the lyrics of a Monty Python song that repeats the word *spam* over and over.

**2.** 15 U.S.C. Sections 7701 *et seq.*

located in other nations increased. These cross-border spammers generally were able to escape detection and legal sanctions because the Federal Trade Commission (FTC) lacked the authority to investigate foreign spamming.

Congress sought to rectify the situation by enacting the U.S. Safe Web Act (also known as the Undertaking Spam, Spyware, and Fraud Enforcement with Enforcers Beyond Borders Act).[3] The act allows the FTC to cooperate and share information with foreign agencies in investigating and prosecuting those involved in spamming, spyware, and various Internet frauds and deceptions.

The Safe Web Act also provides a "safe harbor" for **Internet service providers (ISPs)**—that is, organizations that provide access to the Internet. The safe harbor gives ISPs immunity from liability for supplying information to the FTC concerning possible unfair or deceptive conduct in foreign jurisdictions.

## Domain Names

As e-commerce expanded worldwide, one issue that emerged involved the rights of a trademark owner to use the mark as part of a domain name. A **domain name** is part of an Internet address, such as "**cengage.com**."

**STRUCTURE OF DOMAIN NAMES** Every domain name ends with a generic top-level domain (TLD), which is the part of the name to the right of the period that often indicates the type of entity that operates the site. For instance, *com* is an abbreviation for *commercial,* and *edu* is short for *education.*

The second-level domain (SLD)—the part of the name to the left of the period—is chosen by the business entity or individual registering the domain name. Competition for SLDs among firms with similar names and products has led to numerous disputes. By using an identical or similar domain name, parties have attempted to profit from a competitor's **goodwill** (the nontangible value of a business). For instance, a party might use a similar domain name to sell pornography, offer for sale another party's domain name, or otherwise infringe on others' trademarks.

**DISTRIBUTION SYSTEM** The Internet Corporation for Assigned Names and Numbers (ICANN), a nonprofit corporation, oversees the distribution of domain names and operates an online arbitration system. Due

to numerous complaints, ICANN completely overhauled the domain name distribution system.

In 2012, ICANN started selling new generic top-level domain names (gTLDs) for an initial price of $185,000 plus an annual fee of $25,000. Whereas TLDs were limited to only a few terms (such as "com," "net," and "org"), gTLDs can take any form. By 2013, many companies and corporations had acquired gTLDs based on their brands, such as .aol, .bmw, .canon, .gap, .target, .toyota, and .walmart. Some companies have numerous gTLDs. Google's gTLDs, for instance, include .android, .chrome, .gmail, .goog, and .YouTube.

## Cybersquatting

One of the goals of the new gTLD system is to alleviate the problem of *cybersquatting*. **Cybersquatting** occurs when a person registers a domain name that is the same as, or confusingly similar to, the trademark of another and then offers to sell the domain name back to the trademark owner.

▶ **Case in Point 9.2** Apple, Inc., has repeatedly sued cybersquatters that registered domain names similar to its products, such as iphone4s.com and ipods.com. In 2012, Apple won a judgment in litigation at the World Intellectual Property Organization (WIPO—see Chapter 24) against a company that was squatting on the domain name iPhone5.com.[4] ◀

**ANTICYBERSQUATTING LEGISLATION** Because cybersquatting has led to so much litigation, Congress enacted the Anticybersquatting Consumer Protection Act (ACPA),[5] which amended the Lanham Act—the federal law protecting trademarks, discussed in Chapter 8. The ACPA makes cybersquatting illegal when both of the following are true:

1. The name is identical or confusingly similar to the trademark of another.
2. The one registering, trafficking in, or using the domain name has a "bad faith intent" to profit from that trademark.

**THE ONGOING PROBLEM OF CYBERSQUATTING** Despite the ACPA, cybersquatting continues to present a problem for businesses, largely because more TLDs and gTLDs are now available and many more companies are registering domain names. Indeed, domain name registrars have proliferated. Registrar compa-

---

3. Pub. L. No. 109-455, 120 Stat. 3372 (2006), codified in various sections of 15 U.S.C. and 12 U.S.C. Section 3412.

4. WIPO Case No. D2012-0951.
5. 15 U.S.C. Section 1129.

nies charge a fee to businesses and individuals to register new names and to renew annual registrations (often through automated software). Many of these companies also buy and sell expired domain names.

All domain name registrars are supposed to relay information about these transactions to ICANN and other companies that keep a master list of domain names, but this does not always occur. The speed at which domain names change hands and the difficulty in tracking mass automated registrations have created an environment where cybersquatting can flourish.

▶ **Case in Point 9.3**  OnNet USA, Inc., owns the English-language rights to 9Dragons, a game with a martial arts theme, and operates a Web site for its promotion. When a party known as "Warv0x" began to operate a pirated version of the game at Play9D. com, OnNet filed an action under the ACPA in a federal court. OnNet was unable to obtain contact information for the owner of Play9D.com through its Australian domain name registrar, however, and thus could not complete service of process (see Chapter 3). Therefore, the federal court allowed OnNet to serve the defendant by publishing a notice of the suit in a newspaper in Gold Coast, Australia.[6] ◀

**TYPOSQUATTING**  Cybersquatters have also developed new tactics, such as **typosquatting,** or registering a name that is a misspelling of a popular brand, such as googl.com or appple.com. Because many Internet users are not perfect typists, Web pages using these misspelled names receive a lot of traffic.

More traffic generally means increased profit (advertisers often pay Web sites based on the number of unique visits, or hits), which in turn provides incentive for more cybersquatters. Also, if the misspelling is significant, the trademark owner may have difficulty proving that the name is identical or confusingly similar to the trademark of another as the ACPA requires.

Cybersquatting is costly for businesses, which must attempt to register all variations of a name to protect their domain name rights from would-be cybersquatters and typosquatters. Large corporations may have to register thousands of domain names across the globe just to protect their basic brands and trademarks.

**APPLICABILITY AND SANCTIONS OF THE ACPA**  The ACPA applies to all domain name registrations of

trademarks. Successful plaintiffs in suits brought under the act can collect actual damages and profits, or they can elect to receive statutory damages ranging from $1,000 to $100,000.

Although some companies have been successful suing under the ACPA, there are roadblocks to pursuing such lawsuits. Some domain name registrars offer privacy services that hide the true owners of Web sites, making it difficult for trademark owners to identify cybersquatters. Thus, before bringing a suit, a trademark owner has to ask the court for a subpoena to discover the identity of the owner of the infringing Web site. Because of the high costs of court proceedings, discovery, and even arbitration, many disputes over cybersquatting are settled out of court.

## Meta Tags

Search engines compile their results by looking through a Web site's key-word field. As noted in Chapter 4, *meta tags* are key words that are inserted into the HTML (hypertext markup language) code to tell Internet browsers specific information about a Web page. Meta tags increase the likelihood that a site will be included in search engine results, even though the site may have nothing to do with the key words. Using this same technique, one site may appropriate the key words of other sites with more frequent hits so that the appropriating site will appear in the same search engine results as the more popular sites.

Using another's trademark in a meta tag without the owner's permission, however, normally constitutes trademark infringement. Some uses of another's trademark as a meta tag may be permissible if the use is reasonably necessary and does not suggest that the owner authorized or sponsored the use.

▶ **Case in Point 9.4**  Farzad and Lisa Tabari are auto brokers—the personal shoppers of the automotive world. They contact authorized dealers, solicit bids, and arrange for customers to buy from the dealer offering the best combination of location, availability, and price. The Tabaris offered this service at the Web sites **buy-a-lexus.com** and **buyorleaselexus.com**. Toyota Motor Sales U.S.A., Inc., the exclusive distributor of Lexus vehicles and the owner of the Lexus mark, objected to the Tabaris' practices. The Tabaris removed Toyota's photographs and logo from their site and added a disclaimer in large type at the top, but they refused to give up their domain names. Toyota sued for infringement. The court forced the Tabaris to stop using any "domain name, service mark, trademark,

---

6. *OnNet USA, Inc. v. Play9D.com,* ___ F.Supp.2d ___, 2013 WL 120319 (N.D.Cal. 2013).

trade name, meta tag or other commercial indication of origin that includes the mark LEXUS."[7] ◄

## Trademark Dilution in the Online World

As discussed in Chapter 8, trademark *dilution* occurs when a trademark is used, without authorization, in a way that diminishes the distinctive quality of the mark.

---

7. *Toyota Motor Sales, U.S.A., Inc. v. Tabari*, 610 F.3d 171 (9th Cir. 2011).

Unlike trademark infringement, a claim of dilution does not require proof that consumers are likely to be confused by a connection between the unauthorized use and the mark. For this reason, the products involved need not be similar, as the following *Spotlight Case* illustrates.

## SP⬤TLIGHT on Internet Porn

### Case 9.1   Hasbro, Inc. v. Internet Entertainment Group, Ltd.

United States District Court, Western District of Washington, ___ F.Supp.2d ___ (1996).

**BACKGROUND AND FACTS**   In 1949, Hasbro, Inc.—then known as the Milton Bradley Company—published its first version of Candy Land, a children's board game. Hasbro is the owner of the trademark "Candy Land," which has been registered with the U.S. Patent and Trademark Office since 1951. Over the years, Hasbro has produced several versions of the game, including Candy Land puzzles, a travel version, a computer game, and a handheld electronic version. In the mid-1990s, Brian Cartmell and his employer, the Internet Entertainment Group, Ltd., used the term *candyland.com* as a domain name for a sexually explicit Internet site. Anyone who performed an online search using the word *candyland* was directed to this adult Web site. Hasbro filed a trademark dilution claim in a federal court, seeking a permanent injunction to prevent the defendants from using the Candy Land trademark.

**DECISION AND RATIONALE**   The federal district court granted Hasbro a permanent injunction and ordered the defendants to remove all content from the *candyland.com* Web site and to stop using the Candyland mark. Hasbro had shown that the defendants' use of the Candyland mark and the domain name *candyland.com* in connection with their Internet site was causing irreparable injury to Hasbro. As required to obtain an injunction, Hasbro had demonstrated a likelihood of prevailing on its claims that the defendants' conduct violated both the federal and the Washington State statutes against trademark dilution. "The probable harm to Hasbro from defendants' conduct outweighs any inconvenience that defendants will experience if they are required to stop using the CANDYLAND name."

**THE ECONOMIC DIMENSION**   *How can companies protect themselves from others who create Web sites that have similar domain names, and what limits each company's ability to be fully protected?*

**WHAT IF THE FACTS WERE DIFFERENT?**   *Suppose that the site using* candyland.com *had not been sexually explicit but had sold candy. Would the result have been the same? Explain.*

---

## Licensing

Recall from Chapter 8 that a company may permit another party to use a trademark (or other intellectual property) under a license. A licensor might grant a license allowing its trademark to be used as part of a domain name, for example.

Indeed, licensing is ubiquitous in the online world. When you download an application on your smartphone, tablet, or other mobile device, for instance, you are typically entering into to a license agreement. You are obtaining only a *license* to use that app and not ownership rights in it. Apps published on Google Play, for instance, may use its licensing service to prompt users to agree to a license at the time of installation and use.

Licensing agreements frequently include restrictions that prohibit licensees from sharing the file and using it to create similar software applications. The license may also limit the use of the application to a specific device or give permission to the user for a certain time period. For further discussion of licensing and e-contracts, see Chapter 12.

### SECTION 2
# COPYRIGHTS IN DIGITAL INFORMATION

Copyright law is probably the most important form of intellectual property protection on the Internet. This is because much of the material on the Internet (including software and database information) is copyrighted, and in order to transfer that material online, it must be "copied." Generally, whenever a party downloads software or music into a computer's random access memory, or RAM, without authorization, a copyright is infringed. Technology has vastly increased the potential for copyright infringement.

▶ **Case in Point 9.5**   In one case, a rap song that was included in the sound track of a movie had used only a few seconds from the guitar solo of another's copyrighted sound recording without permission. Nevertheless, a federal court held that digitally sampling a copyrighted sound recording of any length constitutes copyright infringement.[8] ◀

Some other federal courts have not found that digital sampling is always illegal. Some courts have allowed the defense of fair use (see Chapter 8), while others have not. ▶ **Example 9.6**   Hip hop stars Jay-Z and Kanye West were sued for digitally sampling music by soul musician Syl Johnson. Given the uncertain outcome of the litigation, they ended up settling the suit in 2012 for an undisclosed amount. ◀

Initially, criminal penalties for copyright violations could be imposed only if unauthorized copies were exchanged for financial gain. Yet much piracy of copyrighted materials online was "altruistic" in nature—unauthorized copies were made simply to be shared with others. Then, Congress amended the law and extended criminal liability for the piracy of copyrighted materials to persons who exchange unauthorized copies of copyrighted works without realizing a profit.

## Digital Millennium Copyright Act

In 1998, Congress passed further legislation to protect copyright holders—the Digital Millennium Copyright Act (DMCA).[9] The DMCA gave significant protection to owners of copyrights in digital information. Among other things, the act established civil and criminal penalties for anyone who circumvents (bypasses) encryption software or other technological antipiracy protection. Also prohibited are the manufacture, import, sale, and distribution of devices or services for circumvention.

The DMCA provides for exceptions to fit the needs of libraries, scientists, universities, and others. In general, the law does not restrict the "fair use" of circumvention methods for educational and other noncommercial purposes. For instance, circumvention is allowed to test computer security, to conduct encryption research, to protect personal privacy, and to enable parents to monitor their children's use of the Internet. The exceptions are to be reconsidered every three years.

The DMCA also limits the liability of Internet service providers (ISPs). Under the act, an ISP is not liable for copyright infringement by its customer *unless* the ISP is aware of the subscriber's violation. An ISP may be held liable only if it fails to take action to shut down the subscriber after learning of the violation. A copyright holder must act promptly, however, by pursuing a claim in court, or the subscriber has the right to be restored to online access.

## MP3 and File-Sharing Technology

Soon after the Internet became popular, a few enterprising programmers created software to compress large data files, particularly those associated with music. The best-known compression and decompression system is MP3, which enables music fans to download songs or entire CDs onto their computers or onto portable listening devices, such as iPods. The MP3 system also made it possible for music fans to access other fans' files by engaging in file-sharing via the Internet.

**METHODS OF FILE-SHARING**   File-sharing is accomplished through **peer-to-peer (P2P) networking.** The concept is simple. Rather than going through a central Web server, P2P networking uses numerous personal computers (PCs) that are connected to

---

**8.** *Bridgeport Music, Inc. v. Dimension Films,* 410 F.3d 792 (6th Cir. 2005).

**9.** 17 U.S.C. Sections 512, 1201–1205, 1301–1332; and 28 U.S.C. Section 4001.

the Internet. Individuals on the same network can access files stored on one another's PCs through a **distributed network.** Parts of the network may be distributed all over the country or the world, which offers an unlimited number of uses. Persons scattered throughout the country or the world can work together on the same project by using file-sharing programs.

A newer method of sharing files via the Internet is called **cloud computing,** which is essentially a subscription-based or pay-per-use service that extends a computer's software or storage capabilities. Cloud computing can deliver a single application through a browser to multiple users. Alternatively, cloud computing might be a utility program to pool resources and provide data storage and virtual servers that can be accessed on demand. Amazon, Facebook, Google, IBM, and Sun Microsystems are using and developing more cloud computing services.

**SHARING STORED MUSIC FILES** When file-sharing is used to download others' stored music files, copyright issues arise. Recording artists and their labels stand to lose large amounts of royalties and revenues if relatively few digital downloads or CDs are purchased and then made available on distributed networks. Anyone can get the music for free on these networks.

▶ **Case in Point 9.7** The issue of file-sharing infringement has been the subject of an ongoing debate since the highly publicized cases against two companies (Napster, Inc. and Grokster, Ltd.) that created software used for copyright infringement. In the first case, Napster operated a Web site with free software that enabled users to copy and transfer MP3 files via the Internet. Firms in the recording industry sued Napster. Ultimately, the court held that Napster was liable for contributory and vicarious[10] (indirect) copyright infringement.

As technology evolved, Grokster, Ltd., and several other companies created and distributed new types of file-sharing software. This software did not maintain a central index of content, but allowed P2P network users to share stored music files. The court held that because the companies distributed file-sharing software "with the object of promoting its use to infringe the copyright," they were liable for the resulting acts of infringement by the software's users.[11] ◀

In the following case, a group of recording companies sued an Internet user who had downloaded a number of copyrighted songs from the Internet. The user then shared the audio files with others via a P2P network. One of the issues before the court was whether the user was an "innocent infringer." In other words, was she innocent of copyright infringement because she was unaware that the works were copyrighted?

---

**10.** *Vicarious (indirect) liability* exists when one person is subject to liability for another's actions. A common example occurs in the employment context, when an employer is held vicariously liable by third parties for torts committed by employees in the course of their employment.

**11.** *A&M Records, Inc. v. Napster, Inc.,* 239 F.3d 1004 (9th Cir. 2001); and *Metro-Goldwyn-Mayer Studios, Inc. v. Grokster, Ltd.,* 545 U.S. 913, 125 S.Ct. 2764, 162 L.Ed.2d 781 (2005). Grokster, Ltd., later settled this dispute out of court and stopped distributing its software.

## CASE 9.2

### Maverick Recording Co. v. Harper
United States Court of Appeals, Fifth Circuit, 598 F.3d 193 (2010).

**COMPANY PROFILE** Recording star Madonna, others in the music business, and Time Warner created Maverick Records in 1992. Initially, the company saw great success with Alanis Morissette, The Prodigy, Candlebox, and the Deftones. It also created the sound track for the movie *The Matrix.* In a dispute over management of the company, Madonna and another co-owner were bought out. Today, Maverick is a wholly owned subsidiary of Warner Music Group.

**BACKGROUND AND FACTS** Maverick Recording Company and several other music-recording firms (the plaintiffs) hired MediaSentry to investigate the infringement of their copyrights over the Internet. During its investigation, MediaSentry discovered that Whitney Harper was using a file-sharing program to share digital audio files with other users of a peer-to-peer network. The shared audio files included a number of the plaintiffs' copyrighted works. The plaintiffs brought an action in a federal court against Harper for copyright infringement. They sought $750 per infringed work, the minimum amount of damages set forth in Section 504(c)(1) of the Copyright Act.

CASE 9.2 CONTINUED      Harper asserted that her infringement was "innocent" and that therefore Section 504(c)(2) of the Copyright Act should apply. That section provides that when an infringer was not aware, and had no reason to believe, that his or her acts constituted copyright infringement, "the court in its discretion may reduce the award of statutory damages to a sum of not less than $200." The trial court granted summary judgment for the plaintiffs on the issue of copyright infringement and enjoined Harper from further downloading and sharing of copyrighted works. The court, however, awarded the plaintiffs only $200 for each infringed work. Both parties appealed. Harper claimed that there was insufficient evidence of copyright infringement. The plaintiffs argued that the district court had erred by failing to rule out the innocent infringer defense as a matter of law.

**DECISION AND RATIONALE**  The U.S. Court of Appeals for the Fifth Circuit affirmed the trial court's finding of copyright liability and reversed its finding that the innocent infringer defense presented an issue for trial. The court remanded the case for further proceedings consistent with its opinion.  The court concluded that Harper was not an innocent infringer and that the district court had therefore erred in awarding damages of only $200 per infringement. "The innocent infringer defense is limited by [Section 402(d) of the Copyright Act]:  with one exception not relevant here, when a proper copyright notice 'appears on the published . . . phonorecords to which a defendant . . . had access, then no weight shall be given to such a defendant's interposition of a defense based on innocent infringement in mitigation of actual or statutory damages.'" Furthermore, the defendant's reliance on her own understanding of copyright law—or lack thereof—was irrelevant in the context of the Copyright Act. That statute "shows that the infringer's knowledge or intent does not affect its application. Lack of legal sophistication cannot overcome a properly asserted limitation to the innocent infringer defense." The federal appellate court ruled that the plaintiffs must be awarded statutory damages of $750 per infringed work.

**THE ETHICAL DIMENSION**  *In this and other cases involving similar rulings, the courts have held that when the published phonorecordings from which audio files were taken contained copyright notices, the innocent infringer defense does not apply. It is irrelevant that the notice is not provided in the online file. Is this fair? Explain.*

**MANAGERIAL IMPLICATIONS**  *Owners and managers of firms in the business of recording and distributing music face a constant challenge in protecting their copyrights.  This is particularly true for audio files in the online environment, where Internet users can easily download a copyrighted song and make it available to P2P file-sharing networks. Among other things, this means that recording companies must be ever vigilant in searching the Web to find infringing uses of any works distributed online. Today, it is not uncommon for companies to hire antipiracy firms to investigate the illegal downloading of their copyrighted materials.*

---

**DVDs AND FILE-SHARING** File-sharing also creates problems for the motion picture industry, which loses significant amounts of revenue annually as a result of pirated DVDs. Numerous Web sites offer software that facilitates the illegal copying of movies, such as BitTorrent, which enables users to download high-quality files from the Internet.

▶ **Case in Point 9.8** TorrentSpy, a popular BitTorrent indexing Web site, enabled users to locate and exchange files. The Motion Picture Association of America (MPAA) and Columbia Pictures, Inc., brought a lawsuit against the operators of TorrentSpy for facilitating copyright infringement. The MPAA also claimed that the operators had destroyed evidence that would reveal the identity of individual infringers. The operators had ignored a court order to keep server logs of the Internet addresses of people who facilitated the trading of files via the site. Because TorrentSpy's operators had willfully destroyed evidence, a federal court found in favor of the MPAA and ordered the defendants to pay a judgment of $111 million.[12] ◀

**SECTION 3**
# SOCIAL MEDIA

**Social media** provide a means by which people can create, share, and exchange ideas and comments via the Internet. Social networking sites, such as Facebook, Google+, MySpace, LinkedIn, Pinterest, and Tumblr,

---

12. *Columbia Pictures Industries, v. Bunnell,* 2007 WL 4877701 (C.D.Cal. 2007).

have become ubiquitous. Studies show that Internet users spend more time on social networks than at any other sites. The amount of time people spend accessing social networks on their smartphones and other mobile devices has increased every year (by nearly 37 percent in 2012 alone).

▶ **Example 9.9** Facebook, which was launched in 2004, had more than a billion active users by 2013. Individuals of all ages use Facebook to maintain social contacts, update friends on events, and distribute images to others. Facebook members often share common interests based on their school, location, or recreational affiliation, such as a sports team. ◀

## Legal Issues

The emergence of Facebook and other social networking sites has created a number of legal and ethical issues for businesses. For instance, a firm's rights in valuable intellectual property may be infringed if users post trademarked images or copyrighted materials on these sites without permission.

Social media posts now are routinely included in discovery in litigation (see Chapter 3) because they can provide damaging information that establishes a person's intent or what she or he knew at a particular time. Like e-mail, posts on social networks can be the smoking gun that leads to liability.

Tweets and other social media posts can also be used to reduce damages awards. ▶ **Example 9.10** Omeisha Daniels sued for injuries she sustained in a car accident. She claimed that her injuries made it impossible for her to continue working as a hairstylist. The jury originally awarded her $237,000, but when the jurors saw Daniels's tweets and photographs of her partying in New Orleans and vacationing on the beach, they reduced the damages to $142,000. ◀

**CRIMINAL INVESTIGATIONS** Law enforcement uses social media to detect and prosecute criminals. ▶ **Example 9.11** A nineteen-year-old posts a message on Facebook bragging about how drunk he was on New Year's Eve and apologizing to the owner of the parked car that he hit. The next day, police officers arrest him for drunk driving and leaving the scene of an accident. ◀

**ADMINISTRATIVE AGENCIES** Federal regulators also use social media posts in their investigations into illegal activities. ▶ **Example 9.12** Reed Hastings, the top executive of Netflix, stated on Facebook that Netflix subscribers had watched a billion hours of video the previous month. As a result, Netflix's stock price rose, which prompted a federal agency investigation. Because such a statement is considered to be material information to investors, it must be disclosed to all investors at the same time under securities law. The agency ultimately concluded that it could not hold Hastings responsible for any wrongdoing because the agency's policy on social media use was not clear. The agency then issued new guidelines that allow companies to disclose material information through social media if the investors have been notified in advance. ◀

The decision in a hearing before an administrative law judge can turn on the content of two Facebook posts, as occurred in the following case.

---

## CASE 9.3

### In re O'Brien
Superior Court of New Jersey, Appellate Division, 2013 WL 132508 (2013).

**BACKGROUND AND FACTS** Jennifer O'Brien was a tenured teacher at School No. 21 in Paterson, New Jersey, when she posted the following messages on her Facebook page: "I'm not a teacher—I'm a warden for future criminals!" and "They had a scared straight program in school—why couldn't I bring first graders?" Not surprisingly, outraged parents protested. The deputy superintendent of schools filed a complaint against O'Brien with the commissioner of education, charging her with conduct unbecoming a teacher. After a hearing, an administrative law judge (ALJ) ordered that O'Brien be removed from her teaching position. The commissioner issued a final decision, concluding that removal was the appropriate penalty. O'Brien appealed to a state court.

**DECISION AND RATIONALE** The state intermediate appellate court affirmed the commissioner's final decision to remove O'Brien from her position. The court was "satisfied" with this outcome for the reasons stated by the administrative law judge and the commissioner in their decisions.

CASE 9.3 CONTINUED    O'Brien argued that her Facebook postings were protected by the First Amendment and could not be used to discipline or discharge her, but the reviewing court disagreed. "To determine whether a public employee's statements are protected by the First Amendment, we balance the employee's interest as a citizen, in commenting upon matters of public concern, and the interest of the State, as an employer, in promoting the efficiency of the public services it performs through its employees." Both the administrative law judge and the commissioner determined that her Facebook statements were driven by her dissatisfaction with her job and the conduct of some of her students. Accordingly, "O'Brien failed to establish that her Facebook postings were protected speech . . . ." The seriousness of O'Brien's conduct "warranted her removal from her tenured position in the district."

**THE LEGAL DIMENSION**  *Certain interests of public employees and their employer are balanced to determine whether the First Amendment protects an employee's Facebook posts. What are those interests?*

**WHAT IF THE FACTS WERE DIFFERENT?**  *Would the outcome have been different if O'Brien had apologized? Discuss.*

---

**EMPLOYERS' SOCIAL MEDIA POLICIES** Employees who use social media in a way that violates their employer's stated policies may be disciplined or fired from their jobs. (Many large corporations have established specific guidelines on creating a social media policy in the workplace.) Courts and employment agencies usually uphold an employer's right to terminate a person based on his or her violation of a social media policy.

▶ **Case in Point 9.13**  Virginia Rodriquez worked for Wal-Mart Stores, Inc., for almost twenty years and had been promoted to management. Then she was disciplined for violating the company's policies by having a fellow employee use Rodriquez's password to alter the price of an item that she purchased. Under Wal-Mart's rules, another violation within a year would mean termination.

Nine months later, on Facebook, Rodriquez publicly chastised employees under her supervision for calling in sick to go to a party. The posting violated Wal-Mart's "Social Media Policy," which was "to avoid public comment that adversely affects employees." Wal-Mart terminated Rodriquez. She filed a lawsuit, alleging discrimination, but the court issued a summary judgment in Wal-Mart's favor.[13] ◀ Note, however, that employees' posts on social media may be protected under labor law, as discussed in *Example 5.3* in Chapter 5.

# The Electronic Communications Privacy Act

The Electronic Communications Privacy Act (ECPA)[14] amended federal wiretapping law to cover electronic forms of communications. Although Congress enacted the ECPA many years before social media networks existed, it nevertheless applies to communications through social media.

The ECPA prohibits the intentional interception of any wire, oral, or electronic communication. It also prohibits the intentional disclosure or use of the information obtained by the interception.

**EXCLUSIONS** Excluded from the ECPA's coverage are any electronic communications through devices that an employer provides for its employee to use "in the ordinary course of its business." Consequently, if a company provides the electronic device (cell phone, laptop, tablet) to the employee for ordinary business use, the company is not prohibited from intercepting business communications made on it.

This "business-extension exception" to the ECPA permits employers to monitor employees' electronic communications made in the ordinary course of business. It does not, however, permit employers to monitor employees' personal communications. Another exception allows an employer to avoid liability under the act if the employees consent to having their electronic communications monitored by the employer.

---

13. *Rodriquez v. Wal-Mart Stores, Inc.,* __F.Supp.2d __, 2013 WL 102674 (N.D.Tex. 2013).

14. 18 U.S.C. Sections 2510–2521.

**STORED COMMUNICATIONS** Part of the ECPA is known as the Stored Communications Act (SCA).[15] The SCA prohibits intentional and unauthorized access to *stored* electronic communications and sets forth criminal and civil sanctions for violators. A person can violate the SCA by intentionally accessing a stored electronic communication. The SCA also prevents "providers" of communication services (such as cell phone companies and social media networks) from divulging private communications to certain entities and individuals.

▶ **Case in Point 9.14** Two restaurant employees, Brian Pietrylo and Doreen Marino, were fired after their manager uncovered their password-protected MySpace group. The group's communications, stored on MySpace's Web site, contained sexual remarks about customers and management, and comments about illegal drug use and violent behavior. One employee said the group's purpose was to "vent about any BS we deal with out of work without any outside eyes spying on us."

The restaurant learned about the private MySpace group when a hostess showed it to a manager who requested access. The hostess was not explicitly threatened with termination but feared she would lose her job if she did not comply. The court allowed the employees' SCA claim, and the jury awarded them $17,003 in compensatory and punitive damages.[16] ◀

## Protection of Social Media Passwords

In recent years, employees and applicants for jobs or colleges have sometimes been asked to divulge their social media passwords. Employers and schools have sometimes looked at an individual's Facebook or other account to see if it included controversial postings such as racially discriminatory remarks or photos of drug parties. Such postings can have a negative effect on a person's prospects even though they were made years earlier or have been taken out of context.

By 2013, four states (California, Illinois, Maryland, and Michigan) had enacted legislation to protect individuals from having to disclose their social media passwords. Each state's law is slightly different. Some states, such as Michigan, prohibit employers from taking adverse action against an employee or job applicant based on what the person has posted online. Michigan's law also applies to e-mail and cloud stor-

age accounts. The federal government is also considering legislation that would prohibit employers and schools from demanding passwords to social media accounts.

Even if legislation is passed, however, it will not completely prevent employers and others from taking actions against a person based on his or her social network postings. Management and human resources personnel are unlikely to admit that they looked at someone's Facebook page and that it influenced their decision. How would a person who does not get a job be able to prove that she or he was rejected because the employer accessed social media? Also, the employer or school may use private browsing, which enables people to keep their Web browsing activities confidential.

## Company-wide Social Media Networks

Many companies, including Dell, Inc., and Nikon Instruments, form their own internal social media networks. Software companies offer a variety of systems, including Salesforce.com's Chatter, Microsoft's Yammer, and Cisco Systems' WebEx Social. Posts on these internal networks are quite different from the typical posts on Facebook, LinkedIn, and Twitter. Employees use these intranets to exchange messages about topics related to their work such as deals that are closing, new products, production flaws, how a team is solving a problem, and the details of customer orders. Thus, the tone is businesslike.

**PROTECTION OF TRADE SECRETS** An important advantage to using an internal system for employee communications is that the company can better protect its trade secrets. The company usually decides which employees can see particular intranet files and which employees will belong to each specific "social" group within the company. Companies providing internal social media networks often keep the resulting data on their own servers in secure "clouds."

**OTHER ADVANTAGES** Internal social media systems also offer additional benefits such as real-time information about important issues, such as production glitches. Additionally, posts can include tips on how to best sell new products or deal with difficult customers, as well as information about competitors' products and services.

---

15. 18 U.S.C. Sections 2701–2711.
16. *Pietrylo v. Hillstone Restaurant Group,* 2009 WL 3128420 (D.N.J. 2009).

Another major benefit of intranets is a significant reduction in the use of e-mail. Rather than wasting fellow employees' time reading mass e-mailings, workers can post messages or collaborate on presentations via the company's social network.

## SECTION 4
# ONLINE DEFAMATION

**Cyber torts** are torts that arise from online conduct. One of the most prevalent cyber torts is online defamation. Recall from Chapter 6 that defamation is wrongfully hurting a person's reputation by communicating false statements about that person to others. Because the Internet enables individuals to communicate with large numbers of people simultaneously (via a blog or tweet, for instance), online defamation has become a problem in today's legal environment.

▶ **Example 9.15** Courtney Love was sued for defamation based on remarks she posted about fashion designer Dawn Simorangkir on Twitter. Love claimed that her statements were opinion (rather than statements of fact, as required) and therefore were not actionable as defamation. Nevertheless, Love ended up paying $430,000 to settle the case out of court. ◀

## Identifying the Author of Online Defamation

An initial issue raised by online defamation is simply discovering who is committing it. In the real world, identifying the author of a defamatory remark generally is an easy matter. Suppose, though, that a business firm has discovered that defamatory statements about its policies and products are being posted in an online forum. Such forums allow anyone—customers, employees, or crackpots—to complain about a firm that they dislike while remaining anonymous.

Therefore, a threshold barrier to anyone who seeks to bring an action for online defamation is discovering the identity of the person who posted the defamatory message. An Internet service provider (ISP) can disclose personal information about its customers only when ordered to do so by a court. Consequently, businesses and individuals are increasingly bringing lawsuits against "John Does" (John Doe, Jane Doe, and the like are fictitious names used in lawsuits when the identity of a party is not known or when

a party wishes to conceal his or her name for privacy reasons). Then, using the authority of the courts, the plaintiffs can obtain from the ISPs the identity of the persons responsible for the defamatory messages.

## Liability of Internet Service Providers

Recall from the discussion of defamation in Chapter 6 that normally one who repeats or otherwise republishes a defamatory statement is subject to liability as if he or she had originally published it. Thus, newspapers, magazines, and television and radio stations are subject to liability for defamatory content that they publish or broadcast, even though the content was prepared or created by others.

Applying this rule to cyberspace, however, raises an important issue: Should ISPs be regarded as publishers and therefore be held liable for defamatory messages that are posted by their users in online forums or other arenas?

**GENERAL RULE** The Communications Decency Act (CDA) states that "[n]o provider or user of an interactive computer service shall be treated as the publisher or speaker of any information provided by another information content provider."[17] Thus, under the CDA, ISPs usually are treated differently from publishers in print and other media and are not liable for publishing defamatory statements that come from a third party.

**EXCEPTIONS** Although the courts generally have construed the CDA as providing a broad shield to protect ISPs from liability for third party content, some courts have started establishing some limits to this immunity. ▶ **Case in Point 9.16** Roommate.com, LLC, operates an online roommate-matching Web site that helps individuals find roommates based on their descriptions of themselves and their roommate preferences. Users respond to a series of online questions, choosing from answers in drop-down and select-a-box menus.

Some of the questions asked users to disclose their sex, family status, and sexual orientation—which is not permitted under the federal Fair Housing Act. When a nonprofit housing organization sued Roommate.com, the company claimed it was immune from liability under the CDA. A federal appellate court

---

17. 47 U.S.C. Section 230.

disagreed and ruled that Roommate.com was not immune from liability. Roommate.com was ordered to pay nearly $500,000 for prompting discriminatory preferences from users and matching users based on these criteria in violation of federal law.[18] ◄

---

## SECTION 5
# PRIVACY

---

Facebook, Google, and Yahoo have all been accused of violating users' privacy rights. As discussed in Chapter 4, the courts have held that the right to privacy is guaranteed by the Bill of Rights, and some state constitutions guarantee it as well. To maintain a suit for the invasion of privacy, though, a person must have a reasonable expectation of privacy in the particular situation (see Chapter 6). People clearly have a reasonable expectation of privacy when they enter their personal banking or credit-card information online. They also have a reasonable expectation that online companies will follow their own privacy policies. But it is probably not reasonable to expect privacy in statements made on Twitter.

Sometimes, people are confused and mistakenly believe that they are making statements or posting photos in a private forum. ▶ **Example 9.17** Randi Zuckerberg, the older sister of Mark Zuckerberg (the founder of Facebook), used a mobile app called "Poke" to post a "private" photo on Facebook of their family gathering during the holidays. Poke allows the sender to decide how long the photo can be seen by others. Facebook allows users to configure their privacy settings to limit access to photos, which Randi thought she had done. Nonetheless, the photo showed up in the Facebook feed of Callie Schweitzer, who then put it on Twitter where it eventually went viral. Schweitzer apologized and removed the photo, but it had already gone public for the world to see. ◄

## Data Collection and Cookies

Whenever a consumer purchases items from an online retailer, such as Amazon.com, or a retailer that sells both offline and online, such as Best Buy, the retailer collects information about the consumer. **Cookies** are invisible files that computers, smartphones, and other mobile devices create to track a user's Web browsing activities. Cookies provide detailed information to marketers about an individual's behavior and preferences, which is then used to personalize online services.

Over time, the retailer can amass considerable data about a person's shopping habits. Does collecting this information violate a consumer's right to privacy? Should retailers be able to pass on the data they have collected to their affiliates? Should they be able to use the information to predict what a consumer might want and then create online "coupons" customized to fit the person's buying history?

▶ **Example 9.18** Facebook, Inc., recently settled a lawsuit over its use of a targeted advertising technique called "Sponsored Stories." An ad would display a Facebook friend's name, profile picture, and a statement that the friend "likes" the company sponsoring the advertisement, alongside the company's logo. A group of plaintiffs filed suit, claiming that Facebook had used their pictures for advertising without their permission. When a federal court refused to dismiss the case, Facebook agreed to settle. ◄

## Internet Companies' Privacy Policies

The Federal Trade Commission (FTC) investigates consumer complaints of privacy violations. The FTC has forced many companies, including Google, Facebook, Twitter, and MySpace, to enter a consent decree that gives the FTC broad power to review their privacy and data practices. It can then sue companies that violate the terms of the decree.

▶ **Example 9.19** In 2012, Google settled a suit brought by the FTC alleging that it had misused data from Apple's Safari users. Google allegedly had used cookies to trick the Safari browser on iPhones and iPads so that Google could monitor users who had blocked such tracking. This violated the consent decree with the FTC. Google agreed to pay $22.5 million to settle the suit without admitting liability. ◄

Facebook has faced a number of complaints about its privacy policy and has changed its policy several times to satisfy its critics and ward off potential government investigations. Other companies, including mobile app developers, have also changed their privacy policies to provide more information to consumers. Consequently, it is frequently the companies, rather than courts or legislatures, that are defining the privacy rights of their online users.

---

**18.** *Fair Housing Council of San Fernando Valley v. Roommate.com, LLC,* 666 F.3d 1216 (9th Cir. 2012).

## The Consumer Privacy Bill of Rights

To protect consumers' personal information, the Obama administration has proposed a consumer privacy bill of rights (see Exhibit 9–1 below). The goal is to ensure that personal information is safe online.

If this proposed privacy bill of rights becomes law, retailers will have to change some of their procedures. Retailers will have to give customers better choices about what data are collected and how the data are used for marketing. They may also have to take into account consumers' expectations about how their information will be used once it is collected.

---

**EXHIBIT 9–1  The Proposed Consumer Privacy Bill of Rights**

1. Individual Control—Consumers have a right to exercise control over what personal data organizations collect from them and how they use it.

2. Transparency—Consumers have the right to easily understandable information about privacy and security practices.

3. Respect for Context—Consumers have a right to expect that organizations will collect, use, and disclose personal data in ways that are consistent with the context in which consumers provide the data.

4. Security—Consumers have the right to secure and responsible handling of personal data.

5. Access and Accuracy—Consumers have a right to access and correct personal data in usable formats, in a manner that is appropriate to the sensitivity of the data and the risk of adverse consequences to consumers if the data are inaccurate.

6. Focus Collection—Consumers have a right to reasonable limits on the personal data that companies collect and retain.

7. Accountability—Consumers have a right to have personal data handled by companies with appropriate measures in place to assure that they adhere to the Consumer Privacy Bill of Rights.

---

## Reviewing: Internet Law, Social Media, and Privacy

While he was in high school, Joel Gibb downloaded numerous songs to his smartphone from an unlicensed file-sharing service. He used portions of the copyrighted songs when he recorded his own band and posted videos on YouTube and Facebook. Gibb also used BitTorrent to download several movies from the Internet. Now he has applied to Boston University. The admissions office has requested access to his Facebook password, and he has complied. Using the information presented in the chapter, answer the following questions.

1. What laws, if any, did Gibb violate by downloading the music and videos from the Internet?
2. Was Gibb's use of portions of copyrighted songs in his own music illegal?  Explain.
3. Can individuals legally post copyrighted content on their Facebook pages? Why or why not?
4. Did Boston University violate any laws when it asked Joel to provide his Facebook password? Explain.

**DEBATE THIS . . .** *Internet service providers should be subject to the same defamation laws as newspapers, magazines, and television and radio stations.*

## Terms and Concepts

| | | |
|---|---|---|
| cookie 174 | distributed network 168 | peer-to-peer (P2P) networking 167 |
| cloud computing 168 | domain name 164 | social media 169 |
| cyber tort 173 | goodwill 164 | spam 163 |
| cybersquatting 164 | Internet service provider (ISP) 164 | typosquatting 165 |

## Issue Spotters

1. Karl self-publishes a cookbook titled *Hole Foods,* in which he sets out recipes for donuts, Bundt cakes, tortellini, and other foods with holes. To publicize the book, Karl designs the Web site **holefoods.com**. Karl appropriates the key words of other cooking and cookbook sites with more frequent hits so that **holefoods.com** will appear in the same search engine results as the more popular sites. Has Karl done anything wrong? Explain. **(See page 164.)**

2. Eagle Corporation began marketing software in 2001 under the mark "Eagle." In 2013, Eagle.com, Inc., a different company selling different products, begins to use *eagle* as part of its URL and registers it as a domain name. Can Eagle Corporation stop this use of *eagle?* If so, what must the company show? **(See page 164.)**

• **Check your answers to the Issue Spotters against the answers provided in Appendix E at the end of this text.**

## Business Scenarios

**9–1. Domain Names.** Tony owns Antonio's, a pub in a small town in Iowa. Universal Dining, Inc., opens a chain of pizza parlors in California called "Antonio's." Without Tony's consent, Universal uses "antoniosincalifornia" as part of the domain name for the chain's Web site. Has Universal committed trademark dilution or any other violation of the law? Explain. **(See page 164.)**

**9–2. Internet Service Providers.** CyberConnect, Inc., is an Internet service provider (ISP). Pepper is a CyberConnect subscriber. Market Reach, Inc., is an online advertising company. Using sophisticated software, Market Reach directs its ads to those users most likely to be interested in a particular product. When Pepper receives one of the ads, she objects to the content. Further, she claims that CyberConnect should pay damages for "publishing" the ad. Is the ISP regarded as a publisher and therefore liable for the content of Market Reach's ad? Why or why not? **(See page 173.)**

**9–3. Privacy.** SeeYou, Inc., is an online social network. SeeYou's members develop personalized profiles to interact and share information—photos, videos, stories, activity updates, and other items—with other members. Members post the information that they want to share and decide with whom they want to share it. SeeYou launched a program to allow members to share with others what they do elsewhere online. For example, if a member rents a movie through Netflix, SeeYou will broadcast that information to everyone in the member's online network. How can SeeYou avoid complaints that this program violates its members' privacy? **(See page 174.)**

## Business Case Problems

**9–4. Copyrights in Digital Information.** When she was in college, Jammie Thomas-Rasset wrote a case study on Napster, the online peer-to-peer (P2P) file-sharing network, and knew that it was shut down because it was illegal. Later, Capitol Records, Inc., which owns the copyrights to a large number of music recordings, discovered that "tereastarr"—a user name associated with Thomas-Rasset's Internet protocol address—had made twenty-four songs available for distribution on KaZaA, another P2P network. Capitol notified Thomas-Rasset that she had been identified as engaging in the unauthorized trading of music. She replaced the hard drive on her computer with a new drive that did not contain the songs in dispute. Is Thomas-Rasset liable for copyright infringement? Explain. [*Capitol Records, Inc. v. Thomas-Rasset,* 692 F.3d 899 (8th Cir. 2012)] **(See page 167.)**

**9–5. Domain Names.** Austin Rare Coins, Inc., buys and sells rare coins, bullion, and other precious metals through eight Web sites with different domain names. An unknown individual took control of Austin's servers and transferred the domain names to another registrant without Austin's permission. The new registrant began using the domain names to host malicious content—including hate letters to customers and fraudulent contact information—and to post customers' credit-card numbers and other private information, thereby tarnishing Austin's goodwill. Austin filed a suit in a federal district court against the new registrant under the Anticybersquatting Consumer Protection Act. Is Austin entitled to a transfer of the domain names? Explain. [*Austin Rare Coins, Inc. v. Acoins.com,* ___ F.Supp.2d ___, 2013 WL 85142 (E.D.Va. 2013)] **(See page 164.)**

**9–6. BUSINESS CASE PROBLEM WITH SAMPLE ANSWER: Privacy.**

 *Using special software, South Dakota law enforcement officers found a person who appeared to possess child pornography at a specific Internet protocol address. The officers subpoenaed Midcontinent Communications, the service that assigned the address, for the personal information of its subscriber. With this information, the officers obtained a search warrant for the*

*residence of John Rolfe, where they found a laptop that contained child pornography. Rolfe argued that the subpoenas violated his "expectation of privacy." Did Rolfe have a privacy interest in the information obtained by the subpoenas issued to Midcontinent? Discuss.* [State of South Dakota v. Rolfe, *825 N.W.2d 901 (S.Dak. 2013)]* **(See page 174.)**

- **For a sample answer to Problem 9–6, go to Appendix F at the end of this text.**

**9–7. File-Sharing.** Dartmouth College professor M. Eric Johnson, in collaboration with Tiversa, Inc., a company that monitors peer-to-peer networks to provide security services, wrote an article titled "Data Hemorrhages in the Health-Care Sector." In preparing the article, Johnson and Tiversa searched the networks for data that could be used to commit medical or financial identity theft. They found a document that contained the Social Security numbers, insurance information, and treatment codes for patients of LabMD, Inc. Tiversa notified LabMD of the find in order to solicit its business. Instead of hiring Tiversa, however, LabMD filed a suit in a federal district court against the company, alleging trespass, conversion, and violations of federal statutes. What do these facts indicate about the security of private information? Explain. How should the court rule? [*LabMD, Inc. v. Tiversa, Inc.,* 2013 WL 425983 (11th Cir. 2013)] **(See page 167.)**

**9–8. A QUESTION OF ETHICS: Criminal Investigations.**

*After the unauthorized release and posting of classified U.S. government documents to WikiLeaks. org, allegedly involving Bradley Manning, a U.S. Army private first class, the U.S. government began a criminal investigation. The government obtained a court order to require Twitter, Inc., to turn over subscriber information and communications to and from the e-mail addresses of Birgitta Jonsdottir and others. The court sealed the order and the other documents in the case, reasoning that "there exists no right to public notice of all the types of documents filed in a . . . case." Jonsdottir and the others appealed this decision.* [In re Application of the United States of America for an Order Pursuant to 18 U.S.C. Section 2703(d), *707 F.3d 283 (4th Cir. 2013)]* **(See page 170.)**

(a) Why would the government want to "seal" the documents of an investigation? Why would the individuals under investigation want those documents to be "unsealed"? What factors should be considered in striking a balance between these competing interests?

(b) How does law enforcement use social media to detect and prosecute criminals? Is this use of social media an unethical invasion of individuals' privacy? Discuss.

## Legal Reasoning Group Activity

**9–9. File-Sharing.** James, Chang, and Sixta are roommates. They are music fans and frequently listen to the same artists and songs. They regularly exchange MP3 music files that contain songs from their favorite artists. **(See page 167.)**

(a) One group of students will decide whether the fact that the roommates are transferring files among themselves for no monetary benefit precludes them from being subject to copyright law.

(b) The second group will consider an additional fact. Each roommate regularly buys CDs and rips them to his or her hard drive. Then the roommate gives the CDs to the other roommates to do the same.

# CHAPTER 10

# CRIMINAL LAW AND CYBER CRIME

Criminal law is an important part of the legal environment of business. Various sanctions are used to bring about a society in which individuals engaging in business can compete and flourish. These sanctions include damages for various types of tortious conduct (see Chapters 6 and 7), damages for breach of contract (to be discussed in Chapter 19), and the equitable remedies discussed in Chapter 1. Additional sanctions are imposed under criminal law. Indeed, many statutes regulating business provide for criminal as well as civil penalties.

In this chapter, after explaining some essential differences between criminal law and civil law, we look at how crimes are classified and at the elements that must be present for criminal liability to exist. We then examine the various categories of crimes, the defenses that can be raised to avoid criminal liability, and the rules of criminal procedure.

We conclude the chapter with a discussion of crimes that occur in cyberspace, which are often called *cyber crimes*. Cyber attacks are becoming all too common—even e-mail and data of government agencies and former U.S. presidents have been hacked. Smartphones are being infected by malicious software, which puts users' data at risk, as you will read in a feature later in this chapter.

---

## SECTION 1
## CIVIL LAW AND CRIMINAL LAW

Recall from Chapter 1 that *civil law* pertains to the duties that exist between persons or between persons and their governments. Criminal law, in contrast, has to do with crime. A **crime** can be defined as a wrong against society set forth in a statute and punishable by a fine and/or imprisonment—or, in some cases, death.

As mentioned in Chapter 1, because crimes are *offenses against society as a whole,* they are prosecuted by a public official, such as a district attorney (D.A.) or an attorney general (A.G.), not by the victims. Once a crime has been reported, the D.A.'s office decides whether to file criminal charges and to what extent to pursue the prosecution or carry out additional investigation.

### Key Differences between Civil Law and Criminal Law

Because the state has extensive resources at its disposal when prosecuting criminal cases, there are numerous procedural safeguards to protect the rights of defendants. We look here at one of these safeguards—the higher burden of proof that applies in a criminal case—as well as the harsher sanctions for criminal acts compared with those for civil wrongs. Exhibit 10–1 on the next page summarizes these and other key differences between civil law and criminal law.

**BURDEN OF PROOF** In a civil case, the plaintiff usually must prove his or her case by a *preponderance of the evidence.* Under this standard, the plaintiff must convince the court that based on the evidence presented by both parties, it is more likely than not that the plaintiff's allegation is true.

In a criminal case, in contrast, the state must prove its case **beyond a reasonable doubt.** If the jury views the evidence in the case as reasonably permitting either a guilty or a not guilty verdict, then the jury's verdict must be not guilty. In other words, the government (prosecutor) must prove beyond a reasonable doubt that the defendant has committed every essential element of the offense with which she or he is charged.

If the jurors are not convinced of the defendant's guilt beyond a reasonable doubt, they must find

**EXHIBIT 10-1 Key Differences between Civil Law and Criminal Law**

| Issue | Civil Law | Criminal Law |
|---|---|---|
| Party who brings suit | The person who suffered harm. | The state. |
| Wrongful act | Causing harm to a person or to a person's property. | Violating a statute that prohibits some type of activity. |
| Burden of proof | Preponderance of the evidence. | Beyond a reasonable doubt. |
| Verdict | Three-fourths majority (typically). | Unanimous (almost always). |
| Remedy | Damages to compensate for the harm or a decree to achieve an equitable result. | Punishment (fine, imprisonment, or death). |

the defendant not guilty. Note also that in a criminal case, the jury's verdict normally must be unanimous—agreed to by all members of the jury—to convict the defendant.[1] (In a civil trial by jury, in contrast, typically only three-fourths of the jurors need to agree.)

**CRIMINAL SANCTIONS** The sanctions imposed on criminal wrongdoers are also harsher than those applied in civil cases. Remember from Chapter 6 that the purpose of tort law is to enable a person harmed by a wrongful act to obtain compensation from the wrongdoer, rather than to punish the wrongdoer. In contrast, criminal sanctions are designed to punish those who commit crimes and to deter others from committing similar acts in the future.

Criminal sanctions include fines as well as the much harsher penalty of the loss of one's liberty by incarceration in a jail or prison. Most criminal sanctions also involve probation and sometimes require performance of community service, completion of an educational or treatment program, or payment of restitution. The harshest criminal sanction is, of course, the death penalty.

## Civil Liability for Criminal Acts

Some torts, such as assault and battery, provide a basis for a criminal prosecution as well as a civil action in tort. ▶ **Example 10.1** Carlos is walking down the street, minding his own business, when a person attacks him. In the ensuing struggle, the attacker stabs Carlos several times, seriously injuring him. A police officer restrains and arrests the assailant. In this situation, the attacker may be subject both to criminal prosecution by the state and to a tort lawsuit brought by Carlos to obtain compensation for his injuries. ◀

Exhibit 10–2 on the following page illustrates how the same wrongful act can result in both a civil (tort) action and a criminal action against the wrongdoer.

## Classification of Crimes

Depending on their degree of seriousness, crimes are classified as felonies or misdemeanors. **Felonies** are serious crimes punishable by death or by imprisonment for more than one year.[2] Many states also define different degrees of felony offenses and vary the punishment according to the degree.[3] For instance, most jurisdictions punish a burglary that involves forced entry into a home at night more harshly than a burglary that involves breaking into a nonresidential building during the day.

**Misdemeanors** are less serious crimes, punishable by a fine or by confinement for up to a year. **Petty offenses** are minor violations, such as jaywalking or violations of building codes, considered to be a subset of misdemeanors. Even for petty offenses, however, a guilty party can be put in jail for a few days, fined, or both, depending on state or local law. Whether a crime is a felony or a misdemeanor can determine in which court the case is

---

1. A few states allow jury verdicts that are not unanimous. Arizona, for example, allows six of eight jurors to reach a verdict in criminal cases. Louisiana and Oregon have also relaxed the requirement of unanimous jury verdicts.

2. Some states, such as North Carolina, consider felonies to be punishable by incarceration for at least two years.

3. Although the American Law Institute issued the Model Penal Code in 1962, it is not a uniform code, and each state has developed its own set of laws governing criminal acts. Thus, types of crimes and prescribed punishments may differ from one jurisdiction to another.

**EXHIBIT 10-2  Civil (Tort) Lawsuit and Criminal Prosecution for the Same Act**

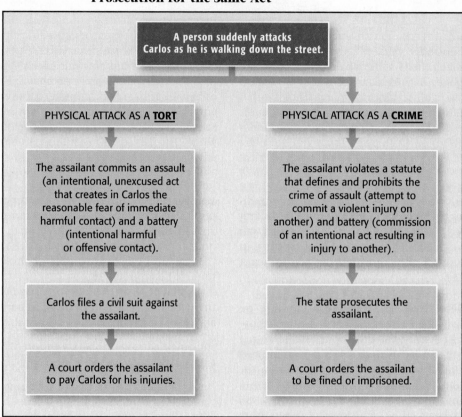

A person suddenly attacks Carlos as he is walking down the street.

| PHYSICAL ATTACK AS A **TORT** | PHYSICAL ATTACK AS A **CRIME** |
|---|---|
| The assailant commits an assault (an intentional, unexcused act that creates in Carlos the reasonable fear of immediate harmful contact) and a battery (intentional harmful or offensive contact). | The assailant violates a statute that defines and prohibits the crime of assault (attempt to commit a violent injury on another) and battery (commission of an intentional act resulting in injury to another). |
| Carlos files a civil suit against the assailant. | The state prosecutes the assailant. |
| A court orders the assailant to pay Carlos for his injuries. | A court orders the assailant to be fined or imprisoned. |

tried and, in some states, whether the defendant has a right to a jury trial.

## SECTION 2
# CRIMINAL LIABILITY

The following two elements normally must exist *simultaneously* for a person to be convicted of a crime:

1. The performance of a prohibited act *(actus reus)*.
2. A specified state of mind, or intent, on the part of the actor *(mens rea)*.

## The Criminal Act

Every criminal statute prohibits certain behavior. Most crimes require an act of *commission*—that is, a person must *do* something in order to be accused of a

crime. In criminal law, a prohibited act is referred to as the **actus reus,**[4] or guilty act. In some instances, an act of omission can be a crime, but only when a person has a legal duty to perform the omitted act, such as filing a tax return.

The *guilty act* requirement is based on one of the premises of criminal law—that a person should be punished for harm done to society. For a crime to exist, the guilty act must cause some harm to a person or to property. Thinking about killing someone or about stealing a car may be morally wrong, but the thoughts do no harm until they are translated into action.

Of course, a person can be punished for *attempting* murder or robbery, but normally only if he or she has taken substantial steps toward the criminal objective. Additionally, the person must have specifically

---

4. Pronounced *ak*-tuhs *ray*-uhs.

intended to commit the crime to be convicted of an attempt.

## State of Mind

A wrongful mental state, or ***mens rea,***[5] also is typically required to establish criminal liability. The required mental state, or intent, is indicated in the applicable statute or law. Murder, for example, involves the guilty act of killing another human being, and the guilty mental state is the desire, or intent, to take another's life. For theft, the guilty act is the taking of another person's property. The mental state involves both the awareness that the property belongs to another and the desire to deprive the owner of it.

**RECKLESSNESS** A court can also find that the required mental state is present when a defendant's acts are reckless or criminally negligent. A defendant is *criminally reckless* if he or she consciously disregards a substantial and unjustifiable risk.

▶ **Example 10.2** A fourteen-year-old New Jersey girl posts a Facebook message saying that she is going to launch a terrorist attack on her high school and asking if anyone wants to help. The police arrest the girl for the crime of making a terrorist threat.  The statute requires the intent to commit an act of violence with "the intent to terrorize" or "in reckless disregard of the risk of causing" terror or inconvenience. Although the girl argues that she had no intent to cause harm, the police can prosecute her under the "reckless disregard" part of the statute. ◀

**CRIMINAL NEGLIGENCE** *Criminal negligence* involves the mental state in which the defendant takes an unjustified, substantial, and foreseeable risk that results in harm. A defendant can negligent even if she or he was not actually aware of the risk but *should have been aware* of it.[6]

A homicide is classified as *involuntary manslaughter* when it results from an act of criminal negligence and there is no intent to kill. ▶ **Example 10.3** Dr. Conrad Murray, the personal physician of pop star Michael Jackson, was convicted of involuntary manslaughter in 2011 for prescribing the drug that led to Jackson's sudden death in 2009. Murray had given Jackson propofol, a powerful anesthetic normally used in surgery, as a sleep aid on the night of his death, even though he knew that Jackson had already taken other sedatives. ◀

**STRICT LIABILITY AND OVERCRIMINALIZATION** An increasing number of laws and regulations impose criminal sanctions for strict liability crimes. Strict liability crimes are offenses that do not require a wrongful mental state to establish criminal liability.

***Federal Crimes.*** The federal criminal code now lists more than four thousand criminal offenses, many of which do not require a specific mental state. There are also at least ten thousand federal rules that can be enforced through criminal sanctions, and many of these rules do not require intent.

▶ **Example 10.4** Eddie Leroy Anderson, a retired logger and former science teacher, and his son went digging for arrowheads near a campground in Idaho. They did not realize that they were on federal land and that it is a felony to remove artifacts from federal land without a permit. Although the crime carries as much as two years in prison, father and son pleaded guilty, and each received a sentence of probation and a $1,500 fine. ◀

Strict liability crimes are particularly common in environmental laws, laws aimed at combatting illegal drugs, and other laws affecting public health, safety, and welfare. Under federal law, for example, tenants can be evicted from public housing if a member of the household or a guest used illegal drugs. The eviction can occur regardless of whether the tenant knew or should have known about the drug activity.[7]

***State Crimes.*** Many states have also enacted laws that punish behavior as criminal without the need to show criminal intent. ▶ **Example 10.5** In Arizona, a hunter who shoots an elk outside the area specified by the hunting permit has committed a crime. The hunter can be convicted of the crime regardless of her or his intent or knowledge of the law. ◀

***Overcriminalization.*** Proponents of strict liability criminal laws argue that they are necessary to protect the public and the environment. Critics say laws that criminalize conduct without any required intent have led to *overcriminalization,* or the use of criminal law as

---

**5.** Pronounced *mehns ray-*uh.
**6.** Model Penal Code Section 2.02(2)(d).

**7.** See, for example, *Department of Housing and Urban Development v. Rucker*, 535 U.S. 125, 122 S.Ct. 1230, 152 L.Ed.2d 258 (2002).

the main tool to solve social problems, such as illegal drug use. They argue that when the requirement of intent is removed, people are more likely to commit crimes unknowingly—and perhaps even innocently. When an honest mistake can lead to a criminal conviction, the idea that crimes are a wrong against society is undermined.

## Corporate Criminal Liability

A corporation is a legal entity created under the laws of a state. At one time, it was thought that a corporation could not incur criminal liability because, although a corporation is a legal person, it can act only through its agents (corporate directors, officers, and employees). Therefore, the corporate entity itself could not "intend" to commit a crime. Over time, this view has changed. Obviously, corporations cannot be imprisoned, but they can be fined or denied certain legal privileges (such as necessary licenses).

**LIABILITY OF THE CORPORATE ENTITY** Today, corporations normally are liable for the crimes committed by their agents and employees within the course and scope of their employment.[8] For liability to be imposed, the prosecutor generally must show that the corporation could have prevented the act or that a supervisor authorized or had knowledge of the act. In addition, corporations can be criminally liable for failing to perform specific duties imposed by law (such as duties under environmental laws or securities laws).

▶ **Case in Point 10.6** A prostitution ring, the Gold Club, was operating out of some motels in West Virginia. A motel manager, who was also a corporate officer, gave discounted rates to Gold Club prostitutes, and they paid him in cash. The corporation received a portion of the funds generated by the Gold Club's illegal operations. A jury found that the corporation was criminally liable because a supervisor within the corporation—the motel manager—had knowledge of the prostitution and the corporation had allowed it to continue.[9] ◀

**LIABILITY OF THE CORPORATE OFFICERS AND DIRECTORS** Corporate directors and officers are personally liable for the crimes they commit, regardless of whether the crimes were committed for their private benefit or on the corporation's behalf. Additionally, corporate directors and officers may be held liable for the actions of employees under their supervision. Under the *responsible corporate officer* doctrine, a court may impose criminal liability on a corporate officer who participated in, directed, or merely knew about a given criminal violation.

▶ **Case in Point 10.7** The Roscoe family owned the Customer Company, which operated an underground storage tank that leaked gasoline. An employee, John Johnson, reported the leak to the state environmental agency, and the Roscoes hired an environmental services firm to clean up the spill. The clean-up did not occur immediately, however. The state sent many notices to John Roscoe, a corporate officer, warning him that the company was violating federal and state environmental laws. Roscoe gave the letters to Johnson, who passed them on to the environmental services firm, but the spill was not cleaned up.

The state eventually filed criminal charges against the corporation and the Roscoes individually. They were convicted under the responsible corporate officer doctrine. The Roscoes were in positions of responsibility, they had influence over the corporation's actions, and their failure to act constituted a violation of environmental laws.[10] ◀

### SECTION 3
# TYPES OF CRIMES

Federal, state, and local laws provide for the classification and punishment of hundreds of thousands of different criminal acts. Generally, though, criminal acts can be grouped into five broad categories: violent crime (crimes against persons), property crime, public order crime, white-collar crime, and organized crime. Note also that many crimes may be committed in cyberspace, as well as the physical world. When they occur in the virtual world, we

---

**8.** See Model Penal Code Section 2.07.
**9.** As a result of the convictions, the motel manager was sentenced to fifteen months in prison, and the corporation was ordered to forfeit the motel property. *United States v. Singh,* 518 F.3d 236 (4th Cir. 2008).

**10.** The Roscoes and the corporation were sentenced to pay penalties of $2,493,250. *People v. Roscoe,* 169 Cal.App.4th 829, 87 Cal.Rptr.3d 187 (3 Dist. 2008).

refer to them as cyber crimes, as discussed later in the chapter.

## Violent Crime

Certain crimes are called *violent crimes,* or crimes against persons, because they cause others to suffer harm or death. Murder is a violent crime. So is sexual assault, or rape. **Robbery**—defined as the taking of money, personal property, or any other article of value from a person by means of force or fear—is also a violent crime. Typically, states have more severe penalties for *aggravated robbery*—robbery with the use of a deadly weapon.

Assault and battery, which were discussed in Chapter 6 in the context of tort law, are also classified as violent crimes. ▶ **Example 10.8** Former rap star Flavor Flav (whose real name is William Drayton) was arrested in Las Vegas in 2012 on assault and battery charges. During an argument with his fiancée, Drayton allegedly threw her to the ground and then grabbed two kitchen knives and chased her son. ◀

Each violent crime is further classified by degree, depending on the circumstances surrounding the criminal act. These circumstances include the intent of the person committing the crime and whether a weapon was used. For crimes other than murder, the level of pain and suffering experienced by the victim is also a factor.

## Property Crime

The most common type of criminal activity is property crime, in which the goal of the offender is some form of economic gain or the damaging of property. Robbery is a form of property crime, as well as a violent crime, because the offender seeks to gain the property of another. We look here at a number of other crimes that fall within the general category of property crime. (Note also that many types of cyber crime, discussed later in this chapter, are forms of property crime as well.)

**BURGLARY** Traditionally, **burglary** was defined as breaking and entering the dwelling of another at night with the intent to commit a felony. This definition was aimed at protecting an individual's home and its occupants. Most state statutes have eliminated some of the requirements found in the common law definition. The time of day at which the breaking and entering occurs, for example, is usually immaterial. State statutes frequently omit the element of breaking, and some states do not require that the building be a dwelling. When a deadly weapon is used in a burglary, the perpetrator can be charged with *aggravated burglary* and punished more severely.

**LARCENY** Under the common law, the crime of **larceny** involved the unlawful taking and carrying away of someone else's personal property with the intent to permanently deprive the owner of possession. Put simply, larceny is stealing, or theft. Whereas robbery involves force or fear, larceny does not. Therefore, picking pockets is larceny, not robbery. Similarly, taking company products and supplies home for personal use without permission is larceny. (Note that a person who commits larceny generally can also be sued under tort law because the act of taking possession of another's property involves the tort of trespass to personal property.)

Most states have expanded the definition of property that is subject to larceny statutes. Stealing computer programs may constitute larceny even though the "property" is not physical (see the discussion of computer crime later in this chapter). So, too, can the theft of natural gas or Internet and television cable service.

**OBTAINING GOODS BY FALSE PRETENSES** Obtaining goods by means of false pretenses is a form of theft that involves trickery or fraud, such as using someone else's credit-card number without permission to purchase an iPad. Statutes dealing with such illegal activities vary widely from state to state. They often apply not only to property, but also to services and cash.

Sometimes, a statute consolidates the crime of obtaining goods by false pretenses with other property offenses, such as larceny and embezzlement, into a single crime called simply "theft." Under such a statute, it is not necessary for a defendant to be charged specifically with larceny, embezzlement, or obtaining goods by false pretenses. *Petty theft* is the theft of a small quantity of cash or low-value goods. *Grand theft* is the theft of a larger amount of cash or higher-value property. In the following case, the sales manager of a sports vehicle dealership was charged under a state statute with grand theft.

## CASE 10.1

### People v. Whitmer

Court of Appeal of California, Second District, Division 4, 213 Cal.App.4th 122, 152 Cal.Rptr.3d 216 (2013).

**BACKGROUND AND FACTS**   Jerome Gilding owned Temple City Power Sports, a business in San Gabriel, California, that sold motorcycles, all terrain vehicles (ATVs), and jet skis. If a customer failed to pay for a vehicle or used a bad credit card, the dealership incurred a "charge back," suffering a loss. To prevent charge backs, the dealership's policy was to require customers to make purchases in person. An "offline" sale occurred when a transaction was recorded but no credit information was sent to a bank until the end of the day. Gilding did not permit offline sales.

Jeffrey Whitmer was the dealership's sales manager. Eric Van Hek and Richard Carlos worked in the finance department. Gilding told Whitmer not to deal with Mordichi Mor, who had previously engaged in a fraudulent transaction at the dealership. Despite this instruction, Whitmer met with Mordichi. Whitmer then began directing the finance department to process "offline" sales involving customers neither Van Hek nor Carlos had met. Whitmer directed other employees to deliver the purchased vehicles to Mordichi.

Months later, Gilding uncovered twenty potentially fraudulent sales of motorcycles and other vehicles. The identification information provided for the buyers was false. The dealership incurred a charge back on each sale, resulting in losses exceeding $250,000. Whitmer was arrested. A jury in a California state court convicted him of twenty counts of grand theft. He appealed to a state intermediate appellate court, contending that he had been unlawfully convicted.

**DECISION AND RATIONALE**   The state intermediate appellate court affirmed the judgment of the lower court. The reviewing court concluded that the record contained sufficient evidence to establish that Whitmer was properly convicted of twenty counts of grand theft. Each transaction involved a different vehicle and those transactions occurred on thirteen different dates. Each transaction involved distinct fictitious buyers and separate paper work and documentation.

Although Whitmer claimed that there was no direct evidence that he intentionally participated in the fraud activities related to the taking of each vehicle, the reviewing court was not convinced. It pointed out, "We do not engage in independent fact finding, but instead affirm the jury's determination if they are supported by any logical inferences grounded in the evidence." After all, Whitmer authorized the offline credit card sales and other violations of dealership policies, obtained the false signatures from the fictitious buyers on the sales documents, and arranged for the delivery of the vehicles. Therefore, "There was ample evidence that appellant directly perpetuated the thefts."

**THE ETHICAL DIMENSION**   *How might the crimes in this case have been avoided? Discuss.*

**THE LEGAL ENVIRONMENT DIMENSION**   *Besides the defendant, who may have committed a crime in this case?*

---

**RECEIVING STOLEN GOODS**   It is a crime to receive goods that a person knows or should have known were stolen or illegally obtained. To be convicted, the recipient of such goods need not know the true identity of the owner or the thief, and need not have paid for the goods. All that is necessary is that the recipient knows or should know that the goods are stolen, which implies an intent to deprive the true owner of those goods.

**ARSON**   The willful and malicious burning of a building (and, in some states, vehicles and other items of personal property) is the crime of **arson.** At common law, arson applied only to burning down another person's house. The law was designed to protect human life. Today, arson statutes have been extended to cover the destruction of any building, regardless of ownership, by fire or explosion.

Every state has a special statute that covers the act of burning a building for the purpose of collecting insurance. (Of course, the insurer need not pay the claim when insurance fraud is proved.)

**FORGERY**   The fraudulent making or altering of any writing (including electronic records) in a way that changes the legal rights and liabilities of another is **forgery**. ▶ **Example 10.9** Without authorization, Severson signs Bennett's name to the back of a check made out to Bennett and attempts to cash it. Severson is committing forgery. ◀ Forgery also includes changing trademarks, falsifying public records, counterfeiting, and altering a legal document.

## Public Order Crime

Historically, societies have always outlawed activities that are considered contrary to public values and morals. Today, the most common public order crimes include public drunkenness, prostitution, gambling, and illegal drug use. These crimes are sometimes referred to as *victimless crimes* because they normally harm only the offender. From a broader perspective, however, they are deemed detrimental to society as a whole because they may create an environment that gives rise to property and violent crimes.

▶ **Example 10.10** A man flying from Texas to California on a commercial airliner becomes angry and yells obscenities at a flight attendant when a beverage cart strikes his knee. After the pilot diverts the plane and makes an unscheduled landing at a nearby airport, police remove the passenger and arrest him. If the man is later found guilty of the public order crime of interfering with a flight crew, he may be sentenced to more than two years in prison. ◀

## White-Collar Crime

Crimes occurring in the business context are popularly referred to as *white-collar crimes,* although this is not an official legal term. Ordinarily, **white-collar crime** involves an illegal act or series of acts committed by an individual or business entity using some nonviolent means to obtain a personal or business advantage.

Usually, this kind of crime takes place in the course of a legitimate business occupation. Corporate crimes fall into this category. Certain property crimes, such as larceny and forgery, may also be white-collar crimes if they occur within the business context. The crimes discussed next normally occur only in the business context.

**EMBEZZLEMENT** When a person who is entrusted with another person's property fraudulently appropriates it, **embezzlement** occurs. Typically, embezzlement is carried out by an employee who steals funds. Banks are particularly prone to this problem, but

embezzlement can occur in any firm. Embezzlement is not larceny because the wrongdoer does not *physically* take the property from the possession of another, and it is not robbery because no force or fear is used. The intent to return the embezzled property—or its actual return—is not a defense to the crime of embezzlement.

Embezzlement occurs whether the embezzler takes the funds directly from the victim or from a third person. If the financial officer of a large corporation pockets checks from third parties that were given to her to deposit into the corporate account, she is embezzling.

Frequently, an embezzler takes a relatively small amount at one time but does so repeatedly over a long period. This might be done by underreporting income or deposits and embezzling the remaining amount or by creating fictitious persons or accounts and writing checks to them from the corporate account. Even an employer's failure to remit state withholding taxes that were collected from employee wages can constitute embezzlement.

**MAIL AND WIRE FRAUD** Among the most potent weapons against white-collar criminals are the federal laws that prohibit mail fraud[11] and wire fraud.[12] These laws make it a federal crime to devise any scheme that uses U.S. mail, commercial carriers (FedEx, UPS), or wire (telegraph, telephone, television, the Internet, e-mail) with the intent to defraud the public. These laws are often applied when persons send out advertisements or e-mails with the intent to fraudulently obtain cash or property by false pretenses.

▶ **Case in Point 10.11** Cisco Systems, Inc., offers a warranty program to authorized resellers of Cisco parts. Iheanyi Frank Chinasa and Robert Kendrick Chambliss devised a scheme to intentionally defraud Cisco with respect to this program and obtain replacement parts to which they were not entitled. The two men planned and used specific language in numerous e-mails and Internet service requests that they sent to Cisco to convince Cisco to ship them new parts via commercial carriers. Ultimately, Chinasa and Chambliss were convicted of mail and wire fraud, and conspiracy to commit mail and wire fraud.[13] ◀

The maximum penalty under these statutes is substantial. Persons convicted of mail, wire, and Internet fraud may be imprisoned for up to twenty years and/or fined. If the violation affects a financial institution or involves fraud in connection with emergency

---

**11.** The Mail Fraud Act of 1990, 18 U.S.C. Sections 1341–1342.
**12.** 18 U.S.C. Section 1343.
**13.** *United States v. Chinasa,* 789 F.Supp.2d 691 (E.D.Va. 2011). See also *United States v. Lyons,* 569 F.3d 995 (9th Cir. 2009).

disaster-relief funds, the violator may be fined up to $1 million, imprisoned for up to thirty years, or both.

**BRIBERY** The crime of bribery involves offering to give something of value to a person in an attempt to influence that person, who is usually, but not always, a public official, to act in a way that serves a private interest. Three types of bribery are considered crimes: bribery of public officials, commercial bribery, and bribery of foreign officials. As an element of the crime of bribery, intent must be present and proved. The bribe itself can be anything the recipient considers to be valuable. Realize that the *crime of bribery occurs when the bribe is offered*—it is not required that the bribe be accepted. *Accepting a bribe* is a separate crime.

Commercial bribery involves corrupt dealings between private persons or businesses. Typically, people make commercial bribes to obtain proprietary information, cover up an inferior product, or secure new business. Industrial espionage sometimes involves commercial bribes. ▶ **Example 10.12** Kent Peterson works at the firm of Jacoby & Meyers. He offers to pay Laurel, an employee in a competing firm, to give him that firm's trade secrets and pricing schedules. Peterson has committed commercial bribery. ◀ So-called kickbacks, or payoffs for special favors or services, are a form of commercial bribery in some situations.

**BANKRUPTCY FRAUD** Federal bankruptcy law allows individuals and businesses to be relieved of oppressive debt through bankruptcy proceedings. Numerous white-collar crimes may be committed during the many phases of a bankruptcy action. A creditor may file a false claim against the debtor, which is a crime. Also, a debtor may fraudulently transfer assets to favored parties before or after the petition for bankruptcy is filed. For instance, a company-owned automobile may be "sold" at a bargain price to a trusted friend or relative. Closely related to the crime of fraudulent transfer of property is the crime of fraudulent concealment of property, such as the hiding of gold coins.

**INSIDER TRADING** An individual who obtains "inside information" about the plans of a publicly listed corporation can often make stock-trading profits by purchasing or selling corporate securities based on this information. *Insider trading* is a violation of securities law. Basically, securities law prohibits a person who possesses inside information and has a duty not to disclose it to outsiders from trading on that infor-

mation. A person may not profit from the purchase or sale of securities based on inside information until the information is made available to the public.

**THEFT OF TRADE SECRETS AND OTHER INTELLECTUAL PROPERTY** As discussed in Chapter 8, trade secrets constitute a form of intellectual property that for many businesses can be extremely valuable. The Economic Espionage Act[14] makes the theft of trade secrets a federal crime. The act also makes it a federal crime to buy or possess another person's trade secrets, knowing that the trade secrets were stolen or otherwise acquired without the owner's authorization.

Violations of the Economic Espionage Act can result in steep penalties: imprisonment for up to ten years and a fine of up to $500,000. A corporation or other organization can be fined up to $5 million. Additionally, the law provides that any property acquired as a result of the violation, such as airplanes and automobiles, is subject to criminal forfeiture, or seizure by the government. Similarly, any property used in the commission of the violation, such as servers and other electronic devices, is subject to forfeiture. A theft of trade secrets conducted via the Internet, for instance, could result in the forfeiture of every computer or other device used to commit or facilitate the violation as well as any assets gained.

## Organized Crime

White-collar crime takes place within the confines of the legitimate business world. *Organized crime,* in contrast, operates *illegitimately* by, among other things, providing illegal goods and services. Traditionally, the preferred markets for organized crime have been gambling, prostitution, illegal narcotics, and loan sharking (lending funds at higher-than-legal interest rates), along with more recent ventures into counterfeiting and credit-card scams.

**MONEY LAUNDERING** The profits from organized crime and illegal activities amount to billions of dollars a year. These profits come from illegal drug transactions and, to a lesser extent, from racketeering, prostitution, and gambling. Under federal law, banks, savings and loan associations, and other financial institutions are required to report currency transactions involving more than $10,000. Consequently, those who engage in illegal activities

---

14. 18 U.S.C. Sections 1831–1839.

face difficulties in depositing their cash profits from illegal transactions.

As an alternative to storing cash from illegal transactions in a safe-deposit box, wrongdoers and racketeers launder "dirty" money through legitimate business to make it "clean." **Money laundering** is engaging in financial transactions to conceal the identity, source, or destination of illegally gained funds.

▶ **Example 10.13**  Leo Harris, a successful drug dealer, becomes a partner with a restaurateur. Little by little, the restaurant shows increasing profits. As a partner in the restaurant, Harris is able to report the "profits" of the restaurant as legitimate income on which he pays federal and state taxes. He can then spend those funds without worrying that his lifestyle may exceed the level possible with his reported income. ◀

**RACKETEERING**  To curb the entry of organized crime into the legitimate business world, Congress enacted the Racketeer Influenced and Corrupt Organizations Act (RICO).[15] The statute makes it a federal crime to:

1.  Use income obtained from racketeering activity to purchase any interest in an enterprise.
2.  Acquire or maintain an interest in an enterprise through racketeering activity.
3.  Conduct or participate in the affairs of an enterprise through racketeering activity.
4.  Conspire to do any of the preceding activities.

**Broad Application of RICO.**  The broad language of RICO has allowed it to be applied in cases that have little or nothing to do with organized crime. RICO incorporates by reference twenty-six separate types of federal crimes and nine types of state felonies.[16] If a person commits two of these offenses, he or she is guilty of "racketeering activity."

Under the criminal provisions of RICO, any individual found guilty is subject to a fine of up to $25,000 per violation, imprisonment for up to twenty years, or both. Additionally, any assets (property or cash) that were acquired as a result of the illegal activity or that were "involved in" or an "instrumentality of" the activity are subject to government forfeiture.

---

**15.** 18 U.S.C. Sections 1961–1968.
**16.** See 18 U.S.C. Section 1961(1)(A). The crimes listed in this section include murder, kidnapping, gambling, arson, robbery, bribery, extortion, money laundering, securities fraud, counterfeiting, dealing in obscene matter, dealing in controlled substances (illegal drugs), and a number of others.

**Civil Liability.**  In the event of a RICO violation, the government can seek civil penalties. The government can seek the divestiture of a defendant's interest in a business or the dissolution of the business. (Divestiture refers to the taking of possession—or forfeiture—of the defendant's interest and its subsequent sale.)

Moreover, in some cases, the statute allows private individuals to sue violators and potentially recover three times their actual losses (treble damages), plus attorneys' fees, for business injuries caused by a RICO violation. This is perhaps the most controversial aspect of RICO and one that continues to cause debate in the nation's federal courts. The prospect of receiving treble damages in civil RICO lawsuits has given plaintiffs a financial incentive to pursue businesses and employers for violations.

See *Concept Summary 10.1* on the following page for a review of the different types of crimes.

---

## SECTION 4
# DEFENSES TO CRIMINAL LIABILITY

Persons charged with crimes may be relieved of criminal liability if they can show that their criminal actions were justified under the circumstances. In certain situations, the law may also allow a person to be excused from criminal liability because she or he lacks the required mental state. We look at several defenses to criminal liability here.

Note that procedural violations (such as obtaining evidence without a valid search warrant) may also operate as defenses. Evidence obtained in violation of a defendant's constitutional rights may not be admitted in court. If the evidence is suppressed, then there may be no basis for prosecuting the defendant.

## Justifiable Use of Force

Probably the best-known defense to criminal liability is **self-defense.** Other situations, however, also justify the use of force: the defense of one's dwelling, the defense of other property, and the prevention of a crime. In all of these situations, it is important to distinguish between deadly and nondeadly force. *Deadly force* is likely to result in death or serious bodily harm. *Nondeadly force* is force that reasonably appears necessary to prevent the imminent use of criminal force.

Generally speaking, people can use the amount of nondeadly force that seems necessary to protect

---

### CONCEPT SUMMARY 10.1
## Types of Crimes

| CRIME CATEGORY | DEFINITION AND EXAMPLES |
|---|---|
| **Violent Crime** | 1. *Definition*—Crime that causes others to suffer harm or death.<br>2. *Examples*—Murder, assault and battery, sexual assault (rape), and robbery. |
| **Property Crime** | 1. *Definition*—Crime in which the goal of the offender is some form of economic gain or the damaging of property; the most common form of crime.<br>2. *Examples*—Burglary, larceny, arson, receiving stolen goods, forgery, and obtaining goods by false pretenses. |
| **Public Order Crime** | 1. *Definition*—Crime that is contrary to public values and morals.<br>2. *Examples*—Public drunkenness, prostitution, gambling, and illegal drug use. |
| **White-Collar Crime** | 1. *Definition*—An illegal act or series of acts committed by an individual or business entity using some nonviolent means to obtain a personal or business advantage; usually committed in the course of a legitimate occupation.<br>2. *Examples*—Embezzlement, mail and wire fraud, bribery, bankruptcy fraud, insider trading, and the theft of intellectual property. |
| **Organized Crime** | 1. *Definition*—A form of crime conducted by groups operating illegitimately to satisfy the public's demand for illegal goods and services (such as gambling and illegal narcotics).<br>2. *Money laundering*—Passing "dirty" money (obtained through criminal activities, such as illegal drug trafficking) through legitimate enterprises so as to "launder" it (make it appear to be legitimate income).<br>3. *RICO*—The Racketeer Influenced and Corrupt Organizations Act (RICO) makes it a federal crime to (a) use income obtained from racketeering activity to purchase any interest in an enterprise, (b) acquire or maintain an interest in an enterprise through racketeering activity, (c) conduct or participate in the affairs of an enterprise through racketeering activity, or (d) conspire to do any of the preceding activities. RICO provides for both civil and criminal liability. |

---

themselves, their dwellings, or other property, or to prevent the commission of a crime. Deadly force can be used in self-defense only when the defender *reasonably believes* that imminent death or grievous bodily harm will otherwise result. In addition, normally the attacker must be using unlawful force, and the defender must not have initiated or provoked the attack.

Many states are expanding the situations in which the use of deadly force can be justified. Florida, for instance, allows the use of deadly force to prevent the commission of a "forcible felony," including robbery, carjacking, and sexual battery.

### Necessity

Sometimes, criminal defendants can be relieved of liability by showing **necessity**—that a criminal act was necessary to prevent an even greater harm.

▶ **Example 10.14** Jake Trevor is a convicted felon and, as such, is legally prohibited from possessing a firearm. While he and his wife are in a convenience store, a man draws a gun, points it at the cashier, and demands all the cash in the register. Afraid that the man will start shooting, Trevor grabs the gun and holds onto it until police arrive. In this situation, if Trevor is charged with possession of a firearm, he can assert the defense of necessity. ◀

### Insanity

A person who suffers from a mental illness may be incapable of the state of mind required to commit a crime. Thus, insanity may be a defense to a criminal charge. Note that an insanity defense does not enable a person to avoid imprisonment. It simply means that if the defendant successfully proves insanity, she or he will be placed in a mental institution.

▶ **Example 10.15** James Holmes opened fire with an automatic weapon in a crowded Colorado movie theater during the screening of *The Dark Knight Rises,* killing twelve people and injuring more than fifty. Holmes had been a graduate student until he suffered from mental health problems. Before the incident, he had no criminal history. Holmes's attorneys have asserted the defense of insanity to try to avoid a possible death penalty. If the defense is successful, Holmes will be confined to a mental institution, rather than a prison. ◄

**MODEL PENAL CODE** The courts have had difficulty deciding what the test for legal insanity should be. Federal courts and some states use the substantial-capacity test set forth in the Model Penal Code:

> A person is not responsible for criminal conduct if at the time of such conduct as a result of mental disease or defect he or she lacks substantial capacity either to appreciate the wrongfulness of his [or her] conduct or to conform his [or her] conduct to the requirements of the law.

**M'NAGHTEN AND OTHER STATE RULES** Some states use the *M'Naghten* test.[17] Under this test, a person is not responsible if, at the time of the offense, he or she did not know the nature and quality of the act or did not know that the act was wrong.

Other states use the irresistible-impulse test. A person operating under an irresistible impulse may know an act is wrong but cannot refrain from doing it. Under any of these tests, proving insanity is extremely difficult. For this reason, the insanity defense is rarely used and usually is not successful. Four states have abolished the insanity defense.

## Mistake

Everyone has heard the saying "Ignorance of the law is no excuse." Ordinarily, ignorance of the law or a mistaken idea about what the law requires is not a valid defense. A *mistake of fact,* however, as opposed to a *mistake of law,* can excuse criminal responsibility if it negates the mental state necessary to commit a crime.

► **Example 10.16** Oliver Wheaton mistakenly walks off with Julie Tyson's briefcase. If Wheaton genuinely thought that the case was his, there is no theft. Theft requires knowledge that the property belongs to another. (If Wheaton's act causes Tyson to incur damages, however, she may sue him in a civil action for trespass to personal property or conversion—torts that were discussed in Chapter 6.) ◄

## Duress

**Duress** exists when the *wrongful threat* of one person induces another person to perform an act that he or she would not otherwise have performed. In such a

situation, duress is said to negate the mental state necessary to commit a crime because the defendant was forced or compelled to commit the act.

Duress can be used as a defense to most crimes except murder. Both the definition of duress and the types of crimes that it can excuse vary among the states, however. Generally, to successfully assert duress as a defense, the defendant must reasonably have believed that he or she was in immediate danger, and the jury (or judge) must conclude that the defendant's belief was reasonable.

## Entrapment

**Entrapment** is a defense designed to prevent police officers or other government agents from enticing persons to commit crimes in order to later prosecute them for those crimes. In the typical entrapment case, an undercover agent *suggests* that a crime be committed and somehow pressures or induces an individual to commit it. The agent then arrests the individual for the crime.

For entrapment to be considered a defense, both the suggestion and the inducement must take place. The defense is not intended to prevent law enforcement agents from setting a trap for an unwary criminal. Rather, its purpose is to prevent them from pushing the individual into a criminal act. The crucial issue is whether the person who committed a crime was predisposed to commit the illegal act or did so only because the agent induced it.

## Statute of Limitations

With some exceptions, such as the crime of murder, statutes of limitations apply to crimes just as they do to civil wrongs. In other words, the state must initiate criminal prosecution within a certain number of years. If a criminal action is brought after the statutory time period has expired, the accused person can raise the statute of limitations as a defense.

The running of the time period in a statute of limitations may be *tolled*—that is, suspended or stopped temporarily—if the defendant is a minor or is not in the jurisdiction. When the defendant reaches the age of majority or returns to the jurisdiction, the statutory time period begins to run again.

## Immunity

Accused persons are understandably reluctant to give information if it will be used to prosecute them, and they cannot be forced to do so. The privilege against **self-incrimination** is guaranteed by a clause in

---

**17.** A rule derived from *M'Naghten's* Case, 8 Eng.Rep. 718 (1843).

the Fifth Amendment to the U.S. Constitution. The clause reads "nor shall [any person] be compelled in any criminal case to be a witness against himself."

When the state wishes to obtain information from a person accused of a crime, the state can grant *immunity* from prosecution. Alternatively, the state can agree to prosecute the accused for a less serious offense in exchange for the information. Once immunity is given, the person has an absolute privilege against self-incrimination and therefore can no longer refuse to testify on Fifth Amendment grounds.

Often, a grant of immunity from prosecution for a serious crime is part of the **plea bargaining** between the defending and prosecuting attorneys. The defendant may be convicted of a lesser offense, while the state uses the defendant's testimony to prosecute accomplices for serious crimes carrying heavy penalties.

## SECTION 5
# CRIMINAL PROCEDURES

Criminal law brings the force of the state, with all of its resources, to bear against the individual. Criminal procedures are designed to protect the constitutional rights of individuals and to prevent the arbitrary use of power on the part of the government.

The U.S. Constitution provides specific safeguards for those accused of crimes. The United States Supreme Court has ruled that most of these safeguards apply not only in federal court but also in state courts by virtue of the due process clause of the Fourteenth Amendment. These protections include the following:

1. The Fourth Amendment protection from unreasonable searches and seizures.
2. The Fourth Amendment requirement that no warrant for a search or an arrest be issued without probable cause.
3. The Fifth Amendment requirement that no one be deprived of "life, liberty, or property without due process of law."
4. The Fifth Amendment prohibition against **double jeopardy** (trying someone twice for the same criminal offense).[18]

5. The Fifth Amendment requirement that no person be required to be a witness against (incriminate) himself or herself.
6. The Sixth Amendment guarantees of a speedy trial, a trial by jury, a public trial, the right to confront witnesses, and the right to a lawyer at various stages in some proceedings.
7. The Eighth Amendment prohibitions against excessive bail and fines and against cruel and unusual punishment.

## Fourth Amendment Protections

The Fourth Amendment protects the "right of the people to be secure in their persons, houses, papers, and effects." Before searching or seizing private property, normally law enforcement officers must obtain a **search warrant**—an order from a judge or other public official authorizing the search or seizure.

Advances in technology allow the authorities to track phone calls and vehicle movements with greater ease and precision. Nevertheless, the use of such technology can still constitute a search within the meaning of the Fourth Amendment. ▶ **Case in Point 10.17** Antoine Jones owned and operated a nightclub. Police suspected that he was also trafficking in narcotics. As part of their investigation, police obtained a warrant to attach a Global Positioning System (GPS) device to his wife's car. Although the warrant specified that the GPS device had to be attached within ten days, officers did not attach it until eleven days later.

Law enforcement then tracked the vehicle's movement for about a month, eventually arresting Jones for possession and intent to distribute cocaine. Jones was convicted. He appealed, arguing that police did not have a warrant for the GPS tracking. The United States Supreme Court held that the attachment of a GPS tracking device to a suspect's vehicle constitutes a Fourth Amendment search. The Court did not rule on whether the search in this case was unreasonable and required a warrant, however, and allowed Jones's conviction to stand.[19] ◀

**PROBABLE CAUSE** To obtain a search warrant, law enforcement officers must convince a judge that they have reasonable grounds, or **probable cause,** to believe a search will reveal a specific illegality. Probable cause requires the officers to have trustworthy evidence that would convince a reasonable

---

18. The prohibition against double jeopardy means that once a criminal defendant is found not guilty of a particular crime, the government may not indict that person again and retry him or her for the same crime. The prohibition does not preclude the crime victim from bringing a *civil* suit against that same person to recover damages, however. Additionally, a state's prosecution of a crime will not prevent a separate federal prosecution of the same crime, and vice versa.

19. *United States v. Jones,* ___ U.S. ___, 132 S.Ct. 945, 181 L.Ed.2d 911 (2012).

person that the proposed search or seizure is more likely justified than not.

**SCOPE OF WARRANT** The Fourth Amendment prohibits general warrants. It requires a particular description of what is to be searched or seized. General searches through a person's belongings are impermissible. The search cannot extend beyond what is described in the warrant. Although search warrants require specificity, if a warrant is issued for a person's residence, items in that residence may be searched even if they do not belong to that individual.

In the following case, police officers obtained a search warrant and conducted a search for weapons in the home of a suspect's foster mother. A judge later ruled that the warrant was not supported by probable cause, and the homeowners sued individual police officers for executing an illegal search warrant.

---

## CASE 10.2

### Messerschmidt v. Millender
Supreme Court of the United States, ___ U.S. ___, 132 S.Ct. 1235, 182 L.Ed.2d 47 (2012).

**BACKGROUND AND FACTS** The Los Angeles County Sheriff's Department was protecting a woman from Jerry Ray Bowen, when he tried to kill her with a shotgun. The woman told the police that she and Bowen used to date, that Bowen was a gang member, and that she thought Bowen was staying at the home of Augusta Millender, his former foster mother. After investigating the incident further, the police prepared a warrant to search the home for all guns and gang-related material, and a magistrate approved it.

When the police, including Curt Messerschmidt, served the search warrant, they discovered that Bowen was not at the home, but they searched it anyway. The homeowners sued individual police officers in federal court for subjecting them to an illegal search. A federal appellate court held that the police lacked probable cause for such a broad search and that the police officers could be held personally liable. The police officers appealed. The United States Supreme Court granted *certiorari* to determine whether the police officers were immune from personal liability.

**DECISION AND RATIONALE** The United States Supreme Court reversed the decision of the federal appellate court and granted the officers immunity from liability. The doctrine of qualified immunity "gives government officials breathing room to make reasonable but mistaken judgments."

The Supreme Court explained that immunity depends on whether an official "acted in an objectively reasonable manner." Here, the police officers acted reasonably, in part, because a neutral judge approved the search warrant. Moreover, a reasonable police officer could have believed that the warrant was proper. For example, even if the warrant was too broad because it authorized a search for all guns rather than just the one Bowen fired, a reasonable police officer could conclude that Bowen had other guns. After all, the Court reasoned, he owned a sawed-off shotgun, he was a known gang member, and he had just tried to kill a woman for calling the police. Similarly, one could reasonably conclude that there was probable cause to search for gang-related material because it would be helpful in prosecuting Bowen for attacking his ex-girlfriend. Finally, the officers conducted a detailed investigation and had the warrant application reviewed three times before submitting it to the judge.

**THE LEGAL ENVIRONMENT DIMENSION** *How would police officers behave if they could always be held personally liable for executing unconstitutional warrants? Would they be more or less inclined to apply for and execute search warrants? Explain.*

**MANAGERIAL IMPLICATIONS** *The principles of this case would also apply in the context of searches of businesses. Businesses may be subject to warrantless administrative searches. Evidence gleaned from a search conducted in reasonable reliance on information that later proves to have been false may still be admissible in court in a case against the business.*

## The Exclusionary Rule

Under what is known as the **exclusionary rule,** any evidence obtained in violation of the constitutional rights spelled out in the Fourth, Fifth, and Sixth Amendments generally is not admissible at trial. All evidence derived from the illegally obtained evidence is known as the "fruit of the poisonous tree," and such evidence normally must also be excluded from the trial proceedings. For instance, if a confession is obtained after an illegal arrest, the arrest is the "poisonous tree," and the confession, if "tainted" by the arrest, is the "fruit."

The purpose of the exclusionary rule is to deter police from conducting warrantless searches and engaging in other misconduct. The rule can sometimes lead to injustice, however. If the evidence of a defendant's guilt was obtained improperly (without a valid search warrant, for instance), it normally cannot be used against the defendant in court.

## The *Miranda* Rule

An important question many courts faced in the 1950s and 1960s was not whether suspects had constitutional rights—that was not in doubt—but how and when those rights could be exercised. Could the right to be silent (under the Fifth Amendment's protection against self-incrimination) be exercised during pretrial interrogation proceedings or only during the trial? Were confessions obtained from suspects admissible in court if the suspects had not been advised of their right to remain silent and other constitutional rights?

To clarify these issues, the United States Supreme Court issued a landmark decision in 1966 in *Miranda v. Arizona,* which we present here. Today, the procedural rights required by the Court in this case are familiar to almost every American.

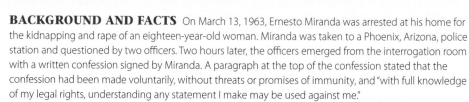

**CLASSIC CASE 10.3**

### Miranda v. Arizona
Supreme Court of the United States, 384 U.S. 436, 86 S.Ct. 1602, 16 L.Ed.2d 694 (1966).

**BACKGROUND AND FACTS** On March 13, 1963, Ernesto Miranda was arrested at his home for the kidnapping and rape of an eighteen-year-old woman. Miranda was taken to a Phoenix, Arizona, police station and questioned by two officers. Two hours later, the officers emerged from the interrogation room with a written confession signed by Miranda. A paragraph at the top of the confession stated that the confession had been made voluntarily, without threats or promises of immunity, and "with full knowledge of my legal rights, understanding any statement I make may be used against me."

Miranda was never advised that he had a right to remain silent and a right to have a lawyer present. The confession was admitted into evidence at his trial, and Miranda was convicted and sentenced to prison for twenty to thirty years. Miranda appealed, claiming that he had not been informed of his constitutional rights. The Supreme Court of Arizona held that Miranda's constitutional rights had not been violated and affirmed his conviction. The *Miranda* case was subsequently reviewed by the United States Supreme Court.

**DECISION AND RATIONALE** The United States Supreme Court reversed Miranda's conviction, holding that he could not be convicted of the crime on the basis of his confession because his confession was inadmissible as evidence. The Court ruled that for any statement made by a defendant to be admissible, the defendant must be informed of certain constitutional rights before a police interrogation. These are (1) that he or she has a right to remain silent; (2) that anything said can and will be used against the individual in court (to warn a person in custody of "the consequences of forgoing" the right to remain silent); (3) that he or she has the right to have an attorney present during questioning; and (4) that if the individual cannot afford an attorney, one will be appointed. If the accused waives his or her rights to remain silent and to have counsel present, the government must be able to demonstrate that the waiver was made knowingly and intelligently.

**IMPACT OF THIS CASE ON TODAY'S LAW** *Despite considerable criticism and later attempts to overrule the* Miranda *decision through legislation, the requirements stated in this case continue to provide the benchmark by which criminal procedures are judged today. Police officers routinely advise suspects*

**CASE 10.3 CONTINUED**

*of their "Miranda rights" on arrest. When Ernesto Miranda himself was later murdered, the suspected murderer was "read his Miranda rights."*

**THE GLOBAL DIMENSION** *The right to remain silent has long been a legal hallmark in Great Britain as well as in the United States. In 1994, however, the British Parliament passed an act that provides that a criminal defendant's silence may be interpreted as evidence of his or her guilt. British police officers are now required, when making an arrest, to inform the suspect, "You do not have to say anything. But if you do not mention now something which you later use in your defense, the court may decide that your failure to mention it now strengthens the case against you. A record will be made of everything you say, and it may be given in evidence if you are brought to trial." Should U.S. law also be changed to allow a defendant's silence during questioning to be considered as an indication of guilt? Why or why not?*

## Exceptions to the *Miranda* Rule

Although the Supreme Court's decision in the *Miranda* case was controversial, it has survived several attempts by Congress to overrule it. Over time, however, the Supreme Court has made a number of exceptions to the *Miranda* ruling. For instance, the Court has recognized a "public safety" exception that allows certain statements to be admitted even if the defendant was not given *Miranda* warnings. A defendant's statements that reveal the location of a weapon would be admissible under this exception.

Additionally, a suspect must unequivocally and assertively ask to exercise her or his right to counsel in order to stop police questioning. Saying, "Maybe I should talk to a lawyer" during an interrogation after being taken into custody is not enough.

## Criminal Process

As mentioned earlier in this chapter, a criminal prosecution differs significantly from a civil case in several respects. These differences reflect the desire to safeguard the rights of the individual against the state. Exhibit 10–3 on the next page summarizes the major steps in processing a criminal case. We now discuss three phases of the criminal process—arrest, indictment or information, and trial—in more detail.

**ARREST** Before a warrant for arrest can be issued, there must be probable cause to believe that the individual in question has committed a crime. As discussed earlier in this chapter, *probable cause* can be defined as a substantial likelihood that the person has committed or is about to commit a crime. Note that probable cause involves a likelihood, not just a possibility. Arrests can be made without a warrant if there is no time to get one, but the action of the arresting officer is still judged by the standard of probable cause.

**INDICTMENT OR INFORMATION** Individuals must be formally charged with having committed specific crimes before they can be brought to trial. If issued by a grand jury, such a charge is called an **indictment.**[20] A **grand jury** does not determine the guilt or innocence of an accused party. Rather, its function is to hear the state's evidence and to determine whether a reasonable basis (probable cause) exists for believing that a crime has been committed and that a trial ought to be held.

Usually, grand juries are called in cases involving serious crimes, such as murder. For lesser crimes, an individual may be formally charged with a crime by an **information,** or criminal complaint. An information will be issued by a government prosecutor if the prosecutor determines that there is sufficient evidence to justify bringing the individual to trial.

**TRIAL** At a criminal trial, the accused person does not have to prove anything. The entire burden of proof is on the prosecutor (the state). As mentioned earlier, the prosecution must show that, based on all the evidence, the defendant's guilt is established *beyond a reasonable doubt.* If there is reasonable doubt as to whether a criminal defendant committed the crime with which she or he has been charged, then the verdict must be "not guilty." A verdict of "not guilty" is not the same as stating that the defendant is innocent. It merely means that not enough evidence was properly presented to the court to prove guilt beyond a reasonable doubt.

Courts have complex rules about what types of evidence may be presented and how the evidence may be brought out in criminal cases, especially in jury

---

**20.** Pronounced in-*dyte*-ment.

**EXHIBIT 10-3  Major Procedural Steps in a Criminal Case**

```
                         ┌─────────────────┐
                         │     ARREST      │
                         └─────────────────┘
                                 │
                         ┌─────────────────┐
                         │     BOOKING     │
                         └─────────────────┘
                                 │
┌───────────────────────────────────────────────────────────────┐
│                    INITIAL APPEARANCE                           │
│  The defendant appears before the judge and is informed of the │
│  charges and of his or her rights. A lawyer may be appointed    │
│  for the defendant. The judge sets bail (conditions under which │
│  a suspect can obtain release pending disposition of the case). │
└───────────────────────────────────────────────────────────────┘
```

| GRAND JURY | PRELIMINARY HEARING |
|---|---|
| A grand jury determines if there is probable cause to believe that the defendant committed the crime. The federal government and about half of the states require grand jury indictments for at least some felonies. | In a court proceeding, a prosecutor presents evidence, and the judge determines if there is probable cause to hold the defendant over for trial. |

| INDICTMENT | INFORMATION |
|---|---|
| An *indictment* is a written document issued by the grand jury to formally charge the defendant with a crime. | An *information* is a formal criminal charge made by the prosecutor. |

**ARRAIGNMENT**
The defendant is brought before the court, informed of the charges, and asked to enter a plea. Usually, the prosecutor will attempt to get the defendant to enter into a plea bargain at this stage. Most defendants plead guilty to a lesser offense or receive a reduced sentence for their crime without ever proceeding to trial.

**TRIAL**
The trial can be either a jury trial or a bench trial. (In a bench trial, there is no jury, and the judge decides questions of fact as well as questions of law.) If the verdict is "guilty," the judge sets a date for the sentencing. Everyone convicted of a crime has the right to an appeal.

trials. These rules are designed to ensure that evidence presented at trials is relevant, reliable, and not prejudicial toward the defendant.

## Federal Sentencing Guidelines

The Sentencing Reform Act created the U.S. Sentencing Commission, which performs the task of standardizing sentences for *federal* crimes. The commission's guidelines establish a range of possible pen-

alties for each federal crime. Originally, the guidelines were mandatory, in that the judge was required to select a sentence from within the set range and was not allowed to deviate from it.

**PROBLEMS WITH CONSTITUTIONALITY** In 2005, the United States Supreme Court held that certain provisions of the federal sentencing guidelines were unconstitutional. ▶ **Case in Point 10.18** Freddie Booker was arrested with 92.5 grams of crack cocaine in his possession. Booker admitted to police that he had sold an additional 566 grams of crack cocaine, but he was never charged with, or tried for, possession of this additional quantity. Nevertheless, under the federal sentencing guidelines the judge was required to sentence Booker to twenty-two years in prison. The Court ruled that this sentence was unconstitutional because a jury did not find beyond a reasonable doubt that Booker had possessed the additional 566 grams of crack.[21] ◄

Essentially, the Court's ruling changed the federal sentencing guidelines from mandatory to advisory. Depending on the circumstances of the case, a federal trial judge may now depart from the guidelines if she or he believes that it is reasonable to do so.

**FACTORS THAT INCREASE CRIMINAL PENALTIES**
Sentencing guidelines still exist and provide for enhanced punishment for certain types of crimes. Penalties can be enhanced for white-collar crimes, violations of the Sarbanes-Oxley Act (mentioned in Chapter 5), and violations of securities laws.[22]

The sentencing judge must take into account the various sentencing factors that apply to an individual defendant before concluding that a particular sentence is reasonable. When the defendant is a business firm, these factors include the company's history of past violations, management's cooperation with federal investigators, and the extent to which the firm has undertaken specific programs and procedures to prevent criminal activities by its employees.

## SECTION 6
# CYBER CRIME

The U.S. Department of Justice broadly defines **computer crime** as any violation of criminal law that involves knowledge of computer technology for its perpetration, investigation, or prosecution. Many computer crimes fall under the broad label of **cyber crime,** which describes any criminal activity occurring via a computer in the virtual community of the Internet.

Most cyber crimes are simply existing crimes, such as fraud and theft of intellectual property, in which the Internet is the instrument of wrongdoing. ▶ **Example 10.19**  Richard O'Dwyer ran TVShack.net, a Web site with links directing users to copyrighted TV shows and movies. U.S. authorities seized his .net domain name, claiming that the site was nothing more than a search engine for pirated content. O'Dwyer simply moved the site to a .cc domain over which the United States apparently has no authority. ◄

Here we look at several types of activities that constitute cyber crimes against persons or property. (Of course, just as computers and the Internet have expanded the scope of crime, they have also provided new ways of detecting and combatting crime. For instance, police are using social media as an investigative tool, as discussed in Chapter 9.)

## Cyber Fraud

As pointed out in Chapter 6, fraud is any misrepresentation knowingly made with the intention of deceiving another and on which a reasonable person would and does rely to her or his detriment. **Cyber fraud** is fraud committed over the Internet.

**ONLINE AUCTION FRAUD**  Online auction fraud, in its most basic form, is a simple process. A person puts up an expensive item for auction, on either a legitimate or a fake auction site, and then refuses to send the product after receiving payment. Or, as a variation, the wrongdoer may send the purchaser an item that is worth less than the one offered in the auction.

The larger online auction sites, such as eBay, try to protect consumers against such schemes by providing warnings about deceptive sellers or offering various forms of insurance. It is nearly impossible to completely block fraudulent auction activity on the Internet, however. Because users can assume multiple identities, it is very difficult to pinpoint fraudulent sellers—they will simply change their screen names with each auction.

**ONLINE RETAIL FRAUD**  Somewhat similar to online auction fraud is online retail fraud, in which consumers pay directly (without bidding) for items that are never delivered. As with other forms of online fraud, it is difficult to determine the actual extent of online sales fraud, but anecdotal evidence suggests that it is a substantial problem.

▶ **Case in Point 10.20**  Jeremy Jaynes grossed more than $750,000 per week selling nonexistent or worthless products such as "penny stock pickers" and "Internet history erasers." By the time he was arrested, he had amassed an estimated $24 million from his various fraudulent schemes.[23] ◄

---

21. *United States v. Booker,* 543 U.S. 220, 125 S.Ct. 738, 160 L.Ed.2d 621 (2005).
22. The sentencing guidelines were amended in 2003, as required under the Sarbanes-Oxley Act, to impose stiffer penalties for corporate securities fraud.

23. *Jaynes v. Commonwealth of Virginia,* 276 Va.App. 443, 666 S.E.2d 303 (2008).

## Cyber Theft

In cyberspace, thieves are not subject to the physical limitations of the "real" world. A thief can steal data stored in a networked computer with Internet access from anywhere on the globe. Only the speed of the connection and the thief's computer equipment limit the quantity of data that can be stolen.

**IDENTITY THEFT** Not surprisingly, there has been a marked increase in identity theft in recent years. **Identity theft** occurs when the wrongdoer steals a form of identification—such as a name, date of birth, or Social Security number—and uses the information to access the victim's financial resources.

The Internet has provided even easier access to private data, as we discussed in Chapter 9. Frequent Web surfers surrender a wealth of information about themselves without knowing it. Most Web sites use "cookies" to collect data on those who visit their sites. Web browsers often store information such as the consumer's name and e-mail address. Finally, every time a purchase is made online, the item is linked to the purchaser's name.

**PHISHING** A distinct form of identity theft known as **phishing** has added a different wrinkle to the practice. In a phishing attack, the perpetrator "fishes" for financial data and passwords from consumers by posing as a legitimate business, such as a bank or credit-card company. The "phisher" sends an e-mail asking the recipient to update or confirm vital information, often with the threat that an account or some other service will be discontinued if the information is not provided. Once the unsuspecting individual enters the information, the phisher can use it to masquerade as that person or to drain his or her bank or credit account.

▶ **Example 10.21**   Customers of Wachovia Bank (now owned by Wells Fargo) received official-looking e-mails telling them to type in personal information on a Web form to complete a mandatory installation of a new Internet security certificate. But the Web site was bogus. When people filled out the forms, their computers were infected and funneled their data to a computer server. The cyber criminals then sold the data. ◀

**EMPLOYMENT FRAUD** Cyber criminals also look for victims at online job-posting sites. Claiming to be an employment officer in a well-known company, the criminal sends bogus e-mail messages to job seekers.

The messages ask the unsuspecting job seekers to reveal enough information to allow for identity theft. As the unemployment rate has remained high, cyber criminals have found many opportunities for employment fraud.

▶ **Example 10.22**   The job site Monster.com once asked 4.5 million users to change their passwords. Cyber thieves had broken into its databases and stolen user identities, passwords, and other data in one of Britain's largest cyber theft cases. ◀

**CREDIT-CARD NUMBERS** Companies take risks by storing their online customers' credit-card numbers. Although the consumer can make a purchase more quickly without entering a lengthy card number, the electronic warehouses that store the numbers are targets for cyber thieves. Stolen credit-card numbers are much more likely to hurt merchants and credit-card issuers (such as banks) than consumers. In most situations, the legitimate holders of credit cards are not held responsible for the costs of purchases made with a stolen number.

## Hacking

A **hacker** is someone who uses one computer to break into another. The danger posed by hackers has increased significantly because of **botnets,** or networks of computers that have been appropriated by hackers without the knowledge of their owners. A hacker may secretly install a program on thousands, if not millions, of personal computer "robots," or "bots," that allows him or her to forward transmissions to an even larger number of systems.

▶ **Example 10.23**   When a hacker broke into Sony Corporation's PlayStation 3 video gaming and entertainment networks, the company had to temporarily shut down its online services. This single hacking incident affected more than 100 million online accounts that provide gaming, chat, and music streaming services. ◀

**MALWARE** Botnets are one of the latest forms of **malware,** a term that refers to any program that is harmful to a computer or, by extension, a computer user. A **worm,** for example, is a software program that is capable of reproducing itself as it spreads from one computer to the next.

▶ **Example 10.24**   Within three weeks, the computer worm called "Conflicker" spread to more than a million personal computers around the world. It was transmitted to some computers through the use of Facebook and Twitter. This worm also infected servers and devices plugged into infected computers, via USB ports, such as iPads, iPhones, and flash drives. ◄

A **virus,** another form of malware, is also able to reproduce itself, but must be attached to an "infested" host file to travel from one computer network to another. For instance, hackers are now capable of corrupting banner ads that use Adobe's Flash Player. When an Internet user clicks on the banner ad, a virus is installed. Worms and viruses can be programmed to perform a number of functions, such as prompting host computers to continually "crash" and reboot, or otherwise infect the system. (For a discussion of how malware is now affecting smartphones, see this chapter's *Insight into the Global Environment* feature below.)

**SERVICE-BASED HACKING** Today, many companies offer "software as a service." Instead of buying

---

# INSIGHT INTO THE GLOBAL ENVIRONMENT
## Even Smartphones Are Vulnerable to International Cyber Attacks

Recent statistics show that the number of bank robberies occurring annually is on the decline. Criminals have learned that it is easier, less risky, and more profitable to steal via the Internet. Advances in the speed and use of the Internet have fostered the growth of a relatively new criminal industry that uses malware to conduct espionage and profit from crime.

### Who Are the Creators of Malware?

While any smart teenager can buy prepackaged hacking software on the Internet, the malware that businesses and governments are worried about is much more sophisticated. There is evidence that malware that can be used for international diplomatic espionage as well as industrial espionage is most often developed by so-called cyber mercenaries. According to Steve Sachs of the cyber security firm FireEye, "There are entire little villages dedicated to malware in Russia, villages in China, very sophisticated, very organized, very well-funded."

### Flame Malware

The most sophisticated globally created and propagated malware has been labeled Flame. Flame was discovered in 2012, although experts believe that it was lying dormant in thousands of computers worldwide for at least five years.

Flame can record screen shots, keyboard strokes, network traffic, and audio. It can also record Skype conversations. It can even turn infected computers into Bluetooth beacons, which can then attempt to download contact information from nearby Bluetooth-enabled devices.

### The Malware Can Infect Smartphones

Many smartphone owners are unaware that their Apple, Nokia, and Microsoft Windows mobile phones can be infected with Flame malware or variants of it without their knowledge. The information that is hacked from smartphones can then be sent on to a series of command-and-control servers and ultimately to members of international criminal gangs.

Once a computer or smartphone is infected with this malware, all information in the device can be transferred. Additionally, files can be deleted, and furthermore, files that have been erased on hard drives can be resurrected. This malware has been responsible for stealing e-mail databases from Microsoft's e-mail program Outlook and has even been able to capture e-mail from remote servers.[a]

Until recently, most attacks involved diplomatic espionage, but cyber technicians at large business enterprises are now worried that industrial espionage may be taking place. In fact, an extensive hacking operation was uncovered in 2013 that was linked to a Chinese military unit (the "Comment Crew"). The wide-ranging cyber attacks involved the theft of hundreds of terabytes of data and intellectual property of more than 140 corporations in twenty different industries. The goal of the attacks was to help Chinese companies better compete against U.S. and foreign firms.[b]

### LEGAL CRITICAL THINKING
**INSIGHT INTO THE TECHNOLOGICAL ENVIRONMENT**

*What entities might pay "cyber mercenaries" to create some of the malware described in this feature?*

---

a. Mark Stevens, "CWI Cryptanalyst Discovers New Cryptographic Attack Variant in Flame Spy Malware," June 7, 2012, **www.cwi.nl/news/2012**.
b. David E. Sanger, David Barboza, and Nicole Perlroth, "Chinese Army Unit Is Seen as Tied to Hacking Against U.S.," **www.nytimes.com/2013**.

software to install on a computer, the user connects to Web-based software. The user can write e-mails, edit spreadsheets, or perform other tasks using his or her Web browser. Cyber criminals have adapted this distribution method to provide "crimeware as a service."

A would-be thief no longer has to be a computer hacker to create a botnet or steal banking information and credit-card numbers. He or she can rent the online services of cyber criminals to do the work for a small price. Fake security software (also known as scareware) is a common example. The thief can even target individual groups, such as U.S. physicians or British attorneys.

**CYBERTERRORISM** Cyberterrorists, as well as hackers, may target businesses. The goals of a hacking operation might include a wholesale theft of data, such as a merchant's customer files, or the monitoring of a computer to discover a business firm's plans and transactions. A cyberterrorist might also want to insert false codes or data. For instance, the processing control system of a food manufacturer could be changed to alter the levels of ingredients so that consumers of the food would become ill.

A cyberterrorist attack on a major financial institution, such as the New York Stock Exchange or a large bank, could leave securities or money markets in flux and seriously affect the daily lives of millions of citizens. Similarly, any prolonged disruption of computer, cable, satellite, or telecommunications systems due to the actions of expert hackers would have serious repercussions on business operations—and national security—on a global level.

## Prosecuting Cyber Crime

Cyber crime has raised new issues in the investigation of crimes and the prosecution of offenders. Determining the "location" of a cyber crime and identifying a criminal in cyberspace present significant challenges for law enforcement.

**JURISDICTION AND IDENTIFICATION CHALLENGES** A threshold issue is, of course, jurisdiction. Jurisdiction is normally based on physical geography, as discussed in Chapter 2. Each state and nation has jurisdiction, or authority, over crimes committed within its boundaries. But geographic boundaries simply do not apply in cyberspace. A person who commits an act against a business in California, where the act is a cyber crime, might never have set foot in California but might instead reside in New York, or even in Canada, where the act may not be a crime.

Identifying the wrongdoer can also be difficult. Cyber criminals do not leave physical traces, such as fingerprints or DNA samples, as evidence of their crimes. Even electronic "footprints" can be hard to find and follow. For instance, e-mail may be sent through a remailer, an online service that guarantees that a message cannot be traced to its source.

For these reasons, laws written to protect physical property are often difficult to apply in cyberspace. Nonetheless, governments at both the state and the federal level have taken significant steps toward controlling cyber crime. California, for instance, which has the highest identity theft rate in the nation, has established a new eCrime unit to investigate and prosecute cyber crimes. Other states, including Florida, Louisiana, and Texas, also have special law enforcement units that focus solely on Internet crimes.

**THE COMPUTER FRAUD AND ABUSE ACT** Perhaps the most significant federal statute specifically addressing cyber crime is the Counterfeit Access Device and Computer Fraud and Abuse Act.[24] This act is commonly known as the Computer Fraud and Abuse Act (CFAA).

Among other things, the CFAA provides that a person who accesses a computer online, without authority, to obtain classified, restricted, or protected data (or attempts to do so) is subject to criminal prosecution. Such data could include financial and credit records, medical records, legal files, military and national security files, and other confidential information. The data can be located in government or private computers. The crime has two elements: accessing a computer without authority and taking the data.

This theft is a felony if it is committed for a commercial purpose or for private financial gain, or if the value of the stolen data (or computer time) exceeds $5,000. Penalties include fines and imprisonment for up to twenty years. A victim of computer theft can also bring a civil suit against the violator to obtain damages, an injunction, and other relief.

---

**24.** 18 U.S.C. Section 1030.

## Reviewing: Criminal Law and Cyber Crime

Edward Hanousek worked for Pacific & Arctic Railway and Navigation Company (P&A) as a roadmaster of the White Pass & Yukon Railroad in Alaska. Hanousek was responsible "for every detail of the safe and efficient maintenance and construction of track, structures and marine facilities of the entire railroad," including special projects. One project was a rock quarry, known as "6-mile," above the Skagway River. Next to the quarry, and just beneath the surface, ran a high-pressure oil pipeline owned by Pacific & Arctic Pipeline, Inc., P&A's sister company. When the quarry's backhoe operator punctured the pipeline, an estimated 1,000 to 5,000 gallons of oil were discharged into the river. Hanousek was charged with negligently discharging a harmful quantity of oil into a navigable water of the United States in violation of the criminal provisions of the Clean Water Act (CWA). Using the information presented in the chapter, answer the following questions.

1. Did Hanousek have the required mental state *(mens rea)* to be convicted of a crime? Why or why not?
2. Which theory discussed in the chapter would enable a court to hold Hanousek criminally liable for violating the statute if he participated in, directed, or merely knew about the specific violation?
3. Could the backhoe operator who punctured the pipeline also be charged with a crime in this situation? Explain.
4. Suppose that at trial, Hanousek argued that he should not be convicted because he was not aware of the requirements of the CWA. Would this defense be successful? Why or why not?

**DEBATE THIS . . .** *Because of overcriminalization, particularly by the federal government, Americans may be breaking the law regularly without knowing it. Should Congress rescind many of the more than four thousand federal crimes now on the books?*

## Terms and Concepts

| | | |
|---|---|---|
| *actus reus* 180 | exclusionary rule 192 | necessity 188 |
| arson 184 | felony 179 | petty offense 179 |
| beyond a reasonable doubt 178 | forgery 185 | phishing 196 |
| botnet 196 | grand jury 193 | plea bargaining 190 |
| burglary 183 | hacker 196 | probable cause 190 |
| computer crime 195 | identity theft 196 | robbery 183 |
| crime 178 | indictment 193 | search warrant 190 |
| cyber crime 195 | information 193 | self-defense 187 |
| cyber fraud 195 | larceny 183 | self-incrimination 189 |
| double jeopardy 190 | malware 196 | virus 197 |
| duress 189 | *mens rea* 181 | white-collar crime 185 |
| embezzlement 185 | misdemeanor 179 | worm 196 |
| entrapment 189 | money laundering 187 | |

## Issue Spotters

1. Dana takes her roommate's credit card without permission, intending to charge expenses that she incurs on a vacation. Her first stop is a gas station, where she uses the card to pay for gas. With respect to the gas station, has she committed a crime? If so, what is it? **(See page 183.)**

2. Without permission, Ben downloads consumer credit files from a computer belonging to Consumer Credit Agency. He then sells the data to Dawn. Has Ben committed a crime? If so, what is it? **(See page 198.)**

- **Check your answers to the Issue Spotters against the answers provided in Appendix E at the end of this text.**

## Business Scenarios

**10–1. Types of Cyber Crimes.** The following situations are similar, but each represents a variation of a particular crime. Identify the crime and point out the differences in the variations. **(See page 195.)**

(a) Chen, posing fraudulently as Diamond Credit Card Co., sends an e-mail to Emily, stating that the company has observed suspicious activity in her account and has frozen the account. The e-mail asks her to reregister her credit-card number and password to reopen the account.

(b) Claiming falsely to be Big Buy Retail Finance Co., Conner sends an e-mail to Dino, asking him to confirm or update his personal security information to prevent his Big Buy account from being discontinued.

(c) Felicia posts her résumé on GotWork.com, an online job-posting site, seeking a position in business and managerial finance and accounting. Hayden, who misrepresents himself as an employment officer with International Bank & Commerce Corp., sends her an e-mail asking for more personal information.

**10–2. Property Crimes.** Which, if any, of the following crimes necessarily involves illegal activity on the part of more than one person? **(See page 183.)**

(a) Bribery.

(b) Forgery.

(c) Embezzlement.

(d) Larceny.

(e) Receiving stolen property.

**10–3. Cyber Scam.** Kayla, a student at Learnwell University, owes $20,000 in unpaid tuition. If Kayla does not pay the tuition, Learnwell will not allow her to graduate. To obtain the funds to pay the debt, she sends e-mails to people that she does not personally know asking for financial help to send Milo, her disabled child, to a special school. In reality, Kayla has no children. Is this a crime? If so, which one? **(See page 196.)**

## Business Case Problems

**10–4. Cyber Crime.** Jiri Klimecek was a member of a group that overrode copyright protection in movies, video games, and software, and made them available for download online. Klimecek bought and installed hardware and software to set up a computer server and paid half of the monthly service charges to connect the server to the Internet. He knew that users around the world could access the server to upload and download copyrighted works. He obtained access to Czech movies and music to make them available. Klimecek was indicted in a federal district court for copyright infringement. He claimed that he did not understand the full scope of the operation. Did Klimecek commit a crime? If so, was he a "minor participant" entitled to a reduced sentence? Explain. [*United States v. Klimecek*, ___ F.3d ___ (7th Cir. 2009)] **(See page 195.)**

**10–5. Fourth Amendment.** Three police officers, including Maria Trevizo, were on patrol in Tucson, Arizona, near a neighborhood associated with the Crips gang, when they pulled over a car with suspended registration. Each officer talked to one of the three occupants. Trevizo spoke with Lemon Johnson, who was wearing clothing consistent with Crips membership. Visible in his jacket pocket was a police scanner, and he said that he had served time in prison for burglary. Trevizo asked him to get out of the car and patted him down "for officer safety." She found a gun. Johnson was charged in an Arizona state court with illegal possession of a weapon. What standard should apply to an officer's patdown of a passenger during a traffic stop? Should a search warrant be required? Could a search proceed solely on the basis of probable cause? Would a reasonable suspicion short of probable cause be sufficient?

Discuss. [*Arizona v. Johnson*, 555 U.S. 323, 129 S.Ct. 781, 172 L.Ed.2d 694 (2009)] **(See page 190.)**

**10–6. Searches.** Charles Byrd was in a minimum-security jail awaiting trial. A team of sheriff's deputies took several inmates into a room for a strip search without any apparent justification. Byrd was ordered to remove all of his clothing except his boxer shorts. A female deputy searched Byrd while several male deputies watched. One of the male deputies videotaped the search. Byrd filed a suit against the sheriff's department. Did the search violate Byrd's rights? Discuss. [*Byrd v. Maricopa County Sheriff's Department*, 629 F.3d 1135 (9th Cir. 2011)] **(See page 190.)**

**10–7. Credit-Card Theft.** Jacqueline Barden was shopping for school clothes with her children when her purse and automobile were taken. In Barden's purse were her car keys, credit and debit cards for herself and her children, as well as the children's Social Security cards and birth certificates needed for enrollment at school. Immediately after the purse and car were stolen, Rebecca Mary Turner attempted to use Barden's credit card at a local Exxon gas station, but the card was declined. The gas station attendant recognized Turner because she had previously written bad checks and used credit cards that did not belong to her.

Turner was later arrested while attempting to use one of Barden's checks to pay for merchandise at a Wal-Mart—where the clerk also recognized Turner from prior criminal activity. Turner claimed that she had not stolen Barden's purse or car, and that a friend had told her he had some checks and credit cards and asked her to try using them at Wal-Mart. Turner was convicted at trial. She appealed, claiming that there was insufficient evidence that she committed credit- and debit-card theft. Was the evidence sufficient to uphold her conviction? Why or why not? [*Turner v. State of Arkansas*, 2012 Ark.App. 150 (2012)] **(See page 183.)**

**10–8. BUSINESS CASE PROBLEM WITH SAMPLE ANSWER: Criminal Liability.**
 *During the morning rush hour, David Green threw bottles and plates from a twenty-sixth-floor hotel balcony overlooking Seventh Avenue in New York City. A video of the incident also showed him doing cartwheels while holding a beer bottle and sprinting toward the balcony while holding a glass steadily in his hand. When he saw police on the street below and on the roof of the building across the street, he suspended his antics but resumed tossing objects off the balcony after the police left. He later admitted that he could recall what he had done, but claimed to have been intoxicated and said his only purpose was to amuse himself and his friends. Did Green have the mental state required to establish criminal liability? Discuss. [State of New York v. Green, 104 A.D.3d 126, 958 N.Y.S.2d 138 (1 Dept. 2013)]* **(See page 181.)**

• **For a sample answer to Problem 10–8, go to Appendix F at the end of this text.**

**10–9. A QUESTION OF ETHICS: Identity Theft.**
 *Twenty-year-old Davis Omole had good grades in high school, where he played on the football and chess teams, and went on to college. Omole worked at a cell phone store where he stole customers' personal information. He used the stolen identities to create a hundred different accounts on eBay, and held more than three hundred auctions listing for sale items that he did not own (including cell phones, plasma televisions, and stereos). From these auctions, he collected $90,000. To avoid getting caught, he continuously closed and opened the eBay accounts, activated and deactivated cell phone and e-mail accounts, and changed mailing addresses and post office boxes. Omole, who had previously been convicted in a state court for Internet fraud, was convicted in a federal district court of identity theft and wire fraud. [United States v. Omole, 523 F.3d 691 (7th Cir. 2008)]* **(See page 196.)**

(a) Omole displayed contempt for the court and ridiculed his victims, calling them stupid for having been cheated. What does this behavior suggest about Omole's ethics?

(b) Under federal sentencing guidelines, Omole could have been imprisoned for more than eight years. He received only three years, however, two of which comprised the mandatory sentence for identity theft. Was this sentence too lenient? Explain.

## Legal Reasoning Group Activity

**10–10. Cyber Crime.** Cyber crime costs consumers millions of dollars per year, and it costs businesses, including banks and other credit-card issuers, even more. Nonetheless, when cyber criminals are caught and convicted, they are rarely ordered to pay restitution or sentenced to long prison terms. **(See page 195.)**

(a) One group should argue that stiffer sentences would reduce the amount of cyber crime.

(b) A second group should determine how businesspersons can best protect themselves from cyber crime and avoid the associated costs.

Ethical and legal concepts are often closely intertwined. This is because the common law, as it evolved in England and then in America, reflected society's values and customs. This connection between law and ethics is clearly evident in the area of tort law, which provides remedies for harms caused by actions that society has deemed wrongful. Criminal law is also rooted in common law concepts of right and wrong behavior, although common law concepts governing criminal acts are now expressed in, or replaced by, federal, state, and local criminal statutes. The number of torts and crimes has continued to expand as new ways to commit wrongs have been discovered.

The laws governing torts, crimes, and intellectual property—the areas of law covered in this unit—constitute an important part of the legal environment of business. In each of these areas, new legal (and ethical) challenges have emerged as a result of developments in technology. In this *Focus on Ethics* feature, we look at the ethical dimensions of selected topics discussed in the preceding chapters, including some issues that are unique to the cyber age.

## Privacy Rights in an Online World

Privacy rights are protected under constitutional law, tort law, and various federal and state statutes. How to protect privacy rights in the online world, though, has been a recurring problem over the past decade. One difficulty is that individuals today often are not even aware that information about their personal lives and preferences is being collected by Internet companies and other online users. Nor do they know how that information will be used.

As discussed in Chapter 9, "cookies" installed in computers may allow users' Web movements to be tracked. Many e-mail services, such as Google's Gmail, automatically scan and save information about users. Persons who purchase goods from online merchants or auctions inevitably must reveal some personal information, often including their credit-card numbers.

In addition, many goods purchased today use radio-frequency identification (RFID) tags to transmit information. Such tags are frequently included in automobiles, clothing, and cell phones. For instance, clothing manufacturers may use RFID tags to track merchandise and see which products are being sold through which retailers. Health-care facilities, hospitals, libraries, museums, and schools may also use RFID tags. The possibility that these tags may be used to read information linked to a person without her or his consent raises privacy concerns.

## The Increased Value of Personal Information

One of the major concerns of consumers in recent years has been the collection and sale of their personal information—sometimes even by third parties with whom the consumers have never had dealings. This information has become increasingly valuable to online marketers, who are willing to pay a high price to those who collect and sell it.

Because of consumers' concerns—and the possibility of lawsuits based on privacy laws—businesses marketing goods online need to exercise care. Today, many online businesses create and post on their Web sites a privacy policy disclosing how any information obtained from their customers will be used.

## Privacy Rights in the Workplace

Another area of concern is the extent to which employees' privacy rights should be protected in the workplace. Traditionally, employees have been afforded a certain "zone of privacy" in the workplace. For example, the courts have concluded that employees have a reasonable expectation of privacy with respect to personal items contained in their desks or in their lockers. Should this zone of privacy extend to personal e-mail sent via the employer's server or social media posts made via a smartphone that the employer provided? This question and others relating to employee privacy rights should be considered by employers today given the increased use of the Internet and social media by employees.

### LEGAL REASONING

1. *Some observers maintain that privacy rights are quickly becoming a thing of the past. In your opinion, is it possible to protect privacy rights in today's online world? Why or why not?*

## Should Civil Liberties Be Sacrificed to Control Crime and Terrorist Activities in the Cyber Age?

The very real and substantial threat posed by criminal conspirators and terrorists today has raised some important questions about what methods should be used to combat them. In 2012, for instance, the movie *Zero Dark Thirty* raised the question of whether it is ever acceptable for the United States to use torture to obtain information about terrorists.

Similarly, as criminals and terrorists use the Internet to communicate and even to recruit new members, the question arises as to whether it is possible to control many types of crime and terrorist activities without sacrificing some civil liberties. Should the U.S. government actively monitor e-mail, social media, and other electronic communications of particular users or groups?

Traditionally, Americans rejected any attempt by the government to monitor Internet use to detect criminal conspiracies or terrorist activities. Immediately after the terrorist attacks of 2001, however, Americans seemed more willing to trade off some of their civil liberties for greater national security. The USA Patriot Act (see Chapter 4) gave law enforcement personnel more authority to conduct electronic surveillance, such as monitoring Web sites and e-mail exchanges. Today, though, many complain that this legislation has gone too far in curbing traditional civil liberties guaranteed by the U.S. Constitution.

### LEGAL REASONING

2. *Many believe that the federal government should not be allowed to monitor the Internet activities and e-mail exchanges of its citizens without obtaining a warrant. Yet others maintain that in some situations, when time is of the essence, such monitoring may be necessary to keep Americans safe from terrorists. Where should the line be drawn between justifiable and unjustifiable governmental interference with American citizens' civil liberties? Discuss fully.*

### Global Companies and Censorship Issues—Google China

Doing business on a global level can sometimes involve serious ethical challenges. Consider the ethical firestorm that erupted when Google, Inc., decided to market "Google China" (**Google.cn**) in 2006. This version of Google's widely used search engine was tailored to the Chinese government's censorship requirements.

In China, Web sites that offer pornography, criticism of the government, or information on sensitive topics, such as the Tiananmen Square massacre in 1989, are censored—that is, they cannot be accessed by Web users. Government agencies enforce the censorship and encourage citizens to inform on one another. Thousands of Web sites are shut down each year, and the sites' operators are subject to potential imprisonment.

The Chinese government insists that in restricting access to certain Web sites, it is merely following the lead of other national governments, which also impose controls on information access. As an example, it cites France, which bans access to any Web sites selling or displaying Nazi paraphernalia. The United States itself prohibits the dissemination of certain types of materials, such as child pornography, over the Internet. Furthermore, the U.S. government monitors Web sites and e-mail communications to protect against terrorist threats. How, ask Chinese officials, can other nations point their fingers at China for engaging in a common international practice?

### Censorship—The Lesser of Two Evils?

Human rights groups came out strongly against Google's decision, maintaining that the company was seeking profits in a lucrative marketplace at the expense of assisting the Chinese Communist Party in suppressing free speech. Google defended its actions by pointing out that its Chinese search engine at least lets users know which sites are being censored. Google China includes the links to censored sites, but when a user tries to access a link, the program states that it is not accessible.

Google claimed that its approach was essentially the "lesser of two evils": if U.S. companies did not cooperate with

the Chinese government, Chinese residents would have less user-friendly Internet access. Moreover, Google asserted that providing Internet access, even if censored, is a step toward more open access in the future because technology is, in itself, a revolutionary force.

### China's Cyberattack and Google's Response

Google's attitude changed when it discovered that its software had been the target of a cyberattack that apparently originated in China. David Drummond, senior vice president of corporate development and Google's chief legal officer, informed the public about the attack in an article on the official Google blog on January 12, 2010. Drummond described the attack as "highly sophisticated" and said that it was not limited to Google—some twenty other large companies were similarly targeted. Drummond believed the goal of the attackers was to access the Gmail accounts of Chinese human rights activists. Google also discovered that the accounts of dozens of human rights advocates in the United States, China, and Europe had routinely been accessed by third parties.

Drummond said that the attacks and the surveillance that the investigation uncovered led Google to announce a change in its China policy: "We have decided we are no longer willing to continue censoring our results on **Google.cn** . . . . We recognize that this may well mean having to shut down **Google.cn**."[1] In 2010, Google stopped operating **Google.cn** and automatically redirected users to its Hong Kong servers at **Google.com.hk** for search services in Chinese.

Although the Chinese government censors results on Google's Hong Kong servers, it nonetheless found Google's auto-redirect policy unacceptable and threatened to revoke Google's license. Then Google again revised its policy so that it no longer auto-redirects Chinese users to the Hong Kong servers. Instead, Google directs Chinese users to a Web page at which they must elect to use the Hong Kong servers. In addition, Google reopened Google China to host minimal searches for content that does not require censorship, such as for maps, music, and translation services.

Proponents of human rights applauded Google's efforts to avoid censorship of its search content, but others are not so sure. If Google and similar companies refuse to cooperate with governments that engage in censorship, will this transform the World Wide Web? Will the information highway of the future be forced to stop at national borders?

### LEGAL REASONING

3. *Do companies that do business on a global level, such as Google, have an ethical duty to foreign citizens not to suppress*

---

1. David Drummond, "A New Approach to China," *The Official Google Blog,* January 12, 2010.

FOCUS ON ETHICS CONTINUES ➡

*free speech? Is it ever acceptable for these companies to censor the information that they provide in other nations at the request of a foreign government? Explain your answer.*

## Do Gun Makers Have a Duty to Warn?

One of the big issues in today's legal environment is how tort law principles apply to harms (injury or death) caused by guns. Many negligence lawsuits have been filed across the nation against gun manufacturers. Plaintiffs often claim that gun makers have a duty to warn users of their products of the dangers associated with gun use. Would it be fair to impose such a requirement on gun manufacturers? Some say no, because such dangers are open and obvious. (Recall from Chapter 6 that, generally, there is no duty to warn of open and obvious dangers.) Others contend that warnings could prevent numerous gun accidents.

State courts addressing this issue have generally ruled that manufacturers have no duty to warn users of the obvious risks associated with gun use. For example, New York's highest court held that a gun manufacturer's duty of care does not extend to those who are injured by the illegal use of handguns.[2] Some courts, however, have held that gun makers whose marketing or sales practices cause a large influx of guns into the illegal secondary market could be liable under a public nuisance theory.[3] Other courts have allowed plaintiffs to sue for negligence when guns are sold to a straw purchaser (a person pretending to be a legitimate buyer) and then distributed to criminals.[4]

### LEGAL REASONING

4. *In your opinion, should gun manufacturers have a duty to warn gun users of the dangers of using guns? Would such a warning be effective in preventing gun-related violence? Discuss.*

## Trademark Protection versus Free Speech Rights

Another legal issue pits the rights of trademark owners against the right to free speech. The question is whether a company's ownership rights in a trademark used as a domain name outweigh the free speech rights of those who use a similar domain name to criticize or parody the company. A common tactic of those critical of a company's goods or services is to add the word *sucks* or *stinks* (or some other disparaging term) to the trademark owner's domain name.

A number of companies have sued the owners of such sites for trademark infringement in the hope that a court or an arbitrating panel will order the site owner to cease using the domain name. To date, though, companies have had little success pursuing this alternative. After all, one of the primary reasons trademarks are protected under U.S. law is to prevent customers from becoming confused about the origin of the goods for sale—and a "sucks" site certainly does not create such confusion.

Furthermore, U.S. courts and arbitrators give extensive protection to free speech rights, including the right to express opinions about companies and their products.[5] Even international arbitration panels, when hearing disputes between U.S. parties, give significant weight to U.S. constitutional law protecting speech.[6]

## Trade Secrets versus Free Speech Rights

Another ongoing issue with ethical dimensions involves the point at which free speech rights come into conflict with the right of copyright holders to protect their property by using encryption technology. This issue came before the California Supreme Court in the case of *DVD Copy Control Association v. Bunner.*[7]

Trade associations in the movie industry sued an Internet Web site operator who had posted the code of a computer program that cracked technology used to encrypt DVDs. This posed a significant threat to the movie industry because, by using the code-cracking software, users would be able to duplicate the copyrighted movies stored on the DVDs.

In their suit, the trade associations claimed that the Web site operator had misappropriated trade secrets. The defendant argued that software programs designed to break encryption programs were a form of constitutionally protected speech. When the case reached the California Supreme Court, the court held that although the First Amendment applies to computer code, computer code is not a form of "pure speech," and the courts can therefore protect it to a lesser extent. The court reinstated a trial court order that enjoined (prevented) the Web site operator from continuing to post the code.

### LEGAL REASONING

5. *Generally, do you believe that the law has struck a fair balance between the rights of intellectual property owners and the rights of the public? Why or why not?*

---

2. *Hamilton v. Beretta U.S.A. Corp.,* 96 N.Y.2d 222, 750 N.E.2d 1055, 727 N.Y.S.2d 7 (2001). See also, *Williams v. Beesmiller, Inc.,* 962 N.Y.S.2d 834, 103 A.D.3d 1191 (2013).

3. *City of New York v. Beretta U.S.A. Corp.,* 524 F.3d 384 (2d Cir. 2008); *Gilland v. Sportsmen's Outpost, Inc.,* 2011 WL 2479693 (Conn.Super. 2011); and *Illeto v. Glock, Inc.,* 349 F.3d 1191 (9th Cir. 2003).

4. *Williams v. Beemiller, Inc.,* 962 N.Y.S.2d 834, 103 A.D.3d 1191 (2013); and *Smith v. Atlantic Gun & Tackle, Inc.,* 376 F.Supp.2d 291 (E.D.N.Y. 2005).

5. Many businesses have concluded that although they cannot control what people say about them, they can make it more difficult for it to be said. Today, businesses commonly register such insulting domain names before the cyber-gripers themselves can register them.

6. See, for example, *Sutherland Institute v. Continuative, LLC,* WIPO Arbitration and Mediation Center, Case No. D2009-0893.

7. 31 Cal.4th 864, 4 Cal.Rptr.3d 69 (2003). See also *VI 4D, LLP v. Crucians in Focus, Inc.,* 2012 WL 6757243 (VI Super. 2012).

MILLER

SUMMARIZED-CASE EDITION

# UNIT THREE

# CONTRACTS AND E-CONTRACTS

## CONTENTS

# CHAPTER 11

# NATURE AND TERMINOLOGY

The noted legal scholar Roscoe Pound once said that "[t]he social order rests upon the stability and predictability of conduct, of which keeping promises is a large item."[1] Contract law deals with, among other things, the formation and keeping of promises. A **promise** is a declaration by a person (the *promisor*) to do or not to do a certain act. As a result, the person to whom the promise is made (the *promisee*) has a right to expect or demand that something either will or will not happen in the future.

Like other types of law, contract law reflects our social values, interests, and expectations at a given point in time. It shows, for instance, to what extent our society allows people to make promises or commitments that are legally binding. It distinguishes between promises that create only *moral* obligations (such as a promise to take a friend to lunch) and promises that are legally binding (such as a promise to pay for merchandise purchased).

Contract law also demonstrates which excuses our society accepts for breaking certain types of promises. In addition, it indicates which promises are considered to be contrary to public policy—against the interests of society as a whole—and therefore legally invalid. When the person making a promise is a child or is mentally incompetent, for example, a question will arise as to whether the promise should be enforced. Resolving such questions is the essence of contract law.

1. Roscoe Pound, *Jurisprudence,* Vol. 3 (St. Paul, Minn.: West Publishing Co., 1959), p. 162.

---

## SECTION 1
## AN OVERVIEW OF CONTRACT LAW

Before we look at the numerous rules that courts use to determine whether a particular promise will be enforced, it is necessary to understand some fundamental concepts of contract law. In this section, we describe the sources and general function of contract law and introduce the objective theory of contracts.

### Sources of Contract Law

The common law governs all contracts except when it has been modified or replaced by statutory law, such as the Uniform Commercial Code (UCC),[2] or by administrative agency regulations. Contracts relating to services, real estate, employment, and insurance,

for instance, generally are governed by the common law of contracts. (For a sample contract with an explanation of its terms, see the *Appendix to Chapter 19: Reading and Analyzing Contracts.*)

Contracts for the sale and lease of goods, however, are governed by the UCC—to the extent that the UCC has modified general contract law. The relationship between general contract law and the law governing sales and leases of goods will be explored in detail in Chapter 20. In the discussion of general contract law that follows, we indicate in footnotes the areas in which the UCC has significantly altered common law contract principles.

### The Function of Contract Law

No aspect of modern life is entirely free of contractual relationships. You acquire rights and obligations, for example, when you borrow funds, buy or lease a house, obtain insurance, and purchase goods or services. Contract law is designed to provide stability and predictability, as well as certainty, for both buyers and sellers in the marketplace.

2. See Chapters 1 and 20 for further discussions of the significance and coverage of the UCC. The UCC is presented in Appendix C at the end of this book.

Contract law assures the parties to private agreements that the promises they make will be enforceable. Clearly, many promises are kept because the parties involved feel a moral obligation to keep them or because keeping a promise is in their mutual self-interest. The **promisor** (the person making the promise) and the **promisee** (the person to whom the promise is made) may also decide to honor their agreement for other reasons. In business agreements, the rules of contract law are often followed to avoid potential disputes.

By supplying procedures for enforcing private contractual agreements, contract law provides an essential condition for the existence of a market economy. Without a legal framework of reasonably assured expectations within which to make long-run plans, businesspersons would be able to rely only on the good faith of others. Duty and good faith are usually sufficient to obtain compliance with a promise. When price changes or adverse economic factors make compliance costly, however, these elements may not be enough. Contract law is necessary to ensure compliance with a promise or to entitle the innocent party to some form of relief.

## The Definition of a Contract

A **contract** is "a promise or a set of promises for the breach of which the law gives a remedy, or the performance of which the law in some way recognizes as a duty."[3] Put simply, a contract is an agreement that can be enforced in court. It is formed by two or more parties who agree to perform or to refrain from performing some act now or in the future.

Generally, contract disputes arise when there is a promise of future performance. If the contractual promise is not fulfilled, the party who made it is subject to the sanctions of a court (see Chapter 19). That party may be required to pay damages for failing to perform the contractual promise. In a few instances, the party may be required to perform the promised act.

---

**3.** *Restatement (Second) of Contracts,* Section 1. As mentioned in Chapter 1, *Restatements of the Law* are scholarly books that restate the existing common law principles distilled from court opinions as a set of rules on a particular topic. Courts often refer to the *Restatements* for guidance. The *Restatement of the Law of Contracts* was compiled by the American Law Institute in 1932. The *Restatement,* which is now in its second edition (a third edition is being drafted), will be referred to throughout the following chapters on contract law.

## The Objective Theory of Contracts

In determining whether a contract has been formed, the element of intent is of prime importance. In contract law, intent is determined by what is called the **objective theory of contracts,** not by the personal or subjective intent, or belief, of a party. (We will also look at the objective theory of contracts in Chapter 12, in the context of contract formation.)

### FACTS AS INTERPRETED BY A REASONABLE PERSON
The theory is that a party's intention to enter into a legally binding agreement, or contract, is judged by outward, objective facts. The facts are as interpreted by a *reasonable* person, rather than by the party's own secret, subjective intentions. Objective facts may include:

1. What the party said when entering into the contract.
2. How the party acted or appeared (intent may be manifested by conduct as well as by oral or written words).
3. The circumstances surrounding the transaction.

▶ **Case in Point 11.1**  Linear Technology Corporation (LTC) makes and sells integrated circuits for use in cell phones and computers. LTC sued its competitor, Micrel, Inc., for infringement of a patent on a particular chip. In its defense, Micrel claimed that LTC's patent was invalid because LTC had offered to sell the chip commercially before the date on which it could be legally sold. The issue was whether LTC had entered into sales contracts when it solicited input on pricing and accepted distributors' purchase orders using a "will advise" procedure before the critical date.

The court ruled that under the objective theory of contracts, no reasonable customer could interpret LTC's requests for information about pricing and potential orders as an offer that could bind LTC to a sale. Therefore, LTC did not violate the ban on sales and could continue its suit against Micrel for patent infringement.[4] ◀

### UNDERLYING MOTIVE NOT IMPORTANT
A party may have many reasons for entering into an agreement—obtaining real property, goods, or services, for example, and profiting from the deal. Any of these purposes may provide a motivation for performing the contract. In the following case, however, one party failed to perform and claimed that he had not intended to enter into the contract when he signed it.

---

**4.** *Linear Technology Corp. v. Micrel, Inc.,* 275 F.3d 1040 (Fed.Cir. 2001).

# CASE 11.1

## Pan Handle Realty, LLC v. Olins
Appellate Court of Connecticut, 140 Conn.App. 556, 59 A.3d 842 (2013).

**BACKGROUND AND FACTS**   Pan Handle Realty, LLC, built a luxury home in Westport, Connecticut. Robert Olins proposed to lease the property. Pan Handle forwarded a draft lease to Olins. On January 17, 2009, the parties met and negotiated changes to the terms. After the final draft of the lease was signed, Olins gave Pan Handle a check for the amount of the annual rent—$138,000—and said that he planned to move into the home on January 28. Before that date, according to the lease, Pan Handle removed all of the furnishings.

On January 27, Olins's bank informed Pan Handle that payment had been stopped on the rental check. Olins then told Pan Handle that he was "unable to pursue any further interest in the property." Pan Handle made substantial efforts to find a new tenant, but was unable to do so. Consequently, Pan Handle filed a lawsuit in a Connecticut state court against Olins, alleging that he had breached the lease. From a decision in Pan Handle's favor—and an award of damages in the amount of $138,000 in unpaid rent, $8,000 in utility fees, interest, and attorneys' fees—Olins appealed.

**DECISION AND RATIONALE**   The state intermediate appellate court affirmed the lower court's judgment. The objective fact, as supported by the evidence, was that the parties intended to be bound by the lease when they signed it. That Olins had a different intent or a later "change of heart" was not persuasive. Olins contended that because material terms were still being negotiated that there was no meeting of the minds, which is required to form a contract. The reviewing court noted that "If there has been a misunderstanding between the parties, or a misapprehension by one of the parties or both so that their minds have never met, no contract has been entered into by them and the court will not make for them a contract for which they themselves did not make." Here, though, Olins and a representative of Pan Handle had made revisions and signed a lease. Olins had tendered a check, on which he noted payment for a one-year lease of the premises.

"The defendant's apparent unilateral changed of heart regarding the lease agreement does not negate the parties' prior meeting of the minds that occurred at the time the lease was executed." The trial court was correct in finding that "the lease agreement was a valid and binding contract which the defendant" breached.

**THE LEGAL ENVIRONMENT DIMENSION**   *How did the objective theory of contracts affect the results of this case? Explain.*

**THE ETHICAL DIMENSION**   *Did the measure of damages assessed in this case place Pan Handle in the same position that it would have been in if the lease had been fully performed? Discuss.*

---

### SECTION 2
# ELEMENTS OF A CONTRACT

The many topics that will be discussed in the following chapters on contract law require an understanding of the basic elements of a valid contract and the way in which a contract is created. It is also necessary to understand the types of circumstances in which even legally valid contracts will not be enforced.

## Requirements of a Valid Contract

The following list briefly describes the four requirements that must be met before a valid contract exists. If any of these elements is lacking, no contract will have been formed. (Each requirement will be explained more fully in subsequent chapters.)

1. *Agreement.* An agreement to form a contract includes an *offer* and an *acceptance*. One party must offer to enter into a legal agreement, and another party must accept the terms of the offer.

2. *Consideration.* Any promises made by the parties to the contract must be supported by legally sufficient and bargained-for *consideration* (something of value received or promised, such as money, to convince a person to make a deal).
3. *Contractual capacity.* Both parties entering into the contract must have the contractual *capacity* to do so. The law must recognize them as possessing characteristics that qualify them as competent parties.
4. *Legality.* The contract's purpose must be to accomplish some goal that is legal and not against public policy.

## Defenses to the Enforceability of a Contract

Even if all of the requirements listed above are satisfied, a contract may be unenforceable if the following requirements are not met. These requirements typically are raised as *defenses* to the enforceability of an otherwise valid contract.

1. *Voluntary consent.* The consent of both parties must be voluntary. For instance, if a contract was formed as a result of fraud, undue influence, mistake, or duress, the contract may not be enforceable (see Chapter 15).
2. *Form.* The contract must be in whatever form the law requires. Some contracts must be in writing to be enforceable (see Chapter 16).

### SECTION 3
# TYPES OF CONTRACTS

There are many types of contracts. They are categorized based on legal distinctions as to their formation, performance, and enforceability.

## Contract Formation

Contracts can be classified according to how and when they are formed. Exhibit 11–1 on the next page shows three such classifications, and the following subsections explain them in greater detail.

**BILATERAL VERSUS UNILATERAL CONTRACTS** Every contract involves at least two parties. The **offeror** is the party making the offer. The **offeree** is the party to whom the offer is made. Whether the contract is classified as *bilateral* or *unilateral* depends on what the offeree must do to accept the offer and bind the offeror to a contract.

*Bilateral Contracts.* If the offeree can accept simply by promising to perform, the contract is a **bilateral contract.** Hence, a bilateral contract is a "promise for a promise." No performance, such as payment of funds or delivery of goods, need take place for a bilateral contract to be formed. The contract comes into existence at the moment the promises are exchanged. (An example of a bilateral contract appears in the *Appendix to Chapter 19.*)

▶ **Example 11.2** Javier offers to buy Ann's smartphone for $200. Javier tells Ann that he will give her the $200 for the smartphone next Friday, when he gets paid. Ann accepts Javier's offer and promises to give him the smartphone when he pays her on Friday. Javier and Ann have formed a bilateral contract. ◀

*Unilateral Contracts.* If the offer is phrased so that the offeree can accept the offer only by completing the contract performance, the contract is a **unilateral contract.** Hence, a unilateral contract is a "promise for an act."[5] In other words, a unilateral contract is formed not at the moment when promises are exchanged but at the moment when the contract is *performed.* ▶ **Example 11.3** Reese says to Celia, "If you drive my car from New York to Los Angeles, I'll give you $1,000." Only on Celia's completion of the act—bringing the car to Los Angeles—does she fully accept Reese's offer to pay $1,000. If she chooses not to accept the offer to drive the car to Los Angeles, there are no legal consequences. ◀

Contests, lotteries, and other competitions involving prizes are examples of offers to form unilateral contracts. If a person complies with the rules of the contest—such as by submitting the right lottery number at the right place and time—a unilateral contract is formed. The organization offering the prize is then bound to a contract to perform as promised in the offer. If the person fails to comply with the contest rules, however, no binding contract is formed. (See this chapter's *Insight into Ethics* feature on page 211 for a discussion of whether a company can change a contest prize from what it originally advertised.)

*Revocation of Offers for Unilateral Contracts.* A problem arises in unilateral contracts when the promisor attempts to *revoke* (cancel) the offer after the promisee

---

5. The phrase *unilateral contract,* if read literally, is a contradiction in terms. A contract cannot be one sided because, by definition, an agreement implies the existence of two or more parties.

## EXHIBIT 11-1 Classifications Based on Contract Formation

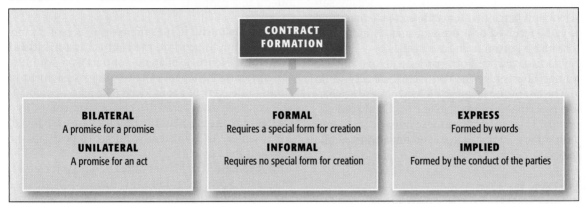

**CONTRACT FORMATION**

| **BILATERAL** | **FORMAL** | **EXPRESS** |
| A promise for a promise | Requires a special form for creation | Formed by words |
| **UNILATERAL** | **INFORMAL** | **IMPLIED** |
| A promise for an act | Requires no special form for creation | Formed by the conduct of the parties |

has begun performance but before the act has been completed. ▶ **Example 11.4** Seiko offers to buy Jin's sailboat, moored in San Francisco, on delivery of the boat to Seiko's dock in Newport Beach, three hundred miles south of San Francisco. Jin rigs the boat and sets sail. Shortly before his arrival at Newport Beach, Jin receives a message from Seiko withdrawing her offer. Seiko's offer was for a unilateral contract, which could be accepted only by Jin's delivery of the sailboat at her dock. ◀

In contract law, offers are normally *revocable* (capable of being taken back, or canceled) until accepted. Under the traditional view of unilateral contracts, Seiko's revocation would terminate the offer. Because of the harsh effect on the offeree of the revocation of an offer to form a unilateral contract, the modern-day view is different. Today, once performance has been *substantially* undertaken, the offeror cannot revoke the offer. Thus, in *Example 11.4* above, even though Jin has not yet accepted the offer by complete performance, Seiko is normally prohibited from revoking it. Jin can deliver the boat and bind Seiko to the contract.

**FORMAL VERSUS INFORMAL CONTRACTS** Another classification system divides contracts into formal contracts and informal contracts. **Formal contracts** are contracts that require a special form or method of creation (formation) to be enforceable.[6] One example is *negotiable instruments*, which include checks, drafts, promissory notes, bills of exchange, and certificates of deposit. Negotiable instruments are formal contracts

because, under the Uniform Commercial Code (UCC), a special form and language are required to create them.

*Letters of credit,* which are frequently used in international sales contracts (see Chapter 24), are another type of formal contract. Letters of credit are agreements to pay contingent on the purchaser's receipt of invoices and *bills of lading* (documents evidencing receipt of, and title to, goods shipped).

**Informal contracts** (also called *simple contracts*) include all other contracts. No special form is required (except for certain types of contracts that must be in writing), as the contracts are usually based on their substance rather than their form. Typically, business-persons put their contracts in writing to ensure that there is some proof of a contract's existence should disputes arise.

**EXPRESS VERSUS IMPLIED CONTRACTS** Contracts may also be categorized as *express* or *implied*. In an **express contract,** the terms of the agreement are fully and explicitly stated in words, oral or written. A signed lease for an apartment or a house is an express written contract. If one classmate calls another on the phone and agrees to buy her textbooks from last semester for $300, an express oral contract has been made.

A contract that is implied from the conduct of the parties is called an **implied contract** (or sometimes an *implied-in-fact contract*). This type of contract differs from an express contract in that the conduct of the parties, rather than their words, creates and defines the terms of the contract.

***Requirements for Implied Contracts.*** For an implied contract to arise, certain requirements must be met.

---

**6.** See *Restatement (Second) of Contracts,* Section 6, which explains that formal contracts include (1) contracts under seal, (2) recognizances, (3) negotiable instruments, and (4) letters of credit.

# INSIGHT INTO ETHICS
## Can a Company That Sponsors a Contest Change the Prize from What It Originally Offered?

Courts have historically treated contests as unilateral contracts, which typically cannot be modified by the offeror after the offeree has begun to perform. But this principle may not always apply to contest terms or advertisements.

John Rogalski entered a poker tournament conducted by Little Poker League, LLC (LPL). The tournament lasted several months as players competed for spots in a winner-take-all final event. During the final event, Rogalski and the other contestants signed a "World Series of Poker (WSOP) Agreement," which stated that LPL would pay the $10,000 WSOP entry fee on the winner's behalf and provide $2,500 for travel-related expenses. The agreement also stated that if the winner did not attend the WSOP, he or she would relinquish the WSOP seat and return the expense money to LPL.

Rogalski won and took the $2,500 for travel expenses, but did not attend the WSOP. He then filed a suit for $10,000 against LPL, arguing that it had advertised that the winner could choose to receive the cash value of the prizes ($12,500) instead of going to the WSOP. Rogalski

claimed that, by participating in the tournament, he had accepted the advertised offer to take the cash in lieu of entering the WSOP. He further claimed that the later agreement was an invalid contract modification. LPL filed a counterclaim to recover the $2,500 in expenses. The court ruled in favor of LPL, finding that the contract was not formed when Rogalski began participating in the contest. Rather, it was formed when he signed the WSOP agreement. Under the contest rules as stated in the WSOP agreement, Rogalski had to return the $2,500 of expenses to LPL.[a]

### LEGAL CRITICAL THINKING
**INSIGHT INTO THE SOCIAL ENVIRONMENT**

*Why would a company that changes its advertised prizes have to worry about its reputation?*

---

a. *Rogalski v. Little Poker League, LLC,* 2011 WL 589636 (Minn.App. 2011).

---

Normally, if the following conditions exist, a court will hold that an implied contract was formed:

1. The plaintiff furnished some service or property.
2. The plaintiff expected to be paid for that service or property, and the defendant knew or should have known that payment was expected.
3. The defendant had a chance to reject the services or property and did not.

▶ **Example 11.5** Oleg, a small-business owner, needs an accountant to complete his tax return. He drops by a local accountant's office, explains his situation to the accountant, and learns what fees she charges. The next day, he returns and gives the receptionist all of the necessary documents to complete his return. Then he walks out without saying anything further to the accountant.

In this situation, Oleg has entered into an implied contract to pay the accountant the usual fees for her services. The contract is implied because of Oleg's conduct and hers. She expects to be paid for completing the tax return, and by bringing in

the records she will need to do the job, Oleg has implied an intent to pay her. ◀

***Contracts with Express and Implied Terms.*** Note that a contract may be a mixture of an express contract and an implied contract. In other words, a contract may contain some express terms, while others are implied. During the constructions of a home, for instance, the homeowner often asks the builder to make changes in the original specifications.

▶ **Case in Point 11.6** Lamar Hopkins hired Uhrhahn Construction & Design, Inc., for several projects in building his home. For each project, the parties signed a written contract that was based on a cost estimate and specifications and that required changes to the agreement to be in writing. While the work was in progress, however, Hopkins repeatedly asked Uhrhahn to deviate from the contract specifications, which Uhrhahn did. None of these requests was made in writing.

One day, Hopkins asked Uhrhahn to use Durisol blocks instead of the cinder blocks specified in the original contract, indicating that the cost would be the same. Uhrhahn used the Durisol blocks but demanded extra payment when it became clear that the Durisol blocks were more complicated to install. Although Hopkins had paid for the other deviations from the contract that he had orally requested, he refused to pay Uhrhahn for the substitution of the Durisol blocks. Uhrhahn sued for breach of contract. The court found that Hopkins, through his conduct, had waived the provision requiring written contract modification and created an implied contract to pay the extra cost of installing the Durisol blocks.[7] ◄

## Contract Performance

Contracts are also classified according to the degree to which they have been performed. A contract that has been fully performed on both sides is called an **executed contract.** A contract that has not been fully performed by the parties is called an **executory contract.** If one party has fully performed but the other has not, the contract is said to be executed on the one side and executory on the other, but the contract is still classified as executory.

▶ **Example 11.7** Jackson, Inc., agreed to buy ten tons of coal from the Northern Coal Company.

---

7. *Uhrhahn Construction & Design, Inc. v. Hopkins,* 179 P.3d 808 (Utah App. 2008).

Northern delivered the coal to Jackson's steel mill, where it is being burned. At this point, the contract is executed on the part of Northern and executory on Jackson's part. After Jackson pays Northern, the contract will be executed on both sides. ◄

## Contract Enforceability

A **valid contract** has the elements necessary to entitle at least one of the parties to enforce it in court. Those elements, as mentioned earlier, consist of (1) an agreement (offer and acceptance) (2) supported by legally sufficient consideration (3) made by parties who have the legal capacity to enter into the contract, and (4) a legal purpose.

As you can see in Exhibit 11–2 below, valid contracts may be enforceable, voidable, or unenforceable. Additionally, a contract may be referred to as a *void contract.* We look next at the meaning of the terms *voidable, unenforceable,* and *void* in relation to contract enforceability.

**VOIDABLE CONTRACTS** A **voidable contract** is a valid contract but one that can be avoided at the option of one or both of the parties. The party having the option can elect either to avoid any duty to perform or to *ratify* (make valid) the contract. If the contract is avoided, both parties are released from it. If it is ratified, both parties must fully perform their respective legal obligations.

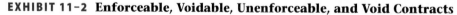

**EXHIBIT 11-2 Enforceable, Voidable, Unenforceable, and Void Contracts**

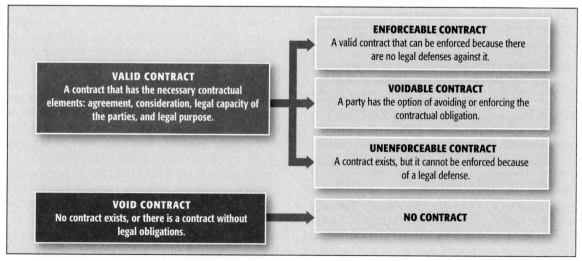

As you will read in Chapter 14, contracts made by minors generally are voidable at the option of the minor (with certain exceptions). Contracts made by mentally incompetent persons and intoxicated persons may also be voidable. Additionally, contracts entered into under fraudulent conditions are voidable at the option of the defrauded party. Contracts entered into under legally defined duress or undue influence are also voidable (see Chapter 15).

**UNENFORCEABLE CONTRACTS** An **unenforceable contract** is one that cannot be enforced because of certain legal defenses against it. It is not unenforceable because a party failed to satisfy a legal requirement of the contract. Rather, it is a valid contract rendered unenforceable by some statute or law. For instance, certain contracts must be in writing (see Chapter 16), and if they are not, they will not be enforceable except in certain exceptional circumstances.

**VOID CONTRACTS** A **void contract** is no contract at all. The terms *void* and *contract* are contradictory. None of the parties have any legal obligations if a contract is void. A contract can be void because one of the parties was determined by a court to mentally incompetent, for instance, or because the purpose of the contract was illegal (see Chapter 14).

To review the various types of contracts, see *Concept Summary 11.1* below.

## SECTION 4
# QUASI CONTRACTS

**Quasi contracts,** or contracts *implied in law,* are not actual contracts. Express contracts and implied contracts are actual or true contracts formed by the words or actions of the parties. The word *quasi* is Latin for "as if" or "analogous to." Quasi contracts are not true contracts because they do not arise from any agreement, express or implied, between the parties themselves. Rather, quasi contracts are fictional contracts that courts can impose on the parties "as if" the parties had entered into an actual contract. They are equitable rather than legal contracts.

Usually, quasi contracts are imposed to avoid the *unjust enrichment* of one party at the expense of another. The doctrine of unjust enrichment is based on the theory that individuals should not be allowed to profit or enrich themselves inequitably at the expense of others. When the court imposes a quasi contract, a plaintiff may recover in ***quantum meruit,***[8] a Latin phrase meaning "as much as he or she deserves." *Quantum meruit* essentially describes the extent of compensation owed under a contract implied in law.

In the following case, the parties did not have an express contract, but one party enjoyed the benefits of the other party's services. The court had to decide if the parties had a quasi contract.

---

**8.** Pronounced *kwahn*-tuhm *mehr*-oo-wit.

---

| | **CONCEPT SUMMARY 11.1** |
|---|---|
| | **Types of Contracts** |
| **ASPECT** | **DEFINITION** |
| **Formation** | 1. *Bilateral*—A promise for a promise.<br>2. *Unilateral*—A promise for an act (acceptance is the completed performance of the act).<br>3. *Formal*—Requires a special form for creation.<br>4. *Informal*—Requires no special form for creation.<br>5. *Express*—Formed by words (oral, written, or a combination).<br>6. *Implied*—Formed by the conduct of the parties. |
| **Performance** | 1. *Executed*—A fully performed contract.<br>2. *Executory*—A contract not fully performed. |
| **Enforceability** | 1. *Valid*—The contract has the necessary contractual elements: agreement (offer and acceptance), consideration, legal capacity of the parties, and legal purpose.<br>2. *Voidable*—One party has the option of avoiding or enforcing the contractual obligation.<br>3. *Unenforceable*—A contract exists, but it cannot be enforced because of a legal defense.<br>4. *Void*—No contract exists, or there is a contract without legal obligations. |

## CASE 11.2

### Seawest Services Association v. Copenhaver

Court of Appeals of Washington, 166 Wash.App. 1006 (2012).

**BACKGROUND AND FACTS** Seawest Services Association owned and operated a water distribution system that served homes both inside and outside a housing development. Seawest had two classes of members. "Full members" owned property in the housing development, and "limited members" received water services for homes outside the development. Both full and limited members paid water bills and, as necessary, assessments for work performed on the water system. In 2001, the Copenhavers purchased a home outside the housing development. They did not have an express contract with Seawest, but they paid water bills for eight years and paid one $3,950 assessment for water system upgrades. In 2009, a dispute arose between the parties, and the Copenhavers began refusing to pay their water bills and assessments. Seawest sued the Copenhavers in a Washington state court. The trial court found that the Copenhavers were limited members of Seawest and thus were liable for the unpaid water bills and assessments. The Copenhavers appealed.

**DECISION AND RATIONALE** The state intermediate appellate court affirmed the decision of the trial court, holding that the Copenhavers were liable to Seawest for breach of a quasi contract. The court explained that a quasi contract exists when a person knowingly receives a benefit from another party and it would be "inequitable for the [person] to retain the benefit without the payment of its value." In this case, the Copenhavers enjoyed the benefits of Seawest's water services and even paid for them before their dispute arose. The reviewing court found that "the Copenhavers would be unjustly enriched if they could retain benefits provided by Seawest without paying for them." After all, the court reasoned, they purchased a home that received water services, and they knew that they could not receive water without being a limited member of Seawest.

**THE ETHICAL DIMENSION** *In recognizing quasi contracts, does the law try to correct for unethical behavior? Why or why not?*

**THE ECONOMIC DIMENSION** *Could the Copenhavers have successfully argued that by forcing them to pay a price to which they had not agreed, Seawest was unjustly enriched at their expense?*

## Limitations on Quasi-Contractual Recovery

Although quasi contracts exist to prevent unjust enrichment, the party obtaining the enrichment is not held liable in some situations. In general, a party who has conferred a benefit on someone else unnecessarily or as a result of misconduct or negligence cannot invoke the principle of quasi contract. The enrichment in those situations will not be considered "unjust."

▶ **Case in Point 11.8** Qwest Wireless, LLC, provides wireless phone services in Arizona and thirteen other states. Qwest marketed and sold handset insurance to its customers, although it did not have a license to sell insurance in Arizona or in any other state. Patrick and Vicki Van Zanen sued Qwest for unjust enrichment based on its receipt of sales commissions for the handset insurance. The court agreed that Qwest had violated the insurance-licensing stat-

ute. Nevertheless, the court found that the commissions did not constitute unjust enrichment because the customers had, in fact, received the insurance. Qwest had not retained a benefit (the commissions) without paying for it (providing insurance).[9] ◀

## When an Actual Contract Exists

The doctrine of quasi contract generally cannot be used when there is an *actual contract* that covers the matter in controversy. A remedy already exists if a party is unjustly enriched as a result of a breach of contract: the nonbreaching party can sue the breaching party for breach of contract.

▶ **Example 11.9** Fung contracts with Cameron to deliver a furnace to a building owned by Grant. Fung delivers the furnace, but Cameron never pays Fung.

---

9. *Van Zanen v. Qwest Wireless, LLC,* 522 F.3d 1127 (10th Cir. 2008).

**EXHIBIT 11-3  Rules of Contract Interpretation**

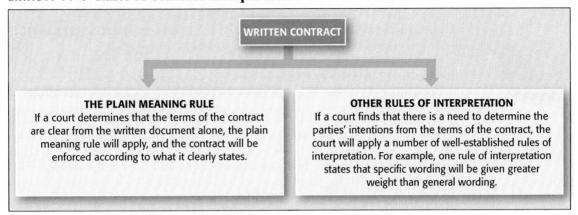

WRITTEN CONTRACT

**THE PLAIN MEANING RULE**
If a court determines that the terms of the contract are clear from the written document alone, the plain meaning rule will apply, and the contract will be enforced according to what it clearly states.

**OTHER RULES OF INTERPRETATION**
If a court finds that there is a need to determine the parties' intentions from the terms of the contract, the court will apply a number of well-established rules of interpretation. For example, one rule of interpretation states that specific wording will be given greater weight than general wording.

Grant has been unjustly enriched in this situation, to be sure. Fung, however, cannot recover from Grant in quasi contract because Fung had an actual contract with Cameron. Fung already has a remedy—he can sue for breach of contract to recover the price of the furnace from Cameron. The court does not need to impose a quasi contract in this situation to achieve justice. ◄

## SECTION 5
# INTERPRETATION OF CONTRACTS

Sometimes, parties agree that a contract has been formed but disagree on its meaning or legal effect. One reason this may happen is that one of the parties is not familiar with the legal terminology used in the contract. To an extent, *plain language* laws (enacted by the federal government and a majority of the states) have helped to avoid this difficulty. Sometimes, though, a dispute may arise over the meaning of a contract simply because the rights or obligations under the contract are not expressed clearly—no matter how "plain" the language used.

In this section, we look at some common law rules of contract interpretation. These rules, which have evolved over time, provide the courts with guidelines for deciding disputes over how contract terms or provisions should be interpreted. Exhibit 11–3 above provides a brief graphic summary of how these rules are applied.

## The Plain Meaning Rule

When a contract's writing is clear and unequivocal, a court will enforce it according to its obvious terms. The meaning of the terms must be determined from the *face of the instrument*—from the written document alone. This is sometimes referred to as the *plain meaning rule*.

The words—and their plain, ordinary meaning—determine the intent of the parties at the time that they entered into the contract. A court is bound to give effect to the contract according to this intent. The importance of each word or phrase in a contract is discussed further in the *Appendix to Chapter 19: Reading and Analyzing Contracts*.

**AMBIGUITY** A court will consider a contract to be ambiguous (unclear) in the following situations:

1. When the intent of the parties cannot be determined from the contract's language.
2. When the contract lacks a provision on a disputed term.
3. When a term is susceptible to more than one interpretation.
4. When there is uncertainty about a provision.

**EXTRINSIC EVIDENCE** If a contract term is ambiguous, a court can consider *extrinsic evidence* (evidence outside the contract), or it may interpret the ambiguity against the party who drafted the term. **Extrinsic evidence** is any evidence not contained in the document itself—such as the testimony of parties and witnesses, additional agreements or communications, or other relevant information.

The admissibility of extrinsic evidence can significantly affect the court's interpretation of ambiguous contractual provisions and thus the outcome of litigation. When a contract is clear and unambiguous, a court cannot consider extrinsic evidence. The following case illustrates these points.

## SPTLIGHT on Columbia Pictures

### Case 11.3 Wagner v. Columbia Pictures Industries, Inc.
California Court of Appeal, Second District, 146 Cal.App.4th 586, 52 Cal.Rptr.3d 898 (2007).

**BACKGROUND AND FACTS** Actor Robert Wagner entered into an agreement with Spelling-Goldberg Productions (SGP) "relating to *Charlie's Angels* (herein called the 'series')." The contract entitled Wagner to 50 percent of the net profits that SGP received from broadcasting the series and from all ancillary, music, and subsidiary rights in connection with the series. SGP hired Ivan Goff and Ben Roberts to write the series, under a contract subject to the Writers Guild of America Minimum Basic Agreement (MBA).[a] The MBA stipulates that the writer of a television show retains the right to make and market films based on the material, subject to the producer's right to buy this right if the writer decides to sell it within five years.

The first *Charlie's Angels* episode aired in 1976. In 1982, SGP sold its rights to the series to Columbia Pictures Industries, Inc. Thirteen years later, Columbia bought the movie rights to the material from Goff's and Roberts's heirs. In 2000 and 2003, Columbia produced and distributed two *Charlie's Angels* films. Wagner filed a suit in a California state court against Columbia, claiming a share of the profits from the films. The court granted Columbia's motion for summary judgment. Wagner appealed to a state intermediate appellate court.

**DECISION AND RATIONALE** The state intermediate appellate court affirmed the lower court's judgment. The contract "unambiguously" stated the conditions under which the parties were to share the films' profits, and those conditions had not occurred. The court reasoned that even if the parties intended Wagner to share in the profits from all sources, "they did not say so in their contract." Under the language of the contract, Wagner was entitled to share in the profits from the exercise of the movie rights to *Charlie's Angels* if those rights were exploited as "ancillary" or "subsidiary" to the primary "right to exhibit photoplays of the series," but not if those rights were acquired separately. SGP's contract with Goff and Roberts was subject to the MBA, under which the writers kept the movie rights, which the producer could buy if the writers opted to sell them within five years. SGP did not acquire the movie rights to *Charlie's Angels* by exercising this right within the five-year period. Columbia obtained those rights independently more than five years later.

**WHAT IF THE FACTS WERE DIFFERENT?** *How might the result in this case have been different if the court had admitted Wagner's evidence of the "Love Song" contract?*

**THE LEGAL ENVIRONMENT DIMENSION** *Under what circumstances would Wagner have been entitled to a share of the profits from the* Charlie's Angels *movies even though the evidence of the* Love Song *contract was irrelevant?*

---

a. The Writers Guild of America is an association of screen and television writers that negotiates industry-wide agreements with motion picture and television producers.

## Other Rules of Interpretation

Generally, a court will interpret the language to give effect to the parties' intent as *expressed in their contract.* This is the primary purpose of the rules of interpretation—to determine the parties' intent from the language used in their agreement and to give effect to that intent. A court normally will not make or remake a contract, nor will it interpret the language according to what the parties *claim* their intent was when they made it.

**RULES THE COURTS USE** The courts use the following rules in interpreting contractual terms:

1. As far as possible, a reasonable, lawful, and effective meaning will be given to all of a contract's terms.
2. A contract will be interpreted as a whole. Individual, specific clauses will be considered subordinate to the contract's general intent. All writings that are a part of the same transaction will be interpreted together.

3. Terms that were the subject of separate negotiation will be given greater consideration than standardized terms and terms that were not negotiated separately.
4. A word will be given its ordinary, commonly accepted meaning, and a technical word or term will be given its technical meaning, unless the parties clearly intended something else.
5. Specific and exact wording will be given greater consideration than general language.
6. Written or typewritten terms will prevail over preprinted ones.
7. Because a contract should be drafted in clear and unambiguous language, a party who uses ambiguous expressions is held to be responsible for the ambiguities. Thus, when the language has more than one meaning, it will be interpreted against the party who drafted the contract.
8. Evidence of *usage of trade, course of dealing,* and *course of performance* may be admitted to clarify the meaning of an ambiguously worded contract. (These terms will be defined and discussed in more detail in Chapter 20.)

**EXPRESS TERMS USUALLY GIVEN THE MOST WEIGHT** Express terms (terms expressly stated in the contract) are given the greatest weight, followed by course of performance, course of dealing, and custom and usage of trade—in that order. When considering custom and usage, a court will look at the trade customs and usage common to the particular business or industry and to the locale in which the contract was made or is to be performed.

▶ **Case in Point 11.10** Jessica Robbins bought a house in Tennessee. U.S. Bank financed the purchase, and Tennessee Farmers Mutual Insurance Company issued the homeowner's insurance policy. The policy included a clause that promised payment to the bank unless the house was lost due to an "increase in hazard" that the bank knew about but did not tell the insurer. When Robbins fell behind on her mortgage payments, the bank started foreclosure proceedings. No one told the insurer. Robbins filed for bankruptcy, which postponed foreclosure.

Meanwhile, the house was destroyed in a fire. The bank filed a claim under the policy, but the insurer refused to pay because it had not been told by the bank of an "increase in hazard"—the foreclosure. The bank then filed a lawsuit. The court found that the plain meaning of the words "increase in hazard" in the policy referred to physical conditions on the property that posed a risk, not to events such as foreclosure. Thus, the bank was not required to notify the insurer under the terms of the policy, and the lack of notice did not invalidate the coverage.[10] ◀

---

10. *U.S. Bank, N.A. v. Tennessee Farmers Mutual Insurance Co.,* 277 S.W.3d 381 (Tenn.Sup.Ct. 2009).

## Reviewing: Nature and Terminology

Mitsui Bank hired Ross Duncan as a branch manager in one of its Southern California locations. At that time, Duncan received an employee handbook informing him that Mitsui would review his performance and salary level annually. In 2012, Mitsui decided to create a new lending program to help financially troubled businesses stay afloat. It hired Duncan to be the credit development officer (CDO) and gave him a written compensation plan. Duncan's compensation was to be based on the program's success and involved a bonus and commissions based on the volume of new loans and sales. The written plan also stated, "This compensation plan will be reviewed and potentially amended after one year and will be subject to such review and amendment annually thereafter."

Duncan's efforts as CDO were successful, and the business-lending program he developed grew to represent 25 percent of Mitsui's business in 2013 and 40 percent in 2014. Nevertheless, Mitsui refused to give Duncan a raise in 2013. Mitsui also amended his compensation plan to significantly reduce his compensation and to change his performance evaluation schedule to every six months. When he had still not received a raise by 2014, Duncan resigned as CDO and filed a lawsuit alleging breach of contract. Using the information presented in the chapter, answer the following questions.

1. What are the four requirements of a valid contract?
2. Did Duncan have a valid contract with Mitsui for employment as CDO? If so, was it a bilateral or a unilateral contract?

*Continued*

3. What are the requirements of an implied contract?
4. Can Duncan establish an implied contract based on the employment manual or the written compensation plan? Why or why not?

**DEBATE THIS . . .** *Companies should be able to make or break employment contracts whenever and however they wish.*

## Terms and Concepts

bilateral contract 209

contract 207

executed contract 212

executory contract 212

express contract 210

extrinsic evidence 215

formal contract 210

implied contract 210

informal contract 210

objective theory of contracts 207

offeree 209

offeror 209

promise 206

promisee 207

promisor 207

*quantum meruit* 213

quasi contract 213

unenforceable contract 213

unilateral contract 209

valid contract 212

void contract 213

voidable contract 212

## Issue Spotters

1. Joli receives a letter from Kerin saying that he has a book at a certain price. Joli signs and returns the letter to Kerin. When Kerin delivers the book, Joli sends it back, claiming that they do not have a contract. Kerin claims they do. What standard determines whether these parties have a contract? **(See page 207.)**

2. Dyna tells Ed that she will pay him $1,000 to set fire to her store so that she can collect under a fire insurance policy. Ed sets fire to the store, but Dyna refuses to pay. Can Ed recover? Why or why not? **(See page 208.)**

• **Check your answers to the Issue Spotters against the answers provided in Appendix E at the end of this text.**

## Business Scenarios

**11–1. Unilateral Contract.** Rocky Mountain Races, Inc., sponsors the "Pioneer Trail Ultramarathon" with an advertised first prize of $10,000. The rules require the competitors to run 100 miles from the floor of Blackwater Canyon to the top of Pinnacle Mountain. The rules also provide that Rocky reserves the right to change the terms of the race at any time. Monica enters the race and is declared the winner. Rocky offers her a prize of $1,000 instead of $10,000. Did Rocky and Monica have a contract? Explain. **(See page 209.)**

**11–2. Implied Contract.** Janine was hospitalized with severe abdominal pain and placed in an intensive care unit. Her doctor told the hospital personnel to order around-the-clock nursing care for Janine. At the hospital's request, a nursing services firm, Nursing Services Unlimited, provided two weeks of in-hospital care and, after Janine was sent home, an additional two weeks of at-home care. During the at-home period of care, Janine was fully aware that she was receiving the benefit of the nursing services. Nursing Services later billed Janine $4,000 for the nursing care, but Janine refused to pay on the ground that she had never contracted for the services, either orally or in writing. In view of the fact that no express contract was ever formed, can Nursing Services recover the $4,000 from Janine? If so, under what legal theory? Discuss. **(See page 210.)**

**11–3. Contract Classification.** For employment with the Firestorm Smokejumpers—a crew of elite paratroopers who parachute into dangerous situations to fight fires—applicants must complete a series of tests. The crew chief sends the most qualified applicants a letter stating that they will be admitted to Firestorm's training sessions if they pass a medical exam. Jake Kurzyniec receives the letter and passes the exam, but a new crew chief changes the selection process and rejects him. Is there a contract between Kurzyniec and Firestorm? If there is a contract, what type of contract is it? **(See page 209.)**

## Business Case Problems

**11–4. Spotlight on Taco Bell—Implied Contract.** Thomas Rinks and Joseph Shields developed Psycho Chihuahua, a caricature of a Chihuahua dog with a "do-not-back-down" attitude. They promoted and marketed the character through their company, Wrench, L.L.C. Ed Alfaro and Rudy Pollak, representatives of Taco Bell Corp., learned of Psycho Chihuahua and met with Rinks and Shields to talk about using the character as a Taco Bell "icon." Wrench sent artwork, merchandise, and marketing ideas to Alfaro, who promoted the character within Taco Bell. Alfaro asked Wrench to propose terms for Taco Bell's use of Psycho Chihuahua. Taco Bell did not accept Wrench's terms, but Alfaro continued to promote the character within the company. Meanwhile, Taco Bell hired a new advertising agency, which proposed an advertising campaign involving a Chihuahua. When Alfaro learned of this proposal, he sent the Psycho Chihuahua materials to the agency. Taco Bell made a Chihuahua the focus of its marketing but paid nothing to Wrench. Wrench filed a suit against Taco Bell in a federal court claiming that it had an implied contract with Taco Bell and that Taco Bell breached that contract. Do these facts satisfy the requirements for an implied contract? Why or why not? [*Wrench, L.L.C. v. Taco Bell Corp.,* 256 F.3d 446 (6th Cir. 2001), cert. denied, 534 U.S. 1114, 122 S.Ct. 921, 151 L.Ed.2d 805 (2002)] **(See page 210.)**

**11–5. Quasi Contract.** Kim Panenka asked to borrow $4,750 from her sister, Kris, to make a mortgage payment. Kris deposited a check for that amount into Kim's bank account. Hours later, Kim asked to borrow another $1,100. Kris took a cash advance on her credit card and deposited this amount into Kim's account. When Kim did not repay the amounts, Kris filed a suit, arguing that she had "loaned" Kim the money. Can the court impose a contract between the sisters? Explain. [*Panenka v. Panenka,* 331 Wis.2d 731, 795 N.W.2d 493 (2011)] **(See page 213.)**

**11–6. Interpretation of Contracts.** Lisa and Darrell Miller had a son, Landon. When the Millers divorced, they entered into a "Joint Plan" (JP). Under the JP, Darrell agreed to "begin setting funds aside for Landon to attend college." After Landon's eighteenth birthday, Lisa asked a court to order Darrell to pay the boy's college expenses based on the JP. Darrell contended that the JP was not clear on this point. Do the rules of contract interpretation support Lisa's request or Darrell's contention? Explain. [*Miller v. Miller,* 1 So.3d 815 (La.App. 2009)] **(See page 215.)**

**11–7. BUSINESS CASE PROBLEM WITH SAMPLE ANSWER: Quasi Contract.**

 *Robert Gutkowski, a sports marketing expert, met numerous times with George Steinbrenner, the owner of the New York Yankees, to discuss the Yankees Entertainment and Sports Network (YES). Gutkowski was paid as a consultant. Later, he filed a suit, seeking an ownership share in YES. There was no written contract for the share, but he claimed that there were discussions about his being a part owner. Does Gutkowski have a valid claim for* payment? Discuss. [Gutkowski v. Steinbrenner, *680 F. Supp.2d 602 (S.D.N.Y. 2010)]* **(See page 213.)**

- **For a sample answer to Problem 11–7, go to Appendix F at the end of this text.**

**11–8. Implied Contracts.** Ralph Ramsey insured his car with Allstate Insurance Co. He also owned a house on which he maintained a homeowner's insurance policy with Allstate. Bank of America had a mortgage on the house and paid the insurance premiums on the homeowner's policy from Ralph's account. After Ralph died, Allstate canceled the car insurance. Ralph's son Douglas inherited the house. The bank continued to pay the premiums on the homeowner's policy, but from Douglas's account, and Allstate continued to renew the insurance. When a fire destroyed the house, Allstate denied coverage, however, claiming that the policy was still in Ralph's name. Douglas filed a suit in a federal district court against the insurer. Was Allstate liable under the homeowner's policy? Explain. [*Ramsey v. Allstate Insurance Co.,* 2013 WL 467327 (6th Cir. 2013)] **(See page 210.)**

**11–9. A QUESTION OF ETHICS: Unilateral Contracts.**

 *International Business Machines Corp. (IBM) hired Niels Jensen in 2000 as a software sales representative. According to the brochure on IBM's "Sales Incentive Plan" (SIP), "the more you sell, the more earnings for you." But "the SIP program does not constitute a promise by IBM. IBM reserves the right to modify the program at any time." Jensen was given a "quota letter" that said he would be paid $75,000 as a base salary and, if he attained his quota, an additional $75,000 as incentive pay. Jensen closed a deal worth more than $24 million to IBM. When IBM paid him less than $500,000 as a commission, Jensen filed a suit. He argued that the SIP was a unilateral offer that became a binding contract when he closed the sale. [Jensen v. International Business Machines Corp., 454 F.3d 382 (4th Cir. 2006)]* **(See page 209.)**

(a) Would it be fair to the employer for the court to hold that the SIP brochure and the quota letter created a unilateral contract if IBM did not *intend* to create such a contract? Would it be fair to the employee to hold that *no* contract was created? Explain.

(b) The "Sales Incentives" section of IBM's brochure included a clause providing that "management will decide if an adjustment to the payment is appropriate" when an employee closes a large transaction. Does this affect your answers to the above questions? From an ethical perspective, would it be fair to hold that a contract exists despite these statements? Why or why not?

## Legal Reasoning Group Activity

**11–10. Contracts.** Review the basic requirements for a valid contract listed at the beginning of this chapter. Now consider the relationship created when a student enrolls in a college or university. **(See page 208.)**

(a) One group should analyze and discuss whether a contract has been formed between the student and the college or university.

(b) A second group should assume that there is a contract and explain whether it is bilateral or unilateral.

# CHAPTER 12

# AGREEMENT IN TRADITIONAL AND E-CONTRACTS

Contract law developed over time to meet society's need to know with certainty what kinds of promises, or contracts, will be enforced and the point at which a valid and binding contract is formed. For a contract to be considered valid and enforceable, the requirements listed in Chapter 11 must be met. In this chapter, we look closely at the first of these requirements, *agreement*.

Agreement is required to form a contract, whether it is formed in the traditional way (on paper) or online. In today's world, many contracts are formed via the Internet—even from smartphones, tablets, and other mobile devices. We discuss online offers and acceptances and examine some laws that have been created to apply to electronic contracts, or *e-contracts*, in the latter part of this chapter.

## AGREEMENT

An essential element for contract formation is **agreement**—the parties must agree on the terms of the contract and manifest to each other their *mutual assent* (agreement) to the same bargain. Ordinarily, agreement is evidenced by two events: an *offer* and an *acceptance*. One party offers a certain bargain to another party, who then accepts that bargain.

The agreement does not necessarily have to be in writing. Both parties, however, must manifest their assent, or voluntary consent, to the same bargain. Once an agreement is reached, if the other elements of a contract (consideration, capacity, and legality—discussed in subsequent chapters) are present, a valid contract is formed. Generally, the contract creates enforceable rights and duties between the parties.

Because words often fail to convey the precise meaning intended, the law of contracts generally adheres to the *objective theory of contracts,* as discussed in Chapter 11. Under this theory, a party's words and conduct are held to mean whatever a reasonable person in the offeree's position would think they meant.

### Requirements of the Offer

An **offer** is a promise or commitment to do or refrain from doing some specified action in the future. As mentioned in Chapter 11, the parties to a contract are the *offeror,* the one who makes an offer or proposal to another party, and the *offeree,* the one to whom the offer or proposal is made. Under the common law, three elements are necessary for an offer to be effective:

1. The offeror must have a serious intention to become bound by the offer.
2. The terms of the offer must be reasonably certain, or definite, so that the parties and the court can ascertain the terms of the contract.
3. The offer must be communicated to the offeree.

Once an effective offer has been made, the offeree's acceptance of that offer creates a legally binding contract (providing the other essential elements for a valid and enforceable contract are present).

**INTENTION** The first requirement for an effective offer is a serious intent on the part of the offeror. Serious intent is not determined by the subjective intentions, beliefs, and assumptions of the offeror. Rather, it is determined by what a reasonable person in the offeree's position would conclude that the offeror's words and actions meant. Offers made in obvious anger, jest, or undue excitement do not meet the serious-and-objective-intent test because a reasonable person would realize that a serious offer was not being made. Because these offers are not effective, an offeree's acceptance does not create an agreement.

▶ **Example 12.1**   Linda and Dena ride to school each day in Dena's new automobile, which has a market value of $20,000. One cold morning, they get into the car, but the car will not start. Dena yells in anger, "I'll sell this car to anyone for $500!" Linda drops $500 on Dena's lap. A reasonable person—taking into consideration Dena's frustration and the obvious difference in value between the market price of the car and the proposed purchase price—would realize that Dena's offer was not made with serious and objective intent. No agreement is formed. ◀

In the classic case presented next, the court considered whether an offer made "after a few drinks" met the serious-and-objective-intent requirement.

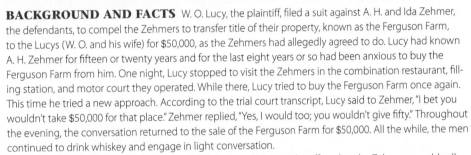

## CLASSIC CASE 12.1

### Lucy v. Zehmer
Supreme Court of Appeals of Virginia, 196 Va. 493, 84 S.E.2d 516 (1954).

**BACKGROUND AND FACTS**   W. O. Lucy, the plaintiff, filed a suit against A. H. and Ida Zehmer, the defendants, to compel the Zehmers to transfer title of their property, known as the Ferguson Farm, to the Lucys (W. O. and his wife) for $50,000, as the Zehmers had allegedly agreed to do. Lucy had known A. H. Zehmer for fifteen or twenty years and for the last eight years or so had been anxious to buy the Ferguson Farm from him. One night, Lucy stopped to visit the Zehmers in the combination restaurant, filling station, and motor court they operated. While there, Lucy tried to buy the Ferguson Farm once again. This time he tried a new approach. According to the trial court transcript, Lucy said to Zehmer, "I bet you wouldn't take $50,000 for that place." Zehmer replied, "Yes, I would too; you wouldn't give fifty." Throughout the evening, the conversation returned to the sale of the Ferguson Farm for $50,000. All the while, the men continued to drink whiskey and engage in light conversation.

Eventually, Lucy enticed Zehmer to write up an agreement to the effect that the Zehmers would sell the Ferguson Farm to Lucy for $50,000 complete. Later, Lucy sued Zehmer to compel him to go through with the sale. Zehmer argued that he had been drunk and that the offer had been made in jest and hence was unenforceable. The trial court agreed with Zehmer, and Lucy appealed.

**DECISION AND RATIONALE**   The Supreme Court of Appeals of Virginia reversed the ruling of the lower court. The state supreme court ordered the Zehmers to carry through with the sale. The court noted that Lucy attempted to testify in detail as to what was said and done the night of the transaction. "Zehmer was not intoxicated to the extent of being unable to comprehend the nature and consequences of the instrument he executed, and hence that instrument is not to be invalidated on that ground."

The court found that the execution of the agreement was a serious business transaction, as evidenced by a number of circumstances. These included the discussion of the contract for forty minutes or more before it was signed, its rewriting to reflect Mrs. Zehmer's interest, the discussion of what was to be included in the sale, the provision for an examination of the title, the completeness of the instrument, and Lucy's taking possession of the agreement without Zehmer's request that he give it back. As the court explained, "We must look to the outward expression of a person as manifesting his intention rather than to his secret and unexpressed intention."

**IMPACT OF THIS CASE ON TODAY'S LAW**   *This is a classic case in contract law because it illustrates so clearly the objective theory of contracts with respect to determining whether a serious offer was intended. Today, the courts continue to apply the objective theory of contracts and routinely cite* Lucy v. Zehmer *as a significant precedent in this area.*

**WHAT IF THE FACTS WERE DIFFERENT?**   *Suppose that the day after Lucy signed the purchase agreement for the farm, he decided that he did not want it after all, and Zehmer sued Lucy to perform the contract. Would this change in the facts alter the court's decision that Lucy and Zehmer had created an enforceable contract? Why or why not?*

**SITUATIONS WHEN INTENT MAY BE LACKING** The concept of intention can be further clarified through an examination of types of statements that are *not* offers. We look at these expressions and statements in the subsections that follow.

***Expressions of Opinion.*** An expression of opinion is not an offer. It does not indicate an intention to enter into a binding agreement.

▶ **Case in Point 12.2** George Hawkins took his son to McGee, a physician, and asked McGee to operate on the son's hand. McGee said that the boy would be in the hospital three or four days and that the hand would *probably* heal a few days later. The son's hand did not heal for a month, but the father did not win a suit for breach of contract. The court held that McGee had not made an offer to heal the son's hand in a few days. He had merely expressed an opinion as to when the hand would heal.[1] ◀

***Statements of Future Intent.*** A statement of an intention to do something in the future is not an offer.

▶ **Example 12.3** Samir says, "I *plan* to sell my stock in Novation, Inc., for $150 per share." If John "accepts" and tenders the $150 per share for the stock, no contract is created. Samir has merely expressed his intention to enter into a future contract for the sale of the stock. No contract is formed because a reasonable person would conclude that Samir was only *thinking about* selling his stock, not *promising* to sell it. ◀

***Preliminary Negotiations.*** A request or invitation to negotiate is not an offer. It only expresses a willingness to discuss the possibility of entering into a contract. Statements such as "Will you sell Blythe Estate?" or "I wouldn't sell my car for less than $5,000" are examples. A reasonable person in the offeree's position would not conclude that these statements indicated an intention to enter into a binding obligation.

Likewise, when the government or private firms require construction work, they invite contractors to submit bids. The *invitation* to submit bids is not an offer, and a contractor does not bind the government or private firm by submitting a bid. (The bids that the contractors submit are offers, however, and the government or private firm can bind the contractor by accepting the bid.)

***Advertisements.*** In general, advertisements (including representations made in mail-order catalogues, price lists, and circulars) are treated not as offers to

contract but as invitations to negotiate.[2] ▶ **Case in Point 12.4** An advertisement on the *Science NOW* Web site asked readers to submit "news tips," which the organization would investigate for possible inclusion in its magazine or on the Web site. Erik Trell, a professor and physician, submitted a manuscript in which he claimed to have solved a famous mathematical problem.

When *Science NOW* did not publish the solution, Trell filed a lawsuit for breach of contract. He claimed that the *Science NOW* ad was an offer, which he had accepted by submitting his manuscript. The court dismissed Trell's suit, holding that the ad was not an offer, but merely an invitation to offer. Responses to the ad were not acceptances. Trell's submission of the manuscript for publication was the offer, which *Science NOW* did not accept.[3] ◀

Price lists are another form of invitation to negotiate or trade. A seller's price list is not an offer to sell at that price. It merely invites the buyer to offer to buy at that price. In fact, the seller usually puts "prices subject to change" on the price list. Only in rare circumstances will a price quotation be construed as an offer.

Although most advertisements and price lists are treated as invitations to negotiate, this does not mean that they can never be an offer. On some occasions, courts have construed advertisements to be offers because the ads contained definite terms that invited acceptance (such as an ad offering a reward for the return of a lost dog).

***Online Auctions.*** The most familiar type of auction today takes place on the Internet. Online auction sites, such as eBay, eBid, and WebStore, provide a forum for buyers and sellers to find or sell almost anything. Like advertisements and price lists, "offers" to sell an item on these sites generally are treated as invitations to negotiate. Unlike live auctions (discussed next), online auctions are automated. Buyers can enter incremental bids on an item (without approving each price increase) up to a specified amount or without a limit, if they want to be assured of making the winning bid.

***Live Auctions.*** In a live auction, a seller "offers" goods for sale through an auctioneer, but this is not an offer to form a contract. Rather, it is an invitation asking bidders to submit offers. In the context of an auction, a bidder is the offeror, and the auctioneer is the offeree. The offer is accepted when the auctioneer strikes the hammer. Before the fall of the hammer, a

---

1. *Hawkins v. McGee,* 84 N.H. 114, 146 A. 641 (1929).

2. *Restatement (Second) of Contracts,* Section 26, Comment b.
3. *Trell v. American Association for the Advancement of Science,* ___ F.Supp.2d ___ (W.D.N.Y. 2007).

bidder may revoke (take back) her or his bid, or the auctioneer may reject that bid or all bids. Typically, an auctioneer will reject a bid that is below the price the seller is willing to accept.

When the auctioneer accepts a higher bid, he or she rejects all previous bids. Because rejection terminates an offer (as will be discussed later), those bids represent offers that have been terminated. Thus, if the highest bidder withdraws her or his bid before the hammer falls, none of the previous bids is reinstated. If the bid is not withdrawn or rejected, the contract is formed when the auctioneer announces, "Going once, going twice, sold!" (or something similar) and lets the hammer fall.

**Auctions with and without Reserve.** Auctions tradition-ally have been referred to as either "with reserve" or "without reserve." In an auction with reserve, the seller (through the auctioneer) may withdraw the goods at any time before the auctioneer closes the sale by announcement or by the fall of the hammer.

All auctions are assumed to be auctions with reserve unless the terms of the auction are explicitly stated to be *without reserve*. In an auction without reserve, the goods cannot be withdrawn by the seller and must be sold to the highest bidder. In auctions with reserve, the seller may reserve the right to confirm or reject the sale even after "the hammer has fallen." In this situation, the seller is obligated to notify those attend-ing the auction that sales of goods made during the auction are not final until confirmed by the seller.[4]

**Agreements to Agree.** Traditionally, agreements to agree—that is, agreements to agree to the material terms of a contract at some future date—were not considered to be binding contracts. The modern view, however, is that agreements to agree may be enforce-able agreements (contracts) if it is clear that the par-ties intended to be bound by the agreements. In other words, under the modern view the emphasis is on the parties' intent rather than on form.

▶ **Case in Point 12.5**   After a person was injured and nearly drowned on a water ride at one of its amusement parks, Six Flags, Inc., filed a lawsuit against the manufacturer that had designed the ride. The defendant manufacturer claimed that the parties did not have a binding contract but had only engaged in preliminary negotiations that were never formal-ized in a construction contract.

The court, however, held that the evidence was suf-ficient to show an intent to be bound. The evidence included a faxed document specifying the details of the water ride, along with the parties' subsequent actions (beginning construction and handwriting notes on the fax). The manufacturer was required to provide insurance for the water ride at Six Flags. Its insurer was required to defend Six Flags in the personal-injury law-suit that arose out of the incident.[5]  ◀

**Preliminary Agreements.** Increasingly, the courts are holding that a preliminary agreement constitutes a binding contract if the parties have agreed on all essen-tial terms and no disputed issues remain to be resolved. In contrast, if the parties agree on certain major terms but leave other terms open for further negotiation, a preliminary agreement is not binding. The parties are bound only in the sense that they have committed themselves to negotiate the undecided terms in good faith in an effort to reach a final agreement.

In the following *Spotlight Case,* the dispute was over an agreement to settle a case during the trial. One party claimed that the agreement formed via e-mail was binding. The other party claimed the e-mail exchange was merely an agreement to work out the terms of a settlement in the future. Can an exchange of e-mails create a complete and unambigu-ous agreement?

---

**4.** These rules apply under both the common law of contracts and the Uniform Commercial Code (UCC)—see UCC 2–328.

**5.** *Six Flags, Inc. v. Steadfast Insurance Co.,* 474 F.Supp.2d 201 (D.Mass. 2007).

**SPOTLIGHT on Amazon.com**

**Case 12.2   Basis Technology Corp. v. Amazon.com, Inc.**
Appeals Court of Massachusetts, 71 Mass.App.Ct. 29, 878 N.E.2d 952 (2008).

**BACKGROUND AND FACTS** Basis Technology Corporation created software and provided tech-nical services for a Japanese-language Web site belonging to Amazon.com, Inc. The agreement between the two companies allowed for separately negotiated contracts for additional services that Basis might provide

CASE 12.2 CONTINUES ▶

CASE 12.2 CONTINUED to Amazon. At the end of 1999, Basis and Amazon entered into stock-purchase agreements. Later, Amazon objected to certain actions related to the securities that Basis sold. Basis sued Amazon for various claims involving these securities and for failing to pay for services performed by Basis that were not included in the original agreement. During the trial, the two parties appeared to reach an agreement to settle out of court via a series of e-mail exchanges outlining the settlement. When Amazon reneged, Basis served a motion to enforce the proposed settlement. The trial judge entered a judgment against Amazon, which appealed.

**DECISION AND RATIONALE** The state intermediate appellate court affirmed the trial court's finding that Amazon intended to be bound by the terms of the e-mail exchanges. The reviewing court examined the evidence consisting of e-mails between the two parties. It pointed out that in open court and on the record, counsel "reported the result of the settlement without specification of the terms." Amazon claimed that the e-mail terms were incomplete and were not definite enough to form an agreement. The reviewing court noted, however, that "provisions are not ambiguous simply because the parties have developed different interpretations of them." In the exchange of e-mails, the essential business terms were indeed resolved. Afterward, the parties were simply proceeding to record the settlement terms, not to create them. The e-mails constituted a complete and unambiguous statement of the parties' desire to be bound by the settlement terms.

**WHAT IF THE FACTS WERE DIFFERENT?** *Suppose that the attorneys for both sides had simply had a phone conversation that included all of the terms to which they actually agreed in their e-mail exchanges. Would the court have ruled differently? Why or why not?*

**THE LEGAL ENVIRONMENT DIMENSION** *What does the result in this case suggest that a businessperson should do before agreeing to a settlement of a legal dispute?*

**DEFINITENESS OF TERMS** The second requirement for an effective offer involves the definiteness of its terms. An offer must have reasonably definite terms so that a court can determine if a breach has occurred and give an appropriate remedy.[6] The specific terms required depend, of course, on the type of contract.

Generally, a contract must include the following terms, either expressed in the contract or capable of being reasonably inferred from it:

1. The identification of the parties.
2. The identification of the object or subject matter of the contract (also the quantity, when appropriate), including the work to be performed, with specific identification of such items as goods, services, and land.
3. The consideration to be paid.
4. The time of payment, delivery, or performance.

An offer may invite an acceptance to be worded in such specific terms that the contract is made definite. ▶ **Example 12.6** Nintendo of America, Inc., contacts your Play 2 Win Games store and offers to sell "from one to twenty-five Nintendo 3DS gaming systems for $75 each. State number desired in acceptance." You agree to buy twenty systems. Because the quantity is specified in the acceptance, the terms are definite, and the contract is enforceable. ◀

When the parties have clearly manifested an intent to form a contract, courts sometimes are willing to supply a missing term in a contract, especially a sales contract.[7] But a court will not rewrite a contract if the parties' expression of intent is too vague or uncertain to be given any precise meaning.

**COMMUNICATION** The third requirement for an effective offer is communication—the offer must be communicated to the offeree. Ordinarily, one cannot agree to a bargain without knowing that it exists. ▶ **Example 12.7** Tolson advertises a reward for the return of her lost cat. Dirk, not knowing of the reward, finds the cat and returns it to Tolson. Usually, Dirk cannot recover the reward because an essential element of a reward contract is that the one who claims the reward must have known it was offered. A few states would allow recovery of the reward, but not on contract principles. Dirk would be allowed to recover on the basis that it would be unfair to deny him the reward just because he did not know about it. ◀

---

6. *Restatement (Second) of Contracts*, Section 33.

7. See UCC 2–204. Note that Article 2 of the UCC specifies different rules relating to the definiteness of terms used in a contract for the sale of goods. In essence, Article 2 modifies general contract law by requiring *less* specificity.

In the following case, a woman hit by a bus signed documents that clearly released her claims against the bus company in exchange for the payment of $1 million from the company's insurer. Did the documents have to be delivered to the company or its insurer for the release and settlement to be binding?

## CASE 12.3

### Gyabaah v. Rivlab Transportation Corp.
New York Supreme Court, Appellate Division, First Department, 102 A.D.3d 451, 958 N.Y.S.2d 109 (2013).

**BACKGROUND AND FACTS** Adwoa Gyabaah was hit by a bus owned by Rivlab Transportation Corporation. She retained attorney Jeffrey Aronsky to represent her in negotiations with Rivlab, and its insurer, National Casualty Company. Gyabaah agreed to pay Aronsky a contingency fee of one-third of the amount of her recovery. (A *contingency fee* is charged by an attorney and is based on a percentage of the final award received by his or her client as a result of litigation.) Aronsky filed a lawsuit on Gyabaah's behalf in a New York state court against the bus company.

In a letter to Aronsky dated October 1, 2010, National Casualty offered $1 million to settle the case. Gyabaah accepted the offer and signed a release (see Chapter 13) on October 5. Aronsky did not deliver the documents to Rivlab or National Casualty, however, because Gyabaah had to make further decisions about the form of the settlement. By December 9, Gyabaah had retained new counsel, Kenneth Wilhelm. Wilhelm told Aronsky that Gyabaah did not wish to settle the case. Aronsky filed a motion with the court to enforce what he contended was a $1 million settlement and to set his contingency fee according to his agreement with Gyabaah. The court denied the motion. Aronsky appealed.

**DECISION AND RATIONALE**   The state intermediate appellate court affirmed the lower court's order denying Aronsky's motion in so far as it sought to enforce a purported settlement and set his fee. Gyabaah's acceptance of National Casulty's offer was never communicated to Rivlab or its insurer. This omission was fatal to Aronsky's claim of a settlement.

Aronsky maintained that Gyabaah's signing of the General Release constituted a binding legal contract. The reviewing court pointed out that "A general release is governed by principles of contract law." Further, "It is essential in any bilateral contract that the fact of acceptance be communicated to the offeror. Therefore, this action was not settled because the executed release was never forwarded to defendant nor was acceptance of the offer otherwise communicated to defendant or its carrier." Just because he might have been "advised of a settlement by his counsel" does not "suffice as evidence that a settlement was effected."

Because there had been no settlement, the amount of Aronsky's fee could not be determined until the final disposition of the case. Aronsky's legal fees should be a percentage of the fee recovered by the Wilhelm firm based on the *pro rata* share of the work the two attorneys performed in obtaining the recovery.

**THE ETHICAL DIMENSION**   *What is the most likely reason that Gyabaah did not wish to settle the case with Rivlab or its insurer according to their terms?*

**WHAT IF THE FACTS WERE DIFFERENT?**   *If Aronsky had informed Rivlab or its insurer that Gyabaah had agreed to the settlement, would her later "change of heart" have been sufficient to set aside the agreement? Explain your answer.*

## Termination of the Offer

The communication of an effective offer to an offeree gives the offeree the power to transform the offer into a binding, legal obligation (a contract) by an acceptance. This power of acceptance does not continue forever, though. It can be terminated either by action of the parties or by operation of law.

**TERMINATION BY ACTION OF THE PARTIES** An offer can be terminated by action of the parties in any of three ways: by revocation, by rejection, or by counteroffer.

**Revocation.** The offeror's act of withdrawing (revoking) an offer is known as **revocation.** Unless an offer is irrevocable, the offeror usually can revoke the offer, as long as the revocation is communicated to the offeree before the offeree accepts. Revocation may be accomplished by either of the following:

1. Express repudiation of the offer (such as "I withdraw my previous offer of October 17").
2. Performance of acts that are inconsistent with the existence of the offer and are made known to the offeree (for instance, selling the offered property to another person in the presence of the offeree).

In most states, a revocation becomes effective when the offeree or the offeree's *agent* (a person acting on behalf of the offeree) actually receives it. Therefore, a revocation sent via FedEx on April 1 and delivered at the offeree's residence or place of business on April 3 becomes effective on April 3.

An offer made to the general public can be revoked in the same manner that the offer was originally communicated. ▶ **Example 12.8** An electronics retailer offers a $10,000 reward to anyone who provides information leading to the arrest of the individuals who broke into its store. The offer is published on the Web sites and in the printed editions of three local papers and of four papers in nearby communities. To revoke the offer, the retailer must publish the revocation in all seven papers in which it published the offer. ◀

**Irrevocable Offers.** Although most offers are revocable, some can be made irrevocable—that is, they cannot be revoked. Increasingly, courts refuse to allow an offeror to revoke an offer when the offeree has changed position because of justifiable reliance on the offer. (The courts apply the doctrine of *detrimental reliance,* or *promissory estoppel,* which will be discussed in Chapter 13.) In some circumstances, "firm offers" made by merchants may also be considered irrevocable—see the discussion of a "merchant's firm offer" in Chapter 20.

Another form of irrevocable offer is an **option contract.** An option contract is created when an offeror promises to hold an offer open for a specified period of time in return for a payment (consideration) given by the offeree. An option contract takes away the offeror's power to revoke the offer for the period of time specified in the option.

Option contracts are frequently used in conjunction with the sale or lease of real estate. ▶ **Example 12.9** Tyrell agrees to lease a house from Jackson, the property owner. The lease contract includes a clause stating that Tyrell is paying an additional $15,000 for an option to purchase the property within a specified period of time. If Tyrell decides not to purchase the house after the specified period has lapsed, he loses the $15,000, and Jackson is free to sell the property to another buyer. ◀

**Rejection.** If the offeree rejects the offer—by words or by conduct—the offer is terminated. Any subsequent attempt by the offeree to accept will be construed as a new offer, giving the original offeror (now the offeree) the power of acceptance. Like a revocation, a rejection of an offer is effective only when it is actually received by the offeror or the offeror's agent.

Merely inquiring about an offer does not constitute rejection. When the offeree merely inquires as to the "firmness" of the offer, there is no reason to presume that he or she intends to reject it.
▶ **Example 12.10** Raymond offers to buy Francie's iPhone 5 for $200, and Francie responds, "Is that your best offer?" or "Will you pay me $275 for it?" A reasonable person would conclude that Francie did not reject the offer but merely made an inquiry about it. She can still accept and bind Raymond to the $200 purchase price. ◀

**Counteroffer.** A **counteroffer** is a rejection of the original offer and the simultaneous making of a new offer. ▶ **Example 12.11** Burke offers to sell his home to Lang for $270,000. Lang responds, "Your price is too high. I'll offer to purchase your house for $250,000." Lang's response is called a counteroffer because it rejects Burke's offer to sell at $270,000 and creates a new offer by Lang to purchase the home at a price of $250,000. ◀

At common law, the **mirror image rule** requires the offeree's acceptance to match the offeror's offer exactly—to mirror the offer. Any change in, or addition to, the terms of the original offer automatically terminates that offer and substitutes the counteroffer. The counteroffer, of course, need not be accepted, but if the original offeror does accept the terms of the counteroffer, a valid contract is created.[8]

---

8. The mirror image rule has been greatly modified in regard to sales contracts. Section 2–207 of the UCC provides that a contract is formed if the offeree makes a definite expression of acceptance (such as signing the form in the appropriate location), even though the terms of the acceptance modify or add to the terms of the original offer (see Chapter 20).

**TERMINATION BY OPERATION OF LAW** The power of the offeree to transform the offer into a binding, legal obligation can be terminated by operation of law through the occurrence of any of the following events:

1. Lapse of time.
2. Destruction of the specific subject matter of the offer.
3. Death or incompetence of the offeror or the offeree.
4. Supervening illegality of the proposed contract. (A statute or court decision that makes an offer illegal automatically terminates the offer.)

***Lapse of Time.*** An offer terminates automatically by law when the period of time *specified in the offer* has passed. If the offer states that it will be left open until a particular date, then the offer will terminate at midnight on that day. If the offer states that it will be open for a number of days, this time period normally begins to run when the offeree *receives* the offer (not when it is formed or sent).

If the offer does not specify a time for acceptance, the offer terminates at the end of a *reasonable* period of time. What constitutes a reasonable period of time depends on the subject matter of the contract, business and market conditions, and other relevant circumstances. An offer to sell farm produce, for example, will terminate sooner than an offer to sell farm equipment because farm produce is perishable. Produce is also subject to greater fluctuations in market value.

***Destruction of the Subject Matter.*** An offer is automatically terminated if the specific subject matter of the offer (such as a smartphone or a house) is destroyed before the offer is accepted.[9] ▶ **Example 12.12** Johnson offers to sell his prize greyhound to Rizzo. If the dog dies before Rizzo can accept, the offer is automatically terminated. Johnson does not have to tell Rizzo that the animal has died for the offer to terminate. ◀

***Death or Incompetence of the Offeror or Offeree.*** An offeree's power of acceptance is terminated when the offeror or offeree dies or is legally incapacitated—*unless the offer is irrevocable.* ▶ **Example 12.13** Sybil Maven offers to sell commercial property to Westside Investment for $2 million. In June, Westside pays Maven $5,000 in exchange for her agreement to hold the offer open for ten months (forming an option contract). If Maven dies in July, her offer is not terminated

because it is irrevocable. Westside can purchase the property anytime within the ten-month period. ◀

A revocable offer is personal to both parties and cannot pass to the heirs, guardian, or estate of either party. This rule applies whether or not the other party had notice of the death or incompetence.

***Supervening Illegality of the Proposed Contract.*** A statute or court decision that makes an offer illegal automatically terminates the offer.[10] ▶ **Example 12.14** Lee offers to lend Kim $10,000 at an annual interest rate of 15 percent. Before Kim can accept the offer, a law is enacted that prohibits interest rates higher than 12 percent. Lee's offer is automatically terminated. (If the statute is enacted after Kim accepts the offer, a valid contract is formed, but the contract may still be unenforceable—see Chapter 14.) ◀

*Concept Summary 12.1* on the next page provides a review of the ways in which an offer can be terminated.

## Acceptance

**Acceptance** is a voluntary act by the offeree that shows assent (agreement) to the terms of an offer. The offeree's act may consist of words or conduct. The acceptance must be unequivocal and must be communicated to the offeror. Generally, only the person to whom the offer is made or that person's agent can accept the offer and create a binding contract.

**UNEQUIVOCAL ACCEPTANCE** To exercise the power of acceptance effectively, the offeree must accept unequivocally. This is the *mirror image rule* previously discussed. An acceptance may be unequivocal even though the offeree expresses dissatisfaction with the contract. For instance, "I accept the offer, but can you give me a better price?" is an effective acceptance.

An acceptance cannot impose new conditions or change the terms of the original offer. If it does, the acceptance may be considered a counteroffer, which is a rejection of the original offer. For instance, the statement "I accept the offer but only if I can pay on ninety days' credit" is a counteroffer and not an unequivocal acceptance.

Certain terms, when included in an acceptance, will not change the offer sufficiently to constitute rejection. ▶ **Example 12.15** In response to an art dealer's offer to sell a painting, the offeree, Ashton Gibbs, replies, "I accept. Please send a written

---

**9.** *Restatement (Second) of Contracts,* Section 36.

**10.** *Restatement (Second) of Contracts,* Section 36.

---

## CONCEPT SUMMARY 12.1
### Methods by Which an Offer Can Be Terminated

**BY ACTION OF THE PARTIES—**

1. *Revocation*—Unless the offer is irrevocable, it can be revoked at any time before acceptance without liability. Revocation is not effective until received by the offeree or the offeree's agent. Some offers, such as a merchant's firm offer and option contracts, are irrevocable. Also, in some situations, an offeree's detrimental reliance or partial performance will cause a court to rule that the offeror cannot revoke the offer.
2. *Rejection*—Accomplished by words or actions that demonstrate a clear intent not to accept the offer; not effective until received by the offeror or the offeror's agent.
3. *Counteroffer*—A rejection of the original offer and the making of a new offer.

**BY OPERATION OF LAW—**

1. *Lapse of time*—The offer terminates at the end of the time period specified in the offer or, if no time period is stated in the offer, at the end of a reasonable time period.
2. *Destruction of the subject matter*—When the specific subject matter of the offer is destroyed before the offer is accepted, the offer automatically terminates.
3. *Death or incompetence of the offeror or offeree*—If the offeror or offeree dies or becomes incompetent, the offer terminates (unless the offer is irrevocable).
4. *Supervening illegality*—When a statute or court decision makes the proposed contract illegal, the offer automatically terminates.

---

contract." Gibbs is requesting a written contract but is not making it a condition for acceptance. Therefore, the acceptance is effective without the written contract. In contrast, if Gibbs replies, "I accept *if* you send a written contract," the acceptance is expressly conditioned on the request for a writing, and the statement is not an acceptance but a counteroffer. (Notice how important each word is!)[11] ◄

**SILENCE AS ACCEPTANCE** Ordinarily, silence cannot constitute acceptance, even if the offeror states, "By your silence and inaction, you will be deemed to have accepted this offer." An offeree should not be obligated to act affirmatively to reject an offer when no consideration (nothing of value) has passed to the offeree to impose such a duty.

In some instances, however, the offeree does have a duty to speak and her or his silence or inaction will operate as an acceptance. Silence may constitute an acceptance in the following circumstances:

1. When an offeree takes the benefit of offered services even though he or she had an opportunity to reject them and knew that they were offered with the expectation of compensation. ▶ **Example 12.16** John is a student who earns extra income by washing store windows. John taps on the window of a store, catches the attention of the store's manager, and points to the window and raises his cleaner, signaling that he will be washing the window. The manager does nothing to stop him. Here, the store manager's silence constitutes an acceptance, and an implied contract is created. The store is bound to pay a reasonable value for John's work. ◄

2. When the offeree has had prior dealings with the offeror. For instance, a merchant routinely receives shipments from a certain supplier and always notifies that supplier when defective goods are rejected. The merchant's silence regarding a particular shipment (failure to reject the goods) will constitute acceptance.

**COMMUNICATION OF ACCEPTANCE** In a bilateral contract, acceptance is in the form of a promise (not performance). Because bilateral contracts are formed when the promise is made (rather than when the act is performed), communication of acceptance is necessary. Communication of acceptance may not be necessary if the offer dispenses with the require-

---

11. As noted in footnote 8, in regard to sales contracts, the UCC provides that an acceptance may still be valid even if some terms are added. The new terms are simply treated as proposed additions to the contract.

ment, however, or if the offer can be accepted by silence.

▶ **Case in Point 12.17**   Powerhouse Custom Homes, Inc., owed $95,260.42 to 84 Lumber Company under a credit agreement. When Powerhouse failed to pay, 84 Lumber filed a suit to collect. During mediation, the parties agreed to a deadline for objections to whatever agreement they might reach. If there were no objections, the agreement would be binding.

Powerhouse then offered to pay less than the amount owed, and 84 Lumber did not respond. Powerhouse argued that 84 Lumber accepted the offer by not objecting to it within the deadline. The court, however, held that for a contract to be formed, an offer must be accepted unequivocally. Although Powerhouse had made an offer of a proposed settlement, 84 Lumber did not communicate its acceptance. Thus, the court reasoned that the parties did not reach an agreement on the proposed settlement.[12] ◀

Because a unilateral contract calls for the full performance of some act, acceptance is usually evident, and notification is therefore unnecessary. Nevertheless, exceptions do exist, such as when the offeror requests notice of acceptance or has no way of determining whether the requested act has been performed.

**MODE AND TIMELINESS OF ACCEPTANCE**   In bilateral contracts, acceptance must be timely. The general rule is that acceptance in a bilateral contract is timely if it is made before the offer is terminated. Problems may arise, though, when the parties involved are not dealing face to face. In such situations, the offeree should use an authorized mode of communication.

***The Mailbox Rule.***   Acceptance takes effect, thus completing formation of the contract, at the time the offeree sends or delivers the communication via the mode expressly or impliedly authorized by the offeror. This is the so-called **mailbox rule,** also called the *deposited acceptance rule,* which the majority of courts follow. Under this rule, if the authorized mode of communication is the mail, then an acceptance becomes valid when it is dispatched (placed in the control of the U.S. Postal Service)—*not* when it is received by the offeror. (Note, however, that if the offer stipulates when acceptance will be effective, then the offer will not be effective until the time specified.)

The mailbox rule does not apply to instantaneous forms of communication, such as when the parties are

dealing face to face, by telephone, by fax, and usually by e-mail. Under the Uniform Electronic Transactions Act (UETA—discussed later in this chapter), e-mail is considered sent when it either leaves the control of the sender or is received by the recipient. This rule takes the place of the mailbox rule when the parties have agreed to conduct transactions electronically and allows an e-mail acceptance to become effective when sent.

***Authorized Means of Acceptance.***   A means of communicating acceptance can be expressly authorized by the offeror or impliedly authorized by the facts and circumstances of the situation.[13] An acceptance sent by means not expressly or impliedly authorized normally is not effective until it is received by the offeror.

When an offeror specifies how acceptance should be made (for example, by overnight delivery), *express authorization* is said to exist. The contract is not formed unless the offeree uses that specified mode of acceptance. Moreover, both offeror and offeree are bound in contract the moment this means of acceptance is employed. ▶ **Example 12.18**   Motorola Mobility, Inc., offers to sell 144 Atrix 4G smartphones and 72 Lapdocks to Call Me Plus phone stores. The offer states that Call Me Plus must accept the offer via FedEx overnight delivery. The acceptance is effective (and a binding contract is formed) the moment that Call Me Plus gives the overnight envelope containing the acceptance to the FedEx driver. ◀

If the offeror does not expressly authorize a certain mode of acceptance, then acceptance can be made by *any reasonable means.*[14] Courts look at the prevailing business usages and the surrounding circumstances to determine whether the mode of acceptance used was reasonable. Usually, the offeror's choice of a particular means in making the offer implies that the offeree can use the *same or a faster means* for acceptance. Thus, if the offer is made via Priority U.S. mail, it would be reasonable to accept the offer via Priority mail or by a faster method, such as signed scanned documents sent as attachments via e-mail or overnight delivery.

***Substitute Method of Acceptance.***   Sometimes, the offeror authorizes a particular method of acceptance, but the offeree accepts by a different means. In that situation, the acceptance may still be effective if the

---

12. *Powerhouse Custom Homes, Inc. v. 84 Lumber Co.,* 307 Ga.App. 605, 705 S.E.2d 704 (2011).

13. *Restatement (Second) of Contracts,* Section 30, provides that an offer invites acceptance "by any medium reasonable in the circumstances," unless the offer specifies the means of acceptance.

14. *Restatement (Second) of Contracts,* Section 30. This is also the rule under UCC 2–206(1)(a).

substituted method serves the same purpose as the authorized means.

The acceptance by a substitute method is not effective on dispatch, though, and no contract will be formed until the acceptance is received by the offeror. For instance, an offer specifies acceptance by FedEx overnight delivery, but the offeree instead accepts by overnight delivery from another carrier. The substitute method of acceptance will still be effective, but the contract will not be formed until the offeror receives it.

# SECTION 2
# AGREEMENT IN E-CONTRACTS

Numerous contracts are formed online. Electronic contracts, or **e-contracts,** must meet the same basic requirements (agreement, consideration, contractual capacity, and legality) as paper contracts. Disputes concerning e-contracts, however, tend to center on contract terms and whether the parties voluntarily agreed to those terms.

Online contracts may be formed not only for the sale of goods and services but also for *licensing.* As mentioned in Chapter 9, the purchase of software generally involves a license, or a right to use the software, rather than the passage of title (ownership rights) from the seller to the buyer. ▶ **Example 12.19**  Galynn downloads an app on her iPad that enables her to work on spreadsheets. During the transaction, she has to select "I agree" several times to indicate that she understands that she is purchasing only the right to use the software under specific terms. After she agrees to these terms (the licensing agreement), she can use the application. ◀

## Online Offers

Sellers doing business via the Internet can protect themselves against contract disputes and legal liability by creating offers that clearly spell out the terms that will govern their transactions if the offers are accepted. All important terms should be conspicuous and easy to view.

**DISPLAYING THE OFFER**  The seller's Web site should include a hypertext link to a page containing the full contract so that potential buyers are made aware of the terms to which they are assenting. The contract generally must be displayed online in a readable format, such as a twelve-point typeface.

All provisions should be reasonably clear. ▶ **Example 12.20**  Netquip sells a variety of heavy equipment, such as trucks and trailers, on its Web site. Because Netquip's pricing schedule is very complex, the schedule must be fully provided and explained on the Web site. In addition, the terms of the sale (such as any warranties and the refund policy) must be fully disclosed. ◀

**PROVISIONS TO INCLUDE**  An important rule to keep in mind is that the offeror (the seller) controls the offer and thus the resulting contract. The seller should therefore anticipate the terms he or she wants to include in a contract and provide for them in the offer. In some instances, a standardized contract form may suffice. At a minimum, an online offer should include the following provisions:

1. *Acceptance of terms.* A clause that clearly indicates what constitutes the buyer's agreement to the terms of the offer, such as a box containing the words "I accept" that the buyer can click. (Mechanisms for accepting online offers will be discussed in detail later in the chapter.)
2. *Payment.* A provision specifying how payment for the goods (including any applicable taxes) must be made.
3. *Return policy.* A statement of the seller's refund and return policies.
4. *Disclaimer.* Disclaimers of liability for certain uses of the goods. For example, an online seller of business forms may add a disclaimer that the seller does not accept responsibility for the buyer's reliance on the forms rather than on an attorney's advice.
5. *Limitation on remedies.* A provision specifying the remedies available to the buyer if the goods are found to be defective or if the contract is otherwise breached. Any limitation of remedies should be clearly spelled out.
6. *Privacy policy.* A statement indicating how the seller will use the information gathered about the buyer.
7. *Dispute resolution.* Provisions relating to dispute settlement, such as an arbitration clause or a *forum-selection clause* (discussed next).

**DISPUTE-SETTLEMENT PROVISIONS**  Online offers frequently include provisions relating to dispute settlement. For example, the offer might include an arbitration clause specifying that any dispute arising under the contract will be arbitrated in a designated forum.

***Forum-Selection Clause.*** Many online contracts contain a **forum-selection clause** indicating the forum, or location (such as a court or jurisdiction), in which contract disputes will be resolved. As discussed in Chapter 2, significant jurisdictional issues may arise when parties are at a great distance, as they often are when they form contracts via the Internet. A forum-selection clause will help to avert future jurisdictional problems and also help to ensure that the seller will not be required to appear in court in a distant state.

▶ **Case in Point 12.21** Before advertisers can place ads through Google, Inc., they must agree to certain terms that are displayed in an online window. These terms include a forum-selection clause, which provides that any dispute is to be "adjudicated in Santa Clara County, California."

Lawrence Feldman, who advertised through Google, complained that he was overcharged and filed a lawsuit against Google in a federal district court in Pennsylvania. The court held that Feldman had agreed to the forum-selection clause in Google's online contract and transferred the case to a court in Santa Clara County.[15] ◀

***Choice-of-Law Clause.*** Some online contracts may also include a *choice-of-law clause* specifying that any contract dispute will be settled according to the law of a particular jurisdiction, such as a state or country. As will be discussed in Chapter 24, choice-of-law clauses are particularly common in international contracts, but they may also appear in e-contracts to specify which state's laws will govern in the United States.

## Online Acceptances

The *Restatement (Second) of Contracts,* which, as noted earlier, is a compilation of common law contract principles, states that parties may agree to a contract "by written or spoken words or by other action or by failure to act."[16] The Uniform Commercial Code (UCC), which governs sales contracts, has a similar provision. Section 2–204 of the UCC states that any contract for the sale of goods "may be made in any manner sufficient to show agreement, including conduct by both parties which recognizes the existence of such a contract."

**CLICK-ON AGREEMENTS** The courts have used the *Restatement* and UCC provisions to conclude that a binding contract can be created by conduct. This includes the act of clicking on a box indicating "I accept" or "I agree" to accept an online offer. The agreement resulting from such an acceptance is often called a **click-on agreement** (sometimes referred to as a *click-on license* or *click-wrap agreement*). Exhibit 12–1 below shows a portion of a typical click-on agreement that accompanies a software package.

Generally, the law does not require that the parties have read all of the terms in a contract for it to be effective. Therefore, clicking on a box that states "I agree" to certain terms can be enough. The terms may be contained on a Web site through which the buyer is obtaining goods or services. They may also appear on a screen when software is loaded from a CD-ROM or DVD or downloaded from the Internet.

▶ **Case in Point 12.22** The "Terms of Use" that govern Facebook users' accounts include a forum-selection clause that provides for the resolution of all disputes in a court in Santa Clara County, California. To sign up for a Facebook account, a person must click on a box indicating that he or she has agreed to this term.

Mustafa Fteja was an active user of facebook.com when his account was disabled. He sued Facebook in a federal court in New York, claiming that it had disabled his Facebook page without justification and for discriminatory reasons. Facebook filed a motion to transfer the case to California under the forum-selection clause. The court found that the clause in

---

**EXHIBIT 12–1 A Sample Click-On Agreement**

This exhibit illustrates an online offer to form a contract. To accept the offer, the user simply scrolls down the page and clicks on the "I Accept" button.

---

15. *Feldman v. Google, Inc.,* 513 F.Supp.2d 229 (E.D.Pa. 2007).
16. *Restatement (Second) of Contracts,* Section 19.

Facebook's online contract was binding and transferred the case. When Fteja clicked on the button to accept the "Terms of Use" and become a Facebook user, he agreed to resolve all disputes with Facebook in Santa Clara County, California.[17] ◀

**SHRINK-WRAP AGREEMENTS** With a **shrink-wrap agreement** (or *shrink-wrap license*), the terms are expressed inside the box in which the goods are packaged. (The term *shrink-wrap* refers to the plastic that covers the box.) Usually, the party who opens the box is told that she or he agrees to the terms by keeping whatever is in the box. Similarly, when a purchaser opens a software package, he or she agrees to abide by the terms of the limited license agreement.

▶ **Example 12.23**   Ava orders a new iMac from Big Dog Electronics, which ships it to her. Along with the iMac, the box contains an agreement setting forth the terms of the sale, including what remedies are available. The document also states that Ava's retention of the iMac for longer than thirty days will be construed as an acceptance of the terms. ◀

In most instances, a shrink-wrap agreement is not between a retailer and a buyer, but between the manufacturer of the hardware or software and the ultimate buyer-user of the product. The terms generally concern warranties, remedies, and other issues associated with the use of the product.

**Shrink-Wrap Agreements and Enforceable Contract Terms.** In some cases, the courts have enforced the terms of shrink-wrap agreements in the same way as the terms of other contracts. These courts have reasoned that by including the terms with the product, the seller proposed a contract. The buyer could accept this contract by using the product after having an opportunity to read the terms. Thus, a buyer's failure to object to terms contained within a shrink-wrapped software package may constitute an acceptance of the terms by conduct.

**Shrink-Wrap Terms That May Not Be Enforced.** Some-times, however, the courts have refused to enforce certain terms included in shrink-wrap agreements because the buyer did not expressly consent to them. An important factor is when the parties formed their contract.

If a buyer orders a product over the telephone, for instance, and is not informed of an arbitration clause or forum-selection clause at that time, the buyer clearly has not expressly agreed to these terms. If the buyer discovers the clauses *after* the parties entered into a contract, a court may conclude that those terms were proposals for additional terms and were not part of the contract.

**BROWSE-WRAP TERMS** Like the terms of click-on agreements, **browse-wrap terms** can occur in transactions conducted over the Internet. Unlike click-on agreements, however, browse-wrap terms do not require Internet users to assent to the terms before downloading or using certain software. In other words, a person can install the software without clicking "I agree" to the terms of a license. Browse-wrap terms are often unenforceable because they do not satisfy the agreement requirement of contract formation.[18]

▶ **Example 12.24**   BrowseNet Corporation provides free downloadable software called "QuickLoad" on its Web site. Users must indicate, by clicking on a designated box, that they wish to obtain it. On the Web site's download page is a reference to a license agreement that users can view only by scrolling to the next screen. In other words, the user does not have to agree to the terms of the license before downloading the software. One of the license terms requires all disputes to be submitted to arbitration in California. If a user sues BrowseNet in Washington state, the arbitration clause might not be enforceable because users were not required to indicate their assent to the agreement. ◀

## E-Signature Technologies

Today, numerous technologies allow electronic documents to be signed. An **e-signature** has been defined as "an electronic sound, symbol, or process attached to or logically associated with a record and executed or adopted by a person with the intent to sign the record."[19] Thus, e-signatures include encrypted digital signatures, names (intended as signatures) at the end of e-mail messages, and clicks on a Web page if the click includes some means of identification.

## Federal Law on E-Signatures and E-Documents

In 2000, Congress enacted the Electronic Signatures in Global and National Commerce Act (E-SIGN Act),[20] which provides that no contract, record, or signature may be "denied legal effect" solely because it is in electronic form. In other words, under this law, an electronic signature is as valid as a signature on paper, and an e-document can be as enforceable as a paper one.

---

**17.** *Fteja v. Facebook, Inc.,* 841 F.Supp.2d 829 (S.D.N.Y. 2012).

**18.** See, for example, *Jesmer v. Retail Magic, Inc.,* 863 N.Y.S.2d 737 (2008).

**19.** This definition is from the Uniform Electronic Transactions Act, which will be discussed later in this chapter.

**20.** 15 U.S.C. Sections 7001 *et seq.*

For an e-signature to be enforceable, the contracting parties must have agreed to use electronic signatures. For an electronic document to be valid, it must be in a form that can be retained and accurately reproduced.

The E-SIGN Act does not apply to all types of documents. Contracts and documents that are exempt include court papers, divorce decrees, evictions, foreclosures, health-insurance terminations, prenuptial agreements, and wills. Also, the only agreements governed by the UCC that fall under this law are those covered by Articles 2 and 2A (sales and lease contracts) and UCC 1–107 and 1–206. Despite these limitations, the E-SIGN Act significantly expanded the possibilities for contracting online.

## Partnering Agreements

One way that online sellers and buyers can prevent disputes over signatures in their e-contracts, as well as disputes over the terms and conditions of those contracts, is to form partnering agreements. In a **partnering agreement,** a seller and a buyer who frequently do business with each other agree in advance on the terms and conditions that will apply to all transactions subsequently conducted electronically. The partnering agreement can also establish special access and identification codes to be used by the parties when transacting business electronically.

A partnering agreement reduces the likelihood that disputes will arise under the contract because the parties have agreed in advance to the terms and conditions that will accompany each sale. Furthermore, if a dispute does arise, a court or arbitration forum will be able to refer to the partnering agreement when determining the parties' intent.

### SECTION 3
# THE UNIFORM ELECTRONIC TRANSACTIONS ACT

Although most states have laws governing e-signatures and other aspects of electronic transactions, these laws vary. In an attempt to create more uniformity among the states, in 1999 the National Conference of Commissioners on Uniform State Laws and the American Law Institute promulgated the Uniform Electronic Transactions Act (UETA). The UETA has been adopted, at least in part, by forty-eight states. Among other things, the UETA declares that a signature may not be denied legal effect or enforceability solely because it is in electronic form.

The primary purpose of the UETA is to remove barriers to e-commerce by giving the same legal effect to electronic records and signatures as is given to paper documents and signatures. As mentioned earlier, the UETA broadly defines an *e-signature* as "an electronic sound, symbol, or process attached to or logically associated with a record and executed or adopted by a person with the intent to sign the record."[21] A **record** is "information that is inscribed on a tangible medium or that is stored in an electronic or other medium and is retrievable in perceivable [visual] form."[22]

## The Scope and Applicability of the UETA

The UETA does not create new rules for electronic contracts but rather establishes that records, signatures, and contracts may not be denied enforceability solely due to their electronic form. The UETA does not apply to all writings and signatures. It covers only electronic records and electronic signatures *relating to a transaction*. A *transaction* is defined as an interaction between two or more people relating to business, commercial, or governmental activities.[23]

The act specifically does not apply to wills or testamentary trusts or to transactions governed by the UCC (other than those covered by Articles 2 and 2A).[24] In addition, the provisions of the UETA allow the states to exclude its application to other areas of law.

The UETA does not apply to a transaction unless each of the parties has previously agreed to conduct transactions by electronic means. The agreement need not be explicit, however. It can be implied by the conduct of the parties and the surrounding circumstances, such as negotiating a contract via e-mail.[25] The parties can agree to opt out of all or some of the terms of the UETA, but if they do not, then the UETA terms will govern their electronic transactions.

## The Federal E-SIGN Act and the UETA

Congress passed the E-SIGN Act in 2000, a year after the UETA was presented to the states for adoption. Thus, a significant issue was to what extent the federal E-SIGN Act preempted the UETA as adopted by the states.

The E-SIGN Act refers explicitly to the UETA and provides that if a state has enacted the uniform

---

**21.** UETA 102(8).
**22.** UETA 102(15).
**23.** UETA 2(12) and 3.
**24.** UETA 3(b).
**25.** UETA 5(b), and Comment 4B.

version of the UETA, it is not preempted by the E-SIGN Act.[26] In other words, if the state has enacted the UETA without modification, state law will govern. The problem is that many states have enacted nonuniform (modified) versions of the UETA, usually to exclude other areas of state law from the UETA's terms. The E-SIGN Act specifies that those exclusions will be preempted to the extent that they are inconsistent with the E-SIGN Act's provisions.

The E-SIGN Act explicitly allows the states to enact alternative requirements for the use of electronic records or electronic signatures. Generally, however, the requirements must be consistent with the provisions of the E-SIGN Act, and the state must not give greater legal status or effect to one specific type of technology. Additionally, if a state enacts alternative requirements after the E-SIGN Act was adopted, the state law must specifically refer to the E-SIGN Act. The relationship between the UETA and the E-SIGN Act is illustrated in Exhibit 12–2 below.

## Signatures on Electronic Records

Under the UETA, if an electronic record or signature is the act of a particular person, the record or signature may be attributed to that person. If a person types her or his name at the bottom of an e-mail purchase

---

26. 15 U.S.C. Section 7002(2)(A)(i).

order, for instance, that name would qualify as a "signature." The signature would therefore be attributed to the person whose name appeared.

The UETA does not contain any express provisions about what constitutes fraud or whether an agent is authorized to enter a contract. Under the UETA, other state laws control if any issues relating to agency, authority, forgery, or contract formation arise. If existing state law requires a document to be notarized, the UETA provides that this requirement is satisfied by the electronic signature of a notary public or other person authorized to verify signatures.

## The Effect of Errors

The UETA encourages, but does not require, the use of security procedures (such as encryption) to verify changes to electronic documents and to correct errors. It does this by providing a benefit to parties who have agreed to a security procedure. If one of the parties does not detect an error because he or she did not follow the procedure, the other party can legally avoid the effect of the change or error. When the parties have not agreed to use a security procedure, then other state laws (including contract law governing mistakes—see Chapter 15) will determine the effect of the error.

To avoid the effect of errors, a party must promptly notify the other party of the error and of her or his

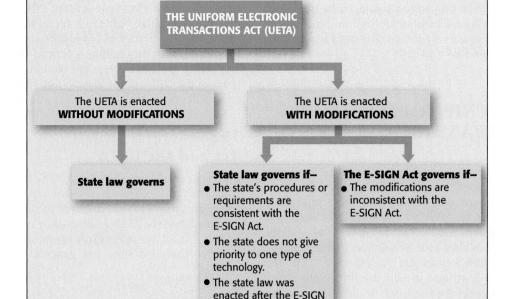

**EXHIBIT 12–2  The E-SIGN Act and the UETA**

THE UNIFORM ELECTRONIC TRANSACTIONS ACT (UETA)

The UETA is enacted **WITHOUT MODIFICATIONS**

The UETA is enacted **WITH MODIFICATIONS**

**State law governs**

**State law governs if—**
- The state's procedures or requirements are consistent with the E-SIGN Act.
- The state does not give priority to one type of technology.
- The state law was enacted after the E-SIGN Act and refers to it.

**The E-SIGN Act governs if—**
- The modifications are inconsistent with the E-SIGN Act.

intent not to be bound by the error. In addition, the party must take reasonable steps to return any benefit received: parties cannot avoid a transaction if they have benefited.

## Timing

An electronic record is considered *sent* when it is properly directed to the intended recipient in a form readable by the recipient's computer system. Once the electronic record leaves the control of the sender or comes under the control of the recipient, the UETA deems it to have been sent. An electronic record is considered *received* when it enters the recipient's processing system in a readable form—*even if no individual is aware of its receipt.*

**SECTION 4**

# INTERNATIONAL TREATIES AFFECTING E-CONTRACTS

Today, much of the e-commerce conducted on a worldwide basis involves buyers and sellers from the United States. The preeminence of U.S. law in this area is likely to be challenged in the future, however, as Internet use continues to expand worldwide. Already, several international organizations have created their own regulations for global Internet transactions.

The United Nations Convention on the Use of Electronic Communications in International Contracts improves commercial certainty by determining an Internet user's location for legal purposes. The convention also establishes standards for creating functional equivalence between electronic communications and paper documents. The convention also provides that e-signatures will be treated as the equivalent of signatures on paper documents.

Another treaty relevant to e-contracts is the Hague Convention on the Choice of Court Agreements. Although it does not specifically mention e-commerce, this convention provides more certainty regarding jurisdiction and recognition of judgments by other nations' courts, thereby facilitating both offline and online transactions.

## Reviewing: Agreement in Traditional and E-Contracts

Shane Durbin wanted to have a recording studio custom-built in his home. He sent invitations to a number of local contractors to submit bids on the project. Rory Amstel submitted the lowest bid, which was $20,000 less than any of the other bids Durbin received. Durbin called Amstel to ascertain the type and quality of the materials that were included in the bid and to find out if he could substitute a superior brand of acoustic tiles for the same bid price. Amstel said he would have to check into the price difference. The parties also discussed a possible start date for construction. Two weeks later, Durbin changed his mind and decided not to go forward with his plan to build a recording studio. Amstel filed a suit against Durbin for breach of contract. Using the information presented in the chapter, answer the following questions.

1. Did Amstel's bid meet the requirements of an offer? Explain.
2. Was there an acceptance of the offer? Why or why not?
3. Suppose that the court determines that the parties did not reach an agreement. Further suppose that Amstel, in anticipation of building Durbin's studio, had purchased materials and refused other jobs so that he would have time in his schedule for Durbin's project. Under what theory discussed in the chapter might Amstel attempt to recover these costs?
4. How is an offer terminated? Assuming that Durbin did not inform Amstel that he was rejecting the offer, was the offer terminated at any time described here? Explain.

**DEBATE THIS . . .** *The terms and conditions in click-on agreements are so long and detailed that no one ever reads the agreements. Therefore, the act of clicking on "I agree" is not really an acceptance.*

## Terms and Concepts

| | | |
|---|---|---|
| acceptance 227 | e-signature 232 | partnering agreement 233 |
| agreement 220 | forum-selection clause 231 | record 233 |
| browse-wrap terms 232 | mailbox rule 229 | revocation 226 |
| click-on agreement 231 | mirror image rule 226 | shrink-wrap agreement 232 |
| counteroffer 226 | offer 220 | |
| e-contract 230 | option contract 226 | |

## Issue Spotters

1. Fidelity Corporation offers to hire Ron to replace Monica, who has given Fidelity a month's notice of intent to quit. Fidelity gives Ron a week to decide whether to accept. Two days later, Monica decides not to quit and signs an employment contract with Fidelity for another year. The next day, Monica tells Ron of the new contract. Ron immediately faxes a formal letter of acceptance to Fidelity. Do Fidelity and Ron have a contract? Why or why not? **(See page 226.)**

2. Applied Products, Inc., does business with Beltway Distributors, Inc., online. Under the Uniform Electronic Transactions Act, what determines the effect of the electronic documents evidencing the parties' deal? Is a party's "signature" necessary? Explain. **(See page 234.)**

• **Check your answers to the Issue Spotters against the answers provided in Appendix E at the end of this text.**

## Business Scenarios

**12–1. Agreement.** Ball e-mails Sullivan and inquires how much Sullivan is asking for a specific forty-acre tract of land Sullivan owns. Sullivan responds, "I will not take less than $60,000 for the forty-acre tract as specified." Ball immediately sends Sullivan a fax stating, "I accept your offer for $60,000 for the forty-acre tract as specified." Discuss whether Ball can hold Sullivan to a contract for the sale of the land. **(See page 220.)**

**12–2. Offer and Acceptance.** Schmidt, the owner of a small business, has a large piece of used farm equipment for sale. He offers to sell the equipment to Barry for $10,000. Discuss the legal effects of the following events on the offer: **(See page 227.)**

  (a) Schmidt dies prior to Barry's acceptance, and at the time he accepts, Barry is unaware of Schmidt's death.

  (b) The night before Barry accepts, fire destroys the equipment.

  (c) Barry pays $100 for a thirty-day option to purchase the equipment. During this period, Schmidt dies, and later Barry accepts the offer, knowing of Schmidt's death.

  (d) Barry pays $100 for a thirty-day option to purchase the equipment. During this period, Barry dies, and Barry's estate accepts Schmidt's offer within the stipulated time period.

**12–3. Online Acceptance.** Anne is a reporter for *Daily Business Journal,* a print publication consulted by investors and other businesspersons. She often uses the Internet to perform research for the articles that she writes for the publication. While visiting the Web site of Cyberspace Investments Corp., Anne reads a pop-up window that states, "Our business newsletter, *E-Commerce Weekly,* is available at a one-year subscription rate of $5 per issue. To subscribe, enter your e-mail address below and click 'SUBSCRIBE.' By subscribing, you agree to the terms of the subscriber's agreement. To read this agreement, click 'AGREEMENT.' " Anne enters her e-mail address, but does not click on "AGREEMENT" to read the terms. Has Anne entered into an enforceable contract to pay for *E-Commerce Weekly?* Explain. **(See page 231.)**

## Business Case Problems

**12–4. Spotlight on Crime Stoppers—Acceptance.** The Baton Rouge Crime Stoppers (BCS) offered a reward for information about the "South Louisiana Serial Killer." The information was to be provided via a hot line. Dianne Alexander had survived an attack by a person suspected of being the killer. She identified a suspect in a police photo lineup and later sought to collect the reward. BCS refused to pay because she did not provide information to them via the hot line. Did Alexander comply with the terms of the offer? Explain. [*Alexander v. Lafayette Crime Stoppers, Inc.,* 38 So.3d 282 (La.App. 3 Dist. 2010) **(See page 227.)**

## 12–5. BUSINESS CASE PROBLEM
## WITH SAMPLE ANSWER: Offer and Acceptance.

*While gambling at Prairie Meadows Casino, Troy Blackford became angry and smashed a slot machine. He was banned from the premises. Despite the ban, he later gambled at the casino and won $9,387. When he tried to collect his winnings, the casino refused to pay. Blackford filed a suit for breach of contract, arguing that he and the casino had a contract because he had accepted its offer to gamble. Did the casino and Blackford have a contract? Discuss.* [Blackford v. Prairie Meadows Racetrack and Casino, *778 N.W.2d 184 (Sup.Ct. Iowa 2010)]* **(See page 220.)**

- **For a sample answer to Problem 12–5, go to Appendix F at the end of this text.**

**12–6. Shrink-Wrap Agreements.** TracFone Wireless, Inc., sells phones and wireless service. The phones are sold for less than their cost, which TracFone recoups by selling prepaid airtime for their use on its network. Software in the phones prohibits their use on other networks. The phones are sold subject to the condition that the buyer agrees "not to tamper with or alter the software." This is printed on the packaging. Bequator Corp. bought at least 18,616 of the phones, disabled the software so that they could be used on other networks, and resold them. Is Bequator liable for breach of contract? Explain. [*TracFone Wireless, Inc. v. Bequator Corp.,* __ F.Supp.2d __ (S.D.Fla. 2011)] **(See page 232.)**

**12–7. Online Acceptances.** Heather Reasonover opted to try Internet service from Clearwire Corp. Clearwire sent her a confirmation e-mail that included a link to its Web site. Clearwire also sent her a modem. In the enclosed written materials, at the bottom of a page, in small type was the Web site URL. When Reasonover plugged in the modem, an "I accept terms" box appeared. Without clicking on the box, Reasonover quit the page. A clause in Clearwire's "Terms of Service," accessible only through its Web site, required its subscribers to submit any dispute to arbitration. Is Reasonover bound to this clause? Why or why not? [*Kwan v. Clearwire Corp.,* 2012 WL 32380 (W.D.Wash. 2012)] **(See page 231.)**

**12–8. Acceptance.** Judy Olsen, Kristy Johnston, and their mother, Joyce Johnston, owned seventy-eight acres of real property on Eagle Creek in Meagher County, Montana. When Joyce died, she left her interest in the property to Kristy. Kristy wrote to Judy, offering to buy Judy's interest or to sell her own interest to Judy. The letter said to "please respond to Bruce Townsend." In a letter to Kristy—

not to Bruce—Judy accepted Kristy's offer to sell her interest. By that time, however, Kristy had made the same offer to sell her interest to their brother Dave, and he had accepted. Did Judy and Kristy have an enforceable binding contract? Or did Kristy's offer specifying one exclusive mode of acceptance mean that Judy's reply was not effective? Discuss. [*Olsen v. Johnston,* 368 Mont. 347, __ P.3d __, (2013)] **(See page 227.)**

## 12–9. A QUESTION OF ETHICS: E-Contract Disputes.

*Dewayne Hubbert, Elden Craft, Chris Grout, and Rhonda Byington bought computers from Dell Corp. through its Web site. Before buying, Hubbert and the others configured their own computers. To make a purchase, each buyer completed forms on five Web pages. On each page, Dell's "Terms and Conditions of Sale" were accessible by clicking on a blue hyperlink. A statement on three of the pages read, "All sales are subject to Dell's Term[s] and Conditions of Sale," but a buyer was not required to click an assent to the terms to complete a purchase. The terms were also printed on the backs of the invoices and on separate documents contained in the shipping boxes with the computers. Among those terms was a "Binding Arbitration" clause.*

*The computers contained Pentium 4 microprocessors, which Dell advertised as the fastest, most powerful Intel Pentium processors then available. In 2002, Hubbert and the others filed a suit in an Illinois state court against Dell, alleging that this marketing was false, misleading, and deceptive. The plaintiffs claimed that the Pentium 4 microprocessor was slower and less powerful, and provided less performance, than either a Pentium III or an AMD Athlon, and at a greater cost. Dell asked the court to compel arbitration.* [Hubbert v. Dell Corp., *359 Ill.App.3d 976, 835 N.E.2d 113, 296 Ill.Dec. 258 (5 Dist. 2005)]* **(See page 230.)**

(a) Should the court enforce the arbitration clause in this case? If you were the judge, how would you rule on this issue?

(b) Do you think shrink-wrap, click-on, and browse-wrap terms impose too great a burden on purchasers? Why or why not?

(c) An ongoing complaint about shrink-wrap, click-on, and browse-wrap terms is that sellers (often large corporations) draft them and buyers (typically individual consumers) do not read them. Should purchasers be bound in contract by terms that they have not even read? Why or why not?

## Legal Reasoning Group Activity

**12–10. E-Contracts.** To download a specific application (app) to your smartphone or tablet device, usually you have to check a box indicating that you agree to the company's terms and conditions. Most individuals do so without ever reading those terms and conditions. Print out a specific set of terms and conditions from a downloaded app to use in this assignment. **(See page 230.)**

(a) One group will determine which of these terms and conditions are favorable to the company.

(b) Another group will determine which of these terms and conditions conceivably will be favorable to the individual.

(c) A third group will determine which terms and conditions, on net, favor the company too much.

# CHAPTER 13

# CONSIDERATION

The fact that a promise has been made does not mean the promise can or will be enforced. Under Roman law, a promise was not enforceable without a *causa*—that is, a reason for making the promise that was also deemed to be a sufficient reason for enforcing it.

Under the common law, a primary basis for the enforcement of promises is consideration. **Consideration** usually is defined as the value (such as cash) given in return for a promise (in a bilateral contract) or in return for a performance (in a unilateral contract). As long as consideration is present, the courts generally do not interfere with contracts based on the amount of consideration paid.

It is up to the contracting parties to determine how much their bargain is worth. Therefore, courts normally enforce a player's contract with a sports team, even if the player does not perform as well as expected or is injured and unable to play. Consequently, no matter how well or how poorly baseball player Prince Fielder performs, his $214 million contract with the Detroit Tigers is enforceable during its nine-year period.

## SECTION 1
# ELEMENTS OF CONSIDERATION

Often, consideration is broken down into two parts: (1) something of *legally sufficient value* must be given in exchange for the promise, and (2) there must be a *bargained-for* exchange.

## Legally Sufficient Value

To be legally sufficient, consideration must be something of value in the eyes of the law. The "something of legally sufficient value" may consist of the following:

1. A promise to do something that one has no prior legal duty to do.
2. The performance of an action that one is otherwise not obligated to undertake.
3. The refraining from an action that one has a legal right to undertake (called a **forbearance**).

Consideration in bilateral contracts normally consists of a promise in return for a promise, as explained in Chapter 11. In a contract for the sale of goods, for instance, the seller promises to ship specific goods to the buyer, and the buyer promises to pay for those goods. Each of these promises constitutes consideration for the contract.

In contrast, unilateral contracts involve a promise in return for a performance. ▶ **Example 13.1** Anita says to her neighbor, "When you finish painting the garage, I will pay you $800." Anita's neighbor paints the garage. The act of painting the garage is the consideration that creates Anita's contractual obligation to pay her neighbor $800. ◀

What if, in return for a promise to pay, a person refrains from pursuing harmful habits (a forbearance), such as the use of tobacco and alcohol? Does such forbearance constitute legally sufficient consideration? This was the issue before the court in the following classic case concerning consideration.

## CLASSIC CASE 13.1

### Hamer v. Sidway

Court of Appeals of New York, Second Division, 124 N.Y. 538, 27 N.E. 256 (1891).

**BACKGROUND AND FACTS**   William E. Story, Sr., was the uncle of William E. Story II. In the presence of family members and others, the uncle promised to pay his nephew $5,000 ($76,000 in today's dollars) if he would refrain from drinking, using tobacco, swearing, and playing cards or billiards for money until he reached the age of twenty-one. (Note that in 1869, when this contract was formed, it was legal in New York to drink and play cards for money before the age of twenty-one.)

The nephew agreed and fully performed his part of the bargain. When he reached the age of twenty-one, he wrote and told his uncle that he had kept his part of the agreement and was therefore entitled to $5,000. The uncle wrote a letter back indicating that he was pleased with his nephew's performance and saying "you shall have five thousand dollars, as I promised you." The uncle also said that the $5,000 was in the bank and that the nephew could "consider this money on interest." The nephew left the $5,000 in the care of his uncle where it would earn interest under the terms and conditions of the letter.

The uncle died about twelve years later without having paid his nephew any part of the $5,000 and interest. The executor of the uncle's estate (Sidway, the defendant in this action) claimed that there had been no valid consideration for the promise. Sidway refused to pay the $5,000 (plus interest) to Hamer, a third party to whom the nephew had transferred his rights in the note. The court reviewed the case to determine whether the nephew had given valid consideration under the law.

**DECISION AND RATIONALE**   The Court of Appeals of New York disagreed with Sidway. The court ruled that the nephew had provided legally sufficient consideration by giving up smoking, drinking alcohol, swearing, and playing cards or billiards for money until he became twenty-one and was therefore entitled to the money. Sidway argued that the nephew had suffered no detriment, because what he had done was in his own best interest.

The court pointed out that "in general a waiver of any legal right at the request of another party is a sufficient consideration for a promise." In this case, the court noted that "the promisee used tobacco, occasionally drank liquor, and he had a legal right to do so. That right he abandoned for a period of years upon the strength of the promise of [his uncle] that for such forbearance he would give him $5,000. . . . It is of no moment whether such performance actually proved a benefit to the promisor."

**IMPACT OF THIS CASE ON TODAY'S LAW**   *Although this case was decided more than a century ago, the principles enunciated by the court remain applicable to contracts formed today, including online contracts. For a contract to be valid and binding, consideration must be given, and that consideration must be something of legally sufficient value.*

**WHAT IF THE FACTS WERE DIFFERENT?**   *If the nephew had not had a legal right to engage in the behavior that he agreed to forgo, would the result in this case have been different? Explain.*

## Bargained-for Exchange

The second element of consideration is that it must provide the basis for the bargain struck between the contracting parties. The item of value must be given or promised by the promisor (offeror) in return for the promisee's promise, performance, or promise of performance.

This element of bargained-for exchange distinguishes contracts from gifts.  ▶ **Example 13.2** Sheng-Li says to his son, "In consideration of the fact that you are not as wealthy as your brothers, I will pay you $5,000." The fact that the word *consideration* is used does not, by itself, mean that consideration has been given. Indeed, Sheng-Li's promise is not enforceable because the son does not have to do anything in order to receive the $5,000 promised. Because the son does not need to give Sheng-Li something of legal value in return for his promise, there is no bargained-for exchange. Rather, Sheng-Li has simply stated his motive for giving his son a gift. ◄

## SECTION 2
# ADEQUACY OF CONSIDERATION

Adequacy of consideration involves how much consideration is given. Essentially, adequacy of consideration concerns the fairness of the bargain.

## The General Rule

On the surface, when the items exchanged are of unequal value, fairness would appear to be an issue. In general, however, a court will not question the adequacy of consideration based solely on the comparative value of the things exchanged.

In other words, the determination of whether consideration exists does not depend on a comparison of the values of the things exchanged. Something need not be of direct economic or financial value to be considered legally sufficient consideration. In many situations, the exchange of promises and potential benefits is deemed to be sufficient consideration.

Under the doctrine of freedom of contract, courts leave it up to the parties to decide what something is worth, and parties are usually free to bargain as they wish. If people could sue merely because they had entered into an unwise contract, the courts would be overloaded with frivolous suits.

## When Voluntary
## Consent May Be Lacking

When there is a large disparity in the amount or value of the consideration exchanged, it may raise a red flag for a court to look more closely at the bargain. Shockingly inadequate consideration can indicate that fraud, duress, or undue influence was involved. It may also cause a judge to question whether the contract is so one sided that it is *unconscionable*,[1] a concept that will be discussed further in Chapter 14.

For instance, an experienced appliance dealer induces a consumer to sign a contract written in

---

**1.** Pronounced un-*kon*-shun-uh-bul.

complicated legal language. If the contract requires the consumer to pay twice the market value of the appliance, the disparity in value may indicate that the sale involved undue influence or fraud. A judge would thus want to make sure that the person voluntarily entered into this agreement.

## SECTION 3
# AGREEMENTS THAT LACK CONSIDERATION

Sometimes, one of the parties (or both parties) to an agreement may think that consideration has been exchanged when in fact it has not. Here, we look at some situations in which the parties' promises or actions do not qualify as contractual consideration.

## Preexisting Duty

Under most circumstances, a promise to do what one already has a legal duty to do does not constitute legally sufficient consideration. The preexisting legal duty may be imposed by law or may arise out of a previous contract. A sheriff, for instance, has a duty to investigate crime and to arrest criminals. Hence, a sheriff cannot collect a reward for providing information leading to the capture of a criminal.

Likewise, if a party is already bound by contract to perform a certain duty, that duty cannot serve as consideration for a second contract. ▶ **Example 13.3** Ajax Contractors begins construction on a seven-story office building and after three months demands an extra $75,000 on its contract. If the extra $75,000 is not paid, the contractor will stop working. The owner of the land, finding no one else to complete the construction, agrees to pay the extra $75,000. The agreement is unenforceable because it is not supported by legally sufficient consideration. Ajax Contractors had a preexisting contractual duty to complete the building. ◄

**UNFORESEEN DIFFICULTIES** The rule regarding preexisting duty is meant to prevent extortion and the so-called holdup game. Nonetheless, if, during performance of a contract, extraordinary difficulties arise that were totally unforeseen at the time the contract was formed, a court may allow an exception to the rule. The key is whether the court finds the modification is fair and equitable in view of circumstances not anticipated by the parties when the contract was made.[2]

---

**2.** *Restatement (Second) of Contracts,* Section 73.

Suppose that in *Example 13.3*, Ajax Contractors had asked for the extra $75,000 because it encountered a rock formation that no one knew existed. If the landowner agrees to pay the extra $75,000 to excavate the rock and the court finds that it is fair to do so, Ajax Contractors can enforce the agreement. If rock formations are common in the area, however, the court may determine that the contractor should have known of the risk. In that situation, the court may choose to apply the preexisting duty rule and prevent Ajax Contractors from obtaining the extra $75,000.

**RESCISSION AND NEW CONTRACT** The law recognizes that two parties can mutually agree to rescind, or cancel, their contract, at least to the extent that it is *executory* (still to be carried out). **Rescission**[3] is the unmaking of a contract so as to return the parties to the positions they occupied before the contract was made.

Sometimes, parties rescind a contract and make a new contract at the same time. When this occurs, it is often difficult to determine whether there was consideration for the new contract, or whether the parties had a preexisting duty under the previous contract. If a court finds there was a preexisting duty, then the new contract will be invalid because there was no consideration.

## Past Consideration

Promises made in return for actions or events that have already taken place are unenforceable. These promises lack consideration in that the element of bargained-for exchange is missing. In short, you can bargain for

something to take place now or in the future but not for something that has already taken place. Therefore, **past consideration** is no consideration.

▶ **Case in Point 13.4** Jamil Blackmon became friends with Allen Iverson when Iverson was a high school student who showed tremendous promise as an athlete. One evening, Blackmon suggested that Iverson use "The Answer" as a nickname in the summer league basketball tournaments. Blackmon said that Iverson would be "The Answer" to all of the National Basketball Association's woes. Later that night, Iverson said that he would give Blackmon 25 percent of any proceeds from the merchandising of products that used "The Answer" as a logo or a slogan. Because Iverson's promise was made in return for past consideration, it was unenforceable. In effect, Iverson stated his intention to give Blackmon a gift.[4] ◀

In a variety of situations, an employer will often ask an employee to sign a *covenant not to compete,* also called a *noncompete agreement.* Under such an agreement, the employee agrees not to compete with the employer for a certain period of time after the employment relationship ends. When a current employee is required to sign a noncompete agreement, his or her employment is not sufficient consideration for the agreement because the individual is already employed. To be valid, the agreement requires new consideration.

In the following case, the court had to decide if new consideration supported a noncompete agreement between physicians and a medical clinic.

---

**3.** Pronounced reh-*sih*-zhen.

**4.** *Blackmon v. Iverson,* 324 F.Supp.2d 602 (E.D.Pa. 2003).

---

## CASE 13.2

### Baugh v. Columbia Heart Clinic, P.A.[a]
Court of Appeals of South Carolina, 402 S.C. 1, 738, S.E.2d 480 (2013).

**BACKGROUND AND FACTS** Columbia Heart Clinic, P.A., in Columbia, South Carolina, provides comprehensive cardiology services. Its physicians are all cardiologists. When Kevin Baugh, M.D., and Barry Feldman, M.D., became employees and shareholders of Columbia Heart, and again several years later, they signed noncompete agreements. Under these agreements, Baugh and Feldman would forfeit certain payments if they competed with Columbia Heart within a year after their employment ended. Specifically, they were not to practice cardiology "within a twenty (20) mile radius of any Columbia Heart office at which [they] routinely provided services." Later, Baugh and Feldman left Columbia Heart and opened a new cardiology practice near one of Columbia Heart's offices. They then filed a suit in a South Carolina state court against Columbia Heart, seeking a ruling that their noncompete agreements were unenforceable. From a judgment in favor of Baugh and Feldman, Columbia Heart appealed.

---

**a.** *P.A.* means "Professional Organization."

CASE 13.2 CONTINUES ▶

CASE 13.2 CONTINUED

**DECISION AND RATIONALE**   A state intermediate court reversed the lower court's finding that the noncompete provisions were unenforceable. The agreements were in fact supported by new consideration because they provided for compensation to physicians who left Columbia Heart so long as they did not compete with the clinic's cardiology practice. To be sure, no separate monetary consideration was paid to any shareholder–physician to sign the noncompete agreement, nor did the agreements change the established compensation system. But it is not correct that those agreements were unenforceable because they were not supported by new consideration.

"When a covenant not to compete is entered into after the inception of employment, separate consideration, in addition to continued at-will employment, is necessary in order for the covenant to be enforceable. There is no consideration when the contract containing the covenant is exacted after several years' employment and the employee's duties and position are left unchanged." But Baugh and another physician signed an agreement that provided that they would be paid $5,000 per month for each of twelve months following termination so long as they did not violate the noncompete agreement. "Consequently, the Agreements are supported by new consideration."

**THE LEGAL DIMENSION**   *When a noncompete agreement is entered into before employment, would additional compensation (beyond the basic salary for the position) constitute sufficient consideration for the agreement? Why or why not?*

**THE ETHICAL DIMENSION**   *When a noncompete agreement is entered into after employment has begun, would continued employment constitute sufficient consideration for the agreement? Explain.*

## Illusory Promises

If the terms of the contract express such uncertainty of performance that the promisor has not definitely promised to do anything, the promise is said to be *illusory*—without consideration and unenforceable. A promise is illusory when it fails to bind the promisor.

▶ **Example 13.5**   The president of Tuscan Corporation says to her employees, "If profits continue to be high, everyone will get a 10 percent bonus at the end of the year—if management agrees." This is an *illusory promise,* or no promise at all, because performance depends solely on the discretion of the president (management). There is no bargained-for consideration. The statement indicates only that management may or may not do something in the future. Therefore, even though the employees work hard and profits remain high, the company is not obligated to pay the bonus now or later. ◀

**OPTION-TO-CANCEL CLAUSES**   Sometimes, option-to-cancel clauses in contracts present problems in regard to consideration. When the promisor has the option to cancel the contract before performance has begun, the promise is illusory. ▶ **Example 13.6**   Abe contracts to hire Chris for one year at $5,000 per month, reserving the right to cancel the contract at any time. On close examination of these words, you can see that Abe has not actually agreed to hire

Chris, as Abe could cancel without liability before Chris started performance. This contract is therefore illusory.

But if Abe instead reserves the right to cancel the contract at any time *after* Chris has begun performance by giving Chris *thirty days' notice,* the promise is not illusory. Abe, by saying that he will give Chris thirty days' notice, is relinquishing the opportunity (legal right) to hire someone else instead of Chris for a thirty-day period. If Chris works for one month and Abe then gives him thirty days' notice, Chris has an enforceable claim for two months' salary ($10,000). ◀

**REQUIREMENTS AND OUTPUT CONTRACTS**   Problems with consideration may also arise in other types of contracts because of uncertainty of performance. Uncertain performance is characteristic of requirements and output contracts, for instance. In a *requirements contract,* a buyer and a seller agree that the buyer will purchase from the seller all of the goods of a designated type that the buyer needs, or requires. In an *output contract,* the buyer and seller agree that the buyer will purchase from the seller all of what the seller produces, or the seller's output. These types of sales contracts will be discussed further in Chapter 20.

*Concept Summary 13.1* on the following page provides a convenient summary of the main aspects of consideration.

---

## CONCEPT SUMMARY 13.1
### Consideration

| | |
|---|---|
| **Elements of Consideration** | Consideration is the value given in exchange for a promise. A contract cannot be formed without sufficient consideration. Consideration is often broken down into two elements:<br>1. *Legal value*—Something of legally sufficient value must be given in exchange for a promise. This may consist of a promise, a performance, or a forbearance.<br>2. *Bargained-for exchange*—There must be a bargained-for exchange. |
| **Adequacy of Consideration** | Adequacy of consideration relates to how much consideration is given and whether a fair bargain was reached. Courts will inquire into the adequacy of consideration (if the consideration is legally sufficient) only when fraud, undue influence, duress, or the lack of a bargained-for exchange may be involved. |
| **Agreements That Lack Consideration** | Consideration is lacking in the following situations:<br>1. *Preexisting duty*—Consideration is not legally sufficient if one is either by law or by contract under a *preexisting duty* to perform the action being offered as consideration for a new contract.<br>2. *Past consideration*—Actions or events that have already taken place do not constitute legally sufficient consideration.<br>3. *Illusory promises*—When the nature or extent of performance is too uncertain, the promise is rendered illusory and unenforceable. |

---

## SECTION 4
# SETTLEMENT OF CLAIMS

Businesspersons and others often enter into contracts to settle legal claims. It is important to understand the nature of consideration given in these kinds of settlement agreements, or contracts. Claims are commonly settled through an *accord and satisfaction,* in which a debtor offers to pay a lesser amount than the creditor purports to be owed. Claims may also be settled by the signing of a *release* or a *covenant not to sue.*

### Accord and Satisfaction

In an **accord and satisfaction,** a debtor offers to pay, and a creditor accepts, a lesser amount than the creditor originally claimed was owed. The *accord* is the agreement. In the accord, one party undertakes to give or perform, and the other to accept, in satisfaction of a claim, something other than that on which the parties originally agreed. *Satisfaction* is the performance (usually payment) that takes place after the accord is executed.

A basic rule is that there can be no satisfaction unless there is first an accord. For accord and satisfaction to occur, the amount of the debt *must be in dispute.*

**LIQUIDATED DEBTS** If a debt is *liquidated,* accord and satisfaction cannot take place. A **liquidated debt** is one whose amount has been ascertained, fixed, agreed on, settled, or exactly determined. ▶ **Example 13.7** Barbara Kwan signs an installment loan contract with her bank. In the contract, Kwan agrees to pay a set rate of interest on a specified amount of borrowed funds at monthly intervals for two years. Because both parties know the precise amount of the total obligation, it is a liquidated debt. ◀

In the majority of states, acceptance of a lesser sum than the entire amount of a liquidated debt is *not* satisfaction, and the balance of the debt is still legally owed. The reason for this rule is that the debtor has given no consideration to satisfy the obligation of paying the balance to the creditor. The debtor had a preexisting legal obligation to pay the entire debt. (Of course, even with liquidated debts, creditors often do negotiate debt settlement agreements with debtors for a lesser amount than was originally owed. Creditors sometimes even forgive or write off a liquidated debt as uncollectable.)

**UNLIQUIDATED DEBTS** An **unliquidated debt** is the opposite of a liquidated debt. The amount of the debt is *not* settled, fixed, agreed on, ascertained, or determined, and reasonable persons may differ over the amount owed. In these circumstances, acceptance of a lesser sum operates as satisfaction, or discharge, of the debt because there is valid consideration. The parties give up a legal right to contest the amount in dispute.

## Release

A **release** is a contract in which one party forfeits the right to pursue a legal claim against the other party. It bars any further recovery beyond the terms stated in the release.

A release will generally be binding if it meets the following requirements:

1. The agreement is made in good faith (honesty).
2. The release contract is in a signed writing (required in many states).
3. The contract is accompanied by consideration.[5]

Clearly, an individual is better off knowing the extent of his or her injuries or damages before signing a release. ▶ **Example 13.8** Lupe's car is damaged in an automobile accident caused by Dexter's negligence. Dexter offers to give her $3,000 if she will

---

5. Under the Uniform Commercial Code (UCC), a written, signed waiver or renunciation by an aggrieved party discharges any further liability for a breach, even without consideration.

release him from further liability resulting from the accident. Lupe agrees and signs the release.

If Lupe later discovers that it will cost $4,200 to repair her car, she cannot recover the additional amount from Dexter. Lupe is limited to the $3,000 specified in the release. Lupe and Dexter both voluntarily agreed to the terms in the release, which was in a signed writing, and sufficient consideration was present. The consideration was the legal right Lupe forfeited to sue to recover damages, should they be more than $3,000, in exchange for Dexter's promise to give her $3,000. ◀

## Covenant Not to Sue

Unlike a release, a **covenant not to sue** does not always bar further recovery. The parties simply substitute a contractual obligation for some other type of legal action based on a valid claim. Suppose in *Example 13.8*, that Lupe agrees with Dexter not to sue for damages in a tort action if he will pay for the damage to her car. If Dexter fails to pay for the repairs, Lupe can bring an action against him for breach of contract.

As the following case illustrates, a covenant not to sue can form the basis for a dismissal of the claims of either party to the covenant.

### Case 13.3   Already, LLC v. Nike, Inc.
Supreme Court of the United States, ___ U.S. ___, 133 S.Ct. 721, 184 L.Ed.2d 553 (2013).

**BACKGROUND AND FACTS** Nike, Inc., designs, makes, and sells athletic footwear, including a line of shoes known as "Air Force 1." Already, LLC, also designs and markets athletic footwear, including the "Sugar" and "Soulja Boy" lines. Nike filed a suit in a federal district court against Already, alleging that Soulja Boys and Sugars infringed the Air Force 1 trademark. Already filed a counterclaim, contending that the Air Force 1 trademark was invalid. While the suit was pending, Nike issued a covenant not to sue, promising not to raise any trademark claims against Already or any affiliated entity based on Already's existing footwear designs, or any future Already designs that constituted a "colorable imitation" of Already's current products. Nike then filed a motion to dismiss its own claims and to dismiss Already's counterclaim. Already opposed the dismissal of its counterclaim, but the court granted Nike's motion. The U.S. Court of Appeals for the Second Circuit affirmed. Already appealed to the United States Supreme Court.

**DECISION AND RATIONALE** The United States Supreme Court affirmed the judgment of the lower courts dismissing both Nike's claims and Already's counterclaims. The Supreme Court looked at the wording of the covenant not to sue to determine whether Already's counterclaim was moot (not legally relevant). Nike had unconditionally and irrevocably promised not to make any trademark infringement claims against Already "relating to the NIKE Mark based on the appearance of *any* of Already's current and/or previous footwear product designs, and *any* colorable [reasonable] imitations thereof."

Under the covenant's broad language, the Court noted, "It is hard to imagine a scenario that would potentially infringe Nike's trademark and yet not fall under the covenant." Therefore, the Court con-

**CASE 13.3 CONTINUED**     cluded that Nike could not file a claim for trademark infringement against Already, and Already could not assert that Nike's trademark was invalid.

**THE ECONOMIC DIMENSION** *Why would any party agree to a covenant not to sue?*

**THE LEGAL ENVIRONMENT DIMENSION** *Which types of contracts are similar to a covenant not to sue? Explain.*

---

## SECTION 5
# EXCEPTIONS TO THE CONSIDERATION REQUIREMENT

There are some exceptions to the rule that only promises supported by consideration are enforceable. The following types of promises may be enforced despite the lack of consideration:

1. Promises that induce detrimental reliance, under the doctrine of *promissory estoppel*.
2. Promises to pay debts that are barred by a statute of limitations.
3. Promises to make charitable contributions.

## Promissory Estoppel

Sometimes, individuals rely on promises to their detriment, and their reliance may form a basis for a court to infer contract rights and duties. Under the doctrine of **promissory estoppel** (also called *detrimental reliance*), a person who has reasonably and substantially relied on the promise of another may be able to obtain some measure of recovery.

Promissory estoppel is applied in a wide variety of contexts in which a promise is otherwise unenforceable, such as when a promise made *without consideration*. Under this doctrine, a court may enforce an otherwise unenforceable promise to avoid the injustice that would otherwise result.

**REQUIREMENTS TO STATE A CLAIM** For the promissory estoppel doctrine to be applied, the following elements are required:

1. There must be a clear and definite promise.
2. The promisor should have expected that the promisee would rely on the promise.
3. The promisee reasonably relied on the promise by acting or refraining from some act.
4. The promisee's reliance was definite and resulted in substantial detriment.
5. Enforcement of the promise is necessary to avoid injustice.

If these requirements are met, a promise may be enforced even though it is not supported by consideration.[6] In essence, the promisor will be **estopped** (prevented) from asserting the lack of consideration as a defense.

Promissory estoppel is similar in some ways to the doctrine of quasi contract that was discussed in Chapter 11. In both situations, a court, acting in the interests of equity, imposes contract obligations on the parties to prevent unfairness even though no actual contract exists. The difference is that with quasi contract, no promise was made at all. In contrast, with promissory estoppel, a promise was made and relied on, but it was unenforceable.

**APPLICATION OF THE DOCTRINE** Promissory estoppel was originally applied to situations involving gifts (I promise to pay you $1,000 a week so that you will not have to work) and donations to charities (I promise to contribute $50,000 a year to the Raising Giants orphanage). Later, courts began to apply the doctrine to avoid inequity or hardship in other situations, including business transactions, some employment relationships, and even disputes among family members.

▶ **Case in Point 13.9** Jeffrey and Kathryn Dow own 125 acres of land in Corinth, Maine. The Dows regarded the land as their children's heritage, and the subject of the children's living on the land was often discussed within the family. With the Dows' permission, their daughter Teresa installed a mobile home and built a garage on the land.

After Teresa married Jarrod Harvey, the Dows agreed to finance the construction of a house on the land for the couple. When Jarrod died in a motorcycle accident, however, Teresa financed the house with his life insurance proceeds. The construction cost about $200,000. Her father, Jeffrey, performed a substantial amount of carpentry and other work on the house.

Teresa then asked her parents for a deed to the property so that she could obtain a mortgage. They refused. Teresa sued her parents for promissory estoppel. Maine's highest court ruled in favor of Teresa's

---

6. *Restatement (Second) of Contracts,* Section 90.

promissory estoppel claim. The court reasoned that the Dows' support and encouragement of their daughter's construction of a house on the land "conclusively demonstrated" their intent to transfer. For years, they had made general promises to convey the land to their children, including Teresa. Teresa had reasonably relied on their promise in financing construction of a house to her detriment ($200,000). The court concluded that enforcing the promise was the only way to avoid injustice in this situation.[7] ◄

## Promises to Pay Debts Barred by a Statute of Limitations

Statutes of limitations in all states require a creditor to sue within a specified period to recover a debt. If the creditor fails to sue in time, recovery of the debt is barred by the statute of limitations.

A debtor who promises to pay a previous debt even though recovery is barred by the statute of limitations makes an enforceable promise. *The promise needs no consideration.* (Some states, however, require that it be in writing.) In effect, the promise extends the limitations period, and the creditor can sue to recover the entire debt or at least the amount

---

7. *Harvey v. Dow,* 2011 ME 4, 11 A.3d 303 (2011).

promised. The promise can be implied if the debtor acknowledges the barred debt by making a partial payment.

## Charitable Subscriptions

A charitable subscription is a promise to make a donation to a religious, educational, or charitable institution. Traditionally, such promises were unenforceable because they are not supported by legally sufficient consideration. A gift, after all, is the opposite of bargained-for consideration. The modern view, however, is to make exceptions to the general rule by applying the doctrine of promissory estoppel.

▶ **Example 13.10** A church solicits and receives pledges (commitments to contribute funds) from church members to erect a new church building. On the basis of these pledges, the church purchases land, hires architects, and makes other contracts that change its position. Because of the church's detrimental reliance, a court may enforce the pledges under the theory of promissory estoppel. Alternatively, a court may find consideration in the fact that each promise was made in reliance on the other promises of support or that the church trustees, by accepting the subscriptions, impliedly promised to complete the proposed undertaking. ◄

---

# Reviewing: Consideration

John operates a motorcycle repair shop from his home but finds that his business is limited by the small size of his garage. Driving by a neighbor's property, he notices a for-sale sign on a large, metal-sided garage. John contacts the neighbor and offers to buy the building, hoping that it can be dismantled and moved to his own property. The neighbor accepts John's payment and makes a generous offer in return: if John will help him dismantle the garage, which will take a substantial amount of time, he will help John reassemble it after it has been transported to John's property. They agree to have the entire job completed within two weeks. John spends every day for a week working with his neighbor to disassemble the building. In his rush to acquire a larger workspace, he turns down several lucrative repair jobs. Once the disassembled building has been moved to John's property, however, the neighbor refuses to help John reassemble it as he originally promised. Using the information presented in the chapter, answer the following questions.

1. Are the basic elements of consideration present in the neighbor's promise to help John reassemble the garage? Why or why not?
2. Suppose that the neighbor starts to help John but then realizes that, because of the layout of John's property, putting the building back together will take much more work than dismantling it took. Under which principle discussed in the chapter might the neighbor be allowed to ask for additional compensation?
3. What if John's neighbor made his promise to help reassemble the garage at the time he and John were moving it to John's property, saying, "Since you helped me take it down, I will help you put it

4. Under what doctrine discussed in the chapter might John seek to recover the profits he lost when he turned down repair jobs for one week?

**DEBATE THIS . . .** *Courts should not be able to rule on the adequacy of consideration. A deal is a deal.*

## Terms and Concepts

accord and satisfaction 243
consideration 238
covenant not to sue 244
estopped 245

forbearance 238
liquidated debt 243
past consideration 241
promissory estoppel 245

release 244
rescission 241
unliquidated debt 243

## Issue Spotters

1. In September, Sharyn agrees to work for Totem Productions, Inc., at $500 a week for a year beginning January 1. In October, Sharyn is offered the same work at $600 a week by Umber Shows, Ltd. When Sharyn tells Totem about the other offer, they tear up their contract and agree that Sharyn will be paid $575. Is the new contract binding? Explain. **(See page 241.)**

2. Before Maria starts her first year of college, Fred promises to give her $5,000 when she graduates. She goes to college, borrowing and spending far more than $5,000. At the beginning of the spring semester of her senior year, she reminds Fred of the promise. Fred sends her a note that says, "I revoke the promise." Is Fred's promise binding? Explain. **(See page 245.)**

• Check your answers to the Issue Spotters against the answers provided in Appendix E at the end of this text.

## Business Scenarios

**13–1. Preexisting Duty.** Tabor is a buyer of file cabinets manufactured by Martin. Martin's contract with Tabor calls for delivery of fifty file cabinets at $40 per cabinet in five equal installments. After delivery of two installments (twenty cabinets), Martin informs Tabor that because of inflation, Martin is losing money and will promise to deliver the remaining thirty cabinets only if Tabor will pay $50 per cabinet. Tabor agrees in writing to do so. Discuss whether Martin can legally collect the additional $100 on delivery to Tabor of the next installment of ten cabinets. **(See page 240.)**

**13–2. Consideration.** Daniel, a recent college graduate, is on his way home for the Christmas holidays from his new job. He gets caught in a snowstorm and is taken in by an elderly couple, who provide him with food and shelter. After the snowplows have cleared the road, Daniel proceeds home. Daniel's father, Fred, is most appreciative of the elderly couple's action and in a letter promises to pay them $500. The elderly couple, in need of funds, accept Fred's offer. Then, because of a dispute between Daniel and Fred, Fred refuses to pay the elderly couple the $500. Discuss whether the couple can hold

Fred liable in contract for the services rendered to Daniel. **(See page 241.)**

**13–3. Illusory Promises.** Costello hired Sagan to drive his racing car in a race. Sagan's friend Gideon promised to pay Sagan $3,000 if she won the race. Sagan won the race, but Gideon refused to pay. Gideon contended that no legally binding contract had been formed because he had received no consideration from Sagan in exchange for his promise to pay the $3,000. Sagan sued Gideon for breach of contract, arguing that winning the race was the consideration given in exchange for Gideon's promise to pay the $3,000. What rule of law discussed in this chapter supports Gideon's claim? **(See page 242.)**

**13–4. Accord and Satisfaction.** Merrick grows and sells blueberries. Maine Wild Blueberry Co. agreed to buy all of Merrick's crop under a contract that left the price unliquidated. Merrick delivered the berries, but a dispute arose over the price. Maine Wild sent Merrick a check with a letter stating that the check was the "final settlement." Merrick cashed the check but filed a suit for breach of contract, claiming that he was owed more. What will the court likely decide in this case? Why? **(See page 243.)**

## Business Case Problems

**13–5. Past Consideration.** Access Organics, Inc., hired Andy Hernandez to sell organic produce. Later, Hernandez signed an agreement not to compete with Access for two years following the termination of his employment. He did not receive a pay increase or any other new benefits in return for signing the agreement. When Access encountered financial trouble, Hernandez left and began to compete with his former employer. Access filed a lawsuit against Hernandez. Is the noncompete agreement enforceable? Discuss. [*Access Organics, Inc. v. Hernandez*, 341 Mont. 73, 175 P.3d 899 (2008)] **(See page 241.)**

**13–6. BUSINESS CASE PROBLEM
WITH SAMPLE ANSWER: Rescission.**

*Farrokh and Scheherezade Sharabianlou signed a purchase agreement to buy a building owned by Berenstein Associates for $2 million. They deposited $115,000 toward the purchase. Before the deal closed, an environmental assessment of the property indicated the presence of chemicals used in dry cleaning. This substantially reduced the property's value. Do the Sharabianlous have a good argument for the return of their deposit and rescission of the contract? Explain your answer.* [Sharabianlou v. Karp, 181 Cal.App.4th 1133, 105 Cal.Rptr.3d 300 (1st Dist. 2010)] **(See page 241.)**

- **For a sample answer to Problem 13–6, go to Appendix F at the end of this text.**

**13–7. Statute of Limitations.** Leonard Kranzler loaned Lewis Saltzman $100,000. Saltzman made fifteen payments on the loan, but this did not repay the entire amount. More than ten years after the date of the loan, but less than two years after the date of the last payment, Kranzler filed a suit against Saltzman to recover the outstanding balance. Saltzman claimed that the suit was barred by a ten-year statute of limitations. Does Kranzler need to prove a new promise with new consideration to collect the unpaid debt? Explain. [*Kranzler v. Saltzman*, 407 Ill. App.3d 24, 942 N.E.2d 722, 347 Ill.Dec. 519 (1 Dist. 2011)] **(See page 246.)**

**13–8. Consideration.** On Brenda Sniezek's first day of work for the Kansas City Chiefs Football Club, she signed a document that purported to compel arbitration of any disputes that she might have with the Chiefs. In the document, Sniezek agreed to comply at all times with and be bound by the constitution and bylaws of the National Football League (NFL). She agreed to refer all disputes to the NFL Commissioner for a binding decision. On the Commissioner's decision, she agreed to release the Chiefs and others from any related claims. Nowhere in the document did the Chiefs agree to do anything. Was there consideration for the arbitration provision? Explain. [*Sniezek v. Kansas City Chiefs Football Club*, __ S.W.3e __, 2013 WL 661632 (Mo.App. W.D. 2013)] **(See page 238.)**

**13–9. A QUESTION OF ETHICS: Promissory Estoppel.**

*Claudia Aceves borrowed from U.S. Bank to buy a home. Two years later, she could no longer afford the monthly payments. The bank notified her that it planned to foreclose (take possession of and sell) on her home. Aceves filed for bankruptcy. The bank offered to modify Aceves's mortgage if she would forgo bankruptcy. She agreed. Once she withdrew the filing, however, the bank foreclosed.* [Aceves v. U.S. Bank, N.A., 192 Cal.App.4th 218, 120 Cal.Rptr.3d 507 (2 Dist. 2011)] **(See page 245.)**

(a) Could Aceves succeed on a claim of promissory estoppel? Why or why not?

(b) Did Aceves or U.S. Bank behave unethically? Discuss.

## Legal Reasoning Group Activity

**13–10. Preexisting Duty.** Melissa Faraj owns a lot and wants to build a house according to a particular set of plans and specifications. She solicits bids from building contractors and receives three bids: one from Carlton for $160,000, one from Feldberg for $158,000, and one from Siegel for $153,000. She accepts Siegel's bid. One month after beginning construction of the house, Siegel contacts Faraj and tells her that because of inflation and a recent price hike for materials, he will not finish the house unless Faraj agrees to pay an extra $13,000. Faraj reluctantly agrees to pay the additional sum. **(See page 240.)**

(a) One group will discuss whether a contractor can ever raise the price of completing construction based on inflation and the rising cost of materials.

(b) A second group will assume that after the house is finished, Faraj refuses to pay the extra $13,000. The group will decide whether Faraj is legally required to pay this additional amount.

(c) A third group will discuss the types of extraordinary difficulties that could arise during construction that would justify a contractor charging more than the original bid.

# CHAPTER 14

# CAPACITY AND LEGALITY

In addition to agreement and consideration, for a contract to be deemed valid, the parties to the contract must have **contractual capacity**—the legal ability to enter into a contractual relationship. Courts generally presume the existence of contractual capacity, but in some situations, as when a person is young or mentally incompetent, capacity may be lacking or questionable. Similarly, contracts calling for the performance of an illegal act are illegal and thus void—they are not contracts at all. In this chapter, we examine contractual capacity and some aspects of illegal bargains.

Realize that capacity and legality are not inherently related other than that they are both contract requirements. We treat these topics in one chapter merely for convenience and reasons of space.

## SECTION 1
## CONTRACTUAL CAPACITY

Historically, the law has given special protection to those who bargain with the inexperience of youth and those who lack the degree of mental competence required by law. A person who has been determined by a court to be mentally incompetent, for instance, cannot form a legally binding contract with another party. In other situations, a party may have the capacity to enter into a valid contract but also have the right to avoid liability under it. Minors—or *infants,* as they are commonly referred to in legal terminology—usually are not legally bound by contracts. In this section, we look at the effect of youth, intoxication, and mental incompetence on contractual capacity.

### Minors

Today, in almost all states, the **age of majority** (when a person is no longer a minor) for contractual purposes is eighteen years.[1] In addition, some states provide for the termination of minority on marriage.

Minority status may also be terminated by a minor's **emancipation,** which occurs when a child's parent or legal guardian relinquishes the legal right to exercise control over the child. Normally, minors who leave home to support themselves are considered emancipated. Several jurisdictions permit minors themselves to petition a court for emancipation. For business purposes, a minor may petition a court to be treated as an adult.

The general rule is that a minor can enter into any contract that an adult can, except contracts prohibited by law for minors (for example, the purchase of tobacco or alcoholic beverages). A contract entered into by a minor, however, is voidable at the option of that minor, subject to certain exceptions. To exercise the option to avoid a contract, a minor need only manifest (clearly show) an intention not to be bound by it. The minor "avoids" the contract by disaffirming it.

**DISAFFIRMANCE** The legal avoidance, or setting aside, of a contractual obligation is referred to as **disaffirmance.** To disaffirm, a minor must express his or her intent, through words or conduct, not to be bound to the contract. The minor must disaffirm the entire contract, not merely a portion of it. For instance, the minor cannot decide to keep part of the goods purchased under a contract and return the remaining goods.

▶ **Case in Point 14.1** Fifteen-year-old Morgan Kelly was a cadet in her high school's Navy Junior

---

1. The age of majority may still be twenty-one for other purposes, such as the purchase and consumption of alcohol.

Reserve Officer Training Corps. As part of the program, she visited a U.S. Marine Corps training facility. To enter the camp, she was required to sign a waiver that exempted the Marines from all liability for any injuries arising from her visit.

While participating in activities on the camp's confidence-building course, Kelly fell from the "Slide for Life" and suffered serious injuries. She filed a suit to recover her medical costs. The Marines asserted that she had signed their waiver of liability. Kelly claimed that she had disaffirmed the waiver when she filed suit. The court ruled in Kelly's favor. Liability waivers are generally enforceable contracts, but a minor can avoid a contract by disaffirming it.[2] ◄

Note that an adult who enters into a contract with a minor cannot avoid his or her contractual duties on the ground that the minor can do so. Unless the minor exercises the option to disaffirm the contract, the adult party normally is bound by it. On disaffirming a contract, a minor can recover any property that he or she transferred to the adult as consideration, even if the property is in the possession of a third party.[3]

***Must Be within a Reasonable Time.*** A contract can ordinarily be disaffirmed at any time during minority[4] or for a reasonable period after reaching majority. What constitutes a "reasonable" time may vary. If an individual fails to disaffirm an executed contract (fully performed) within a reasonable time after reaching the age of majority, a court will likely hold that the contract has been ratified (*ratification* will be discussed shortly).

***Minor's Obligations on Disaffirmance.*** Although all states' laws permit minors to disaffirm contracts (with certain exceptions), states differ on the extent of a minor's obligations on disaffirmance. Courts in most states hold that the minor need only return the goods (or other consideration) subject to the contract, provided the goods are in the minor's possession or control. Even if the minor returns damaged goods, the minor often is entitled to disaffirm the contract and obtain a full refund of the purchase price.

Courts in a growing number of states place an additional duty on the minor to restore the adult party to

the position she or he held before the contract was made. These courts may hold a minor responsible for damage, ordinary wear and tear, and depreciation of goods that the minor used prior to disaffirmance.

▶ **Case in Point 14.2** Sixteen-year-old Joseph Dodson bought a pickup truck from a used-car dealer. Although the truck developed mechanical problems nine months later, Dodson continued to drive it until it stopped running. Then Dodson disaffirmed the contract and attempted to return the truck to the dealer for a full refund. When the dealer refused to accept the pickup or refund the purchase price, Dodson filed a suit. Ultimately, the Tennessee Supreme Court allowed Dodson to disaffirm the contract but required him to compensate the seller for the depreciated value—not the purchase price—of the pickup.[5] ◄

## EXCEPTIONS TO A MINOR'S RIGHT TO DISAFFIRM

State courts and legislatures have carved out several exceptions to the minor's right to disaffirm. Marriage contracts and contracts to enlist in the armed services, for instance, cannot be avoided for public-policy reasons. Some contracts may not be disaffirmed for other reasons, including those discussed here.

***Misrepresentation of Age.*** Ordinarily, minors can disaffirm contracts even when they have misrepresented their age (claimed to be twenty-one years old when they were not). Nevertheless, a growing number of states have enacted laws to prohibit disaffirmance in such situations. In some states, misrepresentation of age is enough to prevent disaffirmance. Other states prohibit disaffirmance by minors who misrepresented their age while engaged in business as an adult.

***Contracts for Necessaries.*** A minor who enters into a contract for necessaries may disaffirm the contract but remains liable for the reasonable value of the goods. **Necessaries** are basic needs, such as food, clothing, shelter, and medical services. What is a necessary for one minor, however, may be a luxury for another, depending on the minors' customary living standard. Contracts for necessaries are enforceable only to the level of value needed to maintain the minor's standard of living.

**RATIFICATION** In contract law, **ratification** is the act of accepting and giving legal force to an obligation

---

**2.** *Kelly v. United States,* 809 F.Supp.2d 429 (E.D.N.C. 2011).

**3.** Section 2–403(1) of the Uniform Commercial Code (UCC) allows an exception if the third party is a "good faith purchaser for value." See Chapter 20.

**4.** In some states, however, a minor who enters into a contract for the sale of land cannot disaffirm the contract until she or he reaches the age of majority.

**5.** *Dodson v. Shrader,* 824 S.W.2d 545 (Tenn.Sup.Ct. 1992) is a seminal case on this subject. See also *Restatement (Third) of Restitution,* Sections 16 and 33.

that previously was not enforceable. A minor who has reached the age of majority can ratify a contract expressly or impliedly. *Express* ratification takes place when the individual, on reaching the age of majority, states orally or in writing that he or she intends to be bound by the contract. *Implied* ratification takes place when the minor, on reaching the age of majority, indicates an intent to abide by the contract.

▶ **Example 14.3** Lin enters into a contract to sell her laptop to Andrew, a minor. If, on reaching the age of majority, Andrew e-mails Lin stating that he still agrees to buy the laptop, he has *expressly* ratified the contract. If, instead, Andrew takes possession of the laptop as a minor and continues to use it well after reaching the age of majority, he has *impliedly* ratified the contract. ◀

If a minor fails to disaffirm a contract within a reasonable time after reaching the age of majority, then the court must determine whether the conduct constitutes ratification or disaffirmance. Generally, courts presume that executed contracts (fully performed) are ratified and that executory contracts (not yet fully performed by both parties) are disaffirmed.

**PARENTS' LIABILITY** As a general rule, parents are not liable for contracts made by minor children acting on their own. As a consequence, businesses ordinarily require parents to cosign any contract made with a minor. The parents then become personally obligated under the contract to perform the conditions of the contract, even if their child avoids liability. (Parents can sometimes be held liable for a minor's torts, however, depending on state law.)

*Concept Summary 14.1* below reviews the rules relating to contracts by minors.

## Intoxication

Intoxication is a condition in which a person's normal capacity to act or think is inhibited by alcohol or some other drug. A contract entered into by an intoxicated person can be either voidable or valid (and thus enforceable).[6]

If the person was sufficiently intoxicated to lack mental capacity, then the agreement may be voidable even if the intoxication was purely voluntary. If, despite intoxication, the person understood the legal consequences of the agreement, the contract will be enforceable.

Courts look at objective indications of the intoxicated person's condition to determine if he or she possessed or lacked the required capacity. It is difficult to prove that a person's judgment was so severely impaired that he or she could not comprehend the legal consequences of entering into a contract. Therefore, courts rarely permit contracts to be avoided due to intoxication.

**DISAFFIRMANCE** If a contract is voidable because one party was intoxicated, that person has the option of disaffirming it while intoxicated and for a reasonable time after becoming sober. The person claiming intoxication typically must be able to return all

---

**6.** Note that if an alcoholic makes a contract while sober, there is no lack of capacity. See *Wright v. Fisher,* 32 N.W. 605 (Mich. 1887).

---

## CONCEPT SUMMARY 14.1
### Contracts by Minors

| CONCEPT | DESCRIPTION |
| --- | --- |
| **General Rule** | Contracts entered into by minors are *voidable* at the option of the minor. |
| **Rules of Disaffirmance** | A minor may disaffirm the contract at any time while still a minor and within a reasonable time after reaching the age of majority. Most states do not require restitution. |
| **Exceptions to Basic Rules of Disaffirmance** | 1. *Misrepresentation of age (or fraud)*—In many jurisdictions, misrepresentation of age prohibits the right of disaffirmance. <br> 2. *Necessaries*—Minors remain liable for the reasonable value of necessaries (goods and services). <br> 3. *Ratification*—After reaching the age of majority, a person can ratify a contract that he or she formed as a minor, thereby becoming fully liable for it. |

consideration received unless the contract involved necessaries. Contracts for necessaries are voidable, but the intoxicated person is liable in quasi contract for the reasonable value of the consideration received (see Chapter 13).

**RATIFICATION** An intoxicated person, after becoming sober, may ratify a contract expressly or impliedly, just as a minor may do on reaching majority. Implied ratification occurs when a person enters into a contract while intoxicated and fails to disaffirm the contract within a *reasonable* time after becoming sober. Acts or conduct inconsistent with an intent to disaffirm—such as the continued use of property purchased under a voidable contract—will also ratify the contract.

See *Concept Summary 14.2* below for a review of the rules relating to contracts by intoxicated persons.

## Mental Incompetence

Contracts made by mentally incompetent persons can be void, voidable, or valid. We look here at the circumstances that determine when each of these classifications applies.

**WHEN THE CONTRACT WILL BE VOID** If a court has previously determined that a person is mentally incompetent, any contract made by that person is *void*—no contract exists. On determining that someone is mentally incompetent, the court appoints a guardian to represent the individual. Only the guardian can enter into binding legal obligations on behalf of the mentally incompetent person.

**WHEN THE CONTRACT WILL BE VOIDABLE** If a court has not previously judged a person to be mentally incompetent but the person was incompetent at the time the contract was formed, the contract may be voidable. A contract is *voidable* if the person did not know he or she was entering into the contract or lacked the mental capacity to comprehend its nature, purpose, and consequences. In such situations, the contract is voidable (or can be ratified) at the option of the mentally incompetent person but not at the option of the other party.

▶ **Example 14.4** Larry agrees to sell his stock in Google, Inc., to Sergey for substantially less than its market value. At the time of the deal, Larry is confused about the purpose and details of the transaction, but he has not been declared incompetent. Nonetheless, if a court finds that Larry did not understand the nature and consequences of the contract due to a lack of mental capacity, he can avoid the sale. ◀

**WHEN THE CONTRACT WILL BE VALID** A contract entered into by a mentally incompetent person (whom a court has not previously declared incompetent) may also be *valid* if the person had capacity *at the time the contract was formed*. Some people who are incompetent due to age or illness have *lucid intervals*—temporary periods of sufficient intelligence, judgment, and will. During such intervals, they will be considered to have legal capacity to enter into contracts.

See *Concept Summary 14.3* on the following page for a review of the rules relating to contracts entered into by mentally incompetent persons.

---

### CONCEPT SUMMARY 14.2
### Contracts by Intoxicated Persons

| CONCEPT | DESCRIPTION |
|---|---|
| **General Rules** | If a person was sufficiently intoxicated to lack the mental capacity to comprehend the legal consequences of entering into the contract, the contract may be *voidable* at the option of the intoxicated person. If, despite intoxication, the person understood these legal consequences, the contract will be enforceable. |
| **Disaffirmance** | An intoxicated person may disaffirm the contract at any time while intoxicated and for a reasonable time after becoming sober but must make full restitution. Contracts for necessaries are voidable, but the intoxicated person is liable for the reasonable value of the goods or services. |
| **Ratification** | After becoming sober, a person can ratify a contract that she or he formed while intoxicated, thereby becoming fully liable for it. |

> ## CONCEPT SUMMARY 14.3
> ### Contracts by Mentally Incompetent Persons
>
> | CONCEPT | DESCRIPTION |
> |---------|-------------|
> | **Void** | If a court has declared a person to be mentally incompetent and has appointed a legal guardian, any contract made by that person is void from the outset. |
> | **Voidable** | If a court has *not* declared a person mentally incompetent, but that person lacked the capacity to comprehend the subject matter, nature, and consequences of the agreement, then the contract is voidable at that person's option. |
> | **Valid** | If a court has *not* declared a person mentally incompetent and that person was able to understand the nature and effect of the contract at the time it was formed, then the contract is valid and enforceable. |

## SECTION 2
# LEGALITY

Legality is the fourth requirement for a valid contract to exist. For a contract to be valid and enforceable, it must be formed for a legal purpose. A contract to do something that is prohibited by federal or state statutory law is illegal and, as such, void from the outset and thus unenforceable. Additionally, a contract to commit a tortious act—such as an agreement to engage in fraudulent misrepresentation (see Chapter 6)—is contrary to public policy and therefore illegal and unenforceable.

## Contracts Contrary to Statute

Statutes often set forth rules specifying which terms and clauses may be included in contracts and which are prohibited. We now examine several ways in which contracts may be contrary to statute and thus illegal.

**CONTRACTS TO COMMIT A CRIME** Any contract to commit a crime is in violation of a statute. Thus, a contract to sell illegal drugs in violation of criminal laws is unenforceable, as is a contract to cover up a corporation's violation of the Dodd-Frank Wall Street Reform and Consumer Protection Act. Similarly, a contract to smuggle undocumented workers from another country into the United States for an employer is illegal, as is a contract to dump hazardous waste in violation of environmental laws.

Sometimes, the object or performance of a contract is rendered illegal by a statute *after* the parties entered into the contract. In that situation, the contract is considered to be discharged by law. (See the discussion of impossibility or impracticability of performance in Chapter 18.)

**USURY** Almost every state has a statute that sets the maximum rate of interest that can be charged for different types of transactions, including ordinary loans. A lender who makes a loan at an interest rate above the lawful maximum commits **usury.** Although usurious contracts are illegal, most states simply limit the interest that the lender may collect on the contract to the lawful maximum interest rate in that state. In a few states, the lender can recover the principal amount of the loan but no interest.

Usury statutes place a ceiling on allowable rates of interest, but states can make exceptions to facilitate business transactions. For instance, many states exempt corporate loans from the usury laws, and nearly all states allow higher interest rate loans for borrowers who could not otherwise obtain funds. In reaction to the latest economic recession, the federal government placed some restrictions on the interest rates and fees that banks and credit-card companies can legally charge consumers.[7]

**GAMBLING** Gambling is the creation of risk for the purpose of assuming it. Any scheme that involves the distribution of property by chance among persons who have paid valuable consideration for the opportunity (chance) to receive the property is gambling. Traditionally, the states have deemed gambling

---

**7.** The Credit Card Accountability, Responsibility, and Disclosure Act of 2009, Pub. L. No. 111-24, 123 Stat. 1734.

contracts illegal and thus void. It is sometimes difficult, however, to distinguish a gambling contract from the risk sharing inherent in almost all contracts.

All states have statutes that regulate gambling, and many states allow certain forms of gambling, such as betting on horse races, poker machines, and charity-sponsored bingo. In addition, nearly all states allow state-operated lotteries as well as gambling on Native American reservations. Even in states that permit certain types of gambling, though, courts often find that gambling contracts are illegal.

▶ **Case in Point 14.5**  Video poker machines are legal in Louisiana, but their use requires the approval of the state video gaming commission. Gaming Venture, Inc., did not obtain this approval before agreeing with Tastee Restaurant Corporation to install poker machines in some of its restaurants. For this reason, when Tastee allegedly reneged on the deal by refusing to install the machines, a state court held that their agreement was an illegal gambling contract and therefore void.[8] ◀

---

8. *Gaming Venture, Inc. v. Tastee Restaurant Corp.*, 996 So.2d 515 (La.App. 5 Cir. 2008).

**LICENSING STATUTES** All states require members of certain professions—including physicians, lawyers, real estate brokers, accountants, architects, electricians, and stockbrokers—to have licenses. Some licenses are obtained only after extensive schooling and examinations, which indicate to the public that a special skill has been acquired. Others require only that the applicant be of good moral character and pay a fee.

Whether a contract with an unlicensed person is legal and enforceable depends on the purpose of the licensing statute. If the statute's purpose is to protect the public from unauthorized practitioners (such as unlicensed attorneys and electricians, for instance), then a contract involving an unlicensed practitioner is generally illegal and unenforceable. If the statute's purpose is merely to raise government revenues, however, a court may enforce the contract and fine the unlicensed person.

Can a member of a profession who is licensed in one jurisdiction recover on a contract to perform professional services in another jurisdiction? What if the contract was the result of a winning entry in an international competition? In the following case, the court had to answer these questions.

---

## CASE 14.1

### Sturdza v. United Arab Emirates
District of Columbia Court of Appeals, 11 A.3d 251 (2011).

**COMPANY PROFILE**  In 1971, six of the Trucial States of the Persian Gulf coast merged to form the United Arab Emirates (UAE). A seventh state joined in 1972. After the discovery of oil in the UAE more than thirty years ago, the nation changed from an expanse of small desert principalities to a modern state with a high standard of living. Today, the UAE has an open economy with a high per capita income comparable to that of Western Europe and an annual trade surplus. Although hit hard by falling oil and real estate prices and the international banking crisis during the recent world recession, the UAE continues to play an important role in the Persian Gulf.

**BACKGROUND AND FACTS**  The UAE held a competition for the design of a new embassy in Washington, D.C. At the conclusion of the competition, the UAE informed Elena Sturdza—an architect licensed in Maryland and Texas but not in the District of Columbia—that she had won. Sturdza and the UAE began to negotiate a contract. For two years, they exchanged proposals. Then, without explanation, the UAE stopped communicating with Sturdza. No contract between the UAE and Sturdza was ever signed. About two years later, Sturdza learned that the UAE had contracted with a District of Columbia architect, Angelos Demetriou, to use his design for its embassy. Believing that Demetriou's design "copied and appropriated many of the design features that had been the hallmark of [my] design," Sturdza filed a suit in a federal district court against the UAE, alleging breach of contract. The court issued a summary judgment in the UAE's favor. Sturdza appealed to the U.S. Court of Appeals for the District of Columbia Circuit. This court asked the District of Columbia Court of Appeals "precisely how D.C. law applies" in this situation.

**DECISION AND RATIONALE** The District of Columbia Court of Appeals answered the question of the U.S. Court of Appeals for the District of Columbia Circuit. An architect cannot recover on a contract to perform architectural services in the District of Columbia if he or she lacks a District of Columbia license. Sturdza argued that the licensing statute should not apply to architects who submit plans in international architectural design competitions. The court held, however, that licensing requirements are necessary to ensure the safety of those who work in and visit buildings in the District of Columbia, as well as the safety of neighboring buildings. Besides, the statute contains no exception for international design competitions or any other type of client or service. "We must apply the statute as it is written and not create *ad hoc* [impromptu] exceptions by judicial decree based on nebulous [unclear] policy considerations."

**THE GLOBAL DIMENSION** *The architectural services at the center of this case were to be performed for a foreign embassy. Should the court have made an exception for such a situation? Why or why not?*

**THE LEGAL ENVIRONMENT DIMENSION** *Should restrictions on the enforcement of contracts with unlicensed practitioners extend beyond the performance of professional services to include negotiations to provide the services? Discuss.*

# Contracts Contrary to Public Policy

Although contracts involve private parties, some are not enforceable because of the negative impact they would have on society. These contracts are said to be *contrary to public policy.* Examples include a contract to commit an immoral act, such as selling a child, and a contract that prohibits marriage. We look here at certain types of business contracts that are often found to be against public policy.

**CONTRACTS IN RESTRAINT OF TRADE** Contracts in restraint of trade (anticompetitive agreements) usually adversely affect the public policy that favors competition in the economy. Typically, such contracts also violate one or more federal or state antitrust statutes.[9]

An exception is recognized when the restraint is reasonable and is contained in an ancillary (secondary or subordinate) clause in a contract. Such restraints often are included in contracts for the sale of an ongoing business and employment contracts.

**Covenants Not to Compete and the Sale of an Ongoing Business.** Many contracts involve a type of restraint called a **covenant not to compete,** or a restrictive covenant (promise). A covenant not to compete may be created when a seller of a store agrees not to open a new store in a certain geographic area surrounding the old business. The agreement enables the purchaser

to buy, and the seller to sell, the goodwill and reputation of an ongoing business without having to worry that the seller will open a competing business a block away. Provided the restrictive covenant is reasonable and is an ancillary part of the sale of an ongoing business, it is enforceable.

**Covenants Not to Compete in Employment Contracts.** Agreements not to compete (also referred to as *noncompete agreements*) are sometimes included in employment contracts (such as the contract between physicians and a medical clinic that was in dispute in Case 13.2 in Chapter 13). People in middle- or upper-level management positions commonly agree not to work for competitors or not to start competing businesses for a specified period of time after termination of employment. (For an example of such a noncompete clause, see paragraph 9 of the sample contract in the appendix following Chapter 19.)

Such agreements are legal in most states so long as the specified period of time (of restraint) is not excessive in duration and the geographic restriction is reasonable. What constitutes a reasonable time period may be shorter in the online environment than in conventional employment contracts because the restrictions apply worldwide.

To be reasonable, a restriction on competition must protect a legitimate business interest and must not be any greater than necessary to protect that interest. ▶ **Case in Point 14.6** Safety and Compliance Management, Inc. (SCMI), provides drug- and alcohol-testing services. When SCMI hired Angela to pick up test specimens, she signed a covenant not to compete "in any area of SCMI

---

**9.** Federal statutes include the Sherman Antitrust Act, the Clayton Act, and the Federal Trade Commission Act.

business." Angela later quit SCMI's employ to work in a hospital where she sometimes collected patient specimens. SCMI claimed this was a breach of their noncompete agreement. A court ruled that the covenant was unreasonable because it imposed a greater restriction on Angela than necessary to protect SCMI.[10]  ◄

10. *Stultz v. Safety and Compliance Management, Inc.*, 285 Ga.App.799, 648 S.E.2d 129 (2007).

The contract in the following *Spotlight Case* provided an exclusive license to open and operate comedy clubs under a certain famous trademark. It included a covenant not to compete. The question was whether the restraint was reasonable.

### SP☉TLIGHT on the Improv

### Case 14.2 Comedy Club, Inc. v. Improv West Associates
United States Court of Appeals, Ninth Circuit, 553 F.3d 1277 (2009).

**BACKGROUND AND FACTS** Improv West Associates is the founder of the Improv Comedy Club and owner of the "Improv" trademark. Comedy Club, Inc. (CCI), owns and operates restaurants and comedy clubs. Improv West granted CCI an exclusive license to open four Improv clubs per year in 2001, 2002, and 2003. Their agreement prohibited CCI from opening any non-Improv comedy clubs "in the contiguous United States" until 2019. When CCI failed to open eight clubs by the end of 2002, Improv West commenced arbitration. In 2005, the arbitrator found that CCI had forfeited its right to open Improv clubs but that the parties' agreement had not terminated and the covenant not to compete was enforceable. Therefore, CCI could not open any new comedy clubs for the agreement's duration. A federal district court confirmed the award, and CCI appealed.

**DECISION AND RATIONALE** The U.S. Court of Appeals for the Ninth Circuit reversed part of the lower court's confirmation of the award and remanded the case. The court said that terminating CCI's exclusive right to open Improv clubs due to its inadequate performance of the parties' contract "makes sense" and that Improv West should be protected from "improper" competition. But the covenant not to compete in this case has "dramatic geographic and temporal [relating to time] scope. . . . For more than fourteen years the entire contiguous United States comedy club market, except for CCI's current Improv clubs, is off limits to CCI."

The effect would be to foreclose competition in a substantial share of the comedy club business. This restraint is "too broad to be countenanced." The covenant should be tailored to cover only the areas in which CCI is operating Improv clubs under the parties' agreement. It should allow CCI to open non-Improv clubs in "all those counties" where it does not operate an Improv club.

**THE ETHICAL DIMENSION** *Should any companies or subsidiaries affiliated with CCI be subject to the covenant not to compete? Would it be unethical to impose such a requirement? Discuss.*

**THE LEGAL ENVIRONMENT DIMENSION** *Why would a business such as Improv West include a covenant not to compete in an agreement such as the contract at issue in this case? Explain.*

**Enforcement Problems.** The laws governing the enforceability of covenants not to compete vary significantly from state to state. In some states, including Texas, such a covenant will not be enforced unless the employee has received some benefit in return for signing the noncompete agreement. This is true even if the covenant is reasonable as to time and area. If

the employee receives no benefit, the covenant will be deemed void. California prohibits altogether the enforcement of covenants not to compete.

Occasionally, depending on the jurisdiction, courts will *reform* covenants not to compete. If a covenant is found to be unreasonable in time or geographic area, the court may convert the terms into reasonable ones and then enforce the reformed covenant. Such court actions present a problem, though, in that the judge implicitly becomes a party to the contract. Consequently, courts usually resort to contract **reformation** only when necessary to prevent undue burdens or hardships.

**UNCONSCIONABLE CONTRACTS OR CLAUSES** A court ordinarily does not look at the fairness or equity of a contract (or inquire into the adequacy of consideration, as discussed in Chapter 13). Persons are assumed to be reasonably intelligent, and the courts will not come to their aid just because they have made an unwise or foolish bargain.

In certain circumstances, however, bargains are so oppressive that the courts relieve innocent parties of part or all of their duties. Such bargains are deemed **unconscionable**[11] because they are so unscrupulous or grossly unfair as to be "void of conscience."

The Uniform Commercial Code (UCC) incorporates the concept of unconscionability in its provisions with regard to the sale and lease of goods.[12] A contract can be unconscionable on either procedural or substantive grounds, as discussed in the following subsections and illustrated graphically in Exhibit 14–1 below.

---

11. Pronounced un-*kon*-shun-uh-bul.
12. See UCC 2–302 and 2A–719.

*Procedural Unconscionability.* *Procedural* unconscionability often involves inconspicuous print, unintelligible language ("legalese"), or the lack of an opportunity to read the contract or ask questions about its meaning. This type of unconscionability typically arises when a party's lack of knowledge or understanding of the contract terms deprived him or her of any meaningful choice.

Procedural unconscionability can also occur when there is such disparity in bargaining power between the two parties that the weaker party's consent is not voluntary. This type of situation often involves an *adhesion* contract (see Chapter 15), which is a contract written exclusively by one party and presented to the other on a take-it-or-leave-it basis.[13] In other words, the party to whom the contract is presented (usually a buyer or borrower) has no opportunity to negotiate its terms. Not all adhesion contracts are unconscionable, only those that unreasonably favor the drafter.[14]

*Substantive Unconscionability.* *Substantive* unconscionability occurs when contracts, or portions of contracts, are oppressive or overly harsh. Courts generally focus on provisions that deprive one party of the

---

13. For a classic case involving an adhesion contract, see *Henningsen v. Bloomfield Motors, Inc.,* 32 N.J. 358, 161 A.2d 69 (1960).
14. See, for example, *Thibodeau v. Comcast Corp.,* 2006 PA Super. 346, 912 A.2d 874 (2006).

**EXHIBIT 14–1  Unconscionability**

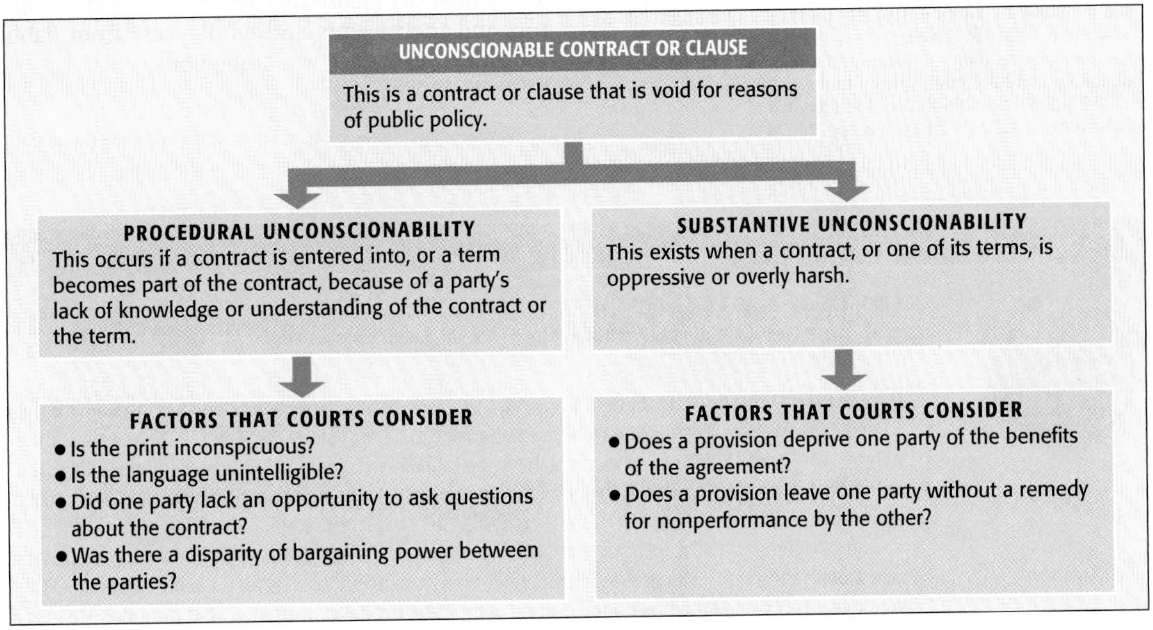

benefits of the agreement or leave that party without a remedy for nonperformance by the other.

Substantive unconscionability can arise in a wide variety of business contexts. For instance, a contract clause that gives the business entity free access to the courts but requires the other party to arbitrate any dispute with the firm may be unconscionable.[15] Similarly, contracts drafted by cell phone providers and insurance companies have been found substantively unconscionable when they included provisions that were overly harsh or one sided.[16]

**EXCULPATORY CLAUSES** Often closely related to the concept of unconscionability are **exculpatory clauses,** which release a party from liability in the event of monetary or physical injury *no matter who is at fault.* Indeed, courts sometimes refuse to enforce such clauses on the ground that they are unconscionable.

*Often Violate Public Policy.* Most courts view exculpatory clauses with disfavor. Exculpatory clauses found in rental agreements for commercial property are frequently held to be contrary to public policy, and such clauses are almost always unenforceable in residential property leases. Courts also usually hold that exculpatory clauses are against public policy in the employment context. Thus, employers frequently cannot enforce exculpatory clauses in contracts with employees or independent contractors (see Chapter 32) to avoid liability for work-related injuries.

---

15. See, for example, *Wisconsin Auto Title Loans, Inc. v. Jones,* 290 Wis.2d 514, 714 N.W.2d 155 (2006).

16. See, for example, *Gatton v. T-Mobile USA, Inc.,* 152 Cal.App.4th 571, 61 Cal.Rptr.3d 344 (2007); *Kinkel v. Cingular Wireless, LLC,* 223 Ill.2d 1, 857 N.E.2d 250, 306 Ill.Dec. 157 (2006); and *Aul v. Golden Rule Insurance Co.,* 737 N.W.2d 24 (Wis.App. 2007).

▶ **Case in Point 14.7** Speedway SuperAmerica, LLC, hired Sebert Erwin to work for its convenience stores. The company required Erwin, who had an eighth-grade education, to sign a contract stating that he was not an employee and had no right to workers' compensation. The contract also included a clause under which Erwin promised not to hold Speedway liable for anything that happened to him while working for the company. When Erwin was later injured on the job and sued Speedway for damages, the court held that the exculpatory clause was invalid because it was against public policy.[17] ◀

*When Courts Will Enforce Exculpatory Clauses.* Courts do enforce exculpatory clauses if they are reasonable, do not violate public policy, and do not protect parties from liability for intentional misconduct. The language used must not be ambiguous, and the parties must have been in relatively equal bargaining positions.

Businesses such as health clubs, racetracks, amusement parks, skiing facilities, horse-rental operations, golf-cart concessions, and skydiving organizations frequently use exculpatory clauses to limit their liability for patrons' injuries. Because these services are not essential, the companies offering them have no relative advantage in bargaining strength, and anyone contracting for their services does so voluntarily. Courts also may enforce reasonable exculpatory clauses in loan documents, real estate contracts, and trust agreements.

In the following case, the court considered whether an exculpatory clause that released "any Event sponsors and their agents and employees" from liability for future negligence was ambiguous.

---

17. *Speedway SuperAmerica, LLC v. Erwin,* 250 S.W.3d 339 (Ky. 2008).

---

**CASE 14.3**

## Holmes v. Multimedia KSDK, Inc.
Missouri Court of Appeals, Eastern District, Division Two, ___ S.W.3d ___, 2013 WL 150809 (2013).

**BACKGROUND AND FACTS** On May 12, 2009, Colleen Holmes signed an entry form for the Susan G. Komen Race for the Cure to be held on June 13, 2009, in St. Louis, Missouri. The form included a "RACE WAIVER AND RELEASE" under which Holmes agreed to "release . . . any Event sponsors and their agents and employees . . . for any injury or damages I might suffer in connection with my participation in this Event . . . . This release applies to any . . . negligence of the [sponsors]."

Later, Multimedia KSDK, Inc., agreed to be one of the sponsors of the event. KSDK also broadcast the race. During the event, Holmes was injured when she tripped and fell over an audiovisual box. KSDK employees had placed the box on the ground without barricades or warnings of its presence. Holmes and

**CASE 14.3 CONTINUED** her husband, Rick, filed a suit in a Missouri state court against KSDK. The court entered a judgment in the defendant's favor. The plaintiffs appealed.

**DECISION AND RATIONALE** A state intermediate appellate court affirmed the lower court's judgment in favor of KSDK. The appellate court held that the language used in the exculpatory clause clearly released all sponsors and their agents and employees without exclusion from liability for future negligence. The reviewing court was not persuaded by the plaintiffs' argument that the language in the release was ambiguous "because it did not specifically name the individuals and entities released." Further, "a release that releases claims against 'any and all persons' is unambiguous and enforceable to bar claims against third parties who were not parties to the release, and it is not necessary that the release identify those persons by name or otherwise."

The reviewing court additionally did not accept that a prospective release "for further acts of negligence" requires more specificity. While public policy disfavors releases of future negligence, it does not prohibit them. All that is necessary is that "There must be no doubt that a reasonable person agreeing to an exculpatory clause actually understands what future claims he or she is waiving." Such was the situation here.

**THE ETHICAL DIMENSION** *When do courts enforce exculpatory clauses?*

**THE SOCIAL DIMENSION** *When Holmes signed the release on May 12, KSDK had not yet become a sponsor of the event. Did this fact render the clause unenforceable? Explain.*

---

**DISCRIMINATORY CONTRACTS** Contracts in which a party promises to discriminate on the basis of race, color, national origin, religion, gender, age, or disability are contrary to both statute and public policy. They are also unenforceable.[18]

For instance, if a property owner promises in a contract not to sell the property to a member of a particular race, the contract is unenforceable. The public policy underlying these prohibitions is very strong, and the courts are quick to invalidate discriminatory contracts.

Exhibit 14–2 on the next page illustrates the types of contracts that may be illegal because they are contrary to statute or public policy.

## Effect of Illegality

In general, an illegal contract is void—that is, the contract is deemed never to have existed, and the courts will not aid either party. In most illegal contracts, both parties are considered to be equally at fault—*in pari delicto*.[19] If the contract is executory (not yet fulfilled), neither party can enforce it. If it has been executed, neither party can recover damages.

The courts are usually not concerned if one wrongdoer in an illegal contract is unjustly enriched at the expense of the other—except under certain circum-

stances. The main reason for this hands-off attitude is the belief that a plaintiff who has broken the law by entering into an illegal bargain should not be allowed to obtain help from the courts. Another justification is the hoped-for deterrent effect: a plaintiff who suffers a loss because of an illegal bargain will presumably be deterred from entering into similar illegal bargains in the future.

There are exceptions to the general rule that neither party to an illegal bargain can sue for breach and neither party can recover for performance rendered. We look at these exceptions next.

**JUSTIFIABLE IGNORANCE OF THE FACTS** When one of the parties is relatively innocent (has no reason to know that the contract is illegal), that party can often recover any benefits conferred in a partially executed contract. In this situation, the courts will not enforce the contract but will allow the parties to return to their original positions.

A court may sometimes permit an innocent party who has fully performed under the contract to enforce the contract against the guilty party. ▶ **Example 14.8** A trucking company contracts with Gillespie to carry crates filled with goods to a specific destination for the normal fee of $5,000. The trucker delivers the crates and later finds out that they contained illegal goods. Although the law specifies that the shipment, use, and sale of the goods were illegal, the trucker, being an innocent party, can still legally collect the $5,000 from Gillespie. ◀

---

**18.** The major federal statute prohibiting discrimination is the Civil Rights Act of 1964, 42 U.S.C. Sections 2000e–2000e-17.

**19.** Pronounced in-*pah*-ree deh-*lick*-tow.

**EXHIBIT 14–2 Contract Legality**

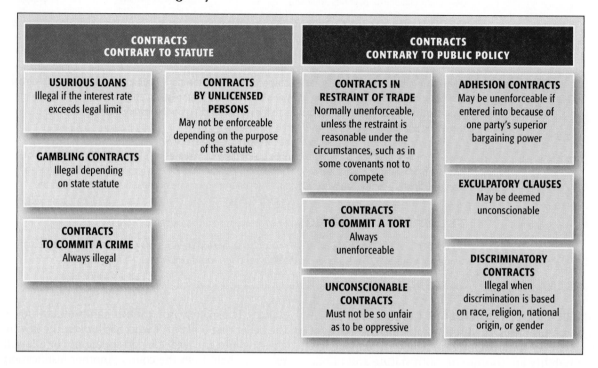

**CONTRACTS CONTRARY TO STATUTE**

**USURIOUS LOANS**
Illegal if the interest rate exceeds legal limit

**CONTRACTS BY UNLICENSED PERSONS**
May not be enforceable depending on the purpose of the statute

**GAMBLING CONTRACTS**
Illegal depending on state statute

**CONTRACTS TO COMMIT A CRIME**
Always illegal

**CONTRACTS CONTRARY TO PUBLIC POLICY**

**CONTRACTS IN RESTRAINT OF TRADE**
Normally unenforceable, unless the restraint is reasonable under the circumstances, such as in some covenants not to compete

**ADHESION CONTRACTS**
May be unenforceable if entered into because of one party's superior bargaining power

**CONTRACTS TO COMMIT A TORT**
Always unenforceable

**EXCULPATORY CLAUSES**
May be deemed unconscionable

**UNCONSCIONABLE CONTRACTS**
Must not be so unfair as to be oppressive

**DISCRIMINATORY CONTRACTS**
Illegal when discrimination is based on race, religion, national origin, or gender

**MEMBERS OF PROTECTED CLASSES** When a statute is clearly designed to protect a certain class of people, a member of that class can enforce a contract in violation of the statute even though the other party cannot. ▶ **Example 14.9** Statutes prohibit certain employees (such as flight attendants and pilots) from working more than a certain number of hours per month. An employee who is required to work more than the maximum can recover for those extra hours of service. ◀

Other examples of statutes designed to protect a particular class of people are state statutes that regulate the sale of insurance. If an insurance company violates a statute when selling insurance, the purchaser can still enforce the policy and recover from the insurer.

**WITHDRAWAL FROM AN ILLEGAL AGREEMENT** If the illegal part of a bargain has not yet been performed, the party rendering performance can withdraw from the contract and recover the performance or its value.
▶ **Example 14.10** Sam and Jim decide to wager (illegally) on the outcome of a boxing match. Each deposits cash with a stakeholder, who agrees to pay the winner of the bet. At this point, each party has performed part of the agreement, but the illegal element of the

agreement will not occur until the funds are paid to the winner. Before that payment occurs, either party is entitled to withdraw from the bargain by giving notice of repudiation to the stakeholder. ◀

**CONTRACT ILLEGAL THROUGH FRAUD, DURESS, OR UNDUE INFLUENCE** Often, one party to an illegal contract is more at fault than the other. When one party uses fraud, duress, or undue influence to induce another party to enter into an illegal bargain, the second party will be allowed to recover for the performance or its value.

**SEVERABLE, OR DIVISIBLE, CONTRACTS** A contract that is *severable*, or divisible, consists of distinct parts that can be performed separately, with separate consideration provided for each part. With an *indivisible* contract, in contrast, complete performance by each party is essential, even if the contract contains a number of seemingly separate provisions.

If a contract is divisible into legal and illegal portions, a court may enforce the legal portion but not the illegal one, so long as the illegal portion does not affect the essence of the bargain. This approach is consistent with the courts' basic policy of enforcing the legal intentions of the contracting parties whenever possible.

▶ **Example 14.11**   Cole signs an employment contract that includes an overly broad and thus illegal covenant not to compete. In that situation, a court might allow the employment contract to be enforceable but reform the unreasonably broad covenant by converting its terms into reasonable ones. Alternatively, the court could declare the covenant illegal (and thus void) and enforce the remaining employment terms. ◀ (A contract might include a clause stating that the parties intend the contract terms to be enforced to "the fullest extent possible." Such a clause indicates that the parties regard their contract as divisible and, in the event of a dispute, want the court to strike out the illegal terms and enforce the rest. For an example, see the *Appendix to Chapter 19: Reading and Analyzing Contracts.*)

## Reviewing: Capacity and Legality

Renee Beaver started racing go-karts competitively in 2012, when she was fourteen. Many of the races required her to sign an exculpatory clause to participate, which she or her parents regularly signed. In 2014, right before her sixteenth birthday, she participated in the annual Elkhart Grand Prix, a series of races in Elkhart, Indiana. During the event in which she drove, a piece of foam padding used as a course barrier was torn from its base and ended up on the track. A portion of the padding struck Beaver in the head, and another portion was thrown into oncoming traffic, causing a multikart collision during which she sustained severe injuries. Beaver filed an action against the race organizers for negligence. The race organizers could not locate the exculpatory clause that Beaver had supposedly signed. The organizers argued that she must have signed one to enter the race, but even if she had not signed one, her actions showed her intent to be bound by its terms. Using the information presented in the chapter, answer the following questions.

1. Did Beaver have the contractual capacity to enter a contract with an exculpatory clause? Why or why not?
2. Assuming that Beaver did, in fact, sign the exculpatory clause, did she later disaffirm or ratify the contract? Explain.
3. Now assume that Beaver stated that she was eighteen years old at the time that she signed the exculpatory clause. How might this affect Beaver's ability to disaffirm or ratify the contract?
4. If Beaver did not actually sign the exculpatory clause, could a court conclude that she impliedly accepted its terms by participating in the race? Why or why not?

**DEBATE THIS . . .** *After agreeing to an exculpatory clause or purchasing some item, such as a computer, minors often seek to avoid the contracts. Today's minors are far from naïve and should not be allowed to avoid their contractual obligations.*

## Terms and Concepts

| | | |
|---|---|---|
| age of majority 249 | emancipation 249 | reformation 257 |
| contractual capacity 249 | exculpatory clause 258 | unconscionable 257 |
| covenant not to compete 255 | necessaries 250 | usury 253 |
| disaffirmance 249 | ratification 250 | |

## Issue Spotters

1. Joan, who is sixteen years old, moves out of her parents' home and signs a one-year lease for an apartment at Kenwood Apartments. Joan's parents tell her that she can return to live with them at any time. Unable to pay the rent, Joan moves back to her parents' home two months later. Can Kenwood enforce the lease against Joan? Why or why not? **(See page 249.)**

2. Sun Airlines, Inc., prints on its tickets that it is not liable for any injury to a passenger caused by the airline's negligence. If the cause of an accident is found to be the airline's negligence, can it use the clause as a defense to liability? Why or why not? **(See page 258.)**

- Check your answers to the Issue Spotters against the answers provided in Appendix E at the end of this text.

## Business Scenarios

**14–1. Covenants Not to Compete.** A famous New York City hotel, Hotel Lux, is noted for its food as well as its luxury accommodations. Hotel Lux contracts with a famous chef, Chef Perlee, to become its head chef at $30,000 per month. The contract states that should Perlee leave the employment of Hotel Lux for any reason, he will not work as a chef for any hotel or restaurant in New York, New Jersey, or Pennsylvania for a period of one year. During the first six months of the contract, Hotel Lux heavily advertises Perlee as its head chef, and business at the hotel is excellent. Then a dispute arises between the hotel's management and Perlee, and Perlee terminates his employment. One month later, he is hired by a famous New Jersey restaurant just across the New York state line. Hotel Lux learns of Perlee's employment through a large advertisement in a New York City newspaper. It seeks to enjoin (prevent) Perlee from working in that restaurant as a chef for one year. Discuss how successful Hotel Lux will be in its action. **(See page 255.)**

**14–2. Capacity.** Joanne is a seventy-five-year-old widow who survives on her husband's small pension. Joanne has become increasingly forgetful, and her family worries that she may have Alzheimer's disease (a brain disorder that seriously affects a person's ability to carry out daily activi-

ties). No physician has diagnosed her, however, and no court has ruled on Joanne's legal competence. One day while she is out shopping, Joanne stops by a store that is having a sale on pianos and enters into a fifteen-year installment contract to buy a grand piano. When the piano arrives the next day, Joanne seems confused and repeatedly asks the delivery person why a piano is being delivered. Joanne claims that she does not recall buying a piano. Explain whether this contract is void, voidable, or valid. Can Joanne avoid her contractual obligation to buy the piano? If so, how? **(See page 252.)**

**14–3. Licensing Statutes.** State X requires that persons who prepare and serve liquor in the form of drinks at commercial establishments be licensed by the state to do so. The only requirement for obtaining a yearly license is that the person be at least twenty-one years old. Mickey, aged thirty-five, is hired as a bartender for the Southtown Restaurant. Gerald, a staunch alumnus of a nearby university, brings twenty of his friends to the restaurant to celebrate a football victory one afternoon. Gerald orders four rounds of drinks, and the bill is nearly $600. When he learns that Mickey has failed to renew his bartender's license, Gerald refuses to pay, claiming that the contract is unenforceable. Discuss whether Gerald is correct. **(See page 254.)**

## Business Case Problems

**14–4. Spotlight on Arbitration Clauses—Unconscionable Contracts or Clauses.** Roberto Basulto and Raquel Gonzalez, who did not speak English, responded to an ad on Spanish-language television sponsored by Hialeah Automotive, LLC, which does business as Potamkin Dodge. Potamkin's staff understood that Basulto and Gonzalez did not speak or read English and conducted the entire transaction in Spanish. They explained the English-language contract, but did not explain an accompanying arbitration agreement. This agreement limited the amount of damages that the buyers could seek in court to less than $5,000, but

did not limit Potamkin's right to pursue greater damages. Basulto and Gonzalez bought a Dodge Caravan and signed the contract in blank (meaning that some parts were left blank). Potamkin later filled in a lower trade-in allowance than agreed and refused to change it. The buyers returned the van—having driven it a total of seven miles—and asked for a return of their trade-in vehicle, but it had been sold. The buyers filed a suit in a Florida state court against Potamkin. The dealer sought arbitration. Was the arbitration agreement unconscionable? Why or why not? [*Hialeah Automotive, LLC v. Basulto,* 156 Fla. 92, 22 So.3d 586 (3 Dist. 2009)] **(See page 257.)**

**14–5. BUSINESS CASE PROBLEM**
**WITH SAMPLE ANSWER: Unconscionable Contracts or Clauses.**

 *Geographic Expeditions, Inc. (GeoEx), which guided climbs up Mount Kilimanjaro, required climbers to sign a release to participate in an expedition. The form mandated the arbitration of any dispute in San Francisco and limited damages to the cost of the trip. GeoEx told climbers that the terms were nonnegotiable and were the same as terms imposed by other travel firms. Jason Lhotka died on a GeoEx climb. His mother filed a suit against GeoEx. GeoEx sought arbitration. Was the arbitration clause unconscionable? Why or why not?* [Lhotka v. Geographic Expeditions, Inc., 181 Cal.App.4th 816, 104 Cal.Rptr.3d 844 (2010)] **(See page 257.)**

- **For a sample answer to Problem 14–5, go to Appendix F at the end of this text.**

**14–6. Mental Incompetence.** Dorothy Drury suffered from dementia and chronic confusion. When she became unable to manage her own affairs, including decisions about medical and financial matters, her son Eddie arranged for her move to an assisted living facility. During admission, she signed a residency agreement, which included an arbitration clause. After she sustained injuries in a fall at the facility, a suit was filed to recover damages. The facility asked the court to compel arbitration. Was Dorothy bound to the residency agreement? Discuss. [Drury v. Assisted Living Concepts, Inc., 245 Or.App. 217, 262 P.3d 1162 (2011)] **(See page 252.)**

**14–7. Licensing Statutes.** PEMS Co. International, Inc., agreed to find a buyer for Rupp Industries, Inc., for a commission of 2 percent of the purchase price, which was to be paid by the buyer. Using PEMS's services, an investment group bought Rupp for $20 million and changed its name to Temp-Air, Inc. PEMS asked Temp-Air to pay a commission on the sale. Temp-Air refused, arguing that PEMS acted as a broker in the deal without a license. The applicable statute defines a broker as any person who deals with the sale of a business. If this statute was intended to protect the public, can PEMS collect its commission? Explain. [PEMS Co. International, Inc. v. Temp-Air, Inc., __ N.W.2d __ (Minn.App. 2011)] **(See page 254.)**

**14–8. Minors.** D.V.G. (a minor) was injured in a one-car auto accident in Hoover, Alabama. The vehicle was covered by an insurance policy issued by Nationwide Mutual Insurance Co. Stan Brobston, D.V.G.'s attorney, accepted Nationwide's offer of $50,000 on D.V.G.'s behalf. Before the settlement could be submitted to an Alabama state court for approval, D.V.G. died from injuries received in a second, unrelated auto accident. Nationwide argued that it was not bound to the settlement because a minor lacks the capacity to contract and so cannot enter into a binding settlement without court approval. Should Nationwide be bound to the settlement? Why or why not? [Nationwide Mutual Insurance Co. v. Wood, __ So.3d __, 2013 WL 646468 (Ala. 2013)] **(See page 249.)**

**14–9. A QUESTION OF ETHICS: Covenants Not to Compete.**

 *Brendan Coleman created and marketed Clinex, a software billing program. Later, Retina Consultants, P.C., a medical practice, hired Coleman as a software engineer. Together, they modified the Clinex program to create Clinex-RE. Coleman signed an agreement to the effect that he owned Clinex, Retina owned Clinex-RE, and he would not market Clinex in competition with Clinex-RE. After Coleman quit Retina, he withdrew funds from a Retina bank account and marketed both forms of the software to other medical practices. At trial, the court entered a judgment enjoining (preventing) Coleman from marketing the software that was in competition with the software he had developed for Retina Consultants. The court also obligated Coleman to return the funds taken from the company's bank account. Coleman appealed.* [Coleman v. Retina Consultants, P.C., 286 Ga. 317, 687 S.E.2d 457 (2009)] **(See page 255.)**

(a) Should the court uphold the noncompete clause? If so, why? If not, why not?

(b) Should the court require Coleman to return the funds he withdrew from the company's accounts? Discuss fully.

(c) Did Coleman's behavior after he left the company influence the court's decision? Explain your answer.

---

## Legal Reasoning Group Activity

**14–10. Covenants Not to Compete.** Assume that you are part of a group of executives at a large software corporation. The company is considering whether to incorporate covenants not to compete into its employment contracts. You know that there are some issues with the enforceability of these covenants and want to make an informed decision. **(See page 255.)**

(a) One group should make a list of what interests are served by enforcing covenants not to compete.

(b) A second group should create a list of what interests are served by refusing to enforce covenants not to compete.

(c) A third group should discuss whether a court should reform (and then enforce) a covenant not to compete that it determines is illegal, and create an argument for and against reformation.

# CHAPTER 15

# MISTAKES, FRAUD, AND VOLUNTARY CONSENT

An otherwise valid contract may still be unenforceable if the parties have not genuinely agreed to its terms. As mentioned in Chapter 11, a lack of *voluntary consent* (assent) can be used as a defense to the contract's enforceability.

**Voluntary consent** may be lacking because of a mistake, misrepresentation, undue influence, or duress—in other words, because there is no true "meeting of the minds." Generally, a party who demonstrates that he or she did not truly agree to the terms of

a contract has a choice. The party can choose either to carry out the contract or to rescind (cancel) it and thus avoid the entire transaction. In this chapter, we examine the kinds of factors that may indicate a lack of voluntary consent.

---

## SECTION 1
# MISTAKES

We all make mistakes, so it is not surprising that mistakes are made when contracts are formed. In certain circumstances, contract law allows a contract to be avoided on the basis of mistake. It is important to distinguish between *mistakes of fact* and *mistakes of value or quality*. Only a mistake of fact makes a contract voidable. Also, the mistake must involve some *material fact*—a fact that a reasonable person would consider important when determining his or her course of action.

▶ **Example 15.1**  Sung buys a violin from Bev for $250. Although the violin is very old, neither party believes that it is valuable. Later, however, an antiques dealer informs the parties that the violin is rare and worth thousands of dollars. Here, both parties were mistaken, but the mistake is a mistake of *value* rather than a mistake of *fact* that warrants contract rescission. Therefore, Bev cannot rescind the contract. ◀

Mistakes of fact occur in two forms—*bilateral* and *unilateral*. A unilateral mistake is made by only *one* of the parties. A bilateral, or mutual, mistake is made by *both* of the contracting parties. We look next at these two types of mistakes and illustrate them graphically in Exhibit 15–1 on the following page.

## Unilateral Mistakes of Fact

A unilateral mistake is made by only one of the parties. In general, a unilateral mistake does not give the mistaken party any right to relief from the contract. Normally, the contract is enforceable.

▶ **Example 15.2**  Elena intends to sell her jet ski for $2,500. When she learns that Chin is interested in buying a used jet ski, she sends him an e-mail offering to sell the jet ski to him. When typing the e-mail, however, she mistakenly keys in the price of $1,500. Chin immediately sends Elena an e-mail reply accepting her offer. Even though Elena intended to sell her personal jet ski for $2,500, she has made a unilateral mistake and is bound by the contract to sell it to Chin for $1,500. ◀

This general rule has at least two exceptions.[1] The contract may be enforceable if:

1. The *other* party to the contract knows or should have known that a mistake of fact was made.
2. The error was due to a substantial mathematical mistake in addition, subtraction, division, or multiplication and was made inadvertently and without gross (extreme) negligence. If, for instance, a contractor's bid was significantly low because he or she made a mistake in addition when totaling

---

1. The *Restatement (Second) of Contracts,* Section 153, liberalizes the general rule to take into account the modern trend of allowing avoidance even though only one party has been mistaken.

### EXHIBIT 15-1   Mistakes of Fact

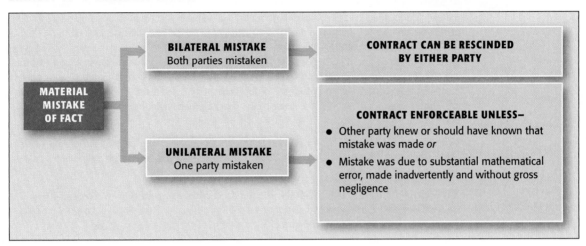

the estimated costs, any contract resulting from the bid normally may be rescinded.

Of course, in both situations, the mistake must still involve some material fact.

## Bilateral (Mutual) Mistakes of Fact

A bilateral mistake is a "mutual misunderstanding concerning a basic assumption on which the contract was made."[2] When both parties are mistaken about

---
**2.** *Restatement (Second) of Contracts,* Section 152.

the same material fact, the contract can be rescinded by either party.

A word or term in a contract may be subject to more than one reasonable interpretation. If the parties to the contract attach materially different meanings to the term, a court may allow the contract to be rescinded because there has been no true "meeting of the minds."

In the following case, the court had to grapple with the question of whether a mutual mistake of fact had occurred.

# CASE 15.1

## L&H Construction Co. v. Circle Redmont, Inc.

District Court of Appeal of Florida, Fifth District, 55 So.3d 630 (2011).

**BACKGROUND AND FACTS**  L&H Construction Company was a general contractor involved in the renovation of the Thomas Edison historic site in West Orange, New Jersey, for the National Park Service. L&H contracted with Circle Redmont, Inc., which is based in Melbourne, Florida, to make a cast-iron staircase and a glass flooring system. Redmont's original proposal was to "engineer, fabricate, and install" the staircase and flooring system.

During negotiations, however, installation and its costs were cut from the deal. In the final agreement, payment was due on "Supervision of Installation" instead of "Completion of Installation." Nevertheless, the final agreement stated that Redmont would "engineer, fabricate, and install." Later, Redmont claimed that this was a mistake. L&H insisted that installation was included. L&H filed a suit in a Florida state court against Redmont. The court found that the word *install* in the phrase "engineer, fabricate, and install" was the result of a mutual mistake. L&H appealed.

CASE 15.1 CONTINUES ➧

**DECISION AND RATIONALE** A state intermediate appellate court upheld the lower court's decision on the question of whether the use of the word *install* in the parties' agreement was a mutual mistake. The appellate court explained that the contract between these parties was ambiguous. The proposal indicated that Redmont would "engineer, fabricate, and install" the staircase and flooring system, but the agreement stated that L&H's final payment was due on "Supervision" of the installation. According to the testimony of Redmont's witnesses, the final agreement stated the parties' understanding—Redmont would only supervise the installation, not perform it. Installation was cut from the contract as a cost-saving measure at the request of L&H's president. The trial court determined that these witnesses were credible. The appellate court reversed the lower court's final judgment in Redmont's favor on other grounds, however.

**WHAT IF THE FACTS WERE DIFFERENT?** *Suppose that Redmont had intentionally misled L&H to believe that installation was included in the price. Would the court's decision on the mutual mistake issue have been different? Discuss.*

**THE ECONOMIC DIMENSION** *The parties performed as agreed, with Redmont working on schedule and L&H making timely payments, until the issue of installation arose. Assuming that no further disputes arose, what might be the appropriate remedy?*

## Mistakes of Value

If a mistake concerns the future market value or quality of the object of the contract, the mistake is one of *value,* and the contract normally is enforceable. The reason for this is that value is variable. Depending on the time, place, and other circumstances, the same item may be worth considerably different amounts.

When parties form a contract, their agreement establishes the value of the object of their transaction—for the moment. Each party is considered to have assumed the risk that the value will change in the future or prove to be different from what he or she thought. Without this rule, almost any party who did not receive what she or he considered a fair bargain could argue mistake.

## SECTION 2
# FRAUDULENT MISREPRESENTATION

Although fraud is a tort (see Chapter 6), it also affects the authenticity of the innocent party's consent to the contract. When an innocent party is fraudulently induced to enter into a contract, the contract normally can be avoided because that party has not *voluntarily* consented to its terms.[3] Ordinarily, the innocent party can either rescind the contract and be

restored to her or his original position or enforce the contract and seek damages for any harms resulting from the fraud.

Generally, fraudulent misrepresentation refers only to misrepresentation that is consciously false and is intended to mislead another. The person making the fraudulent misrepresentation knows or believes that the assertion is false or knows that she or he does not have a basis (stated or implied) for the assertion.[4] Typically, fraudulent misrepresentation consists of the following elements:

1. A misrepresentation of a material fact must occur.
2. There must be an intent to deceive.
3. The innocent party must justifiably rely on the misrepresentation.
4. To collect damages, a party must have been harmed as a result of the misrepresentation.

## Misrepresentation Has Occurred

The first element of proving fraud is to show that misrepresentation of a material fact has occurred. This misrepresentation can occur by words or actions. For instance, the statement "This sculpture was created by Michelangelo" is a misrepresentation of fact if another artist sculpted the statue. Similarly, if a customer asks to see only paintings by the decorative artist Paul Wright and the gallery owner immediately leads the customer over to paintings that were

---

3. *Restatement (Second) of Contracts,* Sections 163 and 164.

4. *Restatement (Second) of Contracts,* Section 162.

not done by Wright, the owner's actions can be a misrepresentation.

**MISREPRESENTATION BY CONDUCT** Misrepresentation also occurs when a party takes specific action to conceal a fact that is material to the contract.[5] Therefore, if a seller, by her or his actions, prevents a buyer from learning of some fact that is material to the contract, such behavior constitutes misrepresentation by conduct.

▶ **Case in Point 15.3** Actor Tom Selleck contracted to purchase a horse named Zorro for his daughter from Dolores Cuenca. Cuenca acted as though Zorro was fit to ride in competitions, when in reality the horse suffered from a medical condition. Selleck filed a lawsuit against Cuenca for wrongfully concealing the horse's condition and won. A jury awarded Selleck more than $187,000 for Cuenca's misrepresentation by conduct.[6] ◀

**STATEMENTS OF OPINION** Statements of opinion and representations of future facts (predictions) generally are not subject to claims of fraud. Every person is expected to exercise care and judgment when entering into contracts. The law will not come to the aid of one who simply makes an unwise bargain.

Statements such as "This land will be worth twice as much next year" or "This car will last for years and years" are statements of opinion, not fact. Contracting parties should recognize them as opinions and not rely on them. A fact is objective and verifiable, whereas an opinion is usually subject to debate.

Nevertheless, in certain situations, such as when a naïve purchaser relies on an opinion from an expert, the innocent party may be entitled to rescission or reformation. (As discussed in Chapter 14, *reformation* occurs when a court alters the terms of a contract to prevent undue hardships or burdens.)

▶ **Case in Point 15.4** In a classic case, an instructor at an Arthur Murray dance school told Audrey Vokes, a widow without family, that she had the potential to become an accomplished dancer. The instructor sold her 2,302 hours of dancing lessons for a total amount of $31,090.45 (equivalent to $142,000 in 2014). When it became clear to Vokes that she did not, in fact, have the potential to be an excellent dancer, she sued the school for fraudulent misrepresentation. The court held that because the dance school had superior knowledge about a person's dance potential, the instructor's statements could be considered statements of fact rather than opinion.[7] ◀

**MISREPRESENTATION OF LAW** Misrepresentation of law *ordinarily* does not entitle a party to relief from a contract. ▶ **Example 15.5** Camara has a parcel of property that she is trying to sell to Pike. Camara knows that a local ordinance prohibits the construction of anything higher than three stories on the property. Nonetheless, she tells Pike, "You can build a condominium a hundred stories high on this land if you want to." Pike buys the land and later discovers that Camara's statement was false. Normally, Pike cannot avoid the contract because people are assumed to know state and local laws. ◀

Exceptions to this rule occur when the misrepresenting party is in a profession that is known to require greater knowledge of the law than the average citizen possesses. For instance, if Camara, in *Example 15.5*, had been a lawyer or a real estate broker, her willful misrepresentation of the area's zoning laws probably would have constituted fraud.

**MISREPRESENTATION BY SILENCE** Ordinarily, neither party to a contract has a duty to come forward and disclose facts. Therefore, courts typically do not set aside contracts because a party did not volunteer pertinent information. ▶ **Example 15.6** Jim is selling a car that has been in an accident and has been repaired. He does not need to volunteer this information to a potential buyer. If, however, the purchaser asks Jim if the car has had extensive bodywork and he lies, he has committed a fraudulent misrepresentation. ◀

In general, if a seller knows of a serious potential problem that the buyer cannot reasonably be expected to discover, the seller may have a duty to speak. Generally, the seller must disclose only **latent defects**—that is, defects that could not readily be ascertained. Because a buyer of a house could easily discover the presence of termites through an inspection, for instance, termites may not qualify as a latent defect. Also, when the parties are in a *fiduciary relationship*—one of trust, such as partners, physician and patient, or attorney and client—they have a duty to disclose material facts. Failure to do so may constitute fraud.

In the following case, a real estate investor claimed that misrepresentation by silence had occurred when a seller of property failed to disclose material facts about its value.

---

5. *Restatement (Second) of Contracts*, Section 160.
6. *Selleck v. Cuenca*, Case No. GIN056909, North County of San Diego, California, decided September 9, 2009.

7. *Vokes v. Arthur Murray, Inc.*, 212 So.2d 906 (Fla.App. 1968).

## CASE 15.2

### Fazio v. Cypress/GR Houston I, LP
Court of Appeals of Texas, First Division, ___ S.W.3d ___ (2012).

**BACKGROUND AND FACTS**  Peter Fazio began talks with Cypress/GR Houston I, LP, to buy retail property whose main tenant was a Garden Ridge store. In performing a background investigation, Fazio and his agents became concerned about Garden Ridge's financial health. Nevertheless, after being assured that Garden Ridge had a positive financial outlook, Fazio sent Cypress a letter of intent to buy the property for $7.67 million "based on the currently reported absolute net income of $805,040." Cypress then agreed to provide all information in its possession, but it failed to disclose that:

1. A consultant for Garden Ridge had recently requested a $240,000 reduction in the annual rent as part of a restructuring of the company's real estate leases.
2. Cypress's bank was so concerned about Garden Ridge's financial health that it had required a personal guaranty of the property's loan.

The parties entered into a purchase agreement, but Garden Ridge went into bankruptcy shortly after the deal closed. Fazio sued Cypress for fraud after he was forced to sell the property for only $3.75 million. A jury found in Fazio's favor, but the trial court awarded judgment *n.o.v.* ("notwithstanding the verdict"— see Chapter 3) to Cypress. Fazio appealed.

**DECISION AND RATIONALE**  A state intermediate appellate court reversed the trial court and held that Cypress was liable to Fazio for fraud. The reviewing court found that before the parties entered into the purchase agreement, Cypress had agreed to provide all information in its possession. Cypress knew that Fazio had been concerned about Garden Ridge's financial health and that he had based the purchase price on the anticipated income from the property.

According to the court, a reasonable person in Fazio's position would have attached significance to Garden Ridge's recent request for a $240,000 rent reduction. A reasonable person would also attach significance to the fact that Cypress had been required to provide a personal guaranty of the property's loan. Therefore, the court concluded "that Cypress's active concealment of this material information, which it was under a duty to disclose as financial information" was fraudulent as a matter of law.

**THE ETHICAL DIMENSION**  *Was Cypress's conduct unethical? Why or why not?*

**THE SOCIAL DIMENSION**  *What does the decision in this case suggest to sellers of commercial real estate and others who engage in business negotiations?*

---

## Intent to Deceive

The second element of fraud is knowledge on the part of the misrepresenting party that facts have been falsely represented. This element, normally called **scienter,**[8] or "guilty knowledge," signifies that there was an *intent to deceive. Scienter* clearly exists if a party knows a fact is not as stated. *Scienter* also exists if a party makes a statement that he or she believes is not true or makes a statement recklessly, without regard to whether it is true or false. Finally, this element is met if a party says or implies that a statement is made on some basis, such as personal knowledge or personal investigation, when it is not.

▶ **Case in Point 15.7**  Robert Sarvis applied for a position as a business law professor two weeks after his release from prison. On his résumé, he said that he had been a corporate president for fourteen years and had taught business law at another college. After he was hired, his probation officer alerted the school to Sarvis's criminal history. The school immediately fired him.

When Sarvis sued the school for breach of his employment contract, the court concluded that by not disclosing his history, Sarvis clearly exhibited an intent to deceive and that the school had justifiably relied on his misrepresentations. Therefore, the school could rescind Sarvis's employment contract.[9] ◀

---

8. Pronounced sy-*en*-ter.

9. *Sarvis v. Vermont State Colleges,* 172 Vt. 76, 772 A.2d 494 (2001).

**INNOCENT MISREPRESENTATION** If a person makes a statement that she or he believes to be true but that actually misrepresents material facts, the person is guilty only of an **innocent misrepresentation**, not of fraud. When an innocent misrepresentation occurs, the aggrieved party can rescind the contract but usually cannot seek damages. ▶ **Example 15.8**  Parris tells Roberta that a tract of land contains 250 acres. Parris is mistaken—the tract contains only 215 acres—but Parris had no knowledge of the mistake. Roberta relies on the statement and contracts to buy the land. Even though the misrepresentation is innocent, Roberta can avoid the contract if the misrepresentation is material. ◀

**NEGLIGENT MISREPRESENTATION** Sometimes, a party will make a misrepresentation through carelessness, believing the statement is true. If the party did not exercise reasonable care in uncovering or disclosing the facts or use the skill and competence that her or his business or profession requires, the misrepresentation may constitute **negligent misrepresentation.** For instance, an operator of a weight scale certifies the weight of Sneed's commodity, even though the scale's accuracy has not been checked for more than three years.

In almost all states, such negligent misrepresentation is equal to *scienter,* or knowingly making a misrepresentation. In effect, negligent misrepresentation is treated as fraudulent misrepresentation, even though the misrepresentation was not purposeful. In negligent misrepresentation, culpable ignorance of the truth supplies the intention to mislead, even if the defendant can claim, "I didn't know."

## Reliance on the Misrepresentation

The third element of fraud is reasonably *justifiable reliance* on the misrepresentation of fact. The deceived party must have a justifiable reason for relying on the misrepresentation. Also, the misrepresentation must be an important factor (but not necessarily the sole factor) in inducing the deceived party to enter into the contract.

Reliance is not justified if the innocent party knows the true facts or relies on obviously extravagant statements (such as, "this pickup truck will get fifty miles to the gallon"). ▶ **Example 15.9**  Meese, a securities broker, offers to sell BIM stock to Packer. Meese assures Packer that BIM shares are blue chip securities—that is, they are stable, have limited risk, and yield a good return on investment over time. In reality, Meese knows nothing about the quality of BIM stock and does not believe the truth of what he is saying. Thus, Meese's statement is an intentional misrepresentation of a material fact. If Packer is induced by Meese's statement to enter into a contract to buy the stock, he probably can avoid the contract. Packer justifiably relied on his broker's misrepresentation of material fact. ◀

The same rule applies to defects in property sold. If the defects would be obvious on inspection, the buyer cannot justifiably rely on the seller's representations. If the defects are hidden or latent, as previously discussed, the buyer is justified in relying on the seller's statements.

In the following case, the receiver for a car wash assured the buyer that the property would be "appropriately winterized," but it was not. Was the buyer justified in relying on the seller's representations? (A *receiver,* also called a *trustee,* is an independent, impartial party appointed by a bankruptcy court to manage property in bankruptcy and dispose of it in an orderly manner for the benefit of the creditors.)

---

## CASE 15.3

### Cronkelton v. Guaranteed Construction Services, LLC
Court of Appeals of Ohio, Third District, __ N.E.2d __, 2013 WL 428734, 2013-Ohio-328 (2013).

**BACKGROUND AND FACTS** A court appointed Patrick Shivley to be a receiver for a foreclosed car wash in Bellefontaine, Ohio. The property was offered for sale by Huntington Bank. Clifford Cronkelton inspected the car wash in November 2009. He knew that some equipment would have to be replaced, but he was concerned that the property needed to be winterized to protect it from damage. In phone calls and e-mail, Shivley assured him that it would be done.

Shivley contacted Guaranteed Construction Services, which hired Strayer Company to winterize the property. Strayer told Shivley that the only way to avoid problems was to leave the heat on, but Shivley

CASE 15.3 CONTINUES ▶

**CASE 15.3 CONTINUED** knew Huntington Bank had shut off the heat because the property was not generating income. In March 2010, Shivley informed the bank of damage to the property caused by freezing. Shivley did not share this information with Cronkelton, who did not become aware of the damage until after he bought the car wash in June. Cronkelton filed a suit in an Ohio state court against Guaranteed Construction Services and Shivley, asserting fraud. From a jury verdict in Cronkelton's favor, and an award of more than $140,000 in damages and attorneys' fees, the defendants appealed.

**DECISION AND RATIONALE** A state intermediate appellate court affirmed the lower court's judgment in Cronkelton's favor. The reviewing court found that the jury verdict was supported by "competent, credible evidence" indicating that Cronkelton reasonably relied on Shivley's representations. No one denied that the damage by freezing was open and obvious upon inspection, and that Conkelton could have again inspected the property before signing the purchase agreement. But Cronkelton testified that the receiver of the foreclosed car wash, Shivley, had guaranteed in an e-mail that everything was taken care of. That the jury found that Cronkelton had reasonably relied on Shivley's representations appears justified.

As a receiver, Shivley had a fiduciary duty to take care of the assets under his control. "Under the circumstances of this case, Cronkleton had a reasonable basis to believe that Shivley, who was acting as an arm of the court, would take the promised steps to winterize the property.

**THE LEGAL DIMENSION** *In evaluating a claim of fraud, what factors does a court consider in determining whether reliance was justifiable?*

**THE ETHICAL DIMENSION** *Did Shively's misrepresentations rise to the level of fraud? Explain.*

## Injury to the Innocent Party

Most courts do not require a showing of injury when the action is to rescind the contract. These courts hold that because rescission returns the parties to the positions they held before the contract was made, a showing of injury to the innocent party is unnecessary.

In contrast, to recover damages caused by fraud, proof of harm is universally required. The measure of damages is ordinarily equal to the property's value had it been delivered as represented, less the actual price paid for the property. (What if someone pretends to be someone else online? Can the victim of the hoax prove injury sufficient to recover for fraudulent misrepresentation? See this chapter's *Insight into Social Media* feature on the following page for a discussion of this topic.)

Additionally, because fraud actions necessarily involve wrongful conduct, courts may also award *punitive damages,* or *exemplary damages.* As discussed in Chapter 6, punitive damages are intended to punish the defendant and are granted to a plaintiff over and above compensation for the proved, actual loss. Because of the potential for punitive damages, which normally are not available in contract actions, plaintiffs often include a claim for fraudulent misrepresentation in their contract disputes.

## SECTION 3
# UNDUE INFLUENCE

Undue influence arises from relationships in which one party can greatly influence another party, thus overcoming that party's free will. A contract entered into under excessive or undue influence lacks voluntary consent and is therefore voidable.[10]

## One Party Dominates the Other

In various types of relationships, one party may have the opportunity to dominate and unfairly influence another party. Minors and elderly people, for instance, are often under the influence of guardians (persons who are legally responsible for another). If a guardian induces a young or elderly ward (a person whom the guardian looks after) to enter into a contract that benefits the guardian, the guardian may have exerted undue influence. Undue influence can arise from a number of fiduciary relationships, such as physician-patient, parent-child, husband-wife, or guardian-ward situations.

The essential feature of undue influence is that the party being taken advantage of does not, in reality, exercise free will in entering into a contract. It is not

---

**10.** *Restatement (Second) of Contracts,* Section 177.

---

# INSIGHT INTO SOCIAL MEDIA
## "Catfishing": Is That Online "Friend" Who You Think It Is?

When you are communicating with a person you have met only online, how do you know that person is who she or he purports to be? After all, the person could turn out to be a "catfish." The term comes from *Catfish,* a 2010 film about a fake online persona.

According to a story told in the film, when live cod were shipped long distances, they were inactive and their flesh became mushy. When catfish were added to the tanks, the cod swam around and stayed in good condition. At the end of the film, a character says of the creator of the fake persona, "There are those people who are catfish in life.  And they keep you on your toes. They keep you guessing, they keep you thinking, they keep you fresh."

### Catfishing Makes National Headlines

Catfishing made headlines in 2012 when a popular Notre Dame football star supposedly fell victim to it. Linebacker Manti Te'o said that his girlfriend Lennay Kekua, a student at Stanford, had died of leukemia after a near-fatal car accident. Although Kekua had Facebook and Twitter accounts and Te'o had communicated with her online and by telephone for several years, reporters could find no evidence of her existence. Te'o later claimed that he had been a victim of a catfishing hoax. Others suggested that his friends created the persona and her tragic death to provide an inspirational story what would increase Te'o's chances of winning the Heisman trophy.

### Is Online Fraudulent Misrepresentation Actionable?

Some victims of catfishing have turned to the courts, but they have had little success. A few have attempted to sue Internet service providers for allowing fake personas, but the courts have generally dismissed these suits.[a] Laws in some states make it a crime to impersonate someone online, but these laws generally do not apply to those who create totally fake personas.

Attempts to recover damages for fraudulent misrepresentation have generally failed to meet the requirement that there must be proof of actual injury. For instance, Paula Bonhomme developed an online romantic relationship with a man called Jesse. Jesse was actually a woman named Janna St. James, who also communicated with Bonhomme using her own name and pretending to be a friend of Jesse's.

St. James created a host of fictional characters, including an ex-wife and a son for Jesse. Bonhomme in turn sent gifts totaling more than $10,000 to Jesse and the other characters. After being told by St. James that Jesse had attempted suicide, Bonhomme suffered such emotional distress that she incurred more than $5,000 in bills for a therapist. Eventually, she was told that Jesse had died of liver cancer. When Bonhomme finally learned the truth, she suffered additional emotional distress, resulting in more expenses for a therapist and lost earnings due to her "affected mental state."

Although Bonhomme had incurred considerable expenses, the Illinois Supreme Court ruled that she could not bring a suit for fraudulent misrepresentation. The case involved only a "purely personal relationship" without any "commercial, transactional, or regulatory component." Bonhomme and St. James "were not engaged in any kind of business dealings or bargaining." Therefore, the truth of representations "made in the context of purely private personal relationships is simply not something the state regulates or in which the state possesses any kind of valid public policy interest."[b]

**LEGAL CRITICAL THINKING**
**INSIGHT INTO THE LEGAL ENVIRONMENT**

*So far, victims of catfishing have had little success in the courts. Under what circumstances might a person be able to collect damages for fraudulent misrepresentation involving online impersonation?"*

---
**a.** See, for example, *Robinson v. Match.com, LLC,* 2012 WL 3263992 (N.D.Tex. 2012).

**b.** *Bonhomme v. St. James,* 970 N.E.2d 1 (Ill. 2012).

---

enough that a person is elderly or suffers from some physical or mental impairment. There must be clear and convincing evidence that the person did not act out of her or his free will.[11] Similarly, the existence of

a fiduciary relationship alone is insufficient to prove undue influence.[12]

---
**11.** See, for example, *Bailey v. Turnbow,* 273 Va. 262, 639 S.E.2d 291 (2007); and *Hooten v. Jensen,* 94 Ark.App. 130, 227 S.W.3d 431 (2006).

**12.** See, for example, *Landers v. Sgouros,* 224 S.W.3d 651 (Mo.App. 2007); and *Ware v. Ware,* 161 P.3d 1188 (Alaska 2007).

## A Presumption of Undue Influence in Certain Situations

When the dominant party in a fiduciary relationship (such as the one between an attorney and a client) benefits from that relationship, a presumption of undue influence arises. The dominant party (the attorney) must exercise the utmost good faith in dealing with the other party. When a contract enriches the dominant party, the court will often *presume* that the contract was made under undue influence.

▶ **Example 15.10**  Erik is the guardian for Kinsley, his ward. On her behalf, he enters into a contract from which he benefits financially. If Kinsley challenges the contract, the court will likely presume that the guardian has taken advantage of his ward. To rebut (refute) this presumption, Erik has to show that he made full disclosure to Kinsley and that consideration was present. He must also show that Kinsley received, if available, independent and competent advice before completing the transaction. Unless the presumption can be rebutted, the contract will be rescinded. ◀

## SECTION 4
# DURESS

Agreement to the terms of a contract is not voluntary if one of the parties is *forced* into the agreement. The use of threats to force a party to enter into a contract is referred to as *duress*. In addition, blackmail or extortion to induce consent to a contract constitutes duress. Duress is both a defense to the enforcement of a contract and a ground for the rescission of a contract.

## The Threatened Act Must Be Wrongful or Illegal

To establish duress, there must be proof of a threat to do something that the threatening party has no right to do. Generally, for duress to occur, the threatened act must be wrongful or illegal, and it must render the person incapable of exercising free will. A threat to exercise a legal right, such as the right to sue someone, ordinarily does not constitute duress.

▶ **Example 15.11**  Joan accidentally drives into Olin's car at a stoplight. Joan has no automobile insurance, but she has substantial assets. At the scene, Olin claims to have suffered whiplash and tells Joan that he will agree not to file a lawsuit against her if she pays him $5,000. Joan initially refuses, but Olin says, "If you don't pay me $5,000 right now, I'm going to sue you for $25,000." Joan then gives Olin a check for $5,000 to avoid the lawsuit. The next day, Joan stops payment on the check. When Olin later sues to enforce their oral settlement agreement for $5,000, Joan claims duress as a defense to its enforcement. In this situation, because Olin had a right to sue Joan, his threat to sue her does not constitute duress. A court normally would not consider the threat of a civil suit to be duress. ◀

## Economic Duress

Economic need generally is not sufficient to constitute duress, even when one party exacts a very high price for an item that the other party needs. If the party exacting the price also creates the need, however, *economic duress* may be found.

▶ **Example 15.12**  The Internal Revenue Service (IRS) assesses a large tax and penalty against Weller. Weller retains Eyman, the accountant who prepared the tax returns on which the assessment was based, to challenge the assessment. Two days before the deadline for filing a reply with the IRS, Eyman declines to represent Weller unless he signs a very expensive contingency-fee agreement for the services.

In this situation, a court might find that the agreement was unenforceable because of economic duress. Although Eyman has threatened only to withdraw his services, something that he is legally entitled to do, he is responsible for delaying the withdrawal until two days before the IRS deadline. It would be impossible at that late date to obtain adequate representation elsewhere. Therefore, Weller could argue that he was forced either to sign the contract or to lose his right to challenge the IRS assessment. ◀

## SECTION 5
# ADHESION CONTRACTS AND UNCONSCIONABILITY

Questions concerning voluntary consent may arise when the terms of a contract are dictated by a party with overwhelming bargaining power and the signer must agree to those terms or go without the commodity or service in question. As explained in Chapter 14, **adhesion contracts** are written *exclusively* by one party and presented to the other party on a take-it-or-leave-it basis. These contracts often use standard forms, which give the adhering party no opportunity to negotiate the contract terms.

## Standard-Form Contracts

Standard-form contracts often contain fine-print provisions that shift a risk ordinarily borne by one party to the other. A variety of businesses use such contracts. Life insurance policies, residential leases, loan agreements, and employment agency contracts are often standard-form contracts. To avoid enforcement of the contract or of a particular clause, the plaintiff normally must show that the contract or particular term is *unconscionable*.

▶ **Case in Point 15.13**  Sherry Simpson signed a standard-form contract with Addy's Harbor Dodge, a car dealership, when she traded in her automobile for a new vehicle. Above the signature line was a statement indicating that there were additional terms and conditions on the opposite page. Simpson did not read these terms, which contained an arbitration clause that also limited the damages she could recover in the event of a dispute.

Simpson later filed a lawsuit, claiming that Addy's had misrepresented the trade-in value of her vehicle, artificially increased the purchase price, and failed to provide all promised rebates. Addy's filed a motion to compel arbitration, which the court denied. The court refused to enforce the arbitration provision on the ground that it was unconscionable. Not only was it oppressive, one sided, and inconspicuous, but it

also required Simpson to give up remedies that were available under the state statute.[13] ◀

## Unconscionability and the Courts

Technically, unconscionability under Section 2–302 of the Uniform Commercial Code (UCC) applies only to contracts for the sale of goods. Many courts, however, have broadened the concept and applied it in other situations.

Although unconscionability was discussed in Chapter 14, it is important to note here that the UCC gives courts a great degree of discretion to invalidate or strike down a contract or clause as being unconscionable. As a result, some states have *not* adopted Section 2–302 of the UCC. In those states, the legislature and the courts prefer to rely on traditional notions of fraud, undue influence, and duress.

See *Concept Summary 15.1* below for a review of all of the factors that may indicate a lack of voluntary consent.

---

**13.** *Simpson v. MSA of Myrtle Beach, Inc.,* 373 S.C. 15, 644 S.E.2d 663 (2007).

---

## CONCEPT SUMMARY 15.1
### Voluntary Consent

| PROBLEMS OF ASSENT | RULE |
|---|---|
| **Mistakes** | 1. *Bilateral (mutual) mistake*—If both parties are mistaken about a material fact, such as the identity of the subject matter, either party can avoid the contract. If the mistake relates to the value or quality of the subject matter, either party can enforce the contract.<br>2. *Unilateral mistake*—Generally, the mistaken party is bound by the contract, unless the other party knows or should have known of the mistake, or the mistake is an inadvertent mathematical error in addition, subtraction, or the like that is committed without gross negligence. |
| **Fraudulent Misrepresentation** | The elements of fraudulent misrepresentation are:<br>1. A misrepresentation of a material fact has occurred.<br>2. There has been an intent to deceive.<br>3. The innocent party has justifiably relied on the misrepresentation.<br>4. To collect damages, a party must have been harmed as a result of the misrepresentation. |
| **Undue Influence and Duress** | 1. *Undue influence*—Arises from special relationships, such as fiduciary relationships, in which one party's free will has been overcome by the undue influence of another. Usually, the contract is voidable.<br>2. *Duress*—Defined as the use of threats to force a party to enter into a contract out of fear; for example, the threat of violence or economic pressure. The party forced to enter into the contract can rescind the contract. |
| **Adhesion Contracts and Unconscionability** | Concerns one-sided bargains in which one party has substantially superior bargaining power and can dictate the terms of a contract. Unconscionability typically occurs as a result of the following:<br>1. *Standard-form contracts*—In which a fine-print provision purports to shift a risk normally borne by one party to the other (for example, a liability disclaimer).<br>2. *Take-it-or-leave-it adhesion contracts*—In which the buyer has no choice but to agree to the seller's dictated terms if the buyer is to procure certain goods or services. |

## Reviewing: Mistakes, Fraud, and Voluntary Consent

Chelene had been a caregiver for Marta's eighty-year-old mother, Janis, for nine years. Shortly before Janis passed away, Chelene convinced her to buy Chelene's house for Marta. The elderly woman died before the papers were signed, however. Four months later, Marta used her inheritance to buy Chelene's house without having it inspected. The house was built in the 1950s, and Chelene said it was in "perfect condition." Nevertheless, one year after the purchase, the basement started leaking. Marta had the paneling removed from the basement walls and discovered that the walls were bowed inward and cracked. Marta then had a civil engineer inspect the basement walls, and he found that the cracks had been caulked and painted over before the paneling was installed. He concluded that the "wall failure" had existed "for at least thirty years" and that the basement walls were "structurally unsound." Using the information presented in the chapter, answer the following questions.

1. Can Marta obtain rescission of the contract based on undue influence? If the sale to Janis had been completed before her death, could Janis have obtained rescission based on undue influence? Explain.
2. Can Marta sue Chelene for fraudulent misrepresentation? Why or why not? What element(s) might be lacking?
3. Now assume that Chelene knew that the basement walls were cracked and bowed and that she had hired someone to install paneling before she offered to sell the house. Did she have a duty to disclose this defect to Marta? Could a court find that Chelene's silence in this situation constituted misrepresentation? Explain.
4. If Chelene knew about the problem with the walls but did not know that the house was structurally unsound, could she be liable for negligent misrepresentation? Why or why not?
5. Can Marta avoid the contract on the ground that both parties made a mistake about the condition of the house? Explain.

**DEBATE THIS...** *The concept of* caveat emptor *("let the buyer beware") should be applied to all sales, including those of real property.*

## Terms and Concepts

| | | |
|---|---|---|
| adhesion contract 272 | latent defects 267 | *scienter* 268 |
| innocent misrepresentation 269 | negligent misrepresentation 269 | voluntary consent 264 |

## Issue Spotters

1. In selling a house, Matt tells Ann that the wiring, fixtures, and appliances are of a certain quality. Matt knows nothing about the quality, but it is not as specified. Ann buys the house. On learning the true quality, Ann confronts Matt. He says he wasn't trying to fool her, he was only trying to make a sale. Can she rescind the deal? Why or why not? **(See page 266.)**

2. Elle, an accountant, certifies several audit reports for Flite Corporation, her client, knowing that Flite in-

tends to use the reports to obtain loans from Good Credit Company (GCC). Elle believes that the reports are true and does not intend to deceive GCC, but she does not check the reports before certifying them. Can Elle be held liable to GCC? Why or why not? **(See page 269.)**

• **Check your answers to the Issue Spotters against the answers provided in Appendix E at the end of this text.**

## Business Scenarios

**15–1. Undue Influence.** Juan is an elderly man who lives with his nephew, Samuel. Juan is totally dependent on Samuel's support. Samuel tells Juan that unless he transfers a tract of land he owns to Samuel for a price 35 percent below its market value, Samuel will no longer support and take care of him. Juan enters into the contract. Discuss fully whether Juan can set aside this contract. **(See page 270.)**

**15–2. Fraudulent Misrepresentation.** Grano owns a forty-room motel on Highway 100. Tanner is interested in purchasing the motel. During the course of negotiations, Grano tells Tanner that the motel netted $30,000 during the previous year and that it will net at least $45,000 the next year. The motel books, which Grano turns over to Tanner before the purchase, clearly show that Grano's motel netted only $15,000 the previous year. Also, Grano fails to tell Tanner that a bypass to Highway 100 is being planned that will redirect most traffic away from the front of the motel. Tanner purchases the motel. During the first year under Tanner's operation, the motel nets only $18,000. At this time, Tanner learns of the motel's previous low profits and the planned bypass. Tanner wants Grano to return the purchase price. Discuss fully Tanner's probable success in getting his funds back. **(See page 266.)**

**15–3. Voluntary Consent.** Discuss whether either of the following contracts will be unenforceable on the ground that voluntary consent is lacking:

(a) Simmons finds a stone in his pasture that he believes to be quartz. Jenson, who also believes that the stone is quartz, contracts to purchase it for $10. Just before delivery, the stone is discovered to be a diamond worth $1,000. **(See page 266.)**

(b) Jacoby's barn is burned to the ground. He accuses Goldman's son of arson and threatens to have the prosecutor bring a criminal action unless Goldman agrees to pay him $5,000. Goldman agrees to pay. **(See page 300.)**

## Business Case Problems

**15–4. Fraudulent Misrepresentation.** Peggy Williams helped eighty-seven-year-old Melvin Kaufman care for Elsie Kaufman, his wife and Williams's great aunt, for several years before her death. Melvin then asked Williams to "take care of him the rest of his life." He conveyed his house to her for "Ten and No/100 Dollars ($10.00), and other good and valuable consideration," according to the deed, and executed a power of attorney in her favor. When Melvin returned from a trip to visit his brother, however, Williams had locked him out of the house. He filed a suit in a Texas state court, alleging fraud. He claimed that he had deeded the house to her in exchange for her promise of care, but that she had not taken care of him and had not paid him the ten dollars. Williams admitted that she had not paid the ten dollars, but argued that she had made no such promise, that Melvin had given her the house when he had been unable to sell it, and that his trip had been intended as a move. Do these facts show fraud? If so, what would be the appropriate remedy? Explain. [*Williams v. Kaufman*, 275 S.W.3d 637 (Tex.App.—Beaumont 2009)] **(See page 266.)**

**15–5. BUSINESS CASE PROBLEM WITH SAMPLE ANSWER: Fraudulent Misrepresentation.**
 *Ricky and Sherry Wilcox hired Esprit Log and Timber Frame Homes to build a log house, which the Wilcoxes intended to sell. They paid Esprit $125,260 for materials and services. They eventually sold the home for $1,620,000 but sued Esprit due to construction delays. The logs were supposed to arrive at the construction site precut and predrilled, but that did not happen. So it took five extra months to build the house while the logs were cut and drilled one by one. The Wilcoxes claimed that the interest they paid on a loan for the extra construction time cost them about $200,000. The jury agreed and awarded them that much in damages, plus $250,000 in punitive damages and $20,000 in attorneys' fees. Esprit appealed, claiming that the evidence did not support the verdict because the Wilcoxes had sold the house for a good price. Is Esprit's argument credible? Why or why not? How should the court rule? [Esprit Log and Timber Frame Homes, Inc. v. Wilcox, 302 Ga.App. 550, 691 S.E.2d 344 (2010)]* **(See page 266.)**

- **For a sample answer to Problem 15–5, go to Appendix F at the end of this text.**

**15–6. Mutual Mistake.** When Steven Simkin divorced Laura Blank, they agreed to split their assets equally. They owned an account with Bernard L. Madoff Investment Securities estimated to be worth $5.4 million. Simkin kept the account and paid Blank more than $6.5 million—including $2.7 million to offset the amount of the funds that they believed were in the account. Later, they learned that the account actually contained no funds due to its manager's fraud. Could their agreement be rescinded on the basis of a mistake? Discuss. [*Simkin v. Blank*, 80 A.D.3d 401, 915 N.Y.S.2d 47 (1 Dept. 2011)] **(See page 265.)**

**15–7. Misrepresentation.** Charter One Bank owned a fifteen-story commercial building. A fire inspector told Charter that the building's drinking-water and fire-suppression systems were linked. Without disclosing this information, Charter sold the building to Northpoint

Properties, Inc. Northpoint spent $280,000 to repair the water and fire-suppression systems and filed a suit against Charter One. Is the seller liable for not disclosing the building's defects? Discuss. [*Northpoint Properties, Inc. v. Charter One Bank*, 2011-Ohio-2512 (Ohio App. 8 Dist. 2011)] **(See page 267.)**

**15–8. Standard-Form Contracts.** David Desgro hired Paul Pack to inspect a house that Desgro wanted to buy. Pack had Desgro sign a standard-form contract that included a twelve-month limit for claims based on the agreement. Pack reported that the house had no major problems, but after Desgro bought it, he discovered issues with the plumbing, insulation, heat pump, and floor support. Thirteen months after the inspection, Desgro filed a suit in a Tennessee state court against Pack. Was Desgro's complaint filed too late, or was the contract's twelve-month limit unenforceable? Discuss. [*Desgro v. Pack*, __ So.3d __, 2013 WL 84899 (Tenn.App. 2013)] **(See page 272.)**

**15–9. A QUESTION OF ETHICS: Mistake.**

*On behalf of BRJM, LLC, Nicolas Kepple offered Howard Engelsen $210,000 for a parcel of land known as lot five on the north side of Barnes Road in Stonington, Connecticut. Engelsen's company, Output Systems, Inc., owned the land. Engelsen had the lot surveyed and obtained an appraisal. The appraiser valued the property at $277,000, after determining that it was 3.0*
*acres in size and thus could not be subdivided because it did not meet the town's minimum legal requirement of 3.7 acres for subdivision. Engelsen responded to Kepple's offer with a counteroffer of $230,000, which Kepple accepted. On May 3, 2002, the parties signed a contract. When Engelsen refused to go through with the deal, BRJM filed a suit in a Connecticut state court against Output, seeking specific performance and other relief. The defendant asserted the defense of mutual mistake on at least two grounds. [BRJM, LLC v. Output Systems, Inc., 100 Conn.App. 153, 917 A.2d 605 (2007)]* **(See page 264.)**

(a) In the counteroffer, Engelsen asked Kepple to remove from their contract a clause requiring written confirmation of the availability of a "free split," which meant that the property could be subdivided without the town's prior approval. Kepple agreed. After signing the contract, Kepple learned that the property was *not* entitled to a free split. Would this circumstance qualify as a mistake on which the defendant could avoid the contract? Discuss.

(b) After signing the contract, Engelsen obtained a second appraisal that established the size of lot five as 3.71 acres, which meant that it could be subdivided, and valued the property at $490,000. Can the defendant avoid the contract on the basis of a mistake in the first appraisal? Explain.

## Legal Reasoning Group Activity

**15–10. Fraudulent Misrepresentation.** Radiah Givens was involved romantically with Joseph Rosenzweig. She moved into an apartment on which he made the down payment. She signed the mortgage, but he made the payments and paid household expenses. They later married. She had their marriage annulled, however, when she learned that he was married to someone else. Rosenzweig then filed a suit against her to collect on the mortgage. **(See page 266.)**

(a) The first group should decide whether Rosenzweig committed fraud.

(b) The second group should evaluate whether Rosenzweig's conduct was deceitful, and if so, whether his deceitfulness should affect the decision in this case.

(c) The third group should consider how fraud is related to ethics. Can a contracting party act ethically and still commit fraud? How?

# CHAPTER 16

# THE WRITING REQUIREMENT AND ELECTRONIC RECORDS

A contract that is otherwise valid may still be unenforceable if it is not in the proper form. Certain types of contracts are required to be in writing or evidenced by a memorandum or electronic record (*record* was defined in Chapter 12). The writing requirement does not mean that an agreement must be a formal written contract. An exchange of e-mails that evidences the parties' agreement usually is sufficient, provided that they are "signed," or agreed to, by the party against whom enforcement is sought.

In this chapter, we examine the kinds of contracts that require a writing and some exceptions to the writing requirement. We also discuss the *parol evidence rule,* which courts follow when determining whether evidence that is extraneous, or external, to written contracts may be admissible at trial. Though not inherently related to the writing requirement, the parol evidence rule has general application in contract law.

---

## WRITING REQUIREMENT: THE STATUTE OF FRAUDS

Every state has a statute that stipulates what types of contracts must be in writing. We refer to such a statute as the **Statute of Frauds.** The origins of these statutes can be traced to early English law.

### Origins of the Statute

At early common law, parties to a contract were not allowed to testify if a dispute arose. This led to the practice of hiring third party witnesses. As early as the seventeenth century, the English recognized that this practice created many problems and enacted a statute to help deal with them.

The statute, passed by the English Parliament in 1677, was known as "An Act for the Prevention of Frauds and Perjuries." The act established that certain types of contracts, to be enforceable, had to be evidenced by a writing and signed by the party against whom enforcement was sought. The primary purpose of the statute was to ensure that, for certain types of contracts, there was reliable evidence of the contracts and their terms.

### State Legislation

Today, although each state has a statute modeled after the English act, the statutes vary slightly from state to state. All states require certain types of contracts to be in writing or evidenced by a written memorandum or an electronic record. In addition, the party or parties against whom enforcement is sought must have signed the contract, unless certain exceptions apply (as discussed later in this chapter). Recall from Chapter 12 that in the context of electronic communications, a party's name typed at the bottom of an e-mail can qualify as a signature.

The actual name of the Statute of Frauds is misleading because the statute does not apply to fraud. Rather, it denies enforceability to certain contracts that do not comply with its writing requirements. The primary purpose of the statute is to prevent harm to innocent parties by requiring written evidence of agreements concerning important transactions. A contract that is oral when it is required to be in writing is normally voidable by a party who later does not wish to follow through with the agreement.

## SECTION 2
# CONTRACTS THAT REQUIRE A WRITING

The following types of contracts are generally required to be in writing or evidenced by a written memorandum or electronic record:

1. Contracts involving interests in land.
2. Contracts that cannot *by their terms* be performed within one year from the day after the date of formation.
3. Collateral, or secondary, contracts, such as promises to answer for the debt or duty of another and promises by the administrator or executor of an estate to pay a debt of the estate personally—that is, out of her or his own pocket.
4. Promises made in consideration of marriage.
5. Under the Uniform Commercial Code (UCC—see Chapter 20), contracts for the sale of goods priced at $500 or more.

## Contracts Involving Interests in Land

A contract calling for the sale of land is not enforceable unless it is in writing or evidenced by a written memorandum. Land is *real property* and includes all physical objects that are permanently attached to the soil, such as buildings, fences, trees, and the soil itself.

The Statute of Frauds operates as a *defense* to the enforcement of an oral contract for the sale of land.

▶ **Example 16.1** Skylar contracts orally to sell his property in Fair Oaks to Beth. If he later decides not to sell, under most circumstances, Beth cannot enforce the contract. ◀

The Statute of Frauds also requires written evidence of contracts for the transfer of other interests in land, such as mortgage agreements and leases. Similarly, an agreement that includes an option to purchase real property must be in writing for the option to be enforced.

Generally, for a land sale contract to be enforceable under the Statute of Frauds, the contract must describe the property being transferred with sufficient certainty for it to be identified. Whether a contract for the sale of land met this requirement was at issue in the following case.

---

## CASE 16.1

### Salim v. Solaiman
Court of Appeals of Georgia, 302 Ga.App. 607, 691 S.E.2d 389 (2010).

**BACKGROUND AND FACTS** Mohammad Salim offered his convenience store and gas station for sale. Talat Solaiman and Sabina Chowdhury offered to buy the property for $975,000. All the parties signed a handwritten document and then later signed a more formal typewritten "Purchase and Sale Agreement" prepared by Solaiman and Chowdhury. The typed agreement described the property simply as "the property and business (known as BP Food Mart) located at 199 Upper Riverdale Road, Jonesboro, GA 30236." The agreement included a $25,000 security deposit, but did not specify what would happen if the sale failed to close on time.

Solaiman and Chowdhury visited the store and spoke to store clerks, vendors, and customers. They ordered a title search, and they paid $2,000 to renew the store's alcoholic beverage license in their names. The closing never occurred. After receiving the title report, Solaiman and Chowdhury notified Salim that they were not going to buy the property and business. They asked for the return of their security deposit and the $2,000 alcohol license renewal fee. Salim refused, and Solaiman and Chowdhury sued to recover the funds. The trial court found that the parties' purchase agreement was unenforceable because "it did not sufficiently describe the real property purchased" and issued a judgment in favor of Solaiman and Chowdhury. Salim filed an appeal.

**DECISION AND RATIONALE** A state intermediate appellate court affirmed the trial court's holding. The issue that the reviewing court addressed was the sufficiency of the description of the prop-

**CASE 16.1 CONTINUED**   erty to be sold. The court stated, "The requirement that a contract to purchase real property include an adequate property description arises under the Statute of Frauds."

To comply with the statute, an agreement for the sale of land "must be in writing and must provide a sufficiently definite description of the property to be sold. Specifically, such a contract must describe the property . . . with the same degree of certainty as that required in a deed conveying realty." This means that a purchase agreement for real property must describe the particular tract of land or provide a key by which it can be located with the aid of outside evidence. The property description in the typewritten agreement "clearly failed to identify the land at issue with the necessary certainty because it only provided a street address."

**WHAT IF THE FACTS WERE DIFFERENT?**   *Suppose that Solaiman and Chowdhury had paid for the property and taken possession, but six months later had tried to rescind the transaction, using the same arguments presented above. Would the result have been the same? Why or why not?*

**THE LEGAL ENVIRONMENT DIMENSION**   *Why does the Statute of Frauds require that a contract for a sale of land include a sufficiently definite description of the property?*

## The One-Year Rule

Contracts that cannot, *by their own terms*, be performed within one year *from the day after* the contract is formed must be in writing to be enforceable.[1] The reason for this rule is that the parties' memory of their contract's terms is not reliable for longer than a year.

**TIME PERIOD STARTS THE DAY AFTER THE CONTRACT IS FORMED**   The one-year period begins to run *the day after the contract is made.* ▶ **Example 16.2**   Superior University forms a contract with Kimi San stating that San will teach three courses in history during the coming academic year (September 15 through June 15). If the contract is formed in March, it must be in writing to be enforceable—because it cannot be performed within one year. If the contract is not formed until July, however, it does not have to be in writing to be enforceable—because it can be performed within one year. ◀

**MUST BE OBJECTIVELY IMPOSSIBLE TO PERFORM WITHIN ONE YEAR**   The test for determining whether an oral contract is enforceable under the one-year rule is whether performance is *possible* within one year. It does not matter whether the agreement is *likely* to be performed during that period.

When performance of a contract is objectively impossible during the one-year period, the oral contract will be unenforceable. ▶ **Example 16.3**   A contract to provide five crops of tomatoes to be grown on a specific farm in Illinois would be objectively impos- sible to perform within one year. No farmer in Illinois can grow five crops of tomatoes in a single year. ◀

If performance is possible within one year under the contract's terms, the contract does not "fall within" or "under" the Statute of Frauds and need not be in writing. ▶ **Example 16.4**   Janine enters a contract to provide security services for a warehouse for as long as the warehouse needs them. The con- tract could be fully performed within a year because the warehouse could go out of business within twelve months. Therefore, the contract need not be in writ- ing to be enforceable. ◀ Similarly, an oral contract for lifetime employment does not fall within the Statute of Frauds because an employee can die within a year, so the contract can be performed within one year.[2]

Exhibit 16–1 on the next page graphically illus- trates the one-year rule.

## Collateral Promises

A **collateral promise,** or secondary promise, is one that is ancillary (subsidiary) to a principal transaction or primary contractual relationship. In other words, a collateral promise is one made by a third party to assume the debts or obligations of a primary party to a contract if that party does not perform. Any collateral promise of this nature falls under the Statute of Frauds and therefore must be in writing to be enforceable.

To understand this concept, it is important to dis- tinguish between primary and secondary promises and obligations.

---

1. *Restatement (Second) of Contracts,* Section 130.

2. See, for example, *Gavegnano v. TLT Construction Corp.,* 67 Mass.App. Ct. 1102, 851 N.E.2d 1133 (2006).

**EXHIBIT 16-1  The One-Year Rule**

Under the Statute of Frauds, contracts that by their terms are impossible to perform within one year from the day after the date of contract formation must be in writing to be enforceable. Put another way, if it is at all possible to perform an oral contract within one year from the day after the contract is made, the contract will fall outside the Statute of Frauds and be enforceable.

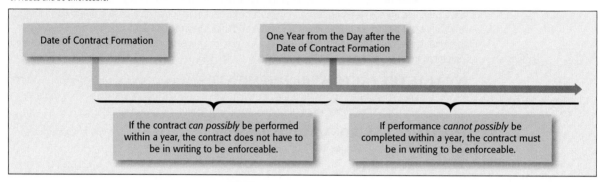

**PRIMARY OBLIGATIONS** A primary obligation is a third party's promise to pay another person's debt (or other obligation) that is not conditioned on the person's failure to pay (or perform). As a general rule, a contract in which a party assumes a primary obligation does not need to be in writing to be enforceable.
▶ **Example 16.5**  Nigel tells Leanne Lu, an orthodontist, that he will pay for the services provided for Nigel's niece. Because Nigel has assumed direct financial responsibility for his niece's debt, this is a primary obligation and need not be in writing to be enforceable. ◀

**SECONDARY OBLIGATIONS** A secondary obligation is a promise to pay another's debt only if that party fails to pay. ▶ **Example 16.6**  Kareem's mother borrows $10,000 from the Medford Trust Company on a promissory note payable in six months. Kareem promises the bank officer handling the loan that he will pay the $10,000 *if his mother does not pay the loan on time.* Kareem, in this situation, becomes what is known as a *guarantor* on the loan. He is guaranteeing to the bank (the creditor) that he will pay the loan if his mother fails to do so. This kind of collateral promise must be in writing to be enforceable. ◀

Exhibit 16–2 on the following page illustrates the concept of a collateral promise. (Notice that the bottom arrow says "Promises to Answer for A's Debt." It does not say "Promises to Pay.")

**AN EXCEPTION—THE "MAIN PURPOSE" RULE** An oral promise to answer for the debt of another is covered by the Statute of Frauds *unless* the guarantor's main purpose in incurring a secondary obligation is to secure a personal benefit. This type of contract need not be in writing.[3] The assumption is that a court can infer from the circumstances of a particular case whether the "leading objective" of the guarantor was to secure a personal benefit. In this situation, the guarantor is, in effect, answering for (guaranteeing) her or his own debt.
▶ **Example 16.7**  Carlie Braswell contracts with Custom Manufacturing Company to have some machines custom-made for her factory. She promises Newform Supply, Custom's supplier, that if Newform continues to deliver the materials to Custom for the production of the custom-made machines, she will guarantee payment. This promise need not be in writing, even though the effect may be to pay the debt of another. This is because Braswell's main purpose in forming the contract is to secure a benefit for herself. ◀

Another typical application of the main purpose rule occurs when one creditor guarantees a debtor's debt to another creditor to forestall litigation. A creditor might do this because it allows the debtor to remain in business long enough to generate profits sufficient to pay *both* creditors. In this situation, the guaranty does not need to be in writing to be enforceable.

## Promises Made in Consideration of Marriage

A unilateral promise to make a monetary payment or to give property in consideration of a promise to marry

---

3. *Restatement (Second) of Contracts,* Section 116.

## EXHIBIT 16–2  Collateral Promises

A collateral (secondary) promise is one made by a third party (C, in this exhibit) to a creditor (B, in this exhibit) to pay the debt of another (A, in this exhibit), who is primarily obligated to pay the debt. Under the Statute of Frauds, collateral promises must be in writing to be enforceable.

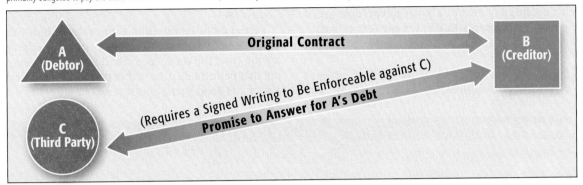

must be in writing. In other words, if a mother promises to pay a man $20,000 if he marries her daughter, that promise must be in writing to be enforceable.

▶ **Example 16.8** Evan promises to buy Celeste a house in Maui if she marries him. Celeste would need written evidence of Evan's promise to enforce it. ◀

The same rule applies to **prenuptial agreements**—agreements made before marriage that define each partner's ownership rights in the other partner's property. Prenuptial agreements must be in writing to be enforceable. ▶ **Example 16.9** Before marrying country singer Keith Urban, actress Nicole Kidman entered into a prenuptial agreement with him. Kidman agreed that if the couple divorced, she would pay Urban $640,000 for every year they had been married, unless Urban had relapsed and used drugs again. In that event, he would receive nothing. ◀

### Contracts for the Sale of Goods

The Uniform Commercial Code (UCC) includes Statute of Frauds provisions that require written evidence or an electronic record of a contract for the sale of goods priced at $500 or more. (This low threshold amount may be increased in the future.)

A writing that will satisfy the UCC requirement need only state the quantity term (such as 6,000 boxes of cotton gauze, for instance). The contract will not be enforceable for any quantity greater than that set forth in the writing. Other agreed-on terms can be omitted or even stated imprecisely in the writing, as long as they adequately reflect both parties' intentions.

A written memorandum or series of communications evidencing a contract will suffice, provided that the writing is signed by the party against whom enforcement is sought. The writing normally need not designate the buyer or the seller, the terms of payment, or the price. Requirements of the Statute of Frauds under the UCC will be discussed in more detail in Chapter 20.

### SECTION 3
# EXCEPTIONS TO THE WRITING REQUIREMENT

Exceptions to the writing requirement are made in certain circumstances. We describe those situations here.

### Partial Performance

When a contract has been partially performed and the parties cannot be returned to their positions prior to the contract, a court may grant *specific performance*. Specific performance is an equitable remedy that requires performance of the contract according to its precise terms (see Chapter 19).

Courts may grant specific performance of an oral contract to transfer an interest in land that has been partially performed. Partial performance can arise when the purchaser has paid part of the price, taken possession of the property, and made permanent improvements to it. Whether a court will enforce an oral contract usually is determined by the degree of harm that would be suffered if the court chose *not* to enforce the oral contract. The parties still must prove that an oral contract existed, however.

In some states, mere reliance on certain types of oral contracts is enough to remove them from the Statute of Frauds.[4] Under the UCC, an oral contract for the sale of goods is enforceable to the extent that a seller accepts payment or a buyer accepts delivery of the goods.[5] ▶ **Example 16.10** Cooper orders twenty chairs from an online seller. After ten chairs have been delivered and accepted, Cooper repudiates (denies the existence of) the contract. In that situation, the seller can enforce the contract (and obtain payment) to the extent of the ten chairs already accepted by Cooper. ◀

Partial performance is an unmistakable indication that one party believes there is a contract. In the following case, the court considered whether by accepting that performance, the other party indicated that it also understood that a contract was in effect.

---

**4.** *Restatement (Second) of Contracts*, Section 129.
**5.** UCC 2–201(3)(c). See Chapter 20.

---

## CASE 16.2

### NYKCool A.B. v. Pacific Fruit, Inc.
United States Court of Appeals, Second Circuit, 2013 WL 163621 (2013).

**COMPANY PROFILE**  NYKCool A.B., based in Stockholm, Sweden, provides maritime transportation for hire. It is a subsidiary of NYKReefers Limited, which operates as a subsidiary of Nippon Yusen Kabushiki Kaisha, one of the world's largest shipping companies. NYKCool has a fleet of more than fifty ships and offices in Argentina, Brazil, Chile, Ecuador, Japan, New Zealand, South Africa, the United Kingdom, and the United States. NYKCool focuses on transporting perishables, especially fruit. To reduce the number of empty containers, the firm disperses its large fleet around the globe in cost-efficient patterns and carries other cargoes on its vessels' return trips.

**BACKGROUND AND FACTS**  Pacific Fruit, Inc., exports cargo from Ecuador. NYKCool and Pacific entered into a written contract with a two-year duration, under which NYKCool agreed to transport weekly shipments of bananas from Ecuador to California and Japan. At the end of the period, the parties agreed to extend the deal. Due to a disagreement over one of the terms, a new contract was never signed, but the parties' trade continued. After nearly four more years of performance between 2005 and 2008, a dispute arose over unused cargo capacity and unpaid freight charges. An arbitration panel of the Society of Maritime Arbitrators found that Pacific Fruit was liable to NYKCool for $8,787,157 for breach of contract. NYKCool filed a petition in a federal district court to confirm the award. Pacific Fruit appealed the judgment in NYKCool's favor, contending that the arbitration panel "manifestly disregarded" the law when it concluded that the parties had an enforceable contract.

**DECISION AND RATIONALE**  The U.S. Court of Appeals for the Second Circuit affirmed the judgment of the lower court. In order to vacate an arbitration award for manifest disregard of the law, a court must find that the arbitrator knew the relevant law and intentionally refused to apply it. The reviewing court could find no shocking impropriety on the part of the arbitration panel, so there could be no review of whether the arbitrator misconstrued a contract.

The appellate court agreed with the arbitration panel's statement that "the parties' substantial partial performance on the contract weighs strongly in favor of contract formation." Moreover, the court noted that the panel's conclusion that the "parties' substantial performance" weighed in favor of contract formation was relatively undisputed. After all, for two years, NYKCool transported 30 million boxes of cargo for Pacific Fruit during over 100 trips and received $70 million in payments even though there was no written contract in place. Clearly, "the parties' behavior during 2005 and 2006 strongly suggests that they believe themselves subject to a binding agreement."

**THE LEGAL ENVIRONMENT DIMENSION**  *What circumstance in this case demonstrates most strongly that Pacific did not truly believe that it had no contract with NYKCool? Explain.*

**THE ECONOMIC DIMENSION**  *How can a carrier avoid losses under a contract that obligates it only to transport cargo one way and not on the return voyage?*

## Admissions

If a party against whom enforcement of an oral contract is sought "admits" under oath that a contract for sale was made, the contract will be enforceable.[6] The party's admission can occur at any stage of the court proceedings, such as during a deposition or other discovery, pleadings, or testimony.

If a party admits a contract subject to the UCC, it is enforceable, but only to the extent of the quantity admitted.[7] ▶ **Example 16.11**   Rachel, the president of Bistro Corporation, admits under oath that an oral agreement was made with Commercial Kitchens, Inc., to buy certain equipment for $10,000. A court will enforce the agreement only to the extent admitted ($10,000), even if Commercial Kitchens claims that the agreement involved $20,000 worth of equipment. ◀

## Promissory Estoppel

An oral contract that would otherwise be unenforceable under the Statute of Frauds may be enforced in some states under the doctrine of promissory estoppel. Recall from Chapter 13 that if a person justifiably relies on another's promise to his or her detriment, a court may *estop* (prevent) the promisor from denying that a contract exists. Section 139 of the *Restatement (Second) of Contracts* provides that in these circumstances, an oral promise can be enforceable notwithstanding the Statute of Frauds.

---

6. *Restatement (Second) of Contracts*, Section 133.
7. UCC 2–201(3)(b).

For the promise to be enforceable, the promisee must have justifiably relied on it to her or his detriment, and the reliance must have been foreseeable to the person making the promise. In addition, there must be no way to avoid injustice except to enforce the promise. (Note the similarities between promissory estoppel and the doctrine of partial performance discussed previously. Both require reasonable reliance and operate to estop a party from claiming that no contract exists.)

## Special Exceptions under the UCC

Special exceptions to the writing requirement apply to sales contracts. Oral contracts for customized goods may be enforced in certain circumstances. Another exception has to do with oral contracts *between merchants* that have been confirmed in a written memorandum. We will examine these exceptions in more detail in Chapter 20, when we discuss the UCC's Statute of Frauds provisions.

Exhibit 16–3 below graphically summarizes the types of contracts that fall under the Statute of Frauds and the various exceptions that apply.

### SECTION 4
# SUFFICIENCY OF THE WRITING

A written contract will satisfy the writing requirement, as will a written memorandum or an electronic record that evidences the agreement and is signed by the party against whom enforcement is sought. The signature

---

**EXHIBIT 16–3   Business Contracts and the Writing Requirement**

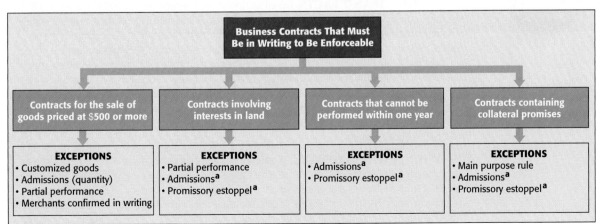

a. Some states follow Section 133 (on admissions) and Section 139 (on promissory estoppel) of the *Restatement (Second) of Contracts*.

need not be placed at the end of the document but can be anywhere in the writing. A signature can consist of a typed name (as discussed in Chapter 12) or even just initials rather than the full name.

## What Constitutes a Writing?

A writing can consist of any order confirmation, invoice, sales slip, check, fax, or e-mail—or such items in combination. The written contract need not consist of a single document in order to constitute an enforceable contract. One document may incorporate another document by expressly referring to it. Several documents may form a single contract if they are physically attached, such as by staple, paper clip, or glue. Several documents may form a single contract even if they are only placed in the same envelope.

▶ **Example 16.12**  Simpson orally agrees to sell some land next to a shopping mall to Terro Properties. Simpson gives Terro an unsigned memo that contains a legal description of the property, and Terro gives Simpson an unsigned first draft of their real estate contract. Simpson sends Terro a signed letter that refers to the memo and to the first and final drafts of the contract. Terro sends Simpson an unsigned copy of the final draft of the contract with a signed check stapled to it. Together, the documents can constitute

a writing sufficient to satisfy the writing requirement and bind both parties to the terms of the contract.  ◀

## What Must Be Contained in the Writing?

A memorandum or note evidencing the oral contract need only contain the essential terms of the contract, not every term. There must, of course, also be some indication that the parties voluntarily agreed to the terms. As mentioned earlier, under the UCC, a writing evidencing a contract for the sale of goods need only state the quantity and be signed by the party against whom enforcement is sought.

Under most state laws, the writing must also name the parties and identify the subject matter, the consideration, and the essential terms with reasonable certainty. In addition, contracts for the sale of land often are required to state the price and describe the property with sufficient clarity to allow them to be determined without reference to outside sources.

Note that because only the party against whom enforcement is sought must have signed the writing, a contract may be enforceable by one of its parties but not by the other. In the following case, the plaintiff sought to enforce a written contract that was missing the signatures of the parties against whom enforcement was being sought.

## CASE 16.3

### Beneficial Homeowner Service Corporation v. Steele
Supreme Court of New York, Suffolk County, 30 Misc.3d 1208(A) (2011).

**BACKGROUND AND FACTS**  Beneficial Homeowner Service Corporation filed a suit in a New York state court against Stephen and Susan Steele to foreclose on a mortgage. (A mortgage is a written instrument that gives a creditor an interest in property that the debtor provides as security for the payment of the loan. In a foreclosure, the lender repossesses and sells the property that secured the loan.) Beneficial (the lender) claimed that the loan was secured by real property in East Hampton, New York. Beneficial sought $91,614.34 in unpaid principal, plus interest. The lender, based on its assertion that both Stephen and Susan Steele had signed the loan agreement, filed a motion for summary judgment. Among the documents that Beneficial filed with the court was a copy of the loan agreement. There were two problems—the agreement identified Stephen Steele as the sole obligor (the party owing the obligation), and it had not been signed.

**DECISION AND RATIONALE**  The New York state court concluded that the agreement was unenforceable and denied Beneficial's motion for summary judgment. Because a mortgage involves the transfer of an interest in real property, the mortgage agreement and its underlying obligation must be in writing to satisfy the Statute of Frauds. To be enforceable, the writings must be signed by the parties to be charged. Beneficial was seeking to foreclose on a mortgage that purportedly constituted security for a certain loan agreement. Beneficial sought to enforce the agreement against two parties— Stephen

**CASE 16.3 CONTINUED**   and Susan Steele—who had not signed it. In fact, Susan was not even mentioned in the agreement as a party to it. The lender's assertions about the document were "painfully obvious misstatements of facts" and meant that the agreement was most likely unenforceable. The court ordered a hearing to determine whether, in presenting the unsigned documents, Beneficial had acted in good faith.

**WHAT IF THE FACTS WERE DIFFERENT?** *Suppose that at the hearing, the Steeles admit they had an obligation to pay the outstanding loan amount. Would the result be different? Explain.*

**THE ECONOMIC DIMENSION** *Why might Beneficial have tried to enforce an unsigned document?*

---

## SECTION 5
# THE PAROL EVIDENCE RULE

Sometimes, a written contract does not include—or contradicts—an oral understanding reached by the parties before or at the time of contracting. For instance, a landlord might tell a person who agrees to rent an apartment that cats are allowed, whereas the lease contract clearly states that no pets are permitted. In deciding such disputes, the courts look to a common law rule governing the admissibility in court of oral evidence, or *parol evidence.*

Under the **parol evidence rule,** if a court finds that a written contract represents the complete and final statement of the parties' agreement, it will not allow either party to present parol evidence. *Parol evidence* is testimony or other evidence of communications between the parties that is not contained in the contract itself. A party normally cannot present evidence of the parties' prior negotiations, prior agreements, or contemporaneous (happening at the same time) oral agreements if that evidence contradicts or varies the terms of the written contract.[8]

▶ **Example 16.13**   TKTS, Inc., sends Gwen an offer to sell season tickets to the Dallas Cowboys football games in Cowboys Stadium. Prices and seat locations are indicated in diagrams in a brochure that accompanies the offer. Gwen responds, listing her seat preference. TKTS sends her the tickets, along with a different diagram showing seat locations. Also enclosed is a document that reads, "This is the entire agreement of the parties," which Gwen signs and returns. When Gwen goes to the first game, she discovers that her seat is not where she expected, based on the brochure. Under the parol evidence rule, however, the brochure is not part of the parties' agreement. The document that Gwen signed was identified as the parties' entire contract. Therefore, she cannot introduce in court any evidence of prior negotiations or agreements that contradict or vary the contract's terms. ◀

## Exceptions to the Parol Evidence Rule

Because of the rigidity of the parol evidence rule, the courts have created the following exceptions:

1. *Contracts subsequently modified.* Evidence of any subsequent modification (oral or written) of a written contract can be introduced in court. Oral modifications may not be enforceable under the Statute of Frauds, however (for instance, a modification that increases the price of the goods being sold to more than $500). Also, oral modifications will not be enforceable if the original contract provides that any modification must be in writing.[9]

2. *Voidable or void contracts.* Oral evidence can be introduced in all cases to show that the contract was voidable or void (for example, induced by mistake, fraud, or misrepresentation). The reason is simple: if deception led one of the parties to agree to the terms of a written contract, oral evidence attesting to the fraud should not be excluded. Courts frown on bad faith and are quick to allow such evidence when it establishes fraud.

3. *Contracts containing ambiguous terms.* When the terms of a written contract are ambiguous and require interpretation, evidence is admissible to show the meaning of the terms.
   ▶ **Case in Point 16.14**   Pamela Watkins bought a home from Sandra Schexnider. Their agreement stated that Watkins would make payments on the mortgage until the note was paid in full, when "the house" would become hers. The agreement also stipulated that she would pay for insurance on

---

**8.** *Restatement (Second) of Contracts,* Section 213.

**9.** UCC 2–209(2), (3).

"the property." The home was destroyed in a hurricane, and the insurance proceeds satisfied (paid off) the mortgage. Watkins claimed that she owned the land, but Schexnider argued that she had sold only the house. The court found that because "the house" term in the contract was ambiguous, parol evidence was admissible. The court also concluded that the parties intended to transfer ownership of both the house and the land, and ordered that title to the property be transferred to Watkins.[10] ◄

4. *Incomplete contracts.* When the written contract is incomplete in that it lacks one or more of the essential terms, the courts allow additional evidence to "fill in the gaps."

5. *Prior dealing, course of performance, or usage of trade.* Under the UCC, evidence can be introduced to explain or supplement a written contract by showing a prior dealing, course of performance, or usage of trade.[11] This is because when buyers and sellers deal with each other over extended periods of time, certain customary practices develop. These practices are often overlooked in writing the contract, so courts allow the introduction of evidence to show how the parties have acted in the past. Usage of trade—practices and customs generally followed in a particular industry—can also shed light on the meaning of certain contract provisions. Thus, evidence of trade usage may be admissible. We will discuss these terms in further detail in Chapter 20, in the context of sales contracts.

6. *Contracts subject to an orally agreed-on condition precedent.* As you will read in Chapter 18, sometimes the parties agree that a condition must be fulfilled before a party is required to perform the contract. This is called a *condition precedent.* If the parties have orally agreed on a condition precedent that does not conflict with the terms of their written agreement, a court may allow parol evidence to prove the oral condition. The parol evidence rule does not apply here because the existence of the entire written contract is subject to an orally agreed-on condition. Proof of the condition does not alter or modify the written terms but affects the *enforceability* of the written contract.

7. *Contracts with an obvious or gross clerical (or typographic) error that clearly would not represent the agreement of the parties.* Parol evidence is admissible to correct an obvious typographic error. ▶ **Example 16.15** Davis agrees to lease office space from Stone Enterprises for $3,000 per month. The signed written lease provides for a monthly payment of $300 rather than the $3,000 agreed to by the parties. Because the error is obvious, Stone Enterprises would be allowed to admit parol evidence to correct the mistake. ◄

## Integrated Contracts

In determining whether to allow parol evidence, courts consider whether the written contract is intended to be the complete and final statement of the terms of the agreement. If it is, the contract is referred to as an **integrated contract,** and extraneous evidence (evidence from outside the contract) is excluded. For an example of an integration clause within a contract, see Paragraph 19 of the sample contract in the *Appendix to Chapter 19: Reading and Analyzing Contracts.*

An integrated contract can be either completely or partially integrated. If it contains all of the terms of the parties' agreement, it is completely integrated. If it contains only some of the terms that the parties agreed on and not others, it is partially integrated. If the contract is only partially integrated, evidence of consistent additional terms is admissible to supplement the written agreement.[12] Note that for both completely and partially integrated contracts, courts exclude any evidence that *contradicts* the writing and allow parol evidence only to add to the terms of a partially integrated contract. Exhibit 16–4 on the following page illustrates the relationship between integrated contracts and the parol evidence rule.

Exhibit 16–4 on the following page

## SECTION 6
# THE STATUTE OF FRAUDS IN THE INTERNATIONAL CONTEXT

As you will read in Chapter 20, the Convention on Contracts for the International Sale of Goods (CISG) governs international sales contracts between citizens of countries that have ratified the convention (agreement). Article 11 of the CISG does not incorporate any Statute of Frauds provisions. Rather, it states that a "contract for sale need not be concluded in or evidenced by writing and is not subject to any other requirements as to form."

---

10. *Watkins v. Schexnider,* 31 So.3d 609 (La.App. 3 Cir. 2010).
11. UCC 1–205, 2–202.

12. *Restatement (Second) of Contracts,* Section 216; and UCC 2–202.

**EXHIBIT 16–4 The Parol Evidence Rule**

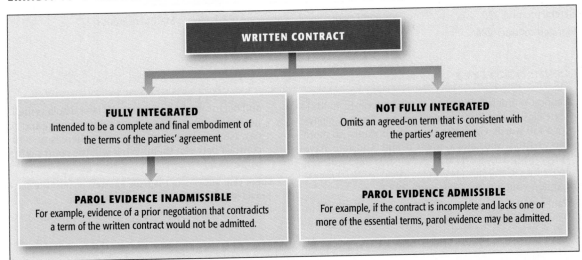

Article 11 accords with the legal customs of most nations, which no longer require contracts to meet certain formal or writing requirements to be enforceable. Ironically, even England, the nation that created the original Statute of Frauds in 1677, has repealed all of it except the provisions relating to collateral promises and to transfers of interests in land. Many other countries that once had such statutes have also repealed all or parts of them. Some countries, such as France, have never required certain types of contracts to be in writing.

## Reviewing: The Writing Requirement and Electronic Records

Charter Golf, Inc., manufactures and sells golf apparel and supplies. Ken Odin had worked as a Charter sales representative for six months when he was offered a position with a competing firm. Charter's president, Jerry Montieth, offered Odin a 10 percent commission "for the rest of his life" if Ken would turn down the offer and stay with Charter. He also promised that Odin would not be fired unless he was dishonest. Odin turned down the competitor's offer and stayed with Charter. Three years later, Charter fired Odin for no reason. Odin sued, alleging breach of contract. Using the information presented in the chapter, answer the following questions.

1. Would a court likely decide that Odin's employment contract falls within the Statute of Frauds? Why or why not?
2. Assume that the court does find that the contract falls within the Statute of Frauds and that the state in which the court sits recognizes every exception to the Statute of Frauds discussed in the chapter. What exception provides Odin with the best chance of enforcing the oral contract in this situation?
3. Now suppose that Montieth had taken out a pencil, written "10 percent for life" on the back of a register receipt, and handed it to Odin. Would this satisfy the Statute of Frauds? Why or why not?
4. Assume that Odin had signed a written employment contract at the time he was hired to work for Charter, but it was not completely integrated. Would a court allow Odin to present parol evidence of Montieth's subsequent promises?

**DEBATE THIS . . .** *Many countries have eliminated the Statute of Frauds except for sales of real estate. The United States should do the same.*

## Terms and Concepts

collateral promise 279

parol evidence rule 285

Statute of Frauds 277

integrated contract 286

prenuptial agreement 281

## Issue Spotters

1. GamesCo orders $800 worth of game pieces from Midstate Plastic, Inc. Midstate delivers, and GamesCo pays for $450 worth. GamesCo then says it wants no more pieces from Midstate. GamesCo and Midstate have never dealt with each other before and have nothing in writing. Can Midstate enforce a deal for $350 more? Explain your answer. **(See page 283.)**

2. Paula orally agrees to work with Next Corporation in New York City for two years. Paula moves her family

and begins work. Three months later, Paula is fired for no stated cause. She sues for reinstatement and back pay. Next Corporation argues that there is no written contract between them. What will the court say? **(See page 283.)**

• Check your answers to the Issue Spotters against the answers provided in Appendix E at the end of this text.

## Business Scenarios

**16–1. The One-Year Rule.** On May 1, by telephone, Yu offers to hire Benson to perform personal services. On May 5, Benson returns Yu's call and accepts the offer. Discuss fully whether this contract falls under the Statute of Frauds in the following circumstances: **(See page 279.)**

(a) The contract calls for Benson to be employed for one year, with the right to begin performance immediately.

(b) The contract calls for Benson to be employed for nine months, with performance of services to begin on September 1.

(c) The contract calls for Benson to submit a written research report, with a deadline of two years for submission.

**16–2. Collateral Promises.** Mallory promises a local hardware store that she will pay for a lawn mower that her brother is purchasing on credit if the brother fails to pay the debt. Must this promise be in writing to be enforceable? Why or why not? **(See page 279.)**

## Business Case Problems

**16–3. The Parol Evidence Rule.** Evangel Temple Assembly of God leased a facility from Wood Care Centers, Inc., to house evacuees who had lost their homes in Hurricane Katrina. One clause in the lease contract said that Evangel could terminate the lease at any time by giving Wood Care notice and paying 10 percent of the balance remaining on the lease. Another clause stated that if the facility was not given a property tax exemption (as a church), Evangel had the option to terminate the lease without making the 10 percent payment. Nine months later, the last of the evacuees left the facility, and Evangel notified Wood Care that it would end the lease. Wood Care demanded the 10 percent payment. Is parol evidence admissible to interpret this lease? Why or why not? [*Wood Care Centers, Inc. v. Evangel Temple Assembly of God of Wichita Falls*, 307 S.W.3d 816 (Tex.App.—Fort Worth 2010)] **(See page 285.)**

**16–4. Sufficiency of the Writing.** Newmark & Co. Real Estate, Inc., contacted 2615 East 17 Street Realty, LLC, to lease certain real property on behalf of a client. Newmark e-mailed

the landlord a separate agreement for the payment of Newmark's commission. The landlord e-mailed it back with a separate demand to pay the commission in installments. Newmark revised the agreement and e-mailed a final copy to the landlord. Does the agreement qualify as a writing under the Statute of Frauds? Explain. [*Newmark & Co. Real Estate, Inc. v. 2615 East 17 Street Realty, LLC*, 80 A.D.3d 476, 914 N.Y.S.2d 162 (1 Dept. 2011)] **(See page 283.)**

**16–5. BUSINESS CASE PROBLEM WITH SAMPLE ANSWER: The Parol Evidence Rule.**

 *Rimma Vaks and her husband, Steven Mangano, executed a written contract with Denise Ryan and Ryan Auction Co. to auction their furnishings. The six-page contract provided a detailed summary of* the parties' agreement. It addressed the items to be auctioned, how reserve prices would be determined, and the amount of Ryan's commission. When a dispute arose between the parties, Vaks and Mangano sued Ryan for breach of contract. Vaks and Mangano asserted that, before they executed the contract, Ryan *made various oral representations that were inconsistent with the terms of their written agreement. Assuming that their written contract was valid, can Vaks and Mangano recover for breach of an oral contract? Why or why not? [Vaks v. Ryan, 2012 WL 194398 (Mass.App. 2012)]* **(See page 285.)**

- **For a sample answer to Problem 16–5, see Appendix F at the end of this text.**

**16–6. Promises Made in Consideration of Marriage.** After twenty-nine years of marriage, Robert and Mary Lou Tuttle were divorced. They admitted in court that before they were married, they had signed a prenuptial agreement. They agreed that the agreement had stated that each would keep his or her own property and anything derived from that property. Robert came into the marriage owning farmland while Mary Lou owned no real estate. During the marriage, ten different parcels of land, totaling about six hundred acres, were acquired, and two corporations, Tuttle Grain, Inc., and Tuttle Farms, Inc., were formed. A copy of the prenuptial agreement could not be found. Can the court enforce the agreement without a writing? Why or why not? [*In re Marriage of Tuttle*, 2013 WL 164035 (Ill. App. 5 Dist. 2013)] **(See page 280.)**

**16–7. A QUESTION OF ETHICS: The Parol Evidence Rule.**

 *Robert Shelborne asked attorney William Williams to represent him in a deal with Robert Tundy. Shelborne expected to receive $31 million and agreed to pay Williams a fee of $1 million. Tundy*

*said that a tax of $100,000 would have to be paid for Shelborne to receive the $31 million. Shelborne asked James Parker to loan him $50,000. Parker, Shelborne, and Williams wired the funds to Tundy. They never heard from him again. No $31 million was transferred. Shelborne then disappeared. Parker filed a suit against Williams, alleging breach of contract. Parker offered as evidence a recording of a phone conversation in which Williams guaranteed Shelborne's loan. [Parker v. Williams, 977 So.2d 476 (Ala. 2007)]* **(See page 285.)**

(a) Is the court likely to rule in Parker's favor on the contract claim? Why or why not? Does Williams have a defense under the Statute of Frauds?

(b) The sham deal at the center of this case is known to law enforcement authorities as advance fee fraud, or a "419 scam." The victim is promised a transfer of funds from an overpaid contract, or some other suspect source, but is asked to pay a tax or other fee first. Among the parties in this case, who, if anyone, behaved ethically? Discuss.

## Legal Reasoning Group Activity

**16–8. The Writing Requirement.** Jason Novell, doing business as Novell Associates, hired Barbara Meade to work for him. The parties orally agreed on the terms of employment, including payment of a share of the company's income to Meade, but they did not put anything in writing. Two years later, Meade quit. Novell then told Meade that she was entitled to $9,602—25 percent of the difference between the accounts receivable and the accounts payable as of Meade's last day of work. Meade disagreed and demanded more than $63,500—25 percent of the revenue from all invoices, less the cost of materials and outside processing, for each of the years that she had worked

for Novell. Meade filed a lawsuit against Novell for breach of contract. **(See page 278.)**

(a) The first group should decide whether the parties had an enforceable contract.

(b) The second group should decide whether that the parties' oral agreement falls within any exception to the Statute of Frauds.

(c) The third group should discuss how the lawsuit would be affected if Novell admitted that the parties had an oral contract under which Meade was entitled to 25 percent of the difference between accounts receivable and payable as of the day Meade quit.

# CHAPTER 17

# THIRD PARTY RIGHTS

O nce it has been determined that a valid and legally enforceable contract exists, attention can turn to the rights and duties of the parties to the contract. A contract is a private agreement between the parties who have entered into it, and traditionally these parties alone have rights and liabilities under the contract. This principle is referred to as **privity of contract** (see Chapter 7). A *third party*—one who is not a direct party to a particular contract—normally does not have rights under that contract.

There are exceptions to the rule of privity of contract. For instance, as discussed in Chapter 7, privity of contract is not required to recover damages under product liability laws. Hence, a person injured by a defective product can still recover damages even though she or he was not the buyer of the product. In this chapter, we look at two other exceptions. One exception allows a party to a contract to transfer the rights or duties arising from the contract to another person through an *assignment* (of rights) or a *delegation* (of duties). The other exception involves a *third party beneficiary contract*—a contract in which the parties to the contract intend that the contract benefit a third party.

## SECTION 1
## ASSIGNMENTS AND DELEGATIONS

In a bilateral contract, the two parties have corresponding rights and duties. One party has a *right* to require the other to perform some task, and the other has a *duty* to perform it. The transfer of contractual *rights* to a third party is known as an **assignment.** The transfer of contractual *duties* to a third party is known as a **delegation.** An assignment or a delegation occurs *after* the original contract was made.

### Assignments

Assignments are important because they are used in many types of business financing. Banks, for instance, frequently assign their rights to receive payments under their loan contracts to other firms, which pay for those rights. If Tia obtains a loan from a bank, she may later receive a notice from the bank stating that it has transferred (assigned) its rights to receive payments on the loan to another firm. When it is time to repay the loan, Tia must make the payments to that other firm.

Financial institutions that make *mortgage* loans (loans to enable prospective home buyers to purchase land or a home) often assign their rights to collect the mortgage payments to a third party, such as PNC Mortgage. Following the assignment, the home buyers are notified that they must make future payments not to the bank that loaned them the funds but to the third party. Billions of dollars change hands daily in the business world in the form of assignments of rights in contracts. If it were not possible to transfer contractual rights, many businesses could not continue to operate.

**THE EFFECT OF AN ASSIGNMENT** In an assignment, the party assigning the rights to a third party is known as the **assignor,**[1] and the party receiving the rights is the **assignee.**[2] Other traditional terms used to describe the parties in assignment relationships are **obligee** (the person to whom a duty, or obligation, is owed) and **obligor** (the person who is obligated to perform the duty).

***Extinguishes the Rights of the Assignor.*** When rights under a contract are assigned unconditionally, the

---

1. Pronounced uh-*sye*-nore.
2. Pronounced uh-*sye*-nee.

rights of the assignor are extinguished.³ The third party (the assignee) has a right to demand performance from the other original party to the contract. The assignee takes only those rights that the assignor originally had, however.

▶ **Example 17.1**   Brower is obligated by contract to pay Horton $1,000. Brower is the obligor because she owes an obligation, or duty, to Horton. Horton is the obligee, the one to whom the obligation, or duty, is owed. If Horton then assigns his right to receive the

———
**3.** *Restatement (Second) of Contracts*, Section 317.

$1,000 to Kuhn, Horton is the assignor and Kuhn is the assignee. Kuhn now becomes the obligee because Brower owes Kuhn the $1,000. Here, a valid assignment of a debt exists. Kuhn (the assignee-obligee) is entitled to enforce payment in court if Brower (the obligor) does not pay him the $1,000. ◀ These concepts are illustrated in Exhibit 17–1 on the following page.

In the following case, a lender assigned its rights to loan payments from a borrower. The court had to decide whether the borrower owed the payments to the assignee.

---

## CASE 17.1

### Hosch v. Colonial Pacific Leasing Corp.
Court of Appeals of Georgia, 313 Ga.App. 873, 722 S.E.2d 778 (2012).

**BACKGROUND AND FACTS**   Edward Hosch entered into four loan agreements with Citicapital Commercial Corporation to finance the purchase of heavy construction equipment. A few months later, Citicapital merged into Citicorp Leasing, Inc., which was then renamed GE Capital Commercial, Inc. One year later, GE Capital assigned the loans to Colonial Pacific Leasing Corporation. When Hosch defaulted on the loans, Colonial provided a notice of default and demanded payment. Hosch failed to repay the loans, so Colonial sued to collect the amount due. The trial court granted summary judgment to Colonial and entered final judgment against Hosch. On appeal, Hosch argued that there was insufficient evidence that the loans had been assigned to Colonial.

**DECISION AND RATIONALE**   The Georgia appellate court affirmed the trial court's judgment in favor of the assignee, Colonial Pacific. The court stated that "a party may assign a contractual right to collect payment, including the right to sue to enforce the right." To be enforceable, the assignment must be in writing. In this case, there was sufficient evidence that GE Capital assigned Hosch's loans to Colonial Pacific. Significantly, the record included a written assignment, other documents showing that the loans had been assigned, and affidavits of a GE litigation specialist. Against that evidence, Hosch merely asserted that he had not been notified of the assignment. Under the loan agreements, however, GE Capital could assign its rights without Hosch's knowledge or consent.

**THE LEGAL ENVIRONMENT DIMENSION**   *Do borrowers benefit from the fact that lenders may freely assign their rights under loan agreements? If so, how?*

**WHAT IF THE FACTS WERE DIFFERENT?**   *Suppose that Hosch had sold the equipment financed by the loans from Citicapital to a third party. Would Hosch still have been liable to Colonial Pacific? Why or why not?*

---

***Assignee's Rights Are Subject to the Same Defenses.***   The assignee's rights are subject to the defenses that the obligor has against the assignor. In other words, the assignee obtains only those rights that the assignor originally had.

▶ **Example 17.2**   In *Example 17.1* discussed earlier, Brower owes Horton the $1,000 under a contract in which Brower agreed to buy Horton's 15-inch MacBook Pro laptop. When Brower decided to purchase the laptop, she relied on Horton's fraudulent misrepresentation that the MacBook had retina display. When Brower discovers that it does not have this feature, she tells Horton that she is going to return the laptop to him and cancel the contract. Even though Horton has assigned his "right" to receive the $1,000 to Kuhn, Brower need not pay Kuhn the $1,000. Brower can raise the defense of Horton's fraudulent misrepresentation to avoid payment. ◀

**EXHIBIT 17–1 Assignment Relationships**

In the assignment relationship illustrated here, Horton assigns his *rights* under a contract that he made with Brower to a third party, Kuhn. Horton thus becomes the *assignor* and Kuhn the *assignee* of the contractual rights. Brower, the *obligor,* now owes performance to Kuhn instead of Horton. Horton's original contract rights are extinguished after assignment.

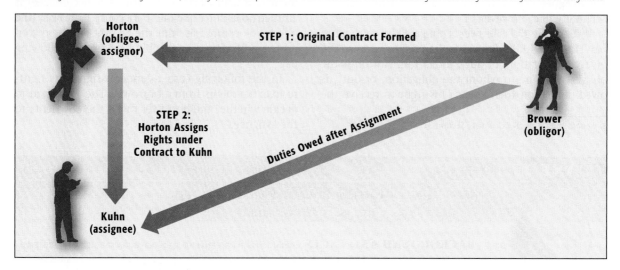

**Form of the Assignment.** In general, an assignment can take any form, oral or written. Naturally, it is more difficult to prove that an oral assignment occurred, so it is advisable to put all assignments in writing. Of course, assignments covered by the Statute of Frauds—such as an assignment of an interest in land—must be in writing to be enforceable. In addition, most states require contracts for the assignment of wages to be in writing.[4]

**RIGHTS THAT CANNOT BE ASSIGNED** As a general rule, all rights can be assigned. Exceptions are made, however, under certain circumstances. Some of these exceptions are listed below and described in more detail in the following subsections:

1. The assignment is prohibited by statute.
2. The contract is personal.
3. The assignment significantly changes the risk or duties of the obligor.
4. The contract prohibits assignment.

**When a Statute Prohibits Assignment.** When a statute expressly prohibits assignment of a particular right, that right cannot be assigned. ▶ **Example 17.3** Quincy is an employee of Specialty Travel, Inc. Specialty is an employer bound by workers' compensation statutes in this state, and thus Quincy is a covered employee. Quincy is injured on the job and begins to collect

monthly workers' compensation checks. In need of a loan, Quincy borrows from Draper, assigning to Draper all of her future workers' compensation benefits. A state statute prohibits the assignment of *future* workers' compensation benefits, and thus such rights cannot be assigned. ◀

**When a Contract Is Personal in Nature.** If a contract is for personal services, the rights under the contract normally cannot be assigned unless all that remains is a monetary payment.[5] ▶ **Example 17.4** Anton signs a contract to be a tutor for Marisa's children. Marisa then attempts to assign to Roberto her right to Anton's services. Roberto cannot enforce the contract against Anton. Roberto's children may be more difficult to tutor than Marisa's. Thus, if Marisa could assign her rights to Anton's services to Roberto, it would change the nature of Anton's obligation. Because personal services are unique to the person rendering them, rights to receive personal services are likewise unique and cannot be assigned. ◀

Note that when legal actions involve personal rights, they are considered personal in nature and cannot be assigned. For instance, personal-injury tort claims generally are nonassignable as a matter of public policy. If Elizabeth is injured by Randy's defamation, she cannot assign to someone else her right to sue Randy for damages.

---

4. See, for example, California Labor Code Section 300. There are other assignments that must be in writing as well.

5. *Restatement (Second) of Contracts,* Sections 317 and 318.

***When an Assignment Will Significantly Change the Risk or Duties of the Obligor.*** A right cannot be assigned if the assignment will significantly increase or alter the risks to or the duties of the obligor (the party owing performance under the contract).[6] ▶ **Example 17.5**  Larson owns a hotel. To insure it, he takes out a policy with Southeast Insurance. The policy insures against fire, theft, floods, and vandalism. Larson attempts to assign the insurance policy to Hewitt, who also owns a hotel.

The assignment is ineffective because it substantially alters Southeast Insurance's *duty of performance.* An insurance company evaluates the particular risk of a certain party and tailors its policy to fit that risk. If the policy is assigned to a third party, the insurance risk is materially altered because the insurance company may have no information on the third party. Therefore, the assignment will not operate to give Hewitt any rights against Southeast Insurance. ◀

***When the Contract Prohibits Assignment.*** When a contract specifically stipulates that a right cannot be assigned, then *ordinarily* it cannot be assigned. (For an example of a contract that prohibits assignment by one party, see Paragraph 12 of the sample contract in the *Appendix to Chapter 19: Reading and Analyzing Contracts.*) Note that restraints on the power to assign operate only against the parties themselves. They do not prohibit an assignment by operation of law, such as an assignment pursuant to bankruptcy or death.

Whether an *antiassignment clause* is effective depends, in part, on how it is phrased. A contract that states that *any* assignment is void effectively prohibits any assignment. ▶ **Example 17.6**  Ramirez agrees to build a house for Carmen. Their contract states "This contract cannot be assigned by Carmen without Ramirez's consent. Any assignment without such consent renders the contract void." This antiassignment clause is effective, and Carmen cannot assign her rights without obtaining Ramirez's consent. ◀

The general rule that a contract can prohibit assignment has several exceptions:

1.  A contract cannot prevent an assignment of the right to receive funds. This exception exists to encourage the free flow of funds and credit in modern business settings.
2.  The assignment of rights in real estate often cannot be prohibited because such a prohibition is contrary to public policy in most states. Prohibitions of this kind are called restraints against **alienation** (transfer of land ownership).

3.  The assignment of *negotiable instruments* (such as checks and promissory notes) cannot be prohibited.
4.  In a contract for the sale of goods, the right to receive damages for breach of contract or payment of an account owed may be assigned even though the sales contract prohibits such an assignment.[7]

**NOTICE OF ASSIGNMENT**  Once a valid assignment of rights has been made, the assignee (the third party to whom the rights have been assigned) should notify the obligor (the one owing performance) of the assignment. For instance, in *Example 17.1* on page 291, when Horton assigns to Kuhn his right to receive the $1,000 from Brower, Kuhn should notify Brower, the obligor, of the assignment.

Giving notice is not legally necessary to establish the validity of the assignment: an assignment is effective immediately, whether or not notice is given. Two major problems arise, however, when notice of the assignment is not given to the obligor:

1.  *Priority issues.* If the assignor assigns the same right to two different persons, the question arises as to which one has priority—that is, which one has the right to the performance by the obligor. The rule most often observed in the United States is that the first assignment in time is the first in right. Nevertheless, some states follow the English rule, which basically gives priority to the first assignee who gives notice. ▶ **Example 17.7**  Jason owes Alexis $5,000 under a contract. Alexis first assigns the claim to Carmen, who does not give notice to Jason, and then assigns it to Dorman, who notifies Jason. In most states, Carmen would have priority because the assignment to her was first in time. In some states, however, Dorman would have priority because he gave first notice. ◀
2.  *Potential for discharge by performance to the wrong party.* Until the obligor has notice of an assignment, the obligor can discharge his or her obligation by performance to the assignor (the obligee). Performance by the obligor to the assignor (obligee) constitutes a discharge to the assignee. Once the obligor receives proper notice, however, only performance to the assignee can discharge the obligor's obligations.

▶ **Example 17.8**  Recall that Alexis, the obligee in *Example 17.7*, assigned to Carmen her right to collect $5,000 from Jason, and Carmen did not give notice to Jason. Jason subsequently pays Alexis the $5,000. Although the assignment was valid, Jason's payment to Alexis is a discharge of

---
**6.** Section 2–210(2) of the Uniform Commercial Code (UCC).

**7.** UCC 2–210(2).

the debt. Carmen's failure to notify Jason of the assignment causes her to lose the right to collect the $5,000 from Jason. (Note that Carmen still has a claim against Alexis for the $5,000.) If Carmen had given Jason notice of the assignment, however, Jason's payment to Alexis would not have discharged the debt. ◄

In the following case, the parties disputed whether the right to buy advertising space in publications at a steep discount was validly assigned from the original owner to companies that he later formed.

## SP🔵TLIGHT on *PC Magazine*

### Case 17.2   Gold v. Ziff Communications Co.
Appellate Court of Illinois, First District, 322 Ill.App.3d 32, 748 N.E.2d 198, 254 Ill.Dec. 752 (2001).

**BACKGROUND AND FACTS**  Ziff Communications Company, a publisher of specialty magazines, bought *PC Magazine* from its founder, Anthony Gold, for more than $10 million. As part of the deal, Ziff gave Gold or a company that he owned and controlled "ad/list rights"—rights to advertise at an 80 percent discount on a limited number of pages in Ziff publications and free use of Ziff's subscriber lists. In 1983, Gold formed Software Communications, Inc. (SCI), a mail-order software business that he wholly owned, to use the ad/list rights. In 1987 and 1988, he formed two new mail-order companies, Hanson & Connors, Inc., and PC Brand, Inc. Gold told Ziff that he was allocating his ad/list rights to Hanson & Connors, which took over most of SCI's business, and to PC Brand, of which Gold owned 90 percent. Ziff's other advertisers complained about this "allocation."

Ziff refused to run large ads for Hanson & Connors or to release its subscriber lists to the company. Ziff also declared PC Brand ineligible for the ad discount because it "was not controlled by Gold." Gold and his companies filed a suit in an Illinois state court against Ziff, alleging breach of contract. The court ordered Ziff to pay the plaintiffs more than $88 million in damages and interest. Ziff appealed to an intermediate state appellate court, arguing, in part, that Gold had not properly assigned the ad/list rights to Hanson & Connors and PC Brand.

**DECISION AND RATIONALE**   A state intermediate appellate court affirmed the lower court's decision in favor of Ziff. The appellate court remanded the case, however, for a new trial on the amount of the damages, reasoning that some parts of the award "were not within the reasonable contemplation of the parties."

The court explained, "We agree with plaintiffs that assignments can be implied from circumstances. No particular mode or form . . . is necessary to effect a valid assignment, and any acts or words are sufficient which show an intention of transferring or appropriating the owner's interest. Furthermore, "it is undisputed that Gold owned 100 [percent] of SCE. In a letter dated May 13, 1988, Gold, as president of SCI, instructed Ziff that he was allocating the ad/list rights to Hanson and PC Brand. Additionally, SCI stopped using the ad/list rights when PC Brand and Hanson were formed. . . . Gold's behavior toward his companies and his conduct toward the obligor, Ziff, implied that the ad/list rights were assigned to PC Brand and Hanson."

**THE SOCIAL DIMENSION**  *Would the assignments in this case have been valid if Gold had not notified Ziff? Why or why not?*

**THE ECONOMIC DIMENSION**  *How might Ziff have effectively avoided both this dispute with Gold and complaints from its other advertisers?*

## Delegations

Just as a party can transfer rights through an assignment, a party can also transfer duties. Duties are not assigned, however, they are *delegated*. The party del-egating the duties is the **delegator,** and the party to whom the duties are delegated is the **delegatee.** Normally, a delegation of duties does not relieve the delegator of the obligation to perform in the event that the delegatee fails to do so.

No special form is required to create a valid delegation of duties. As long as the delegator expresses an intention to make the delegation, it is effective. The delegator need not even use the word *delegate.* Exhibit 17–2 below illustrates delegation relationships.

**DUTIES THAT CANNOT BE DELEGATED** As a general rule, any duty can be delegated. There are, however, some exceptions to this rule. Delegation is prohibited in the circumstances discussed next.

***When the Duties Are Personal in Nature.*** When special trust has been placed in the obligor or when performance depends on the personal skill or talents of the obligor, contractual duties cannot be delegated. ▶ **Example 17.9** O'Brien, who is impressed with Brodie's ability to perform veterinary surgery, contracts with Brodie to have her perform surgery on O'Brien's prize-winning stallion in July. Brodie later decides that she would rather spend the summer at the beach, so she delegates her duties under the contract to Lopez, who is also a competent veterinary surgeon. The delegation is not effective without O'Brien's consent, no matter how competent Lopez is, because the contract is for *personal* performance.

In contrast, nonpersonal duties may be delegated. Assume that Brodie contracts with O'Brien to pick up and deliver a large horse trailer to O'Brien's property. Brodie delegates this duty to Lopez, who owns a towing business. This delegation is effective because the performance required is of a *routine* and *nonpersonal* nature. ◀

***When Performance by a Third Party Will Vary Materially from That Expected by the Obligee.*** When performance by a third party will vary materially from that expected by the obligee under the contract, contractual duties cannot be delegated. ▶ **Example 17.10** Jared, a wealthy investor, established the company Heaven Sent to provide grants of capital to struggling but potentially successful businesses. Jared contracted with Merilyn, whose judgment Jared trusted, to select the recipients of the grants. Later, Merilyn delegated this duty to Donald. Jared did not trust Donald's ability to select worthy recipients. This delegation is not effective because it materially alters Jared's expectations under the contract with Merilyn. ◀

***When the Contract Prohibits Delegation.*** When the contract expressly prohibits delegation by including an *antidelegation clause,* the duties cannot be delegated. ▶ **Example 17.11** Stark, Ltd., contracts with Belisario, a certified public accountant, to perform its annual audits for five years. The contract prohibits delegation. Belisario cannot delegate the duty to

---

**EXHIBIT 17–2 Delegation Relationships**

In the delegation relationship illustrated here, Brower delegates her *duties* under a contract that she made with Horton to a third party, Kuhn. Brower thus becomes the *delegator* and Kuhn the *delegatee* of the contractual duties. Kuhn now owes performance of the contractual duties to Horton. Note that a delegation of duties normally does not relieve the delegator (Brower) of liability if the delegatee (Kuhn) fails to perform the contractual duties.

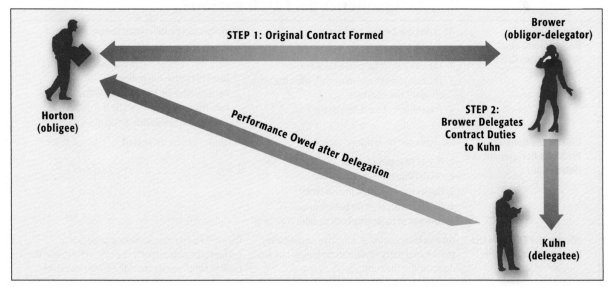

perform the audit to another accountant—not even an accountant at the same firm. ◄

**EFFECT OF A DELEGATION** If a delegation of duties is enforceable, the obligee must accept performance from the delegatee. ▶ **Example 17.12** Bryan has a duty to pick up and deliver metal fabrication equipment to Alicia's property. Bryan delegates his duty to Liam. In this situation, Alicia (the obligee) must accept performance from Liam (the delegatee) because the delegation is effective. ◄ The obligee can legally refuse performance from the delegatee only if the duty is one that cannot be delegated.

As noted, a valid delegation of duties does not relieve the delegator of obligations under the contract. Although there are many exceptions, the general rule today is that the obligee can sue both the delegatee and the delegator. ▶ **Example 17.13** In *Example 17.12,* if Liam (the delegatee) fails to perform, Bryan (the delegator) is still liable to Alicia (the obligee to whom performance is owed). The obligee can also hold the delegatee liable if the delegatee made a promise of performance that will directly benefit the obligee. For instance, if Liam promised Bryan in a contract to deliver the equipment to Alicia's property but fails to do so, Alicia can sue Bryan, Liam, or both. ◄

*Concept Summary 17.1* below outlines the basic principles of the laws governing assignments and delegations.

## Assignment of "All Rights"

When a contract provides for an "assignment of all rights," this wording may create both an assignment of rights and a delegation of duties.[8] Typically, this occurs when general words are used, such as "I assign the contract" or "I assign all my rights under the contract." A court normally will construe such words as implying both an assignment of rights and a delegation of any duties of performance. Thus, the assignor remains liable if the assignee fails to perform the contractual obligations.

### SECTION 2

# THIRD PARTY BENEFICIARIES

Another exception to the doctrine of privity of contract arises when the contract is intended to benefit a third party. When the original parties to the contract agree that the contract performance should be rendered to or directly benefit a third person, the third person becomes an *intended* **third party beneficiary** of the contract. As the **intended beneficiary** of the contract, the third party has legal rights and can sue the promisor directly for breach of the contract.

---

8. *Restatement (Second) of Contracts,* Section 328; UCC 2–210(3), (4).

---

| **CONCEPT SUMMARY 17.1** | | |
|---|---|---|
| **Assignments and Delegations** | | |
| **Which Rights Can Be Assigned, and Which Duties Can Be Delegated?** | All rights can be assigned *unless:*  1. A statute expressly prohibits assignment.  2. The contract is for personal services.  3. The assignment will materially alter the obligor's risk or duties.  4. The contract prohibits assignment. | All duties can be delegated *unless:*  1. Performance depends on the obligor's personal skills or talents or special trust has been placed in the obligor.  2. Performance by a third party will materially vary from that expected by the obligee.  3. The contract prohibits delegation. |
| **What If the Contract Prohibits Assignment or Delegation?** | No rights can be assigned *except:*  1. Rights to receive funds.  2. Ownership rights in real estate.  3. Rights to negotiable instruments.  4. Rights to damages for breach of a sales contract or payments under a sales contract. | No duties can be delegated. |
| **What Is the Effect on the Original Party's Rights?** | On a valid assignment, effective immediately, the original party (assignor) no longer has any rights under the contract. | On a valid delegation, if the delegatee fails to perform, the original party (delegator) is liable to the obligee (who may also hold the delegatee liable). |

## Who Is the Promisor?

Who, though, is the promisor? In a bilateral contract, both parties to the contract make promises that can be enforced, so the court has to determine which party made the promise that benefits the third party. That person is the promisor. In effect, allowing a third party to sue the promisor directly circumvents the "middle person" (the promisee) and thus reduces the burden on the courts. Otherwise, the third party would sue the promisee, who would then sue the promisor.

▶ **Case in Point 17.14** The classic case that gave third party beneficiaries the right to bring a suit directly against a promisor was decided in 1859. The case involved three parties—Holly, Lawrence, and Fox. Holly had borrowed $300 from Lawrence. Shortly thereafter, Holly loaned $300 to Fox, who in return promised Holly that he would pay Holly's debt to Lawrence on the following day. When Lawrence failed to obtain the $300 from Fox, he sued Fox to recover the funds. The court had to decide whether Lawrence could sue Fox directly (rather than suing Holly). The court held that when "a promise [is] made for the benefit of another, he for whose benefit it is made may bring an action for its breach."[9] ◀

## Types of Intended Beneficiaries

The law distinguishes between *intended* beneficiaries and *incidental* beneficiaries. Only intended beneficiaries acquire legal rights in a contract.

**CREDITOR BENEFICIARY** One type of intended beneficiary is a *creditor beneficiary*. Like the plaintiff in the case discussed in *Case in Point 17.14*, a creditor beneficiary benefits from a contract in which one party (the promisor) promises another party (the promisee) to pay a debt that the promisee owes to a third party (the creditor beneficiary).

▶ **Case in Point 17.15** Autumn Allan owned a condominium unit in a Texas complex located directly beneath a condo unit owned by Aslan Koraev. Over the course of two years, Allan's unit suffered eight incidents of water and sewage incursion as a result of plumbing problems and misuse of appliances in Koraev's unit. Allan sued Koraev for breach of contract and won.

Koraev appealed, arguing that he had no contractual duty to Allan. The court found that Allan was an intended third party beneficiary of the contract between Koraev and the condominium owners' association. Because the governing documents stated that each owner had to comply strictly with their provisions,

failure to comply created grounds for an action by the condominium association or an aggrieved (wronged) owner. Here, Allan was clearly an aggrieved owner and could sue Koraev directly for his failure to perform his contract duties to the condominium association.[10] ◀

**DONEE BENEFICIARY** Another type of intended beneficiary is a *donee beneficiary*. When a contract is made for the express purpose of giving a *gift* to a third party, the third party (the donee beneficiary) can sue the promisor directly to enforce the promise.[11]

The most common donee beneficiary contract is a life insurance contract. ▶ **Example 17.16** Ang (the promisee) pays premiums to Standard Life, a life insurance company. Standard Life (the promisor) promises to pay a certain amount upon Ang's death to anyone Ang designates as a beneficiary. The designated beneficiary is a donee beneficiary under the life insurance policy and can enforce the promise made by the insurance company to pay her or him on Ang's death. ◀

Most third party beneficiaries do not fit neatly into either the creditor beneficiary or the donee beneficiary category. Thus, the modern view adopted by the *Restatement (Second) of Contracts* does not draw clear lines between the types of intended beneficiaries. Today, courts frequently distinguish only between *intended beneficiaries* (who can sue to enforce contracts made for their benefit) and *incidental beneficiaries* (who cannot sue, as will be discussed shortly).

## When the Rights of an Intended Beneficiary Vest

An intended third party beneficiary cannot enforce a contract against the original parties until the rights of the third party have *vested*, which means the rights have taken effect and cannot be taken away. Until these rights have vested, the original parties to the contract—the promisor and the promisee—can modify or rescind the contract without the consent of the third party.

When do the rights of third parties vest? The majority of courts hold that the rights vest when any of the following occurs:

1. The third party materially changes his or her position in justifiable reliance on the promise.
2. The third party brings a lawsuit on the promise.
3. The third party demonstrates her or his consent to the promise at the request of the promisor or

---

9. *Lawrence v. Fox,* 20 N.Y. 268 (1859).

10. *Allan v. Nersesova,* 307 S.W.3d 564 (Tx.App.—Dallas 2010).
11. This principle was first enunciated in *Seaver v. Ransom,* 224 N.Y. 233, 120 N.E. 639 (1918).

promisee, such as by sending a letter or e-mail indicating that she or he is aware of and consents to a contract formed for her or his benefit.[12]

If the contract expressly reserves to the contracting parties the right to cancel, rescind, or modify the contract, the rights of the third party beneficiary are subject to any changes that result. If the original contract reserves the right to revoke the promise or change the beneficiary, the vesting of the third party's rights does not terminate that power.[13] In most life insurance contracts, for instance, the policyholder reserves the right to change the designated beneficiary.

## Incidental Beneficiaries

Sometimes, a third person receives a benefit from a contract even though that person's benefit is not the reason the contract was made. Such a person is known as an **incidental beneficiary.** Because the benefit is *unintentional,* an incidental beneficiary cannot sue to enforce the contract.

▶ **Case in Point 17.17**   Spectators at the infamous boxing match in which Mike Tyson was disqualified for biting his opponent's ear sued Tyson and the fight's promoters for a refund on the basis of breach of contract. The spectators claimed that they were third party beneficiaries of the contract between Tyson and the fight's promoters. The court, however, held that the spectators could not sue because they were not in contractual privity with the defendants. Any benefits they received from the contract were incidental to the contract, and according to the court, the spectators got what they paid for: "the right to view whatever event transpired."[14] ◀

## Intended versus Incidental Beneficiaries

In determining whether a third party beneficiary is an intended or an incidental beneficiary, the courts focus on intent, as expressed in the contract language and implied by the surrounding circumstances. Any beneficiary who is not deemed an intended beneficiary is considered incidental. Exhibit 17–3 below illustrates the distinction between intended beneficiaries and incidental beneficiaries.

Although no single test can embrace all possible situations, courts often apply the *reasonable person* test: Would a reasonable person in the position of the beneficiary believe that the promisee intended to confer on the beneficiary the right to enforce the contract? In addition, the presence of one or more of

---

**12.** *Restatement (Second) of Contracts,* Section 311.
**13.** Defenses against third party beneficiaries are given in the *Restatement (Second) of Contracts,* Section 309.

**14.** *Castillo v. Tyson,* 268 A.D.2d 336, 701 N.Y.S.2d 423 (Sup.Ct.App.Div. 2000).

---

**EXHIBIT 17–3   Third Party Beneficiaries**

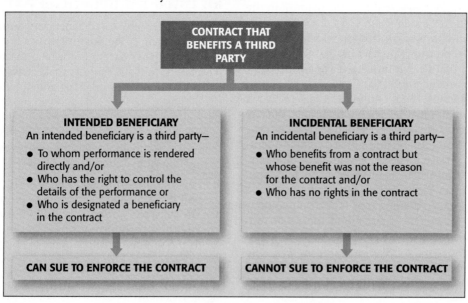

CONTRACT THAT BENEFITS A THIRD PARTY

**INTENDED BENEFICIARY**
An intended beneficiary is a third party—
- To whom performance is rendered directly and/or
- Who has the right to control the details of the performance or
- Who is designated a beneficiary in the contract

**CAN SUE TO ENFORCE THE CONTRACT**

**INCIDENTAL BENEFICIARY**
An incidental beneficiary is a third party—
- Who benefits from a contract but whose benefit was not the reason for the contract and/or
- Who has no rights in the contract

**CANNOT SUE TO ENFORCE THE CONTRACT**

the following factors strongly indicates that the third party is an intended beneficiary to the contract:

1. Performance is rendered directly to the third party.
2. The third party has the right to control the details of performance.

3. The third party is expressly designated as a beneficiary in the contract.

   In the following case, a subcontractor argued that it was a third party beneficiary of a contract between a general contractor and a public entity.

## CASE 17.3

### Lake County Grading Co. v. Village of Antioch

Appellate Court of Illinois, Second District, 2013 IL App (2d) 120474, 368 Ill.App.3d 831, 985 N.E.2d 638 (2013).

**BACKGROUND AND FACTS** Neumann Homes, Inc., entered into a contract to make public improvements for the Village of Antioch, Illinois. Neumann subcontracted the grading work required by the contract to Lake County Grading Company. Lake County completed the work but was not paid in full. When Neumann declared bankruptcy, Lake County was unable to obtain further payment from the general contractor. Lake County then filed a suit in an Illinois state court against the Village to recover. Lake County contended that a state statute and the contract between Neumann and the Village conferred third party beneficiary status on Lake County, thus permitting it to sue the Village for breach for not requiring Neumann to post a payment bond in its benefit. (A *payment bond* guarantees that a contractor will pay what is owed for completion of a project.) The court agreed and issued a summary judgment in Lake County's favor. The Village appealed.

**DECISION AND RATIONALE** A state intermediate appellate court affirmed the summary judgment in Lake County's favor. The reviewing court concluded that Lake County was an intended third party beneficiary of the contract between Neumann and the Village. As a third party beneficiary, Lake County had the right to bring an action for breach of the contract. A person's status as a third-party beneficiary depends on the contract language. "The contract language must show that the contract was made for the direct, not merely incidental, benefit of the third party. Such an intention must be shown by an expressed provision in the contract identifying the third-party beneficiary by name or by description of a class to which the third party belongs."

Illinois law requires that as part of its agreement with a general contractor, any public entity "shall require every contractor for the work to furnish, supply and deliver a bond, and the bond shall be conditioned for the completion of the contract, for the payment of material used in the work, and for all labor performed in the work, including work completed by subcontractors." The Village had agreed that Neuman was to construct the public improvements using subcontractors selected by Neuman and at Neuman's sole discretion. Therefore, the Village breached its contract when it failed to require Neuman to furnish a payment bond for the benefit of subcontractors.

**THE LEGAL ENVIRONMENT DIMENSION** *What do courts focus on when determining whether a third party beneficiary is an intended or an incidental beneficiary?*

**THE ETHICAL DIMENSION** *Did Lake County obtain the remedy that it sought in this case? Explain.*

## Reviewing: Third Party Rights

Myrtle Jackson owns several commercial buildings that she leases to businesses, one of which is a restaurant. The lease states that tenants are responsible for securing all necessary insurance policies but the landlord is obligated to keep the buildings in good repair. The owner of the restaurant, Joe McCall, tells

*Continued*

his restaurant manager to purchase insurance, but the manager never does so. Jackson tells her son-in-law, Rob Dunn, to perform any necessary maintenance for the buildings. Dunn knows that the ceiling in the restaurant needs repair but fails to do anything about it.

One day a customer, Ian Faught, is dining in the restaurant when a chunk of the ceiling falls on his head and fractures his skull. Faught files suit against the restaurant and discovers that there is no insurance policy in effect. Faught then files a suit against Jackson. He argues that he is an intended third party beneficiary of the lease provision requiring the restaurant to carry insurance and thus can sue Jackson for failing to enforce that provision. Using the information presented in the chapter, answer the following questions.

1. Can Jackson delegate her duty to maintain the buildings to Dunn? Why or why not?
2. Who can be held liable for Dunn's failure to fix the ceiling, Jackson or Dunn? Why?
3. Was Faught an intended third party beneficiary of the lease between Jackson and McCall? Why or why not?
4. Suppose that Jackson tells Dan Stryker, a local builder to whom she owes $50,000, that he can collect the rents from the buildings' tenants until the debt is satisfied. Is this a valid assignment? Why or why not?

**DEBATE THIS . . .** *As a matter of public policy, personal-injury tort claims cannot be assigned. This public policy is wrong and should be changed.*

## Terms and Concepts

alienation 293
assignee 290
assignment 290
assignor 290
delegatee 294

delegation 290
delegator 294
incidental beneficiary 298
intended beneficiary 296
obligee 290

obligor 290
privity of contract 290
third party beneficiary 296

## Issue Spotters

1. Brian owes Jeff $100. Ed tells Brian to give him the $100 and he will pay Jeff. Brian gives Ed the $100. Ed never pays Jeff. Can Jeff successfully sue Ed for the $100? Why or why not? **(See page 296.)**
2. Eagle Company contracts to build a house for Frank. The contract states that "any assignment of this contract renders the contract void." After Eagle builds the house, but before Frank pays, Eagle assigns its right to payment to Good Credit Company. Can Good Credit enforce the contract against Frank? Why or why not? **(See page 293.)**

• Check your answers to the Issue Spotters against the answers provided in Appendix E at the end of this text.

## Business Scenarios

**17–1. Third Party Beneficiary.** Alexander has been accepted as a freshman at a college two hundred miles from his home for the fall semester. Alexander's wealthy uncle, Michael, decides to give Alexander a car for Christmas. In November, Michael makes a contract with Jackson Auto Sales to purchase a new car for $18,000 to be delivered to Alexander just before the Christmas holidays, in mid-December. The title to the car is to be in Alexander's name. Michael pays the full purchase price, calls Alexander and tells him about the gift, and takes off for a six-month vacation in Europe. Is Alexander an intended third party beneficiary of the contract between Michael and Jackson Auto Sales? Suppose that Jackson Auto Sales never delivers the car to Alexander. Does Alexander have the right to sue Jackson Auto Sales for breaching its contract with Michael? Explain. **(See page 296.)**

**17–2. Assignment.** Five years ago, Hensley purchased a house. At that time, being unable to pay the full purchase price, she borrowed funds from Thrift Savings and Loan, which in turn took a mortgage at 6.5 percent interest on the house. The mortgage contract did not prohibit the assignment of the mortgage. Then Hensley secured a new job in another city and sold the house to Sylvia. The purchase price included payment to Hensley of the value of her equity and the assumption of the mortgage debt still owed to Thrift. At the time the contract between Hensley and Sylvia was made, Thrift did not know about or consent to the sale. On the basis of these facts, if Sylvia defaults in making the mortgage payments to Thrift, what are Thrift's rights? Discuss. **(See page 290.)**

**17–3. Assignment.** Marsala, a college student, signs a one-year lease agreement that runs from September 1 to August 31. The lease agreement specifies that the lease cannot be assigned without the landlord's consent. In late May, Marsala decides not to go to summer school and assigns the balance of the lease (three months) to a close friend, Fred. The landlord objects to the assignment and denies Fred access to the apartment. Marsala claims that Fred is financially sound and should be allowed the full rights and privileges of an assignee. Discuss fully who is correct, the landlord or Marsala. **(See page 290.)**

**17–4. Delegation.** Inez has a specific set of plans to build a sailboat. The plans are detailed, and any boatbuilder can construct the boat. Inez secures bids, and the low bid is made by the Whale of a Boat Corp. Inez contracts with Whale to build the boat for $4,000. Whale then receives unexpected business from elsewhere. To meet the delivery date in the contract with Inez, Whale delegates its obligation to build the boat, without Inez's consent, to Quick Brothers, a reputable boatbuilder. When the boat is ready for delivery, Inez learns of the delegation and refuses to accept delivery, even though the boat is built to her specifications. Discuss fully whether Inez is obligated to accept and pay for the boat. Would your answer be any different if Inez had not had a specific set of plans but had instead contracted with Whale to design and build a sailboat for $4,000? Explain. **(See page 294.)**

## Business Case Problems

**17–5. Spotlight on Drug Testing—Third Party Beneficiary.** Bath

Iron Works (BIW) offered a job to Thomas Devine, contingent on Devine's passing a drug test. The testing was conducted by NorDx, a subcontractor of Roche Biomedical Laboratories. When NorDx found that Devine's urinalysis showed the presence of opiates, a result confirmed by Roche, BIW refused to offer Devine permanent employment. Devine sued Roche, claiming that the ingestion of poppy seeds can yield a positive result and that he tested positive only because of his daily consumption of poppy seed muffins. Devine argued that he was a third party beneficiary of the contract between his prospective employer (BIW) and NorDx (Roche). Is Devine an intended third party beneficiary of the BIW–NorDx contract? Why or why not? Do drug-testing labs have a duty to the persons being tested to exercise reasonable care in conducting the tests? Explain. [*Devine v. Roche Biomedical Laboratories*, 659 A.2d 868 (Me. 1995)] **(See page 296.)**

**17–6. Assignment.** Senna Hills, Ltd., granted Southern Union Co. the right to distribute propane in a residential subdivision developed by Senna in exchange for a fee. Under their agreement, Senna's "right to receive a Fee shall continue for so long as the Propane System is owned by Southern Union." The agreement also allowed Southern Union to assign the distribution right. Later, Sonterra Energy Corp. bought the distribution system and was assigned the distribution right, but did not pay the fee to Senna. Did Sonterra breach the propane service agreement? Why or why not? [*Senna Hills, Ltd. v. Sonterra Energy Corp.*, __ S.W.3d __ (Tex.App.—Austin 2010)] **(See page 290.)**

**17–7. BUSINESS CASE PROBLEM WITH SAMPLE ANSWER: Duties That Cannot Be Delegated.**

*Bruce Albea Contracting, Inc., was the general contractor on a state highway project. Albea subcontracted the asphalt work to APAC-Southeast, Inc. Their contract prohibited any delegation without Albea's consent. In midproject, APAC delegated its duties to Matthews Contracting Co. Although Albea allowed Matthews to finish the work, Albea did not pay APAC for its work on the project. Albea argued that APAC had violated the antidelegation clause, rendering their contact void. Is Albea correct? Explain.* [Western Surety Co. v. APAC-Southeast, Inc., *302 Ga.App. 654, 691 S.E.2d 234 (2010)*] **(See page 295.)**

- **For a sample answer to Problem 17–7, go to Appendix F at the end of this text.**

**17–8. Notice of Assignment.** Arnold Kazery was the owner of a hotel leased to George Wilkinson. The lease included renewal options of ten years each. When Arnold transferred his interest in the property to his son, Sam, no one notified Wilkinson. For the next twenty years, Wilkinson paid the rent to Arnold and renewed the lease by notice to Arnold. When Wilkinson wrote to Arnold that he was exercising another option to renew, Sam filed a suit against him, claiming that the lease was void. Did Wilkinson give proper notice to renew? Discuss. [*Kazery v. Wilkinson*, 52 So.3d 1270 (Miss.App. 2011)] **(See page 293.)**

**17–9. Third Party Beneficiary.** David and Sandra Dess contracted with Sirva Relocation, LLC, to assist in selling their home. In their contract, the Desses agreed to disclose all information about the property on which Sirva "and other prospective buyers may rely in deciding whether and on what terms to purchase the Property." The Kincaids contracted with Sirva to buy the house. After the closing, they discovered dampness in the walls, defective and rotten windows, mold, and other undisclosed problems. Can the Kincaids bring an action against the Desses for breach of their contract with Sirva? Why or why not? [*Kincaid v. Dess*, 298 P.3d 358 (2013)] **(See page 296.)**

**17–10. A QUESTION OF ETHICS: Assignment and Delegation.**

*Premier Building & Development, Inc., entered a listing agreement giving Sunset Gold Realty, LLC, the exclusive right to find a tenant for some commercial property. The terms of the listing agreement stated that it was binding on both parties and "their . . . assigns." Premier Building did not own the property at the time, but had the option to purchase it. To secure financing for the project, Premier Building established a new company called Cobblestone Associates. Premier Building then bought* the property and conveyed it to Cobblestone the same day. Meanwhile, Sunset Gold found a tenant for the property, and Cobblestone became the landlord. Cobblestone acknowledged its obligation to pay Sunset Gold for finding a tenant, but it later refused to pay Sunset Gold's commission. Sunset Gold then sued Premier Building and Cobblestone for breach of the listing agreement. [*Sunset Gold Realty, LLC v. Premier Building & Development, Inc.*, 36 A.3d 243 (Conn.App.Ct. 2012)] **(See page 290.)**

(a) Is Premier Building relieved of its contractual duties if it assigned the contract to Cobblestone? Why or why not?

(b) Given that Sunset Gold performed its obligations under the listing agreement, did Cobblestone behave unethically in refusing to pay Sunset Gold's commission? Why or why not?

## Legal Reasoning Group Activity

**17–11. Assignment.** The Smiths buy a house. They borrow 80 percent of the purchase price from the local ABC Savings and Loan. Before they make their first payment, ABC transfers the right to receive mortgage payments to Citibank. **(See page 290.)**

(a) The first group will outline what would happen if the Smiths continue to make all their payments to ABC Savings and Loan because ABC never notified them of the assignment.

(b) The second group will describe what would happen if the Smiths were notified by ABC of the assignment, but continued to make payments to ABC.

(c) A third group will determine what would happen if the Smiths fail to make any payments on the loan. Which financial institution would have the right to repossess their house?

## CHAPTER 18

# PERFORMANCE AND DISCHARGE IN TRADITIONAL AND E-CONTRACTS

Just as rules are necessary to determine when a legally enforceable contract exists, so also are they required to determine when one of the parties can justifiably say, "I have fully performed, so I am now discharged from my obligations under this contract." The legal environment of business requires the identification of some point at which the parties can reasonably know that their duties have ended.

The most common way to **discharge,** or terminate, one's contractual duties is by the **performance** of those duties. For example, a buyer and seller enter into an agreement via e-mail for the sale of a 2014 Lexus for $42,000. This contract will be discharged by performance when the buyer pays $42,000 to the seller and the seller transfers possession of the Lexus to the buyer.

The duty to perform under any contract (including e-contracts) may be *conditioned* on the occurrence or nonoccurrence of a certain event, or the duty may be *absolute*. In the first part of this chapter, we look at conditions of performance and the degree of performance required. We then examine some other ways in which a contract can be discharged, including discharge by agreement of the parties and discharge by operation of law.

---

## SECTION 1
## CONDITIONS

In most contracts, promises of performance are not expressly conditioned or qualified. Instead, they are *absolute promises.* They must be performed, or the parties promising the acts will be in breach of contract.
▶ **Example 18.1** Paloma Enterprises contracts to sell a truckload of organic produce to Tran for $10,000. The parties' promises are unconditional: Paloma will deliver the produce to Tran, and Tran will pay $10,000 to Paloma. The payment does not have to be made if the produce is not delivered. ◀

In some situations, however, performance is contingent on the occurrence or nonoccurrence of a certain event. A **condition** is a qualification in a contract based on a possible future event. The occurrence or nonoccurrence of the event will trigger the performance of a legal obligation or terminate an existing obligation under a contract.[1] If the condi-

tion is not satisfied, the obligations of the parties are discharged.

Three types of conditions can be present in contracts: conditions *precedent*, conditions *subsequent,* and *concurrent* conditions. Conditions are also classified as *express* or *implied.*

### Conditions Precedent

A condition that must be fulfilled before a party's performance can be required is called a **condition precedent.** The condition precedes the absolute duty to perform. Life insurance contracts frequently specify that certain conditions, such as passing a physical examination, must be met before the insurance company will be obligated to perform under the contract.

In addition, many contracts are conditioned on an independent appraisal of value. ▶ **Example 18.2** Restoration Motors offers to buy Charlie's 1960 Cadillac limousine only if an expert appraiser estimates that it can be restored for less than a certain price. Thus, the parties' obligations are conditioned on the outcome of the appraisal. If the condition is not satisfied—that is, if the appraiser

---

1. The *Restatement (Second) of Contracts,* Section 224, defines a condition as "an event, not certain to occur, which must occur, unless its nonoccurrence is excused, before performance under a contract becomes due."

deems the cost to be above that price—their obligations are discharged. ◄

Sometimes, a lease of real property includes an option to buy that property. The lease in the following case required timely rent payments as a condition of exercising such an option, but the lessee (the tenant) often failed to make the payments on time. The court had to decide whether the lessee could still exercise the option even though it had not strictly complied with the condition precedent.

---

## CASE 18.1

### Pack 2000, Inc. v. Cushman

Appellate Court of Connecticut, 126 Conn.App. 339, 11 A.3d 181 (2011).

**COMPANY PROFILE** The first Midas muffler repair shop opened in Macon, Georgia, in 1956. Within ten years, Midas had added shock absorber services and expanded beyond the United States into the European market. By 1986, Midas had added brake services and opened shops around the world. Today, with more than 1,700 locations, Midas is a leader in muffler and exhaust services. It also offers comprehensive auto programs for tires, maintenance, and commercial fleet services. Recently, the company has renewed its focus on its franchise and real estate businesses.

**BACKGROUND AND FACTS** Eugene Cushman agreed to transfer two Midas muffler shops to Pack 2000, Inc. The deal included leases for the real estate on which the shops were located. Each lease provided Pack with an option to buy the leased real estate subject to certain conditions. Pack was to pay rent by the first day of each month, make payments on the notes by the eighth day of each month, and pay utilities and other accounts on time. Pack, however, was often late in making these payments. The utility and phone companies threatened to cut off services, an insurance company canceled Pack's liability coverage, and other delinquencies prompted collection calls and letters. When Pack sought to exercise the options to buy the real estate, Cushman responded that Pack had not complied with the conditions. Pack filed a suit in a Connecticut state court against Cushman, seeking specific performance of the options. The court rendered a judgment in Pack's favor. Cushman appealed.

**DECISION AND RATIONALE** A state intermediate appellate court reversed the lower court's judgment and remanded the case for the entry of a judgment for Cushman. A party retains its right to exercise an option to buy real estate only by complying strictly with any conditions precedent to its exercise of the option.

The leases provided Pack with the option to buy the leased real estate. But to take advantage of the options, Pack had to comply with the condition precedent of making periodic payments to Cushman and to certain third parties by specific dates. Pack was often late in making these payments and thus did not strictly comply with the condition. The court reasoned that because of this failure of strict compliance, Pack lost the right to exercise the options to buy the real estate.

**WHAT IF THE FACTS WERE DIFFERENT?** *Suppose that Pack had late payments. Would the result in this case have been different? Explain.*

**THE ECONOMIC DIMENSION** *Why are rent and other payments due under a lease subject to strict time deadlines?*

---

## Conditions Subsequent

When a condition operates to terminate a party's absolute promise to perform, it is called a **condition subsequent.** The condition follows, or is subsequent to, the time that the absolute duty to perform arose. If the condition occurs, the party's duty to perform is discharged. ▶ **Example 18.3** A law firm hires Julie Mendez, a recent law school graduate. Their contract provides that the firm's obligation to continue employing Mendez is discharged if Mendez fails to pass the bar exam by her second attempt. This is a condition subsequent because a failure to pass the exam—and thus to obtain a license to practice law—would discharge a duty (employment) that has already arisen. ◄

Generally, conditions precedent are common, and conditions subsequent are rare. The *Restatement (Second) of Contracts* does not use the terms *condition subsequent* and *condition precedent* but refers to both simply as conditions.[2]

## Concurrent Conditions

When each party's performance is conditioned on the other party's performance or tender of performance (offer to perform), **concurrent conditions** are present. These conditions exist only when the contract expressly or impliedly calls for the parties to perform their respective duties *simultaneously*.

▶ **Example 18.4** If Janet Feibush promises to pay for goods when Hewlett-Packard delivers them, the parties' promises to perform are mutually dependent. Feibush's duty to pay for the goods does not become absolute until Hewlett-Packard either delivers or tenders the goods. Likewise, Hewlett-Packard's duty to deliver the goods does not become absolute until Feibush tenders or actually makes payment. Therefore, neither can recover from the other for breach without first tendering performance. ◀

## Express and Implied Conditions

Conditions can also be classified as express or implied in fact. *Express conditions* are provided for by the parties' agreement. Although no particular words are necessary, express conditions are normally prefaced by the words *if, provided, after,* or *when.*

▶ **Case in Point 18.5** Alejandro Alvarado's automobile insurance policy stated that, if he was involved in an accident, he must cooperate with the insurance company in the defense of any claim or lawsuit. Alvarado was involved in an accident and was sued for negligence. He notified the insurance company, but then failed to cooperate in his defense and did not appear in court for the trial. Although Alvarado was found to have been negligent, the insurance company was not liable for the damages awarded. The court found that the cooperation clause was a condition precedent to coverage under the policy. Therefore, because Alvarado did not cooperate with the insurer, the accident was not covered by the policy.[3] ◀

*Implied conditions* are understood to be part of the agreement, but they are not found in the express language of the agreement. Courts may imply conditions from the purpose of the contract or from the intent of the parties. Conditions are often implied when they are necessarily inherent in the actual performance of the contract.

## SECTION 2
# DISCHARGE BY PERFORMANCE

The great majority of contracts are discharged by performance. The contract comes to an end when both parties fulfill their respective duties by performing the acts they have promised.

Performance can also be accomplished by *tender.* **Tender** is an unconditional offer to perform by a person who is ready, willing, and able to do so. Therefore, a seller who places goods at the disposal of a buyer has tendered delivery and can demand payment. A buyer who offers to pay for goods has tendered payment and can demand delivery of the goods.

Once performance has been tendered, the party making the tender has done everything possible to carry out the terms of the contract. If the other party then refuses to perform, the party making the tender can sue for breach of contract. There are two basic types of performance—*complete performance* and *substantial performance*.

## Complete Performance

When a party performs exactly as agreed, there is no question as to whether the contract has been performed. When a party's performance is perfect, it is said to be complete. Normally, conditions expressly stated in a contract must fully occur in all respects for complete performance (strict performance) of the contract to take place. Any deviation breaches the contract and discharges the other party's obligations to perform.

Most construction contracts, for instance, require the builder to meet certain specifications. If the specifications are conditions, complete performance is required to avoid material breach (*material breach* will be discussed shortly). If the conditions are met, the other party to the contract must then fulfill her or his obligation to pay the builder.

If the parties to the contract did not expressly make the specifications a condition, however, and the builder fails to meet the specifications, performance is not complete. What effect does such a failure have on

---

2. *Restatement (Second) of Contracts*, Section 224.
3. *Progressive County Mutual Insurance Co. v. Trevino*, 202 S.W.3d 811 (Tex. App.—San Antonio 2006).

the other party's obligation to pay? The answer is part of the doctrine of *substantial performance*.

## Substantial Performance

A party who in good faith performs substantially all of the terms of a contract can enforce the contract against the other party under the doctrine of substantial performance. The basic requirements for performance to qualify as substantial performance are as follows:

1. The party must have performed in good faith. Intentional failure to comply with the contract terms is a breach of the contract.
2. The performance must not vary greatly from the performance promised in the contract. An omission, variance, or defect in performance is considered minor if it can easily be remedied by compensation (monetary damages).
3. The performance must create substantially the same benefits as those promised in the contract.

Courts decide whether the performance was substantial on a case-by-case basis, examining all of the facts of the particular situation. ▶ **Case in Point 18.6** Wisconsin Electric Power Company (WEPCO) contracted with Union Pacific Railroad to transport coal to WEPCO from mines in Colorado. The contract required WEPCO to notify Union Pacific monthly of how many tons of coal (below a specified maximum) it wanted to have shipped the next month. Union Pacific was to make "good faith reasonable efforts" to meet the schedule.

The contract also required WEPCO to supply the railcars. When WEPCO did not supply the railcars, Union Pacific used its own railcars and delivered 84 percent of the requested coal. In this situation, a federal court held that the delivery of 84 percent of the contracted amount constituted substantial performance.[4] ◀

**EFFECT ON DUTY TO PERFORM** If performance is substantial, the other party's duty to perform remains absolute (except that the party can sue for damages due to the minor deviations). In other words, the parties must continue performing under the contract (for instance, making payment to the party who substantially performed). If performance is not substantial, there is a *material breach* (to be discussed shortly), and the non-breaching party is excused from further performance.

**MEASURE OF DAMAGES** Because substantial performance is not perfect, the other party is entitled to damages to compensate for the failure to comply with the contract. The measure of the damages is the cost to bring the object of the contract into compliance with its terms, if that cost is reasonable under the circumstances.

If the cost is unreasonable, the measure of damages is the difference in value between the performance that was rendered and the performance that would have been rendered if the contract had been performed completely.

The following case is a classic illustration that there is no exact formula for deciding when a contract has been substantially performed.

---

4. *Wisconsin Electric Power Co. v. Union Pacific Railroad Co.*, 557 F.3d 504 (7th Cir. 2009).

## CLASSIC CASE 18.2

### Jacob & Youngs v. Kent
Court of Appeals of New York, 230 N.Y. 239, 129 N.E. 889 (1921).

**BACKGROUND AND FACTS** The plaintiff, Jacob & Youngs, Inc., was a builder that had contracted with George Kent to construct a country residence for him. A specification in the building contract required that "all wrought-iron pipe must be well galvanized, lap welded pipe of the grade known as 'standard pipe' of Reading manufacture." Jacob & Youngs installed substantially similar pipe that was not of Reading manufacture. When Kent became aware of the difference, he ordered the builder to remove all of the plumbing and replace it with the Reading type. To do so would have required removing finished walls that encased the plumbing—an expensive and difficult task. The builder explained that the plumbing was of the same quality, appearance, value, and cost as Reading pipe. When Kent refused to pay the $3,483.46 still owed for the work, Jacob & Youngs sued to compel payment. The trial court ruled in favor of Kent. The plaintiff appealed, and the appellate court reversed the trial court's decision. Kent then appealed to the Court of Appeals of New York, the state's highest court.

**CASE 18.2 CONTINUED**  **DECISION AND RATIONALE**  The highest state court in New York held that the plaintiff had substantially performed the contract and affirmed the state intermediate appellate court's decision. The reviewing court explained, "The courts never say that one who makes a contract fills the measure of his duty by less than full performance. They do say, however, that an omission, both trivial and innocent, will sometimes be atoned for by allowance of the resulting damage, and will not always be the breach of a condition. . . . The question is one of degree . . . . We must weigh the purpose to be served, the desire to be gratified, the excuse for deviation from the letter, [and] the cruelty of enforced adherence." As for adjusting the contract price, "the measure of the allowance is not the cost of replacement, . . . but the difference in value" (the cost to complete). The builder was entitled to the amount owed to it, less the difference in value between the specified and substituted pipe (which the court stated would be "nominal or nothing").

**IMPACT OF THIS CASE ON TODAY'S LAW**  *At the time of the* Jacob & Youngs *case, some courts did not apply the doctrine of substantial performance to disputes involving breaches of contract. This landmark decision contributed to a developing trend toward equity and fairness in those circumstances. Today, an unintentional and trivial deviation from the terms of a contract will not prevent its enforcement but will permit an adjustment in the value of its performance.*

**THE LEGAL ENVIRONMENT DIMENSION**  *The New York Court of Appeals found that Jacob & Youngs had substantially performed the contract. To what, if any, remedy was Kent entitled?*

## Performance to the Satisfaction of Another

Contracts often state that completed work must personally satisfy one of the parties or a third person. The question then is whether this satisfaction becomes a condition precedent, requiring actual personal satisfaction or approval for discharge, or whether the performance need only satisfy a *reasonable person* (substantial performance).

**WHEN THE CONTRACT IS PERSONAL**  When the subject matter of the contract is *personal*, the obligation is conditional, and performance must actually satisfy the party specified in the contract. For instance, contracts for portraits, works of art, and tailoring are considered personal because they involve matters of personal taste. Therefore, only the personal satisfaction of the party fulfills the condition—unless a court finds that the party is expressing dissatisfaction simply to avoid payment or otherwise is not acting in good faith.

**REASONABLE PERSON STANDARD**  Most other contracts need to be performed only to the satisfaction of a reasonable person unless they *expressly state otherwise*. When the subject matter of the contract is mechanical, courts are more likely to find that the performing party has performed satisfactorily if a reasonable person would be satisfied with what was done. ▶ **Example 18.7**  Mason signs a contract with Jen to mount a new heat pump on a concrete platform to her satisfaction. Such a contract normally need only be performed to the satisfaction of a reasonable person. ◀

When contracts require performance to the satisfaction of a third party with superior knowledge or training in the subject matter—such as a supervising engineer—the courts are divided. A majority of courts require the work to be satisfactory to a reasonable person, but some courts require the personal satisfaction of the third party designated in the contract. (Again, the personal judgment must be made honestly, or the condition will be excused.)

## Material Breach of Contract

A **breach of contract** is the nonperformance of a contractual duty. The breach is *material* when performance is not at least substantial.[5] As mentioned earlier, when there is a material breach, the nonbreaching party is excused from the performance of contractual duties. That party can also sue the breaching party for damages resulting from the breach.

▶ **Example 18.8**  When country singer Garth Brooks's mother died, he donated $500,000 to a hospital in his hometown to build a new women's health center named after his mother. After several years passed and the health center was not built, Brooks demanded a refund. The hospital refused, claiming that while it had promised to honor his mother in some way, it did not promise to build a women's health center.

---

**5.** *Restatement (Second) of Contracts,* Section 241.

Brooks sued for breach of contract. A jury determined that the hospital's failure to build a women's health center and name it after Brooks's mother was a material breach of the contract. The jury awarded Brooks $500,000 in actual damages for the contract breach—plus another $500,000 because it found the hospital guilty of reckless disregard and intentionally acting with malice toward others. ◄

**MATERIAL VERSUS MINOR BREACH** If the breach is *minor* (not material), the nonbreaching party's duty

to perform can sometimes be suspended until the breach has been remedied, but the duty to perform is not entirely excused. Once the minor breach has been cured, the nonbreaching party must resume performance of the contractual obligations.

Both parties in the following case were arguably in breach of their contract. Which party's breach was material?

---

## CASE 18.3

### Kohel v. Bergen Auto Enterprises, L.L.C.

Superior Court of New Jersey, Appellate Division, 2013 WL 439970 (2013).

**BACKGROUND AND FACTS**  Marc and Bree Kohel agreed to buy a used 2009 Mazda from Bergen Auto Enterprises, LLC, doing business as Wayne Mazda, Inc. The Kohels were credited $7,000 as a trade-in for their 2005 Nissan Altima. They still owed about $8,000 on the Nissan, which Wayne Mazda agreed to remit. The Kohels took possession of the Mazda with temporary plates.

Sometime later, after discovering that the Nissan was missing a vehicle identification number (VIN) tag, the dealer refused to make the payment for the Nissan and also refused to give the Kohels permanent plates for the Mazda. The Kohels applied and paid for a replacement VIN tag for the Nissan, but Wayne Mazda refused to take their calls on the matter and continued to refuse to supply permanent plates for the Mazda. The Kohels filed a complaint against the dealer in a New Jersey state court, alleging breach of contract. The court ruled in the plaintiffs' favor, and Wayne Mazda appealed.

**DECISION AND RATIONALE**  A state intermediate appellate court affirmed the judgment in Kohels' favor. While both parties were arguably in breach of their contract, "there is a material distinction in plaintiff's conduct," which was unintentional, "and defendant's refusal to release the permanent plates for which the plaintiffs had paid." After all, the Kohels were not aware that their trade-in Nissan lacked a vehicle identification number (VIN) tag. Moreover, "defendant's representatives examined the car twice before accepting it in trade and did not notice the missing VIN tag until they took the car to an auction where they tried to sell it." The reviewing court found that Wayne Mazda acted only to maintain "leverage." The Kohels applied and paid for a replacement VIN tag. The owner of Wayne Mazda would not take the Kohels calls to discuss the matter. Wayne Mazda acted in an unreasonable manner and the reviewing court could not accept Wayne Mazda's argument that the Kohels' failure to obtain the replacement VIN tag amounted to a repudiation of a contract.

**THE ETHICAL DIMENSION**  *The court suggested that Wayne Mazda might have handled this situation more "adroitly." What could the dealer have done to avoid this dispute?*

**THE LEGAL ENVIRONMENT DIMENSION**  *What is a material breach of contract? When a material breach occurs, what are the nonbreaching party's options?*

---

**DISCHARGES NONBREACHING PARTY FROM FURTHER PERFORMANCE** Any breach entitles the nonbreaching party to sue for damages, but only a material breach discharges the nonbreaching party from the contract. The policy underlying these rules allows a

contract to go forward when only minor problems occur but allows it to be terminated if major difficulties arise.

▶ **Case in Point 18.9**  Su Yong Kim sold an apartment building with substandard plumbing that violated the city's housing code. The contract stated that Kim would have the plumbing fixed (brought up to code) within eight months. A year later, Kim still had not made the necessary repairs, so the buyers stopped making the payments due under the contract. A court found that Kim's failure to make the required repairs was a material breach because it defeated the purpose of the contract—to lease the building to tenants. Because Kim's breach was material, the buyers were no longer obligated to continue making payments under the contract.[6] ◄

## Anticipatory Repudiation

Before either party to a contract has a duty to perform, one of the parties may refuse to carry out his or her contractual obligations. This is called **anticipatory repudiation**[7] of the contract.

**REPUDIATION IS A MATERIAL BREACH** When an anticipatory repudiation occurs, it is treated as a material breach of the contract, and the nonbreaching party is permitted to bring an action for damages immediately. The nonbreaching party can file suit even though the scheduled time for performance under the contract may still be in the future. Until the nonbreaching party treats an early repudiation as a breach, however, the repudiating party can retract her or his anticipatory repudiation by proper notice and restore the parties to their original obligations.[8]

An anticipatory repudiation is treated as a present, material breach for two reasons. First, the nonbreaching party should not be required to remain ready and willing to perform when the other party has already repudiated the contract. Second, the nonbreaching party should have the opportunity to seek a similar contract elsewhere and may have a duty to do so to minimize his or her loss.[9]

**ANTICIPATORY REPUDIATION AND MARKET PRICES** Quite often, anticipatory repudiation occurs when performance of the contract would be extremely unfavorable to one of the parties because of a sharp fluctuation in market prices.

▶ **Example 18.10** Mobile X enters into an e-contract to manufacture and sell 100,000 cell phones to Best Com, a global telecommunications company. Delivery is to be made two months from the date of the contract. One month later, three inventory suppliers raise their prices to Mobile X. Because of these higher prices, Mobile X stands to lose $500,000 if it sells the cell phones to Best Com at the contract price. Mobile X immediately sends an e-mail to Best Com, stating that it cannot deliver the 100,000 cell phones at the contract price. Even though you may sympathize with Mobile X, its e-mail is an anticipatory repudiation of the contract. Best Com can treat the repudiation as a material breach and immediately pursue remedies, even though the contract delivery date is still a month away. ◄

## Time for Performance

If no time for performance is stated in the contract, a *reasonable time* is implied.[10] If a specific time is stated, the parties must usually perform by that time. Unless time is expressly stated to be vital, though, a delay in performance will not destroy the performing party's right to payment.[11]

When time is expressly stated to be "of the essence" or vital, the parties normally must perform within the stated time period because the time element becomes a condition. Even when the contract states that time is of the essence, a court may find that a party who fails to complain about the other party's delay has waived the breach of the time provision.

### SECTION 3
# DISCHARGE BY AGREEMENT

Any contract can be discharged by agreement of the parties. The agreement can be contained in the original contract, or the parties can form a new contract for the express purpose of discharging the original contract.

## Discharge by Mutual Rescission

As mentioned in previous chapters, *rescission* is the process by which a contract is canceled or terminated

---

**6.** *Kim v. Park*, 192 Or.App. 365, 86 P.3d 63 (2004).

**7.** *Restatement (Second) of Contracts,* Section 253; Section 2–610 of the Uniform Commercial Code (UCC).

**8.** See UCC 2–611.

**9.** The doctrine of anticipatory repudiation first arose in the landmark case of *Hochster v. De La Tour*, 2 Ellis and Blackburn Reports 678 (1853). An English court recognized the delay and expense inherent in a rule requiring a nonbreaching party to wait until the time of performance before suing on an anticipatory repudiation.

**10.** See UCC 2–204.

**11.** See, for example, *Manganaro Corp. v. Hitt Contracting, Inc.,* 193 F.Supp.2d 88 (D.D.C. 2002).

and the parties are returned to the positions they occupied prior to forming it. For **mutual rescission** to take place, the parties must make another agreement that also satisfies the legal requirements for a contract. There must be an *offer,* an *acceptance,* and *consideration.* Ordinarily, if the parties agree to rescind the original contract, their promises not to perform the acts stipulated in the original contract will be legal consideration for the second contract (the rescission).

Agreements to rescind most executory contracts (in which neither party has performed) are enforceable, even if the agreement is made orally and even if the original agreement was in writing. Under the Uniform Commercial Code (UCC), however, agreements to rescind a sales contract must be in writing (or contained in an electronic record) when the contract requires a written rescission.[12] Agreements to rescind contracts involving transfers of realty also must be evidenced by a writing or record.

When one party has fully performed, an agreement to cancel the original contract normally will *not* be enforceable unless there is additional consideration. Because the performing party has received no consideration for the promise to call off the original bargain, additional consideration is necessary to support a rescission contract.

## Discharge by Novation

A contractual obligation may also be discharged through novation. A **novation** occurs when both of the parties to a contract agree to substitute a third party for one of the original parties. The requirements of a novation are as follows:

1. A previous valid obligation.
2. An agreement by all parties to a new contract.
3. The extinguishing of the old obligation (discharge of the prior party).
4. A new contract that is valid.

▶ **Example 18.11** Union Corporation contracts to sell its pharmaceutical division to British Pharmaceuticals, Ltd. Before the transfer is completed, Union, British Pharmaceuticals, and a third company, Otis Chemicals, execute a new agreement to transfer all of British Pharmaceuticals' rights and duties in the transaction to Otis Chemicals. As long as the new contract is supported by consideration, the novation will discharge the original contract (between Union and British Pharmaceuticals) and replace it with the new contract (between Union and Otis Chemicals). ◀

A novation expressly or impliedly revokes and discharges a prior contract. The parties involved may expressly state in the new contract that the old contract is now discharged. If the parties do not expressly discharge the old contract, it will be impliedly discharged if the new contract's terms are inconsistent with the old contract's terms. It is this immediate discharge of the prior contract that distinguishes a novation from both an accord and satisfaction, which will be discussed shortly, and an assignment of all rights, discussed in Chapter 17.

## Discharge by Settlement Agreement

A compromise, or settlement agreement, that arises out of a genuine dispute over the obligations under an existing contract will be recognized at law. The agreement will be substituted as a new contract and will either expressly or impliedly revoke and discharge the obligations under the prior contract. In contrast to a novation, a substituted agreement does not involve a third party. Rather, the two original parties to the contract form a different agreement to substitute for the original one.

## Discharge by Accord and Satisfaction

As discussed in Chapter 13, in an accord and satisfaction, the parties agree to accept performance that is different from the performance originally promised. An *accord* is a contract to perform some act to satisfy an existing contractual duty that is not yet discharged.[13] A *satisfaction* is the performance of the accord agreement. An accord and its satisfaction discharge the original contractual obligation.

Once the accord has been made, the original obligation is merely suspended until the accord agreement is fully performed. If it is not performed, the obligee (the one to whom performance is owed) can file a lawsuit based on the original obligation or the accord. ▶ **Example 18.12** Fahreed has a judgment against Ling for $8,000. Later, both parties agree that the judgment can be satisfied by Ling's transfer of his automobile to Fahreed. This agreement to accept the auto in lieu of $8,000 in cash is the accord. If Ling transfers the car to Fahreed, the accord is fully performed, and the debt is discharged. If Ling refuses to transfer the car, the accord is breached. Because the original obligation was merely suspended, Fahreed can sue Ling

---

**12.** UCC 2–209(2), (4).

**13.** *Restatement (Second) of Contracts,* Section 281.

to enforce the original judgment for $8,000 in cash or bring an action for breach of the accord. ◀

## SECTION 4
# DISCHARGE BY OPERATION OF LAW

Under specified circumstances, contractual duties may be discharged by operation of law. These circumstances include material alteration of the contract, the running of the statute of limitations, bankruptcy, and the impossibility or impracticability of performance.

## Material Alteration of the Contract

To discourage parties from altering written contracts, the law allows an innocent party to be discharged when the other party has materially altered a written contract without consent. For instance, a party alters a material term of a contract, such as the stated quantity or price, without the knowledge or consent of the other party. In this situation, the party who was unaware of the alteration can treat the contract as discharged or terminated.

## Statutes of Limitations

As mentioned earlier in this text, statutes of limitations restrict the period during which a party can sue on a particular cause of action. After the applicable limitations period has passed, a suit can no longer be brought. The limitations period for bringing suits for breach of oral contracts usually is two to three years, and for written or otherwise recorded contracts, four to five years. Parties generally have ten to twenty years to file for recovery of amounts awarded in judgments, depending on state law.

Lawsuits for breach of a contract for the sale of goods generally must be brought within four years after the cause of action has accrued.[14] By their original agreement, the parties can reduce this four-year period to not less than one year, but they cannot agree to extend it.

## Bankruptcy

A proceeding in bankruptcy attempts to allocate the debtor's assets to the creditors in a fair and equita-

ble fashion. Once the assets have been allocated, the debtor receives a **discharge in bankruptcy.** A discharge in bankruptcy ordinarily prevents the creditors from enforcing most of the debtor's contracts. Partial payment of a debt *after* discharge in bankruptcy will not revive the debt.

## Impossibility of Performance

After a contract has been made, supervening events (such as a fire) may make performance impossible in an objective sense. This is known as **impossibility of performance** and can discharge a contract.[15] The doctrine of impossibility of performance applies only when the parties could not have reasonably foreseen, at the time the contract was formed, the event that rendered performance impossible. Performance may also become so difficult or costly due to some unforeseen event that a court will consider it commercially unfeasible, or impracticable, as will be discussed later in the chapter.

*Objective impossibility* ("It can't be done") must be distinguished from *subjective impossibility* ("I'm sorry, I simply can't do it"). An example of subjective impossibility occurs when a party cannot deliver goods on time because of freight car shortages or cannot make payment on time because the bank is closed. In effect, in each of these situations the party is saying, "It is impossible for *me* to perform," not "It is impossible for *anyone* to perform." Accordingly, such excuses do not discharge a contract, and the nonperforming party is normally held in breach of contract.

**WHEN PERFORMANCE IS IMPOSSIBLE** Three basic types of situations may qualify as grounds for the discharge of contractual obligations based on impossibility of performance:[16]

1. *When one of the parties to a personal contract dies or becomes incapacitated prior to performance.*
   ▶ **Example 18.13** Frederic, a famous dancer, contracts with Ethereal Dancing Guild to play a leading role in its new ballet. Before the ballet can be performed, Frederic becomes ill and dies. His personal performance was essential to the completion of the contract. Thus, his death discharges the contract and his estate's liability for his nonperformance. ◀

2. *When the specific subject matter of the contract is destroyed.*
   ▶ **Example 18.14** A-1 Farm Equipment agrees to sell Gunther the green tractor on its lot and promises

---

14. Section 2–725 of the UCC contains this four-year limitation period. A cause of action for a sales contract generally accrues when the breach occurs, even if the aggrieved party is not aware of the breach. A breach of warranty normally occurs when the seller delivers the goods to the buyer.

15. *Restatement (Second) of Contracts,* Section 261.
16. *Restatement (Second) of Contracts,* Sections 262–266; UCC 2–615.

to have the tractor ready for Gunther to pick up on Saturday. On Friday night, however, a truck veers off the nearby highway and smashes into the tractor, destroying it beyond repair. Because the contract was for this specific tractor, A-1's performance is rendered impossible owing to the accident. ◄

3. *When a change in law renders performance illegal.*
   ▶ **Example 18.15** Hopper contracts with Playlist, Inc., to create a Web site through which users can post and share movies, music, and other forms of digital entertainment. Hopper goes to work. Before the site is operational, however, Congress passes the No Online Piracy in Entertainment (NOPE) Act. The NOPE Act makes it illegal to operate a Web site on which copyrighted works are posted without the copyright owners' consent. In this situation, the contract is discharged by operation of law. The purpose of the contract has been rendered illegal, and contract performance is objectively impossible. ◄

**TEMPORARY IMPOSSIBILITY** An occurrence or event that makes performance temporarily impossible operates to suspend performance until the impossibility ceases.

***Performance Normally Is Only Delayed.*** Once the temporary event ends, the parties ordinarily must perform the contract as originally planned. ▶ **Case in Point 18.16** Keefe Hurwitz contracted to sell his home in Louisiana to Wesley and Gwendolyn Payne for $241,500. Four days later, Hurricane Katrina made landfall and caused extensive damage to the house. Hurwitz refused to pay the cost ($60,000) for the necessary repairs before the deal closed. The Paynes filed a lawsuit to enforce the contract at the agreed-on price.

Hurwitz argued that Hurricane Katrina had made it impossible for him to perform and had discharged his duties under the contract. The court, however, ruled that Hurricane Katrina had caused only a temporary impossibility. Hurwitz was required to pay for the necessary repairs and to perform the contract as written. He could not obtain a higher purchase price to offset the cost of the repairs.[17] ◄

***Performance Can Be Discharged.*** Sometimes, the lapse of time and the change in circumstances surrounding the contract make it substantially more burdensome for the parties to perform the promised acts. In that situation, the contract is discharged. ▶ **Case in Point 18.17** In 1942, actor Gene Autry was drafted into the U.S. Army.

Being drafted rendered his contract with a Hollywood movie company temporarily impossible to perform, and it was suspended until the end of World War II in 1945. When Autry got out of the army, the purchasing power of the dollar had declined so much that performance of the contract would have been substantially burdensome to him. Therefore, the contract was discharged.[18] ◄

It can be difficult to predict how a court will—or should—rule on whether performance is impossible in a particular situation, as discussed in this chapter's *Insight into Ethics* feature on the following page.

## Commercial Impracticability

Courts may also excuse parties from their performance when it becomes much more difficult or expensive than the parties originally contemplated at the time the contract was formed. For someone to invoke the doctrine of **commercial impracticability** successfully, however, the anticipated performance must become *significantly* difficult or costly.[19]

The added burden of performing not only must be extreme but also *must not have been known by the parties when the contract was made.* In one classic case, for example, a court held that a contract could be discharged because a party would otherwise have to pay ten times more than the original estimate to excavate a certain amount of gravel.[20]

## Frustration of Purpose

Closely allied with the doctrine of commercial impracticability is the doctrine of **frustration of purpose.** In principle, a contract will be discharged if supervening circumstances make it impossible to attain the purpose both parties had in mind when they made the contract. As with commercial impracticability and impossibility, the supervening event must not have been reasonably foreseeable at the time the contract was formed.

There are some differences between the doctrines, however. Commercial impracticability usually involves an event that increases the cost or difficulty of performance. In contrast, frustration of purpose typically involves an event that decreases the value of what a party receives under the contract.[21]

See Exhibit 18–1 on the following page for a summary of the ways in which a contract can be discharged.

---

17. *Payne v. Hurwitz,* 978 So.2d 1000 (La.App. 1st Cir. 2008).

18. *Autry v. Republic Productions,* 30 Cal.2d 144, 180 P.2d 888 (1947).
19. *Restatement (Second) of Contracts,* Section 264.
20. *Mineral Park Land Co. v. Howard,* 172 Cal. 289, 156 P. 458 (1916).
21. See, for example, *East Capitol View Community Development Corp. v. Robinson,* 941 A.2d 1036 (D.C.App. 2008).

## INSIGHT INTO ETHICS
### When Is Impossibility of Performance a Valid Defense?

The doctrine of impossibility of performance is applied only when the parties could not have reasonably foreseen, at the time the contract was formed, the event or events that rendered performance impossible. In some cases, the courts may seem to go too far in holding that the parties should have foreseen certain events or conditions. Thus, the parties cannot avoid their contractual obligations under the doctrine of impossibility of performance.

Actually, courts today are more likely to allow parties to raise this defense than courts in the past, which rarely excused parties from performance under the impossibility doctrine. Indeed, until the latter part of the nineteenth century, courts were reluctant to discharge a contract even when performance appeared to be impossible.

Generally, the courts must balance the freedom of parties to contract (and thereby assume the risks involved) against the injustice that may result when certain contractual obligations are enforced. If the courts allowed parties to raise impossibility of performance as a defense to contractual obligations more often, freedom of contract would suffer.

#### LEGAL CRITICAL THINKING
**INSIGHT INTO THE SOCIAL ENVIRONMENT**

*Why might those entering into contracts be worse off in the long run if the courts increasingly accept impossibility of performance as a defense?*

---

**EXHIBIT 18-1** Contract Discharge

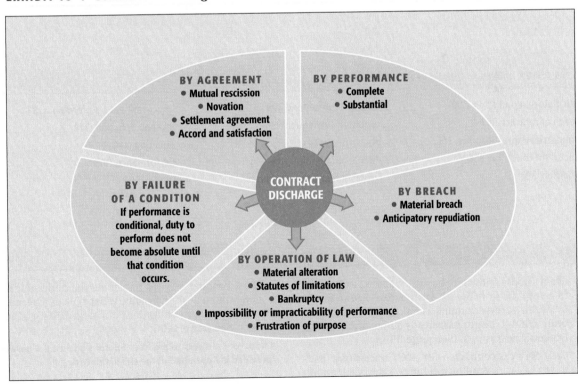

**BY AGREEMENT**
- Mutual rescission
- Novation
- Settlement agreement
- Accord and satisfaction

**BY PERFORMANCE**
- Complete
- Substantial

**BY FAILURE OF A CONDITION**
If performance is conditional, duty to perform does not become absolute until that condition occurs.

**CONTRACT DISCHARGE**

**BY BREACH**
- Material breach
- Anticipatory repudiation

**BY OPERATION OF LAW**
- Material alteration
- Statutes of limitations
- Bankruptcy
- Impossibility or impracticability of performance
- Frustration of purpose

# Reviewing: Performance and Discharge in Traditional and E-Contracts

Val's Foods signs a contract to buy 1,500 pounds of basil from Sun Farms, a small organic herb grower, as long as an independent organization inspects the crop and certifies that it contains no pesticide or herbicide residue. Val's has a contract with several restaurant chains to supply pesto and intends to use Sun Farms' basil in the pesto to fulfill these contracts. While Sun Farms is preparing to harvest the basil, an unexpected hailstorm destroys half the crop. Sun Farms attempts to purchase additional basil from other farms, but it is late in the season and the price is twice the normal market price. Sun Farms is too small to absorb this cost and immediately notifies Val's that it will not fulfill the contract. Using the information presented in the chapter, answer the following questions.

1. Suppose that the basil does not pass the chemical-residue inspection. Which concept discussed in the chapter might allow Val's to refuse to perform the contract in this situation?
2. Under which legal theory or theories might Sun Farms claim that its obligation under the contract has been discharged by operation of law? Discuss fully.
3. Suppose that Sun Farms contacts every basil grower in the country and buys the last remaining chemical-free basil anywhere. Nevertheless, Sun Farms is able to ship only 1,475 pounds to Val's. Would this fulfill Sun Farms' obligations to Val's? Why or why not?
4. Now suppose that Sun Farms sells its operations to Happy Valley Farms. As a part of the sale, all three parties agree that Happy Valley will provide the basil as stated under the original contract. What is this type of agreement called?

**DEBATE THIS . . .** *The doctrine of commercial impracticability should be abolished.*

## Terms and Concepts

anticipatory repudiation 309

breach of contract 307

commercial impracticability 312

concurrent condition 305

condition 303

condition precedent 303

condition subsequent 304

discharge 303

discharge in bankruptcy 311

frustration of purpose 312

impossibility of performance 311

mutual rescission 310

novation 310

performance 303

tender 305

## Issue Spotters

1. Ready Foods contracts to buy two hundred carloads of frozen pizzas from Stealth Distributors. Before Ready or Stealth starts performing, can the parties call off the deal? What if Stealth has already shipped the pizzas? Explain your answers. **(See page 309.)**
2. C&D Services contracts with Ace Concessions, Inc., to service Ace's vending machines. Later, C&D wants Dean Vending Services to assume the duties under a new contract. Ace consents. What type of agreement is this? Are Ace's obligations discharged? Why or why not? **(See page 310.)**

- **Check your answers to the Issue Spotters against the answers provided in Appendix E at the end of this text.**

## Business Scenarios

**18–1. Conditions of Performance.** The Caplans contract with Faithful Construction, Inc., to build a house for them for $360,000. The specifications state "all plumbing bowls and fixtures . . . to be Crane brand." The Caplans leave on vacation, and during their absence, Faithful is unable to buy and install Crane plumbing fixtures. Instead, Faithful installs Kohler brand fixtures, an equivalent in the industry. On completion of the building contract, the Caplans inspect the work, discover the substitution, and refuse to accept the house, claiming Faithful has breached the conditions set forth in the specifications. Discuss fully the Caplans' claim. **(See page 303.)**

**18–2. Discharge by Agreement.** Junior owes creditor Iba $1,000, which is due and payable on June 1. Junior has been in a car accident, has missed a great deal of work, and consequently will not have the funds on June 1. Junior's father, Fred, offers to pay Iba $1,100 in four equal installments if Iba will discharge Junior from any further liability on the debt. Iba accepts. Is this transaction a novation or an accord and satisfaction? Explain. **(See page 309.)**

**18–3. Impossibility of Performance.** In the following situations, certain events take place after the contracts are formed. Discuss which of these contracts are discharged because the events render the contracts impossible to perform. **(See page 311.)**

(a) Jimenez, a famous singer, contracts to perform in your nightclub. He dies prior to performance.

(b) Raglione contracts to sell you her land. Just before title is to be transferred, she dies.

(c) Oppenheim contracts to sell you one thousand bushels of apples from her orchard in the state of Washington. Because of a severe frost, she is unable to deliver the apples.

(d) Maxwell contracts to lease a service station for ten years. His principal income is from the sale of gasoline. Because of an oil embargo by foreign oil-producing nations, gasoline is rationed, cutting sharply into Maxwell's gasoline sales. He cannot make his lease payments.

**18–4. Implied Conditions.** Heublein, Inc., makes wines and distilled spirits. Tarrant Distributors, Inc., agreed to distribute Heublein brands. When problems arose, the parties entered mediation. Under a settlement agreement, Heublein agreed to pay Tarrant the amount of its "net loss" as determined by Coopers & Lybrand, an accounting firm, according to a specified formula. The parties agreed that Coopers & Lybrand's calculation would be "final and binding." Heublein disagreed with Coopers & Lybrand's calculation, however, and refused to pay. The parties asked a court to rule on the dispute. Heublein argued that the settlement agreement included an implied condition precedent that Coopers & Lybrand would correctly apply the specified formula before Heublein would be obligated to pay. Tarrant pointed to the clause stating that the calculation would be "final and binding." With whom will the court agree, and why? **(See page 305.)**

## Business Case Problems

**18–5. Condition Precedent.** Just Homes, LLC (JH), hired Mike Building & Contracting, Inc., to do $1.35 million worth of renovation work on three homes. Community Preservation Corporation (CPC) supervised Mike's work on behalf of JH. The contract stated that in the event of a dispute, JH would have to obtain the project architect's certification to justify terminating Mike. As construction progressed, relations between Mike and CPC worsened.

At a certain point in the project, Mike requested partial payment, and CPC recommended that JH not make it. Mike refused to continue work without further payment. JH evicted Mike from the project. Mike sued for breach of contract. JH contended that it had the right to terminate the contract due to CPC's negative reports and Mike's failure to agree with the project's engineer. Mike moved for summary judgment for the amounts owed for work performed. Mike claimed that JH had not fulfilled the condition precedent—JH never obtained the project architect's certification for Mike's termination. Which of the two parties involved breached the contract? Explain your answer. [*Mike Building & Contracting, Inc. v. Just Homes, LLC,* 27 Misc.3d 833, 901 N.Y.S.2d 458 (2010)] **(See page 303.)**

**18–6. BUSINESS CASE PROBLEM WITH SAMPLE ANSWER: Conditions of Performance.**

 *James Maciel leased an apartment in Regent Village, a university-owned housing facility for Regent University (RU) students in Virginia Beach, Virginia. The lease ran until the end of the fall semester. Maciel had an option to renew the lease semester by semester as long as he maintained his status as an RU student. When Maciel completed his coursework for the spring semester, he told RU that he intended to withdraw. The university told him that he could stay in the apartment until May 31, the final day of the spring semester. Maciel asked for two additional weeks, but the university denied the request. On June 1, RU changed the locks on the apartment. Maciel entered through a window and e-mailed the university that he planned to stay "for another one*

*or two weeks.*" When he was charged with trespassing, Maciel argued that he had "legal authority" to occupy the apartment. Was Maciel correct? Explain. [Maciel v. Commonwealth, __ S.E.2d __ (Va.App. 2011)] **(See page 303.)**

- **For a sample answer to Problem 18–6, go to Appendix F at the end of this text.**

**18–7. Material Breach.** The Northeast Independent School District in Bexar County, Texas, hired STR Constructors, Ltd., to renovate a middle school. STR subcontracted the tile work in the school's kitchen to Newman Tile, Inc. (NTI). The project had already fallen behind schedule. As a result, STR allowed other workers to walk over and damage the newly installed tile before it had cured, forcing NTI to constantly redo its work. Despite NTI's requests for payment, STR remitted only half the amount due under their contract. When the school district refused to accept the kitchen, including the tile work, STR told NTI to quickly make the repairs. A week later, STR terminated their contract. Did STR breach the contract with NTI? Explain. [*STR Constructors, Ltd. v. Newman Tile, Inc.,* __ S.W.3d __, 2013 WL 632969 (Tex.App.—El Paso 2013)] **(See page 307.)**

**18–8. A QUESTION OF ETHICS: Conditions.**

 *King County, Washington, hired Frank Coluccio Construction Co. (FCCC) to act as general contractor for a public works project involving the construction of a small utility tunnel under the Duwamish Waterway. FCCC hired Donald B. Murphy Contractors, Inc. (DBM), as a subcontractor. DBM was responsible for constructing an access shaft at the eastern end of the tunnel. Problems arose during construction, including a "blow-in" of the access shaft that caused it to fill with water, soil, and debris. FCCC and DBM incurred substantial expenses from the repairs and delays. Under the project contract, King*

*County was supposed to buy an insurance policy to "insure against physical loss or damage by perils included under an 'All-Risk' Builder's Risk policy." Any claim under this policy was to be filed through the insured. King County, which had general property damage insurance, did not obtain an all-risk builder's risk policy. For the losses attributable to the blow-in, FCCC and DBM submitted builder's risk claims, which the county denied. FCCC filed a suit in a Washington state court against King County, alleging, among other claims, breach of contract.* [Frank Coluccio Construction Co. v. King County, *136 Wash.App. 751, 150 P.3d 1147 (Div. 1 2007)]* **(See page 303.)**

(a) King County's property damage policy specifically excluded, at the county's request, coverage of tunnels. The county drafted its contract with FCCC to require the all-risk builder's risk policy and authorize itself to "sponsor" claims. When FCCC and DBM filed their claims, the county secretly colluded with its property damage insurer to deny payment. What do these facts indicate about the county's ethics and legal liability in this situation?

(b) Could DBM, as a third party to the contract between King County and FCCC, maintain an action on the contract against King County? Discuss.

(c) All-risk insurance is a promise to pay on the "fortuitous" happening of a loss or damage from any cause except those that are specifically excluded. Payment usually is not made on a loss that, at the time the insurance was obtained, the claimant subjectively knew would occur. If a loss results from faulty workmanship on the part of a contractor, should the obligation to pay under an all-risk policy be discharged? Explain.

## Legal Reasoning Group Activity

**18–9. Anticipatory Repudiation.** ABC Clothiers, Inc., has a contract with Taylor & Sons, a retailer, to deliver one thousand summer suits to Taylor's place of business on or before May 1. On April 1, Taylor receives a letter from ABC informing him that ABC will not be able to make the delivery as scheduled. Taylor is very upset, as he had planned a big ad campaign. **(See page 309.)**

(a) The first group will discuss whether Taylor can immediately sue ABC for breach of contract (on April 2).

(b) Now suppose that Taylor's son, Tom, tells his father that they cannot file a lawsuit until ABC actually fails to deliver the suits on May 1. The second group will decide who is correct, Taylor senior or Tom.

(c) Assume that Taylor & Sons can either file immediately or wait until ABC fails to deliver the goods. The third group will evaluate which course of action is better, given the circumstances.

# CHAPTER 19
# BREACH OF CONTRACT AND REMEDIES

When one party breaches a contract, the other party—the nonbreaching party—can choose one or more of several remedies. (Does changing terms of service on a social networking site constitute a breach of contract? See this chapter's *Insight into Social Media* feature on page 319 for a look at this issue.) A *remedy* is the relief provided for an innocent party when the other party has breached the contract. It is the means employed to enforce a right or to redress an injury.

The most common remedies available to a nonbreaching party include damages, *rescission* and *restitution*, *specific performance*, and *reformation*. As discussed in Chapter 1, a distinction is made between *remedies at law* and *remedies in equity*. Today, the remedy at law normally is monetary damages, which are discussed in the first part of this chapter. Equitable remedies include rescission and restitution, specific performance, and reformation, all of which will be examined later in the chapter. Usually, a court will not award an equitable remedy unless the remedy at law is inadequate.

---

## DAMAGES

A breach of contract entitles the nonbreaching party to sue for monetary damages. As discussed in Chapter 6, tort law damages are designed to compensate a party for harm suffered as a result of another's wrongful act. In the context of contract law, damages compensate the nonbreaching party for the loss of the bargain. Often, courts say that innocent parties are to be placed in the position they would have occupied had the contract been fully performed.[1]

Realize at the outset, though, that collecting damages through a court judgment requires litigation, which can be expensive and time consuming. Also keep in mind that court judgments are often difficult to enforce, particularly if the breaching party does not have sufficient assets to pay the damages awarded (as discussed in Chapter 3). For these reasons, most parties settle their lawsuits for damages (or other remedies) prior to trial.

### Types of Damages

There are four broad categories of damages:

1. Compensatory (to cover direct losses and costs).
2. Consequential (to cover indirect and foreseeable losses).
3. Punitive (to punish and deter wrongdoing).
4. Nominal (to recognize wrongdoing when no monetary loss is shown).

Compensatory and punitive damages were discussed in Chapter 6 in the context of tort law. Here, we look at these types of damages, as well as consequential and nominal damages, in the context of contract law.

**COMPENSATORY DAMAGES** Damages that compensate the nonbreaching party for the *loss of the bargain* are known as *compensatory damages*. These damages compensate the injured party only for damages actually sustained and proved to have arisen directly from the loss of the bargain caused by the breach of contract. They simply replace what was lost because of the wrong or damage and, for this reason, are often said to "make the person whole."

Can an award of damages for a breach of contract elevate the nonbreaching party to a better position than he or she would have been in if the contract had not been breached? That was the question in the following case.

---

1. *Restatement (Second) of Contracts*, Section 347.

## CASE 19.1

# Hallmark Cards, Inc. v. Murley

United States Court of Appeals, Eighth Circuit, 703 F.3d 456 (2013).

**BACKGROUND AND FACTS** Janet Murley served as Hallmark Cards, Inc.'s vice-president of marketing from 1999 to 2002. She was responsible for product and business development, research, and advertising. She had access to confidential information, including Hallmark's business plans, market research, and financial information. In 2002, Murley and the company negotiated a separation agreement. Murley agreed not to work in the greeting card or gift industry for a period of eighteen months or to solicit Hallmark's employees. Further, she agreed not to disclose any proprietary or confidential information or to retain any business records or documents relating to Hallmark. In exchange, Hallmark paid Murley a $735,000 severance fee plus other benefits.

In 2006, after the expiration of her non-compete agreement, Murley accepted a consulting assignment with Recyled Paper Greetings. Murley admitted that she disclosed to Recyled Paper Hallmark confidential information. Hallmark filed suit in a federal district court against Murley, alleging breach of contract. Hallmark sought compensatory damages of $860,000. The jury ruled in favor of Hallmark. Murley appealed.

**DECISION AND RATIONALE** The U.S. Court of Appeals for the Eighth Circuit confirmed that Murley owed $735,000 to Hallmark, but not the monies she earned from Recyled Paper Greetings ($125,000). "Under the circumstances, we cannot characterize the jury's reimbursement of Hallmark's original payment under the separation agreement as grossly excessive or glaringly unwarranted." At trial, Hallmark had presented ample evidence that Murley not only retained, but disclosed Hallmark's confidential materials to a competitor in violation of the "terms and primary purpose of that agreement."

"In an action for breach of contract, a plaintiff may recover the benefit of his or her bargain as well as damages naturally and proximately caused by the breach and the damages that could have been reasonably contemplated by the defendant at the time of the agreement."

**THE LEGAL ENVIRONMENT DIMENSION** *What are compensatory damages? What is the standard measure of compensatory damages?*

**THE SOCIAL DIMENSION** *In this case, what was the basis for Hallmark's suit against Murley? How much did Hallmark seek to recover in the form of damages?*

---

***Standard Measure.*** The standard measure of compensatory damages is the difference between the value of the breaching party's promised performance under the contract and the value of her or his actual performance. This amount is reduced by any loss that the injured party has avoided, however.

▶ **Example 19.1** Randall contracts to perform certain services exclusively for Hernandez during the month of March for $4,000. Hernandez cancels the contract and is in breach. Randall is able to find another job during March but can earn only $3,000. He can sue Hernandez for breach and recover $1,000 as compensatory damages. Randall can also recover from Hernandez the amount that he spent to find the other job. ◀

Expenses that are caused directly by a breach of contract—such as those incurred to obtain performance from another source—are known as **incidental damages.** Note that the measure of compensatory damages often varies by type of contract. Certain types of contracts deserve special mention.

***Sale of Goods.*** In a contract for the sale of goods, the usual measure of compensatory damages is an amount equal to the difference between the contract price and the market price.[2] ▶ **Example 19.2** Medik Laboratories contracts to buy ten model UTS network servers from Cal Industries for $4,000 each. Cal Industries, however, fails to deliver the ten servers to Medik. The market price of the servers at the

---

2. More specifically, the amount is the difference between the contract price and the market price at the time and place at which the goods were to be delivered or tendered. See Sections 2–708 and 2–713 of the Uniform Commercial Code (UCC).

---

# INSIGHT INTO SOCIAL MEDIA
## Was Instagram's Revision of Its Terms of Service a Breach of Contract?

In 2012, Facebook acquired the social networking site Instagram for $715 million. Instagram is a photo-sharing service that also allows users to add filters and effects to the photos.

### The Terms of Service Are a Contract

When you use social media or other services on the Internet or download an app for your mobile devices, you normally have to indicate that you accept the terms of service associated with that service or app. Of course, users rarely, if ever, actually read those terms. They simply click on "accept" and start using the service. By clicking on "accept," however, those users are entering into a contract.

### Instagram Changes Its Terms of Service

In 2013, to the consternation of a number of users, Instagram changed its terms of service to give it the right and ability to transfer and otherwise use user content on the site, apparently without compensation. The new terms also limited users' ability to bring class-action lawsuits against Instagram, limited the damages they could recover to $100, and required arbitration of any disputes.

    Lucy Funes, an Instagram user in California, filed a class-action lawsuit on behalf of herself and other users, claiming breach of contract and breach of the covenant of good faith and fair dealing that a contract implies.[a] Although Instagram subsequently modified the language that appeared to give it the right to use users' photos without compensation, it retained other controversial terms, including the mandatory arbitration clause and a provision allowing it to place ads in conjunction with user content.

---
**a.** *Funes v. Instagram, Inc.,* 3:12-CV06482-WHA (N.D.Cal. 2012).

### Instagram Seeks Dismissal of the Lawsuit

While Funes is contending that Instagram breached their contract by changing its terms of service, Instagram argues that Funes cannot claim breach of contract. The reason is that she—and other users—were given thirty days' notice before the new terms of service took effect. Because Funes continued to use her account after that thirty-day period, Instagram maintains that, in effect, she agreed to the new terms.

### Behind the Change in Terms of Service

In revising its terms of service, Instagram, or rather its new owner Facebook, was trying to monetize, or find a way to make revenue, from the many users of its site. A challenge for Facebook is how to translate its billions of users into profits. This challenge has become particularly acute for Facebook since its initial public offering in 2012. Now that it is a public company, Facebook must answer to its shareholders.

    Facebook has faced a number of class-action lawsuits, including an ongoing suit for $15 billion from users who claim that Facebook has been "improperly tracking the Internet use of its members even after they have logged out of their accounts." As Facebook tries to increase its profits to please its shareholders, it is likely to face even more lawsuits from users who resent the company's efforts to monetize the content on its site.

### LEGAL CRITICAL THINKING
#### INSIGHT INTO THE ETHICAL ENVIRONMENT

*Within Instagram's current terms of service there is a statement, "We may not always identify paid services, sponsored content, or commercial communications as such." Is it ethical for Instagram to act this way? Discuss.*

---

time Medik learns of the breach is $4,500. Therefore, Medik's measure of damages is $5,000 (10 × $500), plus any incidental damages (expenses) caused by the breach. ◄

    When the buyer breaches and the seller has not yet produced the goods, compensatory damages normally equal lost profits on the sale, not the difference between the contract price and the market price.

**Sale of Land.** Ordinarily, because each parcel of land is unique, the remedy for a seller's breach of a contract for a sale of real estate is specific performance. The buyer is awarded the parcel of property for which she or he bargained (*specific performance* will be discussed more fully later in this chapter). When the buyer is the party in breach, the measure of damages is typically the difference between the contract price and the market price of the land. The same measure is used when specific performance is not available (because the seller has sold the property to someone else, for example). The majority of states follow this rule.

A minority of states follow a different rule when the seller breaches the contract and the breach is not deliberate (intentional).[3] These states limit the prospective buyer's damages to a refund of any down payment made plus any expenses incurred (such as fees for title searches, attorneys, and escrows). Thus, the minority rule effectively returns purchasers to the positions they occupied prior to the sale, rather than giving them the benefit of the bargain.

**Construction Contracts.** The measure of damages in a building or construction contract varies depending on which party breaches and when the breach occurs.

1. *Breach by owner.* The owner may breach at three different stages—before performance has begun, during performance, or after performance has been completed. If the owner breaches *before performance has begun,* the contractor can recover only the profits that would have been made on the contract (that is, the total contract price less the cost of materials and labor).

   If the owner breaches *during performance,* the contractor can recover the profits plus the costs incurred in partially constructing the building. If the owner breaches *after the construction has been completed,* the contractor can recover the entire contract price, plus interest.

2. *Breach by contractor.* When the construction contractor breaches the contract—either by failing to begin construction or by stopping work partway through the project—the measure of damages is the cost of completion. The cost of completion includes reasonable compensation for any delay

in performance. If the contractor finishes late, the measure of damages is the loss of use.

3. *Breach by both owner and contractor.* When the performance of both parties—the construction contractor and the owner—falls short of what their contract required, the courts attempt to strike a fair balance in awarding damages.

▶ **Case in Point 19.3** Jamison Well Drilling, Inc., contracted to drill a well for Ed Pfeifer for $4,130. Jamison drilled the well and installed a storage tank. The well did not comply with state health department requirements, however, and failed repeated tests for bacteria. The health department ordered the well to be abandoned and sealed. Pfeifer used the storage tank but paid Jamison nothing. Jamison filed a suit to recover. The court held that Jamison was entitled to $970 for the storage tank but was not entitled to the full contract price because the well was not usable.[4] ◀

The rules concerning the measurement of damages in breached construction contracts are summarized in Exhibit 19–1 below.

**Construction Contracts and Economic Waste.** If the contractor substantially performs, a court may use the cost-of-completion formula, but only if requiring completion will not entail unreasonable economic waste. *Economic waste* occurs when the cost of repairing or completing the performance as required by the contract greatly outweighs the benefit to the owner.

▶ **Example 19.4** Halverson Contracting discovers that it will cost $20,000 to move a large coral rock eleven inches as specified in the contract. Changing the rock's position will alter the appearance of the project only slightly. In this situation, a court would likely conclude that full completion would involve economic waste. Thus, the contractor will not be

---

3. "Deliberate" breaches include the seller's failure to convey (transfer title to) the land because the market price has gone up. "Nondeliberate" breaches include the seller's failure to convey the land because of a problem with the title, such as the discovery of an unknown *easement* that gives another party a right of use over the property.

4. *Jamison Well Drilling, Inc. v. Pfeifer,* 2011 Ohio 521 (2011).

---

**EXHIBIT 19–1 Measurement of Damages—Breach of Construction Contracts**

| Party in Breach | Time of Breach | Measurement of Damages |
|---|---|---|
| Owner | Before construction has begun. | Profits (contract price less cost of materials and labor). |
| Owner | During construction. | Profits, plus costs incurred up to time of breach. |
| Owner | After construction is completed. | Full contract price, plus interest. |
| Contractor | Before construction has begun. | Cost in excess of contract price to complete work. |
| Contractor | Before construction is completed. | Generally, all costs incurred by owner to complete. |

required to incur addition $20,000 in expenses to complete performance. ◀

**CONSEQUENTIAL DAMAGES** Foreseeable damages that result from a party's breach of contract are called **consequential damages,** or *special damages*. They differ from compensatory damages in that they are caused by special circumstances beyond the contract itself. They flow from the consequences, or results, of a breach. When a seller fails to deliver goods, knowing that the buyer is planning to use or resell those goods immediately, a court may award consequential damages for the loss of profits from the planned resale.

▶ **Example 19.5**  Marty contracts to buy a certain quantity of Quench, a specialty sports drink, from Nathan. Nathan knows that Marty has contracted with Ruthie to resell and ship the Quench within hours of its receipt. The beverage will then be sold to fans attending the Super Bowl. Nathan fails to timely deliver the Quench. Marty can recover the consequential damages—the loss of profits from the planned resale to Ruthie—caused by the nondelivery. (If Marty purchases Quench from another vender, he can also recover compensatory damages for the difference between the contract price and the market price.) ◀

For the nonbreaching party to recover consequential damages, the breaching party must have known (or had reason to know) that special circumstances would cause the nonbreaching party to suffer an additional loss. This rule was enunciated in the following classic case. In reading this decision, it is helpful to understand that in the mid-nineteenth century, large flour mills customarily kept more than one main crankshaft on hand in the event that one broke and had to be repaired.

## CLASSIC CASE 19.2

### Hadley v. Baxendale
Court of Exchequer, 156 Eng.Rep. 145 (1854).

**BACKGROUND AND FACTS**  The Hadleys (the plaintiffs) ran a flour mill in Gloucester, England. The main crankshaft attached to the steam engine in the mill broke, causing the mill to shut down. The crankshaft had to be sent to a foundry located in Greenwich so that a new shaft could be made to fit the other parts of the engine. Baxendale, the defendant, was a common carrier that transported the shaft from Gloucester to Greenwich. The freight charges were collected in advance, and Baxendale promised to deliver the shaft the following day. It was not delivered for a number of days, however. As a consequence, the mill was closed for several days. The Hadleys sued to recover the profits lost during that time. Baxendale contended that the loss of profits was "too remote" to be recoverable. The court held for the plaintiffs, and the jury was allowed to take into consideration the lost profits. The defendant appealed.

**DECISION AND RATIONALE**  The Court of Exchequer ordered a new trial. The court explained that if an injury is outside the usual course of events, it must be shown that the breaching party had reason to foresee the injury. According to the court, to collect consequential damages the plaintiffs in this case would have to have given express notice of the special circumstances that caused the loss of profits. The court reasoned that "special circumstances were here never communicated by the plaintiffs to the defendants. It follows, therefore, that the loss of profits here cannot reasonably be considered such a consequence of the breach of contract as could have been fairly and reasonably contemplated by both the parties when they made this contract."

**IMPACT OF THIS CASE ON TODAY'S LAW**  *This case established the rule that consequential damages are awarded only for injuries that the defendant could reasonably have foreseen as a probable result of the usual course of events following a breach. Today, the rule enunciated by the court in this case still applies. To recover consequential damages, the plaintiff must show that the defendant had reason to know or foresee that a particular loss or injury would occur.*

**THE E-COMMERCE DIMENSION**  *If a Web merchant loses business due to a computer system's failure that can be attributed to malfunctioning software, can the merchant recover the lost profits from the software maker? Explain.*

**PUNITIVE DAMAGES** Punitive damages generally are not awarded in lawsuits for breach of contract. Because punitive damages are designed to punish a wrongdoer and set an example to deter similar conduct in the future, they have no legitimate place in contract law. A contract is simply a civil relationship between the parties. The law may compensate one party for the loss of the bargain—no more and no less. When a person's actions cause both a breach of contract and a tort (such as fraud), punitive damages may be available. Overall, though, punitive damages are almost never available in contract disputes.

**NOMINAL DAMAGES** When no actual damage or financial loss results from a breach of contract and only a technical injury is involved, the court may award **nominal damages** to the innocent party. Awards of nominal damages are often small, such as one dollar, but they do establish that the defendant acted wrongfully. Most lawsuits for nominal damages are brought as a matter of principle under the theory that a breach has occurred and some damages must be imposed regardless of actual loss.

▶ **Example 19.6** Jackson contracts to buy potatoes from Stanley at fifty cents a pound. Stanley breaches the contract and does not deliver the potatoes. In the meantime, the price of potatoes has fallen. Jackson is able to buy them in the open market at half the price he contracted for with Stanley. He is clearly better off because of Stanley's breach. Thus, because Jackson sustained only a technical injury and suffered no monetary loss, he is likely to be awarded only nominal damages if he brings a suit for breach of contract. ◀

## Mitigation of Damages

In most situations, when a breach of contract occurs, the innocent injured party is held to a duty to mitigate, or reduce, the damages that he or she suffers. Under this doctrine of **mitigation of damages,** the duty owed depends on the nature of the contract.

**RENTAL AGREEMENTS** Some states require a landlord to use reasonable means to find a new tenant if a tenant abandons the premises and fails to pay rent. If an acceptable tenant is found, the landlord is required to lease the premises to this tenant to mitigate the damages recoverable from the former tenant.

The former tenant is still liable for the difference between the amount of the rent under the original lease and the rent received from the new tenant. If the landlord has not taken reasonable steps to find a new tenant, a court will likely reduce any award made by the amount of rent the landlord could have received had he or she done so.

**EMPLOYMENT CONTRACTS** In the majority of states, a person whose employment has been wrongfully terminated owes a duty to mitigate the damages suffered because of the employer's breach of the employment contract. In other words, a wrongfully terminated employee has a duty to take a similar job if one is available. If the employee fails to do this, the damages awarded will be equivalent to the person's former salary less the income he or she would have received in a similar job obtained by reasonable means.

The employer has the burden of proving that such a job existed and that the employee could have been hired. Normally, the employee is under no duty to take a job of a different type and rank.

## Liquidated Damages versus Penalties

A **liquidated damages** provision in a contract specifies that a certain dollar amount is to be paid in the event of a *future* default or breach of contract. (*Liquidated* means determined, settled, or fixed.)

Liquidated damages differ from penalties. Although a **penalty** also specifies a certain amount to be paid in the event of a default or breach of contract, it is designed to penalize the breaching party, not to make the innocent party whole. Liquidated damages provisions usually are enforceable. In contrast, if a court finds that a provision calls for a penalty, the agreement as to the amount will not be enforced, and recovery will be limited to actual damages.

**ENFORCEABILITY** To determine if a particular provision is for liquidated damages or for a penalty, a court must answer two questions:

1. When the contract was entered into, was it apparent that damages would be difficult to estimate in the event of a breach?
2. Was the amount set as damages a reasonable estimate and not excessive?[5]

If the answers to both questions are yes, the provision normally will be enforced. If either answer is no, the provision usually will not be enforced.

---

5. *Restatement (Second) of Contracts,* Section 356(1).

▶ **Case in Point 19.7** James Haber contracted with B-Sharp Musical Productions, Inc., to provide a particular band to perform at his son's bar mitzvah for $30,000. The contract contained a liquidated damages clause under which if Haber canceled within ninety days of the date of the bar mitzvah, he would still owe $30,000 to B-Sharp. If he canceled more than ninety days beforehand, Haber would owe B-Sharp half of that amount ($15,000).

Haber canceled less than ninety days before the bar mitzvah and refused to pay B-Sharp the $25,000 balance due under the contract. B-Sharp sued. The court held that the liquidated damages clause was enforceable. The court reasoned that the expense and possibility of rebooking a canceled performance could not be determined at the time of contracting and that the clause provided a reasonable amount of damages.[6] ◀

**LIQUIDATED DAMAGES COMMON IN CERTAIN CONTRACTS** Liquidated damages provisions are frequently used in construction contracts. For instance, a provision requiring a construction contractor to pay $300 for every day he or she is late in completing the project is a liquidated damages provision.

Such provisions are also common in contracts for the sale of goods.[7] In addition, contracts with entertainers and professional athletes often include liquidated damages provisions. ▶ **Example 19.8** A television network settled its contract dispute with *Tonight Show* host Conan O'Brien for $33 million. The amount of the settlement was somewhat less than the $40 million O'Brien could have received under a liquidated damages clause in his contract. ◀

## SECTION 2
# EQUITABLE REMEDIES

Sometimes, damages are an inadequate remedy for a breach of contract. In these situations, the nonbreaching party may ask the court for an equitable remedy. Equitable remedies include rescission and restitution, specific performance, and reformation.

## Rescission and Restitution

As discussed in Chapter 18, *rescission* is essentially an action to undo, or terminate, a contract—to return the contracting parties to the positions they occupied prior to the transaction.[8] When fraud, a mistake, duress, undue influence, misrepresentation, or lack of capacity to contract is present, unilateral rescission is available. Rescission may also be available by statute.[9] The failure of one party to perform entitles the other party to rescind the contract. The rescinding party must give prompt notice to the breaching party.

**RESTITUTION** Generally, to rescind a contract, both parties must make **restitution** to each other by returning goods, property, or funds previously conveyed.[10] If the property or goods can be returned, they must be. If the goods or property have been consumed, restitution must be made in an equivalent dollar amount.

Essentially, restitution involves the plaintiff's recapture of a benefit conferred on the defendant that has unjustly enriched her or him. ▶ **Example 19.9** Katie contracts with Mikhail to design a house for her. Katie pays Mikhail $9,000 and agrees to make two more payments of $9,000 (for a total of $27,000) as the design progresses. The next day, Mikhail calls Katie and tells her that he has taken a position with a large architectural firm in another state and cannot design the house. Katie decides to hire another architect that afternoon. Katie can obtain restitution of the $9,000. ◀

**RESTITUTION IS NOT LIMITED TO RESCISSION CASES** Restitution may be appropriate when a contract is rescinded, but the right to restitution is not limited to rescission cases. Because an award of restitution basically returns something to its rightful owner, a party can seek restitution in actions for breach of contract, tort actions, and other types of actions.

Restitution can be obtained when funds or property have been transferred by mistake or because of fraud or incapacity. Similarly, restitution might be available when there has been misconduct by a party

---

6. *B-Sharp Musical Productions, Inc. v. Haber,* 27 Misc.3d 41, 899 N.Y.S.2d 792 (2010).
7. Section 2–718(1) of the UCC specifically authorizes the use of liquidated damages provisions.
8. The rescission discussed here is *unilateral* rescission, in which only one party wants to undo the contract. In mutual rescission, which was discussed in Chapter 18, both parties agree to undo the contract. Mutual rescission discharges the contract. Unilateral rescission generally is available as a remedy for breach of contract.
9. Many states have statutes allowing individuals who enter "home solicitation contracts" to rescind those contracts within three business days for any reason. See, for example, California Civil Code Section 1689.5.
10. *Restatement (Second) of Contracts,* Section 370.

in a confidential or other special relationship. Even in criminal cases, a court can order restitution of funds or property obtained through embezzlement, conversion, theft, or copyright infringement.

## Specific Performance

The equitable remedy of **specific performance** calls for the performance of the act promised in the contract. This remedy is attractive to a nonbreaching party because it provides the exact bargain promised in the contract. It also avoids some of the problems inherent in a suit for damages, such as collecting a judgment and arranging another contract. In addition, the actual performance may be more valuable than the monetary damages.

Normally, however, specific performance will not be granted unless the party's legal remedy (monetary damages) is inadequate.[11] For this reason, contracts for the sale of goods rarely qualify for specific performance. The legal remedy—monetary damages—is ordinarily adequate in such situations because substantially identical goods can be bought or sold in the market. Only if the goods are unique will a court grant specific performance. For instance, paintings, sculptures, or rare books or coins are so unique that monetary damages will not enable a buyer to obtain substantially identical substitutes in the market.

**SALE OF LAND** A court may grant specific performance to a buyer in an action for a breach of contract involving the sale of land. In this situation, the legal remedy of monetary damages may not compensate the buyer adequately because every parcel of land is unique: the same land in the same location obviously cannot be obtained elsewhere. Only when specific performance is unavailable (such as when the seller has sold the property to someone else) will monetary damages be awarded instead.

▶ **Case in Point 19.10** Howard Stainbrook entered into a contract to sell Trent Low forty acres of mostly timbered land for $45,000. Low agreed to pay for a survey of the property and other costs in addition to the price. He gave Stainbrook a check for $1,000 to show his intent to fulfill the contract. One month later, Stainbrook died. His son David became the executor of the estate. After he discovered that the timber on the property was worth more than $100,000, David asked Low to withdraw his offer to buy the forty acres. Low refused and filed a suit

against David seeking specific performance of the contract. The court found that because Low had substantially performed his obligations under the contract and offered to perform the rest, he was entitled to specific performance.[12] ◀

**CONTRACTS FOR PERSONAL SERVICES** Contracts for personal services require one party to work personally for another party. Courts generally refuse to grant specific performance of personal-service contracts because to order a party to perform personal services against his or her will amounts to a type of involuntary servitude.[13]

Moreover, the courts do not want to monitor contracts for personal services, which usually require the exercise of personal judgment or talent. ▶ **Example 19.11** Nicole contracts with a surgeon to perform surgery to remove a tumor on her brain. If he refuses, the court would not compel (nor would Nicole want) the surgeon to perform under those circumstances. A court cannot ensure meaningful performance in such a situation.[14] ◀

If a contract is not deemed personal, the remedy at law of monetary damages may be adequate if substantially identical service (such as lawn mowing) is available from other persons.

## Reformation

**Reformation** is an equitable remedy used when the parties have *imperfectly* expressed their agreement in writing. Reformation allows a court to rewrite the contract to reflect the parties' true intentions.

Exhibit 19–2 on the following page graphically summarizes the remedies, including reformation, that are available to the nonbreaching party.

**WHEN FRAUD OR MUTUAL MISTAKE IS PRESENT** Courts order reformation most often when fraud or mutual mistake (for example, a clerical error) is present. Typically, a party seeks reformation so that some other remedy may then be pursued.

▶ **Example 19.12** If Carson contracts to buy a forklift from Yoshie but their contract mistakenly

---

11. *Restatement (Second) of Contracts*, Section 359.

12. *Stainbrook v. Low*, 842 N.E.2d 386 (Ind.App. 2006).

13. Involuntary servitude, or slavery, is contrary to the public policy expressed in the Thirteenth Amendment to the U.S. Constitution. A court can, however, enter an order (injunction) prohibiting a person who breached a personal-service contract from engaging in similar contracts for a period of time in the future.

14. Similarly, courts often refuse to order specific performance of construction contracts because courts are not set up to operate as construction supervisors or engineers.

**EXHIBIT 19-2  Remedies for Breach of Contract**

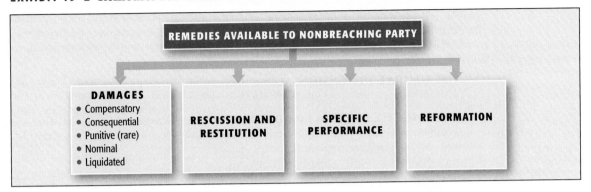

refers to a crane, a mutual mistake has occurred (see Chapter 15). Accordingly, a court can reform the contract so that it conforms to the parties' intentions and accurately refers to the forklift being sold. ◄

**WRITTEN CONTRACT INCORRECTLY STATES THE PARTIES' ORAL AGREEMENT** A court will also reform a contract when two parties enter into a binding oral contract but later make an error when they attempt to put the terms into writing. Normally, a court will allow into evidence the correct terms of the oral contract, thereby reforming the written contract.

**COVENANTS NOT TO COMPETE** Courts also may reform contracts when the parties have executed a written covenant not to compete (see Chapter 14). If the covenant is for a valid and legitimate purpose (such as the sale of a business) but the area or time restraints of the covenant are unreasonable, reformation may occur. Some courts will reform the restraints by making them reasonable and then will enforce the entire contract as reformed. Other courts, however, will throw out the entire restrictive covenant as illegal.

In the following case, a physician claimed that the covenant not to compete he signed was unreasonable and should therefore be declared illegal.

## CASE 19.3

### Emerick v. Cardiac Study Center, Inc.
Court of Appeals of Washington, 166 Wash.App. 1039 (2012).

**BACKGROUND AND FACTS** Cardiac Study Center is a medical practice group of approximately fifteen cardiologists. In 2002, Cardiac hired Dr. Robert Emerick as an employee. In 2004, Emerick became a shareholder of Cardiac. He signed a shareholder agreement and an employment contract that included a covenant not to compete. Under the covenant, any physician who left the group would have to promise not to practice competitively in the surrounding area for a period of five years. In 2005, patients and other medical providers began to complain to Cardiac about Emerick's conduct. Some physicians stopped referring patients to Cardiac as a result. Finally, Cardiac terminated Emerick's employment in 2009. Emerick sued Cardiac seeking a declaration that the covenant not to compete was unenforceable. He prevailed at trial, and Cardiac appealed.

**DECISION AND RATIONALE** A state intermediate appellate court reversed the lower court's decision and held in favor of Cardiac that the covenant not to compete was enforceable. The reviewing court examined the reasonableness of the covenant not to compete in terms of how it protected the employer's business or goodwill. The court pointed out that "an employee who joins an established business gains access to his employer's customers and acquires valuable information as to the nature and character of the business." Further, an employer has a "legitimate interest in protecting its existing client base and prohibiting the employee from taking its clients."

CASE 19.3 CONTINUES ➡

**CASE 19.3 CONTINUED**

Cardiac had provided Emerick with an immediate client base and established referral sources when he moved to the area. Emerick had access to Cardiac's business model and goodwill. Finally, the reviewing court explained that many Washington courts have held that restrictive covenants among physicians are enforceable. Indeed, "restrictive covenants are common among professionals because they allow a new professional to step in to an already established practice while protecting the employer from future competition."

**THE GLOBAL DIMENSION** *Should an employer be able to restrict a former employee from engaging in a competing business on a global level? Why or why not?*

**WHAT IF THE FACTS WERE DIFFERENT?** *Suppose that Emerick had authored a nationally published book,* How to Avoid Cardiac Surgery through Diet and Exercise. *Could Cardiac have blocked the book's distribution in Cardiac's area based on the covenant not to compete?*

---

## SECTION 3
# RECOVERY BASED ON QUASI CONTRACT

In some situations, when no actual contract exists, a court may step in to prevent one party from being unjustly enriched at the expense of another party. As discussed in Chapter 11, quasi contract is a legal theory under which an obligation is imposed in the absence of an agreement.

The legal obligation arises because the law considers that the party accepting the benefits has made an implied promise to pay for them. Generally, when one party has conferred a benefit on another party, justice requires that the party receiving the benefit pay the reasonable value for it. The party conferring the benefit can recover in *quantum meruit,* which means "as much as he or she deserves."

## When Quasi Contract Is Used

Quasi contract allows a court to act as if a contract exists when there is no actual contract or agreement between the parties. A court can also use this theory when the parties entered into a contract, but it is unenforceable for some reason.

Quasi-contractual recovery is often granted when one party has partially performed under a contract that is unenforceable. It provides an alternative to suing for damages and allows the party to recover the reasonable value of the partial performance. Depending on the case, the amount of the recovery may be measured either by the benefit received or by the detriment suffered.

▶ **Example 19.13** Ericson contracts to build two oil derricks for Petro Industries. The derricks are to

be built over a period of three years, but the parties do not make a written contract. Thus, the writing requirement will bar enforcement of the contract.[15] After Ericson completes one derrick, Petro Industries informs him that it will not pay for the derrick. Ericson can sue Petro Industries under the theory of quasi contract. ◀

## The Requirements of Quasi Contract

To recover under the theory of quasi contract, the party seeking recovery must show the following:

1. The party has conferred a benefit on the other party.
2. The party conferred the benefit with the reasonable expectation of being paid.
3. The party did not act as a volunteer in conferring the benefit.
4. The party receiving the benefit would be unjustly enriched if allowed to retain the benefit without paying for it.

Applying these requirements to the scenario discussed in *Example 19.13,* Ericson can sue in quasi contract because all of the conditions for quasi-contractual recovery have been fulfilled. Ericson conferred a benefit on Petro Industries by building the oil derrick. Ericson built the derrick with the reasonable expectation of being paid. He was not intending to act as a volunteer. The derrick conferred an obvious benefit on Petro Industries. Petro Industries would be unjustly enriched if it was allowed to keep the derrick without paying Ericson for the work. Therefore, Ericson should be able to recover in *quantum meruit*

---

**15.** Contracts that by their terms cannot be performed within one year must be in writing to be enforceable (see Chapter 16).

the reasonable value of the oil derrick that was built, which is ordinarily equal to its fair market value.

*Concept Summary 19.1* below reviews all of the equitable remedies, including quasi contract, that may be available in the event that a contract is breached.

## SECTION 4
# WAIVER OF BREACH

Under certain circumstances, a nonbreaching party may be willing to accept a defective performance of the contract. This knowing relinquishment of a legal right (that is, the right to require satisfactory and full performance) is called a **waiver.**

## Consequences of a Waiver of Breach

When a waiver of a breach of contract occurs, the party waiving the breach cannot take any later action on it. In effect, the waiver erases the past breach, and the contract continues as if the breach had never occurred. Of course, the waiver of breach of contract extends only to the matter waived and not to the whole contract.

## Reasons for Waiving a Breach

Businesspersons often waive breaches of contract to obtain whatever benefit is still possible out of the contract. For instance, a seller contracts with a buyer to deliver to the buyer ten thousand tons of coal on or before November 1. The contract calls for the buyer to pay by November 10 for coal delivered. Because of a coal miners' strike, coal is hard to find. The seller breaches the contract by not tendering delivery until November 5. The buyer will likely choose to waive the seller's breach, accept delivery of the coal, and pay as contracted.

## Waiver of Breach and Subsequent Breaches

Ordinarily, a waiver by a contracting party will not operate to waive subsequent, additional, or future breaches of contract. This is always true when the subsequent breaches are unrelated to the first breach.

▶ **Example 19.14** Ashton owns a multimillion-dollar apartment complex that is under construction. Ashton allows the contractor to complete a stage of construction late. By doing so, Ashton waives his right to sue for the delay. Ashton does not, however, waive the right to sue for failure to comply with engineering specifications on the same job. ◀

**PATTERN-OF-CONDUCT EXCEPTION** A waiver can extend to subsequent defective performance if a reasonable person would conclude that similar defective performance in the future will be acceptable. Therefore, a *pattern of conduct* that waives a number of successive breaches will operate as a continued waiver. To change this result, the nonbreaching party

---

### CONCEPT SUMMARY 19.1
#### Equitable Remedies

| REMEDY | DESCRIPTION |
| --- | --- |
| **Rescission and Restitution** | 1. *Rescission*—A remedy whereby a contract is canceled and the parties are restored to the original positions that they occupied prior to the transaction.<br>2. *Restitution*—When a contract is rescinded, both parties must make restitution to each other by returning the goods, property, or funds previously conveyed. |
| **Specific Performance** | An equitable remedy calling for the performance of the act promised in the contract. Only available when monetary damages would be inadequate—such as in contracts for the sale of land or unique goods—and never available in personal-service contracts. |
| **Reformation** | An equitable remedy allowing a contract to be reformed, or rewritten, to reflect the parties' true intentions. Available when an agreement is imperfectly expressed in writing, such as when a mutual mistake has occurred. |
| **Recovery Based on Quasi Contract** | An equitable theory under which a party who confers a benefit on another with the reasonable expectation of being paid can seek a court order for the fair market value of the benefit conferred. |

should give notice to the breaching party that full performance will be required in the future.

**EFFECT ON THE CONTRACT** The party who has rendered defective or less-than-full performance remains liable for the damages caused by the breach of contract. In effect, the waiver operates to keep the contract going. The waiver prevents the nonbreaching party from declaring the contract at an end or rescinding the contract. The contract continues, but the nonbreaching party can recover damages caused by the defective or less-than-full performance.

## SECTION 5
# CONTRACT PROVISIONS LIMITING REMEDIES

A contract may include provisions stating that no damages can be recovered for certain types of breaches or that damages will be limited to a maximum amount. The contract may also provide that the only remedy for breach is replacement, repair, or refund of the purchase price. The contract may also provide that one party can seek injunctive relief if the other party breaches the contract (for an example, see Paragraph 11 in *Appendix to Chapter 19: Reading and Analyzing Contracts,* following this chapter). Provisions stating that no damages can be recovered are called *exculpatory clauses* (see Chapter 14). Provisions that affect the availability of certain remedies are called *limitation-of-liability clauses.*

## The UCC Allows Sales Contracts to Limit Remedies

The Uniform Commercial Code (UCC) provides that in a contract for the sale of goods, remedies can be limited. We will examine the UCC provisions on lim-

ited remedies in Chapter 22, in the context of the remedies available on the breach of a contract for the sale or lease of goods.[16]

## Enforceability of Limitation-of-Liability Clauses

Whether a limitation-of-liability clause in a contract will be enforced depends on the type of breach that is excused by the provision. Normally, a provision excluding liability for fraudulent or intentional injury will not be enforced. Likewise, a clause excluding liability for illegal acts, acts that are contrary to public policy, or violations of law will not be enforced. A clause that excludes liability for negligence may be enforced in some situations when the parties have roughly equal bargaining positions.

▶ **Case in Point 19.15** Engineering Consulting Services, Ltd. (ECS), contracted with RSN Properties, Inc, a real estate developer. ECS was to perform soil studies for $2,200 and render an opinion on the use of septic systems in a particular subdivision being developed. A clause in the contract limited ECS's liability to RSN to the value of the engineering services or the sum of $50,000, whichever was greater.

ECS concluded that most of the lots were suitable for septic systems, so RSN proceeded with the development. RSN constructed the roads and water lines to the subdivision in reliance on ECS's conclusions, which turned out to be incorrect. RSN sued ECS for breach of contract and argued that the limitation of liability was against public policy and unenforceable. The court, however, enforced the limitation-of-liability clause as "a reasonable allocation of risks in an arm's-length business transaction."[17] ◀

---

16. See UCC 2–719(1).
17. *RSN Properties, Inc. v. Engineering Consulting Services, Ltd.,* 301 Ga.App. 52, 686 S.E.2d 853 (2009).

## Reviewing: Breach of Contract and Remedies

Kyle Bruno enters a contract with X Entertainment to be a stuntman in a movie. Bruno is widely known as the best motorcycle stuntman in the business, and the movie to be produced, *Xtreme Riders,* has numerous scenes involving high-speed freestyle street-bike stunts. Filming is set to begin August 1 and end by December 1 so that the film can be released the following summer. Both parties to the contract have stipulated that the filming must end on time to capture the profits from the summer movie market. The contract states that Bruno will be paid 10 percent of the net proceeds from the movie for his stunts.

The contract also includes a liquidated damages provision, which specifies that if Bruno breaches the contract, he will owe X Entertainment $1 million. In addition, the contract includes a limitation-of-liability clause stating that if Bruno is injured during filming, X Entertainment's liability is limited to nominal damages. Using the information presented in the chapter, answer the following questions.

1. One day, while Bruno is preparing for a difficult stunt, he gets into an argument with the director and refuses to perform any stunts at all. Can X Entertainment seek specific performance of the contract? Why or why not?

2. Suppose that while performing a high-speed wheelie on a motorcycle, Bruno is injured by the intentionally reckless act of an X Entertainment employee. Will a court be likely to enforce the limitation-of-liability clause? Why or why not?

3. What factors would a court consider to determine whether the $1 million liquidated damages provision constitutes valid damages or is a penalty?

4. Suppose that there was no liquidated damages provision (or the court refused to enforce it) and X Entertainment breached the contract. The breach caused the release of the film to be delayed until after summer. Could Bruno seek consequential (special) damages for lost profits from the summer movie market in that situation? Explain.

**DEBATE THIS . . .** *Courts should always uphold limitation-of-liability clauses, whether or not the two parties to the contract had equal bargaining power.*

## Terms and Concepts

consequential damages 321

incidental damages 318

liquidated damages 322

mitigation of damages 322

nominal damages 322

penalty 322

reformation 324

restitution 323

specific performance 324

waiver 327

## Issue Spotters

1. Greg contracts to build a storage shed for Haney, who pays Greg in advance, but Greg completes only half the work. Haney pays Ipswich $500 to finish the shed. If Haney sues Greg, what would be the measure of recovery? **(See page 320.)**

2. Lyle contracts to sell his ranch to Marley, who is to take possession on June 1. Lyle delays the transfer un- til August 1. Marley  incurs expenses in providing for cattle that he bought for the ranch. When they made the contract, Lyle had no reason to know of the cattle. Is Lyle liable for Marley's expenses in providing for the cattle? Why or why not? **(See page 321.)**

• **Check your answers to the Issue Spotters against the answers provided in Appendix E at the end of this text.**

## Business Scenarios

**19–1. Liquidated Damages.** Cohen contracts to sell his house and lot to Windsor for $100,000. The terms of the contract call for Windsor to pay 10 percent of the purchase price as a deposit toward the purchase price, or a down payment. The terms further stipulate that if the buyer breaches the contract, Cohen will retain the deposit as liquidated damages. Windsor pays the deposit, but because her expected financing of the $90,000 balance falls through, she breaches the contract. Two weeks later Cohen sells the house and lot to Ballard for $105,000. Windsor demands her $10,000 back, but Cohen refuses, claiming that Windsor's breach and the contract terms entitle him to keep the deposit. Discuss who is correct. **(See page 322.)**

**19–2. Specific Performance.** In which of the following situations would specific performance be an appropriate remedy? Discuss fully. **(See page 324.)**

(a) Thompson contracts to sell her house and lot to Cousteau. Then, on finding another buyer willing to pay a higher purchase price, she refuses to deed the property to Cousteau.

(b) Amy contracts to sing and dance in Fred's nightclub for one month, beginning May 1. She then refuses to perform.

(c) Hoffman contracts to purchase a rare coin owned by Erikson, who is breaking up his coin collection.

At the last minute, Erikson decides to keep his coin collection intact and refuses to deliver the coin to Hoffman.

(d) ABC Corp. has three shareholders: Panozzo, who owns 48 percent of the stock; Chang, who owns another 48 percent; and Ryan, who owns 4 percent. Ryan contracts to sell her 4 percent to Chang. Later, Ryan refuses to transfer the shares to Chang.

## Business Case Problems

**19–3. Quasi Contract.** Middleton Motors, Inc., a struggling Ford dealership in Madison, Wisconsin, sought managerial and financial assistance from Lindquist Ford, Inc., a successful Ford dealership in Bettendorf, Iowa. While the two dealerships negotiated the terms for the services and a cash infusion, Lindquist sent Craig Miller, its general manager, to assume control of Middleton. After about a year, the parties had not agreed on the terms, Lindquist had not invested any funds, Middleton had not made a profit, and Miller was fired without being paid. Lindquist and Miller filed a suit in a federal district court against Middleton based on quasi contract, seeking to recover Miller's pay for his time. What are the requirements to recover on a theory of quasi contract? Which of these requirements is most likely to be disputed in this case? Why? [*Lindquist Ford, Inc. v. Middleton Motors, Inc.*, 557 F.3d 469 (7th Cir. 2009)] **(See page 326.)**

**19–4. Liquidated Damages and Penalties.** Planned Pethood Plus, Inc., is a veterinarian-owned clinic. It borrowed $389,000 from KeyBank at an interest rate of 9.3 percent per year for ten years. The loan had a "prepayment penalty" clause that clearly stated that if the loan was repaid early, a specific formula would be used to assess a lump-sum payment to extinguish the obligation. The sooner the loan was paid off, the higher the prepayment penalty. After a year, the veterinarians decided to pay off the loan. KeyBank invoked a prepayment penalty of $40,525.92, which was equal to 10.7 percent of the balance due. The veterinarians sued, contending that the prepayment requirement was unenforceable because it was a penalty. The bank countered that the amount was not a penalty but liquidated damages and that the sum was reasonable. The trial court agreed with the bank, and the veterinarians appealed. Was the loan's prepayment charge reasonable, and should it have been enforced? Why or why not? [*Planned Pethood Plus, Inc. v. KeyCorp, Inc.*, 228 P.3d 262 (Colo.App. 2010)] **(See page 322.)**

**19–5. Measure of Damages.** Before buying a house, Dean and Donna Testa hired Ground Systems, Inc. (GSI), to inspect the sewage and water disposal system. GSI reported a split system with a watertight septic tank, a wastewater tank, a distribution box, and a leach field. The

Testas bought the house. Later, Dean saw that the system was not as GSI described—there was no distribution box or leach field, and there was only one tank, which was not watertight. The Testas arranged for the installation of a new system and sold the house. Assuming that GSI is liable for breach of contract, what is the measure of damages? [*Testa v. Ground Systems, Inc.*, 206 N.J. 330, 20 A.3d 435 (App.Div. 2011)] **(See page 318.)**

**19–6. BUSINESS CASE PROBLEM WITH SAMPLE ANSWER: Consequential Damages.**

 *After submitting the high bid at a foreclosure sale, David Simard entered into a contract to purchase real property in Maryland for $192,000. Simard defaulted (failed to pay) on the contract. A state court ordered the property to be resold at Simard's expense, as required by state law. The property was then resold for $163,000, but the second purchaser also defaulted on his contract. The court then ordered a second resale, resulting in a final price of $130,000. Assuming that Simard is liable for consequential damages, what is the extent of his liability? Is he liable for losses and expenses related to the first resale? If so, is he also liable for losses and expenses related to the second resale? Why or why not? [*Burson v. Simard*, 35 A.3d 1154 (Md. 2012)] **(See page 321.)**

- **For a sample answer to Problem 19–6, go to Appendix F at the end of this text.**

**19–7. Liquidated Damages.** Cuesport Properties, LLC, sold a condominium in Anne Arundel County, Maryland, to Critical Developments, LLC. As part of the sale, Cuesport agreed to build a wall between Critical Developments' unit and an adjacent unit within thirty days of closing. If Cuesport failed to do so, it was to pay $126 per day until completion. This was an estimate of the amount of rent that Critical Developments would lose until the wall was finished and the unit could be rented. Actual damages were otherwise difficult to estimate at the time of the contract. The wall was built on time, but without a county permit, and it did not comply with the county building code. Critical Developments did not modify the wall to comply with the code until 260 days after the date of the contract deadline for completion of the wall. Does Cuesport have to pay Critical Developments $126 for each of the 260 days? Explain. [*Cuesport Properties, LLC v. Critical Developments, LLC,* 209 Md.App. 607, 61 A.3d 91 (2013)] **(See page 322.)**

**19–8. A QUESTION OF ETHICS: Remedies.**

 *On a weekday, Tamara Cohen, a real estate broker, showed a townhouse owned by Ray and Harriet Mayer to Jessica Seinfeld, the wife of comedian Jerry Seinfeld. On the weekend, when Cohen was unavailable because her religious beliefs prevented her from working, the Seinfelds revisited the townhouse on* their own and agreed to buy it. The contract stated that the "buyers will pay buyer's real estate broker's fees." [Cohen v. Seinfeld, 15 Misc.3d 1118(A), 839 N.Y.S.2d 432 (Sup. 2007)] **(See page 323.)**

(a) Is Cohen entitled to payment even though she was not available to show the townhouse to the Seinfelds on the weekend? Explain.

(b) What obligation do parties involved in business deals owe to each other with respect to their religious beliefs? How might the situation in this case have been avoided?

## Legal Reasoning Group Activity

**19–9. Breach and Remedies.** Frances Morelli agreed to sell Judith Bucklin a house in Rhode Island for $177,000. The sale was supposed to be closed by September 1, when the parties were to exchange the deed for the price. The contract included a provision that "if Seller is unable to convey good, clear, insurable, and marketable title, Buyer shall have the option to: (a) accept such title as Seller is able to convey without reduction of the Purchase Price, or (b) cancel this Agreement and receive a return of all Deposits."

An examination of the public records revealed that the house did not have marketable title. Bucklin offered Morelli additional time to resolve the problem, and the closing did not occur as scheduled. Morelli decided "the deal is over" and offered to return the deposit. Bucklin refused and, in mid-October, decided to exercise her option to accept the house without marketable title. She notified Morelli, who did not respond. She then filed a lawsuit against Morelli in a state court. **(See page 317.)**

(a) One group will discuss whether Morelli breached the contract and will decide in whose favor the court should rule.

(b) A second group will assume that Morelli did breach the contract and will determine what the appropriate remedy is in this situation.

# APPENDIX TO CHAPTER 19

## READING AND ANALYZING CONTRACTS

As the text and cases in this unit have indicated, businesses use contracts to make their transactions more predictable. Contracts allow parties to clarify their obligations in great detail. Businesses also use contracts to resolve anticipated problems or conflicts and to clarify responsibility in the event of a breach. An understanding of what is in a typical contract is crucial to using contracts effectively.

Being able to read and understand a contract takes some practice, however. Contract terms often are highly technical and complex, and sometimes the vocabulary and phrasing can be unfamiliar. Nevertheless, businesspersons need to be able to understand the meaning of various contract provisions so that they will know what their business's obligations and rights are under the contract.

### Reading a Contract

A contract is generally intended to serve two purposes:

1. To achieve some commercial purpose—such as, a sale of goods, a lease of property, or an employment agreement.
2. To prevent future conflict by clarifying the obligations and rights of the parties.

Parties should address the details of the business agreement and also should think strategically about how a conflict should be resolved if something goes awry.

Different types of contracts will have different provisions. Sales contracts should contain information on the products being sold, the quantity, the price, and delivery terms. Employment contracts may contain information on the term of employment, employment duties, confidentiality and nondisclosure of the employer's documents and information, and restrictions on competing with the employer after leaving the position.

Although standard forms exist for many types of contracts, the parties to a particular contract may have specific requirements and thus may need to tailor the contract to fit their transaction. A larger transaction or more specialized goods or real estate will require a more specific and probably a longer contract. For example, a sales contract between Airbus and American Airlines for the sale of an Airbus S.A.S. plane was more than 109 pages, not counting the eleven exhibits that followed the main contract.[1]

Regardless of the specificity of the contract provisions, it is important for a businessperson to read and evaluate the responsibilities or commitments of both parties to the contract. Sometimes, a single word or phrase can make an enormous difference. For example, a rental contract for a house may state that the owner is responsible for any plumbing issues, or it may specify that the renter is the responsible party. If a plumber has to be called to deal with clogged pipes on a holiday, that single phrase in the contract will determine who has to pay the plumber's very high holiday rates.

---

1. "Sample Business Contracts," *Onecle.com*, July 14, 2012.

## Contract Analysis Exercise

The sample contract on pages 334–336 is based on an actual employment-related contract between a company called Boulder Dry and its chief financial officer (CFO). As you read the contract, think about the following questions:

1. Which party seems to have had the stronger bargaining position, and why?
2. Which specific provisions favor the employer?
3. Which specific provisions favor the employee?
4. The parties' main intentions in signing this contract were to protect the firm's confidential information and to explain how the CFO could use that information. Which provisions are related to those two purposes?
5. Which provisions seem entirely unrelated to the main purposes? Why are these other provisions included in the contract? What do they do for the parties?
6. What terms in the contract do you find difficult to understand?
7. As a potential employee being asked to sign this agreement, what concerns might you have?
8. If after one year the employee resigns from Boulder Dry, what provisions of this contract should the employee have reviewed before resigning because they would affect his or her future? When leaving the company, what actions would the employee take to ensure that he or she was in compliance with all obligations?

*SEE SAMPLE CONTRACT ON THE FOLLOWING PAGES.*

# EMPLOYEE NONCOMPETITION AND NONDISCLOSURE AGREEMENT

In consideration of my employment or continued employment, with Boulder Dry (the "Company"), and the compensation received from the Company, I hereby agree as follows:

1. *Proprietary Information and Inventions:* I understand and acknowledge that:

    A. The Company is engaged in research, development, production, marketing, and servicing. I am expected to make new contributions and inventions of value to the Company as part of my employment.

    B. My employment creates a relationship of trust between the Company and me with respect to information that may be made known to me or learned by me during my employment.

    C. The Company possesses information that has been discovered or developed by the Company that has commercial value to the Company and is treated by the Company as confidential. All such information is hereinafter called "Proprietary Information," which term shall include, but shall not be limited to, systems, processes, data, computer programs, discoveries, marketing plans, strategies, forecasts, new products, unpublished financial statements, licenses, and customer and supplier lists. The term "Proprietary Information" shall not include any of the foregoing that is in the public domain.

    D. All existing confidential lists of customers of the Company, and all confidential lists of customers developed during my employment, are the sole and exclusive property of the Company and I shall not have any right, title, or interest therein.

2. *Ownership of Proprietary Information:* All Proprietary Information shall be the sole property of the Company, including patents, copyrights, and trademarks. I hereby assign to the Company any rights I may have or acquire in such Proprietary Information. Both during and after my employment, I will keep in strictest confidence and trust all Proprietary Information. I will not use or disclose any Proprietary Information without the written consent of the Company, except as may be necessary in performing my duties as a Company employee.

3. *Commitment to Company and Other Employment:* During my employment, I will devote substantially all of my time to the Company, and I will not, without the Company's prior written consent, engage in any employment or business other than for the Company.

4. *Documentation:* Upon the termination of my employment, I will deliver to the Company all documents, computer programs, data, and other materials of any nature pertaining to my work with the Company. I will not take any originals or reproductions of the foregoing that are embodied in a tangible medium of expression.

5. *Disclosure of Inventions:* I will promptly disclose to the Company all discoveries, designs, inventions, blueprints, computer programs, and data ("Inventions") made by me, either alone or jointly with others, during my employment. Inventions include by definition those things that are related to the business of the Company or that result from the use of property owned, leased, or contracted for by the Company.

6. *Ownership of Inventions:* All Inventions shall be the sole property of the Company, and the Company shall be the sole owner of all patents, copyrights, trademarks, and other rights. I assign to the Company any rights I may have or acquire in such Inventions. I shall assist the Company to obtain and enforce patents, copyrights, trademarks, and other rights and protections relating to Inventions. This obligation shall continue beyond the termination of my employment, but the Company shall compensate me at a reasonable rate after my termination.

7. *Other Agreements:* I represent and warrant that this Agreement and the performance of it do not breach any other agreement to which I am a party. I have not entered into and shall not enter into any agreement in conflict with this Agreement.

8. *Use of Confidential Information of Other Persons:* I have not brought and will not bring with me to the Company any materials or documents of an employer or a former employer that are not generally available to the public. If I desire or need to use any materials from a prior employer, I will obtain express written authorization from such employer.

9. *Restrictive Covenant:* I hereby acknowledge my possession of Proprietary Information and the highly competitive nature of the business of the Company. I will not, during my employment and for three (3) years following my termination, directly or indirectly engage in any competitive business or assist others in engaging in any competitive business. I understand that this Section is not meant to prevent me from earning a living. It does intend to prevent any competitive business from gaining any unfair advantage from my knowledge of Proprietary Information. I understand that by making my new employer aware of the provisions of this Section 9, that employer can take such action as to avoid my breaching the provisions hereof and to indemnify me in the event of a breach.

# COMMENTS TO CONTRACT PARAGRAPHS

**Paragraph 1A.**  This is essentially a broad description of the employee's role at the company and explains why this agreement is necessary. Often, a clause like this precedes a statement indicating that the employer gets to keep any value that the employee adds to the firm.

**Paragraph 1B.**  This paragraph establishes that a relationship of trust and confidence exists between employer and employee. Through this clause, both parties are agreeing they owe duties to each other related to information that benefits the company. The clause implies that that there will be negative consequences for the employee if he or she breaks that relationship.

**Paragraph 1C.**  This paragraph establishes what the term "Proprietary Information" means. In contracts, terms that are capitalized and placed in quotation marks (sometimes in parentheses as well) are called "defined terms." Whenever the term "Proprietary Information" appears throughout the rest of the contract, it will have the definition set out in this paragraph. The definition is extremely broad and captures almost any intellectual property, data, and similar items. The contract asserts that this information is important to the business and gives the company some strategic advantage.

**Paragraph 1D.**  This clause clarifies that customer lists belong to the employer even if the employee develops or expands the lists in some way. This may become important if the employee leaves the company because the clause clarifies that the employee may not recruit or "steal" customers.

**Paragraph 2.**  Here, we see the defined term "Proprietary Information" again. This paragraph documents that the employer owns all Proprietary Information, as defined, even if it was created by the employee. Further, the employee agrees to give the employer any legal rights that the employee may obtain to any Proprietary Information.

**Paragraph 3.**  In this clause, the employee promises that he or she will work full time for the employer and will not take any additional employment without the employer's permission.

**Paragraph 4.**  This clause further asserts that the company takes the confidential nature of the Proprietary Information seriously. Here, the employee promises that if he or she leaves the company's employment, he or she will turn over any work-related material to the company.

**Paragraph 5.**  If the employee creates something of any kind at work, he or she must tell the employer about it, and the employer will receive any disclosures confidentially. The contract goes out of its way to ensure that almost anything the employee invents at work or that is related to work fits under this paragraph. Such items are given a new term called "Inventions." Note that the definition of inventions includes the same items that are in the definition of Proprietary Information as well as some additional ones. The paragraphs discussing Proprietary Information deal with information that the company already possesses and will continue to possess and that the employee will access or need. This paragraph expands the obligations of the employee to what could be called new proprietary information, defined as "Inventions."

**Paragraph 6.**  Just as the employee agreed to give any right in already existing information (such as a modified customer list) to the employer, here the employee promises to give all legal rights to inventions to the employer. In addition, because the rights may originally belong to the employee, the employee promises to help the employer secure any rights or protections necessary to increase the value of the invention. This obligation to help the employer continues to exist after the employee leaves the firm, and the employer agrees to pay for the work required in that situation. The employer is making sure that it can keep anything the employee invents during work time or with company resources.

**Paragraph 7.**  The employer wants to ensure that this contract does not conflict with any others the employee may have already signed. Here, the employee affirms that he or she has made no conflicting agreements. The clause implies that the employee will be responsible for any consequences that arise from such conflicts.

**Paragraph 8.**  The employer does not want to become involved in a dispute with another company by hiring this employee. In this clause, the employee states that he or she is not bringing the employer any confidential information belonging to someone else.

**Paragraph 9.**  This paragraph is a covenant not to compete, one of the most important provisions from the perspective of the employee. Employers worry that former employees will join a rival company and take their information and expertise with them. A covenant not to compete helps prevent that from happening. In short, a covenant not to compete prohibits an employee from working for a competing business for a specified time. This covenant applies regardless of whether the employee leaves the company or is terminated. Covenants not to compete have to be carefully drafted. A court will not enforce a covenant that is too broad in its coverage or that lasts for too long. Three years, the length of this covenant not to compete, is not unduly long. If the covenant is challenged, however, the employer will have to show that this length of time was necessary to protect its business interests. Employees do not appreciate covenants not to compete, but find that they are an inevitable part of employment in information-sensitive industries.

10. *Agreement Not to Solicit Customers:* During the course of my employment and for a period of three (3) years following my termination, I will not attempt to solicit any person, firm, or corporation that has been a customer account of the Company.

11. *Remedies:* I acknowledge that a remedy at law for any breach or threatened breach of the provisions of this Agreement would be inadequate. I therefore agree that the Company shall be entitled to injunctive relief in addition to any other available rights and remedies in case of any such breach or threatened breach. Nothing contained herein shall be construed as prohibiting the Company from pursuing any other remedies available for any such breach or threatened breach.

12. *Assignment:* This Agreement and the rights and obligations of the parties hereto shall bind and inure to the benefit of any successor(s) of the Company, whether by reorganization, merger, consolidation, sale of assets, or otherwise. Neither this Agreement nor any rights or benefits hereunder may be assigned by me.

13. *Interpretation:* It is the desire and intent of the parties hereto that the provisions of this Agreement shall be enforced to the fullest extent permissible. Accordingly, if any provision of this Agreement shall be adjudicated to be invalid or unenforceable, such provision shall be deemed deleted. Such deletion will apply only to the deleted provision in the particular jurisdiction in which such adjudication is made. If any provision contained herein shall be held to be excessively broad as to duration, geographical scope, activity, or subject, it shall be construed by limiting and reducing it so as to be enforceable.

14. *Notices:* All notices pursuant to this Agreement shall be given by personal delivery or by certified mail, return receipt requested. Notices to the Employee shall be addressed to the Employee at the address of record with the Company. Notices to the Company shall be addressed to its principal office. The date of personal delivery or the date of mailing any such notice shall be deemed to be the date of delivery thereof.

15. *Waivers:* Any waiver of breach of any provision of this Agreement shall not thereby be deemed a waiver of any preceding or succeeding breach of the same or any other provision of this Agreement.

16. *Headings:* The headings of the sections hereof are inserted for convenience only and shall not be deemed to constitute a part hereof nor to affect the meaning hereof.

17. *Governing Law:* This Agreement shall be governed by and construed and enforced in accordance with the laws of the State of New Hampshire.

18. *No Employment Agreement:* I acknowledge that this Agreement does not constitute an employment agreement. This Agreement shall be binding upon me regardless of whether my employment shall continue for any length of time and whether my employment is terminated for any reason whatsoever. This is true whether my employment is terminated by the Company or by me.

19. *Complete Agreement, Amendments, and Prior Agreements:* The foregoing is the entire agreement of the parties with respect to the subject matter hereof and may not be amended, supplemented, canceled, or discharged except by written instrument executed by both parties hereto. This Agreement supersedes any and all prior agreements between the parties hereto with respect to the matters covered hereby.

Date: _____     Employee: _____

Accepted and agreed to as of this date by Company:

Date: _____     By: _____

Name: _____

Title: _____

**Paragraph 10.**  Similar to a covenant not to compete, this clause prohibits an employee from soliciting the company's customers during his or her employment or for up to three years afterward. Without such protection, an employer would be vulnerable to any former employee taking customer lists and using them to solicit customers at a new employer or at his or her own business.

**Paragraph 11.**  This paragraph allows the employer to seek injunctive relief against the employee, should it be necessary. Here, the employee agrees that the employer not only may seek monetary damages from the employee in the event that this agreement is breached but may also prohibit him or her from engaging in whatever behavior violates the contract. Recall that typically the first line of remedies is damages to compensate for injury. Here the parties are acknowledging in advance (for the benefit of any court that later is involved) that the harm caused by a breach of the contract cannot be compensated or corrected with monetary damages.

**Paragraph 12.**  Companies change, and so do their owners. This paragraph states that the contract will survive even if ownership of the company changes due to a merger, reorganization, or other reason. The employee cannot avoid this contract simply because the owner that signed the agreement later sells the company to someone else. This paragraph and many of the subsequent paragraphs are often referred to as "boilerplate language," meaning provisions that appear in some form in many contracts. They are included because conflicts have arisen over these points in the past and courts have interpreted contracts without this language in a way that the parties want to avoid. Boilerplate language can be very dangerous because parties may see the headings and not read further because the language is similar from contract to contract. But boilerplate language can make a difference in which party later wins a dispute (because the language spells out the law that will be used to interpret the contract, where a case must be brought, the proper way to give notice of changes, and the like).

**Paragraph 13.**  Employers know that even the most carefully drafted agreements can sometimes be rendered unenforceable by a reviewing court. Laws change over time, and so do attitudes toward contract terms. This paragraph states that if part of this contract is rendered unenforceable for some reason, the rest of the contract will survive intact (that is, the unenforceable part of the contract is severable). The paragraph specifically references the covenant not to compete and the prohibition against solicitation. If a court rejects those terms as too broad in scope or too lengthy, the parties agree that the court should adjust the clause in order to make it enforceable under the law.

**Paragraph 14.**  This paragraph deals with notices. If the employer or the employee wants to communicate about the contract, the communication must be sent by personal delivery or registered/certified mail. Note that this means that an e-mail is not sufficient notice under this agreeement.

**Paragraph 15.**  This paragraph is meant to protect the employer. Sometimes, through generosity or neglect, employers fail to enforce every clause of a contract. For example, an employer may allow a former employee to start a competing business earlier than the contract states or permit an employee to take a second job. This paragraph ensures that if the employer allows some action that is prohibited in the contract, that does not mean that the contract term is waived forever. Just because the employer does not fully enforce the contract every time does not necessarily mean the employer is barred from doing so in the future.

**Paragraph 16.**  This clause is meant to clarify that the headings are just headings and do not change the interpretation of the language in the paragraphs or the overall meaning of the contract.

**Paragraph 17.**  This contract will be interpreted using the law of the state of New Hampshire. It is likely that the employer selected New Hampshire for some particular reason. Typically, an employer chooses a state where the law provides the most benefits for the employer. For example, employers typically choose the law of a particular state because it is their geographic home state and the employer's lawyers are familiar with its law. Employers may also choose a legal jurisdiction because its laws create a climate that is more favorable to the employer than the employee.

**Paragraph 18.**  In this paragraph, the employee acknowledges that this contract is about nondisclosure of information and does not constitute an employment agreement that promises any length of service or any promise of continued employment.

**Paragraph 19.**  This paragraph states that this contract is the complete agreement between the employer and the employee. Any other side agreements, e-mails, conversations, or other communications are irrelevant. The employee cannot rely on a manager's promise of a particular salary or terms of a covenant not to compete. This agreement is the final statement of the relationship between the employer and the employee.

## Contract Law and the Application of Ethics

Generally, a responsible business manager will evaluate a business transaction on the basis of three criteria—legality, profitability, and ethics (see Chapter 5). But what does acting ethically mean in the area of contracts? If you enter into a contract with an individual who fails to look after her or his own interests, is that your fault? Should you be doing something about it? If the contract happens to be to your advantage and to the other party's detriment, do you have a responsibility to correct the situation?

Suppose that your neighbor puts a "For sale" sign on her car and offers to sell it for $6,000. You learn that she is moving to another state and needs the extra cash to help finance the move. You know that she could easily get $10,000 for the car, and you consider purchasing it and then reselling it at a profit. But you also discover that your neighbor is completely unaware that she has priced the car significantly below its *Blue Book* value. Are you ethically obligated to tell her that she is essentially giving away $4,000 if she sells you the car for only $6,000?

This kind of situation, transplanted into the world of commercial transactions, raises an obvious question: At what point should the sophisticated businessperson cease looking after his or her own economic welfare and become "his or her brother's keeper," so to speak?

## Freedom of Contract and Freedom from Contract

The answer to the question just raised is not simple. On the one hand, a common ethical assumption in our society is that individuals should be held responsible for the consequences of their own actions, including their contractual promises. This principle is expressed in the legal concept of freedom of contract. On the other hand, another common assumption in our society is that individuals should not harm one another by their actions. This is the basis of both tort law and criminal law.

In the area of contract law, ethical behavior often involves balancing these principles. In the above example, if you purchased the car and your neighbor later learned its true value and sued you for the difference, very likely no court of law would find that the contract should be rescinded. At times, however, courts will hold that the principle of freedom *of* contract should give way to the principle of freedom *from* contract, a doctrine based on the assumption that people should not be harmed by the actions of others. We look next at some examples of situations in which parties to contracts may be excused from performance under their contracts to prevent injustice.

**Impossibility of Performance** The doctrine of impossibility of performance is based to some extent on the ethical question of whether one party should suffer economic loss when it is impossible to perform a contract. The rule that one is "bound by his or her contracts" is not followed when performance becomes impossible.

The doctrine, however, is applied only when the parties themselves did not consciously assume the risk of the events that rendered performance impossible. Furthermore, this doctrine rests on the assumption that the party claiming the defense of impossibility has acted ethically.

A contract is discharged, for example, if it calls for the delivery of a particular car and, through no fault of either party, this car is stolen and completely demolished in an accident. Yet the doctrine would not excuse performance if the party who agreed to sell the car caused its destruction by her or his negligence.

Before the late nineteenth century, courts were reluctant to discharge a contract even when performance was literally impossible. Just as society's ethics changes with the passage of time, however, the law also changes to reflect society's new perceptions of ethical behavior.[1]

Today, courts are much more willing to discharge a contract when its performance has become literally impossible. Holding a party in breach of contract, when performance has become impossible through no fault of that party, no longer coincides with society's notions of fairness.

### LEGAL REASONING

1.  *Suppose that you contract to purchase steel at a fixed price per ton. Before the contract is performed, a lengthy steelworkers' strike causes the price of steel to triple from the price specified in the contract. If you demand that the supplier fulfill the contract, the supplier will go out of business. What are your ethical obligations in this situation? What are your legal rights?*

**Unconscionability** The doctrine of unconscionability is a good example of how the law attempts to enforce ethical behavior. Under this doctrine, a contract may be deemed to be so unfair to one party as to be unenforceable—even though that party voluntarily agreed to the contract's terms. Unconscionable action, like unethical action, defies precise definition. Information about the particular facts and specific circumstances surrounding the contract is essential. For example, a court might find that a contract made with a marginally literate consumer was unfair and unenforceable but might uphold the same contract made with a major business firm.

Section 2–302 of the Uniform Commercial Code (to be discussed in Unit Four), incorporates the common law concept of unconscionability. Similarly, it does not define the concept with any precision. Rather, it leaves it to the courts to determine when a contract is so one sided and unfair to one party as to be unconscionable and thus unenforceable.

Usually, courts will do all that they can to save contracts rather than render them unenforceable. Only in extreme situations, as when a contract or clause is so one sided as to "shock the conscience" of the court, will a court hold a contract or contractual clause unconscionable.

---

1. A leading English case in which the court held that a defendant was discharged from the duty to perform due to impossibility of performance is *Taylor v. Caldwell,* 122 Eng.Rep. 309 (K.B. [King's Bench] 1863).

**Exculpatory Clauses**  In some situations, courts have also refused to enforce exculpatory clauses on the ground that they are unconscionable or contrary to public policy. An *exculpatory clause* attempts to excuse a party from liability in the event of monetary or physical injury, no matter who is at fault. In some situations, such clauses are upheld.

***Nonessential Services.***  Generally, the law permits parties to assume, by express agreement, the risks inherent in certain nonessential activities. For example, a health club can require its members to sign a clause releasing the club from any liability for injuries the members might incur while using the club's equipment and facilities. Likewise, an exculpatory clause releasing a ski resort from liability for skiing accidents would likely be enforced.[2] In such situations, exculpatory clauses make it possible for a firm's owner to stay in business—by shifting some of the liability risks from the business to the customer.

***Disparities in Bargaining Power.***  Nonetheless, some jurisdictions take a dubious view of exculpatory clauses, particularly when the agreement is between parties with unequal bargaining power, such as a landlord and a tenant or an employer and an employee. Frequently, courts will hold that an exculpatory clause that attempts to exempt an employer from *all* liability for negligence toward its employees is against public policy and thus void.[3]

The courts reason that disparity in bargaining power and economic necessity force the employee to accept the employer's terms. Also, if a plaintiff can prove that an exculpatory clause is ambiguous, the courts generally will not enforce the clause.[4]

### LEGAL REASONING

2. *In determining whether an exculpatory clause should be enforced, why does it matter whether the contract containing the clause involves essential services (such as transportation) or nonessential services (such as skiing or other leisure-time activities)?*

## Covenants Not to Compete

In today's complicated, technological business world, knowledge learned on the job, including trade secrets, has become a valuable commodity. To prevent this knowledge from falling into the hands of competitors, more and more employers are requiring their employees to sign covenants not to compete. The increasing number of lawsuits over noncompete clauses in employment contracts has caused many courts to reconsider the reasonableness of these covenants.

Generally, the courts have few problems with enforcing a covenant not to compete that is ancillary to the sale of a business as long as the covenant's terms are reasonable. After all, part of what is being sold is the business's reputation and goodwill. If, after the sale, the seller opens a competing business nearby, the value of the original business to the purchaser could be greatly diminished.

More difficult for the courts is determining whether covenants not to compete in the employment context should be enforced. Often, this determination involves balancing the interests of the employer against the interests of the employee. Employers have a legitimate interest in protecting their trade secrets and customer lists. At the same time, employees should not be unreasonably restricted in their ability to work in their chosen profession or trade.

**Jurisdictional Differences in Enforcement**  Jurisdictions vary in their approach to covenants not to compete. Many jurisdictions will enforce noncompete covenants in the employment context if both of the following are true.

1. The limitations placed on an employee are reasonable as to time and geographic area.
2. The limitations do not impose a greater restraint than necessary to protect the goodwill or other business interests of the employer.[5]

In a number of jurisdictions, if a court finds that a restraint in a noncompete covenant is not reasonable in light of the circumstances, it will reform the unreasonable provision and then enforce it. A court might, for instance, rewrite an unreasonable restriction by reducing the time period during which a former employee cannot compete from three years to one year. The court would then enforce the reformed agreement.[6]

Other jurisdictions are not so "employer friendly" and refuse to enforce unreasonable covenants. Under California law, covenants not to compete are illegal, as are a number of other types of agreements that have a similar effect.[7] Other western states also tend to regard noncompete covenants with suspicion. For example, courts in Washington State refuse to reform noncompete covenants that are unreasonable and lacking in consideration.[8] Courts in Arizona and Texas have reached similar conclusions.[9]

---

2. *Myers v. Lutsen Mountains Corp.,* 587 F.3d 891 (8th Cir. 2009).

3. See, for example, *Wallace v. Busch Entertainment Corp., City of Santa Barbara v. Superior Court,* 62 Cal.Rptr.3d 527, 161 P.3d 1095 (2007).

4. See, for example, *Tatman v. Space Coast Kennel Club, Inc.,* 27 So.3d 108 (Fla.App. 5 Dist., 2010).

5. See *Drummond American, LLC v. Share Corp.,* 692 F.Supp.2d 650 (E.D.Tex., 2010); and *TEKsystems, Inc. v. Bolton,* 2010 WL 447782 (D.Md. 2010).

6. See, for example, *Estee Lauder Companies v. Batra,* 430 F.Supp.2d 158 (S.D.N.Y. 2006).

7. See, for example, *SriCom, Inc. v. Ebis Logic, Inc.,* 2012 WL 4051222 (N.D.Cal. 2012); and *Thomas Weisel Partners, LLC v. BNP Paribas,* 2010 WL 1267744 (N.D.Cal. 2010).

8. See, for example, *International Paper Co. v. Stuit,* 2012 WL 187143 (W.D.Wash. 2012); and *EEOC v. Fry's Electronics, Inc.,* 2011 WL 666328 (W.D.Wash. 2011).

9. *Philipello v. Taylor,* 2012 WL 1435171 (Tex.App.—Waco 2012); and *Varsity Gold, Inc. v. Porzio,* 202 Ariz. 355, 45 P.3d 352 (2002).

FOCUS ON ETHICS CONTINUES ▶

**Do Noncompete Covenants Stifle Innovation?** One of the reasons that the courts usually look closely at covenants not to compete and evaluate them on a case-by-case basis is the strong public policy favoring competition in this country. Some scholars claim that covenants not to compete, regardless of how reasonable they are, may stifle competition and innovation.

Consider, for example, the argument put forth some years ago by Ronald Gilson, a Stanford University professor of law and business. He contended that California's prohibition on covenants not to compete helped to explain why technological innovation and economic growth skyrocketed in California's Silicon Valley in the late 1990s, while technological development along Massachusetts's Route 128 languished during the same time period. According to Gilson, the different legal rules regarding covenants not to compete in California and Massachusetts were a "critical" factor in explaining why one area saw so much innovation and transfer of technology knowledge and the other area did not.[10]

### LEGAL REASONING

3. *Employers often include covenants not to compete in employment contracts to protect their trade secrets. What effect, if any, will the growth in e-commerce have on the reasonableness of covenants not to compete?*

## Oral Contracts and Promissory Estoppel

Oral contracts are made every day. Many—if not most—of them are carried out, and no problems arise. Occasionally, however, oral contracts are not performed, and one party decides to sue the other. Sometimes, to prevent injustice, the courts will enforce oral contracts under the theory of promissory estoppel.

Ethical standards certainly underlie this doctrine, under which a person who has reasonably relied on the promise of another to his or her detriment can often obtain some measure of recovery. Essentially, promissory estoppel allows a variety of oral promises to be enforced even though they lack what is formally regarded as consideration.

An oral promise made by an insurance agent to a business owner, for example, may be binding if the owner relies on that promise to her or his detriment. Employees who rely to their detriment on an employer's promise may be able to recover damages under the doctrine of promissory estoppel. If a subcontractor fails to complete specific work at a certain price as promised, the contractor whose bid was based on that promise may be able to recover on the basis of promissory estoppel. These are but a few of the many examples in which the courts,

in the interests of fairness and justice, have estopped a promisor from denying that a contract existed.

## Oral Contracts and the Writing Requirement

The courts sometimes use the theory of promissory estoppel to remove a contract from the writing requirement, thereby making oral contracts enforceable. As you learned in Chapter 16, the Statute of Frauds was originally enacted in England in 1677.

Before the Statute of Frauds was passed, English courts had enforced oral contracts on the strength of oral testimony by witnesses. It was not too difficult to evade justice by procuring "convincing" witnesses to support the claim that a contract had been created and then breached. Moreover, seventeenth-century English courts did not allow oral testimony to be given by the parties to a lawsuit—or by any parties with an interest in the litigation, such as husbands or wives. Only written evidence or the testimony of third parties could be used in actions for breach of contract. These constraints enhanced the possibility of fraud.

**Detrimental Reliance** Under the Statute of Frauds, if a contract is oral when it is required to be in writing, it will not, as a rule, be enforced by the courts. An exception to this rule is made if a party has reasonably relied, to his or her detriment, on the oral contract. Enforcing an oral contract on the basis of a party's reliance arguably undercuts the essence of the Statute of Frauds. The reason that such an exception is made is to prevent the statute—which was created to prevent injustice—from being used to promote injustice. Nevertheless, this use of the doctrine is controversial—as is the Statute of Frauds itself.

**Criticisms of the Statute of Frauds** Since its inception more than three hundred years ago, the Statute of Frauds has been criticized by some. They point out that although the statute was created to protect the innocent, it can also be used as a technical defense by a party breaching a genuine, mutually agreed-on oral contract that happens to fall under the statute. For this reason, some legal scholars believe the act has caused more injustice than it has prevented. Thus, exceptions are sometimes made—such as under the doctrine of promissory estoppel—to prevent unfairness and inequity. Generally, the courts are slow to apply the statute if doing so will result in obvious injustice. In some instances, this has required a good deal of inventiveness on the part of the courts.

### LEGAL REASONING

4. *Many countries have no Statute of Frauds, and even England, the country that created the original act, has repealed it. Should the United States do likewise? What are some of the costs and benefits to society of the Statute of Frauds?*

---

10. Ronald J. Gilson, "The Legal Infrastructure of High Technology Industrial Districts: Silicon Valley, Route 128, and Covenants Not to Compete," *New York University Law Review* (June 1999): 575–579.

# Unit Four

## Domestic and International Sales and Lease Contracts

### Contents

# CHAPTER 20

# THE FORMATION OF SALES AND LEASE CONTRACTS

When we turn to contracts for the sale and lease of goods, we move away from common law principles and into the area of statutory law. State statutory law governing sales and lease transactions is based on the uniform Commercial code (UCC), which, as mentioned in Chapter 1, has been adopted as law by all of the states.[1] Of all the attempts to produce a uniform body of laws relating to commercial transactions in the United States, none has been as successful as the UCC.

1. Louisiana has not adopted Articles 2 and 2A, however.

We open this chapter with a discussion of the UCC's Article 2 (on sales) and Article 2A (on leases) as a background to the topic of this chapter, which is the formation of contracts for the sale and lease of goods. The goal of the UCC is to simplify and to streamline commercial transactions. The UCC allows parties to form sales and lease contracts without observing the same degree of formality used in forming other types of contracts, including those entered into online. We look at the important issue of whether online sales can be taxed in this chapter's *Insight into E-Commerce* feature.

Today, businesses often engage in sales and lease transactions on a global scale. Because international sales transactions are increasingly commonplace, we conclude the chapter with an examination of the United Nations Convention on Contracts for the International Sale of Goods (CISG), which governs international sales contracts. The CISG is a model uniform law that applies only when a nation has adopted it, just as the UCC applies only to the extent that it has been adopted by a state.

---

## THE UNIFORM COMMERCIAL CODE

In the early years of this nation, sales law varied from state to state, and this lack of uniformity complicated the formation of multistate sales contracts. The problems became especially troublesome in the late nineteenth century as multistate contracts became the norm. For this reason, numerous attempts were made to produce a uniform body of laws relating to commercial transactions.

The National Conference of Commissioners on Uniform State Laws (NCCUSL) drafted two uniform ("model") acts that were widely adopted by the states: the Uniform Negotiable Instruments Law (1896) and the Uniform Sales Act (1906). Several other proposed uniform acts followed, although most were not as widely adopted.

In the 1940s, the NCCUSL recognized the need to integrate the half dozen or so uniform acts covering commercial transactions into a single, comprehensive body of statutory law. The NCCUSL developed the Uniform Commercial Code (UCC) to serve that purpose. First issued in 1949, the UCC facilitates commercial transactions by making the laws governing sales and lease contracts clearer, simpler, and more readily applicable to the numerous difficulties that can arise during such transactions.

### Comprehensive Coverage of the UCC

The UCC is the single most comprehensive codification of the broad spectrum of laws involved in a total commercial transaction. The UCC views the entire "commercial transaction for the sale of and payment for goods" as a single legal occurrence having numerous facets. The articles and sections of the UCC are periodically revised or supplemented to clarify certain aspects or to establish new rules as needed when the business environment changes.

You can gain an idea of the UCC's comprehensiveness by looking at the titles of the articles of the UCC in Appendix C. As you will note, Article 1, titled General Provisions, sets forth definitions and general principles applicable to commercial transactions. For instance, there is an obligation to perform in "good faith" all contracts falling under the UCC [UCC 1–304]. Article 1 thus provides the basic groundwork for the remaining articles, each of which focuses on a particular aspect of commercial transactions.

Does the duty of good faith and fair dealing apply to contracts other than contracts for sales of goods? That question arose in the following case.

---

## CASE 20.1

### Amaya v. Brater
Court of Appeals of Indiana, 981 N.E.2d 1235 (2013).

**BACKGROUND AND FACTS** In March 2010, as a third-year medical student at Indiana University School of Medicine (IUSM) in Indianapolis, Peter Amaya took a group examination covering several subjects. Three professors observed Amaya and concluded that he was cheating by looking at the paper of another student. After the exam, two of the professors confronted Amaya. He denied cheating and maintained that he was merely looking over at the clock on the wall. In August, IUSM Dean Craig Brater dismissed Amaya from the school. Amaya filed a complaint in an Indiana state court against the dean and IUSM, alleging breach of contract and breach of the duty of good faith and fair dealing. The court granted IUSM's motion for summary judgment. Amaya appealed.

**DECISION AND RATIONALE** A state intermediate appellate court affirmed the judgment in IUSM's favor. Amaya's separate causes of action for alleged breaches of contract and the duty of good faith and fair dealing were inappropriate. "The duty of good faith and fair dealing is a concept created by the Uniform Commercial Code and restricted to contracts for the sale of goods . . . ." With respect to the claim of breach of contract, the reviewing court pointed out that the legal relationship between a student and her or his university is one of *implied* contract. "The courts' approach has been similar to that used with contracts conditioned upon the satisfaction of one party. The university requires that the student's academic performance be satisfactory to the university in its honest judgment." The University's conclusion that Amaya failed to maintain acceptable professional standards was a "rational determination arrived after much deliberation and after Amaya had numerous opportunities to be heard."

**THE ETHICAL DIMENSION** *The UCC's duty of good faith and fair dealing may not apply to the contract that exists between a university and its students, but the school cannot act in bad faith. How is "bad faith" defined? To whom else might a school owe this duty?*

**THE LEGAL DIMENSION** *What type of contract was at the center of this case?*

---

## A Single, Integrated Framework for Commercial Transactions

The UCC attempts to provide a consistent and integrated framework of rules to deal with all the phases *ordinarily arising* in a commercial sales transaction from start to finish. For an example how several articles of the UCC can apply to a single commercial transaction, see Exhibit 20–1 on the following page.

SECTION 2

## THE SCOPE OF ARTICLES 2 (SALES) AND 2A (LEASES)

Article 2 of the UCC sets forth the requirements for *sales contracts*, as well as the duties and obligations of the parties involved in the sales contract. Article 2A covers similar issues for *lease contracts*. Bear in mind, however, that

**EXHIBIT 20-1  How Several Articles of the UCC Can Apply to a Single Transaction**

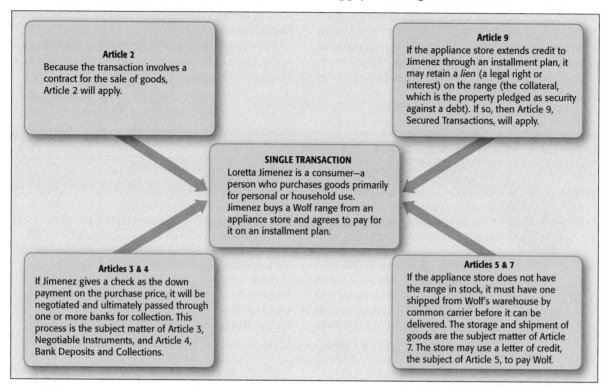

**Article 2**
Because the transaction involves a contract for the sale of goods, Article 2 will apply.

**Article 9**
If the appliance store extends credit to Jimenez through an installment plan, it may retain a *lien* (a legal right or interest) on the range (the collateral, which is the property pledged as security against a debt). If so, then Article 9, Secured Transactions, will apply.

**SINGLE TRANSACTION**
Loretta Jimenez is a consumer—a person who purchases goods primarily for personal or household use. Jimenez buys a Wolf range from an appliance store and agrees to pay for it on an installment plan.

**Articles 3 & 4**
If Jimenez gives a check as the down payment on the purchase price, it will be negotiated and ultimately passed through one or more banks for collection. This process is the subject matter of Article 3, Negotiable Instruments, and Article 4, Bank Deposits and Collections.

**Articles 5 & 7**
If the appliance store does not have the range in stock, it must have one shipped from Wolf's warehouse by common carrier before it can be delivered. The storage and shipment of goods are the subject matter of Article 7. The store may use a letter of credit, the subject of Article 5, to pay Wolf.

the parties to sales or lease contracts are free to agree to terms different from those stated in the UCC.

## Article 2—The Sale of Goods

Article 2 of the UCC (as adopted by state statutes) governs **sales contracts,** or contracts for the sale of goods. To facilitate commercial transactions, Article 2 modifies some of the common law contract requirements that were discussed in the previous chapters.

To the extent that it has not been modified by the UCC, however, the common law of contracts also applies to sales contracts. In other words, the common law requirements for a valid contract—agreement consideration, capacity, and legality—that were discussed in previous chapters are also applicable to sales contracts.

In general, the rule is that whenever a conflict arises between a common law contract rule and the state statutory law based on the UCC, the UCC controls. Thus, when a UCC provision addresses a certain

issue, the UCC rule governs. When the UCC is silent, the common law governs.

The relationship between general contract law and the law governing sales of goods is illustrated in Exhibit 20–2 on the facing page.

In regard to Article 2, keep two points in mind.

1. Article 2 deals with the sale of *goods*. It does not deal with real property (real estate), services, or intangible property such as stocks and bonds. Thus, if the subject matter of a dispute is goods, the UCC governs. If it is real estate or services, the common law applies.

2. In some situations, the rules can vary depending on whether the buyer or the seller is a *merchant*.

We look now at how the UCC defines a *sale, goods,* and *merchant status.*

**WHAT IS A SALE?**  The UCC defines a **sale** as "the passing of title [evidence of ownership rights] from the seller to the buyer for a price" [UCC 2–106(1)]. The price may be payable in cash or in other goods or ser-

## EXHIBIT 20-2 The Law Governing Contracts

This exhibit graphically illustrates the relationship between general contract law and statutory law (UCC Articles 2 and 2A) governing contracts for the sale and lease of goods. Sales contracts are not governed exclusively by Article 2 of the UCC but are also governed by general contract law whenever it is relevant and has not been modified by the UCC.

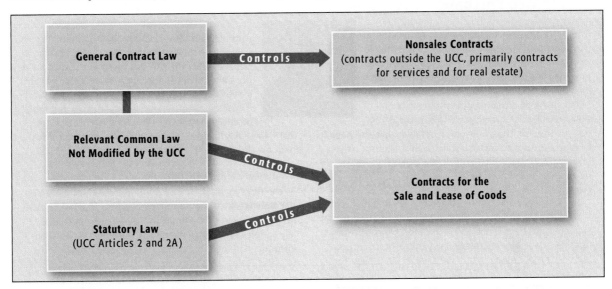

vices. (See this chapter's *Insight into E-Commerce* on the following page for a discussion of whether states can impose taxes on online sales.)

**WHAT ARE GOODS?** To be characterized as a *good,* an item of property must be *tangible,* and it must be *movable.* **Tangible property** has physical existence— it can be touched or seen. **Intangible property**— such as corporate stocks and bonds, patents and copyrights, and ordinary contract rights—has only conceptual existence and thus does not come under Article 2. A *movable* item can be carried from place to place. Hence, real estate is excluded from Article 2.

*Goods Associated with Real Estate.* Goods *associated* with real estate often do fall within the scope of Article 2, however [UCC 2–107]. For instance, a contract for the sale of minerals, oil, or gas is a contract for the sale of goods if *severance, or separation, is to be made by the seller.* Similarly, a contract for the sale of growing crops or timber to be cut is a contract for the sale of goods *regardless of who severs them from the land.*

▶ **Case in Point 20.1** Homeowners in Colorado installed underground radiant heating systems to warm indoor flooring or melt snow and ice under driveways and sidewalks. The systems began to leak as a result of the hardening of a hose called Entran II. The homeowners sued Goodyear Tire and Rubber

Company, the maker of the hose, asserting claims under Colorado's version of the UCC. The court held that because the hose was a tangible and movable good at the time the contract was made, it was a "good" under the UCC. Therefore, the UCC applied to the contract even though the hose was later incorporated into real property (under flooring).[2] ◀

*Goods and Services Combined.* When contracts involve a combination of goods and services, courts generally use the **predominant-factor test** to determine whether a contract is primarily for the sale of goods or the sale of services.[3] If a court decides that a mixed contract is primarily a goods contract, *any* dispute, even a dispute over the services portion, will be decided under the UCC.

▶ **Case in Point 20.2** Gene and Martha Jannusch agreed to sell Festival Foods, a concessions business, to Lindsey and Louann Naffziger for a price of $150,000. The deal included a truck, a trailer, freezers, roasters, chairs, tables, a fountain service, signs, and lighting. The Naffzigers paid $10,000 down with the balance

---

2. *Loughridge v. Goodyear Tire and Rubber Co.,* 192 F.Supp.2d 1175 (D.Colo. 2002).

3. UCC 2–314(1) does stipulate that serving food or drinks is a "sale of goods" for purposes of the implied warranty of merchantability, as will be discussed in Chapter 23. The UCC also specifies that selling unborn animals or rare coins qualifies as a "sale of goods."

# INSIGHT INTO E-COMMERCE
## Taxing Web Purchases

In 1992, the United States Supreme Court ruled that an individual state cannot compel an out-of-state business that lacks a substantial physical presence within that state to collect and remit state taxes.[a] Although Congress has the power to pass legislation requiring out-of-state corporations to collect and remit state sales taxes, it has not yet done so. Thus, only online retailers that also have a physical presence within a state must collect state taxes on any Web sales made to residents of that state. (State residents are supposed to self-report their purchases and pay use taxes to the state, which they rarely do.)

### Redefining Physical Presence

Several states have found a way to collect taxes on Internet sales made to state residents by out-of-state corporations—by redefining *physical presence*. In 2008, New York changed its tax laws in this manner. Now, an online retailer that pays any party within New York to solicit business for its products is considered a physical presence in the state and must collect state taxes. Since then, at least seventeen other states have made similar changes in their laws in an effort to increase their revenues by collecting sales tax from online retailers.

These new laws, often called the "Amazon tax" because they are largely aimed at Amazon.com, affect all online sellers, including Overstock.com and Drugstore.com. These tax laws especially affect those retailers that pay affiliates to direct traffic to their Web sites. These laws allow states to tax online commerce even though, to date, Congress has explicitly chosen not to tax Internet sales.

### Local Governments Sue Online Travel Companies

Travelocity, Priceline.com, Hotels.com, and Orbitx.com are online travel companies (OTCs) that offer, among other things, hotel booking services. By 2013, more than twenty cities, including Atlanta, Charleston, Philadelphia, and San Antonio, had filed suits claiming that the OTCs owed taxes on hotel reservations that they had booked. All of the cities involved in the suits impose a hotel occupancy tax, which is essentially a sales tax.

Initially, some cities won their cases, but more recently, they have been losing in court.[b] As of 2013, the OTCs had prevailed in fifteen of nineteen cases nationwide.

### The Market Place Fairness Act

By the time you read this, online sales taxes may have become a reality for every online business that has annual revenues in excess of $1 million. For several years now, legislation called the Market Place Fairness Act has been introduced in the U.S. Senate. The act would allow states to collect sales taxes from online retailers for transactions within the state.

There are several problems with such legislation. The current tax system involves 9,600 taxing jurisdictions. Even one zip code may cover multiple taxing entities such as different cities and counties. Just consider that the Dallas–Fort Worth airport includes six separate taxing jurisdictions. Current software solutions for retailers that allow them to collect and remit sales taxes for different jurisdictions are extremely costly to install and operate. Overstock.com, for example, spent $1.3 million to add just one state to its sales tax collection system.

### LEGAL CRITICAL THINKING
#### INSIGHT INTO ETHICS

*Some argue that if online retailers are required to collect and pay sales taxes in jurisdictions in which they have no physical presence, they have no democratic way to fight high taxes in those places. Is this an instance of taxation without representation? Discuss.*

---

a. *Quill Corp. v. North Dakota,* 504 U.S. 298, 112 S.Ct. 1904, 119 L.Ed.2d 91 (1992).

b. *Travelscape, LLC v. South Carolina Department of Revenue,* 391 S.C. 89, 705 S.E.2d 28 (2011).

---

to come from a bank loan. They took possession of the equipment and began to use it immediately in Festival Foods operations at various events.

After six events, the Naffzigers returned the truck and all the equipment, and wanted out of the deal because the business did not generate as much income as they expected. The Jannusches sued the Naffzigers for the balance due on the purchase price, claiming that the Naffzigers could no longer reject the goods under the UCC. The Naffzigers claimed that the UCC did not apply because the deal primarily involved the sale of a business rather than the sale of goods.

The court found that the UCC governed under the predominant-factor test. The primary value of the contract was in the goods, not the value of the business. The parties had agreed on the essential terms of the contract (such as the price). Thus, a contract had been formed, and the Naffzigers had breached it. The Naffzigers took possession and control of all of the physical aspects of the business. Therefore, they had no right to return them.[4] ◄

**WHO IS A MERCHANT?** Article 2 governs the sale of goods in general. It applies to sales transactions between all buyers and sellers. In a limited number of instances, though, the UCC presumes that special business standards ought to be imposed because of merchants' relatively high degree of commercial expertise.[5] Such standards do not apply to the casual or inexperienced seller or buyer (consumer).

Section 2–104 sets forth three ways in which merchant status can arise:

1. A merchant is a person who *deals in goods of the kind* involved in the sales contract. Thus, a retailer, a wholesaler, or a manufacturer is a merchant of the goods sold in his or her business. A merchant for one type of goods is not necessarily a merchant for another type. For instance, a sporting goods retailer is a merchant when selling tennis rackets but not when selling a used computer.

2. A merchant is a person who, by occupation, *holds himself or herself out as having knowledge and skill* unique to the practices or goods involved in the transaction. This broad definition may include banks or universities as merchants.

3. A person who *employs a merchant as a broker, agent, or other intermediary* has the status of merchant in that transaction. Hence, if an art collector hires a broker to purchase or sell art for her, the collector is considered a merchant in the transaction.

In summary, a person is a **merchant** when she or he, acting in a mercantile capacity, possesses or uses an expertise specifically related to the goods being sold. This basic distinction is not always clear-cut. For instance, state courts appear to be split on whether farmers should be considered merchants.

---

4. *Jannusch v. Naffziger,* 379 Ill.App.3d 381, 883 N.E.2d 711 (2008).
5. The provisions that apply only to merchants deal principally with the Statute of Frauds, firm offers, confirmatory memoranda, warranties, and contract modification. These special rules reflect expedient business practices commonly known to merchants in the commercial setting. They will be discussed later in this chapter.

# Article 2A—Leases

Leases of personal property (goods such as automobiles and industrial equipment) have become increasingly common. In this context, a lease is a transfer of the right to possess and use goods for a period of time in exchange for payment. Article 2A of the UCC was created to fill the need for uniform guidelines in this area.

Article 2A covers any transaction that creates a lease of goods or a sublease of goods [UCC 2A–102, 2A–103(1)(k)]. Article 2A is essentially a repetition of Article 2, except that it applies to leases of goods rather than sales of goods and thus varies to reflect differences between sales and lease transactions. (Note that Article 2A is not concerned with leases of real property, such as land or buildings.)

**DEFINITION OF A LEASE AGREEMENT** Article 2A defines a **lease agreement** as a lessor's and lessee's bargain with respect to the lease of goods, as found in their language and as implied by other circumstances [UCC 2A–103(1)(k)]. A **lessor** is one who transfers the right to the possession and use of goods under a lease [UCC 2A–103(1)(p)]. A **lessee** is one who acquires the right to the possession and use of goods under a lease [UCC 2A–103(1)(o)]. In other words, the lessee is the party who is leasing the goods from the lessor.

Article 2A applies to all types of leases of goods. Special rules apply to certain types of leases, however, including consumer leases and finance leases.

**CONSUMER LEASES** A *consumer lease* involves three elements:

1. A lessor who regularly engages in the business of leasing or selling.
2. A lessee (except an organization) who leases the goods "primarily for a personal, family, or household purpose."
3. Total lease payments that are less than $25,000 [UCC 2A–103(1)(e)].

To ensure special protection for consumers, certain provisions of Article 2A apply only to consumer leases. For instance, one provision states that a consumer may recover attorneys' fees if a court determines that a term in a consumer lease contract is unconscionable [UCC 2A–108(4)(a)].

**FINANCE LEASES** A *finance lease* involves a lessor, a lessee, and a supplier. The lessor buys or leases goods from the supplier and leases or subleases them to the lessee [UCC 2A–103(1)(g)]. Typically, in a finance lease, the lessor is simply financing the transaction.

▶ **Example 20.3** Marlin Corporation wants to lease a crane for use in its construction business. Marlin's bank agrees to purchase the equipment from Jenco, Inc., and lease the equipment to Marlin. In this situation, the bank is the lessor-financer, Marlin is the lessee, and Jenco is the supplier. ◀

Article 2A, unlike ordinary contract law, makes the lessee's obligations under a finance lease irrevocable and independent from the financer's obligations [UCC 2A–407]. In other words, the lessee must perform and continue to make lease payments even if the leased equipment turns out to be defective. The lessee must look almost entirely to the supplier for any recovery.

▶ **Example 20.4** McKessen Company obtains surgical ophthalmic equipment from a manufacturer and leases it to Vasquez for use at his medical eye center. When the equipment turns out to be defective, Vasquez stops making the lease payments. McKessen sues. Because the lease clearly qualifies as a finance lease under Article 2A, a court would hold in favor of McKessen. Vasquez is obligated to make all payments due under the lease regardless of the condition or performance of the leased equipment. Vasquez can sue the manufacturer of the defective equipment, however. ◀

**SECTION 3**

# THE FORMATION OF SALES AND LEASE CONTRACTS

In regard to the formation of sales and lease contracts, the UCC modifies the common law in several ways. We look here at how Articles 2 and 2A of the UCC modify common law contract rules. Remember, though, that parties to sales and lease contracts are basically free to establish whatever terms they wish.

The UCC comes into play when the parties either fail to provide certain terms in their contract or wish to change the effect of the UCC's terms in the contract's application. The UCC makes this very clear by its repeated use of such phrases as "unless the parties otherwise agree" and "absent a contrary agreement by the parties."

## Offer

In general contract law, the moment a definite offer is met by an unqualified acceptance, a binding con-

tract is formed. In commercial sales transactions, the verbal exchanges, correspondence, and actions of the parties may not reveal exactly when a binding contractual obligation arises. The UCC states that an agreement sufficient to constitute a contract can exist even if the moment of its making is undetermined [UCC 2–204(2), 2A–204(2)].

**OPEN TERMS** According to general contract law, an offer must be definite enough for the parties (and the courts) to ascertain its essential terms when it is accepted. In contrast, the UCC states that a sales or lease contract will not fail for indefiniteness even if one or more terms are left open as long as *both* of the following are true:

1. The parties intended to make a contract.
2. There is a reasonably certain basis for the court to grant an appropriate remedy [UCC 2–204(3), 2A–204(3)].

The UCC provides numerous *open-term* provisions (discussed next) that can be used to fill the gaps in a contract. Thus, if a dispute occurs, all that is necessary to prove the existence of a contract is an indication (such as a purchase order) that there is a contract. Missing terms can be proved by evidence, or a court can presume that the parties intended whatever is reasonable under the circumstances.

Keep in mind, though, that if too many terms are left open, a court may find that the parties did not intend to form a contract. Also, the *quantity* of goods involved usually must be expressly stated in the contract. If the quantity term is left open, the courts will have no basis for determining a remedy.

**Open Price Term.** If the parties have not agreed on a price, the court will determine a "reasonable price at the time for delivery" [UCC 2–305(1)]. If either the buyer or the seller is to determine the price, the price is to be decided in good faith [UCC 2–305(2)]. Under the UCC, *good faith* means honesty in fact and the observance of reasonable commercial standards of fair dealing in the trade [UCC 2–103(1)(b)]. The concepts of *good faith* and *commercial reasonableness* permeate the UCC.

Sometimes, the price fails to be set through the fault of one of the parties. In that situation, the other party can treat the contract as canceled or determine a reasonable price. ▶ **Example 20.5** Perez and Merrick enter into a contract for the sale of goods and agree that Perez will determine the price. Perez refuses to specify the price. Merrick can either treat the contract as canceled or set a reasonable price [UCC 2–305(3)]. ◄

**Open Payment Term.** When the parties do not specify payment terms, payment is due at the time and place at which the buyer is to receive the goods [UCC 2–310(a)]. The buyer can tender payment using any commercially normal or acceptable means, such as a check or credit card. If the seller demands payment in cash, however, the buyer must be given a reasonable time to obtain it [UCC 2–511(2)]. This is especially important when the contract states a definite and final time for performance.

▶ **Case in Point 20.6** Max Alexander agreed to purchase hay from Wagner's farm. Alexander left his truck and trailer at the farm for the seller to load the hay. Nothing was said about when payment was due, and the parties were unaware of the UCC's rules. When Alexander came back to get the hay, a dispute broke out. Alexander claimed that he had been given less hay than he had ordered and argued that he did not have to pay at that time. Wagner refused to release the hay (or the vehicles on which the hay was loaded) until Alexander paid for it. Eventually, Alexander jumped into his truck and drove off without paying for the hay—for which he was later prosecuted for the crime of theft (see Chapter 10). Because the parties had failed to specify when payment was due, UCC 2–310(a) controlled, and payment was due at the time Alexander picked up the hay.[6] ◄

**Open Delivery Term.** When no delivery terms are specified, the buyer normally takes delivery at the seller's place of business [UCC 2–308(a)]. If the seller has no place of business, the seller's residence is used. When goods are located in some other place and both parties know it, delivery is made there. If the time for shipment or delivery is not clearly specified in the sales contract, then the court will infer a "reasonable" time for performance [UCC 2–309(1)].

**Duration of an Ongoing Contract.** A single contract might specify successive performances but not indicate how long the parties are required to deal with each other. In this situation, either party may terminate the ongoing contractual relationship. Nevertheless, principles of good faith and sound commercial practice call for reasonable notification before termination so as to give the other party sufficient time to seek a substitute arrangement [UCC 2–309(2), (3)].

**Options and Cooperation with Regard to Performance.** When the contract contemplates shipment of the goods but does not specify the shipping arrangements, the *seller* has the right to make these arrangements in good faith, using commercial reasonableness in the situation [UCC 2–311].

When a sales contract omits terms relating to the assortment of goods, the *buyer* can specify the assortment. ▶ **Example 20.7** Petry Drugs agrees to purchase one thousand toothbrushes from Marconi's Dental Supply. The toothbrushes come in a variety of colors, but the contract does not specify color. Petry, the buyer, has the right to take six hundred blue toothbrushes and four hundred green ones if it wishes. Petry, however, must exercise good faith and commercial reasonableness in making the selection [UCC 2–311]. ◄

**REQUIREMENTS AND OUTPUT CONTRACTS** Normally, as mentioned earlier, if the parties do not specify a quantity, no contract is formed. A court will have no basis for determining a remedy because there is almost no way to determine objectively what is a reasonable quantity of goods for someone to buy. (In contrast, a court can objectively determine a reasonable price for particular goods by looking at the market for like goods.) The UCC recognizes two exceptions to this rule in requirements and output contracts [UCC 2–306(1)].

**Requirements Contracts.** Requirements contracts are common in the business world and normally are enforceable. In a **requirements contract,** the buyer agrees to purchase and the seller agrees to sell all or up to a stated amount of what the buyer requires.

▶ **Example 20.8** Newport Cannery forms a contract with Victor Tu. The cannery agrees to purchase from Tu, and Tu agrees to sell to the cannery all of the green beans that the cannery requires during the following summer. ◄ There is implicit consideration in a requirements contract because the buyer (the cannery, in *Example 20.8*) gives up the right to buy from any other seller, and this forfeited right creates a legal detriment (consideration).

If, however, the buyer promises to purchase only if he or she *wishes* to do so, the promise is illusory (without consideration) and unenforceable by either party.[7] Similarly, if the buyer reserves the right to buy the goods from someone other than the seller, the

---

6. *State v. Alexander*, 186 Or.App. 600, 64 P.3d 1148 (2003).

7. See, for example, *In re Anchor Glass Container Corp.*, 345 Bankr. 765 (M.D.Fla. 2006).

promise is unenforceable (illusory) as a requirements contract.

### Output Contracts.
In an **output contract,** the seller agrees to sell and the buyer agrees to buy all or up to a stated amount of what the seller *produces.*

▶ **Example 20.9** Ruth Sewell has planted two acres of organic tomatoes. Bella Union, a local restaurant, agrees to buy all of the tomatoes that Sewell produces that year to use at the restaurant. ◀ Again, because the seller essentially forfeits the right to sell goods to another buyer, there is implicit consideration in an output contract.

The UCC imposes a *good faith limitation* on requirements and output contracts. The quantity under such contracts is the amount of requirements or the amount of output that occurs during a *normal* production period. The actual quantity purchased or sold cannot be unreasonably disproportionate to normal or comparable prior requirements or output [UCC 2–306(1)].

**MERCHANT'S FIRM OFFER** Under regular contract principles, an offer can be revoked at any time before acceptance. The major common law exception is an *option contract* (discussed in Chapter 12), in which the offeree pays consideration for the offeror's irrevocable promise to keep the offer open for a stated period. The UCC creates a second exception for *firm offers* made by a merchant concerning the sale or lease of goods (regardless of whether or not the offeree is a merchant).

### When a Merchant's Firm Offer Arises.
A **firm offer** arises when a merchant-offeror gives *assurances in a signed writing* that the offer will remain open. The merchant's firm offer is irrevocable without the necessity of consideration[8] for the stated period or, if no definite period is stated, a reasonable period (neither to exceed three months) [UCC 2–205, 2A–205].

▶ **Example 20.10** Osaka, a used-car dealer, e-mails a letter to Gomez on January 1, stating, "I have a used 2013 Toyota RAV4 on the lot that I'll sell you for $22,000 any time between now and January 31." This e-mail creates a firm offer, and Osaka will be liable for breach of contract if he sells the RAV4 to another person before January 31. ◀

### Requirements for a Firm Offer.
To qualify as a firm offer, the offer must be:

1. *Written* (or electronically recorded, such as in an e-mail).
2. *Signed* by the offeror.[9]

When a firm offer is contained in a form contract prepared by the offeree, the offeror must also sign a separate assurance of the firm offer. The requirement of a separate signature ensures that the offeror will be made aware of the firm offer.

For instance, an offeree might respond to an initial offer by sending its own form contract containing a clause stating that the offer will remain open for three months. If the firm offer is buried amid copious language on the last page of the offeree's form contract, the offeror may inadvertently sign the contract without realizing that it contains a firm offer. This would defeat the purpose of the rule—which is to give effect to a merchant's *deliberate* intent to be bound to a firm offer.

## Acceptance

Acceptance of an offer to buy, sell, or lease goods generally may be made in any reasonable manner and by any reasonable means. The UCC permits acceptance of an offer to buy goods "either by a prompt *promise* to ship or by the prompt or current shipment of conforming or nonconforming goods" [UCC 2–206(1)(b)]. *Conforming goods* accord with the contract's terms, whereas *nonconforming goods* do not.

The prompt shipment of nonconforming goods constitutes both an acceptance, which creates a contract, and a breach of that contract. This rule does not apply if the seller **seasonably** (within a reasonable amount of time) notifies the buyer that the nonconforming shipment is offered only as an *accommodation,* or as a favor. The notice of accommodation must clearly indicate to the buyer that the shipment does not constitute an acceptance and that, therefore, no contract has been formed.

▶ **Example 20.11** McFarren Pharmacy orders five cases of Johnson & Johnson 3-by-5-inch gauze pads from H.T. Medical Supply, Inc. If H.T. ships five cases of Xeroform 3-by-5-inch gauze pads instead, the shipment acts as both an acceptance of McFarren's offer

---

**8.** If the offeree pays consideration, then an option contract (not a merchant's firm offer) is formed.

**9.** *Signed* includes any symbol executed or adopted by a party with a present intention to authenticate a writing [UCC 1–201(37)]. A complete signature is not required.

and a *breach* of the resulting contract. McFarren may sue H.T. for any appropriate damages. If, however, H.T. notifies McFarren that the Xeroform gauze pads are being shipped *as an accommodation*—because H.T. has only Xeroform pads in stock—the shipment will constitute a counteroffer, not an acceptance. A contract will be formed only if McFarren accepts the Xeroform gauze pads.  ◄

**COMMUNICATION OF ACCEPTANCE** Under the common law, because a unilateral offer invites acceptance by performance, the offeree need not notify the offeror of performance unless the offeror would not otherwise know about it. In other words, a unilateral offer can be accepted by beginning performance.

The UCC is more stringent than the common law in this regard because it requires notification. Under the UCC, if the offeror is not notified within a reasonable time that the offeree has accepted the contract by beginning performance, then the offeror can treat the offer as having lapsed before acceptance [UCC 2–206(2), 2A–206(2)].

**ADDITIONAL TERMS** Recall from Chapter 12 that under the common law, the mirror image rule requires that the terms of the acceptance exactly match those of the offer. ▶ **Example 20.12** Aldrich e-mails an offer to sell twenty Samsung Galaxy model 7.0 tablets to Beale. If Beale accepts the offer but changes it to require model 8.9 tablets, then there is no contract. ◄

To avoid these problems, the UCC dispenses with the mirror image rule. Under the UCC, a contract is formed if the offeree's response indicates a *definite* acceptance of the offer, *even if the acceptance includes terms additional to or different from those contained in the offer* [UCC 2–207(1)]. Whether the additional terms become part of the contract depends, in part, on whether the parties are nonmerchants or merchants.

**Rules When One Party or Both Parties Are Nonmerchants.** If one (or both) of the parties is a *nonmerchant,* the contract is formed according to the terms of the original offer and does not include any of the additional terms in the acceptance [UCC 2–207(2)].

▶ **Case in Point 20.13** OfficeSupplyStore.com sells office supplies on the Web. Employees of the Kansas City School District in Missouri ordered $17,642.54 worth of office supplies—without the authority or approval of their employer—from the Web site. The invoices accompanying the goods contained a *forum-selection clause* (see Chapter 12) that required all disputes to be resolved in California.

When the goods were not paid for, Office Supply filed suit in California. The Kansas City School District objected, arguing that the forum-selection clause was not binding. The court held that the forum-selection clause was not part of the parties' contract. The clause was an additional term included in the invoices delivered to a nonmerchant buyer (the school district) with the purchased goods. Therefore, the clause did not become part of the contract unless the buyer expressly agreed, which did not happen in this case.[10] ◄

**Rules When Both Parties Are Merchants.** The drafters of the UCC created a special rule for merchants to avoid the "battle of the forms," which occurs when two merchants exchange separate standard forms containing different contract terms.

Under UCC 2–207(2), in contracts *between merchants,* the additional terms *automatically* become part of the contract *unless* one of the following conditions arises:

1. The original offer expressly limited acceptance to its terms.
2. The new or changed terms materially alter the contract.
3. The offeror objects to the new or changed terms within a reasonable period of time.

When determining whether an alteration is material, courts consider several factors. Generally, if the modification does not involve any unreasonable element of surprise or hardship for the offeror, a court will hold that the modification did not materially alter the contract. Courts also consider the parties' prior dealings.

In the following case, a party conditioned its acceptance of an offer on the other parties' agreement to additional terms by a specific date. When the parties agreed to the most important terms after the deadline, the court had to decide if there was an enforceable contract.

10. *OfficeSupplyStore.com v. Kansas City School Board,* 334 S.W.3d 574 (Kan. 2011).

## CASE 20.2

### WPS, Inc. v. Expro Americas, LLC
Court of Appeals of Texas, First District, 369 S.W.3d 384 (2012).

**BACKGROUND AND FACTS** In April 2006, WPS, Inc., submitted a formal proposal to manufacture equipment for Expro Americas, LLC, and Surface Production Systems, Inc. (SPS). Expro and SPS then submitted two purchase orders. WPS accepted the first purchase order in part, and it accepted the second order conditionally. Among other things, WPS required that, by April 28, 2006, Expro and SPS give their "full release to proceed" and agree to "pay all valid costs associated with any order cancellation." The parties' negotiations continued, and Expro and SPS eventually submitted a third purchase order on May 9, 2006.

The third purchase order did not comply with all of WPS's requirements, but it did give WPS full permission to proceed and agreed that Expro and SPS would pay all cancellation costs. With Expro and SPS's knowledge, WPS then began work under the third purchase order. Expro and SPS soon canceled the order, however, so WPS sent them an invoice charging them for the cancellation costs. At trial, the jury and court concluded that there was a contract and found in WPS's favor. Expro and SPS appealed.

**DECISION AND RATIONALE** A state intermediate appellate court affirmed the judgment for WPS. The court found that the parties had a contract based on WPS's conditional acceptance and Expro and SPS's third purchase order. It did not matter that Expro and SPS submitted the third purchase order after WPS's deadline of April 28, 2006. Regardless of what WPS originally required, the parties continued their negotiations and "operated as if they had additional time to resolve the outstanding differences." Moreover, Expro and SPS agreed to nearly everything that WPS requested. Most important, they gave WPS "full release to proceed" and agreed "to pay all valid costs associated with any order cancellation." Those terms had been holding up the contract, and SPS's vice president conceded that the "release to proceed" "basically means that one party is in agreement." A jury could have reasonably concluded that, since the parties were in agreement, WPS was contractually obligated to move forward with its work.

**THE LEGAL ENVIRONMENT DIMENSION** *In allowing a party to condition its acceptance on additional terms, does contract law make negotiations more or less efficient? Explain your answer.*

**THE ECONOMIC DIMENSION** *Why would a manufacturer like WPS want its purchase orders to include terms such as those at issue in this case? Why would a buyer like Expro or SPS want to exclude such terms?*

---

**Conditioned on Offeror's Assent.** Regardless of merchant status, the UCC provides that the offeree's response cannot be construed as an acceptance if it contains additional or different terms and is expressly *conditioned* on the offeror's assent to those terms [UCC 2–207(1)].

▶ **Example 20.14** Philips offers to sell Hundert 650 pounds of turkey thighs at a specified price and with specified delivery terms. Hundert responds, "I accept your offer for 650 pounds of turkey thighs *on the condition that you agree to give me ninety days to pay for them.*" Hundert's response will be construed not as an acceptance but as a counteroffer, which Philips may or may not accept. ◀

**Additional Terms May Be Stricken.** The UCC provides yet another option for dealing with conflicting terms in the parties' writings. Section 2–207(3) states that conduct by both parties that recognizes the existence of a contract is sufficient to establish a contract for sale even though the writings of the parties do not otherwise establish a contract. In this situation, "the terms of the particular contract will consist of those terms on which the writings of the parties agree, together with any supplementary terms incorporated under any other provisions of this Act." In a dispute over contract terms, this provision allows a court simply to strike from the contract those terms on which the parties do not agree.

▶ **Example 20.15** SMT Marketing orders goods over the phone from Brigg Sales, Inc., which ships the goods to SMT with an acknowledgment form (confirming the order). SMT accepts and pays for the goods. The parties' writings do not establish a contract, but there is no question that a contract exists. If a dispute arises over the terms, such as the extent of any warranties, UCC 2–207(3) provides the governing rule. ◀

As noted previously, the fact that a merchant's acceptance frequently contains terms that add to or even conflict with those of the offer is often referred to as the "battle of the forms." Although the UCC tries to eliminate this battle, the problem of differing contract terms still arises in commercial settings, particularly when standard forms (for placing and confirming orders) are used.

## Consideration

The common law rule that a contract requires consideration also applies to sales and lease contracts. Unlike the common law, however, the UCC does not require a contract modification to be supported by new consideration. The UCC states that an agreement modifying a contract for the sale or lease of goods "needs no consideration to be binding" [UCC 2–209(1), 2A–208(1)]. Of course, any contract modification must be made in good faith [UCC 1–304].

In some situations, an agreement to modify a sales or lease contract without consideration must be in writing to be enforceable. For instance, if the contract itself specifies that any changes to the contract must be in a signed writing, only those changes agreed to in a signed writing are enforceable.

Sometimes, when a consumer (nonmerchant) is buying goods from a merchant-seller, the merchant supplies a form that contains a prohibition against oral modification. In those situations, the consumer must sign a separate acknowledgment of the clause for it to be enforceable [UCC 2–209(2), 2A–208(2)]. Also, any modification that makes a sales contract come under Article 2's writing requirement (its Statute of Frauds, discussed next) usually requires a writing (or electronic record) to be enforceable.

## The Statute of Frauds

The UCC contains Statute of Frauds provisions covering sales and lease contracts. Under these provisions, sales contracts for goods priced at $500 or more and lease contracts requiring total payments of $1,000 or more must be in writing to be enforceable [UCC 2–201(1), 2A–201(1)]. (These low threshold amounts may eventually be raised.)

**SUFFICIENCY OF THE WRITING** A writing, e-mail, or other electronic record will be sufficient to satisfy the UCC's Statute of Fraud as long as it:

1. Indicates that the parties intended to form a contract.
2. Is signed by the party (or agent of the party) against whom enforcement is sought. (Remember that a typed name can qualify as a signature on an electronic record, as discussed in Chapter 9.)

The contract normally will not be enforceable beyond the quantity of goods shown in the writing, however. All other terms can be proved in court by oral testimony. For leases, the writing must reasonably identify and describe the goods leased and the lease term.

**SPECIAL RULES FOR CONTRACTS BETWEEN MERCHANTS** The UCC provides a special rule for merchants in sales transactions (there is no corresponding rule that applies to leases under Article 2A). Merchants can satisfy the Statute of Frauds if, after the parties have agreed orally, one of the merchants sends a signed written (or electronic) confirmation to the other merchant within a reasonable time.

The communication must indicate the terms of the agreement, and the merchant receiving the confirmation must have reason to know of its contents. Unless the merchant who receives the confirmation gives written notice of objection to its contents within ten days after receipt, the writing is sufficient against the receiving merchant, even though she or he has not signed it [UCC 2–201(2)].

▶ **Example 20.16** Alfonso is a merchant-buyer in Cleveland. He contracts over the telephone to purchase $6,000 worth of spare aircraft parts from Goldstein, a merchant-seller in New York City. Two days later, Goldstein e-mails a signed confirmation detailing the terms of the oral contract, and Alfonso subsequently receives it. Alfonso does not notify Goldstein in writing (or e-mail) that he objects to the contents of the confirmation within ten days of receipt. Therefore, Alfonso cannot raise the Statute of Frauds as a defense against the enforcement of the oral contract. ◀

**EXCEPTIONS** The UCC defines three exceptions to the writing requirements of the Statute of Frauds. An oral contract for the sale of goods priced at $500 or more or the lease of goods involving total payments of $1,000 or more will be enforceable despite the absence of a writing in the circumstances described next [UCC 2–201(3), 2A–201(4)].

***Specially Manufactured Goods.*** An oral contract for the sale or lease of custom-made goods will be enforceable if:

1. The goods are *specially manufactured* for a particular buyer or specially manufactured or obtained for a particular lessee.
2. The goods are *not suitable for resale or lease* to others in the ordinary course of the seller's or lessor's business.
3. The seller or lessor has *substantially started to manufacture* the goods or has made commitments for the manufacture or procurement of the goods.

In these situations, once the seller or lessor has taken action, the buyer or lessee cannot repudiate the agreement claiming the Statute of Frauds as a defense.

▶ **Example 20.17** Womach orders custom window treatments to use at a day spa business for $6,000 from Hunter Douglas. The contract is oral. When Hunter Douglas manufactures the window coverings and tenders delivery to Womach, she refuses to pay for them, even though the job has been completed on time. Womach claims that she is not liable because the contract was oral. If the unique style, size, and color of the window treatments make it improbable that Hunter Douglas can find another buyer, Womach is liable to Hunter Douglas. ◀

***Admissions.*** An oral contract for the sale or lease of goods is enforceable if the party against whom enforcement is sought admits in pleadings, testimony, or other court proceedings that a sales or lease contract was made. In this situation, the contract will be enforceable even though it was oral, but enforceability will be limited to the quantity of goods admitted.

▶ **Case in Point 20.18** Gerald Lindgren, a farmer, agreed by phone to sell his crops to Glacial Plains Cooperative. The parties reached four oral agreements: two for the delivery of soybeans and two for the delivery of corn. Lindgren made the soybean deliveries and part of the first corn delivery, but he sold the rest of his corn to another dealer. Glacial Plains bought corn elsewhere, paying a higher price, and then sued Lindgren for breach of contract. In papers filed with the court, Lindgren acknowledged his oral agreements with Glacial Plains and admitted

that he did not fully perform. The court applied the admissions exception and held that the four agreements were enforceable.[11] ◀

***Partial Performance.*** An oral contract for the sale or lease of goods is enforceable if payment has been made and accepted or goods have been received and accepted. This is the "partial performance" exception. The oral contract will be enforced at least to the extent that performance actually took place.

▶ **Case in Point 20.19** Quality Pork International formed an oral contract with Rupari Food Services, Inc., which buys food products and sells them to retail operations. Quality was to ship three orders of pork to Star Food Processing, Inc., and Rupari was to pay for the products. Quality shipped the goods to Star and sent invoices to Rupari. Rupari billed Star for all three orders but paid Quality only for the first two. Quality filed a suit against Rupari to recover $44,051.98, the cost of the third order.

Rupari argued that because the parties did not have a written agreement, there was no enforceable contract. The court held that even though Rupari had not signed a written contract or purchase order, it had accepted the goods and partially performed the contract by paying for the first two shipments. Rupari's conduct was sufficient to prove the existence of a contract, and the court required Rupari to pay for the last shipment.[12] ◀

The exceptions just discussed and other ways in which sales law differs from general contract law are summarized in Exhibit 20–3 on the following page.

## Parol Evidence

Recall from Chapter 16 that parol evidence consists of evidence outside the contract such as evidence of the parties' prior negotiations, prior agreements, or contemporaneous (simultaneous) oral agreements. When a contract completely sets forth all the terms and conditions agreed to by the parties and is intended as a final statement of their agreement, it is considered fully *integrated* (see Chapter 16). The terms of a **fully integrated contract** cannot be contradicted by evidence of any prior agreements or contemporaneous oral agreements.

If, however, the writing contains some of the terms the parties agreed on but not others, then the contract

---

11. *Glacial Plains Cooperative v. Lindgren,* 759 N.W.2d 661 (Min.App. 2009).
12. *Quality Pork International v. Rupari Food Services, Inc.,* 267 Neb. 474, 675 N.W.2d 642 (2004).

**EXHIBIT 20-3  Major Differences between Contract Law and Sales Law**

|  | Contract Law | Sales Law |
|---|---|---|
| **Contract Terms** | Contract must contain all material terms. | Open terms are acceptable if parties intended to form a contract, but the contract is not enforceable beyond quantity term. |
| **Acceptance** | Mirror image rule applies. If additional terms are added in acceptance, a counteroffer is created. | Additional terms will not negate acceptance unless acceptance is expressly conditioned on assent to the additional terms. |
| **Contract Modification** | Modification requires consideration. | Modification does not require consideration. |
| **Irrevocable Offers** | Option contracts (with consideration). | Merchants' firm offers (without consideration). |
| **Statute of Frauds Requirements** | All material terms must be included in the writing. | Writing is required only for sale of goods priced at $500 or more, but the contract is not enforceable beyond the quantity specified. Merchants can satisfy the writing by a confirmation evidencing their agreement.<br><br>*Exceptions:*<br>1. Specially manufactured goods.<br>2. Admissions by party against whom enforcement is sought.<br>3. Partial performance. |

is not fully integrated. When a court finds that a contract is *not fully integrated,* then the court may allow evidence of *consistent additional terms* to explain or supplement the terms in the contract. The court may also allow the parties to submit evidence of *course of dealing, usage of trade,* or *course of performance* [UCC 2–202, 2A–202].

**COURSE OF DEALING AND USAGE OF TRADE** Under the UCC, the meaning of any agreement, evidenced by the language of the parties and by their actions, must be interpreted in light of commercial practices and other surrounding circumstances. In interpreting a commercial agreement, a court will assume that the course of dealing between the parties and the general usage of trade were taken into account when the agreement was phrased.

***Course of Dealing.*** A **course of dealing** is a sequence of actions and communications between the parties to a particular transaction that establishes a common basis for their understanding [UCC 1–303(b)]. A course of dealing is restricted to the sequence of conduct between the parties in their transactions prior to the agreement.

Under the UCC, a course of dealing between the parties is relevant in ascertaining the meaning of the

parties' agreement. It "may give particular meaning to specific terms of the agreement, and may supplement or qualify the terms of the agreement" [UCC 1–303(d)].

***Usage of Trade.*** Any practice or method of dealing that is so regularly observed in a place, vocation, or trade as to justify an expectation by the parties that it will be observed in their transaction is a **usage of trade** [UCC 1–303(c)].

▶ **Example 20.20** Phat Khat Loans, Inc., hires Fleet Title Review Company to search the public records for prior claims on potential borrrowers' assets. Fleet's invoice states, "Liability limited to amount of fee." In the title search industry, liability limits are common. After conducting many searches for Phat Khat, Fleet reports that there are no claims with respect to Main Street Autos. Phat Khat loans $100,000 to Main, with payment guaranteed by Main's assets.

When Main defaults on the loan, Phat Khat learns that another lender has priority to Main's assets under a previous claim. If Phat Khat sues Fleet Title for breach of contract, Fleet's liability will normally be limited to the amount of its fee. The statement in the invoice was part of the contract between Phat Khat and Fleet, according to the usage of trade in the industry and the parties' course of dealing. ◀

**COURSE OF PERFORMANCE** The conduct that occurs under the terms of a particular agreement is called a **course of performance** [UCC 1–303(a)]. Presumably, the parties themselves know best what they meant by their words. Thus, the course of performance actually carried out under the parties' agreement is the best indication of what they meant [UCC 2–208(1), 2A–207(1)].

▶ **Example 20.21** Janson's Lumber Company contracts with Lopez to sell Lopez a specified number of two-by-fours. The lumber in fact does not measure exactly 2 inches by 4 inches but rather 1⅞ inches by 3¾ inches. Janson's agrees to deliver the lumber in five deliveries, and Lopez, without objection, accepts the lumber in the first three deliveries. On the fourth delivery, however, Lopez objects that the two-by-fours do not measure precisely 2 inches by 4 inches.

The course of performance in this transaction—that is, the fact that Lopez accepted three deliveries without objection under the agreement—is relevant in determining that here a "two-by-four" actually means a "1⅞-by-3¾." Janson's can also prove that two-by-fours need not be exactly 2 inches by 4 inches by applying usage of trade, course of dealing, or both. Janson's can, for example, show that in previous transactions, Lopez took 1⅞-inch-by-3¾-inch lumber without objection. In addition, Janson's can show that in the trade, two-by-fours are commonly 1⅞ inches by 3¾ inches. ◀

**RULES OF CONSTRUCTION** The UCC provides *rules of construction* for interpreting contracts. Express terms, course of performance, course of dealing, and usage of trade are to be construed to be consistent with each other whenever reasonable. When such a construction is unreasonable, however, the UCC establishes the following order of priority [UCC 1–303(e), 2–208(2), 2A–207(2)]:

1. Express terms.
2. Course of performance.
3. Course of dealing.
4. Usage of trade.

## Unconscionability

As discussed in Chapters 14 and 15, an unconscionable contract is one that is so unfair and one sided that it would be unreasonable to enforce it. The UCC allows a court to evaluate a contract or any clause in a contract, and if the court deems it to have been unconscionable *at the time it was made,* the court can do any of the following [UCC 2–302, 2A–108]:

1. Refuse to enforce the contract.
2. Enforce the remainder of the contract without the unconscionable part.
3. Limit the application of the unconscionable term to avoid an unconscionable result.

The following classic case illustrates an early application of the UCC's unconscionability provisions.

## CLASSIC CASE 20.3

### Jones v. Star Credit Corp.
Supreme Court of New York, Nassau County, 59 Misc.2d 189, 298 N.Y.S.2d 264 (1969).

**BACKGROUND AND FACTS** In August 1965, Clifton and Cora Jones agreed to buy a freezer for $900 as the result of a visit to their home from a salesperson representing Your Shop At Home Service, Inc. The parties signed a "Retail Installment Contract" that included time credit charges, credit life insurance, credit property insurance, and sales tax. The purchase price totaled $1,234.80. The freezer's retail value was approximately $300. In June 1966, the parties discharged their agreement through a *novation* (see Chapter 18), replacing Your Shop At Home Service with Star Credit Corporation. After the Joneses had paid $619.88 on the contract, they filed a suit in a New York state court against Star Credit, asking that the contract be reformed on the ground that it was unconscionable. Star Credit claimed that, with various credit charges added for an extension of time, there was a balance due of $819.81.

**DECISION AND RATIONALE** The state trial court ruled in favor of the Joneses. The contract was reformed so that they were required to make no further payments. The court relied on UCC 2–302(1), which states that if "the court as a matter of law finds the contract or any clause of the contract to have been unconscionable at the time it was made the court may . . . so limit the application of any unconscionable clause as to avoid any unconscionable result." The court considered the disparity between

**CASE 20.3 CONTINUED** the $900 purchase price and the $300 retail value, the fact that the credit charges alone exceeded the retail value, and the seller's knowledge of the buyers' limited resources sufficient to declare the contract unconscionable.

**IMPACT OF THIS CASE ON TODAY'S LAW** *This early classic case illustrates the approach that many courts take today when deciding whether a sales contract is unconscionable—an approach that focuses on "excessive" price and unequal bargaining power. Most of the litigants who have used UCC 2–302 successfully could demonstrate both an absence of meaningful choice and that the contract terms were unreasonably favorable to the other party.*

**THE SOCIAL DIMENSION** *Why would the seller's knowledge of the buyers' limited resources support a finding of unconscionability?*

---

*Concept Summary 20.1* on the next page reviews the concepts and rules related to the formation of sales and lease contracts.

## SECTION 4
# CONTRACTS FOR THE INTERNATIONAL SALE OF GOODS

International sales contracts between firms or individuals located in different countries may be governed by the 1980 United Nations Convention on Contracts for the International Sale of Goods (CISG). The CISG governs international contracts only if the countries of the parties to the contract have ratified the CISG and if the parties have not agreed that some other law will govern their contract.

As of 2013, the CISG had been adopted by seventy-eight countries, including the United States, Canada, some Central and South American countries, China, most European nations, Japan, and Mexico. That means that the CISG is the uniform international sales law of countries that account for more than two-thirds of all global trade. (For an example of an international sales contract, see the appendix to this chapter.)

Essentially, the CISG is to international sales contracts what Article 2 of the UCC is to domestic sales contracts. In domestic transactions, the UCC applies when the parties to a contract for a sale of goods have failed to specify in writing some important term, such as the price or delivery. Similarly, whenever the parties to international transactions have failed to specify in writing the precise terms of a contract, the CISG will be applied.

Unlike the UCC, *the CISG does not apply to consumer sales.* Neither the UCC nor the CISG applies to contracts for services.

## A Comparison of CISG and UCC Provisions

The provisions of the CISG, although similar for the most part to those of the UCC, differ from them in some respects. If the CISG and the UCC conflict, the CISG applies (because it is a treaty of the U.S. national government and therefore is supreme—see the discussion of the supremacy clause in Chapter 4).

The major differences between the CISG and the UCC in regard to contract formation concern the mirror image rule, irrevocable offers, the Statute of Frauds, and the time of contract formation. We discuss these differences in the subsections that follow. CISG provisions relating to risk of loss, performance, remedies, and warranties will be discussed in the following chapters as those topics are examined.

**THE MIRROR IMAGE RULE** Under the UCC, a definite expression of acceptance that contains additional terms can still result in the formation of a contract, unless the additional terms are conditioned on the assent of the offeror. In other words, the UCC does away with the mirror image rule in domestic sales contracts.

Article 19 of the CISG provides that a contract can be formed even though the acceptance contains additional terms, unless the additional terms materially alter the contract. Under the CISG, however, the definition of a "material alteration" includes almost any change in the terms. If an additional term relates to payment, quality, quantity, price, time and place of delivery, extent of one party's liability to the other,

---

### CONCEPT SUMMARY 20.1

## The Formation of Sales and Lease Contracts

| CONCEPT | DESCRIPTION |
|---|---|
| **Offer and Acceptance** | 1. *Offer—*<br>  a. Not all terms have to be included for a contract to be formed.<br>  b. The price does not have to be included for a contract to be formed.<br>  c. Particulars of performance can be left open.<br>  d. An offer by a merchant in a signed writing with assurances that the offer will not be withdrawn is irrevocable without consideration (for up to three months).<br>2. *Acceptance—*<br>  a. Acceptance may be made by any reasonable means of communication. It is effective when dispatched.<br>  b. The acceptance of a unilateral offer can be made by a promise to ship or by the shipment of conforming or nonconforming goods.<br>  c. Acceptance by performance requires notice within a reasonable time. Otherwise, the offer can be treated as lapsed.<br>  d. A definite expression of acceptance creates a contract even if the terms of the acceptance modify the terms of the offer. |
| **Consideration** | A modification of a contract for the sale of goods does not require consideration. |
| **Requirements under the Statute of Frauds** | 1. All contracts for the sale of goods priced at $500 or more must be in writing. A writing is sufficient as long as it indicates a contract between the parties and is signed by the party against whom enforcement is sought. A contract is not enforceable beyond the quantity shown in the writing.<br>2. When written confirmation of an oral contract between merchants is not objected to in writing by the receiver within ten days, the oral contract is enforceable.<br>3. Exceptions to the requirement of a writing exist in the following situations:<br>  a. When the oral contract is for specially manufactured or obtained goods not suitable for resale or lease to others and the seller or lessor has made commitments for the manufacture or procurement of the goods.<br>  b. If the defendant admits in pleadings, testimony, or other court proceedings that an oral contract for the sale or lease of goods was made, then the contract will be enforceable to the extent of the quantity of goods admitted.<br>  c. The oral agreement will be enforceable to the extent that payment has been received and accepted or to the extent that goods have been received and accepted. |
| **Parol Evidence Rule** | 1. The terms of a clearly and completely worded written contract cannot be contradicted by evidence of prior agreements or contemporaneous oral agreements.<br>2. Evidence is admissible to clarify the terms of a writing in the following situations:<br>  a. If the contract terms are ambiguous.<br>  b. If evidence of course of dealing, usage of trade, or course of performance is necessary to learn or to clarify the intentions of the parties to the contract. |

---

or the settlement of disputes, the CISG considers the added term a material alteration. In effect, then, the CISG requires that the terms of the acceptance mirror those of the offer.

Therefore, as a practical matter, businesspersons undertaking international sales transactions should not use the sale or purchase forms that they customarily use for transactions within the United States.

Instead, they should draft specific forms to suit the needs of the particular transaction.

**IRREVOCABLE OFFERS** UCC 2–205 provides that a merchant's firm offer is irrevocable, even without consideration, if the merchant gives assurances in a signed writing. In contrast, under the CISG, an offer can become irrevocable without a signed writing.

Article 16(2) of the CISG provides that an offer will be irrevocable if:

1. The offeror states orally that the offer is irrevocable.
2. The offeree reasonably relies on the offer as being irrevocable.

In both of these situations, the offer will be irrevocable even without a writing and without consideration.

**THE WRITING REQUIREMENT** As discussed previously, the UCC has a Statute of Frauds provision. UCC 2–201 requires contracts for the sale of goods priced at $500 or more to be evidenced by a written or electronic record signed by the party against whom enforcement is sought.

Article 11 of the CISG, however, states that a contract of sale "need not be concluded in or evidenced by writing and is not subject to any other requirements as to form. It may be proved by any means, including witnesses." Article 11 of the CISG accords with the legal customs of most nations, which no longer require contracts to meet certain formal or writing requirements to be enforceable.

**TIME OF CONTRACT FORMATION** Under the common law of contracts and the UCC, an acceptance is effective on dispatch, so a contract is created when the acceptance is transmitted. Under the CISG, in contrast, a contract is created not at the time the acceptance is transmitted but only on its *receipt* by the offeror. (The offer becomes *irrevocable*, however, when the acceptance is sent.)

Article 18(2) states that an acceptance by return promise (a unilateral contract—see Chapter 11) "becomes effective at the moment the indication of assent reaches the offeror." Under Article 18(3), the offeree may also bind the offeror by performance even without giving any notice to the offeror. The acceptance becomes effective "at the moment the act is performed." Thus, it is the offeree's reliance, rather than the communication of acceptance to the offeror, that creates the contract.

## Special Provisions in International Contracts

Language and legal differences among nations can create various problems for parties to international contracts when disputes arise. It is possible to avoid these problems by including in a contract special provisions relating to choice of language, choice of forum, choice of law, and the types of events that may excuse the parties from performance.

**CHOICE OF LANGUAGE** A deal struck between a U.S. company and a company in another country frequently involves two languages. One party may not understand complex contractual terms that are written in the other party's language. Translating the terms poses its own problems, as typically many phrases are not readily translatable into another language.

To make sure that no disputes arise out of this language problem, an international sales contract should include a **choice-of-language clause,** designating the official language by which the contract will be interpreted in the event of disagreement. The clause might also specify that the agreement is to be translated into, say, Spanish, and that the translation is to be approved by both parties so that they can rely on it. If arbitration is anticipated, an additional clause must be added to indicate the official language that will be used at the arbitration proceeding.

**CHOICE OF FORUM** A forum-selection clause designates the forum (place, or court) in which any disputes that arise under the contract will be litigated. Including a forum-selection clause in an international contract is especially important because when several countries are involved, litigation may be sought in courts in different nations. There are no universally accepted rules regarding the jurisdiction of a particular court over subject matter or parties to a dispute, although the adoption of the 2005 Choice of Court Convention helps resolve certain issues.

A forum-selection clause should indicate the specific court that will have jurisdiction. The forum does not necessarily have to be within the geographic boundaries of either party's nation.

Under certain circumstances, a forum-selection clause will not be valid. Specifically, if the clause denies one party an effective remedy, or is the product of fraud or unconscionable conduct, the clause will not be enforced. Similarly, if the designated forum causes substantial inconvenience to one of the parties, or violates public policy, the clause may not be enforced.

**CHOICE OF LAW** A contractual provision designating the applicable law, called a **choice-of-law clause,** is typically included in every international contract. At common law (and in European civil law systems—see Chapter 24), parties are allowed to choose the law that will govern their contractual relationship.

There must normally be some connection between the chosen law and the contracting parties to show that the parties are not merely trying to avoid the laws of their own jurisdictions. ▶ **Example 20.22** A U.S. automaker contracts with a German company. The parties cannot choose the law of China to govern their agreement if neither the contract nor the parties have anything to do with China. The choice of Chinese law in that situation might reflect an attempt to avoid consumer, environmental, or employment laws that would otherwise apply to the transaction. ◀

Under the UCC, parties may choose the law that will govern the contract as long as the choice is "reasonable." Article 6 of the CISG, however, imposes no limitation on the parties in their choice of what law will govern the contract. The 1986 Hague Convention on the Law Applicable to Contracts for the International Sale of Goods—often referred to as the

Choice-of-Law Convention—allows unlimited autonomy in the choice of law. Whenever a choice of law is not specified in a contract, the Hague Convention indicates that the law of the country where the seller's place of business is located will govern.

**FORCE MAJEURE CLAUSE** Every contract, and particularly those involving international transactions, should have a **force majeure clause.** The meaning of the French term *force majeure* is "impossible or irresistible force"—sometimes loosely defined as "an act of God." *Force majeure* clauses commonly stipulate that in addition to acts of God, a number of other eventualities (such as governmental orders or regulations, embargoes, or extreme shortages of materials) may excuse a party from liability for nonperformance.

## Reviewing: The Formation of Sales and Lease Contracts

Guy Holcomb owns and operates Oasis Goodtime Emporium, an adult entertainment establishment. Holcomb wanted to create an adult Internet system for Oasis that would offer customers adult theme videos and "live" chat room programs using performers at the club. On May 10, Holcomb signed a work order authorizing Thomas Consulting Group (TCG) "to deliver a working prototype of a customer chat system, demonstrating the integration of live video and chatting in a Web browser." In exchange for creating the prototype, Holcomb agreed to pay TCG $64,697. On May 20, Holcomb signed an additional work order in the amount of $12,943 for TCG to install a customized firewall system. The work orders stated that Holcomb would make monthly installment payments to TCG, and both parties expected the work would be finished by September.

Due to unforeseen problems largely attributable to system configuration and software incompatibility, the project required more time than anticipated. By the end of the summer, the Web site was still not ready, and Holcomb had fallen behind in his payments to TCG. TCG threatened to cease work and file a suit for breach of contract unless the bill was paid. Rather than make further payments, Holcomb wanted to abandon the Web site project. Using the information presented in the chapter, answer the following questions.

1. Would a court be likely to decide that the transaction between Holcomb and TCG was covered by the Uniform Commercial Code (UCC)? Why or why not?
2. Would a court be likely to consider Holcomb a merchant under the UCC? Why or why not?
3. Did the parties have a valid contract under the UCC? Were any terms left open in the contract? If so, which terms? How would a court deal with open terms?
4. Suppose that Holcomb and TCG meet in October in an attempt to resolve their problems. At that time, the parties reach an oral agreement that TCG will continue to work without demanding full payment of the past due amounts and Holcomb will pay TCG $5,000 per week. Assuming the contract falls under the UCC, is the oral agreement enforceable? Why or why not?

**DEBATE THIS...** *The UCC should require the same degree of definiteness of terms, especially with respect to price and quantity, as contract law does.*

## Terms and Concepts

| | | |
|---|---|---|
| choice-of-language clause 359 | intangible property 345 | requirements contract 349 |
| choice-of-law clause 359 | lease agreement 347 | sale 344 |
| course of dealing 355 | lessee 347 | sales contract 344 |
| course of performance 356 | lessor 347 | seasonably 350 |
| firm offer 350 | merchant 347 | tangible property 345 |
| *force majeure* clause 360 | output contract 350 | usage of trade 355 |
| fully integrated contract 354 | predominant-factor test 345 | |

## Issue Spotters

1. E-Design, Inc., orders 150 computer desks. Fav-O-Rite Supplies, Inc., ships 150 printer stands. Is this an acceptance of the offer or a counteroffer? If it is an acceptance, is it a breach of the contract? Why or why not? What if Fav-O-Rite told E-Design it was sending the printer stands as "an accommodation"? **(See page 350.)**

2. Truck Parts, Inc. (TPI), often sells supplies to United Fix-It Company (UFC), which services trucks. Over the phone, they negotiate for the sale of eighty-four sets of tires. TPI sends a letter to UFC detailing the terms and two weeks later ships the tires. Is there an enforceable contract between them? Why or why not? **(See page 353.)**

- **Check your answers to the Issue Spotters against the answers provided in Appendix E at the end of this text.**

## Business Scenarios

**20–1. The Statute of Frauds.** Fresher Foods, Inc., orally agreed to purchase one thousand bushels of corn for $1.25 per bushel from Dale Vernon, a farmer. Fresher Foods paid $125 down and agreed to pay the remainder of the purchase price on delivery, which was scheduled for one week later. When Fresher Foods tendered the balance of $1,125 on the scheduled day of delivery and requested the corn, Vernon refused to deliver it. Fresher Foods sued Vernon for damages, claiming that Vernon had breached their oral contract. Can Fresher Foods recover? If so, to what extent? **(See page 353.)**

**20–2. Additional Terms.** Strike offers to sell Bailey one thousand shirts for a stated price. The offer declares that shipment will be made by Dependable Truck Line. Bailey replies, "I accept your offer for one thousand shirts at the price quoted. Delivery to be by Yellow Express Truck Line." Both Strike and Bailey are merchants. Three weeks later, Strike ships the shirts by Dependable Truck Line, and Bailey refuses to accept delivery. Strike sues for breach of contract. Bailey claims that there never was a contract because his reply, which included a modification of carriers, did not constitute an acceptance. Bailey further claims that even if there had been a contract, Strike would have been in breach because Strike shipped the shirts by Dependable, contrary to the contract terms. Discuss fully Bailey's claims. **(See page 351.)**

## Business Case Problems

**20–3. Spotlight on Goods and Services—The Statute of Frauds.**

Fallsview Glatt Kosher Caterers ran a business that provided travel packages, including food, entertainment, and lectures on religious subjects, to customers during the Passover holiday at a New York resort. Willie Rosenfeld verbally agreed to pay Fallsview $24,050 for the Passover package for himself and his family. Rosenfeld did not appear at the resort and never paid the amount owed. Fallsview sued Rosenfeld for breach of contract. Rosenfeld claimed that the contract was unenforceable because it was not in writing and violated the UCC's Statute of Frauds. Is the contract valid? Explain.

[*Fallsview Glatt Kosher Caterers, Inc. v. Rosenfeld*, 794 N.Y.S.2d 790 (N.Y.Super. 2005)] **(See page 353.)**

**20–4. BUSINESS CASE PROBLEM WITH SAMPLE ANSWER: Additional Terms.**

*B.S. International, Ltd. (BSI), makes costume jewelry. JMAM, LLC, is a wholesaler of costume jewelry. JMAM sent BSI a letter with the terms for orders, including the necessary procedure for obtaining credit for items that customers rejected. The letter stated, "By signing below, you agree to the terms." Steven Baracsi, BSI's owner, signed the letter and returned it. For six*

*years, BSI made jewelry for JMAM, which resold it. Items rejected by customers were sent back to JMAM, but were never returned to BSI. BSI filed a suit against JMAM, claiming $41,294.21 for the unreturned items. BSI showed the court a copy of JMAM's terms. Across the bottom had been typed a "PS" requiring the return of rejected merchandise. Was this "PS" part of the contract? Discuss. [B.S. International, Ltd. v. JMAM, LLC, 13 A.3d 1057 (R.I. 2011)]* **(See page 351.)**

• **For a sample answer to Problem 20–4, go to Appendix F at the end of this text.**

**20–5. Partial Performance and the Statute of Frauds.** After a series of e-mails, Jorge Bonilla, the sole proprietor of a printing company in Uruguay, agreed to buy a used printer from Crystal Graphics Equipment, Inc., in New York. Crystal Graphics, through its agent, told Bonilla that the printing press was fully operational, contained all of its parts, and was in excellent condition except for some damage to one of the printing towers. Bonilla paid $95,000. Crystal Graphics sent him a signed, stamped invoice reflecting this payment. The invoice was dated six days after Bonilla's conversation with the agent. When the printing press arrived, Bonilla discovered that it was missing parts and was damaged. Crystal Graphics sent replacement parts, but they did not work. Ultimately, Crystal Graphics was never able to make the printer operational. Bonilla sued, alleging breach of contract, breach of the implied covenant of good faith and fair dealing, breach of express warranty, and breach of implied warranty. Crystal Graphics claimed that the contract was not enforceable because it did not satisfy the Statute of Frauds. Can Crystal Graphics prevail on this basis? Why or why not? [*Bonilla v. Crystal Graphics Equipment, Inc.,* 2012 WL 360145 (S.D.Fla. 2012)] **(See page 354.)**

**20–6. The Statute of Frauds.** Kendall Gardner agreed to buy from B&C Shavings, a specially built shaving mill to produce wood shavings for poultry processors. B&C faxed an invoice to Gardner reflecting a purchase price of $86,200, with a 30 percent down payment and the "balance due before shipment." Gardner paid the down payment. B&C finished the mill and wrote Gardner a letter telling him to

"pay the balance due or you will lose the down payment." By then, Gardner had lost his customers for the wood shavings, could not pay the balance due, and asked for the return of his down payment. Did these parties have an enforceable contract under the Statute of Frauds? Explain. [*Bowen v. Gardner,* 2013 Ark.App. 52, __ S.W.3d __ (2013)] **(See page 353.)**

**20–7. A QUESTION OF ETHICS: Contract Terms.**

 *Daniel Fox owned Fox & Lamberth Enterprises, Inc., a kitchen and bath remodeling business, in Dayton, Ohio. Fox leased a building from Carl and Bellulah Hussong. Craftsmen Home Improvement, Inc., also remodeled baths and kitchens. When Fox planned to close his business, Craftsmen expressed an interest in buying his showroom assets. Fox set a price of $50,000. Craftsmen's owners agreed and gave Fox a list of the desired items and "A Bill of Sale" that set the terms for payment. The parties did not discuss Fox's arrangement with the Hussongs, but Craftsmen expected to negotiate a new lease and extensively modified the premises, including removing some of the displays to its own showroom. When the Hussongs and Craftsmen could not agree on new terms, Craftsmen told Fox that the deal was off. [Fox & Lamberth Enterprises, Inc. v. Craftsmen Home Improvement, Inc., __ Ohio App.3d __, __ N.E.2d __ (2 Dist. 2006)]* **(See page 353.)**

(a) In Fox's suit in an Ohio state court for breach of contract, Craftsmen raised the Statute of Frauds as a defense. What are the requirements of the Statute of Frauds? Did the deal between Fox and Craftsmen meet these requirements? Did it fall under one of the exceptions? Explain.

(b) Craftsmen also claimed that the predominant factor of its agreement with Fox was a lease for the Hussongs' building. What is the "predominant-factor" test? Does it apply here? In any event, is it fair to hold a party to a contract to buy a business's assets when the buyer cannot negotiate a favorable lease of the premises on which the assets are located? Discuss.

## Legal Reasoning Group Activity

**20–8. Parol Evidence.** Mountain Stream Trout Co. agreed to buy "market size" trout from trout grower Lake Farms, LLC. Their five- year contract did not define *market size*. At the time, in the trade, *market size* referred to fish of one-pound live weight. After three years, Mountain Stream began taking fewer, smaller deliveries of larger fish, claiming that *market size* varied according to whatever its customers demanded and that its customers now demanded larger fish. Lake Farms filed a suit for breach of contract. **(See page 354.)**

(a) The first group will decide whether parol (outside) evidence is admissible to explain the terms of this contract. Are there any exceptions that could apply?

(b) A second group will determine the impact of course of dealing and usage of trade on the interpretation of contract terms.

(c) A third group will discuss how parties to a commercial contract can avoid the possibility that a court will interpret the contract terms in accordance with trade usage.

**①**

OVERLAND COFFEE IMPORT CONTRACT
OF THE
GREEN COFFEE ASSOCIATION
OF
NEW YORK CITY, INC.*

**②**

Contract Seller's No.: __504617__
Buyer's No.: __P9264__
Date: __10/11/15__

SOLD BY: __XYZ Co.__
TO: __Starbucks__

**③**

QUANTITY: __Five Hundred__ (__500__) Tons of (Bags) __Mexican__ coffee weighing about __152.117 lbs.__ per bag.

PACKAGING: Coffee must be packed in clean sound bags of uniform size made of sisal, henequen, jute, burlap, or similar woven material, without inner lining or outer covering of any material properly sewn by hand and/or machine. Bulk shipments are allowed if agreed by mutual consent of Buyer and Seller.

**④**

DESCRIPTION: __High grown Mexican Altura__

**⑤**

PRICE: At __Ten/$10.00 dollars__ U.S. Currency, per __lb.__ net, (U.S. Funds)
Upon delivery in Bonded Public Warehouse at __Laredo, TX__
(City and State)

PAYMENT: __Cash against warehouse receipts__

**⑥**

Bill and tender to DATE when all import requirements and governmental regulations have been satisfied, and coffee delivered or discharged (as per contract terms). Seller is obliged to give the Buyer two (2) calendar days free time in Bonded Public Warehouse following but not including date of tender.

**⑦**

ARRIVAL: During __December__ via __truck__
(Period)                    (Method of Transportation)
from __Mexico__ for arrival at __Laredo, TX, USA__
(Country of Exportation)          (Country of Importation)
Partial shipments permitted.

**⑧**

ADVICE OF ARRIVAL: Advice of arrival with warehouse name and location, together with the quantity, description, marks and place of entry, must be transmitted directly, or through Seller's Agent/Broker, to the Buyer or his Agent/ Broker. Advice will be given as soon as known but not later than the fifth business day following arrival at the named warehouse. Such advice may be given verbally with written confirmation to be sent the same day.

**⑨**

WEIGHTS: (1) DELIVERED WEIGHTS: Coffee covered by this contract is to be weighed at location named in tender. Actual tare to be allowed.
(2) SHIPPING WEIGHTS: Coffee covered by this contract is sold on shipping weights. Any loss in weight exceeding __1/2__ percent at location named in tender is for account of Seller at contract price.
(3) Coffee is to be weighed within fifteen (15) calendar days after tender. Weighing expenses, if any, for account of __Seller__ (Seller or Buyer)

**⑩**

MARKINGS: Bags to be branded in English with the name of Country of Origin and otherwise to comply with laws and regulations of the Country of Importation, in effect at the time of entry, governing marking of import merchandise. Any expense incurred by failure to comply with these regulations to be borne by Exporter/Seller.

**⑪**

RULINGS: The "Rulings on Coffee Contracts" of the Green Coffee Association of New York City, Inc., in effect on the date this contract is made, is incorporated for all purposes as a part of this agreement, and together herewith, constitute the entire contract. No variation or addition hereto shall be valid unless signed by the parties to the contract.
Seller guarantees that the terms printed on the reverse hereof, which by reference are made a part hereof, are identical with the terms as printed in By-Laws and Rules of the Green Coffee Association of New York City, Inc., heretofore adopted.
Exceptions to this guarantee are:
ACCEPTED:                                    COMMISSION TO BE PAID BY:
__XYZ Co.__                                   __Seller__
                        Seller
BY_____ _DM_____
                        Agent

**⑫**

__Starbucks__
                        Buyer
BY_____
                        Agent        __ABC Brokerage__
                                          Broker(s)

**⑬**

When this contract is executed by a person acting for another, such person hereby represents that he is fully authorized to commit his principal.

* Reprinted with permission of The Green Coffee Association of New York City, Inc.

Shutterstock.com/Sergii Figurnyi

(Continued)

# An Example of a Contract for the International Sale of Coffee

**①** This is a contract for a sale of coffee to be *imported* internationally. If the parties have their principal places of business located in different countries, the contract may be subject to the United Nations Convention on Contracts for the International Sale of Goods (CISG). If the parties' principal places of business are located in the United States, the contract may be subject to the Uniform Commercial Code (UCC).

**②** Quantity is one of the most important terms to include in a contract. Without it, a court may not be able to enforce the contract. See Chapter 20.

**③** Weight per unit (bag) can be exactly stated or approximately stated. If it is not so stated, usage of trade in international contracts determines standards of weight.

**④** Packaging requirements can be conditions for acceptance and payment. Bulk shipments are not permitted without the consent of the buyer.

**⑤** A description of the coffee and the "Markings" constitute express warranties. Warranties in contracts for domestic sales of goods are discussed generally in Chapter 23. International contracts rely more heavily on descriptions and models or samples.

**⑥** Under the UCC, parties may enter into a valid contract even though the price is not set. Under the CISG, a contract must provide for an exact determination of the price.

**⑦** The terms of payment may take one of two forms: credit or cash. Credit terms can be complicated. A cash term can be simple, and payment can be made by any means acceptable in the ordinary course of business (for example, a personal check or a letter of credit). If the seller insists on actual cash, the buyer must be given a reasonable time to get it. See Chapter 22.

**⑧** *Tender* means the seller has placed goods that conform to the contract at the buyer's disposition. What constitutes a valid tender is explained in Chapter 21. This contract requires that the coffee meet all import regulations and that it be ready for pickup by the buyer at a "Bonded Public Warehouse." (A *bonded warehouse* is a place in which goods can be stored without payment of taxes until the goods are removed.)

**⑨** The delivery date is significant because, if it is not met, the buyer may hold the seller in breach of the contract. Under this contract, the seller is given a "period" within which to deliver the goods, instead of a specific day. The seller is also given some time to rectify goods that do not pass inspection (see the "Guarantee" clause on page two of the contract). For a discussion of the remedies of the buyer and seller, see Chapter 22.

**⑩** As part of a proper tender, the seller (or its agent) must inform the buyer (or its agent) when the goods have arrived at their destination.

**⑪** In some contracts, delivered and shipping weights can be important. During shipping, some loss can be attributed to the type of goods (spoilage of fresh produce, for example) or to the transportation itself. A seller and buyer can agree on the extent to which either of them will bear such losses.

**⑫** Documents are often incorporated in a contract by reference, because including them word for word can make a contract difficult to read. If the document is later revised, the entire contract might have to be reworked. Documents that are typically incorporated by reference include detailed payment and delivery terms, special provisions, and sets of rules, codes, and standards.

**⑬** In international sales transactions, and for domestic deals involving certain products, brokers are used to form the contracts. When so used, the brokers are entitled to a commission.

# An Example of a Contract for the International Sale of Coffee

## TERMS AND CONDITIONS

**14 ARBITRATION:** All controversies relating to, in connection with, or arising out of this contract, its modification, making or the authority or obligations of the signatories hereto, and whether involving the principals, agents, brokers, or others who actually subscribe hereto, shall be settled by arbitration in accordance with the "Rules of Arbitration" of the Green Coffee Association of New York City, Inc., as they exist at the time of the arbitration (including provisions as to payment of fees and expenses). Arbitration is the sole remedy hereunder, and it shall be held in accordance with the law of New York State, and judgment of any award may be entered in the courts of that State, or in any other court of competent jurisdiction. All notices or judicial service in reference to arbitration or enforcement shall be deemed given if transmitted as required by the aforesaid rules.

**15 GUARANTEE:** (a) If all or any of the coffee is refused admission into the country of importation by reason of any violation of governmental laws or acts, which violation existed at the time the coffee arrived at Bonded Public Warehouse, seller is required, as to the amount not admitted and as soon as possible, to deliver replacement coffee in conformity to all terms and conditions of this contract, excepting only the Arrival terms, but not later than thirty (30) days after the date of the violation notice. Any payment made and expenses incurred for any coffee denied entry shall be refunded within ten (10) calendar days of denial of entry, and payment shall be made for the replacement delivery in accordance with the terms of this contract. Consequently, if Buyer removes the coffee from the Bonded Public Warehouse, Seller's responsibility as to such portion hereunder ceases.
(b) Contracts containing the overstamp "No Pass-No Sale" on the face of the contract shall be interpreted to mean: If any or all of the coffee is not admitted into the country of Importation in its original condition by reason of failure to meet requirements of the government's laws or Acts, the contract shall be deemed null and void as to that portion of the coffee which is not admitted in its original condition. Any payment made and expenses incurred for any coffee denied entry shall be refunded within ten (10) calendar days of denial of entry.

**16 CONTINGENCY:** This contract is not contingent upon any other contract.

**17 CLAIMS:** Coffee shall be considered accepted as to quality unless within *fifteen* (15) calendar days after delivery at Bonded Public Warehouse or within *fifteen* (15) calendar days after all Government clearances have been received, whichever is later, either:
(a) Claims are settled by the parties hereto, or,
(b) Arbitration proceedings have been filed by one of the parties in accordance with the provisions hereof.
(c) If neither (a) nor (b) has been done in the stated period or if any portion of the coffee has been removed from the Bonded Public Warehouse before representative sealed samples have been drawn by the Green Coffee Association of New York City, Inc., in accordance with its rules, Seller's responsibility for quality claims ceases for that portion so removed.
(d) Any question of quality submitted to arbitration shall be a matter of allowance only, unless otherwise provided in the contract.

**18 DELIVERY:** (a) No more than three (3) chops may be tendered for each lot of 250 bags.
(b) Each chop of coffee tendered is to be uniform in grade and appearance. All expense necessary to make coffee uniform shall be for account of seller.
(c) Notice of arrival and/or sampling order constitutes a tender, and must be given not later than the fifth business day following arrival at Bonded Public Warehouse stated on the contract.

**INSURANCE:** Seller is responsible for any loss or damage, or both, until Delivery and Discharge of coffee at the Bonded Public Warehouse in the Country of Importation.

All Insurance Risks, costs and responsibility are for Seller's Account until Delivery and Discharge of coffee at the Bonded Public Warehouse in the Country of Importation.

Buyer's insurance responsibility begins from the day of importation or from the day of tender, whichever is later.

**19 FREIGHT:** Seller to provide and pay for all transportation and related expenses to the Bonded Public Warehouse in the Country of Importation.

**20 EXPORT DUTIES/TAXES:** Exporter is to pay all Export taxes, duties or other fees or charges, if any, levied because of exportation.

**IMPORT DUTIES/TAXES:** Any Duty or Tax whatsoever, imposed by the government or any authority of the Country of Importation, shall be borne by the Importer/Buyer.

**21 INSOLVENCY OR FINANCIAL FAILURE OF BUYER OR SELLER:** If, at any time before the contract is fully executed, either party hereto shall meet with creditors because of inability generally to make payment of obligations when due, or shall suspend such payments, fail to meet his general trade obligations in the regular course of business, shall file a petition in bankruptcy or, for an arrangement, shall become insolvent, or commit an act of bankruptcy, then the other party may at his option, expressed in writing, declare the aforesaid to constitute a breach and default of this contract, and may, in addition to other remedies, decline to deliver further or make payment or may sell or purchase for the defaulter's account, and may collect damage for any injury or loss, or shall account for the profit, if any, occasioned by such sale or purchase.

This clause is subject to the provisions of (11 USC 365 (e) 1) if invoked.

**22 BREACH OR DEFAULT OF CONTRACT:** In the event either party hereto fails to perform, or breaches or repudiates this agreement, the other party shall subject to the specific provisions of this contract be entitled to the remedies and relief provided for by the Uniform Commercial Code of the State of New York. The computation and ascertainment of damages, or the determination of any other dispute as to relief, shall be made by the arbitrators in accordance with the Arbitration Clause herein.

**23** Consequential damages shall not, however, be allowed.

*(Continued)*

# An Example of a Contract for the International Sale of Coffee

**(14)** Arbitration is the settling of a dispute by submitting it to a disinterested party (other than a court), which renders a decision. The procedures and costs can be provided for in an arbitration clause or incorporated through other documents. To enforce an award rendered in an arbitration, the winning party can "enter" (submit) the award in a court "of competent jurisdiction." For a general discussion of arbitration and other forms of dispute resolution (other than courts), see Chapter 2.

**(15)** When goods are imported internationally, they must meet certain import requirements before being released to the buyer. See Chapter 24. Because of this, buyers frequently want a guaranty clause that covers the goods not admitted into the country and that either requires the seller to replace the goods within a stated time or allows the contract for those goods not admitted to be void.

**(16)** In the "Claims" clause, the parties agree that the buyer has a certain time within which to reject the goods. The right to reject is a right by law and does not need to be stated in a contract. If the buyer does not exercise the right within the time specified in the contract, the goods will be considered accepted. See Chapter 22.

**(17)** Many international contracts include definitions of terms so that the parties understand what they mean. Some terms are used in a particular industry in a specific way. Here, the word *chop* refers to a unit of like-grade coffee beans. The buyer has a right to inspect ("sample") the coffee. If the coffee does not conform to the contract, the seller must correct the nonconformity. See Chapter 22.

**(18)** The "Delivery," "Insurance," and "Freight" clauses, with the "Arrival" clause on page one of the contract, indicate that this is a destination contract. The seller has the obligation to deliver the goods to the destination, not simply deliver them into the hands of a carrier. Under this contract, the destination is a "Bonded Public Warehouse" in a specific location. The seller bears the risk of loss until the goods are delivered at their destination. Typically, the seller will have bought insurance to cover the risk. See Chapter 21 for a discussion of delivery terms and the risk of loss.

**(19)** Delivery terms are commonly placed in all sales contracts. Such terms determine who pays freight and other costs and, in the absence of an agreement specifying otherwise, who bears the risk of loss. International contracts may use these delivery terms, or they may use INCOTERMS, which are published by the International Chamber of Commerce. For example, the INCOTERM DDP (delivered duty paid) requires the seller to arrange shipment, obtain and pay for import or export permits, and get the goods through customs to a named destination.

**(20)** Exported and imported goods are subject to duties, taxes, and other charges imposed by the governments of the countries involved. International contracts spell out who is responsible for these charges.

**(21)** This clause protects a party if the other party should become financially unable to fulfill the obligations under the contract. Thus, if the seller cannot afford to deliver, or the buyer cannot afford to pay, for the stated reasons, the other party can consider the contract breached. This right is subject to "11 USC 365(e)(1)," which refers to a specific provision of the U.S. Bankruptcy Code dealing with executory contracts.

**(22)** In the "Breach or Default of Contract" clause, the parties agree that the remedies under this contract are the remedies (except for consequential damages) provided by the UCC, as in effect in the state of New York. The amount and "ascertainment" of damages, as well as other disputes about relief, are to be determined by arbitration. Breach of contract and contractual remedies in general are explained in Chapter 22. Arbitration is discussed in Chapter 2.

**(23)** Three clauses frequently included in international contracts (see Chapter 20) are omitted here. There is no choice-of-language clause designating the official language to be used in interpreting the contract terms. There is no choice-of-forum clause designating the place in which disputes will be litigated, except for arbitration (law of New York State). Finally, there is no *force majeure* clause relieving the sellers or buyers from nonperformance due to events beyond their control.

# CHAPTER 21

# TITLE, RISK, AND INSURABLE INTEREST

Before the creation of the Uniform Commercial Code (UCC), *title*—the right of ownership—was the central concept in sales law. Title controlled all issues of rights and remedies of the parties to a sales contract. There were numerous problems with this concept, however. Anything can happen between the time a contract is signed and the time the goods are transferred to the buyer's or lessee's possession. It was frequently difficult to determine when title actually passed from the seller to the buyer.

Therefore, it was also difficult to predict which party a court would decide had title at the time of a loss.

Because of such problems, the UCC divorced the question of title as completely as possible from the question of the rights and obligations of buyers, sellers, and third parties (such as subsequent purchasers, creditors, or the tax collector). Nevertheless, in some situations, title is still relevant under the UCC, and the UCC has special rules for assigning title. These rules will be discussed in the sections that follow. In

most situations, however, the UCC has replaced the concept of title with three other concepts: identification, risk of loss, and insurable interest.

In lease contracts, of course, the lessor-owner of the goods retains title. Hence, the UCC's provisions relating to passage of title do not apply to leased goods. Other concepts discussed in this chapter, though, including identification, risk of loss, and insurable interest, relate to lease contracts as well as to sales contracts.

---

### SECTION 1
## IDENTIFICATION

Before any interest in specific goods can pass from the seller or lessor to the buyer or lessee, the goods must be (1) in existence and (2) identified as the specific goods designated in the contract [UCC 2–105(2)]. **Identification** takes place when specific goods are designated as the subject matter of a sales or lease contract.

Title and risk of loss cannot pass to the buyer from the seller unless the goods are identified to the contract. (As mentioned, title to leased goods remains with the lessor—or, if the owner is a third party, with that party.) Identification is significant because it gives the buyer or lessee the right to insure (or to have an insurable interest in) the goods and the right to recover from third parties who damage the goods.

The parties can agree in their contract on when identification will take place (although it will not effectively pass title and risk of loss to the buyer on

future goods, such as unborn cattle). If the parties do not so specify, however, the UCC provisions discussed here determine when identification takes place [UCC 2–501(1), 2A–217].

### Existing Goods

If the contract calls for the sale or lease of specific and ascertained goods that are already in existence, identification takes place at the time the contract is made.
▶ **Example 21.1** Litco Company contracts to lease a fleet of five cars designated by their vehicle identification numbers (VINs). Because the cars are identified by their VINs, identification has taken place, and Litco acquires an insurable interest in the cars at the time of contracting. ◀

### Future Goods

Any goods that are not in existence at the time of contracting are known as future goods. If a sale or lease involves unborn animals to be born within twelve months after contracting, identification takes place when the animals are conceived.

If a sale involves crops that are to be harvested within twelve months (or the next harvest season occurring after contracting, whichever is longer), identification takes place when the crops are planted. Otherwise, identification takes place when the crops begin to grow. (See this chapter's *Insight into the Global Environment* feature below for a discussion of how contracts for agricultural products can benefit the environment.)

In a sale or lease of any other future goods, identification occurs when the seller or lessor ships, marks, or otherwise designates the goods as those to which the contract refers. ▶ **Case in Point 21.2** Gordon Bonner contracted with Ronnie Carman to build a forty-six-foot motorboat for $278,950. The contract required progress payments but did not contain any specific provisions regarding delivery (which, as you will read shortly, can determine when title to the goods passes to the buyer). After nearly three years, with the boat still not completed, Carman filed for bankruptcy. The bankruptcy trustee wanted to sell the unfinished boat to pay Carman's creditors, but Bonner claimed that the boat—which was still on Carman's business premises—was his.

The court held that under the UCC, the boat constituted future goods because it did not exist at the time the contract was signed. In addition, title had not passed to Bonner because the boat had not been identified to the contract. The boat could have been identified by listing its hull number in the contract or by later marking or designating it as Bonner's, but no such steps were taken. Therefore, the bankruptcy trustee could sell the boat and distribute the funds to Carman's creditors.[1] ◀

---

**1.** *In re Carman,* 399 Bankr. 158 (D.Md. 2009). For another case in which a boat was held to be future goods, see *Gonsalves v. Montgomery,* 2006 WL 2711540 (N.D.Cal. 2006).

# INSIGHT INTO THE GLOBAL ENVIRONMENT
## Contracts with Fair Trade Pricing Can Promote Environmental Sustainability

Most sales contracts have price terms that are mutually agreed to by the buyer and seller. But sales contracts can do more than that. Thanks to the Fair Trade movement, they can also benefit poor farmers in developing nations and can promote environmentally sustainable farming practices.

**The Fair Trade Movement**

The Fair Trade movement originated during the 1980s. Today, the Fair Trade Labelling Organizations International determines minimum "fair prices that ensure that small producers can earn a living wage." It urges importers to pay these fair prices for the products they obtain.

Under the Fair Trade system, low-income farmers and artisans in developing countries form alliances with importers and marketers in western Europe and North America. Participants must agree to certain basic principles:

- Producers must receive a stable minimum price for their products.
- Producers will not use forced or child labor.
- Production methods will be environmentally friendly.

When these standards are met, international certification bodies allow the products to carry a Fair Trade logo, such as the well-known label borne by some coffee imported into the United States. Retailers are free to charge any price they wish, but because they necessarily pay more for Fair Trade products, they pass on the higher costs to their customers.

**The Fair Trade Sustainability Alliance**

The Fair Trade Sustainability Alliance (FairTSA), a nonprofit organization that promotes socially responsible development in emerging countries, has taken the Fair Trade concept to another level. FairTSA attempts to ensure that the community development associated with its work is accountable and sustainable. In addition to promoting sustainable development, FairTSA monitors suppliers and certifies those that practice ethical and accountable supply chain management.

FairTSA will certify a producer of any type of agricultural products. To win certification, a producer must accept professional standards and be open for audits and inspections.

### LEGAL CRITICAL THINKING
**INSIGHT INTO ETHICS**

*Why might marketing managers of large retail companies, particularly grocery chains, want to purchase Fair Trade products?*

## Goods That Are
## Part of a Larger Mass

Goods that are part of a larger mass are identified when the goods are marked, shipped, or somehow designated by the seller or lessor as the particular goods to pass under the contract. ▶ **Example 21.3**  A buyer orders 10,000 pairs of men's jeans from a lot that contains 90,000 articles of clothing for men, women, and children. Until the seller separates the 10,000 pairs of men's jeans from the other items, title and risk of loss remain with the seller. ◀

A common exception to this rule involves fungible goods. **Fungible goods** are goods that are alike naturally, by agreement, or by trade usage. Typical examples include specific grades or types of wheat, petroleum, and cooking oil, which usually are stored in large containers. If the owners of these goods hold title as *tenants in common* (owners with an undivided share of the whole), a seller-owner can pass title and risk of loss to the buyer without actually separating the goods. The buyer replaces the seller as an owner in common [UCC 2–105(4)].

▶ **Example 21.4**  Alvarez, Braudel, and Carpenter are farmers. They deposit, respectively, 5,000 bushels, 3,000 bushels, and 2,000 bushels of grain of the same grade and quality in a grain elevator. The three become owners in common, with Alvarez owning 50 percent of the 10,000 bushels, Braudel 30 percent, and Carpenter 20 percent. Alvarez contracts to sell her 5,000 bushels of grain to Treyton. Because the goods are fungible, she can pass title and risk of loss to Treyton without physically separating the 5,000 bushels. Treyton now becomes an owner in common with Braudel and Carpenter. ◀

## SECTION 2
# WHEN TITLE PASSES

Once goods exist and are identified, the provisions of UCC 2–401 apply to the passage of title. In nearly all subsections of UCC 2–401, the words "unless otherwise explicitly agreed" appear, meaning that any explicit understanding between the buyer and the seller determines when title passes.

Without an explicit agreement to the contrary, *title passes to the buyer at the time and the place the seller performs by delivering the goods* [UCC 2–401(2)]. ▶ **Example 21.5**  Joshua buys cattle at a livestock auction. Title will pass when the cattle are physically delivered to him (unless, of course, the parties agree otherwise). ◀

If a seller gives up possession or control of goods, but keeps a "certificate of origin" supposedly showing ownership, has there been a delivery sufficient to pass title? That was the question in the following case.

---

## CASE 21.1

### United States v. 2007 Custom Motorcycle
United States District Court, District of Arizona, 2011 WL 232331 (2011).

**BACKGROUND AND FACTS**  Timothy Allen commissioned a custom motorcycle from Indy Route 66 Cycles, Inc. Indy built the motorcycle and issued a "Certificate of Origin." Two years later, federal law enforcement officers arrested Allen on drug charges and seized his home and other property. The officers also seized the Indy-made motorcycle from the garage at the home of Allen's sister, Tena. The government alleged that the motorcycle was subject to forfeiture as the proceeds of drug trafficking. Indy filed a claim against the government, arguing that it owned the motorcycle, as evidenced by the "Certificate of Origin," which the company still possessed. Indy claimed that it had been keeping the motorcycle in storage. The government filed a motion to strike the claim, asserting that title to the motorcycle had passed when it was delivered to Allen.

**DECISION AND RATIONALE**  The federal district court issued a ruling in the government's favor and granted the motion to strike Indy's claim. Under UCC 2–401(2), "unless otherwise explicitly agreed, title passes to the buyer at the time and place at which the seller completes his performance with reference to the physical delivery of the goods." In the sales transaction in this case, the parties did not "otherwise explicitly agree" to different terms. Thus, the critical question was whether Indy had delivered the cycle to Allen. Testimony by Indy's former vice president, Vince Ballard, was "inconclusive" but implied that Indy had delivered the motorcycle to Allen. The cycle was found in Tena's garage, which also indicated that Indy had delivered it to Allen. Thus, Indy had given up possession of the cycle to Allen. This was sufficient to pass title even though Indy had kept a "Certificate of Origin." As a consequence, the motorcycle was subject to forfeiture as the proceeds of drug trafficking.

**WHAT IF THE FACTS WERE DIFFERENT?**   *Suppose that Indy had given the "Certificate of Origin" to Allen and had kept the motorcycle. Would the result have been different? Explain.*

**THE LEGAL ENVIRONMENT DIMENSION**   *Should the passage of title be tied so closely to the possession of the goods? Discuss.*

## Shipment and Destination Contracts

Unless otherwise agreed, delivery arrangements can determine when title passes from the seller to the buyer. In a **shipment contract,** the seller is required or authorized to ship goods by carrier, such as a trucking company. Under a shipment contract, the seller is required only to deliver the goods into the hands of a carrier, and title passes to the buyer at the time and place of shipment [UCC 2–401(2)(a)]. Generally, *all contracts are assumed to be shipment contracts if nothing to the contrary is stated in the contract.*

In a **destination contract,** the seller is required to deliver the goods to a particular destination, usually directly to the buyer, but sometimes to another party designated by the buyer. Title passes to the buyer when the goods are *tendered* at that destination [UCC 2–401(2)(b)]. As you will read in Chapter 22, *tender of delivery* occurs when the seller places or holds conforming goods at the buyer's disposal (with any necessary notice), enabling the buyer to take possession [UCC 2–503(1)].

## Delivery without Movement of the Goods

Sometimes, a sales contract does not call for the seller to ship or deliver the goods (such as when the buyer is to pick up the goods). In that situation, the passage of title depends on whether the seller must deliver a **document of title,** such as a bill of lading or a warehouse receipt, to the buyer. A *bill of lading*[2] is a receipt for goods that is signed by a carrier and serves as a contract for the transportation of the goods. A *warehouse receipt* is a receipt issued by a warehouser for goods stored in a warehouse.

**WHEN A TITLE DOCUMENT IS REQUIRED**   When a title document is required, title passes to the buyer *when and where the document is delivered.* Thus, if the goods are stored in a warehouse, title passes to the buyer when the appropriate documents are delivered to the buyer. The goods never move. In fact, the buyer can choose to leave the goods at the same warehouse for a period of time, and the buyer's title to those goods will be unaffected.

**WHEN A TITLE DOCUMENT IS NOT REQUIRED**   When no document of title is required and the goods are identified to the contract, title passes at the time and place the sales contract is made. If the goods have not been identified, title does not pass until identification occurs.

▶ **Example 21.6**   Juarez sells lumber to Bodan. They agree that Bodan will pick up the lumber at the yard. If the lumber has been identified (segregated, marked, or in any other way distinguished from all other lumber), title passes to Bodan when the contract is signed. If the lumber is still in large storage bins at the mill, title does not pass to Bodan until the particular pieces of lumber to be sold under this contract are identified [UCC 2–401(3)]. ◀

## Sales or Leases by Nonowners

Problems occur when persons who acquire goods with imperfect titles attempt to sell or lease them. Sections 2–402 and 2–403 of the UCC deal with the rights of two parties who lay claim to the same goods sold with imperfect titles. Generally, a buyer acquires at least whatever title the seller has to the goods sold.

---

**2.** The term *bill of lading* has been used by international carriers for many years. It derives from *bill,* which historically referred to a schedule of costs for services, and the verb *to lade,* which means to load cargo onto a ship or other form of transportation.

These same UCC sections also protect lessees. Obviously, a lessee does not acquire whatever title the lessor has to the goods. Rather, the lessee acquires a right to possess and use the goods—that is, a *leasehold interest*. A lessee acquires whatever leasehold interest the lessor has or has the power to transfer, subject to the lease contract [UCC 2A–303, 2A–304, 2A–305].

**VOID TITLE** A buyer may unknowingly purchase goods from a seller who is not the owner of the goods. If the seller is a thief, the seller's title is *void*—legally, no title exists. Thus, the buyer acquires no title, and the real owner can reclaim the goods from the buyer. If the goods were leased instead, the same result would occur because the lessor would have no leasehold interest to transfer.

▶ **Example 21.7** If Saki steals a valuable necklace owned by Shannon, Saki has a *void title* to that necklace. If Saki sells the necklace to Valdez, Shannon can reclaim it from Valdez even though Valdez acted in good faith and honestly was not aware that the necklace was stolen. (Note that Valdez may file a tort claim against Saki under these circumstances, but here we are only discussing title to the goods.) ◀ Article 2A contains similar provisions for leases.

**VOIDABLE TITLE** A seller has a *voidable title* to goods obtained by fraud, paid for with a check that was later dishonored, purchased from a minor, or purchased on credit when the seller was **insolvent.** (Under the UCC, insolvency occurs when a person ceases to pay debts in the ordinary course of business, cannot pay debts as they become due, or is insolvent under federal bankruptcy law [UCC 1–201(23)].)

***Good Faith Purchasers.*** In contrast to a seller with void title, a seller with voidable title has the power to transfer good title to a good faith purchaser for value. A **good faith purchaser** is one who buys without knowledge of circumstances that would make an ordinary person inquire about the validity of the seller's title to the goods. One who purchases *for value* gives legally sufficient consideration (value) for the goods purchased. The original owner normally cannot recover goods from a good faith purchaser for value [UCC 2–403(1)].[3]

If the buyer is not a good faith purchaser for value, the actual owner can reclaim the goods from the buyer (or from the seller, if the goods are still in the seller's possession). Exhibit 21–1 below illustrates these concepts.

---

**3.** The real owner could sue the person who initially obtained voidable title to the goods.

---

### EXHIBIT 21–1  Void and Voidable Titles

If goods are transferred from their owner to another by theft, the thief acquires no ownership rights. Because the thief's title is *void,* a later buyer can acquire no title, and the owner can recover the goods. If the transfer occurs by fraud, the transferee acquires a *voidable* title. A later good faith purchaser for value can acquire good title, and the original owner cannot recover the goods.

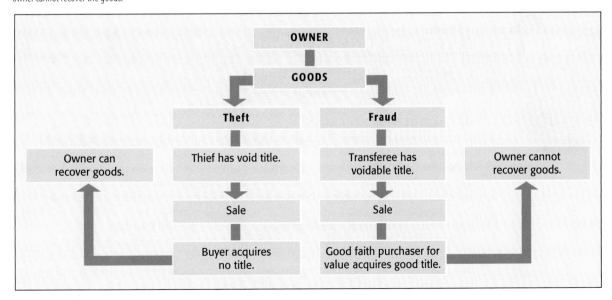

***Voidable Title and Leases.***  The same rules apply in situations involving leases. A lessor with voidable title has the power to transfer a valid leasehold interest to a good faith lessee for value. The real owner cannot recover the goods, except as permitted by the terms of the lease. The real owner can, however, receive all proceeds arising from the lease. The owner can also obtain a transfer of the rights that the lessor had under the lease, including the right to the return of the goods when the lease expires [UCC 2A–305(1)].

**THE ENTRUSTMENT RULE**  Entrusting goods to a merchant *who deals in goods of that kind* gives the merchant the power to transfer all rights to *a buyer in the ordinary course of business* [UCC 2–403(2)]. This is known as the **entrustment rule.** Entrusting includes both turning over the goods to the merchant and leaving purchased goods with the merchant for later delivery or pickup [UCC 2–403(3)]. Article 2A provides a similar rule for leased goods [UCC 2A–305(2)]. Under the UCC, a person is a **buyer in the ordinary course of business** if:

1.  She or he buys goods in good faith (honestly).
2.  The goods are purchased without knowledge that the sale violates the rights of another person in the goods.
3.  The goods are purchased in the ordinary course from a merchant (other than a pawnbroker) in the business of selling goods of that kind.

4.  The sale to that person comports with the usual or customary practices in the kind of business in which the seller is engaged [UCC 1–201(9)].

The entrustment rule basically allows innocent buyers to obtain legitimate title to goods purchased from merchants even if the merchants do not have good title.  ▶ **Example 21.8**  Jan leaves her watch with a jeweler to be repaired. The jeweler sells both new and used watches. The jeweler sells Jan's watch to Kim, a customer who is unaware that the jeweler has no right to sell it. Kim, as a good faith buyer, gets good title against Jan's claim of ownership.[4] Kim, however, obtains only those rights held by the person entrusting the goods (Jan).

Now suppose that Jan had stolen the watch from Greg and left it with the jeweler to be repaired. The jeweler then sold it to Kim. Kim would obtain good title against Jan, who entrusted the watch to the jeweler, but not against Greg (the real owner), who neither entrusted the watch to Jan nor authorized Jan to entrust it.  ◀

A nonowner's sale of *Red Elvis,* an artwork by Andy Warhol, was at the center of the dispute over title in the following case.

---

4.  Jan can sue the jeweler for the tort of conversion (or trespass to personal property) to obtain damages equivalent to the cash value of the watch (see Chapter 6).

## SP TLIGHT on Andy Warhol

### Case 21.2   Lindholm v. Brant
Supreme Court of Connecticut, 283 Conn. 65, 925 A.2d 1048 (2007).

**BACKGROUND AND FACTS**  In 1987, Kerstin Lindholm of Greenwich, Connecticut, bought a silkscreen by Andy Warhol titled *Red Elvis* from Anders Malmberg, a Swedish art dealer, for $300,000. In 1998, Lindholm loaned *Red Elvis* to the Guggenheim Museum in New York City for an exhibition to tour Europe. Peter Brant, who was on the museum's board of trustees and also a Greenwich resident, believed that Lindholm was the owner. Stellan Holm, a Swedish art dealer who had bought and sold other Warhol works with Brant, told him, however, that Malmberg had bought it and would sell it for $2.9 million. Malmberg refused Brant's request to provide a copy of an invoice between Lindholm and himself on the ground that such documents normally and customarily are not disclosed in art deals.

To determine whether Malmberg had good title, Brant hired an attorney to search the Art Loss Register (an international database of stolen and missing artworks) and other sources. No problems were found, but Brant was cautioned that this provided only "minimal assurances." Brant's attorney drafted a formal contract, which conditioned payment on the delivery of *Red Elvis* to a warehouse in Denmark. The

**CASE 21.2 CONTINUED**

exchange took place in April 2000.[a] Lindholm filed a suit in a Connecticut state court against Brant, alleging conversion, among other things. The court issued a judgment in Brant's favor. Lindholm appealed to the Connecticut Supreme Court.

**DECISION AND RATIONALE** The Connecticut Supreme Court affirmed the judgment of the lower court. The appellate court pointed out that "a person buys goods in good faith if there is honesty in fact and the observance of reasonable commercial standards of fair dealing in the conduct or transaction concerned." In most art transactions, the buyer has no reason for concern about the seller's ability to convey good title. Such transactions are completed by a handshake and an invoice exchange. Sophisticated buyers and sellers normally do not obtain signed invoices from the original seller to the dealer prior to a transaction. "Nor is it an ordinary or customary practice to request the underlying invoice corroborating [substantiating] information as to a dealer's authority to convey title." In sum, it is customary to rely on representations made by "respected dealers regarding their authority to sell works of art." The state supreme court concluded that "on the basis of all the circumstances surrounding this sale," Brant was a buyer in the ordinary course of business and therefore took all rights to *Red Elvis* under UCC 2–403(2).

**THE ETHICAL DIMENSION** *How did the "usual and customary" methods of dealing in the art business help Malmberg deceive the other parties in this case? What additional steps might those parties have taken to protect themselves from such deceit?*

**THE GLOBAL DIMENSION** *Considering the international locales in this case, why was Lindholm able to bring an action against Brant in Connecticut?*

---

a. Unaware of this deal, Lindholm accepted a Japanese buyer's offer of $4.6 million for *Red Elvis*. The funds were wired to Malmberg, who kept them. Lindholm filed a criminal complaint against Malmberg in Sweden. In 2003, a Swedish court convicted Malmberg of "gross fraud embezzlement." The court awarded Lindholm $4.6 million and other relief.

---

## SECTION 3
# RISK OF LOSS

At the various stages of a sale or lease transaction, the question may arise as to who bears the risk of loss. In other words, who suffers the financial loss if the goods are damaged, destroyed, or lost in transit? Under the UCC, risk of loss does not necessarily pass with title. When risk of loss passes from a seller or lessor to a buyer or lessee is generally determined by the contract between the parties.

Sometimes, the contract states expressly when the risk of loss passes. At other times, it does not, and a court must interpret the existing terms to determine whether the risk has passed. When no provision in the contract indicates when risk passes, the UCC provides special rules, based on delivery terms, to guide the courts.

Like risk of loss, the risk of liability that arises from the goods does not necessarily require the passage of title. And like risk of loss, when this risk passes from a seller to a buyer is generally determined by the contract between the parties, as in the following case.

---

# CASE 21.3

## Person v. Bowman
Court of Appeals of Washington, 2013 WL 663726 (2013).

**BACKGROUND AND FACTS** Tammy Herring and Stacy Bowman signed an agreement titled "Bill of Sale—Purchase Agreement" involving a horse named Toby. The agreement defined Herring as the "buyer" and Stacy and Gregory Bowman, who owned Summit Stables in Puyallup, Washington, as the "seller." It required Herring to make monthly payments until she paid $2,200 in total for Toby, to board Toby

**CASE 21.3 CONTINUES ▶**

at Summit Stables until the balance was paid, and to cover incidental costs, such as veterinary expenses. The Bowmans were to provide Toby's registration papers to Herring only when she had paid in full. Diana Person was injured when she was thrown from a buggy drawn by Toby and driven by Herring's daughter, Alex. Person and her husband, Robert, filed a suit in a Washington state court against the Bowmans to recover for Person's injuries. The court ruled in the defendants' favor, and the Persons appealed.

**DECISION AND RATIONALE** A state intermediate appellate court affirmed the judgment in the Bowmans' favor. Herring (not the Bowmans) owned Toby at the time of the accident that resulted in Person's injuries. Washington state "follows the objective manifestation theory of contract interpretation, under which courts try to ascertain the parties' intent by focusing on the objective manifestations of the agreement, rather than on the unexpressed subjective intent of the parties." The contract clearly showed that Herring owned Toby. Just because Herring asserted that she believed she would not own Toby until she paid the full contract price does not negate her ownership rights in the horse. No statements actually demonstrated that the parties intended to lease Toby. "Each statement acknowledged that the Bowmans retained a security interest in Toby." Herring's subjective belief may have been that she did not own Toby and that this was a lease-like agreement, but "the parties' objective manifestations are consistent with this being a sale, not a lease."

**THE LEGAL ENVIRONMENT DIMENSION** *What did the contract between Herring and the Bowmans require Herring to do? What is the significance of these provisions?*

**WHAT IF THE FACTS WERE DIFFERENT?** *If the agreement between Herring and the Bowmans had been a lease, would the result have been the same? Explain.*

---

## Delivery with Movement of the Goods—Carrier Cases

When the contract involves movement of the goods via a common carrier but does not specify when risk of loss passes, the courts first look for specific delivery terms in the contract. The terms that have traditionally been used in contracts within the United States are listed and defined in Exhibit 21–2 on page 375. *Unless the parties agree otherwise,* these terms will determine which party will pay the costs of delivering the goods and who will bear the risk of loss. If the contract does not include these terms, then the courts must decide whether the contract is a shipment or a destination contract.

**SHIPMENT CONTRACTS** In a shipment contract, the seller or lessor is required or authorized to ship goods by carrier, but is not required to deliver them to a particular destination. The risk of loss in a shipment contract passes to the buyer or lessee when the goods are delivered to the carrier [UCC 2–509(1)(a), 2A–219(2)(a)].

▶ **Example 21.9** Pitman, a seller in Texas, sells five hundred cases of grapefruit to a buyer in New York, F.O.B. Houston (free on board in Houston). This term means that the buyer pays the transportation charges from Houston—see Exhibit 21–2 on the facing page.

The contract authorizes shipment by carrier. It does not require that the seller tender the grapefruit in New York. Risk passes to the buyer when conforming goods are properly placed in the possession of the carrier. If the goods are damaged in transit, the loss is the buyer's. (Actually, buyers have recourse against carriers, subject to certain limitations, and they usually insure the goods from the time the goods leave the seller.) ◀

**DESTINATION CONTRACTS** In a destination contract, the risk of loss passes to the buyer or lessee when the goods are tendered to the buyer or lessee at the specified destination [UCC 2–509(1)(b), 2A–219(2)(b)]. In *Example 21.9* above, if the contract had been a destination contract, F.O.B. New York, risk of loss during transit to New York would have been the seller's. Risk of loss would not have passed to the buyer until the carrier tendered the grapefruit to the buyer in New York.

Whether a contract is a shipment contract or a destination contract can have significant consequences for the parties. When an agreement is ambiguous as to whether it is a shipment or a destination contract, courts normally will presume that it is a shipment contract. Thus, the parties must use clear and explicit language to overcome this presumption and create a destination contract.

**EXHIBIT 21–2  Contract Terms—Definitions**

The contract terms listed and defined in this exhibit help to determine which party will bear the costs of delivery and when risk of loss will pass from the seller to the buyer.

**F.O.B.** (free on board)—Indicates that the selling price of goods includes transportation costs to the specific F.O.B. place named in the contract. The seller pays the expenses and carries the risk of loss to the F.O.B. place named [UCC 2–319(1)]. If the named place is the place from which the goods are shipped (for example, the seller's city or place of business), the contract is a shipment contract. If the named place is the place to which the goods are to be shipped (for example, the buyer's city or place of business), the contract is a destination contract.

**F.A.S.** (free alongside)—Requires that the seller, at his or her own expense and risk, deliver the goods alongside the carrier before risk passes to the buyer [UCC 2–319(2)]. An F.A.S. contract is essentially an F.O.B. contract for ships.

**C.I.F.** or **C.&F.** (cost, insurance, and freight or just cost and freight)—Requires, among other things, that the seller "put the goods in possession of a carrier" before risk passes to the buyer [UCC 2–320(2)]. (These are basically pricing terms, and the contracts remain shipment contracts, not destination contracts.)

**Delivery ex-ship** (delivery from the carrying vessel)—Means that risk of loss does not pass to the buyer until the goods are properly unloaded from the ship or other carrier [UCC 2–322].

## Delivery without Movement of the Goods

The UCC also addresses situations in which the contract does not require the goods to be shipped or moved. Frequently, the buyer or lessee is to pick up the goods from the seller or lessor, or the goods are to be held by a bailee. A **bailment** is a temporary delivery of personal property, without passage of title, into the care of another, called a *bailee*. Under the UCC, a bailee is a party who—by a bill of lading, warehouse receipt, or other document of title—acknowledges possession of goods and/or contracts to deliver them. For instance, a warehousing company or a trucking company may be a bailee.[5]

**GOODS HELD BY THE SELLER** When the seller keeps the goods for pickup, a document of title usually is not used. If the seller is not a merchant, the risk of loss to goods held by the seller passes to the buyer on *tender of delivery* [UCC 2–509(3)]. Thus, the seller bears the risk of loss until he or she makes the goods available to the buyer and notifies the buyer that the goods are ready to be picked up.

**Merchants.** If the seller is a merchant, risk of loss to goods held by the seller passes to the buyer when the buyer *actually takes physical possession of the goods* [UCC 2–509(3)]. In other words, the merchant bears the risk of loss between the time the contract is formed and the time the buyer picks up the goods.

▶ **Case in Point 21.10** Henry Ganno purchased a twelve-foot beam at a lumberyard. The lumberyard loaded the beam onto Ganno's truck, but did not tie it down (it was policy not to secure loads for customers). After he drove onto the highway, the beam fell out of Ganno's truck, and he was injured while trying to retrieve it. Ganno sued the lumberyard for negligence, but the court held that Ganno—not the lumberyard—bore the risk of loss and injury after he left the lumberyard's premises. Once the truck was loaded, the risk of loss passed to Ganno under the UCC because he had taken physical possession of the goods.[6] ◀

**Leases.** Except in a finance lease (in which the lessor acquires goods to supply the lessee—see Chapter 20), the lessor normally retains the risk of loss [UCC 2A–219]. If a lease contract provides that risk of loss is to pass to the lessee but does not specify when, then it depends on whether the lessor is a merchant. If the lessor is a merchant, the risk of loss passes to the lessee on the lessee's receipt of the goods. If the lessor is not a merchant, the risk passes to the lessee on tender of delivery (when goods are made available for pickup) [UCC 2A–219(2)(c)].

▶ **Example 21.11** Erikson Crane leases a helicopter from Jevis, Ltd., which is in the business of renting aircraft. While Erikson's pilot is on the way to Idaho to pick up the helicopter, the helicopter is damaged during an unexpected storm. In this situation, Jevis is a merchant-lessor, so it bears the risk of loss to the leased helicopter until Erikson takes possession of the helicopter. ◀

---

5. The law requires bailees to take appropriate care of the bailed goods.

6. *Ganno v. Lanoga Corp.*, 119 Wash.App. 310, 80 P.3d 180 (2003).

**GOODS HELD BY A BAILEE** When a bailee is holding goods that are to be delivered under a contract without being moved, the goods are usually represented by a document of title. The title document may be written or evidenced by an electronic record.

***Negotiability of Title Document.*** A document of title is either *negotiable* or *nonnegotiable,* depending on whether the transferee is a buyer or lessee, and how it is transferred. Negotiable and nonnegotiable documents may transfer different rights to the goods that the documents cover.

With a negotiable document of title, a party can transfer the rights by signing and delivering, or in some situations simply delivering, the document. The rights to the goods—free of any claims against the party that issued the document—pass with the document to the transferee. With a nonnegotiable document of title, the transferee obtains only the rights goods that the party transferring it had, subject to any prior claims.

***When Risk of Loss Passes.*** When goods are held by a bailee, risk of loss passes to the buyer when one of the following occurs:

1. The buyer receives a negotiable document of title for the goods.
2. The bailee acknowledges the buyer's right to possess the goods.
3. The buyer receives a nonnegotiable document of title, *and* the buyer has had a *reasonable time* to present the document to the bailee and demand the goods. If the bailee refuses to honor the document, the risk of loss remains with the seller [UCC 2–503(4)(b), 2–509(2)].

With respect to leases, if goods held by a bailee are to be delivered without being moved, the risk of loss passes to the lessee on acknowledgment by the bailee of the lessee's right to possession of the goods [UCC 2A–219(2)(b)].

*Concept Summary 21.1* below reviews the rules for when title and risk of loss pass to the buyer or lessee when the seller or lessor is not required to ship or deliver the goods.

## Conditional Sales

Buyers and sellers sometimes form sales contracts that are conditioned either on the buyer's approval of

---

### CONCEPT SUMMARY 21.1
## Delivery without Movement of the Goods

| CONCEPT | DESCRIPTION |
|---|---|
| **Goods Not Represented by a Document of Title** | Unless otherwise agreed, if the goods are not represented by a document of title, title and risk pass as follows:<br>1. Title passes on the formation of the contract [UCC 2–401(3)(b)].<br>2. Risk of loss passes to the buyer or lessee:<br>   a. if the seller or lessor is a merchant, risk passes on the buyer's or lessee's *receipt* of the goods.<br>   b. If the seller or lessor is a nonmerchant, risk passes to the buyer or lessee on the seller's or lessor's *tender* of delivery of the goods [UCC 2–509(3), 2A–219(2)(c)]. |
| **Goods Represented by a Document of Title** | Unless otherwise agreed, if the goods are represented by a document of title, title and risk pass to the buyer when any of the following occurs:<br>1. The buyer receives a negotiable document of title for the goods.<br>2. The bailee acknowledges the buyer's right to possess the goods.<br>3. The buyer receives a nonnegotiable document of title or a writing (record) directing the bailee to hand over the goods, and the buyer has had a reasonable time to present the document to the bailee and demand the goods [UCC 2–503(4)(b), 2–509(2)]. |
| **Leased Goods Held by a Bailee** | If leased goods held by a bailee are to be delivered without being moved, the risk of loss passes to the lessee on acknowledgment by the bailee of the lessee's right to possession of the goods [UCC 2A–219(2)(b)]. |

the goods or on the buyer's resale of the goods. The UCC states that (unless otherwise agreed) if the goods are for the buyer to use, the transaction is a *sale on approval*. If the goods are for the buyer to resell, the transaction is a *sale or return*.

**SALE ON APPROVAL** When a seller offers to sell goods to a buyer and permits the buyer to take the goods on a trial basis, a **sale on approval** is made. The goods are delivered primarily so that the prospective buyer can use the goods and be convinced of their appearance or performance. The term *sale* here is misleading, however, because only an *offer* to sell has been made, along with a bailment created by the buyer's possession.

Title and risk of loss (from causes beyond the buyer's control) remain with the seller until the buyer accepts (approves) the offer. Acceptance can be made expressly or by any act inconsistent with the *trial purpose* or the seller's ownership (such as reselling the goods). Thus, the buyer's decision not to return the goods within the trial period will be considered acceptance. If the buyer does not wish to accept, the buyer must notify the seller, and the return is made at the seller's expense and risk [UCC 2–327(1)]. Goods held on approval are not subject to the claims of the buyer's creditors until acceptance.

▶ **Example 21.12** Brad orders a Bowflex Tread-Climber online, and the manufacturer allows him to try it risk-free for thirty days. If Brad decides to keep the TreadClimber, then the sale is complete, but if he returns it within thirty days, there will be no sale and he will not be charged. If Brad files for bankruptcy within the thirty-day period and still has the TreadClimber in his possession, his creditors may not yet attach (seize) the TreadClimber because he has not accepted it. ◀

**SALE OR RETURN** In a **sale or return,** in contrast, the sale is completed, but the buyer has an option to return the goods and undo the sale. Sale-or-return contracts often arise when a merchant purchases goods primarily for resale. The merchant has the right to return part or all of the goods in lieu of payment if the goods fail to be resold. Basically, a sale or return is a sale of goods in the present that may be undone at the buyer's option within a specified time period.

▶ **Example 21.13** Freedom Press, a publisher, delivers forty cases of a best-selling book to Powell's Books, a retailer. If Freedom Press agrees that Powell's can return any unsold copies of the books at the end of a year, the transaction is a sale or return. ◀

Because the buyer receives possession at the time of the sale, title and risk of loss pass to the buyer and remain with the buyer unless the goods are returned within the time period specified. If the buyer decides to return the goods within this time period, the return is made at the buyer's risk and expense. Goods held under a sale-or-return contract are subject to the claims of the buyer's creditors while they are in the buyer's possession.

## Risk of Loss When a Sales or Lease Contract Is Breached

When a sales or lease contract is breached, the transfer of risk operates differently depending on which party breaches. Generally, the party in breach bears the risk of loss.

**WHEN THE SELLER OR LESSOR BREACHES** If the seller or lessor breaches by supplying goods that are so nonconforming that the buyer has the right to reject them, the risk of loss does not pass to the buyer.

▶ **Example 21.14** Lowe's orders stainless steel refrigerators from Whirlpool, F.O.B. Whirlpool's plant. Whirlpool ships white refrigerators instead. The white refrigerators (nonconforming goods) are damaged in transit. The risk of loss falls on Whirlpool. Had it shipped stainless steel refrigerators (conforming goods) instead, the risk would have fallen on Lowe's [UCC 2–510(1)]. ◀

With nonconforming goods, the risk of loss does not pass to the buyer until either:

1. The defects are *cured* (that is, the goods are repaired, replaced, or discounted in price by the seller—see Chapter 22).
2. The buyer accepts the goods in spite of their defects (thus waiving the right to reject).

***When Acceptance Is Revoked.*** If a buyer accepts a shipment of goods and later discovers a defect, acceptance can be revoked. The revocation allows the buyer to pass the risk of loss back to the seller, at least to the extent that the buyer's insurance does not cover the loss [UCC 2–510(2)].

***Leases.*** Article 2A provides a similar rule for leases. If the tender or delivery of goods is so nonconforming that the lessee has the right to reject them, the risk of loss remains with the lessor (or the supplier) until cure or acceptance [UCC 2A–220(1)(a)]. If the lessee accepts the goods and then rightfully revokes acceptance, the risk of loss passes back to the lessor to the extent that the lessee's insurance does not cover the loss [UCC 2A–220(1)(b)].

**WHEN THE BUYER OR LESSEE BREACHES** The general rule is that when a buyer or lessee breaches a contract, the risk of loss *immediately shifts* to the buyer or lessee. This rule has three important limitations [UCC 2–510(3), 2A–220(2)]:

1. The seller or lessor must have already identified the contract goods.
2. The buyer or lessee bears the risk for only a *commercially reasonable time* after the seller or lessor has learned of the breach.
3. The buyer or lessee is liable only to the extent of any deficiency in the seller's or lessor's insurance coverage.

See *Concept Summary 21.2* below for a review of the rules on who bears the risk of loss when a contract is breached.

## SECTION 4
# INSURABLE INTEREST

Parties to sales and lease contracts often obtain insurance coverage to protect against damage, loss, or destruction of goods. Any party purchasing insurance, however, must have a sufficient interest in the insured item to obtain a valid policy. Insurance laws—not the UCC—determine sufficiency. The UCC is helpful, though, because it contains certain rules regarding insurable interests in goods.

## Insurable Interest of the Buyer or Lessee

A buyer or lessee has an **insurable interest** in *identified goods*. The moment the contract goods are identified by the seller or lessor, the buyer or lessee has a property interest in them. That interest allows the buyer or lessee to obtain insurance coverage for those goods even before the risk of loss has passed [UCC 2–501(1), 2A–218(1)]. Identification can be made at any time and in any manner agreed to by the parties.

When the parties do not explicitly agree on identification in their contract, then the UCC provisions on identification discussed on page 367 of this chapter apply. Buyers obtain an insurable interest in crops at the time of identification. ▶ **Example 21.15** In March, a farmer sells a cotton crop that she hopes to harvest in October. If the contract does not specify otherwise, the buyer acquires an insurable interest in the crop when it is planted because the goods (the cotton crop) are identified to the sales contract at that time [UCC 2–501(1)(c)]. ◀

## Insurable Interest of the Seller or Lessor

A seller has an insurable interest in goods as long as he or she retains title to the goods. Even after title passes to a buyer, a seller who has a *security interest* (a right to secure payment) in the goods still has an

---

### CONCEPT SUMMARY 21.2
### Risk of Loss When a Sales or Lease Contract Is Breached

| CONCEPT | DESCRIPTION |
|---|---|
| **When the Seller or Lessor Breaches the Contract** | If the seller or lessor breaches by tendering nonconforming goods that the buyer or lessee has a right to reject, the risk of loss does not pass to the buyer or lessee until the defects are cured or the buyer accepts the goods (thus waiving the right to reject) [UCC 2–510(1), 2A–220(1)]. |
| **When the Buyer or Lessee Breaches the Contract** | If the buyer or lessee breaches the contract, the risk of loss to identified goods immediately shifts to the buyer or lessee. Limitations to this rule are as follows [UCC 2–510(3), 2A–220(2)]:<br>1. The seller or lessor must have already identified the contract goods.<br>2. The buyer or lessee bears the risk for only a commercially reasonable time after the seller or lessor has learned of the breach.<br>3. The buyer or lessee is liable only to the extent of any deficiency in the seller's or lessor's insurance coverage. |

insurable interest and can insure the goods [UCC 2–501(2)].

Thus, both the buyer and the seller can have an insurable interest in identical goods at the same time. Of course, the buyer or seller must sustain an actual loss to have the right to recover from an insurance company. In regard to leases, the lessor retains an insurable interest in leased goods unless the lessee exercises an option to buy, in which event the risk of loss passes to the lessee [UCC 2A–218(3)].

---

## Reviewing: Title, Risk, and Insurable Interest

In December, Mendoza agreed to buy the broccoli grown on one hundred acres of Willow Glen's one-thousand-acre broccoli farm. The sales contract specified F.O.B. Willow Glen's field by Falcon Trucking. The broccoli was to be planted in February and harvested in March of the following year. Using the information presented in the chapter, answer the following questions.

1. At what point is a crop of broccoli identified to the contract under the Uniform Commercial Code? Why is identification significant?
2. When does title to the broccoli pass from Willow Glen to Mendoza under the contract terms? Why?
3. Suppose that while in transit, Falcon's truck overturns and spills the entire load. Who bears the loss, Mendoza or Willow Glen?
4. Suppose that instead of buying fresh broccoli, Mendoza had contracted with Willow Glen to purchase one thousand cases of frozen broccoli from Willow Glen's processing plant. The highest grade of broccoli is packaged under the "FreshBest" label, and everything else is packaged under the "FamilyPac" label. Further suppose that although the contract specified that Mendoza was to receive FreshBest broccoli, Falcon Trucking delivered FamilyPac broccoli to Mendoza. If Mendoza refuses to accept the broccoli, who bears the loss?

**DEBATE THIS . . .** *The distinction between shipment and destination contracts for the purpose of deciding who will bear the risk of loss should be eliminated in favor of a rule that always requires the buyer to obtain insurance for the goods being shipped.*

---

## Terms and Concepts

bailment 375
buyer in the ordinary course of business 372
destination contract 370
document of title 370

entrustment rule 372
fungible goods 369
good faith purchaser 371
identification 367
insolvent 371

insurable interest 378
sale on approval 377
sale or return 377
shipment contract 370

---

## Issue Spotters

1. Adams Textiles in Kansas City sells certain fabric to Silk & Satin Stores in Oklahoma City. Adams packs the fabric and ships it by rail to Silk. While the fabric is in transit across Kansas, a tornado derails the train and shreds and scatters the fabric across miles of cornfields. What are the consequences if Silk bore the risk? If Adams bore the risk? **(See page 378.)**

2. Karlin takes her television set for repair to Orken, a merchant who sells new and used television sets. By accident, one of Orken's employees sells the set to Grady, an innocent purchaser-customer, who takes possession. Karlin wants her set back from Grady. If Karlin files a lawsuit, will she prevail? Why or why not? **(See page 372.)**

• **Check your answers to the Issue Spotters against the answers provided in Appendix E at the end of this text.**

## Business Scenarios

**21–1. Risk of Loss.** Mackey orders from Pride one thousand cases of Greenie brand peas from lot A at list price to be shipped F.O.B. Pride's city via Fast Freight Lines. Pride receives the order and immediately sends Mackey an acceptance of the order with a promise to ship promptly. Pride later separates the one thousand cases of Greenie peas and prints Mackey's name and address on each case. The peas are placed on Pride's dock, and Fast Freight is notified to pick up the shipment. The night before the pickup by Fast Freight, through no fault of Pride's, a fire destroys the one thousand cases of peas. Pride claims that title passed to Mackey at the time the contract was made and that risk of loss passed to Mackey when the goods were marked with Mackey's name and address. Discuss Pride's contentions. **(See page 374.)**

**21–2. Risk of Loss.** On May 1, Sikora goes into Carson's retail clothing store to purchase a suit. Sikora finds a suit he likes for $190 and buys it. The suit needs alterations. Sikora is to pick up the altered suit at Carson's store on May 10. Consider the following separate sets of circumstances: **(See page 375.)**

(a) One of Carson's major creditors obtains a judgment on the debt Carson owes and has the court issue a writ of execution (a court order to seize a debtor's property to satisfy a debt) to collect on that judgment all clothing in Carson's possession. Discuss Sikora's rights in the suit under these circumstances.

(b) On May 9, through no fault of Carson's, the store burns down, and all contents are a total loss. Between Carson and Sikora, who suffers the loss of the suit destroyed by the fire? Explain.

**21–3. Sale or Return.** Zeke, who sells lawn mowers, tells Stasio, a regular customer, about a special promotional campaign. On receipt of a $50 down payment, Zeke will sell Stasio a new Universal lawn mower for $200, even though it normally sells for $350. Zeke also says that if Stasio does not like the performance of the lawn mower, he can return it within thirty days, and Zeke will refund the $50 down payment. Stasio pays the $50 and takes the mower. On the tenth day, the lawn mower is stolen through no fault of Stasio's. Stasio calls Zeke and demands the return of his $50. Zeke claims that Stasio should suffer the risk of loss and that he still owes Zeke $150 for the rest of the purchase price. Discuss who is correct, Stasio or Zeke. **(See page 377.)**

## Business Case Problems

**21–4. Delivery without Movement of the Goods.** Aleris International, Inc., signed a contract to buy a John Deere loader from Holt Equipment Co. The agreement provided that "despite physical delivery of the equipment, title shall remain in the seller until" Aleris paid the full price. The next month, Aleris filed for bankruptcy. Holt filed a claim with the court to repossess the loader. Holt asserted that it was the owner. Who is entitled to the loader, and why? [*In re Aleris International, Ltd.*, __ Bankr. __ (D.Del. 2011)] **(See page 375.)**

**21–5. Goods Held by the Seller or Lessor.** Douglas Singletary bought a manufactured home from Andy's Mobile Home and Land Sales. The contract stated that the buyer accepted the home "as is where is." Singletary paid the full price, and his crew began to ready the home to relocate it to his property. The night before the home was to be moved, however, it was destroyed by fire. Who suffered the loss? Explain. [*Singletary, III v. P&A Investments, Inc.*, 712 S.E.2d 681 (N.C.App. 2011)] **(See page 375.)**

**21–6. BUSINESS CASE PROBLEM**
**WITH SAMPLE ANSWER: Passage of Title.**

 *Kenzie Godfrey, a college student majoring in physics, was a passenger in a taxi when it collided with a car driven by Dawn Altieri. Altieri had originally leased the car from G.E. Capital Auto Lease, Inc. By the time of the accident, she had bought it, but*

*she had not fully paid for it or completed the transfer-of-title paperwork. Godfrey suffered a brain injury and sought to recover damages from the owner of the car that Altieri was driving. Who had title to the car at the time of the accident? Explain.* [Godfrey v. G.E. Capital Auto Lease, Inc., 89 A.D.3d 471, 933 N.Y.S.2d 208 (1 Dept. 2011)] **(See page 369.)**

• **For a sample answer to Problem 21–6, go to Appendix F at the end of this text.**

**21–7. Risk of Loss.** Ethicon, Inc., a pharmaceutical company, entered into an agreement with UPS Supply Chain Solutions, Inc., to transport pharmaceuticals. Under a contract with UPS's subsidiary, Worldwide Dedicated Services, Inc., (WDS), the drivers were provided by International Management Services Co. (IMSCO). During the transport of a shipment from Ethicon's facility in Texas to buyers "F.O.B. Tennessee," one of the trucks collided with a concrete barrier near Little Rock, Arkansas, and caught fire, damaging the goods. Who was liable for the loss? Why? [*Royal & Sun Alliance Insurance, PLC v. International Management Services Co.*, 703 F.3d 604 (2d Cir. 2013)] **(See page 374.)**

**21–8. A QUESTION OF ETHICS: Void and Voidable Titles.**

 *Kenneth West agreed to sell his car, a 1975 Corvette, to a man representing himself as Robert Wilson. In exchange for a cashier's check, West signed over the Corvette's title to Wilson and gave*

*him the car. Ten days later, when West learned that the cashier's check was a forgery, he filed a stolen vehicle report with the police. The police could not immediately locate Wilson or the Corvette, however, and the case grew cold. Nearly two and a half years later, the police found the Corvette in the possession of Tammy Roberts, who also had the certificate of title. She said that she had bought the car from her brother, who had obtained it through an ad in a newspaper. West filed a suit in a Colorado state court against Roberts to reclaim the car. The court applied Colorado Revised Statutes Section 4-2-403 (Colorado's version of Section 2–403 of the Uniform Commercial Code) to determine the vehicle's rightful owner. [West v. Roberts, 143 P.3d 1037 (Colo. 2006)]* **(See page 371.)**

(a) Under UCC 2–403, what title, if any, to the Corvette did "Wilson" acquire? What was the status of Roberts's title, if any, assuming that she bought the car without knowledge of circumstances that would make a person of ordinary prudence inquire about the validity of the seller's title? In whose favor should the court rule? Explain.

(b) If the original owner of a vehicle relinquishes it due to fraud, should he or she be allowed to recover the vehicle from a good faith purchaser? If not, which party or parties might the original owner sue for recovery? What is the ethical principle underlying your answer to these questions? Discuss.

## Legal Reasoning Group Activity

**21–9. Shipment Contracts.** Professional Products, Inc. (PPI), bought three pallets of computer wafers from Omneon Video Graphics. (A computer wafer is a thin, round slice of silicon from which microchips are made.) Omneon agreed to ship the wafers to the City University of New York "FOB Omneon's dock." Shipment was arranged through Haas Industries, Inc. The "conditions of carriage" on the back of the bill of lading stated that Haas's liability for lost goods was limited to fifty cents per pound. When the shipment arrived, it included only two pallets. **(See page 370.)**

(a) The first group will determine who suffers the loss in this situation.

(b) The second group will discuss whether it is it fair for a carrier to limit its liability for lost goods.

# CHAPTER 22

# PERFORMANCE AND BREACH OF SALES AND LEASE CONTRACTS

The performance that is required of the parties under a sales or lease contract consists of the duties and obligations each party has under the terms of the contract. The basic obligation of the seller or lessor is to transfer and deliver the goods as stated in the contract, and the basic duty of the buyer or lessee is to accept and pay for the goods.

Keep in mind that "duties and obligations" under the terms of the contract include those specified by the agreement, by custom, and by the Uniform Commercial Code (UCC). Thus, parties to a sales or lease contract may be bound not only by terms they expressly agreed on, but also by terms implied by custom, such as a customary method of weighing or measuring particular goods.

Sometimes, circumstances make it difficult for a person to carry out the promised performance, leading to a breach of the contract. When a breach occurs, the aggrieved (wronged) party looks for remedies—which we examine in the second half of the chapter. Note that in contrast to the common law of contracts, remedies under the UCC are *cumulative* in nature—meaning that the aggrieved party is not limited to one exclusive remedy.

## SECTION 1
## PERFORMANCE OBLIGATIONS

As discussed in previous chapters, the obligations of good faith and commercial reasonableness underlie every sales and lease contract.

### The UCC's Good Faith Provision

The UCC's good faith provision, which can never be disclaimed, reads as follows: "Every contract or duty within this Act imposes an obligation of good faith in its performance or enforcement" [UCC 1–304]. *Good faith* means honesty in fact. For a merchant, it means honesty in fact and the observance of reasonable commercial standards of fair dealing in the trade [UCC 2–103(1)(b)]. In other words, merchants are held to a higher standard of performance or duty than are nonmerchants.

### Good Faith and
### Contract Performance

The principle of good faith applies to both parties and provides a framework for the entire agreement. If a sales contract leaves open some particulars of perfor-

mance, for instance, the parties must exercise good faith and commercial reasonableness when later specifying the details. The *Focus on Ethics* feature at the end of this unit explores the ethical implications of the UCC's good faith standard.

In performing a sales or lease contract, the basic obligation of the seller or lessor is to *transfer and deliver conforming goods*. The basic obligation of the buyer or lessee is to *accept and pay for conforming goods* in accordance with the contract [UCC 2–301, 2A–516(1)]. Overall performance of a sales or lease contract is controlled by the agreement between the parties. When the contract is unclear and disputes arise, the courts look to the UCC and impose standards of good faith and commercial reasonableness.

## SECTION 2
## OBLIGATIONS OF
## THE SELLER OR LESSOR

As stated, the basic duty of the seller or lessor is to deliver the goods called for under the contract to the buyer or lessee.

## Tender of Delivery

Goods that conform to the contract description in every way are called **conforming goods.** To fulfill the contract, the seller or lessor must either deliver or tender delivery of conforming goods to the buyer or lessee. **Tender of delivery** occurs when the seller or lessor makes conforming goods available and gives the buyer or lessee whatever notification is reasonably necessary to enable the buyer or lessee to take delivery [UCC 2–503(1), 2A–508(1)].

Tender must occur at a *reasonable hour* and in a *reasonable manner.* For example, a seller cannot call the buyer at 2:00 A.M. and say, "The goods are ready. I'll give you twenty minutes to get them." Unless the parties have agreed otherwise, the goods must be tendered for delivery at a reasonable hour and kept available for a reasonable time to enable the buyer to take possession [UCC 2–503(1)(a)].

Normally, all goods called for by a contract must be tendered in a single delivery—unless the parties have agreed on delivery in several lots or *installments* (to be discussed shortly) [UCC 2–307, 2–612, 2A–510]. ▶ **Example 22.1** An order for 1,000 Under Armour men's shirts cannot be delivered two shirts at a time. If, however, the parties agree that the shirts will be delivered in four orders of 250 each as they are produced (for summer, fall, winter, and spring inventory), then tender of delivery may occur in this manner. ◀

## Place of Delivery

The buyer and seller (or lessor and lessee) may agree that the goods will be delivered to a particular destination where the buyer or lessee will take possession. If the contract does not indicate where the goods will be delivered, then the place for delivery will be one of the following:

1. The *seller's place of business.*
2. The *seller's residence,* if the seller has no business location [UCC 2–308(a)].
3. The *location of the goods,* if both parties know at the time of contracting that the goods are located somewhere other than the seller's business [UCC 2–308(b)].

▶ **Example 22.2** Li Wan and Boyd both live in San Francisco. In San Francisco, Li Wan contracts to sell Boyd five used trucks, which both parties know are located in a Chicago warehouse. If nothing more is specified in the contract, the place of delivery for the trucks is Chicago. Li Wan may tender delivery by giving Boyd either a negotiable or a nonnegotiable document of title. Alternatively, Li Wan may obtain the bailee's (warehouser's) acknowledgment that Boyd is entitled to possession.[1] ◀

## Delivery via Carrier

In many instances, it is clear from the surrounding circumstances or delivery terms in the contract (such as F.O.B. or F.A.S. terms; see Exhibit 21–2 on page 375) that the parties intended the goods to be moved by a carrier. In carrier contracts, the seller fulfills the obligation to deliver the goods through either a shipment contract or a destination contract.

**SHIPMENT CONTRACTS** Recall from Chapter 21 that a *shipment contract* requires or authorizes the seller to ship goods by a carrier, rather than to deliver them at a particular destination [UCC 2–319, 2–509(1)(a)]. Under a shipment contract, unless otherwise agreed, the seller must do the following:

1. Place the goods into the hands of the carrier.
2. Make a contract for their transportation that is reasonable according to the nature of the goods and their value. (For example, certain types of goods need refrigeration in transit.)
3. Obtain and promptly deliver or tender to the buyer any documents necessary to enable the buyer to obtain possession of the goods from the carrier.
4. Promptly notify the buyer that shipment has been made [UCC 2–504].

If the seller does not make a reasonable contract for transportation or notify the buyer of the shipment, the buyer can reject the goods, but only if a *material loss* or a *significant delay* results. ▶ **Example 22.3** Zigi's Organic Fruits sells strawberries to Lozier under a shipment contract. If Zigi's does not arrange for refrigerated transportation and the berries spoil during transport, a material loss will likely result because Lozier will be unable to sell them. ◀ (Of course, the parties are free to make agreements that alter the UCC's rules and allow the buyer to reject goods for other reasons.)

**DESTINATION CONTRACTS** In a *destination contract,* the seller agrees to deliver conforming goods to the

---

1. Unless the buyer objects, the seller may also tender delivery by instructing the bailee in a writing (record) to release the goods to the buyer without the bailee's acknowledgment of the buyer's rights [UCC 2–503(4)]. Risk of loss, however, does not pass until the buyer has had a reasonable amount of time in which to present the document or the instructions. See Chapter 21.

buyer at a particular destination. The goods must be tendered at a reasonable hour and held at the buyer's disposal for a reasonable length of time. The seller must also give the buyer appropriate notice and any necessary documents to enable the buyer to obtain delivery from the carrier [UCC 2–503].

## The Perfect Tender Rule

As previously noted, the seller or lessor has an obligation to ship or tender *conforming goods,* which the buyer or lessee is then obligated to accept and pay for according to the terms of the contract [UCC 2–507].

Under the common law, the seller was obligated to deliver goods that conformed with the terms of the contract in every detail. This is called the **perfect tender rule.**

The UCC preserves the perfect tender doctrine. It states that if goods or tender of delivery fails *in any respect* to conform to the contract, the buyer or lessee may accept the goods, reject the entire shipment, or accept part and reject part [UCC 2–601, 2A–509].

The corollary to this rule is that if the goods conform in every respect, the buyer or lessee does not have a right to reject the goods, as the following case illustrates.

---

## CASE 22.1

### Wilson Sporting Goods Co. v. U.S. Golf and Tennis Centers, Inc.
Court of Appeals of Tennessee, 2012 WL 601804 (2012).

**BACKGROUND AND FACTS** U.S. Golf & Tennis Centers, Inc., operates two retail sporting goods stores that specialize in golf and tennis equipment. U.S. Golf agreed to buy 96,000 golf balls from Wilson Sporting Goods Company for a total price of $20,000. The parties negotiated the agreement via fax, and Wilson represented that U.S. Golf was receiving the lowest price ($5 per two-dozen unit) "that Wilson offered to any one in the market."

Wilson shipped golf balls to U.S. Golf that conformed to the contract in quantity and quality, but it did not receive payment. U.S. Golf claimed that it had learned that Wilson had sold the product for $2 a unit to another buyer and asked Wilson to reduce the contract price of the balls to $4 per unit (for a total of $16,000). Wilson refused and filed a suit to collect the $20,000. The trial court entered a judgment in favor of Wilson for $33,099.28, which included the contract price, interest, attorneys' fees, and certain allowable expenses. U.S. Golf appealed.

**DECISION AND RATIONALE** A state appellate court affirmed the lower court's judgment in favor of Wilson. When a seller tenders conforming goods, the buyer is obligated to accept and pay for the goods. Because it was undisputed that the shipment of golf balls conformed in quantity and quality to the contract specifications, U.S. Golf was obligated to accept the goods and pay the agreed-on price. U.S. Golf argued that Wilson had breached the contract by misrepresenting the price of the golf balls as its lowest price, but the court was not convinced. Evidence showed that the parties had agreed on a price of $20,000. U.S. Golf did not present any evidence to contradict the price term in the parties' agreement or to establish that Wilson had engaged in misrepresentation. Therefore, the perfect tender rule applied, and U.S. Golf was not entitled to reject the goods or cancel the contract.

**WHAT IF THE FACTS WERE DIFFERENT?** *Suppose that U.S. Golf had presented as evidence a contract between Wilson and another buyer a month after this shipment was delivered to U.S. Golf. In that contract, Wilson agreed to sell the same golf balls for $4 per unit to a different buyer. Would the court have ruled differently in this dispute? Why or why not?*

**THE LEGAL ENVIRONMENT DIMENSION** *According to the UCC, what are a buyer's options if the goods do not conform to the contract? Does a buyer have those same options if the goods conform in every respect? Explain.*

# Exceptions to the Perfect Tender Rule

Because of the rigidity of the perfect tender rule, several exceptions to the rule have been created, some of which we discuss here.

**AGREEMENT OF THE PARTIES** Exceptions to the perfect tender rule may be established by agreement. If the parties have agreed, for instance, that defective goods or parts will not be rejected if the seller or lessor is able to repair or replace them within a reasonable period of time, the perfect tender rule does not apply.

**CURE** The UCC does not specifically define the term **cure,** but it refers to the right of the seller or lessor to repair, adjust, or replace defective or nonconforming goods [UCC 2–508, 2A–513].

The seller or lessor has a right to attempt to "cure" a defect when the following are true:

1. A delivery is rejected because the goods were nonconforming.
2. The time for performance has not yet expired.
3. The seller or lessor provides timely notice to the buyer or lessee of the intention to cure.
4. The cure can be made *within the contract time for performance.*

*Reasonable Grounds.* Once the time for performance under the contract has expired, the seller or lessor no longer has a right to cure. Nevertheless, the seller or lessor can still cure if he or she has *reasonable grounds to believe that the nonconforming tender will be acceptable to the buyer or lessee* [UCC 2–508(2), 2A–513(2)].

▶ **Example 22.4** In the past, EZ Office Supply has frequently accepted blue pens when the seller, Baxter's Wholesale, did not have black pens in stock. In this context, Baxter's has reasonable grounds to believe that EZ will again accept such a substitute. Even if EZ rejected the substituted goods on one particular occasion, Baxter's has reasonable grounds to believe that blue pens will be acceptable. Therefore, if EZ indicates that it will not accept blue pens, Baxter's normally will have a reasonable time to obtain and tender black pens. ◀

A seller or lessor will sometimes tender nonconforming goods with some type of price allowance (discount). A discounted price can serve as the "reasonable grounds" to believe that the buyer or lessee will accept the nonconforming tender.

*Limits Right to Reject Goods.* The right to cure substantially restricts the right of the buyer or lessee to reject goods. To reject, the buyer or lessee must inform the seller or lessor of the particular defect. If the defect is not disclosed, the buyer or lessee cannot later assert the defect as a defense if the defect is one that the seller or lessor could have cured. Generally, buyers and lessees must act in good faith and state specific reasons for refusing to accept goods [UCC 2–605, 2A–514].

**SUBSTITUTION OF CARRIERS** Sometimes, an agreed-on manner of delivery (such as the use of a particular carrier to transport the goods) becomes impracticable or unavailable through no fault of either party. In that situation, if a commercially reasonable substitute is available, this substitute performance is sufficient tender to the buyer and must be used [UCC 2–614(1)]. The seller or lessor is required to arrange for a substitute carrier and normally is responsible for any additional shipping costs (unless the contract states otherwise).

▶ **Example 22.5** A sales contract calls for a large generator to be shipped by Mac's Trucking on or before June 1. The contract terms clearly state the importance of the delivery date. The employees of Mac's go on strike. The seller must make a reasonable substitute tender, by another trucking company or perhaps by rail, if it is available. ◀

**INSTALLMENT CONTRACTS** An **installment contract** is a single contract that requires or authorizes delivery in two or more separate lots to be accepted and paid for separately. With an installment contract, a buyer or lessee can reject an installment *only if the nonconformity substantially impairs the value* of the installment and cannot be cured [UCC 2–307, 2–612(2), 2A–510(1)]. If the buyer or lessee fails to notify the seller or lessor of the rejection, however, and subsequently accepts a nonconforming installment, the contract is reinstated [UCC 2–612(3), 2A–510(2)].

Unless the contract provides otherwise, the entire installment contract is breached only when one or more nonconforming installments *substantially* impair the value of the *whole contract.* ▶ **Example 22.6** A contract calls for the parts of a machine to be delivered in installments. The first part is necessary for the operation of the machine, but when it is delivered, it is irreparably defective. The failure of this first installment will be a breach of the whole contract because the machine will not operate without the first part.

Suppose that, instead, the contract had called for twenty carloads of plywood and only 6 percent of one carload had deviated from the thickness specifications in the contract. It is unlikely that a court would find that a defect in 6 percent of one installment substantially impaired the value of the whole contract. ◄

The point to remember is that the UCC significantly alters the right of the buyer or lessee to reject the entire contract if the contract requires delivery to be made in several installments. The UCC strictly limits rejection to instances of *substantial* nonconformity.

**COMMERCIAL IMPRACTICABILITY** As discussed in Chapter 18, occurrences unforeseen by either party when a contract was made may make performance commercially impracticable. When this occurs, the perfect tender rule no longer applies. The seller or lessor must, however, notify the buyer or lessee as soon as practicable that there will be a delay or nondelivery.

▶ **Example 22.7** Houston Oil Company, which receives its oil from the Middle East, has a contract to supply Northwest Fuels with one hundred thousand barrels of oil. Because of an oil embargo by the Organization of Petroleum Exporting Countries, Houston is unable to secure oil from the Middle East or any other source to meet the terms of the contract. This situation comes fully under the commercial impracticability exception to the perfect tender doctrine. ◄

***An Unforeseeable Contingency.*** The doctrine of commercial impracticability does not extend to problems that could have been foreseen—such as an increase in cost resulting from inflation. The nonoccurrence of the contingency must have been a basic assumption on which the contract was made [UCC 2–615, 2A–405].

Can unanticipated increases in a seller's costs that make performance "impracticable" constitute a valid defense to performance on the basis of commercial impracticability? The court dealt with this question in the following classic case.

---

## CLASSIC CASE 22.2

### Maple Farms, Inc. v. City School District of Elmira
Supreme Court of New York, 76 Misc.2d 1080, 352 N.Y.S.2d 784 (1974).

**BACKGROUND AND FACTS** On June 15, 1973, Maple Farms, Inc., formed an agreement with the city school district of Elmira, New York, to supply the school district with milk for the 1973–1974 school year. The agreement was in the form of a requirements contract, under which Maple Farms would sell to the school district all the milk the district required at a fixed price. The specified price was the June market price of milk. By December 1973, the price of raw milk had increased by 23 percent over the price specified in the contract.

This meant that if the terms of the contract were fulfilled, Maple Farms would lose $7,350. Because it had similar contracts with other school districts, Maple Farms stood to lose a great deal if it was held to the price stated in the contracts. The school district refused to release Maple Farms from its contract. Therefore, Maple Farms brought an action in a New York state court for a declaratory judgment (a determination of the parties' rights under a contract). Maple Farms contended that when the parties formed their contract, they had not contemplated such a substantial increase in the price of raw milk. Given the increased price, performance of the contract was commercially impracticable.

**DECISION AND RATIONALE** The state trial court ruled that inflation and fluctuating prices did not render performance in this case impracticable and granted summary judgment in favor of the school district. Commercial impracticability arises when an event occurs that is totally unexpected and unforeseeable by the parties. An increase in the price of milk was not unexpected because the previous year, the price had risen 10 percent and the price of milk had traditionally varied. Also, general inflation should have been anticipated. Maple Farms had reason to know these facts and could have provided "in the contract an exculpatory clause to excuse it from performance in the event of a substantial rise in the price of raw milk." The court also noted that the school district's primary purpose in forming the contract was to protect itself (for budgeting reasons) against price fluctuations.

**IMPACT OF THIS CASE ON TODAY'S LAW** *This classic case illustrates the UCC's commercial impracticability doctrine as courts still apply it today. Under this doctrine, increased cost alone does not*

CASE 22.2 CONTINUED          *excuse performance unless the rise in cost is due to some unforeseen contingency that alters the essential nature of the performance.*

**WHAT IF THE FACTS WERE DIFFERENT?** *Suppose that the court had ruled in the plaintiff's favor. How might that ruling have affected the plaintiff's contracts with other parties?*

---

*Partial Performance.* Sometimes, the unforeseen event only *partially* affects the capacity of the seller or lessor to perform. Therefore, the seller or lessor can *partially* fulfill the contract but cannot tender total performance. In this event, the seller or lessor is required to distribute any remaining goods or deliveries fairly and reasonably among the parties to whom it is contractually obligated to deliver the goods [UCC 2–615(b), 2A–405(b)]. The buyer or lessee must receive notice of the allocation and has the right to accept or reject it [UCC 2–615(c), 2A–405(c)].

▶ **Example 22.8** A Florida orange grower, Best Citrus, Inc., contracts to sell this season's crop to a number of customers, including Martin's grocery chain. Martin's contracts to purchase two thousand crates of oranges. Best Citrus has sprayed *some* of its orange groves with a chemical called Karmoxin. The U.S. Department of Agriculture discovers that persons who eat products sprayed with Karmoxin may develop cancer and issues an order prohibiting the sale of these products.

Best Citrus picks all the oranges not sprayed with Karmoxin, but the quantity is insufficient to meet all the contracted-for deliveries. In this situation, Best Citrus is required to allocate its production. It notifies Martin's that it cannot deliver the full quantity specified in the contract and indicates the amount it will be able to deliver. Martin's can either accept or reject the allocation, but Best Citrus has no further contractual liability. ◀

**DESTRUCTION OF IDENTIFIED GOODS** Sometimes, an unexpected event, such as a fire, totally destroys goods through no fault of either party before risk passes to the buyer or lessee. In such a situation, *if the goods were identified at the time the contract was formed,* the parties are excused from performance [UCC 2–613, 2A–221]. If the goods are only partially destroyed, however, the buyer or lessee can inspect them and either treat the contract as void or accept the damaged goods with a reduction in the contract price.

▶ **Example 22.9** Atlas Sporting Equipment agrees to lease to River Bicycles sixty bicycles of a particular model that has been discontinued. No other bicy-cles of that model are available. River specifies that it needs the bicycles to rent to tourists. Before Atlas can deliver the bicycles, they are destroyed by a fire. In this situation, Atlas is not liable to River for failing to deliver the bicycles. Through no fault of either party, the goods were destroyed before the risk of loss passed to the lessee. The loss was total, so the contract is avoided. Clearly, Atlas has no obligation to tender the bicycles, and River has no obligation to make the lease payments for them. ◀

**ASSURANCE AND COOPERATION** Two other exceptions to the perfect tender doctrine apply equally to both parties to sales and lease contracts: the right of assurance and the duty of cooperation.

*The Right of Assurance.* The UCC provides that if one party has "reasonable grounds" to believe that the other party will not perform, the first party may *in writing* "demand adequate assurance of due performance" from the other party. Until such assurance is received, the first party may "suspend" further performance without liability. What constitutes "reasonable grounds" is determined by commercial standards. If such assurances are not forthcoming within a reasonable time (not to exceed thirty days), the failure to respond may be treated as a repudiation of the contract [UCC 2–609, 2A–401].

▶ **Case in Point 22.10** Two companies that made road-surfacing materials, Koch Materials and Shore Slurry Seal, Inc., entered into a contract. Koch obtained a license to use Novachip, a special material made by Shore, and Shore agreed to buy all of its asphalt from Koch for the next seven years. A few years into the contract term, Shore notified Koch that it planned to sell its assets to Asphalt Paving Systems, Inc. Koch demanded assurances that Asphalt Paving would continue the deal, but Shore refused to provide assurances. The court held that Koch could treat Shore's failure to give assurances as a repudiation and sue Shore for breach of contract.[2] ◀

---

2. *Koch Materials Co. v. Shore Slurry Seal, Inc.,* 205 F.Supp.2d 324 (D.N.J. 2002).

***The Duty of Cooperation.*** Sometimes, the performance of one party depends on the cooperation of the other. The UCC provides that when cooperation is not forthcoming, the other party can suspend performance without liability and hold the uncooperative party in breach or proceed to perform the contract in any reasonable manner [UCC 2–311(3)].

▶ **Example 22.11** Aman is required by contract to deliver 1,200 LG washing machines to various locations in California on or before October 1. Frieda, the buyer, is to specify the locations for delivery. Aman repeatedly requests the delivery locations, but Frieda does not respond. The washing machines are ready for shipment on October 1, but Frieda still refuses to give Aman the delivery locations. If Aman does not ship on October 1, he cannot be held liable. Aman is excused for any resulting delay of performance because of Frieda's failure to cooperate. ◀

## SECTION 3
# OBLIGATIONS OF THE BUYER OR LESSEE

The main obligation of the buyer or lessee under a sales or lease contract is to pay for the goods tendered in accordance with the contract. Once the seller or lessor has adequately tendered delivery, the buyer or lessee is obligated to accept the goods and pay for them according to the terms of the contract.

## Payment

In the absence of any specific agreements, the buyer or lessee must make payment at the time and place the goods are *received* [UCC 2–310(a), 2A–516(1)]. When a sale is made on credit, the buyer is obligated to pay according to the specified credit terms (for example, 60, 90, or 120 days), not when the goods are received. The credit period usually begins on the *date of shipment* [UCC 2–310(d)]. Under a lease contract, a lessee must make the lease payment that was specified in the contract [UCC 2A–516(1)].

Payment can be made by any means agreed on between the parties—cash or any other method generally acceptable in the commercial world. If the seller demands cash, the seller must permit the buyer reasonable time to obtain it [UCC 2–511].

## Right of Inspection

Unless the parties otherwise agree, or for C.O.D. (collect on delivery) transactions, the buyer or lessee has an absolute right to inspect the goods before making payment. This right allows the buyer or lessee to verify that the goods tendered or delivered conform to the contract. If the goods are not as ordered, the buyer or lessee has no duty to pay. *An opportunity for inspection is therefore a condition precedent to the right of the seller or lessor to enforce payment* [UCC 2–513(1), 2A–515(1)].

Inspection can take place at any reasonable place and time and in any reasonable manner. Generally, what is reasonable is determined by custom of the trade, past practices of the parties, and the like. The buyer bears the costs of inspecting the goods but can recover the costs from the seller if the goods do not conform and are rejected [UCC 2–513(2)].

## Acceptance

After having had a reasonable opportunity to inspect the goods, the buyer or lessee can demonstrate acceptance in any of the following ways:

1. The buyer or lessee indicates (by words or conduct) to the seller or lessor that the goods are conforming or that he or she will retain them in spite of their nonconformity [UCC 2–606(1)(a), 2A–515(1)(a)].
2. The buyer or lessee *fails to reject* the goods within a reasonable period of time [UCC 2–602(1), 2–606(1)(b), 2A–515(1)(b)].
3. In sales contracts, the buyer will be deemed to have accepted the goods if he or she *performs any act inconsistent with the seller's ownership*. For instance, any use or resale of the goods—except for the limited purpose of testing or inspecting the goods—generally constitutes an acceptance [UCC 2–606(1)(c)].

## Partial Acceptance

If some of the goods delivered do not conform to the contract and the seller or lessor has failed to cure, the buyer or lessee can make a *partial* acceptance [UCC 2–601(c), 2A–509(1)]. The same is true if the nonconformity was not reasonably discoverable before acceptance. (In the latter situation, the buyer or lessee may be able to revoke the acceptance, as will be discussed later in this chapter.)

A buyer or lessee cannot accept less than a single commercial unit, however. The UCC defines a *commercial unit* as a unit of goods that, by commercial usage, is viewed as a "single whole" for purposes of sale and that cannot be divided without materially impairing the character of the unit, its market value, or its use [UCC 2–105(6), 2A–103(1)(c)]. A commercial unit can be a single article (such as a machine), a set of articles (such as a suite of furniture), a quantity (such as a bale, a gross, or a carload), or any other unit treated in the trade as a single whole.

See *Concept Summary 22.1* below for a review of the obligations of both parties to a sales or lease contract.

## SECTION 4
# ANTICIPATORY REPUDIATION

What if, before the time for contract performance, one party clearly communicates to the other the intention *not* to perform? As discussed in Chapter 18, such an action is a breach of the contract by *anticipatory repudiation.*

## Suspension of Performance Obligations

When anticipatory repudiation occurs, the non-breaching party has a choice of two responses:

1. Treat the repudiation as a final breach by pursuing a remedy.
2. Wait to see if the repudiating party will decide to honor the contract despite the avowed intention to renege [UCC 2–610, 2A–402].

In either situation, the nonbreaching party may suspend performance.

---

## CONCEPT SUMMARY 22.1
### Performance of Sales and Lease Contracts

| CONCEPT | DESCRIPTION |
|---|---|
| **Obligations of the Seller or Lessor** | 1. The seller or lessor must tender *conforming* goods to the buyer or lessee at a *reasonable hour* and in a *reasonable manner*. Under the perfect tender doctrine, the seller or lessor must tender goods that conform exactly to the terms of the contract [UCC 2–503(1), 2A–508(1)].<br>2. If the seller or lessor tenders nonconforming goods and the buyer or lessee rejects them, the seller or lessor may *cure* (repair or replace the goods) within the contract time for performance [UCC 2–508(1), 2A–513(1)]. Even if the time for performance under the contract has expired, the seller or lessor has a reasonable time to substitute conforming goods without liability if the seller or lessor has reasonable grounds to believe the nonconforming tender will be acceptable to the buyer or lessee [UCC 2–508(2), 2A–513(2)].<br>3. If the agreed-on means of delivery becomes impracticable or unavailable, the seller must substitute an alternative means (such as a different carrier) if a reasonable one is available [UCC 2–614(1)].<br>4. If a seller or lessor tenders nonconforming goods in any one installment under an installment contract, the buyer or lessee may reject the installment only if the nonconformity substantially impairs its value and cannot be cured. The entire installment contract is breached only when one or more installments *substantially* impair the value of the *whole* contract [UCC 2–612, 2A–510].<br>5. When performance becomes commercially impracticable owing to circumstances unforeseen when the contract was formed, the perfect tender rule no longer applies [UCC 2–615, 2A–405]. |
| **Obligations of the Buyer or Lessee** | 1. On tender of delivery by the seller or lessor, the buyer or lessee must pay for the goods at the time and place the goods are *received,* unless the sale is made on credit. Payment can be made by any method generally acceptable in the commercial world, but the seller can demand cash [UCC 2–310, 2–511].<br>2. Unless otherwise agreed or in C.O.D. shipments, the buyer or lessee has an absolute right to inspect the goods before acceptance [UCC 2–513(1), 2A–515(1)].<br>3. The buyer or lessee can manifest acceptance of delivered goods in words or by conduct, such as by failing to reject the goods after having had a reasonable opportunity to inspect them. A buyer will be deemed to have accepted goods if he or she performs any act inconsistent with the seller's ownership [UCC 2–606(1), 2A–515(1)]. |

## A Repudiation May Be Retracted

The UCC permits the breaching party to "retract" his or her repudiation (subject to some limitations). This can be done by any method that clearly indicates the party's intent to perform. Once retraction is made, the rights of the repudiating party under the contract are reinstated. There can be no retraction, however, if since the time of the repudiation the other party has canceled or materially changed position or otherwise indicated that the repudiation is final [UCC 2–611, 2A–403].

▶ **Example 22.12** On April 1, Cora Lyn, who owns a small inn, purchases a suite of furniture from Tom Horton, proprietor of Horton's Furniture Warehouse. The contract states that "delivery must be made on or before May 1." On April 10, Horton informs Lyn that he cannot make delivery until May 10 and asks her to consent to the modified delivery date.

In this situation, Lyn has two options. She can either treat Horton's notice of late delivery as a final breach of contract and pursue a remedy or agree to the later delivery date. Suppose that Lyn does neither for two weeks. On April 24, Horton informs Lyn that he will be able to deliver the furniture by May 1 after all. In effect, Horton has retracted his repudiation, reinstating the rights and obligations of the parties under the original contract. Note that if Lyn had told Horton that she was canceling the contract after he repudiated, he would not have been able to retract his repudiation. ◀

## SECTION 5
# REMEDIES OF THE SELLER OR LESSOR

When the buyer or lessee is in breach, the seller or lessor has numerous remedies under the UCC. Generally, the remedies available to the seller or lessor depend on the circumstances existing at the time of the breach. The most pertinent considerations are which party has possession of the goods, whether the goods are in transit, and whether the buyer or lessee has rejected or accepted the goods.

## When the Goods Are in the Possession of the Seller or Lessor

Under the UCC, if the buyer or lessee breaches the contract before the goods have been delivered, the seller or lessor has the right to pursue the following remedies:

1. Cancel (rescind) the contract.
2. Resell the goods and sue to recover damages.
3. Sue to recover the purchase price or lease payments due.
4. Sue to recover damages for the buyer's nonacceptance of goods.

**THE RIGHT TO CANCEL THE CONTRACT** If the buyer or lessee breaches the contract, the seller or lessor can choose to simply cancel the contract [UCC 2–703(f), 2A–523(1)(a)]. The seller or lessor must notify the buyer or lessee of the cancellation, and at that point all remaining obligations of the seller or lessor are discharged. The buyer or lessee is not discharged from all remaining obligations, however. She or he is in breach, and the seller or lessor can pursue remedies available under the UCC for breach.

**THE RIGHT TO WITHHOLD DELIVERY** In general, sellers and lessors can withhold delivery or discontinue performance of their obligations under sales or lease contracts when the buyers or lessees are in breach. This is true whether a buyer or lessee has wrongfully rejected or revoked acceptance of contract goods (discussed later in this chapter), failed to make a payment, or repudiated the contract [UCC 2–703(a), 2A–523(1)(c)]. The seller or lessor can also refuse to deliver the goods to a buyer or lessee who is insolvent (unable to pay debts as they become due) unless the buyer or lessee pays in cash [UCC 2–702(1), 2A–525(1)].

**THE RIGHT TO RESELL OR DISPOSE OF THE GOODS** When a buyer or lessee breaches or repudiates the contract while the seller or lessor is in possession of the goods, the seller or lessor can resell or dispose of the goods. The seller can retain any profits made as a result of the sale and can hold the buyer or lessee liable for any loss [UCC 2–703(d), 2–706(1), 2A–523(1)(e), 2A–527(1)].

The seller must give the original buyer reasonable notice of the resale, unless the goods are perishable or will rapidly decline in value [UCC 2–706(2), (3)]. The resale can be private or public, and the goods can be sold as a unit or in parcels. A good faith purchaser at the resale takes the goods free of any of the rights of the original buyer [UCC 2–706(5)].

*When the Goods Are Unfinished.* When the goods contracted for are unfinished at the time of the breach, the seller or lessor can do either of the following:

1. Cease manufacturing the goods and resell them for scrap or salvage value.
2. Complete the manufacture and resell or dispose of the goods, and hold the buyer or lessee liable for any deficiency.

In choosing between these two alternatives, the seller or lessor must exercise reasonable commercial judgment in order to mitigate the loss and obtain maximum value from the unfinished goods [UCC 2–704(2), 2A–524(2)]. Any resale of the goods must be made in good faith and in a commercially reasonable manner.

***When the Resale Price Is Insufficient.*** In sales transactions, the seller can recover any deficiency between the resale price and the contract price. The seller can also recover *incidental damages* (see Chapter 19), defined as the costs to the seller resulting from the breach [UCC 2–706(1), 2–710].

In lease transactions, the lessor may lease the goods to another party and recover damages from the original lessee. Damages include any unpaid lease payments up to the beginning date of the lease term under the new lease. The lessor can also recover any deficiency between the lease payments due under the original lease contract and those under the new lease contract, along with incidental damages [UCC 2A–527(2)].

**THE RIGHT TO RECOVER THE PURCHASE PRICE OR LEASE PAYMENTS DUE** Under the UCC, an unpaid seller or lessor can bring an action to recover the purchase price or the payments due under the lease contract, plus incidental damages [UCC 2–709(1), 2A–529(1)]. If a seller or lessor is unable to resell or dispose of the goods and sues for the contract price or lease payments due, the goods must be held for the buyer or lessee. The seller or lessor can resell the goods at any time before collecting the judgment from the buyer or lessee. If the goods are resold, the net proceeds from the sale must be credited to the buyer or lessee because of the duty to mitigate damages.

▶ **Example 22.13** Southern Realty contracts with Gem Point, Inc., to purchase one thousand pens with Southern Realty's name inscribed on them. Gem Point tenders delivery of the pens, but Southern Realty wrongfully refuses to accept them. In this situation, Gem Point can bring an action for the purchase price because it delivered conforming goods, and Southern Realty refused to accept or pay for the goods.

Gem Point obviously cannot resell the pens inscribed with the buyer's business name, so this situation falls under UCC 2–709. Gem Point is required to make the pens available for Southern Realty, but can resell them (in the event that it can find a buyer) at any time prior to collecting the judgment from Southern Realty. ◀

**THE RIGHT TO RECOVER DAMAGES FOR THE BUYER'S NONACCEPTANCE** If a buyer or lessee repudiates a contract or wrongfully refuses to accept the goods, a seller or lessor can bring an action to recover the damages sustained. Ordinarily, the amount of damages equals the difference between the contract price or lease payments and the market price or lease payments at the time and place of tender of the goods, plus incidental damages [UCC 2–708(1), 2A–528(1)].

When the ordinary measure of damages is inadequate to put the seller or lessor in as good a position as the buyer's or lessee's performance would have, the UCC provides an alternative. In that situation, the proper measure of damages is the lost profits of the seller or lessor, including a reasonable allowance for overhead and other expenses [UCC 2–708(2), 2A–528(2)].

## When the Goods Are in Transit

When the seller or lessor has delivered the goods to a carrier or a bailee but the buyer or lessee has not yet received them, the goods are said to be *in transit*.

**EFFECT OF INSOLVENCY AND BREACH** If the seller or lessor learns that the buyer or lessee is insolvent, the seller or lessor can stop the delivery of the goods still in transit, regardless of the quantity of goods shipped. A different rule applies if the buyer or lessee is in breach but is not insolvent. In this situation, the seller or lessor can stop the goods in transit only if the quantity shipped is at least a carload, a truckload, a planeload, or a larger shipment [UCC 2–705(1), 2A–526(1)].

▶ **Example 22.14** Arturo Ortega orders a truckload of lumber from Timber Products, Inc., to be shipped to Ortega six weeks later. Ortega, who has not paid Timber Products for a past shipment, promises to pay the debt immediately and to pay for the current shipment as soon as it is received. After the lumber has been shipped, a bankruptcy court judge notifies Timber Products that Ortega has filed a petition in bankruptcy and listed Timber Products as one of his creditors. If the goods are still in transit, Timber Products can stop the carrier from delivering the lumber to Ortega. ◀

**REQUIREMENTS FOR STOPPING DELIVERY** To stop delivery, the seller or lessor must *timely notify* the carrier or other bailee that the goods are to be returned or held for the seller or lessor. If the carrier has sufficient time to stop delivery, the goods must be held and delivered according to the instructions of the seller or lessor. The seller or lessor is liable to the carrier for any additional costs incurred [UCC 2–705(3), 2A–526(3)].

The seller or lessor has the right to stop delivery of the goods under UCC 2–705(2) and 2A–526(2) until the time when:

1. The buyer or lessee receives the goods.
2. The carrier or the bailee acknowledges the rights of the buyer or lessee in the goods (by reshipping or holding the goods for the buyer or lessee, for example).
3. A negotiable document of title covering the goods has been properly transferred to the buyer in a sales transaction, giving the buyer ownership rights in the goods [UCC 2–705(2)].

Once the seller or lessor reclaims the goods in transit, she or he can pursue the remedies allowed to sellers and lessors when the goods are in their possession.

## When the Goods Are in the Possession of the Buyer or Lessee

When the buyer or lessee breaches the contract while the goods are in his or her possession, the seller or lessor can sue. The seller or lessor can recover the purchase price of the goods or the lease payments due, plus incidental damages [UCC 2–709(1), 2A–529(1)].

In some situations, a seller may also have a right to reclaim the goods from the buyer. For instance, in a sales contract, if the buyer has received the goods on credit and the seller discovers that the buyer is insolvent, the seller can demand the return of the goods [UCC 2–702(2)]. Ordinarily, the demand must be made within ten days of the buyer's receipt of the goods.[3] The seller's right to reclaim the goods is subject to the rights of a good faith purchaser or other subsequent buyer in the ordinary course of business who purchases the goods from the buyer before the seller reclaims them.

In regard to lease contracts, if the lessee is in default (fails to make payments that are due, for instance),

the lessor may reclaim the leased goods that are in the lessee's possession [UCC 2A–525(2)].

---

### SECTION 6
# REMEDIES OF THE BUYER OR LESSEE

When the seller or lessor breaches the contract, the buyer or lessee has numerous remedies available under the UCC. Like the remedies available to sellers and lessors, the remedies available to buyers and lessees depend on the circumstances existing at the time of the breach. Relevant factors include whether the seller has refused to deliver conforming goods or delivered nonconforming goods.

## When the Seller or Lessor Refuses to Deliver the Goods

If the seller or lessor refuses to deliver the goods to the buyer or lessee, the basic remedies available to the buyer or lessee include the right to:

1. Cancel (rescind) the contract.
2. Obtain goods that have been paid for if the seller or lessor is insolvent.
3. Sue to obtain specific performance if the goods are unique or if damages are an inadequate remedy.
4. Buy other goods (obtain *cover*—defined on page 393) and recover damages from the seller.
5. Sue to obtain identified goods held by a third party (*replevy* goods—defined on page 393).
6. Sue to obtain damages.

**THE RIGHT TO CANCEL THE CONTRACT** When a seller or lessor fails to make proper delivery or repudiates the contract, the buyer or lessee can cancel, or rescind, the contract. The buyer or lessee is relieved of any further obligations under the contract but retains all rights to other remedies against the seller or lessor [UCC 2–711(1), 2A–508(1)(a)]. (The right to cancel the contract is also available to a buyer or lessee who has rightfully rejected goods or revoked acceptance, as will be discussed shortly.)

**THE RIGHT TO OBTAIN THE GOODS UPON INSOLVENCY** If a buyer or lessee has partially or fully paid for goods that are in the possession of a seller or lessor who becomes insolvent, the buyer or lessee can obtain the goods. The seller or lessor must have become insol-

---

3. The seller can demand and reclaim the goods at any time, though, if the buyer misrepresented his or her solvency in writing within three months prior to the delivery of the goods.

vent within ten days after receiving the first payment, and the goods must be identified to the contract. To exercise this right, the buyer or lessee must pay the seller or lessor any unpaid balance of the purchase price or lease payments [UCC 2–502, 2A–522].

**THE RIGHT TO OBTAIN SPECIFIC PERFORMANCE** A buyer or lessee can obtain specific performance if the goods are unique or the remedy at law (monetary damages) is inadequate [UCC 2–716(1), 2A–521(1)]. Ordinarily, an award of damages is sufficient to place a buyer or lessee in the position she or he would have occupied if the seller or lessor had fully performed.

When the contract is for the purchase of a particular work of art or a similarly unique item, however, damages may not be sufficient. Under these circumstances, equity requires that the seller or lessor perform exactly by delivering the particular goods identified to the contract (the remedy of specific performance).

▶ **Case in Point 22.15**   Together, Doreen Houseman and Eric Dare bought a house and a pedigreed dog. When the couple separated, they agreed that Dare would keep the house (and pay Houseman for her interest in it) and that Houseman would keep the dog. Houseman allowed Dare to take the dog for visits, but after one visit, Dare kept the dog. Houseman filed a lawsuit seeking specific performance of their agreement. The court found that because pets have special subjective value to their owners, a dog can be considered a unique good. Thus, an award of specific performance was appropriate.[4] ◀

**THE RIGHT OF COVER**  In certain situations, buyers and lessees can protect themselves by obtaining **cover**— that is, by buying or leasing substitute goods for those that were due under the contract. This option is available when the seller or lessor repudiates the contract or fails to deliver the goods, or when a buyer or lessee has rightfully rejected goods or revoked acceptance.

In purchasing or leasing substitute goods, the buyer or lessee must act in good faith and without unreasonable delay [UCC 2–712, 2A–518]. The buyer or lessee can recover from the seller or lessor:

1. The difference between the cost of cover and the contract price (or lease payments).
2. Incidental damages that resulted from the breach.
3. *Consequential damages* to compensate for indirect losses (such as lost profits) resulting from the breach that were reasonably foreseeable at the time of contract formation. The amount of consequen-

tial damages is reduced by any amount the buyer or lessee saved as a result of the breach (such as when a buyer obtains cover without having to pay delivery charges that were part of the original sales contract).

Buyers and lessees are not required to cover, and failure to do so will not bar them from using any other remedies available under the UCC. A buyer or lessee who fails to cover, however, risks collecting a lower amount of consequential damages. A court may reduce the consequential damages by the amount of the loss that could have been avoided had the buyer or lessee purchased or leased substitute goods.

**THE RIGHT TO REPLEVY GOODS**  Buyers and lessees also have the right to replevy goods. **Replevin**[5] is an action to recover identified goods in the hands of a party who is unlawfully withholding them. Under the UCC, a buyer or lessee can replevy goods identified to the contract if the seller or lessor has repudiated or breached the contract. To maintain an action to replevy goods, buyers and lessees must usually show that they were unable to cover for the goods after making a reasonable effort [UCC 2–716(3), 2A–521(3)].

**THE RIGHT TO RECOVER DAMAGES**  If a seller or lessor repudiates the contract or fails to deliver the goods, the buyer or lessee can sue for damages. For the buyer, the measure of recovery is the difference between the contract price and the market price of the goods at the time the buyer *learned* of the breach. For the lessee, the measure is the difference between the lease payments and the lease payments that could be obtained for the goods at the time the lessee learned of the breach.

The market price or market lease payments are determined at the place where the seller or lessor was supposed to deliver the goods. The buyer or lessee can also recover incidental and consequential damages less the expenses that were saved as a result of the breach [UCC 2–713, 2A–519].

▶ **Case in Point 22.16**   Les Entreprises Jacques Defour & Fils, Inc., contracted to buy a thirty-thousand-gallon industrial tank from Dinsick Equipment Corporation for $70,000. Les Entreprises hired Xaak Transport, Inc., to pick up the tank, but when Xaak arrived at the pickup location, there was no tank. Les Entreprises paid Xaak $7,459 for its services and filed a suit against Dinsick. The court awarded compensatory damages of $70,000 for the tank and incidental damages of $7,459 for the transport. To

4. *Houseman v. Dare*, 405 N.J.Super. 538, 966 A.2d 24 (2009).

5. Pronounced ruh-*pleh*-vun, derived from the Old French word *plevir*, meaning "to pledge."

establish a breach of contract requires an enforceable contract, substantial performance by the nonbreaching party, a breach by the other party, and damages. In this case, Les Entreprises agreed to buy a tank and paid the price. Dinsick failed to tender or deliver the tank, or to refund the price. The shipping costs were a necessary part of performance, so this was a reasonable expense.[6] ◄

## When the Seller or Lessor Delivers Nonconforming Goods

When the seller or lessor delivers nonconforming goods, the buyer or lessee has several remedies available under the UCC.

**THE RIGHT TO REJECT THE GOODS** If either the goods or their tender fails to conform to the contract in any respect, the buyer or lessee can reject all of the goods or any commercial unit of the goods [UCC 2–601, 2A–509]. On rejecting the goods, the buyer or lessee may obtain cover or cancel the contract, and may seek damages just as if the seller or lessor had refused to deliver the goods. (See the earlier discussion of these remedies.)

▶ **Case in Point 22.17**   Jorge Jauregui contracted to buy a new Kawai RX5 piano for $24,282 from Bobb's Piano Sales & Service, Inc. When the piano was delivered with "unacceptable damage," Jauregui rejected it and filed a lawsuit for breach of contract. The court ruled that Bobb's had breached the contract by delivering nonconforming goods. Jauregui was entitled to damages equal to the contract price with interest, plus the sales tax, delivery charge, and attorneys' fees.[7] ◄

*Timeliness and Reason for Rejection Are Required.* The buyer or lessee must reject the goods within a reasonable amount of time after delivery or tender of delivery and must seasonably (timely) notify the seller or lessor [UCC 2–602(1), 2A–509(2)]. If the buyer or lessee fails to reject the goods within a reasonable amount of time, acceptance will be presumed.

When rejecting goods, the buyer or lessee must also designate defects that are ascertainable by reasonable inspection. Failure to do so precludes the buyer or lessee from using such defects to justify rejection or to establish breach when the seller or lessor could

have cured the defects if they had been disclosed seasonably [UCC 2–605, 2A–514].

*Duties of Merchant-Buyers and Lessees When Goods Are Rejected.* Sometimes, a *merchant-buyer or lessee* rightfully rejects goods, and the seller or lessor has no agent or business at the place of rejection. In that situation, the merchant-buyer or lessee has a good faith obligation to follow any reasonable instructions received from the seller or lessor with respect to the goods [UCC 2–603, 2A–511]. The buyer or lessee is entitled to be reimbursed for the care and cost entailed in following the instructions. The same requirements apply if the buyer or lessee rightfully revokes her or his acceptance of the goods at some later time [UCC 2–608(3), 2A–517(5)]. (Revocation of acceptance will be discussed shortly.)

If no instructions are forthcoming and the goods are perishable or threaten to decline in value quickly, the buyer or lessee can resell the goods. The buyer or lessee must exercise good faith and can take appropriate reimbursement and a selling commission (not to exceed 10 percent of the gross proceeds) from the proceeds [UCC 2–603(1), (2); 2A–511(1)]. If the goods are not perishable, the buyer or lessee may store them for the seller or lessor or reship them to the seller or lessor [UCC 2–604, 2A–512].

**REVOCATION OF ACCEPTANCE** Acceptance of the goods precludes the buyer or lessee from exercising the right of rejection, but it does not necessarily prevent the buyer or lessee from pursuing other remedies. In certain circumstances, a buyer or lessee is permitted to *revoke* his or her acceptance of the goods.

Acceptance of a lot or a commercial unit can be revoked if the nonconformity *substantially* impairs the value of the lot or unit *and* if one of the following factors is present:

1. Acceptance was based on the reasonable assumption that the nonconformity would be cured, and it has not been cured within a reasonable period of time [UCC 2–608(1)(a), 2A–517(1)(a)].
2. The failure of the buyer or lessee to discover the nonconformity was reasonably induced by either the difficulty of discovery before acceptance or by assurances made by the seller or lessor [UCC 2–608(1)(b), 2A–517(1)(b)].

Revocation of acceptance is not effective until notice is given to the seller or lessor. Notice must occur within a reasonable time after the buyer or

---

6. *Les Enterprises Jacques Defour & Fils, Inc. v. Dinsick Equipment Corp.,* 2011 WL 307501 (N.D.Ill. 2011).
7. *Jauregui v. Bobb's Piano Sales & Service, Inc.,* 922 So.2d 303 (Fla.App. 2006).

lessee either discovers or *should have discovered* the grounds for revocation. Additionally, revocation must occur before the goods have undergone any substantial change (such as spoilage) not caused by their own defects [UCC 2–608(2), 2A–517(4)]. Once acceptance is revoked, the buyer or lessee can pursue remedies, just as if the goods had been rejected.

**THE RIGHT TO RECOVER DAMAGES FOR ACCEPTED GOODS** A buyer or lessee who has accepted nonconforming goods may also keep the goods and recover damages [UCC 2–714(1), 2A–519(3)]. To do so, the buyer or lessee must notify the seller or lessor of the breach within a reasonable time after the defect was or should have been discovered. Failure to give notice of the defects (breach) to the seller or lessor bars the buyer or lessee from pursuing any remedy [UCC 2–607(3), 2A–516(3)]. In addition, the parties to a sales or lease contract can insert into the

contract a provision requiring the buyer or lessee to give notice of any defects in the goods within a prescribed period.

When the goods delivered are not as promised, the measure of damages equals the difference between the value of the goods as accepted and their value if they had been delivered as warranted, unless special circumstances show proximately caused damages of a different amount [UCC 2–714(2), 2A–519(4)]. The buyer or lessee is also entitled to incidental and consequential damages when appropriate [UCC 2–714(3), 2A–519]. With proper notice to the seller or lessor, the buyer or lessee can also deduct all or any part of the damages from the price or lease payments still due under the contract [UCC 2–717, 2A–516(1)].

Is two years after a sale of goods a reasonable time period in which to discover a defect in those goods and notify the seller of a breach? That was the question in the following case.

## SP TLIGHT on Baseball Cards

### Case 22.3   Fitl v. Strek
Supreme Court of Nebraska, 269 Neb. 51, 690 N.W.2d 605 (2005).

**BACKGROUND AND FACTS** In 1995, James Fitl attended a sports-card show in San Francisco, California, where he met Mark Strek, doing business as Star Cards of San Francisco, an exhibitor at the show. Later, on Strek's representation that a certain 1952 Mickey Mantle Topps baseball card was in near-mint condition, Fitl bought the card from Strek for $17,750. Strek delivered it to Fitl in Omaha, Nebraska, and Fitl placed it in a safe-deposit box.

In May 1997, Fitl sent the card to Professional Sports Authenticators (PSA), a sports-card grading service. PSA told Fitl that the card was ungradable because it had been discolored and doctored. Fitl complained to Strek, who replied that Fitl should have initiated a return of the card within "a typical grace period for the unconditional return of a card, . . . 7 days to 1 month" of its receipt. In August, Fitl sent the card to ASA Accugrade, Inc. (ASA), another grading service, for a second opinion of the value. ASA also concluded that the card had been refinished and trimmed. Fitl filed a suit in a Nebraska state court against Strek, seeking damages. The court awarded Fitl $17,750, plus his court costs. Strek appealed to the Nebraska Supreme Court.

**DECISION AND RATIONALE** The state supreme court affirmed the lower court's decision in favor of Fitl. Section 2–607(3)(a) of the UCC states, "Where a tender has been accepted . . . the buyer must within a reasonable time after he discovers or should have discovered any breach notify the seller of breach or be barred from any remedy." "What is a reasonable time for taking any action depends on the nature, purpose and circumstances of such action" [UCC 1–205(a)].

The state's highest court concluded that the buyer (Fitl) had reasonably relied on the seller's (Strek's) representation that the goods were "authentic," which they were not, and when their defects were discovered, Fitl had given timely notice. The court reasoned that "the policies behind the notice requirement, to allow the seller to correct a defect, to prepare for negotiation and litigation, and to protect against stale claims at a time beyond which an investigation can be completed, were not unfairly prejudiced by the lack of an earlier notice to Strek. Any problem Strek may have had with the party from whom he obtained

CASE 22.3 CONTINUES ▶

CASE 22.3 CONTINUED the baseball card was a separate matter from his transaction with Fitl, and an investigation into the source of the altered card would not have minimized Fitl's damages."

**WHAT IF THE FACTS WERE DIFFERENT?** *Suppose that Fitl and Strek had included in their deal a written clause requiring Fitl to give notice of any defect in the card within "7 days to 1 month" of its receipt. Would the result have been different? Why or why not?*

**THE LEGAL ENVIRONMENT DIMENSION** *What might a court award to a buyer who prevails in a dispute such as the one in this case?*

---

## SECTION 7
# ADDITIONAL PROVISIONS AFFECTING REMEDIES

The parties to a sales or lease contract can vary their respective rights and obligations by contractual agreement. For instance, a seller and buyer can expressly provide for remedies in addition to those provided in the UCC. They can also specify remedies in lieu of those provided in the UCC (including liquidated damages clauses—see Chapter 19), or they can change the measure of damages. A seller can provide that the buyer's only remedy on the seller's breach will be repair or replacement of the item. Alternatively, the seller can limit the buyer's remedy to return of the goods and refund of the purchase price.

In sales and lease contracts, an agreed-on remedy is in addition to those provided in the UCC unless the parties expressly agree that the remedy is exclusive of all others [UCC 2–719(1), 2A–503(1),(2)].

## Exclusive Remedies

If the parties state that a remedy is *exclusive,* then it is the sole (only) remedy. ▶ **Example 22.18** Standard Tool Company agrees to sell a pipe-cutting machine to United Pipe & Tubing Corporation. The contract limits United's remedy exclusively to repair or replacement of any defective parts. Thus, repair or replacement of defective parts is the buyer's only remedy under this contract. ◀

When circumstances cause an exclusive remedy to fail in its essential purpose, however, it is no longer exclusive, and the buyer or lessee may pursue other remedies available under the UCC [UCC 2–719(2), 2A–503(2)]. In *Example 22.18,* suppose that Standard Tool Company was unable to repair a defective part, and no replacement parts were available. In this situation, because the exclusive remedy failed in its essen-

tial purpose (to provide recovery), the buyer could pursue other remedies available under the UCC. (See the *Managerial Strategy* feature on the facing page for guidelines on what to do when a contract is breached.)

## Consequential Damages

As discussed earlier, consequential damages are special damages that compensate for indirect losses (such as lost profits) resulting from a breach of contract that were reasonably foreseeable. Under the UCC, parties to a contract can limit or exclude consequential damages, provided the limitation is not unconscionable.

When the buyer or lessee is a consumer, any limitation of consequential damages for personal injuries resulting from consumer goods is *prima facie* (presumed to be) unconscionable. The limitation of consequential damages is not necessarily unconscionable when the loss is commercial in nature—for example, lost profits and property damage [UCC 2–719(3), 2A–503(3)].

## Statute of Limitations

An action for breach of contract under the UCC must be commenced *within four years after the cause of action accrues* [UCC 2–725(1)]. This means that a buyer or lessee must file the lawsuit within four years after the breach occurs.[8] The parties can agree in their contract to reduce this period to not less than one year, but cannot extend it beyond four years [UCC 2–725(1), 2A–506(1)].

If a buyer or lessee has accepted nonconforming goods, that party has a reasonable time to notify the seller or lessor of the breach. Failure to provide notice will bar the buyer or lessee from pursuing any remedy [UCC 2–607(3) (a), 2A–516(3)].

---

8. For breach of warranty, to be discussed in Chapter 23, the cause of action arises when the seller or lessor delivers the contracted goods [UCC 2–725(2), 2A–506(2)]. Thus, the buyer or lessee has four years from the delivery date to file a suit for breach of warranty.

## MANAGERIAL STRATEGY

### Facing a Breach of Contract

A contract for the sale of goods has been breached. Can the dispute be settled without a trip to court? The answer, of course, depends on the willingness of the parties to agree on an appropriate remedy.

#### A Store Policy against Refunds

As the manager of a retail outlet, you may wish to establish a policy of not providing refunds. Instead, you will offer only to repair or replace items that are defective. Does this mean that you will never have to provide a refund if a customer purchases a good (or service) that turns out to be defective and cannot be repaired? That was the question facing a court in New York when a store cited its no-refund policy in declining to provide a dissatisfied customer with a full refund.

Sarah Milligan purchased a wig from Shuly Wigs, Inc., but discovered that the wig was defective. Shuly twice tried to repair the wig, but both attempts failed. Milligan purchased another wig and asked Shuly for a refund. When Shuly refused, Milligan sued. A small claims court ruled in Milligan's favor. On appeal, the reviewing court affirmed the ruling. The court observed that when "a vendor prohibits refunds and limits the purchaser's remedies to repair or replacement of its goods, the remedy fails of its essential purpose if a delay or failure adequately to repair or replace the goods in a reasonable time deprives the plaintiff of a substantial benefit of her bargain."[a]

#### Contractual Clauses Concerning Applicable Remedies

Often, the parties to sales and lease contracts agree in advance in their contracts on what remedies will be applicable in the event of a breach. This may take the form of a contract provision restricting or expanding remedies available under Section 2–719 of the Uniform Commercial Code (UCC). Such clauses help to reduce uncertainty and the necessity for costly litigation.

#### When the Contract Is Silent on Applicable Remedies

If your agreement does not cover a breach and you are the nonbreaching party, the UCC gives you a variety of alternatives. You need to determine the available remedies, analyze them, rank them in order of priority, and then predict how successful you might be in pursuing each remedy if you decide to go to court. Before going to court, however, consider the position of the breaching party to determine if you can negotiate a settlement.

For example, when defective goods are delivered and accepted, usually it is preferable for the buyer and seller to reach an agreement on a reduced purchase price. Practically speaking, though, the buyer may be unable to obtain a partial refund from the seller. In this situation, UCC 2–717 allows the buyer to give notice of the intention to deduct the damages from any part of the purchase price not yet paid. If you are a buyer who has accepted defective goods and has not yet paid in full, you may wish to exercise your rights under UCC 2–717 and deduct appropriate damages from your final payment. Remember that most breaches of contract do not end up in court—they are settled beforehand.

#### MANAGERIAL IMPLICATIONS

Of course, the best way to avoid having to go to court to settle a dispute about a breached contract is to specify in the contract itself what remedies will be available to each party in the event of a breach. Nothing in the UCC prevents parties from expanding the remedies available under it, as UCC 2–719 points out. In general, the more clearly remedies for breach are outlined in a sales contract, the less chance there will be a lawsuit.

#### BUSINESS QUESTIONS

1. *Under what circumstances is a negotiated settlement for a breach preferable to litigation?*

2. *Assume that you are in a dispute over a breach of contract and you discover that the contract does not explicitly mention any remedies. What do you do now?*

---

a. *Milligan v. Shuly Wigs, Inc.,* 34 Misc.3d. 128(A), 941 N.Y.S.2d 539 (2011).

---

## SECTION 8
## DEALING WITH INTERNATIONAL CONTRACTS

Buyers and sellers (or lessees and lessors) engaged in international business transactions may be separated by thousands of miles. Special precautions are often taken to ensure performance under international contracts. Sellers and lessors want to avoid delivering goods for which they might not be paid. Buyers and lessees desire the assurance that sellers and lessors will not be paid until there is evidence that the goods have been shipped. Thus, **letters of credit** frequently are used to facilitate international business transactions.

## Letter-of-Credit Transactions

In a simple letter-of-credit transaction, the *issuer* (a bank or other financial institution) agrees to issue a letter of credit and to ascertain whether the *beneficiary* (seller or lessor) performs certain acts. In return, the *account party* (buyer or lessee) promises to reimburse the issuer for the amount paid to the beneficiary. The transaction may also involve an *advising bank* that transmits information and a *paying bank* that expedites payment under the letter of credit. See Exhibit 22–1 below for an illustration of a letter-of-credit transaction.

**PAYMENT UNDER A LETTER OF CREDIT** Under a letter of credit, the issuer is bound to pay the beneficiary (seller or lessor) when the beneficiary has complied with the terms and conditions of the letter of credit. The letter of credit assures the beneficiary of payment at the same time as it assures the account party (buyer or lessee) of performance. Typically, a letter of credit will require that the beneficiary deliver a *bill of lading* (the carrier's contract) to prove that shipment has been made.

**THE VALUE OF A LETTER OF CREDIT** The basic principle behind letters of credit is that payment is made against the documents presented by the beneficiary and not against the facts that the documents purport to reflect. Thus, in a letter-of-credit transaction, the

**EXHIBIT 22–1 A Letter-of-Credit Transaction**

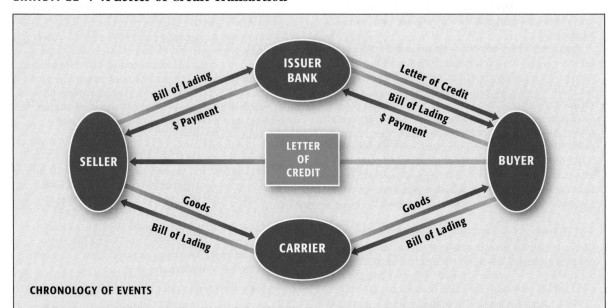

**CHRONOLOGY OF EVENTS**

1. Buyer contracts with issuer bank to issue a letter of credit. This sets forth the bank's obligation to pay on the letter of credit and buyer's obligation to pay the bank.

2. Letter of credit is sent to seller informing seller that on compliance with the terms of the letter of credit (such as presentment of necessary documents—in this example, a bill of lading), the bank will issue payment for the goods.

3. Seller delivers goods to carrier and receives a bill of lading.

4. Seller delivers the bill of lading to issuer bank and, if the document is proper, receives payment.

5. Issuer bank delivers the bill of lading to buyer.

6. Buyer delivers the bill of lading to carrier.

7. Carrier delivers the goods to buyer.

8. Buyer settles with issuer bank.

issuer (bank) does not police the underlying contract. The letter of credit is independent of the underlying contract between the buyer and the seller.

Eliminating the need for the bank (issuer) to inquire into whether actual contractual conditions have been satisfied greatly reduces the costs of letters of credit. Moreover, the use of a letter of credit protects both buyers and sellers.

## Remedies for Breach of International Sales Contracts

The United Nations Convention on Contracts for the International Sale of Goods (CISG) provides international sellers and buyers with remedies very similar to those available under the UCC. Article 74 of the CISG provides for money damages, including foreseeable consequential damages, on a contract's breach. As under the UCC, the measure of damages normally is the difference between the contract price and the market price of the goods.

Under Article 49, the buyer is permitted to avoid obligations under the contract if the seller breaches the contract or fails to deliver the goods during the time specified in the contract or later agreed on by the parties. Similarly, under Article 64, the seller can avoid obligations under the contract if the buyer breaches the contract, fails to accept delivery of the goods, or fails to pay for the goods.

The CISG also allows for specific performance as a remedy under Article 28, which provides that "one party is entitled to require performance of any obligation by the other party." Nevertheless, a court may grant specific performance under Article 28 only if it would do so "under its own [national] law." As already discussed, U.S. courts normally grant specific performance only if no adequate remedy at law (monetary damages) is available and the goods are unique in nature. In other countries, such as Germany, however, specific performance is a commonly granted remedy for breach of contract.

## Reviewing: Performance and Breach of Sales and Lease Contracts

GFI, Inc., a Hong Kong company, makes audio decoder chips, an essential component in the manufacture of MP3 players. Egan Electronics contracts with GFI to buy 10,000 chips on an installment contract, with 2,500 chips to be shipped every three months, F.O.B. Hong Kong, via Air Express. At the time for the first delivery, GFI delivers only 2,400 chips but explains to Egan that although the shipment is less than 5 percent short, the chips are of a higher quality than those specified in the contract and are worth 5 percent more than the contract price. Egan accepts the shipment and pays GFI the contract price. At the time for the second shipment, GFI makes a shipment identical to the first. Egan again accepts and pays for the chips. At the time for the third shipment, GFI ships 2,400 of the same chips, but this time GFI sends them via Hong Kong Air instead of Air Express. While in transit, the chips are destroyed. When it is time for the fourth shipment, GFI again sends 2,400 chips, but this time Egan rejects the chips without explanation. Using the information presented in the chapter, answer the following questions.

1. Did GFI have a legitimate reason to expect that Egan would accept the fourth shipment? Why or why not?
2. Did the substitution of carriers in the third shipment constitute a breach of the contract by GFI? Explain.
3. Suppose that the silicon used for the chips becomes unavailable for a period of time. Consequently, GFI cannot manufacture enough chips to fulfill the contract, but does ship as many as it can to Egan. Under what doctrine might a court release GFI from further performance of the contract?
4. Under the UCC, does Egan have a right to reject the fourth shipment? Why or why not?

**DEBATE THIS . . .** *If a contract specifies a particular carrier, then the shipper must use that carrier or be in breach of the contract—no exceptions should ever be allowed.*

## Terms and Concepts to Review

conforming goods 383

cover 393

cure 385

installment contract 385

letter of credit 397

perfect tender rule 384

replevin 393

tender of delivery 383

## Issue Spotters

1. Country Fruit Stand orders eighty cases of peaches from Downey Farms. Without stating a reason, Downey delivers thirty cases instead of eighty at the wrong time. Does Country have the right to reject the shipment? Explain. **(See page 384.)**

2. Brite Images agrees to sell Poster Planet five thousand posters of celebrities, to be delivered on May 1. On April 1, Brite repudiates the contract. Poster Planet informs Brite that it expects delivery. Can Poster Planet sue Brite without waiting until May 1? Why or why not? **(See page 389.)**

• Check your answers to the Issue Spotters against the answers provided in Appendix E at the end of this text.

## Business Scenarios

**22–1. Anticipatory Repudiation.** Moore contracted in writing to sell her 2012 Hyundai Santa Fe to Hammer for $16,500. Moore agreed to deliver the car on Wednesday, and Hammer promised to pay the $16,500 on the following Friday. On Tuesday, Hammer informed Moore that he would not be buying the car after all. By Friday, Hammer had changed his mind again and tendered $16,500 to Moore. Moore, although she had not sold the car to another party, refused the tender and refused to deliver. Hammer claimed that Moore had breached their contract. Moore contended that Hammer's repudiation released her from her duty to perform under the contract. Who is correct, and why? **(See page 389.)**

**22–2. Remedies of the Buyer or Lessee.** Lehor collects antique cars. He contracts to purchase spare parts for a 1938 engine from Beem. These parts are not made anymore and are scarce. To obtain the contract with Beem, Lehor agrees to pay 50 percent of the purchase price in advance. Lehor sends the payment on May 1, and Beem receives it on May 2. On May 3, Beem, having found another buyer willing to pay substantially more for the parts, informs Lehor that he will not deliver as contracted. That same day, Lehor learns that Beem is insolvent. Discuss fully any possible remedies available to Lehor to enable him to take possession of these parts. **(See page 392.)**

## Business Case Problems

**22–3. Spotlight on Revocation of Acceptance—Remedies of the**  **Buyer.** L.V.R.V., Inc., sells recreational vehicles (RVs) in Las Vegas, Nevada, as Wheeler's Las Vegas RV. In September 1997, Wheeler's sold a Santara RV made by Coachmen Recreational Vehicle Co. to Arthur and Roswitha Waddell. The Waddells hoped to spend two or three years driving around the country, but almost immediately—and repeatedly—they experienced problems with the RV. Its entry door popped open. Its cooling and heating systems did not work properly. Its batteries did not maintain a charge. Most significantly, its engine overheated when ascending a moderate grade. The Waddells brought it to Wheeler's service department for repairs. Over the next year and a half, the RV spent more than seven months at Wheeler's. In March 1999, the Waddells filed a complaint in a Nevada state court against the dealer to revoke their acceptance of the RV. What are the requirements for a buyer's revocation of acceptance? Were the requirements met in this case? In whose favor should the court rule? Why? [*Waddell v. L.V.R.V., Inc.*, 122 Nev. 15, 125 P.3d 1160 (2006)] **(See page 394.)**

**22–4. Obligations of the Seller.** Flint Hills Resources, LP, a crude oil refiner, agreed to buy "approximately 1,000 barrels per day" of Mexican natural gas condensate from JAG Energy, Inc., an oil broker. Four months into the contract, Pemex, the only authorized seller of freshly extracted Mexican condensate, warned Flint Hills that some companies might be selling stolen Mexican condensate. Fearing potential criminal liability, Flint Hills refused to accept more deliveries from JAG without proof of the title to its product. JAG promised to forward documents showing its chain of title. After several weeks, when JAG did not produce the documents, Flint Hills canceled their agreement.

JAG filed a suit in a federal district court against Flint Hills, alleging breach of contract. Did Flint Hills have a right to demand assurance of JAG's title to its product? If so, did Flint Hills act reasonably in exercising that right? Explain. [*Flint Hills Resources LP v. Jag Energy, Inc.,* 559 F.3d 373 (5th Cir. 2009)] **(See page 382.)**

**22–5. Breach and Damages.** Utility Systems of America, Inc., was doing roadwork when Chad DeRosier, a nearby landowner, asked Utility to dump 1,500 cubic yards of fill onto his property. Utility agreed but exceeded DeRosier's request by dumping 6,500 cubic yards. Utility offered to remove the extra fill for $9,500. DeRosier paid a different contractor $46,629 to remove the fill and do certain other work. He then filed a suit against Utility. Because Utility charged nothing for the fill, was there a breach of contract? If so, would the damages be greater than $9,500? Could consequential damages be justified? Discuss. [*DeRosier v. Utility Systems of America, Inc.,* 780 N.W.2d 1 (Minn.App. 2010)] **(See page 394.)**

**22–6. Right of Inspection.** Jessie Romero offered to deliver two trade-in vehicles—a 2003 Mitsubishi Montero SP and a 2002 Chevrolet Silverado pickup—to Scoggin-Dickey Chevrolet Buick, Inc., in exchange for a 2006 Silverado pickup. Scoggin-Dickey agreed. The parties negotiated a price, including a value for the trade-in vehicles, plus cash. Romero paid the cash and took the new Silverado. On inspecting the trade-in vehicles, however, Scoggin-Dickey found that they had little value. The dealer repossessed the Silverado. Did the dealership have the right to inspect the goods and reject them when it did? Why or why not? [*Romero v. Scoggin-Dickey Chevrolet Buick, Inc.,* __ S.W.3d __ (Tex.Civ.App.—Amarillo 2010)] **(See page 388.)**

**22–7. The Right to Recover Damages.** Woodridge USA Properties, L.P., bought eighty-seven commercial truck trailers from Southeast Trailer Mart, Inc. (STM). Gerald McCarty, an independent sales agent who arranged the deal, showed Woodridge the documents of title. They did not indicate that Woodridge was the buyer. Woodridge asked McCarty to sell the trailers, and within three months they were sold, but McCarty did not give the proceeds to Woodridge. Woodridge—without mentioning the title documents—asked STM to refund the contract price. STM refused. Does Woodridge have a right to recover damages from STM? Explain. [*Woodridge USA Properties, L.P. v. Southeast Trailer Mart, Inc.,* __ F.3d __ (11th Cir. 2011)] **(See page 393.)**

**22–8. BUSINESS CASE PROBLEM WITH SAMPLE ANSWER: Nonconforming Goods.**

 *Padma Paper Mills, Ltd., converts waste paper into usable paper. In 2007, Padma entered into a contract with Universal Exports, Inc., under which Universal Exports certified that it would ship white envelope cuttings, and Padma paid $131,000 for the paper. When the shipment arrived, however, Padma discovered that Universal Exports had sent multicolored paper plates and other brightly colored paper products. Padma accepted the goods but notified Universal Exports that they did not conform to the contract. Can Padma recover even though it accepted the goods knowing that they were nonconforming? If so, how? [Padma Paper Mills, Ltd. v. Universal Exports, Inc., 34 Misc.3d 1236(A) (N.Y.Sup. 2012)]* **(See page 395.)**

• **For a sample answer for Problem 22–8, go to Appendix F at the end of this text.**

**22–9. A QUESTION OF ETHICS: Revocation of Acceptance.**

 *Scotwood Industries, Inc., sells calcium chloride flake for use in ice melt products. Between July and September 2004, Scotwood delivered thirty-seven shipments of flake to Frank Miller & Sons, Inc. After each delivery, Scotwood billed Miller, which paid thirty-five of the invoices and processed 30 to 50 percent of the flake. In August, Miller began complaining about the product's quality. Scotwood assured Miller that it would remedy the situation. Finally, in October, Miller told Scotwood, "This is totally unacceptable. We are willing to discuss Scotwood picking up the material." Miller claimed that the flake was substantially defective because it was chunked. Calcium chloride maintains its purity for up to five years, but if it is exposed to and absorbs moisture, it chunks and becomes unusable. Scotwood sued to collect payment on the unpaid invoices. In response, Miller filed a counterclaim in a federal district court for breach of contract, seeking to recover based on revocation of acceptance, among other things. [Scotwood Industries, Inc. v. Frank Miller & Sons, Inc., 435 F.Supp.2d 1160 (D.Kan. 2006)]* **(See page 394.)**

(a) What is revocation of acceptance? How does a buyer effectively exercise this option? Do the facts in this case support this theory as a ground for Miller to recover damages? Why or why not?

(b) Is there an ethical basis for allowing a buyer to revoke acceptance of goods and recover damages? If so, is there an ethical limit to this right? Discuss.

## Legal Reasoning Group Activity

**22–10. Performance Obligations.** Kodiak agrees to sell 1,000 espresso machines to Lin to be delivered on May 1. Due to a strike during the last week of April, there is a temporary shortage of delivery vehicles. Kodiak can deliver the espresso makers 200 at a time over a period of ten days, with the first delivery on May 1. **(See page 383.)**

(a) The first group will determine if Kodiak has the right to deliver the goods in five lots. What happens if Lin objects to delivery in lots?

(b) A second group will analyze whether the doctrine of commercial impracticability applies to this scenario, and if it does, what the result will be.

# CHAPTER 23

# WARRANTIES

Most goods are covered by some type of warranty designed to protect buyers. In sales and lease law, a warranty is an assurance or guarantee by the seller or lessor about the quality and features of the goods being sold or leased.

The Uniform Commercial Code (UCC) has numerous rules governing product warranties as they occur in sales and lease contracts. Articles 2 (on sales) and 2A (on leases) designate several types of warranties that can arise in a sales or lease contract, including warranties of title, express warranties, and implied warranties. In this chapter, we discuss these types of warranties as well as a federal statute that is designed to prevent deception and make warranties more understandable.

Because a warranty imposes a duty on the seller or lessor, a breach of warranty is a breach of the seller's or lessor's promise. Assuming that the parties have not agreed to limit or modify the remedies available, if the seller or lessor breaches a warranty, the buyer or lessee can sue to recover damages from the seller or lessor. Under some circumstances, a breach of warranty can allow the buyer or lessee to rescind (cancel) the agreement.

## SECTION 1
## WARRANTIES OF TITLE

Under the UCC, three types of title warranties—*good title, no liens,* and *no infringements*—can automatically arise in sales and lease contracts [UCC 2–312, 2A–211]. Normally, a seller or lessor can disclaim or modify these title warranties only by including *specific language* in the contract. For example, sellers may assert that they are transferring only such rights, title, and interest as they have in the goods.

### Good Title

In most sales, sellers warrant that they have good and valid title to the goods sold and that the transfer of the title is rightful [UCC 2–312(1)(a)]. If the buyer subsequently learns that the seller did not have valid title to the goods that were purchased, the buyer can sue the seller for breach of this warranty.

▶ **Example 23.1** Alexis steals two iPads from Camden and sells them to Emma, who does not know that they are stolen. If Camden discovers that Emma has the iPads, then he has the right to reclaim them from her. When Alexis sold Emma the iPads, Alexis *automatically* warranted to Emma that the title conveyed was valid and that its transfer was rightful. Because a thief has no title to stolen goods, Alexis breached the warranty of title imposed by UCC 2–312(1)(a) and became liable to Emma for appropriate damages. (See Chapter 21 for a detailed discussion of sales by nonowners.) ◀

### No Liens

A second warranty of title protects buyers and lessees who are *unaware* of any encumbrances (claims, charges, or liabilities—usually called *liens*[1]) against goods at the time the contract is made [UCC 2–312(1)(b), 2A–211(1)].

This warranty protects buyers who, for instance, unknowingly purchase goods that are subject to a creditor's security interest. (A *security interest* in this context is an interest in the goods that secures payment or performance of an obligation.) If a creditor legally repossesses the goods from a buyer *who had no actual knowledge of the security interest,* the buyer can recover from the seller for breach of warranty.

---

**1.** Pronounced *leens.*

(In contrast, a buyer who has *actual knowledge of a security interest* has no recourse against a seller.)

▶ **Example 23.2**   Henderson buys a used boat from Loring for cash. A month later, Barish proves that she has a valid security interest in the boat and that Loring, who has missed five payments, is in default. Barish then repossesses the boat from Henderson. Henderson demands his cash back from Loring. Under Section 2–312(1)(b), Henderson has legal grounds to recover from Loring because the seller of goods warrants that the goods are delivered free from any security interest or other lien of which the buyer has no knowledge. ◀

Article 2A affords similar protection for lessees. Section 2A–211(1) provides that during the term of the lease, no claim of any third party will interfere with the lessee's enjoyment of the leasehold interest.

## No Infringements

A third type of warranty of title arises automatically when the seller or lessor is a merchant. A merchant-seller or lessor warrants that the buyer or lessee takes the goods *free of infringements* from any copyright, trademark, or patent claims of a third person[2] [UCC 2–312(3), 2A–211(2)].

**NOTICE REQUIRED IN SALES CONTRACTS**   If the buyer is subsequently sued by a third party holding copyright, trademark, or patent rights in the goods, then this warranty is breached. The buyer *must notify the seller* of the litigation within a reasonable time to enable the seller to decide whether to defend the lawsuit. The seller then decides whether to defend the buyer and bear all expenses in the action.

If the seller agrees in a writing (or record) to defend and to pay the expenses, then the buyer must turn over control of the litigation to the seller. Otherwise, the buyer is barred from any remedy against the seller for liability established by the litigation [UCC 2–607(3)(b), 2–607(5)(b)]. Thus, if a buyer wins at trial but did not notify the seller of the litigation, the buyer cannot sue the seller to recover the expenses of the lawsuit.

**NOTICE IN LEASE CONTRACTS**   In situations that involve leases rather than sales, Article 2A provides

for the same notice of infringement litigation [UCC 2A–516(3)(b), 2A–516(4)(b)]. After being notified of the lawsuit, the lessor (or supplier, in a finance lease) who agrees to pay all expenses can demand that the lessee turn over the control of the litigation. Failure to provide notice normally bars any subsequent remedy against the lessor for liability established by the litigation.

There is an exception for leases to individual consumers for personal, family, or household purposes. A consumer who fails to notify the lessor within a reasonable time does not lose his or her remedy against the lessor for whatever liability is established in the litigation [UCC 2A–516(3)(b)].

## SECTION 2
# EXPRESS WARRANTIES

A seller or lessor can create an **express warranty** by making representations concerning the quality, condition, description, or performance potential of the goods.

## Statements That Create Express Warranties

Under UCC 2–313 and 2A–210, express warranties arise when a seller or lessor indicates any of the following:

1. That the goods conform to any *affirmation* (declaration that something is true) *of fact* or *promise* that the seller or lessor makes to the buyer or lessee about the goods. Such affirmations or promises are usually made during the bargaining process. ▶ **Example 23.3**   D. J. Vladick, a salesperson at Home Depot, tells a customer, "These drill bits will *easily* penetrate stainless steel—and without dulling." Vladick's statement is an express warranty. ◀

2. That the goods conform to any *description* of them. ▶ **Example 23.4**   A label reads "Crate contains one Kawasaki 750 4X4 ATV," and a contract calls for the delivery of a "wool coat." Both statements create express warranties that the content of the goods sold conforms to the description. ◀

3. That the goods conform to any *sample or model* of the goods shown to the buyer or lessee. ▶ **Example 23.5**   Melissa Faught orders a stainless steel 5500 Super Angel juicer for $1,100 after

---

**2.** Recall from Chapter 20 that a *merchant* is defined in UCC 2–104(1) as a person who deals in goods of the kind involved in the sales contract or who, by occupation, presents himself or herself as having knowledge or skill peculiar to the goods involved in the transaction.

seeing a dealer demonstrate its use at a raw foods health fair. The Super Angel is shipped to her. When the juicer arrives, it is an older model, not the 5500 model. This is a breach of an express warranty because the dealer warranted that the juicer would be the same model used in the demonstration. ◄

Express warranties can be found in a seller's or lessor's advertisement, brochure, or promotional materials, in addition to being made orally or in an express warranty provision in a sales or lease contract.

## Basis of the Bargain

To create an express warranty, a seller or lessor does not have to use formal words such as *warrant* or *guarantee*. It is only necessary that a reasonable buyer or lessee would regard the representation as being part of the basis of the bargain [UCC 2–313(2), 2A–210(2)].

The UCC does not explicitly define the phrase "basis of the bargain." Generally, it means that the buyer or lessee must have relied on the representation at the time of entering into the agreement. Therefore, a court must determine in each case whether a representation was made at such a time and in such a way that it induced the buyer or lessee to enter into the contract.

## Statements of Opinion and Value

Only statements of fact create express warranties. A seller or lessor who makes a statement that merely relates to the value or worth of the goods, or states an opinion about or recommends the goods, does not create an express warranty [UCC 2–313(2), 2A–210(2)].

▶ **Example 23.6** A car salesperson claims that "this is the best used car to come along in years. It has four new tires and a 250-horsepower engine just rebuilt this year." The seller has made several *affirmations of fact* that can create a warranty. The automobile has an engine. It is a 250-horsepower engine and was rebuilt this year. There are four tires on the car and the tires are new.

The seller's *opinion* that the vehicle is "the best used car to come along in years," however, is known as "puffery" and creates no warranty. (*Puffery* is an expression of opinion by a seller or lessor that is not made as a representation of fact.) ◄

A statement about the value of the goods, such as "this is worth a fortune" or "anywhere else you'd pay $10,000 for it," usually does not create a warranty.

**OPINIONS BY EXPERTS** Ordinarily, statements of opinion do not create warranties. If the seller or lessor is an expert, however, and gives an opinion as an expert to a layperson, then a warranty may be created. ▶ **Example 23.7** Stephen is an art dealer and an expert in seventeenth-century paintings. If Stephen tells Lauren, a purchaser, that in his opinion a particular painting is by Rembrandt, Stephen has warranted the accuracy of his opinion. ◄

**REASONABLE RELIANCE** It is not always easy to determine whether a statement constitutes an express warranty or puffery. The reasonableness of the buyer's or lessee's reliance appears to be the controlling criterion in many cases. ▶ **Example 23.8** A salesperson's statements that a ladder will "never break" and will "last a lifetime" are so clearly improbable that they do not create a warranty. No reasonable buyer would rely on such statements. ◄

Additionally, the context in which a statement is made may be relevant in determining the reasonableness of a buyer's or lessee's reliance. A reasonable person is more likely to rely on a written statement made in an advertisement than on a statement made orally by a salesperson.

▶ **Case in Point 23.9** A tobacco farmer read an advertisement for Chlor-O-Pic, a chemical fumigant. The ad stated that, if applied as directed, Chlor-O-Pic would give "season-long control with application in fall, winter, or spring" against black shank disease, a fungal disease that destroys tobacco crops. The farmer bought Chlor-O-Pic and applied it as directed to his tobacco crop. Nonetheless, the crop developed black shank disease.

The farmer sued the manufacturer of Chlor-O-Pic, arguing that he had purchased the product in reliance on a "strong promise" of "season-long control." The court found that the manufacturer's strong promise had created an express warranty and that the farmer was entitled to the value of the damaged crop.[3] ◄

## SECTION 3
# IMPLIED WARRANTIES

An **implied warranty** is one that *the law derives* by inference from the nature of the transaction or the relative situations or circumstances of the parties.

---

3. *Triple E, Inc. v. Hendrix & Dail, Inc.*, 344 S.C. 186, 543 S.E.2d 245 (2001). See also *Nomo Agroindustrial Sa De CV v. Enza Zaden North America, Inc.*, 492 F.Supp.2d 1175 (D.Ariz. 2007).

Under the UCC, merchants impliedly warrant that the goods they sell or lease are merchantable and, in certain circumstances, fit for a particular purpose. In addition, an implied warranty may arise from a course of dealing or usage of trade. We examine these three types of implied warranties in the following subsections.

## Implied Warranty of Merchantability

Every sale or lease of goods made by a merchant who deals in goods of the kind sold or leased automatically gives rise to an **implied warranty of merchantability** [UCC 2–314, 2A–212]. Thus, a merchant who is in the business of selling ski equipment makes an implied warranty of merchantability every time he sells a pair of skis. A neighbor selling her skis at a garage sale does not (because she is not in the business of selling goods of this type).

**MERCHANTABLE GOODS** To be *merchantable,* goods must be "reasonably fit for the ordinary purposes for which such goods are used." They must be of at least average, fair, or medium-grade quality. The quality must be comparable to quality that will pass without objection in the trade or market for goods of the same description.

To be merchantable, the goods must also be adequately packaged and labeled, and they must conform to the promises or affirmations of fact made on the container or label, if any. Of course, merchants are not absolute insurers against *all* accidents arising in connection with the goods. A bar of soap is not unmerchantable merely because a user could slip and fall by stepping on it.

The warranty of merchantability may be breached even though the merchant did not know or could not have discovered that a product was defective (not merchantable). ▶ **Example 23.10** Christine contracts to purchase a log home package from Milde, a log home dealer. The dealer provides the logs and other materials and constructs the home. Immediately after Christine moves into the house, she finds that when it rains, water seeps through the exterior walls, staining and discoloring the interior walls. The problem occurs because a defective waterproofing product was used on the logs. Even though Milde did not know that the product was defective, he can be held liable because the waterproofing product was not reasonably fit for its ordinary purpose—that is, making the house waterproof. ◀

If the buyer of a product that requires a significant number of repairs sells the item before filing a complaint against its manufacturer, is the sale evidence of the product's merchantability? That was the question in the following case.

## SP☉TLIGHT on DaimlerChrysler

### Case 23.1   Shoop v. DaimlerChrysler Corp.
Appellate Court of Illinois, First District, 371 Ill.App.3d 1058, 864 N.E.2d 785, 309 Ill.Dec. 544 (2007).

**COMPANY PROFILE** In 1920, Walter Chrysler, the head of manufacturing operations for General Motors Corporation(GMC), was dissatisfied with its management and quit. He took over Maxwell Motor Company and renamed it Chrysler Corporation. For most of its history, Chrysler ranked third in vehicle sales among the "Big 3" U.S. automakers—GMC, Ford Motor Company, and Chrysler. In 1998, the German company Daimler-Benz AG, maker of Mercedes-Benz vehicles, bought Chrysler and created DaimlerChrysler AG. The new entity proved less successful than its investors had hoped, and in 2007, Chrysler was sold to Cerberus Capital Management, which renamed it Chrysler, LLC (**www.chrysler.com**). Its vehicles are made and sold under the Chrysler, Dodge, Jeep, and Mopar brands.

**BACKGROUND AND FACTS** In April 2002, Darrell Shoop bought a 2002 Dodge Dakota truck for $28,000 from Dempsey Dodge in Chicago, Illinois. DaimlerChrysler Corporation had manufactured the Dakota. Problems with the truck arose almost immediately. Defects in the engine, suspension, steering, transmission, and other components required repairs twelve times within the first eighteen months, including at least five times for the same defect, which remained uncorrected. In May 2005, after having driven the Dakota 39,000 miles, Shoop accepted $16,500 for the trade-in value of the truck as part of a purchase of a new vehicle. At the time, a comparable vehicle in average condition would have had an

**CASE 23.1 CONTINUED**

average trade-in value of $14,425 and an average retail value of $17,225. Shoop filed a suit in an Illinois state court against DaimlerChrysler, alleging, among other things, a breach of the implied warranty of merchantability. DaimlerChrysler countered, in part, that Shoop's sale of the Dakota was evidence of its merchantability. The court issued a summary judgment in DaimlerChrysler's favor. Shoop appealed to a state intermediate appellate court.

**DECISION AND RATIONALE**  The state intermediate appellate court reversed the lower court's summary judgment and remanded the case for trial. For automobiles, fitness for the ordinary purpose of driving implies that the vehicle should be in safe condition and free from defects. The reviewing court stated that, in addition, "breach of an implied warranty of merchantability may also occur when the warrantor has unsuccessfully attempted to repair or replace defective parts. Whether an implied warranty has been breached is a question of fact." The facts in this case were clear: the plaintiff was required to take the truck to the Chrysler dealership twelve times within eighteen months. The dealership was unable to cure the defects after a reasonable number of attempts. The state intermediate appellate court concluded that "a genuine issue of material fact existed as to whether Chrysler breached the implied warranty of merchantability."

**THE ETHICAL DIMENSION**  *Should Shoop's trade-in of the Dakota preclude his recovery in this case? Why or why not?*

**THE LEGAL ENVIRONMENT DIMENSION**  *If Shoop is allowed to recover damages for breach of warranty, what should be the measure of those damages?*

---

**MERCHANTABLE FOOD**  The serving of food or drink to be consumed on or off the premises is also treated as a sale of goods and subject to the implied warranty of merchantability [UCC 2–314(1)]. "Merchantable" food is food that is fit to eat.

Courts generally determine whether food is fit to eat on the basis of consumer expectations. Consumers should reasonably expect to find on occasion bones in fish fillets, cherry pits in cherry pie, a nutshell in a package of shelled nuts, and the like—because such substances are natural to the ingredients or the finished food product. In contrast, consumers would not reasonably expect to find an inchworm in a can of peas or a piece of glass in a soft drink—because these substances are *not* natural to the food product.

In the following classic case, the court had to determine whether one should reasonably expect to find a fish bone in fish chowder.

## CLASSIC CASE 23.2

### Webster v. Blue Ship Tea Room, Inc.
Supreme Judicial Court of Massachusetts, 347 Mass. 421 198 N.E.2d 309 (1964).

**BACKGROUND AND FACTS**  Blue Ship Tea Room, Inc., was located in Boston in an old building overlooking the ocean. Webster, who had been born and raised in New England, went to the restaurant and ordered fish chowder. The chowder was milky in color. After three or four spoonfuls, she felt something lodged in her throat. As a result, she underwent two esophagoscopies (procedures in which a telescope-like instrument is used to look into the throat). In the second esophagoscopy, a fish bone was found and removed. Webster filed a suit against the restaurant in a Massachusetts state court for breach of the implied warranty of merchantability. The jury rendered a verdict for Webster, and the restaurant appealed to the state's highest court.

**DECISION AND RATIONALE**  The Supreme Judicial Court of Massachusetts "sympathized with a plaintiff who has suffered a peculiarly New England injury," but it entered a judgment for Blue Ship Tea Room. The court concluded that no breach of warranty had occurred. The question was whether a fish bone made chowder unfit for eating. The court stated that "The joys of life in New England include the ready availability of fresh fish chowder. We should be prepared to cope with the hazards of fish bones, the

CASE 23.2 CONTINUED occasional presence of which in chowders is, it seems to us, to be anticipated, and which, in the light of a hallowed tradition, do not impair their fitness or merchantability."

**IMPACT OF THIS CASE ON TODAY'S LAW**  *This classic case, phrased in memorable language, was an early application of the UCC's implied warranty of merchantability to food products. The case established the rule that consumers should expect to find, on occasion, elements of food products that are natural to the product (such as fish bones in fish chowder). Courts today still apply this rule.*

**THE E-COMMERCE DIMENSION**  *If Webster had made the chowder herself from a recipe that she had found on the Internet, could she have successfully brought an action against its author for a breach of the implied warranty of merchantability? Explain.*

---

## Implied Warranty of Fitness for a Particular Purpose

The **implied warranty of fitness for a particular purpose** arises in the sale or lease of goods when a seller or lessor (merchant or nonmerchant) knows *both* of the following:

1. The particular purpose for which a buyer or lessee will use the goods.
2. That the buyer or lessee is relying on the skill and judgment of the seller or lessor to select suitable goods [UCC 2–315, 2A–213].

**PARTICULAR VERSUS ORDINARY PURPOSE**  A "particular purpose" of the buyer or lessee differs from the "ordinary purpose for which goods are used" (merchantability). Goods can be merchantable but unfit for a particular purpose.

▶ **Example 23.11**  Shakira needs a gallon of paint to match the color of her living room walls—a light shade somewhere between coral and peach. She takes a sample to Sherwin-Williams and requests a gallon of paint of that color. Instead, the salesperson gives her a gallon of bright blue paint.

Here, the salesperson has not breached any warranty of implied merchantability—the bright blue paint is of high quality and suitable for interior walls. The salesperson has breached an implied warranty of fitness for a particular purpose, though, because the paint is not the right color for Shakira's purpose (to match her living room walls). ◀

**KNOWLEDGE AND RELIANCE REQUIREMENTS**  A seller or lessor need not have actual knowledge of the buyer's or lessee's particular purpose. It is sufficient if a seller or lessor "has reason to know" the purpose. For an implied warranty to be created, however, the buyer or lessee must have *relied* on the skill or judgment of the seller or lessor in selecting or furnishing suitable goods. Moreover, the seller or lessor must have reason to know that the buyer or lessee is relying on her or his judgment or skill.

▶ **Example 23.12**  Carlos Fuentes tells Tyrone, a salesperson at GamerPC, that he is looking to buy a new PC, such as the Cyberpower Black Pearl or Velocity Raptor Signature Edition, to use for gaming. Fuentes's statement implies that he needs a PC with a video card that is capable of running fast-paced video games with detailed graphics. Tyrone recommends and sells Carlos a computer that does not have a video card and is too slow to run such video games. By doing so, Tyrone has breached the implied warranty of fitness for a particular purpose. ◀

## Warranties Implied from Prior Dealings or Trade Custom

Implied warranties can also arise (or be excluded or modified) as a result of course of dealing or usage of trade [UCC 2–314(3), 2A–212(3)]. Without evidence to the contrary, when both parties to a sales or lease contract have knowledge of a well-recognized trade custom, the courts will infer that both parties intended for that custom to apply to their contract.

▶ **Example 23.13**  Industry-wide custom is to lubricate a new car before it is delivered. If a dealer fails to lubricate a car, the dealer can be held liable to a buyer for damages resulting from the breach of an implied warranty. (This, of course, would also be negligence on the part of the dealer.) ◀

## Lemon Laws

Purchasers of defective automobiles—called "lemons"—may have remedies in addition to those offered by the UCC. All of the states and the District of Columbia have enacted *lemon laws*.

Basically, state lemon laws provide remedies to consumers who buy automobiles that repeatedly fail to meet standards of quality and performance because they are "lemons." Although lemon laws vary by state, typically they apply to automobiles under warranty that are defective in a way that significantly affects the vehicle's value or use. Lemon laws do not necessarily cover used-car purchases (unless the car is covered by a manufacturer's extended warranty) or vehicles that are leased.[4]

### SELLER HAS HAD OPPORTUNITY TO REMEDY DEFECT

Generally, the seller or manufacturer is given a number of opportunities to remedy the defect (usually four). If the seller fails to cure the problem despite a reasonable number of attempts (as specified by state law), the buyer is entitled to a new car, replacement of defective parts, or return of all consideration paid. Buyers who prevail in a lemon-law dispute may also be entitled to reimbursement of their attorneys' fees.

**ARBITRATION OFTEN REQUIRED** In most states, lemon laws require the owner of the vehicle to notify the dealer or manufacturer of the problem and to provide the dealer or manufacturer with an opportunity to solve it. If the problem remains, the owner must then submit complaints to the arbitration program specified in the manufacturer's warranty before taking the case to court.

Decisions by arbitration panels are binding on the manufacturer—that is, cannot be appealed by the manufacturer to the courts—but usually are not binding on the purchaser. Most major automobile companies operate their own arbitration panels. All arbitration boards must meet state and/or federal standards of impartiality, and some states have established mandatory government-sponsored arbitration programs for lemon-law disputes.

## Magnuson-Moss Warranty Act

The Magnuson-Moss Warranty Act of 1975[5] was designed to prevent deception in warranties by making them easier to understand.

**APPLIES ONLY TO CONSUMER TRANSACTIONS** The Magnuson-Moss Warranty Act modifies UCC warranty rules to some extent when *consumer* transactions are involved. The UCC, however, remains the primary codification of warranty rules for commercial transactions.

Under the Magnuson-Moss Act, no seller is *required* to give a written warranty for consumer goods sold. If a seller chooses to make an express written warranty, however, and the cost of the consumer goods is more than $25, the warranty must be labeled as either "full" or "limited."

A *full warranty* requires free repair or replacement of any defective part. If the product cannot be repaired within a reasonable time, the consumer has the choice of a refund or a replacement without charge. A full warranty can be for an unlimited or limited time period, such as a "full twelve-month warranty."

A *limited warranty* is one in which the buyer's recourse is limited in some fashion, such as to replacement of an item. The fact that only a limited warranty is being given must be conspicuously stated.

**REQUIRES CERTAIN DISCLOSURES** The Magnuson-Moss Act further requires the warrantor to make certain disclosures fully and conspicuously in a single document in "readily understood language." The seller must disclose the name and address of the warrantor, specifically what is warranted, and the procedures for enforcing the warranty. The seller must also clarify that the buyer has legal rights and explain limitations on warranty relief.

See *Concept Summary 23.1* on the following page for a review of the various types of warranties.

### SECTION 4
# OVERLAPPING WARRANTIES

Sometimes, two or more warranties are made in a single transaction. An implied warranty of merchantability, an implied warranty of fitness for a particular purpose, or both can exist in addition to an express warranty. ▶ **Example 23.14** A sales contract for a new car states that "this car engine is warranted to be free from defects for 36,000 miles or thirty-six months, whichever occurs first." This statement creates an express warranty against all defects, as well as an implied warranty that the car will be fit for normal use. ◀

## When the Warranties Are Consistent

The rule under the UCC is that express and implied warranties are construed as *cumulative* if they are consistent with one another [UCC 2–317, 2A–215].

---

4. Note that in some states, such as California, these laws may extend beyond automobile purchases and apply to other consumer goods.
5. 15 U.S.C. Sections 2301–2312.

## CONCEPT SUMMARY 23.1
### Types of Warranties

| CONCEPT | DESCRIPTION |
|---|---|
| **Warranties of Title** | The UCC provides for the following warranties of title [UCC 2–312, 2A–211]:<br>1. *Good title*—A seller warrants that he or she has the right to pass good and rightful title to the goods.<br>2. *No liens*—A seller warrants that the goods sold are free of any encumbrances (claims, charges, or liabilities—usually called *liens*). A lessor warrants that the lessee will not be disturbed in her or his possession of the goods by the claims of a third party.<br>3. *No infringements*—A merchant-seller warrants that the goods are free of infringement claims (claims that a patent, trademark, or copyright has been infringed) by third parties. Lessors make similar warranties. |
| **Express Warranties** | An express warranty arises under the UCC when a seller or lessor indicates any of the following as part of the sale or bargain [UCC 2–313, 2A–210]:<br>1. An affirmation of fact or promise.<br>2. A description of the goods.<br>3. A sample or model shown as conforming to the contract goods. |
| **Implied Warranty of Merchantability** | When a seller or lessor is a merchant who deals in goods of the kind sold or leased, the seller or lessor warrants that the goods sold or leased are properly packaged and labeled, are of proper quality, and are reasonably fit for the ordinary purposes for which such goods are used [UCC 2–314, 2A–212]. |
| **Implied Warranty of Fitness for a Particular Purpose** | An implied warranty of fitness for a particular purpose arises when the buyer's or lessee's purpose or use is known by the seller or lessor, and the buyer or lessee purchases or leases the goods in reliance on the seller's or lessor's selection [UCC 2–315, 2A–213]. |
| **Other Implied Warranties** | Other implied warranties can arise as a result of course of dealing or usage of trade [UCC 2–314(3), 2A–212(3)]. |
| **Magnuson-Moss Warranty Act** | An express written warranty covering consumer goods priced at more than $25, *if made,* must be labeled as either a full warranty or a limited warranty. A full warranty requires free repair or replacement of defective parts and refund or replacement for goods that cannot be repaired in a reasonable time. A limited warranty is one in which the buyer's recourse is limited in some fashion, such as to replacement of an item. Sellers must make certain disclosures to buyers and must state any limitations on a warranty clearly, conspicuously, and in readily understood language. |

In other words, courts interpret two or more warranties as being in agreement with each other unless this construction is unreasonable. If it is unreasonable for the two warranties to be consistent, then the court looks at the intention of the parties to determine which warranty is dominant.

## Conflicting Warranties

If the warranties are *inconsistent,* the courts usually apply the following rules to interpret which warranty is most important:

1. *Express* warranties displace inconsistent *implied* warranties, except implied warranties of fitness for a particular purpose.
2. Samples take precedence over inconsistent general descriptions.
3. Exact or technical specifications displace inconsistent samples or general descriptions.

▶ **Example 23.15** Innova, Ltd., leases a high-speed server from Vernon Sources. The contract contains an express warranty concerning the speed of the CPU and the application programs that the server is capable of running. Innova does not realize that the speed expressly warranted in the contract is insufficient for its needs until it tries to run the software and the server slows to a crawl.

Because Innova made it clear that it was leasing the server to perform certain tasks, Innova files an action against Vernon for breach of the implied warranty of fitness for a particular purpose. In this situation, Innova normally will prevail. Although the express warranty on CPU speed takes precedence over the implied warranty of merchantability, it normally does not take precedence over an implied warranty of fitness for a particular purpose. ◀

## SECTION 5
# WARRANTY DISCLAIMERS AND LIMITATIONS ON LIABILITY

The UCC generally permits warranties to be disclaimed or limited by specific and unambiguous language, provided that this is done in a manner that protects the buyer or lessee from surprise. Because each type of warranty is created in a different way, the manner in which a seller or lessor can disclaim warranties varies with the type of warranty.

## Express Warranties

A seller or lessor can disclaim all oral express warranties by including in the contract a written (or an electronically recorded) disclaimer. The disclaimer must be in language that is clear and conspicuous, and called to a buyer's or lessee's attention [UCC 2–316(1), 2A–214(1)]. This allows the seller or lessor to avoid false allegations that oral warranties were made, and it ensures that only representations made by properly authorized individuals are included in the bargain.

Note, however, that a buyer or lessee must be made aware of any warranty disclaimers or modifications *at the time the contract is formed.* In other words, the seller or lessor cannot modify any warranties or disclaimers made during the bargaining process without the consent of the buyer or lessee.

## Implied Warranties

Generally, unless circumstances indicate otherwise, the implied warranties of merchantability and fitness are disclaimed by an expression such as "as is" or "with all faults." Both parties must be able to clearly understand from the language used that there are no implied warranties [UCC 2–316(3)(a), 2A–214(3)(a)]. (Note, however, that some states have passed consumer protection statutes that forbid "as is" sales or make it illegal to disclaim warranties of merchantability on consumer goods.)

▶ **Case in Point 23.16** Mandy Morningstar advertised a "lovely, eleven-year-old mare" with extensive jumping ability for sale. After examining the horse twice, Sue Hallett contracted to buy the horse. She signed a contract that described the horse as an eleven-year-old mare and as being sold "as is." Shortly after the purchase, a veterinarian determined that the horse was actually sixteen years old and in no condition for jumping. Hallett stopped payment, and Morningstar filed a lawsuit for breach of contract.

The court held that the statement in the contract describing the horse as eleven years old constituted an express warranty, which Morningstar had breached. Although the "as is" clause effectively disclaimed any implied warranties (of merchantability and fitness for a particular purpose, such as jumping), the court ruled that it did not disclaim the express warranty concerning the horse's age.[6] ◀

In the following case, the court explained the rationale behind the effect of an "as is" clause.

---

6. *Morningstar v. Hallett,* 858 A.2d 125 (Pa.Super.Ct. 2004).

## CASE 23.3

### Roberts v. Lanigan Auto Sales
Court of Appeals of Kentucky, __ S.W.3d __, 2013 WL 44020 (2013).

**BACKGROUND AND FACTS** Evan Roberts bought a used car from Lanigan Auto Sales in Elsmere, Kentucky. Roberts and Lanigan signed a contract that contained a clause stating the vehicle was "sold as is . . . without any guarantee express or implied." After the sale, Roberts obtained a report that indicated the car had previously been in an accident and suffered damage to the undercarriage. Roberts filed a suit in a Kentucky state court against Lanigan, alleging fraud. Lanigan argued that it never represented

**CASE 23.3 CONTINUED**
the vehicle had *not* been damaged or involved in an accident and filed a motion to dismiss. The trial court granted the motion on the basis of the "as is" clause in the parties' contract. Roberts appealed.

**DECISION AND RATIONALE** A state intermediate appellate court affirmed the trial court's decision in favor of granting Lanigan Auto Sales' motion to dismiss. The reviewing court looked at Kentucky's version the Uniform Commercial Code, which provides that "unless the circumstances indicate otherwise, all implied warranties are excluded by expressions like 'as is,' 'with all faults' or other language which in common understanding calls the buyer's attention to the exclusion of warranties." The court pointed out that "a valid 'as is' agreement prevents a buyer from holding a seller liable if the thing sold turns out to be worth less than the price paid, because it is impossible for the buyer's injury on account of this disparity to have been caused by the seller and the sole cause of the buyer's injury is the buyer himself or herself."

In other words, the effect of a "sold as is" clause in a sales contract is to shift the assumption of risk regarding the condition of the vehicle to the buyer. Roberts explicitly agreed to make his own assessment of the condition of the vehicle and therefore cannot later claim that he reasonably relied on the seller's representations when agreeing to purchase it.

**THE LEGAL ENVIRONMENT DIMENSION** *What language in a sales contract excludes all implied warranties?*

**THE SOCIAL DIMENSION** *How does an "as is" clause in a sales contract affect the bargain between the buyer and the seller?*

---

**DISCLAIMER OF THE IMPLIED WARRANTY OF MERCHANTABILITY** To specifically disclaim an implied warranty of merchantability, a seller or lessor must mention the word *merchantability*. The disclaimer need not be written, but if it is, the writing (or record) must be conspicuous [UCC 2–316(2), 2A–214(4)].

Under the UCC, a term or clause is conspicuous when it is written or displayed in such a way that a reasonable person would notice it. Conspicuous terms include words set in capital letters, in a larger font size, or in a different color so as to be set off from the surrounding text.

**DISCLAIMER OF THE IMPLIED WARRANTY OF FITNESS** To disclaim an implied warranty of fitness for a particular purpose, the disclaimer must be in a writing (or record) and must be conspicuous. The writing does not have to mention the word *fitness*. It is sufficient if, for instance, the disclaimer states, "There are no warranties that extend beyond the description on the face hereof.

## Buyer's or Lessee's Examination or Refusal to Inspect

If a buyer or lessee examines the goods (or a sample or model) as fully as desired, *there is no implied warranty with respect to defects that a reasonable examination would reveal or defects that are found on examination* [UCC 2–316(3)(b), 2A–214(2)(b)]. Also, if a buyer or lessee refuses to examine the goods on the seller's or lessor's request that he or she do so, there is no implied warranty with respect to reasonably evident defects.

▶ **Example 23.17** Janna buys a table at Gershwin's Home Store. No express warranties are made. Gershwin asks Janna to inspect the table before buying it, but she refuses. Had Janna inspected the table, she would have noticed that one of its legs was obviously cracked, which made it unstable.

Janna takes the table home and sets a lamp on it. The table later collapses, and the lamp starts a fire that causes significant damage. Janna normally will not be able to hold Gershwin's liable for breach of the warranty of merchantability because she refused to examine the table as Gershwin requested. Janna therefore assumed the risk that the table was defective. ◀

## Warranty Disclaimers and Unconscionability

The UCC sections dealing with warranty disclaimers do not refer specifically to unconscionability as a factor. Ultimately, however, the courts will test warranty disclaimers with reference to the UCC's unconscionability standards [UCC 2–302, 2A–108]. Factors such as lack of bargaining position, "take-it-or-leave-it" choices, and a buyer's or lessee's failure to understand or know of a warranty disclaimer will be relevant to the issue of unconscionability.

## Statutes of Limitations

As discussed in Chapter 22, a cause of action for breach of contract under the UCC must be commenced within four years after the breach occurs (unless the parties agree to a shorter period). An action for breach of warranty accrues when the seller or lessor *tenders* delivery, even if the buyer or lessee is unaware of the breach at that time [UCC 2–725(2), 2A–506(2)]. In addition, the nonbreaching party usually must notify the breaching party within a reasonable time after discovering the breach or be barred from pursuing any remedy [UCC 2–607(3)(a), 2A–516(3)].

## Reviewing: Warranties

Shalene Kolchek bought a Great Lakes spa from Val Porter, a dealer who was selling spas at the state fair. Porter told Kolchek that Great Lakes spas were "top of the line" and "the Cadillac of spas" and indicated that the spa she was buying was "fully warranted for three years." Kolchek signed an installment contract. Then, Porter handed her the manufacturer's paperwork and arranged for the spa to be delivered and installed for her. Three months later, Kolchek noticed that one corner of the spa was leaking onto her new deck and causing damage. She complained to Porter, but he did nothing about the problem. Kolchek's family continued to use the spa. Using the information presented in the chapter, answer the following questions.

1. Did Porter's statement that the spa was "top of the line" and "the Cadillac of spas" create any type of warranty? Why or why not?
2. If the paperwork provided to Kolchek after her purchase indicated that the spa had no warranty, would this be an effective disclaimer under the Uniform Commercial Code? Explain.
3. Can Kolchek sue Porter for breach of the implied warranty of merchantability because the spa leaked? Explain.
4. Suppose that one year later, Pacific Credit Union contacted Kolchek and claimed that it had a security interest in the spa. Would this be a breach of any of the title warranties discussed in the chapter? Explain.

**DEBATE THIS . . .** *No express warranties should be created by the oral statements made by salespersons about a product.*

## Terms and Concepts

express warranty 403
implied warranty 404

implied warranty of fitness for a particular purpose 407

implied warranty of merchantability 405

## Issue Spotters

1. General Construction Company (GCC) tells Industrial Supplies, Inc., that it needs an adhesive to do a particular job. Industrial provides a five-gallon bucket of a certain brand. When it does not perform to GCC's specifications, GCC sues Industrial, which claims, "We didn't expressly promise anything." What should GCC argue? **(See page 407.)**
2. Stella bought a cup of coffee at the Roasted Bean Drive-Thru. The coffee had been heated to 190 degrees and consequently had dissolved the inside of the cup. When Stella lifted the lid, the cup collapsed, spilling the contents on her lap. To recover for third-degree burns on her thighs, Stella filed a suit against the Roasted Bean. Can Stella recover for breach of the implied warranty of merchantability? Why or why not? **(See page 405.)**

• **Check your answers to the Issue Spotters against the answers provided in Appendix E at the end of this text.**

## Business Scenarios

**23–1. Implied Warranties.** Moon, a farmer, needs to install a two-thousand-pound piece of equipment in his barn. This will require lifting the equipment thirty feet up into a hayloft. Moon goes to Davidson Hardware and tells Davidson that he needs some heavy-duty rope to be used on his farm. Davidson recommends a one-inch-thick nylon rope, and Moon purchases two hundred feet of it. Moon ties the rope around the piece of equipment; puts the rope through a pulley; and, with a tractor, lifts the equipment off the ground. Suddenly, the rope breaks. The equipment crashes to the ground and is severely damaged. Moon files a suit against Davidson for breach of the implied warranty of fitness for a particular purpose. Discuss how successful Moon will be in his suit. **(See page 404.)**

**23–2. Warranty Disclaimers.** Tandy purchased a washing machine from Marshall Appliances. The sales contract included a provision explicitly disclaiming all express or implied warranties, including the implied warranty of merchantability. The disclaimer was printed in the same size and color as the rest of the contract. The machine never functioned properly. Tandy sought a refund of the purchase price, claiming that Marshall had breached the implied warranty of merchantability. Can Tandy recover the purchase price, notwithstanding the warranty disclaimer in the contract? Explain. **(See page 410.)**

## Business Case Problems

### 23–3. BUSINESS CASE PROBLEM WITH SAMPLE ANSWER: Express Warranties.

*Videotape is recorded magnetically. The magnetic particles that constitute the recorded image are bound to the tape's polyester base. The binder that holds the particles to the base breaks down over time. This breakdown, which is called sticky shed syndrome, causes the image to deteriorate. The Walt Disney Co. made many of its movies available on tape. Buena Vista Home Entertainment, Inc., sold the tapes, which it described as part of a "Gold Collection" or "Masterpiece Collection." The advertising included such statements as "Give Your Children the memories of a lifetime—Collect Each Timeless Masterpiece!" and "Available for a Limited Time Only!" Charmaine Schreib and others who bought the tapes filed a suit in an Illinois state court against Disney and Buena Vista, alleging, among other things, breach of warranty. The plaintiffs claimed that the defendants' marketing promised the tapes would last for generations. In reality, the tapes were as subject to sticky shed syndrome as other tapes. Did the ads create an express warranty? In whose favor should the court rule on this issue? Explain. [Schreib v. The Walt Disney Co., __ N.E.2d __, 2006 WL 573008 (Ill.App. 1 Dist. 2006)]* **(See page 403.)**

- **For a sample answer to Problem 23–3, go to Appendix F at the end of this text.**

**23–4. Implied Warranties.** Peter and Tanya Rothing operated Diamond R Stables near Belgrade, Montana, where they bred, trained, and sold horses. Arnold Kallestad owned a ranch in Gallatin County, Montana, where he grew hay and grain, and raised Red Angus cattle. For more than twenty years, Kallestad had sold between three hundred and one thousand tons of hay annually, sometimes advertising it for sale in the *Bozeman Daily Chronicle*. In 2001, the Rothings bought hay from Kallestad for $90 a ton. They received delivery on April 23. In less than two weeks, at least nine of the Rothings' horses exhibited symptoms of poisoning that was diagnosed as botulism. Before the outbreak was over, nineteen animals had died. Robert Whitlock, associate professor of medicine and the director of the Botulism Laboratory at the University of Pennsylvania, concluded that Kallestad's hay was the source. The Rothings filed a suit in a Montana state court against Kallestad, claiming, in part, breach of the implied warranty of merchantability. Kallestad asked the court to dismiss this claim on the ground that, if botulism had been present, it had been in no way foreseeable. Should the court grant this request? Why or why not? [*Rothing v. Kallestad*, 337 Mont. 193, 159 P.3d 222 (2007)] **(See page 404.)**

**23–5. Spotlight on Apple—Implied Warranties.** Alan Vitt purchased an iBook G4 laptop computer from Apple, Inc. Shortly after the one-year warranty expired, the laptop failed to work due to a weakness in the product manufacture. Vitt sued Apple, arguing that the laptop should have lasted "at least a couple of years," which Vitt believed was a reasonable consumer expectation for a laptop. Vitt claimed that Apple's descriptions of the laptop as "durable," "rugged," "reliable," and "high performance" were affirmative statements concerning the quality and performance of the laptop, which Apple did not meet. How should the court rule? Why? [*Vitt v. Apple Computer, Inc.*, 2012 WL 627702 (9th Cir. 2011)] **(See page 407.)**

**23–6. Implied Warranties.** Bariven, S.A., agreed to buy 26,000 metric tons of powdered milk for $123.5 million from Absolute Trading Corp. to be delivered in shipments from China to Venezuela. After the first three shipments, China halted dairy exports due to the presence of melamine in some products. Absolute assured Bariven that its milk was safe, and when China resumed dairy exports, Absolute delivered sixteen more shipments. Tests of samples of the milk revealed that it contained dangerous levels of melamine. Did Absolute breach any implied warranties? Discuss. [*Absolute Trading Corp. v. Bariven S.A.*, 2013 WL 49735 (11th Cir. 2013)] **(See page 404.)**

**23–7. A QUESTION OF ETHICS: Lemon Laws.**

 *Randal Schweiger bought a 2008 Kia Spectra EX from Kia Motors America, Inc., for his stepdaughter, April Kirichkow. The cost was $17,231, plus sales tax, fees, and other items. April had trouble starting the car. The Kia dealership replaced different parts of the motor several times, but was unable to fix the problem. Schweiger sought a refund under the state's lemon law. When they could not agree on the amount, Schweiger filed a suit in a Wisconsin state court against Kia. From a judgment in Schweiger's favor, Kia appealed. [Schweiger v. Kia Motors America, Inc., __ Wis.2d __, __ N.W.2d __, 2013 WL 1149765 (2013)]* **(See page 407.)**

(a) Kia offered a refund of $3,306.24. Should this offer bar Schweiger's claim for a refund? Why or why not?

(b) Schweiger claimed that Kia's offer did not include the $1,301 cost of a service contract. Kia argued that the "payoff to the lender" of $13,060.16, which Schweiger agreed was the correct amount, "would by definition refund the cost of the service contract." The court found "no logical basis" for this argument. Is it ethical for a party to argue a position for which there is no logical basis? Discuss.

## Legal Reasoning Group Activity

**23–8. Warranties.** Milan purchased saffron extract, marketed as "America's Hottest New Way to a Flat Belly," online from Dr. Chen. The Web site stated that recently published studies showed a significant weight loss (more than 25 percent) for people who used pure saffron extract as a supplement *without diet and exercise*. Dr. Chen said that the saffron suppresses appetite by increasing levels of serotonin, which reduces emotional eating. Milan took the extract as directed without any resulting weight loss. **(See page 403.)**

(a) The first group will determine whether Dr. Chen's Web site made any express warranty on the saffron extract or its effectiveness in causing weight loss.

(b) The second group will discuss whether the implied warranty of merchantability applies to the purchase of weight-loss supplements.

(c) The third group will decide if Dr. Chen's sale of saffron extract breached the implied warranty of fitness for a particular purpose.

## CHAPTER 24

# INTERNATIONAL LAW IN A GLOBAL ECONOMY

International business transactions are not unique to the modern world. Commerce has always crossed national borders. What is new in our day is the dramatic growth in world trade and the emergence of a global business community. Exchanges of goods, services, and ideas (intellectual property) on a global level are now routine. Therefore, students of business law and the legal environment should be familiar with the laws pertaining to international business transactions.

Laws affecting the international legal environment of business include both international law and national law. **International law** can be defined as a body of law—formed as a result of international customs, treaties, and organizations—that governs relations among or between nations.

International law may be public, creating standards for the nations themselves. It may also be private, establishing international standards for private transactions that cross national borders. (Can officials legally search electronic devices, including laptops and smartphones, of persons who cross national borders? See this chapter's *Insight into the Global Environment* feature on the following page for the answer.) **National law** is the law of a particular nation, such as Brazil, Germany, Japan, or the United States. In this chapter, we examine how both international law and national law frame business operations in the global context.

## SECTION 1
## INTERNATIONAL LAW

The major difference between international law and national law is that government authorities can enforce national law. What government, however, can enforce international law? By definition, a *nation* is a sovereign entity—which means that there is no higher authority to which that nation must submit.

▶ **Example 24.1** In February 2013, North Korea performed its third underground nuclear weapons test in violation of United Nations Security Council resolutions. Although world leaders uniformly condemned North Korea's action, the United Nations had no ready means of enforcing its resolutions. ◀

If a nation violates an international law and persuasive tactics fail, other countries or international organizations have no recourse except to take coercive actions. Coercive actions might include economic sanctions, severance of diplomatic relations, boycotts, and, as a last resort, war against the violating nation.

International law attempts to reconcile each country's need to be the final authority over its own affairs with the desire of nations to benefit economically from trade and harmonious relations with one another. Sovereign nations can, and do, voluntarily agree to be governed in certain respects by international law, usually for the purpose of facilitating international trade and commerce. As a result, a body of international law has evolved.

### Sources of International Law

Basically, there are three sources of international law: international customs, treaties and international agreements, and international organizations and conferences. We look at each of these sources here.

**INTERNATIONAL CUSTOMS** One important source of international law consists of the international customs that have evolved among nations in their relations with one another. Article 38(1) of the Statute of the International Court of Justice refers to an international custom as "evidence of a general practice accepted as law." The legal principles and doctrines that you will read about shortly are rooted in international customs and traditions that have evolved over time in the international arena.

# INSIGHT INTO THE GLOBAL ENVIRONMENT
## Border Searches of Your Electronic Devices

Every year, tens of millions of travelers arrive at U.S. borders where they are subject to a search. Of these travelers, about 12 million undergo a secondary screening, and approximately five thousand of these screenings involve an electronic device. About three hundred devices—computers, BlackBerrys, tablets, and smartphones—are sent to the Immigration and Customs Enforcement forensics laboratory in Fairfax, Virginia, for further examination.

The U.S. government has historically had a broad power to search travelers and their property when they enter this country. That power includes the right to inspect papers and other physical documents in the possession of anyone entering the United States, including U.S. citizens.

### A Legal Challenge to Extensive Searches of Electronic Devices

Increasingly, however, instead of being carried in physical form, documents are carried on the hard drives of laptop computers, in tablets, or in smartphones. Indeed, a person might have thousands and thousands of photos, e-mails, video clips, and documents on the hard drive of a laptop. Does the government's power to conduct border searches give it the right to rummage through all of the data on an electronic device? Several recent lawsuits have raised this issue.

When Pascal Abidor, a Ph.D. student who has dual U.S. and French citizenship, traveled by train from Canada to New York, U.S. Customs and Border Control agents pulled him aside and required him to log on to his computer. They then examined much of its contents. Abidor was released after a few hours, but the Department of Homeland Security kept his laptop for eleven days. Abidor challenged the search. His complaint alleged:

> [A government policy that authorizes] the suspicionless search of the contents of Americans' laptops, cell phones, cameras, and other electronic devices at the international border . . . violates the constitutional rights of American citizens to keep the private and expressive details of their lives, as well as sensitive information obtained or created in the course of their work, free from unwarranted government scrutiny.

Although the lawsuit was filed several years ago, as we go to press, there is no information available on the verdict.[a]

### Protecting Attorney-Client Privilege

Border searches present a special problem for attorneys because they have a duty to protect the attorney-client privilege by preventing anyone, including the government, from accessing client communications. To avoid this problem, attorneys should never keep client files on a digital device that they are taking abroad. If the attorneys will need the files during the trip abroad, they can be put on a server in the "cloud."

#### LEGAL CRITICAL THINKING
#### INSIGHT INTO THE TECHNOLOGICAL ENVIRONMENT

*What are some steps that businesspersons can take to avoid any issues at the border with respect to the contents of their electronic devices?*

---

**a.** *Abidor v. Napolitano,* 10-cv-04059-ERK (E.D.N.Y.).

---

**TREATIES AND INTERNATIONAL AGREEMENTS** Treaties and other explicit agreements between or among foreign nations provide another important source of international law. A **treaty** is an agreement or contract between two or more nations that must be authorized and ratified by the supreme power of each nation. Under Article II, Section 2, of the U.S. Constitution, the president has the power "by and with the Advice and Consent of the Senate, to make Treaties, provided two-thirds of the Senators present concur."

A *bilateral* agreement, as the term implies, is an agreement formed by two nations to govern their commercial exchanges or other relations with one another. A *multilateral* agreement is formed by several nations. For instance, regional trade associations such as the Andean Community, the Association of Southeast Asian Nations, and the European Union are the result of multilateral trade agreements.

**INTERNATIONAL ORGANIZATIONS** The term **international organization** generally refers to an organization composed mainly of officials of member nations and usually established by treaty. The United States is a member of more than one hundred multilateral and bilateral organizations, including at least twenty through the United Nations.

***Adopt Resolutions.*** These organizations adopt resolutions, declarations, and other types of standards that often require nations to behave in a particular manner. The General Assembly of the United Nations, for instance, has adopted numerous nonbinding resolutions and declarations that embody principles of international law. Disputes with respect to these resolutions and declarations may be brought before the International Court of Justice. That court, however, normally has authority to settle legal disputes only when nations voluntarily submit to its jurisdiction.

***Create Uniform Rules.*** The United Nations Commission on International Trade Law has made considerable progress in establishing uniformity in international law as it relates to trade and commerce. One of the commission's most significant creations to date is the 1980 Convention on Contracts for the International Sale of Goods (CISG).

Recall from Chapters 20 through 22 that the CISG is similar to Article 2 of the Uniform Commercial Code in that it is designed to settle disputes between parties to sales contracts. It spells out the duties of international buyers and sellers that will apply if the parties have not agreed otherwise in their contracts. The CISG governs only sales contracts between trading partners in nations that have ratified the CISG, however.

## Common Law and Civil Law Systems

Companies operating in foreign nations are subject to the laws of those nations. In addition, international disputes are often resolved through the court systems of foreign nations. Therefore, businesspersons should understand that legal systems around the globe generally are divided into *common law* and *civil law* systems. Exhibit 24–1 below indicates some of the nations that use civil law systems and some that use common law systems.

**EXHIBIT 24–1 The Legal Systems of Selected Nations**

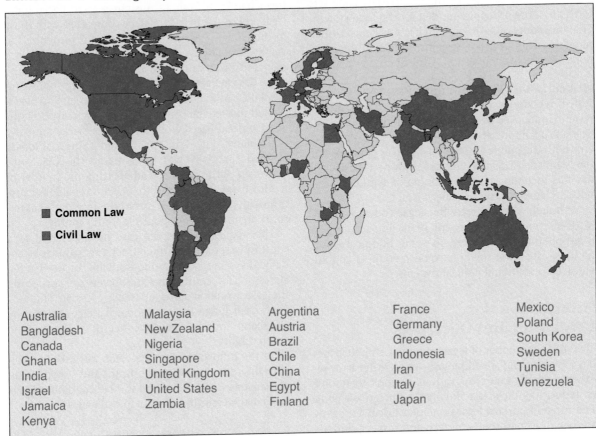

■ Common Law
■ Civil Law

| | | | | |
|---|---|---|---|---|
| Australia | Malaysia | Argentina | France | Mexico |
| Bangladesh | New Zealand | Austria | Germany | Poland |
| Canada | Nigeria | Brazil | Greece | South Korea |
| Ghana | Singapore | Chile | Indonesia | Sweden |
| India | United Kingdom | China | Iran | Tunisia |
| Israel | United States | Egypt | Italy | Venezuela |
| Jamaica | Zambia | Finland | Japan | |
| Kenya | | | | |

**COMMON LAW SYSTEMS** As discussed in Chapter 1, in a common law system, the courts independently develop the rules governing certain areas of law, such as torts and contracts. These common law rules apply to all areas not covered by statutory law. Although the common law doctrine of *stare decisis* obligates judges to follow precedential decisions in their jurisdictions, courts may modify or even overturn precedents when deemed necessary.

**CIVIL LAW SYSTEMS** In contrast to common law countries, most European nations, as well as nations in Latin America, Africa, and Asia, base their legal systems on Roman civil law, or "code law." The term *civil law,* as used here, refers not to civil as opposed to criminal law but to *codified* law—an ordered grouping of legal principles enacted into law by a legislature or other governing body.

In a **civil law system,** the primary source of law is a statutory code. Courts interpret the code and apply the rules to individual cases, but courts may not depart from the code and develop their own laws. Judicial precedents are not binding, as they are in a common law system. In theory, the law code sets forth all of the principles needed for the legal system. Trial procedures also differ in civil law systems. Unlike judges in common law systems, judges in civil systems often actively question witnesses.

**ISLAMIC LEGAL SYSTEMS** A third, less prevalent, legal system is common in Islamic countries, where the law is often influenced by *sharia,* the religious law of Islam. *Sharia* is a comprehensive code of principles that governs both the public and the private lives of persons of the Islamic faith. *Sharia* directs many aspects of day-to-day life, including politics, economics, banking, business law, contract law, and social issues.

Although *sharia* affects the legal codes of many Muslim countries, the extent of its impact and its interpretation vary widely. In some Middle Eastern nations, aspects of *sharia* have been codified and are enforced by national judicial systems.

# International Principles and Doctrines

Over time, a number of legal principles and doctrines have evolved and are employed—to a greater or lesser extent—by the courts of various nations to resolve or reduce conflicts that involve a foreign element. The three important legal principles discussed below are based primarily on courtesy and respect, and are applied in the interests of maintaining harmonious relations among nations.

One way to understand two of these principles—*comity* and the *act of state doctrine*—is to consider the relationships among the states in our federal form of government. Each state honors (gives "full faith and credit" to) the contracts, property deeds, wills, and other legal obligations formed in other states, as well as judicial decisions with respect to such obligations. On a global basis, nations similarly attempt to honor judgments rendered in other countries when it is feasible to do so. Of course, in the United States the states are constitutionally required to honor other states' actions, whereas international law does not *require* nations to honor the actions of other nations.

**THE PRINCIPLE OF COMITY** The principle of **comity** basically refers to legal reciprocity. One nation will defer and give effect to the executive, legislative, and judicial acts of another country, as long as the acts are consistent with the law and public policy of the accommodating nation. For instance, a U.S. court ordinarily will recognize and enforce a default judgment (see Chapter 3) from an Australian court because the legal procedures in Australia are compatible with those in the United States. Nearly all nations recognize the validity of marriage decrees (at least those between a man and a woman) issued in another country.

▶ **Case in Point 24.2** Karen Goldberg's husband was killed in a terrorist bombing in Israel. She filed a lawsuit in a federal court in New York against UBS AG, a Switzerland-based global financial services company with many offices in the United States. Goldberg claimed that UBS was liable under the U.S. Anti-Terrorism Act for aiding and abetting the murder of her husband. She argued that UBS was liable because it provided financial services to the international terrorist organizations responsible for his murder.

UBS requested that the case be transferred to a court in Israel, which would offer a remedy "substantially the same" as the one available in the United States. The court refused, however. Transferring the case would require an Israeli court to take evidence and judge the emotional damage suffered by Goldberg, "raising distinct concerns of comity and enforceability."[1] ◀

In the following case, the court was asked to balance interests that were significant and serious to all of the parties. The defendant wanted the court to give particular weight to the principle of comity.

---

1. *Goldberg v. UBS AG,* 690 F.Supp.2d 92 (E.D.N.Y. 2010).

# CASE 24.1

## Linde v. Arab Bank, PLCᵃ
United States Court of Appeals, Second Circuit, 706 F.3d 92 (2013).

**COMPANY PROFILE** Founded in 1930, Arab Bank is one of the largest financial institutions in the Middle East. Headquartered in Jordan, it serves clients in more than 500 branches in thirty countries, including branches in Australia, New York, and Switzerland. The bank is a major economic engine in Jordan and throughout the Middle East/Northern Africa, providing modern banking services and capital, and facilitating development and trade throughout the region.

**BACKGROUND AND FACTS** Victims of terrorist attacks that were committed in Israel between 1995 and 2004—during a period commonly referred to as the Second Intifada—filed a suit in a federal district court against Arab Bank, PLC, seeking damages under the Anti-Terrorism Act (ATA) and the Alien Tort Claims Act. According to plaintiffs, Arab Bank provided financial services and support to the terrorists. Over several years and despite multiple discovery orders, the bank failed to produce certain documents relevant to the case. As a result, the court issued an order imposing sanctions. Arab Bank appealed, arguing that the order was an abuse of discretion.

**DECISION AND RATIONALE** The U.S. Court of Appeals for the Second Circuit affirmed the lower court's decision and order. The Bank argued that the requested documents were covered by foreign bank secrecy laws such that their disclosure would subject the Bank to criminal prosecution and in several foreign jurisdictions. The trial court had noted that the documents that plaintiffs had already obtained "tended to support the inference that Arab Bank knew that its services benefitted terrorists." Therefore, the court reasoned that the lower court had not abused its discretion in concluding that the interest of other nations in enforcing bank secrecy laws are outweighed by the need to impede terrorism.

Arab Bank further argued that the trial court's order to produce the documents should be vacated because they offend "international comity." "This argument derives from the notion that the sanctions force foreign authorities either to waive enforcement of their bank secrecy laws or to enforce those laws, and in so doing create an allegedly devastating financial liability for the leading financial institutions in their region." The reviewing court stated that international comity "requires a particularized analysis of the respective interests of the foreign nation and the requesting nation." Therefore, the analysis requires a weighing of all of the relevant interests of all of the nations affected by the court's decision. The reviewing court pointed out that the trial court did take into account the United States' interests in the effective prosecution of civil claims under the Anti-Terrorism Act and such an analysis did not "so obviously offend international comity."

**THE ETHICAL DIMENSION** *Is it unethical to give the interest of fighting terrorism precedence over an international legal principle? Discuss.*

**THE LEGAL ENVIRONMENT DIMENSION** *What interests were at stake in the dispute at the heart of this case?*

---

**a.** *PLC* stands for "public liability company," which is a publicly traded company in England and Ireland. This business form is the equivalent to a publicly traded corporation in the United States.

---

**THE ACT OF STATE DOCTRINE** The **act of state doctrine** provides that the judicial branch of one country will not examine the validity of public acts committed by a recognized foreign government within the latter's own territory.

▶ **Case in Point 24.3** Spectrum Stores, Inc., a gasoline retailer in the United States, filed a lawsuit in a U.S. court against Citgo Petroleum Corporation, which is owned by the government of Venezuela. Spectrum alleged that Citgo had conspired with other oil companies in Venezuela and Saudi Arabia to limit production of crude oil and thereby fix the prices of petroleum products sold in the United States.

Because Citgo is owned by a foreign government, the U.S. court dismissed the case under the act of state doctrine. A government controls the natural resources, such as oil reserves, within its territory. A U.S. court will not rule on the validity of a foreign government's acts within its own territory.[2] ◄

**When a Foreign Government Takes Private Property.** The act of state doctrine can have important consequences for individuals and firms doing business with, and investing in, other countries. This doctrine is frequently employed in cases involving expropriation or confiscation.

**Expropriation** occurs when a government seizes a privately owned business or privately owned goods for a proper public purpose and awards just compensation. When a government seizes private property for an illegal purpose and without just compensation, the taking is referred to as a **confiscation.** The line between these two forms of taking is sometimes blurred because of differing interpretations of what is illegal and what constitutes just compensation.

▶ **Example 24.4** Flaherty, Inc., a U.S. company, owns a mine in Brazil. The government of Brazil seizes the mine for public use and claims that the profits Flaherty has already realized from the mine constitute just compensation. Flaherty disagrees, but the act of state doctrine may prevent the company's recovery in a U.S. court. ◄ Note that in a case alleging that a foreign government has wrongfully taken the plaintiff's property, the defendant government has the burden of proving that the taking was an expropriation, not a confiscation.

**Doctrine May Immunize a Foreign Government's Actions.** When applicable, both the act of state doctrine and the doctrine of *sovereign immunity,* which we discuss next, tend to shield foreign nations from the jurisdiction of U.S. courts. As a result, firms or individuals who own property overseas generally have little legal protection against government actions in the countries where they operate.

**THE DOCTRINE OF SOVEREIGN IMMUNITY** When certain conditions are satisfied, the doctrine of **sovereign immunity** exempts foreign nations from the jurisdiction of the U.S. courts. In 1976, Congress codified this rule in the Foreign Sovereign Immunities Act (FSIA).[3]

The FSIA exclusively governs the circumstances in which an action may be brought in the United States

against a foreign nation, including attempts to attach a foreign nation's property. Because the law is jurisdictional in nature, a plaintiff generally has the burden of showing that a defendant is not entitled to sovereign immunity.

**When a Foreign State Will Not Be Immune.** Section 1605 of the FSIA sets forth the major exceptions to the jurisdictional immunity of a foreign state. A foreign state is not immune from the jurisdiction of U.S. courts in the following situations:

1. When the foreign state has waived its immunity either explicitly or by implication.
2. When the foreign state has engaged in commercial activity within the United States or in commercial activity outside the United States that has "a direct effect in the United States."
3. When the foreign state has committed a tort in the United States or has violated certain international laws.

**Application of the Act.** When courts apply the FSIA, questions frequently arise as to whether an entity is a "foreign state" and what constitutes a "commercial activity." Under Section 1603 of the FSIA, a *foreign state* includes both a political subdivision of a foreign state and an instrumentality (department or agency of any branch of a government) of a foreign state.

Section 1603 broadly defines a *commercial activity* as a regular course of commercial conduct, transaction, or act that is carried out by a foreign state within the United States. Section 1603, however, does not describe the particulars of what constitutes a commercial activity. Thus, the courts are left to decide whether a particular activity is governmental or commercial in nature.

**SECTION 2**

# DOING BUSINESS INTERNATIONALLY

A U.S. domestic firm can engage in international business transactions in a number of ways. The simplest way is for U.S. firms to **export** their goods and services to foreign markets. Alternatively, a U.S. firm can establish foreign production facilities to be closer to the foreign market or markets in which its products are sold. The advantages may include lower labor

---

2. *Spectrum Stores, Inc. v. Citgo Petroleum Corp.,* 632 F.3d 938 (5th Cir. 2011).
3. 28 U.S.C. Sections 1602–1611.

costs, fewer government regulations, and lower taxes and trade barriers. A domestic firm can also obtain revenues by licensing its technology to an existing foreign company or by selling franchises to overseas entities.

## Exporting

Exporting can take two forms: direct exporting and indirect exporting. In *direct exporting,* a U.S. company signs a sales contract with a foreign purchaser that provides for the conditions of shipment and payment for the goods. (International contracts for the purchase and sale of goods, as well as the use of letters of credit to make payments, were discussed in Chapters 20 through 22.)

If sufficient business develops in a foreign country, a U.S. company may establish a specialized marketing organization there by appointing a foreign agent or a foreign distributor. This is called *indirect exporting.*

When a U.S. firm wishes to limit its involvement in an international market, it will typically establish an *agency relationship* with a foreign firm. The foreign firm then acts as the U.S. firm's agent and can enter contracts in the foreign location on behalf of the principal (the U.S. company).

**DISTRIBUTORSHIPS** When a foreign country represents a substantial market, a U.S. firm may wish to appoint a distributor located in that country. The U.S. firm and the distributor enter into a **distribution agreement.** This is a contract setting out the terms and conditions of the distributorship, such as price, currency of payment, guarantee of supply availability, and method of payment. Disputes concerning distribution agreements may involve jurisdictional or other issues, as well as contract law.

**THE NATIONAL EXPORT INITIATIVE** Although the United States is one of the world's major exporters, exports make up a much smaller share of annual output in the United States than they do in our most important trading partners. In the past, the United States has not promoted exports as actively as many other nations have.

In an effort to increase U.S. exports, the Obama administration created the National Export Initiative (NEI) with a goal of doubling U.S. exports by 2015. Some commentators believe that another goal of the NEI is to reduce outsourcing—the practice of having manufacturing or other activities performed in lower-wage countries such as China and India.

***Export Promotion.*** An important component of the NEI is the Export Promotion Cabinet, which includes officials from sixteen government agencies and departments. All cabinet members must submit detailed plans to the president, outlining the steps that they will take to increase U.S. exports.

The U.S. Commerce Department plays a leading role in the NEI, and hundreds of its trade experts serve as advocates to help some twenty thousand U.S. companies increase their export sales. In addition, the Commerce Department and other Export Promotion Cabinet members work to promote U.S. exports in the high-growth developing markets of Brazil, China, and India. The members also identify market opportunities in fast-growing sectors, such as environmental goods and services, biotechnology, and renewable energy.

***Increased Export Financing.*** Under the NEI, the Export-Import Bank of the United States increased the financing that it makes available to small and medium-sized businesses by 50 percent. In the initial phase, the bank added hundreds of new small-business clients that sell a wide variety of products, from sophisticated polymers to date palm trees and nanotechnology-based cosmetics.

## Manufacturing Abroad

An alternative to direct or indirect exporting is the establishment of foreign manufacturing facilities. Typically, U.S. firms establish manufacturing plants abroad when they believe that by doing so they will reduce costs. Costs for labor, shipping, and raw materials may be lower in foreign nations, which can enable the business to compete more effectively in foreign markets.

Foreign firms have done the same in the United States. Sony, Nissan, and other Japanese manufacturers have established U.S. plants to avoid import duties that the U.S. Congress may impose on Japanese products entering this country.

**LICENSING** A U.S. firm may license a foreign manufacturing company to use its copyrighted, patented, or trademarked intellectual property or trade secrets. Basically, licensing allows the foreign firm to use an established brand name for a fee. A licensing agreement with a foreign-based firm is much the same as any other licensing agreement (see Chapters 8, 9, and 12). Its terms require a payment of royalties on some basis—such as so many cents per unit produced or a certain percentage of profits from units sold in a particular geographic territory.

▶ **Example 24.5** The Coca-Cola Bottling Company licenses firms worldwide to use (and keep confidential) its secret formula for the syrup used in its soft drink. In return, the company receives a percentage of the income gained from the sale of Coca-Cola by those firms. ◀

The firm that receives the license can take advantage of an established reputation for quality. The firm that grants the license receives income from the foreign sales of its products and also establishes a global reputation. Once a firm's trademark is known worldwide, the demand for other products manufactured or sold by that firm may increase—obviously, an important consideration.

**FRANCHISING** Franchising is a well-known form of licensing and is evident the world over. The owner of a trademark, trade name, or copyright (the franchisor) licenses another (the franchisee) to use the mark, name, or copyright, under certain conditions or limitations, in the selling of goods or services. Franchising allows the franchisor to maintain greater control over the business operation than is possible with most other licensing agreements. In return, the franchisee pays a fee, usually based on a monthly percentage of gross or net sales. Examples of international franchises include Holiday Inn and Hertz.

**INVESTING IN A WHOLLY OWNED SUBSIDIARY OR A JOINT VENTURE** Another way to expand into a foreign market is to establish a wholly owned subsidiary firm in a foreign country. In many European countries, a subsidiary would likely take the form of a *société anonyme* (S.A.), which is similar to a U.S. corporation. In German-speaking nations, it would be called an *Aktiengesellschaft* (A.G.).

When a wholly owned subsidiary is established, the parent company remains in the United States. The parent maintains complete ownership of all of the facilities in the foreign country, as well as total authority and control over all phases of the operation.

A U.S. firm can also expand into international markets through a *joint venture*. In a joint venture, the U.S. company owns only part of the operation. The rest is owned either by local owners in the foreign country or by another foreign entity. All of the firms involved in a joint venture share responsibilities, as well as profits and liabilities.

# REGULATION OF SPECIFIC BUSINESS ACTIVITIES

Doing business abroad can affect the economies, foreign policies, domestic politics, and other national interests of the countries involved. For this reason, nations impose laws to restrict or facilitate international business. Controls may also be imposed by international agreements.

## Investment Protections

Firms that invest in foreign nations face the risk that the foreign government may expropriate the investment property. Expropriation, as mentioned earlier in this chapter, occurs when property is taken and the owner is paid just compensation for what is taken. This generally does not violate accepted principles of international law.

Confiscating property without compensation (or without adequate compensation), in contrast, normally violates international law. Few remedies are available for confiscation of property by a foreign government. Claims are often resolved by lump-sum settlements after negotiations between the United States and the taking nation.

Because the possibility of confiscation may deter potential investors, many countries guarantee compensation to foreign investors if their property is taken. A guaranty can be in the form of national constitutional or statutory laws or provisions in international treaties. As further protection for foreign investments, some countries provide insurance for their citizens' investments abroad.

## Export Controls

Article I, Section 9, of the U.S. Constitution provides that "No Tax or Duty shall be laid on Articles exported from any State." Thus, Congress cannot impose any export taxes.

Congress can, however, use a variety of other devices to restrict or encourage exports, including the following:

1. *Export quotas.* Congress sets export quotas on various items, such as grain being sold abroad.
2. *Restrictions on technology exports.* Under the Export Administration Act of 1979,[4] the flow of techno-

---

**4.** 50 U.S.C. Sections 2401–2420.

logically advanced products and technical data can be restricted.

3. *Incentives and subsidies.* The United States (and other nations) also uses incentives and subsidies to stimulate other exports and thereby aid domestic businesses. ▶ **Example 24.6**  Under the Export Trading Company Act of 1982,[5] U.S. banks are encouraged to invest in export trading companies, which are formed when exporting firms join together to export a line of goods. The Export-Import Bank of the United States provides financial assistance, primarily in the form of credit guaranties given to commercial banks that in turn lend funds to U.S. exporting companies. ◀

## Import Controls

All nations have restrictions on imports, and the United States is no exception. Restrictions include strict prohibitions, quotas, and tariffs.

**PROHIBITED GOODS**  Under the Trading with the Enemy Act of 1917,[6] no goods may be imported from nations that have been designated enemies of the United States. Other laws prohibit the importation of illegal drugs, books that urge insurrection against the United States,[7] and agricultural products that pose dangers to domestic crops or animals.

The importation of goods that infringe U.S. patents is also prohibited. The International Trade Commission is the government agency that investigates allegations that imported goods infringe U.S. patents and imposes penalties if necessary.

▶ **Case in Point 24.7**  Fuji Photo Film Company owned numerous patents for disposable cameras, including the plastic shell covering. Jazz Photo Corporation collected used plastic shells in the United States, shipped them abroad to have new film inserted, and imported the refurbished shells back into the United States for sale. The International Trade Commission (ITC) determined that Jazz's resale of shells originally sold outside the United States infringed Fuji's patents. The ITC ordered Jazz to stop the imports. When Jazz imported and sold 27 million more refurbished shells, Fuji complained to the ITC, which fined Jazz more than $13.5 million.[8] ◀

---

5. 15 U.S.C. Sections 4001, 4003.
6. 12 U.S.C. Section 95a.
7. Because numerous resources that advocate the overthrow of the U.S. government are available on the Internet, this prohibition against importing books that urge insurrection is rather meaningless.
8. *Fuji Photo Film Co. v. International Trade Commission,* 474 F.3d 1281 (Fed.Cir. 2007).

**QUOTAS AND TARIFFS**  Limits on the amounts of goods that can be imported are known as **quotas.** At one time, the United States had legal quotas on the number of automobiles that could be imported from Japan. Today, Japan "voluntarily" restricts the number of automobiles exported to the United States.

**Tariffs** are taxes on imports. A tariff is usually a percentage of the value of the import, but it can be a flat rate per unit (such as per barrel of oil). Tariffs raise the prices of imported goods, causing some consumers to purchase domestically manufactured goods instead of imports.

**POLITICAL FACTORS**  Sometimes, countries impose tariffs on goods from a particular nation in retaliation for political acts. ▶ **Example 24.8**  In 2009, Mexico imposed tariffs of 10 to 20 percent on ninety products exported from the United States in retaliation for the Obama administration's cancellation of a cross-border trucking program.  The program had been instituted to comply with a provision in the North American Free Trade Agreement (to be discussed shortly) that called for Mexican trucks to eventually be granted full access to U.S. highways.

U.S. truck drivers opposed the program, however, and consumer protection groups claimed that the Mexican trucks posed safety issues. Because the Mexican tariffs were imposed on $2.4 billion of U.S. goods annually, in 2011 President Barack Obama negotiated a deal that allowed Mexican truckers to enter the United States. In exchange, Mexico agreed to suspend half of the tariffs immediately and the remainder when the first Mexican hauler complied with the new U.S. requirements. ◀

**ANTIDUMPING DUTIES**  The United States has laws specifically directed at what it sees as unfair international trade practices. **Dumping,** for example, is the sale of imported goods at "less than fair value." *Fair value* is usually determined by the price of the goods in the exporting country. Foreign firms that engage in dumping in the United States hope to undersell U.S. businesses and obtain a larger share of the U.S. market. To prevent this, an extra tariff—known as an *antidumping duty*—may be assessed on the imports.

Two U.S. government agencies are instrumental in imposing antidumping duties: the International Trade Commission (ITC) and the International Trade Administration (ITA). The ITC assesses the effects of dumping on domestic businesses and then makes recommendations to the president concerning temporary import restrictions.

The ITA, which is part of the Department of Commerce, decides whether imports were sold at less than fair value. The ITA's determination establishes the amount of antidumping duties, which are set to equal the difference between the price charged in the United States and the price charged in the exporting country. A duty may be retroactive to cover past dumping.

## Minimizing Trade Barriers

Restrictions on imports are also known as *trade barriers*. The elimination of trade barriers is sometimes seen as essential to the world's economic well-being. Most of the world's leading trading nations are members of the World Trade Organization (WTO), which was established in 1995 to minimize trade barriers among nations.

Each member country of the WTO is required to grant **normal trade relations (NTR) status** (formerly known as *most-favored-nation status*) to other member countries. This means that each member is obligated to treat other members at least as well as it treats the country that receives its most favorable treatment with regard to imports or exports. Various regional trade agreements and associations also help to minimize trade barriers between nations.

**THE EUROPEAN UNION (EU)** The European Union (EU) arose out of the 1957 Treaty of Rome, which created the Common Market, a free trade zone comprising the nations of Belgium, France, Italy, Luxembourg, the Netherlands, and West Germany. Today, the EU is a single integrated trading unit made up of twenty-eight European nations.

The EU has gone a long way toward creating a new body of law to govern all of the member nations—although some of its efforts to create uniform laws have been confounded by nationalism. Its governing authorities issue regulations, or directives, that define EU law in various areas, such as environmental law, product liability, anticompetitive practices, and corporations. The directives normally are binding on all member countries.

**THE NORTH AMERICAN FREE TRADE AGREEMENT (NAFTA)** The North American Free Trade Agreement (NAFTA) created a regional trading unit consisting of Canada, Mexico, and the United States. The goal of NAFTA was to eliminate tariffs among these three nations on substantially all goods by reducing the tariffs incrementally over a period of time.

NAFTA gives the three countries a competitive advantage by retaining tariffs on goods imported from countries outside the NAFTA trading unit. Additionally, NAFTA provides for the elimination of barriers that traditionally have prevented the cross-border movement of services, such as financial and transportation services. NAFTA also attempts to eliminate citizenship requirements for the licensing of accountants, attorneys, physicians, and other professionals.

**THE CENTRAL AMERICA–DOMINICAN REPUBLIC–UNITED STATES FREE TRADE AGREEMENT (CAFTA-DR)** The Central America–Dominican Republic–United States Free Trade Agreement (CAFTA-DR) was formed by Costa Rica, the Dominican Republic, El Salvador, Guatemala, Honduras, Nicaragua, and the United States. Its purpose is to reduce trade tariffs and improve market access among all of the signatory nations, including the United States. Legislatures from all seven countries have approved the CAFTA-DR, despite significant opposition in certain nations.

**THE REPUBLIC OF KOREA–UNITED STATES FREE TRADE AGREEMENT (KORUS FTA)** In 2011, the United States ratified its first free trade agreement with South Korea—the Republic of Korea–United States Free Trade Agreement (KORUS FTA). The treaty's provisions will eliminate 95 percent of each nation's tariffs on industrial and consumer exports within five years.

KORUS is the largest free trade agreement that the United States has entered into since NAFTA. It is expected to boost U.S. exports by more than $10 billion a year and will benefit U.S. automakers, farmers, ranchers, and manufacturers by enabling them to compete in new markets.

Also in 2011, Congress ratified free trade agreements with Colombia and Panama. The Colombian trade agreement includes a provision requiring an exchange of tax information, and the Panama bill incorporates assurances on labor rights. The treaties are expected to increase U.S. exports and reduce prices for consumers. The Obama administration hopes that the agreements will also provide impetus for negotiations of the trans-Pacific trade initiative, aimed at increasing exports to Japan and other Asian nations.

## SECTION 4
# INTERNATIONAL DISPUTE RESOLUTION

International contracts frequently include arbitration clauses. By means of such clauses, the parties agree in advance to be bound by the decision of a specified third party in the event of a dispute, as discussed in Chapter 3.

## The New York Convention

The United Nations Convention on the Recognition and Enforcement of Foreign Arbitral Awards (often referred to as the New York Convention) assists in the enforcement of arbitration clauses, as do provisions in specific treaties among nations. Basically, the convention requires courts in nations that have signed it to honor private agreements to arbitrate and recognize arbitration awards made in other contracting states. The New York Convention has been implemented in nearly one hundred countries, including the United States.

Under the New York Convention, a court will compel the parties to arbitrate their dispute if all of the following are true:

1. There is a written (or recorded) agreement to arbitrate the matter.
2. The agreement provides for arbitration in a convention signatory nation.
3. The agreement arises out of a commercial legal relationship.
4. One party to the agreement is not a U.S. citizen. In other words, both parties cannot be U.S. citizens.

In the following case, the parties had agreed to arbitrate any disputes in Guernsey, which is a British Crown dependency in the English Channel. The court had to decide whether the agreement was enforceable even though one party was a U.S. company and the other party may have had its principal place of business in the United States.

---

## CASE 24.2

### S & T Oil Equipment & Machinery, Ltd. v. Juridica Investments, Ltd.
United States Court of Appeals, Fifth Circuit, 2012 WL 28242 (2012).

**BACKGROUND AND FACTS** Juridica Investments, Ltd. (JIL), entered into a financing contract with S & T Oil Equipment & Machinery, Ltd., a U.S. company. The contract included an arbitration provision stating that any disputes would be arbitrated "in St. Peter Port, Guernsey, Channel Islands." The contract also stated that it was executed in Guernsey and would be fully performed there. When a dispute arose between the parties, JIL initiated arbitration in Guernsey. Nevertheless, S & T filed a suit in federal district court in the United States. When JIL filed a motion to dismiss in favor of arbitration, the court granted the motion and compelled arbitration under the Convention on the Recognition and Enforcement of Foreign Arbitral Awards. S & T appealed.

**DECISION AND RATIONALE** The U.S. Court of Appeals for the Fifth Circuit affirmed the district court's judgment compelling arbitration. The court explained that the Convention requires arbitration if "(1) there is a written agreement to arbitrate the matter; (2) the agreement provides for arbitration in a Convention signatory nation; (3) the agreement arises out of a commercial legal relationship; and (4) a party to the agreement is not an American citizen."

Here, the first three requirements were clearly satisfied, but there was some question about whether JIL was an American citizen based on its principal place of business. Nevertheless, under the statute implementing the Convention, an arbitration agreement between American citizens is enforceable if it "involves property abroad, envisages performance or enforcement abroad, or has some other reasonable relation with one or more foreign states." The court reasoned that in this case, JIL and S & T executed their contract in Guernsey and agreed that it would be fully performed there. Thus, the parties had a reasonable relation with a foreign state beyond the arbitration agreement itself. Arbitration was therefore required under the Convention.

**THE GLOBAL DIMENSION** *What would happen if Congress did not require a reasonable relationship with a foreign state for arbitration agreements between U.S. citizens doing business abroad? Would there be more or fewer agreements to arbitrate disputes abroad?*

**THE TECHNOLOGICAL DIMENSION** *How might these parties have avoided the time and expense of settling their dispute in a foreign jurisdiction?*

## Effect of Choice-of-Law and Choice-of-Forum Clauses

If a sales contract does not include an arbitration clause, litigation may occur. When the contract contains forum-selection and choice-of-law clauses (see Chapter 20), the lawsuit will be heard by a court in the specified forum and decided according to that forum's law.

▶ **Case in Point 24.9** Intermax Trading Corporation, a New York firm, contracted to act as the North American sales agent for Garware Polyester, Ltd., based in Mumbai, India. The parties executed a series of contracts with provisions stating that the courts of Mumbai, India, would have exclusive jurisdiction over any disputes relating to the agreements. When Intermax fell behind in its payments to Garware, Garware filed a lawsuit in a U.S. court to collect the balance due. Garware claimed that the forum-selection clause did not apply to sales of warehoused goods, but the court sided with Intermax. Because the forum-selection clause was valid and enforceable, Garware had to bring its complaints against Intermax in a court in India.[9] ◀

If the contract does not specify a forum and choice of law, proceedings will be more complex and legally uncertain. Litigation may take place in two or more countries, with each country applying its own choice-of-law rules to determine the substantive law that will be applied to the particular transactions. Even if a plaintiff wins a favorable judgment in its own country, there is no way to predict whether courts in the defendant's country will enforce the judgment.

## SECTION 5
# U.S. LAWS IN A GLOBAL CONTEXT

The globalization of business raises questions about the extraterritorial application of a nation's laws—that is, the effect of the country's laws outside its boundaries. To what extent do U.S. domestic laws apply to other nations' businesses? To what extent do U.S. domestic laws apply to U.S. firms doing business abroad? Here, we discuss the extraterritorial application of certain U.S. laws, including antitrust laws, tort laws, and laws prohibiting employment discrimination.

## U.S. Antitrust Laws

U.S. antitrust laws have a wide application. They may *subject* firms in foreign nations to their provisions, as well as *protect* foreign consumers and competitors from violations committed by U.S. citizens. Section 1 of the Sherman Act—the most important U.S. antitrust law—provides for the extraterritorial effect of the U.S. antitrust laws.

The United States is a major proponent of free competition in the global economy. Thus, any conspiracy that has a *substantial effect* on U.S. commerce is within the reach of the Sherman Act. The law applies even if the violation occurs outside the United States, and foreign governments as well as businesses can be sued for violations. Before U.S. courts will exercise jurisdiction and apply antitrust laws, however, it must be shown that the alleged violation had a substantial effect on U.S. commerce.

▶ **Example 24.10** An investigation by the U.S. government revealed that a Tokyo-based auto-parts supplier, Furukawa Electric Company, and its executives conspired with competitors in an international price-fixing agreement (an agreement to set prices). The agreement lasted more than ten years and resulted in automobile manufacturers paying noncompetitive higher prices for parts in cars sold to U.S. consumers.

Because the conspiracy had a substantial effect on U.S. commerce, the United States had jurisdiction to prosecute the case. In 2011, Furukawa agreed to plead guilty and pay a $200 million fine. The Furukawa executives from Japan also agreed to serve up to eighteen months in a U.S. prison and to cooperate fully with the ongoing investigation. ◀

## International Tort Claims

The international application of tort liability is growing in significance and controversy. An increasing number of U.S. plaintiffs are suing foreign (or U.S.) entities for torts that these entities have allegedly committed overseas. Often, these cases involve human rights violations by foreign governments. The Alien Tort Claims Act (ATCA),[10] allows even foreign citizens to bring civil suits in U.S. courts for injuries caused by violations of the law of nations or a treaty of the United States.

Since 1980, foreign plaintiffs have increasingly used this act to bring actions against companies operating in nations such as Colombia, Ecuador, Egypt,

---

**9.** *Garware Polyester, Ltd. v. Intermax Trading Corp.*, 2001 WL 1035134 (S.D.N.Y. 2001).

**10.** 28 U.S.C. Section 1350.

Guatemala, India, Indonesia, Nigeria, and Saudi Arabia. Some of these cases have involved alleged environmental destruction. Others have involved human rights violations.[11] In addition, mineral com-

panies in Southeast Asia have been sued for collaborating with oppressive government regimes.

In the following *Spotlight Case,* the United States Supreme Court considers the parameters of the ATCA (which the Court refers to as the Alien Tort Statute, or ATS). The question is whether the statute allows courts to recognize a cause of action for violations of the law of nations occurring within the territory of a sovereign other than the United States.

---

11. See, for example, *Khulumani v. Barclay National Bank, Ltd.,* 504 F.3d 254 (2007), in which plaintiffs claimed that hundreds of corporations "aided and abetted" the government of South Africa in maintaining its apartheid (racially discriminatory) regime.

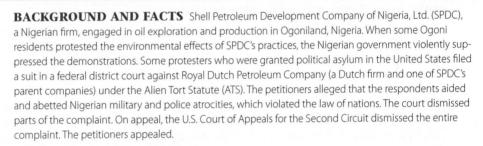

## SP TLIGHT on International Torts

### Case 24.3   Kiobel v. Royal Dutch Petroleum Co.
Supreme Court of the United States, __ U.S. __, 133 S.Ct. 1659, ___L.Ed. ___ (2013).

**BACKGROUND AND FACTS**  Shell Petroleum Development Company of Nigeria, Ltd. (SPDC), a Nigerian firm, engaged in oil exploration and production in Ogoniland, Nigeria. When some Ogoni residents protested the environmental effects of SPDC's practices, the Nigerian government violently suppressed the demonstrations. Some protesters who were granted political asylum in the United States filed a suit in a federal district court against Royal Dutch Petroleum Company (a Dutch firm and one of SPDC's parent companies) under the Alien Tort Statute (ATS). The petitioners alleged that the respondents aided and abetted Nigerian military and police atrocities, which violated the law of nations. The court dismissed parts of the complaint. On appeal, the U.S. Court of Appeals for the Second Circuit dismissed the entire complaint. The petitioners appealed.

**DECISION AND RATIONALE**  The United States Supreme Court affirmed the lower court's judgment dismissing the case. The presumption against extraterritoriality applies to claims under the Alien Tort Statute (ATS). Nothing in the statute rebuts that presumption, and all the conduct about which the petitioners complained took place *outside* the United States. "When a statute gives no clear indication of an extraterritoriality application, it has none and reflects the presumption that the United States law governs domestically, but does not rule the world."

The Supreme Court further pointed out that the ATS "covers actions by aliens for violations of the law of nations, but does not imply extraterritorial reach—such violations affecting aliens can occur within or outside the United States." The Court found no support for the proposition that Congress expected causes of action under the statute to be brought for violations of the law of nations occurring abroad. "There is no indication that the ATS was passed to make the United States a uniquely hospitable forum for the enforcement of international norms." Therefore, the lower court had properly concluded that the case should be dismissed.

**THE LEGAL ENVIRONMENT DIMENSION**  *What are the ramifications of the ruling in this case for the respondents (Royal Dutch Petroleum)?*

**THE GLOBAL DIMENSION**  *If the Court had adopted the petitioners' view, how might U.S. citizens have been affected?*

---

## Antidiscrimination Laws

As you probably already know, federal laws in the United States prohibit discrimination on the basis of race, color, national origin, religion, gender, age, and disability. These laws, as they affect employment relationships, generally apply extraterritorially.

▶ **Example 24.11**  The Age Discrimination in Employment Act protects U.S. employees working abroad for U.S. employers. The Americans with Disabilities Act, which requires employers to accommodate the needs of workers with disabilities, also applies to U.S. nationals working abroad for U.S. firms. ◀

In addition, the major U.S. law regulating employment discrimination—Title VII of the Civil Rights Act of 1964—also applies extraterritorially to all U.S. employees working for U.S. employers abroad. Generally, U.S. employers must abide by U.S. discrimination laws unless to do so would violate the laws of the country where their workplaces are located. This "foreign laws exception" allows employers to avoid being subjected to conflicting laws.

## Reviewing: International Law in a Global Economy

Robco, Inc., was a Florida arms dealer. The armed forces of Honduras contracted to purchase weapons from Robco over a six-year period. After the government was replaced and a democracy installed, the Honduran government sought to reduce the size of its military, and its relationship with Robco deteriorated. Honduras refused to honor the contract and purchase the inventory of arms, which Robco could sell only at a much lower price. Robco filed a suit in a federal district court in the United States to recover damages for this breach of contract by the government of Honduras. Using the information presented in the chapter, answer the following questions.

1. Should the Foreign Sovereign Immunities Act (FSIA) preclude this lawsuit? Why or why not?
2. Does the act of state doctrine bar Robco from seeking to enforce the contract? Explain.
3. Suppose that prior to this lawsuit, the new government of Honduras had enacted a law making it illegal to purchase weapons from foreign arms dealers. What doctrine of deference might lead a U.S. court to dismiss Robco's case in that situation?
4. Now suppose that the U.S. court hears the case and awards damages to Robco, but the government of Honduras has no assets in the United States that can be used to satisfy the judgment. Under which doctrine might Robco be able to collect the damages by asking another nation's court to enforce the U.S. judgment?

**DEBATE THIS . . .** *The U.S. federal courts are accepting too many lawsuits initiated by foreigners that concern matters not relevant to this country.*

## Terms and Concepts

| | | |
|---|---|---|
| act of state doctrine 419 | export 420 | quota 423 |
| civil law system 418 | expropriation 420 | sovereign immunity 420 |
| comity 418 | international law 415 | tariff 423 |
| confiscation 420 | international organization 416 | treaty 416 |
| distribution agreement 421 | national law 415 | |
| dumping 423 | normal trade relations (NTR) status 424 | |

## Issue Spotters

1. Café Rojo, Ltd., an Ecuadoran firm, agrees to sell coffee beans to Dark Roast Coffee Company, a U.S. firm. Dark Roast accepts the beans but refuses to pay. Café Rojo sues Dark Roast in an Ecuadoran court and is awarded damages, but Dark Roast's assets are in the United States. Under what circumstances would a U.S. court enforce the judgment of the Ecuadoran court? **(See page 418.)**

2. Gems International, Ltd., is a foreign firm that has a 12 percent share of the U.S. market for diamonds. To capture a larger share, Gems offers its products at a below-cost discount to U.S. buyers (and inflates the prices in its own country to make up the difference). How can this attempt to undersell U.S. businesses be defeated? **(See page 423.)**

- **Check your answers to the Issue Spotters against the answers provided in Appendix E at the end of this text.**

## Business Scenarios

**24–1. Doing Business Internationally.** Macrotech, Inc., develops an innovative computer chip and obtains a patent on it. The firm markets the chip under the trade-marked brand name "Flash." Macrotech wants to sell the chip to Nitron, Ltd., in Pacifica, a foreign country. Macrotech is concerned, however, that after an initial purchase, Nitron will duplicate the chip, pirate it, and sell the pirated version to computer manufacturers in Pacifica. To avoid this possibility, Macrotech could establish its own manufacturing facility in Pacifica, but it does not want to do this. How can Macrotech, without establishing a manufacturing facility in Pacifica, protect Flash from being pirated by Nitron? **(See page 420.)**

**24–2. Dumping.** The U.S. pineapple industry alleged that producers of canned pineapple from the Philippines were selling their canned pineapple in the United States for less than its fair market value (dumping). The Philippine producers also exported other products, such as pineapple juice and juice concentrate. These products used separate parts of the same fresh pineapple, so they shared raw material costs with the canned fruit, according to the producers' own financial records. To determine fair value and antidumping duties, the pineapple industry argued that a court should calculate the Philippine producers' cost of production and allocate a portion of the shared fruit costs to the canned fruit. The result of this allocation showed that more than 90 percent of the canned fruit sales were below the cost of production. Is this a reasonable approach to determining the production costs and fair market value of canned pineapple in the United States? Why or why not? **(See page 423.)**

**24–3. Sovereign Immunity.** Taconic Plastics, Ltd., is a manufacturer incorporated in Ireland with its principal place of business in New York. Taconic enters into a contract with a German firm, Werner Voss Architects and Engineers, acting as an agent for the government of Saudi Arabia. The contract calls for Taconic to supply special material for tents designed to shelter religious pilgrims visiting holy sites in Saudi Arabia. Most of the material is made in, and shipped from, New York. The German company does not pay Taconic and files for bankruptcy. Taconic files a suit in a U.S. court against the government of Saudi Arabia, seeking to collect $3 million. The defendant files a motion to dismiss the suit based on the doctrine of sovereign immunity. Under what circumstances does this doctrine apply? What are its exceptions? Should this suit be dismissed? Explain. **(See page 420.)**

## Business Case Problems

**24–4. Dumping.** Nuclear power plants use low-enriched uranium (LEU) as a fuel. LEU consists of feed uranium enriched by energy to a certain assay—the percentage of the isotope necessary for a nuclear reaction. The amount of energy required is described by an industry standard as a "separative work unit" (SWU). A nuclear utility may buy LEU from an enricher, or the utility may provide an enricher with feed uranium and pay for the SWUs necessary to produce LEU. Under an SWU contract, the LEU returned to the utility may not be exactly the uranium the utility provided. This is because feed uranium is fungible and trades like a commodity (such as wheat or corn), and profitable enrichment requires the constant processing of undifferentiated stock. Foreign enrichers, including Eurodif, S.A., allegedly exported LEU to the United States and sold it for "less than fair value." Did this constitute dumping? Explain. If so, what could be done to prevent it? [*United States v. Eurodif, S.A.*, 555 U.S. 305, 129 S.Ct. 878, 172 L.Ed.2d 679 (2009)] **(See page 423.)**

**24–5. International Agreements and Jurisdiction.** U.S. citizens who were descendants of victims of the Holocaust (the mass murder of 6 million Jews by the Nazis during World War II) in Europe filed a claim for breach of contract in the United States against an Italian insurance company, Assicurazioni Generali, S.P.A. (Generali). Before the Holocaust, the plaintiffs' ancestors had purchased insurance policies from Generali, but Generali refused to pay them benefits under the policies. Due to certain agreements among nations after World War II, such lawsuits could not be filed for many years. In 2000, however, the United States agreed that Germany could establish a foundation—the International Commission on Holocaust-Era Insurance Claims, or ICHEIC—that would compensate victims who had suffered losses at the hands of the Germans during the war. Whenever a German company was sued in a U.S. court based on a Holocaust-era claim, the U.S. government would inform the court that the matter should be referred to the ICHEIC as the exclusive forum and remedy for the resolution. There was no such agreement with Italy, however, so the federal district court dismissed the suit. The plaintiffs appealed. Did the plaintiffs have to take their claim to the ICHEIC rather than sue in a U.S. court? Why or why not? [*In re Assicurazioni Generali, S.P.A.*, 592 F.3d 113 (2d Cir. 2010)] **(See page 420.)**

**24–6. BUSINESS CASE PROBLEM
WITH SAMPLE ANSWER: Sovereign Immunity.**

*Bell Helicopter Textron, Inc., designs, makes, and sells helicopters with distinctive and famous trade dress that identifies them as Bell aircraft. Bell also owns the helicopters' design patents. Bell's Model*

*206 Series includes the Jet Ranger. Thirty-six years after Bell developed the Jet Ranger, the Islamic Republic of Iran began to make and sell counterfeit Model 206 Series helicopters and parts. Iran's counterfeit versions—the Shahed 278 and the Shahed 285—used Bell's* trade dress *(see Chapter 8). The Shahed aircraft was promoted at an international air show in Iran to aircraft customers. Bell filed a suit in a U.S. district court against Iran, alleging violations of trademark and patent laws. Is Iran—a foreign nation—exempt in these circumstances from the jurisdiction of U.S. courts? Explain. [Bell Helicopter Textron, Inc. v. Islamic Republic of Iran, 764 F.Supp.2d 122 (D.D.C. 2011)]* **(See page 420.)**

- **For a sample answer to Problem 24–6, go to Appendix F at the end of this text.**

**24–7. Commercial Activity Exception.** Technology Incubation and Entrepreneurship Training Society (TIETS) entered into a joint-venture agreement with Mandana Farhang and M.A. Mobile to develop and market certain technology for commercial purposes. Farhang and M.A. Mobile filed a suit in a federal district court in California, where they both were based, alleging claims under the joint-venture agreement and a related nondisclosure agreement. The parties agreed that TIETS was a "foreign state" covered by the Foreign Sovereign Immunities Act (FSIA) because it was a part of the Indian government. Nevertheless, Farhang and M.A. Mobile argued that TIETS did not enjoy sovereign immunity because it had engaged in a commercial activity that has a direct effect in the United States. Could TIETS still be subject to the jurisdiction of U.S. courts under the commercial activities exception even though the joint venture was to take place outside the United States? If so, how? *[Farhang v. Indian Institute of Technology, 2012 WL113739 (N.D.Cal. 2012)]* **(See page 420.)**

**24–8. Sovereign Immunity.** In 1954, the government of Bolivia began expropriating land from Francisco Loza for public projects, including an international airport. The government directed the payment of compensation in exchange for at least some of his land. But the government never paid the full amount. Decades later, his heirs, Genoveva and Marcel Loza, who were both U.S. citizens, filed a suit in a federal district court in the United States against the government of Bolivia, seeking damages for

the taking. Can the court exercise jurisdiction? Explain. *[Santivanez v. Estado Plurinacional de Bolivia, 2013 WL 879983 (11th Cir. 2013)]* **(See page 420.)**

**24–9. A QUESTION OF ETHICS: Terrorism.**

*On December 21, 1988, Pan Am Flight 103 exploded 31,000 feet in the air over Lockerbie, Scotland, killing all 259 passengers and crew on board and 11 people on the ground. Among those killed was Roger Hurst, a U.S. citizen. An investigation determined that a portable radio-cassette player packed in a brown Samsonite suitcase smuggled onto the plane was the source of the explosion. The explosive device was constructed with a digital timer specially made for, and bought by, Libya. Abdel Basset Ali Al-Megrahi, a Libyan government official and an employee of the Libyan Arab Airline (LAA), was convicted by the Scottish High Court of Justiciary on criminal charges that he planned and executed the bombing in association with members of the Jamahiriya Security Organization (JSO) (an agency of the Libyan government that performed security and intelligence functions) or the Libyan military. Members of the victims' families filed a suit in a U.S. district court against the JSO, the LAA, Al-Megrahi, and others. The plaintiffs claimed violations of U.S. federal law, including the Anti-Terrorism Act, and state law, including the intentional infliction of emotional distress. [Hurst v. Socialist People's Libyan Arab Jamahiriya, 474 F.Supp.2d 19 (D.D.C. 2007)]* **(See page 419.)**

(a) Under what doctrine, codified in which federal statute, might the defendants claim to be immune from the jurisdiction of a U.S. court? Should this law include an exception for "state-sponsored terrorism"? Why or why not?

(b) The defendants agreed to pay $2.7 billion, or $10 million per victim, to settle all claims for "compensatory death damages." The families of eleven victims, including Hurst, were excluded from the settlement because they were "not wrongful death beneficiaries under applicable state law." These plaintiffs continued the suit. The defendants filed a motion to dismiss. Should the motion be granted on the ground that the settlement bars the plaintiffs' claims? Explain.

## Legal Reasoning Group Activity

**24–10. Globalization.** Assume that you are manufacturing iPad accessories and that your business is becoming more successful. You are now considering expanding operations into another country. **(See page 420.)**

(a) One group will explore the costs and benefits of advertising on the Internet.

(b) Another group will consider whether to take in a partner from a foreign nation and will explain the benefits and risks of having a foreign partner.

(c) A third group will discuss what problems may arise if you want to manufacture in a foreign location.

Transactions involving the sale or lease of goods make up a great deal of the business activity in the commercial and manufacturing sectors of our economy. Articles 2 and 2A of the Uniform Commercial Code (UCC) govern the sale or lease of goods in every state except Louisiana. Many of the UCC's provisions express our ethical standards.

## Good Faith and Commercial Reasonableness

The concepts of good faith and commercial reasonableness permeate the UCC and help to prevent unethical behavior by businesspersons. These two key concepts are read into every contract and impose certain duties on all parties. Additionally, reasonableness in the formation, performance, and termination of contracts underlies almost all of the UCC's provisions.

As an example, consider the UCC's approach to open terms. Section 2–311(1) states that when a term is to be specified by one of the parties, "any such specification must be made in within limits set by commercial reasonableness." The requirement of commercial reasonableness means that the term subsequently supplied by one party should not come as a surprise to the other. The party filling in the missing term may not use the opportunity to take advantage of the other party. For instance, the party may not add a term that will be beneficial to himself or herself (and detrimental to the other party) and then demand that the other party perform the contract.

Under the UCC, the party filling in the missing term is not allowed to deviate from what is commercially reasonable in the context of the transaction. Courts frequently look to course of dealing, usage of trade, and the surrounding circumstances in determining what is commercially reasonable in a given situation.

### LEGAL REASONING

1. *How can a court objectively measure good faith and commercial reasonableness?*

**Good Faith in Output and Requirements Contracts** The obligation of good faith is particularly important in so-called output and requirements contracts. UCC 2–306 states that "quantity" in these contracts "means such actual output or requirements as may occur in good faith." For example, Mandrow's Machines, which assembles personal computers, has a requirements contract with Advanced Tech Circuit Boards, under which Advanced Tech is to supply Mandrow's with all of the circuit boards it needs. If Mandrow's suddenly quadruples the size of its business, it cannot insist that Advanced Tech supply all of its requirements, as specified in the original contract.

As another example, assume that the market price of the goods subject to a requirements contract rises rapidly and

dramatically because of an extreme shortage of materials necessary to their production. The buyer could claim that she needs all of the seller's output and buy the entire output at the contract price (which is substantially below the market price). Then, the buyer could turn around and sell the goods that she does not need at the higher market price. Under the UCC, this type of unethical behavior is prohibited, even though the buyer in this instance has not technically breached the contract.

**Bad Faith Not Required for Breach** A party can breach the obligation of good faith under the UCC even if the party did not show "bad faith"—that is, even when there is no proof that the party was dishonest. For example, a large manufacturer of recreational boats, Genmar Holdings, Inc., purchased Horizon, a small company that produced a particular type of fishing boat. At the time of the purchase, Genmar promised that Horizon boats would be the company's "champion" and vowed to keep Horizon's key employees on as managers. The contract required Genmar to pay Horizon a lump sum in cash and also to pay "earn-out consideration" under a specified formula for five years. The "earn-out" amount would depend on the number of Horizon brand boats sold and on annual gross revenues.

One year after the sale, Genmar renamed the Horizon brand boats "Nova" and told employees to give priority to producing Genmar brand boats over the Nova boats. Because the Genmar boats were more difficult and time consuming to make than the Nova boats, gross revenues and production decreased, and Genmar was not required to pay the "earn-out" amounts. Eventually, Genmar fired the former Horizon employees and stopped manufacturing the Nova boats entirely. The former employees filed a suit alleging that Genmar had breached the implied covenant of good faith and fair dealing. Genmar argued that it could not have violated good faith because there was no proof that it had engaged in fraud, deceit, or misrepresentation. The court held for the plaintiffs, however, and the decision was affirmed on appeal.[1] It is possible for a party to breach its good faith obligations under the UCC even if the party did not engage in fraud, deceit, or misrepresentation.

**Commercial Reasonableness** Under the UCC, the concept of good faith is closely linked to commercial reasonableness. All commercial actions—including the performance and enforcement of contract obligations—must display commercial reasonableness. A merchant is expected to act in a reasonable manner according to reasonable commercial customs. The reliance of the UCC's drafters on commercial customs, or usage of trade, as a guideline to reasonable behavior in a given trade or

---

1. *O'Tool v. Genmar Holdings, Inc.,* 387 F.3d 1188 (10th Cir. 2004).

FOCUS ON ETHICS CONTINUES ➧

industry indicates the importance of good faith and commercial reasonableness in sales law.

The concept of commercial reasonableness is clearly expressed in the doctrine of commercial impracticability, which is related to the common law doctrine of impossibility of performance. Under the commercial impracticability doctrine, a party's nonperformance of a contractual obligation may be excused when performance of the contract becomes impracticable because of unforeseen circumstances. The courts make clear, however, that performance will not be excused under this doctrine unless the nonperforming party has made every reasonable effort to fulfill his or her obligations.

### LEGAL REASONING

**2.** *Generally, the courts determine what constitutes "reasonable" behavior in disputes between contract parties over whether a party has demonstrated commercial reasonableness. Should the UCC be more specific in defining what will be deemed reasonable in particular circumstances so that the courts do not have to decide the issue? Why or why not?*

## The Concept of the Good Faith Purchaser

The concept of the good faith purchaser reflects the UCC's emphasis on protecting innocent parties. Suppose, for example, that you innocently and in good faith purchase a boat for a fair market price from someone who appears to have good title. Under the UCC, you are protected from the possibility that the real owner—from whom the seller may have fraudulently obtained the boat—will later appear and demand his boat back. (Note that nothing prevents the true owner from bringing suit against the party who defrauded him.)

Ethical questions arise, though, when both parties to a dispute over title to goods are good faith purchasers. For example, suppose that a car dealer purchases a used car in good faith for value and sells it to a customer, also a good faith purchaser. If it turns out that there was actually a lien on the vehicle and the true owner claims title to the car, which of these two good faith purchasers should lose out? Here, a court would likely look to trade usage for guidance. In one case involving this situation, the court noted that in the used-car industry, it is customary for the seller to reimburse the buyer when the seller cannot deliver good title to a vehicle. According to the court, this custom is consistent with public policy. Car dealers are better able than buyers to investigate irregularities in title, so the risk of forged title documents "can and should be borne by dealers rather than purchasers."[2]

Another ethical issue is raised when the purchaser of goods is not quite so innocent. Suppose that the purchaser

has reason to suspect that the seller may not have good title to the goods being sold but nonetheless goes ahead with the transaction because it is a "good deal." Has this buyer crossed the boundary that separates the good faith purchaser from one who purchases in bad faith? This boundary is important in the law of sales because the UCC will not be a refuge for those who purchase in bad faith. The term *good faith purchaser* means just that—one who purchases goods without knowing, or having any reason to know, that there is anything shady or illegal about the deal.

### LEGAL REASONING

**3.** *Why does the UCC protect innocent persons (good faith purchasers) who buy goods from sellers with voidable title but not innocent persons who buy goods from sellers with void title?*

## Unconscionability

The doctrine of unconscionability is a good example of how the law attempts to enforce ethical behavior. This doctrine suggests that some contracts may be so unfair to one party as to be unenforceable, even though that party originally agreed to the contract's terms. Under UCC Section 2–302, a court will consider a contract's fairness and may hold that the contract or a clause in it was unconscionable at the time the contract was made. If a court makes such a determination, it may refuse to enforce the contract, enforce the contract without the unconscionable clause, or limit the clause's application so as to avoid an unconscionable result.

**The Test for Unconscionability** The UCC does not define the term *unconscionability*. The drafters of the UCC, however, have added explanatory comments to the relevant sections, and these comments serve as guidelines for applying the UCC. Comment 1 to Section 2–302 discusses the basic test for unconscionability. The test is whether, under the circumstances existing at the time of the contract's formation, the clause in question was so one sided as to be unconscionable. This test is to be applied against the general commercial background of the contract.

**Unconscionability—A Case Example** In one case applying Section 2–302, a New York appellate court held that an arbitration clause was unconscionable and refused to enforce it. Gateway 2000, Inc., which sold computers and software directly to consumers, included an arbitration clause in its retail agreements. The clause specified that any dispute arising out of the contract had to be arbitrated in Chicago, Illinois, in accordance with the arbitration rules of the International Chamber of Commerce (ICC).

A number of consumers who had purchased Gateway products became incensed when they learned that the ICC

---

2. *Superior, Inc. v. Arrington*, 2009 Ark.App. 875 (2009).

rules required advance fees of $4,000 (more than the cost of most Gateway products). Furthermore, the $2,000 registration fee was nonrefundable—even if the consumer prevailed at the arbitration. Additionally, the consumers would have to pay travel expenses to Chicago. In the class-action litigation against Gateway that followed, the New York court agreed with the consumers that the "egregiously [flagrantly] oppressive" arbitration clause was unconscionable. The clause barred consumers from resorting to the courts and made arbitration financially prohibitive, leaving consumers "with no forum at all in which to resolve a dispute."[3]

## Warranties

A seller or lessor has not only a legal obligation to provide safe products but also an ethical one. When faced with the possibility of increasing safety at no extra cost, every ethical businessperson will certainly opt for a safer product. An ethical issue arises, however, when producing a safer product means higher costs. To some extent, our warranty laws serve to protect consumers from sellers who may be tempted to neglect ethical concerns if what they are doing is both legal and profitable.

**Express and Implied Warranties** The UCC recognizes both express and implied warranties. Under UCC 2–314 and 2A–212, goods sold by a merchant or leased by a lessor must be fit for the ordinary purposes for which such goods are used, be of proper quality, and be properly labeled and packaged.

The UCC injects greater fairness into contractual situations by recognizing descriptions as express warranties. Hence, a seller or lessor of goods may be held to have breached a contract if the goods fail to conform to the description. In this way, the UCC acknowledges that a buyer or lessee may often reasonably believe that a seller or lessor is warranting his or her product, even though the word *warrant* or *guarantee* was not used. Thus, the law imposes an ethical obligation on sellers and lessors in a statutory form.

**Warranty Disclaimers** The UCC requirement that warranty disclaimers be sufficiently conspicuous to catch the eye of a reasonable purchaser is based on the ethical premise that sellers of goods should not take advantage of unwary consumers. Buyers may not always read the "fine print" on standard purchase order forms. As discussed in Chapter 23, if a seller's or lessor's warranty disclaimer fails to meet the specific requirements imposed by the UCC, the warranties will not be effectively disclaimed. Before the UCC was adopted by the states, purchasers of automobiles frequently signed standard-form purchase agreements drafted by the auto manufacturer without learning the meaning of all the fine print until later.

**Freedom of Contract versus Freedom from Contract— Revisited** Although freedom of contract reflects a basic ethical principle in our society, courts have made it clear that when such freedom leads to gross unfairness, it should be curbed. (Several examples of the exceptions to freedom of contract that courts will make were offered in the *Focus on Ethics* feature at the end of Unit Three.)

Nonetheless, before the UCC was in effect, courts generally would not intervene in cases involving warranty disclaimers in fine print or otherwise "hidden" in a standard purchase order form. Exceptions were made only when the resulting unfairness "shocked the conscience" of the court. By establishing specific requirements for warranty disclaimers, the UCC has made dealing fairly with buyers and lessees—already an ethical obligation of all sellers and lessors—a legal obligation as well.

Today, if a warranty disclaimer unfairly "surprises" a purchaser or a lessee, chances are that the disclaimer was not sufficiently conspicuous. In this situation, the unfairness of the bargain need not be so great as to "shock the court's conscience" before a remedy will be granted.

### LEGAL REASONING

4. *Review the UCC provisions that apply to the topics discussed in Chapters 20 through 23. Discuss fully how various UCC provisions, excluding the provisions discussed above, reflect social values and ethical standards.*

## International Transactions

Conducting business internationally presents unique challenges including, at times, ethical challenges. This is understandable, given that laws and cultures vary from one country to another. Consider the role of women.

In the United States, equal employment opportunity is a fundamental public policy. This policy is clearly expressed in Title VII of the Civil Rights Act of 1964, which prohibits discrimination against women in the employment context. Some other countries, however, largely reject any professional role for women. Consequently, U.S. women conducting business transactions in those countries may encounter difficulties. For example, when the World Bank sent a delegation that included women to negotiate with the Central Bank of Korea, the Koreans were surprised and offended. They thought that the presence of women meant that the negotiations were not being taken seriously.

There are also some important ethical differences among nations. In Islamic countries, for example, the consumption of

---

3. *Brower v. Gateway 2000, Inc.*, 246 A.D.2d 246, 676 N.Y.S.2d 569 (1998). See also *DeFontes v. Dell, Inc.*, 984 A.2d 1061 (R.I. 2009).

FOCUS ON ETHICS CONTINUES ➡

alcohol and certain foods is forbidden by the Islamic religion. Thus, it would be thoughtless and imprudent to invite a Saudi Arabian business contact out for a drink.

Additionally, in many foreign nations, gift giving is a common practice between contracting companies or between companies and government officials. To Americans, such gift giving may look suspiciously like an unethical (and possibly illegal) bribe. This cultural difference has been an important source of friction in international business, particularly since the U.S. Congress passed the Foreign Corrupt Practices Act in 1977 (discussed in Chapters 5 and 10). This act prohibits U.S.

business firms from offering certain side payments to foreign officials to secure favorable contracts.

### LEGAL REASONING

5. *Should U.S. firms doing business internationally send female employees to foreign nations that reject any role for women in business? Why or why not? How can a U.S. company accommodate the culture of foreign nations and still treat its own employees equally?*

# MILLER
## SUMMARIZED-CASE EDITION

## UNIT FIVE

# AGENCY AND EMPLOYMENT

## CONTENTS

# CHAPTER 25

# AGENCY FORMATION AND DUTIES

One of the most common, important, and pervasive legal relationships is that of **agency.** In an agency relationship involving two parties, one of the parties, called the *agent,* agrees to represent or act for the other, called the *principal.* The principal has the right to control the agent's conduct in matters entrusted to the agent. By using agents, a principal can conduct multiple business operations simultaneously in various locations. Thus, for example, contracts that bind the principal can be made at different places with different persons at the same time.

A familiar example of an agent is a corporate officer who serves in a representative capacity for the owners of the corporation. In this capacity, the officer has the authority to bind the principal (the corporation) to a contract. In fact, agency law is essential to the existence and operation of a corporate entity because only through its agents can a corporation function and enter into contracts.

Most employees are also considered to be agents of their employers. Thus, some of the concepts of employment law that you will learn about in Chapters 27 and 28 are based on agency law. Indeed, agency relationships permeate the business world. For that reason, an understanding of the law of agency is crucial to understanding business law.

## SECTION 1
## AGENCY RELATIONSHIPS

Section 1(1) of the *Restatement (Third) of Agency*[1] defines *agency* as "the fiduciary relation [that] results from the manifestation of consent by one person to another that the other shall act in his [or her] behalf and subject to his [or her] control, and consent by the other so to act." In other words, in a principal-agent relationship, the parties have agreed that the agent will act *on behalf and instead of* the principal in negotiating and transacting business with third parties.

The term **fiduciary** is at the heart of agency law. This term can be used both as a noun and as an adjective. When used as a noun, it refers to a person having a duty created by his or her undertaking to act primarily for another's benefit in matters connected with the undertaking. When used as an adjective, as in the phrase *fiduciary relationship,* it means that the relationship involves trust and confidence.

Agency relationships commonly exist between employers and employees. Agency relationships may sometimes also exist between employers and independent contractors who are hired to perform special tasks or services.

### Employer-Employee Relationships

Normally, all employees who deal with third parties are deemed to be agents. A salesperson in a department store, for instance, is an agent of the store's owner (the principal) and acts on the owner's behalf. Any sale of goods made by the salesperson to a customer is binding on the principal. Similarly, most representations of fact made by the salesperson with respect to the goods sold are binding on the principal.

Because employees who deal with third parties generally are deemed to be agents of their employers, agency law and employment law overlap considerably. Agency relationships, though, as will become apparent, can exist outside an employer-employee relationship, and thus agency law has a broader reach than employment law does.

Employment laws (state and federal) apply only to the employer-employee relationship. Thus, statutes that govern Social Security, withholding taxes, workers' compensation, unemployment compensation, and workplace safety apply only when an employer-

---

**1.** The *Restatement (Third) of Agency* is an authoritative summary of the law of agency and is often referred to by judges in their decisions and opinions.

employee relationship exists (see Chapter 27). Similarly, laws that prohibit employment discrimination (see Chapter 28) apply only to employers and employees. *These laws do not apply to an independent contractor.*

## Employer–Independent Contractor Relationships

Independent contractors are not employees because, by definition, those who hire them have no control over the details of their work performance. Section 2 of the *Restatement (Third) of Agency* defines an **independent contractor** as follows:

> [An independent contractor is] a person who contracts with another to do something for him [or her] but who is not controlled by the other nor subject to the other's right to control with respect to his [or her] physical conduct in the performance of the undertaking. He [or she] may or may not be an agent.

Building contractors and subcontractors are independent contractors. A property owner who hires a contractor and subcontractors to complete a project does not control the details of the way they perform their work. Truck drivers who own their vehicles and hire out on a per-job basis are independent contractors, but truck drivers who drive company trucks on a regular basis usually are employees.

The relationship between a principal and an independent contractor may or may not involve an agency relationship. To illustrate: A homeowner who hires a real estate broker to sell her house has not only contracted with an independent contractor (the broker) but also established an agency relationship for the specific purpose of selling the property. Another example is an insurance agent, who is both an independent contractor and an agent of the insurance company for which he sells policies. (Note that an insurance *broker,* in contrast, normally is an agent of the person obtaining insurance and not of the insurance company.)

## Determination of Employee Status

The courts are frequently asked to determine whether a particular worker is an employee or an independent contractor. How a court decides this issue can have a significant effect on the rights and liabilities of the parties. For instance, employers are required to pay certain taxes, such as Social Security and unemployment taxes, for employees but not for independent contractors.

**CRITERIA USED BY THE COURTS**  In deciding whether a worker is categorized as an employee or an independent contractor, courts often consider the following questions:

1. *How much control does the employer exercise over the details of the work?* If the employer exercises considerable control over the details of the work and the day-to-day activities of the worker, this indicates employee status. This is perhaps the most important factor weighed by the courts in determining employee status.
2. *Is the worker engaged in an occupation or business distinct from that of the employer?* If so, this points to independent-contractor, not employee, status.
3. *Is the work usually done under the employer's direction or by a specialist without supervision?* If the work is usually done under the employer's direction, this indicates employee status.
4. *Does the employer supply the tools at the place of work?* If so, this indicates employee status.
5. *For how long is the person employed?* If the person is employed for a long period of time, this indicates employee status.
6. *What is the method of payment—by time period or at the completion of the job?* Payment by time period, such as once every two weeks or once a month, indicates employee status.
7. *What degree of skill is required of the worker?* If a great degree of skill is required, this may indicate that the person is an independent contractor hired for a specialized job and not an employee.

*Disputes Involving Employment Law.*  Sometimes, workers may benefit from having employee status—for tax purposes and to be protected under certain employment laws, for example. As mentioned earlier, federal statutes governing employment discrimination apply only when an employer-employee relationship exists. Protection under employment-discrimination statutes provides a significant incentive for workers to claim that they are employees rather than independent contractors.

▶ **Case in Point 25.1**  A Puerto Rican television station, WIPR, contracted with Victoria Alberty-Vélez to cohost a television show. Alberty signed a new contract for each episode and was committed to work for WIPR only during the filming of the episodes. WIPR paid her a lump sum for each contract and did not withhold any taxes.

When Alberty became pregnant, WIPR stopped contracting with her. She filed a lawsuit claiming that WIPR was discriminating against her in violation of federal antidiscrimination laws, but the court found in favor of WIPR. Because the parties had used repeated fixed-length contracts and had described Alberty as an independent contractor on tax documents, she could not maintain an employment-discrimination suit.[2] ◄

***Disputes Involving Tort Liability.*** Whether a worker is an employee or an independent contractor can also affect the employer's liability for the worker's actions. ▶ **Case in Point 25.2**   El Palmar Taxi, Inc., requires its drivers to supply their own cabs, which must display El Palmar's logo. The drivers pay gas, maintenance, and insurance costs, and a fee to El Palmar. They are expected to comply with the law, including licensing regulations, but they can work when they want for as long as they want. Mario Julaju drove a taxi under

a contract with El Palmar that described him as an independent contractor.

El Palmar sent Julaju to pick up Maria Lopez and her children. During the ride, Julaju's cab collided with a truck. To recover for their injuries, the Lopezes sued El Palmar. The employer argued that it was not liable because Julaju was an independent contractor. The court held in favor of El Palmar. An employer normally is not responsible for the actions of an independent contractor with whom the employer contracts. Here, the employment contract had clearly specified that Julaju was an independent contractor, and there were no facts indicating that he was an employee (or that the employer controlled his activities).[3] ◄

In the following case, the court had to determine the status of an auto service company and its tow truck driver who assaulted the passenger of a vehicle the company had been hired to tow.

---

2. *Alberty-Vélez v. Corporación de Puerto Rico para la Difusión Pública,* 361 F.3d 1 (1st Cir. 2004).

3. *Lopez v. El Palmar Taxi, Inc.,* 297 Ga.App. 121, 676 S.E.2d 460 (2009).

---

## CASE 25.1

### Coker v. Pershad

Superior Court of New Jersey, Appellate Division, 2013 WL 1296271 (2013).

**BACKGROUND AND FACTS**   AAA North Jersey, Inc., contracted with Five Star Auto Service to perform towing and auto repair services for AAA. Terence Pershad, the driver of a tow truck for Five Star, responded to a call to AAA for assistance by the driver of a car involved in an accident in Hoboken, New Jersey. Pershad got into a fight with Nicholas Coker, a passenger in the car, and assaulted Coker with a knife. Coker filed a suit in a New Jersey state court against Pershad, Five Star, and AAA. The court determined that Pershad was Five Star's employee and that Five Star was an independent contractor, not AAA's employee. Thus, AAA was "not responsible for the alleged negligence of its independent contractor, defendant Five Star, in hiring Mr. Pershad." Five Star entered into a settlement with Coker. Coker appealed the ruling in AAA's favor.

**DECISION AND RATIONALE**   A state intermediate appellate court affirmed the lower court's ruling. AAA could not be held liable for the actions of Five Star, its independent contractor.  Under the circumstances of this case, "the important difference between an employee and an independent contractor is that one who hires an independent contractor has no right of control in the manner in which the work is to be done." It is clear from the evidence that AAA did not control the manner and means of Five Star's work. "The agreement specifically stated Five Star was an independent contractor. Five Star purchased its own trucks and any other necessary equipment." Five Star completed its work without any supervision by AAA. AAA had used Five Star to provide towing service for its members for eight years. There was nothing "in the record to demonstrate it lacked the skill needed to provide these services."

**THE LEGAL ENVIRONMENT DIMENSION**   *Five Star's contract with AAA required Five Star to be available to provide service for AAA members. Does this support Coker's argument that Five Star was AAA's employee? Why or why not?*

**MANAGERIAL IMPLICATIONS**   *When an employment contract clearly designates one party as an independent contractor, the relationship between the parties is presumed to be that of employer and inde-*

**CASE 25.1 CONTINUED**   *pendent contractor. But this is only a presumption. Evidence can be introduced to show that the employer exercised sufficient control to establish the other party as an employee. The Internal Revenue Service is increasingly pursuing employers that it claims have wrongly classified employees as independent contractors. Thus, from a tax perspective, business managers need to ensure that all independent contractors fully control their own work.*

**CRITERIA USED BY THE IRS** The Internal Revenue Service (IRS) has established its own criteria for determining whether a worker is an independent contractor or an employee. The most important factor is the degree of control the business exercises over the worker.

The IRS tends to closely scrutinize a firm's classification of its workers because, as mentioned, employers can avoid certain tax liabilities by hiring independent contractors instead of employees. Even when a firm has classified a worker as an independent contractor, the IRS may decide that the worker is actually an employee.

If the IRS decides that an employee is misclassified, the employer will be responsible for paying any applicable Social Security, withholding, and unemployment taxes. Microsoft Corporation, for instance, was once ordered to pay back payroll taxes for hundreds of temporary workers who had contractually agreed to work for Microsoft as independent contractors.[4]

**EMPLOYEE STATUS AND "WORKS FOR HIRE"** Under the Copyright Act, any copyrighted work created by an employee within the scope of her or his employment at the request of the employer is a "work for hire." The employer owns the copyright to the work. In contrast, when an employer hires an independent contractor—a freelance artist, writer, or computer programmer, for example—the independent contractor normally owns the copyright. An exception is made if the parties agree in writing that the work is a "work for hire" and the work falls into one of nine specific categories, including audiovisual and other works.

▶ **Case in Point 25.3** Artisan House, Inc., hired a professional photographer, Steven H. Lindner, owner of SHL Imaging, Inc., to take pictures of its products for the creation of color slides to be used by Artisan's sales force. Lindner controlled his own work and carefully chose the lighting and angles used in the photographs. When Artisan published the photographs in a catalogue and brochures without Lindner's permission, SHL filed a lawsuit for copyright infringement. Artisan claimed that its publication of the photographs was authorized because they were works for hire. The court, however, decided that SHL was an independent contractor and owned the copyright to the photographs. Because SHL had not given Artisan permission (a license) to reproduce the photographs in other publications, Artisan was liable for copyright infringement.[5] ◀

**SECTION 2**

# FORMATION OF THE AGENCY RELATIONSHIP

Agency relationships normally are *consensual*—that is, they come about by voluntary consent and agreement between the parties. Generally, the agreement need not be in writing,[6] and consideration is not required.

A person must have contractual capacity to be a principal.[7] Those who cannot legally enter into contracts directly should not be allowed to do so indirectly through an agent. Any person can be an agent, however, regardless of whether he or she has the capacity to contract (including minors).

An agency relationship can be created for any legal purpose. An agency relationship created for a purpose that is illegal or contrary to public policy is unenforceable. ▶ **Example 25.4** Archer (as principal) contracts with Burke (as agent) to sell illegal narcotics. The agency relationship is unenforceable because selling illegal narcotics is a felony and is contrary to public policy. If Burke sells the narcotics and keeps the profits, Archer cannot sue to enforce the agency agreement. ◀

An agency relationship can arise in four ways: by agreement of the parties, by ratification, by estoppel, and by operation of law.

---

4. *Vizcaino v. U.S. District Court for the Western District of Washington,*173 F.3d 713 (9th Cir. 1999).

5. *SHL Imaging, Inc. v. Artisan House, Inc.,* 117 F.Supp.2d 301 (S.D.N.Y. 2000).

6. There are two main exceptions to the statement that agency agreements need not be in writing: (1) Under the *equal dignity rule* (discussed in the next chapter), an agreement must be in writing if it empowers the agent to enter into a contract that the Statute of Frauds requires to be in writing. (2) An agreement that gives an agent power of attorney must also be in writing.

7. Note that some states allow a minor to be a principal. When a minor is permitted to be a principal, any resulting contracts will be voidable by the minor principal but *not* by the adult third party.

## Agency by Agreement

Most agency relationships are based on an express or implied agreement that the agent will act for the principal and that the principal agrees to have the agent so act. An agency agreement can take the form of an express written contract or be created by an oral agreement. ▶ **Example 25.5**   Rees asks Grace, a gardener, to contract with others for the care of his lawn on a regular basis. If Grace agrees, an agency relationship exists between Reese and Grace for the lawn care. ◀

An agency agreement can also be implied by conduct. ▶ **Example 25.6**   A hotel expressly allows only Boris Renke to park cars, but Renke has no employment contract there. The hotel's manager tells Renke when to work, as well as where and how to park the cars. The hotel's conduct manifests a willingness to have Renke park its customers' cars, and Renke can infer from the hotel's conduct that he has authority to act as a parking valet. Thus, there is an implied agreement that Renke is an agent of the hotel and provides valet parking services for hotel guests. ◀

At issue in the following case was whether an agency relationship arose when a man, who was being hospitalized, asked his wife to sign the admissions papers for him.

---

# CASE 25.2

## Laurel Creek Health Care Center v. Bishop
Court of Appeals of Kentucky, 2010 WL 985299 (2010).

**BACKGROUND AND FACTS**   Gilbert Bishop was admitted to Laurel Creek Health Care Center suffering from various physical ailments. During an examination, Bishop told Laurel Creek staff that he could not use his hands well enough to write or hold a pencil, but he was otherwise found to be mentally competent. Bishop's sister, Rachel Combs, testified that when she arrived at the facility, she offered to sign the admissions forms. Laurel Creek employees told her, however, that it was their policy to have the patient's spouse sign the admissions papers if the patient was unable to do so. Combs also testified that Gilbert asked her to get his wife, Anna, so that she could sign his admissions papers.

Combs then brought Anna to the hospital, and Anna signed the admissions paperwork, which contained a provision for mandatory arbitration. Subsequently, Bishop went into cardiopulmonary arrest and died. Following his death, Bishop's family brought an action in a Kentucky state court against Laurel Creek for negligence. Laurel Creek asked the trial court to order the parties to proceed to arbitration in accordance with the mandatory arbitration provision contained in the admissions paperwork signed by Anna. The trial court denied the request on the ground that Anna was not Bishop's agent and had no legal authority to make decisions for him. Laurel Creek appealed.

**DECISION AND RATIONALE**   The state intermediate appellate court reversed the trial court's judgment and remanded the case for further proceedings consistent with its opinion. An actual agency relationship between Bishop and his wife, Anna, had been formed, and the trial court had erred when it found otherwise. The court pointed out that "according to his sister, Rachel, Gilbert specifically asked that his wife be brought to the nursing home so that she could sign the admissions documents for him, and [his wife] acted upon that delegation of authority and signed the admissions papers." The court then cited several sections of the *Restatement (Third) of Agency*, and concluded, "clearly here, [Gilbert's wife's] actions affected Gilbert's relations with Laurel Creek, a third party. . . . Gilbert had created an agency relationship upon which Laurel Creek justifiably relied."

**THE ECONOMIC DIMENSION**   *Which party benefited from the court's ruling? Why?*

**THE LEGAL ENVIRONMENT DIMENSION**   *Laurel Creek argued that even if there was no actual agency relationship, an implied agency relationship existed. Is this argument valid? Why or why not?*

## Agency by Ratification

On occasion, a person who is in fact not an agent (or who is an agent acting outside the scope of her or his authority) may make a contract on behalf of another (a principal). If the principal approves or affirms that contract by word or by action, an agency relationship is created by *ratification*. Ratification involves a question of intent, and intent can be expressed by either words or conduct. The basic requirements for ratification will be discussed in Chapter 26.

## Agency by Estoppel

Sometimes, a principal causes a third person to believe that another person is the principal's agent, and the third person acts to his or her detriment in reasonable reliance on that belief. When this occurs, the principal is "estopped to deny" (prevented from denying) the agency relationship. An agency by estoppel arises when the principal's actions have created the *appearance* of an agency that does not in fact exist.

**THE THIRD PARTY'S RELIANCE MUST BE REASONABLE**
The third person must prove that he or she *reasonably* believed that an agency relationship existed, however.[8] Facts and circumstances must show that an ordinary, prudent person familiar with business practice and custom would have been justified in concluding that the agent had authority.

▶ **Case in Point 25.7**   Marsha and Jerry Wiedmaier owned Wiedmaier, Inc., a corporation that operated a truck stop. Their son, Michael, did not own any interest in the corporation but had worked at the truck stop as a fuel operator. Michael decided to form his own business called Extreme Diecast, LLC. To obtain a line of credit with Motorsport Marketing, Inc., which sells racing memorabilia, Michael asked his mother to sign the credit application form.

After Marsha had signed as "Secretary-Owner" of Wiedmaier, Inc., Michael added his name to the list of corporate owners and faxed the form to Motorsport. Later, when Michael stopped making payments on the merchandise he had ordered, Motorsport sued Wiedmaier, Inc., for the unpaid balance. The court ruled that Michael was an apparent agent of Wiedmaier, Inc., because the credit application had caused Motorsport to reasonably believe that Michael was acting as Wiedmaier's agent in ordering merchandise.[9] ◀

**CREATED BY THE PRINCIPAL'S CONDUCT**  Note that the acts or declarations of a purported *agent* in and of themselves do not create an agency by estoppel. Rather, it is the deeds or statements of the *principal* that create an agency by estoppel. Thus, in *Case in Point 25.7*, if Marsha Wiedmaier had not signed the credit application on behalf of the principal-corporation, then Motorsport would not have been justified in believing that Michael was Wiedmaier's agent.

## Agency by Operation of Law

The courts may find an agency relationship in the absence of a formal agreement in other situations as well. This may occur in family relationships, such as when one spouse purchases certain basic necessaries and charges them to the other spouse's account. The courts often rule that a spouse is liable for payment for the necessaries because of either a social policy or a legal duty to supply necessaries to family members.

Agency by operation of law may also occur in emergency situations. If an agent cannot contact the principal and failure to act would cause the principal substantial loss, the agent may take steps beyond the scope of her or his authority. For example, a railroad engineer may contract on behalf of his or her employer for medical care for an injured motorist hit by the train.

See *Concept Summary 25.1* on the following page for a review of the various ways that agencies are formed.

SECTION 3
# DUTIES OF AGENTS AND PRINCIPALS

Once the principal-agent relationship has been created, both parties have duties that govern their conduct. As discussed previously, the principal-agent relationship is *fiduciary*—based on trust. In a fiduciary relationship, each party owes the other the duty to act with the utmost good faith. In this section, we examine the various duties of agents and principals.

---

**8.** These concepts also apply when a person who is in fact an agent undertakes an action that is beyond the scope of her or his authority, as will be discussed in Chapter 26.

**9.** *Motorsport Marketing, Inc. v. Wiedmaier, Inc.*, 195 S.W.3d 492 (Mo.App. 2006).

---

### CONCEPT SUMMARY 25.1
## Formation of the Agency Relationship

| METHOD OF FORMATION | DESCRIPTION |
|---|---|
| **By Agreement** | The agency relationship is formed through express consent (oral or written) or implied by conduct. |
| **By Ratification** | The principal either by act or by agreement ratifies the conduct of a person who is not in fact an agent. |
| **By Estoppel** | The principal causes a third person to believe that another person is the principal's agent, and the third person acts to his or her detriment in reasonable reliance on that belief. |
| **By Operation of Law** | The agency relationship is based on a social or legal duty (such as the need to support family members) or formed in emergency situations when the agent is unable to contact the principal and failure to act outside the scope of the agent's authority would cause the principal substantial loss. |

---

## Agent's Duties to the Principal

Generally, the agent owes the principal five duties—performance, notification, loyalty, obedience, and accounting.

**PERFORMANCE** An implied condition in every agency contract is the agent's agreement to use reasonable diligence and skill in performing the work. When an agent fails to perform his or her duties, liability for breach of contract may result.

***Standard of Care.*** The degree of skill or care required of an agent is usually that expected of a reasonable person under similar circumstances. Generally, this is interpreted to mean ordinary care. If an agent has represented herself or himself as possessing special skills, however, the agent is expected to exercise the degree of skill claimed. Failure to do so constitutes a breach of the agent's duty.

***Gratuitous Agents.*** Not all agency relationships are based on contract. In some situations, an agent acts gratuitously—that is, without payment. A gratuitous agent cannot be liable for breach of contract because there is no contract. He or she is subject only to tort liability. Once a gratuitous agent has begun to act in an agency capacity, he or she has the duty to continue to perform in that capacity. A gratuitous agent must perform in an acceptable manner and is subject to the same standards of care and duty to perform as other agents.
▶ **Example 25.8** Bower's friend Alcott is a real estate broker. Alcott offers to sell Bower's vacation home at no charge. If Alcott never attempts to sell

the home, Bower has no legal cause of action to force her to do so. If Alcott does attempt to sell the home to Friedman, but then performs so negligently that the sale falls through, Bower can sue Alcott for negligence. ◀

**NOTIFICATION** An agent is required to notify the principal of all matters that come to her or his attention concerning the subject matter of the agency. This is the *duty of notification,* or the duty to inform.
▶ **Example 25.9** Perez, an artist, is about to negotiate a contract to sell a series of paintings to Barber's Art Gallery for $25,000. Perez's agent learns that Barber is insolvent and will be unable to pay for the paintings. The agent has a duty to inform Perez of Barber's insolvency because it is relevant to the subject matter of the agency, which is the sale of Perez's paintings. ◀

Generally, the law assumes that the principal is aware of any information acquired by the agent that is relevant to the agency—regardless of whether the agent actually passes on this information to the principal. It is a basic tenet of agency law that notice to the agent is notice to the principal.

**LOYALTY** Loyalty is one of the most fundamental duties in a fiduciary relationship. Basically, the agent has the duty to act *solely for the benefit of his or her principal* and not in the interest of the agent or a third party. For instance, an agent cannot represent two principals in the same transaction unless both know of the dual capacity and consent to it.

***Maintain Confidentiality.*** The duty of loyalty also means that any information or knowledge acquired through the agency relationship is confidential. It is a breach of loyalty to disclose such information either during the agency relationship or after its termination. Typical examples of confidential information are trade secrets and customer lists compiled by the principal.

***Actions Must Benefit the Principal.*** The agent's loyalty must be undivided. The agent's actions must be strictly for the benefit of the principal and must not result in any secret profit for the agent.

▶ **Case in Point 25.10** Don Cousins contracted with Leo Hodgins, a real estate agent, to negotiate the purchase of an office building. While working for Cousins, Hodgins discovered that the property owner would sell the building only as a package deal with another parcel. Hodgins therefore bought the two properties intending to resell the building to Cousins. When Cousins found out, he sued.

The court held that Hodgins had breached his fiduciary duties. As a real estate agent, Hodgins had a duty to communicate all offers to his principal and not to secretly purchase the property and then resell it to his principal. Hodgins was required to act in Cousins's best interests and could only become the purchaser in this situation with Cousins's knowledge and approval.[10] ◀

In the following case, an employer alleged that a former employee had breached his duty of loyalty by planning a competing business while still working for the employer.

---

10. *Cousins v. Realty Ventures, Inc.*, 844 So.2d 860 (La.App. 5 Cir. 2003).

## CASE 25.3

### Taser International, Inc. v. Ward
Court of Appeals of Arizona, Division 1, 224 Ariz. 389, 231 P.3d 921 (2010).

**BACKGROUND AND FACTS** Taser International, Inc., develops and makes electronic control devices, known as stun guns, and accessories for them that include video and audio recording devices (such as the TASER CAM). Steve Ward was Taser's vice president of marketing when he began to explore the possibility of developing and marketing devices of his own design, including a clip-on camera. Ward talked to patent attorneys and a product development company and completed most of a business plan before he resigned from Taser. He then formed Vievu, LLC, to market the clip-on camera. Taser filed a suit against Ward in an Arizona state court alleging, among other things, that Ward had breached his duty of loyalty to Taser. Taser moved for summary judgment in its favor, which the court granted. Ward appealed.

**DECISION AND RATIONALE** A state intermediate appellate court reversed the lower court's decision that granted summary judgment in favor of Taser. An employee may not actively compete with his or her employer prior to the termination of employment. Ward argued that his pre-termination activities did not constitute active competition but were merely lawful preparation for a future business venture. The court stated, "The line separating mere preparation from active competition may be difficult to discern in some cases, and we must 'focus on the nature of the defendant's preparations to compete.'" Ward did not solicit or recruit Taser's customers or employees during his employment, but he did begin developing a business plan, speaking with patent attorneys, and developing a design for a device that could compete with Taser's products.

Nevertheless, the reviewing court also agreed with Ward "that certain of his pre-termination activities are qualitatively different than 'direct competition' and cannot form the basis for liability." Therefore, summary judgment was improper because a genuine issue of material fact existed as to the extent of Ward's pre-termination design and development efforts. The reviewing court remanded the case back to the lower court for further proceedings.

**WHAT IF THE FACTS WERE DIFFERENT?** *Suppose that Ward's planning and development efforts were focused on a product that would in no way compete with Taser's products. Would such efforts have breached his duty of loyalty to Taser in any way? Explain fully.*

**THE LEGAL ENVIRONMENT DIMENSION** *If the judgment in the case on remand is again in Taser's favor, what might be an appropriate remedy?*

**OBEDIENCE** When acting on behalf of the principal, an agent has a duty to follow all lawful and clearly stated instructions of the principal. Any deviation from such instructions is a violation of this duty.

During emergency situations, however, when the principal cannot be consulted, the agent may deviate from the instructions without violating this duty. Whenever instructions are not clearly stated, the agent can fulfill the duty of obedience by acting in good faith and in a manner reasonable under the circumstances.

**ACCOUNTING** Unless the agent and principal agree otherwise, the agent must keep and make available to the principal an account of all property and funds received and paid out on the principal's behalf. This includes gifts from third parties in connection with the agency. For instance, a gift from a customer to a salesperson for prompt deliveries made by the salesperson's firm, in the absence of a company policy to the contrary, belongs to the firm.

The agent has a duty to maintain a separate account for the principal's funds and must not intermingle these funds with the agent's personal funds. If a licensed professional (such as an attorney) violates this duty, he or she may be subject to disciplinary proceedings carried out by the appropriate regulatory institution (such as the state bar association). Of course, the professional will also be liable to the principal (the professional's client) for failure to account.

## Principal's Duties to the Agent

The principal also has certain duties to the agent. These duties relate to compensation, reimbursement and indemnification, cooperation, and safe working conditions.

**COMPENSATION** In general, when a principal requests certain services from an agent, the agent reasonably expects payment. The principal therefore has a duty to pay the agent for services rendered. For instance, when an accountant or an attorney is asked to act as an agent, an agreement to compensate the agent for this service is implied.

The principal also has a duty to pay that compensation in a timely manner. Unless the agency relationship is gratuitous and the agent does not act in exchange for payment, the principal must pay the agreed-on value for the agent's services. If no amount has been expressly agreed on, then the principal owes the agent the customary compensation for such services.

**REIMBURSEMENT AND INDEMNIFICATION** The principal has a duty to reimburse the agent for any funds disbursed at the principal's request. The principal must also reimburse the agent for any necessary expenses incurred in the course of the reasonable performance of her or his agency duties.[11] Agents cannot recover for expenses incurred as a result of their own misconduct or negligence, though.

Subject to the terms of the agency agreement, the principal has the duty to *indemnify* (compensate) an agent for liabilities incurred because of authorized and lawful acts and transactions. For instance, if the agent, on the principal's behalf, forms a contract with a third party, and the principal fails to perform the contract, the third party may sue the agent for damages. In this situation, the principal is obligated to compensate the agent for any costs incurred by the agent as a result of the principal's failure to perform the contract.

Additionally, the principal must indemnify the agent for the value of benefits that the agent confers on the principal. The amount of indemnification usually is specified in the agency contract. If it is not, the courts will look to the nature of the business and the type of loss to determine the amount. Note that this rule applies to acts by gratuitous agents as well.

**COOPERATION** A principal has a duty to cooperate with the agent and to assist the agent in performing his or her duties. The principal must do nothing to prevent that performance.

For instance, when a principal grants an agent an exclusive territory, the principal creates an **exclusive agency,** in which the principal cannot compete with the agent or appoint or allow another agent to compete. If the principal does so, he or she violates the exclusive agency and is exposed to liability for the agent's lost profits.

▶ **Example 25.11** River City Times Company (the principal) grants Emir (the agent) the right to sell its newspapers at a busy downtown intersection to the exclusion of all other vendors. This creates an exclusive territory within which only Emir has the right to sell those newspapers. If River City Times allows another vendor to sell its papers in that area, Emir can sue for lost profits. ◀

**SAFE WORKING CONDITIONS** The common law requires the principal to provide safe working prem-

---

11. This principle applies to acts by gratuitous agents as well. If a finder of a dog that becomes sick takes the dog to a veterinarian and pays the veterinarian's fees, the gratuitous agent is entitled to be reimbursed by the dog's owner.

ises, equipment, and conditions for all agents and employees. The principal has a duty to inspect working areas and to warn agents and employees about any unsafe situations. When the agent is an employee, the employer's liability is frequently covered by state workers' compensation insurance. In addition, federal and state statutes often require the employer to meet certain safety standards (see Chapter 27).

## SECTION 4
# RIGHTS AND REMEDIES OF AGENTS AND PRINCIPALS

In general, for every duty of the principal, the agent has a corresponding right, and vice versa. When one party to the agency relationship violates his or her duty to the other party, the remedies available to the nonbreaching party arise out of contract and tort law. These remedies include monetary damages, termination of the agency relationship, an injunction, and required accountings.

## Agent's Rights and Remedies against the Principal

The agent has the right to be compensated, to be reimbursed and indemnified, and to have a safe working environment. An agent also has the right to perform agency duties without interference by the principal.

**TORT AND CONTRACT REMEDIES** Remedies of the agent for breach of duty by the principal follow normal contract and tort remedies. ▶ **Example 25.12** Aaron Hart, a builder who has just constructed a new house, contracts with a real estate agent, Fran Boller, to sell the house. The contract calls for the agent to have an exclusive ninety-day listing and to receive 6 percent of the selling price when the home is sold. Boller holds several open houses and shows the home to a number of potential buyers.

One month before the ninety-day listing terminates, Hart agrees to sell the house to another buyer— not one to whom Boller has shown the house—after the ninety-day listing expires. Hart and the buyer agree that Hart will reduce the price of the house by 3 percent because he will sell it directly and thus will not have to pay Boller's commission. In this situation, if Boller learns of Hart's actions, she can terminate the agency relationship and sue Hart for damages, includ-

ing the 6 percent commission she should have earned on the sale of the house. ◀

**DEMAND FOR AN ACCOUNTING** An agent can also withhold further performance and demand that the principal give an accounting. For instance, a sales agent may demand an accounting if the agent and principal disagree on the amount of commissions the agent should have received for sales made during a specific period of time.

**NO RIGHT TO SPECIFIC PERFORMANCE** When the principal-agent relationship is not contractual, the agent has no right to specific performance. An agent can recover for past services and future damages but cannot force the principal to allow him or her to continue acting as an agent.

## Principal's Rights and Remedies against the Agent

In general, a principal has contract remedies for an agent's breach of fiduciary duties. The principal also has tort remedies if the agent engages in misrepresentation, negligence, deceit, libel, slander, or trespass. In addition, any breach of a fiduciary duty by an agent may justify the principal's termination of the agency. The main actions available to the principal are constructive trust, avoidance, and indemnification.

**CONSTRUCTIVE TRUST** Anything that an agent obtains by virtue of the employment or agency relationship belongs to the principal. An agent commits a breach of fiduciary duty if he or she secretly retains benefits or profits that, by right, belong to the principal. ▶ **Example 25.13** Lee, a purchasing agent for Metcalf, receives cash rebates from a customer. If Lee keeps the rebates for himself, he violates his fiduciary duty to his principal, Metcalf. On finding out about the cash rebates, Metcalf can sue Lee and recover them. ◀

**AVOIDANCE** When an agent breaches the agency agreement or agency duties under a contract, the principal has a right to avoid any contract entered into with the agent. This right of avoidance is at the election of the principal.

**INDEMNIFICATION** In certain situations, when a principal is sued by a third party for an agent's negligent conduct, the principal can sue the agent for indemnification—that is, for an equal amount of damages. The same holds true if the agent violates the principal's instructions.

▶ **Example 25.14** Parker (the principal) owns a used-car lot where Moore (the agent) works as a salesperson. Parker tells Moore to make no warranties for the used cars. Moore is eager to make a sale to Walters, a customer, and adds a 50,000-mile warranty for the car's engine. Parker may still be liable to Walters for engine failure, but if Walters sues Parker, Parker normally can then sue Moore for indemnification for violating his instructions. ◀

Sometimes, it is difficult to distinguish between instructions of the principal that limit an agent's authority and those that are merely advice.

▶ **Example 25.15** Gutierrez (the principal) owns an office supply company, and Logan (the agent) is the manager. Gutierrez tells Logan, "Don't purchase any more inventory this month." Gutierrez goes on vacation. A large order comes in from a local business, and the inventory on hand is insufficient to meet it. What is Logan to do? In this situation, Logan probably has the inherent authority to purchase more inventory despite Gutierrez's command. It is unlikely that Logan would be required to indemnify Gutierrez in the event that the local business subsequently canceled the order. ◀

## Reviewing: Agency Formation and Duties

James Blatt hired Marilyn Scott to sell insurance for the Massachusetts Mutual Life Insurance Company. Their contract stated, "Nothing in this contract shall be construed as creating the relationship of employer and employee." The contract was terminable at will by either party. Scott financed her own office and staff, was paid according to performance, had no taxes withheld from her checks, and could legally sell products of Massachusetts Mutual's competitors. Blatt learned that Scott was simultaneously selling insurance for Perpetual Life Insurance Corporation, one of Massachusetts Mutual's fiercest competitors. Blatt therefore withheld client contact information from Scott that would have assisted her insurance sales for Massachusetts Mutual. Scott complained to Blatt that he was inhibiting her ability to sell insurance for Massachusetts Mutual. Blatt subsequently terminated their contract. Scott filed a suit in a New York state court against Blatt and Massachusetts Mutual. Scott claimed that she had lost sales for Massachusetts Mutual—and her commissions—as a result of Blatt's withholding contact information from her. Using the information presented in the chapter, answer the following questions.

1. Who is the principal and who is the agent in this scenario? By which method was an agency relationship formed between Scott and Blatt?
2. What facts would the court consider most important in determining whether Scott was an employee or an independent contractor?
3. How would the court most likely rule on Scott's employee status? Why?
4. Which of the four duties that Blatt owed Scott in their agency relationship has probably been breached?

**DEBATE THIS . . .** *All works created by independent contractors should be considered works for hire under copyright law.*

## Terms and Concepts

agency 436

fiduciary 436

independent contractor 437

exclusive agency 444

## Issue Spotters

1. Winona contracted with XtremeCast, a broadcast media firm, to cohost an Internet-streaming sports program. Winona and XtremeCast signed a new contract for each episode. In each contract, Winona agreed to work a certain number of days for a certain salary. During each broadcast, Winona was free to improvise her performance. She had no other obligation to work for XtremeCast. Was Winona an independent contractor? **(See page 437.)**

2. Dimka Corporation wants to build a new mall on a specific tract of land. Dimka contracts with Nadine to buy the property. When Nadine learns of the difference between the price that Dimka is willing to pay and the price at which the owner is willing to sell, she wants to buy the land and sell it to Dimka herself. Can she do this? Discuss. **(See page 442.)**

- **Check your answers to the Issue Spotters against the answers provided in Appendix E at the end of this text.**

## Business Scenarios

**25–1. Agency Formation.** Paul Gett is a well-known, wealthy financial expert living in the city of Torris. Adam Wade, Gett's friend, tells Timothy Brown that he is Gett's agent for the purchase of rare coins. Wade even shows Brown a local newspaper clipping mentioning Gett's interest in coin collecting. Brown, knowing of Wade's friendship with Gett, contracts with Wade to sell a rare coin valued at $25,000 to Gett. Wade takes the coin and disappears with it. On the payment due date, Brown seeks to collect from Gett, claiming that Wade's agency made Gett liable. Gett does not deny that Wade was a friend, but he claims that Wade was never his agent. Discuss fully whether an agency was in existence at the time the contract for the rare coin was made. **(See page 439.)**

**25–2. Duty of Loyalty.** Peter hires Alice as an agent to sell a piece of property he owns. The price is to be at least $30,000. Alice discovers that the fair market value of Peter's property is actually at least $45,000 and could be higher because a shopping mall is going to be built nearby. Alice forms a real estate partnership with her cousin Carl. Then she prepares for Peter's signature a contract for the sale of the property to Carl for $32,000. Peter signs the contract. Just before closing and passage of title, Peter learns about the shopping mall and the increased fair market value of his property. Peter refuses to deed the property to Carl. Carl claims that Alice, as Peter's agent, solicited a price above that agreed on when the agency was created and that the contract is therefore binding and enforceable. Discuss fully whether Peter is bound to this contract. **(See page 442.)**

**25–3. Employee versus Independent Contractor.** Stephen Hemmerling was a driver for the Happy Cab Co. Hemmerling paid certain fixed expenses and abided by a variety of rules relating to the use of the cab, the hours that could be worked, and the solicitation of fares, among other things. Rates were set by the state. Happy Cab did not withhold taxes from Hemmerling's pay. While driving the cab, Hemmerling was injured in an accident and filed a claim for workers' compensation benefits in a state court. Such benefits are not available to independent contractors. On what basis might the court hold that Hemmerling was an employee? Explain. **(See page 437.)**

## Business Case Problems

**25–4. Spotlight on Agency—Independent Contractors.** Frank  Frausto delivered newspapers under a renewable six-month contract called a "Delivery Agent Agreement." The agreement identified Frausto as an independent contractor. The company collected payment from customers and took complaints about delivery. Frausto was given the route for his paper delivery and was required to deliver the paper within a certain time period each day. Frausto delivered the papers using his own vehicle and had to provide proof of insurance to the company. The company provided health and disability insurance but did not withhold taxes from Frausto's weekly income. One morning, Frausto was delivering papers and collided with Santiago on his motor-cycle. Santiago filed a negligence action against Frausto and the newspaper company. The newspaper company argued that it should not be liable because Frausto was an independent contractor. What was the result? Why? [*Santiago v. Phoenix Newspapers, Inc.,* 794 P.2d 138 (Ariz. 1990)] **(See page 437.)**

**25–5. Agency Formation.** Ford Motor Credit Co. is a subsidiary of Ford Motor Co. with its own offices, officers, and directors. Ford Credit buys contracts and leases of automobiles entered into by dealers and consumers. Ford Credit also provides inventory financing for dealers' purchases of Ford and non-Ford vehicles and makes loans to Ford and non-Ford dealers. Dealers and consumers are not required to finance their purchases or leases of Ford vehicles through Ford Credit. Ford Motor is not a party to the agreements between Ford Credit and its customers and does not directly receive any payments under those agreements. Also, Ford Credit is not subject to any agreement with Ford Motor "restricting or conditioning" its ability to finance the dealers' inventories or the consumers' purchases or leases of vehicles. A number of plaintiffs filed a product liability suit in a Missouri state court against Ford Motor. Ford Motor claimed that the court did not have venue. The plaintiffs asserted that Ford Credit, which had an office in the jurisdiction, acted as Ford's "agent for the transaction of its usual and customary business" there. Is Ford Credit an agent of Ford Motor? Discuss. *[State ex rel. Ford Motor Co. v. Bacon,* 63 S.W.3d 641 (Mo. 2002)] **(See page 439.)**

**25–6. Agency by Ratification.** Wesley Hall, an independent contractor managing property for Acree Investments, Ltd., lost control of a fire he had set to clear ten acres of Acree land. The runaway fire burned seventy-eight acres of Earl Barrs's property. Russell Acree, one of the owners of Acree Investments, had previously owned the ten acres, but he had put it into the company and was no longer the principal owner. Hall had worked for Russell Acree in the past and had told the state forestry department that he was burning the land for Acree. Barrs sued Russell Acree for the acts of his agent, Hall. In his suit, Barrs noted that Hall had been an employee of Russell Acree, Hall had talked about burning the land "for Acree," and Russell Acree had apologized to Barrs for the fire. Barrs also pointed out that Acree Investments had not been identified as the principal property owner until Barrs filed his lawsuit. Barrs argued that those facts were sufficient to create an agency by ratification to impose liability on Russell Acree. Was Barrs's agency by ratification claim valid? Why or why not? *[Barrs v. Acree,* 691 S.E.2d 575 (Ga.App. 2010)] **(See page 441.)**

**25–7. BUSINESS CASE PROBLEM**
**WITH SAMPLE ANSWER: Employment Relationships.**

William Moore owned Moore Enterprises, a wholesale tire business. William's son, Jonathan, worked as a Moore Enterprises employee while he was in high school. Later, Jonathan started his own business, called Morecedes Tire. Morecedes regrooved tires and sold them to businesses, including Moore Enterprises. A decade after Jonathan started Morecedes, William offered him work with Moore Enterprises. On the first day, William told Jonathan to load certain tires on a trailer but did not tell him how to do it. Was Jonathan an independent contractor? Discuss. *[Moore v. Moore,* 152 Idaho 245, 269 P.3d 802 (2011)]* **(See page 437.)**

• **For a sample answer to Problem 25–7, go to Appendix F at the end of this text.**

**25–8. Agent's Duties to Principal.** William and Maxine Miller were shareholders of Claimsco International, Inc. They filed a suit against the other shareholders, Michael Harris and Kenneth Hoxie, and the accountant who worked for all of them—John Verchota. The Millers alleged that Verchota had breached a duty that he owed them. They claimed that at Harris's instruction, Verchota had adjusted Claimsco's books to maximize the Millers' financial liabilities, falsely reflect income to them without actually transferring that income, and unfairly disadvantage them compared to the other shareholders. Which duty are the Millers referring to? If the allegations can be proved, did Verchota breach this duty? Explain. *[Miller v. Harris,* 2013 IL App (2d) 120512, 985 N.E.2d 671 (Ill.App. 2 Dist. 2013)] **(See page 442.)**

**25–9. A QUESTION OF ETHICS: Agency Formation and Duties.**

*Western Fire Truck, Inc., contracted with Emergency One, Inc. (EO), to be its exclusive dealer in Colorado and Wyoming through December 2003. James Costello, a Western salesperson, was authorized to order EO vehicles for his customers. Without informing Western, Costello e-mailed EO about Western's difficulties in obtaining cash to fund its operations. He asked about the viability of Western's contract and his possible employment with EO. On EO's request, and in disregard of Western's instructions, Costello sent some payments for EO vehicles directly to EO. In addition, Costello, with EO's help, sent a competing bid to a potential Western customer. EO's representative e-mailed Costello, "You have my permission to kick [Western's] ass." In April 2002, EO terminated its contract with Western, and, after reviewing Costello's e-mail, fired Costello. Western filed a suit in a Colorado state court, alleging that Costello breached his duty as an agent and that EO aided and abetted the breach. [Western Fire Truck, Inc. v. Emergency One, Inc., 134 P.3d 570 (Colo. App. 2006)]* **(See page 439.)**

(a) Was there an agency relationship between Western and Costello? Western required monthly reports from its sales staff, but Costello did not report regularly. Does this indicate that Costello was not Western's agent? In determining whether an agency relationship exists, is the right to control or the fact of control more important? Explain.

(b) Did Costello owe Western a duty? If so, what was the duty? Did Costello breach it? If so, how?

(c) A Colorado state statute allows a court to award punitive damages in "circumstances of fraud, malice, or willful and wanton conduct." Did any of these circumstances exist in this case? Should punitive damages be assessed against either defendant? Why or why not?

## Legal Reasoning Group Activity

**25–10. Agent's Duties to Principal.** John Warren wanted to buy a condominium in California. Hildegard Merrill was the agent for the seller. Because Warren's credit rating was poor, Merrill told him he needed a co-borrower to obtain a mortgage at a reasonable rate. Merrill said that her daughter Charmaine would "go on title" until the loan and sale were complete if Warren would pay her $10,000. Merrill also offered to defer her commission on the sale as a loan to Warren so that he could make a 20 percent down payment on the property. He agreed to both plans.

Merrill secured the mortgage in Charmaine's name alone by misrepresenting her daughter's address, business, and income. To close the sale, Merrill had Warren remove his name from the title to the property. In October, Warren moved into the condominium, repaid Merrill the amount of her deferred commission, and began paying the mortgage. Within a few months, Merrill had Warren evicted. Warren subsequently filed a suit against Merrill and Charmaine. **(See page 442.)**

(a) The first group will determine who among these parties was in an agency relationship.

(b) The second group will discuss the basic duty that an agent owes a principal and decide whether that duty was breached here.

# CHAPTER 26
# AGENCY LIABILITY TO THIRD PARTIES AND TERMINATION

I n the discussion of agency in the previous chapter, we focused on how the relationship between a principal and an agent is formed and the duties of the principal and agent in that relationship. This chapter deals with another important aspect of agency law—the liability of principals and agents to third parties.

We look first at the liability of principals for contracts formed by agents with third parties. Generally, the liability of the principal will depend on whether the agent was authorized to form the contract. The second part of the chapter deals with an agent's liability to third parties in contract and tort, and the principal's liability to third parties because of an agent's torts. The chapter concludes with a discussion of how agency relationships are terminated.

## SECTION 1
## SCOPE OF AGENT'S AUTHORITY

The liability of a principal to third parties with whom an agent contracts depends on whether the agent had the authority to enter into legally binding contracts on the principal's behalf. An agent's authority can be either *actual* (express or implied) or *apparent*. If an agent contracts outside the scope of his or her authority, the principal may still become liable by ratifying the contract.

### Express Authority

**Express authority** is authority declared in clear, direct, and definite terms. Express authority can be given orally or in writing.

**THE EQUAL DIGNITY RULE** In most states, the **equal dignity rule** requires that if the contract being executed is or must be in writing, then the agent's authority must also be in writing. Failure to comply with the equal dignity rule can make a contract voidable *at the option of the principal*. The law regards the contract at that point as a mere offer. If the principal decides to accept the offer, the acceptance must be ratified, or affirmed, in writing (or in an electronic record).
▶ **Example 26.1** Paloma (the principal) orally asks Austin (the agent) to sell a ranch that Paloma owns. Austin finds a buyer and signs a sales contract (a contract for an interest in realty must be in writing) on behalf of Paloma to sell the ranch. The buyer cannot enforce the contract unless Paloma subsequently ratifies Austin's agency status *in writing*. Once the sales contract is ratified, either party can enforce rights under the contract. ◀

Modern business practice allows several exceptions to the equal dignity rule:

1. An executive officer of a corporation normally can conduct *ordinary* business transactions without obtaining written authority from the corporation (see Chapter 32).
2. When the agent acts in the presence of the principal, the rule does not apply.
3. When the agent's act of signing is merely a formality, then the agent does not need written authority to sign. ▶ **Example 26.2** Sandra Healy (the principal) negotiates a contract but is called out of town the day it is to be signed. If Healy orally authorizes Santini to sign, the oral authorization is sufficient. ◀

**POWER OF ATTORNEY** Giving an agent a **power of attorney** confers express authority.[1] The power of attorney is a written document and is usually notarized. (A document is notarized when a **notary public**—a public official authorized to attest to the

---

1. An agent who holds a power of attorney is called an *attorney-in-fact* for the principal. The holder does not have to be an attorney-at-law (and often is not).

authenticity of signatures—signs and dates the document and imprints it with her or his seal of authority.) Most states have statutory provisions for creating a power of attorney.

A power of attorney can be *special* (permitting the agent to perform specified acts only), or it can be *general* (permitting the agent to transact all business for the principal). Because of the extensive authority granted to an agent by a general power of attorney (see Exhibit 26–1 below), it should be used with great caution and usually only in exceptional circumstances. Ordinarily, a power of attorney terminates

**EXHIBIT 26-1  A Sample General Power of Attorney**

---

## GENERAL POWER OF ATTORNEY

### Know All Men by These Presents:

That I, _____ , hereinafter referred to as PRINCIPAL, in the County of _____
State of _____ , do(es) appoint _____ as my true and lawful attorney.

In principal's name, and for principal's use and benefit, said attorney is authorized hereby;

(1) To demand, sue for, collect, and receive all money, debts, accounts, legacies, bequests, interest, dividends, annuities, and demands as are now or shall hereafter become due, payable, or belonging to principal, and take all lawful means, for the recovery thereof and to compromise the same and give discharges for the same;

(2) To buy and sell land, make contracts of every kind relative to land, any interest therein or the possession thereof, and to take possession and exercise control over the use thereof;

(3) To buy, sell, mortgage, hypothecate, assign, transfer, and in any manner deal with goods, wares and merchandise, choses in action, certificates or shares of capital stock, and other property in possession or in action, and to make, do, and transact all and every kind of business of whatever nature;

(4) To execute, acknowledge, and deliver contracts of sale, escrow instructions, deeds, leases including leases for minerals and hydrocarbon substances and assignments of leases, covenants, agreements and assignments of agreements, mortgages and assignments of mortgages, conveyances in trust, to secure indebtedness or other obligations, and assign the beneficial interest thereunder, subordinations of liens or encumbrances, bills of lading, receipts, evidences of debt, releases, bonds, notes, bills, requests to reconvey deeds of trust, partial or full judgments, satisfactions of mortgages, and other debts, and other written instruments of whatever kind and nature, all upon such terms and conditions as said attorney shall approve.

GIVING AND GRANTING to said attorney full power and authority to do all and every act and thing whatsoever requisite and necessary to be done relative to any of the foregoing as fully to all intents and purposes as principal might or could do if personally present.

All that said attorney shall lawfully do or cause to be done under the authority of this power of attorney is expressly approved.

Dated: _____        /s/_____

State of _____        }  SS.
  County of _____
On _____ , before me, the undersigned, a Notary Public in and for said
State, personally appeared _____

known to me to be the person _____ whose name _____ subscribed
to the within instrument and acknowledged that _____ executed the same.

Witness my hand and official seal.        (Seal) _____
                                                    Notary Public in and for said State.

on the incapacity or death of the person giving the power.[2]

## Implied Authority

An agent has the **implied authority** to do what is reasonably necessary to carry out express authority and accomplish the objectives of the agency. Authority can also be implied by custom or inferred

---

2. A *durable* power of attorney, however, continues to be effective despite the principal's incapacity. An elderly person, for example, might grant a durable power of attorney to provide for the handling of property and investments or specific health-care needs should he or she become incompetent.

from the position the agent occupies. (For a discussion of what happens when an employee-agent makes unauthorized use of the employer's computer data, see this chapter's *Insight into Ethics* feature below.)

▶ **Example 26.3** Archer is employed by Packard Grocery to manage one of its stores. Packard has not expressly stated that Archer has authority to contract with third persons. Nevertheless, authority to manage a business implies authority to do what is reasonably required (as is customary or can be inferred from a manager's position) to operate the business. It is reasonable to imply the authority to form contracts to hire employees, to buy merchandise and equipment, and to advertise the products sold in the store. ◀

---

# INSIGHT INTO ETHICS
## The Ethical and Legal Implications of Breaching Company Policy on the Use of Electronic Data

Suppose that an employee-agent who is authorized to access company trade secrets contained in computer files takes those secrets to a competitor for whom the employee is about to begin working. Clearly, the agent has violated the ethical—and legal—duty of loyalty to the principal. Does this breach of loyalty mean that the employee's act of accessing the trade secrets was unauthorized?

The question has significant implications for both parties. If the action was unauthorized, the employee will be subject to state and federal laws prohibiting unauthorized access to computer information and data, including the Computer Fraud and Abuse Act (CFAA, discussed in Chapter 10). If the action was authorized, these laws will not apply.

### Does Exceeding Authorized Access to a Company's Database Violate the Law?

David Nosal once worked for Korn/Ferry and had access to the company's confidential database. When he left, he encouraged several former colleagues who still worked there to join him in starting a competing firm. He asked them to access Korn/Ferry's database and download source lists, names, and client contact information before they quit. The employees had authority to access the database, but Korn/Ferry's policy forbade disclosure of confidential information.

The government filed charges against Nosal and his colleagues for violating the CFAA, among other things.

### A Court Rules That Violating an Employer's Use Restrictions Is Not a Crime

The U.S. Court of Appeals for the Ninth Circuit refused to find that the defendants had violated the CFAA. The court ruled that the phrase "exceed authorized access" in the CFAA refers to restrictions on access, not restrictions on use. The court reasoned that Congress's intent in enacting the CFAA was to prohibit people from hacking into computers without authorization.

The court also stated that the CFAA should not be used to criminally prosecute persons who use data in an unauthorized or unethical way. The court pointed out that "adopting the government's interpretation would turn vast numbers of teens and pre-teens into juvenile delinquents—and their parents and teachers into delinquency contributors." Furthermore, "the effect this broad construction of the CFAA has on workplace conduct pales by comparison with its effect on everyone else who uses a computer, smart-phone, iPad, Kindle, Nook, X-box, Blu-Ray player or any other Internet-enabled device."[a]

### LEGAL CRITICAL THINKING
#### INSIGHT INTO THE LEGAL ENVIRONMENT

*If an employee accesses Facebook at work even though personal use of a workplace computer is against the employer's stated policies, can the employee be criminally prosecuted? Why or why not?*

---

a. *United States. v. Nosal*, 675 F.3d 854 (9th Cir. 2012).

Note, however, that an agent's implied authority cannot contradict his or her express authority. Thus, if a principal has limited an agent's express authority, then the fact that the agent customarily would have such authority is irrelevant. ▶ **Example 26.4** Juanita Alvarez is the owner of six Baja Tacos restaurants. Alvarez (the principal) strictly forbids the managers (agents) of her taco shops from entering into contracts to hire additional workers. Therefore, the fact that managers customarily would have authority to hire employees is immaterial. ◀

## Apparent Authority

Actual authority (express or implied) arises from what the principal makes clear *to the agent.* Apparent authority, in contrast, arises from what the principal causes a third party to believe. An agent has **apparent authority** when the principal, by either word or action, causes a *third party* reasonably to believe that the agent has authority to act, even though the agent has no express or implied authority.

**A PATTERN OF CONDUCT** Apparent authority usually comes into existence through a principal's pattern of conduct over time. ▶ **Example 26.5** Bailey is a traveling salesperson with the authority to solicit orders for the goods of Carlon Industries (the principal). Because she does not carry any goods with her, she normally would not have the implied authority to collect payments from customers on Carlon's behalf.

Suppose that Bailey does accept payments from Jayco Enterprises, however, and submits them to Carlon's accounting department for processing. If Carlon does nothing to stop Bailey from continuing this practice, a pattern develops over time. Thus, the principal confers apparent authority on Bailey to accept payments from Jayco. ◀

At issue in the following *Spotlight Case* was whether the manager of a horse breeding operation had the authority to bind the farm's owner in a contract guaranteeing breeding rights.

---

## SP★TLIGHT on Apparent Authority

### Case 26.1 Lundberg v. Church Farm, Inc.

Court of Appeals of Illinois, 151 Ill.App.3d 452, 502 N.E.2d 806 (1986).

**BACKGROUND AND FACTS** Gilbert Church owned a horse breeding farm managed by Herb Bagley. Advertisements for the breeding rights to one of Church Farm's stallions, Imperial Guard, directed all inquiries to "Herb Bagley, Manager." Vern and Gail Lundberg bred Thoroughbred horses. The Lundbergs contacted Bagley and executed a preprinted contract giving them breeding rights to Imperial Guard "at Imperial Guard's location," subject to approval of the mares by Church. Bagley handwrote a statement on the contract that guaranteed the Lundbergs "six live foals in the first two years." He then signed it "Gilbert G. Church by H. Bagley."

The Lundbergs bred four mares, which resulted in one live foal. Church then moved Imperial Guard from Illinois to Oklahoma. The Lundbergs sued Church for breaching the contract by moving the horse. Church claimed that Bagley was not authorized to sign contracts for Church or to change or add terms, but only to present preprinted contracts to potential buyers. Church testified that although Bagley was his farm manager and the contact person for breeding rights, Bagley had never before modified the preprinted forms or signed Church's name on these contracts. The jury found in favor of the Lundbergs and awarded $147,000 in damages. Church appealed.

**DECISION AND RATIONALE** A state intermediate appellate court affirmed the lower court's award of $147,000 to the Lundbergs. Because Church allowed circumstances to lead the Lundbergs to believe Bagley had authority, Church was bound by Bagley's actions. A principal may be bound by the unauthorized acts of an agent if the principal leads a third party to believe, or allows a third party to believe, that the agent has authority to perform the act. In this case, Church approved the advertisement listing Bagley as Church Farm's manager and point of contact. Bagley generally was the only person available to visitors to the farm. Bagley answered the farm's phone, and the breeding contract had a preprinted

CASE 26.1 CONTINUES ▶

signature line for him. Church was not engaged in the actual negotiation or signing of the contracts but left that business for Bagley to complete. Based on Church's actions, a reasonable third party would believe that Bagley had authority to sign and modify contracts.

**THE LEGAL ENVIRONMENT DIMENSION** *The court held that Church had allowed the Lundbergs to believe that Bagley was his agent. What steps could Church have taken to protect himself against a finding of apparent authority?*

**THE ETHICAL DIMENSION** *Does a principal have an ethical responsibility to inform an unaware third party that an apparent agent does not in fact have the authority to act on the principal's behalf? Explain.*

---

**APPARENT AUTHORITY AND ESTOPPEL** A court can apply the doctrine of agency by estoppel (discussed in Chapter 25) when a principal has given a third party reason to believe that an agent has authority to act. If the third party honestly relies on the principal's representations to his or her detriment, the principal may be *estopped* (prevented) from denying that the agent had authority.

▶ **Case in Point 26.6** Francis Azur was president and chief executive officer of ATM Corporation of America. Michelle Vanek, Azur's personal assistant at ATM, reviewed his credit-card statements, among other duties. For seven years, Vanek took unauthorized cash advances from Azur's credit-card account with Chase Bank. The charges appeared on at least sixty-five monthly statements. When Azur discovered Vanek's fraud, he fired her and closed the account. He filed a suit against Chase, arguing that the bank should not have allowed Vanek to take cash advances. The court concluded that Azur (the principal) had given the bank reason to believe that Vanek (the agent) had authority. Therefore, Azur was estopped (prevented) from denying Vanek's authority.[3] ◀

## Emergency Powers

When an unforeseen emergency demands action by the agent to protect or preserve the property and rights of the principal, but the agent is unable to communicate with the principal, the agent has emergency power.

▶ **Example 26.7** Rob Fulsom is an engineer for Pacific Drilling Company. While Fulsom is acting within the scope of his employment, he is severely injured in an accident at an oil rig many miles from home. Acosta, the rig supervisor, directs Thompson, a physician, to give medical aid to Fulsom and to charge Pacific for the medical services. Acosta, an agent, has no express or implied authority to bind the princi-

pal, Pacific Drilling, for Thompson's medical services. Because of the emergency situation, however, the law recognizes Acosta as having authority to act appropriately under the circumstances. ◀

## Ratification

**Ratification** occurs when the principal affirms, or accepts responsibility for, an agent's *unauthorized* act. When ratification occurs, the principal is bound to the agent's act, and the act is treated as if it had been authorized by the principal *from the outset*. Ratification can be either express or implied.

If the principal does not ratify the contract, the principal is not bound, and the third party's agreement with the agent is viewed as merely an unaccepted offer. Because the third party's agreement is an unaccepted offer, the third party can revoke it at any time, without liability, before the principal ratifies the contract. The agent, however, may be liable to the third party for misrepresenting her or his authority.

The requirements for ratification can be summarized as follows:

1. The agent must have acted on behalf of an identified principal who subsequently ratifies the action.
2. The principal must know all of the material facts involved in the transaction. If a principal ratifies a contract without knowing all of the facts, the principal can rescind (cancel) the contract.[4]
3. The principal must affirm the agent's act in its entirety.
4. The principal must have the legal capacity to authorize the transaction at the time the agent engages in the act and at the time the principal ratifies. The third party must also have the legal capacity to engage in the transaction.

---

3. *Azur v. Chase Bank, USA, N.A.*, 601 F.3d 212 (3d Cir. 2010).

4. If the third party has changed position in reliance on the apparent contract, however, the principal can rescind but must reimburse the third party for any costs.

5. The principal's affirmation (ratification) must occur before the third party withdraws from the transaction.

6. The principal must observe the same formalities when ratifying the act as would have been required to authorize it initially.

*Concept Summary 26.1* below summarizes the rules concerning an agent's authority to bind the principal and a third party.

## SECTION 2
# LIABILITY FOR CONTRACTS

Liability for contracts formed by an agent depends on how the principal is classified and on whether the actions of the agent were authorized or unauthorized. Principals are classified as disclosed, partially disclosed, or undisclosed.[5]

1. A **disclosed principal** is a principal whose identity is known by the third party at the time the contract is made by the agent.

2. A **partially disclosed principal** is a principal whose identity is not known by the third party. Nevertheless, the third party knows that the agent is or *may* be acting for a principal at the time the contract is made. ▶ **Example 26.8** Eileen has

contracted with a real estate agent to sell certain property. She wishes to keep her identity a secret, but the agent makes it clear to potential buyers of the property that the agent is acting in an agency capacity. In this situation, Eileen is a partially disclosed principal. ◀

3. An **undisclosed principal** is a principal whose identity is totally unknown by the third party. In addition, the third party has no knowledge that the agent is acting in an agency capacity at the time the contract is made.

## Authorized Acts

If an agent acts within the scope of her or his authority, normally the principal is obligated to perform the contract regardless of whether the principal was disclosed, partially disclosed, or undisclosed.

Whether the *agent may also be held liable* under the contract, however, depends on the disclosed, partially disclosed, or undisclosed status of the principal.

**DISCLOSED OR PARTIALLY DISCLOSED PRINCIPAL** A disclosed or partially disclosed principal is liable to a third party for a contract made by the agent. If the principal is disclosed, the agent has no contractual liability for the nonperformance of the principal or the third party. If the principal is partially disclosed, in most states the agent is also treated as a party to the

---

5. *Restatement (Third) of Agency,* Section 1.04(2).

---

| CONCEPT SUMMARY 26.1 | | |
|---|---|---|
| **Authority of an Agent to Bind the Principal and a Third Party** | | |
| **AUTHORITY OF AGENT** | **DEFINITION** | **EFFECT ON PRINCIPAL AND THIRD PARTY** |
| **Express Authority** | Authority expressly given by the principal to the agent. | Principal and third party are bound in contract. |
| **Implied Authority** | Authority implied (1) by custom, (2) from the position in which the principal has placed the agent, or (3) because such authority is necessary if the agent is to carry out expressly authorized duties and responsibilities. | Principal and third party are bound in contract. |
| **Apparent Authority** | Authority created when the conduct of the principal leads a third party to believe that the principal's agent has authority. | Principal and third party are bound in contract. |
| **Unauthorized Acts** | Acts committed by an agent that are outside the scope of his or her express, implied, or apparent authority. | Principal and third party are not bound in contract—*unless* the principal ratifies prior to the third party's withdrawal. |

contract, and the third party can hold the agent liable for contractual nonperformance.[6]

▶ **Case in Point 26.9** Walgreens leased commercial property at a mall owned by Kedzie Plaza Associates. Kedzie used Taxman Corporation, a property management company. Taxman signed the lease with Walgreens on behalf of the principal, Kedzie. The lease required the landlord to keep the sidewalks free of snow and ice. Therefore, Taxman, on behalf of Kedzie, contracted with another company to remove ice and snow from the sidewalks surrounding the Walgreens store.

When a Walgreens employee slipped on ice outside the store and was injured, she sued Taxman, among others, for negligence. Because the identity of the principal (Kedzie) was fully disclosed in the snow-removal contract, however, the court ruled that the agent, Taxman, could not be held liable. Taxman did not assume a contractual obligation to remove the snow but merely retained a contractor to do so on behalf of the owner.[7] ◀

**UNDISCLOSED PRINCIPAL** When neither the fact of an agency relationship nor the identity of the principal is disclosed, the undisclosed principal is bound to perform just as if the principal had been fully disclosed at the time the contract was made.

---

6. *Restatement (Third) of Agency,* Section 6.02.
7. *McBride v. Taxman Corp.,* 327 Ill.App.3d 992, 765 N.E.2d 51 (2002).

When a principal's identity is undisclosed and the agent is forced to pay the third party, the agent is entitled to be *indemnified* (compensated) by the principal. The principal had a duty to perform, even though his or her identity was undisclosed,[8] and failure to do so will make the principal ultimately liable. Once the undisclosed principal's identity is revealed, the third party generally can elect to hold either the principal or the agent liable on the contract.

Conversely, the undisclosed principal can require the third party to fulfill the contract, *unless* one of the following is true:

1. The undisclosed principal was expressly excluded as a party in the written contract.
2. The contract is a negotiable instrument signed by the agent with no indication of signing in a representative capacity.[9]
3. The performance of the agent is personal to the contract, thus allowing the third party to refuse the principal's performance.

In the following case, three parties involved in an auto sales transaction were embroiled in a dispute over who was liable when the car's engine caught fire.

---

8. If the agent is a gratuitous agent, and the principal accepts the benefits of the agent's contract with a third party, then the principal will be liable to the agent on the theory of quasi contract (see Chapter 11).
9. Under the Uniform Commercial Code (UCC), only the agent is liable if the instrument neither names the principal nor shows that the agent signed in a representative capacity [UCC 3–402(b)(2)].

---

## CASE 26.2

### Williams v. Pike
Court of Appeal of Louisiana, Second Circuit, 58 So.3d 525 (2011).

**BACKGROUND AND FACTS** Bobby Williams bought a car for $3,000 at Sherman Henderson's auto repair business in Monroe, Louisiana. Although the car's owner was Joe Pike, the owner of Justice Wrecker Service, Henderson negotiated the sale, accepted Williams's payment, and gave him two receipts. Williams drove the car to Memphis, Tennessee, where his daughter was a student. Three days after the sale, the car began to emit smoke and flames from under the hood. Williams extinguished the blaze and contacted Henderson. The next day, Williams's daughter had the vehicle towed at her expense to her apartment's parking lot, from which it was soon stolen. Williams filed a suit in a Louisiana state court against Pike and Henderson. The court awarded Williams $2,000, plus the costs of the suit, adding that if Williams had returned the car, it would have awarded him the entire price. Pike and Henderson appealed.

**DECISION AND RATIONALE** A state intermediate appellate court affirmed the ruling of the lower court and added the costs of the appeal to the amount that the lower court had awarded. Both Pike and Henderson were liable to Williams. A state permit to sell the car had been issued to Pike and showed that Justice Wrecker was the owner. The car was displayed for sale at Henderson's business, however, and he actually sold it. This made Pike the principal and Henderson his agent. The fact that their agency relationship was not made clear to Williams made Pike an undisclosed principal. Williams could thus choose

**CASE 26.2 CONTINUED**   to hold either Pike or Henderson liable for the condition of the car, which constituted a breach of implied warranty because the car did not fulfill the purpose for which it was intended. The loss of the use of the car, the "inconvenience" caused by the defect, the price, and the cost of the tow were among the factors that supported the award.

**WHAT IF THE FACTS WERE DIFFERENT?** *Suppose that Henderson had fully disclosed the fact of his agency relationship and the identity of his principal. Would the result have been different? Why or why not?*

**THE LEGAL ENVIRONMENT DIMENSION** *Is Henderson entitled to be compensated by Pike for any portion of the judgment that he pays to Williams? Explain.*

## Unauthorized Acts

If an agent has no authority but nevertheless contracts with a third party, the *principal* cannot be held liable on the contract. It does not matter whether the principal was disclosed, partially disclosed, or undisclosed. The *agent* is liable, however.

▶ **Example 26.10**   Chu signs a contract for the purchase of a truck, purportedly acting as an agent under authority granted by Navarro. In fact, Navarro has not given Chu any such authority. Navarro refuses to pay for the truck, claiming that Chu had no authority to purchase it. The seller of the truck is entitled to hold Chu liable for payment. ◀

**IMPLIED WARRANTY** If the principal is disclosed or partially disclosed, and the agent contracts with a third party without authorization, the agent is liable to the third party who relied on the agency status. The agent's liability here is based on his or her breach of the *implied warranty of authority,* not on the breach of the contract itself.[10] An agent impliedly warrants that he or she has the authority to enter a contract on behalf of the principal.

▶ **Example 26.11**   Pinnell, a reclusive artist, hires Auber to solicit offers for particular paintings from various galleries, but does not authorize her to enter into sales agreements. Olaf, a gallery owner, offers to buy two of Pinnell's paintings for an upcoming show. If Auber draws up a sales contract with Olaf, she impliedly warrants that she has the authority to enter into sales contracts on behalf of Pinnell. If Pinnell does not agree to ratify Auber's sales contract, Olaf cannot hold Pinnell liable, but he can hold Auber liable for breaching the implied warranty of authority. ◀

**THIRD PARTY'S KNOWLEDGE** Note that if the third party knows at the time the contract is made that the

agent does not have authority, then the agent is not liable. Similarly, if the agent expressed to the third party *uncertainty* as to the extent of her or his authority, the agent is not personally liable.

## Actions by E-Agents

Although in the past standard agency principles applied only to *human* agents, today these same agency principles also apply to e-agents. An electronic agent, or **e-agent,** is a semiautonomous computer program that is capable of executing specific tasks. For instance, software that can search through many databases and retrieve only relevant information for the user is an e-agent.

The Uniform Electronic Transactions Act (UETA), which was discussed in Chapter 12, sets forth provisions relating to the principal's liability for the actions of e-agents. According to Section 15 of the UETA, e-agents can enter into binding agreements on behalf of their principals—at least, in those states that have adopted the act. Thus, if consumers place an order over the Internet, and the company (principal) takes the order via an e-agent, the company cannot later claim that it did not receive the order.

The UETA also stipulates that if an e-agent does not provide an opportunity to prevent errors at the time of the transaction, the other party to the transaction can avoid the transaction. Therefore, if an e-agent fails to provide an on-screen confirmation of a purchase or sale, the other party can avoid the effect of any errors. ▶ **Example 26.12**   Bigelow wants to purchase three copies of three different books (a total of nine items). The e-agent mistakenly records an order for thirty-three of a single book and does not provide an on-screen verification of the order. If thirty-three books are then sent to Bigelow, he can avoid the contract to purchase them. ◀

---

**10.** The agent is not liable on the contract because the agent was never intended personally to be a party to the contract.

## SECTION 3
# LIABILITY FOR TORTS AND CRIMES

Obviously, any person, including an agent, is liable for his or her own torts and crimes. Whether a principal can also be held liable for an agent's torts and crimes depends on several factors, which we examine here. In some situations, a principal may be held liable not only for the torts of an agent but also for torts committed by an independent contractor.

## Principal's Tortious Conduct

A principal who acts through an agent may be liable for harm resulting from the principal's own negligence or recklessness. Thus, a principal may be liable if he or she gives improper instructions, authorizes the use of improper materials or tools, or establishes improper rules that result in the agent's committing a tort.
▶ **Example 26.13** Parker knows that Audrey's driver's license has been suspended but nevertheless tells her to use the company truck to deliver some equipment to a customer. If someone is injured as a result, Parker will be liable for his own negligence in instructing Audrey to drive without a valid license. ◀

## Principal's Authorization of Agent's Tortious Conduct

Similarly, a principal who authorizes an agent to commit a tort may be liable to persons or property injured thereby, because the act is considered to be the principal's. ▶ **Example 26.14** Pedro directs his agent, Andy, to cut the corn on specific acreage, which neither of them has the right to do. The harvest is therefore a trespass (a tort), and Pedro is liable to the owner of the corn. ◀

Note that an agent acting at the principal's direction can be liable as a *tortfeasor* (one who commits a wrong, or tort), along with the principal, for committing the tortious act even if the agent was unaware that the act was wrong. Assume in *Example 26.14* that Andy, the agent, did not know that Pedro lacked the right to harvest the corn. Andy can still be held liable to the owner of the field for damages, along with Pedro, the principal.

## Liability for Agent's Misrepresentation

A principal is exposed to tort liability whenever a third person sustains a loss due to the agent's mis-representation. The principal's liability depends on whether the agent was actually or apparently authorized to make representations and whether the representations were made within the scope of the agency. The principal is always directly responsible for an agent's misrepresentation made within the scope of the agent's authority.
▶ **Example 26.15** Ainsley is a demonstrator for Pavlovich's products. Pavlovich sends Ainsley to a home show to demonstrate the products and to answer questions from consumers. Pavlovich has given Ainsley authority to make statements about the products. If Ainsley makes only true representations, all is fine. But if he makes false claims, Pavlovich will be liable for any injuries or damages sustained by third parties in reliance on Ainsley's false representations. ◀

**APPARENT IMPLIED AUTHORITY** When a principal has placed an agent in a position of apparent authority—making it possible for the agent to defraud a third party—the principal may also be liable for the agent's fraudulent acts. For instance, partners in a partnership generally have the apparent implied authority to act as agents of the firm, as will be discussed in Chapter 30. Thus, if one of the partners commits a tort or a crime, the partnership itself—and often the other partners personally—can be held liable for the loss.
▶ **Case in Point 26.16** Selheimer & Company, a securities broker-dealer that operated as a partnership, provided various financial services. The managing partner, Perry Selheimer, embezzled funds that clients had turned over to the firm for investment. After Selheimer was convicted, other partners in the firm claimed that they were not liable for losses resulting from his illegal activities. The court, however, held that Selheimer had apparent implied authority to act in the ordinary course of the partnership's business. Thus, the firm, as principal, was liable, and under the law of partnerships the personal assets of the individual partners could be used to cover the firm's liability.[11] ◀

**INNOCENT MISREPRESENTATION** Tort liability based on fraud requires proof that a material misstatement was made knowingly and with the intent to deceive. An agent's *innocent* misstatements in a contract or warranty transaction can also provide grounds for the third party's rescission of the contract and the award of damages. Justice dictates that when a principal

---

11. *In re Selheimer & Co.*, 319 Bankr. 395 (E.D.Pa. 2005).

knows that an agent is not accurately advised of facts but does not correct either the agent's or the third party's impressions, the principal is responsible. The point is that the principal is always directly responsible for an agent's misrepresentation made within the scope of authority.

## Liability for Agent's Negligence

Under the doctrine of ***respondeat superior*** (a Latin term meaning "let the master respond),"[12] a principal may also be liable for harm that his or her agent causes to a third party. This doctrine imposes **vicarious liability,** or indirect liability, on an employer that is similar to strict liability (see Chapter 7), in that both are imposed regardless of fault. Under this doctrine, the employer is liable for torts committed by an employee acting within the course or scope of employment. (Of course, the employee is also liable for any torts that she or he commits.)

Third parties injured through the negligence of an employee can sue either that employee or the employer, if the employee's negligent conduct occurred while the employee was acting within the scope of employment. ▶ **Case in Point 26.17** Aegis Communications hired Southwest Desert Images (SDI) to provide landscaping services for its property. An herbicide sprayed by SDI employee David Hoggatt entered the Aegis building through the air-conditioning system and caused Catherine Warner, an Aegis employee, to suffer a heart attack. Warner sued SDI and Hoggatt for negligence, but the lower court dismissed the suit against Hoggatt. On appeal, the court found that Hoggatt was also liable. An agent is not excused from responsibility for tortious conduct just because he is working for a principal. Both the agent and the principal are liable.[13] ◀

**THE DOCTRINE OF *RESPONDEAT SUPERIOR*** At early common law, a servant (employee) was viewed as the master's (employer's) property. The master was deemed to have absolute control over the servant's acts and was held strictly liable for them, no matter how carefully the master supervised the servant. Although employers today are not masters of their employees, control is still a central concept to liability.

***Underlying Rationale.*** The rationale for the doctrine of *respondeat superior* is based on the social duty that requires every person to manage his or her affairs so as not to injure another. This duty applies even when a person acts through an agent (controls the conduct of another).

***Public Policy.*** Generally, public policy requires that an injured person be afforded effective relief, and a business enterprise is usually better able to provide that relief than is an individual employee. Employers normally carry liability insurance to cover any damages awarded as a result of such lawsuits. They are also able to spread the cost of risk over the entire business enterprise.

The courts have applied the doctrine of *respondeat superior* for nearly two centuries. It continues to have practical implications in all situations involving principal-agent (employer-employee) relationships. Today, the small-town grocer with one clerk and the multinational corporation with thousands of employees are equally subject to the doctrine. (Keep this principle in mind when you read Chapters 27 and 28.)

**DETERMINING THE SCOPE OF EMPLOYMENT** The key to determining whether a principal may be liable for the torts of an agent under the doctrine of *respondeat superior* is whether the torts are committed within the scope of the agency or employment. Courts may consider the following factors in determining whether a particular act occurred within the course and scope of employment:

1. Whether the employee's act was authorized by the employer.
2. The time, place, and purpose of the act.
3. Whether the act was one commonly performed by employees on behalf of their employers.
4. The extent to which the employer's interest was advanced by the act.
5. The extent to which the private interests of the employee were involved.
6. Whether the employer furnished the means or instrumentality (for example, a truck or a machine) by which an injury was inflicted.
7. Whether the employer had reason to know that the employee would perform the act in question and whether the employee had done it before.
8. Whether the act involved the commission of a serious crime.

Whether a real estate salesperson's actions in connection with certain real estate transactions fell within the salesperson's scope of employment was at issue in the following case.

---

12. Pronounced ree-*spahn*-dee-uht soo-*peer*-ee-your. The doctrine of *respondeat superior* applies not only to employer-employee relationships but also to other principal-agent relationships in which the principal has the right of control over the agent.
13. *Warner v. Southwest Desert Images, LLC,* 218 Ariz. 121, 180 P.3d 986 (2008).

## CASE 26.3

### Auer v. Paliath

Court of Appeals of Ohio, Second District, 2013 -Ohio- 391, 986 N.E.2d 1052 (2013).

**BACKGROUND AND FACTS** Jamie Paliath worked as a real estate salesperson for Home Town Realty of Vandalia, LLC, in Dayton, Ohio. Torri Auer, a California resident, relied on Paliath's advice and assistance to buy rental property at 117 Belton Street, as well as 1111 and 1115 Richmond Avenue. Before the sales, Paliath represented that each property was worth approximately twice as much as what Auer would pay, and there was a waiting list of prospective tenants. Additionally, Paliath stated that all of the property needed work and agreed to do it for certain prices. Nearly a year later, when substantial work was still needed, and only a few of the units had been rented, Auer filed a suit in an Ohio state court against Paliath and Home Town Realty, alleging fraud in the sale of the property. A jury found Paliath and Home Town Realty liable to Auer for $135,200 each. Home Town Realty appealed.

**DECISION AND RATIONALE** A state intermediate appellate court affirmed the lower court's judgment. Paliath had acted within the scope of her employment as a real estate salesperson with Home Town Realty when she committed fraud in the sale of property to Auer. Home Town Realty was thus vicariously (indirectly) liable for Paliath's fraud. Under Ohio law, Home Town Realty qualified as a real estate broker. All real estate salespersons can only collect money in connection for a real estate transaction in the name of and with consent of the licensed real estate broker. "A real estate broker will be held vicariously liable for intentional torts commented by salesmen acting within the scope of their authority. Vicariously liability is appropriate because a real estate salesman has no independent status or right to conclude a sale and can only function through the broker with whom he is associated." As a matter of law, a real estate salesperson acting in connection with the type of real estate transaction for which she or he was hired is acting within the scope of that salesperson's employment. Finally, Home Town Realty was listed as the real estate broker on the purchase contract and it received a commission for each sale.

**THE ETHICAL DIMENSION** *What is the ethical basis for imposing vicarious liability on a principal for an agent's tort?*

**THE LEGAL ENVIRONMENT DIMENSION** *What factors did the court apply to determine liability in this case?*

---

**THE DISTINCTION BETWEEN A "DETOUR" AND A "FROLIC"** A useful insight into the concept of "scope of employment" may be gained from Judge Baron Parke's classic distinction between a "detour" and a "frolic" in the case of *Joel v. Morison* (1834).[14] In this case, the English court held that if a servant merely took a detour from his master's business, the master will be responsible. If, however, the servant was on a "frolic of his own" and not in any way "on his master's business," the master will not be liable.

▶ **Example 26.18** Mandel, a traveling salesperson, while driving his employer's vehicle to call on a customer, decides to stop at the post office—which

is one block off his route—to mail a personal letter. As Mandel approaches the post office, he negligently runs into a parked vehicle owned by Chan. In this situation, because Mandel's detour from the employer's business is not substantial, he is still acting within the scope of employment, and the employer is liable.

The result would be different, though, if Mandel had decided to pick up a few friends for drinks in another city and in the process had negligently run his vehicle into Chan's. In that circumstance, the departure from the employer's business would be substantial, and the employer normally would not be liable to Chan for damages. Mandel would be considered to have been on a "frolic" of his own. ◀

---

**14.** 6 Car. & P. 501, 172 Eng.Rep. 1338 (1834).

**EMPLOYEE TRAVEL TIME** An employee going to and from work or to and from meals usually is considered to be outside the scope of employment. In contrast, all travel time of traveling salespersons or others whose jobs require travel is normally considered to be within the scope of employment for the duration of the business trip, including the return trip home.

**NOTICE OF DANGEROUS CONDITIONS** The employer is charged with knowledge of any dangerous conditions discovered by an employee and pertinent to the employment situation. ▶ **Example 26.19** Brad, a maintenance employee in an apartment building, notices a lead pipe protruding from the ground in the building's courtyard. Brad neglects either to fix the pipe or to inform his employer of the danger. John trips on the pipe and is injured.

The employer is charged with knowledge of the dangerous condition regardless of whether Brad actually informed the employer. That knowledge is imputed to the employer by virtue of the employment relationship. ◀

## Liability for Agent's Intentional Torts

Most intentional torts that individuals commit have no relation to their employment, and their employers will not be held liable. Nevertheless, under the doctrine of *respondeat superior,* the employer can be liable for intentional torts that an employee commits within the course and scope of employment. For instance, an employer is liable when an employee (such as a "bouncer" at a nightclub or a security guard at a department store) commits the tort of assault and battery or false imprisonment while acting within the scope of employment.

In addition, an employer who knows or should know that an employee has a propensity for committing tortious acts is liable for the employee's acts even if they would not ordinarily be considered within the scope of employment. ▶ **Example 26.20** Chaz, the owner of the Comedy Club, hires Alec as a bouncer for the club even though he knows that Alec has a history of arrests for criminal assault and battery. In this situation, Chaz may be liable if Alec viciously attacks a customer in the parking lot after hours. ◀

An employer is also liable for permitting an employee to engage in reckless actions that can injure others. ▶ **Example 26.21** The owner of Bates Trucking observes an employee smoking while filling containerized trucks with highly flammable liquids. Failure to stop the employee will cause the employer to be liable for any injuries that result if a truck explodes. ◀ Needless to say, most employers purchase liability insurance to cover their potential liability for employee conduct in many situations.

## Liability for Independent Contractor's Torts

Generally, an employer is not liable for physical harm caused to a third person by the negligent act of an independent contractor in the performance of the contract. This is because the employer does not have *the right to control* the details of an independent contractor's performance.

Courts make an exception to this rule when the contract involves unusually hazardous activities, such as blasting operations, the transportation of highly volatile chemicals, or the use of poisonous gases. In these situations, strict liability (discussed in Chapter 7) is imposed, so an employer cannot be shielded from liability merely by using an independent contractor.

## Liability for Agent's Crimes

An agent is liable for his or her own crimes. A principal or employer normally is *not* liable for an agent's crime even if the crime was committed within the scope of authority or employment. An exception to this rule is made when the principal or employer participated in the crime by conspiracy or other action.

Also, in some jurisdictions, a principal may be liable under specific statutes if an agent, in the course and scope of employment, violates certain regulations. For instance, a principal might be liable for an agent's violation of sanitation rules or regulations governing prices, weights, and the sale of liquor.

### SECTION 4
# TERMINATION OF AN AGENCY

Agency law is similar to contract law in that both an agency and a contract may be terminated *by an act of the parties or by operation of law.* Once the relationship between the principal and the agent has ended, the agent no longer has the right (*actual* authority) to bind the principal. For an agent's *apparent* authority to be terminated, though, third persons may also need to be notified that the agency has been terminated.

## Termination by Act of the Parties

An agency relationship may be terminated by act of the parties in any of the following ways:

1. *Lapse of time.* When an agency agreement specifies the time period during which the agency relationship will exist, the agency ends when that time period expires. If no definite time is stated, then the agency continues for a reasonable time and can be terminated at will by either party. What constitutes a reasonable time depends on the circumstances and the nature of the agency relationship.
2. *Purpose achieved.* If an agent is employed to accomplish a particular objective, such as the purchase of breeding stock for a cattle rancher, the agency automatically ends after the cattle have been purchased. If more than one agent is employed to accomplish the same purpose, such as the sale of real estate, the first agent to complete the sale automatically terminates the agency relationship for all the others.
3. *Occurrence of a specific event.* When an agency relationship is to terminate on the happening of a certain event, the agency automatically ends when the event occurs. ▶ **Example 26.22** If Posner appoints Rubik to handle her business affairs while she is away, the agency automatically terminates when Posner returns. ◀
4. *Mutual agreement.* The parties to an agency can cancel (rescind) their contract by mutually agreeing to terminate the agency relationship, even if it was for a specific (longer) duration.
5. *Termination by one party.* As a general rule, either party can terminate the agency relationship. The act of termination is called *revocation* if done by the principal and *renunciation* if done by the agent. Although both parties may have the *power* to terminate the agency, they may not possess the right and therefore may be liable for breach of contract or *wrongful termination.*

**WRONGFUL TERMINATION** Wrongful termination can subject the canceling party to a lawsuit for breach of contract. ▶ **Example 26.23** Rawlins has a one-year employment contract with Munro to act as agent in return for $65,000. Although Munro has the *power* to discharge Rawlins before the contract period expires, if he does so, he can be sued for breaching the contract because he had no *right* to terminate the agency. ◀

Even in an agency at will—in which either party may terminate at any time—the principal who wishes to terminate must give the agent *reasonable* notice. The notice must be at least sufficient to allow the agent to recoup his or her expenses and, in some situations, to make a normal profit.

**AGENCY COUPLED WITH AN INTEREST** A special rule applies to an *agency coupled with an interest.* In an **agency coupled with an interest,** the agent has some legal right to (an interest in) the property that is the subject of the agency. For instance, a principal might provide inventory for the agent to sell and then to keep the profits. Because the agent has an additional interest in the property beyond the normal commission for selling it, the agent's position cannot be terminated until the agent's interest ends.

This type of agency is not an agency in the usual sense because it is created for the agent's benefit instead of for the principal's benefit. ▶ **Example 26.24** Julie borrows $5,000 from Rob, giving Rob some of her jewelry and signing a letter authorizing him to sell the jewelry as her agent if she fails to repay the loan. After Julie receives the $5,000 from Rob, she attempts to revoke his authority to sell the jewelry as her agent. Julie will not succeed in this attempt because a principal cannot revoke an agency created for the agent's benefit. ◀

An agency coupled with an interest should not be confused with a situation in which the agent merely derives proceeds or profits from the sale of the subject matter. Many agents are paid a commission for their services, but the agency relationship involved does not constitute an agency coupled with an interest. For instance, a real estate agent who merely receives a commission from the sale of real property does not have a beneficial interest in the property itself.

**NOTICE OF TERMINATION** When the parties terminate an agency, it is the principal's duty to inform any third parties who know of the existence of the agency that it has been terminated. No particular form is required for notice of termination of the principal-agent relationship to be effective. The principal can personally notify the agent, or the agent can learn of the termination through some other means.

Although an agent's actual authority ends when the agency is terminated, an agent's *apparent authority* continues until the third party receives notice (from any source) that such authority has been terminated. ▶ **Example 26.25** Manning bids on a shipment of steel, and Stone is hired as an agent to arrange transportation for the shipment. When Stone learns that Manning has lost the bid, Stone's authority to make the transportation arrangement terminates. ◀

If the principal knows that a third party has dealt with the agent, the principal is expected to notify that person *directly*. For third parties who have heard about the agency but have not yet dealt with the agent, *constructive notice* is sufficient.[15] If the agent's authority is written, however, normally it must be revoked in writing (unless the written document contained an expiration date).

## Termination by Operation of Law

Certain events terminate agency authority automatically because their occurrence makes it impossible for the agent to perform or improbable that the principal would continue to want performance. We look at these events here. Note that when an agency terminates by operation of law, there is no duty to notify third persons—unless the agent's authority is coupled with an interest.

1. *Death or insanity.* The general rule is that the death or insanity of either the principal or the agent automatically and immediately terminates an ordinary agency relationship.[16] Knowledge of the death or insanity is not required. ▶ **Example 26.26** Grey sends Bosley to Japan to purchase a rare book. Before Bosley makes the purchase, Grey dies. Bosley's agent status is terminated at the moment of Grey's death, even though Bosley does not know that Grey has died. ◀

   (Some states, however, have enacted statutes that change the common law rule to require an agent's knowledge of the principal's death before termination.)

2. *Impossibility.* When the specific subject matter of an agency is destroyed or lost, the agency terminates. ▶ **Example 26.27** Tsang employs Arnez to sell Tsang's house. Prior to any sale, the house is destroyed by fire. Arnez's agency and authority to sell the house terminate. ◀ Similarly, when it is impossible for the agent to perform the agency lawfully because of a change in the law, the agency terminates.

3. *Changed circumstances.* Sometimes, an event occurs that has such an unusual effect on the subject matter of the agency that the agent can reasonably infer that the principal will not want the agency to continue. In such situations, the agency terminates. ▶ **Example 26.28** Baird hires Joslen to sell a tract of land for $40,000. Subsequently, Joslen learns that there is oil under the land and that the land is therefore worth $1 million. The agency and Joslen's authority to sell the land for $40,000 are terminated. ◀

4. *Bankruptcy.* If either the principal or the agent petitions for bankruptcy, the agency is *usually* terminated. In certain circumstances, such as when the agent's financial status is irrelevant to the purpose of the agency, the agency relationship may continue. *Insolvency* (the inability to pay debts when they come due or when liabilities exceed assets), as distinguished from bankruptcy, does not necessarily terminate the relationship.

5. *War.* When the principal's country and the agent's country are at war with each other, the agency is terminated. In this situation, the agency is automatically suspended or terminated because there is no way to enforce the legal rights and obligations of the parties.

See *Concept Summary 26.2* on the next page for a synopsis of the rules governing the termination of an agency.

---

15. With *constructive notice* of a fact, knowledge of the fact is imputed by law to a person if he or she could have discovered the fact by proper diligence. Constructive notice is often accomplished by publication in a newspaper.

16. An exception to this rule exists in the bank-customer relationship. A bank, as agent, can continue to exercise specific types of authority even after the customer's death or insanity, and can continue to pay checks drawn by the customer for ten days after death.

---

## CONCEPT SUMMARY 26.2
### Termination of an Agency

| METHOD OF TERMINATION | RULES | TERMINATION OF AGENT'S AUTHORITY |
|---|---|---|
| **Act of the Parties** | | |
| 1. Lapse of time. | Automatic at end of the stated time. | |
| 2. Purpose achieved. | Automatic on the completion of the purpose. | |
| 3. Occurrence of a specific event. | Normally automatic on the happening of the event. | **Notice to Third Parties Required—** 1. Direct to those who have dealt with agency. 2. Constructive to all others. |
| 4. Mutual agreement. | Mutual consent required. | |
| 5. At the option of one party (revocation, if by principal, renunciation, if by agent). | Either party normally has a right to terminate the agency but may lack the power to do so, which can lead to liability for breach of contract. | |
| **Operation of Law** | | |
| 1. Death or insanity. | Automatic on the death or insanity of either the principal or the agent (except when the agency is coupled with an interest). | |
| 2. Impossibility— destruction of the specific subject matter. | Applies any time the agency cannot be performed because of an event beyond the parties' control. | |
| 3. Changed circumstances. | Events so unusual that it would be inequitable to allow the agency to continue to exist. | **No Notice Required—** Automatic on the happening of the event. |
| 4. Bankruptcy. | Bankruptcy petition (not mere insolvency) usually terminates the agency. | |
| 5. War between principal's country and agent's country. | Automatically suspends or terminates agency—no way to enforce legal rights. | |

---

# Reviewing: Agency Liability to Third Parties and Termination

Lynne Meyer, on her way to a business meeting and in a hurry, stopped at a Buy-Mart store for a new car charger for her smartphone. There was a long line at one of the checkout counters, but a cashier, Valerie Watts, opened another counter and began loading the cash drawer. Meyer told Watts that she was in a hurry and asked Watts to work faster. Instead, Watts slowed her pace. At this point, Meyer hit Watts.

It is not clear whether Meyer hit Watts intentionally or, in an attempt to retrieve the car charger, hit her inadvertently. In response, Watts grabbed Meyer by the hair and hit her repeatedly in the back of the head, while Meyer screamed for help. Management personnel separated the two women and questioned them about the incident. Watts was immediately fired for violating the store's no-fighting policy. Meyer subsequently sued Buy-Mart, alleging that the store was liable for the tort (assault and battery) committed by its employee. Using the information presented in the chapter, answer the following questions.

1. Under what doctrine discussed in this chapter might Buy-Mart be held liable for the tort committed by Watts?
2. What is the key factor in determining whether Buy-Mart is liable under this doctrine?
3. How is Buy-Mart's potential liability affected by whether Watts's behavior constituted an intentional tort or a tort of negligence?
4. Suppose that when Watts applied for the job at Buy-Mart, she disclosed in her application that she had previously been convicted of felony assault and battery. Nevertheless, Buy-Mart hired Watts as a cashier. How might this fact affect Buy-Mart's liability for Watts's actions?

**DEBATE THIS . . .** *The doctrine of respondeat superior should be modified to make agents solely liable for their tortious (wrongful) acts committed within the scope of employment.*

## Terms and Concepts

agency coupled with an interest 462
apparent authority 453
disclosed principal 455
e-agent 457
equal dignity rule 450

express authority 450
implied authority 452
notary public 450
partially disclosed principal 455
power of attorney 450

ratification 454
*respondeat superior* 459
undisclosed principal 455
vicarious liability 459

## Issue Spotters

1. Davis contracts with Estee to buy a certain horse on her behalf. Estee asks Davis not to reveal her identity. Davis makes a deal with Farmland Stables, the owner of the horse, and makes a down payment. Estee does not pay the rest of the price. Farmland Stables sues Davis for breach of contract. Can Davis hold Estee liable for whatever damages he has to pay? Why or why not? **(See page 455.)**

2. Vivian, owner of Wonder Goods Company, employs Xena as an administrative assistant. In Vivian's absence, and without authority, Xena represents herself as Vivian and signs a promissory note in Vivian's name. In what circumstance is Vivian liable on the note? **(See page 454.)**

- Check your answers to the Issue Spotters against the answers provided in Appendix E at the end of this text.

## Business Scenarios

**26–1. Unauthorized Acts.** Janell Arden is a purchasing agent-employee for the A&B Coal Supply partnership. Arden has authority to purchase the coal needed by A&B to satisfy the needs of its customers. While Arden is leaving a coal mine from which she has just purchased a large quantity of coal, her car breaks down. She walks into a small roadside grocery store for help. While there, she encounters Will Wilson, who owns 360 acres back in the mountains with all mineral rights. Wilson, in need of cash, offers to sell Arden the property for $1,500 per acre.

On inspection of the property, Arden forms the opinion that the subsurface contains valuable coal deposits.

Arden contracts to purchase the property for A&B Coal Supply, signing the contract "A&B Coal Supply, Janell Arden, agent." The closing date is August 1. Arden takes the contract to the partnership. The managing partner is furious, as A&B is not in the property business. Later, just before closing, both Wilson and the partnership learn that the value of the land is at least $15,000 per acre. Discuss the rights of A&B and Wilson concerning the land contract. **(See page 457.)**

**26–2. Ratification by Principal.** Springer was a political candidate running for Congress. He was operating on a tight budget and instructed his campaign staff not to purchase any campaign materials without his explicit authorization. In spite of these instructions, one of his campaign workers ordered Dubychek Printing Co. to print some promotional materials for Springer's campaign. When the printed materials arrived, Springer did not return them but instead used them during his campaign. When Springer failed to pay for the materials, Dubychek sued for recovery of the price. Springer contended that he was not liable on the sales contract because he had not authorized his agent to purchase the printing services. Dubychek argued that the campaign worker was Springer's agent and that the worker had authority to make the printing contract. Additionally, Dubychek claimed that even if the purchase was unauthorized, Springer's use of the materials constituted ratification of his agent's unauthorized purchase. Is Dubychek correct? Explain. **(See page 454.)**

26–3. *Respondeat Superior.* ABC Tire Corp. hires Arnez as a traveling salesperson and assigns him a geographic area and time schedule in which to solicit orders and service customers. Arnez is given a company car to use in covering the territory. One day, Arnez decides to take his personal car to cover part of his territory. It is 11:00 A.M., and Arnez has just finished calling on all customers in the city of Tarrytown. His next appointment is at 2:00 P.M. in the city of Austex, twenty miles down the road.

Arnez starts out for Austex, but halfway there he decides to visit a former college roommate who runs a farm ten miles off the main highway. Arnez is enjoying his visit with his former roommate when he realizes that it is 1:45 P.M. and that he will be late for the appointment in Austex. Driving at a high speed down the country road to reach the main highway, Arnez crashes his car into a tractor, severely injuring Thomas, the driver of the tractor. Thomas claims that he can hold ABC Tire Corp. liable for his injuries. Discuss fully ABC's liability in this situation. **(See page 459.)**

## Business Case Problems

**26–4. Undisclosed Principal.** Homeowners Jim and Lisa Criss hired Kevin and Cathie Pappas, doing business as Outside Creations, to undertake a landscaping project. Kevin signed the parties' contract as "Outside Creations Rep." The Crisses made payments on the contract with checks payable to Kevin, who deposited them in his personal account—there was no Outside Creations account. Later, alleging breach of contract, the Crisses filed a suit in a Georgia state court against the Pappases. The defendants contended that they could not be liable because the contract was not with them personally. They claimed that they were the agents of Forever Green Landscaping and Irrigation, Inc., which had been operating under the name "Outside Creations" at the time of the contract and had since filed for bankruptcy. The Crisses pointed out that the name "Forever Green" was not in the contract. Can the Pappases be liable on this contract? Why or why not? [*Pappas v. Criss*, 296 Ga.App. 803, 676 S.E.2d 21 (2009)] **(See page 456.)**

**26–5. Liability Based on Actual or Apparent Authority.** Summerall Electric Co. and other subcontractors were hired by National Church Services, Inc. (NCS), which was the general contractor on a construction project for the Church of God at Southaven. As work progressed, payments from NCS to the subcontractors were late and eventually stopped altogether. The church had paid NCS in full for the entire project beforehand, but apparently NCS had mismanaged the project. When payments from NCS stopped, the subcontractors filed *mechanic's liens* (see Glossary) for the value of the work they had performed but for which they had not been paid. The subcontractors sued the church, contending that it was liable for the payments because NCS was its agent on the basis of either actual or apparent authority. Was NCS an agent for the church, thereby making the church liable to the subcontractors? Explain your reasoning. [*Summerall Electric Co. v. Church of God at Southaven*, 25 So.3d 1090 (App.Miss. 2010)] **(See page 450.)**

**26–6. Disclosed Principal.** To display desserts in restaurants, Mario Sclafani ordered refrigeration units from Felix Storch, Inc. Felix faxed a credit application to Sclafani. The application was faxed back with a signature that appeared to be Sclafani's. Felix delivered the units. When they were not paid for, Felix filed a suit against Sclafani to collect. Sclafani denied that he had seen the application or signed it. He testified that he referred all credit questions to "the girl in the office." Who was the principal? Who was the agent? Who is liable on the contract? Explain. [*Felix Storch, Inc. v. Martinucci Desserts USA, Inc.*, 30 Misc.2d 1217, 924 N.Y.S.2d 308 (Suffolk Co. 2011)] **(See page 455.)**

**26–7. BUSINESS CASE PROBLEM**
**WITH SAMPLE ANSWER: Liability for Contracts.**

*Thomas Huskin and his wife entered into a contract to have their home remodeled by House Medic Handyman Service. Todd Hall signed the contract as an authorized representative of House Medic. It turned out that House Medic was a fictitious name for Hall Hauling, Ltd. The contract did not indicate this, however, and Hall did not inform the Huskins about Hall Hauling. When a contract dispute later arose, the Huskins sued Todd Hall per-*

*sonally for breach of contract. Can Hall be held personally liable? Why or why not? [Huskin v. Hall, 2012 WL 553136 (Ohio Ct.App. 2012)]* **(See page 455.)**

- **For a sample answer to Problem 26–7, go to Appendix F at the end of this text.**

**26–8. Agent's Authority.** Basic Research, L.L.C., advertised its products on television networks owned by Rainbow Media Holdings, Inc., through an ad agency, Icebox Advertising, Inc. As Basic's agent, Icebox had the express authority to buy ads from Rainbow on Basic's behalf, but the authority was limited to buying ads with cash in advance. Despite this limit, Rainbow sold ads to Basic through Icebox on credit. Basic paid Icebox for the ads, but Icebox did not pass all of the payments on to Rainbow. Icebox filed for bankruptcy. Can Rainbow recoup the unpaid amounts from Basic? Explain. [*American Movie Classics v. Rainbow Media Holdings*, 2013 WL 323229 (10th Cir. 2013)] **(See page 451.)**

**26–9. A QUESTION OF ETHICS: Power of Attorney.**

*Warren Davis lived with Renee Brandt in a house that Davis owned in Virginia Beach, Virginia. At Davis's request, attorney Leigh Ansell prepared, and Davis acknowledged, a durable power of attorney appointing Ansell to act as Davis's attorney-in-fact. Ansell was authorized to sign "any . . . instrument of . . . deposit" and "any contract . . . relating to . . . personal property." Ansell*
*could act "in any circumstances as fully and effectively as I could do as part of my normal, everyday business affairs if acting personally." A few days later, at Davis's direction, Ansell prepared, and Davis signed, a will that gave Brandt the right to occupy, rent-free, the house in which she and Davis lived "so long as she lives in the premises." The will's other chief beneficiaries were Davis's daughters, Sharon Jones and Jody Clark. According to Ansell, Davis intended to "take care of [Brandt] outside of this will" and asked Ansell to designate Brandt the beneficiary "payable on death" (POD) of Davis's $250,000 certificate of deposit (CD). The CD had no other named beneficiary. Less than two months later, Davis died. A suit between Brandt and Davis's daughters ensued in a Virginia state court. [Jones v. Brandt, 645 S.E.2d 312 (Va. 2007)]* **(See page 451.)**

- (a) Should the language in a power of attorney be interpreted broadly or strictly? Why?
- (b) In this case, did Ansell have the authority under the power of attorney to change the beneficiary of Davis's CD? Explain.
- (c) Ansell advised Davis by letter that he had complied with the instruction to designate Brandt the beneficiary of the CD. Davis made no objection. Based on these facts, what theory might apply to validate the designation?

## Legal Reasoning Group Activity

**26–10. Liability for Independent Contractor's Torts.** Dean Brothers Corp. owns and operates a steel drum manufacturing plant. Lowell Wyden, the plant superintendent, hired Best Security Patrol, Inc. (BSP), a security company, to guard Dean property and "deter thieves and vandals." Some BSP security guards, as Wyden knew, carried firearms. Pete Sidell, a BSP security guard, was not certified as an armed guard but nevertheless came to work with his gun (in a briefcase). While working at the Dean plant on October 31, 2014, Sidell fired his gun at Tyrone Gaines, in the belief

that Gaines was an intruder. The bullet struck and killed Gaines. Gaines's mother filed a lawsuit claiming that her son's death was the result of BSP's negligence, for which Dean was responsible. **(See page 458.)**

- (a) The first group will determine what the plaintiff's best argument is to establish that Dean is responsible for BSP's actions.
- (b) The second group will discuss Dean's best defense and formulate arguments in support of it.

# CHAPTER 27

# EMPLOYMENT, IMMIGRATION, AND LABOR LAW

**U**ntil the early 1900s, most employer-employee relationships were governed by the common law. Even today, under the common law *employment-at-will doctrine,* private employers have considerable freedom to hire and fire workers at will, regardless of the employees' performance.

In addition, however, numerous statutes and administrative agency regulations now govern the workplace.

Thus, to a large extent, statutory law has displaced common law doctrines. In this chapter and the next, we look at the most significant laws regulating employment relationships.

In this chapter, we discuss federal statutes that regulate various aspects of the workplace, including employee wages, hours, medical leave, safety, and pension and health plans. We consider employee privacy rights and such issues as the use of electronic

monitoring by employers and drug testing.

We also examine immigration law, a topic of special importance to employers in our diverse society. We conclude the chapter with coverage of labor laws, which continue to have an impact on the employment environment. As you will read in this chapter's *Managerial Strategy* feature, rules that arise in the context of labor unions sometimes can apply to *all* employees, not just to union workers.

---

## SECTION 1
## EMPLOYMENT AT WILL

Employment relationships have traditionally been governed by the common law doctrine of **employment at will.** Under this doctrine, either party may terminate the employment relationship at any time and for any reason, unless doing so violates an employee's statutory or contractual rights.

Today, the majority of U.S. workers continue to have the legal status of "employees at will." In other words, this common law doctrine is still in widespread use, and only one state (Montana) does not apply it.

Nonetheless, federal and state statutes governing employment relationships prevent the doctrine from being applied in a number of circumstances. An employer may not fire an employee if doing so would violate a federal or state statute, such as one prohibiting employment discrimination (see Chapter 28).

Note that the distinction made under agency law (see Chapter 25) between employee status and independent-contractor status is important here. The employment laws that will be discussed in this chapter and in Chapter 28 apply only to the

employer-employee relationship. They do not apply to independent contractors.

### Exceptions to the Employment-at-Will Doctrine

Because of the harsh effects of the employment-at-will doctrine for employees, courts have carved out various exceptions to it. These exceptions are based on contract theory, tort theory, and public policy.

**EXCEPTIONS BASED ON CONTRACT THEORY** Some courts have held that an *implied* employment contract exists between the employer and the employee. If the employee is fired outside the terms of the implied contract, he or she may succeed in an action for breach of contract even though no written employment contract exists.

▶ **Example 27.1** BDI Enterprise's employment manual and personnel bulletin both state that, as a matter of policy, workers will be dismissed only for good cause. Jing Chin is an employee at BDI. If Chin reasonably expects BDI to follow this policy, a court may find that there is an implied contract based on the terms stated in the manual and bulletin. ◀ Generally, the key consideration in determining whether an employment manual creates an implied contractual obligation is the employee's reasonable expectations.

Courts in a few states have gone further and held that all employment contracts contain an implied covenant of good faith. This means that both sides promise to abide by the contract in good faith. If an employer fires an employee for an arbitrary or unjustified reason, the employee can claim that the employer breached the covenant of good faith and violated the contract.

**EXCEPTIONS BASED ON TORT THEORY** In some situations, the discharge of an employee may give rise to an action for wrongful discharge under tort theories. Abusive discharge procedures may result in a lawsuit for intentional infliction of emotional distress or defamation.

In addition, some courts have permitted workers to sue under the tort theory of fraud when an employer made false promises to a prospective employee. ▶ **Example 27.2** Goldfinch Consulting, Inc., induces Brianna to leave a lucrative job and move to another state by offering her "a long-term job with a thriving business." In fact, Goldfinch is not only having significant financial problems but is also planning a merger that will result in the elimination of the position offered to Brianna. If she takes the job in reliance on Goldfinch's representations and is fired shortly thereafter, Brianna may be able to bring an action against the employer for fraud. ◀

**EXCEPTIONS BASED ON PUBLIC POLICY** The most common exception to the employment-at-will doctrine is made on the basis that the employer's reason for firing the employee violates a fundamental public policy of the jurisdiction. Generally, the courts require that the public policy involved be expressed clearly in the statutory law governing the jurisdiction.

The public-policy exception may apply to an employee who is discharged for **whistleblowing**— that is, telling government authorities, upper-level managers, or the media that her or his employer is engaged in some unsafe or illegal activity.

▶ **Case in Point 27.3** Rebecca Wendeln was the staff coordinator at a nursing home. She discovered that a patient at the home had been improperly moved and had been injured as a result. Wendeln reported the incident to state authorities, as she was required to do by state law. Her supervisor was angry about the report, and Wendeln was fired shortly thereafter. When Wendeln sued, the court held that although she was an employee at will, she was protected in this instance from retaliatory firing because a clear mandate of public policy had been violated.[1] ◀ (Normally, whistleblowers seek protection from retaliatory discharge under federal and state statutes, such as the Whistleblower Protection Act of 1989.[2])

In the following case, an employer fired an employee after he complained about how his supervisor performed her job. The court had to decide whether the employee was protected by the employer's whistleblower policy even though it was implemented after he was hired.

---

1. *Wendeln v. The Beatrice Manor, Inc.*, 271 Neb. 373, 712 N.W.2d 226 (2006).
2. 5 U.S.C. Section 1201.

## CASE 27.1

### Waddell v. Boyce Thompson Institute for Plant Research, Inc.

Supreme Court of New York, Appellate Division, 92 A.D.3d 1172, 940 N.Y.S.2d 331 (2012).

**BACKGROUND AND FACTS** Donald Waddell worked as a business office supervisor for the Boyce Thompson Institute for Plant Research. Waddell did not have an employment contract for a fixed term. The Institute's employee manual said that his job was "terminable at the will of either the employee or [the Institute], at any time, with or without cause." Several months after hiring Waddell, the Institute implemented a whistleblower policy designed to encourage "the highest standards of financial reporting and lawful and ethical behavior." The whistleblower policy stated that the Institute would not retaliate against an employee for making a complaint "in good faith pursuant to this policy."

Beginning in May 2010, Waddell repeatedly complained that his supervisor, Sophia Darling, needed to file certain financial documents more promptly. In August 2010, Darling fired Waddell, telling him that his disrespectful and insubordinate conduct violated the Institute's Code of Conduct. Waddell then sued the

CASE 27.1 CONTINUES ▶

CASE 27.1 CONTINUED

Institute, and the trial court held that he failed to state a proper claim for breach of an implied contract. Waddell appealed.

**DECISION AND RATIONALE** A New York state intermediate appellate court affirmed the lower court's judgment that Waddell did not state a claim for breach of an implied contract based on the institute's whistleblower policy. Because Waddell did not have an employment contract with a fixed term, the reviewing court presumed that he was employed at will. An employee may overcome a presumption of employment at will if "the employer made the employee aware of [an] express written policy limiting its rights of discharge and . . . the employee detrimentally relied on that policy in accepting the employment." In this case, the institute had a written whistleblower policy, but it was implemented several months after Waddell was hired. Moreover, Waddell failed to allege that he passed up other job opportunities based on the policy. Because Waddell could not prove that he detrimentally relied on the whistleblower policy, he was employed at will. Waddell therefore failed to state a claim for breach of an implied contract and the lower court's dismissal was proper.

**THE LEGAL ENVIRONMENT DIMENSION** *If Waddell had been allowed to bring a claim for breach of contract, how might his supervisor, Sophia Darling, have defended her conduct? Explain your answer.*

**THE ETHICAL DIMENSION** *Is the at-will employment doctrine fair to employees? Why or why not?*

## Wrongful Discharge

Whenever an employer discharges an employee in violation of an employment contract or a statutory law protecting employees, the employee may bring an action for **wrongful discharge.** Even if an employer's actions do not violate any express employment contract or statute, the employer may still be subject to liability under a common law doctrine, such as a tort theory or agency. For instance, if an employer discharges a female employee while publicly disclosing private facts about her sex life to her co-workers, the employee could bring a wrongful discharge suit based on an invasion of privacy (see Chapter 6).

### SECTION 2
## WAGES, HOURS, AND LAYOFFS

In the 1930s, Congress enacted several laws to regulate the wages and working hours of employees, including the following:

1. The Davis-Bacon Act[3] requires contractors and subcontractors working on federal government construction projects to pay "prevailing wages" to their employees.
2. The Walsh-Healey Act[4] applies to U.S. government contracts. It requires that a minimum wage, as well as overtime pay at 1.5 times regular pay rates, be paid to employees of manufacturers or suppliers entering into contracts with agencies of the federal government.
3. The Fair Labor Standards Act (FLSA)[5] extended wage-hour requirements to cover all employers engaged in interstate commerce or in producing goods for interstate commerce, plus selected other types of businesses. The FLSA, as amended, provides the most comprehensive federal regulation of wages and hours today.

## Child Labor

The FLSA prohibits oppressive child labor. Children under fourteen years of age are allowed to do only certain types of work, such as deliver newspapers, work for their parents, and be employed in entertainment and (with some exceptions) agriculture. Children aged fourteen and fifteen are allowed to work, but not in hazardous occupations. There are also numerous restrictions on how many hours per day and per week children can work.

Working times and hours are not restricted for persons between the ages of sixteen and eighteen, but they cannot be employed in hazardous jobs. None of these restrictions apply to those over the age of eighteen.

---

**3.** 40 U.S.C. Sections 276a–276a-5.
**4.** 41 U.S.C. Sections 35–45.

**5.** 29 U.S.C. Sections 201–260.

# Minimum Wages

The FLSA provides that a **minimum wage** of $7.25 per hour must be paid to employees in covered industries (by the time you read this text, the minimum wage may be higher). Congress periodically revises this minimum wage. Additionally, many states have minimum wages. When the state minimum wage is greater than the federal minimum wage, the employee is entitled to the higher wage.

When an employee receives tips while on the job, the employer is required to pay only $2.13 an hour in direct wages—if that amount, plus the tips received, equals at least the federal minimum wage. If an employee's tips and direct wages do not equal the federal minimum wage, the employer must make up the difference. If employers pay at least the federal minimum wage, the FLSA allows them to take employee tips and make other arrangements for their distribution.

# Overtime Provisions and Exemptions

Under the FLSA, any employee who works more than forty hours per week must be paid no less than 1.5 times her or his regular pay for all hours over forty. The FLSA overtime provisions apply only after an employee has worked more than forty hours per *week*, so employees who work ten hours a day, four days per week, are not entitled to overtime pay.

Certain employees—usually administrative, executive, and professional employees, as well as outside salespersons and computer programmers—are exempt from the FLSA's overtime provisions. Employers are not required to pay overtime wages to exempt employees. An employer can voluntarily pay overtime to ineligible employees but cannot waive or reduce the overtime requirements of the FLSA.

**EXECUTIVE EMPLOYEES** An executive employee is one whose primary duty is management. An employee's primary duty is determined by what he or she does that is of principal value to the employer, not by how much time the employee spends doing particular tasks. An employer cannot deny overtime wages based only on an employee's job title, however, and must be able to show that the employee's primary duty qualifies her or him for an exemption.[6]

▶ **Case in Point 27.4**  Kevin Keevican, a manager at a Starbucks store, worked seventy hours a week for $650 to $800, a 10 to 20 percent bonus, and paid sick leave. Keevican (and other former managers) filed a claim against Starbucks for unpaid overtime. Keevican claimed that he had spent 70 to 80 percent of his time waiting on customers and thus was not an executive employee. The court, however, found that Keevican was "the single highest-ranking employee" in his particular store. He was responsible on site for that store's day-to-day overall operations. Because his primary duty was managerial, Starbucks was not required to pay overtime.[7]  ◀

**ADMINISTRATIVE EMPLOYEES** To qualify under the administrative employee exemption, the employee must be paid a salary, not hourly wages, and have a primary duty directly related to management or the employer's general business operations. In addition, the employee's primary duty must include the exercise of discretion and independent judgment with respect to matters of significance.

▶ **Case in Point 27.5**  Patty Lee Smith was a pharmaceutical sales representative at Johnson and Johnson (J&J). She traveled to ten physicians' offices a day to promote the benefits of J&J's drug Concerta. Smith's work was unsupervised, she controlled her own schedule, and she received a salary of $66,000. When she filed a claim for overtime pay, the court held that she was an administrative employee and therefore exempt from the FLSA's overtime provisions.[8]  ◀

# Layoffs

During the latest economic recession, millions of workers were laid off from their jobs as companies reduced costs by restructuring their operations and downsizing their workforces. In this section, we discuss the laws pertaining to employee layoffs, an area that is increasingly the subject of litigation.

**THE WORKER ADJUSTMENT AND RETRAINING NOTIFICATION ACT** The Worker Adjustment and Retraining Notification (WARN) Act[9] applies to employers with at least one hundred full-time employees. It requires an employer to provide sixty days' notice before implementing a mass layoff or closing a plant that employs more than fifty full-time

---

6. See, for example, *Slusser v. Vantage Builders, Inc.,* 576 F.Supp.2d 1207 (D.N.M. 2008).

7. *Mims v. Starbucks Corp.,* 2007 WL 10369 (S.D.Tex. 2007).
8. *Smith v. Johnson and Johnson,* 593 F.3d 280 (3d Cir. 2010).
9. 29 U.S.C. Sections 2101 *et seq.*

workers. A mass layoff is a layoff of at least one-third of the full-time employees at a particular job site.

**Notification Requirements.** Employers must provide advance notice of the layoff to the affected workers *or* their representative (if the workers are members of a labor union). Employers must also notify state and local government authorities so that they can provide resources, such as job training, to displaced workers. Any part-time and seasonal employees who are being laid off must be notified, even though these workers do not count in determining whether the act's provisions are triggered. Even companies that anticipate filing for bankruptcy normally must provide notice under the WARN Act before implementing a mass layoff.

**Remedies for Violations.** If sued, an employer that orders a mass layoff or plant closing in violation of the WARN Act can be fined up to $500 for each day of the violation. Employees can recover back pay for each day of the violation (up to sixty days), plus reasonable attorneys' fees. An employee can also recover benefits under an employee benefit plan, including the cost of medical expenses that would have been covered by the plan.

Because the WARN Act applies to large employers that lay off thousands of workers, lawsuits can be expensive. The amount that an employer must pay grows larger each day and is multiplied by the number of employees involved in the suit.

### STATE LAWS MAY ALSO REQUIRE LAYOFF NOTICES

Many states also have statutes requiring employers to provide notice before initiating mass layoffs. These laws may have requirements different from and even stricter than those in the WARN Act. In New York, for instance, companies with fifty or more employees must provide ninety days' notice before any layoff that affects twenty-five or more full-time employees.

## SECTION 3
# FAMILY AND MEDICAL LEAVE

In 1993, Congress passed the Family and Medical Leave Act (FMLA)[10] to allow employees to take time off work for family or medical reasons. A majority of the states also have legislation allowing for family or medical leave. Many employers maintain private family-leave plans for their workers.

The FMLA does not supersede any state or local law that provides more generous family- or medical-leave protection. Additional categories of FMLA leave were created in 2009 for military caregivers and for qualifying exigencies that arise due to military service.

## Coverage and Application

The FMLA requires employers that have fifty or more employees to provide an employee with up to twelve weeks of unpaid family or medical leave during any twelve-month period. The FMLA expressly covers private and public (government) employees who have worked for their employers for at least a year.

An eligible employee may take up to *twelve weeks of leave* within a twelve-month period for any of the following reasons:

1. To care for a newborn baby within one year of birth.
2. To care for an adopted or foster child within one year of the time the child is placed with the employee.
3. To care for the employee's spouse, child, or parent who has a serious health condition.
4. If the employee suffers from a serious health condition and is unable to perform the essential functions of her or his job.
5. For any qualifying exigency (nonmedical emergency) arising out of the fact that the employee's spouse, son, daughter, or parent is a covered military member on active duty.[11] For instance, an employee can take leave to arrange for child care or to deal with financial or legal matters when a spouse is being deployed to Korea.

In addition, an employee may take up to *twenty-six weeks of military caregiver leave* within a twelve-month period to care for a family member with a serious injury or illness incurred as a result of military duty.[12]

## Benefits and Protections

When an employee takes FMLA leave, the employer must continue the worker's health-care coverage on the same terms as if the employee had continued to work. On returning from FMLA leave, most employ-

---

**10.** 29 U.S.C. Sections 2601, 2611–2619, 2651–2654.

**11.** 29 C.F.R. Section 825.126.
**12.** 29 C.F.R. Section 825.200.

ees must be restored to their original position or to a comparable position (with nearly equivalent pay and benefits, for example). An important exception allows the employer to avoid reinstating a *key employee*—defined as an employee whose pay falls within the top 10 percent of the firm's workforce.

## Violations

An employer that violates the FMLA can be required to provide various remedies, including the following:

1. Damages to compensate the employee for lost wages and benefits, denied compensation, and actual monetary losses (such as the cost of providing for care of a family member). Compensatory damages are available up to an amount equivalent to the employee's wages for twelve weeks.
2. Job reinstatement.
3. Promotion, if a promotion has been denied.

A successful plaintiff is also entitled to court costs and attorneys' fees. If bad faith on the part of the employer is shown, the plaintiff can receive twice the amount of damages awarded by the judge or jury. Supervisors can also be held personally liable, as employers, for violations of the act.

Employers generally are required to notify employees when an absence will be counted against FMLA leave. If an employer fails to provide such notice, and the employee consequently incurs costs or is otherwise harmed because he or she did not receive notice, the employer may be sanctioned.[13]

### SECTION 4
# WORKER HEALTH AND SAFETY

Under the common law, employees who were injured on the job had to file lawsuits against their employers to obtain recovery. Today, numerous state and federal statutes protect employees from the risk of accidental injury, death, or disease resulting from their employment.

## The Occupational Safety and Health Act

At the federal level, the primary legislation protecting employees' health and safety is the Occupational Safety and Health Act,[14] which is administered by the Occupational Safety and Health Administration (OSHA). The act imposes on employers a general duty to keep the workplace safe.

To this end, OSHA has established specific safety standards that employers must follow depending on the industry. For instance, OSHA regulations require the use of safety guards on certain mechanical equipment and set maximum levels of exposure to substances in the workplace that may be harmful to a worker's health.

**NOTICES, RECORDS, AND REPORTS** The act requires that employers post certain notices in the workplace, maintain specific records, and submit reports. Employers with eleven or more employees are required to keep occupational injury and illness records for each employee. Each record must be made available for inspection when requested by an OSHA compliance officer.

Whenever a work-related injury or disease occurs, employers must make reports directly to OSHA. If an employee dies or three or more employees are hospitalized because of a work-related incident, the employer must notify OSHA within eight hours. A company that fails to do so will be fined. Following the incident, a complete inspection of the premises is mandatory.

**INSPECTIONS** OSHA compliance officers may enter and inspect the facilities of any establishment covered by the Occupational Safety and Health Act. Employees may also file complaints of violations. Under the act, an employer cannot discharge an employee who files a complaint or who, in good faith, refuses to work in a high-risk area if bodily harm or death might result.

## State Workers' Compensation Laws

State **workers' compensation laws** establish an administrative procedure for compensating workers injured on the job. Instead of suing, an injured worker files a claim with the state agency or board that administers local workers' compensation claims.

Most workers' compensation statutes are similar. No state covers all employees. Typically, domestic workers, agricultural workers, temporary employees, and employees of common carriers (companies that

---

**13.** *Ragsdale v. Wolverine World Wide, Inc.,* 535 U.S. 81, 122 S.Ct. 1155, 152 L.Ed.2d 167 (2002).

**14.** 29 U.S.C. Sections 553, 651–678.

provide transportation services to the public) are excluded, but minors are covered.

Usually, the statutes allow employers to purchase insurance from a private insurer or a state fund to pay workers' compensation benefits in the event of a claim. Most states also allow employers to be *self-insured*—that is, employers that show an ability to pay claims do not need to buy insurance.

**WORKERS' COMPENSATION REQUIREMENTS** In general, the only requirements to recover benefits under state workers' compensation laws are:

1. The existence of an employment relationship.
2. An *accidental* injury that *occurred on the job or in the course of employment,* regardless of fault. (An injury that occurs while an employee is commuting to or from work usually is not covered because it did not occur on the job or in the course of employment.)

An injured employee must notify her or his employer promptly (usually within thirty days of the accident). Generally, an employee must also file a workers' compensation claim within a certain period (sixty days to two years) from the time the injury is first noticed, rather than from the time of the accident.

**WORKERS' COMPENSATION VERSUS LITIGATION** If an employee accepts workers' compensation benefits, he or she may not sue for injuries caused by the employer's negligence. By barring lawsuits for negligence, workers' compensation laws also prevent employers from avoiding liability by using defenses, such as contributory negligence or assumption of risk. A worker may sue an employer who *intentionally* injures the worker, however.

## SECTION 5
# INCOME SECURITY

Federal and state governments participate in insurance programs designed to protect employees and their families from the financial impact of retirement, disability, death, hospitalization, and unemployment. The key federal law on this subject is the Social Security Act.[15]

## Social Security

The Social Security Act provides for old-age (retirement), survivors', and disability insurance. The act is therefore often referred to as OASDI. Both employers and employees must "contribute" under the Federal Insurance Contributions Act (FICA)[16] to help pay for benefits that will partially make up for the employees' loss of income on retirement.

The basis for the employee's and the employer's contribution is the employee's annual wage base—the maximum amount of the employee's wages that is subject to the tax. The employer withholds the employee's FICA contribution from the employee's wages and then matches this contribution.

The annual wage base is adjusted each year as needed to take into account the rising cost of living. In 2013, employers were required to withhold 6.2 percent of each employee's wages, up to a maximum wage base of $113,700, and to match this contribution.

Retired workers are eligible to receive monthly payments from the Social Security Administration, which administers the Social Security Act. Social Security benefits are fixed by statute but increase automatically with increases in the cost of living.

## Medicare

Medicare is a federal government health-insurance program administered by the Social Security Administration for people sixty-five years of age and older and for some under age sixty-five who are disabled. It originally had two parts, one pertaining to hospital costs and the other to nonhospital medical costs, such as visits to physicians' offices.

**ADDITIONAL COVERAGE OPTIONS** Medicare now offers additional coverage options and a prescription-drug plan. People who have Medicare hospital insurance can obtain additional federal medical insurance if they pay small monthly premiums.

**TAX CONTRIBUTIONS** Like Social Security, Medicare is funded by "contributions" from the employer and the employee, but there is no cap on the amount of wages subject to the Medicare tax. In 2013, both the employer and the employee were required to pay 1.45 percent of *all* wages and salaries to finance Medicare.

Thus, for Social Security and Medicare together, in 2013 the employer and employee each paid 7.65 percent of the first $113,700 of income (6.2 percent

---

15. 42 U.S.C. Sections 301–1397e.

16. 26 U.S.C. Sections 3101–3125.

for Social Security + 1.45 percent for Medicare), for a combined total of 15.3 percent. In addition, all wages and salaries above $113,700 were taxed at a combined (employer and employee) rate of 2.9 percent for Medicare.[17] Self-employed persons pay both the employer and the employee portions of the Social Security and Medicare taxes.

In addition, as of 2013, a Medicare tax of 3.8 percent is applied to all investment income for single wage earners making more than $200,000 and married couples making more than $250,000.

## Private Pension Plans

The major federal statute that regulates employee retirement plans is the Employee Retirement Income Security Act (ERISA).[18] Its provisions governing employers who have private pension funds for their employees are enforced by the U.S. Department of Labor.

ERISA created the Pension Benefit Guaranty Corporation (PBGC), an independent federal agency, to provide timely and uninterrupted payment of voluntary private pension benefits. The pension plans pay annual insurance premiums (at set rates adjusted for inflation) to the PBGC, which then pays benefits to participants in the event that a plan is unable to do so.

ERISA does *not* require an employer to establish a pension plan. When a plan exists, however, ERISA provides standards for its management. ERISA also imposes detailed record-keeping and reporting requirements.

**VESTING** A key provision of ERISA concerns vesting. **Vesting** gives an employee a legal right to receive pension benefits at some future date when she or he stops working. Before ERISA was enacted, some employees who had worked for companies for as long as thirty years received no pension benefits when their employment terminated because those benefits had not vested.

ERISA establishes complex vesting rules. Generally, however, all of an employee's contributions to a pension plan vest immediately, and the employee's rights to the employer's contributions vest after five years of employment.

**INVESTMENT OF PENSION FUNDS** In an attempt to prevent mismanagement of pension funds, ERISA established rules on how they must be invested.

Managers must choose investments cautiously and must diversify the plan's investments to minimize the risk of large losses.

## Unemployment Insurance

The Federal Unemployment Tax Act (FUTA)[19] created a state-administered system that provides unemployment compensation to eligible individuals who have lost their jobs. The FUTA and state laws require employers that fall under the provisions of the act to pay unemployment taxes at regular intervals. The proceeds from these taxes are then paid out to qualified unemployed workers.

To be eligible for unemployment compensation, a worker must be willing and able to work. Workers who have been fired for misconduct or who have voluntarily left their jobs are not eligible for benefits. Normally, workers must be actively seeking employment to continue receiving benefits. Temporary measures recently enacted in response to persistent high unemployment rates also allow some jobless persons to retain unemployment benefits while pursuing additional education and training.

## COBRA

Federal law also enables employees to continue health-care coverage after their jobs have been terminated and they are no longer eligible for group health-insurance plans. The Consolidated Omnibus Budget Reconciliation Act (COBRA)[20] prohibits an employer from eliminating a worker's medical, vision, or dental insurance on the voluntary or involuntary termination of the worker's employment.

Employers, with some exceptions, must inform employees of COBRA's provisions when they face termination or a reduction of hours that would affect their eligibility for coverage under the plan. Only workers fired for gross misconduct are excluded. An employer that does not comply with COBRA risks substantial penalties, such as a tax of up to 10 percent of the annual cost of the group plan or $500,000, whichever is less.

**PROCEDURES** A worker has sixty days (from the date that the group coverage would stop) to decide whether to continue with the employer's group insurance plan. If the worker chooses to discontinue the coverage, the employer has no further obligation.

---

**17.** As a result of the Health Care and Education Reconciliation Act of 2010, Medicare tax rates will rise, and the applicable compensation base will include more than just salary incomes.

**18.** 29 U.S.C. Sections 1001 *et seq.*

**19.** 26 U.S.C. Sections 3301–3310.

**20.** 29 U.S.C. Sections 1161–1169.

If the worker chooses to continue coverage, the employer is obligated to keep the policy active for up to eighteen months (twenty-nine months if the worker is disabled). The coverage must be the same as that provided to the worker prior to the termination or reduction of work. If family members were originally included, COBRA prohibits their exclusion.

**PAYMENT** Generally, an employer can require the employee to pay all of the premiums, plus a 2 percent administrative charge. If the worker fails to pay the premiums, becomes eligible for Medicare, or obtains coverage under another plan (or if the employer completely eliminates its group plan), the employer is relieved of further responsibility.

## Employer-Sponsored Group Health Plans

The Health Insurance Portability and Accountability Act (HIPAA),[21] discussed in Chapter 4, also affects employer-sponsored group health plans. HIPAA does not require employers to provide health insurance, but it does establish requirements for those that do. Under HIPAA, employers must give credit to employees for previous health coverage (including COBRA coverage) to decrease any waiting period before their coverage becomes effective.

In addition, HIPAA restricts the manner in which employers collect, use, and disclose the health information of employees and their families. Employers must train employees, designate privacy officials, and distribute privacy notices to ensure that employees' health information is not disclosed to unauthorized parties.

Failure to comply with HIPAA regulations can result in civil penalties of up to $100 per person per violation (with a cap of $25,000 per year). The employer is also subject to criminal prosecution for certain types of HIPAA violations and can face up to $250,000 in criminal fines and imprisonment for up to ten years if convicted.

## Affordable Care Act

Under the Affordable Care Act[22] (ACA, commonly referred to as Obamacare), most employers with fifty or more full-time employees are required to offer health-

---

21. 29 U.S.C. Sections 1181 *et seq.*
22. Pub. L. No. 111-148, 124 Stat. 119, March 23, 2010, codified in various sections of 42 U.S.C.

insurance benefits. There is no requirement to provide health benefits if fewer than fifty people are employed. Any business offering health benefits to its employees (even if not legally required to do so) may be eligible for tax credits of up to 35 percent to offset the costs.

An employer who fails to provide health benefits as required under the statute can be fined up to $2,000 for each employee after the first thirty people. (This is known as the 50/30 rule: employers with fifty employees must provide insurance, and those failing to do so will be fined for each employee after the first thirty.) An employer who offers a plan that costs an employee more than 9.5 percent of the employee's income may receive a penalty of $3,000.

Employers will be fined for failing to provide benefits only if one of their employees receives a federal subsidy to buy health insurance through a state health-insurance exchange. The act provided for these exchanges to establish a marketplace where business owners and individuals can compare premiums and purchase policies.

## SECTION 6
# EMPLOYEE PRIVACY RIGHTS

In the last thirty years, concerns about the privacy rights of employees have arisen as employers purportedly use invasive tactics to monitor and screen workers. Perhaps the greatest privacy concern in employment today involves electronic monitoring of employees' activities.

## Electronic Monitoring

More than half of employers engage in some form of electronic monitoring of their employees. Many employers review employees' e-mail, blogs, instant messages, and tweets, as well as their social media, smartphone, and Internet use. Employers may also video their employees at work, record and listen to their telephone conversations and voice mail, and read their text messages and social media posts.

**EMPLOYEE PRIVACY PROTECTION** Employees of private (nongovernment) employers have some privacy protection under tort law (see Chapter 6) and state constitutions. In addition, state and federal statutes may limit an employer's conduct in certain respects. For instance, as discussed in Chapter 9, the Electronic

Communications Privacy Act prohibits employers from intercepting an employee's personal electronic communications unless they are made on devices and systems furnished by the employer. Nonetheless, employers do have considerable leeway to monitor employees in the workplace.

Private employers generally are free to use filtering software (discussed in Chapter 4) to block access to certain Web sites, such as sites containing sexually explicit images. The First Amendment's protection of free speech prevents only *government employers* from restraining speech by blocking Web sites.

**WAS THERE A REASONABLE EXPECTATION OF PRIVACY?** When determining whether an employer should be held liable for violating an employee's privacy rights, the courts generally weigh the employer's interests against the employee's reasonable expectation of privacy. Normally, if employees have been informed that their communications are being monitored, they cannot reasonably expect those interactions to be private. Also, if the employer provided the e-mail system or blog that the employee used for communications, a court will typically hold that the employee did not have a reasonable expectation of privacy.

If employees are *not* informed that certain communications are being monitored, however, the employer may be held liable for invading their privacy. Most employers that engage in electronic monitoring notify their employees about the monitoring. Nevertheless, a general policy may not sufficiently protect an employer who monitors forms of communications that the policy fails to mention. For instance, notifying employees that their e-mails and phone calls may be monitored does not necessarily protect an employer who monitors social media posts or text messages.

## Other Types of Monitoring

In addition to monitoring their employees' online activities, employers also engage in other types of employee screening and monitoring. The practices discussed next have often been challenged as violations of employee privacy rights.

**LIE-DETECTOR TESTS** At one time, many employers required employees or job applicants to take polygraph examinations (lie-detector tests). Today, the Employee Polygraph Protection Act[23] generally pro-

hibits employers from requiring employees or job applicants to take lie-detector tests or suggesting or requesting that they do so. The act also restricts employers' ability to use or ask about the results of any lie-detector test or to take any negative employment action based on the results.

Certain employers are exempt from these prohibitions. Federal, state, and local government employers, and certain security service firms, may conduct polygraph tests. In addition, companies that manufacture and distribute controlled substances may perform lie-detector tests. Other employers may use polygraph tests when investigating losses attributable to theft, including embezzlement and the theft of trade secrets.

**DRUG TESTING** In the interests of public safety and to reduce unnecessary costs, many employers, including the government, require their employees to submit to drug testing.

***Public Employers.*** Government (public) employers are constrained in drug testing by the Fourth Amendment to the U.S. Constitution, which prohibits unreasonable searches and seizures (see Chapter 4). Drug testing of public employees is allowed by statute for transportation workers. Courts normally uphold drug testing of certain employees when drug use in a particular job may threaten public safety. Also, when there is a reasonable basis for suspecting public employees of drug use, courts often find that drug testing does not violate the Fourth Amendment.

***Private Employers.*** The Fourth Amendment does not apply to drug testing conducted by private employers. Hence, the privacy rights and drug testing of private-sector employees are governed by state law, which varies from state to state. Many states have statutes that allow drug testing by private employers but put restrictions on when and how the testing may be performed. A collective bargaining agreement (discussed later in this chapter) may also provide protection against (or authorize) drug testing.

The permissibility of a private employee's drug test often hinges on whether the employer's testing was reasonable. Random drug tests and even "zero-tolerance" policies (which deny a "second chance" to employees who test positive for drugs) have been held to be reasonable.[24]

---

**23.** 29 U.S.C. Sections 2001 *et seq.*

**24.** See *CITGO Asphalt Refining Co. v. Paper, Allied-Industrial, Chemical, and Energy Workers International Union Local No. 2-991*, 385 F.3d 809 (3d Cir. 2004).

Many workers at U.S. government facilities are employees of private contractors, not of the government. Until recently, these workers generally were not subject to the drug testing and background checks that are applied to federal government employees. In the following case, several contract workers claimed that their privacy rights had been violated by new standards that required them to submit to background checks.

## CASE 27.2

### National Aeronautics and Space Administration v. Nelson

Supreme Court of the United States, ___ U.S. ___, 131 S.Ct. 746, 178 L.Ed.2d 667 (2011).

**COMPANY PROFILE**   The National Aeronautics and Space Administration (NASA) is an independent federal agency charged with planning and conducting "space activities." One of NASA's facilities is the Jet Propulsion Laboratory (JPL), which develops and runs most U.S. unmanned space missions—from the Explorer 1 satellite in 1958 to the Mars rovers of this century. The JPL is owned by NASA but is operated by the California Institute of Technology and is staffed exclusively by contract employees.

**BACKGROUND AND FACTS**   In 2007, under newly implemented standards, contract employees with long-term access to federal facilities were ordered to complete a standard background check. The National Agency Check with Inquiries (NACI) performs background checks for the government. The NACI is designed to obtain information on such issues as counseling and treatment, as well as mental and financial stability. Robert Nelson and other JPL employees filed a lawsuit in a federal district court against NASA, claiming that the NACI violated their privacy rights. The court denied the plaintiffs' request to prohibit use of the NACI, but the U.S. Court of Appeals for the Ninth Circuit reversed this decision. NASA appealed to the United States Supreme Court, arguing that the Privacy Act of 1974 provides sufficient protection for employees' privacy. This act allows the government to retain information only for "relevant and necessary" purposes, requires written consent before the information may be disclosed, and imposes criminal liability for violations.

**DECISION AND RATIONALE**   The United States Supreme Court reversed the judgment of the federal appellate court and remanded the case. The inquiries made by the NACI are reasonable and do not violate an individual's right to privacy. The Privacy Act protects against the disclosure of private information. The Court reasoned that even presuming that the government's inquiries implicated a constitutional right to privacy, that does not prevent the government from asking reasonable questions as part of an employment background check. The Privacy Act provides safeguards against the public disclosure of an individual's private information without the individual's consent. The government has conducted employment investigations of applicants for the federal civil service for more than fifty years, and it simply extended this requirement to contract employees with long-term access to federal facilities. "Reasonable investigations of applicants and employees aid the Government in ensuring the security of its facilities and in employing a competent, reliable workforce." The Court concluded that a government employer's reasonable questions as part of a background check do not violate the right to privacy.

**WHAT IF THE FACTS WERE DIFFERENT?**   *Suppose that after the decision in this case, a JPL employee refused to cooperate in an NACI background check. What would be the most likely consequences?*

**THE LEGAL ENVIRONMENT DIMENSION**   *The U.S. Constitution does not explicitly mention a general right to privacy. From what sources does the Court infer this right? (Hint: See the section on "Privacy Rights" in Chapter 4.)*

**GENETIC TESTING** A serious privacy issue arose when some employers began conducting genetic testing of employees or prospective employees in an effort to identify individuals who might develop significant health problems in the future. To prevent the improper use of genetic information by employers and health-insurance providers, in 2008 Congress passed the Genetic Information Nondiscrimination Act (GINA).[25]

Under GINA, employers cannot make decisions about hiring, firing, job placement, or promotion based on the results of genetic testing. GINA also prohibits group health plans and insurers from denying coverage or charging higher premiums based solely on a genetic predisposition to develop a disease in the future.

## SECTION 7
# IMMIGRATION LAW

The United States did not have any laws restricting immigration until the late nineteenth century. Today, the most important laws affecting the employment relationship are the Immigration Reform and Control Act (IRCA) of 1986[26] and the Immigration Act of 1990.[27]

Immigration law has become increasingly important in recent years. An estimated 12 million undocumented immigrants now live in the United States, many of whom came to find jobs. Because U.S. employers face serious penalties if they hire undocumented workers, it is necessary for businesspersons to have an understanding of immigration laws.

## The Immigration Reform and Control Act

When the IRCA was enacted in 1986, it provided amnesty to certain groups of aliens living illegally in the United States at the time. It also established a system that sanctions employers that hire immigrants who lack work authorization.

The IRCA makes it illegal to hire, recruit, or refer for a fee someone not authorized to work in this country. Through Immigration and Customs Enforcement officers, the federal government conducts random compliance audits and engages in enforcement actions against employers who hire undocumented workers.

**I-9 EMPLOYMENT VERIFICATION** To comply with IRCA requirements, an employer must perform **I-9 verifications** for new hires, including those hired as "contractors" or "day workers" if they work under the employer's direct supervision. The employer must complete Form I-9, Employment Eligibility Verification, which is available from U.S. Citizenship and Immigration Services,[28] for each worker *within three days* of his or her commencement of employment. The three-day period allows the employer to check the form's accuracy and to review and verify documents establishing the prospective worker's identity and eligibility for employment in the United States.

***Documentation.*** The employer must declare, under penalty of perjury, that an employee produced documents establishing his or her identity and legal employability. Acceptable documents include a U.S. passport establishing the person's citizenship or a document authorizing a foreign citizen to work in the United States, such as a permanent resident card or an *Alien Registration Receipt* (discussed on the next page).

***Legal Actions.*** Most legal actions alleging violations of I-9 rules are brought against employees. An employee must state on the I-9 form that she or he is a U.S. citizen or otherwise authorized to work in the United States. If the employee enters false information on the form or presents false documentation, the employer can fire the worker, who then may be subject to deportation. Nevertheless, employers must be honest when verifying an employee's documentation: if an employer "should have known" that the worker was unauthorized, the employer has violated the rules.

**ENFORCEMENT** U.S. Immigration and Customs Enforcement (ICE) is the largest investigative arm of the U.S. Department of Homeland Security. ICE has a general inspection program that conducts random compliance audits. Other audits may occur if the agency receives a written complaint alleging that an employer has committed violations. Government inspections include a review of an employer's file of I-9 forms. The government does not need a subpoena or a warrant to conduct such an inspection.

---

25. 26 U.S.C. Section 9834; 42 U.S.C. Sections 300gg-53, 1320d-9, 2000ff-1 to 2000ff-11.
26. 29 U.S.C. Section 1802.
27. This act amended various provisions of the Immigration and Nationality Act of 1952, 8 U.S.C. Sections 1101 *et seq.*

---

28. U.S. Citizenship and Immigration Services is a federal agency that is part of the U.S. Department of Homeland Security.

If an investigation reveals a possible violation, ICE will bring an administrative action and issue a Notice of Intent to Fine, which sets out the charges against the employer. The employer has a right to a hearing on the enforcement action if it files a request within thirty days. This hearing is conducted before an *administrative law judge* (one who presides over an administrative agency hearing), and the employer has a right to counsel and to *discovery* (see Chapter 3). The typical defense in such actions is good faith or substantial compliance with the documentation provisions.

**PENALTIES** An employer who violates the law by hiring an unauthorized worker is subject to substantial penalties. The employer can be fined up to $2,200 for each unauthorized employee for a first offense, $5,000 per employee for a second offense, and up to $11,000 for subsequent offenses.

Employers who have engaged in a "pattern or practice of violations" are subject to criminal penalties, which include additional fines and imprisonment for up to ten years. A company may also be barred from future government contracts.

In determining the penalty, ICE considers the seriousness of the violation (such as intentional falsification of documents) and the employer's past compliance. ICE regulations also identify factors that will mitigate or aggravate the penalty under certain circumstances, such as whether the employer cooperated in the investigation or is a small business.

## The Immigration Act

Often, U.S. businesses find that they cannot hire sufficient domestic workers with specialized skills. For this reason, U.S. immigration laws have long made provisions for businesses to hire specially qualified foreign workers. The Immigration Act of 1990 placed caps on the number of visas (entry permits) that can be issued to immigrants each year.

Most temporary visas are set aside for workers who can be characterized as "persons of extraordinary ability," members of the professions holding advanced degrees, or other skilled workers and professionals. To hire such an individual, an employer must submit a petition to U.S. Citizenship and Immigration Services, which determines whether the job candidate meets the legal standards. Each visa is for a specific job, and there are legal limits on the employee's ability to switch jobs once he or she is in the United States.

**I-551 ALIEN REGISTRATION RECEIPTS** A company seeking to hire a noncitizen worker may do so if the worker is self-authorized. This means that the worker either is a lawful permanent resident or has a valid temporary Employment Authorization Document. A lawful permanent resident can prove his or her status to an employer by presenting an **I-551 Alien Registration Receipt,** known as a green card, or a properly stamped foreign passport.

Many immigrant workers are not already self-authorized, and an employer that wishes to hire them can attempt to obtain labor certification, or green cards, for them. To gain authorization for hiring a foreign worker, the employer must show that no U.S. worker is qualified, willing, and able to take the job. Approximately fifty thousand new green cards are issued each year. A green card can be obtained only for a person who is being hired for a permanent, full-time position. (A separate authorization system provides for the temporary entry and hiring of non-immigrant visa workers.)

The government has detailed regulations governing the advertising of positions as well as the certification process.[29] Any U.S. applicants who meet the stated job qualifications must be interviewed for the position. The employer must also be able to show that the qualifications required for the job are a business necessity.

**THE H-1B VISA PROGRAM** The most common and controversial visa program today is the H-1B visa system. To obtain an H1-B visa, the potential employee must be qualified in a "specialty occupation," which is defined as involving highly specialized knowledge and the attainment of a bachelor's or higher degree or its equivalent. Individuals with H-1B visas can stay in the United States for three to six years and work only for the sponsoring employer.

The recipients of these visas include many high-tech workers, such as computer programmers and electronics specialists. A maximum of sixty-five thousand H-1B visas are set aside each year for new immigrants. That limit is typically reached within the first few weeks of the year. Consequently, many companies, such as Microsoft, continue to lobby Congress to expand the number of H-1B visas available to immigrants. These companies contend that the H-1B system is keeping some of the world's brightest scientific and engineering minds out of the United States.

---

**29.** The most relevant regulations can be found at 20 C.F.R. Section 655 (for temporary employment) and 20 C.F.R. Section 656 (for permanent employment).

In 2013, frustrated by the shortage of visas, several Silicon Valley entrepreneurs started a colony of foreign-born individuals who live and work on a cruise ship stationed in international waters off the coast of California. The ship, called *Blueseed,* stays outside U.S. jurisdiction so that its residents can start or work for companies near Silicon Valley without having to obtain H-1B visas.

**LABOR CERTIFICATION** Before submitting an H-1B application, an employer must file a Labor Certification application on a form known as ETA 9035. The employer must agree to provide a wage level at least equal to the wages offered to other individuals with similar experience and qualifications. The employer must also show that the hiring will not adversely affect other workers similarly employed. The employer is required to inform U.S. workers of the intent to hire a foreign worker by posting the form. The U.S. Department of Labor reviews the applications and may reject them for omissions or inaccuracies.

**H-2, O, L, AND E VISAS** Other specialty temporary visas are available for other categories of employees. H-2 visas provide for workers performing agricultural labor of a seasonal nature. O visas provide entry for persons who have "extraordinary ability in the sciences, arts, education, business or athletics which has been demonstrated by sustained national or international acclaim." L visas allow a company's foreign managers or executives to work inside the United States. E visas permit the entry of certain foreign investors or entrepreneurs.

## State Immigration Legislation

Until 2010, immigration and the treatment of illegal immigrants were governed exclusively by federal laws. Then Arizona enacted a law that required Arizona law enforcement officials to identify, charge, and potentially deport immigrants living in Arizona who are there illegally. Among other things, that law required immigrants to carry their papers at all times and allowed police to check a person's immigration status during any law enforcement action.

**PREEMPTION ISSUES** The federal government, however, insisted that federal immigration laws preempt state legislation. The United States Supreme Court ruled on the legality of the Arizona law in 2012. By that time, several other states had passed similar legislation.

In the *Arizona v. United States*[30] case, the Supreme Court upheld the controversial "show-me-your-papers" provision that requires police to check the immigration status of persons stopped for another violation. All other provisions of Arizona's law were struck down because they were preempted by federal laws.

**THE FUTURE OF STATE LEGISLATION** The Supreme Court's decision does not prohibit states from enacting laws related to immigration, but it does set some limits. States are prohibited from making it a crime for immigrants not to carry their registration documents or for those without work permits to seek employment.

States also cannot authorize law enforcement to arrest anyone based solely on a reasonable suspicion that the person is in the country illegally. States can, however, require individuals to show documentation of their immigration status to law enforcement when requested to do so during a lawful stop for other reasons.

### SECTION 8
# LABOR UNIONS

In the 1930s, in addition to the wage and hour laws discussed earlier, Congress enacted several other laws regulating employment relationships. These laws protect employees' rights to join labor unions, to bargain with management over the terms and conditions of employment, and to conduct strikes.

## Federal Labor Laws

Federal labor laws governing union-employer relations have developed considerably since the first law was enacted in 1932. Initially, the laws were concerned with protecting the rights and interests of workers. Subsequent legislation placed some restraints on unions and granted rights to employers. We look here at four major federal statutes regulating union-employer relations.

**NORRIS-LAGUARDIA ACT** Congress protected peaceful strikes, picketing, and boycotts in 1932 in the Norris-LaGuardia Act.[31] The statute restricted the power of

---

**30.** ___ U.S. ___, 132 S.Ct. 2492, 183 L.Ed.2d 351 (2012).
**31.** 29 U.S.C. Sections 101–110, 113–115.

federal courts to issue injunctions against unions engaged in peaceful strikes. In effect, this act declared a national policy permitting employees to organize.

**NATIONAL LABOR RELATIONS ACT** One of the foremost statutes regulating labor is the National Labor Relations Act (NLRA) of 1935.[32] This act established the rights of employees to engage in collective bargaining and to strike.

The act also specifically defined a number of employer practices as unfair to labor:

1. Interference with the efforts of employees to form, join, or assist labor organizations or to engage in concerted activities for their mutual aid or protection.
2. An employer's domination of a labor organization or contribution of financial or other support to it.
3. Discrimination in the hiring of or the awarding of tenure to employees for reason of union affiliation.
4. Discrimination against employees for filing charges under the act or giving testimony under the act.
5. Refusal to bargain collectively with the duly designated representative of the employees.

*The National Labor Relations Board.* The NLRA also created the National Labor Relations Board (NLRB) to oversee union elections and to prevent employers from engaging in unfair and illegal union activities and unfair labor practices. (To learn how recent NLRB rulings have affected social media policies, see this chapter's *Managerial Strategy* feature on the next page.)

The NLRB has the authority to investigate employees' charges of unfair labor practices and to file complaints against employers in response to these charges. When violations are found, the NLRB may issue a **cease-and-desist order** compelling the employer to stop engaging in the unfair practices. Cease-and-desist orders can be enforced by a federal appellate court if necessary. After the NLRB rules on claims of unfair labor practices, its decision may be appealed to a federal court.

▶ **Case in Point 27.6** Roundy's, Inc., which operates a chain of stores in Wisconsin, became involved in a dispute with a local construction union. When union members started distributing "extremely unflattering" flyers outside the stores, Roundy's ejected them from the property. The NLRB filed a complaint against Roundy's for unfair labor practices. An administrative law judge ruled that Roundy's had violated the law by discriminating against the union, and a

federal appellate court affirmed. It is an unfair labor practice for an employer to prohibit union members from distributing flyers outside a store when it allows nonunion members to do so.[33] ◀

*Good Faith Bargaining.* Under the NLRA, employers and unions have a duty to bargain in good faith. Bargaining over certain subjects is mandatory, and a party's refusal to bargain over these subjects is an unfair labor practice that can be reported to the NLRB. In one case, for example, an employer was required to bargain with the union over the use of hidden video surveillance cameras.[34]

*Workers Protected by the NLRA.* To be protected under the NLRA, an individual must be an employee or a job applicant (otherwise, the NLRA's ban on discrimination in regard to hiring would mean little). Additionally, the United States Supreme Court has held that individuals who are hired by a union to organize a company (union organizers) are to be considered employees of the company for NLRA purposes.[35]

**LABOR-MANAGEMENT RELATIONS ACT** The Labor-Management Relations Act (LMRA or Taft-Hartley Act) of 1947[36] was passed to proscribe certain unfair union practices, such as the *closed shop*. A **closed shop** is a firm that requires union membership as a condition of employment.

Although the act made the closed shop illegal, it preserved the legality of the union shop. A **union shop** is a firm that does not require union membership as a prerequisite for employment but can, and usually does, require that workers join the union after a specified amount of time on the job.

The LMRA also prohibited unions from refusing to bargain with employers, engaging in certain types of picketing, and *featherbedding* (causing employers to hire more employees than necessary). In addition, the act allowed individual states to pass their own **right-to-work laws**—laws making it illegal for union membership to be required for *continued* employment in any establishment. Thus, union shops are technically illegal in the twenty-four states that have right-to-work laws.

---

**33.** *Roundy's, Inc. v. NLRB,* 647 F.3d 638 (7th Cir. 2012).
**34.** *National Steel Corp. v. NLRB,* 324 F.3d 928 (7th Cir. 2003).
**35.** *NLRB v. Town & Country Electric, Inc.,* 516 U.S. 85, 116 S.Ct. 450, 133 L.Ed.2d 371 (1995).
**36.** 29 U.S.C. Sections 141 *et seq.*

---

**32.** 20 U.S.C. Sections 151–169.

## MANAGERIAL STRATEGY

# Many Companies Have to Revise Their Social Media Policies

Over the past few years, many companies have created social media policies for their employees. For example, Costco's policy used to read as follows:

> Any communication transmitted, stored or displayed electronically must comply with the policies outlined in the Costco Employee Agreement. Employees should be aware that statements posted electronically that damage the company, defame any individual or damage any person's reputation, or violate the policies outlined in the Costco Employee Agreement, may be subject to discipline up to and including termination of employment."

Since a ruling by the National Labor Relations Board (NLRB) in 2012, however, many companies have had to revise their policies.

### The NLRB Rules on Protected "Concerted Activities"

Section 7 of the National Labor Relations Act states: "Employees shall have the right to self-organization, to form, join, or assist labor organizations . . . and to engage in other *concerted activities* for the purpose of collective bargaining or *other mutual aid or protection*." [Emphasis added.]

When employees challenged Costco's social media policy, the NLRB found that the policy violated the National Labor Relations Act because it was overly broad and did not specifically reference Section 7 activity. The ruling stated: "The broad prohibition against making statements that 'damage the company, defame any individual or damage any person's reputation' clearly encompasses concerted communications protesting the Respondent's [Costco's] treatment of its employees."[a]

### The NLRB Continues to Strike Down Broad Prohibitions in Social Media Policies

Since the ruling on Costco's social media policy, the NLRB has struck down similar policies at several companies,

including EchoStar Technologies and Dish Network. The NLRB's general counsel has also issued three reports concluding that many companies' social media policies illegally restrict workers' exercise of their rights.

In one case, Karl Knauz BMW, a car dealership, had told its employees to always be "polite and friendly to our customers, vendors, and suppliers, as well as to your fellow employees." The NLRB found that this policy, like the one at Costco, was "unlawful because employees would reasonably construe its broad prohibition against disrespectful conduct and language which injures the image or reputation of the dealership" as encompassing Section 7 activity. In other words, the policy was overly broad because it could apply to discussions in which employees objected to their working conditions and sought the support of others in improving those conditions—which are protected activities.[b]

### MANAGERIAL IMPLICATIONS

All companies that have social media policies should include a statement that any employee communications protected by Section 7 of the National Labor Relations Act are excluded from those policies. Companies can no longer have a policy that states that all social media posts must be "completely accurate and not misleading" because such a policy would be considered overbroad. Note also that companies cannot require their employees to report any unusual or inappropriate internal social media activity.

### BUSINESS QUESTIONS

1. Employees meeting around the water cooler or coffee machine have always had the right to discuss work-related matters. Is a social media outlet simply a digital water cooler? Why or why not?

2. If your company instituted a policy stating that employees should "think carefully about 'friending' co-workers," would that policy be lawful? Why or why not?

a. *Costco Wholesale Corporation and United Food and Commercial Workers Union, Local 371*, Case 34-CA-01242, September 7, 2012, decision and order from NLRB (available at www.nlrb.gov/case/34–CA-012421).

b. www.nlrb.gov/category/case-number/13-CA-046452.

**LABOR-MANAGEMENT REPORTING AND DISCLOSURE ACT** The Labor-Management Reporting and Disclosure Act (LMRDA)[37] established an employee bill of rights and reporting requirements for union activi-

ties. The act regulates unions' internal business procedures, including elections. For instance, the LMRDA requires unions to hold regularly scheduled elections of officers using secret ballots. Former convicts are prohibited from holding union office. Moreover, union officials are accountable for union property

**37.** 29 U.S.C. Sections 401 *et seq.*

and funds. Members have the right to attend and to participate in union meetings, to nominate officers, and to vote in most union proceedings.

The act also outlawed **hot-cargo agreements,** in which employers voluntarily agree with unions not to handle, use, or deal in goods of other employers produced by nonunion employees.

The LMRDA holds union officers to a high standard of responsibility and ethical conduct in administering the affairs of their union. This standard was at the core of the dispute in the following case.

## CASE 27.3

### Services Employees International Union v. National Union of Healthcare Workers

United States Court of Appeals, Ninth Circuit, 711 F.3d 970 (2013).

**BACKGROUND AND FACTS** The Services Employees International Union (SEIU) consists of 2.2 million members who work in healthcare, public services, and property services. United Health Workers (UHW) is affiliated with SEIU and represents 150,000 healthcare workers in California. The SEIU, under its constitution, has the authority to realign local unions. The SEIU constitution also grants the SEIU the authority to place a local union into trusteeship "to protect the interests of the membership."

The SEIU proposed moving 150,000 long-term care workers from three separate unions, including 65,000 from the UHW, into a new union chartered by SEIU. The UHW opposed the move. The SEIU placed the UHW into trusteeship. UHW officials blocked access to its buildings to prevent the trustees from entering, removed UHW property from the buildings, and instructed its members not to recognize the trustees' authority.

Meanwhile, the UHW officials, while still on the UHW payroll, created and promoted a new union—the National Union of Healthcare Workers (NUHW). The SEIU filed a suit in a federal district court against the NUHW and the UHW officials for breach of fiduciary duties. The jury returned a verdict against the NUHW and the UHW, on which the court entered a judgment. The defendants appealed.

**DECISION AND RATIONALE** The U.S. Court of Appeals for the Ninth Circuit affirmed the lower court's judgment. Section 501 of the LMRDA creates a fiduciary duty owed by union officials to the union as an organization, not only the union's rank-and-file members. Officials who divert union resources to establish a new competing union breach this duty. The reviewing court pointed out that officers of labor unions are required to uphold the highest standards "of responsibility and ethical conduct in administrating the affairs of the union."

The reviewing court was not swayed by the defendants' statement that they believed that their actions assisted those union members by establishing a more democratic union with localized control. The reality was that the defendants diverted union resources to weaken their own union and to form a rival union because they did not agree with the constitutionally permissible decision of the international union. "Because no construction of the LMRDA allows such conduct based merely on the defendants' subjective motives, we reject the defendants' argument." The judgment of liability "was properly entered when a correctly instructed jury, on a sufficient factual record, found the defendants in breach of their fiduciary duties."

**THE ETHICAL DIMENSION** *What standard was at the core of the dispute in this case?*

**WHAT IF THE FACTS WERE DIFFERENT?** *If the defendants in this case had only expressed their opinions against the SEIU's imposition of trusteeship and charter of a new union, could they have been held liable for a breach of fiduciary duty? Discuss.*

# Union Organization

Typically, the first step in organizing a union at a particular firm is to have the workers sign authorization cards. An **authorization card** usually states that the worker desires to have a certain union, such as the United Auto Workers, represent the workforce. If a majority of the workers sign authorization cards, the union organizers (unionizers) present the cards to the employer and ask for formal recognition of the union.

The employer is not required to recognize the union at this point in the process, but it may do so voluntarily on a showing of majority support. (Under proposed legislation, the employer would have to recognize the union as soon as a majority of the workers had signed authorization cards—without holding an election, as described next.)[38]

**UNION ELECTIONS** If the employer refuses to voluntarily recognize the union after a majority of the workers sign authorization cards, the union organizers present the cards to the NLRB with a petition for an election. If less than 50 percent of the workers sign the cards, the unionizers may still petition for an election. For an election to be held, they must demonstrate that at least 30 percent of the workers to be represented support a union or an election on unionization.

The proposed union must represent an *appropriate bargaining unit*. Not every group of workers can form a single union. One key requirement to being an appropriate bargaining unit is a *mutuality of interest* among all the workers to be represented by the union. Factors considered in determining whether there is a mutuality of interest include the *similarity of the jobs* of all the workers to be unionized and their physical location.

If all of these requirements are met, an election is held. The NLRB supervises the election and ensures secret voting and voter eligibility. If the proposed union receives majority support in a fair election, the NLRB certifies the union as the bargaining representative for the employees.

**UNION ELECTION CAMPAIGNS** Many disputes between labor and management arise during union election campaigns. Generally, the employer has control over unionizing activities that take place on company property and during working hours. Thus, the employer may limit the campaign activities of union supporters as long as the employer has a legitimate business reason for doing so. The employer may

also reasonably limit the times and places that union solicitation occurs, provided that the employer is not discriminating against the union.

▶ **Example 27.7** A union is seeking to organize clerks at a department store owned by Amanti Enterprises. Amanti can prohibit all union solicitation in areas of the store open to the public because the unionizing activities could interfere with the store's business. It can also restrict union-related activities to coffee breaks and lunch hours. If Amanti allows solicitation for charitable causes in the workplace, however, it may not prohibit union solicitation. ◀

An employer may campaign among its workers against the union, but the NLRB carefully monitors and regulates the tactics used by management. If the employer issued threats ("If the union wins, you'll all be fired") or engaged in other unfair labor practices, the NLRB may certify the union even though it lost the election. Alternatively, the NLRB may ask a court to order a new election.

# Collective Bargaining

If the NLRB certifies the union, the union becomes the *exclusive bargaining representative* of the workers. The central legal right of a union is to engage in collective bargaining on the members' behalf. **Collective bargaining** is the process by which labor and management negotiate the terms and conditions of employment.

**NEGOTIATING TERMS AND CONDITIONS** Wages, hours of work, and certain other conditions of employment may be discussed during collective bargaining sessions. For instance, subjects for negotiation may include workplace safety, employee discounts, healthcare plans, pension funds, and apprentice and scholarship programs.

Management need not bargain over a decision to shut down certain facilities. It must bargain, however, over the economic consequences of this decision. Thus, issues such as *severance pay* (pay given to an employee on termination) in the event of plant shutdown or rights of transfer to other plants are considered mandatory subjects of collective bargaining.

**GOOD FAITH** Both the employer and the union must negotiate in good faith and make a reasonable effort to come to an agreement. They are not obligated to reach an agreement, but they must at least try to reach a compromise.

Although good faith is a matter of subjective intent, a party's actions can be used to evaluate the

---

**38.** If the proposed Employee Free Choice Act (or Card Check Bill) ever becomes law, some of the information here may change.

party's good or bad faith. Excessive delaying tactics may be proof of bad faith, as is insistence on obviously unreasonable contract terms. The following actions constitute bad faith in bargaining:

1. Rejecting a proposal without offering a counterproposal.
2. Engaging in a campaign among workers to undermine the union.
3. Unilaterally changing wages or terms and conditions of employment during the bargaining process.
4. Constantly shifting positions on disputed contract terms.
5. Sending bargainers who lack authority to commit the company to a contract.

If an employer (or a union) refuses to bargain in good faith without justification, it has committed an unfair labor practice, and the other party may petition the NLRB for an order requiring good faith bargaining.

## Strikes

Even when labor and management have bargained in good faith, they may be unable to reach a final agreement. When extensive collective bargaining has been conducted and an impasse results, the union may call a strike against the employer to pressure it into making concessions. In a **strike,** the unionized employees leave their jobs and refuse to work. The workers also typically picket the workplace, walking or standing outside the facility with signs stating their complaints.

A strike is an extreme action. Striking workers lose their rights to be paid, and management loses production and may lose customers when orders cannot be filled. Labor law regulates the circumstances and conduct of strikes.

Most strikes take the form of "economic strikes," which are initiated because the union wants a better contract. ▶ **Example 27.8**  The Chicago Teachers Union engaged in an economic strike in 2012 after contract negotiations with the school district failed to bring an agreement on pay and performance. Classes were canceled for 350,000 public school students during the strike. ◀

**THE RIGHT TO STRIKE**  The right to strike is guaranteed by the NLRA, within limits. Strike activities, such as picketing, are protected by the free speech guarantee of the First Amendment to the U.S. Constitution. Persons who are not employees have a right to participate in picketing an employer.

The NLRA also gives workers the right to refuse to cross a picket line of fellow workers who are engaged in a lawful strike. Employers are permitted to hire replacement workers to substitute for the striking workers.

**ILLEGAL STRIKES**  In the following situations, the conduct of the strikers may cause the strikes to be illegal:

1. *Violent strikes.* The use of violence (including the threat of violence) against management employees or substitute workers is illegal.
2. *Massed picketing.* If the strikers form a barrier and deny management or other nonunion workers access to the plant, the strike is illegal.
3. *Sit-down strikes.* Strikes in which employees simply stay in the plant without working are illegal.
4. *No-strike clause.* A strike may be illegal if it contravenes a no-strike clause that was in the previous collective bargaining agreement between the employer and the union.
5. *Secondary boycotts.* A **secondary boycott** is an illegal strike that is directed against someone other than the strikers' employer, such as the companies that sell materials to the employer. ▶ **Example 27.9**  The unionized workers of SemiCo go out on strike. To increase their economic leverage, the workers picket the leading suppliers and customers of SemiCo in an attempt to hurt the company's business. SemiCo is considered the primary employer, and its suppliers and customers are considered secondary employers. Picketing of the suppliers or customers is a secondary boycott, which was made illegal by the Labor-Management Relations Act. ◀
6. *Wildcat strikes.* A wildcat strike occurs when a small number of workers, perhaps dissatisfied with a union's representation, call their own strike. The union is the exclusive bargaining representative of a group of workers, and only the union can call a strike. Therefore, a wildcat strike, unauthorized by the certified union, is illegal.

**STRIKERS' RIGHTS AFTER A STRIKE ENDS**  An important issue concerns the rights of strikers after a strike ends. In a typical economic strike, the employer has a right to hire permanent replacements during the strike. The employer need not terminate the replacement workers when the strikers seek to return to work. In other words, striking workers are not guaranteed the right to return to their jobs after the strike if satisfactory replacement workers have been found.

If the employer has not hired replacement workers to fill the strikers' positions, however, then the employer must rehire economic strikers to fill any vacancies. Employers may not discriminate against former economic strikers, and those who are rehired retain their seniority rights. Different rules apply when a union strikes because the employer has engaged in unfair labor practices. In this situation, the employer may still hire replacements but must give the strikers back their jobs once the strike is over.

## Lockouts

Lockouts are the employer's counterpart to the workers' right to strike. A **lockout** occurs when the employer shuts down to prevent employees from working. Lockouts usually are used when the employer believes that a strike is imminent. A lockout may be a legal employer response when a union and an employer have reached a stalemate in collective bargaining.

▶ **Example 27.10** In 2011, the owners of the National Football League (NFL) teams imposed a lock-out on the NFL players' union after negotiations on a new collective bargaining agreement broke down. The NFL owners had proposed to reduce players' salaries and extend the season by two games because of decreased profits due to the struggling economy. When the lockout was imposed, the union requested decertification, which cleared the way for a group of players to file an antitrust lawsuit. A settlement was reached before the start of the 2011 football season. The players accepted 3 percent less of the revenue generated (47 percent rather than 50 percent) in exchange for better working conditions and more retirement benefits. The owners agreed to keep the same number of games per season. ◀

Some lockouts are illegal, however. An employer may not use a lockout as a tool to break the union and pressure employees into decertification. An employer must be able to show some economic justification.

---

## Reviewing: Employment, Immigration, and Labor Law

Rick Saldona began working as a traveling salesperson for Aimer Winery in 2008. Sales constituted 90 percent of Saldona's work time. Saldona worked an average of fifty hours per week but received no overtime pay. In June 2014, Saldona's new supervisor, Caesar Braxton, claimed that Saldona had been inflating his reported sales calls and required Saldona to submit to a polygraph test. Saldona reported Braxton to the U.S. Department of Labor, which prohibited Aimer from requiring Saldona to take a polygraph test for this purpose.

In August 2014, Saldona's wife, Venita, fell from a ladder and sustained a head injury while employed as a full-time agricultural harvester. Saldona presented Aimer's Human Resources Department with a letter from his wife's physician indicating that she would need daily care for several months, and Saldona took leave until December 2014. Aimer had sixty-three employees at that time. When Saldona returned to Aimer, he was informed that his position had been eliminated because his sales territory had been combined with an adjacent territory. Using the information presented in the chapter, answer the following questions.

1. Would Saldona have been legally entitled to receive overtime pay at a higher rate? Why or why not?
2. What is the maximum length of time Saldona would have been allowed to take leave to care for his injured spouse?
3. Under what circumstances would Aimer have been allowed to require an employee to take a polygraph test?
4. Would Aimer likely be able to avoid reinstating Saldona under the *key employee* exception? Why or why not?

**DEBATE THIS . . .** *The U.S. labor market is highly competitive, so state and federal laws that require overtime pay are unnecessary and should be abolished.*

## Terms and Concepts

| | | |
|---|---|---|
| authorization card 485 | I-9 verification 479 | strike 486 |
| cease-and-desist order 482 | I-551 Alien Registration Receipt 480 | union shop 482 |
| closed shop 482 | lockout 487 | vesting 475 |
| collective bargaining 485 | minimum wage 471 | whistleblowing 469 |
| employment at will 468 | right-to-work law 482 | workers' compensation law 473 |
| hot-cargo agreement 484 | secondary boycott 486 | wrongful discharge 470 |

## Issue Spotters

1. Erin, an employee of Fine Print Shop, is injured on the job. For Erin to obtain workers' compensation, does her injury have to have been caused by Fine Print's negligence? Does it matter whether the action causing the injury was intentional? Explain. **(See page 473.)**

2. Onyx applies for work with Precision Design Company, which tells her that it requires union membership as a condition of employment. She applies for work with Quality Engineering, Inc., which does not require union membership as a condition of employment but requires employees to join a union after six months on the job. Are these conditions legal? Why or why not? **(See page 482.)**

- **Check your answers to the Issue Spotters against the answers provided in Appendix E at the end of this text.**

## Business Scenarios

**27–1. Unfair Labor Practices.** Consolidated Stores is undergoing a unionization campaign. Prior to the union election, management states that the union is unnecessary to protect workers. Management also provides bonuses and wage increases to the workers during this period. The employees reject the union. Union organizers protest that the wage increases during the election campaign unfairly prejudiced the vote. Should these wage increases be regarded as an unfair labor practice? Discuss. **(See page 482.)**

**27–2. Wrongful Discharge.** Denton and Carlo were employed at an appliance plant. Their job required them to perform occasional maintenance work while standing on a wire mesh twenty feet above the plant floor. Other employees had fallen through the mesh, and one of them had been killed by the fall. When their supervisor told them to perform tasks that would likely involve walking on the mesh, Denton and Carlo refused because they feared they might suffer bodily injury or death. Because they refused to do the requested work, the two employees were fired from their jobs. Was their discharge wrongful? If so, under what federal employment law? To what federal agency or department should they turn for assistance? **(See page 470.)**

## Business Case Problems

**27–3. Employment at Will.** Thomas Ellis signed an agreement with the BlueSky Charter School to serve as its director for one year, from July 1 to June 30. A sentence in bold type stated that the employment was "at will." The agreement included a provision for automatic annual renewal unless the school's board acted before April 15. On May 7, the board terminated the arrangement. Was Ellis an at-will employee? If so, what effect did this status have on the board's authority to terminate his employment? [*Ellis v. BlueSky Charter School,* __ N.W.2d __ (Mn.App. 2010)] **(See page 468.)**

**27–4. Minimum Wage.** Misty Cumbie worked as a waitress at the Vita Café in Portland, Oregon. The café was owned and operated by Woody Woo, Inc. Woody Woo paid its servers an hourly wage that was higher than the state's minimum wage, but the servers were required to contribute their tips to a "tip pool." Approximately one-third of the tip-pool funds went to the servers, and the rest was distributed to kitchen staff members, who otherwise rarely received tips for their services. Did this tip-pooling arrangement violate the minimum wage provisions of the Fair Labor Standards Act? Explain. [*Cumbie v. Woody Woo, Inc.,* 596 F.3d 577 (9th Cir. 2010)] **(See page 471.)**

**27–5. Unfair Labor Practices.** The Laborers' International Union of North America, Local 578, and Shaw Stone & Webster Construction, Inc., agreed on a provision in their collective bargaining agreement that required all employees to pay dues to the union. Sebedeo Lopez went to work for Shaw Stone without paying the union dues. When the union pressed the company to fire him, Lopez agreed to pay. The union continued to demand his discharge, however, and Shaw Stone fired him. Was the union guilty of unfair labor practices? Why or why not? [*Laborers' International Union of North America, Local 578 v. National Labor Relations Board,* 594 F.3d 732 (10th Cir. 2010)] **(See page 482.)**

**27–6. BUSINESS CASE PROBLEM
WITH SAMPLE ANSWER: Workers' Compensation.**

 *As a safety measure, Dynea USA, Inc., required an employee, Tony Fairbanks, to wear steel-toed boots. One of the boots caused a sore on Fairbanks's leg. The skin over the sore broke, and within a week, Fairbanks was hospitalized with a methicillin-resistant staphylococcus aureus (MRSA) infection. He filed a workers' compensation claim. Dynea argued that the MRSA bacteria that caused the infection had been on Fairbanks's skin before he came to work. What are the requirements to recover workers' compensation benefits? Does this claim qualify? Explain. [Dynea USA, Inc. v. Fairbanks, 241 Or.App. 311, 250 P.3d 389 (2011)]* **(See page 470.)**

- **For a sample answer to Problem 27–6, go to Appendix F at the end of this text.**

**27–7. Exceptions to the Employment-at-Will Doctrine.** Li Li worked for Packard Bioscience, and Mark Schmeizl was her supervisor. In March 2000, Schmeizl told Li to call Packard's competitors, pretend to be a potential customer, and request "pricing information and literature." Li refused to perform the assignment. She told Schmeizl that she thought the work was illegal and recommended that he contact Packard's legal department. Although a lawyer recommended against the practice, Schmeizl insisted that Li perform the calls. Moreover, he later wrote negative performance reviews because she was unable to get the requested information when she called competitors and identified herself as a Packard employee. On June 1, 2000, Li was terminated on Schmeizl's recommendation. Can Li bring a claim for wrongful discharge? Why or why not? [*Li v. Canberra Industries*, 39 A.3d 789 (Conn.App. 2012)] **(See page 468.)**

**27–8. Collective Bargaining.** SDBC Holdings, Inc., acquired Stella D'oro Biscuit Co., a bakery in New York City. At the time, a collective bargaining agreement existed between Stella D'oro and Local 50, Bakery, Confectionary, Tobacco Workers and Grain Millers International Union. During negotiations to renew the agreement, Stella D'oro refused to give the union a copy of the company's financial statement. Stella D'oro did allow Local 50 to examine and take notes on the financial statement and offered the union an opportunity to make its own copy. Did Stella D'oro engage in an unfair labor practice? Discuss. [*SDBC Holdings, Inc. v. National Labor Relations Board*, 711 F.3d 281 (2d Cir. 2013)] **(See page 485.)**

**27–9. A QUESTION OF ETHICS: Workers' Compensation Law.**

 *In 1999, after working for Atchison Leather Products, Inc., in Kansas for ten years, Beverly Tull began to complain of hand, wrist, and shoulder pain. Atchison recommended that she contact a certain physician, who in April 2000 diagnosed the condition as carpal tunnel syndrome "severe enough" for surgery. In August, Tull filed a claim with the state workers' compensation board. Because Atchison changed workers' compensation insurance companies every year, a dispute arose as to which company should pay Tull's claim. Fearing liability, no insurer would authorize treatment, and Tull was forced to delay surgery until December. The board granted her temporary total disability benefits for the subsequent six weeks that she missed work. On April 23, 2002, Berger Co. bought Atchison. The new employer adjusted Tull's work so that it was less demanding and stressful, but she continued to suffer pain. In July, a physician diagnosed her condition as permanent. The board granted her permanent partial disability benefits. By May 2005, the bickering over the financial responsibility for Tull's claim involved five insurers—four of which had each covered Atchison for a single year and one of which covered Berger. [Tull v. Atchison Leather Products, Inc., 37 Kan.App.2d 87, 150 P.3d 316 (2007)]* **(See page 470.)**

(a) When an injured employee files a claim for workers' compensation, a proceeding is held to assess the injury and determine the amount of compensation. Should a dispute between insurers over the payment of the claim be resolved in the same proceeding? Why or why not?

(b) The board designated April 23, 2002, as the date of Tull's injury. What is the reason for determining the date of a worker's injury? Should the board in this case have selected this date or a different date? Why?

(c) How should the board assess liability for the payment of Tull's medical expenses and disability benefits? Would it be appropriate to impose joint and several liability on the insurers (holding each of them responsible for the full amount of damages), or should the individual liability of each of them be determined? Explain.

## Legal Reasoning Group Activity

**27–10. Immigration.** Nicole Tipton and Sadik Seferi owned and operated a restaurant in Iowa. Acting on a tip from the local police, agents of Immigration and Customs Enforcement executed search warrants at the restaurant and at an apartment where some restaurant workers lived. The agents discovered six undocumented aliens working at the restaurant and living together. When the I-9 forms for the restaurant's employees were reviewed, none were found for the six aliens. They were paid in cash while other employees were paid by check. Tipton and Seferi were charged with hiring and harboring undocumented aliens. **(See page 479.)**

(a) The first group will develop an argument that Tipton and Seferi were guilty of hiring and harboring illegal aliens.

(b) The second group will assess whether Tipton and Seferi can assert a defense by claiming that they did not know that the workers were unauthorized aliens.

# CHAPTER 28

# EMPLOYMENT DISCRIMINATION AND DIVERSITY

Out of the 1960s civil rights movement to end racial and other forms of discrimination grew a body of law protecting employees against discrimination in the workplace. Legislation, judicial decisions, and administrative agency actions restrict employers from discriminating against workers on the basis of race, color, religion, national origin, gender, age, or disability. A class of persons defined by one or more of these criteria is known as a **protected class.**

Several federal statutes prohibit **employment discrimination** against members of protected classes. The most important statute is Title VII of the Civil Rights Act of 1964.[1] Title VII prohibits employment discrimination on the basis of race, color, religion, national origin, and gender. The Age Discrimination in Employment Act of 1967[2] and the Americans with Disabilities Act of 1990[3] prohibit discrimination on the basis of age and disability, respectively. The protections afforded under these laws also extend to U.S. citizens who are working abroad for U.S. firms or for companies that are controlled by U.S. firms (see Chapter 24).

This chapter focuses on the kinds of discrimination prohibited by these federal statutes. Note, however, that discrimination against employees on the basis of any of the above-mentioned criteria may also violate state human rights statutes or other state laws prohibiting discrimination. By encouraging employment of members of protected classes, these laws also promote diversity in the workplace.

---

**1.** 42 U.S.C. Sections 2000e–2000e-17.
**2.** 29 U.S.C. Sections 621–634.
**3.** 42 U.S.C. Sections 12102–12118.

---

## SECTION 1
## TITLE VII OF THE CIVIL RIGHTS ACT OF 1964

Title VII of the Civil Rights Act of 1964 and its amendments prohibit job discrimination against employees, applicants, and union members on the basis of race, color, national origin, religion, and gender at any stage of employment. It prohibits discrimination in the hiring process, discipline procedures, discharge, promotion, and benefits.

Title VII applies to employers with fifteen or more employees, labor unions with fifteen or more members, labor unions that operate hiring halls (to which members go regularly to be assigned jobs as they become available), employment agencies, and state and local governing units or agencies. The United States Supreme Court has ruled that an employer with fewer than fifteen employees is not automatically shielded from a lawsuit filed under Title VII.[4] In addition, the act prohibits discrimination in most federal government employment. When Title VII applies to the employer, any employee—including an undocumented (alien) worker—can bring an action for employment discrimination.

### The Equal Employment Opportunity Commission

The Equal Employment Opportunity Commission (EEOC) monitors compliance with Title VII. An employee alleging discrimination must file a claim with the EEOC before a lawsuit can be brought against the employer. The EEOC may investigate the dispute and attempt to obtain the parties' voluntary consent to an out-of-court settlement. If a voluntary

---

**4.** *Arbaugh v. Y&H Corp.,* 546 U.S. 500, 126 S.Ct. 1235, 163 L.Ed.2d 1097 (2006).

agreement cannot be reached, the EEOC may file a suit against the employer on the employee's behalf.

The EEOC does not investigate every claim of employment discrimination. Generally, it takes only "priority cases," such as cases that affect many workers and those involving retaliatory discharge (firing an employee in retaliation for submitting a claim to the EEOC). If the EEOC decides not to investigate a claim, the employee may bring his or her own lawsuit against the employer.

## Limitations on Class Actions

In 2011, the United States Supreme Court limited the rights of employees to bring discrimination claims against their employer as a group, or class. The decision did not affect the rights of individual employees to sue under Title VII, however.

▶ **Case in Point 28.1**   A group of female employees sued Wal-Mart, the nation's largest private employer. The employees alleged that store managers who had discretion over pay and promotions were biased against women and disproportionately favored men. The Supreme Court ruled in favor of Wal-Mart, effectively blocking the class action (a lawsuit in which a small number of plaintiffs sue on behalf of a larger group). The Court held that the women had failed to prove a company-wide policy of discrimination that had a common effect on all women included in the class. Therefore, they could not maintain a class action.[5] ◀

## Intentional and Unintentional Discrimination

Title VII of the Civil Rights Act of 1964 prohibits both intentional and unintentional discrimination.

---

5. *Wal-Mart Stores, Inc. v. Dukes,* ___ U.S. ___, 131 S.Ct. 2541, 180 L.Ed.2d 374 (2011).

**INTENTIONAL DISCRIMINATION** Intentional discrimination by an employer against an employee is known as **disparate-treatment discrimination.** Because intent may sometimes be difficult to prove, courts have established certain procedures for resolving disparate-treatment cases.

▶ **Example 28.2**   Samantha applies for employment with a construction firm and is rejected. If she sues on the basis of disparate-treatment discrimination in hiring, she must show that:

1. She is a member of a protected class.
2. She applied and was qualified for the job in question.
3. She was rejected by the employer.
4. The employer continued to seek applicants for the position or filled the position with a person not in a protected class.

If Samantha can meet these relatively easy requirements, she has made out a ***prima facie* case** of illegal discrimination. This means that she has met her initial burden of proof and will win unless the employer can present a legally acceptable defense. (Defenses to claims of employment discrimination will be discussed later in this chapter.)

The burden then shifts to the employer-defendant, who must articulate a legal reason for not hiring the plaintiff. For instance, the employer might say that Samantha was not hired because she lacked sufficient experience or training. To prevail, the plaintiff must then show that the employer's reason is a *pretext* (not the true reason) and that discriminatory intent actually motivated the employer's decision. ◀

In the following case, the trial court assumed that the plaintiff had established a *prima facie* case of discrimination before considering the defendant's evidence of a nondiscriminatory reason for its decision to discharge the plaintiff. The reviewing court had to consider whether to uphold the trial court's finding.

---

## CASE 28.1

### Dees v. United Rentals North America, Inc.
United States Court of Appeals, Ninth Circuit, 2013 WL 28405 (2013).

**COMPANY PROFILE**   United Rentals North America, Inc., rents, sells, and services equipment for underground construction, temporary power, climate control, disaster recovery, and more. Since its founding in 1997, United Rentals has grown to become the world's largest rental equipment provider, with more than $7 billion of inventory available at more than 830 locations and online. The company's customer base

CASE 28.1 CONTINUES ▶

**CASE 28.1 CONTINUED** includes construction and industrial companies, government agencies, local governments, and individual homeowners.

**BACKGROUND AND FACTS** In 2006, Ellis Dees, an African-American, applied to United Rentals for employment and was offered a service technician position in St. Rose, Louisiana. Dees accepted. The first two years of his employment went smoothly, but his performance began to deteriorate in 2009. With increasing frequency, he marked equipment as fit, even though it was not working. His managers coached him, noted the incidents in his performance reviews, and gave him written warnings. After a final warning and a further incident, Dees was fired. He was sixty-two years old at the time. He filed a charge with the Equal Employment Opportunity Commission, alleging employment discrimination based on his race and age in violation of Title VII of the Civil Rights Act and the Age Discrimination in Employment Act (ADEA). After receiving a "right to sue" notice, he filed a suit in a federal district court against United Rentals. The court granted summary judgment in the employer's favor. Dees appealed.

**DECISION AND RATIONALE** The federal appellate court affirmed the lower court's decision in favor of United Rentals. The appellate court reasoned that "Dees failed to submit any evidence of discrimination and that this is fatal to his claims under Title VII and the ADEA." Under those laws, Dees first had to make a *prima facie* case of discrimination based on age or race. If Dees had made a *prima facie* case, "the burden then shifts to United Rentals to articulate a legitimate, non-discriminatory reason for firing him." The trial court determined that United Rentals "had provided extensive evidence of a legitimate, non-discriminatory reason for Dees' termination—namely unsatisfactory job performance." The reviewing court agreed with the trial court's finding. Dees was unable to produce evidence that United Rentals' reason for firing him was a pretext for discrimination. The reviewing court stated that "Dees' subjective belief that United Rentals discriminated against him is clearly insufficient to demonstrate pretext."

**WHAT IF THE FACTS WERE DIFFERENT?** *If Dees had been laid off due to a reduction in the force of all workers whose performance did not meet the defendant's standards, would the result in this case have been different? Explain.*

**THE LEGAL ENVIRONMENT DIMENSION** *On what did both the trial court and the appellate court focus their analysis?*

---

**UNINTENTIONAL DISCRIMINATION** Employers often use interviews and tests to choose from among a large number of applicants for job openings. Minimum educational requirements are also common. Some employer practices, such as those involving educational requirements, may have an unintended discriminatory impact on a protected class.

**Disparate-impact discrimination** occurs when a protected group of people is adversely affected by an employer's practices, procedures, or tests, even though they do not appear to be discriminatory. In a disparate-impact discrimination case, the complaining party must first show statistically (using the methods discussed next) that the employer's practices, procedures, or tests are discriminatory in effect. Once the plaintiff has made out a *prima facie* case, the burden of proof shifts to the employer to show that the practices or procedures in question were justified.

There are two ways of proving that disparate-impact discrimination exists.

*Pool of Applicants.* A plaintiff can prove a disparate impact by comparing the employer's workforce to the pool of qualified individuals available in the local labor market. The plaintiff must show that (1) as a result of educational or other job requirements or hiring procedures, (2) the percentage of nonwhites, women, or members of other protected classes in the employer's workforce (3) does not reflect the percentage of that group in the pool of qualified applicants. If the plaintiff can show a connection between the practice and the disparity, he or she has made out a *prima facie* case and need not provide evidence of discriminatory intent.

*Rate of Hiring.* A plaintiff can also prove disparate-impact discrimination by comparing the *selection rates* of whites and nonwhites (or members of another protected class), regardless of the racial balance in the employer's workforce. When an educational or other job requirement or hiring procedure excludes members of a protected class from an employer's workforce at a substantially higher rate than for nonmembers, discrimination occurs.

Under EEOC guidelines, a selection rate for a protected class that is less than four-fifths, or 80 percent, of the rate for the group with the highest rate of hiring generally will be regarded as evidence of disparate impact. ▶ **Example 28.3** One hundred white applicants take an employment test, and fifty pass the test and are hired. One hundred minority group applicants take the test, and twenty pass the employment test and are hired. Because twenty is less than four-fifths (80 percent) of fifty, the test would be considered discriminatory under the EEOC guidelines. ◀

## Discrimination Based on Race, Color, and National Origin

Title VII prohibits employers from discriminating against employees or job applicants on the basis of race, color, or national origin. Race is interpreted broadly to apply to the ancestry or ethnic characteristics of a group of persons, such as Native Americans. National origin refers to discrimination based on a person's birth in another country or his or her ancestry or culture, such as Hispanic. (For a discussion of whether employers can legally discriminate against employees based on their appearance, see this chapter's *Insight into Ethics* below.)

If an employer's standards or policies for selecting or promoting employees have a discriminatory effect on employees or job applicants in these protected classes, then a presumption of illegal discrimination arises. To avoid liability, the employer must show that its standards or policies have a substantial, demonstrable relationship to realistic qualifications for the job in question.

▶ **Case in Point 28.4** Jiann Min Chang was an instructor at Alabama Agricultural and Mechanical

---

# INSIGHT INTO ETHICS
## Appearance-Based Discrimination

Research has shown that short men make statistically less income than tall men. It has also shown that compared with attractive individuals, less attractive people generally receive poorer performance reviews, lower salaries, and smaller damages awards if they win lawsuits. Should something be done about this?

### Can "Lookism" Be Prohibited?

Although there is certainly evidence that appearance-based discrimination exists in the workplace and elsewhere, it is not so clear that it can be prohibited. In the 1970s, Michigan decided to do something about "lookism" and passed a law barring various kinds of appearance-based discrimination.[a] Whether because of the cost or the difficulty of proving this type of discrimination, however, only a few lawsuits based on the law have been filed each year. At least six cities have similar laws, but these laws also have not given rise to many lawsuits.

Federal and state laws prohibit discrimination against people who are clinically obese, but discrimination against those who are merely overweight is usually not illegal. Given that one study found that more than 40 percent of overweight women felt stigmatized by their employers, this remains a serious problem.

### A Double Standard for Grooming

Women sometimes complain that they are held to different grooming standards in the workplace than their male counterparts. A female bartender at a casino in Nevada brought a lawsuit after she was fired for not complying with rules that required her to wear makeup and teased hair while male bartenders were just told to "look neat." The court ruled, however, that these allegations were not enough to outweigh an at-will employment contract.[b]

At the same time, women in senior management positions find that they can look "too sexy." A few years ago, a Citibank employee made headlines when she claimed that she was fired for her excessive sexiness, which supposedly distracted her male co-workers.

### LEGAL CRITICAL THINKING
**INSIGHT INTO SOCIAL MEDIA**

*The majority of workers today post photographs of themselves, their families, and their friends on Facebook and other social media. How might this practice affect appearance-based discrimination in the workplace?*

---

**a.** Michigan Compiled Laws Section 37.2202.

**b.** *Jespersen v. Harrah's Operating Co.*, 444 F.3d 1104 (9th Cir. 2006).

University (AAMU). When AAMU terminated his employment, Chang filed a lawsuit claiming discrimination based on national origin. Chang established a *prima facie* case because he (1) was a member of a protected class, (2) was qualified for the job, (3) suffered an adverse employment action, and (4) was replaced by someone outside his protected class (a non-Asian instructor). When the burden of proof shifted to the employer, however, AAMU showed that Chang had argued with a vice president and refused to comply with her instructions. The court ruled that the university had not renewed Chang's contract for a legitimate reason—insubordination—and therefore was not liable for unlawful discrimination.[6] ◄

**REVERSE DISCRIMINATION** Note that Title VII also protects against *reverse discrimination*—that is, discrimination against majority group individuals, such as white males. ▶ **Case in Point 28.5** An African American woman fired four white men from their management positions at a school district. She claimed that the terminations were part of a reorganization plan to cut costs in the department. The men sued for (reverse) racial discrimination and won. They were awarded nearly $3 million in damages.[7] ◄

In 2009, the United States Supreme Court issued a decision that has had a significant impact on disparate-impact and reverse discrimination litigation. ▶ **Case in Point 28.6** The fire department in New Haven, Connecticut, administered a test to identify which firefighters were eligible for promotions. No African Americans and only two Hispanic firefighters passed the test. Fearing that it would be sued for racial discrimination if it used the test results for promotions, the city refused to use the results.

The white firefighters (and one Hispanic) who had passed the test then sued the city, claiming reverse discrimination. The Supreme Court held that the city's actions were not justified. Mere fear of litigation was not a sufficient reason for the city to discard its test results.[8] The city subsequently certified the test results and promoted all the firefighters involved in the lawsuit. ◄

**POTENTIAL SECTION 1981 CLAIMS** Victims of racial or ethnic discrimination may also have a cause of action

under 42 U.S.C. Section 1981. This section, which was enacted as part of the Civil Rights Act of 1866 to protect the rights of freed slaves, prohibits discrimination on the basis of race or ethnicity in the formation or enforcement of contracts. Because employment is often a contractual relationship, Section 1981 can provide an alternative basis for a plaintiff's action and is potentially advantageous because it does not place a cap on damages.

## Discrimination Based on Religion

Title VII of the Civil Rights Act of 1964 also prohibits government employers, private employers, and unions from discriminating against persons because of their religion. Employers cannot treat their employees more or less favorably based on their religious beliefs or practices and cannot require employees to participate in any religious activity (or forbid them from participating in one).

▶ **Example 28.7** Jason Sewell claims that his employer, a car dealership, fired him for not attending the weekly prayer meetings of dealership employees. If the dealership does require its employees to attend prayer gatherings and fired Sewell for not attending, he has a valid claim of religious discrimination. ◄

**REASONABLE ACCOMMODATION** An employer must "reasonably accommodate" the religious practices of its employees, unless to do so would cause undue hardship to the employer's business. An employee's religion might prohibit her or him from working on a certain day of the week, for instance, or at a certain type of job. The employer must make a reasonable attempt to accommodate the employee's sincerely held religious belief. Reasonable accommodation is required even if the belief is not based on the doctrines of a traditionally recognized religion, such as Christianity or Judaism, or of a denomination, such as Baptist.

**UNDUE HARDSHIP** A reasonable attempt to accommodate does not necessarily require the employer to make every change an employee requests or to make a permanent change for an employee's benefit. An employer is not required to make an accommodation that would cause the employer undue hardship. ▶ **Case in Point 28.8** Miguel Sánchez-Rodríguez sold cell phones at kiosks in shopping malls for AT&T in Puerto Rico. After six years, Sánchez informed his supervisors that he had become a Seventh Day

---

6. *Jiann Min Chang v. Alabama Agricultural and Mechanical University,* 2009 WL 3403180 (11th Cir. 2009).

7. *Johnston v. School District of Philadelphia,* 2006 WL 999966 (E.D.Pa. 2006). The damages awarded by a jury were reduced slighted by the appellate court.

8. *Ricci v. DeStefano,* 557 U.S. 557, 129 S.Ct. 2658, 174 L.Ed.2d 490 (2009).

Adventist and could no longer work on Saturdays for religious reasons. AT&T responded that his position required rotating Saturday shifts and that his inability to work on Saturdays would cause it hardship.

As a reasonable accommodation, the company suggested that Sánchez swap schedules with others and offered him two other positions that would not require work on Saturdays. Sánchez was unable to find workers to swap shifts with him, however, and declined the other jobs because they would result in less income (no commissions). He began missing work on Saturdays. After a time, AT&T indicated that it would discipline him for any additional Saturdays that he missed. Eventually, he was placed on active disciplinary status. Sánchez resigned and filed a religious discrimination lawsuit. The court found in favor of AT&T, and a federal appellate court affirmed. The company had made adequate efforts at accommodation by allowing Sánchez to swap shifts and offering him other positions that did not require work on Saturdays.[9] ◄

## Discrimination Based on Gender

Under Title VII and other federal acts, employers are forbidden from discriminating against employees on the basis of gender. Employers are prohibited from classifying or advertising jobs as male or female unless the employer can prove that the gender of the applicant is essential to the job. Employers also cannot have separate male and female seniority lists or refuse to promote employees based on their gender.

**GENDER MUST BE A DETERMINING FACTOR** Generally, to succeed in a suit for gender discrimination, a plaintiff must demonstrate that gender was a determining factor in the employer's decision to hire, fire, or promote him or her. Typically, this involves looking at all of the surrounding circumstances.

► **Case in Point 28.9** Wanda Collier worked for Turner Industries Group, LLC, in the maintenance department. She complained to her supervisor that Jack Daniell, the head of the department, treated her unfairly. Her supervisor told her that Daniell had a problem with her gender and was harder on women. The supervisor talked to Daniell about Collier's complaint, but did not take any disciplinary action.

A month later, Daniell confronted Collier, pushing her up against a wall and berating her. After this incident, Collier filed a formal complaint and kept a male co-worker with her at all times. A month later, she was fired. She subsequently filed a lawsuit alleging gender discrimination. The court allowed Collier's clam to go to a jury because there was sufficient evidence that gender was a determining factor in Daniell's conduct.[10] ◄

**PREGNANCY DISCRIMINATION** The Pregnancy Discrimination Act[11] amended Title VII and expanded the definition of gender discrimination to include discrimination based on pregnancy. Women affected by pregnancy, childbirth, or related medical conditions must be treated—for all employment-related purposes, including the receipt of benefits under employee benefit programs—the same as other persons not so affected but similar in ability to work.

**WAGE DISCRIMINATION** Several laws prohibit employers from engaging in gender-based wage discrimination. The Equal Pay Act[12] requires equal pay for male and female employees working at the same establishment doing similar work (a barber and a hair stylist, for example).

To determine whether the Equal Pay Act has been violated, a court will look to the primary duties of the two jobs—the job content rather than the job description controls.[13] If a court finds that the wage differential is due to "any factor other than gender," such as a seniority or merit system, then it does not violate the Equal Pay Act.

In 2009, Congress enacted the Lilly Ledbetter Fair Pay Act, which made discriminatory wages actionable under federal law regardless of when the discrimination began.[14] This act countered a previous decision by the United States Supreme Court that had limited the time period in which plaintiffs could file a wage-discrimination complaint to 180 days after the employer's decision.[15] Today, if a plaintiff continues to work for the employer while receiving discriminatory wages, the time period for filing a complaint is practically unlimited.

---

9. *Sánchez-Rodríguez v. AT&T Mobility Puerto Rico, Inc.*, 673 F.3d 1 (1st Cir. 2012).

10. *Collier v. Turner Industries Group, LLC*, 797 F.Supp.2d 1029 (D. Idaho 2011).

11. 42 U.S.C. Section 2000e(k).

12. 29 U.S.C. Section 206(d).

13. For an illustration of the factors courts consider in wage-discrimination claims under the Equal Pay Act, see *Beck-Wilson v. Principi*, 441 F.3d 353 (6th Cir. 2006).

14. Pub. L. No. 111-2, 123 Stat. 5 (January 5, 2009), amending 42 U.S.C. Section 2000e-5[e].

15. *Ledbetter v. Goodyear Tire Co.*, 550 U.S. 618, 127 S.Ct. 2162, 167 L.Ed.2d 982 (2007).

## Constructive Discharge

The majority of Title VII complaints involve unlawful discrimination in decisions to hire or fire employees. In some situations, however, employees who leave their jobs voluntarily can claim that they were "constructively discharged" by the employer. **Constructive discharge** occurs when the employer causes the employee's working conditions to be so intolerable that a reasonable person in the employee's position would feel compelled to quit.

**PROVING CONSTRUCTIVE DISCHARGE** The employee must present objective proof of intolerable working conditions, which the employer knew or had reason to know about yet failed to correct within a reasonable time period. Courts generally also require the employee to show causation—that the employer's unlawful discrimination caused the working conditions to be intolerable. Put a different way, the employee's resignation must be a foreseeable result of the employer's discriminatory action. Courts weigh the facts on a case-by-case basis.

Employee demotion is one of the most frequently cited reasons for a finding of constructive discharge, particularly when the employee was subjected to humiliation. ▶ **Example 28.10** Khalil's employer humiliates him by informing him in front of his co-workers that he is being demoted to an inferior position. Khalil's co-workers then continually insult him, harass him, and make derogatory remarks to him about his national origin (he is from Iran). The employer is aware of this discriminatory treatment but does nothing to remedy the situation, despite repeated complaints from Khalil. After several months, Khalil quits his job and files a Title VII claim. In this situation, Khalil would likely have sufficient evidence to maintain an action for constructive discharge in violation of Title VII. ◀

**APPLIES TO ALL TITLE VII DISCRIMINATION** Plaintiffs can use constructive discharge to establish any type of discrimination claims under Title VII, including race, color, national origin, religion, gender, and pregnancy, but it is most commonly asserted in cases involving sexual harassment. Constructive discharge may also be used in cases involving discrimination based on age or disability (discussed later in this chapter).

When constructive discharge is claimed, the employee can pursue damages for loss of income, including back pay. These damages ordinarily are not available to an employee who left a job voluntarily.

## Sexual Harassment

Title VII also protects employees against **sexual harassment** in the workplace. Sexual harassment can take two forms:

1. *Quid pro quo* harassment occurs when sexual favors are demanded in return for job opportunities, promotions, salary increases, or other benefits. *Quid pro quo* is a Latin phrase that is often translated as "something in exchange for something else."

2. *Hostile-environment* harassment occurs when a pattern of sexually offensive conduct runs throughout the workplace and the employer has not taken steps to prevent or discourage it. In the words of the United States Supreme Court, hostile-environment harassment exists when "the workplace is permeated with discriminatory intimidation, ridicule, and insult, that is sufficiently severe or pervasive to alter the conditions of the victim's employment and create an abusive working environment."[16]

The courts determine whether the sexually offensive conduct was sufficiently severe or pervasive to create a hostile environment on a case-by-case basis. Typically, a single incident of sexually offensive conduct is not enough to permeate the work environment (although there have been exceptions when the conduct was particularly objectionable).[17]

If the employee who is alleging sexual harassment has signed an employment contract containing an arbitration clause (see Chapter 3), she or he will most likely be required to arbitrate the claim.[18] In other words, the dispute will not be litigated in court.

**HARASSMENT BY SUPERVISORS** For an employer to be held liable for a supervisor's sexual harassment, the supervisor normally must have taken a *tangible employment action* against the employee. A **tangible employment action** is a significant change in employment status or benefits, such as when an employee is fired, refused a promotion, demoted, or reassigned to a position with significantly different responsibilities. Only a supervisor, or another person acting with the authority of the employer, can cause

---

16. *Harris v. Forklift Systems,* 510 U.S. 17, 114 S.Ct. 367, 126 L.Ed.2d 295 (1993). See also *Baker v. Via Christi Regional Medical Center,* 491 F.Supp.2d 1040 (D.Kan. 2007).

17. See, for example, *Pomales v. Celulares Telefonica, Inc.,* 447 F.3d 79 (1st Cir. 2006); and *Fontanez-Nunez v. Janssen Ortho, LLC,* 447 F.3d 50 (1st Cir. 2006).

18. See, for example, *EEOC v. Cheesecake Factory, Inc.,* 2009 WL 1259359 (D.Ariz. 2009).

this sort of harm. A constructive discharge also qualifies as a tangible employment action.[19]

#### THE *ELLERTH/FARAGHER* AFFIRMATIVE DEFENSE In

1998, the United States Supreme Court issued several important rulings that have had a lasting impact on cases involving alleged sexual harassment by supervisors.[20] The Court held that an employer (a city) was liable for a supervisor's harassment of employees even though the employer was unaware of the behavior. Although the city had a written policy against sexual harassment, it had not distributed the policy to its employees and had not established any complaint procedures for employees who felt that they had been sexually harassed. In another case, the Court held that an employer can be liable for a supervisor's sexual harassment even though the employee does not suffer adverse job consequences.

The Court's decisions in these cases established what has become known as the *Ellerth/Faragher* affirmative defense to charges of sexual harassment. The defense has two elements:

1. The employer must have taken reasonable care to prevent and promptly correct any sexually harassing behavior (by establishing effective harassment policies and complaint procedures, for instance).
2. The plaintiff-employee must have unreasonably failed to take advantage of preventive or corrective opportunities provided by the employer to avoid harm.

An employer that can prove both elements normally will not be liable for a supervisor's harassment.

#### RETALIATION BY EMPLOYERS Employers sometimes

retaliate against employees who complain about sexual harassment or other Title VII violations. Retaliation can take many forms. An employer might demote or fire the person, or otherwise change the terms, conditions, and benefits of employment. Title VII prohibits retaliation, and employees can sue their employers when it occurs.

In a *retaliation claim,* an individual asserts that she or he has suffered harm as a result of making a charge, testifying, or participating in a Title VII investigation or proceeding. Plaintiffs do not have to prove that the challenged action adversely affected their workplace or employment. Instead, plaintiffs must show that the action would likely have dissuaded a reasonable worker from making or supporting a charge of discrimination.

Title VII's retaliation protection extends to an employee who speaks out about discrimination against another employee during an employer's internal investigation.[21] The Supreme Court has also held that Title VII protected an employee who was fired after his fiancée filed a gender discrimination claim against their employer.[22]

In the following case, a law professor lost her job after she complained about comments made by her dean and colleagues. The court had to decide whether she had been retaliated against for engaging in protected conduct.

---

19. See, for example, *Pennsylvania State Police v. Suders,* 542 U.S. 129, 124 S.Ct. 2342, 159 L.Ed.2d 204 (2004).
20. *Burlington Industries, Inc. v. Ellerth,* 524 U.S. 742, 118 S.Ct. 2257, 141 L.Ed.2d 633 (1998); and *Faragher v. City of Boca Raton,* 524 U.S. 775, 118 S.Ct. 2275, 141 L.Ed.2d 662 (1998).

21. *Crawford v. Metropolitan Government of Nashville and Davidson County, Tennessee,* 555 U.S. 271, 129 S.Ct. 846, 172 L.Ed.2d 650 (2009).
22. See *Thompson v. North American Stainless, LP,* ___ U.S. ___, 131 S.Ct. 863, 178 L.Ed.2d 694 (2011).

---

## CASE 28.2

### Morales-Cruz v. University of Puerto Rico
United States Court of Appeals, First Circuit, 676 F.3d 220 (2012).

**BACKGROUND AND FACTS** In 2003, Myrta Morales-Cruz began a tenure-track teaching position at the University of Puerto Rico School of Law. During Morales-Cruz's probationary period, one of her colleagues in a law school clinic had an affair with one of their students that resulted in a pregnancy. In 2008, Morales-Cruz wanted the university's administrative committee to approve a one-year extension for her tenure review. The law school's dean asked Morales-Cruz about her colleague's affair and criticized her for failing to report it. He later recommended granting the extension but called Morales-Cruz "insecure," "immature," and "fragile." Similarly, a law school committee recommended granting the extension. Nevertheless, a dissenting professor commented that in dealing with her colleague's affair, Morales-Cruz

CASE 28.2 CONTINUES ➡

had shown poor judgment, exhibited "personality flaws," and demonstrated that she had trouble with "complex and sensitive" situations.

Morales-Cruz soon learned about the dean's and the dissenting professor's comments and complained in writing to the university's chancellor. As a result, the dean then recommended denying the one-year extension, and the administrative committee ultimately did just that. When her employment was terminated, Morales-Cruz sued the university under Title VII. Among other things, she asserted that the dean had retaliated against her for complaining to the chancellor. The district court found that Morales-Cruz had not stated a proper retaliation claim under Title VII.

**DECISION AND RATIONALE** The U.S. Court of Appeals for the First Circuit affirmed the district court's judgment in favor of the University of Puerto Rico. Under Title VII, an employer may not retaliate against an employee because he or she has opposed a practice prohibited by Title VII. In this case, Morales-Cruz argued that the dean recommended against the one-year extension because she had complained about "discriminatory" comments. The reviewing court found that Morales-Cruz did not allege any facts that could be construed as gender-based discrimination. While the comments were hardly flattering, they were entirely gender-neutral. After all, the dean and dissenting professor said only that Morales-Cruz had shown poor judgment, had personality flaws, and was fragile, insecure, and immature. Thus, even if the dean retaliated against Morales-Cruz, it was not for engaging in conduct protected by Title VII.

**THE ETHICAL DIMENSION** *Could Morales-Cruz's dean have had legitimate reasons for changing his mind about the one-year extension? If so, what might they have been?*

**THE LEGAL ENVIRONMENT DIMENSION** *What steps should employers take to reduce the likelihood that supervisors will retaliate against employees who make or support discrimination claims?*

---

**HARASSMENT BY CO-WORKERS AND OTHERS** When the harassment of co-workers, rather than supervisors, creates a hostile working environment, an employee may still have a cause of action against the employer. Normally, though, the employer will be held liable only if it knew or should have known about the harassment and failed to take immediate remedial action.

Occasionally, a court may also hold an employer liable for harassment by *nonemployees* if the employer knew about the harassment and failed to take corrective action. ▶ **Example 28.11** Jordan, who owns and manages a Great Bites restaurant, knows that one of his regular customers, Dean, repeatedly harasses Kaylia, a waitress. If Jordan does nothing and permits the harassment to continue, he may be liable under Title VII even though Dean is not an employee of the restaurant. ◀

**SAME-GENDER HARASSMENT** In *Oncale v. Sundowner Offshore Services, Inc.,*[23] the United States Supreme Court held that Title VII protection extends to individuals who are sexually harassed by members of the same gender. Proving that the harassment in same-gender cases is "based on sex" can be difficult,

though. It is easier to establish a case of same-gender harassment when the harasser is homosexual.[24]

**SEXUAL ORIENTATION HARASSMENT** Federal law (Title VII) does not prohibit discrimination or harassment based on a person's sexual orientation. Nonetheless, a growing number of states have enacted laws that prohibit sexual orientation discrimination in private employment.[25] Some states, such as Michigan, explicitly prohibit discrimination based on a person's gender identity or expression. Many companies have also voluntarily established nondiscrimination policies that include sexual orientation.

## Online Harassment

Employees' online activities can create a hostile working environment in many ways. Racial jokes, ethnic slurs, or other comments contained in e-mail, texts, blogs, and social media can lead to a claim of hostile-environment harassment or other forms of discrimination. A worker who regularly sees sexually explicit images on a co-worker's computer screen may find the images offensive and claim that they create a hostile working environment.

---

**23.** 523 U.S. 75, 118 S.Ct. 998, 140 L.Ed.2d 207 (1998).

**24.** See, for example, *Tepperwien v. Entergy Nuclear Operations, Inc.,* 606 F.Supp.2d 427 (S.D.N.Y. 2009).

**25.** See, for example, 775 Illinois Compiled Statutes 5/1–103.

Nevertheless, employers may be able to avoid liability for online harassment by taking prompt remedial action.

## Remedies under Title VII

Employer liability under Title VII may be extensive. If the plaintiff successfully proves that unlawful discrimination occurred, he or she may be awarded reinstatement, back pay, retroactive promotions, and damages.

Compensatory damages are available only in cases of intentional discrimination. Punitive damages may be recovered against a private employer only if the employer acted with malice or reckless indifference to an individual's rights. The statute limits the total amount of compensatory and punitive damages that plaintiffs can recover from specific employers, depending on the size of the employer. For instance, there is a $50,000 cap on damages from employers with one hundred or fewer employees.

**SECTION 2**

# DISCRIMINATION BASED ON AGE

Age discrimination is potentially the most widespread form of discrimination because anyone—regardless of race, color, national origin, or gender—could be a victim at some point in life. The Age Discrimination in Employment Act[26] (ADEA), as amended, prohibits employment discrimination on the basis of age against individuals forty years of age or older. The act also prohibits mandatory retirement for nonmanagerial workers.

The United States Supreme Court has ruled that the ADEA encompasses not only claims of age discrimination, but also claims of retaliation for complaining

---

**26.** 29 U.S.C. Sections 621–634.

about age discrimination.[27] Thus, the ADEA protects federal and private-sector employees from retaliation based on age-related complaints.

For the act to apply, an employer must have twenty or more employees, and the employer's business activities must affect interstate commerce. The EEOC administers the ADEA, but the act also permits private causes of action against employers for age discrimination.

## Procedures under the ADEA

The burden-shifting procedure under the ADEA differs from the procedure under Title VII as a result of a 2009 United States Supreme Court decision, which dramatically changed the burden of proof in age discrimination cases.[28] As explained earlier, if the plaintiff in a Title VII case can show that the employer was motivated, at least in part, by unlawful discrimination, the burden of proof shifts to the employer to articulate a legitimate nondiscriminatory reason for the challenged action. Thus, in cases in which the employer has a "mixed motive" for discharging an employee, the employer has the burden of proving its reason was legitimate.

Under the ADEA, in contrast, a plaintiff must show that the unlawful discrimination was not just *a* reason but *the* reason for the adverse employment action. In other words, the employee has the burden of establishing *but for* causation—that is, "but for" the employee's age, the action would not have been taken.

Thus, to establish a *prima facie* case, the plaintiff must show that she or he (1) was a member of the protected age group, (2) was qualified for the position from which she or he was discharged, and (3) was discharged because of age discrimination. Then the burden shifts to the employer. If the employer offers a legitimate reason for its action, the plaintiff must show that the stated reason is only a pretext for the employer's decision. The following case illustrates this process.

---

**27.** *Gomez-Perez v. Potter,* 553 U.S. 474, 128 S.Ct. 1931, 170 L.Ed.2d 887 (2008).

**28.** *Gross v. FBL Financial Services, Inc.,* 557 U.S. 167, 129 S.Ct. 2343, 174 L.Ed.2d 119 (2009).

---

## CASE 28.3

### Mora v. Jackson Memorial Foundation, Inc.
United States Court of Appeals, Eleventh Circuit, 597 F.3d 1201 (2010).

**BACKGROUND AND FACTS** Josephine Mora, a fund-raiser for Jackson Memorial Foundation, Inc., was sixty-two years old when the foundation's chief executive officer (CEO) fired her, citing errors and issues with professionalism. Mora filed a suit against the foundation, alleging age discrimination. She

**CASE 28.3 CONTINUES ➡**

CASE 28.3 CONTINUED

asserted that when she was fired, the CEO told her, "I need someone younger I can pay less." She had a witness who heard that statement and also heard the CEO say that Mora was "too old to be working here anyway." The foundation moved for summary judgment, arguing that Mora was fired chiefly because she was incompetent. The district court granted the motion, and Mora appealed.

**DECISION AND RATIONALE** The U.S. Court of Appeals for the Eleventh Circuit vacated (set aside) the decision of the trial court and remanded the case for further proceedings. Because there was a "disputed question of material fact" as to whether Mora had been fired because of her age, the foundation was not entitled to summary judgment. The reviewing court explained that the Supreme Court had excluded the whole idea of a "mixed motive" age discrimination claim. Therefore, the argument that the same decision would have been made regardless of the alleged discrimination was inapplicable. The employer either acted because of the plaintiff's age, or it did not. The district court should not have examined the question of whether Mora would have been fired no matter what her age was simply because she had become incompetent. In reviewing the case, the appellate court focused instead on "whether a material factual question exists on this record about whether Defendant discriminated against her." The court concluded, "The resolution of this case depends on whose account of the pertinent conversations a jury would credit. . . . We conclude that a reasonable juror could accept that Rodriguez made the discriminatory-sounding remarks and that the remarks are sufficient evidence of a discriminatory motive. . . . Summary judgment for Defendant was therefore incorrect."

**THE ETHICAL DIMENSION** *Is the court's decision in this case fair to employers? Why or why not?*

**MANAGERIAL IMPLICATIONS** *Business owners and supervisory personnel should be careful to avoid statements regarding an employee's age that may sound discriminatory. If the employee later has to be dismissed due to poor performance, comments about his or her age may become the basis for an age discrimination lawsuit.*

## Replacing Older Workers with Younger Workers

Numerous age discrimination cases have been brought against employers who, to cut costs, replaced older, higher-salaried employees with younger, lower-salaried workers. Whether a firing is discriminatory or simply part of a rational business decision to prune the company's ranks is not always clear.

A plaintiff must prove that the discharge was motivated by age bias. The plaintiff does not need to prove that she or he was replaced by a person "outside the protected class" (under the age of forty years), as long as the replacement worker is younger than the plaintiff. Nevertheless, the bigger the age gap, the more likely the plaintiff will succeed in showing age discrimination.

## State Employees Not Covered by the ADEA

Generally, the states are immune under the Eleventh Amendment from lawsuits brought by private individuals in federal court—unless a state consents to the suit. This immunity stems from the United States Supreme Court's interpretation of the Eleventh Amendment (see Appendix B).

State immunity under the Eleventh Amendment is not absolute, however. In some situations, such as when fundamental rights are at stake, Congress has the power to abrogate (abolish) state immunity to private suits through legislation that unequivocally shows Congress's intent to subject states to private suits.[29]

Generally, though, the Court has found that state employers are immune from private suits brought by employees under the ADEA (for age discrimination), the Americans with Disabilities Act (for disability-based discrimination),[30] and the Fair Labor Standards Act.[31] As explained in Chapter 27, state employers are not immune from the requirements of the Family and Medical Leave Act.[32]

---

29. *Tennessee v. Lane,* 541 U.S. 509, 124 S.Ct. 1978, 158 L.Ed.2d 820 (2004).
30. *Board of Trustees of the University of Alabama v. Garrett,* 531 U.S. 356, 121 S.Ct. 955, 148 L.Ed.2d 866 (2001).
31. *Alden v. Maine,* 527 U.S. 706, 119 S.Ct. 2240, 144 L.Ed.2d 636 (1999).
32. *Nevada Department of Human Resources v. Hibbs,* 538 U.S. 721, 123 S.Ct. 1972, 155 L.Ed.2d 953 (2003).

## SECTION 3

# DISCRIMINATION BASED ON DISABILITY

The Americans with Disabilities Act (ADA) of 1990[33] prohibits disability-based discrimination in all workplaces with fifteen or more workers. An exception is state government employers, who are generally immune under the Eleventh Amendment, as just discussed. Basically, the ADA requires that employers "reasonably accommodate" the needs of persons with disabilities unless to do so would cause the employer to suffer an "undue hardship." The ADA Amendments Act[34] broadened the coverage of the ADA's protections, as discussed shortly.

## Procedures under the ADA

To prevail on a claim under the ADA, a plaintiff must show that he or she (1) has a disability, (2) is otherwise qualified for the employment in question, and (3) was excluded from the employment solely because of the disability. As in Title VII cases, the plaintiff must pursue the claim through the EEOC before filing an action in court for a violation of the ADA.

The EEOC may decide to investigate and perhaps even sue the employer on behalf of the employee. The EEOC can bring a suit on behalf of the employee under the ADA even if the employee signed an arbitration agreement with the employer.[35] If the EEOC decides not to sue, then the employee may do so.

Plaintiffs in lawsuits brought under the ADA may seek many of the same remedies that are available under Title VII. These include reinstatement, back pay, a limited amount of compensatory and punitive damages (for intentional discrimination), and certain other forms of relief. Repeat violators may be ordered to pay fines of up to $100,000.

## What Is a Disability?

The ADA is broadly drafted to cover persons with physical or mental impairments that "substantially limit" their everyday activities. Specifically, the ADA defines a *disability* as including any of the following:

1. A physical or mental impairment that substantially limits one or more of the major life activities of the affected individual.
2. A record of having such an impairment.
3. Being regarded as having such an impairment.

**TYPES OF DISABILITY** Health conditions that have been considered disabilities under federal law include blindness, alcoholism, heart disease, cancer, muscular dystrophy, cerebral palsy, paraplegia, diabetes, acquired immune deficiency syndrome (AIDS), testing positive for the human immunodeficiency virus (HIV, the virus that causes AIDS), and morbid obesity (which exists when an individual's weight is twice the normal weight for his or her height).

The ADA includes a separate provision that prevents employers from taking adverse employment actions based on stereotypes or assumptions about individuals who associate with people who have disabilities.[36] An employer cannot, for instance, refuse to hire the parent of a child with a disability based on the assumption that the person will miss work too often or be unreliable.[37]

**CORRECTABLE CONDITIONS** At one time, the courts focused on whether a person had a disability *after* the use of corrective devices or medication. A person with severe myopia (nearsightedness), which can be corrected with lenses, for instance, did not qualify as having a disability because that individual's major life activities were not substantially impaired.

In 2008, Congress amended the ADA to strengthen its protections and prohibit employers from considering mitigating measures or medications when determining if an individual has a disability. Disability is now determined on a case-by-case basis. A condition may fit the definition of disability in one set of circumstances, but not in another.

## Reasonable Accommodation

The ADA does not require that employers accommodate the needs of job applicants or employees with disabilities who are not otherwise qualified for the work. If a job applicant or an employee with a disability, with reasonable accommodation, can perform essential job functions, however, the employer must make the accommodation.

---

**33.** 42 U.S.C. Sections 12103–12118.
**34.** 42 U.S.C. Sections 12103 and 12205a.
**35.** This was the Supreme Court's ruling in *EEOC v. Waffle House, Inc.*, 534 U.S. 279, 122 S.Ct. 754, 151 L.Ed.2d 755 (2002).

**36.** 42 U.S.C. Section 12112(b)(4).
**37.** See, for example, *Francin v. Mosby, Inc.*, 248 S.W.3d 619 (Mo. 2008).

Required modifications may include installing ramps for a wheelchair, establishing flexible working hours, creating or modifying job assignments, and designing or improving training materials and procedures. Generally, employers should give primary consideration to employees' preferences in deciding what accommodations should be made.

**UNDUE HARDSHIP** Employers who do not accommodate the needs of persons with disabilities must demonstrate that the accommodations would cause *undue hardship* in terms of being significantly difficult or expensive for the employer. Usually, the courts decide whether an accommodation constitutes an undue hardship on a case-by-case basis.

▶ **Example 28.12** Bryan Lockhart, who uses a wheelchair, works for a cell phone company that provides parking for its employees. Lockhart informs his supervisor that the parking spaces are so narrow that he is unable to extend the ramp on his van that allows him to get in and out of the vehicle. Lockhart therefore requests that the company reasonably accommodate his needs by paying a monthly fee for him to use a larger parking space in an adjacent lot. In this situation, a court would likely find that it would *not* be an undue hardship for the employer to pay for additional parking for Lockhart. ◀

**JOB APPLICATIONS AND PHYSICAL EXAMS** Employers must modify their job-application and selection process so that those with disabilities can compete for jobs with those who do not have disabilities. For instance, a job announcement might be modified to allow applicants to respond by e-mail or letter, as well as by telephone, so that it does not discriminate against potential applicants with hearing impairments.

Employers are restricted in the kinds of questions they may ask on job-application forms and during preemployment interviews. In addition, employers cannot require persons with disabilities to submit to preemployment physicals unless such exams are required of all other applicants. An employer can disqualify the applicant only if the medical problems discovered during a preemployment physical would make it impossible for the applicant to perform the job.

▶ **Example 28.13** Abba Freight Systems runs a trucking operation. When filling the position of delivery truck driver, Abba cannot screen out all applicants who are unable to meet the U.S. Department of Transportation's hearing standard. Abba would first have to prove that drivers who are deaf are not qualified to perform the essential job function of driving

safely and pose a higher risk of accidents than drivers who are not deaf.[38] ◀

**SUBSTANCE ABUSERS** Drug addiction is considered a disability under the ADA because it is a substantially limiting impairment. The act does not protect individuals who are actually using illegal drugs, however. Instead, the ADA protects only persons with *former* drug addictions—those who have completed or are now in a supervised drug-rehabilitation program. Individuals who have used drugs casually in the past also are not protected under the act. They are not considered addicts and therefore do not have a disability (addiction).

People suffering from alcoholism are protected by the ADA. Employers cannot legally discriminate against employees simply because they suffer from alcoholism. Of course, employers can prohibit the use of alcohol in the workplace and require that employees not be under the influence of alcohol while working. Employers can also fire or refuse to hire a person who is an alcoholic if (1) he or she poses a *substantial risk of harm* either to himself or herself or to others, and (2) the risk cannot be reduced by reasonable accommodation.

**HEALTH-INSURANCE PLANS** Workers with disabilities must be given equal access to any health insurance provided to other employees. An employer can put a limit, or cap, on health-care payments under its group health policy, however, as long as the cap is applied equally to all insured employees and does not discriminate on the basis of disability. Whenever a group health-care plan makes a disability-based distinction in its benefits, the plan violates the ADA. (An exception exists if the employer can justify its actions under the business necessity defense, as discussed in the next section.)

### SECTION 4
# DEFENSES TO EMPLOYMENT DISCRIMINATION

The first line of defense for an employer charged with employment discrimination is to assert that the plaintiff has failed to meet his or her initial burden of proving that discrimination occurred. As noted, plaintiffs bringing age discrimination claims may find it difficult to meet this initial burden because they must

---

**38.** See, for example, *Bates v. United Parcel Service, Inc.,* 465 F.3d 1069 (9th Cir. 2006).

prove that age discrimination was the reason for their employer's decision.

Once a plaintiff succeeds in proving that discrimination occurred, the burden shifts to the employer to justify the discriminatory practice. Possible justifications include that the discrimination was the result of a business necessity, a bona fide occupational qualification, or a seniority system. In some situations, as noted earlier, an effective antiharassment policy and prompt remedial action when harassment occurs may shield employers from liability for sexual harassment under Title VII.

## Business Necessity

An employer may defend against a claim of disparate-impact (unintentional) discrimination by asserting that a practice that has a discriminatory effect is a **business necessity.** ▶ **Example 28.14** Jiffy Mart requires its employees to have a high school diploma. If this requirement is shown to have a discriminatory effect, Jiffy might argue that a high school education is necessary for workers to perform the job at a required level of competence. If Jiffy can demonstrate to the court's satisfaction that a definite connection exists between a high school education and job performance, then Jiffy normally will succeed in this business necessity defense. ◀

## Bona Fide Occupational Qualification

Another defense applies when discrimination against a protected class is essential to a job—that is, when a particular trait is a **bona fide occupational qualification (BFOQ).** Race, color, and national origin, however, can never be BFOQs.

Generally, courts have restricted the BFOQ defense to instances in which the employee's gender or religion is essential to the job. ▶ **Example 28.15** Urban Minx, a women's clothing store, might legitimately hire only female salespersons if part of a salesperson's job involves assisting clients in the store's dressing rooms. Similarly, the Federal Aviation Administration can legitimately impose age limits for airline pilots—but an airline cannot impose weight limits only on female flight attendants. ◀

## Seniority Systems

An employer with a history of discrimination may have no members of protected classes in upper-level positions. Even if the employer now seeks to be unbiased, it may face a lawsuit from members of protected classes claiming that they should be promoted ahead

of schedule to compensate for past discrimination. If no present intent to discriminate is shown, however, and if promotions or other job benefits are distributed according to a fair **seniority system** (in which workers with more years of service are promoted first or laid off last), the employer normally has a good defense against the suit.

According to the United States Supreme Court, this defense may also apply to claims of discrimination under the ADA. ▶ **Case in Point 28.16** A baggage handler who had injured his back requested an assignment to a mailroom position at U.S. Airways, Inc. The airline refused to give the employee the position because another employee had seniority. The Court sided with U.S. Airways. If an employee with a disability requests an accommodation that conflicts with an employer's seniority system, the accommodation generally will not be considered "reasonable" under the ADA.[39] ◀

## After-Acquired Evidence of Employee Misconduct

In some situations, employers have attempted to avoid liability for employment discrimination on the basis of "after-acquired evidence"—that is, evidence that the employer discovers after a lawsuit is filed—of an employee's misconduct. ▶ **Example 28.17** An employer fires a worker, Ravi, who then sues the employer for employment discrimination. During pretrial investigation, the employer learns that Ravi made material misrepresentations on his employment application—misrepresentations that, had the employer known about them, would have served as a ground to fire the individual. ◀

According to the United States Supreme Court, after-acquired evidence of wrongdoing cannot be used to shield an employer entirely from liability for employment discrimination. It may, however, be used to limit the amount of damages for which the employer is liable.[40]

### SECTION 5
# AFFIRMATIVE ACTION

Federal statutes and regulations providing for equal opportunity in the workplace were designed to reduce or eliminate discriminatory practices with respect

---

**39.** *U.S. Airways, Inc. v. Barnett,* 535 U.S. 391, 122 S.Ct. 1516, 152 L.Ed.2d 589 (2002).
**40.** *McKennon v. Nashville Banner Publishing Co.,* 513 U.S. 352, 115 S.Ct. 879, 130 L.Ed.2d 852 (1995). See also *EEOC v. Dial Corp.,* 469 F.3d 735 (8th Cir. 2006).

to hiring, retaining, and promoting employees. **Affirmative action** programs go a step further and attempt to "make up" for past patterns of discrimination by giving members of protected classes preferential treatment in hiring or promotion.

These programs also promote diversity in schools and workplaces. During the 1960s, all federal and state government agencies, private companies that contracted to do business with the federal government, and institutions that received federal funding were required to implement affirmative action policies.

Title VII of the Civil Rights Act of 1964 neither requires nor prohibits affirmative action. Thus, most private companies and organizations have not been required to implement affirmative action policies, though many have done so voluntarily. Affirmative action programs have been controversial, however, particularly when they result in reverse discrimination against members of a majority group, such as white males.

## Constitutionality of Affirmative Action Programs

Because of their inherently discriminatory nature, affirmative action programs may violate the equal protection clause of the Fourteenth Amendment to the U.S. Constitution. The United States Supreme Court has held that any federal, state, or local government affirmative action program that uses racial or ethnic classifications as the basis for making decisions is subject to strict scrutiny by the courts.[41] Recall from Chapter 4 that strict scrutiny is the highest standard, which means that most programs do not survive a court's analysis under this test.

Today, an affirmative action program normally is constitutional only if it attempts to remedy past discrimination and does not make use of quotas or preferences. Furthermore, once such a program has succeeded in the goal of remedying past discrimination, it must be changed or dropped.

## Affirmative Action in Schools

Most of the affirmative action cases that have reached the United States Supreme Court in the last twenty years have involved university admissions programs and schools, rather than business employers.

**RACE AS A "PLUS" FACTOR** Generally, the Court has found that a school admissions policy that *auto-*

*matically* awards minority group applicants a specified number of points violates the equal protection clause.[42] A school can, however, "consider race or ethnicity more flexibly as a 'plus' factor in the context of individualized consideration of each and every applicant."[43] In other words, it is unconstitutional for schools to apply a mechanical formula that gives "diversity bonuses" based on race or ethnicity.

▶ **Case in Point 28.18** School districts in Seattle, Washington, and Jefferson County, Kentucky, adopted plans that relied on race to assign certain children to schools. The Seattle plan classified children as "white" or "nonwhite" and used racial classifications as a "tie-breaker" to determine which school students would attend. The school district in Jefferson County classified students as "black" or "other" to assign children to elementary schools.

Parent groups filed lawsuits claiming that the racial preferences violated the equal protection clause. The United States Supreme Court held that the school districts had failed to show that the use of racial classifications in their student assignment plans was necessary to achieve their stated goal of racial diversity. Hence, the affirmative action programs of both school districts were unconstitutional.[44] ◀

**A 2013 CHALLENGE TO RACE-CONSCIOUS POLICIES** In 2013, the Supreme Court issued a ruling in the case of *Fisher v. University of Texas*.[45] The case involved Abigail Fisher, a white woman who claimed that her rights to equal protection had been violated when she was denied admission to the University of Texas. The university's affirmative action program followed the guidelines previously set forth by the Court and considered race merely as a plus factor. Although many thought that the Supreme Court would use this case to invalidate race-conscious affirmative action programs, that did not occur. Instead, the Court held that the lower court had applied the wrong standard when it did not hold the university to the demanding burden of strict scrutiny articulated in the Court's prior decisions. The case was therefore remanded for further proceedings.

---

41. See the landmark decision in *Adarand Constructors, Inc. v. Peña*, 515 U.S. 200, 115 S.Ct. 2097, 132 L.Ed.2d 158 (1995).

42. *Gratz v. Bollinger*, 539 U.S. 244, 123 S.Ct. 2411, 156 L.Ed.2d 257 (2003).

43. *Grutter v. Bollinger*, 539 U.S. 306, 123 S.Ct. 2325, 156 L.Ed.2d 304 (2003).

44. The Court consolidated the two cases and issued one opinion for both. See *Parents Involved in Community Schools v. Seattle School District No. 1*, 551 U.S. 701, 127 S.Ct. 2738, 168 L.Ed.2d 508 (2007).

45. ___ U.S. ___, 133 S.Ct. 2411, 186 L.Ed.2d 474 (2013).

# Reviewing: Employment Discrimination and Diversity

Amaani Lyle, an African American woman, was hired by Warner Brothers Television Productions to be a scriptwriters' assistant for the writers of *Friends*, a popular, adult-oriented television series. One of her essential job duties was to type detailed notes for the scriptwriters during brainstorming sessions in which they discussed jokes, dialogue, and story lines. The writers then combed through Lyle's notes after the meetings for script material. During these meetings, the three male scriptwriters told lewd and vulgar jokes and made sexually explicit comments and gestures. They often talked about their personal sexual experiences and fantasies, and some of these conversations were then used in episodes of *Friends*.

During the meetings, Lyle never complained that she found the writers' conduct offensive. After four months, Lyle was fired because she could not type fast enough to keep up with the writers' conversations during the meetings. She filed a suit against Warner Brothers, alleging sexual harassment and claiming that her termination was based on racial discrimination. Using the information presented in the chapter, answer the following questions.

1. Would Lyle's claim of racial discrimination be for intentional (disparate-treatment) or unintentional (disparate-impact) discrimination? Explain.
2. Can Lyle establish a *prima facie* case of racial discrimination? Why or why not?
3. When Lyle was hired, she was told that typing speed was extremely important to the position. At the time, she maintained that she could type eighty words per minute, so she was not given a typing test. It later turned out that Lyle could type only fifty words per minute. What impact might typing speed have on Lyle's lawsuit?
4. Lyle's sexual-harassment claim is based on the hostile working environment created by the writers' sexually offensive conduct at meetings that she was required to attend. The writers, however, argue that their behavior was essential to the "creative process" of writing for *Friends*, a show that routinely contained sexual innuendos and adult humor. Which defense discussed in the chapter might Warner Brothers assert using this argument?

**DEBATE THIS . . .** *Members of minority groups and women have made enough economic progress in the last several decades that they no longer need special legislation to protect them.*

## Terms and Concepts

affirmative action 504

bona fide occupational
   qualification (BFOQ) 503

business necessity 503

constructive discharge 496

disparate-impact discrimination 492

disparate-treatment discrimination 491

employment discrimination 490

*prima facie* case 491

protected class 490

seniority system 503

sexual harassment 496

tangible employment action 496

## Issue Spotters

1. Ruth is a supervisor for a Subs & Suds restaurant. Tim is a Subs & Suds employee. The owner announces that some employees will be discharged. Ruth tells Tim that if he has sex with her, he can keep his job. Is this sexual harassment? Why or why not? **(See page 496.)**

2. Koko, a person with a disability, applies for a job at Lively Sales Corporation for which she is well qualified, but she is rejected. Lively continues to seek applicants and eventually fills the position with a person who does not have a disability. Could Koko succeed in a suit against Lively for discrimination? Explain. **(See page 501.)**

• Check your answers to the Issue Spotters against the answers provided in Appendix E at the end of this text.

## Business Scenarios

**28–1. Title VII Violations.** Discuss fully whether either of the following actions would constitute a violation of Title VII of the 1964 Civil Rights Act, as amended: **(See page 490.)**

(a) Tennington, Inc., is a consulting firm and has ten employees. These employees travel on consulting jobs in seven states. Tennington has an employment record of hiring only white males.

(b) Novo Films is making a movie about Africa and needs to employ approximately one hundred extras for this picture. To hire these extras, Novo advertises in all major newspapers in Southern California. The ad states that only African Americans need apply.

**28–2. Religious Discrimination.** Gina Gomez, a devout Roman Catholic, worked for Sam's Department Stores, Inc., in Phoenix, Arizona. Sam's considered Gomez a pro-

ductive employee because her sales exceeded $200,000 per year. At the time, the store gave its managers the discretion to grant unpaid leave to employees but prohibited vacations or leave during the holiday season—October through December.

Gomez felt that she had a "calling" to go on a "pilgrimage" in October to Bosnia where some persons claimed to have had visions of the Virgin Mary. The Catholic Church had not designated the site an official pilgrimage site, the visions were not expected to be stronger in October, and tours were available at other times. The store managers denied Gomez's request for leave, but she had a nonrefundable ticket and left anyway. Sam's terminated her employment, and she could not find another job. Can Gomez establish a *prima facie* case of religious discrimination? Explain. **(See page 494.)**

## Business Case Problems

**28–3. Spotlight on Title VII of the Civil Rights Act of 1964—**

**Discrimination Based on Gender.** Burlington Coat Factory Warehouse, Inc., had a dress code that required male salesclerks to wear business attire consisting of slacks, shirt, and a necktie. Female salesclerks, by contrast, were required to wear a smock so that customers could readily identify them. Karen O'Donnell and other female employees refused to wear the smock. Instead they reported to work in business attire and were suspended. After numerous suspensions, the female employees were fired for violating Burlington's dress code policy. All other conditions of employment, including salary, hours, and benefits, were the same for female and male employees. Was the dress code policy discriminatory? Why or why not? [*O'Donnell v. Burlington Coat Factory Warehouse, Inc.*, 656 F.Supp. 263 (S.D. Ohio 1987)] **(See page 495.)**

**28–4. Discrimination Based on Gender.** Brenda Lewis had been employed for two years at Heartland Inns of America, LLC, and gradually worked her way up the management ladder. Lewis, who described herself as a tomboy, was commended for her good work. When she moved to a different Heartland hotel, the director of operations, Barbara Cullinan, told one of the owners that Lewis was not a "good fit" for the front desk because she was not feminine enough. Cullinan told various people that the hotel wanted "pretty" girls at the front desk. Cullinan then informed Lewis that her hiring had not been done properly and that she would need to undergo another interview. Soon after the interview, Cullinan fired Lewis. The reason given in a letter was that Lewis was hostile during the interview. Lewis sued Heartland for gender discrimina-

tion based on unlawful gender stereotyping. The district court dismissed the suit. Lewis appealed. Does her claim fall under Title VII's prohibition against discrimination based on gender? Why or why not? [*Lewis v. Heartland Inns of America, LLC*, 591 F.3d 1033 (8th Cir. 2010)] **(See page 495.)**

**28–5. BUSINESS CASE PROBLEM**
**WITH SAMPLE ANSWER: Retaliation by Employers.**

*Entek International hired Shane Dawson, a male homosexual. Some of Dawson's co-workers, including his supervisor, made derogatory comments about his sexual orientation. Dawson's work deteriorated. He filed a complaint with Entek's human resources department. Two days later, he was fired. State law made it unlawful for an employer to discriminate against an individual based on sexual orientation. Could Dawson establish a claim for retaliation? Explain. [Dawson v. Entek International, 630 F.3d 928 (9th Cir. 2011)]* **(See page 497.)**

- **For a sample answer to Problem 28–5, go to Appendix F at the end of this text.**

**28–6. Sexual Harassment by Co-Worker.** Billie Bradford worked for the Kentucky Department of Community Based Services (DCBS). One of Bradford's co-workers, Lisa Stander, routinely engaged in extreme sexual behavior (such as touching herself and making crude comments) in Bradford's presence. Bradford and others regularly complained about Stander's conduct to their supervisor, Angie Taylor. Rather than resolve the problem, Taylor nonchalantly told Stander to stop, encouraged Bradford to talk to Stander, and suggested that Stander was just having fun. Assuming that

Bradford was subjected to a hostile work environment, could DCBS be liable? Why or why not? *[Bradford v. Department of Community Based Services, 2012 WL 360032 (E.D.Ky. 2012)]* **(See page 498.)**

**28–7. Age Discrimination.** Beginning in 1986, Paul Rangel was a sales professional for the pharmaceutical company sanofi-aventis U.S. LLC (S-A). Rangel had satisfactory performance reviews until 2006, when S-A issued new "Expectations" guidelines with sales call quotas and other standards that he failed to meet. After two years of negative performance reviews, Rangel—who was then more than forty years old—was terminated as part of a nationwide reduction in force of all sales professionals who had not met the "Expectations" guidelines, including younger workers. Did S-A engage in age discrimination? Discuss. *[Rangel v. sanofi aventis U.S. LLC, 2013 WL 142040 (10th Cir. 2013)]* **(See page 499.)**

**28–8. A QUESTION OF ETHICS:**
**Discrimination Based on Disability.**

 *Titan Distribution, Inc., employed Quintak, Inc., to run its tire mounting and distribution operation in Des Moines, Iowa. Robert Chalfant worked for Quintak as a second shift supervisor at Titan. He suffered a heart attack in 1992 and underwent heart bypass surgery in 1997. He also had arthritis. In July 2002, Titan decided to fire Quintak. Chalfant applied to work at Titan. On his application, he described himself as disabled. After a physical exam, Titan's physician concluded that Chalfant could work in his current capacity, and he was notified that he would be hired. Despite the notice, Nadis Barucic, a Titan employee, wrote "not pass px" at the top of Chalfant's application, and he was not hired. He took a job with AMPCO Systems, a parking ramp management company. This work involved walking up to five miles a day and lifting more weight than he had at Titan. In September, Titan eliminated its second shift. Chalfant filed a suit in a federal district court against Titan, in part, under the Americans with Disabilities Act (ADA). Titan argued that it had not hired Chalfant because he did not pass the physical, but no one—including Barucic—could explain why she had written "not pass px" on his application. Later, Titan claimed that Chalfant was not hired because the entire second shift was going to be eliminated. [Chalfant v. Titan Distribution, Inc., 475 F.3d 982 (8th Cir. 2007)]* **(See page 501.)**

(a) What must Chalfant establish to make his case under the ADA? Can he meet these requirements? Explain.

(b) In employment-discrimination cases, punitive damages can be appropriate when an employer acts with malice or reckless indifference toward an employee's protected rights. Would an award of punitive damages to Chalfant be appropriate in this case? Discuss.

## Legal Reasoning Group Activity

**28–9. Racial Discrimination.** Two African American plaintiffs sued the producers of the reality television series *The Bachelor* and *The Bachelorette* for racial discrimination. The plaintiffs claimed that the shows have never featured persons of color in the lead roles. The plaintiffs also alleged that the producers failed to provide people of color who auditioned for the lead roles with the same opportunities to compete as white people who auditioned. **(See page 491.)**

(a) The first group will assess whether the plaintiffs can establish a *prima facie* case of disparate-treatment (intentional) discrimination.

(b) The second group will consider whether the plaintiffs can establish disparate-impact discrimination.

(c) The third group will assume that the plaintiffs established a *prima facie* case and that the burden has shifted to the employer to articulate a legal reason for not hiring the plaintiffs. What legitimate reasons might the employer assert for not hiring the plaintiffs in this situation? Should the law require television producers to hire persons of color for lead roles in reality television shows? Discuss.

# UNIT FIVE Focus on Ethics

## Agency and Employment

Ethical principles—and challenging ethical issues—pervade the areas of agency and employment. As you read in Chapter 25, when one person agrees to act on behalf of another, as an agent does in an agency relationship, both that person and the principal assume certain ethical responsibilities and duties. In essence, agency law gives legal force to the ethical duties arising in an agency relationship. Although agency law also focuses on the rights of agents and principals, those rights are framed by the concept of duty—that is, an agent's duty becomes a right for the principal, and vice versa. Significantly, many of the duties of the principal and agent are negotiable. When they form their contract, the principal and the agent can extend or abridge many of the ordinary duties owed in such a relationship.

Employees who deal with third parties are also deemed to be agents and thus share the ethical (and legal) duties imposed under agency law. It is not always possible for an employee to negotiate favorable employment terms, however. Often, a person who is offered a job must either accept the job on the employer's terms or look elsewhere for a position. Although numerous federal and state statutes protect employees, in some situations employees still have little recourse against their employers. At the same time, employers complain that statutes regulating employment relationships impose so many requirements that they find it hard to exercise a reasonable amount of control over their workplaces.

## The Agent's Duty to the Principal

The principal-agent relationship is based on trust. Because of the nature of this relationship, which we call a fiduciary relationship, an agent is considered to owe certain duties to the principal. These duties include being loyal and obedient, informing the principal of important facts concerning the agency, accounting to the principal for property or funds received, and performing with reasonable diligence and skill.

The ethical conduct expected of an agent has evolved into rules that, if breached, cause the agent to be held legally liable. Thus, an agent may not represent two principals in the same transaction, make a secret profit from the agency relationship, or fail to disclose his or her interest in property being purchased by the principal.

**Does an Agent Also Have a Duty to Society?** A question that sometimes arises is whether an agent's obligation includes a duty to society as well as to the principal.

Consider, for example, the situation faced by an employee who knows that her employer is engaging in an unethical—or even illegal—practice, such as marketing an unsafe product. Does the employee's duty to the principal include keeping silent about this practice, which may harm users of the product? Does the employee have a duty to protect consumers by

disclosing this information to the public, even if she loses her job as a result? Some scholars have argued that many of the greatest evils in the past thirty years were carried out in the name of duty to the principal.

### LEGAL REASONING

1. *How much obedience and loyalty does an agent-employee owe to an employer? What if the employer engages in an activity—or requests that the employee engage in an activity—that violates the employee's ethical standards but does not necessarily violate any public policy or law? In this situation, does an employee's duty to abide by her or his own ethical standards override the employee's duty of loyalty to the employer? Discuss.*

**Does an Agent's Breach of Loyalty Terminate the Agent's Authority?** Several cases in recent years have involved employee-agents who breached the duty of loyalty by taking their employer's trade secrets to a competitor. The employees obtained the secrets from computer files that they were authorized to access. The question for the courts is whether the act of accessing the trade secrets was unauthorized because of the employees' breach of loyalty. If the accessing was unauthorized, the employees could be subject to severe penalties under statutes prohibiting unauthorized access to computer data.

To date, most courts have ruled that an agent's authority continues, even though there was a breach of loyalty. In one case, for example, three employees of Lockheed Martin Corporation copied confidential information and trade secrets from Lockheed's computer network onto compact discs and BlackBerries (personal digital assistants). Lockheed had authorized the employee-agents to access these files but was understandably upset when the three resigned and went to work for a competitor, taking the trade secrets with them. Lockheed sued the former employees under the Computer Fraud and Abuse Act (discussed in Chapter 10), arguing that they had accessed the data without authorization. The federal district court, however, held that the individuals did not lose their authorization to access the computer network when they breached the duty of loyalty. Therefore, the court dismissed the case.[1]

### LEGAL REASONING

2. *When an agent acts in violation of his or her ethical or legal duty to the principal, should that action terminate the agent's authority to act on behalf of the principal? Why or why not?*

---

1. *Lockheed Martin Corp. v. Speed*, 2006 WL 2683058 (M.D.Fla. 2006). See also *Clarity Services, Inc. v. Barney*, 698 F.Supp.2d 1309 (M.D.Fla. 2010).

### The Principal's Duty to the Agent

Just as agents owe certain duties to their principals, so do principals owe duties to their agents, such as compensation and reimbursement for job-related expenses. Principals also owe their agents a duty of cooperation. One might expect principals to cooperate with their agents out of self-interest, but this does not always happen. Suppose that a principal hires an agent on commission to sell a building, and the agent puts considerable time and expense into finding a buyer. If the principal changes his mind and decides to retain the building, he may try to prevent the agent from completing the sale. Is such an action ethical? Does it violate the principal's duty of cooperation? What alternatives would the principal have?

Although a principal is legally obligated to fulfill certain duties to the agent, these duties do not include any specific duty of loyalty. Some argue that employers' failure to be loyal to their employees has resulted in a reduction in employee loyalty to employers. After all, why should an employee be loyal to an employer's interests over the years when the employee knows that the employer has no corresponding legal duty to be loyal to the employee's interests? Employers who do show a sense of loyalty toward their employees—for example, by not laying off longtime employees when business is slow or replacing them with younger workers at lower cost—base that loyalty primarily on ethical, not legal, considerations.

### *Respondeat Superior*

Agency relationships have ethical ramifications for third parties as well as for agents and principals. A legal concept that addresses the effect of agency relationships on third parties is the doctrine of *respondeat superior*. This doctrine raises a significant ethical question: Why should innocent employers be required to assume responsibility for the tortious, or wrongful, actions of their agent-employees? One reason has to do with the courts' perception that when one of two innocent parties must suffer a loss, the party in the better position to prevent that loss should bear the burden. Thus, because the employer has more control over an employee's behavior than a third party does, the employer should bear the cost of that behavior.

Another reason is that the employer is assumed to be better able to pay for any damage incurred by a third party. One of our society's shared beliefs is that an injured party should be afforded the most effective relief possible. Thus, even though an employer may be entirely innocent, the employer has "deeper pockets" than the employee and will be more likely to have the funds necessary to make the injured party whole.

### LEGAL REASONING

3. *If an agent-employee injures a third party during the course of employment, the doctrine of* respondeat superior *applies.*

The employer may be held liable for the employee's action even though the employer did not authorize the action and was not even aware of it. Is it fair to hold the employer liable in this situation? Would it be more equitable if the employee alone was held liable for his or her tortious actions to third parties, even when the actions were committed within the scope of employment? Why or why not?

### Immigration Reform

Unauthorized workers make up 5 percent of the total U.S. workforce and 12 percent of the workers in the construction industry. Not long ago, the federal government significantly stepped up enforcement actions (raids) to combat the growing number of unauthorized immigrants. The raids targeted workers in many industries, including food-processing and packaging firms, contractors (landscape, cleaning, and janitorial services), construction firms, temporary employment services, and fast-food restaurants. Often, the unauthorized workers were performing jobs that no one else wanted because the jobs paid low wages or involved substandard conditions.

As a result of these raids, many immigrant workers were detained and deported, their families were torn apart, the businesses for which they worked were disrupted, and some managers faced prison terms. The impact of these raids on immigrants—in a nation founded by immigrants—has led many U.S. citizens to believe that reforming the immigration laws is a moral imperative. Many believe that it is unethical to imprison and deport these impoverished and unrepresented workers—who often were already being exploited by their U.S. employers.

When President Barack Obama took office, he promised to reform immigration law. The goal was to decrease bureaucracy, increase efficiency, and boost the number of immigrant workers with legal status in the United States. Nevertheless, Congress has not yet reached a consensus on the specific changes necessary. The comprehensive immigration reforms suggested by a bipartisan group of senators in early 2013 were quickly rejected.[2]

### LEGAL REASONING

4. *How should immigration law be reformed? Does the United States have any ethical duties to undocumented aliens who come here to work? How can the law be fair and balance the rights of immigrants, their families, the companies that employ them, and U.S. citizens?*

### Problems with I-9 Verification

Verifying a person's eligibility to work in the United States can be a complicated and costly process for employers. The most

---

2. The Border Security, Economic Opportunity, and Immigration Modernization Act of 2013, Senate Bill 744.

FOCUS ON ETHICS CONTINUES ➡

recent I-9 form (see Chapter 27) specifies the documents that an employer may accept to verify employment eligibility and identification.

At the same time, it is illegal for an employer to discriminate against foreign-born workers by requiring them to provide a driver's license or Social Security card to prove their identity. If an employer relies on the documents a worker provides to prove identity and eligibility (such as a school photo identification card) and these documents later prove to be fraudulent or invalid, the employer can be sanctioned for hiring a person that the employer "should have known" was unauthorized.

Thus, employers are forced to choose between violating antidiscrimination laws and risking sanctions for violating immigration laws. It is an ethical dilemma with no easy answer.

## Discrimination against Transgender Persons

Although some states have laws that specifically ban discrimination based on gender identity, most courts have held that federal law (Title VII, discussed in Chapter 28) does *not* protect transgender persons from discrimination. The situation may be changing, however, now that one federal court has extended Title VII protection against gender discrimination to transsexuals.

Diane Schroer (previously David Schroer) was born male but always identified with the female gender. Schroer, who has master's degrees in history and international relations, served twenty-five years in the military and was a commander of special forces. After retiring with top-secret clearance, Schroer applied for a terrorism specialist position at the Library of Congress. At the job interview, Schroer dressed as a man and received the highest interview score of all eighteen candidates. The selection committee unanimously voted to offer the job to Schroer.

Schroer then met with her future supervisor and explained that she had been diagnosed with gender identity disorder and was planning to have sex reassignment surgery. The next day, the Library of Congress withdrew its offer to hire Schroer. When Schroer sued alleging gender discrimination, the Library claimed that it had withdrawn its offer because Schroer was untrustworthy and would be unable to receive the needed security clearance.

The court, however, found that these reasons were pretexts (excuses) and ruled in favor of Schroer. The court held that the Library had refused to hire Schroer because her appearance and background did not comport with the selection committee's stereotypes about how women and men should act and appear. The court concluded that the revocation of the job offer violated Title VII and constituted discrimination "because of sex" even though Title VII does not include transsexuals as a protected class. Schroer was awarded nearly $500,000 in back pay and damages.[3]

### LEGAL REASONING

**5.** *Should the law prohibit discrimination against transgender persons? Why or why not?*

---

3. *Schroer v. Billington,* 577 F.Supp.2d 293 (D.D.C. 2008). See also *Glenn v. Brumby,* 724 F.Supp.2d 1284 (N.D.Ga. 2010).

# MILLER

## SUMMARIZED-CASE EDITION

---

## UNIT SIX

# BUSINESS ORGANIZATIONS

### CONTENTS

# CHAPTER 29

# SOLE PROPRIETORSHIPS AND FRANCHISES

One of the goals of many business students is to become an **entrepreneur,** one who initiates and assumes the financial risk of a new business enterprise and undertakes to provide or control its management. One of the first decisions an entrepreneur must make is which form of business organization will be most appropriate for the new endeavor.

In selecting an organizational form, the entrepreneur will consider a number of factors, including (1) ease of creation, (2) the liability of the owners, (3) tax considerations, and (4) the ability to raise capital. Keep these factors in mind as you read this unit and learn about the various forms of business organization. Remember, too, in considering these business forms that the

primary motive of an entrepreneur is to make profits.

Traditionally, entrepreneurs have used three major business forms—the sole proprietorship, the partnership, and the corporation. In this chapter, we examine sole proprietorships and also look at franchises. Although the franchise is not strictly speaking a business organizational form, it is widely used today by entrepreneurs.

---

## SECTION 1
## SOLE PROPRIETORSHIPS

The simplest form of business is a **sole proprietorship.** In this form, the owner is the business. Thus, anyone who does business without creating a separate business organization has a sole proprietorship. More than two-thirds of all U.S. businesses are sole proprietorships. They are usually small enterprises—about 99 percent of the sole proprietorships in the United States have revenues of less than $1 million per year. Sole proprietors can own and manage any type of business from an informal, home-office or Web-based undertaking to a large restaurant or construction firm.

### Advantages of the Sole Proprietorship

A major advantage of the sole proprietorship is that the proprietor owns the entire business and receives all of the profits (because she or he assumes all of the risk). In addition, starting a sole proprietorship is often easier and less costly than starting any other kind of business, as few legal formalities are required.

Generally, no documents need to be filed with the government to start a sole proprietorship.[1]

**FLEXIBILITY** This form of business organization also offers more flexibility than does a partnership or a corporation. The sole proprietor is free to make any decision he or she wishes concerning the business—such as whom to hire, when to take a vacation, and what kind of business to pursue.

The sole proprietor can sell or transfer all or part of the business to another party at any time and does not need approval from anyone else. (In contrast, approval is typically required from partners in a partnership and from shareholders in a corporation.)

Sometimes, a sole proprietor can even benefit in a lawsuit from the fact that the business is indistinguishable from the owner. ▶ **Case in Point 29.1** James Ferguson operated "Jim's 11-E Auto Sales" as a sole proprietorship and obtained insurance from Consumers Insurance Company. The policy was issued to "Jim Ferguson, Jim's 11-E Auto Sales." Later,

---

1. Although starting a sole proprietorship involves fewer legal formalities than other business organizational forms, even a small sole proprietorship may need to comply with zoning requirements, obtain a state business license, and the like.

Ferguson bought a motorcycle in his own name, intending to repair and sell it through his dealership. One day when he was riding the motorcycle, he was struck by a car and seriously injured.

When Ferguson sued Consumers Insurance, the insurer argued that because Ferguson bought the motorcycle in his own name and was riding it at the time of the accident, it was his personal vehicle and was not covered under the dealership's policy. The court, however, held that the policy covered Ferguson's injuries. "Because the business is operated as a sole proprietorship, Jim Ferguson and 'Jim's 11-E Auto Sales' are one and the same."[2] ◄

**TAXES** A sole proprietor pays only personal income taxes (including Social Security and Medicare taxes—see Chapter 27) on the business's profits, which are

reported as personal income on the proprietor's personal income tax return. Sole proprietors are also allowed to establish certain retirement accounts that are tax-exempt until the funds are withdrawn.

## Disadvantages of the Sole Proprietorship

The major disadvantage of the sole proprietorship is that the proprietor alone bears the burden of any losses or liabilities incurred by the business enterprise. In other words, the sole proprietor has unlimited liability, or legal responsibility, for all obligations that arise in doing business. Any lawsuit against the business or its employees can lead to unlimited personal liability for the owner of a sole proprietorship.

The personal liability of the owner of a sole proprietorship was at issue in the following case.

---

2. *Ferguson v. Jenkins,* 204 S.W.3d 779 (Tenn.App. 2006).

---

## CASE 29.1

### Quality Car & Truck Leasing, Inc. v. Sark
Court of Appeals of Ohio, Fourth District, 2013 -Ohio- 44, 2013 WL 139359 (2013).

**BACKGROUND AND FACTS** Michael Sark operated a logging business as a sole proprietorship. To acquire equipment for the business, Sark and his wife, Paula, borrowed funds from Quality Car & Truck Leasing, Inc. When his business encountered financial difficulties, Sark became unable to pay his creditors, including Quality. The Sarks sold their house (valued at $203,500) to their son, Michael, Jr., for one dollar but continued to live in it. Three months later, Quality obtained a judgment in an Ohio state court against the Sarks for $150,481.85 and then filed a claim to set aside the transfer of the house to Michael, Jr., as a fraudulent conveyance. From a decision in Quality's favor, the Sarks appealed, arguing that they did not intend to defraud Quality and that they were not actually Quality's debtors.

**DECISION AND RATIONALE** A state intermediate appellate court affirmed the lower court's judgment in Quality's favor. "Reasonable minds can come to only one conclusion, and that conclusion is adverse to the Sarks," said the court. The Sarks "are clearly judgment debtors to Quality Leasing and . . . the judgment has not been satisfied." The reviewing court accepted the trial court's view that "Michael Senior and Paula made a transfer without the exchange of reasonably equivalent value and the debtor was engaged or was about to engage in a business transaction for which the remaining assets of the debtor were unreasonably small in relation to the business or transaction."

Under Ohio law, a creditor need not show that a transfer was made with the intent to defraud in order to prevail. "Thus, the Sarks cannot defeat summary judgment showing that they did not act with fraudulent intent when Michael Senior and Paula transferred the Property to Michael Junior." Further, the Sarks did not challenge the validity of the judgment against them nor did they show that the judgment had been satisfied. Consequently, there was no "genuine issue of material fact regarding whether Paula and Michael Senior are debtors to Quality Leasing."

**THE ECONOMIC DIMENSION** *What might the Sarks have done to avoid this dispute, as well as the loss of their home and their apparently declining business?*

**THE ETHICAL DIMENSION** *Why did the Sarks take the unethical step of fraudulently conveying their home to their son? What should they have done instead?*

**PERSONAL ASSETS AT RISK** Creditors can pursue the owner's personal assets to satisfy any business debts. Although sole proprietors may obtain insurance to protect the business, liability can easily exceed policy limits. This unlimited liability is a major factor to be considered in choosing a business form.

▶ **Example 29.2** Sheila Fowler operates a golf shop near a world-class golf course as a sole proprietorship. One of Fowler's employees fails to secure a display of golf clubs. They fall on Dean Maheesh, a professional golfer, and seriously injure him. If Maheesh sues Fowler's shop and wins, Fowler's personal liability could easily exceed the limits of her insurance policy. Fowler could lose not only her business, but also her house, car, and any other personal assets that can be attached to pay the judgment. ◀

**LACK OF CONTINUITY** The sole proprietorship also has the disadvantage of lacking continuity after the death of the proprietor. When the owner dies, so does the business—it is automatically dissolved. Another disadvantage is that in raising capital, the proprietor is limited to his or her personal funds and funds from any loans that he or she can obtain for the business.

## SECTION 2
# FRANCHISES

Instead of setting up a sole proprietorship to market their own products or services, many entrepreneurs opt to purchase a franchise. A **franchise** is an arrangement in which the owner of intellectual property—such as a trademark, a trade name, or a copyright—licenses others to use it in the selling of goods or services. A **franchisee** (a purchaser of a franchise) is generally legally independent of the **franchisor** (the seller of the franchise). At the same time, the franchisee is economically dependent on the franchisor's integrated business system.

In other words, a franchisee can operate as an independent businessperson but still obtain the advantages of a regional or national organization. Today, franchising companies and their franchisees account for a significant portion of all retail sales in this country. Well-known franchises include McDonald's, 7-Eleven, and Holiday Inn. Franchising has also become a popular way for businesses to expand their operations internationally without violating the legal restrictions that many nations impose on foreign ownership of businesses.

## Types of Franchises

Many different kinds of businesses now sell franchises, and numerous types of franchises are available. Generally, though, franchises fall into one of three classifications: distributorships, chain-style business operations, and manufacturing arrangements.

**DISTRIBUTORSHIP** In a *distributorship,* a manufacturer (the franchisor) licenses a dealer (the franchisee) to sell its product. Often, a distributorship covers an exclusive territory. Automobile dealerships and beer distributorships are common examples.

▶ **Example 29.3** Black Butte Beer Company distributes its brands of beer through a network of authorized wholesale distributors, each with an assigned territory. Marik signs a distributorship contract for the area from Gainesville to Ocala, Florida. If the contract states that Marik is the exclusive distributor in that area, then no other franchisee may distribute Black Butte beer in that region. ◀

**CHAIN-STYLE BUSINESS OPERATION** In a *chain-style business operation,* a franchise operates under a franchisor's trade name and is identified as a member of a select group of dealers that engage in the franchisor's business. The franchisee is generally required to follow standardized or prescribed methods of operation. Often, the franchisor insists that the franchisee maintain certain standards of performance.

In addition, the franchisee may be required to obtain materials and supplies exclusively from the franchisor. McDonald's and most other fast-food chains are examples of this type of franchise. Chain-style franchises are also common in service-related businesses, including real estate brokerage firms, such as Century 21, and tax-preparing services, such as H&R Block, Inc.

**MANUFACTURING ARRANGEMENT** In a *manufacturing,* or *processing-plant, arrangement,* the franchisor transmits to the franchisee the essential ingredients or formula to make a particular product. The franchisee then markets the product either at wholesale or at retail in accordance with the franchisor's standards. Examples of this type of franchise include Pepsi-Cola and other soft-drink bottling companies.

## Laws Governing Franchising

Because a franchise relationship is primarily a contractual relationship, it is governed by contract law.

If the franchise exists primarily for the sale of products manufactured by the franchisor, the law governing sales contracts as expressed in Article 2 of the Uniform Commercial Code applies (see Chapters 20 through 23).

Additionally, the federal government and most states have enacted laws governing certain aspects of franchising. Generally, these laws are designed to protect prospective franchisees from dishonest franchisors and to prevent franchisors from terminating franchises without good cause.

**FEDERAL REGULATION OF FRANCHISES** The federal government regulates franchising through laws that apply to specific industries and through the Franchise Rule, created by the Federal Trade Commission (FTC).

*Industry-Specific Standards.* Congress has enacted laws that protect franchisees in certain industries, such as automobile dealerships and service stations. These laws protect the franchisee from unreasonable demands and bad faith terminations of the franchise by the franchisor.

An automobile manufacturer–franchisor cannot make unreasonable demands of dealer-franchisees or set unrealistically high sales quotas. If an automobile manufacturer–franchisor terminates a franchise because of a dealer-franchisee's failure to comply with unreasonable demands, the manufacturer may be liable for damages.[3]

Similarly, federal law prescribes the conditions under which a franchisor of service stations can terminate the franchise.[4] Federal antitrust laws also apply in certain circumstances to prohibit certain types of anticompetitive agreements.

*The Franchise Rule.* The FTC's Franchise Rule requires franchisors to disclose certain material facts that a prospective franchisee needs in order to make an informed decision concerning the purchase of a franchise.[5] The Franchise Rule requires the following:

1. *Written (or electronically recorded) disclosures.* The franchisor must make numerous disclosures, such as the range of goods and services included and the value and estimated profitability of the franchise. Disclosures can be in writing or done electronically online. Prospective franchisees must be able to download or save all electronic disclosure documents.

2. *Reasonable basis for any representations.* To prevent deception, all representations made to a prospective franchisee must have a reasonable basis at the time they are made.

3. *Projected earnings figures.* If a franchisor provides projected earnings figures, the franchisor must indicate whether the figures are based on actual data or hypothetical examples. (The Franchise Rule does not require franchisors to provide potential earnings figures, however, as discussed in the *Insight into Ethics* feature on the following page.)

4. *Actual data.* If a franchisor makes sales or earnings projections based on actual data for a specific franchise location, the franchisor must disclose the number and percentage of its existing franchises that have achieved this result.

5. *Explanation of terms.* Franchisors are also required to explain termination, cancellation, and renewal provisions of the franchise contract to potential franchisees before the agreement is signed.

Those who violate the Franchise Rule are subject to substantial civil penalties, and the FTC can sue on behalf of injured parties to recover damages.

**STATE REGULATION OF FRANCHISING** State legislation varies but often is aimed at protecting franchisees from unfair practices and bad faith terminations by franchisors.

*State Disclosures.* Approximately fifteen states have laws similar to the federal rules that require franchisors to provide presale disclosures to prospective franchisees.[6] Many state laws also require that a disclosure document (known as the Franchise Disclosure Document, or FDD) be registered or filed with a state official. State laws may also require that a franchisor submit advertising aimed at prospective franchisees to the state for approval.

To protect franchisees, a state law might require the disclosure of information such as the actual costs of operation, recurring expenses, and profits earned, along with facts substantiating these figures. State deceptive trade practices acts may also apply and prohibit certain types of actions by franchisors.

---

3. Automobile Dealers' Franchise Act of 1965, also known as the Automobile Dealers' Day in Court Act, 15 U.S.C. Sections 1221 *et seq.*
4. Petroleum Marketing Practices Act (PMPA) of 1979, 15 U.S.C. Sections 2801 *et seq.* See Case Analysis Case 29.2 on pages 565 and 566.
5. 16 C.F.R. Section 436.1.

6. These states include California, Hawaii, Illinois, Indiana, Maryland, Michigan, Minnesota, New York, North Dakota, Oregon, Rhode Island, South Dakota, Virginia, Washington, and Wisconsin.

## INSIGHT INTO ETHICS
### Should Franchisors Have to Give Prospective Franchisees Information about Potential Earnings?

Entrepreneurs who are thinking about investing in a franchise almost invariably ask, "How much will I make?" Surprisingly, current law does not require franchisors to provide any information about the earnings potential of a franchise.

**Voluntary Disclosure of Earnings Data**

Franchisors can voluntarily choose to provide projected earnings in their disclosures but are not required to do so. If franchisors do include earnings data, they must indicate whether these figures are actual or hypothetical and have a reasonable basis for these claims. About 75 percent of franchisors choose *not* to provide information about earnings potential.

**Franchisee Complaints**

The failure of the FTC's Franchise Rule to require disclosure of earnings potential has led to many complaints from franchisees. After all, some franchisees invest their life savings in franchises that ultimately fail because of unrealistic earnings expectations. Moreover, the franchisee may be

legally obliged to continue paying the franchisor even when the business is not turning a profit.

For instance, Thomas Anderson asked the franchisor, Rocky Mountain Chocolate Factory, Inc. (RMCF), and five of its franchisees for earnings information before he entered into a franchise agreement, but he did not receive any data. Although his chocolate franchise failed to become profitable, a court ordered Anderson and his partner to pay $33,109 in past due royalties and interest to RMCF (plus court costs and expenses).[a]

---

**LEGAL CRITICAL THINKING**

**INSIGHT INTO THE BUSINESS ENVIRONMENT**

*If the law required franchisors to provide estimates of potential earnings, would there be more or less growth in the number of franchises? Explain your answer.*

---

a. *Rocky Mountain Chocolate Factory, Inc. v. SDMS, Inc.,* 2009 WL 579516 (D.Colo. 2009).

---

***May Require Good Cause to Terminate the Franchise.*** To protect franchisees against arbitrary or bad faith terminations, state law may prohibit termination without "good cause" or require that certain procedures be followed in terminating a franchise. ▶ **Case in Point 29.4** FMS, Inc., entered into a franchise agreement with Samsung Construction Equipment North America to become an authorized dealership selling Samsung construction equipment. Then Samsung sold its equipment business to Volvo Construction Equipment North America, Inc., which was to continue selling Samsung brand equipment.

Later, Volvo rebranded the construction equipment under its own name and canceled FMS's franchise. FMS sued, claiming Volvo had terminated the franchise without "good cause" in violation of state law. Because Volvo was no longer manufacturing the Samsung brand equipment, however, the court found that Volvo had good cause to terminate FMS's franchise. If Volvo had continued making the Samsung equipment, though, it could not have terminated the franchise.[7] ◀

---

7. *FMS, Inc. v. Volvo Construction Equipment North America, Inc.,* 557 F.3d 758 (7th Cir. 2009).

## The Franchise Contract

The franchise relationship is defined by the contract between the franchisor and the franchisee. The franchise contract specifies the terms and conditions of the franchise and spells out the rights and duties of the franchisor and the franchisee.

If either party fails to perform its contractual duties, that party may be subject to a lawsuit for breach of contract. Furthermore, if a franchisee is induced to enter into a franchise contract by the franchisor's fraudulent misrepresentation, the franchisor may be liable for damages. Generally, statutes and the case law governing franchising tend to emphasize the importance of good faith and fair dealing in franchise relationships.

Because each type of franchise relationship has its own characteristics, franchise contracts tend to differ. Nonetheless, certain major issues typically are addressed in a franchise contract. We look at some of them next.

**PAYMENT FOR THE FRANCHISE** The franchisee ordinarily pays an initial fee or lump-sum price for the franchise license (the privilege of being granted a franchise). This fee is separate from the various products that the franchisee purchases from or through the franchisor. The franchise agreement may also require the franchisee to pay a percentage of the franchisor's advertising costs and certain administrative expenses.

In some industries, the franchisor relies heavily on the initial sale of the franchise for realizing a profit. In other industries, the continued dealing between the parties brings profit to both. Generally, the franchisor receives a stated percentage of the annual (or monthly) sales or volume of business done by the franchisee.

**BUSINESS PREMISES** The franchise agreement may specify whether the premises for the business must be leased or purchased outright. Sometimes, a building must be constructed to meet the terms of the agreement. The agreement will specify whether the franchisor or the franchisee is responsible for supplying equipment and furnishings for the premises.

**LOCATION OF THE FRANCHISE** Typically, the franchisor determines the territory to be served. Some franchise contracts give the franchisee exclusive rights, or "territorial rights," to a certain geographic area. Other franchise contracts, while defining the territory allotted to a particular franchise, either specifically state that the franchise is nonexclusive or are silent on the issue of territorial rights.

Many franchise cases involve disputes over territorial rights, and the implied covenant of good faith and fair dealing often comes into play in this area of franchising. If the franchise contract does not grant the franchisee exclusive territorial rights and the franchisor allows a competing franchise to be established nearby, the franchisee may suffer a significant loss in profits. In this situation, a court may hold that the franchisor breached an implied covenant of good faith and fair dealing.

**BUSINESS ORGANIZATION** The franchisor may require that the business use a particular organizational form and capital structure. The franchise agreement may also set out standards such as sales quotas and record-keeping requirements. Additionally, a franchisor may retain stringent control over the training of personnel involved in the operation and over administrative aspects of the business.

**QUALITY CONTROL** The day-to-day operation of the franchise business normally is left up to the franchisee. Nonetheless, the franchise agreement may specify that the franchisor will provide some degree of supervision and control so that it can protect the franchise's name and reputation.

***Means of Control.*** When the franchise prepares a product, such as food, or provides a service, such as motel accommodations, the contract often states that the franchisor will establish certain standards for the facility. Typically, the contract will state that the franchisor is permitted to make periodic inspections to ensure that the standards are being maintained.

As a means of controlling quality, franchise agreements also typically limit the franchisee's ability to sell the franchise to another party. ▶ **Example 29.5** Mark Keller, Inc., an authorized Jaguar franchise, contracts to sell its dealership to Henrique Autos West. A Jaguar franchise generally cannot be sold without Jaguar Cars' permission. Prospective franchisees must meet Jaguar's customer satisfaction standards. If Henrique Autos fails to meet those standards, Jaguar can refuse to allow the sale and can terminate the franchise.[8] ◀

***Degree of Control.*** As a general rule, the validity of a provision permitting the franchisor to establish and enforce certain quality standards is unquestioned. The franchisor has a legitimate interest in maintaining the quality of the product or service to protect its name and reputation.

If a franchisor exercises too much control over the operations of its franchisees, however, the franchisor risks potential liability. A franchisor may occasionally be held liable—under the doctrine of *respondeat superior* (see Chapter 26)—for the tortious acts of the franchisees' employees.

**PRICING ARRANGEMENTS** Franchises provide the franchisor with an outlet for the firm's goods and services. Depending on the nature of the business, the franchisor may require the franchisee to purchase certain supplies from the franchisor at an established price.[9] A franchisor cannot, however, set the prices at which the franchisee will resell the goods because such price setting may be a violation of state or federal

---

8. For example, see *Midwest Automotive III, LLC v. Iowa Department of Transportation,* 646 N.W.2d 417 (Iowa 2002).

9. Although a franchisor can require franchisees to purchase supplies from it, requiring a franchisee to purchase exclusively from the franchisor may violate federal antitrust laws.

antitrust laws, or both. A franchisor can suggest retail prices but cannot mandate them.

SECTION 3

# FRANCHISE TERMINATION

The duration of the franchise is a matter to be determined between the parties. Sometimes, a franchise relationship starts with a short trial period, such as a year, so that the franchisee and the franchisor can determine whether they want to stay in business with each another. Other times, the duration of the franchise contract correlates with the term of the lease for the business premises, and both are renewable at the end of that period.

## Grounds for Termination Set by Franchise Contract

Usually, the franchise agreement specifies that termination must be "for cause" and then defines the grounds for termination. Cause might include, for instance, the death or disability of the franchisee, insolvency of the franchisee, breach of the franchise agreement, or failure to meet specified sales quotas.

**NOTICE REQUIREMENTS** Most franchise contracts provide that notice of termination must be given. If no set time for termination is specified, then a reasonable time, with notice, is implied. A franchisee must be given reasonable time to wind up the business—that is, to do the accounting and return the copyright or trademark or any other property of the franchisor.

**OPPORTUNITY TO CURE A BREACH** A franchise agreement may state that the franchisee may attempt to cure an ordinary, curable breach within a certain period of time after notice so as to postpone, or even avoid, the termination of the contract. Even when a contract contains a notice-and-cure provision, however, a franchisee's breach of the duty of honesty and fidelity may be enough to allow the franchisor to terminate the franchise.

▶ **Case in Point 29.6**   Pilot Air Freight Corporation is a franchisor that moves freight through its network of operations at airports and other sites. LJL

Transportation, Inc., was a franchisee. The franchise agreement required LJL to assign all shipments to the Pilot network. The agreement also provided that "Pilot shall allow Franchisee an opportunity to cure a default within ninety (90) days of receipt of written notice." After eight years as a Pilot franchisee, LJL began to divert shipments to Northeast Transportation, a competing service owned by LJL's owners. Pilot then terminated the franchise agreement. LJL filed a lawsuit claiming that it should be allowed to cure its breach, but the court ruled in favor of Pilot. A franchise agreement may be terminated immediately when there is a material breach so serious that it goes directly to the heart and essence of the contract.[10] ◀

## Wrongful Termination

Because a franchisor's termination of a franchise often has adverse consequences for the franchisee, much franchise litigation involves claims of wrongful termination. Generally, the termination provisions of contracts are more favorable to the franchisor than to the franchisee. This means that the franchisee, who normally invests a substantial amount of time and financial resources in making the franchise operation successful, may receive little or nothing for the business on termination. The franchisor owns the trademark and hence the business.

It is in this area that statutory and case law become important. The federal and state laws discussed earlier attempt, among other things, to protect franchisees from the arbitrary or unfair termination of their franchises by the franchisors.

In the following case, a group of service-station franchisees claimed that their franchisor had violated the Petroleum Marketing Practices Act (PMPA) of 1979, which limits the circumstances in which petroleum franchisors may terminate a franchise. The franchisees contended that changes in the rental provisions of the franchise contract had effectively increased their fuel costs, thereby "constructively" (in effect) terminating the franchises. The franchisees, however, had continued to operate their service stations. Under the PMPA, must a franchisee abandon its franchise in order to recover for constructive termination? That was the issue facing the United States Supreme Court.

---

10. *LJL Transportation, Inc. v. Pilot Air Freight Corp.*, 599 Pa. 546, 962 A.2d 639 (Pa.Sup.Ct. 2009).

## CASE 29.2

### Mac's Shell Service, Inc. v. Shell Oil Products Co.
Supreme Court of the United States, 559 U.S. 175, 130 S.Ct. 1251, 176 L.Ed.2d 36 (2010).

**BACKGROUND AND FACTS**   Shell Oil Company, a petroleum franchisor, had franchise agreements with various gasoline stations in Massachusetts. Each franchisee was required to pay monthly rent to Shell for use of the service-station premises. Shell offered the franchisees a rent subsidy based on how much gas they sold each month. Shell renewed the subsidies annually through notices that provided for cancellation with 30 days' notice. In 1998, Shell joined with two other oil companies to create Motiva Enterprises, LLC, a joint venture that combined the companies' petroleum-marketing operations in the United States. Shell assigned its rights and obligations under the relevant franchise agreements to Motiva.

On January 1, 2000, Motiva ended all volume-based rent subsidies. Sixty-three Shell franchisees filed a lawsuit against Shell and Motiva in federal district court. They alleged that the discontinuation of the rent subsidies constituted a breach of contract under state law, as well as under the Petroleum Marketing Practices Act (PMPA). They maintained that by eliminating the rent subsidies, Shell and Motiva had "constructively terminated" their franchises in violation of federal law. At trial, the jury found against Shell and Motiva on all claims. Shell and Motiva moved for summary judgment, arguing that they could not be found liable for constructive termination because none of the dealers had abandoned their franchises when the rent subsidies had been eliminated. The district court denied the motion. Shell and Motiva appealed to the U.S. Court of Appeals for the Fifth Circuit, which affirmed the district court's judgment. Shell and Motiva then appealed to the United States Supreme Court.

**DECISION AND RATIONALE**   The United States Supreme Court reversed the federal appellate court's affirmation of the district court's judgment. The Court examined the question of whether a service-station franchisee may recover for constructive termination when the franchisor's allegedly wrongful conduct did not force the franchisee to abandon its franchise. "We conclude that a necessary element of any constructive termination claim . . . is that the franchisor's conduct forced an end to the franchisee's use of the franchisor's trademark, purchase of the franchisor's fuel, or occupation of the franchisor's service station." The Court stated that the PMPA could be violated "only if an agreement for the use of a trademark, purchase of motor fuel, or lease of a premises is 'put [to] an end.' . . . Conduct that does not force an end to the franchise, in contrast, is not prohibited by the Act's plain terms."

**WHAT IF THE FACTS WERE DIFFERENT?**   *Suppose that some of the service-station franchisees, on the expiration of their contracts with Shell, signed a renewal agreement with Motiva, even though the franchisees believed that the rental terms of the new agreement were unacceptable. Given the Court's reasoning on the issue of constructive termination, would the franchisees have been likely to succeed in a suit against the franchisor for "constructive nonrenewal" of the franchise agreement? Why or why not?*

**THE POLITICAL DIMENSION**   *The PMPA regulates only the circumstances in which service-station franchisors may terminate a franchise or decline to renew a franchise relationship. Are there any reasons why Congress might have limited the scope of the PMPA to just these two aspects of franchising? Explain.*

## The Importance of Good Faith and Fair Dealing

Generally, both statutory law and case law emphasize the importance of good faith and fair dealing in terminating a franchise relationship. In determining whether a franchisor has acted in good faith when terminating a franchise agreement, the courts usually try to balance the rights of both parties.

▶ **Case in Point 29.7**   Chic Miller's Chevrolet is a General Motors Corporation (GM) dealership. Chic Miller's entered into lending agreements, commonly known as floor plan financing, to enable it to buy new vehicles from GM. At first, the dealership had floor plan financing through GM, but then it switched to Chase Manhattan Bank. Later, Chase declined to provide further financing, and Chic Miller's was unable to obtain a loan from any other lender, including GM.

Under the franchise's "Dealer Sales and Service Agreement," GM could terminate a dealership for "Failure of Dealer to maintain the line of credit." GM therefore terminated Chic Miller's franchise. Chic Miller's sued, claiming that GM had failed to act in good faith in terminating the franchise, but the court held in GM's favor. GM had good cause to terminate the dealership because Chic Miller's failed to maintain floor plan financing, which was a material requirement under the franchise agreement.[11] ◄

11. *Chic Miller's Chevrolet, Inc. v. General Motors, Inc.*, 352 F.Supp.2d 251 (D.Conn. 2005).

If a court perceives that a franchisor has arbitrarily or unfairly terminated a franchise, the franchisee will be provided with a remedy for wrongful termination. If a franchisor's decision to terminate a franchise was made in the normal course of business, however, and reasonable notice of termination was given, a court will be less likely to consider the termination wrongful. The importance of good faith and fair dealing in a franchise relationship is underscored by the consequences of the franchisor's acts in the following case.

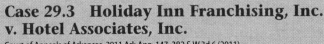

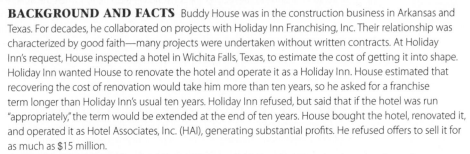

### Case 29.3 Holiday Inn Franchising, Inc. v. Hotel Associates, Inc.

Court of Appeals of Arkansas, 2011 Ark.App. 147, 382 S.W.3d 6 (2011).

**BACKGROUND AND FACTS** Buddy House was in the construction business in Arkansas and Texas. For decades, he collaborated on projects with Holiday Inn Franchising, Inc. Their relationship was characterized by good faith—many projects were undertaken without written contracts. At Holiday Inn's request, House inspected a hotel in Wichita Falls, Texas, to estimate the cost of getting it into shape. Holiday Inn wanted House to renovate the hotel and operate it as a Holiday Inn. House estimated that recovering the cost of renovation would take him more than ten years, so he asked for a franchise term longer than Holiday Inn's usual ten years. Holiday Inn refused, but said that if the hotel was run "appropriately," the term would be extended at the end of ten years. House bought the hotel, renovated it, and operated it as Hotel Associates, Inc. (HAI), generating substantial profits. He refused offers to sell it for as much as $15 million.

Before the ten years had passed, Greg Aden, a Holiday Inn executive, developed a plan to license a different local hotel as a Holiday Inn instead of renewing House's franchise license. Aden stood to earn a commission from licensing the other hotel. No one informed House of Aden's plan. When the time came, HAI applied for an extension of its franchise, and Holiday Inn asked for major renovations. HAI spent $3 million to comply with this request. Holiday Inn did not renew HAI's license, however, but instead granted a franchise to the other hotel. HAI sold its hotel for $5 million and filed a suit in an Arkansas state court against Holiday Inn, asserting fraud. The court awarded HAI compensatory and punitive damages. Holiday Inn appealed.

**DECISION AND RATIONALE** A state intermediate appellate court affirmed the lower court's judgment. A failure to volunteer information normally does not constitute fraud. But silence can amount to fraud when parties are in a relationship of trust and there is an "inequality" of knowledge between them—for example, when one party has information that the other party is justified in assuming does not exist. In this case, House's relationship with Holiday Inn was characterized by "honesty, trust, and the free flow of pertinent information." With respect to the Wichita Falls hotel, Holiday Inn assured HAI that its franchise would be renewed after ten years if the hotel were run "appropriately." House was thus justified in assuming that his franchise was not in jeopardy. Holiday Inn, however, knew of Aden's plan to license a different facility in the same area and did not inform House. In these circumstances, the failure to inform was

**CASE 29.3 CONTINUED**   fraud. Even Holiday Inn personnel, including Aden, admitted that House should have been informed. The appellate court also upheld the lower court's award of compensatory damages and increased the amount of punitive damages, citing Holiday Inn's "degree of reprehensibility."

**THE LEGAL ENVIRONMENT DIMENSION**   *Why should House and HAI have been advised of Holiday Inn's plan to grant a franchise to a different hotel in their territory?*

**THE ECONOMIC DIMENSION**   *A jury awarded HAI $12 million in punitive damages. The court reduced this award to $1 million, but the appellate court reinstated the original award. What is the purpose of punitive damages? Did Holiday Inn's conduct warrant this award? Explain.*

---

## Reviewing: Sole Proprietorships and Franchises

Carlos Del Rey decided to open a Mexican fast-food restaurant and signed a franchise contract with a national chain called La Grande Enchilada. The contract required the franchisee to strictly follow the franchisor's operating manual and stated that failure to do so would be grounds for terminating the franchise contract. The manual set forth detailed operating procedures and safety standards, and provided that a La Grande Enchilada representative would inspect the restaurant monthly to ensure compliance. Nine months after Del Rey began operating his restaurant, a spark from the grill ignited an oily towel in the kitchen. No one was injured, but by the time firefighters were able to put out the fire, the kitchen had sustained extensive damage. The cook told the fire department that the towel was "about two feet from the grill" when it caught fire. This was in compliance with the franchisor's manual that required towels be placed at least one foot from the grills. Nevertheless, the next day La Grande Enchilada notified Del Rey that his franchise would terminate in thirty days for failure to follow the prescribed safety procedures. Using the information presented in the chapter, answer the following questions.

1. What type of franchise was Del Rey's La Grande Enchilada restaurant?
2. If Del Rey operates the restaurant as a sole proprietorship, who bears the loss for the damaged kitchen?  Explain.
3. Assume that Del Rey files a lawsuit against La Grande Enchilada, claiming that his franchise was wrongfully terminated. What is the main factor that a court would consider in determining whether the franchise was wrongfully terminated?
4. Would a court be likely to rule that La Grande Enchilada had good cause to terminate Del Rey's franchise in this situation?  Why or why not?

**DEBATE THIS . . .** *All franchisors should be required by law to provide a comprehensive estimate of the profitability of a prospective franchise based on the experiences of their existing franchisees.*

---

## Terms and Concepts

entrepreneur 512

franchise 514

franchisee 514

franchisor 514

sole proprietorship 512

## Issue Spotters

1. Frank plans to open a sporting goods store and to hire Gogi and Hap. Frank will invest only his own funds. He expects that he will not make a profit for at least eighteen months and will make only a small profit in the three years after that. He hopes to expand eventually. Would a sole proprietorship be an appropriate form for Frank's business? Why or why not? **(See page 512.)**

2. Anchor Bottling Company and U.S. Beverages, Inc. (USB), enter into a franchise agreement that states the franchise may be terminated at any time "for cause." Anchor fails to meet USB's specified sales quota. Does this constitute "cause" for termination? Why or why not? **(See page 518.)**

• **Check your answers to the Issue Spotters against the answers provided in Appendix E at the end of this text.**

## Business Scenarios

**29–1. Franchising.** Maria, Pablo, and Vicky are recent college graduates who would like to go into business for themselves. They are considering purchasing a franchise. If they enter into a franchising arrangement, they would have the support of a large company that could answer any questions they might have. Also, a firm that has been in business for many years would be experienced in dealing with some of the problems that novice businesspersons might encounter. These and other attributes of franchises can lessen some of the risks of the marketplace. What other aspects of franchising—positive and negative—should Maria, Pablo, and Vicky consider before committing themselves to a particular franchise? **(See page 514.)**

**29–2. Control of a Franchise.** National Foods, Inc., sells franchises to its fast-food restaurants, known as Chicky–D's.

Under the franchise agreement, franchisees agree to hire and train employees strictly according to Chicky-D's standards. Chicky-D's regional supervisors are required to approve all job candidates before they are hired and all general policies affecting those employees. Chicky-D's reserves the right to terminate a franchise for violating the franchisor's rules. In practice, however, Chicky-D's regional supervisors routinely approve new employees and individual franchisees' policies. After several incidents of racist comments and conduct by Tim, a recently hired assistant manager at a Chicky-D's, Sharon, a counterperson at the restaurant, resigns. Sharon files a suit in a federal district court against National. National files a motion for summary judgment, arguing that it is not liable for harassment by franchise employees. Will the court grant National's motion? Why or why not? **(See page 517.)**

## Business Case Problems

**29–3. Spotlight on McDonald's—Franchise Termination.** J.C.,  Inc., had a franchise agreement with McDonald's Corp to operate McDonald's restaurants in Lancaster, Ohio. The agreement required J.C. to make monthly payments of certain percentages of the gross sales to McDonald's. If any payment was more than thirty days late, McDonald's had the right to terminate the franchise. The agreement also stated that even if McDonald's accepted a late payment, that would not "constitute a waiver of any subsequent breach."

McDonald's sometimes accepted J.C.'s late payments, but when J.C. defaulted on the payments in July 2010, McDonald's gave notice of thirty days to comply or surrender possession of the restaurants. J.C. missed the deadline. McDonald's demanded that J.C. vacate the restaurants, but J.C. refused. McDonald's alleged that J.C. had violated the franchise agreement. J.C. claimed that McDonald's had breached the implied covenant of good faith and fair dealing. Which party should prevail and why? [*McDonald's Corp. v. C.B. Management Co.,*13 F.Supp.2d 705 (N.D.Ill. 1998)] **(See page 518.)**

**29–4. Franchise Disclosure.** Peaberry Coffee, Inc., owned and operated about twenty company stores in the Denver area. The company began a franchise program and pre-

pared a disclosure document as required by the Federal Trade Commission (FTC). Peaberry sold ten franchises, and each franchisee received a disclosure document. Later, when the franchises did not do well, the franchisees sued Peaberry, claiming that its FTC disclosure document had been fraudulent. Specifically, the franchisees claimed that Peaberry had not disclosed that most of the company stores were unprofitable and that its parent company had suffered significant financial losses over the years. In addition, Peaberry had included in the franchisees' information packets, an article from the *Denver Business Journal* in which an executive had said that Peaberry was profitable. The FTC disclosure document had also contained an *exculpatory clause* (see Chapter 14), which said the buyers should not rely on any material that was not in the franchise contract itself. Can a franchisor disclaim the relevance of the information it provides to franchisees? Why or why not? [*Colorado Coffee Bean, LLC v. Peaberry Coffee, Inc.,* 251 P.3d 9 (Colo.App. 2010)] **(See page 515.)**

**29–5. The Franchise Contract.** Kubota Tractor Corp. makes farm, industrial, and outdoor equipment. Its franchise contracts allow Kubota to enter into dealership agreements with "others at any location." Kejzar Motors, Inc., is a Kubota dealer in Nacogdoches and Jasper, Texas. These two Kejzar stores operate as one dealership with two locations. Kubota granted a dealership to Michael Hammer in Lufkin, Texas, which lies between Kejzar's two store locations. Kejzar filed a suit in a Texas state court against Kubota. Kejzar asked for an injunction to prevent Kubota from locating a dealership in the same market area. Kejzar argued that the new location would cause it to suffer a significant loss of profits. Which party in a franchise relationship typically determines the territory served by a franchisee? Which legal principles come into play in this area? How do these concepts most likely apply in this case? Discuss. [*Kejzar Motors, Inc. v. Kubota Tractor Corp.*, 334 S.W.3d 351 (Tex.App.—Tyler 2011)] **(See page 517.)**

**29–6. BUSINESS CASE PROBLEM**
**WITH SAMPLE ANSWER: Franchise Termination.**

 *George Oshana and GTO Investments, Inc., operated a Mobil gas station franchise in Itasca, Illinois. In 2010, Oshana and GTO became involved in a rental dispute with Buchanan Energy,* to which Mobil had assigned the lease. In November 2011, Buchanan terminated the franchise because Oshana and GTO had failed to pay the rent. Oshana and GTO, however, alleged that they were "ready, willing, and able to pay the rent" but that Buchanan failed to accept their electronic fund transfer. Have Oshana and GTO stated a claim for wrongful termination of their franchise? Why or why not? [Oshana v. Buchanan Energy, *2012 WL 426921 (N.D.Ill. 2012)]* **(See page 518.)**

• **For a sample answer to Problem 29–6, go to Appendix F at the end of this text.**

**29–7. Quality Control.** JTH Tax, Inc., doing business as Liberty Tax Service, provides tax preparation and related loan services through company-owned and franchised stores. Liberty's agreement with its franchisees reserved the right to control their ads. In operations manuals, Liberty provided step-by-step instructions, directions, and limitations regarding the franchisees' ads and retained the right to unilaterally modify the steps at any time. The California attorney general filed a suit in a California state court against Liberty, alleging that its franchisees had used misleading or deceptive ads regarding refund anticipation loans and e-refund checks. Can Liberty be held liable? Discuss. [*People v. JTH Tax, Inc.*, 212 Cal.App.4th 1219, 151 Cal.Rptr.3d 728 (1 Dist. 2013)] **(See page 517.)**

**29–8. A QUESTION OF ETHICS: Sole Proprietorship.**

 *In August 2004, Ralph Vilardo contacted Travel Center, Inc., in Cincinnati, Ohio, to buy a trip to Florida in December for his family to celebrate his fiftieth wedding anniversary. Vilardo paid $6,900 to David Sheets, the sole proprietor of Travel Center. Vilardo also paid $195 to Sheets for a separate trip to Florida in February 2005. Sheets assured Vilardo that everything was set, but in fact no arrangements were made. Later, two unauthorized charges for travel services totaling $1,182.35 appeared on Vilardo's credit-card statement. Vilardo filed a suit in an Ohio state court against Sheets and his business, alleging, among other things, fraud and violations of the state consumer protection law. Vilardo served Sheets and Travel Center with copies of the complaint, the summons, a request for admissions, and other documents filed with the court, including a motion for summary judgment. Each of these filings asked for a response within a certain time period. Sheets responded once on his own behalf with a denial of all of Vilardo's claims. Travel Center did not respond. [*Vilardo v. Sheets, 2006 WL 1843585 (12 Dist. 2006)]* **(See page 512.)**

(a) Almost four months after Vilardo filed his complaint, Sheets decided that he was unable to adequately represent himself and retained an attorney, who asked the court for more time. Should the court grant this request? Why or why not? Ultimately, what should the court rule?

(b) Sheets admitted that Travel Center, Inc., was a sole proprietorship. He also argued that liability might be imposed on his business but not on himself. How would you rule with respect to this argument? Why? Would there be anything unethical about allowing Sheets to avoid liability on this basis? Explain.

## Legal Reasoning Group Activity

**29–9. Franchise Termination.** Walid Elkhatib, an Arab American, bought a Dunkin' Donuts franchise in Illinois. Ten years later, Dunkin' Donuts began offering breakfast sandwiches with bacon, ham, or sausage through its franchises. Elkhatib refused to sell these items at his store on the ground that his religion forbade the handling of pork. Elkhatib then opened a second franchise, at which he also refused to sell pork products.

The next year, at both locations, Elkhatib began selling meatless sandwiches. He also opened a third franchise. When he proposed to relocate this franchise, Dunkin' Donuts refused to approve the new location and informed him that it would not renew any of his franchise agreements because he did not carry the full sandwich line. Elkhatib filed a lawsuit against Dunkin' Donuts. **(See page 518.)**

(a) The first group will argue on behalf of Elkhatib that Dunkin' Donuts wrongfully terminated his franchises.

(b) The second group will take the side of Dunkin' Donuts and justify its decision to terminate the franchises.

(c) The third group will assess whether Dunkin' Donuts acted in good faith in its relationship with Elkhatib. Also, consider whether Dunkin' Donuts should be required to accommodate Elkhatib's religious beliefs and allow him not to serve pork in these three locations.

# CHAPTER 30

# PARTNERSHIPS AND LIMITED LIABILITY PARTNERSHIPS

Historically, two or more persons entering into business together have most commonly organized their business as a partnership or a corporation. A *partnership* arises from an agreement, express or implied, between two or more persons to carry on a business for a profit. Partners are co-owners of the business and have joint control over its operation and the right to share in its profits. In this chapter, we

examine several forms of partnership. (Corporations will be discussed in Chapter 32.)

We begin with an examination of traditional partnerships, or *general partnerships,* and the rights and duties of partners in this business entity.

We then examine some special forms of partnerships known as *limited partnerships* and *limited liability partnerships,* which receive different treatment under the law.

Although general partnerships are less common today than in the past, the limited liability forms of partnership are quite prevalent. Accountants, attorneys, and architects frequently organize as limited liability partnerships. DLA Piper, the second-largest U.S. law firm, for instance, is structured as two limited liability partnerships— DLA Piper U.S., LLP, and DLA Piper International, LLP—both run by a single management board.

## SECTION 1
## BASIC PARTNERSHIP CONCEPTS

Partnerships are governed both by common law concepts—in particular, those relating to agency—and by statutory law. As in so many other areas of business law, the National Conference of Commissioners on Uniform State Laws has drafted uniform laws for partnerships, and these have been widely adopted by the states.

### Agency Concepts and Partnership Law

When two or more persons agree to do business as partners, they enter into a special relationship with one another. To an extent, their relationship is similar to an agency relationship because each partner is deemed to be the agent of the other partners and of the partnership. The agency concepts that were discussed in Chapters 25 and 26 thus apply—specifically, the imputation of knowledge of, and responsibility for, acts carried out within the scope of the partnership

relationship. In their relationships with one another, partners, like agents, are bound by fiduciary ties.

In one important way, however, partnership law differs from agency law. The partners in a partnership agree to commit funds or other assets, labor, and skills to the business with the understanding that profits and losses will be shared. Thus, each partner has an *ownership interest* in the firm. In a nonpartnership agency relationship, the agent usually does not have an ownership interest in the business and is not obligated to bear a portion of ordinary business losses.

### The Uniform Partnership Act

The Uniform Partnership Act (UPA) governs the operation of partnerships *in the absence of express agreement* and has done much to reduce controversies in the law relating to partnerships. A majority of the states have enacted the most recent version of the UPA (as amended in 1997) to provide limited liability for partners in a limited liability partnership.[1] We therefore

---

1. At the time this book went to press, more than two-thirds of the states, as well as the District of Columbia, Puerto Rico, and the U.S. Virgin Islands, had adopted the UPA with the 1997 amendments.

CHAPTER 30  Partnerships and Limited Liability Partnerships  **525**

base our discussion of the UPA in this chapter on the 1997 version of the act and refer to older versions of the UPA in footnotes when appropriate.

## Definition of a Partnership

The UPA defines a **partnership** as "an association of two or more persons to carry on as co-owners a business for profit" [UPA 101(6)]. Note that the UPA's definition of *person* includes corporations, so a corporation can be a partner in a partnership [UPA 101(10)]. The *intent* to associate is a key element of a partnership, and one cannot join a partnership unless all other partners consent [UPA 401(i)].

## Essential Elements of a Partnership

Conflicts sometimes arise over whether a business enterprise is a legal partnership, especially when there is no formal, written partnership agreement. To determine whether a partnership exists, courts usually look for the following three essential elements, which are implicit in the UPA's definition:

1. A sharing of profits or losses.
2. A joint ownership of the business.
3. An equal right to be involved in the management of the business.

If the evidence in a particular case is insufficient to establish all three factors, the UPA provides a set of guidelines to be used.

**THE SHARING OF PROFITS AND LOSSES** The sharing of both profits and losses from a business creates a presumption (legal inference) that a partnership exists. ▶ **Example 30.1** Syd and Drake start a business that sells fruit smoothies near a college campus. They open a joint bank account from which they pay for supplies and expenses, and they share the proceeds (and losses) that the smoothie stand generates. If a conflict arises as to their business relationship, a court will assume that a partnership exists unless the parties prove otherwise. ◀

A court will not presume that a partnership exists, however, if shared profits were received as payment of any of the following [UPA 202(c)(3)]:

1. A debt by installments or interest on a loan.
2. Wages of an employee or for the services of an independent contractor.
3. Rent to a landlord.

4. An annuity to a surviving spouse or representative of a deceased partner.
5. A sale of the **goodwill** (the valuable reputation of a business viewed as an intangible asset) of a business or property.

▶ **Example 30.2** Mason Snopel owes a creditor, Alice Burns, $5,000 on an unsecured debt. They agree that Mason will pay 10 percent of his monthly business profits to Alice until the loan with interest has been repaid. Although Mason and Alice are sharing profits from the business, they are not presumed to be partners. ◀

**JOINT PROPERTY OWNERSHIP** Joint ownership of property does not in and of itself create a partnership [UPA 202(c)(1) and (2)]. The parties' intentions are key. ▶ **Example 30.3** Chiang and Burke jointly own farmland and lease it to a farmer for a share of the profits from the farming operation in lieu of fixed rental payments. This arrangement normally would not make Chiang, Burke, and the farmer partners. ◀

## Entity versus Aggregate

At common law, a partnership was treated only as an aggregate of individuals and never as a separate legal entity. Thus, at common law a lawsuit could never be brought by or against the firm in its own name. Each individual partner had to sue or be sued.

Today, in contrast, a majority of the states follow the UPA and treat a partnership as an entity for most purposes. For instance, a partnership usually can sue or be sued, collect judgments, and have all accounting performed in the name of the partnership entity [UPA 201, 307(a)].

As an entity, a partnership may hold the title to real or personal property in its name rather than in the names of the individual partners. Additionally, federal procedural laws permit the partnership to be treated as an entity in suits in federal courts and bankruptcy proceedings.

## Tax Treatment of Partnerships

Modern law does treat a partnership as an aggregate of the individual partners rather than a separate legal entity in one situation—for federal income tax purposes. The partnership is a pass-through entity and not a taxpaying entity. A **pass-through entity** is a business entity that has no tax liability—the entity's income is passed through to the owners of the entity, who pay income taxes on it.

Thus, the income or losses the partnership incurs are "passed through" the entity framework and attributed to the partners on their individual tax returns. The partnership itself pays no taxes and is responsible only for filing an **information return** with the Internal Revenue Service.

A partner's profit from the partnership (whether distributed or not) is taxed as individual income to the individual partner. Similarly, partners can deduct a share of the partnership's losses on their individual tax returns (in proportion to their partnership interests).

## SECTION 2
# PARTNERSHIP FORMATION AND OPERATION

As a general rule, agreements to form a partnership can be *oral, written,* or *implied by conduct.* Some partnership agreements, however, such as one authorizing partners to transfer interests in real property, must be in writing (or in an electronic record) to be legally enforceable (see Chapter 16).

A partnership agreement, also known as **articles of partnership,** can include almost any terms that the parties wish, unless they are illegal or contrary to public policy or statute [UPA 103]. The terms commonly included in a partnership agreement are listed in Exhibit 30–1 on the next page.

The rights and duties of partners are governed largely by the specific terms of their partnership agreement. In the absence of provisions to the contrary in the partnership agreement, the law imposes certain rights and duties, as discussed in the following subsections. The character and nature of the partnership business generally influence the application of these rights and duties.

## Duration of the Partnership

The partnership agreement can specify the duration of the partnership by stating that it will continue until a designated date or until the completion of a particular project. This is called a *partnership for a term.* Generally, withdrawal from a partnership for a term prematurely (before the expiration date) constitutes a breach of the agreement, and the responsible partner can be held liable for any resulting losses [UPA 602(b)(2)]. If no fixed duration is specified, the partnership is a *partnership at will,* which means that the partnership can be dissolved at any time.

## Partnership by Estoppel

Occasionally, persons who are not partners nevertheless hold themselves out as partners and make representations that third parties rely on in dealing with them.

**LIABILITY IMPOSED** When a third person has reasonably and detrimentally relied on the representation that a nonpartner was part of a partnership, a court may conclude that a **partnership by estoppel** exists and impose liability—but not partnership *rights*—on the alleged partner. Similarly, a partnership by estoppel may be imposed when a partner represents, expressly or impliedly, that a nonpartner is a member of the firm.

**NONPARTNER AGENTS** When a partnership by estoppel is deemed to exist, the nonpartner is regarded as an agent whose acts are binding on the partnership [UPA 308].

▶ **Case in Point 30.4** Jackson Paper Manufacturing Company makes paper that is used by Stonewall Packaging, LLC. Jackson and Stonewall have officers and directors in common, and they share employees, property, and equipment. In reliance on Jackson's business reputation, Best Cartage, Inc., agreed to provide transportation services for Stonewall and bought thirty-seven tractor-trailers to use in fulfilling the contract. Best provided the services until Stonewall terminated the agreement.

Best filed a suit for breach of contract against Stonewall and Jackson, seeking $500,678 in unpaid invoices and consequential damages of $1,315,336 for the tractor-trailers it had purchased. Best argued that Stonewall and Jackson had a partnership by estoppel. The court agreed, finding that "defendants combined labor, skills, and property to advance their alleged business partnership." Jackson had negotiated the agreement on Stonewall's behalf, and a news release stated that Jackson had sought tax incentives for Stonewall. Jackson also had bought real estate, equipment, and general supplies for Stonewall with no expectation of payment from Stonewell to Jackson. This was sufficient to prove a partnership by estoppel.[2] ◀

---

2. *Best Cartage, Inc. v. Stonewall Packaging, LLC,* 727 S.E.2d 291 (N.C.App. 2012).

## EXHIBIT 30-1  Common Terms Included in a Partnership Agreement

| Term | Description |
| --- | --- |
| **Basic Structure** | 1. Name of the partnership.<br>2. Names of the partners.<br>3. Location of the business and the state law under which the partnership is organized.<br>4. Purpose of the partnership.<br>5. Duration of the partnership. |
| **Capital Contributions** | 1. Amount of capital that each partner is contributing.<br>2. The agreed-on value of any real or personal property that is contributed instead of cash.<br>3. How losses and gains on contributed capital will be allocated, and whether contributions will earn interest. |
| **Sharing of Profits and Losses** | 1. Percentage of the profits and losses of the business that each partner will receive.<br>2. When distributions of profit will be made and how net profit will be calculated. |
| **Management and Control** | 1. How management responsibilities will be divided among the partners.<br>2. Name(s) of the managing partner or partners, and whether other partners have voting rights. |
| **Accounting and Partnership Records** | 1. Name of the bank in which the partnership will maintain its business and checking accounts.<br>2. Statement that an accounting of partnership records will be maintained and that any partner or her or his agent can review these records at any time.<br>3. The dates of the partnership's fiscal year (if used) and when the annual audit of the books will take place. |
| **Dissociation and Dissolution** | 1. Events that will cause the dissociation of a partner or dissolve the partnership, such as the retirement, death, or incapacity of any partner.<br>2. How partnership property will be valued and apportioned on dissociation and dissolution.<br>3. Whether an arbitrator will determine the value of partnership property on dissociation and dissolution and whether that determination will be binding. |
| **Arbitration** | 1. Whether arbitration is required for any dispute relating to the partnership agreement. |

## Rights of Partners

The rights of partners in a partnership relate to the following areas: management, interest in the partnership, compensation, inspection of books, accounting, and property.

**MANAGEMENT RIGHTS** In a general partnership, all partners have equal rights in managing the partnership [UPA 401(f)]. Unless the partners agree otherwise, each partner has one vote in management matters *regardless of the proportional size of his or her interest in the firm.* In a large partnership, partners often agree to delegate daily management responsibilities to a management committee made up of one or more of the partners.

***For Ordinary Decisions.*** The majority rule controls decisions on ordinary matters connected with partnership business, unless otherwise specified in the agreement. Decisions that significantly affect the nature of the partnership or that are outside the ordinary course of the partnership business, however, require the *unanimous* consent of the partners [UPA 301(2), 401(i), 401(j)].

***When Unanimous Consent May Be Required.*** Unanimous consent is likely to be required for any decision to:

1. Alter the essential nature of the firm's business as expressed in the partnership agreement.
2. Change the capital structure of the partnership.
3. Amend the terms of the partnership agreement.
4. Admit a new partner.
5. Engage in a completely new business.
6. Assign partnership property to a trust for the benefit of creditors, or allow a creditor to enter a judgment against the partnership, for an agreed sum, without the use of legal proceedings.
7. Dispose of the partnership's *goodwill* (defined on page 525).
8. Submit partnership claims to arbitration.

9. Undertake any act that would make further conduct of the partnership business impossible.

**INTEREST IN THE PARTNERSHIP** Each partner is entitled to the proportion of business profits and losses that is specified in the partnership agreement. If the agreement does not apportion profits (indicate how the profits will be shared), the UPA provides that profits will be shared equally. If the agreement does not apportion losses, losses will be shared in the same ratio as profits [UPA 401(b)].

▶ **Example 30.5** Rimi and Brett form a partnership. The partnership agreement provides for capital contributions of $60,000 from Rimi and $40,000 from Brett, but it is silent as to how they will share profits or losses. In this situation, they will share both profits and losses equally. If their partnership agreement had provided that they would share profits in the same ratio as capital contributions, however, 60 percent of the profits would go to Rimi, and 40 percent would go to Brett. If the agreement was silent as to losses, losses would be shared in the same ratio as profits (60 percent and 40 percent, respectively). ◀

**COMPENSATION** Devoting time, skill, and energy to partnership business is a partner's duty and generally is not a compensable service. Rather, as mentioned, a partner's income from the partnership takes the form of a distribution of profits according to the partner's share in the business.

Partners can, of course, agree otherwise. For instance, the managing partner of a law firm often receives a salary—in addition to her or his share of profits—for performing special administrative or managerial duties.

**INSPECTION OF THE BOOKS** Partnership books and records must be kept accessible to all partners. Each partner has the right to receive (and the corresponding duty to produce) full and complete information concerning the conduct of all aspects of partnership business [UPA 403]. Each firm retains books for recording and securing such information. Partners contribute the information, and a bookkeeper typically has the duty to preserve it.

The partnership books must be kept at the firm's principal business office (unless the partners agree otherwise). Every partner is entitled to inspect all books and records on demand and can make copies of the materials. The personal representative of a deceased partner's estate has the same right of access to partnership books and records that the decedent would have had [UPA 403].

**ACCOUNTING OF PARTNERSHIP ASSETS OR PROFITS** An accounting of partnership assets or profits is required to determine the value of each partner's share in the partnership. An accounting can be performed voluntarily, or it can be compelled by court order. Under UPA 405(b), a partner has the right to bring an action for an accounting during the term of the partnership, as well as on the partnership's dissolution and winding up.

**PROPERTY RIGHTS** Property acquired *by* a partnership is the property of the partnership and not of the partners individually [UPA 203]. Partnership property includes all property that was originally contributed to the partnership and anything later purchased by the partnership or in the partnership's name (except in rare circumstances) [UPA 204].

A partner may use or possess partnership property only on behalf of the partnership [UPA 401(g)]. A partner is *not* a co-owner of partnership property and has no right to sell, mortgage, or transfer partnership property to another [UPA 501].[3]

In other words, partnership property is owned by the partnership as an entity and not by the individual partners. Thus, partnership property cannot be used to satisfy the personal debt of an individual partner. That partner's creditor, however, can petition a court for a **charging order** to attach the partner's *interest* in the partnership to satisfy the partner's obligation [UPA 502]. A partner's interest in the partnership includes her or his proportionate share of the profits and losses and the right to receive distributions. (A partner can also assign her or his right to a share of the partnership profits to another to satisfy a debt.)

## Duties and Liabilities of Partners

The duties and liabilities of partners are derived from agency law. Each partner is an agent of every other partner and acts as both a principal and an agent in any business transaction within the scope of the partnership agreement.

Each partner is also a general agent of the partnership in carrying out the usual business of the firm "or

---

**3.** Under the previous version of the UPA, partners were *tenants in partnership*. This meant that every partner was a co-owner with all other partners of the partnership property. The current UPA does not recognize this concept.

business of the kind carried on by the partnership" [UPA 301(1)]. Thus, every act of a partner concerning partnership business and "business of the kind" and every contract signed in the partnership's name bind the firm.

**FIDUCIARY DUTIES** The fiduciary duties that a partner owes to the partnership and the other partners are the duty of care and the duty of loyalty [UPA 404(a)]. Under the UPA, a partner's *duty of care* is limited to refraining from "grossly negligent or reckless conduct, intentional misconduct, or a knowing violation of law" [UPA 404(c)].[4] A partner is not liable

---

4. The previous version of the UPA touched only briefly on the duty of loyalty and left the details of the partners' fiduciary duties to be developed under the law of agency.

to the partnership for simple negligence or honest errors in judgment in conducting partnership business.

The *duty of loyalty* requires a partner to account to the partnership for "any property, profit, or benefit" derived by the partner in the conduct of the partnership's business or from the use of its property. A partner must also refrain from competing with the partnership in business or dealing with the firm as an adverse party [UPA 404(b)].

The duty of loyalty can be breached by self-dealing, misusing partnership property, disclosing trade secrets, or usurping a partnership business opportunity. The following case is a classic example.

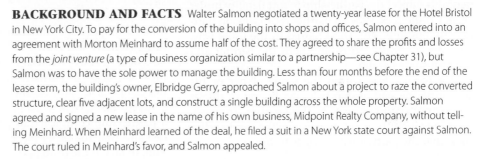

## CLASSIC CASE 30.1

### Meinhard v. Salmon
Court of Appeals of New York, 249 N.Y. 458, 164 N.E. 545 (1928).

**BACKGROUND AND FACTS** Walter Salmon negotiated a twenty-year lease for the Hotel Bristol in New York City. To pay for the conversion of the building into shops and offices, Salmon entered into an agreement with Morton Meinhard to assume half of the cost. They agreed to share the profits and losses from the *joint venture* (a type of business organization similar to a partnership—see Chapter 31), but Salmon was to have the sole power to manage the building. Less than four months before the end of the lease term, the building's owner, Elbridge Gerry, approached Salmon about a project to raze the converted structure, clear five adjacent lots, and construct a single building across the whole property. Salmon agreed and signed a new lease in the name of his own business, Midpoint Realty Company, without telling Meinhard. When Meinhard learned of the deal, he filed a suit in a New York state court against Salmon. The court ruled in Meinhard's favor, and Salmon appealed.

**DECISION AND RATIONALE** The Court of Appeals of New York held that Salmon had breached his fiduciary duty by failing to inform Meinhard of the business opportunity and secretly taking advantage of it himself. The court stated, "Joint adventurers, like copartners, owe to one another, while the enterprise continues, the duty of the finest loyalty." Salmon's conduct excluded Meinhard from any chance to compete and from any chance to enjoy the opportunity for benefit. As a partner, Salmon was bound by his "obligation to his copartners in such dealings not to separate his interest from theirs, but, if he acquires any benefit, to communicate it to them." Salmon was also the managing co-adventurer, and thus the court found that "for him and for those like him the rule of undivided loyalty is relentless and supreme." The court therefore granted Meinhard an interest "measured by the value of half of the entire lease."

**WHAT IF THE FACTS WERE DIFFERENT?** *Suppose that Salmon had disclosed Gerry's proposal to Meinhard, who had said that he was not interested. Would the result in this case have been different? Explain.*

**IMPACT OF THIS CASE ON TODAY'S LAW** *This classic case involved a joint venture, not a partnership. At the time, a member of a joint venture had only the duty to refrain from actively subverting the rights of the other members. The decision in this case imposed the highest standard of loyalty on joint-venture members. The duty is now the same in both joint ventures and partnerships. The eloquent language in this case that describes the standard of loyalty is frequently quoted approvingly by courts in cases involving partnerships.*

**BREACH AND WAIVER OF FIDUCIARY DUTIES** A partner's fiduciary duties may not be waived or eliminated in the partnership agreement. In fulfilling them, each partner must act consistently with the obligation of good faith and fair dealing [UPA 103(b), 404(d)]. The agreement can specify acts that the partners agree will violate a fiduciary duty.

Note that a partner may pursue his or her own interests without automatically violating these duties [UPA 404(e)]. The key is whether the partner has disclosed the interest to the other partners. ▶ **Example 30.6** Jayne Trell, a partner at Jacoby & Meyers, owns a shopping mall. Trell may vote against a partnership proposal to open a competing mall, provided that she has fully disclosed her interest in the existing shopping mall to the other partners at the firm. ◀ A partner cannot make secret profits or put self-interest before his or her duty to the interest of the partnership, however.

**AUTHORITY OF PARTNERS** The UPA affirms general principles of agency law that pertain to a partner's authority to bind a partnership in contract. A partner may also subject the partnership to tort liability under agency principles. When a partner is carrying on partnership business with third parties in the usual way, apparent authority exists, and both the partner and the firm share liability.

If a partner acts within the scope of her or his authority, the partnership is legally bound to honor the partner's commitments to third parties. The partnership will not be liable, however, if the third parties *know* that the partner has no such authority.

*Limitations on Authority.* A partnership may limit a partner's capacity to act as the firm's agent or transfer property on its behalf by filing a "statement of partnership authority" in a designated state office [UPA 105, 303]. Such limits on a partner's authority normally are effective only with respect to third parties who are notified of the limitation. (An exception is made in real estate transactions when the statement has been recorded with the appropriate state office.)

*The Scope of Implied Powers.* The agency concepts relating to apparent authority, actual authority, and ratification that were discussed in Chapter 26 also apply to partnerships. The extent of *implied authority generally is broader for partners than for ordinary agents,* however.

In an ordinary partnership, the partners can exercise all implied powers reasonably necessary and customary to carry on that particular business. Some customarily implied powers include the authority to make warranties on goods in the sales business and the power to enter into contracts consistent with the firm's regular course of business.

▶ **Example 30.7** Jamie Schwab is a partner in a firm that operates a retail tire store. He regularly promises that "each tire will be warranted for normal wear for 40,000 miles." Because Schwab has authority to make warranties, the partnership is bound to honor the warranty. Schwab would not, however, have the authority to sell the partnership's office equipment or other property without the consent of all of the other partners. ◀

**LIABILITY OF PARTNERS** One significant disadvantage associated with a traditional partnership is that the partners are *personally* liable for the debts of the partnership. Moreover, in most states, the liability is essentially unlimited because the acts of one partner in the ordinary course of business subject the other partners to personal liability [UPA 305].

*Joint Liability.* At one time, each partner in a partnership generally was jointly liable for the partnership's obligations. **Joint liability** means that a third party must sue all of the partners as a group, but each partner can be held liable for the full amount.[5]

If, for instance, a third party sued one partner on a partnership contract, that partner has the right to demand that the other partners be sued with her or him. In fact, if the third party does not name all of the partners in the lawsuit, the assets of the partnership cannot be used to satisfy the judgment. With joint liability, the partnership's assets must be exhausted before creditors can reach the partners' individual assets.[6]

*Joint and Several Liability.* In the majority of the states, under UPA 306(a), partners are both jointly and severally (separately, or individually) liable for all partnership obligations, including contracts, torts, and breaches of trust. **Joint and several liability** means that a third party has the option of suing all of the partners together (jointly) or one or more of the partners separately (severally).

---

5. Under the prior version of the UPA, which is still in effect in a few states, partners were subject to joint liability on partnership debts and contracts, but not on partnership debts arising from torts.

6. For a case applying joint liability to a partnership, see *Shar's Cars, LLC v. Elder,* 97 P.3d 724 (Utah App. 2004).

All partners in a partnership can be held liable even if a particular partner did not participate in, know about, or ratify the conduct that gave rise to the cause of action. Normally, though, the partnership's assets must be exhausted before a creditor can enforce a judgment against a partner's separate assets [UPA 307(d)].

A judgment against one partner severally (separately) does not extinguish the others' liability. (Similarly, a release of one partner does not discharge the partners' several liability.) Those not sued in the first action normally may be sued subsequently, unless the court in the first action held that the partnership was in no way liable. If a plaintiff is successful in a suit against a partner or partners, he or she may collect on the judgment only against the assets of those partners named as defendants.

**Indemnification.** With joint and several liability, a partner who commits a tort can be required to indemnify (reimburse) the partnership for any damages it pays. Indemnification will typically be granted *unless* the tort was committed in the ordinary course of the partnership's business.

▶ **Case in Point 30.8** Nicole Moren was a partner in Jax Restaurant. After work one day, Moren was called back to the restaurant to help in the kitchen. She brought her two-year-old son, Remington, and placed him on the kitchen counter. While she was making pizzas, Remington reached into the dough press. His hand was crushed, causing permanent injuries. Through his father, Remington filed a suit against the partnership for negligence.

The partnership filed a complaint against Moren, arguing that it was entitled to indemnification from her for her negligence. The court held in favor of Moren and ordered the partnership to pay damages to Remington. Moren was not required to indemnify the partnership because her negligence occurred in the ordinary course of the partnership's business.[7] ◀

**Liability of Incoming Partners.** A partner newly admitted to an existing partnership is not personally liable for any partnership obligations incurred before the person became a partner [UPA 306(b)]. In other words, the new partner's liability to existing creditors of the partnership is limited to her or his capital contribution to the firm.

▶ **Example 30.9** Smartclub, an existing partnership with four members, admits a new partner, Alex Jaff. He contributes $100,000 to the partnership. Smartclub has debts amounting to $600,000 at the time Jaff joins the firm. Although Jaff's capital contribution of $100,000 can be used to satisfy Smartclub's obligations, Jaff is not personally liable for partnership debts incurred before he became a partner. Thus, his personal assets cannot be used to satisfy the partnership's preexisting debt.

If, however, the partnership incurs additional debts after Jaff becomes a partner, he will be personally liable for those amounts, along with all the other partners. ◀

## SECTION 3
# DISSOCIATION OF A PARTNER

**Dissociation** occurs when a partner ceases to be associated in the carrying on of the partnership business. Although a partner always has the *power* to dissociate from the firm, he or she may not have the *right* to dissociate.

Dissociation normally entitles the partner to have his or her interest purchased by the partnership. It also terminates the partner's actual authority to act for the partnership and to participate in running its business. The partnership may continue to do business without the dissociated partner.[8]

## Events That Cause Dissociation

Under UPA 601, a partner can be dissociated from a partnership in any of the following ways:

1. By the partner's voluntarily giving notice of an "express will to withdraw." (When a partner gives notice of intent to withdraw, the remaining partners must decide whether to continue the partnership business. If they decide not to continue, the voluntary dissociation of a partner will dissolve the firm [UPA 801(1)].)
2. By the occurrence of an event specified in the partnership agreement.
3. By a unanimous vote of the other partners under certain circumstances, such as when a partner transfers substantially all of her or his interest in the partnership, or when it becomes unlawful to carry on partnership business with that partner.

---

7. *Moren v. Jax Restaurant,* 679 N.W.2d 165 (Minn.App. 2004).

8. Under the previous version of the UPA, when a partner withdrew from a partnership, the partnership was considered dissolved, and the business had to end. The new UPA dramatically changed the law governing partnership breakups by no longer requiring that a partnership end if one partner dissociates.

4. By order of a court or arbitrator if the partner has engaged in wrongful conduct that affects the partnership business. The court may order dissociation if a partner breached the partnership agreement, violated a duty owed to the partnership or the other partners, or engaged in conduct that makes it "not reasonably practicable to carry on the business in partnership with the partner" [UPA 601(5)].
5. By the partner's declaring bankruptcy, assigning his or her interest in the partnership for the benefit of creditors, or becoming physically or mentally incapacitated, or by the partner's death.

## Wrongful Dissociation

As mentioned, a partner has the power to dissociate from a partnership at any time, but if she or he lacks the right to dissociate, then the dissociation is considered wrongful under the law [UPA 602]. When a partner's dissociation breaches a partnership agreement, for instance, it is wrongful.

▶ **Example 30.10** Jenkins & Whalen's partnership agreement states that it is a breach of the agreement for any partner to assign partnership property to a creditor without the consent of the other partners. If Kenzie, a partner, makes such an assignment, she has not only breached the agreement but has also wrongfully dissociated from the partnership. ◀

A partner who wrongfully dissociates is liable to the partnership and to the other partners for damages caused by the dissociation. This liability is in addition to any other obligation of the partner to the partnership or to the other partners.

## Effects of Dissociation

Dissociation (rightful or wrongful) terminates some of the rights of the dissociated partner, requires that the partnership purchase his or her interest, and alters the liability of the parties to third parties.

**RIGHTS AND DUTIES** On a partner's dissociation, his or her right to participate in the management and conduct of the partnership business terminates [UPA 603]. The partner's duty of loyalty also ends. A partner's duty of care continues only with respect to events that occurred before dissociation, unless the partner participates in winding up the partnership's business (discussed shortly).

▶ **Example 30.11** Debbie Pearson, a partner who leaves the accounting firm Bubb & Flint, can imme-

diately compete with that firm for new clients. She must exercise care in completing ongoing client transactions, however. Pearson must also account to Bubb & Flint for any fees received from the old clients based on those transactions. ◀

**BUYOUTS** After a partner's dissociation, his or her interest in the partnership must be purchased according to the rules in UPA 701. The **buyout price** is based on the amount that would have been distributed to the partner if the partnership had been wound up on the date of dissociation. Offset against the price are amounts owed by the partner to the partnership, including damages for wrongful dissociation.

▶ **Case in Point 30.12** Wilbur and Dee Warnick and their son Randall bought a ranch for $335,000 and formed a partnership to operate it. The partners' initial capital contributions totaled $60,000, of which Randall paid 34 percent. Over the next twenty years, each partner contributed funds to the operation and received cash distributions from the partnership. In 1999, Randall dissociated from the partnership.

When the parties could not agree on a buyout price, Randall filed a lawsuit. The court awarded Randall $115,783.13—the amount of his cash contributions, plus 34 percent of the increase in the value of the partnership's assets above all partners' cash contributions. Randall's parents appealed, arguing that $50,000 should be deducted from the appraised value of the assets for the estimated expenses of selling them. The court affirmed the buyout price, however, because "purely hypothetical costs of sale are not a required deduction in valuing partnership assets" to determine a buyout price.[9] ◀

**LIABILITY TO THIRD PARTIES** For two years after a partner dissociates from a continuing partnership, the partnership may be bound by the acts of the dissociated partner based on apparent authority [UPA 702]. In other words, if a third party reasonably believed at the time of a transaction that the dissociated partner was still a partner, the partnership may be liable. Also, a dissociated partner may be liable for partnership obligations entered into during a two-year period following dissociation [UPA 703].

To avoid this possible liability, a partnership should notify its creditors, customers, and clients of a partner's dissociation. In addition, either the partnership or the dissociated partner can file a statement of dissociation in the appropriate state office to limit the

---

9. *Warnick v. Warnick*, 2006 WY 58, 133 P.3d 997 (2006).

dissociated partner's authority to ninety days after the filing [UPA 704]. Filing this statement helps to minimize the firm's potential liability for the former partner and vice versa.

SECTION 4

# SECTION 4
# PARTNERSHIP TERMINATION

The same events that cause dissociation can result in the end of the partnership if the remaining partners no longer wish to (or are unable to) continue the partnership business. Only certain departures of a partner will end the partnership, though, and generally the partnership can continue if the remaining partners consent [UPA 801].

The termination of a partnership is referred to as **dissolution,** which essentially means the commencement of the winding up process. **Winding up** is the actual process of collecting, liquidating, and distributing the partnership assets.

## Dissolution

Dissolution of a partnership generally can be brought about by acts of the partners, by operation of law, or by judicial decree [UPA 801]. Any partnership (including one for a fixed term) can be dissolved by the partners' agreement.

If the partnership agreement states that it will dissolve on a certain event, such as a partner's death or bankruptcy, then the occurrence of that event will dissolve the partnership. A partnership for a fixed term or a particular undertaking is dissolved by operation of law at the expiration of the term or on the completion of the undertaking.

**ILLEGALITY OR IMPRACTICALITY** Any event that makes it unlawful for the partnership to continue its business will result in dissolution [UPA 801(4)]. Under the UPA, a court may order dissolution when it becomes obviously impractical for the firm to continue—for instance, if the business can only be operated at a loss [UPA 801(5)]. Even when one partner has brought a court action seeking to dissolve a partnership, the partnership continues to exist until it is legally dissolved by the court or by the parties' agreement.[10]

In the following case, a family partnership began to experience serious problems because of a dispute between two partners. The court had to decide whether it could be judicially dissolved because its economic purpose was being frustrated.

---

10. See, for example, *Curley v. Kaiser,* 112 Conn.App. 213, 962 A.2d 167 (2009).

## CASE 30.2

### Russell Realty Associates v. Russell
Supreme Court of Virginia, 724 S.E.2d 690 (2012).

**BACKGROUND AND FACTS** In 1978, members of the Russell family began operating Russell Realty Associates (RRA) as a partnership. Eddie Russell enjoyed decision-making authority over the partnership's business, which involved buying, holding, leasing, and selling investment properties. After several years, Eddie and his sister, Nina Russell, became involved in several heated disputes over whether to develop or sell particular properties and whether and how to include Nina's son in the partnership.

Nina began to routinely question Eddie's business decisions. She insisted on recording business meetings and editing the partnership's official minutes. Because of their disagreements, RRA experienced two years of delays relating to zoning approval and appraisals before it could sell one piece of property. It also was unable to accept an attractive offer for another property. Despite the siblings' disputes, RRA continued to profit and make distributions to its partners. Nevertheless, in 2008, Eddie filed a complaint seeking a judicial dissolution of the partnership. The circuit court granted the dissolution, and Nina appealed.

**DECISION AND RATIONALE** The Virginia Supreme Court affirmed the judgment of the lower court dissolving the firm. Under Virginia law, a partnership may be judicially dissolved if, among other reasons, the "economic purpose of the partnership is likely to be unreasonably frustrated" or it "is not . . . reasonably practicable to carry on the partnership business in conformity with the partnership agreement."

CASE 30.2 CONTINUES ➡

CASE 30.2 CONTINUED

The state's highest court found that Russell Realty's economic purpose was unreasonably frustrated because the partnership could no longer conduct its business "in an efficient and productive manner." Although the firm continued to profit, it experienced a significant delay in selling one piece of property and failed to accept a lucrative offer for another. Eddie and Nina's dispute also imposed several additional costs for the partnership, including costs associated with addressing litigation and having business meetings recorded. Moreover, the court concluded that it was not reasonably practicable to carry on the partnership business in conformity with the partnership agreement. Despite Eddie's decision-making authority under the agreement, the partnership operated very slowly and inefficiently. There was no reason to believe that Eddie and Nina's relationship would improve, so judicial dissolution was appropriate.

**THE ETHICAL DIMENSION** *Does the judicial power to dissolve partnerships encourage partners to be more respectful toward each other? Why or why not?*

**THE LEGAL ENVIRONMENT DIMENSION** *Eddie petitioned for the dissolution of Russell Realty rather than dissociating from the firm because the partnership agreement prohibited the withdrawal of any partner. How might Eddie have divested himself of his interest in the firm without petitioning for its dissolution?*

**GOOD FAITH** Each partner must exercise good faith when dissolving a partnership. Some state statutes allow partners injured by another partner's bad faith to file a tort claim for wrongful dissolution of a partnership.

▶ **Case in Point 30.13** Attorneys Randall Jordan and Mary Helen Moses formed a two-member partnership. Although the partnership was for an indefinite term, Jordan ended the partnership three years later and asked the court for declarations concerning the partners' financial obligations. Moses, who had objected to ending the partnership, filed a claim against Jordan for wrongful dissolution and for appropriating $180,000 in fees that should have gone to the partnership. Ultimately, the court held in favor of Moses.

A claim for wrongful dissolution of a partnership may be based on the excluded partner's loss of "an existing, or continuing, business opportunity" or of income and material assets. Because Jordan had attempted to appropriate partnership assets through dissolution, Moses could sue for wrongful dissolution.[11] ◀

## Winding Up and Distribution of Assets

After dissolution, the partnership continues for the limited purpose of winding up the business. The partners cannot create new obligations on behalf of the partnership. They have authority only to complete transactions begun but not finished at the time of dissolution and to wind up the business of the partnership [UPA 803, 804(1)].

**DUTIES AND COMPENSATION** *Winding up* includes collecting and preserving partnership assets, discharging liabilities (paying debts), and accounting to each partner for the value of his or her interest in the partnership. Partners continue to have fiduciary duties to one another and to the firm during this process.

UPA 401(h) provides that a partner is entitled to compensation for services in winding up partnership affairs above and apart from his or her share in the partnership profits. A partner may also receive reimbursement for expenses incurred in the process.

**CREDITORS' CLAIMS** Both creditors of the partnership and creditors of the individual partners can make claims on the partnership's assets. In general, partnership creditors share proportionately with the partners' individual creditors in the partners' assets, which include their interests in the partnership. A partnership's assets are distributed according to the following priorities [UPA 807]:

1. Payment of debts, including those owed to partner and nonpartner creditors.
2. Return of capital contributions and distribution of profits to partners.[12]

---

11. *Jordan v. Moses,* 291 Ga. 39, 727 S.E.2d 469 (2012).

12. Under the previous version of the UPA, creditors of the partnership had priority over creditors of the individual partners. Also, in distributing partnership assets, third party creditors were paid before partner creditors, and capital contributions were returned before profits.

If the partnership's liabilities are greater than its assets, the partners bear the losses—in the absence of a contrary agreement—in the same proportion in which they shared the profits (rather than, for example, in proportion to their contributions to the partnership's capital).

## Partnership Buy-Sell Agreements

Before entering into a partnership, partners should agree on how the assets will be valued and divided in the event that the partnership dissolves. A **buy-sell agreement,** sometimes called simply a *buyout agreement,* provides for one or more partners to buy out the other or others, should the situation warrant.

Agreeing beforehand on who buys what, under what circumstances, and, if possible, at what price may eliminate costly negotiations or litigation later.

Alternatively, the agreement may specify that one or more partners will determine the value of the interest being sold and that the other or others will decide whether to buy or sell.

Under UPA 701(a), if a partner's dissociation does not result in a dissolution of the partnership, a buyout of the partner's interest is mandatory. The UPA contains an extensive set of buyout rules that apply when the partners do not have a buyout agreement. Basically, a withdrawing partner receives the same amount through a buyout that he or she would receive if the business were winding up [UPA 701(b)].

In the following case, one of the three partners in an agricultural partnership died. Despite provisions in the partnership agreement that required its dissolution on a certain date or on a partner's death, whichever came first, the remaining partners did not dissolve the firm and did not liquidate the assets.

---

## CASE 30.3

### Estate of Webster v. Thomas

Appellate Court of Illinois, Fifth District, 2013 IL App (5th) 120121-U, 2013 WL 164041 (2013).

**BACKGROUND AND FACTS**  Clyde Webster, James Theis, and Larry Thomas formed T&T Agri-Partners Company to own and farm 180 acres in Christian County, Illinois. Under the partnership agreement, the firm was to continue until January 31, 2010, unless it was dissolved. The death of any partner would dissolve the partnership. Webster died in 2002, but Theis and Thomas did not liquidate T&T and distribute its assets. Webster's estate through its personal representative, Joseph Webster, filed a complaint in an Illinois state circuit court against Theis, Thomas, and the partnership. In December 2009, the court ordered the defendants to dissolve the partnership and liquidate its assets. When this did not happen, the case went to trial. In 2011, after the trial, the court found that the partnership had expired by its own terms on January 31, 2010, and again ordered the partnership dissolved. The court also ordered the defendants to pay the Webster's attorneys' fees. The defendants appealed.

**DECISION AND RATIONALE**  A state intermediate appellate court affirmed the lower court's orders in favor of Webster's estate. The trial court had properly determined that Theis and Thomas had failed to liquidate and distribute the company's assets per the partnership agreement and the court order. "The partnership agreement clearly provided that upon Clyde's death and the partners' failure to vote to continue the partnership, the partnership dissolved. Pursuant to the plain language of the partnership agreement, the assets upon dissolution were to be liquidated and distributed by paying the partners in proportion to their capital accounts. Yet, the defendants failed to do so." The reviewing court pointed out that despite the agreement's language and despite the circuit court's order, the defendants did nothing. The defendants therefore violated the partnership agreement and were liable for the plaintiff's attorney fees pursuant to the same agreement.

**THE LEGAL ENVIRONMENT DIMENSION**  *What lesson might the partners in other partnerships learn from the events of this case and its outcome?*

**THE ETHICAL DIMENSION**  *What might the defendants have done to avoid the dispute that arose from the circumstances of this case?*

# LIMITED LIABILITY PARTNERSHIPS

The **limited liability partnership (LLP)** is a hybrid form of business designed mostly for professionals who normally do business as partners in a partnership. Almost all of the states have enacted LLP statutes.

The major advantage of the LLP is that it allows a partnership to continue as a pass-through entity for tax purposes but limits the personal liability of the partners. The LLP is especially attractive for professional service firms and family businesses. All of the "Big Four" accounting firms—the four largest international accountancy and professional services firms—are organized as LLPs, including Ernst & Young, LLP, and PricewaterhouseCoopers, LLP.

## Formation of an LLP

LLPs must be formed and operated in compliance with state statutes, which may include provisions of the UPA. The appropriate form must be filed with a central state agency, usually the secretary of state's office, and the business's name must include either "Limited Liability Partnership" or "LLP" [UPA 1001, 1002]. An LLP must file an annual report with the state to remain qualified as an LLP in that state [UPA 1003].

In most states, it is relatively easy to convert a traditional partnership into an LLP because the firm's basic organizational structure remains the same. Additionally, all of the statutory and common law rules governing partnerships still apply (apart from those modified by the LLP statute). Normally, LLP statutes are simply amendments to a state's already existing partnership law.

## Liability in an LLP

An LLP allows professionals, such as attorneys and accountants, to avoid personal liability for the malpractice of other partners. A partner in an LLP is still liable for her or his own wrongful acts, such as negligence, however. Also liable is the partner who supervised the individual who committed a wrongful act. (This generally is true for all types of partners and partnerships, not just LLPs.)

▶ **Example 30.14** Five lawyers operate a law firm as an LLP. One of the attorneys, Dan Kolcher, is sued for malpractice and loses. The firm's malpractice insurance is insufficient to pay the judgment. If the firm had been organized as a traditional (general) partnership, the personal assets of the other attorneys could be used to satisfy the obligation. Because the firm is organized as an LLP, however, no other partner at the law firm can be held *personally* liable for Kolcher's malpractice, unless she or he acted as Kolcher's supervisor. In the absence of a supervisor, only Kolcher's personal assets can be used to satisfy the judgment. ◀

Although LLP statutes vary from state to state, generally each state statute limits the liability of partners in some way. For instance, Delaware law protects each innocent partner from the "debts and obligations of the partnership arising from negligence, wrongful acts, or misconduct." The UPA more broadly exempts partners from personal liability for any partnership obligation, "whether arising in contract, tort, or otherwise" [UPA 306(c)].

**LIABILITY FROM STATE TO STATE** When an LLP formed in one state wants to do business in another state, it may be required to register in the second state—for example, by filing a statement of foreign qualification [UPA 1102]. Because state LLP statutes are not uniform, a question sometimes arises as to which law applies if the LLP statutes in the two states provide different liability protection. Most states apply the law of the state in which the LLP was formed, even when the firm does business in another state, which is also the rule under UPA 1101.

**SHARING LIABILITY AMONG PARTNERS** When more than one partner in an LLP is negligent, there is a question as to how liability should be shared. Some states provide for proportionate liability—that is, for separate determinations of the negligence of the partners.

▶ **Example 30.15** Accountants Zach and Lyla are partners in an LLP, with Zach supervising Lyla. Lyla negligently fails to file a tax return for a client, Centaur Tools. Centaur files a suit against Zach and Lyla. Under a proportionate liability statute, Zach will be liable for no more than his portion of the responsibility for the missed tax deadline. In a state that does not allow for proportionate liability, Zach can be held liable for the entire loss. ◀

## Family Limited Liability Partnerships

A **family limited liability partnership (FLLP)** is a limited liability partnership in which the partners are related to each other—for example, as spouses, parents and children, siblings, or cousins. A person acting in a fiduciary capacity for persons so related can also be a partner. All of the partners must be natural persons or persons acting in a fiduciary capacity for the benefit of natural persons.

Probably the most significant use of the FLLP form of business organization is in agriculture. Family-owned farms sometimes find this form to their benefit. The FLLP offers the same advantages as other LLPs with certain additional advantages, such as, in Iowa, an exemption from real estate transfer taxes when partnership real estate is transferred among partners.[13]

## SECTION 6
# LIMITED PARTNERSHIPS

We now look at a business organizational form that limits the liability of *some* of its owners—the **limited partnership (LP).** Limited partnerships originated in medieval Europe and have been in existence in the United States since the early 1800s. Limited partnerships differ from traditional (general) partnerships in several ways.

A limited partnership consists of at least one **general partner** and one or more **limited partners.** A general partner assumes management responsibility for the partnership and has full responsibility for the partnership and for all its debts. A limited partner contributes cash or other property and owns an interest in the firm but is not involved in management responsibilities and is not personally liable for partnership debts beyond the amount of his or her investment. A limited partner can forfeit limited liability by taking part in the management of the business. A comparison of traditional partnerships and limited partnerships appears in Exhibit 30–2 on the following page.[14]

Most states and the District of Columbia have adopted the Revised Uniform Limited Partnership Act (RULPA), which we refer to in the following discussion. A minority of states have adopted some amendments that were proposed in 2001 to make the RULPA more flexible.

---

**13.** Iowa Statutes Section 428A.2.

**14.** Under the UPA, a general partnership can be converted into a limited partnership and vice versa [UPA 902, 903]. The UPA also provides for the merger of a general partnership with one or more general or limited partnerships [UPA 905].

## Formation of a Limited Partnership

In contrast to the informal, private, and voluntary agreement that usually suffices for a traditional partnership, the formation of a limited partnership is a public and formal proceeding that must follow statutory requirements. Not only must a limited partnership have at least one general partner and one limited partner, but the partners must also sign a **certificate of limited partnership.** This certificate must include certain information such as the name, mailing address, and capital contribution of each general and limited partner. The certificate must be filed with the designated state official—under the RULPA, the secretary of state. The certificate is usually open to public inspection.

## Liabilities of Partners in a Limited Partnership

General partners, unlike limited partners, are personally liable to the partnership's creditors. Thus, at least one general partner is necessary in a limited partnership so that someone has personal liability. This policy can be circumvented in states that allow a corporation to be the general partner in a partnership. Because the corporation has limited liability by virtue of corporation statutes, if a corporation is the general partner, no one in the limited partnership has personal liability.

The liability of a limited partner, as mentioned, is limited to the capital that she or he contributes or agrees to contribute to the partnership [RULPA 502]. Limited partners enjoy this limited liability only so long as they do not participate in management [RULPA 303].

A limited partner who participates in management will be just as liable as a general partner to any creditor who transacts business with the limited partnership. Liability arises when the creditor believes, based on the limited partner's conduct, that the limited partner is a general partner [RULPA 303]. The extent of review and advisement that a limited partner can engage in before being exposed to liability is not always clear, though.

## Rights and Duties in a Limited Partnership

With the exception of the right to participate in management, limited partners have essentially the same rights as general partners. Limited partners have a right of access to the partnership's books and to information regarding partnership business.

**EXHIBIT 30-2  A Comparison of General Partnerships and Limited Partnerships**

| Characteristic | General Partnership (UPA) | Limited Partnership (RULPA) |
|---|---|---|
| Creation | By agreement of two or more persons to carry on a business as co-owners for profit. | By agreement of two or more persons to carry on a business as co-owners for profit. Must include one or more general partners and one or more limited partners. Filing of a certificate with the secretary of state is required. |
| Sharing of Profits and Losses | By agreement. In the absence of agreement, profits are shared equally by the partners, and losses are shared in the same ratio as profits. | Profits are shared as required in the certificate agreement, and losses are shared likewise, up to the amount of the limited partners' capital contributions. In the absence of a provision in the certificate agreement, profits and losses are shared on the basis of percentages of capital contributions. |
| Liability | Unlimited personal liability of all partners. | Unlimited personal liability of all general partners; limited partners liable only to the extent of their capital contributions. |
| Capital Contribution | No minimum or mandatory amount; set by agreement. | Set by agreement. |
| Management | By agreement. In the absence of agreement, all partners have an equal voice. | Only the general partner (or the general partners). Limited partners have no voice or else are subject to liability as general partners (but only if a third party has reason to believe that the limited partner is a general partner). A limited partner may act as an agent or employee of the partnership and vote on amending the certificate or on the sale or dissolution of the partnership. |
| Duration | Terminated by agreement of the partners, but can continue to do business even when a partner dissociates from the partnership. | Terminated by agreement in the certificate or by retirement, death, or mental incompetence of a general partner in the absence of the right of the other general partners to continue the partnership. Death of a limited partner does not terminate the partnership, unless he or she is the only remaining limited partner. |
| Distribution of Assets on Liquidation— Order of Priorities | 1. Payment of debts, including those owed to partner and nonpartner creditors.<br>2. Return of capital contributions and distribution of profit to partners. | 1. Outside creditors and partner creditors.<br>2. Partners and former partners entitled to distributions of partnership assets.<br>3. Unless otherwise agreed, return of capital contributions and distribution of profit to partners. |

On dissolution of the partnership, limited partners are entitled to a return of their contributions in accordance with the partnership certificate [RULPA 201(a)(10)]. They can also assign their interests subject to the certificate [RULPA 702, 704]. In addition, limited partners can sue an outside party on behalf of the firm if the general partners with authority to do so have refused to file suit [RULPA 1001].

## Dissociation and Dissolution

A general partner has the power to voluntarily dissociate, or withdraw, from a limited partnership unless the partnership agreement specifies otherwise. A limited partner theoretically can withdraw from the partnership by giving six months' notice unless the partnership agreement specifies a term, as most do. Also, some states have passed laws prohibiting the withdrawal of limited partners.

**EVENTS THAT CAUSE DISSOCIATION**  In a limited partnership, a general partner's voluntary dissociation from the firm normally will lead to dissolution *unless* all partners agree to continue the business. Similarly, the bankruptcy, retirement, death, or mental incompetence of a general partner will cause the dissociation of that partner and the dissolution of the limited partnership unless the other members agree to continue the firm [RULPA 801].

Bankruptcy of a limited partner, however, does not dissolve the partnership unless it causes the bankruptcy of the firm. Death or an assignment of the interest of a limited partner does not dissolve a limited partnership [RULPA 702, 704, 705]. A limited partnership can be dissolved by court decree [RULPA 802].

**DISTRIBUTION OF ASSETS** On dissolution, creditors' claims, including those of partners who are creditors, take first priority. After that, partners and former partners receive unpaid distributions of partnership assets. Unless otherwise agreed, they are also entitled to a return of their contributions in the proportions in which the partners share in distributions [RULPA 804].

**VALUATION OF ASSETS** Disputes commonly arise about how the partnership's assets should be valued and distributed and whether the business should be sold. ▶ **Case in Point 30.16** Actor Kevin Costner was a limited partner in Midnight Star Enterprises, LP, which runs a casino, bar, and restaurant in South Dakota. There were two other limited partners, Carla and Francis Caneva, who owned a small percentage of the partnership (3.25 units each) and received salaries for managing its operations. Another company owned by Costner, Midnight Star Enterprises, Limited (MSEL), was the general partner. Costner thus controlled a majority of the partnership (93.5 units).

When communications broke down between the partners, MSEL asked a court to dissolve the partnership. MSEL's accountant determined that the firm's fair market value was $3.1 million. The Canevas presented evidence that a competitor would buy the business for $6.2 million. The Canevas wanted the court to force Costner to either buy the business for that price within ten days or sell it on the open market to the highest bidder. Ultimately, the state's highest court held in favor of Costner. A partner cannot force the sale of a limited partnership when the other partners want to continue the business. The court also accepted the $3.1 million buyout price of MSEL's accountant and ordered Costner to pay the Canevas the value of their 6.5 partnership units.[15] ◀

## Limited Liability Limited Partnerships

A **limited liability limited partnership (LLLP)** is a type of limited partnership. An LLLP differs from a limited partnership in that a general partner in an LLLP has the same liability as a limited partner in a limited partnership. In other words, the liability of all partners is limited to the amount of their investments in the firm.

A few states provide expressly for LLLPs.[16] In states that do not provide for LLLPs but do allow for limited partnerships and limited liability partnerships, a limited partnership should probably still be able to register with the state as an LLLP.

---

15. *In re Dissolution of Midnight Star Enterprises, LP,* 2006 SD 98, 724 N.W.2d 334 (N.D.Sup.Ct. 2006).
16. See, for example, Colorado Revised Statutes Annotated Section 7-62-109. Other states that provide for LLLPs include Delaware, Florida, Georgia, Kentucky, Maryland, Nevada, Texas, and Virginia.

## Reviewing: Partnerships and Limited Liability Partnerships

Grace Tarnavsky and her sons, Manny and Jason, bought a ranch known as the Cowboy Palace in March 2009, and the three verbally agreed to share the business for five years. Grace contributed 50 percent of the investment, and each son contributed 25 percent. Manny agreed to handle the livestock, and Jason agreed to handle the bookkeeping. The Tarnavskys took out joint loans and opened a joint bank account into which they deposited the ranch's proceeds and from which they made payments for property, cattle, equipment, and supplies. In September 2013, Manny severely injured his back while baling hay and became permanently unable to handle livestock. Manny therefore hired additional laborers to tend the livestock, causing the Cowboy Palace to incur significant debt. In September 2014, Al's Feed Barn filed a lawsuit against Jason to collect $32,400 in unpaid debts. Using the information presented in the chapter, answer the following questions.

1. Was this relationship a partnership for a term or a partnership at will?

*Continued*

2. Did Manny have the authority to hire additional laborers to work at the ranch after his injury? Why or why not?

3. Under the current UPA, can Al's Feed Barn bring an action against Jason individually for the Cowboy Palace's debt? Why or why not?

4. Suppose that after his back injury in 2013, Manny sent his mother and brother a notice indicating his intent to withdraw from the partnership. Can he still be held liable for the debt to Al's Feed Barn? Why or why not?

**DEBATE THIS...** *A partnership should automatically end when one partner dissociates from the firm.*

## Terms and Concepts

articles of partnership 526
buyout price 532
buy-sell agreement 535
certificate of limited partnership 537
charging order 528
dissociation 531
dissolution 533
family limited liability
   partnership (FLLP) 536

general partner 537
goodwill 525
information return 526
joint and several liability 530
joint liability 530
limited liability limited
   partnership (LLLP) 539
limited liability partnership (LLP) 536

limited partner 537
limited partnership (LP) 537
partnership 525
partnership by estoppel 526
pass-through entity 525
winding up 533

## Issue Spotters

1. Darnell and Eliana are partners in D&E Designs, an architectural firm. When Darnell dies, his widow claims that as Darnell's heir, she is entitled to take his place as Eliana's partner or to receive a share of the firm's assets. Is she right? Why or why not? **(See page 532.)**

2. Finian and Gloria are partners in F&G Delivery Service. When business is slow, without Gloria's knowledge, Finian leases the delivery vehicles as moving vans. Because the vehicles would otherwise be sitting idle in a parking lot, can Finian keep the income resulting from the leasing of the delivery vehicles? Explain your answer. **(See page 529.)**

- **Check your answers to the Issue Spotters against the answers provided in Appendix E at the end of this text.**

## Business Scenarios

**30–1. Partnership Formation.** Daniel is the owner of a chain of shoe stores. He hires Rubya to be the manager of a new store, which is to open in Grand Rapids, Michigan. Daniel, by written contract, agrees to pay Rubya a monthly salary and 20 percent of the profits. Without Daniel's knowledge, Rubya represents himself to Classen as Daniel's partner and shows Classen the agreement to share profits. Classen extends credit to Rubya. Rubya defaults. Discuss whether Classen can hold Daniel liable as a partner. **(See page 526.)**

**30–2. Dissolution of a Limited Partnership.** Dorinda, Luis, and Elizabeth form a limited partnership. Dorinda is a general partner, and Luis and Elizabeth are limited part-

ners. Consider the separate events below, and discuss fully whether each event constitutes a dissolution of the limited partnership. **(See page 538.)**

(a) Luis assigns his partnership interest to Ashley.

(b) Elizabeth is petitioned into involuntary bankruptcy.

(c) Dorinda dies.

**30–3. Distribution of Partnership Assets.** Shawna and David formed a partnership. At the time of the partnership's formation, Shawna's capital contribution was $10,000, and David's was $15,000. Later, Shawna made a $10,000 loan to the partnership when it needed working capital. The partnership agreement provided that profits were to be shared with 40 percent for Shawna and 60 percent for David. The partnership was dissolved after David's death. At the end of the dissolution and the winding up of the partnership, the partnership's assets were $50,000, and the partnership's debts were $8,000. Discuss fully how the assets should be distributed. **(See page 534.)**

## Business Case Problems

**30–4. Limited Partnership.** James Carpenter contracted with Austin Estates, LP, to buy property in Texas. Carpenter asked Sandra McBeth to invest in the deal. He admitted that a dispute had arisen with the city of Austin over water for the property, but he assured her that it would not be a significant obstacle. McBeth agreed to invest $800,000 to hold open the option to buy the property. She became a limited partner in StoneLake Ranch, LP. Carpenter acted as the firm's general partner. Despite his assurances to McBeth, the purchase was delayed due to the water dispute. Unable to complete the purchase in a timely manner, Carpenter paid the $800,000 to Austin Estates without notifying McBeth. Later, Carpenter and others—excluding McBeth—bought the property and sold it at a profit. McBeth filed a suit in a Texas state court against Carpenter. What is the nature of the fiduciary duty that a general partner owes a limited partner? Did Carpenter breach that duty in this case? Explain. [*McBeth v. Carpenter,* 565 F.3d 171 (5th Cir. 2009)] **(See page 537.)**

**30–5. Partnership Dissolution.** George Chaney and William Dickerson were partners in Bowen's Mill Landing, which purchased a large piece of land in the 1980s. The partners had planned to develop the property, but nothing was ever done. Chaney died in 1990, and his wife inherited his interest. When she died in 2004, her two sons, John and Dewey Lynch, inherited the half-interest in the partnership. Dickerson died in 1995, and his daughter, Billie Thompson, inherited his half-interest. In 2006, the Lynches filed a petition for partition, asking that a commission be appointed to make a fair division of the land, giving the Lynches half and Thompson half. In 2007, the commission reported on how to divide the land into two parts. Thompson objected that the land belonged to Bowen's Mill Landing and could not be divided. The trial court ordered Thompson to "effectuate the dissolution of any partnership entity and . . . to wind up the business and affairs of any partnership" so that the land could be divided. Thompson appealed. Can the court order the partnership to dissolve? Why or why not? [*Thompson v. Lynch,* 990 A.2d 432 (Sup.Ct.Del. 2010)] **(See page 533.)**

**30–6. Fiduciary Duties of Partners.** Karl Horvath, Hein Rüsen, and Carl Thomas formed a partnership, HRT Enterprises, to buy a manufacturing plant. Rüsen and Thomas leased the plant to their own company, Merkur Steel. Merkur then sublet the premises to other companies owned by Rüsen and Thomas. The rent that these companies paid to Merkur was higher than the rent that Merkur paid to HRT. Rüsen and Thomas did not tell Horvath about the subleases. Did Rüsen and Thomas breach their fiduciary duties to HRT and Horvath? Discuss. [*Horvath v. HRT Enterprises,* 489 Mich.App. 992, 800 N.W.2d 595 (2011)] **(See page 529.)**

**30–7. BUSINESS CASE PROBLEM WITH SAMPLE ANSWER: Partnership Formation.**

 *Patricia Garcia and Bernardo Lucero were in a romantic relationship. While they were seeing each other, Garcia and Lucero acquired an electronics service center, paying $30,000 apiece. Two years later, they purchased an apartment complex. The property was deeded to Lucero, but neither Garcia nor Lucero made a down payment. The couple considered both properties to be owned "50/50," and they agreed to share profits, losses, and management rights. When the couple's romantic relationship ended, Garcia asked a court to declare that she had a partnership with Lucero. In court, Lucero argued that the couple did not have a written partnership agreement. Did they have a partnership? Why or why not? [Garcia v. Lucero, 366 S.W.3d 275 (Tex.App. 2012)]* **(See page 526.)**

- **For a sample answer to Problem 30–7, go to Appendix F at the end of this text.**

**30–8. Winding Up and Distribution of Assets.** Dan and Lori Cole operated a Curves franchise exercise facility in Angola, Indiana, as a partnership. The firm leased commercial space from Flying Cat, LLC, for a renewable three-year term and renewed the lease for a second three-year term. But two years after the renewal, the Coles divorced. By the end of the second term, Flying Cat was owed more than $21,000 on the lease. Without telling the landlord about the divorce, Lori signed another extension. More rent went unpaid. Flying Cat obtained a judgment in an Indiana state court against the partnership for almost $50,000. Can Dan be held liable? Why or why not? [*Curves for Women Angola v. Flying Cat, LLC,* 983 N.E.2d 629 (Ind. App. 2013)] **(See page 534.)**

**30–9. A QUESTION OF ETHICS: Wrongful Dissociation.**

 *Elliot Willensky and Beverly Moran formed a partnership to buy, renovate, and sell a house. Moran agreed to finance the effort, which was to cost no more than $60,000. Willensky agreed to oversee the work, which was to be done in six months. Willensky lived in the house during the renovation. As the project progressed, Willensky incurred excessive and unnecessary expenses, misappropriated funds for his personal use, did not pay bills on time, and did not keep Moran informed of the costs. More than a year later, the renovation was still not completed, and Willensky*

walked off the project. Moran completed the renovation, which ultimately cost $311,222, and sold the house. Moran then sued to dissolve the partnership and recover damages from Willensky for breach of contract and wrongful dissociation. [Moran v. Willensky, 395 S.W.3d 651 (Tenn.Ct.App. 2010)] **(See page 532.)**

(a) Moran alleged that Willensky had wrongfully dissociated from the partnership. When did this dissociation occur? Why was his dissociation wrongful?

(b) Which of Willensky's actions simply represent unethical behavior or bad management, and which constitute a breach of the agreement?

## Legal Reasoning Group Activity

**30–10. Liability of Partners.** At least six months before the Summer Olympic Games in Atlanta, Georgia, Stafford Fontenot and four others agreed to sell Cajun food at the games and began making preparations. On May 19, the group (calling themselves "Prairie Cajun Seafood Catering of Louisiana") applied for a business license from the county health department. Later, Ted Norris sold a mobile kitchen to them for $40,000. They gave Norris an $8,000 check drawn on the "Prairie Cajun Seafood Catering of Louisiana" account and two promissory notes, one for $12,000 and the other for $20,000. The notes, which were dated June 12, listed only Fontenot "d/b/a Prairie Cajun Seafood" as the maker (d/b/a is an abbreviation for "doing business as").

On July 31, Fontenot and his friends signed a partnership agreement, which listed specific percentages of profits and losses. They drove the mobile kitchen to Atlanta, but business was "disastrous." When the notes were not paid, Norris filed a suit in a Louisiana state court against Fontenot, seeking payment. **(See page 526.)**

(a) The first group will discuss the elements of a partnership and determine whether a partnership exists among Fontenot and the others.

(b) The second group will determine who can be held liable on the notes and why.

# CHAPTER 31

# OTHER ORGANIZATIONAL FORMS FOR SMALL BUSINESSES

The U.S. Small Business Administration (SBA) reports that small businesses employ half of all private-sector employees in the country. In addition, small businesses generate more than half of the nation's gross domestic product, hire 43 percent of high-tech workers, and obtain a disproportionate number of patents. Nevertheless, more than half of small businesses fail within four years—in part, because of a lack of understanding of legal issues and how to respond to them.

We have already discussed sole proprietorships, partnerships, and several forms of limited partnerships in previous chapters. Here, we examine a relatively new form of business organization called the *limited liability company (LLC)*, which has become the organizational form of choice among many small businesses.

In this chapter, we look in detail at the LLC and its advantages and disadvantages. We also discuss the operation and management options in an LLC.

Next, we consider a variety of other special business forms, including joint ventures, syndicates, joint stock companies, business trusts, and cooperatives. These business forms can be used by businesses of any size, but several of them—like LLCs—are especially attractive to small businesses. We conclude the chapter with a discussion of factors that anyone starting a small business should consider, including organizational forms, protection of intellectual property, and financing.

## SECTION 1
## THE LIMITED LIABILITY COMPANY

A **limited liability company (LLC)** is a hybrid that combines the limited liability aspects of a corporation and the tax advantages of a partnership. The LLC has been available for only a few decades, but it has become the preferred structure for many small businesses.

LLCs are governed by state statutes, which vary from state to state. In an attempt to create more uniformity, the National Conference of Commissioners on Uniform State Laws issued the Uniform Limited Liability Company Act (ULLCA). Less than one-fifth of the states have adopted it, though. Thus, the law governing LLCs remains far from uniform.

Some provisions are common to most state statutes, however, and we base our discussion of LLCs in this section on these common elements.

## The Nature of the LLC

LLCs share many characteristics with corporations. Like corporations, LLCs must be formed and operated in compliance with state law. Like the shareholders of a corporation, the owners of an LLC, who are called **members,** enjoy limited liability [ULLCA 303].[1]

**LIMITED LIABILITY OF MEMBERS** Members of LLCs are shielded from personal liability in many situations, even sometimes when sued by employees of the firm. ▶ **Case in Point 31.1** Penny McFarland was the activities director at a retirement community in Virginia that was owned by an LLC. Her supervisor told her to take the residents outside for a walk when the temperature was 95 degrees. McFarland complained to the state health department and was fired from her job. She sued a number

---

1. Members of an LLC can also bring derivative actions on behalf of the LLC [ULLCA 101]. As with a corporate shareholder's derivative suit, any damages recovered go to the LLC, not to the members personally.

of managers and members of the LLC for wrongful discharge.

The court held that under Virginia state law, members, managers, and agents of an LLC are not responsible for its liabilities "solely" by virtue of their status. Only those who "have played a key role in contributing to the company's tortious conduct" can be part of a wrongful discharge claim. The court therefore dismissed the action against all but one defendant.[2] ◄

---

**2.** *McFarland v. Virginia Retirement Services of Chesterfield, LLC,* 477 F.Supp.2d 727 (2007).

**LIABILITY UNDER THE ALTER-EGO THEORY** Sometimes, when a corporation is deemed to be merely an "alter ego" of the shareholder-owner, a court will *pierce the corporate veil* and hold the shareholder-owner personally liable (see Chapter 32). A court may apply the alter-ego theory when a shareholder commingles personal and corporate funds or fails to observe required corporate formalities.

Whether the alter-ego theory should be applied to an LLC was at issue in the following case.

---

## CASE 31.1

### ORX Resources, Inc. v. MBW Exploration, LLC
Court of Appeal of Louisiana, Fourth Circuit, 32 So.3d 931 (2010).

**BACKGROUND AND FACTS** ORX Resources, Inc., purchased oil and gas interests in a tract of land located in Lafourche Parish, Louisiana. ORX partnered with other entities, including MBW Exploration, LLC, to share in the expenses and in the potential profits of the venture to explore and develop the oil and gas interests. On behalf of MBW, Mark Washauer signed participation agreements with ORX. He indicated that he was signing on behalf of MBW in his capacity as "managing member." In reality, MBW Exploration, LLC, did not come into existence until several years later, when its articles of organization were filed with the Louisiana secretary of state. ORX later submitted an authorization for expenditures to MBW for approval, which Washauer signed in his own name. He paid MBW's participation fee with a check drawn on another entity, MBW Properties, LLC. He also paid ORX an additional amount with a personal check. When the first well proved to be unsuccessful, it was plugged.

MBW's share of unpaid expenses amounted to approximately $84,000. ORX demanded payment from Washauer, but it did not receive any funds. ORX filed a lawsuit for breach of contract against both MBW and Washauer. The trial court determined that Washauer had operated MBW as his alter ego, and it allowed ORX to "pierce the veil" of the LLC. The court granted summary judgment in favor of ORX, holding Washauer and MBW jointly and severally liable for the $84,000. Washauer and MBW appealed the judgment. The appellate court had to address the issue of whether the alter-ego theory of corporate veil piercing applied to Louisiana LLCs.

**DECISION AND RATIONALE** A state intermediate appellate court affirmed the judgment of the lower court in favor of ORX. The reviewing court determined that "piercing the veil of an LLC is justified to prevent the use of the LLC form to defraud creditors." Washauer had used MBW as a shell and had attempted to avoid paying a legitimate debt of the LLC. "We find that Washauer's activities on behalf of MBW do merit the piercing of the veil of this LLC." Washauer had commingled (mixed together) the MBW funds with his personal funds and those of a separate company. MBW had not even had a separate bank account to transact its own affairs. "Furthermore, when MBW began contracting with ORX, it had not yet been recognized as an LLC by the Louisiana Secretary of State." Washauer was operating MBW "at his leisure and discretion" and could be held personally liable jointly and severally with MBW.

**THE LEGAL ENVIRONMENT DIMENSION** *What does "jointly and severally" mean in terms of liability? Would ORX prefer that Washauer and MBW be held personally liable jointly and severally, rather than that Washauer alone be held personally liable? Explain.*

**THE ETHICAL DIMENSION** *One of the advantages of the LLC is that its members enjoy limited personal liability for the company's obligations. In view of this fact, does the possibility that a court may hold an LLC member personally liable for the LLC's debts reduce the utility of the LLC form of business organization? Explain.*

**OTHER SIMILARITIES TO CORPORATIONS** Another similarity between corporations and LLCs is that LLCs are legal entities apart from their owners. As a legal person, the LLC can sue or be sued, enter into contracts, and hold title to property [ULLCA 201]. The terminology used to describe LLCs formed in other states or nations is also similar to that used in corporate law. For instance, an LLC formed in one state but doing business in another state is referred to in the second state as a *foreign LLC*.

## The Formation of the LLC

LLCs are creatures of statute and thus must follow state statutory requirements. To form an LLC, **articles of organization** must be filed with a central state agency—usually the secretary of state's office [ULLCA 202].[3]

**CONTENTS OF THE ARTICLES** Typically, the articles of organization must include the name of the business, its principal address, the name and address of a registered agent, the members' names, and how the LLC will be managed [ULLCA 203]. The business's name must include the words *Limited Liability Company* or the initials *LLC* [ULLCA 105(a)]. Although a majority of the states permit one-member LLCs, some states require at least two members.

**PREFORMATION CONTRACTS** Businesspersons sometimes enter into contracts on behalf of a business organization that is not yet formed. As you will read in Chapter 32, persons who are forming a corporation may enter into contracts during the process of incorporation but before the corporation becomes a legal entity. These contracts are referred to as *preincorporation contracts*. Once the corporation is formed and adopts the preincorporation contracts (by means of a *novation*, discussed in Chapter 18), it can enforce the contract terms.

In dealing with the preorganization contracts of LLCs, courts may apply the well-established principles of corporate law relating to preincorporation contracts. ▶ **Case in Point 31.2** 607 South Park, LLC, entered into an agreement to sell a hotel to 607 Park View Associates, Ltd., which then assigned the rights to the purchase to another company, 02 Development, LLC. At the time, 02 Development did not yet exist—

it was legally created several months later. 607 South Park subsequently refused to sell the hotel to 02 Development, and 02 Development sued for breach of the purchase agreement.

A California appellate court ruled that LLCs should be treated the same as corporations with respect to preorganization contracts. Although 02 Development did not exist when the agreement was executed, once it came into existence, it could enforce any preorganization contract made on its behalf.[4] ◀

## Jurisdictional Requirements

As we have seen, LLCs and corporations share several characteristics, but a significant difference between these organizational forms involves federal jurisdictional requirements. Under the federal jurisdiction statute, a corporation is deemed to be a citizen of the state where it is incorporated and maintains its principal place of business. The statute does not mention the state citizenship of partnerships, LLCs, and other unincorporated associations, but the courts have tended to regard these entities as citizens of every state of which their members are citizens.

The state citizenship of an LLC may come into play when a party sues the LLC based on diversity of citizenship. Remember from Chapter 2 that when parties to a lawsuit are from different states and the amount in controversy exceeds $75,000, a federal court can exercise diversity jurisdiction. *Total* diversity of citizenship must exist, however.

▶ **Example 31.3** Jen Fong, a citizen of New York, wishes to bring a suit against Skycel, an LLC formed under the laws of Connecticut. One of Skycel's members also lives in New York. Fong will not be able to bring a suit against Skycel in federal court on the basis of diversity jurisdiction because the defendant LLC is also a citizen of New York. The same would be true if Fong was bringing a suit against multiple defendants and one of the defendants lived in New York. ◀

## Advantages of the LLC

The LLC offers many advantages to businesspersons, which is why this form of business organization has become increasingly popular.

**LIMITED LIABILITY** A key advantage of the LLC is that the liability of members is limited to the

---

**3.** In addition to requiring articles of organization to be filed, a few states require that a notice of the intention to form an LLC be published in a local newspaper.

**4.** *02 Development, LLC v. 607 South Park, LLC,* 159 Cal.App.4th 609, 71 Cal.Rptr.3d 608 (2008).

amount of their investments. Although the LLC as an entity can be held liable for any loss or injury caused by the wrongful acts or omissions of its members, the members themselves generally are not personally liable.

**FLEXIBILITY IN TAXATION** Another advantage of the LLC is its flexibility in regard to taxation. An LLC that has *two or more members* can choose to be taxed as either a partnership or a corporation. As will be discussed in Chapter 32, a corporate entity must pay income taxes on its profits, and the shareholders pay personal income taxes on profits distributed as dividends. An LLC that wants to distribute profits to its members may prefer to be taxed as a partnership to avoid the "double taxation" that is characteristic of the corporate entity.

Unless an LLC indicates that it wishes to be taxed as a corporation, the Internal Revenue Service (IRS) automatically taxes it as a partnership. This means that the LLC, as an entity, pays no taxes. Rather, as in a partnership, profits are "passed through" the LLC to the members, who then personally pay taxes on the profits. If an LLC's members want to reinvest profits in the business rather than distribute the profits to members, however, they may prefer to be taxed as a corporation. Corporate income tax rates may be lower than personal tax rates. Part of the attractiveness of the LLC is this flexibility with respect to taxation.

An LLC that has only *one member* cannot be taxed as a partnership. For federal income tax purposes, one-member LLCs are automatically taxed as sole proprietorships unless they indicate that they wish to be taxed as corporations. With respect to state taxes, most states follow the IRS rules.

**MANAGEMENT AND FOREIGN INVESTORS** Another advantage of the LLC for businesspersons is the flexibility it offers in terms of business operations and management—as will be discussed shortly. Foreign investors are allowed to become LLC members, so organizing as an LLC can enable a business to attract investors from other countries.

## Disadvantages of the LLC

The main disadvantage of the LLC is that state LLC statutes are not uniform. Therefore, businesses that operate in more than one state may not receive consistent treatment in these states.

Generally, most states apply to a foreign LLC (an LLC formed in another state) the law of the state where the LLC was formed. Difficulties can arise, though, when one state's court must interpret and apply another state's laws.

## LLC MANAGEMENT AND OPERATION

The members of an LLC have considerable flexibility in managing and operating the business. Here, we discuss management options, fiduciary duties owed, and the operating agreement and general operating procedures of LLCs.

## Management of an LLC

Basically, LLC members have two options for managing the firm. It can be either a "member-managed" LLC or a "manager-managed" LLC. Most state LLC statutes and the ULLCA provide that unless the articles of organization specify otherwise, an LLC is assumed to be member managed [ULLCA 203(a)(6)].

In a *member-managed* LLC, all of the members participate in management, and decisions are made by majority vote [ULLCA 404(a)]. In a *manager-managed* LLC, the members designate a group of persons to manage the firm. The management group may consist of only members, both members and nonmembers, or only nonmembers.

## Fiduciary Duties

Under the ULLCA, managers in a manager-managed LLC owe fiduciary duties (the duty of loyalty and the duty of care) to the LLC and its members [ULLCA 409(a), 409(h)]. (As you will read in Chapter 32, this same rule applies in corporate law—corporate directors and officers owe fiduciary duties to the corporation and its shareholders.) Because not all states have adopted the ULLCA, though, some state statutes provide that managers owe fiduciary duties only to the LLC and not to the LLC's members. Although to whom the duty is owed may seem insignificant at first glance, it can have a dramatic effect on the outcome of litigation.

In Alabama, where the following case arose, managers owe fiduciary duties to the LLC and to its members.

## CASE 31.2

### Polk v. Polk
Court of Civil Appeals of Alabama, 70 So.3d 363 (2011).

**BACKGROUND AND FACTS**   Leslie Polk and his children, Yurii and Dusty Polk and Lezanne Proctor, formed Polk Plumbing, LLC, in Alabama. Leslie, Dusty, and Yurii performed commercial plumbing work, and Lezanne, an accountant, maintained the financial records and served as the office manager. After a couple of years, Yurii quit the firm. Eighteen months later, Leslie "fired" Dusty and Lezanne. He denied them access to the LLC's books and offices but continued to operate the business.

Dusty and Lezanne filed a suit in an Alabama state court against Leslie, claiming breach of fiduciary duty. The court submitted the claim to a jury with the instruction that in Alabama employment relationships are "at will" (see Chapter 27). The court also told the jury that it could not consider the plaintiffs' "firing" as part of their claim. The jury awarded Dusty and Lezanne one dollar each in damages. They appealed, arguing that the judge's instructions to the jury were prejudicial—that is, that the instructions had substantially affected the outcome of the trial.

**DECISION AND RATIONALE**   A state intermediate appellate court reversed the lower court's judgment on the claim for breach of fiduciary duty and remanded the case for a new trial. The lower court had committed reversible errors and had "probably injuriously affected substantial rights of Dusty and Lezanne." The court erred by instructing the jury that the plaintiffs' employment as managers was at will and by failing to instruct the jury that it could consider their "firing" as evidence in support of their claim. Dusty and Lezanne served as managers of the LLC.

The reviewing court reasoned that the operating agreement provided that managers served until replaced or recalled by a vote of the majority of the members. In other words, their employment as managers was not at will. Because no vote had been taken to recall or replace Dusty and Lezanne, their father did not have the authority to terminate their employment. His attempted "firing" of them was in violation of the LLC's operating agreement. If the jury had considered all of this evidence, the amount of damages might have been higher.

**WHAT IF THE FACTS WERE DIFFERENT?**   *Suppose that Leslie owned a majority of Polk Plumbing. Could his "firing" of Dusty and Lezanne still be considered as evidence of a breach of fiduciary duty? Explain.*

**THE LEGAL ENVIRONMENT DIMENSION**   *Under what circumstances might the employment-at-will doctrine apply to the members of an LLC?*

## The LLC Operating Agreement

The members of an LLC can decide how to operate the various aspects of the business by forming an **operating agreement** [ULLCA 103(a)]. In many states, an operating agreement is not required for an LLC to exist, and if there is one, it need not be in writing. Generally, though, LLC members should protect their interests by creating a written operating agreement.

Operating agreements typically contain provisions relating to the following areas:

1. Management and how future managers will be chosen or removed. (Although most LLC statutes are silent on this issue, the ULLCA provides that members may choose and remove managers by majority vote [ULLCA 404(b)(3)].)
2. How profits will be divided.
3. How membership interests may be transferred.
4. Whether the dissociation of a member, such as by death or departure, will trigger dissolution of the LLC.
5. Whether formal members' meetings will be held.
6. How voting rights will be apportioned. (If the agreement does not cover voting, LLC statutes in most states provide that voting rights are apportioned according to each member's capital contributions.[5] Some states provide that, in the absence

---
**5.** In contrast, partners in a partnership generally have equal rights in management and equal voting rights unless they specify otherwise in their partnership agreement (see Chapter 30).

of an agreement to the contrary, each member has one vote.)

**STATE STATUTES FILL IN GAPS** If the agreement does not cover a topic, such as how profits will be divided, the state LLC statute will govern. Most LLC statutes provide that if the members have not specified how profits will be divided, they will be divided equally among the members.

**PARTNERSHIP LAW MAY APPLY** If a dispute arises and the state's LLC statute does not cover the issue, courts sometimes apply the principles of partnership law. ▶ **Case in Point 31.4** Clifford Kuhn, Jr., and Joseph Tumminelli formed Touch of Class Limousine Service as an LLC. They did not create a written operating agreement but orally agreed that Kuhn would provide the financial backing and that Tumminelli would manage the day-to-day operations. Tumminelli embezzled $283,000 from the company after cashing customers' checks at Quick Cash, Inc., a local check-cashing service.

Kuhn sued Tumminelli and Quick Cash to recover the embezzled funds. He argued that Quick Cash was liable because Tumminelli did not have the authority to cash the company's checks. The court, however, held that in the absence of a written operating agreement to the contrary, a member of an LLC, like a partner in a partnership, has the authority to cash a firm's checks. Therefore, Kuhn's claim against Quick Cash was dismissed.[6] ◀

## SECTION 3
# DISSOCIATION AND DISSOLUTION OF AN LLC

As mentioned earlier in Chapter 30, *dissociation* in a partnership occurs when a partner ceases to be associated in the carrying on of the partnership business. The same concept applies to LLCs. A member of an LLC has the *power* to dissociate from the LLC at any time, but he or she may not have the *right* to dissociate.

Under the ULLCA, the events that trigger a member's dissociation from an LLC are similar to the events causing a partner to be dissociated under the Uniform Partnership Act (UPA). These include voluntary withdrawal, expulsion by other members or by court order,

incompetence, and death. Generally, if a member dies or otherwise dissociates from an LLC, the other members may continue to carry on the LLC business, unless the operating agreement provides otherwise.

## Effect of Dissociation

When a member dissociates from an LLC, he or she loses the right to participate in management and the right to act as an agent for the LLC. The member's duty of loyalty to the LLC also terminates, and the duty of care continues only with respect to events that occurred before dissociation.

Generally, the dissociated member also has a right to have his or her interest in the LLC bought out by the other members. The LLC's operating agreement may contain provisions establishing a buyout price, but if it does not, the member's interest is usually purchased at a fair value. In states that have adopted the ULLCA, the LLC must purchase the interest at fair value within 120 days after the dissociation.

If the member's dissociation violates the LLC's operating agreement, it is considered legally wrongful, and the dissociated member can be held liable for damages caused by the dissociation. ▶ **Example 31.5** Chadwick and Barrow are members in an LLC. Chadwick manages the accounts, and Barrow, who has many connections in the community and is a skilled investor, brings in the business. If Barrow wrongfully dissociates from the LLC, the LLC's business will suffer, and Chadwick can hold Barrow liable for the loss of business resulting from her withdrawal. ◀

## Dissolution

Regardless of whether a member's dissociation was wrongful or rightful, normally the dissociated member has no right to force the LLC to dissolve. The remaining members can opt either to continue or to dissolve the business.

Members can also stipulate in their operating agreement that certain events will cause dissolution, or they can agree that they have the power to dissolve the LLC by vote. As with partnerships, a court can order an LLC to be dissolved in certain circumstances. For instance, a court might order dissolution when the members have engaged in illegal or oppressive conduct, or when it is no longer feasible to carry on the business.

In the following case, the court had to decide whether an LLC could be dissolved because continuing the business was impracticable.

---

6. *Kuhn v. Tumminelli*, 366 N.J.Super. 431, 841 A.2d 496 (2004).

## CASE 31.3

### Venture Sales, LLC v. Perkins
Supreme Court of Mississippi, 86 So. 3d 910 (2012).

**BACKGROUND AND FACTS**   Walter Perkins, Gary Fordham, and David Thompson formed Venture Sales, LLC, to develop a subdivision in Petal, Mississippi. All three members contributed land and funds to Venture Sales, resulting in total holdings of 466 acres of land and about $158,000 in cash.

Perkins was an assistant coach for the Cleveland Browns, so he trusted Fordham and Thompson to develop the property. Over a decade later, however, Fordham and Thompson still had not done anything with the property, although they had developed at least two other subdivisions in the area. Fordham and Thompson said that they did not know when they could develop the property and that they had been unable to get the additional $8 million they needed to proceed. Fordham and Thompson suggested selling the property, but Perkins did not agree with the proposed listing price of $3.5 million. Perkins then sought a judicial dissolution of Venture Sales in Mississippi state court. The trial court ordered the company dissolved. Fordham, Thompson, and Venture Sales appealed.

**DECISION AND RATIONALE**   The Mississippi Supreme Court affirmed the judgment of the trial court dissolving the company. Under Mississippi law, an LLC may be judicially dissolved if, among other reasons, "it is not reasonably practicable to carry on the business in conformity with . . . the limited liability company agreement." The statute does not explain when continuing an LLC is "not reasonably practicable." The state's highest court therefore followed decisions from other jurisdictions recognizing that dissolution is appropriate when an LLC "is not meeting the economic purpose for which it was established."

According to Venture Sales' operating agreement, the company's purpose was "to initially acquire, develop and [sell] commercial and residential properties near Petal, Forrest County, Mississippi." Nevertheless, more than a decade later, the LLC's property remained undeveloped. Fordham and Thompson pointed to a number of reasons, including the financial crisis and Hurricane Katrina. But regardless of the reasons, Fordham and Thompson lacked the funds needed to proceed and did not know when they could develop the property as planned. Finally, it was immaterial that Perkins did not agree to other business opportunities, such as possibly selling the whole property for $3.5 million. After all, Venture Sales was formed to develop a subdivision. Because the LLC was not meeting that purpose, dissolution was warranted.

**THE LEGAL ENVIRONMENT DIMENSION**   *Would dissolution be appropriate if the parties had formed a partnership rather than an LLC? Explain your answer.*

**MANAGERIAL IMPLICATIONS**   *To avoid the type of dispute in which the members of Venture Sales became embroiled, the managers of an LLC or other business organization should take care to act on the firm's "economic purpose" within a reasonable time. To ensure that they will be able to do so, the managers should draw up plans and determine the full cost of the project. They should also ascertain how the needed funds will be obtained. If bank loans or other funding will not be available, as occurred in this case, the LLC should require a higher level of contributions from its members to ensure that there will be sufficient funds to complete the project successfully.*

---

## Winding Up

When an LLC is dissolved, any members who did not wrongfully dissociate may participate in the winding up process. To wind up the business, members must collect, liquidate, and distribute the LLC's assets.

Members may preserve the assets for a reasonable time to optimize their return, and they continue to have the authority to perform reasonable acts in conjunction with winding up. In other words, the LLC will be bound by the reasonable acts of its members during the winding up process.

Once all of the LLC's assets have been sold, the proceeds are distributed to pay off debts to creditors first (including debts owed to members who are creditors of the LLC). The members' capital contributions are returned next, and any remaining amounts are then distributed to members in equal shares or according to their operating agreement.

## SECTION 4
# SPECIAL BUSINESS FORMS

In addition to the LLC and the other traditional business forms discussed in this unit, several other forms can be used to organize a business. Many of these special business forms, such as joint ventures and syndicates, are particularly attractive to small businesses. For the most part, they are hybrid organizations— that is, they combine features of other organizational forms such as partnerships and corporations.

## Joint Venture

In a **joint venture,** two or more persons or business entities combine their efforts or their property for a single transaction or project or a related series of transactions or projects. Unless otherwise agreed, joint venturers share profits and losses equally and have an equal voice in controlling the project. For instance, when several contractors combine their resources to build and sell houses in a single development, their relationship is a joint venture.

Joint ventures range in size from very small activities to multimillion-dollar joint actions carried out by some of the world's largest corporations. Large organizations often form joint ventures with other enterprises to produce new products or services. ▶ **Example 31.6** Intel Corporation and Micron Technology, Inc., formed a joint venture to manufacture NAND flash memory. NAND is a data-storage chip widely used in digital cameras, cell phones, and portable music players. ◀

**SIMILARITIES TO PARTNERSHIPS** A joint venture resembles a partnership and is taxed like a partnership. For this reason, most courts apply the same principles to joint ventures as they apply to partnerships. Joint venturers owe each other the same fiduciary duties, including the duty of loyalty, that partners owe each other. Thus, if one of the venturers secretly buys land that was to be acquired by the joint venture, the other joint venturers may be awarded damages for the breach of loyalty.

*Liability and Management Rights.* A joint venturer can be held personally liable for the venture's debts (because joint venturers share profits and losses). Like partners, joint venturers have equal rights to manage the activities of the enterprise, but they can agree to give control of the operation to one of the members.

*Authority to Enter Contracts.* Joint venturers also have authority as agents to enter into contracts for the business that will bind the joint venture. ▶ **Case in Point 31.7** Murdo Cameron developed components for replicas of vintage P-51 Mustang planes. Cameron and Douglas Anderson agreed in writing to collaborate on the design and manufacture of two P-51s, one for each of them.

Without Cameron's knowledge, Anderson borrowed funds from SPW Associates, LLP, to finance the construction, using the first plane as security for the loan. After Anderson built one plane, he defaulted on the loan. SPW filed a lawsuit to obtain possession of the aircraft. The court ruled that Anderson and Cameron had entered into a joint venture and that the plane was the venture's property. Under partnership law, partners have the power as agents to bind the partnership. Because this principle applies to joint ventures, Anderson had the authority to grant SPW a security interest in the plane, and SPW was entitled to take possession of the plane.[7] ◀

**DIFFERENCES FROM PARTNERSHIPS** Joint ventures also differ from partnerships in several important ways. The members of a joint venture have less implied and apparent authority than the partners in a partnership. In part, this reduced authority is because a joint venture is typically created for a single project or series of transactions, whereas a partnership usually (though not always) involves an ongoing business. As discussed in Chapter 30, each partner is treated as an agent of the other partners.

Because the activities of a joint venture are more limited than the business of a partnership, the members of a joint venture are presumed to have less power to bind their co-venturers. In *Case in Point 31.7*, for instance, if Anderson's loan agreement with SPW had not been directly related to the business of building vintage planes, the court might have concluded that Anderson lacked the authority to bind the joint ven-

---

7. *SPW Associates, LLP v. Anderson*, 2006 ND 159, 718 N.W.2d 580 (N.D.Sup.Ct. 2006).

ture. Also, unlike most partnerships, a joint venture normally terminates when the project or transaction for which it was formed is completed.

## Syndicate

In a **syndicate,** or *investment group,* several individuals or firms join together to finance a particular project, such as the construction of a shopping center or the purchase of a professional basketball franchise. The form of such entities varies considerably. A syndicate may be organized as a corporation or as a general or limited partnership. In some instances, the members do not have a legally recognized business arrangement but merely purchase and own property jointly.

## Joint Stock Company

A **joint stock company** is a true hybrid of a partnership and a corporation. It has many characteristics of a corporation in that (1) its ownership is represented by transferable shares of stock, (2) it is managed by directors and officers of the company or association, and (3) it can have a perpetual existence.

Most of its other features, however, are more characteristic of a partnership, and it generally is treated as a partnership. Like a partnership, a joint stock company is formed by agreement (not statute). Property usually is held in the names of the owners, who are called shareholders, and they have personal liability. In a joint stock company, however, shareholders are not considered to be agents of each other, as they would be in a true partnership.

## Business Trust

A **business trust** is created by a written trust agreement that sets forth the interests of the beneficiaries and the obligations and powers of the trustees. The business trust form of organization was started in Massachusetts in an attempt to obtain the limited liability advantage of corporate status. Legal ownership and management of the trust's property stay with one or more of the trustees, and the profits are distributed to the beneficiaries.

A business trust resembles a corporation in many respects. Beneficiaries of the trust, for instance, are not personally responsible for the trust's debts or obligations. In fact, in a number of states, business trusts must pay corporate taxes.

## Cooperative

A **cooperative** is an association that is organized to provide an economic service to its members (or shareholders). It may or may not be incorporated. Most cooperatives are organized under state statutes for cooperatives, general business corporations, or LLCs.

The cooperative form of business is generally adopted by groups of individuals who wish to pool their resources to gain some advantage in the marketplace. *Consumer purchasing co-ops* are formed to obtain lower prices through quantity discounts. *Seller marketing co-ops* are formed to control the market and thereby enable members to sell their goods at higher prices. Co-ops range in size from small, local consumer cooperatives to national businesses such as Ace Hardware and Land O'Lakes, a well-known producer of dairy products.

**INCORPORATED CO-OPS** Generally, an incorporated cooperative will distribute dividends, or profits, to its owners on the basis of their transactions with the cooperative rather than on the basis of the amount of capital they contributed. Members of incorporated cooperatives have limited liability, as do shareholders of corporations and members of LLCs.

**UNINCORPORATED CO-OPS** Cooperatives that are not incorporated are often treated like partnerships. The members have joint liability for the cooperative's acts.

See *Concept Summary 31.1* on the next page for a review of the types of special business forms discussed in this chapter.

### SECTION 5
# GENERAL CONSIDERATIONS FOR SMALL BUSINESS

In the earliest stages, a small business may operate as a sole proprietorship, which requires few legal formalities. The law considers all new, single-owner businesses to be sole proprietorships, unless the owner affirmatively adopts some other form.

Once business is under way, however, the sole proprietorship form may become problematic if additional investors are needed or the personal financial risks of the business become too great. The owner and any additional investors will then want to establish a more formal organization, such as a limited partnership (LP), a limited liability partnership (LLP), a limited liability company (LLC), or a corporation.

## CONCEPT SUMMARY 31.1
### Special Business Forms

| CONCEPT | DESCRIPTION |
|---|---|
| Joint Venture | An organization created by two or more persons in contemplation of a limited activity or a single transaction; similar to a partnership in many respects. |
| Syndicate | An investment group that undertakes to finance a particular project; may be organized as a corporation or as a general or limited partnership. |
| Joint Stock Company | A business form similar to a corporation in some respects (transferable shares of stock, management by directors and officers, perpetual existence) but otherwise resembling a partnership. |
| Business Trust | A business form created by a written trust agreement that sets forth the interests of the beneficiaries and the obligations and powers of the trustee(s). A business trust is similar to a corporation in many respects. Beneficiaries are not personally liable for the debts or obligations of the business trust. |
| Cooperative | An association organized to provide an economic service, without profit, to its members. A cooperative can take the form of a corporation or a partnership. |

Each business form has its own advantages and disadvantages. Factors to consider when choosing a business form include liability, taxation, continuity of life, and the legal formalities and costs associated with organizing the business. Small businesses also need to consider employment laws, applicable environmental or health regulations, licensing requirements, zoning codes, and intellectual property rights. Of course, they also need to protect their hard-earned profits from cyber thieves. See this chapter's *Managerial Strategy* feature on the facing page for a discussion of new developments in this area.

## Limitations on Liability

A key consideration in starting a business is whether the business form chosen will limit the owner's personal liability for business debts and obligations. If you form a limited liability entity, you normally can avoid personal liability if, say, a customer slips and breaks his ankle in your store, sues, and is awarded damages by a court. Although the business entity may be liable for damages, you and the other owners normally will not be personally liable beyond the extent of your contributions to the firm. Legal limited liability generally is necessary for those who wish to raise outside capital.

Corporate business forms offer limited liability to the shareholder-owners. In a traditional partnership, however, there is no limited liability. Each partner is personally liable for the debts and obligations of the partnership. In a limited partnership, the limited partners have limited liability, but there must be at least one general partner who remains personally liable for the partnership's obligations.

Today, all states permit businesspersons to conduct their business operations as LLCs, and most states provide for limited liability partnership (LLPs) (see Chapter 30). These increasingly popular business forms also offer the advantage of limited personal liability for business debts and obligations.

**MAINTAIN INSURANCE** Note that limited personal liability does not obviate the need to obtain insurance for significant business liability risks. Limited liability organizations protect only personal assets, and a substantial uninsured liability can bankrupt the business and cause the owners to lose their entire investments.

**CONDUCT OF OWNERS** Moreover, limited personal liability may be lost by contract. For instance, when an individual personally guarantees payment of a business loan, the individual is personally liable for the business's obligation. In addition, if a small-business owner fails to comply with the rules for a business form, such as by commingling personal and business funds, the business can lose its shield from personal liability (see the discussion of *piercing the corporate veil* in Chapter 32).

## Tax Considerations

Taxes are another critical factor to be considered in choosing a small-business form. A sole proprietorship

## MANAGERIAL STRATEGY

### Small-Business Owners Now Have Recourse When Cyber Thieves Empty Their Bank Accounts

Between 150 and 200 cyber attacks on business organizations occur every day. Most of these attacks are initiated by cyber thieves in other countries, especially China and Russia. Thirty percent of the attacks are aimed at small businesses (those with fewer than 250 employees).

**Who Is Responsible for the Loss due to a Fraudulent Fund Transfer?**

If cyber thieves cause you, an individual, to lose the funds in your bank account, usually your bank is responsible for the loss. The laws that protect individuals' bank accounts do not extend to small businesses, however. Nevertheless, some recent court decisions have allowed businesses to recover from their banks when their funds were fraudulently transferred.

In 2009, an employee at Experi-Metal, Inc., received an e-mail containing a link to a Web page with a Comerica Bank business connect form. Knowing that Comerica was the company's bank, the employee followed a further link and filled in the requested information. Experi-Metal had just been the victim of a phishing attack—the most common method used by cyber thieves to obtain the information needed for fraudulent fund transfers. Within minutes, cyber thieves transferred almost $2 million from Experi-Metal's account to bank accounts in China, Estonia, and Russia.

Experi-Metal sued Comerica, arguing, among other things, that the bank had not observed good faith when it accepted the online command for the wire transfers. Ultimately, the court found that the bank's employees had failed to meet reasonable commercial standards of fair dealing in not questioning the unusual size of the transfers and their destinations.[a]

**A Small Business Wins an Appeal**

Pacto Construction Company did its banking with Ocean Bank (later acquired by People's United Bank). In 2009, cyber thieves installed malware in Pacto's computers. The malware recorded the keystrokes of Pacto's employees, thereby enabling the thieves to obtain the answers to the security questions posed by Ocean Bank for wire transfers. Over a five-day period, Ocean Bank approved wire transfers from Pacto's account for hundreds of thousands of dollars. The funds were sent to numerous individuals, none of whom had ever done business with Pacto. Although the bank's high-risk alert system indicated that the transfers might be fraudulent, the bank continued to allow them. Pacto sued the bank to recover its lost funds, but a U.S. district court ruled against Pacto.

On appeal, however, the reviewing court agreed with Pacto that Ocean Bank had not monitored the transactions effectively and should have notified Pacto before allowing them to be completed. These failures and others "rendered Ocean Bank's security procedures commercially unreasonable."[b]

### MANAGERIAL IMPLICATIONS

Small-business owners now have some recourse if cyber thieves steal funds from their bank accounts. Nonetheless, small-business owners are well advised to be aware of potential cyber threats when they use banks' security procedures. Even though precedent makes recovery of funds stolen by cyber thieves now possible, few small companies have the resources to pursue a lawsuit against their banks.

### BUSINESS QUESTIONS

1. *Might there be any repercussions against small businesses because of recent decisions in their favor in cases involving cyber theft?*

2. *Why is it so difficult for banks to recover funds stolen online from their small-business customers?*

---

a. *Experi-Metal, Inc. v. Comerica Bank*, 2011 WL 2433383 (E.D.Mich. 2011).

b. *Pacto Construction Co. v. People's United Bank, d/b/a Ocean Bank*, 684 F.3d 197 (1st Cir. 2012).

---

is not a separate legal entity, and the owner pays taxes on business income as an individual. All revenues are taxable, but business expenses can be deducted, so the owner is taxed only once on the business's profits.

All corporations must pay certain state and local taxes, but the key consideration involves corporate income taxes. As mentioned earlier, the corporate form entails *double taxation*. The company pays a corporate income tax on its profits, and the shareholder-owners also pay individual income tax on any distributions of the remaining profits that they receive from the corporation. Double taxation is limited to distributions of profits, though, so corporations are taxed only once on retained earnings. (See Chapter 32 for a complete discussion of corporate taxation).

Partnerships, LLCs, LLPs, and S corporations (see Chapter 32) avoid double taxation and provide for "pass-through" taxation—that is, profits are passed through to the partners, members, or owners and are taxed only on their individual returns, not at the business level.

## Continuity of Life

Continuity of life is another concern in selecting a business form. A business should prepare for the possibility that an owner may die, resign, be expelled, or become incapacitated. Corporations have continuity of life—that is, they survive their owners—except in the unusual event that the corporate documents provide otherwise. Normally, on the death of a corporate shareholder-owner, that shareholder's ownership interest simply passes to his or her heirs.

In many states, a partnership will not terminate on the death or withdrawal of a partner, unless the partners have expressly provided otherwise. (In those states that have not adopted the most recent version of the Uniform Partnership Act, however, the death of a partner will automatically dissolve the partnership—see Chapter 30.) By definition, a sole proprietorship terminates with the death of the sole proprietor.

## Legal Formality and Expense

Additionally, businesspersons need to consider the legal formalities and expenses involved in starting a business. The requirements and costs associated with forming and operating as a corporation can be considerable. The expense of establishing an LLP may also be significant. For these reasons, some individuals initially operate their businesses as sole proprietorships or traditional partnerships. By doing so, they run considerable financial risk because of the personal liability associated with each of these business forms. Start-up formalities and costs generally are less extensive for LLCs than for corporations or limited partnerships.

## Requirements for All Business Forms

Any business, whatever its form, has to meet a variety of legal requirements, which typically relate to the following:

1. Business name registration.

2. Occupational licensing.
3. State tax registration (for instance, to obtain permits for collecting and remitting sales taxes).
4. Health and environmental permits.
5. Zoning and building codes.
6. Import/export regulations.

If the business has employees, the owner must also comply with a host of laws governing the workplace (see Chapters 27 and 28). Some small businesses that have only a few employees are exempted from certain laws. For instance, recent health-care legislation imposes a fine on employers that do not provide health insurance for their employees. Companies with fewer than fifty employees, however, are exempt from this requirement. Moreover, small businesses that help pay for employees' insurance are eligible for tax credits under the legislation.

## Converting an LLC into a Corporation

If a small business begins as an LLC and thrives, the owners may wish to convert it to a corporation. By incorporating, the larger business can attract more outside capital with public offerings of its equity. Because the company will likely be retaining its earnings to fund future growth, rather than distributing them to the owners, it will not experience the double-taxation disadvantage of the corporate form. In addition, the corporate structure facilitates the use of equity-based employee incentive plans, such as grants of stock options, and a more expansive management structure.

If the LLC agreement does not provide otherwise, this conversion may require the unanimous consent of the members. The LLC must then file articles of dissolution with the state. The members will agree on a process to assign ownership interests in the new corporation by shareholdings. Then, they will go about forming the successor corporation.

## Protecting Intellectual Property

Protecting rights in intellectual property is the central concern for some businesses. For instance, software companies depend on their copyrights and patents to protect their investments in the research and development required to create new programs.

Without copyright or patent protection, a competitor or a customer could simply copy the software. Laws governing rights in intellectual property were discussed in detail in Chapter 8. Here, we examine some aspects of intellectual property law that individuals should consider at the outset of any business venture.

**TRADEMARKS** Choosing a trademark or service mark and making sure that it can be protected under trademark law can be crucial to the success of a new business venture. A factor to consider in choosing a name for your business entity is whether you will use your business name as a trademark.

If you decide to use your business (trade) name as a trademark, then you need to follow the principles of trademark law. The general rule is that your trademark cannot be the same as another's mark or so similar that confusion might result.

*Registration.* Historically, the first business that actually used a trademark in the marketplace owned it. Today, for national trademark protection, the business must be the first to register the trademark with the U.S. Patent and Trademark Office (PTO) in Washington, D.C. First use still takes some precedence over federal registration, however.

Suppose that you have used a particular trademark for two years but have not registered the mark with the PTO. If another company then registers the same mark with the PTO, you will probably have the traditional common law right to continue using that mark, but only in the geographic region in which you have been operating. Outside that region, the federal registrant will own the mark.

*Use of Symbols.* After registering your trademark, you must protect it. If your mark is federally registered, you may use the symbol ® with your mark. This well-known symbol puts others on notice of your registration and helps to prevent trademark infringement. Even if you have not registered, you can use the symbol ™ with your mark.

Five years after you initially register your mark, you should renew your registration with the PTO. Thereafter, you can renew at ten-year intervals. Filing for renewal informs the PTO that your mark is still in use and ensures that others cannot contest its validity.

**TRADE SECRETS** Much of the value of a business may lie in its trade secrets. As discussed in Chapter 8, trade secrets are business secrets that have value and might be appropriated by another company, such as a competitor. Trade secrets may include information concerning product development, production pro-

cesses and techniques, or customer lists. Preserving the secrecy of the information is necessary for legal protections.

As a practical matter, trade secrets must be divulged to key employees. Thus, any business runs the risk that those employees might disclose the secrets to competitors—or even set up competing businesses themselves. Generally, protecting against the possibility that valuable trade secrets will fall into the hands of others, especially competitors, presents an ongoing challenge for businesses, including new enterprises.

*Nondisclosure and Noncompete Agreements.* To protect their trade secrets, companies may require employees who have access to trade secrets to agree in their employment contracts never to divulge those secrets. A small business may also choose to include a covenant not to compete in an employment contract. A noncompete covenant will help to protect against the possibility that a key employee will go to work for a competitor or set up a competing business—situations in which the company's trade secrets will likely be disclosed.

*Misappropriation.* As discussed in Chapter 8, trade secrets are protected under the common law.[8] Thus, a company can sue an individual or a firm that has misappropriated its trade secrets. ▶ **Example 31.8** Two engineers, Gavin LaRue and Kaoru Matsuo, develop new software for their company, Tanaka Enterprises, LLP, in Chicago. Six months later, LaRue and Matsuo leave to work at KCI Technologies, LLC, a New York firm, where they develop a similar product. Tanaka sues. In this situation, a court may find that LaRue and Matsuo misappropriated Tanaka's trade secrets. ◀

## SECTION 6
# FINANCIAL CAPITAL

Raising financial capital is critical to the growth of most small businesses. In the early days of a business, the sole proprietor or partners may be able to contribute sufficient capital, but if the business becomes successful, more funds may be needed. The owner or owners may want to raise capital from external sources to expand the business. One way to do this is to borrow funds. Another is to exchange equity (ownership rights) in the company in return for funds,

---

**8.** The theft of trade secrets is also a federal crime under the Economic Espionage Act (see Chapter 10).

either through private arrangements or through public stock offerings.

## Loans

A small business may find it beneficial to obtain a bank loan because raising capital in this way allows the founder to retain full ownership and control of the business. Note, though, that the bank may place some restrictions on future business decisions as a condition of granting the loan.

In addition, bank loans may not be available for some businesses. Banks are usually reluctant to lend significant sums to businesses that are not yet established. Even if a bank is willing to make such a loan, the bank may require personal guaranty contracts from the owners, putting their personal assets at risk.

Loans with desirable terms may be available from the U.S. Small Business Administration (SBA). One SBA program provides loans of up to $25,000 to businesspersons who are women, low-income individuals, or members of minority groups. Be aware that the SBA requires business owners to put some of their own funds at risk in the business.

Some entrepreneurs have even used their credit cards to obtain initial capital. In addition, many states offer small-business grants to individuals starting a business.

## Venture Capital

As will be discussed in Chapter 32, many new businesses raise needed capital by exchanging equity in the firm for venture capital. In other words, an outsider contributes funds in exchange for an ownership interest in the company. **Venture capitalists,** often organized into major firms, seek out promising enterprises and fund them in exchange for equity stakes. Akin to venture capitalists are *angels*—that is, individuals who typically invest somewhat smaller sums in new businesses.

**THE PROS AND CONS OF VENTURE CAPITAL FINANCING**
In addition to providing needed financing, venture capitalists offer other advantages for businesses. Venture capitalists are often experienced managers who can provide invaluable assistance to entrepreneurs with respect to strategic business decisions, marketing, and important business contacts. Obtaining this assistance may be crucial to a new company's success.

The disadvantage is that a venture capitalist with a substantial equity stake will demand a corresponding degree of operational control over the company and a similar proportion of future profits.

**REQUIRES A BUSINESS PLAN** To attract outside venture capital, you will need a **business plan** that describes the company, its products, and its anticipated future performance. The plan should be relatively concise (typically fewer than fifty pages). After considering your plan, a venture capitalist may decide to investigate your venture further. This step may require you to disclose trade secrets, and you should insist that the potential investor sign a confidentiality agreement. If all goes well, you will then negotiate the terms of financing. A key point to be negotiated is how much ownership and control the venture capitalist will receive in exchange for the capital contribution.

## Crowdfunding

Although venture capitalists are a source of financing for young companies, there are not enough venture capitalists to fund all of the small businesses looking for help. Now, start-ups that are unable to attract venture capitalists have a new way to obtain funding—crowdfunding.

**Crowdfunding** is a cooperative activity in which people network and pool funds and other resources via the Internet to assist a cause or invest in a venture. Sometimes, crowdfunding is used to raise funds for charitable purposes, such as disaster relief, but increasingly it is being used to finance budding entrepreneurs. Several rock bands have financed tours in this way, and now ventures of all kinds are trying to raise funds through crowdfunding.

**SPECIALIZED CROWDFUNDING SITES** In a very short time, crowdfunding Web sites have proliferated. They offer partial ownership of start-ups in exchange for cash investments. At first, there were mostly general-purpose sites, such as Profounder.com and Startup Addict, but now the sites have become specialized. If you are interested only in new mobile apps, for example, you can go to the Apps Funder (**www.appsfunder.com**).

As you might imagine, many of the apps are games, but this site also has a serious side. For instance, one new app that was funded involves sharing music scores. Another site, NewJelly (**www.newjelly.com**), raises funds for "dream" projects for artists and filmmakers.

**LESS REGULATION ENCOURAGES CROWDFUNDING**
Crowdfunding has taken off in many other countries, including France and Germany. Other countries'

investor protection laws and regulations are often less stringent than U.S. laws, so many future crowdfunding sites are likely to be based abroad.

In 2012, President Barack Obama signed the JOBS Act (the acronym stands for "Jump-start Our Business Start-ups"), which relieved some regulatory burdens. Before this legislation, start-ups could look for financing only from investors who were "accredited," meaning that they had investment experience and

a high net worth. If companies sought investment funds from the general public, they had to meet expensive and lengthy disclosure requirements. In 2013, the Securities and Exchange Commission removed the decades-old ban on public solicitation for private investments. In essence, this means that companies finally can advertise investment opportunities to the public, which will encourage growth of crowdfunding.

## Reviewing: Other Organizational Forms for Small Businesses

The city of Papagos, Arizona, had a deteriorating bridge in need of repair on a prominent public roadway. The city posted notices seeking proposals for an artistic bridge design and reconstruction. Davidson Masonry, LLC, which was owned and managed by Carl Davidson and his wife, Marilyn Rowe, decided to submit a bid to create a decorative concrete structure that incorporated artistic metalwork. They contacted Shana Lafayette, a local sculptor who specialized in large-scale metal creations, to help them design the bridge. The city selected their bridge design and awarded them the contract for a commission of $184,000. Davidson Masonry and Lafayette then entered into an agreement to work together on the bridge project. Davidson Masonry agreed to install and pay for concrete and structural work, and Lafayette agreed to install the metalwork at her expense. They agreed that overall profits would be split, with 25 percent going to Lafayette and 75 percent going to Davidson Masonry. Lafayette designed numerous metal sculptures of trout that were incorporated into colorful decorative concrete forms designed by Rowe, while Davidson performed the structural engineering. The group worked together successfully until the completion of the project. Using the information presented in the chapter, answer the following questions.

1. Would Davidson Masonry automatically be taxed as a partnership or a corporation?
2. Is Davidson Masonry member managed or manager managed?
3. When Davidson Masonry and Lafayette entered an agreement to work together, what kind of special business form was created? Explain.
4. Suppose that during construction, Lafayette had entered into an agreement to rent space in a warehouse that was close to the bridge so that she could work on her sculptures near the site where they would eventually be installed. She entered into the contract without the knowledge or consent of Davidson Masonry. In this situation, would a court be likely to hold that Davidson Masonry was bound by the contract that Lafayette entered? Why or why not?

**DEBATE THIS...** *Because LLCs are essentially just partnerships with limited liability for members, all partnership laws should apply.*

## Terms and Concepts

## Issue Spotters

1. Gabriel, Harris, and Ida are members of Jeweled Watches, LLC. What are their options with respect to the management of their firm? **(See page 546.)**

2. Greener Delivery Company and Hiway Trucking, Inc., form a business trust. Insta Equipment Company and Jiffy Supply Corporation form a joint stock company.

Kwik Mart, Inc., and Luscious Produce, Inc., form an incorporated cooperative. What do these forms of business organization have in common? **(See page 550.)**

• **Check your answers to the Issue Spotters against the answers provided in Appendix E at the end of this text.**

## Business Scenarios

**31–1. Limited Liability Companies.** John, Lesa, and Tabir form a limited liability company. John contributes 60 percent of the capital, and Lesa and Tabir each contribute 20 percent. Nothing is decided about how profits will be divided. John assumes that he will be entitled to 60 percent of the profits, in accordance with his contribution. Lesa and Tabir, however, assume that the profits will be divided equally. A dispute over the profits arises, and ultimately a court has to decide the issue. What law will the court apply? In most states, what will result? How could this dispute have been avoided in the first place? Discuss fully. **(See page 547.)**

**31–2. Special Business Forms.** Bateson Corp. is considering entering into two contracts—one with a joint stock company that distributes home products east of the Mississippi River and the other with a business trust formed by a number of sole proprietors who are sellers of home products on the West Coast. Both contracts will require Bateson to make large capital outlays in order to supply the businesses with restaurant equipment. In both business organizations, at least two shareholders or beneficiaries are personally wealthy, but both organizations have limited financial resources. The owner-managers of Bateson are not familiar with either form of business organization. Because each form resembles a corporation, they are concerned about potential limits on liability in the event that either business organization breaches the contract by failing to pay for the equipment. Discuss fully Bateson's concern. **(See page 550.)**

## Business Case Problems

**31–3. Joint Venture.** Holiday Isle Resort & Marina, Inc., operated four restaurants, five bars, and various food kiosks at its resort in Islamorada, Florida. Holiday entered into a "joint-venture agreement" with Rip Tosun to operate a fifth restaurant called "Rip's—A Place for Ribs." The agreement gave Tosun authority over the employees and "full authority as to the conduct of the business." It also prohibited Tosun from competing with Rip's without Holiday's approval but did not prevent Holiday from competing. Later, Tosun sold half of his interest in Rip's to Thomas Hallock.

Soon, Tosun and Holiday opened the Olde Florida Steakhouse next to Rip's. Holiday stopped serving breakfast at Rip's and diverted employees and equipment from Rip's to the Steakhouse, which then started offering breakfast. Hallock filed a suit in a Florida state court against Holiday. Did Holiday breach the joint-venture agreement? Did it breach the duties that joint venturers owe each other? Explain. [*Hallock v. Holiday Isle Resort & Marina, Inc.,* 4 So.3d 17 (Fla.App. 3 Dist. 2009)] **(See page 550.)**

**31–4. Limited Liability Companies.** Coco Investments, LLC, and other investors participated in a condominium conversion project to be managed by Zamir Manager River Terrace, LLC. The participants entered into a new LLC

agreement for the project. The investors subsequently complained that Zamir had failed to disclose its plans for dramatic changes involving higher-than-expected construction costs and delays, had failed to provide financial information, and had restructured loans in a manner that allowed Zamir representatives to avoid personal liability. The investors sued Zamir on various grounds, including breach of contract and breach of fiduciary duty. Zamir moved for summary judgment. How should the court rule? Explain. [*Coco Investments, LLC v. Zamir Manager River Terrace, LLC,* 26 Misc.3d 1231 (N.Y.Sup. 2010)] **(See page 546.)**

**31–5. LLC Dissolution.** Walter Van Houten and John King formed 1545 Ocean Avenue, LLC, with each managing 50 percent of the business. Its purpose was to renovate an existing building and construct a new commercial building. Van Houten and King quarreled over many aspects of the work on the properties. King claimed that Van Houten paid the contractors too much for the work performed.

As the projects neared completion, King demanded that the LLC be dissolved and that Van Houten agree to a buyout. Because the parties could not agree on a buyout, King sued for dissolution. The trial court enjoined (prevented) further work on the projects until the dispute was settled. As the ground for dissolution, King cited the fights over management decisions. There was no claim of fraud or frustration of purpose. The trial court ordered that the LLC be dissolved, and Van Houten appealed. Should either of the owners be forced to dissolve the LLC before the completion of its purpose—that is, before the building projects are finished? Explain. [*In re 1545 Ocean Avenue, LLC*, 893 N.Y.S.2d 590 (N.Y.A.D. 2 Dept. 2010)] **(See page 548.)**

### 31–6. BUSINESS CASE PROBLEM WITH SAMPLE ANSWER: LLC Operation.

*After Hurricane Katrina, James Williford, Patricia Mosser, Marquetta Smith, and Michael Floyd formed Bluewater Logistics, LLC, to bid on construction contracts. Under Mississippi law, every member of a member-managed LLC is entitled to participate in managing the business. The operating agreement provided for a "super majority" 75 percent vote to remove a member "under any other circumstances that would jeopardize the company status" as a contractor. After Bluewater had completed more than $5 million in con- tracts, Smith told Williford that she, Mosser, and Floyd were exercising their "super majority" vote to fire him. No reason was provided. Williford sued Bluewater and the other members. Did Smith, Mosser, and Floyd breach the state LLC statute, their fiduciary duties, or the Bluewater operating agreements? Discuss.* [Bluewater Logistics, LLC v. Williford, 55 So.3d 148 (Miss. 2011)] **(See page 546.)**

• **For a sample answer to Problem 31–6, go to Appendix F at the end of this text.**

**31–7. Jurisdictional Requirements.** Fadal Machining Centers, LLC, and MAG Industrial Automation Centers, LLC, sued a New Jersey–based corporation, Mid-Atlantic CNC, Inc., in federal district court. Ten percent of MAG was owned by SP MAG Holdings, a Delaware LLC. SP MAG had six members, including a Delaware limited partnership called Silver Point Capital Fund and a Delaware LLC called SPCP Group III. In turn, Silver Point and SPCP Group had a common member, Robert O'Shea, who was a New Jersey citizen. Assuming that the amount in controversy exceeds

$75,000, does the district court have diversity jurisdiction? Why or why not? [*Fadal Machining Centers, LLC v. Mid-Atlantic CNC, Inc.*, 2012 WL 8669 (9th Cir. 2012)] **(See page 545.)**

### 31–8. A QUESTION OF ETHICS: Limited Liability Companies.

*Blushing Brides, LLC, a publisher of wedding planning magazines in Columbus, Ohio, opened an account with Gray Printing Co. in July 2000. On behalf of Blushing Brides, Louis Zacks, the firm's member-manager, signed a credit agreement that identified the firm as the "purchaser" and required payment within thirty days. Despite the agreement, Blushing Brides typically took up to six months to pay the full amount for its orders. Gray printed and shipped 10,000 copies of a fall/winter 2001 issue for Blushing Brides but had not been paid when the firm ordered 15,000 copies of a spring/summer 2002 issue. Gray refused to print the new order without an assurance of payment. On May 22, Zacks signed a promissory note payable to Gray within thirty days for $14,778, plus interest at 6 percent per year. Gray printed the new order but by October had been paid only $7,500. Gray filed a suit in an Ohio state court against Blushing Brides and Zacks to collect the balance.* [Gray Printing Co. v. Blushing Brides, LLC, 2006 WL 832587 (Ohio App. 2006)] **(See page 543.)**

(a) Under what circumstances is a member of an LLC liable for the firm's debts? In this case, is Zacks personally liable under the credit agreement for the unpaid amount on Blushing Brides' account? Did Zacks's promissory note affect the parties' liability on the account? Explain.

(b) Should a member of an LLC assume an ethical responsibility to meet the obligations of the firm? Discuss.

(c) Gray shipped only 10,000 copies of the spring/summer 2002 issue of Blushing Brides' magazine, waiting for the publisher to identify a destination for the other 5,000 copies. The magazine had a retail price of $4.50 per copy. Did Gray have a legal or ethical duty to "mitigate the damages" by attempting to sell or otherwise distribute these copies itself? Why or why not?

## Legal Reasoning Group Activity

**31–9. Fiduciary Duties in LLCs.** Newbury Properties Group owns, manages, and develops real property. Jerry Stoker and the Stoker Group, Inc. (the Stokers), also develop real property. Newbury entered into agreements with the Stokers concerning a large tract of property in Georgia. The parties formed Bellemare, LLC, to develop various parcels of the tract for residential purposes. The operating agreement of Bellemare indicated that "no Member shall be accountable to the LLC or to any other Member with respect to any other business or activity even if the business or activity competes with the LLC's business." Later,

when the Newbury group contracted with other parties to develop parcels within the tract in competition with Bellemare, LLC, the Stokers sued, alleging breach of fiduciary duty. **(See page 546.)**

(a) The first group will discuss and outline the fiduciary duties that the members of an LLC owe to each other.

(b) The second group will determine whether the terms of an operating agreement can alter these fiduciary duties.

(c) The last group will decide in whose favor the court should rule in this situation.

## CHAPTER 32

# CORPORATE FORMATION AND FINANCING

The corporation is a creature of statute. A corporation is an artificial being, existing only in law and neither tangible nor visible. Its existence generally depends on state law, although some corporations, especially public organizations, are created under federal law. Each state has its own body of corporate law, and these laws are not entirely uniform.

The Model Business Corporation Act (MBCA) is a codification of modern corporation law that has been influential in shaping state corporation statutes. Today, the majority of state statutes are guided by the most recent version of the MBCA, often referred to as the Revised Model Business Corporation Act (RMBCA).

Keep in mind, however, that there is considerable variation among the laws of states that have used the MBCA or the RMBCA as a basis for their statutes. In addition, several states do not follow either act. Consequently, individual state corporation laws should be relied on to determine corporate law rather than the MBCA or RMBCA.

## SECTION 1
## THE NATURE AND CLASSIFICATION OF CORPORATIONS

A corporation is a legal entity created and recognized by state law. This business entity can have one or more owners (called shareholders), and it operates under a name distinct from the names of its owners. The owners may be individuals, or *natural persons* (as opposed to the artificial *legal person* of the corporation), or other businesses. Although the corporation substitutes itself for its shareholders when conducting corporate business and incurring liability, its authority to act and the liability for its actions are separate and apart from the individuals who own it.

A corporation is recognized as a "person," and it enjoys many of the same rights and privileges under state and federal law that U.S. citizens enjoy. For instance, corporations possess the same right of access to the courts as citizens and can sue or be sued. The constitutional guarantees of due process, free speech, and freedom from unreasonable searches and seizures also apply to corporations.

## Corporate Personnel

In a corporation, the responsibility for the overall management of the firm is entrusted to a *board of directors,* whose members are elected by the shareholders. The board of directors makes the policy decisions and hires *corporate officers* and other employees to run the daily business operations of the corporation.

When an individual purchases a share of stock in a corporation, that person becomes a shareholder and an owner of the corporation. Unlike the partners in a partnership, the body of shareholders can change constantly without affecting the continued existence of the corporation.

A shareholder can sue the corporation, and the corporation can sue a shareholder. Additionally, under certain circumstances, a shareholder can sue on behalf of a corporation.

## The Limited Liability of Shareholders

One of the key advantages of the corporate form is the limited liability of its owners. Normally, corporate shareholders are not personally liable for the obligations of the corporation beyond the extent of their investments.

In certain limited situations, however, a court can *pierce the corporate veil* (see page 572) and impose liability on shareholders for the corporation's obligations. Additionally, creditors often will not extend credit to small companies unless the shareholders assume personal liability, as guarantors, for corporate obligations.

## Corporate Earnings and Taxation

When a corporation earns profits, it can either pass them on to shareholders in the form of **dividends** or retain them as profits. These **retained earnings,** if invested properly, will yield higher corporate profits in the future and thus cause the price of the company's stock to rise. Individual shareholders can then reap the benefits of these retained earnings in the capital gains that they receive when they sell their stock.

**CORPORATE TAXATION** Whether a corporation retains its profits or passes them on to the shareholders as dividends, those profits are subject to income tax by various levels of government. Failure to pay taxes can lead to severe consequences. The state can suspend the entity's corporate status until the taxes are paid or even dissolve the corporation for failing to pay taxes. (Businesses today, including corporations, may also be required to collect state sales taxes on goods or services sold via the Internet, as discussed in the *Insight into E-Commerce* feature in Chapter 20.)

Another important aspect of corporate taxation is that corporate profits can be subject to double taxation. The company pays tax on its profits. Then, if the profits are passed on to the shareholders as dividends, the shareholders must also pay income tax on them (unless the dividends represent distributions of capital). The corporation normally does not receive a tax deduction for dividends it distributes. This double-taxation feature is one of the major disadvantages of the corporate form.

**HOLDING COMPANIES** Some U.S. corporations use holding companies to reduce or defer their U.S. income taxes. At its simplest, a **holding company** (sometimes referred to as a *parent company*) is a company whose business activity consists of holding shares in another company. Typically, the holding company is established in a low-tax or no-tax offshore jurisdiction, such as the Cayman Islands, Dubai, Hong Kong, Luxembourg, Monaco, or Panama.

Sometimes, a U.S. corporation sets up a holding company in a low-tax offshore environment and then transfers its cash, bonds, stocks, and other investments to the holding company. In general, any profits received by the holding company on these investments are taxed at the rate of the offshore jurisdiction where the company is registered. In other words, holding company profits are not taxed at the rates applicable to the parent company or its shareholders in their country of residence. Thus, deposits of cash, for instance, may earn interest that is taxed at only a minimal rate.

Once the profits are brought "onshore," though, they are taxed at the federal corporate income tax rate, and any payments received by the shareholders are also taxable at the full U.S. rates.

## Tort Liability

A corporation is liable for the torts committed by its agents or officers within the course and scope of their employment. This principle applies to a corporation exactly as it applies to the ordinary agency relationships discussed in Chapter 26. It follows the doctrine of *respondeat superior.*

The following case arose from a fraudulent scheme perpetrated by the officer of an investment firm through a separate investment fund that the officer controlled and managed. When investors in the fund filed a suit to recover the funds they had lost, the court had to determine whether the corporate employer of the officer could be liable for his actions.

## CASE 32.1

### Belmont v. MB Investment Partners, Inc.
United States Court of Appeals, Third Circuit, 708 F.3d 470 (2013).

**BACKGROUND AND FACTS** In 1997, Mark Bloom formed North Hills, LP, as a stock investment fund. Bloom had sole authority over the fund's investments. Between 2001 and 2007, Bloom raised nearly $30 million from investors for the fund. At the time, Bloom was also an investment adviser and an officer and a director of MB Investment Partners, Inc. Investments in North Hills were administered by Bloom and

CASE 32.1 CONTINUES ▶

CASE 32.1 CONTINUED other MB personnel, using MB's offices, computers, filing facilities, and office equipment. MB officers and directors were aware that Bloom was operating North Hills while he was also working at MB. In 2008, two investors in North Hills requested a full redemption of their investments. By that time, however, most of the money that had been invested in North Hills was gone. Bloom was arrested, and MB terminated him. Barry Belmont and other North Hills Investors filed a suit in a federal district court against MB, alleging fraud. From a summary judgment in MB's favor, the investors appealed.

**DECISION AND RATIONALE** The U.S. Court of Appeals for the Third Circuit vacated the summary judgment in MB's favor and remanded the case for trial with respect to the investors' claims against MB. Liability can be attributed to a corporation for the acts of its agent committed within the scope of his or her authority.

The appellate court pointed out that the North Hills investment vehicle was a Ponzi scheme that Bloom used to finance his lavish personal lifestyle. Over time, he diverted at least $20 million dollars from North Hills for his own personal use. During this period, MB "did not have in place basic compliance procedures employed throughout the investment advising industry to identify and prevent fraud and self–dealing by MB employees and affiliates." Further, "MB officers and directors failed to make basic inquiries about Bloom's operation of North Hills, and did not collect any information on North Hills or monitor sales of investments in North Hills to MB's own customers."

Whenever the fraud of an officer of a corporation is involved, it is imputed to the corporation when the officer's fraudulent contact was in the course of his employment and for the benefit of the corporation. It did not matter that Bloom's conduct was unauthorized. His conduct was "clothed with apparent authority of the corporation."

**THE LEGAL ENVIRONMENT DIMENSION** *What circumstances in this case suggest that MB should be held liable for Bloom's fraud?*

**THE SOCIAL DIMENSION** *MB, which was already in financial distress, had to cease operations as a result of Bloom's fraud. How might MB have discovered the fraud before it grew so large as to have such dire effects?*

---

## Criminal Acts

Under modern criminal law (see Chapter 10), a corporation may also be held liable for the criminal acts of its agents and employees, provided the punishment is one that can be applied to the corporation. Although corporations cannot be imprisoned, they can be fined. (Of course, corporate directors and officers can be imprisoned, and some have been in recent years.) In addition, under sentencing guidelines for crimes committed by corporate employees (white-collar crimes), corporate lawbreakers can face fines amounting to hundreds of millions of dollars.[1]

▶ **Case in Point 32.1** Brian Gauthier drove a dump truck for Angelo Todesca Corporation. The truck was missing its back-up alarm, but Angelo allowed Gauthier to continue driving it. At a worksite, Gauthier backed up to dump a load and struck and killed a police officer who was directing traffic. The state charged Angelo and Gauthier with the crime of vehicular homicide.

Angelo argued that a corporation could not be guilty of vehicular homicide because it cannot operate a vehicle. The court ruled that if an employee commits a crime "while engaged in corporate business that the employee has been authorized to conduct," the corporation can be held liable for the crime. Hence, the court held that Angelo Todesca Corporation was liable for Gauthier's negligent operation of its truck, which resulted in a person's death.[2] ◀

## Classification of Corporations

Corporations can be classified in several ways. The classification of a corporation normally depends on its location, purpose, and ownership characteristics, as described in the following subsections.

---

**1.** Note that the Sarbanes-Oxley Act of 2002 (see Chapter 5) stiffened the penalties for certain types of corporate crime and ordered the U.S. Sentencing Commission to revise the sentencing guidelines accordingly.

**2.** *Commonwealth v. Angelo Todesca Corp.*, 446 Mass. 128, 842 N.E.2d 930 (2006).

**DOMESTIC, FOREIGN, AND ALIEN CORPORATIONS** A corporation is referred to as a **domestic corporation** by its home state (the state in which it incorporates). A corporation formed in one state but doing business in another is referred to in the second state as a **foreign corporation.** A corporation formed in another country (say, Mexico) but doing business in the United States is referred to in the United States as an **alien corporation.**

A corporation does not have an automatic right to do business in a state other than its state of incorporation. In some instances, it must obtain a *certificate of authority* in any state in which it plans to do business. Once the certificate has been issued, the corporation generally can exercise in that state all of the powers conferred on it by its home state. If a foreign corporation does business in a state without obtaining a certificate of authority, the state can impose substantial fines and sanctions on that corporation.

Note that most state statutes specify certain activities, such as soliciting orders via the Internet, that are not considered "doing business" within the state. Thus, a foreign corporation normally does not need a certificate of authority to sell goods or services via the Internet or by mail.

**PUBLIC AND PRIVATE CORPORATIONS** A **public corporation** is a corporation formed by the government to meet some political or governmental purpose. Cities and towns that incorporate are common examples. In addition, many federal government organizations, such as the U.S. Postal Service, the Tennessee Valley Authority, and AMTRAK, are public corporations.

Note that a public corporation is not the same as a *publicly held* corporation. A **publicly held corporation** (often called a *public company*) is any corporation whose shares are publicly traded in a securities market, such as the New York Stock Exchange or the NASDAQ (an electronic stock exchange founded by the National Association of Securities Dealers).

In contrast to public corporations (*not* public companies), private corporations are created either wholly or in part for private benefit—that is, for profit. Most corporations are private. Although they may serve a public purpose, as a public electric or gas utility does, they are owned by private persons rather than by a government.[3]

**NONPROFIT CORPORATIONS** Corporations formed for purposes other than making a profit are called *nonprofit* or *not-for-profit* corporations. Private hospitals, educational institutions, charities, and religious organizations, for example, are frequently organized as nonprofit corporations. The nonprofit corporation is a convenient form of organization that allows various groups to own property and to form contracts without exposing the individual members to personal liability.

**CLOSE CORPORATIONS** Most corporate enterprises in the United States fall into the category of close corporations. A **close corporation** is one whose shares are held by members of a family or by relatively few persons. Close corporations are also referred to as *closely held, family,* or *privately held* corporations. Usually, the members of the small group constituting the shareholders of a close corporation are personally known to each other. Because the number of shareholders is so small, there is no trading market for the shares.

In practice, a close corporation is often operated like a partnership. Some states have enacted special statutory provisions that apply to these corporations and allow them to depart significantly from certain formalities required by traditional corporation law.[4]

Additionally, the RMBCA gives a close corporation considerable flexibility in determining its rules of operation [RMBCA 7.32]. If all of a corporation's shareholders agree in writing, the corporation can operate without directors and bylaws. In addition, the corporation can operate without annual or special shareholders' or directors' meetings, stock certificates, or formal records of shareholders' or directors' decisions.[5]

***Management of Close Corporations.*** Management of a close corporation resembles that of a sole proprietorship or a partnership, in that a single shareholder or a tightly knit group of shareholders usually hold the positions of directors and officers. As a corporation, however, the firm must meet all specific legal requirements set forth in state statutes.

To prevent a majority shareholder from dominating the company, a close corporation may require that more than a simple majority of the directors approve any action taken by the board. Typically, this would apply only to extraordinary actions, such as changing

**3.** The United States Supreme Court first recognized the property rights of private corporations and clarified the distinction between public and private corporations in the landmark case *Trustees of Dartmouth College v. Woodward,* 17 U.S. (4 Wheaton) 518, 4 L.Ed. 629 (1819).

**4.** For example, in some states (such as Maryland), a close corporation need not have a board of directors.

**5.** Shareholders cannot agree, however, to eliminate certain rights of shareholders, such as the right to inspect corporate books and records or the right to bring *derivative actions* (lawsuits on behalf of the corporation).

the amount of dividends or dismissing an employee-shareholder, and not to ordinary business decisions.

**Transfer of Shares in Close Corporations.** By definition, a close corporation has a small number of shareholders. Thus, the transfer of one shareholder's shares to someone else can cause serious management problems. The other shareholders may find themselves required to share control with someone they do not know or like.

▶ **Example 32.2**   Three brothers, Terry, Damon, and Henry Johnson, are the only shareholders of Johnson's Car Wash, Inc. Terry and Damon do not want Henry to sell his shares to an unknown third person. To avoid this situation, the corporation could restrict the transferability of shares to outside persons. Shareholders could be required to offer their shares to the corporation or the other shareholders before selling them to an outside purchaser.

In fact, a few states have statutes that prohibit the transfer of close corporation shares unless certain persons—including shareholders, family members, and the corporation—are first given the opportunity to purchase the shares for the same price. ◀

**Shareholder Agreement to Restrict Stock Transfers.** Control of a close corporation can also be stabilized through the use of a *shareholder agreement.* A shareholder agreement can provide for proportional control when one of the original shareholders dies. The decedent's shares of stock in the corporation would be divided in such a way that the proportionate holdings of the survivors, and thus their proportionate control, would be maintained.

Agreements between shareholders can also restrict the transfer of a close corporation's stock in other ways. For instance, shareholders might agree that existing shareholders will have an option to purchase stock before it is sold or transferred to an outside party.

**Misappropriation of Close Corporation Funds.** Sometimes, a majority shareholder in a close corporation takes advantage of his or her position and misappropriates company funds. In such situations, the normal remedy for the injured minority shareholders is to have their shares appraised and to be paid the fair market value for them.

In the following case, a minority shareholder alleged that the majority shareholders paid themselves excessive compensation in breach of their fiduciary duty.

---

## CASE 32.2

### Rubin v. Murray
Appeals Court of Massachusetts, 79 Mass.App.Ct. 64, 943 N.E.2d 949 (2011).

**BACKGROUND AND FACTS**   Olympic Adhesives, Inc., makes and sells industrial adhesives. John Murray, Stephen Hopkins, and Paul Ryan were the controlling shareholders of the company, as well as officers, directors, and employees. Merek Rubin was a minority shareholder. Murray, Hopkins, and Ryan were paid salaries. Under Olympic's profit-sharing plan, one-third of its net operating income was paid into a fund that was distributed to employees, including Murray, Hopkins, and Ryan.

Twice a year, Murray, Hopkins, and Ryan also paid themselves additional compensation—a percentage of the net profits after profit sharing, allocated according to their stock ownership. Over a fifteen-year period, the percentage grew from 75 percent to between 92 and 98 percent. During this time, the additional compensation totaled nearly $15 million. Rubin filed a suit in a Massachusetts state court against Murray, Hopkins, and Ryan, alleging that they had paid themselves excessive compensation and deprived him of his share of Olympic's profits in violation of their fiduciary duty to him as a minority shareholder. The court ordered the defendants to repay Olympic nearly $6 million to be distributed among its shareholders. The defendants appealed.

**DECISION AND RATIONALE**   A state intermediate appellate court affirmed the lower court's judgment. The trial court had discretion to determine what constituted reasonable compensation for the defendants, and its findings were based on sufficient evidence. The compensation of these majority shareholders was excessive and deprived Rubin of his share of Olympic profits in breach of their fiduciary duty to him as a minority shareholder.

**CASE 32.2 CONTINUED**    The reviewing court reasoned that a salary should reasonably relate to a corporate officer's ability and the quantity and quality of services the officer renders. Profits resulting from an officer's performance may also affect the amount of compensation. In this case, the trial judge found that a reasonable amount of compensation for each officer would have been 4 to 7 percent of net sales, plus a "success premium" related to individual contributions, for a total of 10 percent of Olympic's average annual net sales. This amount was comparable to the average compensation for officers in similar firms. The appellate court also pointed out that Murray was vague when he attempted to explain the basis for distributing the profits among the defendants. Those amounts seemed to correspond only to the percentage of the officers' stock ownership, rather than to any aspect of their performance.

**WHAT IF THE FACTS WERE DIFFERENT?**  *Suppose that Murray could have pinpointed a job-related basis for the distribution of the net profits among the defendants. Would the result have been different? Explain.*

**THE ECONOMIC DIMENSION**  *What are the tax consequences of passing corporate profits on to shareholders as dividends?*

---

**S CORPORATIONS**  A close corporation that meets the qualifying requirements specified in Subchapter S of the Internal Revenue Code can choose to operate as an **S corporation.** (A corporation will automatically be taxed under Subchapter C unless it elects S corporation status.) If a corporation has S corporation status, it can avoid the imposition of income taxes at the corporate level while retaining many of the advantages of a corporation, particularly limited liability.

**Important Requirements.** Among the numerous requirements for S corporation status, the following are the most important:

1. The corporation must be a domestic corporation.
2. The corporation must not be a member of an affiliated group of corporations.
3. The shareholders of the corporation must be individuals, estates, or certain trusts and tax-exempt organizations.
4. The corporation must have no more than one hundred shareholders.
5. The corporation must have only one class of stock, although all shareholders do not need to have the same voting rights.
6. No shareholder of the corporation may be a nonresident alien.

**Effect of S Election.** An S corporation is treated differently than a regular corporation for tax purposes. An S corporation is taxed like a partnership, so the corporate income passes through to the shareholders, who pay personal income tax on it. This treatment enables the S corporation to avoid the double taxation imposed on regular corporations.

In addition, the shareholders' tax brackets may be lower than the tax bracket that the corporation would have been in if the tax had been imposed at the corporate level. The resulting tax saving is particularly attractive when the corporation wants to accumulate earnings for some future business purpose. If the corporation has losses, the S election allows the shareholders to use the losses to offset other income.

Nevertheless, because the limited liability company (see Chapter 31) and the limited liability partnership (see Chapter 30) offer similar tax advantages and greater flexibility, the S corporation has lost much of its appeal.

**PROFESSIONAL CORPORATIONS**  Professionals such as physicians, lawyers, dentists, and accountants can incorporate. Professional corporations are typically identified by the letters *P.C.* (professional corporation), *S.C.* (service corporation), or *P.A.* (professional association).

In general, the laws governing the formation and operation of professional corporations are similar to those governing ordinary business corporations. There are some differences in terms of liability, however, because the shareholder-owners are professionals who are held to a higher standard of conduct.

For liability purposes, some courts treat a professional corporation somewhat like a partnership and hold each professional liable for any malpractice committed within the scope of the business by the others in the firm. With the exception of malpractice or a breach of duty to clients or patients, a shareholder in a professional corporation generally cannot be held liable for the torts committed by other professionals at the firm.

**BENEFIT CORPORATIONS** A growing number of states have enacted legislation that creates a new corporate form called a *benefit corporation*. A **benefit corporation** is a for-profit corporation that seeks to have a material positive impact on society and the environment. Benefit corporations differ from traditional corporations in the following three ways:

1. *Purpose.* Although the corporation is designed to make a profit, its purpose is to benefit the public as a whole (rather than just to provide long-term shareholder value, as in ordinary corporations). The directors of a benefit corporation must, during the decision-making process, consider the impact of their decisions on society and the environment.
2. *Accountability.* Shareholders of a benefit corporation determine whether the company has achieved a material positive impact. Shareholders also have a right of private action, called a *benefit enforcement*

*proceeding,* enabling them to sue the corporation if it fails to pursue or create public benefit.
3. *Transparency.* A benefit corporation must issue an annual benefit report on its overall social and environmental performance that uses a recognized third-party standard to assess its performance. The report must be delivered to the shareholders and posted on a public Web site.

See *Concept Summary 32.1* below for a review of the ways in which corporations are classified.

## SECTION 2
# CORPORATE FORMATION

Many Fortune 500 companies started as sole proprietorships or partnerships and then converted to cor-

## CONCEPT SUMMARY 32.1
### Classification of Corporations

| CLASSIFICATION | DESCRIPTION |
| --- | --- |
| **Domestic, Foreign, and Alien Corporations** | A corporation is referred to as a *domestic corporation* in its home state (the state in which it incorporates). A corporation is referred to as a *foreign corporation* by any state that is not its home state. A corporation is referred to as an *alien corporation* if it originates in another country but does business in the United States. |
| **Public and Private Corporations** | A *public corporation* is formed by a government (for example, a city, town, or public project). A *private corporation* is formed wholly or in part for private benefit. Most corporations are private corporations. |
| **Nonprofit Corporation** | A corporation formed without a profit-making purpose (for example, charitable, educational, and religious organizations and hospitals). |
| **Close Corporation** | A corporation that is owned by a family or a relatively small number of individuals. Because the number of shareholders is small and the transfer of shares is usually restricted, the shares are not traded in a public securities market. (Sometimes called a closely held corporation.) |
| **S Corporation** | A small domestic corporation (must have no more than one hundred shareholders) that, under Subchapter S of the Internal Revenue Code, is given special tax treatment. S corporations allow shareholders to enjoy the limited legal liability of the corporate form but avoid its double-taxation feature. (Shareholders pay taxes on the income at personal income tax rates, and the S corporation is not taxed separately.) |
| **Professional Corporation** | A corporation formed by professionals (for instance, physicians or lawyers) to obtain the advantages of incorporation (such as tax benefits and limited liability). A professional corporation functions like an ordinary corporation but is treated differently in terms of liability. Courts may treat the shareholders like partners with regard to malpractice liability. |
| **Benefit Corporation** | A type of corporation designed for businesses that want to consider society and the environment in addition to profit. Shareholders have a right to sue the corporation in enforcement proceedings if it fails to benefit the public. The corporation must issue annual benefit reports. |

porate entities as the businesses grew and needed to obtain additional capital by issuing shares of stock. Incorporating a business is much simpler today than it was twenty years ago, and many states allow businesses to incorporate via the Internet. Here, we examine the process by which a corporation comes into existence. (Corporate financing will be discussed later in this chapter.)

## Promotional Activities

In the past, preliminary steps were taken to organize and promote the business prior to incorporating. Contracts were made with investors and others on behalf of the future corporation. Today, due to the relative ease of forming a corporation in most states, persons incorporating their business rarely, if ever, engage in preliminary promotional activities.

Nevertheless, it is important for businesspersons to understand that they are personally liable for all preincorporation contracts made with investors, accountants, or others on behalf of the future corporation. Personal liability continues until the newly formed corporation assumes liability for the preincorporation contracts through a *novation* (see Chapter 18).

▶ **Example 32.3** Jade Sorrel contracts with an accountant, Ray Cooper, to provide tax advice for a proposed corporation, Blackstone, Inc. Cooper provides the services to Sorrel, knowing that the corporation has not yet been formed. Once Blackstone, Inc., is formed, Cooper sends an invoice to the corporation and to Sorrel personally, but the bill is not paid.

Because Sorrel is personally liable for the preincorporation contract, Cooper can sue Sorrel for breach of the contract. Cooper cannot seek to hold Blackstone, Inc., liable unless he has entered into a contract with the corporation through a novation. ◀

## Incorporation Procedures

Exact procedures for incorporation differ among states, but the basic steps are as follows: (1) select a state of incorporation, (2) secure the corporate name, (3) prepare the articles of incorporation, and (4) file the articles of incorporation with the secretary of state. These steps are discussed in more detail in the following subsections.

**SELECT THE STATE OF INCORPORATION** The first step in the incorporation process is to select a state in which to incorporate. Because state laws differ, individuals

may look for the states that offer the most advantageous tax or incorporation provisions. Another consideration is the fee that a particular state charges to incorporate, as well as the annual fees and the fees for specific transactions (such as stock transfers).

Delaware has historically had the least restrictive laws and provisions that favor corporate management. Consequently, many corporations, including a number of the largest, have incorporated there. Delaware's statutes permit firms to incorporate in that state and conduct business and locate their operating headquarters elsewhere. Most other states now permit this as well.

Note, though, that close corporations, particularly those of a professional nature, generally incorporate in the state where their principal shareholders live and work. For reasons of convenience and cost, businesses often choose to incorporate in the state in which most of the corporation's business will be conducted.

**SECURE THE CORPORATE NAME** The choice of a corporate name is subject to state approval to ensure against duplication or deception. State statutes usually require that the secretary of state run a check on the proposed name in the state of incorporation.

Some states require that the persons incorporating a firm run a check on the proposed name at their own expense. A check can often be made via the Internet. If a firm is likely to do business in other states—or over the Internet—the incorporators should check existing corporate names in those states as well.

Once cleared, a name can be reserved for a short time, for a fee, pending the completion of the articles of incorporation. All states require the corporation's name to include the word *Corporation (Corp.)*, *Incorporated (Inc.)*, *Company (Co.)*, or *Limited (Ltd.)*.[6]

*First Check Available Domain Names.* All corporations need to have an online presence to compete effectively in today's business climate. The corporate name should be one that can be used as the business's Internet domain name. Therefore, it is advisable to check what domain names are available *before* securing a corporate name with the state.

Incorporators can do this by going to one of the many companies that issue domain names, such as Network Solutions (**www.whois.com/whois**), and finding out if the preferred name is available. If another business is using that name, the incorporators can select an alternative name that can be used as

---

6. Failure to use one of these abbreviations to disclose corporate status may be grounds for holding an individual incorporator liable for corporate contracts under agency law (see Chapter 26).

the business's URL, and then seek approval from the state for the name.

***Trade Name Disputes.*** A new corporation's name cannot be the same as (or deceptively similar to) the name of an existing corporation doing business within the same state. If a firm does business under a name that is the same as or deceptively similar to an existing company's name, it may be liable for trade name infringement (see Chapter 8).

▶ **Example 32.4** An existing corporation is named Digital Synergy, Inc. The state is not likely to allow a new corporation to use the name Digital Synergy Company. That name is deceptively similar to the first and could cause confusion. The use of too similar a name could also transfer part of the goodwill established by the first corporate user to the second, thus infringing on the first company's trademark rights. ◀

**PREPARE THE ARTICLES OF INCORPORATION** The primary document needed to incorporate a business is the **articles of incorporation** (for an example, see Exhibit 32–1 below). The articles include basic information about the corporation and serve as a primary source of authority for its future organiza-

**EXHIBIT 32–1 Sample Articles of Incorporation**

**ARTICLE ONE** The name of the corporation is _____ .

**ARTICLE TWO** The period of its duration is _____ (may be a number of years or until a certain date).

**ARTICLE THREE** The purpose (or purposes) for which the corporation is organized is (are) _____ _____ _____ .

**ARTICLE FOUR** The aggregate number of shares that the corporation shall have the authority to issue is _____ with the par value of _____ dollar(s) each (or without par value).

**ARTICLE FIVE** The corporation will not commence business until it has received for the issuance of its shares consideration of the value of $1,000 (can be any sum not less than $1,000).

**ARTICLE SIX** The address of the corporation's registered office is _____ , and the name of its registered agent at such address is _____ _____ .

**ARTICLE SEVEN** The number of initial directors is _____ , and the names and addresses of the directors are _____ _____ .

**ARTICLE EIGHT** The names and addresses of the incorporators are

_____        _____        _____
(Name)                 (Address)              (Signature)

_____        _____        _____
(Name)                 (Address)              (Signature)

_____        _____        _____
(Name)                 (Address)              (Signature)

Sworn to on _____ by the above-named incorporators.
            (Date)

_____
Notary Public

(Notary Seal)

tion and business functions. The person or persons who execute (sign) the articles are the *incorporators*.

Generally, the articles of incorporation *must* include the following information [RMBCA 2.02].

1. The name of the corporation.
2. The number of shares the corporation is authorized to issue.
3. The name and street address of the corporation's initial registered agent and registered office.
4. The name and address of each incorporator.

In addition, the articles *may* set forth other information, such as the names and addresses of the initial members of the board of directors, and the duration and purpose of the corporation.

Articles of incorporation vary widely depending on the jurisdiction and the size and type of the corporation. Frequently, the articles do not provide much detail about the firm's operations, which are spelled out in the company's **bylaws** (internal rules of management adopted by the corporation at its first organizational meeting).

***Shares of the Corporation.*** The articles must specify the number of shares of stock the corporation is authorized to issue [RMBCA 2.02(a)]. For instance, a company might state that the aggregate number of shares that the corporation has the authority to issue is five thousand. Large corporations often state a par value for each share, such as $.20 per share, and specify the various types or classes of stock authorized for issuance (see the discussion of *common* and *preferred stock* later in this chapter).

Sometimes, the articles set forth the capital structure of the corporation and other relevant information. To allow for the raising of additional capital in the future, the articles of incorporation often authorize many more shares of stock than will initially be issued.

***Registered Office and Agent.*** The corporation must indicate the location and street address of its registered office within the state. Usually, the registered office is also the principal office of the corporation.

The corporation must also give the name and address of a specific person who has been designated as an *agent*. The registered agent is the person who can receive legal documents (such as orders to appear in court) on behalf of the corporation.

***Incorporators.*** Each incorporator must be listed by name and address. The incorporators need not have

any interest at all in the corporation, and sometimes signing the articles is their only duty. Many states do not have residency or age requirements for incorporators. It can be as few as one or as many as three. Incorporators frequently participate in the first organizational meeting of the corporation.

***Duration and Purpose.*** A corporation has perpetual existence unless the articles state otherwise. The RMBCA does not require a specific statement of purpose to be included in the articles. A corporation can be formed for any lawful purpose.

Some incorporators choose to specify the intended business activities (such as "to engage in the production and sale of agricultural products"). It is increasingly common, though, for the articles to include only a general statement of purpose. The articles may indicate that the corporation is organized for "any legal business." By not mentioning specifics, the corporation avoids the need for future amendments to the corporate articles [RMBCA 2.02(b)(2)(i), 3.01].

***Internal Organization.*** The articles can describe the corporation's internal management structure, although this usually is included in the bylaws adopted after the corporation is formed. The articles of incorporation commence the corporation, whereas the bylaws are formed after commencement by the board of directors. Bylaws cannot conflict with the incorporation statute or the articles of incorporation [RMBCA 2.06].

Under the RMBCA, shareholders may amend or repeal the bylaws. The board of directors may also amend or repeal the bylaws unless the articles of incorporation or state statutory provisions reserve this power to the shareholders exclusively [RMBCA 10.20].

The bylaws typically describe such matters as voting requirements for shareholders, the election of the board of directors, and the methods of replacing directors. Bylaws also frequently outline the manner and time of holding shareholders' and board meetings.

**FILE THE ARTICLES WITH THE STATE** Once the articles of incorporation have been prepared and signed, they are sent to the appropriate state official, usually the secretary of state, along with the required filing fee. In most states, the secretary of state then stamps the articles "Filed" and returns a copy of the articles to the incorporators. Once this occurs, the corporation officially exists.

# First Organizational Meeting to Adopt Bylaws

After incorporation, the first organizational meeting must be held. Usually, the most important function of this meeting is the adoption of bylaws, which, as mentioned, are the internal rules of management for the corporation. If the articles of incorporation named the initial board of directors, then the directors, by majority vote, call the meeting to adopt the bylaws and complete the company's organization.

If the articles did not name the directors (as is typical), then the incorporators hold the meeting to elect the directors and adopt bylaws. The incorporators may also complete the routine business of incorporation (such as authorizing the issuance of shares and hiring employees) at this meeting. The business transacted depends on the requirements of the state's corporation statute, the nature of the corporation, the provisions made in the articles, and the desires of the incorporators.

# Improper Incorporation

The procedures for incorporation are very specific. If they are not followed precisely, others may be able to challenge the existence of the corporation. Errors in incorporation procedures can become important when, for instance, a third party who is attempting to enforce a contract or bring a suit for a tort injury learns of them.

**DE JURE CORPORATIONS** If a corporation has substantially complied with all conditions precedent to incorporation, the corporation is said to have *de jure* (rightful and lawful) existence. In most states and under RMBCA 2.03(b), the secretary of state's filing of the articles of incorporation is conclusive proof that all mandatory statutory provisions have been met [RMBCA 2.03(b)].

Sometimes, the incorporators fail to comply with all statutory mandates. If the defect is minor, such as an incorrect address listed on the articles of incorporation, most courts will overlook the defect and find that a corporation (*de jure*) exists.

**DE FACTO CORPORATIONS** If the defect in formation is substantial, however, such as a corporation's failure to hold an organizational meeting to adopt bylaws, the outcome will vary depending on the jurisdiction. Some states, including Mississippi, New York, Ohio, and Oklahoma, still recognize the common law doctrine of *de facto* corporation.[7] In those states, the

courts will treat a corporation as a legal corporation despite the defect in its formation if the following three requirements are met:

1. A state statute exists under which the corporation can be validly incorporated.
2. The parties have made a good faith attempt to comply with the statute.
3. The parties have already undertaken to do business as a corporation.

Many state courts, however, have interpreted their states' version of the RMBCA as abolishing the common law doctrine of *de facto* corporations. These states include Alaska, Arizona, Minnesota, New Mexico, Oregon, South Dakota, Tennessee, Utah, and Washington, as well as the District of Columbia. In those jurisdictions, if there is a substantial defect in complying with the incorporation statute, the corporation does not legally exist, and the incorporators are personally liable.

# Corporation by Estoppel

Sometimes, a business association holds itself out to others as being a corporation when it has made no attempt to incorporate. In those situations, the firm normally will be estopped (prevented) from denying corporate status in a lawsuit by a third party. The estoppel doctrine most commonly applies when a third party contracts with an entity that claims to be a corporation but has not filed articles of incorporation. It may also apply when a third party contracts with a person claiming to be an agent of a corporation that does not in fact exist.

When justice requires, courts in some states will treat an alleged corporation as if it were an actual corporation for the purpose of determining the rights and liabilities in particular circumstances.[8] Recognition of corporate status does not extend beyond the resolution of the problem at hand.

▶ **Case in Point 32.5** W.P. Media, Inc., and Alabama MBA, Inc., agreed to form a wireless Internet services company. W.P. Media was to create a wireless network, and Alabama MBA was to contribute the capital. Hugh Brown signed the parties' contract on behalf of Alabama MBA as the chair of its board. At the time, however, Alabama MBA's articles of incorporation had not yet been filed. Brown filed the articles of incorporation the following year.

---

7. See, for example, *In re Hausman*, 13 N.Y.3d 408, 921 N.E.2d 191, 893 N.Y.S.2d 499 (2009).

8. Some states have expressly rejected the common law theory of corporation by estoppel, finding that it is inconsistent with their statutory law. Other states have abolished only the doctrines of *de facto* and *de jure* corporations. See, for example, *Stone v. Jetmar Properties, LLC*, 733 N.W.2d 480 (Minn.App. 2007).

Later, Brown and Alabama MBA filed a suit alleging that W.P. Media had breached their contract by not building the wireless network. The Supreme Court of Alabama held that because W.P. Media had treated Alabama MBA as a corporation, W.P. Media was estopped from denying Alabama MBA's corporate existence.[9] ◀

## SECTION 3
# CORPORATE POWERS

When a corporation is created, the express and implied powers necessary to achieve its purpose also come into existence. The express powers of a corporation are found in its articles of incorporation, in the law of the state of incorporation, and in the state and federal constitutions.

Corporate bylaws and the resolutions of the corporation's board of directors also establish the express powers of the corporation. Because state corporation statutes frequently provide default rules that apply if the company's bylaws are silent on an issue, it is important that the bylaws set forth the specific operating rules of the corporation. In addition, after the bylaws are adopted, the corporation's board of directors will pass resolutions that also grant or restrict corporate powers.

The following order of priority is used if a conflict arises among the various documents involving a corporation:

1. The U.S. Constitution.
2. State constitutions.
3. State statutes.
4. The articles of incorporation.
5. Bylaws.
6. Resolutions of the board of directors.

## Implied Powers

When a corporation is created, certain implied powers arise. In the absence of express constitutional, statutory, or other prohibitions, the corporation has the implied power to perform all acts reasonably necessary to accomplish its corporate purposes. For this reason, a corporation has the implied power to borrow funds within certain limits, lend funds, and extend credit to those with whom it has a legal or contractual relationship.

To borrow funds, the corporation acts through its board of directors to authorize the loan. Most often, the president or chief executive officer of the corporation will execute the necessary documents on behalf of the corporation. Corporate officers such as these have the implied power to bind the corporation in matters directly connected with the *ordinary* business affairs of the enterprise.

There is a limit to what a corporate officer can do, though. A corporate officer does not have the authority to bind the corporation to an action that will greatly affect the corporate purpose or undertaking, such as the sale of substantial corporate assets.

## *Ultra Vires* Doctrine

The term **ultra vires** means "beyond the power." In corporate law, acts of a corporation that are beyond its express or implied powers are *ultra vires* acts.

**WHEN A CORPORATION'S ACTIONS EXCEED ITS STATED PURPOSE** In the past, most cases dealing with *ultra vires* acts involved contracts made for unauthorized purposes. Now, however, most private corporations are organized for "any legal business" and do not state a specific purpose, so the *ultra vires* doctrine has declined in importance.

Today, cases that allege *ultra vires* acts usually involve nonprofit corporations or municipal (public) corporations. ▶ **Case in Point 32.6** Four men formed a nonprofit corporation to create the Armenian Genocide Museum & Memorial (AGM&M). The bylaws appointed them as trustees (similar to corporate directors) for life. One of the trustees, Gerard L. Cafesjian, became the chair and president of AGM&M. Eventually, the relationship among the trustees deteriorated, and Cafesjian resigned.

The corporation then brought a suit claiming that Cafesjian had engaged in numerous *ultra vires* acts, self-dealing, and mismanagement. Although the bylaws required an 80 percent affirmative vote of the trustees to take action, Cafesjian had taken many actions without the board's approval. He had also entered into contracts for real estate transactions in which he had a personal interest. Because Cafesjian had taken actions that exceeded his authority and had failed to follow the rules set forth in the bylaws for board meetings, the court ruled that the corporation could go forward with its suit.[10] ◀

---

9. *Brown v. W.P. Media, Inc.*, 17 So.3d 1167 (2009).

10. *Armenian Assembly of America, Inc. v. Cafesjian*, 692 F.Supp.2d 20 (D.C. 2010).

**REMEDIES FOR *ULTRA VIRES* ACTS** Under Section 3.04 of the RMBCA, the shareholders can seek an injunction from a court to prevent (or stop) the corporation from engaging in *ultra vires* acts. The attorney general in the state of incorporation can also bring an action to obtain an injunction against the *ultra vires* transactions or to seek dissolution of the corporation. The corporation or its shareholders (on behalf of the corporation) can seek damages from the officers and directors who were responsible for the *ultra vires* acts.

## SECTION 4
# PIERCING THE CORPORATE VEIL

Occasionally, the owners use a corporate entity to perpetrate a fraud, circumvent the law, or in some other way accomplish an illegitimate objective. In these situations, the courts will ignore the corporate structure and **pierce the corporate veil,** exposing the shareholders to personal liability [RMBCA 2.04].

Generally, courts pierce the veil when the corporate privilege is abused for personal benefit or when the corporate business is treated so carelessly that it is indistinguishable from that of a controlling shareholder. When the facts show that great injustice would result from the use of a corporation to avoid individual responsibility, a court will look behind the corporate structure to the individual shareholders.

## Factors That Lead Courts to Pierce the Corporate Veil

The following are some of the factors that frequently cause the courts to pierce the corporate veil:

1. A party is tricked or misled into dealing with the corporation rather than the individual.
2. The corporation is set up never to make a profit or always to be insolvent, or it is too "thinly" capitalized. That is, it has insufficient capital at the time it is formed to meet its prospective debts or potential liabilities.
3. The corporation is formed to evade an existing legal obligation.
4. Statutory corporate formalities, such as holding required corporation meetings, are not followed.
5. Personal and corporate interests are mixed together, or **commingled,** to such an extent that the corporation has no separate identity.

Although state corporation codes usually do not prohibit a shareholder from lending funds to her or his corporation, courts will scrutinize the transaction closely if the loan comes from an officer, director, or majority shareholder. Loans from persons who control the corporation must be made in good faith and for fair value.

## A Potential Problem for Close Corporations

The potential for corporate assets to be used for personal benefit is especially great in a close corporation, in which the shares are held by a single person or by only a few individuals, usually family members. In such a situation, the separate status of the corporate entity and the sole shareholder (or family-member shareholders) must be carefully preserved.

Certain practices invite trouble for the one-person or family-owned (close) corporation, including any of the following:

1. The commingling of corporate and personal funds.
2. The failure to hold board of directors' meetings and record the minutes.
3. The shareholders' continuous personal use of corporate property (for instance, company-owned vehicles).

In the following case, when a close corporation failed to pay its legal fees, its attorneys sought to hold the shareholders personally liable. The court had to decide whether to pierce the corporate veil.

## CASE 32.3

### Brennan's, Inc. v. Colbert
Court of Appeal of Louisiana, 85 So. 3d 787 (2012).

**BACKGROUND AND FACTS** Pip, Jimmy, and Theodore Brennan are brothers and shareholders of Brennan's, Inc., which owns and operates New Orleans's famous Brennan's Restaurant. In 1998, the Brennan brothers retained attorney Edward Colbert and his firm, Kenyon & Kenyon, L.L.P., to represent

CASE 32.3 CONTINUED

Brennan's, Inc., in a dispute with another family member. All bills were sent to Brennan's, Inc., and the payments came from the company's checking accounts.

As a close corporation, Brennan's, Inc., did not hold formal corporate meetings with agendas and minutes, but it did maintain corporate books, hold corporate bank accounts, and file corporate tax returns. In 2005, Brennan's, Inc., sued Colbert and his law firm for legal malpractice. In its answer, Kenyon & Kenyon demanded unpaid legal fees both from Brennan's, Inc., and from the Brennan brothers personally. The trial court found that the Brennan brothers could not be held personally liable. Kenyon & Kenyon appealed. The law firm argued that the court should pierce the corporate veil because Brennan's, Inc., did not observe corporate formalities and because the Brennan brothers did not honor their promises to pay their legal bills.

**DECISION AND RATIONALE**   A state intermediate appellate court affirmed the trial court's judgment for the Brennan brothers. Corporate shareholders generally may not be held personally liable, but a court may pierce the corporate veil if the shareholders fail to observe corporate formalities or use the corporation to perpetrate a fraud.

In this case, the Brennan brothers never agreed to personally pay Kenyon & Kenyon's legal fees. Instead, they simply spoke as shareholders for the firm's real client, Brennan's, Inc. Moreover, Kenyon & Kenyon knew that Brennan's, Inc., was a close corporation that operated somewhat informally. Although the corporation did not hold formal corporate meetings, it maintained corporate books, held corporate bank accounts, filed corporate tax returns, and even paid Kenyon & Kenyon with its own checks. Finally, the Brennan brothers did not defraud Kenyon & Kenyon by failing to pay their legal fees. "If a broken promise to pay was sufficient establish fraud," the court reasoned, "then every lawsuit against a corporation for a debt would automatically allow for the piercing of the corporate veil."

**THE ETHICAL DIMENSION**   *Should the Brennan brothers be held personally liable because they misled their attorneys? Why or why not?*

**THE ECONOMIC DIMENSION**   *Do corporations benefit from shareholders' limited liability? If so, how?*

## The Alter-Ego Theory

Sometimes, courts pierce the corporate veil under the theory that the corporation was not operated as a separate entity, but was just another side (or alter ego) of the individual or group that actually controlled the corporation. This is called the alter-ego theory, which was discussed in the context of limited liability companies in Chapter 31.

The alter-ego theory is applied when a corporation is so dominated and controlled by an individual or group that the separate identities of the person (or group) and the corporation are no longer distinct. Courts use the alter-ego theory to avoid injustice or fraud that would result if wrongdoers were allowed to hide behind the protection of limited liability. ▶ **Case in Point 32.7** Harvey and Barbara Jacobson owned Aqua Clear Technologies, Inc., which installed and serviced home water-softening systems. The Jacobsons consistently took funds out of the business for their personal expenses, including payments for their home, cars, health-insurance premiums, and credit cards.

Three weeks after Aqua filed a bankruptcy petition, Harvey formed another corporation called Discount Water Services, Inc. Discount appropriated Aqua's equipment and inventory (without buying it) and continued to service water-softening systems for Aqua's customers, even using the same phone number. The trustee appointed to Aqua's bankruptcy case sought to recover Aqua's assets on the ground that Discount was Aqua's alter ego. The court ruled that Discount was simply a continuation of Aqua's business (its alter ego) under a new name, and therefore held Discount liable for the claims asserted against Aqua in bankruptcy (totaling $108,732.64).[11] ◀

## SECTION 5
# CORPORATE FINANCING

Corporations are financed by the issuance and sale of corporate **securities,** which include stocks and bonds. **Stocks,** or *equity securities*, represent the purchase of ownership in the business firm. **Bonds**

---

**11.** *In re Aqua Clear Technologies, Inc.,* 361 Bankr. 567 (S.D.Fla. 2007).

(debentures), or *debt securities,* represent the borrowing of funds by firms (and governments).

Of course, not all debt is in the form of debt securities. For instance, some debt is in the form of accounts payable and notes payable, which typically are short-term debts. Bonds are simply a way for corporations to split up their long-term debt so that it can be more easily marketed.

## Bonds

Bonds are issued by business firms and by governments at all levels as evidence of the funds they are borrowing from investors. Bonds normally have a designated *maturity date*—the date when the principal, or face amount, of the bond (or loan) is returned to the investor. They are sometimes referred to as *fixed-income securities* because their owners (that is, the creditors) receive fixed-dollar interest payments, usually semiannually, during the period of time prior to maturity.

Because debt financing represents a legal obligation of the corporation, various features and terms of a particular bond issue are specified in a lending agreement, called a **bond indenture.** A corporate trustee, often a commercial bank trust department, represents the collective well-being of all bondholders in ensuring that the corporation meets the terms of the bond issue. The bond indenture specifies the maturity date of the bond and the pattern of interest payments until maturity.

## Stocks

Issuing stocks is another way for corporations to obtain financing [RMBCA 6.01]. The ways in which stocks differ from bonds are summarized in Exhibit 32–2 on the top of the next page. Exhibit 32–3 on the following page offers a summary of the types of stocks issued by corporations. The two major types are *common stock* and *preferred stock.*

**COMMON STOCK** The true ownership of a corporation is represented by **common stock.** Common stock provides a proportionate interest in the corporation with regard to (1) control, (2) earnings, and (3) net assets. A shareholder's interest is generally in proportion to the number of shares he or she owns out of the total number of shares issued.

*Voting Rights.* Any person who purchases common stock acquires voting rights—one vote per share held. Voting rights in a corporation apply to the election of the firm's board of directors and to any proposed changes in the ownership structure of the firm. For

instance, a holder of common stock generally has the right to vote in a decision on a proposed merger, as mergers can change the proportion of ownership. State corporation law specifies the types of actions for which shareholder approval must be obtained.

*Earnings.* Firms are not obligated to return a principal amount per share to each holder of common stock because no firm can ensure that the market price per share of its common stock will not decline over time. The issuing firm also does not have to guarantee a dividend. Indeed, some corporations never pay dividends.

Holders of common stock are investors who assume a *residual* position in the overall financial structure of the business. In terms of receiving returns on their investments, they are last in line. They are entitled to the earnings that are left after federal and state taxes are paid and after preferred stockholders, bondholders, suppliers, employees, and other groups have been paid. Once those groups are paid, however, the owners of common stock may be entitled to *all* the remaining earnings. (The board of directors normally is not under any duty to declare the remaining earnings as dividends, however.)

**PREFERRED STOCK** **Preferred stock** is an equity security with *preferences.* Usually, this means that holders of preferred stock have priority over holders of common stock as to dividends and payment on dissolution of the corporation. The preferences must be stated in the articles of incorporation. Holders of preferred stock may or may not have the right to vote.

Preferred stock is not included among the liabilities of a business because it is equity. Like other equity securities, preferred shares have no fixed maturity date on which the firm must pay them off. Although firms occasionally buy back preferred stock, they are not legally obligated to do so.

Holders of preferred stock are investors who have assumed a rather cautious position. They have a stronger position than common shareholders with respect to dividends and claims on assets, but they do not share in the full prosperity of the firm if its earnings grow over time. Preferred stockholders do receive fixed dividends periodically, however, and they may benefit to some extent from changes in the market price of the shares.

## Venture Capital and Private Equity Capital

Corporations traditionally obtain financing through issuing and selling securities (stocks and bonds) in the

## EXHIBIT 32-2 How Do Stocks and Bonds Differ?

| Stocks | Bonds |
|---|---|
| 1. Stocks represent ownership. | 1. Bonds represent debt. |
| 2. Stocks (common) do not have a fixed dividend rate. | 2. Interest on bonds must always be paid, whether or not any profit is earned. |
| 3. Stockholders can elect the board of directors, which controls the corporation. | 3. Bondholders usually have no voice in or control over management of the corporation. |
| 4. Stocks do not have a maturity date. The corporation usually does not repay the stockholder. | 4. Bonds have a maturity date, when the corporation is to repay the bondholder the face value of the bond. |
| 5. All corporations issue or offer to sell stocks. This is the usual definition of a corporation. | 5. Corporations do not necessarily issue bonds. |
| 6. Stockholders have a claim against the property and income of the corporation after all creditors' claims have been met. | 6. Bondholders have a claim against the property and income of the corporation that must be met before the claims of stockholders. |

capital market. Many investors do not want to purchase stock in a business that lacks a track record, however, and banks generally are reluctant to extend loans to high-risk enterprises. Numerous corporations fail because they are undercapitalized. Therefore, to obtain sufficient financing, many entrepreneurs seek alternative financing.

**VENTURE CAPITAL** Start-up businesses and high-risk enterprises often obtain venture capital financing. As discussed in Chapter 31, *venture capital* is capital provided to new businesses by professional, outside investors, usually in exchange for an ownership interest in the business.

Venture capital investments are high risk—the investors must be willing to lose their invested funds—but offer the potential for well-above-average returns at some point in the future. Many Internet-based companies, such as Google and Amazon, were initially financed by venture capital.

**PRIVATE EQUITY CAPITAL** Private equity firms obtain their capital from wealthy investors in private markets. The firms use their **private equity capital** to invest in existing corporations. Usually, a private equity firm buys an entire corporation and may later reorganize it as a publicly held corporation. Sometimes, divisions of the purchased company are sold off to pay down debt.

Ultimately, the private equity firm may sell shares in the reorganized (and perhaps more profitable)

## EXHIBIT 32-3 Types of Stocks

| Type | Definition |
|---|---|
| **Common Stock** | Voting shares that represent ownership interest in a corporation. Common stock has the lowest priority with respect to payment of dividends and distribution of assets on the corporation's dissolution. |
| **Preferred Stock** | Shares of stock that have priority over common-stock shares as to payment of dividends and distribution of assets on dissolution. Dividend payments are usually a fixed percentage of the face value of the share. Preferred shares may or may not be voting shares. |
| **Cumulative Preferred Stock** | Preferred shares on which required dividends not paid in a given year must be paid in a subsequent year before any common-stock dividends can be paid. |
| **Participating Preferred Stock** | Preferred shares entitling the owner to receive (1) the preferred-stock dividend and (2) additional dividends after the corporation has paid dividends on common stock. |
| **Convertible Preferred Stock** | Preferred shares that, under certain conditions, can be converted into a specified number of common shares either in the issuing corporation or, sometimes, in another corporation. |
| **Redeemable, or Callable, Preferred Stock** | Preferred shares issued with the express condition that the issuing corporation has the right to repurchase the shares as specified. |

company to the public in an *initial public offering* (usually called an IPO). In this way, the private equity firm can make profits by selling its shares in the company to the public.

### SECTION 6
# MAJOR BUSINESS FORMS COMPARED

As mentioned earlier in Chapter 29, when deciding which form of business organization to choose, businesspersons normally consider several factors,

including ease of creation, the liability of the owners, tax considerations, and the ability to raise capital. Each major form of business organization offers distinct advantages and disadvantages with respect to these and other factors.

Exhibit 32–4 on this and the next page summarizes the essential advantages and disadvantages of each of the forms of business organization discussed in Chapters 29 through 32.

**EXHIBIT 32-4 Major Forms of Business Compared**

| Characteristic | Sole Proprietorship | Partnership | Corporation |
|---|---|---|---|
| **Method of Creation** | Created at will by owner. | Created by agreement of the parties. | Authorized by the state under the state's corporation law. |
| **Legal Position** | Not a separate entity; owner is the business. | A general partnership is a separate legal entity in most states. | Always a legal entity separate and distinct from its owners—a legal fiction for the purposes of owning property and being a party to litigation. |
| **Liability** | Unlimited liability. | Unlimited liability. | Limited liability of shareholders—shareholders are not liable for the debts of the corporation. |
| **Duration** | Determined by owner; automatically dissolved on owner's death. | Terminated by agreement of the partners, but can continue to do business even when a partner dissociates from the partnership. | Can have perpetual existence. |
| **Transferability of Interest** | Interest can be transferred, but individual's proprietorship then ends. | Although partnership interest can be assigned, assignee does not have full rights of a partner. | Shares of stock can be transferred. |
| **Management** | Completely at owner's discretion. | Each partner has a direct and equal voice in management unless expressly agreed otherwise in the partnership agreement. | Shareholders elect directors, who set policy and appoint officers. |
| **Taxation** | Owner pays personal taxes on business income. | Each partner pays pro rata share of income taxes on net profits, whether or not they are distributed. | Double taxation—corporation pays income tax on net profits, with no deduction for dividends, and shareholders pay income tax on disbursed dividends they receive. |
| **Organizational Fees, Annual License Fees, and Annual Reports** | None or minimal. | None or minimal. | All required. |
| **Transaction of Business in Other States** | Generally no limitation. | Generally no limitation.[a] | Normally must qualify to do business and obtain certificate of authority. |

a. A few states have enacted statutes requiring that foreign partnerships qualify to do business there.

## EXHIBIT 32-4  Major Forms of Business Compared—Continued

| Charactistic | Limited Partnership | Limited Liability Company | Limited Liability Partnership |
|---|---|---|---|
| **Method of Creation** | Created by agreement to carry on a business for profit. At least one party must be a general partner and the other(s) limited partner(s). Certificate of limited partnership is filed. Charter must be issued by the state. | Created by an agreement of the member-owners of the company. Articles of organization are filed. Charter must be issued by the state. | Created by agreement of the partners. A statement of qualification for the limited liability partnership is filed. |
| **Legal Position** | Treated as a legal entity. | Treated as a legal entity. | Generally, treated same as a general partnership. |
| **Liability** | Unlimited liability of all general partners. Limited partners are liable only to the extent of capital contributions. | Member-owners' liability is limited to the amount of capital contributions or investments. | Varies, but under the Uniform Partnership Act, liability of a partner for acts committed by other partners is limited. |
| **Duration** | By agreement in certificate, or by termination of the last general partner (retirement, death, and the like) or last limited partner. | Unless a single-member LLC, can have perpetual existence (same as a corporation). | Remains in existence until cancellation or revocation. |
| **Transferability of Interest** | Interest can be assigned (same as a general partnership), but if assignee becomes a member with consent of other partners, certificate must be amended. | Member interests are freely transferable. | Interest can be assigned same as in a general partnership. |
| **Management** | General partners have equal voice or by agreement. Limited partners may not retain limited liability if they actively participate in management. | Member-owners can fully participate in management or can designate a group of persons to manage on behalf of the members. | Same as a general partnership. |
| **Taxation** | Generally taxed as a partnership. | LLC is not taxed, and members are taxed personally on profits "passed through" the LLC. | Same as a general partnership. |
| **Organizational Fees, Annual License Fees, and Annual Reports** | Organizational fee required; usually not others. | Organizational fee required. Others vary with states. | Fees are set by each state for filing statements of qualification, statements of foreign qualification, and annual reports. |
| **Transaction of Business in Other States** | Generally no limitations. | Generally no limitations, but may vary depending on state. | Must file a statement of foreign qualification before doing business in another state. |

# Reviewing: Corporate Formation and Financing

William Sharp was the sole shareholder and manager of Chickasaw Club, Inc., an S corporation that operated a popular nightclub of the same name in Columbus, Georgia. Sharp maintained a corporate checking account but paid the club's employees, suppliers, and entertainers in cash out of the club's proceeds. Sharp owned the property on which the club was located. He rented it to the club but made

*Continued*

mortgage payments out of the club's proceeds and often paid other personal expenses with Chickasaw corporate funds.

At 12:45 A.M. on July 31, eighteen-year-old Aubrey Lynn Pursley, who was already intoxicated, entered the Chickasaw Club. A city ordinance prohibited individuals under the age of twenty-one from entering nightclubs, but Chickasaw employees did not check Pursley's identification to verify her age. Pursley drank more alcohol at Chickasaw and was visibly intoxicated when she left the club at 3:00 A.M. with a beer in her hand. Shortly afterward, Pursley lost control of her car, struck a tree, and was killed. Joseph Dancause, Pursley's stepfather, filed a tort lawsuit in a Georgia state court against Chickasaw Club, Inc., and William Sharp, seeking damages. Using the information presented in the chapter, answer the following questions.

1. Under what theory might the court in this case make an exception to the limited liability of shareholders and hold Sharp personally liable for the damages? What factors would be relevant to the court's decision?

2. Suppose that Chickasaw's articles of incorporation failed to describe the corporation's purpose or management structure as required by state law. Would the court be likely to rule that Sharp is personally liable to Dancause on that basis? Why or why not?

3. Suppose that the club extended credit to its regular patrons in an effort to maintain a loyal clientele, although neither the articles of incorporation nor the corporate bylaws authorized this practice. Would the corporation likely have the power to engage in this activity? Explain.

4. How would the court classify the Chickasaw Club corporation—domestic or foreign, public or private? Why?

**DEBATE THIS . . .** *The sole shareholder of an S corporation should not be able to avoid liability for the torts of her or his employees.*

## Terms and Concepts

| | | |
|---|---|---|
| alien corporation 563 | common stock 574 | public corporation 563 |
| articles of incorporation 568 | dividends 561 | publicly held corporation 563 |
| benefit corporation 566 | domestic corporation 563 | retained earnings 561 |
| bond 573 | foreign corporation 563 | S corporation 565 |
| bond indenture 574 | holding company 561 | securities 573 |
| bylaws 569 | pierce the corporate veil 572 | stock 573 |
| close corporation 563 | preferred stock 574 | *ultra vires* 571 |
| commingle 572 | private equity capital 575 | |

## Issue Spotters

1. Northwest Brands, Inc., is a small business incorporated in Minnesota. Its one class of stock is owned by twelve members of a single family. Ordinarily, corporate income is taxed at the corporate and shareholder levels. Is there a way for Northwest Brands to avoid this double taxation? Explain your answer. **(See page 565.)**

2. The incorporators of Consumer Investments, Inc., want their new corporation to have the authority to transact nearly any conceivable type of business. Can they grant this authority to their firm? If so, how? If not, why not? **(See page 569.)**

• Check your answers to the Issue Spotters against the answers provided in Appendix E at the end of this text.

## Business Scenarios

**32–1. Incorporation.** Jonathan, Gary, and Ricardo are active members of a partnership called Swim City. The partnership manufactures, sells, and installs outdoor swimming pools in the states of Arkansas and Texas. The partners want to continue to be active in management and to expand the business into other states as well. They are also concerned about rather large recent judgments entered against swimming pool companies throughout the United States. Based on these facts only, discuss whether the partnership should incorporate. **(See page 560.)**

**32–2. Preincorporation.** Cummings, Okawa, and Taft are recent college graduates who want to form a corporation to manufacture and sell digital tablets. Peterson tells them he will set in motion the formation of their corporation. First, Peterson makes a contract with Owens for the purchase of a piece of land for $20,000. Owens does not know of the prospective corporate formation at the time the contract is signed. Second, Peterson makes a contract with Babcock to build a small plant on the property being purchased. Babcock's contract is conditional on the corporation's formation. Peterson secures all necessary sub-

scription agreements and capitalization, and he files the articles of incorporation. **(See page 567.)**

(a) Discuss whether the newly formed corporation, Peterson, or both are liable on the contracts with Owens and Babcock.

(b) Discuss whether the corporation is automatically liable to Babcock on formation.

**32–3. Corporate Powers.** Oya Paka and two business associates formed a corporation called Paka Corp. for the purpose of selling computer services. Oya, who owned 50 percent of the corporate shares, served as the corporation's president. Oya wished to obtain a personal loan from her bank for $250,000, but the bank required the note to be cosigned by a third party. Oya cosigned the note in the name of the corporation. Later, Oya defaulted on the note, and the bank sued the corporation for payment. The corporation asserted, as a defense, that Oya had exceeded her authority when she cosigned the note on behalf of the corporation. Had she? Explain. **(See page 571.)**

## Business Case Problems

**32–4. Spotlight on Smart Inventions—Piercing the Corporate Veil.** Thomas Persson and Jon Nokes founded Smart Inventions, Inc., to market household consumer products. The success of their first product, the Smart Mop, continued with later products, which were sold through infomercials and other means. Persson and Nokes were the firm's officers and equal shareholders. Persson was responsible for product development, and Nokes was in charge of day-to-day operations. By 1998, they had become dissatisfied with each other's efforts. Nokes represented the firm as financially "dying," "in a grim state, . . . worse than ever," and offered to buy all of Persson's shares for $1.6 million. Persson accepted.

On the day that they signed the agreement to transfer the shares, Smart Inventions began marketing a new product—the Tap Light. It was an instant success, generating millions of dollars in revenues. In negotiating with Persson, Nokes had intentionally kept the Tap Light a secret. Persson sued Smart Inventions, asserting fraud and other claims. Under what principle might Smart Inventions be liable for Nokes's fraud? Is Smart Inventions liable in this case? Explain. [*Persson v. Smart Inventions, Inc.,* 125 Cal.App.4th 1141, 23 Cal.Rptr.3d 335 (2 Dist. 2005)] **(See page 572.)**

**32–5. Improper Incorporation.** Denise Rubenstein and Christopher Mayor agreed to form Bayshore Sunrise Corp. (BSC) in New York to rent certain premises and operate a

laundromat. BSC entered into a twenty-year commercial lease with Bay Shore Property Trust on April 15. Mayor signed the lease as the president of BSC, but the articles of incorporation were not filed until the next day—April 16. Three years later, BSC defaulted on the lease, which resulted in its termination.

Rubenstein and BSC sued Mayor, his brother-in-law Thomas Castellano, and Planet Laundry, Inc., claiming wrongful interference with a contractual relationship. The plaintiffs alleged that Mayor and Castellano conspired to squeeze Rubenstein out of BSC and arranged the default on the lease so that Mayor and Castellano could form and operate their own business, Planet Laundry, at the same address. The defendants argued that they could not be liable on the plaintiffs' claim because there had never been an enforceable lease—BSC lacked the capacity to enter into contracts on April 15. What theory might Rubenstein and BSC assert to refute this argument? Discuss. [*Rubenstein v. Mayor,* 41 A.D.3d 826, 839 N.Y.S.2d 170 (2 Dept. 2007)] **(See page 570.)**

**32–6. Piercing the Corporate Veil.** Smith Services, Inc., a trucking business owned by Tony Smith, charged its fuel purchases to an account at Laker Express. When Smith Services was not paid on several contracts, it ceased doing business and was dissolved. Smith continued to provide trucking services, however, as a sole proprietor. Laker Express sought to recover Smith Services' unpaid fuel charges, which amounted to about $35,000, from Smith.

He argued that he was not personally liable for a corporate debt. Should the court pierce the corporate veil? Explain. [*Bear, Inc. v. Smith*, 303 S.W.3d 137 (Ky.App. 2010)] **(See page 572.)**

**32–7. BUSINESS CASE PROBLEM WITH SAMPLE ANSWER: Close Corporations.**

*Mark Burnett and Kamran Pourgol were the only shareholders in a corporation that built and sold a house. When the buyers discovered that the house exceeded the amount of square footage allowed by* the building permit, Pourgol agreed to renovate the house to conform to the permit. No work was done, however, and Burnett filed a suit against Pourgol. Burnett claimed that, without his knowledge, Pourgol had submitted incorrect plans to obtain the building permit, misrepresented the extent of the renovation, and failed to fix the house. Was Pourgol guilty of misconduct? If so, how might it have been avoided? Discuss. [Burnett v. Pourgol, 83 A.D.3d 756, 921 N.Y.S.2d 280 (2 Dept. 2011)] **(See page 563.)**

- **For a sample answer to Problem 32–7, go to Appendix F at the end of this text.**

**32–8. Piercing the Corporate Veil.** In 1997, Leon Greenblatt, Andrew Jahelka, and Richard Nichols incorporated Loop Corp. with only $1,000 of capital. Three years later, Banco Panamericano, Inc., which was run entirely by Greenblatt and owned by a Greenblatt family trust, extended a large line of credit to Loop. Loop's subsidiaries then participated in the credit, giving $3 million to Loop while acquiring a security interest in Loop itself. Loop then opened an account with Wachovia Securities, LLC, to buy stock shares using credit provided by Wachovia. When the stock values plummeted, Loop owed Wachovia $1.89 million. Loop also defaulted on its loan from Banco, but Banco agreed to lend Loop millions of dollars more.

Rather than repay Wachovia with the influx of funds, Loop gave the funds to closely related entities and "compensated" Nichols and Jahelka without issuing any W-2 forms (forms reporting compensation to the Internal Revenue Service). The evidence also showed that Loop made loans to other related entities and shared office space, equipment, and telephone and fax numbers with related entities. Loop also moved employees among related entities, failed to file its tax returns on time (or sometimes at all), and failed to follow its own bylaws. In a lawsuit brought by Wachovia, can the court hold Greenblatt,

Jahelka, and Nichols personally liable by piercing the corporate veil? Why or why not? [*Wachovia Securities, LLC v. Banco Panamericano, Inc.*, 674 F.3d 743 (9th Cir. 2012)] **(See page 572.)**

**32–9. A QUESTION OF ETHICS: Improper Incorporation.**

*Mike Lyons incorporated Lyons Concrete, Inc., in Montana, but did not file its first annual report, so the state involuntarily dissolved the firm in 1996. Unaware of the dissolution, Lyons continued to do* business as Lyons Concrete. In 2003, he signed a written contract with William Weimar to form and pour a certain amount of concrete on Weimar's property in Lake County for $19,810. Weimar was in a rush to complete the entire project, and he and Lyons orally agreed to additional work on a time-and-materials basis. When scheduling conflicts arose, Weimar had his own employees set some of the forms, which proved deficient. Weimar also directed Lyons to pour concrete in the rain, which undercut its quality. In mid-project, Lyons submitted an invoice for $14,389, which Weimar paid. After the work was complete, Lyons sent Weimar an invoice for $25,731, but he refused to pay, claiming that the $14,389 covered everything. To recover the unpaid amount, Lyons filed a mechanic's lien as "Mike Lyons d/b/a Lyons Concrete, Inc." against Weimar's property. Weimar filed a suit in a Montana state court to strike the lien, and Lyons filed a counterclaim to reassert it. [Weimar v. Lyons, 338 Mont. 242, 164 P.3d 922 (2007)] **(See page 570.)**

(a) Before the trial, Weimar asked for a change of venue on the ground that a sign on the courthouse lawn advertised "Lyons Concrete." How might the sign affect a trial on the parties' dispute? Should the court grant this request? Why or why not?

(b) Weimar asked the court to dismiss the counterclaim on the ground that the state had dissolved Lyons Concrete in 1996. Lyons immediately filed new articles of incorporation for "Lyons Concrete, Inc." Under what doctrine might the court rule that Weimar could not deny the existence of Lyons Concrete? What ethical values underlie this doctrine? Should the court make this ruling? Explain.

(c) At the trial, Weimar argued, in part, that there was no "fixed price" contract between the parties and that even if there were, the poor quality of the work, which required repairs, amounted to a breach, excusing Weimar's further performance. Should the court rule in Weimar's favor on this basis? Why or why not?

## Legal Reasoning Group Activity

**32–10. Corporate versus LLC Form of Business.** Although a limited liability company (LLC—see Chapter 31) may be the best organizational form for most businesses, a significant number of firms may be better off as a corporation or some other form of organization. **(See page 560.)**

(a) The first group will outline several reasons why a firm might be better off as a corporation than as an LLC.

(b) The second group will discuss the differences between corporations and LLCs in terms of their management structure.

Business owners and managers today need to be ever conscious of the ethical implications of doing business. A company's business decisions and ethical practices can affect not only on its employees and shareholders, but also the general public. In this last *Focus on Ethics,* we examine the fiduciary duties of individuals in the various business organizations discussed in the preceding unit.

The law of agency, as outlined in Chapter 25, permeates nearly all relationships within any partnership or corporation. An important duty that arises in the law of agency, and applies to all partners and corporate directors, officers, and management personnel, is the duty of loyalty. As caretakers of the shareholders' wealth, corporate directors and officers also have a fiduciary duty to exercise care when making decisions affecting the corporate enterprise.

### The Duty of Loyalty

Every individual has personal interests, which may at times conflict with the interests of the partnership or corporation with which he or she is affiliated. In particular, partners or corporate officers and directors may face a conflict between personal interests and the interests of the business entity.

**Acquiring Assets.**   Corporate officers and directors may find themselves in a position to acquire assets that would also benefit the corporation if acquired in the corporation's name. If an officer does purchase the asset without offering the opportunity to the corporation, however, she or he may be liable for usurping a corporate opportunity.[1]

**Disclosure.**   Most courts also hold that a corporate officer or director has a fiduciary duty to disclose improper conduct to the corporation. For example, a leading case on the issue involved Thomas Coughlin, a top executive in theft prevention at Wal-Mart. He had held several other high-level positions prior to becoming a member of the board of directors. When he retired, Coughlin signed an agreement and release of claims with Wal-Mart under which he was to receive millions of dollars in benefits over the years.

Then Wal-Mart discovered that Coughlin, before his retirement, had abused his position of authority. He had conspired with subordinates to misappropriate hundreds of thousands of dollars in property and cash through various fraudulent schemes. Wal-Mart sued Coughlin alleging that he had breached his fiduciary duty of loyalty by failing to disclose his misconduct before entering a self-dealing contract.

Ultimately, the Supreme Court of Arkansas agreed and held that the director's fiduciary duty obligated him to divulge material facts of *past* fraud to the corporation before entering the contract. The court stated, "We are persuaded, in addition,

that the majority view is correct, which is that the failure of a fiduciary to disclose material facts of his fraudulent conduct to his corporation prior to entering into a self-dealing contract with that corporation will void that contract."[2]

### The Duty of Care

In addition to the duty of loyalty, every corporate director or officer owes a duty of care. *Due care* means that officers and directors must keep themselves informed and make businesslike judgments. Officers have a duty to disclose material information that shareholders need for competent decision making.

Some courts have even suggested that corporate directors have a duty to detect and "ferret out" wrongdoing within the corporation.[3] In fact, a number of courts applying Delaware law have recognized that directors may be held liable for failing to exercise proper oversight.[4] For example, one Delaware court held that shareholders of Citigroup, Inc., could sue the directors and officers for failure to exercise due care to adequately protect the corporation from exposure to the subprime lending market.[5] Corporate law also creates other structures to protect shareholder interests, such as the right to inspect books and records.

Although traditionally the duty of care did not require directors to monitor the behavior of corporate employees to detect and prevent wrongdoing, the tide may be changing. The corporate sentencing guidelines give courts the power to impose substantial penalties on corporations and corporate directors for criminal wrongdoing. Moreover, since the Sarbanes-Oxley Act required the sentencing commission to revise these guidelines, the penalties for white-collar crimes, such as federal mail and wire fraud, have increased dramatically. The guidelines allow these penalties to be mitigated, though, if a company can show that it has an effective compliance program in place to detect and prevent wrongdoing by corporate personnel.

### LEGAL REASONING

1.  *Three decades ago, corporations and corporate directors were rarely prosecuted for crimes, and penalties for corporate crimes were relatively light. Today, this is no longer true. Under*

---

1.  For a landmark case on this issue, see *Guth v. Loft, Inc.,* 5 A.2d 503 (Del. 1939).

2.  *Wal-Mart Stores, Inc. v. Coughlin,* 369 Ark. 365, 255 S.W.3d 424 (2007). See also *Blankenship v. USA Truck, Inc.,* 601 F.3d 852 (8th Cir. 2010), interpreting Arkansas law by applying the *Wal-Mart* case; and *Mazak Corp. v. King,* 2012 WL 3590817 (6th Cir. 2012), in which a federal court recognized that the *Wal-Mart* case stated the rule in the majority of states.

3.  *In re China Agritech, Inc. Shareholder Derivative Litigation,* 2013 WL 2181514 (Del.Ch. 2013); and *In re Caremark International, Inc. Derivative Litigation,* 698 A.2d 959 (Del.Ch. 1996).

4.  See, for example, *McCall v. Scott,* 239 F.3d 808 (6th Cir. 2001); *Guttman v. Huang,* 823 A.2d 492 (Del.Ch. 2003); *Landy v. D'Alessandro,* 316 F.Supp.2d 49 (D.Mass. 2004); and *Miller v. U.S. Foodservice, Inc.,* 361 F.Supp.2d 470 (D.Md. 2005).

5.  *In re Citigroup, Inc. Shareholder Derivative Litigation,* 964 A.2d 106 (Del.Ch. 2009).

FOCUS ON ETHICS CONTINUES ➡

the corporate sentencing guidelines, corporate wrongdoers can receive substantial penalties. Do these developments mean that corporations are committing more crimes today than in the past? Will stricter laws be effective in curbing corporate criminal activity? How can a company avoid liability for crimes committed by its employees?

## Fiduciary Duties to Creditors

It is a long-standing principle that corporate directors ordinarily owe fiduciary duties only to a corporation's shareholders. Directors who have favored the interests of other corporate "stakeholders," such as creditors, over those of the shareholders have been held liable for breaching these duties.

The picture changes, however, when a corporation approaches insolvency. At this point, the shareholders' equity interests in the corporation may be worthless, while the interests of creditors become paramount. In this situation, do the fiduciary duties of loyalty and care extend to the corporation's creditors as well as to the shareholders?

The answer to this question, according to some courts, is yes. In one case, a Delaware court held that when a corporation is on the brink of insolvency, the directors assume a fiduciary duty to other stakeholders that sustain the corporate entity, including creditors.[6] When a corporation is insolvent, courts may require directors to consider the best interests of the whole corporate enterprise, including all its constituent groups, and not to give preference to the interests of any one group.[7]

## LEGAL REASONING

2. *Do you agree that when a corporation is approaching insolvency, the directors' fiduciary obligations should extend to the corporation's creditors as well as to the shareholders? Why or why not?*

---

6. *Credit Lyonnais Bank Nederland N.V. v. Pathe Communications Corp.,* 1991 WL 277613 (Del.Ch. 1991). See also *Production Resources Group, LLC v. NCT Group, Inc.,* 863 A.2d 772 (Del.Ch. 2004); and *In re USDigital, Inc.,* 443 Bankr. 22 (D.Del. 2011).

7. See *Berg & Berg Enterprises, LLC v. Boyle,* 178 Cal.App.4th 1020, 100 Cal.Rptr.3d 875 (2009); *In re Moeller,* 466 Bankr. 525 (S.D.Cal. 2012); and *Scouler & Co., LLC v. Schwartz,* 2012 WL 1502762 (N.D.Cal. 2012).

## How to Brief Cases

To fully understand the law with respect to business, you need to be able to read and understand court decisions. To make this task easier, you can use a method of case analysis that is called *briefing*. There is a fairly standard procedure that you can follow when you "brief" any court case. You must first read the case opinion carefully. When you feel you understand the case, you can prepare a brief of it.

Although the format of the brief may vary, typically it will present the essentials of the case under headings such as those listed below.

1. **Citation.** Give the full citation for the case, including the name of the case, the date it was decided, and the court that decided it.
2. **Facts.** Briefly indicate (a) the reasons for the lawsuit; (b) the identity and arguments of the plaintiff(s) and defendant(s), respectively; and (c) the lower court's decision—if appropriate.
3. **Issue.** Concisely phrase, in the form of a question, the essential issue before the court. (If more than one issue is involved, you may have two—or even more—questions here.)
4. **Decision.** Indicate here—with a "yes" or "no," if possible—the court's answer to the question (or questions) in the *Issue* section above.
5. **Reason.** Summarize as briefly as possible the reasons given by the court for its decision (or decisions) and the case or statutory law relied on by the court in arriving at its decision.

## An Example of a Briefed Sample Court Case

As an example of the format used in briefing cases, we present here a briefed version of the sample court case that was presented in Chapter 1 in Exhibit 1–6.

### APPLE INC. v. AMAZON.COM INC.
United States District Court, Northern District of California, __ F.Supp.2d __, 2013 WL 11896 (2013).

**FACTS** In July 2008, Apple Inc. began to sell applications for its mobile devices through its APP STORE service. In March 2011, Amazon.com Inc. launched the Amazon Appstore for Android. Apple filed a suit in a federal district court against Amazon in the same month, asserting false advertising. Apple alleged that that by using the word "Appstore" in the name of Amazon's store, Amazon implied that its store was affili-

ated with or sponsored by Apple. Apple argued that Amazon's service did not have the characteristics and qualities that the public had come to expect from the name APP STORE. For this reason, Apple contended, Amazon's use of "Appstore" misled the public. Amazon filed a motion for summary judgment.

**ISSUE** Can a vendor use the term "Appstore" to designate a site for buying apps without representing that the nature, characteristics, or quality of the site is the same as that of another vendor's "APP STORE"?

**DECISION** Yes. The court granted Amazon's motion for summary judgment.

**REASON** The court pointed out that a false advertising claim requires either a false statement of fact in an ad or evidence showing "exactly what message was conveyed that was sufficient to constitute false advertising." Here, Apple failed to show that Amazon made any false statement and presented no evidence that consumers were misled. Apple did not show that consumers understood "app store" to include specific qualities, characteristics, or attributes of the Apple APP STORE or were otherwise misled by Amazon's use of the term. Nothing indicated that a consumer would expect the two sites to be identical—especially considering that Apple sold apps solely for Apple devices and Amazon sold apps solely for Android and Kindle devices. Apple did not make clear how Amazon's use of Appstore constituted a "statement" that implied something false about Apple's APP STORE. Apple "made no showing that such (implied) statement deceived or had a tendency to deceive users of Amazon's Appstore."

## Review of Sample Court Case

Here we provide a review of the briefed version to indicate the kind of information that is contained in each section.

**CITATION** The name of the case is *Apple Inc. v. Amazon.com Inc.* Apple is the plaintiff. Amazon is the defendant. The U.S. District Court for the Northern District of California (a trial court) decided this case in 2013. The citation states that this case can be found in volume __ of the *Federal Supplement, Second Series*, on page __, and on Westlaw® at 2013 WL 11896.

**FACTS** The *Facts* section identifies the plaintiff and the defendant, describes the events leading up to this suit and the allegations made by the plaintiff in the suit. If this case were a decision of one of the U.S. courts of appeals, the lower court's ruling, the party appealing, and the appellant's contention on appeal would also be included here.

**ISSUE** The *Issue* section presents the central issue (or issues) decided by the court. This case involves a false advertising claim. The court considers whether a vendor can use the term "Appstore" to designate a site for buying apps without representing that the nature, characteristics, or quality of the site is the same as that of another vendor's "APP STORE."

**DECISION** The *Decision* section includes the court's decision on the issues before it. The decision reflects the opinion of the judge or justice hearing the case. Here, the court determined that consumers were not deceived by the two vendors' use of the same term. There was no evidence that consumers understood "app store" to include specific qualities, characteristics, or attributes or were otherwise misled by the use of the term. Decisions by appellate courts are frequently phrased in reference to the lower court's decision. That is, the appellate court may "affirm" the lower court's ruling or "reverse" it.

**REASON** The *Reason* section includes references to the relevant laws and legal principles that were applied in coming to the conclusion arrived at in the case before the court. The relevant law here included the principle that a false advertising claim requires either a false statement of fact in an ad or evidence showing "exactly what message was conveyed that was sufficient to constitute false advertising." This section also explains the court's application of the law to the facts in this case.

## Analyzing Case Problems

In addition to learning how to brief cases, students of business law and the legal environment also find it helpful to know how to analyze case problems. Part of the study of business law and the legal environment usually involves analyzing case problems, such as those included in this text at the end of each chapter.

For each case problem in this book, we provide the relevant background and facts of the lawsuit and the issue before the court. When you are assigned one of these problems, your job will be to determine how the court should decide the issue, and why. In other words, you will need to engage in legal analysis and reasoning. Here, we offer some suggestions on how to make this task less daunting. We begin by presenting a sample problem:

> While Janet Lawson, a famous pianist, was shopping in Quality Market, she slipped and fell on a wet floor in one of the aisles. The floor had recently been mopped by one of the store's employees, but there were no signs warning customers that the floor in that area was wet. As a result of the fall, Lawson injured her right arm and was unable to perform piano concerts for the next six months. Had she been able to perform the scheduled concerts, she would have earned approximately $60,000 over that period of time. Lawson sued Quality Market for this amount, plus another $10,000 in medical expenses. She claimed that the store's failure to warn customers of the wet floor constituted

negligence and therefore the market was liable for her injuries. Will the court agree with Lawson? Discuss.

## Understand the Facts

This may sound obvious, but before you can analyze or apply the relevant law to a specific set of facts, you must clearly understand those facts. In other words, you should read through the case problem carefully—more than once, if necessary—to make sure you understand the identity of the plaintiff(s) and defendant(s) in the case and the progression of events that led to the lawsuit.

In the sample case problem just given, the identity of the parties is fairly obvious. Janet Lawson is the one bringing the suit; therefore, she is the plaintiff. Quality Market, against whom she is bringing the suit, is the defendant. Some of the case problems you may work on have multiple plaintiffs or defendants. Often, it is helpful to use abbreviations for the parties. To indicate a reference to a plaintiff, for example, the *pi* symbol—π—is often used, and a defendant is denoted by a *delta*—Δ—a triangle.

The events leading to the lawsuit are also fairly straightforward. Lawson slipped and fell on a wet floor, and she contends that Quality Market should be liable for her injuries because it was negligent in not posting a sign warning customers of the wet floor.

When you are working on case problems, realize that the facts should be accepted as they are given. For example, in our sample problem, it should be accepted that the floor was wet and that there was no sign. In other words, avoid making conjectures, such as "Maybe the floor wasn't too wet," or "Maybe an employee was getting a sign to put up," or "Maybe someone stole the sign." Questioning the facts as they are presented only adds confusion to your analysis.

## Legal Analysis and Reasoning

Once you understand the facts given in the case problem, you can begin to analyze the case. Recall from Chapter 1 that the IRAC method is a helpful tool to use in the legal analysis and reasoning process. IRAC is an acronym for Issue, Rule, Application, Conclusion. Applying this method to our sample problem would involve the following steps:

1. First, you need to decide what legal **issue** is involved in the case. In our sample case, the basic issue is whether Quality Market's failure to warn customers of the wet floor constituted negligence. As discussed in Chapter 6, negligence is a *tort*—a civil wrong. In a tort lawsuit, the plaintiff seeks to be compensated for another's wrongful act. A defendant will be deemed negligent if he or she breached a duty of care owed to the plaintiff and the breach of that duty caused the plaintiff to suffer harm.
2. Once you have identified the issue, the next step is to determine what **rule of law** applies to the issue. To make this determination, you will want to review carefully the text of the chapter in which the relevant rule of law for the problem appears. Our sample case problem involves the tort of

negligence, which is covered in Chapter 6. The applicable rule of law is the tort law principle that business owners owe a duty to exercise reasonable care to protect their customers ("business invitees"). Reasonable care, in this context, includes either removing—or warning customers of—*foreseeable* risks about which the owner *knew* or *should have known.* Business owners need not warn customers of "open and obvious" risks, however. If a business owner breaches this duty of care (fails to exercise the appropriate degree of care toward customers), and the breach of duty causes a customer to be injured, the business owner will be liable to the customer for the customer's injuries.

3. The next—and usually the most difficult—step in analyzing case problems is the **application** of the relevant rule of law to the specific facts of the case you are studying. In our sample problem, applying the tort law principle just discussed presents few difficulties. An employee of the store had mopped the floor in the aisle where Lawson slipped and fell, but no sign was present indicating that the floor was wet. That a customer might fall on a wet floor is clearly a foreseeable risk. Therefore, the failure to warn customers about the wet floor was a breach of the duty of care owed by the business owner to the store's customers.

4. Once you have completed Step 3 in the IRAC method, you should be ready to draw your **conclusion.** In our sample problem, Quality Market is liable to Lawson for her injuries, because the market's breach of its duty of care caused Lawson's injuries.

The fact patterns in the case problems presented in this text are not always as simple as those presented in our sample problem. Often, for example, a case has more than one plaintiff or defendant. A case may also involve more than one issue and have more than one applicable rule of law. Furthermore, in some case problems the facts may indicate that the general rule of law should not apply. For example, suppose that a store employee advised Lawson not to walk on the floor in the aisle because it was wet, but Lawson decided to walk on it anyway. This fact could alter the outcome of the case because the store could then raise the defense of assumption of risk (see Chapter 7). Nonetheless, a careful review of the chapter should always provide you with the knowledge you need to analyze the problem thoroughly and arrive at accurate conclusions.

## Preamble

We the People of the United States, in Order to form a more perfect Union, establish Justice, insure domestic Tranquility, provide for the common defence, promote the general Welfare, and secure the Blessings of Liberty to ourselves and our Posterity, do ordain and establish this Constitution for the United States of America.

## Article I

**Section 1.** All legislative Powers herein granted shall be vested in a Congress of the United States, which shall consist of a Senate and House of Representatives.

**Section 2.** The House of Representatives shall be composed of Members chosen every second Year by the People of the several States, and the Electors in each State shall have the Qualifications requisite for Electors of the most numerous Branch of the State Legislature.

No Person shall be a Representative who shall not have attained to the Age of twenty five Years, and been seven Years a Citizen of the United States, and who shall not, when elected, be an Inhabitant of that State in which he shall be chosen.

Representatives and direct Taxes shall be apportioned among the several States which may be included within this Union, according to their respective Numbers, which shall be determined by adding to the whole Number of free Persons, including those bound to Service for a Term of Years, and excluding Indians not taxed, three fifths of all other Persons. The actual Enumeration shall be made within three Years after the first Meeting of the Congress of the United States, and within every subsequent Term of ten Years, in such Manner as they shall by Law direct. The Number of Representatives shall not exceed one for every thirty Thousand, but each State shall have at Least one Representative; and until such enumeration shall be made, the State of New Hampshire shall be entitled to chuse three, Massachusetts eight, Rhode Island and Providence Plantations one, Connecticut five, New York six, New Jersey four, Pennsylvania eight, Delaware one, Maryland six, Virginia ten, North Carolina five, South Carolina five, and Georgia three.

When vacancies happen in the Representation from any State, the Executive Authority thereof shall issue Writs of Election to fill such Vacancies.

The House of Representatives shall chuse their Speaker and other Officers; and shall have the sole Power of Impeachment.

**Section 3.** The Senate of the United States shall be composed of two Senators from each State, chosen by the Legislature thereof, for six Years; and each Senator shall have one Vote.

Immediately after they shall be assembled in Consequence of the first Election, they shall be divided as equally as may be into three Classes. The Seats of the Senators of the first Class shall be vacated at the Expiration of the second Year, of the second Class at the Expiration of the fourth Year, and of the third Class at the Expiration of the sixth Year, so that one third

may be chosen every second Year; and if Vacancies happen by Resignation, or otherwise, during the Recess of the Legislature of any State, the Executive thereof may make temporary Appointments until the next Meeting of the Legislature, which shall then fill such Vacancies.

No Person shall be a Senator who shall not have attained to the Age of thirty Years, and been nine Years a Citizen of the United States, and who shall not, when elected, be an Inhabitant of that State for which he shall be chosen.

The Vice President of the United States shall be President of the Senate, but shall have no Vote, unless they be equally divided.

The Senate shall chuse their other Officers, and also a President pro tempore, in the Absence of the Vice President, or when he shall exercise the Office of President of the United States.

The Senate shall have the sole Power to try all Impeachments. When sitting for that Purpose, they shall be on Oath or Affirmation. When the President of the United States is tried, the Chief Justice shall preside: And no Person shall be convicted without the Concurrence of two thirds of the Members present.

Judgment in Cases of Impeachment shall not extend further than to removal from Office, and disqualification to hold and enjoy any Office of honor, Trust, or Profit under the United States: but the Party convicted shall nevertheless be liable and subject to Indictment, Trial, Judgment, and Punishment, according to Law.

**Section 4.** The Times, Places and Manner of holding Elections for Senators and Representatives, shall be prescribed in each State by the Legislature thereof; but the Congress may at any time by Law make or alter such Regulations, except as to the Places of chusing Senators.

The Congress shall assemble at least once in every Year, and such Meeting shall be on the first Monday in December, unless they shall by Law appoint a different Day.

**Section 5.** Each House shall be the Judge of the Elections, Returns, and Qualifications of its own Members, and a Majority of each shall constitute a Quorum to do Business; but a smaller Number may adjourn from day to day, and may be authorized to compel the Attendance of absent Members, in such Manner, and under such Penalties as each House may provide.

Each House may determine the Rules of its Proceedings, punish its Members for disorderly Behavior, and, with the Concurrence of two thirds, expel a Member.

Each House shall keep a Journal of its Proceedings, and from time to time publish the same, excepting such Parts as may in their Judgment require Secrecy; and the Yeas and Nays of the Members of either House on any question shall, at the Desire of one fifth of those Present, be entered on the Journal.

Neither House, during the Session of Congress, shall, without the Consent of the other, adjourn for more than three days, nor to any other Place than that in which the two Houses shall be sitting.

**Section 6.** The Senators and Representatives shall receive a Compensation for their Services, to be ascertained by Law, and paid out of the Treasury of the United States. They shall in all Cases, except Treason, Felony and Breach of the Peace, be privileged from Arrest during their Attendance at the Session of their respective Houses, and in going to and returning from the same; and for any Speech or Debate in either House, they shall not be questioned in any other Place.

No Senator or Representative shall, during the Time for which he was elected, be appointed to any civil Office under the Authority of the United States, which shall have been created, or the Emoluments whereof shall have been increased during such time; and no Person holding any Office under the United States, shall be a Member of either House during his Continuance in Office.

**Section 7.** All Bills for raising Revenue shall originate in the House of Representatives; but the Senate may propose or concur with Amendments as on other Bills.

Every Bill which shall have passed the House of Representatives and the Senate, shall, before it become a Law, be presented to the President of the United States; If he approve he shall sign it, but if not he shall return it, with his Objections to the House in which it shall have originated, who shall enter the Objections at large on their Journal, and proceed to reconsider it. If after such Reconsideration two thirds of that House shall agree to pass the Bill, it shall be sent together with the Objections, to the other House, by which it shall likewise be reconsidered, and if approved by two thirds of that House, it shall become a Law. But in all such Cases the Votes of both Houses shall be determined by Yeas and Nays, and the Names of the Persons voting for and against the Bill shall be entered on the Journal of each House respectively. If any Bill shall not be returned by the President within ten Days (Sundays excepted) after it shall have been presented to him, the Same shall be a Law, in like Manner as if he had signed it, unless the Congress by their Adjournment prevent its Return in which Case it shall not be a Law.

Every Order, Resolution, or Vote, to which the Concurrence of the Senate and House of Representatives may be necessary (except on a question of Adjournment) shall be presented to the President of the United States; and before the Same shall take Effect, shall be approved by him, or being disapproved by him, shall be repassed by two thirds of the Senate and House of Representatives, according to the Rules and Limitations prescribed in the Case of a Bill.

**Section 8.** The Congress shall have Power To lay and collect Taxes, Duties, Imposts and Excises, to pay the Debts and provide for the common Defence and general Welfare of the United States; but all Duties, Imposts and Excises shall be uniform throughout the United States;

To borrow Money on the credit of the United States;

To regulate Commerce with foreign Nations, and among the several States, and with the Indian Tribes;

To establish an uniform Rule of Naturalization, and uniform Laws on the subject of Bankruptcies throughout the United States;

To coin Money, regulate the Value thereof, and of foreign Coin, and fix the Standard of Weights and Measures;

To provide for the Punishment of counterfeiting the Securities and current Coin of the United States;

To establish Post Offices and post Roads;

To promote the Progress of Science and useful Arts, by securing for limited Times to Authors and Inventors the exclusive Right to their respective Writings and Discoveries;

To constitute Tribunals inferior to the supreme Court;

To define and punish Piracies and Felonies committed on the high Seas, and Offenses against the Law of Nations;

To declare War, grant Letters of Marque and Reprisal, and make Rules concerning Captures on Land and Water;

To raise and support Armies, but no Appropriation of Money to that Use shall be for a longer Term than two Years;

To provide and maintain a Navy;

To make Rules for the Government and Regulation of the land and naval Forces;

To provide for calling forth the Militia to execute the Laws of the Union, suppress Insurrections and repel Invasions;

To provide for organizing, arming, and disciplining, the Militia, and for governing such Part of them as may be employed in the Service of the United States, reserving to the States respectively, the Appointment of the Officers, and the Authority of training the Militia according to the discipline prescribed by Congress;

To exercise exclusive Legislation in all Cases whatsoever, over such District (not exceeding ten Miles square) as may, by Cession of particular States, and the Acceptance of Congress, become the Seat of the Government of the United States, and to exercise like Authority over all Places purchased by the Consent of the Legislature of the State in which the Same shall be, for the Erection of Forts, Magazines, Arsenals, dock-Yards, and other needful Buildings;—And

To make all Laws which shall be necessary and proper for carrying into Execution the foregoing Powers, and all other Powers vested by this Constitution in the Government of the United States, or in any Department or Officer thereof.

**Section 9.** The Migration or Importation of such Persons as any of the States now existing shall think proper to admit, shall not be prohibited by the Congress prior to the Year one thousand eight hundred and eight, but a Tax or duty may be imposed on such Importation, not exceeding ten dollars for each Person.

The privilege of the Writ of Habeas Corpus shall not be suspended, unless when in Cases of Rebellion or Invasion the public Safety may require it.

No Bill of Attainder or ex post facto Law shall be passed.

No Capitation, or other direct, Tax shall be laid, unless in Proportion to the Census or Enumeration herein before directed to be taken.

No Tax or Duty shall be laid on Articles exported from any State.

No Preference shall be given by any Regulation of Commerce or Revenue to the Ports of one State over those of another: nor shall Vessels bound to, or from, one State be obliged to enter, clear, or pay Duties in another.

No Money shall be drawn from the Treasury, but in Consequence of Appropriations made by Law; and a regular Statement and Account of the Receipts and Expenditures of all public Money shall be published from time to time.

No Title of Nobility shall be granted by the United States: And no Person holding any Office of Profit or Trust under them, shall, without the Consent of the Congress, accept of any present, Emolument, Office, or Title, of any kind whatever, from any King, Prince, or foreign State.

**Section 10.** No State shall enter into any Treaty, Alliance, or Confederation; grant Letters of Marque and Reprisal; coin Money; emit Bills of Credit; make any Thing but gold and silver Coin a Tender in Payment of Debts; pass any Bill of Attainder, ex post facto Law, or Law impairing the Obligation of Contracts, or grant any Title of Nobility.

No State shall, without the Consent of the Congress, lay any Imposts or Duties on Imports or Exports, except what may be absolutely necessary for executing its inspection Laws: and the net Produce of all Duties and Imposts, laid by any State on Imports or Exports, shall be for the Use of the Treasury of the United States; and all such Laws shall be subject to the Revision and Controul of the Congress.

No State shall, without the Consent of Congress, lay any Duty of Tonnage, keep Troops, or Ships of War in time of Peace, enter into any Agreement or Compact with another State, or with a foreign Power, or engage in War, unless actually invaded, or in such imminent Danger as will not admit of delay.

## Article II

**Section 1.** The executive Power shall be vested in a President of the United States of America. He shall hold his Office during the Term of four Years, and, together with the Vice President, chosen for the same Term, be elected, as follows:

Each State shall appoint, in such Manner as the Legislature thereof may direct, a Number of Electors, equal to the whole Number of Senators and Representatives to which the State may be entitled in the Congress; but no Senator or Representative, or Person holding an Office of Trust or Profit under the United States, shall be appointed an Elector.

The Electors shall meet in their respective States, and vote by Ballot for two Persons, of whom one at least shall not be an Inhabitant of the same State with themselves. And they shall make a List of all the Persons voted for, and of the Number of Votes for each; which List they shall sign and certify, and transmit sealed to the Seat of the Government of the United States, directed to the President of the Senate. The President of the Senate shall, in the Presence of the Senate and House of Representatives, open all the Certificates, and the Votes shall then be counted. The Person having the greatest Number of Votes shall be the President, if such Number be a Majority of the whole Number of Electors appointed; and if there be more than one who have such Majority, and have an equal Number of Votes, then the House of Representatives shall immediately chuse by Ballot one of them for President; and if no Person have a Majority, then from the five highest on the List the said House shall in like Manner chuse the President. But in chusing the President, the Votes shall be taken by States, the Representation from each State having one Vote; A quorum for this Purpose shall consist of a Member or Members from two thirds of the States, and a Majority of all the States shall be necessary to a Choice. In every Case, after the Choice of the President, the Person having the greater Number of Votes of the Electors shall be the Vice President. But if there should remain two or more who have equal Votes, the Senate shall chuse from them by Ballot the Vice President.

The Congress may determine the Time of chusing the Electors, and the Day on which they shall give their Votes; which Day shall be the same throughout the United States.

No person except a natural born Citizen, or a Citizen of the United States, at the time of the Adoption of this Constitution, shall be eligible to the Office of President; neither shall any Person be eligible to that Office who shall not have attained to the Age of thirty five Years, and been fourteen Years a Resident within the United States.

In Case of the Removal of the President from Office, or of his Death, Resignation or Inability to discharge the Powers and Duties of the said Office, the same shall devolve on the Vice President, and the Congress may by Law provide for the Case of Removal, Death, Resignation or Inability, both of the President and Vice President, declaring what Officer shall then act as President, and such Officer shall act accordingly, until the Disability be removed, or a President shall be elected.

The President shall, at stated Times, receive for his Services, a Compensation, which shall neither be increased nor diminished during the Period for which he shall have been elected, and he shall not receive within that Period any other Emolument from the United States, or any of them.

Before he enter on the Execution of his Office, he shall take the following Oath or Affirmation: "I do solemnly swear (or affirm) that I will faithfully execute the Office of President of the United States, and will to the best of my Ability, preserve, protect and defend the Constitution of the United States."

**Section 2.** The President shall be Commander in Chief of the Army and Navy of the United States, and of the Militia of the several States, when called into the actual Service of the United States; he may require the Opinion, in writing, of the principal Officer in each of the executive Departments, upon any Subject relating to the Duties of their respective Offices, and he shall have Power to grant Reprieves and Pardons for Offenses against the United States, except in Cases of Impeachment.

He shall have Power, by and with the Advice and Consent of the Senate to make Treaties, provided two thirds of the Senators present concur; and he shall nominate, and by and with the Advice and Consent of the Senate, shall appoint Ambassadors, other public Ministers and Consuls, Judges of the supreme Court, and all other Officers of the United States, whose Appointments are not herein otherwise provided for, and which shall be established by Law; but the Congress may by Law vest the Appointment of such inferior Officers, as they think proper, in the President alone, in the Courts of Law, or in the Heads of Departments.

The President shall have Power to fill up all Vacancies that may happen during the Recess of the Senate, by granting Commissions which shall expire at the End of their next Session.

**Section 3.** He shall from time to time give to the Congress Information of the State of the Union, and recommend to their Consideration such Measures as he shall judge necessary and expedient; he may, on extraordinary Occasions, convene both Houses, or either of them, and in Case of Disagreement between them, with Respect to the Time of Adjournment, he may adjourn them to such Time as he shall think proper; he shall receive Ambassadors and other public Ministers; he shall take Care that the Laws be faithfully executed, and shall Commission all the Officers of the United States.

**Section 4.** The President, Vice President and all civil Officers of the United States, shall be removed from Office on Impeachment for, and Conviction of, Treason, Bribery, or other high Crimes and Misdemeanors.

## Article III

**Section 1.** The judicial Power of the United States, shall be vested in one supreme Court, and in such inferior Courts as the Congress may from time to time ordain and establish. The Judges, both of the supreme and inferior Courts, shall hold their Offices during good Behaviour, and shall, at stated Times, receive for their Services a Compensation, which shall not be diminished during their Continuance in Office.

**Section 2.** The judicial Power shall extend to all Cases, in Law and Equity, arising under this Constitution, the Laws of the United States, and Treaties made, or which shall be made, under their Authority;—to all Cases affecting Ambassadors, other public Ministers and Consuls;—to all Cases of admiralty and maritime Jurisdiction;—to Controversies to which the United States shall be a Party;—to Controversies between two or more States;—between a State and Citizens of another State;—between Citizens of different States;—between Citizens of the same State claiming Lands under Grants of different States, and between a State, or the Citizens thereof, and foreign States, Citizens or Subjects.

In all Cases affecting Ambassadors, other public Ministers and Consuls, and those in which a State shall be a Party, the supreme Court shall have original Jurisdiction. In all the other Cases before mentioned, the supreme Court shall have appellate Jurisdiction, both as to Law and Fact, with such Exceptions, and under such Regulations as the Congress shall make.

The Trial of all Crimes, except in Cases of Impeachment, shall be by Jury; and such Trial shall be held in the State where the said Crimes shall have been committed; but when not committed within any State, the Trial shall be at such Place or Places as the Congress may by Law have directed.

**Section 3.** Treason against the United States, shall consist only in levying War against them, or, in adhering to their Enemies, giving them Aid and Comfort. No Person shall be convicted of Treason unless on the Testimony of two Witnesses to the same overt Act, or on Confession in open Court.

The Congress shall have Power to declare the Punishment of Treason, but no Attainder of Treason shall work Corruption of Blood, or Forfeiture except during the Life of the Person attainted.

## Article IV

**Section 1.** Full Faith and Credit shall be given in each State to the public Acts, Records, and judicial Proceedings of every other State. And the Congress may by general Laws prescribe the Manner in which such Acts, Records and Proceedings shall be proved, and the Effect thereof.

**Section 2.** The Citizens of each State shall be entitled to all Privileges and Immunities of Citizens in the several States.

A Person charged in any State with Treason, Felony, or other Crime, who shall flee from Justice, and be found in another State, shall on Demand of the executive Authority of the State from which he fled, be delivered up, to be removed to the State having Jurisdiction of the Crime.

No Person held to Service or Labour in one State, under the Laws thereof, escaping into another, shall, in Consequence of any Law or Regulation therein, be discharged from such Service or Labour, but shall be delivered up on Claim of the Party to whom such Service or Labour may be due.

**Section 3.** New States may be admitted by the Congress into this Union; but no new State shall be formed or erected within the Jurisdiction of any other State; nor any State be formed by the Junction of two or more States, or Parts of States, without the Consent of the Legislatures of the States concerned as well as of the Congress.

The Congress shall have Power to dispose of and make all needful Rules and Regulations respecting the Territory or other Property belonging to the United States; and nothing in this Constitution shall be so construed as to Prejudice any Claims of the United States, or of any particular State.

**Section 4.** The United States shall guarantee to every State in this Union a Republican Form of Government, and shall protect each of them against Invasion; and on Application of the Legislature, or of the Executive (when the Legislature cannot be convened) against domestic Violence.

## Article V

The Congress, whenever two thirds of both Houses shall deem it necessary, shall propose Amendments to this Constitution, or, on the Application of the Legislatures of two thirds of the several States, shall call a Convention for proposing Amendments, which, in either Case, shall be valid to all Intents and Purposes, as part of this Constitution, when ratified by the Legislatures of three fourths of the several States, or by Conventions in three fourths thereof, as the one or the other Mode of Ratification may be proposed by the Congress; Provided that no Amendment which may be made prior to the Year One thousand eight hundred and eight shall in any Manner affect the first and fourth Clauses in the Ninth Section of the first Article; and that no State, without its Consent, shall be deprived of its equal Suffrage in the Senate.

## Article VI

All Debts contracted and Engagements entered into, before the Adoption of this Constitution shall be as valid against the United States under this Constitution, as under the Confederation.

This Constitution, and the Laws of the United States which shall be made in Pursuance thereof; and all Treaties made, or which shall be made, under the Authority of the United States, shall be the supreme Law of the Land; and the Judges in every State shall be bound thereby, any Thing in the Constitution or Laws of any State to the Contrary notwithstanding.

The Senators and Representatives before mentioned, and the Members of the several State Legislatures, and all executive and judicial Officers, both of the United States and of the several States, shall be bound by Oath or Affirmation, to support this Constitution; but no religious Test shall ever be required as a Qualification to any Office or public Trust under the United States.

## Article VII

The Ratification of the Conventions of nine States shall be sufficient for the Establishment of this Constitution between the States so ratifying the Same.

## Amendment I [1791]

Congress shall make no law respecting an establishment of religion, or prohibiting the free exercise thereof; or abridging the freedom of speech, or of the press; or the right of the people peaceably to assembly, and to petition the Government for a redress of grievances.

## Amendment II [1791]

A well regulated Militia, being necessary to the security of a free State, the right of the people to keep and bear Arms, shall not be infringed.

## Amendment III [1791]

No Soldier shall, in time of peace be quartered in any house, without the consent of the Owner, nor in time of war, but in a manner to be prescribed by law.

## Amendment IV [1791]

The right of the people to be secure in their persons, houses, papers, and effects, against unreasonable searches and seizures, shall not be violated, and no Warrants shall issue, but upon probable cause, supported by Oath or affirmation, and particularly describing the place to be searched, and the persons or things to be seized.

## Amendment V [1791]

No person shall be held to answer for a capital, or otherwise infamous crime, unless on a presentment or indictment of a Grand Jury, except in cases arising in the land or naval forces, or in the Militia, when in actual service in time of War or public danger; nor shall any person be subject for the same offence to be twice put in jeopardy of life or limb; nor shall be compelled in any criminal case to be a witness against himself, nor be deprived of life, liberty, or property, without due process of law; nor shall private property be taken for public use, without just compensation.

## Amendment VI [1791]

In all criminal prosecutions, the accused shall enjoy the right to a speedy and public trial, by an impartial jury of the State and district wherein the crime shall have been committed, which district shall have been previously ascertained by law, and to be informed of the nature and cause of the accusation; to be confronted with the witnesses against him; to have compulsory process for obtaining witnesses in his favor, and to have the Assistance of Counsel for his defence.

## Amendment VII [1791]

In Suits at common law, where the value in controversy shall exceed twenty dollars, the right of trial by jury shall be preserved, and no fact tried by jury, shall be otherwise re-examined in any Court of the United States, than according to the rules of the common law.

## Amendment VIII [1791]

Excessive bail shall not be required, nor excessive fines imposed, nor cruel and unusual punishments inflicted.

## Amendment IX [1791]

The enumeration in the Constitution, of certain rights, shall not be construed to deny or disparage others retained by the people.

## Amendment X [1791]

The powers not delegated to the United States by the Constitution, nor prohibited by it to the States, are reserved to the States respectively, or to the people.

## Amendment XI [1798]

The Judicial power of the United States shall not be construed to extend to any suit in law or equity, commenced or prosecuted against one of the United States by Citizens of another State, or by Citizens or Subjects of any Foreign State.

## Amendment XII [1804]

The Electors shall meet in their respective states, and vote by ballot for President and Vice-President, one of whom, at least, shall not be an inhabitant of the same state with themselves; they shall name in their ballots the person voted for as President, and in distinct ballots the person voted for as Vice-President, and they shall make distinct lists of all persons voted for as President, and of all persons voted for as Vice-President, and of the number of votes for each, which lists they shall sign and certify, and transmit sealed to the seat of the government of the United States, directed to the President of the Senate;—The President of the Senate shall, in the presence of the Senate and House of Representatives, open all the certificates and the votes shall then be counted;—The person having the greatest number of votes for President, shall be the President, if such number be a majority of the whole number of Electors appointed; and if no person have such majority, then from the persons having the highest numbers not exceeding three on the list of those voted for as President, the House of Representatives shall choose immediately, by ballot, the President. But in choosing the President, the votes shall be taken by states, the representation from each state having one vote; a quorum for this purpose shall consist of a member or members from two-thirds of the states, and a majority of all states shall be necessary to a choice. And if the House of Representatives shall not choose a President whenever the right of choice shall devolve upon them, before the fourth day of March next following, then the Vice-President shall act as President, as in the case of the death or other constitutional disability of the President.—The person having the greatest number of votes as Vice-President, shall be the Vice-President, if such number be a majority of the whole number of Electors appointed, and if no person have a majority, then from the two highest numbers on the list, the Senate shall choose the Vice-President; a quorum for the purpose shall consist of two-thirds of the whole number of Senators, and a majority of the whole number shall be necessary to a choice. But no person constitutionally ineligible to the office of President shall be eligible to that of Vice-President of the United States.

## Amendment XIII [1865]

**Section 1.** Neither slavery nor involuntary servitude, except as a punishment for crime whereof the party shall have been duly convicted, shall exist within the United States, or any place subject to their jurisdiction.

**Section 2.** Congress shall have power to enforce this article by appropriate legislation.

## Amendment XIV [1868]

**Section 1.** All persons born or naturalized in the United States, and subject to the jurisdiction thereof, are citizens of the United States and of the State wherein they reside. No State shall make or enforce any law which shall abridge the privileges or immunities of citizens of the United States; nor shall any State deprive any person of life, liberty, or property, without due process of law; nor deny to any person within its jurisdiction the equal protection of the laws.

**Section 2.** Representatives shall be apportioned among the several States according to their respective numbers, counting the whole number of persons in each State, excluding Indians not taxed. But when the right to vote at any election for the choice of electors for President and Vice President of the United States, Representatives in Congress, the Executive and Judicial officers of a State, or the members of the Legislature thereof, is denied to any of the male inhabitants of such State, being twenty-one years of age, and citizens of the United States, or in any way abridged, except for participation in rebellion, or other crime, the basis of representation therein shall be reduced in the proportion which the number of such male citizens shall bear to the whole number of male citizens twenty-one years of age in such State.

**Section 3.** No person shall be a Senator or Representative in Congress, or elector of President and Vice President, or hold any office, civil or military, under the United States, or under any State, who having previously taken an oath, as a member of Congress, or as an officer of the United States, or as a member of any State legislature, or as an executive or judicial officer of any State, to support the Constitution of the United States, shall have engaged in insurrection or rebellion against the same, or given aid or comfort to the enemies thereof. But Congress may by a vote of two-thirds of each House, remove such disability.

**Section 4.** The validity of the public debt of the United States, authorized by law, including debts incurred for payment of pensions and bounties for services in suppressing insurrection or rebellion, shall not be questioned. But neither the United States nor any State shall assume or pay any debt or obligation incurred in aid of insurrection or rebellion against

the United States, or any claim for the loss or emancipation of any slave; but all such debts, obligations and claims shall be held illegal and void.

**Section 5.** The Congress shall have power to enforce, by appropriate legislation, the provisions of this article.

## Amendment XV [1870]

**Section 1.** The right of citizens of the United States to vote shall not be denied or abridged by the United States or by any State on account of race, color, or previous condition of servitude.

**Section 2.** The Congress shall have power to enforce this article by appropriate legislation.

## Amendment XVI [1913]

The Congress shall have power to lay and collect taxes on incomes, from whatever source derived, without apportionment among the several States, and without regard to any census or enumeration.

## Amendment XVII [1913]

**Section 1.** The Senate of the United States shall be composed of two Senators from each State, elected by the people thereof, for six years; and each Senator shall have one vote. The electors in each State shall have the qualifications requisite for electors of the most numerous branch of the State legislatures.

**Section 2.** When vacancies happen in the representation of any State in the Senate, the executive authority of such State shall issue writs of election to fill such vacancies: *Provided,* That the legislature of any State may empower the executive thereof to make temporary appointments until the people fill the vacancies by election as the legislature may direct.

**Section 3.** This amendment shall not be so construed as to affect the election or term of any Senator chosen before it becomes valid as part of the Constitution.

## Amendment XVIII [1919]

**Section 1.** After one year from the ratification of this article the manufacture, sale, or transportation of intoxicating liquors within, the importation thereof into, or the exportation thereof from the United States and all territory subject to the jurisdiction thereof for beverage purposes is hereby prohibited.

**Section 2.** The Congress and the several States shall have concurrent power to enforce this article by appropriate legislation.

**Section 3.** This article shall be inoperative unless it shall have been ratified as an amendment to the Constitution by the legislatures of the several States, as provided in the Constitution, within seven years from the date of the submission hereof to the States by the Congress.

## Amendment XIX [1920]

**Section 1.** The right of citizens of the United States to vote shall not be denied or abridged by the United States or by any State on account of sex.

**Section 2.** Congress shall have power to enforce this article by appropriate legislation.

## Amendment XX [1933]

**Section 1.** The terms of the President and Vice President shall end at noon on the 20th day of January, and the terms of Senators and Representatives at noon on the 3d day of January, of the years in which such terms would have ended if this article had not been ratified; and the terms of their successors shall then begin.

**Section 2.** The Congress shall assemble at least once in every year, and such meeting shall begin at noon on the 3d day of January, unless they shall by law appoint a different day.

**Section 3.** If, at the time fixed for the beginning of the term of the President, the President elect shall have died, the Vice President elect shall become President. If the President shall not have been chosen before the time fixed for the beginning of his term, or if the President elect shall have failed to qualify, then the Vice President elect shall act as President until a President shall have qualified; and the Congress may by law provide for the case wherein neither a President elect nor a Vice President elect shall have qualified, declaring who shall then act as President, or the manner in which one who is to act shall be selected, and such person shall act accordingly until a President or Vice President shall have qualified.

**Section 4.** The Congress may by law provide for the case of the death of any of the persons from whom the House of Representatives may choose a President whenever the right of choice shall have devolved upon them, and for the case of the death of any of the persons from whom the Senate may choose a Vice President whenever the right of choice shall have devolved upon them.

**Section 5.** Sections 1 and 2 shall take effect on the 15th day of October following the ratification of this article.

**Section 6.** This article shall be inoperative unless it shall have been ratified as an amendment to the Constitution by the legislatures of three-fourths of the several States within seven years from the date of its submission.

## Amendment XXI [1933]

**Section 1.** The eighteenth article of amendment to the Constitution of the United States is hereby repealed.

**Section 2.** The transportation or importation into any State, Territory, or possession of the United States for delivery or use therein of intoxicating liquors, in violation of the laws thereof, is hereby prohibited.

**Section 3.** This article shall be inoperative unless it shall have been ratified as an amendment to the Constitution by conventions in the several States, as provided in the Constitution, within seven years from the date of the submission hereof to the States by the Congress.

## Amendment XXII [1951]

**Section 1.** No person shall be elected to the office of the President more than twice, and no person who has held the office of President, or acted as President, for more than two years of a term to which some other person was elected President shall be elected to the office of President more than once. But this Article shall not apply to any person holding the office of President when this Article was proposed by the Congress, and shall not prevent any person who may be holding the office of President, or acting as President, during the term within which this Article becomes operative from holding the office of President or acting as President during the remainder of such term.

**Section 2.** This article shall be inoperative unless it shall have been ratified as an amendment to the Constitution by the legislatures of three-fourths of the several States within seven years from the date of its submission to the States by the Congress.

## Amendment XXIII [1961]

**Section 1.** The District constituting the seat of Government of the United States shall appoint in such manner as the Congress may direct:

A number of electors of President and Vice President equal to the whole number of Senators and Representatives in Congress to which the District would be entitled if it were a State, but in no event more than the least populous state; they shall be in addition to those appointed by the states, but they shall be considered, for the purposes of the election of President and Vice President, to be electors appointed by a state; and they shall meet in the District and perform such duties as provided by the twelfth article of amendment.

**Section 2.** The Congress shall have power to enforce this article by appropriate legislation.

## Amendment XXIV [1964]

**Section 1.** The right of citizens of the United States to vote in any primary or other election for President or Vice President, for electors for President or Vice President, or for Senator or Representative in Congress, shall not be denied or abridged by the United States, or any State by reason of failure to pay any poll tax or other tax.

**Section 2.** The Congress shall have power to enforce this article by appropriate legislation.

## Amendment XXV [1967]

**Section 1.** In case of the removal of the President from office or of his death or resignation, the Vice President shall become President.

**Section 2.** Whenever there is a vacancy in the office of the Vice President, the President shall nominate a Vice President who shall take office upon confirmation by a majority vote of both Houses of Congress.

**Section 3.** Whenever the President transmits to the President pro tempore of the Senate and the Speaker of the House of Representatives his written declaration that he is unable to discharge the powers and duties of his office, and until he transmits to them a written declaration to the contrary, such powers and duties shall be discharged by the Vice President as Acting President.

**Section 4.** Whenever the Vice President and a majority of either the principal officers of the executive departments or of such other body as Congress may by law provide, transmit to the President pro tempore of the Senate and the Speaker of the House of Representatives their written declaration that the President is unable to discharge the powers and duties of his office, the Vice President shall immediately assume the powers and duties of the office as Acting President.

Thereafter, when the President transmits to the President pro tempore of the Senate and the Speaker of the House of Representatives his written declaration that no inability exists, he shall resume the powers and duties of his office unless the Vice President and a majority of either the principal officers of the executive department or of such other body as Congress may by law provide, transmit within four days to the President pro tempore of the Senate and the Speaker of the House of Representatives their written declaration that the President is unable to discharge the powers and duties of his office. Thereupon Congress shall decide the issue, assembling within forty-eight hours for that purpose if not in session. If the Congress, within twenty-one days after receipt of the latter written declaration, or, if Congress is not in session, within twenty-one days after Congress is required to assemble, deter-mines by two-thirds vote of both Houses that the President is unable to discharge the powers and duties of his office, the Vice President shall continue to discharge the same as Acting President; otherwise, the President shall resume the powers and duties of his office.

## Amendment XXVI [1971]

**Section 1.** The right of citizens of the United States, who are eighteen years of age or older, to vote shall not be denied or abridged by the United States or by any State on account of age.

**Section 2.** The Congress shall have power to enforce this article by appropriate legislation.

## Amendment XXVII [1992]

No law, varying the compensation for the services of the Senators and Representatives, shall take effect, until an election of Representatives shall have intervened.

(Adopted in fifty-two jurisdictions—all fifty States, although Louisiana has adopted only Articles 1, 3, 4, 7, 8, and 9; the District of Columbia; and the Virgin Islands.)

The Code consists of the following articles:

**Article**
1. General Provisions
2. Sales
2A. Leases
3. Negotiable Instruments
4. Bank Deposits and Collections
4A. Funds Transfers
5. Letters of Credit
6. Repealer of Article 6—Bulk Transfers and [Revised] Article 6—Bulk Sales
7. Warehouse Receipts, Bills of Lading and Other Documents of Title
8. Investment Securities
9. Secured Transactions
10. Effective Date and Repealer
11. Effective Date and Transition Provisions

## ARTICLE 1: GENERAL PROVISIONS

### Part 1—General Provisions

#### § 1–101. Short Titles.

(a) This [Act] may be cited as Uniform Commercial Code.

(b) This article may be cited as Uniform Commercial Code-Uniform Provisions.

#### § 1–102. Scope of Article.

This article applies to a transaction to the extent that it is governed by another article of [the Uniform Commercial Code].

#### § 1–103. Construction of [Uniform Commercial Code] to Promote Its Purpose and Policies; Applicability of Supplemental Principles of Law.

(a) [The Uniform Commercial Code] must be liberally construed and applied to promote its underlying purposes and policies, which are:

(1) to simplify, clarify, and modernize the law govern-ing commercial transactions;

(2) to permit the continued expansion of commercial practices through custom, usage, and agreement of the parties; and

(3) to make uniform the law among the various jurisdictions.

(b) Unless displaced by the particular provisions of [the Uniform Commercial Code], the principles of law and equity, including the law merchant and the law relative to capacity to

contract, principal and agent, estoppel, fraud, misrepresentation, duress, coercion, mistake, bankruptcy, and other validating or invalidating cause, supplement its provisions.

#### § 1–104. Construction Against Implicit Repeal.

This Act being a general act intended as a unified coverage of its subject matter, no part of it shall be deemed to be impliedly repealed by subsequent legislation if such construction can reasonably be avoided.

#### § 1–105. Severability.

If any provision or clause of [the Uniform Commercial Code] or its application to any person or circumstance is held invalid, the invalidity does not affect other provisions or applications of [the Uniform Commercial Code] which can be given effect without the invalid provision or application, and to this end the provisions of [the Uniform Commercial Code] are severable.

#### § 1–106. Use of Singular and Plural; Gender.

In [the Uniform Commercial Code], unless the statutory context otherwise requires:

(1) words in the singular number include the plural, and those in the plural include the singular; and

(2) words of any gender also refer to any other gender.

#### § 1–107. Section Captions.

Section captions are part of [the Uniform Commercial Code].

#### § 1–108. Relation to Electronic Signatures in Global and National Commerce Act.

This article modifies, limits, and supersedes the Federal Electronic Signatures in Global and National Commerce Act, 15 U.S.C. Sections 7001 *et seq.*, except that nothing in this article modifies, limits, or supersedes Section 7001(c) of that act or authorizes electronic delivery of any of the notices described in Section 7003(b) of that Act.

### Part 2—General Definitions and Principles of Interpretation

#### § 1–201. General Definitions.

Subject to additional definitions contained in the subsequent Articles of this Act which are applicable to specific Articles or Parts thereof, and unless the context otherwise requires, in this Act:

(1) "Action", in the sense of a judicial proceeding, includes recoupment, counterclaim, set-off, suit in equity, and any other proceedings in which rights are determined.

(2) "Aggrieved party" means a party entitled to resort to a remedy.

(3) "Agreement", as distinguished from "contract", means the bargain of the parties in fact, as found in their language or by implication from other circumstances, including course of performance, course of dealing, or usage of trade as provided in Section 1–303.

(4) "Bank" means a person engaged in the business of banking and includes a savings bank, savings and loan association, credit union, and trust company.

**(5)** "Bearer" means a person in control of a negotiable electronic document of title or a person in possession of a negotiable instrument, negotiable tangible document of title, or certificated security that is payable to bearer or indorsed in blank.

**(6)** "Bill of lading" means a document of title evidencing the receipt of goods for shipment issued by a person engaged in the business of directly or indirectly transporting or forwarding goods. The term does not include a warehouse receipt.

**(7)** "Branch" includes a separately incorporated foreign branch of a bank.

**(8)** "Burden of establishing" a fact means the burden of persuading the trier of fact that the existence of the fact is more probable than its nonexistence.

**(9)** "Buyer in ordinary course of business" means a person that buys goods in good faith, without knowledge that the sale violates the rights of another person in the goods, and in the ordinary course from a person, other than a pawnbroker, in the business of selling goods of that kind. A person buys goods in the ordinary course if the sale to the person comports with the usual or customary practices in the kind of business in which the seller is engaged or with the seller's own usual or customary practices. A person that sells oil, gas, or other minerals at the wellhead or minehead is a person in the business of selling goods of that kind. A buyer in ordinary course of business may buy for cash, by exchange of other property, or on secured or unsecured credit, and may acquire goods or documents of title under a pre-existing contract for sale. Only a buyer that takes possession of the goods or has a right to recover the goods from the seller under Article 2 may be a buyer in ordinary course of business. A person that acquires goods in a transfer in bulk or as security for or in total or partial satisfaction of a money debt is not a buyer in ordinary course of business.

**(10)** "Conspicuous", with reference to a term, means so written, displayed, or presented that a reasonable person against which it is to operate ought to have noticed it. Whether a term is "conspicuous" or not is a decision for the court. Conspicuous terms include the following:

(A) a heading in capitals equal to or greater in size than the surrounding text, or in contrasting type, font, or color to the surrounding text of the same or lesser size; and

(B) language in the body of a record or display in larger type than the surrounding text, or in contrasting type, font, or color to the surrounding text of the same size, or set off from surrounding text of the same size by symbols or other marks that call attention to the language.

**(11)** "Consumer" means an individual who enters into a transaction primarily for personal, family, or household purposes.

**(12)** "Contract", as distinguished from "agreement", means the total legal obligation that results from the parties' agreement as determined by [the Uniform Commercial Code] as supplemented by any other laws.

**(13)** "Creditor" includes a general creditor, a secured creditor, a lien creditor and any representative of creditors, including an assignee for the benefit of creditors, a trustee in bankruptcy, a receiver in equity and an executor or administrator of an insolvent debtor's or assignor's estate.

**(14)** "Defendant" includes a person in the position of defendant in a counterclaim, cross-action, or third-party claim.

**(15)** "Delivery" with respect to an electronic document of title means voluntary transfer of control and with respect to an instrument, a tangible document of title, or chattel paper means voluntary transfer of possession.

**(16)** "Document of title" means a record (i) that in regular course of business or financing is treated as adequately evidencing that the person in possession or control of the record is entitled to receive, control, hold, and dispose of the record and the goods the record covers and (ii) that purports to be issued by or addressed to a bailee and to cover goods in the bailee's possession which are either identified or are fungible portions of an identified mass. The term includes a bill of lading, transport document, dock warrant, dock receipt, warehouse receipt, and order for delivery of goods. An electronic document of title means a document of title evidenced by a record consisting of information stored in an electronic medium. A tangible document of title means a document of title evidenced by a record consisting of information that is inscribed on a tangible medium.

**(17)** "Fault" means a default, breach, or wrongful act or omission.

**(18)** "Fungible goods" means:

(A) goods of which any unit, by nature or usage of trade, is the equivalent of any other like unit; or

(B) goods that by agreement are treated as equivalent.

**(19)** "Genuine" means free of forgery or counterfeiting.

**(20)** "Good faith," except as otherwise provided in Article 5, means honesty in fact and the observance of reasonable commercial standards of fair dealing.

**(21)** "Holder" means:

(A) the person in possession of a negotiable instrument that is payable either to bearer or to an identified person that is the person in possession;

(B) the person in possession of a negotiable tangible document of title if the goods are deliverable either to bearer or to the order of the person in possession; or

(C) the person in control of a negotiable electronic document of title.

**(22)** "Insolvency proceeding" includes an assignment for the benefit of creditors or other proceeding intended to liquidate or rehabilitate the estate of the person involved.

**(23)** "Insolvent" means:

(A) having generally ceased to pay debts in the ordinary course of business other than as a result of bona fide dispute;

(B) being unable to pay debts as they become due; or

(C) being insolvent within the meaning of federal bankruptcy law.

**(24)** "Money" means a medium of exchange currently authorized or adopted by a domestic or foreign government. The term includes a monetary unit of account established by an intergovernmental organization or by agreement between two or more countries.

**(25)** "Organization" means a person other than an individual.

**(26)** "Party", as distinguished from "third party", means a person that has engaged in a transaction or made an agreement subject to [the Uniform Commercial Code].

**(27)** "Person" means an individual, corporation, business trust, estate, trust, partnership, limited liability company, association, joint venture, government, governmental subdivision, agency, or instrumentality, public corporation, or any other legal or commercial entity.

**(28)** "Present value" means the amount as of a date certain of one or more sums payable in the future, discounted to the date certain by use of either an interest rate specified by the parties if that rate is not manifestly unreasonable at the time the transaction is entered into or, if an interest rate is not so specified, a commercially reasonable rate that takes into account the facts and circumstances at the time the transaction is entered into.

**(29)** "Purchase" means taking by sale, lease, discount, negotiation, mortgage, pledge, lien, security interest, issue or reissue, gift, or any other voluntary transaction creating an interest in property.

**(30)** "Purchaser" means a person that takes by purchase.

**(31)** "Record" means information that is inscribed on a tangible medium or that is stored in an electronic or other medium and is retrievable in perceivable form.

**(32)** "Remedy" means any remedial right to which an aggrieved party is entitled with or without resort to a tribunal.

**(33)** "Representative" means a person empowered to act for another, including an agent, an officer of a corporation or association, and a trustee, executor, or administrator of an estate.

**(34)** "Right" includes remedy.

**(35)** "Security interest" means an interest in personal property or fixtures which secures payment or performance of an obligation. "Security interest" includes any interest of a consignor and a buyer of accounts, chattel paper, a payment intangible, or a promissory note in a transaction that is subject to Article 9. "Security interest" does not include the special property interest of a buyer of goods on identification of those goods to a contract for sale under Section 2–401, but a buyer may also acquire a "security interest" by complying with Article 9. Except as otherwise provided in Section 2–505, the right of a seller or lessor of goods under Article 2 or 2A to retain or acquire possession of the goods is not a "security interest", but a seller or lessor may also acquire a "security interest" by complying with Article 9. The retention or reservation of title by a seller of goods notwithstanding shipment or delivery to the buyer under Section 2–401 is limited in effect to a reservation of a "security interest." Whether a transaction in the form of a lease creates a "security interest" is determined pursuant to Section 1–203.

**(36)** "Send" in connection with a writing, record, or notice means:

**(A)** to deposit in the mail or deliver for transmission by any other usual means of communication with postage or cost of transmission provided for and properly addressed and, in the case of an instrument, to an address specified thereon or otherwise agreed, or if there be none to any address reasonable under the circumstances; or

**(B)** in any other way to cause to be received any record or notice within the time it would have arrived if properly sent.

**(37)** "Signed" includes using any symbol executed or adopted with present intention to adopt or accept a writing.

**(38)** "State" means a State of the United States, the District of Columbia, Puerto Rico, the United States Virgin Islands, or any territory or insular possession subject to the jurisdiction of the United States.

**(39)** "Surety" includes a guarantor or other secondary obligor.

**(40)** "Term" means a portion of an agreement that relates to a particular matter.

**(41)** "Unauthorized signature" means a signature made without actual, implied, or apparent authority. The term includes a forgery.

**(42)** "Warehouse receipt" means a document of title issued by a person engaged in the business of storing goods for hire.

**(43)** "Writing" includes printing, typewriting, or any other intentional reduction to tangible form. "Written" has a corresponding meaning.

As amended in 2003.

## § 1–202. Notice; Knowledge.

**(a)** Subject to subsection (f), a person has "notice" of a fact if the person:

**(1)** has actual knowledge of it;

**(2)** has received a notice or notification of it; or

**(3)** from all the facts and circumstances known to the person at the time in question, has reason to know that it exists.

**(b)** "Knowledge" means actual knowledge. "Knows" has a corresponding meaning.

**(c)** "Discover", "learn", or words of similar import refer to knowledge rather than to reason to know.

**(d)** A person "notifies" or "gives" a notice or notification to another person by taking such steps as may be reasonably required to inform the other person in ordinary course, whether or not the other person actually comes to know of it.

**(e)** Subject to subsection (f), a person "receives" a notice or notification when:

**(1)** it comes to that person's attention; or

**(2)** it is duly delivered in a form reasonable under the circumstances at the place of business through which the contract was made or at another location held out by that person as the place for receipt of such communications.

**(f)** Notice, knowledge, or a notice or notification received by an organization is effective for a particular transaction from the time it is brought to the attention of the individual conducting that transaction and, in any event, from the time it would have been brought to the individual's attention if the organization had exercised due diligence. An organization exercises due diligence if it maintains reasonable routines for communicating significant information to the person conducting the transaction and there is reasonable compliance with the routines. Due diligence does not require an individual acting for the organization to communicate information unless the communication is part of the individual's regular duties or the individual has reason to know of the transaction and that the transaction would be materially affected by the information.

## § 1–203. Lease Distinguished from Security Interest.

**(a)** Whether a transaction in the form of a lease creates a lease or security interest is determined by the facts of each case.

**(b)** A transaction in the form of a lease creates a security interest if the consideration that the lessee is to pay the lessor for the right to possession and use of the goods is an obligation for the term of the lease and is not subject to termination by the lessee, and:

    (1) the original term of the lease is equal to or greater than the remaining economic life of the goods;

    (2) the lessee is bound to renew the lease for the remaining economic life of the goods or is bound to become the owner of the goods;

    (3) the lessee has an option to renew the lease for the remaining economic life of the goods for no additional consideration or for nominal additional consideration upon compliance with the lease agreement; or

    (4) the lessee has an option to become the owner of the goods for no additional consideration or for nominal additional consideration upon compliance with the lease agreement.

(c) A transaction in the form of a lease does not create a security interest merely because:

    (1) the present value of the consideration the lessee is obligated to pay the lessor for the right to possession and use of the goods is substantially equal to or is greater than the fair market value of the goods at the time the lease is entered into;

    (2) the lessee assumes risk of loss of the goods;

    (3) the lessee agrees to pay, with respect to the goods, taxes, insurance, filing, recording, or registration fees, or service or maintenance costs;

    (4) the lessee has an option to renew the lease or to become the owner of the goods;

    (5) the lessee has an option to renew the lease for a fixed rent that is equal to or greater than the reasonably predictable fair market rent for the use of the goods for the term of the renewal at the time the option is to be performed; or

    (6) the lessee has an option to become the owner of the goods for a fixed price that is equal to or greater than the reasonably predictable fair market value of the goods at the time the option is to be performed.

(d) Additional consideration is nominal if it is less than the lessee's reasonably predictable cost of performing under the lease agreement if the option is not exercised. Additional consideration is not nominal if:

    (1) when the option to renew the lease is granted to the lessee, the rent is stated to be the fair market rent for the use of the goods for the term of the renewal determined at the time the option is to be performed; or

    (2) when the option to become the owner of the goods is granted to the lessee, the price is stated to be the fair market value of the goods determined at the time the option is to be performed.

(e) The "remaining economic life of the goods" and "reasonably predictable" fair market rent, fair market value, or cost of performing under the lease agreement must be determined with reference to the facts and circumstances at the time the transaction is entered into.

### § 1–204. Value.

Except as otherwise provided in Articles 3, 4, [and] 5, [and 6], a person gives value for rights if the person acquires them:

    (1) in return for a binding commitment to extend credit or for the extension of immediately available credit, whether or not drawn upon and whether or not a charge-back is provided for in the event of difficulties in collection;

    (2) as security for, or in total or partial satisfaction of, a preexisting claim;

    (3) by accepting delivery under a preexisting contract for purchase; or

    (4) in return for any consideration sufficient to support a simple contract.

### § 1–205. Reasonable Time; Seasonableness.

(a) Whether a time for taking an action required by [the Uniform Commercial Code] is reasonable depends on the nature, purpose, and circumstances of the action.

(b) An action is taken seasonably if it is taken at or within the time agreed or, if no time is agreed, at or within a reasonable time.

### § 1–206. Presumptions.

Whenever [the Uniform Commercial Code] creates a "presumption" with respect to a fact, or provides that a fact is "presumed," the trier of fact must find the existence of the fact unless and until evidence is introduced that supports a finding of its nonexistence.

### Part 3—Territorial Applicability and General Rules

### § 1–301. Territorial Applicability; Parties' Power to Choose Applicable Law.

(a) In this section:

    (1) "Domestic transaction" means a transaction other than an international transaction.

    (2) "International transaction" means a transaction that bears a reasonable relation to a country other than the United States.

(b) This section applies to a transaction to the extent that it is governed by another article of the [Uniform Commercial Code].

(c) Except as otherwise provided in this section:

    (1) an agreement by parties to a domestic transaction that any or all of their rights and obligations are to be determined by the law of this State or of another State is effective, whether or not the transaction bears a relation to the State designated; and

    (2) an agreement by parties to an international transaction that any or all of their rights and obligations are to be determined by the law of this State or of another State or country is effective, whether or not the transaction bears a relation to the State or country designated.

(d) In the absence of an agreement effective under subsection (c), and except as provided in subsections (e) and (g), the rights and obligations of the parties are determined by the law that would be selected by application of this State's conflict of laws principles.

(e) If one of the parties to a transaction is a consumer, the following rules apply:

    (1) An agreement referred to in subsection (c) is not effective unless the transaction bears a reasonable relation to the State or country designated.

    (2) Application of the law of the State or country determined pursuant to subsection (c) or (d) may not deprive

the consumer of the protection of any rule of law governing a matter within the scope of this section, which both is protective of consumers and may not be varied by agreement: (A) of the State or country in which the consumer principally resides, unless subparagraph (B) applies; or (B) if the transaction is a sale of goods, of the State or country in which the consumer both makes the contract and take delivery of those goods, if such State or country is not the State or country in which the consumer principally resides.

**(f)** An agreement otherwise effective under subsection (c) is not effective to the extent that application of the law of the State or country designated would be contrary to a fundamental policy of the State or country whose law would govern in the absence of agreement under subsection (d).

**(g)** To the extent that [the Uniform Commercial Code] governs a transaction, if one of the following provisions of [the Uniform Commercial Code] specifies the applicable law, that provision governs and a contrary agreement is effective only to the extent permitted by the law so specified: (1) Section 2–402; (2) Sections 2A–105 and 2A–106; (3) Section 4–102; (4) Section 4A–507; (5) Section 5–116; [(6) Section 6–103;] (7) Section 8–110; (8) Sections 9–301 through 9–307.

### § 1–302. Variation by Agreement.

**(a)** Except as otherwise provided in subsection (b) or elsewhere in [the Uniform Commercial Code], the effect of provisions of [the Uniform Commercial Code] may be varied by agreement.

**(b)** The obligations of good faith, diligence, reasonableness, and care prescribed by [the Uniform Commercial Code] may not be disclaimed by agreement. The parties, by agreement, may determine the standards by which the performance of those obligations is to be measured if those standards are not manifestly unreasonable. Whenever [the Uniform Commercial Code] requires an action to be taken within a reasonable time, a time that is not manifestly unreasonable may be fixed by agreement.

**(c)** The presence in certain provisions of [the Uniform Commercial Code] of the phrase "unless otherwise agreed", or words of similar import, does not imply that the effect of other provisions may not be varied by agreement under this section.

### § 1–303. Course of Performance, Course of Dealing, and Usage of Trade.

**(a)** A "course of performance" is a sequence of conduct between the parties to a particular transaction that exists if:

(1) the agreement of the parties with respect to the transaction involves repeated occasions for performance by a party; and

(2) the other party, with knowledge of the nature of the performance and opportunity for objection to it, accepts the performance or acquiesces in it without objection.

**(b)** A "course of dealing" is a sequence of conduct concerning previous transactions between the parties to a particular transaction that is fairly to be regarded as establishing a common basis of understanding for interpreting their expressions and other conduct.

**(c)** A "usage of trade" is any practice or method of dealing having such regularity of observance in a place, vocation, or trade as to justify an expectation that it will be observed with respect to the transaction in question. The existence and scope of such a usage must be proved as facts. If it is established that such a usage is embodied in a trade code or similar record, the interpretation of the record is a question of law.

**(d)** A course of performance or course of dealing between the parties or usage of trade in the vocation or trade in which they are engaged or of which they are or should be aware is relevant in ascertaining the meaning of the parties' agreement, may give particular meaning to specific terms of the agreement, and may supplement or qualify the terms of the agreement. A usage of trade applicable in the place in which part of the performance under the agreement is to occur may be so utilized as to that part of the performance.

**(e)** Except as otherwise provided in subsection (f), the express terms of an agreement and any applicable course of performance, course of dealing, or usage of trade must be construed whenever reasonable as consistent with each other. If such a construction is unreasonable:

(1) express terms prevail over course of performance, course of dealing, and usage of trade;

(2) course of performance prevails over course of dealing and usage of trade; and

(3) course of dealing prevails over usage of trade.

**(f)** Subject to Section 2–209 and Section 2A–208, a course of performance is relevant to show a waiver or modification of any term inconsistent with the course of performance.

**(g)** Evidence of a relevant usage of trade offered by one party is not admissible unless that party has given the other party notice that the court finds sufficient to prevent unfair surprise to the other party.

### § 1–304. Obligation of Good Faith.

Every contract or duty within [the Uniform Commercial Code] imposes an obligation of good faith in its performance and enforcement.

### § 1–305. Remedies to be Liberally Administered.

**(a)** The remedies provided by [the Uniform Commercial Code] must be liberally administered to the end that the aggrieved party may be put in as good a position as if the other party had fully performed but neither consequential or special damages nor penal damages may be had except as specifically provided in [the Uniform Commercial Code] or by other rule of law.

**(b)** Any right or obligation declared by [the Uniform Commercial Code] is enforceable by action unless the provision declaring it specifies a different and limited effect.

### § 1–306. Waiver or Renunciation of Claim or Right After Breach.

A claim or right arising out of an alleged breach may be discharged in whole or in part without consideration by agreement of the aggrieved party in an authenticated record.

### § 1–307. *Prima Facie* Evidence by Third-Party Documents.

A document in due form purporting to be a bill of lading, policy or certificate of insurance, official weigher's or inspector's certificate, consular invoice, or any other document authorized or required by the contract to be issued by a third party is *prima facie* evidence of its own authenticity and genuineness and of the facts stated in the document by the third party.

## § 1–308. Performance or Acceptance Under Reservation of Rights.

(a) A party that with explicit reservation of rights performs or promises performance or assents to performance in a manner demanded or offered by the other party does not thereby prejudice the rights reserved. Such words as "without prejudice," "under protest," or the like are sufficient.

(b) Subsection (a) does not apply to an accord and satisfaction.

## § 1–309. Option to Accelerate at Will.

A term providing that one party or that party's successor in interest may accelerate payment or performance or require collateral or additional collateral "at will" or when the party "deems itself insecure," or words of similar import, means that the party has power to do so only if that party in good faith believes that the prospect of payment or performance is impaired. The burden of establishing lack of good faith is on the party against which the power has been exercised.

## § 1–310. Subordinated Obligations.

An obligation may be issued as subordinated to performance of another obligation of the person obligated, or a creditor may subordinate its right to performance of an obligation by agreement with either the person obligated or another creditor of the person obligated. Subordination does not create a security interest as against either the common debtor or a subordinated creditor.

## ARTICLE 2: SALES

### Part 1—Short Title, General Construction and Subject Matter

### § 2–101. Short Title.

This Article shall be known and may be cited as Uniform Commercial Code—Sales.

### § 2–102. Scope; Certain Security and Other Transactions Excluded From This Article.

Unless the context otherwise requires, this Article applies to transactions in goods; it does not apply to any transaction which although in the form of an unconditional contract to sell or present sale is intended to operate only as a security transaction nor does this Article impair or repeal any statute regulating sales to consumers, farmers or other specified classes of buyers.

### § 2–103. Definitions and Index of Definitions.

(1) In this Article unless the context otherwise requires

    (a) "Buyer" means a person who buys or contracts to buy goods.

    (b) "Good faith" in the case of a merchant means honesty in fact and the observance of reasonable commercial standards of fair dealing in the trade.

    (c) "Receipt" of goods means taking physical possession of them.

    (d) "Seller" means a person who sells or contracts to sell goods.

(2) Other definitions applying to this Article or to specified Parts thereof, and the sections in which they appear are:

"Acceptance". Section 2–606.
"Banker's credit". Section 2–325.
"Between merchants". Section 2–104.
"Cancellation". Section 2–106(4).
"Commercial unit". Section 2–105.
"Confirmed credit". Section 2–325.
"Conforming to contract". Section 2–106.
"Contract for sale". Section 2–106.
"Cover". Section 2–712.
"Entrusting". Section 2–403.
"Financing agency". Section 2–104.
"Future goods". Section 2–105.
"Goods". Section 2–105.
"Identification". Section 2–501.
"Installment contract". Section 2–612.
"Letter of Credit". Section 2–325.
"Lot". Section 2–105.
"Merchant". Section 2–104.
"Overseas". Section 2–323.
"Person in position of seller". Section 2–707.
"Present sale". Section 2–106.
"Sale". Section 2–106.
"Sale on approval". Section 2–326.
"Sale or return". Section 2–326.
"Termination". Section 2–106.

(3) The following definitions in other Articles apply to this Article:

"Check". Section 3–104.
"Consignee". Section 7–102.
"Consignor". Section 7–102.
"Consumer goods". Section 9–109.
"Dishonor". Section 3–507.
"Draft". Section 3–104.

(4) In addition Article 1 contains general definitions and principles of construction and interpretation applicable throughout this Article.

As amended in 1994 and 1999.

### § 2–104. Definitions: "Merchant"; "Between Merchants"; "Financing Agency".

(1) "Merchant" means a person who deals in goods of the kind or otherwise by his occupation holds himself out as having knowledge or skill peculiar to the practices or goods involved in the transaction or to whom such knowledge or skill may be attributed by his employment of an agent or broker or other intermediary who by his occupation holds himself out as having such knowledge or skill.

(2) "Financing agency" means a bank, finance company or other person who in the ordinary course of business makes advances against goods or documents of title or who by arrangement with either the seller or the buyer intervenes in ordinary course to make or collect payment due or claimed under the contract for sale, as by purchasing or paying the seller's draft or making advances against it or by merely taking it for collection whether or not documents of title accompany the draft. "Financing agency" includes also a bank or other person who similarly intervenes between persons who are in the position of seller and buyer in respect to the goods (Section 2–707).

(3) "Between merchants" means in any transaction with respect to which both parties are chargeable with the knowledge or skill of merchants.

## § 2–105. Definitions: Transferability; "Goods"; "Future" Goods; "Lot"; "Commercial Unit".

**(1)** "Goods" means all things (including specially manufactured goods) which are movable at the time of identification to the contract for sale other than the money in which the price is to be paid, investment securities (Article 8) and things in action. "Goods" also includes the unborn young of animals and growing crops and other identified things attached to realty as described in the section on goods to be severed from realty (Section 2–107).

**(2)** Goods must be both existing and identified before any interest in them can pass. Goods which are not both existing and identified are "future" goods. A purported present sale of future goods or of any interest therein operates as a contract to sell.

**(3)** There may be a sale of a part interest in existing identified goods.

**(4)** An undivided share in an identified bulk of fungible goods is sufficiently identified to be sold although the quantity of the bulk is not determined. Any agreed proportion of such a bulk or any quantity thereof agreed upon by number, weight or other measure may to the extent of the seller's interest in the bulk be sold to the buyer who then becomes an owner in common.

**(5)** "Lot" means a parcel or a single article which is the subject matter of a separate sale or delivery, whether or not it is sufficient to perform the contract.

**(6)** "Commercial unit" means such a unit of goods as by commercial usage is a single whole for purposes of sale and division of which materially impairs its character or value on the market or in use. A commercial unit may be a single article (as a machine) or a set of articles (as a suite of furniture or an assortment of sizes) or a quantity (as a bale, gross, or carload) or any other unit treated in use or in the relevant market as a single whole.

## § 2–106. Definitions: "Contract"; "Agreement"; "Contract for Sale"; "Sale"; "Present Sale"; "Conforming" to Contract; "Termination"; "Cancellation".

**(1)** In this Article unless the context otherwise requires "contract" and "agreement" are limited to those relating to the present or future sale of goods. "Contract for sale" includes both a present sale of goods and a contract to sell goods at a future time. A "sale" consists in the passing of title from the seller to the buyer for a price (Section 2–401). A "present sale" means a sale which is accomplished by the making of the contract.

**(2)** Goods or conduct including any part of a performance are "conforming" or conform to the contract when they are in accordance with the obligations under the contract.

**(3)** "Termination" occurs when either party pursuant to a power created by agreement or law puts an end to the contract otherwise than for its breach. On "termination" all obligations which are still executory on both sides are discharged but any right based on prior breach or performance survives.

**(4)** "Cancellation" occurs when either party puts an end to the contract for breach by the other and its effect is the same as that of "termination" except that the cancelling party also retains any remedy for breach of the whole contract or any unperformed balance.

## § 2–107. Goods to Be Severed From Realty: Recording.

**(1)** A contract for the sale of minerals or the like (including oil and gas) or a structure or its materials to be removed from realty is a contract for the sale of goods within this Article if they are to be severed by the seller but until severance a purported present sale thereof which is not effective as a transfer of an interest in land is effective only as a contract to sell.

**(2)** A contract for the sale apart from the land of growing crops or other things attached to realty and capable of severance without material harm thereto but not described in subsection (1) or of timber to be cut is a contract for the sale of goods within this Article whether the subject matter is to be severed by the buyer or by the seller even though it forms part of the realty at the time of contracting, and the parties can by identification effect a present sale before severance.

**(3)** The provisions of this section are subject to any third party rights provided by the law relating to realty records, and the contract for sale may be executed and recorded as a document transferring an interest in land and shall then constitute notice to third parties of the buyer's rights under the contract for sale. As amended in 1972.

## Part 2—Form, Formation and Readjustment of Contract

### § 2–201. Formal Requirements; Statute of Frauds.

**(1)** Except as otherwise provided in this section a contract for the sale of goods for the price of $500 or more is not enforceable by way of action or defense unless there is some writing sufficient to indicate that a contract for sale has been made between the parties and signed by the party against whom enforcement is sought or by his authorized agent or broker. A writing is not insufficient because it omits or incorrectly states a term agreed upon but the contract is not enforceable under this paragraph beyond the quantity of goods shown in such writing.

**(2)** Between merchants if within a reasonable time a writing in confirmation of the contract and sufficient against the sender is received and the party receiving it has reason to know its contents, its satisfies the requirements of subsection (1) against such party unless written notice of objection to its contents is given within ten days after it is received.

**(3)** A contract which does not satisfy the requirements of subsection (1) but which is valid in other respects is enforceable

    **(a)** if the goods are to be specially manufactured for the buyer and are not suitable for sale to others in the ordinary course of the seller's business and the seller, before notice of repudiation is received and under circumstances which reasonably indicate that the goods are for the buyer, has made either a substantial beginning of their manufacture or commitments for their procurement; or

    **(b)** if the party against whom enforcement is sought admits in his pleading, testimony or otherwise in court that a contract for sale was made, but the contract is not enforceable under this provision beyond the quantity of goods admitted; or

    **(c)** with respect to goods for which payment has been made and accepted or which have been received and accepted (Sec. 2–606).

### § 2–202. Final Written Expression: Parol or Extrinsic Evidence.

Terms with respect to which the confirmatory memoranda of the parties agree or which are otherwise set forth in a writing intended by the parties as a final expression of their agreement with respect to such terms as are included therein may not be contradicted by evidence of any prior agreement or of a contemporaneous oral agreement but may be explained or supplemented

> **(a)** by course of dealing or usage of trade (Section 1–205) or by course of performance (Section 2–208); and
>
> **(b)** by evidence of consistent additional terms unless the court finds the writing to have been intended also as a complete and exclusive statement of the terms of the agreement.

### § 2–203.  Seals Inoperative.

The affixing of a seal to a writing evidencing a contract for sale or an offer to buy or sell goods does not constitute the writing a sealed instrument and the law with respect to sealed instruments does not apply to such a contract or offer.

### § 2–204.  Formation in General.

**(1)** A contract for sale of goods may be made in any manner sufficient to show agreement, including conduct by both parties which recognizes the existence of such a contract.

**(2)** An agreement sufficient to constitute a contract for sale may be found even though the moment of its making is undetermined.

**(3)** Even though one or more terms are left open a contract for sale does not fail for indefiniteness if the parties have intended to make a contract and there is a reasonably certain basis for giving an appropriate remedy.

### § 2–205.  Firm Offers.

An offer by a merchant to buy or sell goods in a signed writing which by its terms gives assurance that it will be held open is not revocable, for lack of consideration, during the time stated or if no time is stated for a reasonable time, but in no event may such period of irrevocability exceed three months; but any such term of assurance on a form supplied by the offeree must be separately signed by the offeror.

### § 2–206.  Offer and Acceptance in Formation of Contract.

**(1)** Unless other unambiguously indicated by the language or circumstances

> **(a)** an offer to make a contract shall be construed as inviting acceptance in any manner and by any medium reasonable in the circumstances;
>
> **(b)** an order or other offer to buy goods for prompt or current shipment shall be construed as inviting acceptance either by a prompt promise to ship or by the prompt or current shipment of conforming or nonconforming goods, but such a shipment of non-conforming goods does not constitute an acceptance if the seller seasonably notifies the buyer that the shipment is offered only as an accommodation to the buyer.

**(2)** Where the beginning of a requested performance is a reasonable mode of acceptance an offeror who is not notified of acceptance within a reasonable time may treat the offer as having lapsed before acceptance.

### § 2–207.  Additional Terms in Acceptance or Confirmation.

**(1)** A definite and seasonable expression of acceptance or a written confirmation which is sent within a reasonable time oper-

ates as an acceptance even though it states terms additional to or different from those offered or agreed upon, unless acceptance is expressly made conditional on assent to the additional or different terms.

**(2)** The additional terms are to be construed as proposals for addition to the contract. Between merchants such terms become part of the contract unless:

> **(a)** the offer expressly limits acceptance to the terms of the offer;
>
> **(b)** they materially alter it; or
>
> **(c)** notification of objection to them has already been given or is given within a reasonable time after notice of them is received.

**(3)** Conduct by both parties which recognizes the existence of a contract is sufficient to establish a contract for sale although the writings of the parties do not otherwise establish a contract. In such case the terms of the particular contract consist of those terms on which the writings of the parties agree, together with any supplementary terms incorporated under any other provisions of this Act.

### § 2–208.  Course of Performance or Practical Construction.

**(1)** Where the contract for sale involves repeated occasions for performance by either party with knowledge of the nature of the performance and opportunity for objection to it by the other, any course of performance accepted or acquiesced in without objection shall be relevant to determine the meaning of the agreement.

**(2)** The express terms of the agreement and any such course of performance, as well as any course of dealing and usage of trade, shall be construed whenever reasonable as consistent with each other; but when such construction is unreasonable, express terms shall control course of performance and course of performance shall control both course of dealing and usage of trade (Section 1–205).

**(3)** Subject to the provisions of the next section on modification and waiver, such course of performance shall be relevant to show a waiver or modification of any term inconsistent with such course of performance.

### § 2–209.  Modification, Rescission and Waiver.

**(1)** An agreement modifying a contract within this Article needs no consideration to be binding.

**(2)** A signed agreement which excludes modification or rescission except by a signed writing cannot be otherwise modified or rescinded, but except as between merchants such a requirement on a form supplied by the merchant must be separately signed by the other party.

**(3)** The requirements of the statute of frauds section of this Article (Section 2–201) must be satisfied if the contract as modified is within its provisions.

**(4)** Although an attempt at modification or rescission does not satisfy the requirements of subsection (2) or (3) it can operate as a waiver.

**(5)** A party who has made a waiver affecting an executory portion of the contract may retract the waiver by reasonable notification received by the other party that strict performance will be required of any term waived, unless the retraction would be unjust in view of a material change of position in reliance on the waiver.

## § 2–210. Delegation of Performance; Assignment of Rights.

(1) A party may perform his duty through a delegate unless otherwise agreed or unless the other party has a substantial interest in having his original promisor perform or control the acts required by the contract. No delegation of performance relieves the party delegating of any duty to perform or any liability for breach.

(2) Except as otherwise provided in Section 9–406, unless otherwise agreed, all rights of either seller or buyer can be assigned except where the assignment would materially change the duty of the other party, or increase materially the burden or risk imposed on him by his contract, or impair materially his chance of obtaining return performance. A right to damages for breach of the whole contract or a right arising out of the assignor's due performance of his entire obligation can be assigned despite agreement otherwise.

(3) The creation, attachment, perfection, or enforcement of a security interest in the seller's interest under a contract is not a transfer that materially changes the duty of or increases materially the burden or risk imposed on the buyer or impairs materially the buyer's chance of obtaining return performance within the purview of subsection (2) unless, and then only to the extent that, enforcement actually results in a delegation of material performance of the seller. Even in that event, the creation, attachment, perfection, and enforcement of the security interest remain effective, but (i) the seller is liable to the buyer for damages caused by the delegation to the extent that the damages could not reasonably by prevented by the buyer, and (ii) a court having jurisdiction may grant other appropriate relief, including cancellation of the contract for sale or an injunction against enforcement of the security interest or consummation of the enforcement.

(4) Unless the circumstances indicate the contrary a prohibition of assignment of "the contract" is to be construed as barring only the delegation to the assignee of the assignor's performance.

(5) An assignment of "the contract" or of "all my rights under the contract" or an assignment in similar general terms is an assignment of rights and unless the language or the circumstances (as in an assignment for security) indicate the contrary, it is a delegation of performance of the duties of the assignor and its acceptance by the assignee constitutes a promise by him to perform those duties. This promise is enforceable by either the assignor or the other party to the original contract.

(6) The other party may treat any assignment which delegates performance as creating reasonable grounds for insecurity and may without prejudice to his rights against the assignor demand assurances from the assignee (Section 2–609). As amended in 1999.

## Part 3—General Obligation and Construction of Contract

### § 2–301. General Obligations of Parties.

The obligation of the seller is to transfer and deliver and that of the buyer is to accept and pay in accordance with the contract.

## § 2–302. Unconscionable Contract or Clause.

(1) If the court as a matter of law finds the contract or any clause of the contract to have been unconscionable at the time it was made the court may refuse to enforce the contract, or it may enforce the remainder of the contract without the unconscionable clause, or it may so limit the application of any unconscionable clause as to avoid any unconscionable result.

(2) When it is claimed or appears to the court that the contract or any clause thereof may be unconscionable the parties shall be afforded a reasonable opportunity to present evidence as to its commercial setting, purpose and effect to aid the court in making the determination.

## § 2–303. Allocations or Division of Risks.

Where this Article allocates a risk or a burden as between the parties "unless otherwise agreed", the agreement may not only shift the allocation but may also divide the risk or burden.

## § 2–304. Price Payable in Money, Goods, Realty, or Otherwise.

(1) The price can be made payable in money or otherwise. If it is payable in whole or in part in goods each party is a seller of the goods which he is to transfer.

(2) Even though all or part of the price is payable in an interest in realty the transfer of the goods and the seller's obligations with reference to them are subject to this Article, but not the transfer of the interest in realty or the transferor's obligations in connection therewith.

## § 2–305. Open Price Term.

(1) The parties if they so intend can conclude a contract for sale even though the price is not settled. In such a case the price is a reasonable price at the time for delivery if

    (a) nothing is said as to price; or

    (b) the price is left to be agreed by the parties and they fail to agree; or

    (c) the price is to be fixed in terms of some agreed market or other standard as set or recorded by a third person or agency and it is not so set or recorded.

(2) A price to be fixed by the seller or by the buyer means a price for him to fix in good faith.

(3) When a price left to be fixed otherwise than by agreement of the parties fails to be fixed through fault of one party the other may at his option treat the contract as cancelled or himself fix a reasonable price.

(4) Where, however, the parties intend not to be bound unless the price be fixed or agreed and it is not fixed or agreed there is no contract. In such a case the buyer must return any goods already received or if unable so to do must pay their reasonable value at the time of delivery and the seller must return any portion of the price paid on account.

## § 2–306. Output, Requirements and Exclusive Dealings.

(1) A term which measures the quantity by the output of the seller or the requirements of the buyer means such actual output or requirements as may occur in good faith, except that no quantity unreasonably disproportionate to any stated estimate or in the absence of a stated estimate to any normal or other-

wise comparable prior output or requirements may be tendered or demanded.

**(2)** A lawful agreement by either the seller or the buyer for exclusive dealing in the kind of goods concerned imposes unless otherwise agreed an obligation by the seller to use best efforts to supply the goods and by the buyer to use best efforts to promote their sale.

### § 2–307.  Delivery in Single Lot or Several Lots.

Unless otherwise agreed all goods called for by a contract for sale must be tendered in a single delivery and payment is due only on such tender but where the circumstances give either party the right to make or demand delivery in lots the price if it can be apportioned may be demanded for each lot.

### § 2–308.  Absence of Specified Place for Delivery.

Unless otherwise agreed

  **(a)** the place for delivery of goods is the seller's place of business or if he has none his residence; but

  **(b)** in a contract for sale of identified goods which to the knowledge of the parties at the time of contracting are in some other place, that place is the place for their delivery; and

  **(c)** documents of title may be delivered through customary banking channels.

### § 2–309.  Absence of Specific Time Provisions; Notice of Termination.

**(1)** The time for shipment or delivery or any other action under a contract if not provided in this Article or agreed upon shall be a reasonable time.

**(2)** Where the contract provides for successive performances but is indefinite in duration it is valid for a reasonable time but unless otherwise agreed may be terminated at any time by either party.

**(3)** Termination of a contract by one party except on the happening of an agreed event requires that reasonable notification be received by the other party and an agreement dispensing with notification is invalid if its operation would be unconscionable.

### § 2–310.  Open Time for Payment or Running of Credit; Authority to Ship Under Reservation.

Unless otherwise agreed

  **(a)** payment is due at the time and place at which the buyer is to receive the goods even though the place of shipment is the place of delivery; and

  **(b)** if the seller is authorized to send the goods he may ship them under reservation, and may tender the documents of title, but the buyer may inspect the goods after their arrival before payment is due unless such inspection is inconsistent with the terms of the contract (Section 2–513); and

  **(c)** if delivery is authorized and made by way of documents of title otherwise than by subsection (b) then payment is due at the time and place at which the buyer is to receive the documents regardless of where the goods are to be received; and

  **(d)** where the seller is required or authorized to ship the goods on credit the credit period runs from the time of shipment but post-dating the invoice or delaying its dis-

patch will correspondingly delay the starting of the credit period.

### § 2–311.  Options and Cooperation Respecting Performance.

**(1)** An agreement for sale which is otherwise sufficiently definite (subsection (3) of Section 2–204) to be a contract is not made invalid by the fact that it leaves particulars of performance to be specified by one of the parties. Any such specification must be made in good faith and within limits set by commercial reasonableness.

**(2)** Unless otherwise agreed specifications relating to assortment of the goods are at the buyer's option and except as otherwise provided in subsections (1)(c) and (3) of Section 2–319 specifications or arrangements relating to shipment are at the seller's option.

**(3)** Where such specification would materially affect the other party's performance but is not seasonably made or where one party's cooperation is necessary to the agreed performance of the other but is not seasonably forthcoming, the other party in addition to all other remedies

  **(a)** is excused for any resulting delay in his own performance; and

  **(b)** may also either proceed to perform in any reasonable manner or after the time for a material part of his own performance treat the failure to specify or to cooperate as a breach by failure to deliver or accept the goods.

### § 2–312.  Warranty of Title and Against Infringement; Buyer's Obligation Against Infringement.

**(1)** Subject to subsection (2) there is in a contract for sale a warranty by the seller that

  **(a)** the title conveyed shall be good, and its transfer rightful; and

  **(b)** the goods shall be delivered free from any security interest or other lien or encumbrance of which the buyer at the time of contracting has no knowledge.

**(2)** A warranty under subsection (1) will be excluded or modified only by specific language or by circumstances which give the buyer reason to know that the person selling does not claim title in himself or that he is purporting to sell only such right or title as he or a third person may have.

**(3)** Unless otherwise agreed a seller who is a merchant regularly dealing in goods of the kind warrants that the goods shall be delivered free of the rightful claim of any third person by way of infringement or the like but a buyer who furnishes specifications to the seller must hold the seller harmless against any such claim which arises out of compliance with the specifications.

### § 2–313.  Express Warranties by Affirmation, Promise, Description, Sample.

**(1)** Express warranties by the seller are created as follows:

  **(a)** Any affirmation of fact or promise made by the seller to the buyer which relates to the goods and becomes part of the basis of the bargain creates an express warranty that the goods shall conform to the affirmation or promise.

  **(b)** Any description of the goods which is made part of the basis of the bargain creates an express warranty that the goods shall conform to the description.

**(c)** Any sample or model which is made part of the basis of the bargain creates an express warranty that the whole of the goods shall conform to the sample or model.

**(2)** It is not necessary to the creation of an express warranty that the seller use formal words such as "warrant" or "guarantee" or that he have a specific intention to make a warranty, but an affirmation merely of the value of the goods or a statement purporting to be merely the seller's opinion or commendation of the goods does not create a warranty.

### § 2–314. Implied Warranty: Merchantability; Usage of Trade.

**(1)** Unless excluded or modified (Section 2–316), a warranty that the goods shall be merchantable is implied in a contract for their sale if the seller is a merchant with respect to goods of that kind. Under this section the serving for value of food or drink to be consumed either on the premises or elsewhere is a sale.

**(2)** Goods to be merchantable must be at least such as
    **(a)** pass without objection in the trade under the contract description; and
    **(b)** in the case of fungible goods, are of fair average quality within the description; and
    **(c)** are fit for the ordinary purposes for which such goods are used; and
    **(d)** run, within the variations permitted by the agreement, of even kind, quality and quantity within each unit and among all units involved; and
    **(e)** are adequately contained, packaged, and labeled as the agreement may require; and
    **(f)** conform to the promises or affirmations of fact made on the container or label if any.

**(3)** Unless excluded or modified (Section 2–316) other implied warranties may arise from course of dealing or usage of trade.

### § 2–315. Implied Warranty: Fitness for Particular Purpose.

Where the seller at the time of contracting has reason to know any particular purpose for which the goods are required and that the buyer is relying on the seller's skill or judgment to select or furnish suitable goods, there is unless excluded or modified under the next section an implied warranty that the goods shall be fit for such purpose.

### § 2–316. Exclusion or Modification of Warranties.

**(1)** Words or conduct relevant to the creation of an express warranty and words or conduct tending to negate or limit warranty shall be construed wherever reasonable as consistent with each other; but subject to the provisions of this Article on parol or extrinsic evidence (Section 2–202) negation or limitation is inoperative to the extent that such construction is unreasonable.

**(2)** Subject to subsection (3), to exclude or modify the implied warranty of merchantability or any part of it the language must mention merchantability and in case of a writing must be conspicuous, and to exclude or modify any implied warranty of fitness the exclusion must be by a writing and conspicuous. Language to exclude all implied warranties of fitness is sufficient if it states, for example, that "There are no warranties which extend beyond the description on the face hereof."

**(3)** Notwithstanding subsection (2)
    **(a)** unless the circumstances indicate otherwise, all implied warranties are excluded by expressions like "as is", "with all faults" or other language which in common understanding calls the buyer's attention to the exclusion of warranties and makes plain that there is no implied warranty; and
    **(b)** when the buyer before entering into the contract has examined the goods or the sample or model as fully as he desired or has refused to examine the goods there is no implied warranty with regard to defects which an examination ought in the circumstances to have revealed to him; and
    **(c)** an implied warranty can also be excluded or modified by course of dealing or course of performance or usage of trade.

**(4)** Remedies for breach of warranty can be limited in accordance with the provisions of this Article on liquidation or limitation of damages and on contractual modification of remedy (Sections 2–718 and 2–719).

### § 2–317. Cumulation and Conflict of Warranties Express or Implied.

Warranties whether express or implied shall be construed as consistent with each other and as cumulative, but if such construction is unreasonable the intention of the parties shall determine which warranty is dominant. In ascertaining that intention the following rules apply:
    **(a)** Exact or technical specifications displace an inconsistent sample or model or general language of description.
    **(b)** A sample from an existing bulk displaces inconsistent general language of description.
    **(c)** Express warranties displace inconsistent implied warranties other than an implied warranty of fitness for a particular purpose.

### § 2–318. Third Party Beneficiaries of Warranties Express or Implied.

Note: If this Act is introduced in the Congress of the United States this section should be omitted. (States to select one alternative.)

**Alternative A**

A seller's warranty whether express or implied extends to any natural person who is in the family or household of his buyer or who is a guest in his home if it is reasonable to expect that such person may use, consume or be affected by the goods and who is injured in person by breach of the warranty. A seller may not exclude or limit the operation of this section.

**Alternative B**

A seller's warranty whether express or implied extends to any natural person who may reasonably be expected to use, consume or be affected by the goods and who is injured in person by breach of the warranty. A seller may not exclude or limit the operation of this section.

**Alternative C**

A seller's warranty whether express or implied extends to any person who may reasonably be expected to use, consume or be affected by the goods and who is injured by breach of the warranty. A seller may not exclude or limit the operation of this section with respect to injury to the person of an individual to whom the warranty extends.

As amended 1966.

### § 2–319. F.O.B. and F.A.S. Terms.

**(1)** Unless otherwise agreed the term F.O.B. (which means "free on board") at a named place, even though used only in connection with the stated price, is a delivery term under which

(a) when the term is F.O.B. the place of shipment, the seller must at that place ship the goods in the manner provided in this Article (Section 2–504) and bear the expense and risk of putting them into the possession of the carrier; or

(b) when the term is F.O.B. the place of destination, the seller must at his own expense and risk transport the goods to that place and there tender delivery of them in the manner provided in this Article (Section 2–503);

(c) when under either (a) or (b) the term is also F.O.B. vessel, car or other vehicle, the seller must in addition at his own expense and risk load the goods on board. If the term is F.O.B. vessel the buyer must name the vessel and in an appropriate case the seller must comply with the provisions of this Article on the form of bill of lading (Section 2–323).

**(2)** Unless otherwise agreed the term F.A.S. vessel (which means "free alongside") at a named port, even though used only in connection with the stated price, is a delivery term under which the seller must

(a) at his own expense and risk deliver the goods alongside the vessel in the manner usual in that port or on a dock designated and provided by the buyer; and

(b) obtain and tender a receipt for the goods in exchange for which the carrier is under a duty to issue a bill of lading.

**(3)** Unless otherwise agreed in any case falling within subsection (1)(a) or (c) or subsection (2) the buyer must seasonably give any needed instructions for making delivery, including when the term is F.A.S. or F.O.B. the loading berth of the vessel and in an appropriate case its name and sailing date. The seller may treat the failure of needed instructions as a failure of cooperation under this Article (Section 2–311). He may also at his option move the goods in any reasonable manner preparatory to delivery or shipment.

**(4)** Under the term F.O.B. vessel or F.A.S. unless otherwise agreed the buyer must make payment against tender of the required documents and the seller may not tender nor the buyer demand delivery of the goods in substitution for the documents.

### § 2–320. C.I.F. and C. & F. Terms.

**(1)** The term C.I.F. means that the price includes in a lump sum the cost of the goods and the insurance and freight to the named destination. The term C. & F. or C.F. means that the price so includes cost and freight to the named destination.

**(2)** Unless otherwise agreed and even though used only in connection with the stated price and destination, the term C.I.F. destination or its equivalent requires the seller at his own expense and risk to

(a) put the goods into the possession of a carrier at the port for shipment and obtain a negotiable bill or bills of lading covering the entire transportation to the named destination; and

(b) load the goods and obtain a receipt from the carrier (which may be contained in the bill of lading) showing that the freight has been paid or provided for; and

(c) obtain a policy or certificate of insurance, including any war risk insurance, of a kind and on terms then current at the port of shipment in the usual amount, in the currency of the contract, shown to cover the same goods covered by the bill of lading and providing for payment of loss to the order of the buyer or for the account of whom it may concern; but the seller may add to the price the amount of the premium for any such war risk insurance; and

(d) prepare an invoice of the goods and procure any other documents required to effect shipment or to comply with the contract; and

(e) forward and tender with commercial promptness all the documents in due form and with any indorsement necessary to perfect the buyer's rights.

**(3)** Unless otherwise agreed the term C. & F. or its equivalent has the same effect and imposes upon the seller the same obligations and risks as a C.I.F. term except the obligation as to insurance.

**(4)** Under the term C.I.F. or C. & F. unless otherwise agreed the buyer must make payment against tender of the required documents and the seller may not tender nor the buyer demand delivery of the goods in substitution for the documents.

### § 2–321. C.I.F. or C. & F.: "Net Landed Weights"; "Payment on Arrival"; Warranty of Condition on Arrival.

Under a contract containing a term C.I.F. or C. & F.

**(1)** Where the price is based on or is to be adjusted according to "net landed weights", "delivered weights", "out turn" quantity or quality or the like, unless otherwise agreed the seller must reasonably estimate the price. The payment due on tender of the documents called for by the contract is the amount so estimated, but after final adjustment of the price a settlement must be made with commercial promptness.

**(2)** An agreement described in subsection (1) or any warranty of quality or condition of the goods on arrival places upon the seller the risk of ordinary deterioration, shrinkage and the like in transportation but has no effect on the place or time of identification to the contract for sale or delivery or on the passing of the risk of loss.

**(3)** Unless otherwise agreed where the contract provides for payment on or after arrival of the goods the seller must before payment allow such preliminary inspection as is feasible; but if the goods are lost delivery of the documents and payment are due when the goods should have arrived.

### § 2–322. Delivery "Ex-Ship".

**(1)** Unless otherwise agreed a term for delivery of goods "ex-ship" (which means from the carrying vessel) or in equivalent language is not restricted to a particular ship and requires delivery from a ship which has reached a place at the named port of destination where goods of the kind are usually discharged.

**(2)** Under such a term unless otherwise agreed

(a) the seller must discharge all liens arising out of the carriage and furnish the buyer with a direction which puts the carrier under a duty to deliver the goods; and

(b) the risk of loss does not pass to the buyer until the goods leave the ship's tackle or are otherwise properly unloaded.

### § 2–323. Form of Bill of Lading Required in Overseas Shipment; "Overseas".

(1) Where the contract contemplates overseas shipment and contains a term C.I.F. or C. & F. or F.O.B. vessel, the seller unless otherwise agreed must obtain a negotiable bill of lading stating that the goods have been loaded on board or, in the case of a term C.I.F. or C. & F., received for shipment.

(2) Where in a case within subsection (1) a bill of lading has been issued in a set of parts, unless otherwise agreed if the documents are not to be sent from abroad the buyer may demand tender of the full set; otherwise only one part of the bill of lading need be tendered. Even if the agreement expressly requires a full set

(a) due tender of a single part is acceptable within the provisions of this Article on cure of improper delivery (subsection (1) of Section 2–508); and

(b) even though the full set is demanded, if the documents are sent from abroad the person tendering an incomplete set may nevertheless require payment upon furnishing an indemnity which the buyer in good faith deems adequate.

(3) A shipment by water or by air or a contract contemplating such shipment is "overseas" insofar as by usage of trade or agreement it is subject to the commercial, financing or shipping practices characteristic of international deep water commerce.

### § 2–324. "No Arrival, No Sale" Term.

Under a term "no arrival, no sale" or terms of like meaning, unless otherwise agreed,

(a) the seller must properly ship conforming goods and if they arrive by any means he must tender them on arrival but he assumes no obligation that the goods will arrive unless he has caused the non-arrival; and

(b) where without fault of the seller the goods are in part lost or have so deteriorated as no longer to conform to the contract or arrive after the contract time, the buyer may proceed as if there had been casualty to identified goods (Section 2–613).

### § 2–325. "Letter of Credit" Term; "Confirmed Credit".

(1) Failure of the buyer seasonably to furnish an agreed letter of credit is a breach of the contract for sale.

(2) The delivery to seller of a proper letter of credit suspends the buyer's obligation to pay. If the letter of credit is dishonored, the seller may on seasonable notification to the buyer require payment directly from him.

(3) Unless otherwise agreed the term "letter of credit" or "banker's credit" in a contract for sale means an irrevocable credit issued by a financing agency of good repute and, where the shipment is overseas, of good international repute. The term "confirmed credit" means that the credit must also carry the direct obligation of such an agency which does business in the seller's financial market.

### § 2–326. Sale on Approval and Sale or Return; Rights of Creditors.

(1) Unless otherwise agreed, if delivered goods may be returned by the buyer even though they conform to the contract, the transaction is

(a) a "sale on approval" if the goods are delivered primarily for use, and

(b) a "sale or return" if the goods are delivered primarily for resale.

(2) Goods held on approval are not subject to the claims of the buyer's creditors until acceptance; goods held on sale or return are subject to such claims while in the buyer's possession.

(3) Any "or return" term of a contract for sale is to be treated as a separate contract for sale within the statute of frauds section of this Article (Section 2–201) and as contradicting the sale aspect of the contract within the provisions of this Article or on parol or extrinsic evidence (Section 2–202).

As amended in 1999.

### § 2–327. Special Incidents of Sale on Approval and Sale or Return.

(1) Under a sale on approval unless otherwise agreed

(a) although the goods are identified to the contract the risk of loss and the title do not pass to the buyer until acceptance; and

(b) use of the goods consistent with the purpose of trial is not acceptance but failure seasonably to notify the seller of election to return the goods is acceptance, and if the goods conform to the contract acceptance of any part is acceptance of the whole; and

(c) after due notification of election to return, the return is at the seller's risk and expense but a merchant buyer must follow any reasonable instructions.

(2) Under a sale or return unless otherwise agreed

(a) the option to return extends to the whole or any commercial unit of the goods while in substantially their original condition, but must be exercised seasonably; and

(b) the return is at the buyer's risk and expense.

### § 2–328. Sale by Auction.

(1) In a sale by auction if goods are put up in lots each lot is the subject of a separate sale.

(2) A sale by auction is complete when the auctioneer so announces by the fall of the hammer or in other customary manner. Where a bid is made while the hammer is falling in acceptance of a prior bid the auctioneer may in his discretion reopen the bidding or declare the goods sold under the bid on which the hammer was falling.

(3) Such a sale is with reserve unless the goods are in explicit terms put up without reserve. In an auction with reserve the auctioneer may withdraw the goods at any time until he announces completion of the sale. In an auction without reserve, after the auctioneer calls for bids on an article or lot, that article or lot cannot be withdrawn unless no bid is made within a reasonable time. In either case a bidder may retract his bid until the auctioneer's announcement of completion of the sale, but a bidder's retraction does not revive any previous bid.

(4) If the auctioneer knowingly receives a bid on the seller's behalf or the seller makes or procures such as bid, and notice has not been given that liberty for such bidding is reserved, the buyer may at his option avoid the sale or take the goods at the price of the last good faith bid prior to the completion of the sale. This subsection shall not apply to any bid at a forced sale.

## Part 4—Title, Creditors and Good Faith Purchasers

### § 2–401. Passing of Title; Reservation for Security; Limited Application of This Section.

Each provision of this Article with regard to the rights, obligations and remedies of the seller, the buyer, purchasers or other third parties applies irrespective of title to the goods except where the provision refers to such title. Insofar as situations are not covered by the other provisions of this Article and matters concerning title became material the following rules apply:

(1) Title to goods cannot pass under a contract for sale prior to their identification to the contract (Section 2–501), and unless otherwise explicitly agreed the buyer acquires by their identification a special property as limited by this Act. Any retention or reservation by the seller of the title (property) in goods shipped or delivered to the buyer is limited in effect to a reservation of a security interest. Subject to these provisions and to the provisions of the Article on Secured Transactions (Article 9), title to goods passes from the seller to the buyer in any manner and on any conditions explicitly agreed on by the parties.

(2) Unless otherwise explicitly agreed title passes to the buyer at the time and place at which the seller completes his performance with reference to the physical delivery of the goods, despite any reservation of a security interest and even though a document of title is to be delivered at a different time or place; and in particular and despite any reservation of a security interest by the bill of lading

> (a) if the contract requires or authorizes the seller to send the goods to the buyer but does not require him to deliver them at destination, title passes to the buyer at the time and place of shipment; but

> (b) if the contract requires delivery at destination, title passes on tender there.

(3) Unless otherwise explicitly agreed where delivery is to be made without moving the goods,

> (a) if the seller is to deliver a document of title, title passes at the time when and the place where he delivers such documents; or

> (b) if the goods are at the time of contracting already identified and no documents are to be delivered, title passes at the time and place of contracting.

(4) A rejection or other refusal by the buyer to receive or retain the goods, whether or not justified, or a justified revocation of acceptance revests title to the goods in the seller. Such revesting occurs by operation of law and is not a "sale".

### § 2–402. Rights of Seller's Creditors Against Sold Goods.

(1) Except as provided in subsections (2) and (3), rights of unsecured creditors of the seller with respect to goods which have been identified to a contract for sale are subject to the buyer's rights to recover the goods under this Article (Sections 2–502 and 2–716).

(2) A creditor of the seller may treat a sale or an identification of goods to a contract for sale as void if as against him a retention of possession by the seller is fraudulent under any rule of law of the state where the goods are situated, except that retention of possession in good faith and current course of trade by a merchant-seller for a commercially reasonable time after a sale or identification is not fraudulent.

(3) Nothing in this Article shall be deemed to impair the rights of creditors of the seller

> (a) under the provisions of the Article on Secured Transactions (Article 9); or

> (b) where identification to the contract or delivery is made not in current course of trade but in satisfaction of or as security for a pre-existing claim for money, security or the like and is made under circumstances which under any rule of law of the state where the goods are situated would apart from this Article constitute the transaction a fraudulent transfer or voidable preference.

### § 2–403. Power to Transfer; Good Faith Purchase of Goods; "Entrusting".

(1) A purchaser of goods acquires all title which his transferor had or had power to transfer except that a purchaser of a limited interest acquires rights only to the extent of the interest purchased. A person with voidable title has power to transfer a good title to a good faith purchaser for value. When goods have been delivered under a transaction of purchase the purchaser has such power even though

> (a) the transferor was deceived as to the identity of the purchaser, or

> (b) the delivery was in exchange for a check which is later dishonored, or

> (c) it was agreed that the transaction was to be a "cash sale", or

> (d) the delivery was procured through fraud punishable as larcenous under the criminal law.

(2) Any entrusting of possession of goods to a merchant who deals in goods of that kind gives him power to transfer all rights of the entruster to a buyer in ordinary course of business.

(3) "Entrusting" includes any delivery and any acquiescence in retention of possession regardless of any condition expressed between the parties to the delivery or acquiescence and regardless of whether the procurement of the entrusting or the possessor's disposition of the goods have been such as to be larcenous under the criminal law.

(4) The rights of other purchasers of goods and of lien creditors are governed by the Articles on Secured Transactions (Article 9), Bulk Transfers (Article 6) and Documents of Title (Article 7). As amended in 1988.

## Part 5—Performance

### § 2–501. Insurable Interest in Goods; Manner of Identification of Goods.

(1) The buyer obtains a special property and an insurable interest in goods by identification of existing goods as goods to which the contract refers even though the goods so identified are non-conforming and he has an option to return or reject them. Such identification can be made at any time and in any manner explicitly agreed to by the parties. In the absence of explicit agreement identification occurs

> (a) when the contract is made if it is for the sale of goods already existing and identified;

> (b) if the contract is for the sale of future goods other than those described in paragraph (c), when goods are shipped,

marked or otherwise designated by the seller as goods to which the contract refers;

(c) when the crops are planted or otherwise become growing crops or the young are conceived if the contract is for the sale of unborn young to be born within twelve months after contracting or for the sale of crops to be harvested within twelve months or the next normal harvest season after contracting whichever is longer.

(2) The seller retains an insurable interest in goods so long as title to or any security interest in the goods remains in him and where the identification is by the seller alone he may until default or insolvency or notification to the buyer that the identification is final substitute other goods for those identified.

(3) Nothing in this section impairs any insurable interest recognized under any other statute or rule of law.

### § 2–502. **Buyer's Right to Goods on Seller's Insolvency.**

(1) Subject to subsections (2) and (3) and even though the goods have not been shipped a buyer who has paid a part or all of the price of goods in which he has a special property under the provisions of the immediately preceding section may on making and keeping good a tender of any unpaid portion of their price recover them from the seller if:

(a) in the case of goods bought for personal, family, or household purposes, the seller repudiates or fails to deliver as required by the contract; or

(b) in all cases, the seller becomes insolvent within ten days after receipt of the first installment on their price.

(2) The buyer's right to recover the goods under subsection (1)(a) vests upon acquisition of a special property, even if the seller had not then repudiated or failed to deliver.

(3) If the identification creating his special property has been made by the buyer he acquires the right to recover the goods only if they conform to the contract for sale.

As amended in 1999.

### § 2–503. **Manner of Seller's Tender of Delivery.**

(1) Tender of delivery requires that the seller put and hold conforming goods at the buyer's disposition and give the buyer any notification reasonably necessary to enable him to take delivery. The manner, time and place for tender are determined by the agreement and this Article, and in particular

(a) tender must be at a reasonable hour, and if it is of goods they must be kept available for the period reasonably necessary to enable the buyer to take possession; but

(b) unless otherwise agreed the buyer must furnish facilities reasonably suited to the receipt of the goods.

(2) Where the case is within the next section respecting shipment tender requires that the seller comply with its provisions.

(3) Where the seller is required to deliver at a particular destination tender requires that he comply with subsection (1) and also in any appropriate case tender documents as described in subsections (4) and (5) of this section.

(4) Where goods are in the possession of a bailee and are to be delivered without being moved

(a) tender requires that the seller either tender a negotiable document of title covering such goods or procure acknowledgment by the bailee of the buyer's right to possession of the goods; but

(b) tender to the buyer of a non-negotiable document of title or of a written direction to the bailee to deliver is sufficient tender unless the buyer seasonably objects, and receipt by the bailee of notification of the buyer's rights fixes those rights as against the bailee and all third persons; but risk of loss of the goods and of any failure by the bailee to honor the non-negotiable document of title or to obey the direction remains on the seller until the buyer has had a reasonable time to present the document or direction, and a refusal by the bailee to honor the document or to obey the direction defeats the tender.

(5) Where the contract requires the seller to deliver documents

(a) he must tender all such documents in correct form, except as provided in this Article with respect to bills of lading in a set (subsection (2) of Section 2–323); and

(b) tender through customary banking channels is sufficient and dishonor of a draft accompanying the documents constitutes non-acceptance or rejection.

### § 2–504. **Shipment by Seller.**

Where the seller is required or authorized to send the goods to the buyer and the contract does not require him to deliver them at a particular destination, then unless otherwise agreed he must

(a) put the goods in the possession of such a carrier and make such a contract for their transportation as may be reasonable having regard to the nature of the goods and other circumstances of the case; and

(b) obtain and promptly deliver or tender in due form any document necessary to enable the buyer to obtain possession of the goods or otherwise required by the agreement or by usage of trade; and

(c) promptly notify the buyer of the shipment.

Failure to notify the buyer under paragraph (c) or to make a proper contract under paragraph (a) is a ground for rejection only if material delay or loss ensues.

### § 2–505. **Seller's Shipment under Reservation.**

(1) Where the seller has identified goods to the contract by or before shipment:

(a) his procurement of a negotiable bill of lading to his own order or otherwise reserves in him a security interest in the goods. His procurement of the bill to the order of a financing agency or of the buyer indicates in addition only the seller's expectation of transferring that interest to the person named.

(b) a non-negotiable bill of lading to himself or his nominee reserves possession of the goods as security but except in a case of conditional delivery (subsection (2) of Section 2–507) a non-negotiable bill of lading naming the buyer as consignee reserves no security interest even though the seller retains possession of the bill of lading.

(2) When shipment by the seller with reservation of a security interest is in violation of the contract for sale it constitutes an improper contract for transportation within the preceding section but impairs neither the rights given to the buyer by shipment and identification of the goods to the contract nor the seller's powers as a holder of a negotiable document.

### § 2–506. **Rights of Financing Agency.**

(1) A financing agency by paying or purchasing for value a draft which relates to a shipment of goods acquires to the extent of the payment or purchase and in addition to its own rights under the draft and any document of title securing it any rights of the shipper in the goods including the right to stop delivery and the shipper's right to have the draft honored by the buyer.

(2) The right to reimbursement of a financing agency which has in good faith honored or purchased the draft under commitment to or authority from the buyer is not impaired by subsequent discovery of defects with reference to any relevant document which was apparently regular on its face.

### § 2–507. **Effect of Seller's Tender; Delivery on Condition.**

(1) Tender of delivery is a condition to the buyer's duty to accept the goods and, unless otherwise agreed, to his duty to pay for them. Tender entitles the seller to acceptance of the goods and to payment according to the contract.

(2) Where payment is due and demanded on the delivery to the buyer of goods or documents of title, his right as against the seller to retain or dispose of them is conditional upon his making the payment due.

### § 2–508. **Cure by Seller of Improper Tender or Delivery; Replacement.**

(1) Where any tender or delivery by the seller is rejected because non-conforming and the time for performance has not yet expired, the seller may seasonably notify the buyer of his intention to cure and may then within the contract time make a conforming delivery.

(2) Where the buyer rejects a non-conforming tender which the seller had reasonable grounds to believe would be acceptable with or without money allowance the seller may if he seasonably notifies the buyer have a further reasonable time to substitute a conforming tender.

### § 2–509. **Risk of Loss in the Absence of Breach.**

(1) Where the contract requires or authorizes the seller to ship the goods by carrier

    (a) if it does not require him to deliver them at a particular destination, the risk of loss passes to the buyer when the goods are duly delivered to the carrier even though the shipment is under reservation (Section 2–505); but

    (b) if it does require him to deliver them at a particular destination and the goods are there duly tendered while in the possession of the carrier, the risk of loss passes to the buyer when the goods are there duly so tendered as to enable the buyer to take delivery.

(2) Where the goods are held by a bailee to be delivered without being moved, the risk of loss passes to the buyer

    (a) on his receipt of a negotiable document of title covering the goods; or

    (b) on acknowledgment by the bailee of the buyer's right to possession of the goods; or

    (c) after his receipt of a non-negotiable document of title or other written direction to deliver, as provided in subsection (4)(b) of Section 2–503.

(3) In any case not within subsection (1) or (2), the risk of loss passes to the buyer on his receipt of the goods if the seller is a merchant; otherwise the risk passes to the buyer on tender of delivery.

(4) The provisions of this section are subject to contrary agreement of the parties and to the provisions of this Article on sale on approval (Section 2–327) and on effect of breach on risk of loss (Section 2–510).

### § 2–510. **Effect of Breach on Risk of Loss.**

(1) Where a tender or delivery of goods so fails to conform to the contract as to give a right of rejection the risk of their loss remains on the seller until cure or acceptance.

(2) Where the buyer rightfully revokes acceptance he may to the extent of any deficiency in his effective insurance coverage treat the risk of loss as having rested on the seller from the beginning.

(3) Where the buyer as to conforming goods already identified to the contract for sale repudiates or is otherwise in breach before risk of their loss has passed to him, the seller may to the extent of any deficiency in his effective insurance coverage treat the risk of loss as resting on the buyer for a commercially reasonable time.

### § 2–511. **Tender of Payment by Buyer; Payment by Check.**

(1) Unless otherwise agreed tender of payment is a condition to the seller's duty to tender and complete any delivery.

(2) Tender of payment is sufficient when made by any means or in any manner current in the ordinary course of business unless the seller demands payment in legal tender and gives any extension of time reasonably necessary to procure it.

(3) Subject to the provisions of this Act on the effect of an instrument on an obligation (Section 3–310), payment by check is conditional and is defeated as between the parties by dishonor of the check on due presentment.

As amended in 1994.

### § 2–512. **Payment by Buyer Before Inspection.**

(1) Where the contract requires payment before inspection non-conformity of the goods does not excuse the buyer from so making payment unless

    (a) the non-conformity appears without inspection; or

    (b) despite tender of the required documents the circumstances would justify injunction against honor under this Act (Section 5–109(b)).

(2) Payment pursuant to subsection (1) does not constitute an acceptance of goods or impair the buyer's right to inspect or any of his remedies.

As amended in 1995.

### § 2–513. **Buyer's Right to Inspection of Goods.**

(1) Unless otherwise agreed and subject to subsection (3), where goods are tendered or delivered or identified to the contract for sale, the buyer has a right before payment or acceptance to inspect them at any reasonable place and time and in any reasonable manner. When the seller is required or authorized to send the goods to the buyer, the inspection may be after their arrival.

(2) Expenses of inspection must be borne by the buyer but may be recovered from the seller if the goods do not conform and are rejected.

(3) Unless otherwise agreed and subject to the provisions of this Article on C.I.F. contracts (subsection (3) of Section 2–321), the buyer is not entitled to inspect the goods before payment of the price when the contract provides

(a) for delivery "C.O.D." or on other like terms; or

(b) for payment against documents of title, except where such payment is due only after the goods are to become available for inspection.

(4) A place or method of inspection fixed by the parties is presumed to be exclusive but unless otherwise expressly agreed it does not postpone identification or shift the place for delivery or for passing the risk of loss. If compliance becomes impossible, inspection shall be as provided in this section unless the place or method fixed was clearly intended as an indispensable condition failure of which avoids the contract.

### § 2–514. When Documents Deliverable on Acceptance; When on Payment.

Unless otherwise agreed documents against which a draft is drawn are to be delivered to the drawee on acceptance of the draft if it is payable more than three days after presentment; otherwise, only on payment.

### § 2–515. Preserving Evidence of Goods in Dispute.

In furtherance of the adjustment of any claim or dispute

(a) either party on reasonable notification to the other and for the purpose of ascertaining the facts and preserving evidence has the right to inspect, test and sample the goods including such of them as may be in the possession or control of the other; and

(b) the parties may agree to a third party inspection or survey to determine the conformity or condition of the goods and may agree that the findings shall be binding upon them in any subsequent litigation or adjustment.

## Part 6—Breach, Repudiation and Excuse

### § 2–601. Buyer's Rights on Improper Delivery.

Subject to the provisions of this Article on breach in installment contracts (Section 2–612) and unless otherwise agreed under the sections on contractual limitations of remedy (Sections 2–718 and 2–719), if the goods or the tender of delivery fail in any respect to conform to the contract, the buyer may

(a) reject the whole; or

(b) accept the whole; or

(c) accept any commercial unit or units and reject the rest.

### § 2–602. Manner and Effect of Rightful Rejection.

(1) Rejection of goods must be within a reasonable time after their delivery or tender. It is ineffective unless the buyer seasonably notifies the seller.

(2) Subject to the provisions of the two following sections on rejected goods (Sections 2–603 and 2–604),

(a) after rejection any exercise of ownership by the buyer with respect to any commercial unit is wrongful as against the seller; and

(b) if the buyer has before rejection taken physical possession of goods in which he does not have a security interest under the provisions of this Article (subsection (3) of Section 2–711), he is under a duty after rejection to hold them with reasonable care at the seller's disposition for a time sufficient to permit the seller to remove them; but

(c) the buyer has no further obligations with regard to goods rightfully rejected.

(3) The seller's rights with respect to goods wrongfully rejected are governed by the provisions of this Article on Seller's remedies in general (Section 2–703).

### § 2–603. Merchant Buyer's Duties as to Rightfully Rejected Goods.

(1) Subject to any security interest in the buyer (subsection (3) of Section 2–711), when the seller has no agent or place of business at the market of rejection a merchant buyer is under a duty after rejection of goods in his possession or control to follow any reasonable instructions received from the seller with respect to the goods and in the absence of such instructions to make reasonable efforts to sell them for the seller's account if they are perishable or threaten to decline in value speedily. Instructions are not reasonable if on demand indemnity for expenses is not forthcoming.

(2) When the buyer sells goods under subsection (1), he is entitled to reimbursement from the seller or out of the proceeds for reasonable expenses of caring for and selling them, and if the expenses include no selling commission then to such commission as is usual in the trade or if there is none to a reasonable sum not exceeding ten per cent on the gross proceeds.

(3) In complying with this section the buyer is held only to good faith and good faith conduct hereunder is neither acceptance nor conversion nor the basis of an action for damages.

### § 2–604. Buyer's Options as to Salvage of Rightfully Rejected Goods.

Subject to the provisions of the immediately preceding section on perishables if the seller gives no instructions within a reasonable time after notification of rejection the buyer may store the rejected goods for the seller's account or reship them to him or resell them for the seller's account with reimbursement as provided in the preceding section. Such action is not acceptance or conversion.

### § 2–605. Waiver of Buyer's Objections by Failure to Particularize.

(1) The buyer's failure to state in connection with rejection a particular defect which is ascertainable by reasonable inspection precludes him from relying on the unstated defect to justify rejection or to establish breach

(a) where the seller could have cured it if stated seasonably; or

(b) between merchants when the seller has after rejection made a request in writing for a full and final written statement of all defects on which the buyer proposes to rely.

(2) Payment against documents made without reservation of rights precludes recovery of the payment for defects apparent on the face of the documents.

### § 2–606. What Constitutes Acceptance of Goods.

(1) Acceptance of goods occurs when the buyer

(a) after a reasonable opportunity to inspect the goods signifies to the seller that the goods are conforming or that he will take or retain them in spite of their nonconformity; or

**(b)** fails to make an effective rejection (subsection (1) of Section 2–602), but such acceptance does not occur until the buyer has had a reasonable opportunity to inspect them; or

**(c)** does any act inconsistent with the seller's ownership; but if such act is wrongful as against the seller it is an acceptance only if ratified by him.

**(2)** Acceptance of a part of any commercial unit is acceptance of that entire unit.

### § 2–607. Effect of Acceptance; Notice of Breach; Burden of Establishing Breach After Acceptance; Notice of Claim or Litigation to Person Answerable Over.

**(1)** The buyer must pay at the contract rate for any goods accepted.

**(2)** Acceptance of goods by the buyer precludes rejection of the goods accepted and if made with knowledge of a non-conformity cannot be revoked because of it unless the acceptance was on the reasonable assumption that the non-conformity would be seasonally cured but acceptance does not of itself impair any other remedy provided by this Article for non-conformity.

**(3)** Where a tender has been accepted

**(a)** the buyer must within a reasonable time after he discovers or should have discovered any breach notify the seller of breach or be barred from any remedy; and

**(b)** if the claim is one for infringement or the like (subsection (3) of Section 2–312) and the buyer is sued as a result of such a breach he must so notify the seller within a reasonable time after he receives notice of the litigation or be barred from any remedy over for liability established by the litigation.

**(4)** The burden is on the buyer to establish any breach with respect to the goods accepted.

**(5)** Where the buyer is sued for breach of a warranty or other obligation for which his seller is answerable over

**(a)** he may give his seller written notice of the litigation. If the notice states that the seller may come in and defend and that if the seller does not do so he will be bound in any action against him by his buyer by any determination of fact common to the two litigations, then unless the seller after seasonable receipt of the notice does come in and defend he is so bound.

**(b)** if the claim is one for infringement or the like (subsection (3) of Section 2–312) the original seller may demand in writing that his buyer turn over to him control of the litigation including settlement or else be barred from any remedy over and if he also agrees to bear all expense and to satisfy any adverse judgment, then unless the buyer after seasonable receipt of the demand does turn over control the buyer is so barred.

**(6)** The provisions of subsections (3), (4) and (5) apply to any obligation of a buyer to hold the seller harmless against infringement or the like (subsection (3) of Section 2–312).

### § 2–608. Revocation of Acceptance in Whole or in Part.

**(1)** The buyer may revoke his acceptance of a lot or commercial unit whose non-conformity substantially impairs its value to him if he has accepted it

**(a)** on the reasonable assumption that its nonconformity would be cured and it has not been seasonably cured; or

**(b)** without discovery of such non-conformity if his acceptance was reasonably induced either by the difficulty of discovery before acceptance or by the seller's assurances.

**(2)** Revocation of acceptance must occur within a reasonable time after the buyer discovers or should have discovered the ground for it and before any substantial change in condition of the goods which is not caused by their own defects. It is not effective until the buyer notifies the seller of it.

**(3)** A buyer who so revokes has the same rights and duties with regard to the goods involved as if he had rejected them.

### § 2–609. Right to Adequate Assurance of Performance.

**(1)** A contract for sale imposes an obligation on each party that the other's expectation of receiving due performance will not be impaired. When reasonable grounds for insecurity arise with respect to the performance of either party the other may in writing demand adequate assurance of due performance and until he receives such assurance may if commercially reasonable suspend any performance for which he has not already received the agreed return.

**(2)** Between merchants the reasonableness of grounds for insecurity and the adequacy of any assurance offered shall be determined according to commercial standards.

**(3)** Acceptance of any improper delivery or payment does not prejudice the party's right to demand adequate assurance of future performance.

**(4)** After receipt of a justified demand failure to provide within a reasonable time not exceeding thirty days such assurance of due performance as is adequate under the circumstances of the particular case is a repudiation of the contract.

### § 2–610. Anticipatory Repudiation.

When either party repudiates the contract with respect to a performance not yet due the loss of which will substantially impair the value of the contract to the other, the aggrieved party may

**(a)** for a commercially reasonable time await performance by the repudiating party; or

**(b)** resort to any remedy for breach (Section 2–703 or Section 2–711), even though he has notified the repudiating party that he would await the latter's performance and has urged retraction; and

**(c)** in either case suspend his own performance or proceed in accordance with the provisions of this Article on the seller's right to identify goods to the contract notwithstanding breach or to salvage unfinished goods (Section 2–704).

### § 2–611. Retraction of Anticipatory Repudiation.

**(1)** Until the repudiating party's next performance is due he can retract his repudiation unless the aggrieved party has since the repudiation cancelled or materially changed his position or otherwise indicated that he considers the repudiation final.

**(2)** Retraction may be by any method which clearly indicates to the aggrieved party that the repudiating party intends to perform, but must include any assurance justifiably demanded under the provisions of this Article (Section 2–609).

**(3)** Retraction reinstates the repudiating party's rights under the contract with due excuse and allowance to the aggrieved party for any delay occasioned by the repudiation.

### § 2–612. "Installment Contract"; Breach.

**(1)** An "installment contract" is one which requires or authorizes the delivery of goods in separate lots to be separately accepted, even though the contract contains a clause "each delivery is a separate contract" or its equivalent.

**(2)** The buyer may reject any installment which is non-conforming if the non-conformity substantially impairs the value of that installment and cannot be cured or if the non-conformity is a defect in the required documents; but if the non-conformity does not fall within subsection (3) and the seller gives adequate assurance of its cure the buyer must accept that installment.

**(3)** Whenever non-conformity or default with respect to one or more installments substantially impairs the value of the whole contract there is a breach of the whole. But the aggrieved party reinstates the contract if he accepts a non-conforming installment without seasonably notifying of cancellation or if he brings an action with respect only to past installments or demands performance as to future installments.

### § 2–613. Casualty to Identified Goods.

Where the contract requires for its performance goods identified when the contract is made, and the goods suffer casualty without fault of either party before the risk of loss passes to the buyer, or in a proper case under a "no arrival, no sale" term (Section 2–324) then

(a) if the loss is total the contract is avoided; and

(b) if the loss is partial or the goods have so deteriorated as no longer to conform to the contract the buyer may nevertheless demand inspection and at his option either treat the contract as voided or accept the goods with due allowance from the contract price for the deterioration or the deficiency in quantity but without further right against the seller.

### § 2–614. Substituted Performance.

**(1)** Where without fault of either party the agreed berthing, loading, or unloading facilities fail or an agreed type of carrier becomes unavailable or the agreed manner of delivery otherwise becomes commercially impracticable but a commercially reasonable substitute is available, such substitute performance must be tendered and accepted.

**(2)** If the agreed means or manner of payment fails because of domestic or foreign governmental regulation, the seller may withhold or stop delivery unless the buyer provides a means or manner of payment which is commercially a substantial equivalent. If delivery has already been taken, payment by the means or in the manner provided by the regulation discharges the buyer's obligation unless the regulation is discriminatory, oppressive or predatory.

### § 2–615. Excuse by Failure of Presupposed Conditions.

Except so far as a seller may have assumed a greater obligation and subject to the preceding section on substituted performance:

(a) Delay in delivery or non-delivery in whole or in part by a seller who complies with paragraphs (b) and (c) is not a breach of his duty under a contract for sale if performance as agreed has been made impracticable by the occurrence of a contingency the nonoccurrence of which was a basic assumption on which the contract was made or by compliance in good faith with any applicable foreign or domestic governmental regulation or order whether or not it later proves to be invalid.

(b) Where the causes mentioned in paragraph (a) affect only a part of the seller's capacity to perform, he must allocate production and deliveries among his customers but may at his option include regular customers not then under contract as well as his own requirements for further manufacture. He may so allocate in any manner which is fair and reasonable.

(c) The seller must notify the buyer seasonably that there will be delay or non-delivery and, when allocation is required under paragraph (b), of the estimated quota thus made available for the buyer.

### § 2–616. Procedure on Notice Claiming Excuse.

**(1)** Where the buyer receives notification of a material or indefinite delay or an allocation justified under the preceding section he may by written notification to the seller as to any delivery concerned, and where the prospective deficiency substantially impairs the value of the whole contract under the provisions of this Article relating to breach of installment contracts (Section 2–612), then also as to the whole,

(a) terminate and thereby discharge any unexecuted portion of the contract; or

(b) modify the contract by agreeing to take his available quota in substitution.

**(2)** If after receipt of such notification from the seller the buyer fails so to modify the contract within a reasonable time not exceeding thirty days the contract lapses with respect to any deliveries affected.

**(3)** The provisions of this section may not be negated by agreement except in so far as the seller has assumed a greater obligation under the preceding section.

### Part 7—Remedies

### § 2–701. Remedies for Breach of Collateral Contracts Not Impaired.

Remedies for breach of any obligation or promise collateral or ancillary to a contract for sale are not impaired by the provisions of this Article.

### § 2–702. Seller's Remedies on Discovery of Buyer's Insolvency.

**(1)** Where the seller discovers the buyer to be insolvent he may refuse delivery except for cash including payment for all goods theretofore delivered under the contract, and stop delivery under this Article (Section 2–705).

**(2)** Where the seller discovers that the buyer has received goods on credit while insolvent he may reclaim the goods upon demand made within ten days after the receipt, but if misrepresentation of solvency has been made to the particular seller in writing within three months before delivery the ten day limitation does not apply. Except as provided in this subsection the seller may not base a right to reclaim goods on the buyer's fraudulent or innocent misrepresentation of solvency or of intent to pay.

**(3)** The seller's right to reclaim under subsection (2) is subject to the rights of a buyer in ordinary course or other good faith purchaser under this Article (Section 2–403). Successful reclamation of goods excludes all other remedies with respect to them.

### § 2–703. Seller's Remedies in General.

Where the buyer wrongfully rejects or revokes acceptance of goods or fails to make a payment due on or before delivery or repudiates with respect to a part or the whole, then with respect to any goods directly affected and, if the breach is of the whole contract (Section 2–612), then also with respect to the whole undelivered balance, the aggrieved seller may

**(a)** withhold delivery of such goods;

**(b)** stop delivery by any bailee as hereafter provided (Section 2–705);

**(c)** proceed under the next section respecting goods still unidentified to the contract;

**(d)** resell and recover damages as hereafter provided (Section 2–706);

**(e)** recover damages for non-acceptance (Section 2–708) or in a proper case the price (Section 2–709);

**(f)** cancel.

### § 2–704. Seller's Right to Identify Goods to the Contract Notwithstanding Breach or to Salvage Unfinished Goods.

**(1)** An aggrieved seller under the preceding section may

    **(a)** identify to the contract conforming goods not already identified if at the time he learned of the breach they are in his possession or control;

    **(b)** treat as the subject of resale goods which have demonstrably been intended for the particular contract even though those goods are unfinished.

**(2)** Where the goods are unfinished an aggrieved seller may in the exercise of reasonable commercial judgment for the purposes of avoiding loss and of effective realization either complete the manufacture and wholly identify the goods to the contract or cease manufacture and resell for scrap or salvage value or proceed in any other reasonable manner.

### § 2–705. Seller's Stoppage of Delivery in Transit or Otherwise.

**(1)** The seller may stop delivery of goods in the possession of a carrier or other bailee when he discovers the buyer to be insolvent (Section 2–702) and may stop delivery of carload, truckload, planeload or larger shipments of express or freight when the buyer repudiates or fails to make a payment due before delivery or if for any other reason the seller has a right to withhold or reclaim the goods.

**(2)** As against such buyer the seller may stop delivery until

    **(a)** receipt of the goods by the buyer; or

    **(b)** acknowledgment to the buyer by any bailee of the goods except a carrier that the bailee holds the goods for the buyer; or

    **(c)** such acknowledgment to the buyer by a carrier by reshipment or as warehouseman; or

    **(d)** negotiation to the buyer of any negotiable document of title covering the goods.

**(3)** (a) To stop delivery the seller must so notify as to enable the bailee by reasonable diligence to prevent delivery of the goods.

    **(b)** After such notification the bailee must hold and deliver the goods according to the directions of the seller but the seller is liable to the bailee for any ensuing charges or damages.

    **(c)** If a negotiable document of title has been issued for goods the bailee is not obliged to obey a notification to stop until surrender of the document.

    **(d)** A carrier who has issued a non-negotiable bill of lading is not obliged to obey a notification to stop received from a person other than the consignor.

### § 2–706. Seller's Resale Including Contract for Resale.

**(1)** Under the conditions stated in Section 2–703 on seller's remedies, the seller may resell the goods concerned or the undelivered balance thereof. Where the resale is made in good faith and in a commercially reasonable manner the seller may recover the difference between the resale price and the contract price together with any incidental damages allowed under the provisions of this Article (Section 2–710), but less expenses saved in consequence of the buyer's breach.

**(2)** Except as otherwise provided in subsection (3) or unless otherwise agreed resale may be at public or private sale including sale by way of one or more contracts to sell or of identification to an existing contract of the seller. Sale may be as a unit or in parcels and at any time and place and on any terms but every aspect of the sale including the method, manner, time, place and terms must be commercially reasonable. The resale must be reasonably identified as referring to the broken contract, but it is not necessary that the goods be in existence or that any or all of them have been identified to the contract before the breach.

**(3)** Where the resale is at private sale the seller must give the buyer reasonable notification of his intention to resell.

**(4)** Where the resale is at public sale

    **(a)** only identified goods can be sold except where there is a recognized market for a public sale of futures in goods of the kind; and

    **(b)** it must be made at a usual place or market for public sale if one is reasonably available and except in the case of goods which are perishable or threaten to decline in value speedily the seller must give the buyer reasonable notice of the time and place of the resale; and

    **(c)** if the goods are not to be within the view of those attending the sale the notification of sale must state the place where the goods are located and provide for their reasonable inspection by prospective bidders; and

    **(d)** the seller may buy.

**(5)** A purchaser who buys in good faith at a resale takes the goods free of any rights of the original buyer even though the seller fails to comply with one or more of the requirements of this section.

**(6)** The seller is not accountable to the buyer for any profit made on any resale. A person in the position of a seller (Section 2–707) or a buyer who has rightfully rejected or justifiably revoked acceptance must account for any excess over the amount of his security interest, as hereinafter defined (subsection (3) of Section 2–711).

### § 2–707. "Person in the Position of a Seller".

**(1)** A "person in the position of a seller" includes as against a principal an agent who has paid or become responsible for the price of goods on behalf of his principal or anyone who otherwise holds a security interest or other right in goods similar to that of a seller.

**(2)** A person in the position of a seller may as provided in this Article withhold or stop delivery (Section 2–705) and resell (Section 2–706) and recover incidental damages (Section 2–710).

### § 2–708. Seller's Damages for Non-Acceptance or Repudiation.

**(1)** Subject to subsection (2) and to the provisions of this Article with respect to proof of market price (Section 2–723), the measure of damages for non-acceptance or repudiation by the buyer is the difference between the market price at the time and place for tender and the unpaid contract price together with any incidental damages provided in this Article (Section 2–710), but less expenses saved in consequence of the buyer's breach.

**(2)** If the measure of damages provided in subsection (1) is inadequate to put the seller in as good a position as performance would have done then the measure of damages is the profit (including reasonable overhead) which the seller would have made from full performance by the buyer, together with any incidental damages provided in this Article (Section 2–710), due allowance for costs reasonably incurred and due credit for payments or proceeds of resale.

### § 2–709. Action for the Price.

**(1)** When the buyer fails to pay the price as it becomes due the seller may recover, together with any incidental damages under the next section, the price

   **(a)** of goods accepted or of conforming goods lost or damaged within a commercially reasonable time after risk of their loss has passed to the buyer; and

   **(b)** of goods identified to the contract if the seller is unable after reasonable effort to resell them at a reasonable price or the circumstances reasonably indicate that such effort will be unavailing.

**(2)** Where the seller sues for the price he must hold for the buyer any goods which have been identified to the contract and are still in his control except that if resale becomes possible he may resell them at any time prior to the collection of the judgment. The net proceeds of any such resale must be credited to the buyer and payment of the judgment entitles him to any goods not resold.

**(3)** After the buyer has wrongfully rejected or revoked acceptance of the goods or has failed to make a payment due or has repudiated (Section 2–610), a seller who is held not entitled to the price under this section shall nevertheless be awarded damages for non-acceptance under the preceding section.

### § 2–710. Seller's Incidental Damages.

Incidental damages to an aggrieved seller include any commercially reasonable charges, expenses or commissions incurred in stopping delivery, in the transportation, care and custody of goods after the buyer's breach, in connection with return or resale of the goods or otherwise resulting from the breach.

### § 2–711. Buyer's Remedies in General; Buyer's Security Interest in Rejected Goods.

**(1)** Where the seller fails to make delivery or repudiates or the buyer rightfully rejects or justifiably revokes acceptance then with respect to any goods involved, and with respect to the whole if the breach goes to the whole contract (Section 2–612), the buyer may cancel and whether or not he has done so may in addition to recovering so much of the price as has been paid

   **(a)** "cover" and have damages under the next section as to all the goods affected whether or not they have been identified to the contract; or

   **(b)** recover damages for non-delivery as pro-vided in this Article (Section 2–713).

**(2)** Where the seller fails to deliver or repudiates the buyer may also

   **(a)** if the goods have been identified recover them as pro-vided in this Article (Section 2–502); or

   **(b)** in a proper case obtain specific performance or replevy the goods as provided in this Article (Section 2–716).

**(3)** On rightful rejection or justifiable revocation of acceptance a buyer has a security interest in goods in his possession or control for any payments made on their price and any expenses reasonably incurred in their inspection, receipt, transportation, care and custody and may hold such goods and resell them in like manner as an aggrieved seller (Section 2–706).

### § 2–712. "Cover"; Buyer's Procurement of Substitute Goods.

**(1)** After a breach within the preceding section the buyer may "cover" by making in good faith and without unreasonable delay any reasonable purchase of or contract to purchase goods in substitution for those due from the seller.

**(2)** The buyer may recover from the seller as damages the difference between the cost of cover and the contract price together with any incidental or consequential damages as hereinafter defined (Section 2–715), but less expenses saved in consequence of the seller's breach.

**(3)** Failure of the buyer to effect cover within this section does not bar him from any other remedy.

### § 2–713. Buyer's Damages for Non-Delivery or Repudiation.

**(1)** Subject to the provisions of this Article with respect to proof of market price (Section 2–723), the measure of damages for non-delivery or repudiation by the seller is the difference between the market price at the time when the buyer learned of the breach and the contract price together with any incidental and consequential damages provided in this Article (Section 2–715), but less expenses saved in consequence of the seller's breach.

**(2)** Market price is to be determined as of the place for tender or, in cases of rejection after arrival or revocation of acceptance, as of the place of arrival.

### § 2–714. Buyer's Damages for Breach in Regard to Accepted Goods.

**(1)** Where the buyer has accepted goods and given notification (subsection (3) of Section 2–607) he may recover as damages for any non-conformity of tender the loss resulting in the ordinary course of events from the seller's breach as determined in any manner which is reasonable.

**(2)** The measure of damages for breach of warranty is the difference at the time and place of acceptance between the value of the goods accepted and the value they would have had if they had been as warranted, unless special circumstances show proximate damages of a different amount.

(3) In a proper case any incidental and consequential damages under the next section may also be recovered.

### § 2–715. Buyer's Incidental and Consequential Damages.

(1) Incidental damages resulting from the seller's breach include expenses reasonably incurred in inspection, receipt, transportation and care and custody of goods rightfully rejected, any commercially reasonable charges, expenses or commissions in connection with effecting cover and any other reasonable expense incident to the delay or other breach.

(2) Consequential damages resulting from the seller's breach include

(a) any loss resulting from general or particular requirements and needs of which the seller at the time of contracting had reason to know and which could not reasonably be prevented by cover or otherwise; and

(b) injury to person or property proximately resulting from any breach of warranty.

### § 2–716. Buyer's Right to Specific Performance or Replevin.

(1) Specific performance may be decreed where the goods are unique or in other proper circumstances.

(2) The decree for specific performance may include such terms and conditions as to payment of the price, damages, or other relief as the court may deem just.

(3) The buyer has a right of replevin for goods identified to the contract if after reasonable effort he is unable to effect cover for such goods or the circumstances reasonably indicate that such effort will be unavailing or if the goods have been shipped under reservation and satisfaction of the security interest in them has been made or tendered. In the case of goods bought for personal, family, or household purposes, the buyer's right of replevin vests upon acquisition of a special property, even if the seller had not then repudiated or failed to deliver.
As amended in 1999.

### § 2–717. Deduction of Damages From the Price.

The buyer on notifying the seller of his intention to do so may deduct all or any part of the damages resulting from any breach of the contract from any part of the price still due under the same contract.

### § 2–718. Liquidation or Limitation of Damages; Deposits.

(1) Damages for breach by either party may be liquidated in the agreement but only at an amount which is reasonable in the light of the anticipated or actual harm caused by the breach, the difficulties of proof of loss, and the inconvenience or nonfeasibility of otherwise obtaining an adequate remedy. A term fixing unreasonably large liquidated damages is void as a penalty.

(2) Where the seller justifiably withholds delivery of goods because of the buyer's breach, the buyer is entitled to restitution of any amount by which the sum of his payments exceeds

(a) the amount to which the seller is entitled by virtue of terms liquidating the seller's damages in accordance with subsection (1), or

(b) in the absence of such terms, twenty per cent of the value of the total performance for which the buyer is obligated under the contract or $500, whichever is smaller.

(3) The buyer's right to restitution under subsection (2) is subject to offset to the extent that the seller establishes

(a) a right to recover damages under the provisions of this Article other than subsection (1), and

(b) the amount or value of any benefits received by the buyer directly or indirectly by reason of the contract.

(4) Where a seller has received payment in goods their reasonable value or the proceeds of their resale shall be treated as payments for the purposes of subsection (2); but if the seller has notice of the buyer's breach before reselling goods received in part performance, his resale is subject to the conditions laid down in this Article on resale by an aggrieved seller (Section 2–706).

### § 2–719. Contractual Modification or Limitation of Remedy.

(1) Subject to the provisions of subsections (2) and (3) of this section and of the preceding section on liquidation and limitation of damages,

(a) the agreement may provide for remedies in addition to or in substitution for those provided in this Article and may limit or alter the measure of damages recoverable under this Article, as by limiting the buyer's remedies to return of the goods and repayment of the price or to repair and replacement of nonconforming goods or parts; and

(b) resort to a remedy as provided is optional unless the remedy is expressly agreed to be exclusive, in which case it is the sole remedy.

(2) Where circumstances cause an exclusive or limited remedy to fail of its essential purpose, remedy may be had as provided in this Act.

(3) Consequential damages may be limited or excluded unless the limitation or exclusion is unconscionable. Limitation of consequential damages for injury to the person in the case of consumer goods is *prima facie* unconscionable but limitation of damages where the loss is commercial is not.

### § 2–720. Effect of "Cancellation" or "Rescission" on Claims for Antecedent Breach.

Unless the contrary intention clearly appears, expressions of "cancellation" or "rescission" of the contract or the like shall not be construed as a renunciation or discharge of any claim in damages for an antecedent breach.

### § 2–721. Remedies for Fraud.

Remedies for material misrepresentation or fraud include all remedies available under this Article for non-fraudulent breach. Neither rescission or a claim for rescission of the contract for sale nor rejection or return of the goods shall bar or be deemed inconsistent with a claim for damages or other remedy.

## § 2–722. Who Can Sue Third Parties for Injury to Goods.

Where a third party so deals with goods which have been identified to a contract for sale as to cause actionable injury to a party to that contract

**(a)** a right of action against the third party is in either party to the contract for sale who has title to or a security interest or a special property or an insurable interest in the goods; and if the goods have been destroyed or converted a right of action is also in the party who either bore the risk of loss under the contract for sale or has since the injury assumed that risk as against the other;

**(b)** if at the time of the injury the party plaintiff did not bear the risk of loss as against the other party to the contract for sale and there is no arrangement between them for disposition of the recovery, his suit or settlement is, subject to his own interest, as a fiduciary for the other party to the contract;

**(c)** either party may with the consent of the other sue for the benefit of whom it may concern.

## § 2–723. Proof of Market Price: Time and Place.

**(1)** If an action based on anticipatory repudiation comes to trial before the time for performance with respect to some or all of the goods, any damages based on market price (Section 2–708 or Section 2–713) shall be determined according to the price of such goods prevailing at the time when the aggrieved party learned of the repudiation.

**(2)** If evidence of a price prevailing at the times or places described in this Article is not readily available the price prevailing within any reasonable time before or after the time described or at any other place which in commercial judgment or under usage of trade would serve as a reasonable substitute for the one described may be used, making any proper allowance for the cost of transporting the goods to or from such other place.

**(3)** Evidence of a relevant price prevailing at a time or place other than the one described in this Article offered by one party is not admissible unless and until he has given the other party such notice as the court finds sufficient to prevent unfair surprise.

## § 2–724. Admissibility of Market Quotations.

Whenever the prevailing price or value of any goods regularly bought and sold in any established commodity market is in issue, reports in official publications or trade journals or in newspapers or periodicals of general circulation published as the reports of such market shall be admissible in evidence. The circumstances of the preparation of such a report may be shown to affect its weight but not its admissibility.

## § 2–725. Statute of Limitations in Contracts for Sale.

**(1)** An action for breach of any contract for sale must be commenced within four years after the cause of action has accrued. By the original agreement the parties may reduce the period of limitation to not less than one year but may not extend it.

**(2)** A cause of action accrues when the breach occurs, regardless of the aggrieved party's lack of knowledge of the breach. A breach of warranty occurs when tender of delivery is made, except that where a warranty explicitly extends to future performance of the goods and discovery of the breach must await the time of such performance the cause of action accrues when the breach is or should have been discovered.

**(3)** Where an action commenced within the time limited by subsection (1) is so terminated as to leave available a remedy by another action for the same breach such other action may be commenced after the expiration of the time limited and within six months after the termination of the first action unless the termination resulted from voluntary discontinuance or from dismissal for failure or neglect to prosecute.

**(4)** This section does not alter the law on tolling of the statute of limitations nor does it apply to causes of action which have accrued before this Act becomes effective.

## ARTICLE 2A: LEASES

### Part 1—General Provisions

### § 2A–101. Short Title.

This Article shall be known and may be cited as the Uniform Commercial Code—Leases.

### § 2A–102. Scope.

This Article applies to any transaction, regardless of form, that creates a lease.

### § 2A–103. Definitions and Index of Definitions.

**(1)** In this Article unless the context otherwise requires:

**(a)** "Buyer in ordinary course of business" means a person who in good faith and without knowledge that the sale to him [or her] is in violation of the ownership rights or security interest or leasehold interest of a third party in the goods buys in ordinary course from a person in the business of selling goods of that kind but does not include a pawnbroker. "Buying" may be for cash or by exchange of other property or on secured or unsecured credit and includes receiving goods or documents of title under a preexisting contract for sale but does not include a transfer in bulk or as security for or in total or partial satisfaction of a money debt.

**(b)** "Cancellation" occurs when either party puts an end to the lease contract for default by the other party.

**(c)** "Commercial unit" means such a unit of goods as by commercial usage is a single whole for purposes of lease and division of which materially impairs its character or value on the market or in use. A commercial unit may be a single article, as a machine, or a set of articles, as a suite of furniture or a line of machinery, or a quantity, as a gross or carload, or any other unit treated in use or in the relevant market as a single whole.

**(d)** "Conforming" goods or performance under a lease contract means goods or performance that are in accordance with the obligations under the lease contract.

**(e)** "Consumer lease" means a lease that a lessor regularly engaged in the business of leasing or selling makes to a lessee who is an individual and who takes under the lease primarily for a personal, family, or household purpose [, if the total payments to be made under the lease contract, excluding payments for options to renew or buy, do not exceed $_____].

**(f)** "Fault" means wrongful act, omission, breach, or default.

**(g)** "Finance lease" means a lease with respect to which:

(i) the lessor does not select, manufacture or supply the goods;

(ii) the lessor acquires the goods or the right to possession and use of the goods in connection with the lease; and

(iii) one of the following occurs:

**(A)** the lessee receives a copy of the contract by which the lessor acquired the goods or the right to possession and use of the goods before signing the lease contract;

**(B)** the lessee's approval of the contract by which the lessor acquired the goods or the right to possession and use of the goods is a condition to effectiveness of the lease contract;

**(C)** the lessee, before signing the lease contract, receives an accurate and complete statement designating the promises and warranties, and any disclaimers of warranties, limitations or modifications of remedies, or liquidated damages, including those of a third party, such as the manufacturer of the goods, provided to the lessor by the person supplying the goods in connection with or as part of the contract by which the lessor acquired the goods or the right to possession and use of the goods; or

**(D)** if the lease is not a consumer lease, the lessor, before the lessee signs the lease contract, informs the lessee in writing (a) of the identity of the person supplying the goods to the lessor, unless the lessee has selected that person and directed the lessor to acquire the goods or the right to possession and use of the goods from that person, (b) that the lessee is entitled under this Article to any promises and warranties, including those of any third party, provided to the lessor by the person supplying the goods in connection with or as part of the contract by which the lessor acquired the goods or the right to possession and use of the goods, and (c) that the lessee may communicate with the person supplying the goods to the lessor and receive an accurate and complete statement of those promises and warranties, including any disclaimers and limitations of them or of remedies.

**(h)** "Goods" means all things that are movable at the time of identification to the lease contract, or are fixtures (Section 2A–309), but the term does not include money, documents, instruments, accounts, chattel paper, general intangibles, or minerals or the like, including oil and gas, before extraction. The term also includes the unborn young of animals.

**(i)** "Installment lease contract" means a lease contract that authorizes or requires the delivery of goods in separate lots to be separately accepted, even though the lease contract contains a clause "each delivery is a separate lease" or its equivalent.

**(j)** "Lease" means a transfer of the right to possession and use of goods for a term in return for consideration, but a sale, including a sale on approval or a sale or return, or retention or creation of a security interest is not a lease. Unless the context clearly indicates otherwise, the term includes a sublease.

**(k)** "Lease agreement" means the bargain, with respect to the lease, of the lessor and the lessee in fact as found in their language or by implication from other circumstances including course of dealing or usage of trade or course of performance as provided in this Article. Unless the context clearly indicates otherwise, the term includes a sublease agreement.

**(l)** "Lease contract" means the total legal obligation that results from the lease agreement as affected by this Article and any other applicable rules of law. Unless the context clearly indicates otherwise, the term includes a sublease contract.

**(m)** "Leasehold interest" means the interest of the lessor or the lessee under a lease contract.

**(n)** "Lessee" means a person who acquires the right to possession and use of goods under a lease. Unless the context clearly indicates otherwise, the term includes a sublessee.

**(o)** "Lessee in ordinary course of business" means a person who in good faith and without knowledge that the lease to him [or her] is in violation of the ownership rights or security interest or leasehold interest of a third party in the goods, leases in ordinary course from a person in the business of selling or leasing goods of that kind but does not include a pawnbroker. "Leasing" may be for cash or by exchange of other property or on secured or unsecured credit and includes receiving goods or documents of title under a pre-existing lease contract but does not include a transfer in bulk or as security for or in total or partial satisfaction of a money debt.

**(p)** "Lessor" means a person who transfers the right to possession and use of goods under a lease. Unless the context clearly indicates otherwise, the term includes a sublessor.

**(q)** "Lessor's residual interest" means the lessor's interest in the goods after expiration, termination, or cancellation of the lease contract.

**(r)** "Lien" means a charge against or interest in goods to secure payment of a debt or performance of an obligation, but the term does not include a security interest.

**(s)** "Lot" means a parcel or a single article that is the subject matter of a separate lease or delivery, whether or not it is sufficient to perform the lease contract.

**(t)** "Merchant lessee" means a lessee that is a merchant with respect to goods of the kind subject to the lease.

**(u)** "Present value" means the amount as of a date certain of one or more sums payable in the future, discounted to the date certain. The discount is determined by the interest rate specified by the parties if the rate was not manifestly unreasonable at the time the transaction was entered into; otherwise, the discount is determined by a commercially reasonable rate that takes into account the facts and circumstances of each case at the time the transaction was entered into.

**(v)** "Purchase" includes taking by sale, lease, mortgage, security interest, pledge, gift, or any other voluntary transaction creating an interest in goods.

**(w)** "Sublease" means a lease of goods the right to possession and use of which was acquired by the lessor as a lessee under an existing lease.

**(x)** "Supplier" means a person from whom a lessor buys or leases goods to be leased under a finance lease.

**(y)** "Supply contract" means a contract under which a lessor buys or leases goods to be leased.

**(z)** "Termination" occurs when either party pursuant to a power created by agreement or law puts an end to the lease contract otherwise than for default.

**(2)** Other definitions applying to this Article and the sections in which they appear are:

"Accessions". Section 2A–310(1).
"Construction mortgage". Section 2A–309(1)(d).
"Encumbrance". Section 2A–309(1)(e).
"Fixtures". Section 2A–309(1)(a).
"Fixture filing". Section 2A–309(1)(b).
"Purchase money lease". Section 2A–309(1)(c).

**(3)** The following definitions in other Articles apply to this Article:

"Accounts". Section 9–106.
"Between merchants". Section 2–104(3).
"Buyer". Section 2–103(1)(a).
"Chattel paper". Section 9–105(1)(b).
"Consumer goods". Section 9–109(1).
"Document". Section 9–105(1)(f).
"Entrusting". Section 2–403(3).
"General intangibles". Section 9–106.
"Good faith". Section 2–103(1)(b).
"Instrument". Section 9–105(1)(i).
"Merchant". Section 2–104(1).
"Mortgage". Section 9–105(1)(j).
"Pursuant to commitment". Section 9–105(1)(k).
"Receipt". Section 2–103(1)(c).
"Sale". Section 2–106(1).
"Sale on approval". Section 2–326.
"Sale or return". Section 2–326.
"Seller". Section 2–103(1)(d).

**(4)** In addition Article 1 contains general definitions and principles of construction and interpretation applicable throughout this Article.
As amended in 1990 and 1999.

### § 2A–104. Leases Subject to Other Law.

**(1)** A lease, although subject to this Article, is also subject to any applicable:

    **(a)** certificate of title statute of this State: (list any certificate of title statutes covering automobiles, trailers, mobile homes, boats, farm tractors, and the like);

    **(b)** certificate of title statute of another jurisdiction (Section 2A–105); or

    **(c)** consumer protection statute of this State, or final consumer protection decision of a court of this State existing on the effective date of this Article.

**(2)** In case of conflict between this Article, other than Sections 2A–105, 2A–304(3), and 2A–305(3), and a statute or decision referred to in subsection (1), the statute or decision controls.

**(3)** Failure to comply with an applicable law has only the effect specified therein.
As amended in 1990.

### § 2A–105. Territorial Application of Article to Goods Covered by Certificate of Title.

Subject to the provisions of Sections 2A–304(3) and 2A–305(3), with respect to goods covered by a certificate of title issued under a statute of this State or of another jurisdiction, compliance and the effect of compliance or noncompliance with a certificate of title statute are governed by the law (including the conflict of laws rules) of the jurisdiction issuing the certificate until the earlier of (a) surrender of the certificate, or (b) four months after the goods are removed from that jurisdiction and thereafter until a new certificate of title is issued by another jurisdiction.

### § 2A–106. Limitation on Power of Parties to Consumer Lease to Choose Applicable Law and Judicial Forum.

**(1)** If the law chosen by the parties to a consumer lease is that of a jurisdiction other than a jurisdiction in which the lessee resides at the time the lease agreement becomes enforceable or within 30 days thereafter or in which the goods are to be used, the choice is not enforceable.

**(2)** If the judicial forum chosen by the parties to a consumer lease is a forum that would not otherwise have jurisdiction over the lessee, the choice is not enforceable.

### § 2A–107. Waiver or Renunciation of Claim or Right After Default.

Any claim or right arising out of an alleged default or breach of warranty may be discharged in whole or in part without consideration by a written waiver or renunciation signed and delivered by the aggrieved party.

### § 2A–108. Unconscionability.

**(1)** If the court as a matter of law finds a lease contract or any clause of a lease contract to have been unconscionable at the time it was made the court may refuse to enforce the lease contract, or it may enforce the remainder of the lease contract without the unconscionable clause, or it may so limit the application of any unconscionable clause as to avoid any unconscionable result.

**(2)** With respect to a consumer lease, if the court as a matter of law finds that a lease contract or any clause of a lease contract has been induced by unconscionable conduct or that unconscionable conduct has occurred in the collection of a claim arising from a lease contract, the court may grant appropriate relief.

**(3)** Before making a finding of unconscionability under subsection (1) or (2), the court, on its own motion or that of a party, shall afford the parties a reasonable opportunity to present evidence as to the setting, purpose, and effect of the lease contract or clause thereof, or of the conduct.

**(4)** In an action in which the lessee claims unconscionability with respect to a consumer lease:

    **(a)** If the court finds unconscionability under subsection (1) or (2), the court shall award reasonable attorney's fees to the lessee.

    **(b)** If the court does not find unconscionability and the lessee claiming unconscionability has brought or maintained an action he [or she] knew to be groundless, the court shall award reasonable attorney's fees to the party against whom the claim is made.

(c) In determining attorney's fees, the amount of the recovery on behalf of the claimant under subsections (1) and (2) is not controlling.

### § 2A-109. Option to Accelerate at Will.

(1) A term providing that one party or his [or her] successor in interest may accelerate payment or performance or require collateral or additional collateral "at will" or "when he [or she] deems himself [or herself] insecure" or in words of similar import must be construed to mean that he [or she] has power to do so only if he [or she] in good faith believes that the prospect of payment or performance is impaired.

(2) With respect to a consumer lease, the burden of establishing good faith under subsection (1) is on the party who exercised the power; otherwise the burden of establishing lack of good faith is on the party against whom the power has been exercised.

### Part 2—Formation and Construction of Lease Contract

### § 2A-201. Statute of Frauds.

(1) A lease contract is not enforceable by way of action or defense unless:

(a) the total payments to be made under the lease contract, excluding payments for options to renew or buy, are less than $1,000; or

(b) there is a writing, signed by the party against whom enforcement is sought or by that party's authorized agent, sufficient to indicate that a lease contract has been made between the parties and to describe the goods leased and the lease term.

(2) Any description of leased goods or of the lease term is sufficient and satisfies subsection (1)(b), whether or not it is specific, if it reasonably identifies what is described.

(3) A writing is not insufficient because it omits or incorrectly states a term agreed upon, but the lease contract is not enforceable under subsection (1)(b) beyond the lease term and the quantity of goods shown in the writing.

(4) A lease contract that does not satisfy the requirements of subsection (1), but which is valid in other respects, is enforceable:

(a) if the goods are to be specially manufactured or obtained for the lessee and are not suitable for lease or sale to others in the ordinary course of the lessor's business, and the lessor, before notice of repudiation is received and under circumstances that reasonably indicate that the goods are for the lessee, has made either a substantial beginning of their manufacture or commitments for their procurement; (b) if the party against whom enforcement is sought admits in that party's pleading, testimony or otherwise in court that a lease contract was made, but the lease contract is not enforceable under this provision beyond the quantity of goods admitted; or

(c) with respect to goods that have been received and accepted by the lessee.

(5) The lease term under a lease contract referred to in subsection (4) is:

(a) if there is a writing signed by the party against whom enforcement is sought or by that party's authorized agent specifying the lease term, the term so specified;

(b) if the party against whom enforcement is sought admits in that party's pleading, testimony, or otherwise in court a lease term, the term so admitted; or

(c) a reasonable lease term.

### § 2A-202. Final Written Expression: Parol or Extrinsic Evidence.

Terms with respect to which the confirmatory memoranda of the parties agree or which are otherwise set forth in a writing intended by the parties as a final expression of their agreement with respect to such terms as are included therein may not be contradicted by evidence of any prior agreement or of a contemporaneous oral agreement but may be explained or supplemented:

(a) by course of dealing or usage of trade or by course of performance; and

(b) by evidence of consistent additional terms unless the court finds the writing to have been intended also as a complete and exclusive statement of the terms of the agreement.

### § 2A-203. Seals Inoperative.

The affixing of a seal to a writing evidencing a lease contract or an offer to enter into a lease contract does not render the writing a sealed instrument and the law with respect to sealed instruments does not apply to the lease contract or offer.

### § 2A-204. Formation in General.

(1) A lease contract may be made in any manner sufficient to show agreement, including conduct by both parties which recognizes the existence of a lease contract.

(2) An agreement sufficient to constitute a lease contract may be found although the moment of its making is undetermined.

(3) Although one or more terms are left open, a lease contract does not fail for indefiniteness if the parties have intended to make a lease contract and there is a reasonably certain basis for giving an appropriate remedy.

### § 2A-205. Firm Offers.

An offer by a merchant to lease goods to or from another person in a signed writing that by its terms gives assurance it will be held open is not revocable, for lack of consideration, during the time stated or, if no time is stated, for a reasonable time, but in no event may the period of irrevocability exceed 3 months. Any such term of assurance on a form supplied by the offeree must be separately signed by the offeror.

### § 2A-206. Offer and Acceptance in Formation of Lease Contract.

(1) Unless otherwise unambiguously indicated by the language or circumstances, an offer to make a lease contract must be construed as inviting acceptance in any manner and by any medium reasonable in the circumstances.

(2) If the beginning of a requested performance is a reasonable mode of acceptance, an offeror who is not notified of acceptance within a reasonable time may treat the offer as having lapsed before acceptance.

## § 2A–207. Course of Performance or Practical Construction.

**(1)** If a lease contract involves repeated occasions for performance by either party with knowledge of the nature of the performance and opportunity for objection to it by the other, any course of performance accepted or acquiesced in without objection is relevant to determine the meaning of the lease agreement.

**(2)** The express terms of a lease agreement and any course of performance, as well as any course of dealing and usage of trade, must be construed whenever reasonable as consistent with each other; but if that construction is unreasonable, express terms control course of performance, course of performance controls both course of dealing and usage of trade, and course of dealing controls usage of trade.

**(3)** Subject to the provisions of Section 2A–208 on modification and waiver, course of performance is relevant to show a waiver or modification of any term inconsistent with the course of performance.

## § 2A–208. Modification, Rescission and Waiver.

**(1)** An agreement modifying a lease contract needs no consideration to be binding.

**(2)** A signed lease agreement that excludes modification or rescission except by a signed writing may not be otherwise modified or rescinded, but, except as between merchants, such a requirement on a form supplied by a merchant must be separately signed by the other party.

**(3)** Although an attempt at modification or rescission does not satisfy the requirements of subsection (2), it may operate as a waiver.

**(4)** A party who has made a waiver affecting an executory portion of a lease contract may retract the waiver by reasonable notification received by the other party that strict performance will be required of any term waived, unless the retraction would be unjust in view of a material change of position in reliance on the waiver.

## § 2A–209. Lessee under Finance Lease as Beneficiary of Supply Contract.

**(1)** The benefit of the supplier's promises to the lessor under the supply contract and of all warranties, whether express or implied, including those of any third party provided in connection with or as part of the supply contract, extends to the lessee to the extent of the lessee's leasehold interest under a finance lease related to the supply contract, but is subject to the terms warranty and of the supply contract and all defenses or claims arising therefrom.

**(2)** The extension of the benefit of supplier's promises and of warranties to the lessee (Section 2A–209(1)) does not: (i) modify the rights and obligations of the parties to the supply contract, whether arising therefrom or otherwise, or (ii) impose any duty or liability under the supply contract on the lessee.

**(3)** Any modification or rescission of the supply contract by the supplier and the lessor is effective between the supplier and the lessee unless, before the modification or rescission, the supplier has received notice that the lessee has entered into a finance lease related to the supply contract. If the modification or rescission is effective between the supplier and the lessee, the lessor is deemed to have assumed, in addition to the obligations of the lessor to the lessee under the lease contract, promises of the supplier to the lessor and warranties that were so modified or rescinded as they existed and were available to the lessee before modification or rescission.

**(4)** In addition to the extension of the benefit of the supplier's promises and of warranties to the lessee under subsection (1), the lessee retains all rights that the lessee may have against the supplier which arise from an agreement between the lessee and the supplier or under other law.
As amended in 1990.

## § 2A–210. Express Warranties.

**(1)** Express warranties by the lessor are created as follows:

(a) Any affirmation of fact or promise made by the lessor to the lessee which relates to the goods and becomes part of the basis of the bargain creates an express warranty that the goods will conform to the affirmation or promise.

(b) Any description of the goods which is made part of the basis of the bargain creates an express warranty that the goods will conform to the description.

(c) Any sample or model that is made part of the basis of the bargain creates an express warranty that the whole of the goods will conform to the sample or model.

**(2)** It is not necessary to the creation of an express warranty that the lessor use formal words, such as "warrant" or "guarantee," or that the lessor have a specific intention to make a warranty, but an affirmation merely of the value of the goods or a statement purporting to be merely the lessor's opinion or commendation of the goods does not create a warranty.

## § 2A–211. Warranties Against Interference and Against Infringement; Lessee's Obligation Against Infringement.

**(1)** There is in a lease contract a warranty that for the lease term no person holds a claim to or interest in the goods that arose from an act or omission of the lessor, other than a claim by way of infringement or the like, which will interfere with the lessee's enjoyment of its leasehold interest.

**(2)** Except in a finance lease there is in a lease contract by a lessor who is a merchant regularly dealing in goods of the kind a warranty that the goods are delivered free of the rightful claim of any person by way of infringement or the like.

**(3)** A lessee who furnishes specifications to a lessor or a supplier shall hold the lessor and the supplier harmless against any claim by way of infringement or the like that arises out of compliance with the specifications.

## § 2A–212. Implied Warranty of Merchantability.

**(1)** Except in a finance lease, a warranty that the goods will be merchantable is implied in a lease contract if the lessor is a merchant with respect to goods of that kind.

**(2)** Goods to be merchantable must be at least such as

(a) pass without objection in the trade under the description in the lease agreement;

(b) in the case of fungible goods, are of fair average quality within the description;

(c) are fit for the ordinary purposes for which goods of that type are used;

(d) run, within the variation permitted by the lease agreement, of even kind, quality, and quantity within each unit and among all units involved;

(e) are adequately contained, packaged, and labeled as the lease agreement may require; and

(f) conform to any promises or affirmations of fact made on the container or label.

(3) Other implied warranties may arise from course of dealing or usage of trade.

### § 2A–213. Implied Warranty of Fitness for Particular Purpose.

Except in a finance of lease, if the lessor at the time the lease contract is made has reason to know of any particular purpose for which the goods are required and that the lessee is relying on the lessor's skill or judgment to select or furnish suitable goods, there is in the lease contract an implied warranty that the goods will be fit for that purpose.

### § 2A–214. Exclusion or Modification of Warranties.

(1) Words or conduct relevant to the creation of an express warranty and words or conduct tending to negate or limit a warranty must be construed wherever reasonable as consistent with each other; but, subject to the provisions of Section 2A–202 on parol or extrinsic evidence, negation or limitation is inoperative to the extent that the construction is unreasonable.

(2) Subject to subsection (3), to exclude or modify the implied warranty of merchantability or any part of it the language must mention "merchantability", be by a writing, and be conspicuous. Subject to subsection (3), to exclude or modify any implied warranty of fitness the exclusion must be by a writing and be conspicuous. Language to exclude all implied warranties of fitness is sufficient if it is in writing, is conspicuous and states, for example, "There is no warranty that the goods will be fit for a particular purpose".

(3) Notwithstanding subsection (2), but subject to subsection (4),

(a) unless the circumstances indicate otherwise, all implied warranties are excluded by expressions like "as is" or "with all faults" or by other language that in common understanding calls the lessee's attention to the exclusion of warranties and makes plain that there is no implied warranty, if in writing and conspicuous;

(b) if the lessee before entering into the lease contract has examined the goods or the sample or model as fully as desired or has refused to examine the goods, there is no implied warranty with regard to defects that an examination ought in the circumstances to have revealed; and

(c) an implied warranty may also be excluded or modified by course of dealing, course of performance, or usage of trade.

(4) To exclude or modify a warranty against interference or against infringement (Section 2A–211) or any part of it, the language must be specific, be by a writing, and be conspicuous, unless the circumstances, including course of performance, course of dealing, or usage of trade, give the lessee reason to know that the goods are being leased subject to a claim or interest of any person.

### § 2A–215. Cumulation and Conflict of Warranties Express or Implied.

Warranties, whether express or implied, must be construed as consistent with each other and as cumulative, but if that construction is unreasonable, the intention of the parties determines which warranty is dominant. In ascertaining that intention the following rules apply:

(a) Exact or technical specifications displace an inconsistent sample or model or general language of description.

(b) A sample from an existing bulk displaces inconsistent general language of description.

(c) Express warranties displace inconsistent implied warranties other than an implied warranty of fitness for a particular purpose.

### § 2A–216. Third-Party Beneficiaries of Express and Implied Warranties.

**Alternative A**

A warranty to or for the benefit of a lessee under this Article, whether express or implied, extends to any natural person who is in the family or household of the lessee or who is a guest in the lessee's home if it is reasonable to expect that such person may use, consume, or be affected by the goods and who is injured in person by breach of the warranty. This section does not displace principles of law and equity that extend a warranty to or for the benefit of a lessee to other persons. The operation of this section may not be excluded, modified, or limited, but an exclusion, modification, or limitation of the warranty, including any with respect to rights and remedies, effective against the lessee is also effective against any beneficiary designated under this section.

**Alternative B**

A warranty to or for the benefit of a lessee under this Article, whether express or implied, extends to any natural person who may reasonably be expected to use, consume, or be affected by the goods and who is injured in person by breach of the warranty. This section does not displace principles of law and equity that extend a warranty to or for the benefit of a lessee to other persons. The operation of this section may not be excluded, modified, or limited, but an exclusion, modification, or limitation of the warranty, including any with respect to rights and remedies, effective against the lessee is also effective against the beneficiary designated under this section.

**Alternative C**

A warranty to or for the benefit of a lessee under this Article, whether express or implied, extends to any person who may reasonably be expected to use, consume, or be affected by the goods and who is injured by breach of the warranty. The operation of this section may not be excluded, modified, or limited with respect to injury to the person of an individual to whom the warranty extends, but an exclusion, modification, or limitation of the warranty, including any with respect to rights and remedies, effective against the lessee is also effective against the beneficiary designated under this section.

### § 2A–217. Identification.

Identification of goods as goods to which a lease contract refers may be made at any time and in any manner explicitly agreed to by the parties. In the absence of explicit agreement, identification occurs:

(a) when the lease contract is made if the lease contract is for a lease of goods that are existing and identified;

**(b)** when the goods are shipped, marked, or otherwise designated by the lessor as goods to which the lease contract refers, if the lease contract is for a lease of goods that are not existing and identified; or

**(c)** when the young are conceived, if the lease contract is for a lease of unborn young of animals.

### § 2A–218. Insurance and Proceeds.

**(1)** A lessee obtains an insurable interest when existing goods are identified to the lease contract even though the goods identified are nonconforming and the lessee has an option to reject them.

**(2)** If a lessee has an insurable interest only by reason of the lessor's identification of the goods, the lessor, until default or insolvency or notification to the lessee that identification is final, may substitute other goods for those identified.

**(3)** Notwithstanding a lessee's insurable interest under subsections (1) and (2), the lessor retains an insurable interest until an option to buy has been exercised by the lessee and risk of loss has passed to the lessee.

**(4)** Nothing in this section impairs any insurable interest recognized under any other statute or rule of law.

**(5)** The parties by agreement may determine that one or more parties have an obligation to obtain and pay for insurance covering the goods and by agreement may determine the beneficiary of the proceeds of the insurance.

### § 2A–219. Risk of Loss.

**(1)** Except in the case of a finance lease, risk of loss is retained by the lessor and does not pass to the lessee. In the case of a finance lease, risk of loss passes to the lessee.

**(2)** Subject to the provisions of this Article on the effect of default on risk of loss (Section 2A–220), if risk of loss is to pass to the lessee and the time of passage is not stated, the following rules apply:

  **(a)** If the lease contract requires or authorizes the goods to be shipped by carrier

  **(i)** and it does not require delivery at a particular destination, the risk of loss passes to the lessee when the goods are duly delivered to the carrier; but

  **(ii)** if it does require delivery at a particular destination and the goods are there duly tendered while in the possession of the carrier, the risk of loss passes to the lessee when the goods are there duly so tendered as to enable the lessee to take delivery.

  **(b)** If the goods are held by a bailee to be delivered without being moved, the risk of loss passes to the lessee on acknowledgment by the bailee of the lessee's right to possession of the goods.

  **(c)** In any case not within subsection (a) or (b), the risk of loss passes to the lessee on the lessee's receipt of the goods if the lessor, or, in the case of a finance lease, the supplier, is a merchant; otherwise the risk passes to the lessee on tender of delivery.

### § 2A–220. Effect of Default on Risk of Loss.

**(1)** Where risk of loss is to pass to the lessee and the time of passage is not stated:

  **(a)** If a tender or delivery of goods so fails to conform to the lease contract as to give a right of rejection, the risk of their

loss remains with the lessor, or, in the case of a finance lease, the supplier, until cure or acceptance.

  **(b)** If the lessee rightfully revokes acceptance, he [or she], to the extent of any deficiency in his [or her] effective insurance coverage, may treat the risk of loss as having remained with the lessor from the beginning.

**(2)** Whether or not risk of loss is to pass to the lessee, if the lessee as to conforming goods already identified to a lease contract repudiates or is otherwise in default under the lease contract, the lessor, or, in the case of a finance lease, the supplier, to the extent of any deficiency in his [or her] effective insurance coverage may treat the risk of loss as resting on the lessee for a commercially reasonable time.

### § 2A–221. Casualty to Identified Goods.

If a lease contract requires goods identified when the lease contract is made, and the goods suffer casualty without fault of the lessee, the lessor or the supplier before delivery, or the goods suffer casualty before risk of loss passes to the lessee pursuant to the lease agreement or Section 2A–219, then:

**(a)** if the loss is total, the lease contract is avoided; and

**(b)** if the loss is partial or the goods have so deteriorated as to no longer conform to the lease contract, the lessee may nevertheless demand inspection and at his [or her] option either treat the lease contract as avoided or, except in a finance lease that is not a consumer lease, accept the goods with due allowance from the rent payable for the balance of the lease term for the deterioration or the deficiency in quantity but without further right against the lessor.

## Part 3—Effect of Lease Contract

### § 2A–301. Enforceability of Lease Contract.

Except as otherwise provided in this Article, a lease contract is effective and enforceable according to its terms between the parties, against purchasers of the goods and against creditors of the parties.

### § 2A–302. Title to and Possession of Goods.

Except as otherwise provided in this Article, each provision of this Article applies whether the lessor or a third party has title to the goods, and whether the lessor, the lessee, or a third party has possession of the goods, notwithstanding any statute or rule of law that possession or the absence of possession is fraudulent.

### § 2A–303. Alienability of Party's Interest Under Lease Contract or of Lessor's Residual Interest in Goods; Delegation of Performance; Transfer of Rights.

**(1)** As used in this section, "creation of a security interest" includes the sale of a lease contract that is subject to Article 9, Secured Transactions, by reason of Section 9–109(a)(3).

**(2)** Except as provided in subsections (3) and Section 9–407, a provision in a lease agreement which (i) prohibits the voluntary or involuntary transfer, including a transfer by sale, sublease, creation or enforcement of a security interest, or attachment, levy, or other judicial process, of an interest of a party under the lease contract or of the lessor's residual interest in the goods, or (ii) makes such a transfer an event of default, gives rise to the rights and remedies provided in subsection (4), but a transfer that is prohibited or is an event of default under the lease agreement is otherwise effective.

(3) A provision in a lease agreement which (i) prohibits a transfer of a right to damages for default with respect to the whole lease contract or of a right to payment arising out of the transferor's due performance of the transferor's entire obligation, or (ii) makes such a transfer an event of default, is not enforceable, and such a transfer is not a transfer that materially impairs the propsect of obtaining return performance by, materially changes the duty of, or materially increases the burden or risk imposed on, the other party to the lease contract within the purview of subsection (4).

(4) Subject to subsection (3) and Section 9–407:

(a) if a transfer is made which is made an event of default under a lease agreement, the party to the lease contract not making the transfer, unless that party waives the default or otherwise agrees, has the rights and remedies described in Section 2A–501(2);

(b) if paragraph (a) is not applicable and if a transfer is made that (i) is prohibited under a lease agreement or (ii) materially impairs the prospect of obtaining return performance by, materially changes the duty of, or materially increases the burden or risk imposed on, the other party to the lease contract, unless the party not making the transfer agrees at any time to the transfer in the lease contract or otherwise, then, except as limited by contract, (i) the transferor is liable to the party not making the transfer for damages caused by the transfer to the extent that the damages could not reasonably be prevented by the party not making the transfer and (ii) a court having jurisdiction may grant other appropriate relief, including cancellation of the lease contract or an injunction against the transfer.

(5) A transfer of "the lease" or of "all my rights under the lease", or a transfer in similar general terms, is a transfer of rights and, unless the language or the circumstances, as in a transfer for security, indicate the contrary, the transfer is a delegation of duties by the transferor to the transferee. Acceptance by the transferee constitutes a promise by the transferee to perform those duties. The promise is enforceable by either the transferor or the other party to the lease contract.

(6) Unless otherwise agreed by the lessor and the lessee, a delegation of performance does not relieve the transferor as against the other party of any duty to perform or of any liability for default.

(7) In a consumer lease, to prohibit the transfer of an interest of a party under the lease contract or to make a transfer an event of default, the language must be specific, by a writing, and conspicuous.

As amended in 1990 and 1999.

### § 2A–304. Subsequent Lease of Goods by Lessor.

(1) Subject to Section 2A–303, a subsequent lessee from a lessor of goods under an existing lease contract obtains, to the extent of the leasehold interest transferred, the leasehold interest in the goods that the lessor had or had power to transfer, and except as provided in subsection (2) and Section 2A–527(4), takes subject to the existing lease contract. A lessor with voidable title has power to transfer a good leasehold interest to a good faith subsequent lessee for value, but only to the extent set forth in the preceding sentence. If goods have been delivered under a transaction of purchase the lessor has that power even though:

(a) the lessor's transferor was deceived as to the identity of the lessor;

(b) the delivery was in exchange for a check which is later dishonored;

(c) it was agreed that the transaction was to be a "cash sale"; or

(d) the delivery was procured through fraud punishable as larcenous under the criminal law.

(2) A subsequent lessee in the ordinary course of business from a lessor who is a merchant dealing in goods of that kind to whom the goods were entrusted by the existing lessee of that lessor before the interest of the subsequent lessee became enforceable against that lessor obtains, to the extent of the leasehold interest transferred, all of that lessor's and the existing lessee's rights to the goods, and takes free of the existing lease contract.

(3) A subsequent lessee from the lessor of goods that are subject to an existing lease contract and are covered by a certificate of title issued under a statute of this State or of another jurisdiction takes no greater rights than those provided both by this section and by the certificate of title statute.

As amended in 1990.

### § 2A–305. Sale or Sublease of Goods by Lessee.

(1) Subject to the provisions of Section 2A–303, a buyer or sublessee from the lessee of goods under an existing lease contract obtains, to the extent of the interest transferred, the leasehold interest in the goods that the lessee had or had power to transfer, and except as provided in subsection (2) and Section 2A–511(4), takes subject to the existing lease contract. A lessee with a voidable leasehold interest has power to transfer a good leasehold interest to a good faith buyer for value or a good faith sublessee for value, but only to the extent set forth in the preceding sentence. When goods have been delivered under a transaction of lease the lessee has that power even though:

(a) the lessor was deceived as to the identity of the lessee;

(b) the delivery was in exchange for a check which is later dishonored; or

(c) the delivery was procured through fraud punishable as larcenous under the criminal law.

(2) A buyer in the ordinary course of business or a sublessee in the ordinary course of business from a lessee who is a merchant dealing in goods of that kind to whom the goods were entrusted by the lessor obtains, to the extent of the interest transferred, all of the lessor's and lessee's rights to the goods, and takes free of the existing lease contract.

(3) A buyer or sublessee from the lessee of goods that are subject to an existing lease contract and are covered by a certificate of title issued under a statute of this State or of another jurisdiction takes no greater rights than those provided both by this section and by the certificate of title statute.

### § 2A–306. Priority of Certain Liens Arising by Operation of Law.

If a person in the ordinary course of his [or her] business furnishes services or materials with respect to goods subject to a lease contract, a lien upon those goods in the possession of that person given by statute or rule of law for those materials or services takes priority over any interest of the lessor or lessee under the lease contract or this Article unless the lien is created by statute and the statute provides otherwise or unless the lien is created by rule of law and the rule of law provides otherwise.

### § 2A–307. Priority of Liens Arising by Attachment or Levy on, Security Interests in, and Other Claims to Goods.

(1) Except as otherwise provided in Section 2A–306, a creditor of a lessee takes subject to the lease contract.

(2) Except as otherwise provided in subsection (3) and in Sections 2A–306 and 2A–308, a creditor of a lessor takes subject to the lease contract unless the creditor holds a lien that attached to the goods before the lease contract became enforceable.

(3) Except as otherwise provided in Sections 9–317, 9–321, and 9–323, a lessee takes a leasehold interest subject to a security interest held by a creditor of the lessor.

As amended in 1990 and 1999.

### § 2A–308. Special Rights of Creditors.

(1) A creditor of a lessor in possession of goods subject to a lease contract may treat the lease contract as void if as against the creditor retention of possession by the lessor is fraudulent under any statute or rule of law, but retention of possession in good faith and current course of trade by the lessor for a commercially reasonable time after the lease contract becomes enforceable is not fraudulent.

(2) Nothing in this Article impairs the rights of creditors of a lessor if the lease contract (a) becomes enforceable, not in current course of trade but in satisfaction of or as security for a pre-existing claim for money, security, or the like, and (b) is made under circumstances which under any statute or rule of law apart from this Article would constitute the transaction a fraudulent transfer or voidable preference.

(3) A creditor of a seller may treat a sale or an identification of goods to a contract for sale as void if as against the creditor retention of possession by the seller is fraudulent under any statute or rule of law, but retention of possession of the goods pursuant to a lease contract entered into by the seller as lessee and the buyer as lessor in connection with the sale or identification of the goods is not fraudulent if the buyer bought for value and in good faith.

### § 2A–309. Lessor's and Lessee's Rights When Goods Become Fixtures.

(1) In this section:

(a) goods are "fixtures" when they become so related to particular real estate that an interest in them arises under real estate law;

(b) a "fixture filing" is the filing, in the office where a mortgage on the real estate would be filed or recorded, of a financing statement covering goods that are or are to become fixtures and conforming to the requirements of Section 9–502(a) and (b);

(c) a lease is a "purchase money lease" unless the lessee has possession or use of the goods or the right to possession or use of the goods before the lease agreement is enforceable;

(d) a mortgage is a "construction mortgage" to the extent it secures an obligation incurred for the construction of an improvement on land including the acquisition cost of the land, if the recorded writing so indicates; and

(e) "encumbrance" includes real estate mortgages and other liens on real estate and all other rights in real estate that are not ownership interests.

(2) Under this Article a lease may be of goods that are fixtures or may continue in goods that become fixtures, but no lease exists under this Article of ordinary building materials incorporated into an improvement on land.

(3) This Article does not prevent creation of a lease of fixtures pursuant to real estate law.

(4) The perfected interest of a lessor of fixtures has priority over a conflicting interest of an encumbrancer or owner of the real estate if:

(a) the lease is a purchase money lease, the conflicting interest of the encumbrancer or owner arises before the goods become fixtures, the interest of the lessor is perfected by a fixture filing before the goods become fixtures or within ten days thereafter, and the lessee has an interest of record in the real estate or is in possession of the real estate; or

(b) the interest of the lessor is perfected by a fixture filing before the interest of the encumbrancer or owner is of record, the lessor's interest has priority over any conflicting interest of a predecessor in title of the encumbrancer or owner, and the lessee has an interest of record in the real estate or is in possession of the real estate.

(5) The interest of a lessor of fixtures, whether or not perfected, has priority over the conflicting interest of an encumbrancer or owner of the real estate if:

(a) the fixtures are readily removable factory or office machines, readily removable equipment that is not primarily used or leased for use in the operation of the real estate, or readily removable replacements of domestic appliances that are goods subject to a consumer lease, and before the goods become fixtures the lease contract is enforceable; or

(b) the conflicting interest is a lien on the real estate obtained by legal or equitable proceedings after the lease contract is enforceable; or

(c) the encumbrancer or owner has consented in writing to the lease or has disclaimed an interest in the goods as fixtures; or

(d) the lessee has a right to remove the goods as against the encumbrancer or owner. If the lessee's right to remove terminates, the priority of the interest of the lessor continues for a reasonable time.

(6) Notwithstanding paragraph (4)(a) but otherwise subject to subsections (4) and (5), the interest of a lessor of fixtures, including the lessor's residual interest, is subordinate to the conflicting interest of an encumbrancer of the real estate under a construction mortgage recorded before the goods become fixtures if the goods become fixtures before the completion of the construction. To the extent given to refinance a construction mortgage, the conflicting interest of an encumbrancer of the real estate under a mortgage has this priority to the same extent as the encumbrancer of the real estate under the construction mortgage.

**(7)** In cases not within the preceding subsections, priority between the interest of a lessor of fixtures, including the lessor's residual interest, and the conflicting interest of an encumbrancer or owner of the real estate who is not the lessee is determined by the priority rules governing conflicting interests in real estate.

**(8)** If the interest of a lessor of fixtures, including the lessor's residual interest, has priority over all conflicting interests of all owners and encumbrancers of the real estate, the lessor or the lessee may (i) on default, expiration, termination, or cancellation of the lease agreement but subject to the agreement and this Article, or (ii) if necessary to enforce other rights and remedies of the lessor or lessee under this Article, remove the goods from the real estate, free and clear of all conflicting interests of all owners and encumbrancers of the real estate, but the lessor or lessee must reimburse any encumbrancer or owner of the real estate who is not the lessee and who has not otherwise agreed for the cost of repair of any physical injury, but not for any diminution in value of the real estate caused by the absence of the goods removed or by any necessity of replacing them. A person entitled to reimbursement may refuse permission to remove until the party seeking removal gives adequate security for the performance of this obligation.

**(9)** Even though the lease agreement does not create a security interest, the interest of a lessor of fixtures, including the lessor's residual interest, is perfected by filing a financing statement as a fixture filing for leased goods that are or are to become fixtures in accordance with the relevant provisions of the Article on Secured Transactions (Article 9).

As amended in 1990 and 1999.

### § 2A–310. Lessor's and Lessee's Rights When Goods Become Accessions.

**(1)** Goods are "accessions" when they are installed in or affixed to other goods.

**(2)** The interest of a lessor or a lessee under a lease contract entered into before the goods became accessions is superior to all interests in the whole except as stated in subsection (4).

**(3)** The interest of a lessor or a lessee under a lease contract entered into at the time or after the goods became accessions is superior to all subsequently acquired interests in the whole except as stated in subsection (4) but is subordinate to interests in the whole existing at the time the lease contract was made unless the holders of such interests in the whole have in writing consented to the lease or disclaimed an interest in the goods as part of the whole.

**(4)** The interest of a lessor or a lessee under a lease contract described in subsection (2) or (3) is subordinate to the interest of

   **(a)** a buyer in the ordinary course of business or a lessee in the ordinary course of business of any interest in the whole acquired after the goods became accessions; or

   **(b)** a creditor with a security interest in the whole perfected before the lease contract was made to the extent that the creditor makes subsequent advances without knowledge of the lease contract.

**(5)** When under subsections (2) or (3) and (4) a lessor or a lessee of accessions holds an interest that is superior to all interests in the whole, the lessor or the lessee may (a) on default,

expiration, termination, or cancellation of the lease contract by the other party but subject to the provisions of the lease contract and this Article, or (b) if necessary to enforce his [or her] other rights and remedies under this Article, remove the goods from the whole, free and clear of all interests in the whole, but he [or she] must reimburse any holder of an interest in the whole who is not the lessee and who has not otherwise agreed for the cost of repair of any physical injury but not for any diminution in value of the whole caused by the absence of the goods removed or by any necessity for replacing them. A person entitled to reimbursement may refuse permission to remove until the party seeking removal gives adequate security for the performance of this obligation.

### § 2A–311. Priority Subject to Subordination.

Nothing in this Article prevents subordination by agreement by any person entitled to priority.

As added in 1990.

### Part 4—Performance of Lease Contract: Repudiated, Substituted and Excused

### § 2A–401. Insecurity: Adequate Assurance of Performance.

**(1)** A lease contract imposes an obligation on each party that the other's expectation of receiving due performance will not be impaired.

**(2)** If reasonable grounds for insecurity arise with respect to the performance of either party, the insecure party may demand in writing adequate assurance of due performance. Until the insecure party receives that assurance, if commercially reasonable the insecure party may suspend any performance for which he [or she] has not already received the agreed return.

**(3)** A repudiation of the lease contract occurs if assurance of due performance adequate under the circumstances of the particular case is not provided to the insecure party within a reasonable time, not to exceed 30 days after receipt of a demand by the other party.

**(4)** Between merchants, the reasonableness of grounds for insecurity and the adequacy of any assurance offered must be determined according to commercial standards.

**(5)** Acceptance of any nonconforming delivery or payment does not prejudice the aggrieved party's right to demand adequate assurance of future performance.

### § 2A–402. Anticipatory Repudiation.

If either party repudiates a lease contract with respect to a performance not yet due under the lease contract, the loss of which performance will substantially impair the value of the lease contract to the other, the aggrieved party may:

**(a)** for a commercially reasonable time, await retraction of repudiation and performance by the repudiating party;

**(b)** make demand pursuant to Section 2A–401 and await assurance of future performance adequate under the circumstances of the particular case; or

**(c)** resort to any right or remedy upon default under the lease contract or this Article, even though the aggrieved party has notified the repudiating party that the aggrieved party would await the repudiating party's performance and assurance and has urged retraction. In addition, whether or not the aggrieved party is pursuing one of the foregoing remedies, the aggrieved party may suspend performance or, if the aggrieved party is the lessor, proceed in accordance with the provisions of this Article on the lessor's right to identify goods to the lease contract notwithstanding default or to salvage unfinished goods (Section 2A–524).

### § 2A–403. Retraction of Anticipatory Repudiation.

**(1)** Until the repudiating party's next performance is due, the repudiating party can retract the repudiation unless, since the repudiation, the aggrieved party has cancelled the lease contract or materially changed the aggrieved party's position or otherwise indicated that the aggrieved party considers the repudiation final.

**(2)** Retraction may be by any method that clearly indicates to the aggrieved party that the repudiating party intends to perform under the lease contract and includes any assurance demanded under Section 2A–401.

**(3)** Retraction reinstates a repudiating party's rights under a lease contract with due excuse and allowance to the aggrieved party for any delay occasioned by the repudiation.

### § 2A–404. Substituted Performance.

**(1)** If without fault of the lessee, the lessor and the supplier, the agreed berthing, loading, or unloading facilities fail or the agreed type of carrier becomes unavailable or the agreed manner of delivery otherwise becomes commercially impracticable, but a commercially reasonable substitute is available, the substitute performance must be tendered and accepted.

**(2)** If the agreed means or manner of payment fails because of domestic or foreign governmental regulation:

(a) the lessor may withhold or stop delivery or cause the supplier to withhold or stop delivery unless the lessee provides a means or manner of payment that is commercially a substantial equivalent; and

(b) if delivery has already been taken, payment by the means or in the manner provided by the regulation discharges the lessee's obligation unless the regulation is discriminatory, oppressive, or predatory.

### § 2A–405. Excused Performance.

Subject to Section 2A–404 on substituted performance, the following rules apply:

(a) Delay in delivery or nondelivery in whole or in part by a lessor or a supplier who complies with paragraphs (b) and (c) is not a default under the lease contract if performance as agreed has been made impracticable by the occurrence of a contingency the nonoccurrence of which was a basic assumption on which the lease contract was made or by compliance in good faith with any applicable foreign or domestic governmental regulation or order, whether or not the regulation or order later proves to be invalid.

(b) If the causes mentioned in paragraph (a) affect only part of the lessor's or the supplier's capacity to perform, he [or she] shall allocate production and deliveries among his [or her] customers but at his [or her] option may include regular customers not then under contract for sale or lease as well as his [or her] own requirements for further manufacture. He [or she] may so allocate in any manner that is fair and reasonable.

(c) The lessor seasonally shall notify the lessee and in the case of a finance lease the supplier seasonally shall notify the lessor and the lessee, if known, that there will be delay or nondelivery and, if allocation is required under paragraph (b), of the estimated quota thus made available for the lessee.

### § 2A–406. Procedure on Excused Performance.

**(1)** If the lessee receives notification of a material or indefinite delay or an allocation justified under Section 2A–405, the lessee may by written notification to the lessor as to any goods involved, and with respect to all of the goods if under an installment lease contract the value of the whole lease contract is substantially impaired (Section 2A–510):

(a) terminate the lease contract (Section 2A–505(2)); or

(b) except in a finance lease that is not a consumer lease, modify the lease contract by accepting the available quota in substitution, with due allowance from the rent payable for the balance of the lease term for the deficiency but without further right against the lessor.

**(2)** If, after receipt of a notification from the lessor under Section 2A–405, the lessee fails so to modify the lease agreement within a reasonable time not exceeding 30 days, the lease contract lapses with respect to any deliveries affected.

### § 2A–407. Irrevocable Promises: Finance Leases.

**(1)** In the case of a finance lease that is not a consumer lease the lessee's promises under the lease contract become irrevocable and independent upon the lessee's acceptance of the goods.

**(2)** A promise that has become irrevocable and independent under subsection (1):

(a) is effective and enforceable between the parties, and by or against third parties including assignees of the parties, and

(b) is not subject to cancellation, termination, modification, repudiation, excuse, or substitution without the consent of the party to whom the promise runs.

**(3)** This section does not affect the validity under any other law of a covenant in any lease contract making the lessee's promises irrevocable and independent upon the lessee's acceptance of the goods.

As amended in 1990.

### Part 5—Default

### A. In General

### § 2A–501. Default: Procedure.

**(1)** Whether the lessor or the lessee is in default under a lease contract is determined by the lease agreement and this Article.

**(2)** If the lessor or the lessee is in default under the lease contract, the party seeking enforcement has rights and remedies as provided in this Article and, except as limited by this Article, as provided in the lease agreement.

**(3)** If the lessor or the lessee is in default under the lease contract, the party seeking enforcement may reduce the party's claim to judgment, or otherwise enforce the lease contract by self-help or any available judicial procedure or nonjudicial procedure, including administrative proceeding, arbitration, or the like, in accordance with this Article.

**(4)** Except as otherwise provided in Section 1–106(1) or this Article or the lease agreement, the rights and remedies referred to in subsections (2) and (3) are cumulative.

**(5)** If the lease agreement covers both real property and goods, the party seeking enforcement may proceed under this Part as to the goods, or under other applicable law as to both the real property and the goods in accordance with that party's rights and remedies in respect of the real property, in which case this Part does not apply.

As amended in 1990.

### § 2A–502. Notice After Default.

Except as otherwise provided in this Article or the lease agreement, the lessor or lessee in default under the lease contract is not entitled to notice of default or notice of enforcement from the other party to the lease agreement.

### § 2A–503. Modification or Impairment of Rights and Remedies.

**(1)** Except as otherwise provided in this Article, the lease agreement may include rights and remedies for default in addition to or in substitution for those provided in this Article and may limit or alter the measure of damages recoverable under this Article.

**(2)** Resort to a remedy provided under this Article or in the lease agreement is optional unless the remedy is expressly agreed to be exclusive. If circumstances cause an exclusive or limited remedy to fail of its essential purpose, or provision for an exclusive remedy is unconscionable, remedy may be had as provided in this Article.

**(3)** Consequential damages may be liquidated under Section 2A–504, or may otherwise be limited, altered, or excluded unless the limitation, alteration, or exclusion is unconscionable. Limitation, alteration, or exclusion of consequential damages for injury to the person in the case of consumer goods is *prima facie* unconscionable but limitation, alteration, or exclusion of damages where the loss is commercial is not *prima facie* unconscionable.

**(4)** Rights and remedies on default by the lessor or the lessee with respect to any obligation or promise collateral or ancillary to the lease contract are not impaired by this Article.

As amended in 1990.

### § 2A–504. Liquidation of Damages.

**(1)** Damages payable by either party for default, or any other act or omission, including indemnity for loss or diminution of anticipated tax benefits or loss or damage to lessor's residual interest, may be liquidated in the lease agreement but only at an amount or by a formula that is reasonable in light of the then anticipated harm caused by the default or other act or omission.

**(2)** If the lease agreement provides for liquidation of damages, and such provision does not comply with subsection (1), or such provision is an exclusive or limited remedy that circumstances cause to fail of its essential purpose, remedy may be had as provided in this Article.

**(3)** If the lessor justifiably withholds or stops delivery of goods because of the lessee's default or insolvency (Section 2A–525 or 2A–526), the lessee is entitled to restitution of any amount by which the sum of his [or her] payments exceeds:

    **(a)** the amount to which the lessor is entitled by virtue of terms liquidating the lessor's damages in accordance with subsection (1); or

    **(b)** in the absence of those terms, 20 percent of the then present value of the total rent the lessee was obligated to pay for the balance of the lease term, or, in the case of a consumer lease, the lesser of such amount or $500.

**(4)** A lessee's right to restitution under subsection (3) is subject to offset to the extent the lessor establishes:

    **(a)** a right to recover damages under the provisions of this Article other than subsection (1); and

    **(b)** the amount or value of any benefits received by the lessee directly or indirectly by reason of the lease contract.

### § 2A–505. Cancellation and Termination and Effect of Cancellation, Termination, Rescission, or Fraud on Rights and Remedies.

**(1)** On cancellation of the lease contract, all obligations that are still executory on both sides are discharged, but any right based on prior default or performance survives, and the cancelling party also retains any remedy for default of the whole lease contract or any unperformed balance.

**(2)** On termination of the lease contract, all obligations that are still executory on both sides are discharged but any right based on prior default or performance survives.

**(3)** Unless the contrary intention clearly appears, expressions of "cancellation," "rescission," or the like of the lease contract may not be construed as a renunciation or discharge of any claim in damages for an antecedent default.

**(4)** Rights and remedies for material misrepresentation or fraud include all rights and remedies available under this Article for default.

**(5)** Neither rescission nor a claim for rescission of the lease contract nor rejection or return of the goods may bar or be deemed inconsistent with a claim for damages or other right or remedy.

### § 2A–506. Statute of Limitations.

**(1)** An action for default under a lease contract, including breach of warranty or indemnity, must be commenced within 4 years after the cause of action accrued. By the original lease contract the parties may reduce the period of limitation to not less than one year.

**(2)** A cause of action for default accrues when the act or omission on which the default or breach of warranty is based is or should have been discovered by the aggrieved party, or when the default occurs, whichever is later. A cause of action for indemnity accrues when the act or omission on which the claim for indemnity is based is or should have been discovered by the indemnified party, whichever is later.

**(3)** If an action commenced within the time limited by subsection (1) is so terminated as to leave available a remedy by another action for the same default or breach of warranty or indemnity, the other action may be commenced after the expiration of the time limited and within 6 months after the termination of the first action unless the termination resulted from voluntary discontinuance or from dismissal for failure or neglect to prosecute.

**(4)** This section does not alter the law on tolling of the statute of limitations nor does it apply to causes of action that have accrued before this Article becomes effective.

### § 2A–507. Proof of Market Rent: Time and Place.

(1) Damages based on market rent (Section 2A–519 or 2A–528) are determined according to the rent for the use of the goods concerned for a lease term identical to the remaining lease term of the original lease agreement and prevailing at the times specified in Sections 2A–519 and 2A–528.

(2) If evidence of rent for the use of the goods concerned for a lease term identical to the remaining lease term of the original lease agreement and prevailing at the times or places described in this Article is not readily available, the rent prevailing within any reasonable time before or after the time described or at any other place or for a different lease term which in commercial judgment or under usage of trade would serve as a reasonable substitute for the one described may be used, making any proper allowance for the difference, including the cost of transporting the goods to or from the other place.

(3) Evidence of a relevant rent prevailing at a time or place or for a lease term other than the one described in this Article offered by one party is not admissible unless and until he [or she] has given the other party notice the court finds sufficient to prevent unfair surprise.

(4) If the prevailing rent or value of any goods regularly leased in any established market is in issue, reports in official publications or trade journals or in newspapers or periodicals of general circulation published as the reports of that market are admissible in evidence. The circumstances of the preparation of the report may be shown to affect its weight but not its admissibility.

As amended in 1990.

### B. Default by Lessor

### § 2A–508. Lessee's Remedies.

(1) If a lessor fails to deliver the goods in conformity to the lease contract (Section 2A–509) or repudiates the lease contract (Section 2A–402), or a lessee rightfully rejects the goods (Section 2A–509) or justifiably revokes acceptance of the goods (Section 2A–517), then with respect to any goods involved, and with respect to all of the goods if under an installment lease contract the value of the whole lease contract is substantially impaired (Section 2A–510), the lessor is in default under the lease contract and the lessee may:

  (a) cancel the lease contract (Section 2A–505(1));

  (b) recover so much of the rent and security as has been paid and is just under the circumstances;

  (c) cover and recover damages as to all goods affected whether or not they have been identified to the lease contract (Sections 2A–518 and 2A–520), or recover damages for nondelivery (Sections 2A–519 and 2A–520);

  (d) exercise any other rights or pursue any other remedies provided in the lease contract.

(2) If a lessor fails to deliver the goods in conformity to the lease contract or repudiates the lease contract, the lessee may also:

  (a) if the goods have been identified, recover them (Section 2A–522); or

  (b) in a proper case, obtain specific performance or replevy the goods (Section 2A–521).

(3) If a lessor is otherwise in default under a lease contract, the lessee may exercise the rights and pursue the remedies provided in the lease contract, which may include a right to cancel the lease, and in Section 2A–519(3).

(4) If a lessor has breached a warranty, whether express or implied, the lessee may recover damages (Section 2A–519(4)).

(5) On rightful rejection or justifiable revocation of acceptance, a lessee has a security interest in goods in the lessee's possession or control for any rent and security that has been paid and any expenses reasonably incurred in their inspection, receipt, transportation, and care and custody and may hold those goods and dispose of them in good faith and in a commercially reasonable manner, subject to Section 2A–527(5).

(6) Subject to the provisions of Section 2A–407, a lessee, on notifying the lessor of the lessee's intention to do so, may deduct all or any part of the damages resulting from any default under the lease contract from any part of the rent still due under the same lease contract.

As amended in 1990.

### § 2A–509. Lessee's Rights on Improper Delivery; Rightful Rejection.

(1) Subject to the provisions of Section 2A–510 on default in installment lease contracts, if the goods or the tender or delivery fail in any respect to conform to the lease contract, the lessee may reject or accept the goods or accept any commercial unit or units and reject the rest of the goods.

(2) Rejection of goods is ineffective unless it is within a reasonable time after tender or delivery of the goods and the lessee seasonably notifies the lessor.

### § 2A–510. Installment Lease Contracts: Rejection and Default.

(1) Under an installment lease contract a lessee may reject any delivery that is nonconforming if the nonconformity substantially impairs the value of that delivery and cannot be cured or the nonconformity is a defect in the required documents; but if the nonconformity does not fall within subsection (2) and the lessor or the supplier gives adequate assurance of its cure, the lessee must accept that delivery.

(2) Whenever nonconformity or default with respect to one or more deliveries substantially impairs the value of the installment lease contract as a whole there is a default with respect to the whole. But, the aggrieved party reinstates the installment lease contract as a whole if the aggrieved party accepts a nonconforming delivery without seasonably notifying of cancellation or brings an action with respect only to past deliveries or demands performance as to future deliveries.

### § 2A–511. Merchant Lessee's Duties as to Rightfully Rejected Goods.

(1) Subject to any security interest of a lessee (Section 2A–508(5)), if a lessor or a supplier has no agent or place of business at the market of rejection, a merchant lessee, after rejection of goods in his [or her] possession or control, shall follow any reasonable instructions received from the lessor or the supplier with respect to the goods. In the absence of those instructions, a merchant lessee shall make reasonable efforts to sell, lease, or otherwise dispose of the goods for the lessor's account if they threaten to decline in value speedily. Instructions are not reasonable if on demand indemnity for expenses is not forthcoming.

**(2)** If a merchant lessee (subsection (1)) or any other lessee (Section 2A–512) disposes of goods, he [or she] is entitled to reimbursement either from the lessor or the supplier or out of the proceeds for reasonable expenses of caring for and disposing of the goods and, if the expenses include no disposition commission, to such commission as is usual in the trade, or if there is none, to a reasonable sum not exceeding 10 percent of the gross proceeds.

**(3)** In complying with this section or Section 2A–512, the lessee is held only to good faith. Good faith conduct hereunder is neither acceptance or conversion nor the basis of an action for damages.

**(4)** A purchaser who purchases in good faith from a lessee pursuant to this section or Section 2A–512 takes the goods free of any rights of the lessor and the supplier even though the lessee fails to comply with one or more of the requirements of this Article.

### § 2A–512. Lessee's Duties as to Rightfully Rejected Goods.

**(1)** Except as otherwise provided with respect to goods that threaten to decline in value speedily (Section 2A–511) and subject to any security interest of a lessee (Section 2A–508(5)):

    **(a)** the lessee, after rejection of goods in the lessee's possession, shall hold them with reasonable care at the lessor's or the supplier's disposition for a reasonable time after the lessee's seasonable notification of rejection;

    **(b)** if the lessor or the supplier gives no instructions within a reasonable time after notification of rejection, the lessee may store the rejected goods for the lessor's or the supplier's account or ship them to the lessor or the supplier or dispose of them for the lessor's or the supplier's account with reimbursement in the manner provided in Section 2A–511; but

    **(c)** the lessee has no further obligations with regard to goods rightfully rejected.

**(2)** Action by the lessee pursuant to subsection (1) is not acceptance or conversion.

### § 2A–513. Cure by Lessor of Improper Tender or Delivery; Replacement.

**(1)** If any tender or delivery by the lessor or the supplier is rejected because nonconforming and the time for performance has not yet expired, the lessor or the supplier may seasonably notify the lessee of the lessor's or the supplier's intention to cure and may then make a conforming delivery within the time provided in the lease contract.

**(2)** If the lessee rejects a nonconforming tender that the lessor or the supplier had reasonable grounds to believe would be acceptable with or without money allowance, the lessor or the supplier may have a further reasonable time to substitute a conforming tender if he [or she] seasonably notifies the lessee.

### § 2A–514. Waiver of Lessee's Objections.

**(1)** In rejecting goods, a lessee's failure to state a particular defect that is ascertainable by reasonable inspection precludes the lessee from relying on the defect to justify rejection or to establish default:

    **(a)** if, stated seasonably, the lessor or the supplier could have cured it (Section 2A–513); or

    **(b)** between merchants if the lessor or the supplier after rejection has made a request in writing for a full and final written statement of all defects on which the lessee proposes to rely.

**(2)** A lessee's failure to reserve rights when paying rent or other consideration against documents precludes recovery of the payment for defects apparent on the face of the documents.

### § 2A–515. Acceptance of Goods.

**(1)** Acceptance of goods occurs after the lessee has had a reasonable opportunity to inspect the goods and

    **(a)** the lessee signifies or acts with respect to the goods in a manner that signifies to the lessor or the supplier that the goods are conforming or that the lessee will take or retain them in spite of their nonconformity; or

    **(b)** the lessee fails to make an effective rejection of the goods (Section 2A–509(2)).

**(2)** Acceptance of a part of any commercial unit is acceptance of that entire unit.

### § 2A–516. Effect of Acceptance of Goods; Notice of Default; Burden of Establishing Default after Acceptance; Notice of Claim or Litigation to Person Answerable Over.

**(1)** A lessee must pay rent for any goods accepted in accordance with the lease contract, with due allowance for goods rightfully rejected or not delivered.

**(2)** A lessee's acceptance of goods precludes rejection of the goods accepted. In the case of a finance lease, if made with knowledge of a nonconformity, acceptance cannot be revoked because of it. In any other case, if made with knowledge of a nonconformity, acceptance cannot be revoked because of it unless the acceptance was on the reasonable assumption that the nonconformity would be seasonably cured. Acceptance does not of itself impair any other remedy provided by this Article or the lease agreement for nonconformity.

**(3)** If a tender has been accepted:

    **(a)** within a reasonable time after the lessee discovers or should have discovered any default, the lessee shall notify the lessor and the supplier, if any, or be barred from any remedy against the party notified;

    **(b)** except in the case of a consumer lease, within a reasonable time after the lessee receives notice of litigation for infringement or the like (Section 2A–211) the lessee shall notify the lessor or be barred from any remedy over for liability established by the litigation; and

    **(c)** the burden is on the lessee to establish any default.

**(4)** If a lessee is sued for breach of a warranty or other obligation for which a lessor or a supplier is answerable over the following apply:

    **(a)** The lessee may give the lessor or the supplier, or both, written notice of the litigation. If the notice states that the person notified may come in and defend and that if the person notified does not do so that person will be bound in any action against that person by the lessee by any determination of fact common to the two litigations, then unless the person notified after seasonable receipt of the notice does come in and defend that person is so bound.

**(b)** The lessor or the supplier may demand in writing that the lessee turn over control of the litigation including settlement if the claim is one for infringement or the like (Section 2A–211) or else be barred from any remedy over. If the demand states that the lessor or the supplier agrees to bear all expense and to satisfy any adverse judgment, then unless the lessee after seasonable receipt of the demand does turn over control the lessee is so barred.

**(5)** Subsections (3) and (4) apply to any obligation of a lessee to hold the lessor or the supplier harmless against infringement or the like (Section 2A–211).

As amended in 1990.

### § 2A–517. Revocation of Acceptance of Goods.

**(1)** A lessee may revoke acceptance of a lot or commercial unit whose nonconformity substantially impairs its value to the lessee if the lessee has accepted it:

(a) except in the case of a finance lease, on the reasonable assumption that its nonconformity would be cured and it has not been seasonably cured; or

(b) without discovery of the nonconformity if the lessee's acceptance was reasonably induced either by the lessor's assurances or, except in the case of a finance lease, by the difficulty of discovery before acceptance.

**(2)** Except in the case of a finance lease that is not a consumer lease, a lessee may revoke acceptance of a lot or commercial unit if the lessor defaults under the lease contract and the default substantially impairs the value of that lot or commercial unit to the lessee.

**(3)** If the lease agreement so provides, the lessee may revoke acceptance of a lot or commercial unit because of other defaults by the lessor.

**(4)** Revocation of acceptance must occur within a reasonable time after the lessee discovers or should have discovered the ground for it and before any substantial change in condition of the goods which is not caused by the nonconformity. Revocation is not effective until the lessee notifies the lessor.

**(5)** A lessee who so revokes has the same rights and duties with regard to the goods involved as if the lessee had rejected them.

As amended in 1990.

### § 2A–518. Cover; Substitute Goods.

**(1)** After a default by a lessor under the lease contract of the type described in Section 2A–508(1), or, if agreed, after other default by the lessor, the lessee may cover by making any purchase or lease of or contract to purchase or lease goods in substitution for those due from the lessor.

**(2)** Except as otherwise provided with respect to damages liquidated in the lease agreement (Section 2A–504) or otherwise determined pursuant to agreement of the parties (Sections 1–102(3) and 2A–503), if a lessee's cover is by lease agreement substantially similar to the original lease agreement and the new lease agreement is made in good faith and in a commercially reasonable manner, the lessee may recover from the lessor as damages (i) the present value, as of the date of the commencement of the term of the new lease agreement, of the rent under the new lease agreement applicable to that period of the new lease term which is comparable to the then remaining term of the original lease agreement minus the present value as of the same date of the total rent for the then remaining lease term of the original lease agreement, and (ii) any incidental or consequential damages, less expenses saved in consequence of the lessor's default.

**(3)** If a lessee's cover is by lease agreement that for any reason does not qualify for treatment under subsection (2), or is by purchase or otherwise, the lessee may recover from the lessor as if the lessee had elected not to cover and Section 2A–519 governs.

As amended in 1990.

### § 2A–519. Lessee's Damages for Non-Delivery, Repudiation, Default, and Breach of Warranty in Regard to Accepted Goods.

**(1)** Except as otherwise provided with respect to damages liquidated in the lease agreement (Section 2A–504) or otherwise determined pursuant to agreement of the parties (Sections 1–102(3) and 2A–503), if a lessee elects not to cover or a lessee elects to cover and the cover is by lease agreement that for any reason does not qualify for treatment under Section 2A–518(2), or is by purchase or otherwise, the measure of damages for non-delivery or repudiation by the lessor or for rejection or revocation of acceptance by the lessee is the present value, as of the date of the default, of the then market rent minus the present value as of the same date of the original rent, computed for the remaining lease term of the original lease agreement, together with incidental and consequential damages, less expenses saved in consequence of the lessor's default.

**(2)** Market rent is to be determined as of the place for tender or, in cases of rejection after arrival or revocation of acceptance, as of the place of arrival.

**(3)** Except as otherwise agreed, if the lessee has accepted goods and given notification (Section 2A–516(3)), the measure of damages for non-conforming tender or delivery or other default by a lessor is the loss resulting in the ordinary course of events from the lessor's default as determined in any manner that is reasonable together with incidental and consequential damages, less expenses saved in consequence of the lessor's default.

**(4)** Except as otherwise agreed, the measure of damages for breach of warranty is the present value at the time and place of acceptance of the difference between the value of the use of the goods accepted and the value if they had been as warranted for the lease term, unless special circumstances show proximate damages of a different amount, together with incidental and consequential damages, less expenses saved in consequence of the lessor's default or breach of warranty.

As amended in 1990.

### § 2A–520. Lessee's Incidental and Consequential Damages.

**(1)** Incidental damages resulting from a lessor's default include expenses reasonably incurred in inspection, receipt, transportation, and care and custody of goods rightfully rejected or goods the acceptance of which is justifiably revoked, any commercially reasonable charges, expenses or commissions in connection with effecting cover, and any other reasonable expense incident to the default.

**(2)** Consequential damages resulting from a lessor's default include:

(a) any loss resulting from general or particular requirements and needs of which the lessor at the time of contracting had reason to know and which could not reasonably be prevented by cover or otherwise; and

(b) injury to person or property proximately resulting from any breach of warranty.

### § 2A–521. Lessee's Right to Specific Performance or Replevin.

(1) Specific performance may be decreed if the goods are unique or in other proper circumstances.

(2) A decree for specific performance may include any terms and conditions as to payment of the rent, damages, or other relief that the court deems just.

(3) A lessee has a right of replevin, detinue, sequestration, claim and delivery, or the like for goods identified to the lease contract if after reasonable effort the lessee is unable to effect cover for those goods or the circumstances reasonably indicate that the effort will be unavailing.

### § 2A–522. Lessee's Right to Goods on Lessor's Insolvency.

(1) Subject to subsection (2) and even though the goods have not been shipped, a lessee who has paid a part or all of the rent and security for goods identified to a lease contract (Section 2A–217) on making and keeping good a tender of any unpaid portion of the rent and security due under the lease contract may recover the goods identified from the lessor if the lessor becomes insolvent within 10 days after receipt of the first installment of rent and security.

(2) A lessee acquires the right to recover goods identified to a lease contract only if they conform to the lease contract.

### C. Default by Lessee

### § 2A–523. Lessor's Remedies.

(1) If a lessee wrongfully rejects or revokes acceptance of goods or fails to make a payment when due or repudiates with respect to a part or the whole, then, with respect to any goods involved, and with respect to all of the goods if under an installment lease contract the value of the whole lease contract is substantially impaired (Section 2A–510), the lessee is in default under the lease contract and the lessor may:

(a) cancel the lease contract (Section 2A–505(1));

(b) proceed respecting goods not identified to the lease contract (Section 2A–524);

(c) withhold delivery of the goods and take possession of goods previously delivered (Section 2A–525);

(d) stop delivery of the goods by any bailee (Section 2A–526);

(e) dispose of the goods and recover damages (Section 2A–527), or retain the goods and recover damages (Section 2A–528), or in a proper case recover rent (Section 2A–529)

(f) exercise any other rights or pursue any other remedies provided in the lease contract.

(2) If a lessor does not fully exercise a right or obtain a remedy to which the lessor is entitled under subsection (1), the lessor may recover the loss resulting in the ordinary course of events from the lessee's default as determined in any reasonable manner, together with incidental damages, less expenses saved in consequence of the lessee's default.

(3) If a lessee is otherwise in default under a lease contract, the lessor may exercise the rights and pursue the remedies provided in the lease contract, which may include a right to cancel the lease. In addition, unless otherwise provided in the lease contract:

(a) if the default substantially impairs the value of the lease contract to the lessor, the lessor may exercise the rights and pursue the remedies provided in subsections (1) or (2); or

(b) if the default does not substantially impair the value of the lease contract to the lessor, the lessor may recover as provided in subsection (2).

As amended in 1990.

### § 2A–524. Lessor's Right to Identify Goods to Lease Contract.

(1) After default by the lessee under the lease contract of the type described in Section 2A–523(1) or 2A–523(3)(a) or, if agreed, after other default by the lessee, the lessor may:

(a) identify to the lease contract conforming goods not already identified if at the time the lessor learned of the default they were in the lessor's or the supplier's possession or control; and

(b) dispose of goods (Section 2A–527(1)) that demonstrably have been intended for the particular lease contract even though those goods are unfinished.

(2) If the goods are unfinished, in the exercise of reasonable commercial judgment for the purposes of avoiding loss and of effective realization, an aggrieved lessor or the supplier may either complete manufacture and wholly identify the goods to the lease contract or cease manufacture and lease, sell, or otherwise dispose of the goods for scrap or salvage value or proceed in any other reasonable manner.

As amended in 1990.

### § 2A–525. Lessor's Right to Possession of Goods.

(1) If a lessor discovers the lessee to be insolvent, the lessor may refuse to deliver the goods.

(2) After a default by the lessee under the lease contract of the type described in Section 2A–523(1) or 2A–523(3)(a) or, if agreed, after other default by the lessee, the lessor has the right to take possession of the goods. If the lease contract so provides, the lessor may require the lessee to assemble the goods and make them available to the lessor at a place to be designated by the lessor which is reasonably convenient to both parties. Without removal, the lessor may render unusable any goods employed in trade or business, and may dispose of goods on the lessee's premises (Section 2A–527).

(3) The lessor may proceed under subsection (2) without judicial process if that can be done without breach of the peace or the lessor may proceed by action.

As amended in 1990.

### § 2A–526. Lessor's Stoppage of Delivery in Transit or Otherwise.

(1) A lessor may stop delivery of goods in the possession of a carrier or other bailee if the lessor discovers the lessee to be insolvent and may stop delivery of carload, truckload, planeload, or larger shipments of express or freight if the lessee repudiates or fails to make a payment due before delivery, whether for rent, security or otherwise under the lease contract, or for

any other reason the lessor has a right to withhold or take possession of the goods.

**(2)** In pursuing its remedies under subsection (1), the lessor may stop delivery until

    **(a)** receipt of the goods by the lessee;

    **(b)** acknowledgment to the lessee by any bailee of the goods, except a carrier, that the bailee holds the goods for the lessee; or

    **(c)** such an acknowledgment to the lessee by a carrier via reshipment or as warehouseman.

**(3) (a)** To stop delivery, a lessor shall so notify as to enable the bailee by reasonable diligence to prevent delivery of the goods.

    **(b)** After notification, the bailee shall hold and deliver the goods according to the directions of the lessor, but the lessor is liable to the bailee for any ensuing charges or damages.

    **(c)** A carrier who has issued a nonnegotiable bill of lading is not obliged to obey a notification to stop received from a person other than the consignor.

### § 2A–527. Lessor's Rights to Dispose of Goods.

**(1)** After a default by a lessee under the lease contract of the type described in Section 2A–523(1) or 2A–523(3)(a) or after the lessor refuses to deliver or takes possession of goods (Section 2A–525 or 2A–526), or, if agreed, after other default by a lessee, the lessor may dispose of the goods concerned or the undelivered balance thereof by lease, sale, or otherwise.

**(2)** Except as otherwise provided with respect to damages liquidated in the lease agreement (Section 2A–504) or otherwise determined pursuant to agreement of the parties (Sections 1–102(3) and 2A–503), if the disposition is by lease agreement substantially similar to the original lease agreement and the new lease agreement is made in good faith and in a commercially reasonable manner, the lessor may recover from the lessee as damages (i) accrued and unpaid rent as of the date of the commencement of the term of the new lease agreement, (ii) the present value, as of the same date, of the total rent for the then remaining lease term of the original lease agreement minus the present value, as of the same date, of the rent under the new lease agreement applicable to that period of the new lease term which is comparable to the then remaining term of the original lease agreement, and (iii) any incidental damages allowed under Section 2A–530, less expenses saved in consequence of the lessee's default.

**(3)** If the lessor's disposition is by lease agreement that for any reason does not qualify for treatment under subsection (2), or is by sale or otherwise, the lessor may recover from the lessee as if the lessor had elected not to dispose of the goods and Section 2A–528 governs.

**(4)** A subsequent buyer or lessee who buys or leases from the lessor in good faith for value as a result of a disposition under this section takes the goods free of the original lease contract and any rights of the original lessee even though the lessor fails to comply with one or more of the requirements of this Article.

**(5)** The lessor is not accountable to the lessee for any profit made on any disposition. A lessee who has rightfully rejected or justifiably revoked acceptance shall account to the lessor for any excess over the amount of the lessee's security interest (Section 2A–508(5)).

As amended in 1990.

### § 2A–528. Lessor's Damages for Non-acceptance, Failure to Pay, Repudiation, or Other Default.

**(1)** Except as otherwise provided with respect to damages liquidated in the lease agreement (Section 2A–504) or otherwise determined pursuant to agreement of the parties (Section 1–102(3) and 2A–503), if a lessor elects to retain the goods or a lessor elects to dispose of the goods and the disposition is by lease agreement that for any reason does not qualify for treatment under Section 2A–527(2), or is by sale or otherwise, the lessor may recover from the lessee as damages for a default of the type described in Section 2A–523(1) or 2A–523(3)(a), or if agreed, for other default of the lessee, (i) accrued and unpaid rent as of the date of the default if the lessee has never taken possession of the goods, or, if the lessee has taken possession of the goods, as of the date the lessor repossesses the goods or an earlier date on which the lessee makes a tender of the goods to the lessor, (ii) the present value as of the date determined under clause (i) of the total rent for the then remaining lease term of the original lease agreement minus the present value as of the same date of the market rent as the place where the goods are located computed for the same lease term, and (iii) any incidental damages allowed under Section 2A–530, less expenses saved in consequence of the lessee's default.

**(2)** If the measure of damages provided in subsection (1) is inadequate to put a lessor in as good a position as performance would have, the measure of damages is the present value of the profit, including reasonable overhead, the lessor would have made from full performance by the lessee, together with any incidental damages allowed under Section 2A–530, due allowance for costs reasonably incurred and due credit for payments or proceeds of disposition.

As amended in 1990.

### § 2A–529. Lessor's Action for the Rent.

**(1)** After default by the lessee under the lease contract of the type described in Section 2A–523(1) or 2A–523(3)(a) or, if agreed, after other default by the lessee, if the lessor complies with subsection (2), the lessor may recover from the lessee as damages:

    **(a)** for goods accepted by the lessee and not repossessed by or tendered to the lessor, and for conforming goods lost or damaged within a commercially reasonable time after risk of loss passes to the lessee (Section 2A–219), (i) accrued and unpaid rent as of the date of entry of judgment in favor of the lessor (ii) the present value as of the same date of the rent for the then remaining lease term of the lease agreement, and (iii) any incidental damages allowed under Section 2A–530, less expenses saved in consequence of the lessee's default; and

    **(b)** for goods identified to the lease contract if the lessor is unable after reasonable effort to dispose of them at a reasonable price or the circumstances reasonably indicate that effort will be unavailing, (i) accrued and unpaid rent as of the date of entry of judgment in favor of the lessor, (ii) the present value as of the same date of the rent for the then remaining lease term of the lease agreement, and (iii) any incidental damages allowed under Section 2A–530, less expenses saved in consequence of the lessee's default.

**(2)** Except as provided in subsection (3), the lessor shall hold for the lessee for the remaining lease term of the lease agreement any goods that have been identified to the lease contract and are in the lessor's control.

**(3)** The lessor may dispose of the goods at any time before collection of the judgment for damages obtained pursuant to subsection (1). If the disposition is before the end of the remaining lease term of the lease agreement, the lessor's recovery against the lessee for damages is governed by Section 2A–527 or Section 2A–528, and the lessor will cause an appropriate credit to be provided against a judgment for damages to the extent that the amount of the judgment exceeds the recovery available pursuant to Section 2A–527 or 2A–528.

**(4)** Payment of the judgment for damages obtained pursuant to subsection (1) entitles the lessee to the use and possession of the goods not then disposed of for the remaining lease term of and in accordance with the lease agreement.

**(5)** After default by the lessee under the lease contract of the type described in Section 2A–523(1) or Section 2A–523(3)(a) or, if agreed, after other default by the lessee, a lessor who is held not entitled to rent under this section must nevertheless be awarded damages for non-acceptance under Sections 2A–527 and 2A–528.

As amended in 1990.

### § 2A–530. Lessor's Incidental Damages.

Incidental damages to an aggrieved lessor include any commercially reasonable charges, expenses, or commissions incurred in stopping delivery, in the transportation, care and custody of goods after the lessee's default, in connection with return or disposition of the goods, or otherwise resulting from the default.

### § 2A–531. Standing to Sue Third Parties for Injury to Goods.

**(1)** If a third party so deals with goods that have been identified to a lease contract as to cause actionable injury to a party to the lease contract (a) the lessor has a right of action against the third party, and (b) the lessee also has a right of action against the third party if the lessee:

(i) has a security interest in the goods;

(ii) has an insurable interest in the goods; or

(iii) bears the risk of loss under the lease contract or has since the injury assumed that risk as against the lessor and the goods have been converted or destroyed.

**(2)** If at the time of the injury the party plaintiff did not bear the risk of loss as against the other party to the lease contract and there is no arrangement between them for disposition of the recovery, his [or her] suit or settlement, subject to his [or her] own interest, is as a fiduciary for the other party to the lease contract.

**(3)** Either party with the consent of the other may sue for the benefit of whom it may concern.

### § 2A–532. Lessor's Rights to Residual Interest.

In addition to any other recovery permitted by this Article or other law, the lessor may recover from the lessee an amount that will fully compensate the lessor for any loss of or damage to the lessor's residual interest in the goods caused by the default of the lessee.

As added in 1990.

## REVISED ARTICLE 3: NEGOTIABLE INSTRUMENTS

### Part 1—General Provisions and Definitions

### § 3–101. Short Title.

This Article may be cited as Uniform Commercial Code–Negotiable Instruments.

### § 3–102. Subject Matter.

**(a)** This Article applies to negotiable instruments. It does not apply to money, to payment orders governed by Article 4A, or to securities governed by Article 8.

**(b)** If there is conflict between this Article and Article 4 or 9, Articles 4 and 9 govern.

**(c)** Regulations of the Board of Governors of the Federal Reserve System and operating circulars of the Federal Reserve Banks supersede any inconsistent provision of this Article to the extent of the inconsistency.

### § 3–103. Definitions.

**(a)** In this Article:

(1) "Acceptor" means a drawee who has accepted a draft.

(2) "Drawee" means a person ordered in a draft to make payment.

(3) "Drawer" means a person who signs or is identified in a draft as a person ordering payment.

(4) "Good faith" means honesty in fact and the observance of reasonable commercial standards of fair dealing.

(5) "Maker" means a person who signs or is identified in a note as a person undertaking to pay.

(6) "Order" means a written instruction to pay money signed by the person giving the instruction. The instruction may be addressed to any person, including the person giving the instruction, or to one or more persons jointly or in the alternative but not in succession. An authorization to pay is not an order unless the person authorized to pay is also instructed to pay.

(7) "Ordinary care" in the case of a person engaged in business means observance of reasonable commercial standards, prevailing in the area in which the person is located, with respect to the business in which the person is engaged. In the case of a bank that takes an instrument for processing for collection or payment by automated means, reasonable commercial standards do not require the bank to examine the instrument if the failure to examine does not violate the bank's prescribed procedures and the bank's procedures do not vary unreasonably from general banking usage not disapproved by this Article or Article 4.

(8) "Party" means a party to an instrument.

(9) "Promise" means a written undertaking to pay money signed by the person undertaking to pay. An acknowledgment of an obligation by the obligor is not a promise unless the obligor also undertakes to pay the obligation.

(10) "Prove" with respect to a fact means to meet the burden of establishing the fact (Section 1–201(8)).

(11) "Remitter" means a person who purchases an instrument from its issuer if the instrument is payable to an identified person other than the purchaser.

**(b)** [Other definitions' section references deleted.]

**(c)** [Other definitions' section references deleted.]

**(d)** In addition, Article 1 contains general definitions and principles of construction and interpretation applicable throughout this Article.

### § 3–104. Negotiable Instrument.

**(a)** Except as provided in subsections (c) and (d), "negotiable instrument" means an unconditional promise or order to pay a fixed amount of money, with or without interest or other charges described in the promise or order, if it:

> **(1)** is payable to bearer or to order at the time it is issued or first comes into possession of a holder;
>
> **(2)** is payable on demand or at a definite time; and
>
> **(3)** does not state any other undertaking or instruction by the person promising or ordering payment to do any act in addition to the payment of money, but the promise or order may contain (i) an undertaking or power to give, maintain, or protect collateral to secure payment, (ii) an authorization or power to the holder to confess judgment or realize on or dispose of collateral, or (iii) a waiver of the benefit of any law intended for the advantage or protection of an obligor.

**(b)** "Instrument" means a negotiable instrument.

**(c)** An order that meets all of the requirements of subsection (a), except paragraph (1), and otherwise falls within the definition of "check" in subsection (f) is a negotiable instrument and a check.

**(d)** A promise or order other than a check is not an instrument if, at the time it is issued or first comes into possession of a holder, it contains a conspicuous statement, however expressed, to the effect that the promise or order is not negotiable or is not an instrument governed by this Article.

**(e)** An instrument is a "note" if it is a promise and is a "draft" if it is an order. If an instrument falls within the definition of both "note" and "draft," a person entitled to enforce the instrument may treat it as either.

**(f)** "Check" means (i) a draft, other than a documentary draft, payable on demand and drawn on a bank or (ii) a cashier's check or teller's check. An instrument may be a check even though it is described on its face by another term, such as "money order."

**(g)** "Cashier's check" means a draft with respect to which the drawer and drawee are the same bank or branches of the same bank.

**(h)** "Teller's check" means a draft drawn by a bank (i) on another bank, or (ii) payable at or through a bank.

**(i)** "Traveler's check" means an instrument that (i) is payable on demand, (ii) is drawn on or payable at or through a bank, (iii) is designated by the term "traveler's check" or by a substantially similar term, and (iv) requires, as a condition to payment, a countersignature by a person whose specimen signature appears on the instrument.

**(j)** "Certificate of deposit" means an instrument containing an acknowledgment by a bank that a sum of money has been received by the bank and a promise by the bank to repay the sum of money. A certificate of deposit is a note of the bank.

### § 3–105. Issue of Instrument.

**(a)** "Issue" means the first delivery of an instrument by the maker or drawer, whether to a holder or nonholder, for the purpose of giving rights on the instrument to any person.

**(b)** An unissued instrument, or an unissued incomplete instrument that is completed, is binding on the maker or drawer, but nonissuance is a defense. An instrument that is conditionally issued or is issued for a special purpose is binding on the maker or drawer, but failure of the condition or special purpose to be fulfilled is a defense.

**(c)** "Issuer" applies to issued and unissued instruments and means a maker or drawer of an instrument.

### § 3–106. Unconditional Promise or Order.

**(a)** Except as provided in this section, for the purposes of Section 3–104(a), a promise or order is unconditional unless it states (i) an express condition to payment, (ii) that the promise or order is subject to or governed by another writing, or (iii) that rights or obligations with respect to the promise or order are stated in another writing. A reference to another writing does not of itself make the promise or order conditional.

**(b)** A promise or order is not made conditional (i) by a reference to another writing for a statement of rights with respect to collateral, prepayment, or acceleration, or (ii) because payment is limited to resort to a particular fund or source.

**(c)** If a promise or order requires, as a condition to payment, a countersignature by a person whose specimen signature appears on the promise or order, the condition does not make the promise or order conditional for the purposes of Section 3–104(a). If the person whose specimen signature appears on an instrument fails to countersign the instrument, the failure to countersign is a defense to the obligation of the issuer, but the failure does not prevent a transferee of the instrument from becoming a holder of the instrument.

**(d)** If a promise or order at the time it is issued or first comes into possession of a holder contains a statement, required by applicable statutory or administrative law, to the effect that the rights of a holder or transferee are subject to claims or defenses that the issuer could assert against the original payee, the promise or order is not thereby made conditional for the purposes of Section 3–104(a); but if the promise or order is an instrument, there cannot be a holder in due course of the instrument.

### § 3–107. Instrument Payable in Foreign Money.

Unless the instrument otherwise provides, an instrument that states the amount payable in foreign money may be paid in the foreign money or in an equivalent amount in dollars calculated by using the current bank-offered spot rate at the place of payment for the purchase of dollars on the day on which the instrument is paid.

### § 3–108. Payable on Demand or at Definite Time.

**(a)** A promise or order is "payable on demand" if it (i) states that it is payable on demand or at sight, or otherwise indicates that it is payable at the will of the holder, or (ii) does not state any time of payment.

**(b)** A promise or order is "payable at a definite time" if it is payable on elapse of a definite period of time after sight or acceptance or at a fixed date or dates or at a time or times readily ascertainable at the time the promise or order is issued, subject to rights of (i) prepayment, (ii) acceleration, (iii) extension at the option of the holder, or (iv) extension to a further definite time at the option of the maker or acceptor or automatically upon or after a specified act or event.

(c) If an instrument, payable at a fixed date, is also payable upon demand made before the fixed date, the instrument is payable on demand until the fixed date and, if demand for payment is not made before that date, becomes payable at a definite time on the fixed date.

### § 3–109.  Payable to Bearer or to Order.

(a) A promise or order is payable to bearer if it:

(1) states that it is payable to bearer or to the order of bearer or otherwise indicates that the person in possession of the promise or order is entitled to payment;

(2) does not state a payee; or

(3) states that it is payable to or to the order of cash or otherwise indicates that it is not payable to an identified person.

(b) A promise or order that is not payable to bearer is payable to order if it is payable (i) to the order of an identified person or (ii) to an identified person or order. A promise or order that is payable to order is payable to the identified person.

(c) An instrument payable to bearer may become payable to an identified person if it is specially indorsed pursuant to Section 3–205(a). An instrument payable to an identified person may become payable to bearer if it is indorsed in blank pursuant to Section 3–205(b).

### § 3–110.  Identification of Person to Whom Instrument Is Payable.

(a) The person to whom an instrument is initially payable is determined by the intent of the person, whether or not authorized, signing as, or in the name or behalf of, the issuer of the instrument. The instrument is payable to the person intended by the signer even if that person is identified in the instrument by a name or other identification that is not that of the intended person. If more than one person signs in the name or behalf of the issuer of an instrument and all the signers do not intend the same person as payee, the instrument is payable to any person intended by one or more of the signers.

(b) If the signature of the issuer of an instrument is made by automated means, such as a check-writing machine, the payee of the instrument is determined by the intent of the person who supplied the name or identification of the payee, whether or not authorized to do so.

(c) A person to whom an instrument is payable may be identified in any way, including by name, identifying number, office, or account number. For the purpose of determining the holder of an instrument, the following rules apply:

(1) If an instrument is payable to an account and the account is identified only by number, the instrument is payable to the person to whom the account is payable. If an instrument is payable to an account identified by number and by the name of a person, the instrument is payable to the named person, whether or not that person is the owner of the account identified by number.

(2) If an instrument is payable to:

(i) a trust, an estate, or a person described as trustee or representative of a trust or estate, the instrument is payable to the trustee, the representative, or a successor of either, whether or not the beneficiary or estate is also named;

(ii) a person described as agent or similar representative of a named or identified person, the instrument is payable to the represented person, the representative, or a successor of the representative;

(iii) a fund or organization that is not a legal entity, the instrument is payable to a representative of the members of the fund or organization; or

(iv) an office or to a person described as holding an office, the instrument is payable to the named person, the incumbent of the office, or a successor to the incumbent.

(d) If an instrument is payable to two or more persons alternatively, it is payable to any of them and may be negotiated, discharged, or enforced by any or all of them in possession of the instrument. If an instrument is payable to two or more persons not alternatively, it is payable to all of them and may be negotiated, discharged, or enforced only by all of them. If an instrument payable to two or more persons is ambiguous as to whether it is payable to the persons alternatively, the instrument is payable to the persons alternatively.

### § 3–111.  Place of Payment.

Except as otherwise provided for items in Article 4, an instrument is payable at the place of payment stated in the instrument. If no place of payment is stated, an instrument is payable at the address of the drawee or maker stated in the instrument. If no address is stated, the place of payment is the place of business of the drawee or maker. If a drawee or maker has more than one place of business, the place of payment is any place of business of the drawee or maker chosen by the person entitled to enforce the instrument. If the drawee or maker has no place of business, the place of payment is the residence of the drawee or maker.

### § 3–112.  Interest.

(a) Unless otherwise provided in the instrument, (i) an instrument is not payable with interest, and (ii) interest on an interest-bearing instrument is payable from the date of the instrument.

(b) Interest may be stated in an instrument as a fixed or variable amount of money or it may be expressed as a fixed or variable rate or rates. The amount or rate of interest may be stated or described in the instrument in any manner and may require reference to information not contained in the instrument. If an instrument provides for interest, but the amount of interest payable cannot be ascertained from the description, interest is payable at the judgment rate in effect at the place of payment of the instrument and at the time interest first accrues.

### § 3–113.  Date of Instrument.

(a) An instrument may be antedated or postdated. The date stated determines the time of payment if the instrument is payable at a fixed period after date. Except as provided in Section 4–401(c), an instrument payable on demand is not payable before the date of the instrument.

(b) If an instrument is undated, its date is the date of its issue or, in the case of an unissued instrument, the date it first comes into possession of a holder.

### § 3–114. Contradictory Terms of Instrument.

If an instrument contains contradictory terms, typewritten terms prevail over printed terms, handwritten terms prevail over both, and words prevail over numbers.

### § 3–115. Incomplete Instrument.

(a) "Incomplete instrument" means a signed writing, whether or not issued by the signer, the contents of which show at the time of signing that it is incomplete but that the signer intended it to be completed by the addition of words or numbers.

(b) Subject to subsection (c), if an incomplete instrument is an instrument under Section 3–104, it may be enforced according to its terms if it is not completed, or according to its terms as augmented by completion. If an incomplete instrument is not an instrument under Section 3–104, but, after completion, the requirements of Section 3–104 are met, the instrument may be enforced according to its terms as augmented by completion.

(c) If words or numbers are added to an incomplete instrument without authority of the signer, there is an alteration of the incomplete instrument under Section 3–407.

(d) The burden of establishing that words or numbers were added to an incomplete instrument without authority of the signer is on the person asserting the lack of authority.

### § 3–116. Joint and Several Liability; Contribution.

(a) Except as otherwise provided in the instrument, two or more persons who have the same liability on an instrument as makers, drawers, acceptors, indorsers who indorse as joint payees, or anomalous indorsers are jointly and severally liable in the capacity in which they sign.

(b) Except as provided in Section 3–419(e) or by agreement of the affected parties, a party having joint and several liability who pays the instrument is entitled to receive from any party having the same joint and several liability contribution in accordance with applicable law.

(c) Discharge of one party having joint and several liability by a person entitled to enforce the instrument does not affect the right under subsection (b) of a party having the same joint and several liability to receive contribution from the party discharged.

### § 3–117. Other Agreements Affecting Instrument.

Subject to applicable law regarding exclusion of proof of contemporaneous or previous agreements, the obligation of a party to an instrument to pay the instrument may be modified, supplemented, or nullified by a separate agreement of the obligor and a person entitled to enforce the instrument, if the instrument is issued or the obligation is incurred in reliance on the agreement or as part of the same transaction giving rise to the agreement. To the extent an obligation is modified, supplemented, or nullified by an agreement under this section, the agreement is a defense to the obligation.

### § 3–118. Statute of Limitations.

(a) Except as provided in subsection (e), an action to enforce the obligation of a party to pay a note payable at a definite time must be commenced within six years after the due date or dates stated in the note or, if a due date is accelerated, within six years after the accelerated due date.

(b) Except as provided in subsection (d) or (e), if demand for payment is made to the maker of a note payable on demand, an action to enforce the obligation of a party to pay the note must be commenced within six years after the demand. If no demand for payment is made to the maker, an action to enforce the note is barred if neither principal nor interest on the note has been paid for a continuous period of 10 years.

(c) Except as provided in subsection (d), an action to enforce the obligation of a party to an unaccepted draft to pay the draft must be commenced within three years after dishonor of the draft or 10 years after the date of the draft, whichever period expires first.

(d) An action to enforce the obligation of the acceptor of a certified check or the issuer of a teller's check, cashier's check, or traveler's check must be commenced within three years after demand for payment is made to the acceptor or issuer, as the case may be.

(e) An action to enforce the obligation of a party to a certificate of deposit to pay the instrument must be commenced within six years after demand for payment is made to the maker, but if the instrument states a due date and the maker is not required to pay before that date, the six-year period begins when a demand for payment is in effect and the due date has passed.

(f) An action to enforce the obligation of a party to pay an accepted draft, other than a certified check, must be commenced (i) within six years after the due date or dates stated in the draft or acceptance if the obligation of the acceptor is payable at a definite time, or (ii) within six years after the date of the acceptance if the obligation of the acceptor is payable on demand.

(g) Unless governed by other law regarding claims for indemnity or contribution, an action (i) for conversion of an instrument, for money had and received, or like action based on conversion, (ii) for breach of warranty, or (iii) to enforce an obligation, duty, or right arising under this Article and not governed by this section must be commenced within three years after the [cause of action] accrues.

### § 3–119. Notice of Right to Defend Action.

In an action for breach of an obligation for which a third person is answerable over pursuant to this Article or Article 4, the defendant may give the third person written notice of the litigation, and the person notified may then give similar notice to any other person who is answerable over. If the notice states (i) that the person notified may come in and defend and (ii) that failure to do so will bind the person notified in an action later brought by the person giving the notice as to any determination of fact common to the two litigations, the person notified is so bound unless after seasonable receipt of the notice the person notified does come in and defend.

### Part 2—Negotiation, Transfer, and Indorsement

### § 3–201. Negotiation.

(a) "Negotiation" means a transfer of possession, whether voluntary or involuntary, of an instrument by a person other than the issuer to a person who thereby becomes its holder.

(b) Except for negotiation by a remitter, if an instrument is payable to an identified person, negotiation requires transfer of possession of the instrument and its indorsement by the holder. If an instrument is payable to bearer, it may be negotiated by transfer of possession alone.

### § 3–202. Negotiation Subject to Rescission.

(a) Negotiation is effective even if obtained (i) from an infant, a corporation exceeding its powers, or a person without capacity, (ii) by fraud, duress, or mistake, or (iii) in breach of duty or as part of an illegal transaction.

(b) To the extent permitted by other law, negotiation may be rescinded or may be subject to other remedies, but those remedies may not be asserted against a subsequent holder in due course or a person paying the instrument in good faith and without knowledge of facts that are a basis for rescission or other remedy.

### § 3–203. Transfer of Instrument; Rights Acquired by Transfer.

(a) An instrument is transferred when it is delivered by a person other than its issuer for the purpose of giving to the person receiving delivery the right to enforce the instrument.

(b) Transfer of an instrument, whether or not the transfer is a negotiation, vests in the transferee any right of the transferor to enforce the instrument, including any right as a holder in due course, but the transferee cannot acquire rights of a holder in due course by a transfer, directly or indirectly, from a holder in due course if the transferee engaged in fraud or illegality affecting the instrument.

(c) Unless otherwise agreed, if an instrument is transferred for value and the transferee does not become a holder because of lack of indorsement by the transferor, the transferee has a specifically enforceable right to the unqualified indorsement of the transferor, but negotiation of the instrument does not occur until the indorsement is made.

(d) If a transferor purports to transfer less than the entire instrument, negotiation of the instrument does not occur. The transferee obtains no rights under this Article and has only the rights of a partial assignee.

### § 3–204. Indorsement.

(a) "Indorsement" means a signature, other than that of a signer as maker, drawer, or acceptor, that alone or accompanied by other words is made on an instrument for the purpose of (i) negotiating the instrument, (ii) restricting payment of the instrument, or (iii) incurring indorser's liability on the instrument, but regardless of the intent of the signer, a signature and its accompanying words is an indorsement unless the accompanying words, terms of the instrument, place of the signature, or other circumstances unambiguously indicate that the signature was made for a purpose other than indorsement. For the purpose of determining whether a signature is made on an instrument, a paper affixed to the instrument is a part of the instrument.

(b) "Indorser" means a person who makes an indorsement.

(c) For the purpose of determining whether the transferee of an instrument is a holder, an indorsement that transfers a security interest in the instrument is effective as an unqualified indorsement of the instrument.

(d) If an instrument is payable to a holder under a name that is not the name of the holder, indorsement may be made by the holder in the name stated in the instrument or in the holder's name or both, but signature in both names may be required by a person paying or taking the instrument for value or collection.

### § 3–205. Special Indorsement; Blank Indorsement; Anomalous Indorsement.

(a) If an indorsement is made by the holder of an instrument, whether payable to an identified person or payable to bearer, and the indorsement identifies a person to whom it makes the instrument payable, it is a "special indorsement." When specially indorsed, an instrument becomes payable to the identified person and may be negotiated only by the indorsement of that person. The principles stated in Section 3–110 apply to special indorsements.

(b) If an indorsement is made by the holder of an instrument and it is not a special indorsement, it is a "blank indorsement." When indorsed in blank, an instrument becomes payable to bearer and may be negotiated by transfer of possession alone until specially indorsed.

(c) The holder may convert a blank indorsement that consists only of a signature into a special indorsement by writing, above the signature of the indorser, words identifying the person to whom the instrument is made payable.

(d) "Anomalous indorsement" means an indorsement made by a person who is not the holder of the instrument. An anomalous indorsement does not affect the manner in which the instrument may be negotiated.

### § 3–206. Restrictive Indorsement.

(a) An indorsement limiting payment to a particular person or otherwise prohibiting further transfer or negotiation of the instrument is not effective to prevent further transfer or negotiation of the instrument.

(b) An indorsement stating a condition to the right of the indorsee to receive payment does not affect the right of the indorsee to enforce the instrument. A person paying the instrument or taking it for value or collection may disregard the condition, and the rights and liabilities of that person are not affected by whether the condition has been fulfilled.

(c) If an instrument bears an indorsement (i) described in Section 4–201(b), or (ii) in blank or to a particular bank using the words "for deposit," "for collection," or other words indicating a purpose of having the instrument collected by a bank for the indorser or for a particular account, the following rules apply:

(1) A person, other than a bank, who purchases the instrument when so indorsed converts the instrument unless the amount paid for the instrument is received by the indorser or applied consistently with the indorsement.

(2) A depositary bank that purchases the instrument or takes it for collection when so indorsed converts the instrument unless the amount paid by the bank with respect to the instrument is received by the indorser or applied consistently with the indorsement.

(3) A payor bank that is also the depositary bank or that takes the instrument for immediate payment over the counter from a person other than a collecting bank converts the instrument unless the proceeds of the instrument are received by the indorser or applied consistently with the indorsement.

**(4)** Except as otherwise provided in paragraph (3), a payor bank or intermediary bank may disregard the indorsement and is not liable if the proceeds of the instrument are not received by the indorser or applied consistently with the indorsement.

**(d)** Except for an indorsement covered by subsection (c), if an instrument bears an indorsement using words to the effect that payment is to be made to the indorsee as agent, trustee, or other fiduciary for the benefit of the indorser or another person, the following rules apply:

**(1)** Unless there is notice of breach of fiduciary duty as provided in Section 3–307, a person who purchases the instrument from the indorsee or takes the instrument from the indorsee for collection or payment may pay the proceeds of payment or the value given for the instrument to the indorsee without regard to whether the indorsee violates a fiduciary duty to the indorser.

**(2)** A subsequent transferee of the instrument or person who pays the instrument is neither given notice nor otherwise affected by the restriction in the indorsement unless the transferee or payor knows that the fiduciary dealt with the instrument or its proceeds in breach of fiduciary duty.

**(e)** The presence on an instrument of an indorsement to which this section applies does not prevent a purchaser of the instrument from becoming a holder in due course of the instrument unless the purchaser is a converter under subsection (c) or has notice or knowledge of breach of fiduciary duty as stated in subsection (d).

**(f)** In an action to enforce the obligation of a party to pay the instrument, the obligor has a defense if payment would violate an indorsement to which this section applies and the payment is not permitted by this section.

### § 3–207. Reacquisition.

Reacquisition of an instrument occurs if it is transferred to a former holder, by negotiation or otherwise. A former holder who reacquires the instrument may cancel indorsements made after the reacquirer first became a holder of the instrument. If the cancellation causes the instrument to be payable to the reacquirer or to bearer, the reacquirer may negotiate the instrument. An indorser whose indorsement is canceled is discharged, and the discharge is effective against any subsequent holder.

### Part 3—Enforcement of Instruments

### § 3–301. Person Entitled to Enforce Instrument.

"Person entitled to enforce" an instrument means (i) the holder of the instrument, (ii) a nonholder in possession of the instrument who has the rights of a holder, or (iii) a person not in possession of the instrument who is entitled to enforce the instrument pursuant to Section 3–309 or 3–418(d). A person may be a person entitled to enforce the instrument even though the person is not the owner of the instrument or is in wrongful possession of the instrument.

### § 3–302. Holder in Due Course.

**(a)** Subject to subsection (c) and Section 3–106(d), "holder in due course" means the holder of an instrument if:

**(1)** the instrument when issued or negotiated to the holder does not bear such apparent evidence of forgery or alteration or is not otherwise so irregular or incomplete as to call into question its authenticity; and

**(2)** the holder took the instrument (i) for value, (ii) in good faith, (iii) without notice that the instrument is overdue or has been dishonored or that there is an uncured default with respect to payment of another instrument issued as part of the same series, (iv) without notice that the instrument contains an unauthorized signature or has been altered, (v) without notice of any claim to the instrument described in Section 3–306, and (vi) without notice that any party has a defense or claim in recoupment described in Section 3–305(a).

**(b)** Notice of discharge of a party, other than discharge in an insolvency proceeding, is not notice of a defense under subsection (a), but discharge is effective against a person who became a holder in due course with notice of the discharge. Public filing or recording of a document does not of itself constitute notice of a defense, claim in recoupment, or claim to the instrument.

**(c)** Except to the extent a transferor or predecessor in interest has rights as a holder in due course, a person does not acquire rights of a holder in due course of an instrument taken (i) by legal process or by purchase in an execution, bankruptcy, or creditor's sale or similar proceeding, (ii) by purchase as part of a bulk transaction not in ordinary course of business of the transferor, or (iii) as the successor in interest to an estate or other organization.

**(d)** If, under Section 3–303(a)(1), the promise of performance that is the consideration for an instrument has been partially performed, the holder may assert rights as a holder in due course of the instrument only to the fraction of the amount payable under the instrument equal to the value of the partial performance divided by the value of the promised performance.

**(e)** If (i) the person entitled to enforce an instrument has only a security interest in the instrument and (ii) the person obliged to pay the instrument has a defense, claim in recoupment, or claim to the instrument that may be asserted against the person who granted the security interest, the person entitled to enforce the instrument may assert rights as a holder in due course only to an amount payable under the instrument which, at the time of enforcement of the instrument, does not exceed the amount of the unpaid obligation secured.

**(f)** To be effective, notice must be received at a time and in a manner that gives a reasonable opportunity to act on it.

**(g)** This section is subject to any law limiting status as a holder in due course in particular classes of transactions.

### § 3–303. Value and Consideration.

**(a)** An instrument is issued or transferred for value if:

**(1)** the instrument is issued or transferred for a promise of performance, to the extent the promise has been performed;

**(2)** the transferee acquires a security interest or other lien in the instrument other than a lien obtained by judicial proceeding;

**(3)** the instrument is issued or transferred as payment of, or as security for, an antecedent claim against any person, whether or not the claim is due;

**(4)** the instrument is issued or transferred in exchange for a negotiable instrument; or

**(5)** the instrument is issued or transferred in exchange for the incurring of an irrevocable obligation to a third party by the person taking the instrument.

**(b)** "Consideration" means any consideration sufficient to support a simple contract. The drawer or maker of an instrument has a defense if the instrument is issued without consideration. If an instrument is issued for a promise of performance, the issuer has a defense to the extent performance of the promise is due and the promise has not been performed. If an instrument is issued for value as stated in subsection (a), the instrument is also issued for consideration.

### § 3–304. Overdue Instrument.

**(a)** An instrument payable on demand becomes overdue at the earliest of the following times:

**(1)** on the day after the day demand for payment is duly made;

**(2)** if the instrument is a check, 90 days after its date; or

**(3)** if the instrument is not a check, when the instrument has been outstanding for a period of time after its date which is unreasonably long under the circumstances of the particular case in light of the nature of the instrument and usage of the trade.

**(b)** With respect to an instrument payable at a definite time the following rules apply:

**(1)** If the principal is payable in installments and a due date has not been accelerated, the instrument becomes overdue upon default under the instrument for nonpayment of an installment, and the instrument remains overdue until the default is cured.

**(2)** If the principal is not payable in installments and the due date has not been accelerated, the instrument becomes overdue on the day after the due date.

**(3)** If a due date with respect to principal has been accelerated, the instrument becomes overdue on the day after the accelerated due date.

**(c)** Unless the due date of principal has been accelerated, an instrument does not become overdue if there is default in payment of interest but no default in payment of principal.

### § 3–305. Defenses and Claims in Recoupment.

**(a)** Except as stated in subsection (b), the right to enforce the obligation of a party to pay an instrument is subject to the following:

**(1)** a defense of the obligor based on (i) infancy of the obligor to the extent it is a defense to a simple contract, (ii) duress, lack of legal capacity, or illegality of the transaction which, under other law, nullifies the obligation of the obligor, (iii) fraud that induced the obligor to sign the instrument with neither knowledge nor reasonable opportunity to learn of its character or its essential terms, or (iv) discharge of the obligor in insolvency proceedings;

**(2)** a defense of the obligor stated in another section of this Article or a defense of the obligor that would be available if the person entitled to enforce the instrument were enforcing a right to payment under a simple contract; and

**(3)** a claim in recoupment of the obligor against the original payee of the instrument if the claim arose from the transaction that gave rise to the instrument; but the claim of the obligor may be asserted against a transferee of the instrument only to reduce the amount owing on the instrument at the time the action is brought.

**(b)** The right of a holder in due course to enforce the obligation of a party to pay the instrument is subject to defenses of the obligor stated in subsection (a)(1), but is not subject to defenses of the obligor stated in subsection (a)(2) or claims in recoupment stated in subsection (a)(3) against a person other than the holder.

**(c)** Except as stated in subsection (d), in an action to enforce the obligation of a party to pay the instrument, the obligor may not assert against the person entitled to enforce the instrument a defense, claim in recoupment, or claim to the instrument (Section 3–306) of another person, but the other person's claim to the instrument may be asserted by the obligor if the other person is joined in the action and personally asserts the claim against the person entitled to enforce the instrument. An obligor is not obliged to pay the instrument if the person seeking enforcement of the instrument does not have rights of a holder in due course and the obligor proves that the instrument is a lost or stolen instrument.

**(d)** In an action to enforce the obligation of an accommodation party to pay an instrument, the accommodation party may assert against the person entitled to enforce the instrument any defense or claim in recoupment under subsection (a) that the accommodated party could assert against the person entitled to enforce the instrument, except the defenses of discharge in insolvency proceedings, infancy, and lack of legal capacity.

### § 3–306. Claims to an Instrument.

A person taking an instrument, other than a person having rights of a holder in due course, is subject to a claim of a property or possessory right in the instrument or its proceeds, including a claim to rescind a negotiation and to recover the instrument or its proceeds. A person having rights of a holder in due course takes free of the claim to the instrument.

### § 3–307. Notice of Breach of Fiduciary Duty.

**(a)** In this section:

**(1)** "Fiduciary" means an agent, trustee, partner, corporate officer or director, or other representative owing a fiduciary duty with respect to an instrument.

**(2)** "Represented person" means the principal, beneficiary, partnership, corporation, or other person to whom the duty stated in paragraph (1) is owed.

**(b)** If (i) an instrument is taken from a fiduciary for payment or collection or for value, (ii) the taker has knowledge of the fiduciary status of the fiduciary, and (iii) the represented person makes a claim to the instrument or its proceeds on the basis that the transaction of the fiduciary is a breach of fiduciary duty, the following rules apply:

**(1)** Notice of breach of fiduciary duty by the fiduciary is notice of the claim of the represented person.

**(2)** In the case of an instrument payable to the represented person or the fiduciary as such, the taker has notice of the breach of fiduciary duty if the instrument is (i) taken in payment of or as security for a debt known by the taker to be the personal debt of the fiduciary, (ii) taken in a transaction known by the taker to be for the personal benefit of the fiduciary, or (iii) deposited to an account other than an account of the fiduciary, as such, or an account of the represented person.

**(3)** If an instrument is issued by the represented person or the fiduciary as such, and made payable to the fiduciary personally, the taker does not have notice of the breach of fiduciary duty unless the taker knows of the breach of fiduciary duty.

**(4)** If an instrument is issued by the represented person or the fiduciary as such, to the taker as payee, the taker has notice of the breach of fiduciary duty if the instrument is (i) taken in payment of or as security for a debt known by the taker to be the personal debt of the fiduciary, (ii) taken in a transaction known by the taker to be for the personal benefit of the fiduciary, or (iii) deposited to an account other than an account of the fiduciary, as such, or an account of the represented person.

## § 3–308. Proof of Signatures and Status as Holder in Due Course.

**(a)** In an action with respect to an instrument, the authenticity of, and authority to make, each signature on the instrument is admitted unless specifically denied in the pleadings. If the validity of a signature is denied in the pleadings, the burden of establishing validity is on the person claiming validity, but the signature is presumed to be authentic and authorized unless the action is to enforce the liability of the purported signer and the signer is dead or incompetent at the time of trial of the issue of validity of the signature. If an action to enforce the instrument is brought against a person as the undisclosed principal of a person who signed the instrument as a party to the instrument, the plaintiff has the burden of establishing that the defendant is liable on the instrument as a represented person under Section 3–402(a).

**(b)** If the validity of signatures is admitted or proved and there is compliance with subsection (a), a plaintiff producing the instrument is entitled to payment if the plaintiff proves entitlement to enforce the instrument under Section 3–301, unless the defendant proves a defense or claim in recoupment. If a defense or claim in recoupment is proved, the right to payment of the plaintiff is subject to the defense or claim, except to the extent the plaintiff proves that the plaintiff has rights of a holder in due course which are not subject to the defense or claim.

## § 3–309. Enforcement of Lost, Destroyed, or Stolen Instrument.

**(a)** A person not in possession of an instrument is entitled to enforce the instrument if (i) the person was in possession of the instrument and entitled to enforce it when loss of possession occurred, (ii) the loss of possession was not the result of a transfer by the person or a lawful seizure, and (iii) the person cannot reasonably obtain possession of the instrument because the instrument was destroyed, its whereabouts cannot be determined, or it is in the wrongful possession of an unknown person or a person that cannot be found or is not amenable to service of process.

**(b)** A person seeking enforcement of an instrument under subsection (a) must prove the terms of the instrument and the person's right to enforce the instrument. If that proof is made, Section 3–308 applies to the case as if the person seeking enforcement had produced the instrument. The court may not enter judgment in favor of the person seeking enforcement unless it finds that the person required to pay the instrument is adequately protected against loss that might occur by reason of a claim by another person to enforce the instrument. Adequate protection may be provided by any reasonable means.

## § 3–310. Effect of Instrument on Obligation for Which Taken.

**(a)** Unless otherwise agreed, if a certified check, cashier's check, or teller's check is taken for an obligation, the obligation is discharged to the same extent discharge would result if an amount of money equal to the amount of the instrument were taken in payment of the obligation. Discharge of the obligation does not affect any liability that the obligor may have as an indorser of the instrument.

**(b)** Unless otherwise agreed and except as provided in subsection (a), if a note or an uncertified check is taken for an obligation, the obligation is suspended to the same extent the obligation would be discharged if an amount of money equal to the amount of the instrument were taken, and the following rules apply:

**(1)** In the case of an uncertified check, suspension of the obligation continues until dishonor of the check or until it is paid or certified. Payment or certification of the check results in discharge of the obligation to the extent of the amount of the check.

**(2)** In the case of a note, suspension of the obligation continues until dishonor of the note or until it is paid. Payment of the note results in discharge of the obligation to the extent of the payment.

**(3)** Except as provided in paragraph (4), if the check or note is dishonored and the obligee of the obligation for which the instrument was taken is the person entitled to enforce the instrument, the obligee may enforce either the instrument or the obligation. In the case of an instrument of a third person which is negotiated to the obligee by the obligor, discharge of the obligor on the instrument also discharges the obligation.

**(4)** If the person entitled to enforce the instrument taken for an obligation is a person other than the obligee, the obligee may not enforce the obligation to the extent the obligation is suspended. If the obligee is the person entitled to enforce the instrument but no longer has possession of it because it was lost, stolen, or destroyed, the obligation may not be enforced to the extent of the amount payable on the instrument, and to that extent the obligee's rights against the obligor are limited to enforcement of the instrument.

**(c)** If an instrument other than one described in subsection (a) or (b) is taken for an obligation, the effect is (i) that stated in subsection (a) if the instrument is one on which a bank is liable as maker or acceptor, or (ii) that stated in subsection (b) in any other case.

## § 3–311. Accord and Satisfaction by Use of Instrument.

(a) If a person against whom a claim is asserted proves that (i) that person in good faith tendered an instrument to the claimant as full satisfaction of the claim, (ii) the amount of the claim was unliquidated or subject to a bona fide dispute, and (iii) the claimant obtained payment of the instrument, the following subsections apply.

(b) Unless subsection (c) applies, the claim is discharged if the person against whom the claim is asserted proves that the instrument or an accompanying written communication contained a conspicuous statement to the effect that the instrument was tendered as full satisfaction of the claim.

(c) Subject to subsection (d), a claim is not discharged under subsection (b) if either of the following applies:

(1) The claimant, if an organization, proves that (i) within a reasonable time before the tender, the claimant sent a conspicuous statement to the person against whom the claim is asserted that communications concerning disputed debts, including an instrument tendered as full satisfaction of a debt, are to be sent to a designated person, office, or place, and (ii) the instrument or accompanying communication was not received by that designated person, office, or place.

(2) The claimant, whether or not an organization, proves that within 90 days after payment of the instrument, the claimant tendered repayment of the amount of the instrument to the person against whom the claim is asserted. This paragraph does not apply if the claimant is an organization that sent a statement complying with paragraph (1)(i).

(d) A claim is discharged if the person against whom the claim is asserted proves that within a reasonable time before collection of the instrument was initiated, the claimant, or an agent of the claimant having direct responsibility with respect to the disputed obligation, knew that the instrument was tendered in full satisfaction of the claim.

## § 3–312. Lost, Destroyed, or Stolen Cashier's Check, Teller's Check, or Certified Check.*

(a) In this section:

(1) "Check" means a cashier's check, teller's check, or certified check.

(2) "Claimant" means a person who claims the right to receive the amount of a cashier's check, teller's check, or certified check that was lost, destroyed, or stolen.

(3) "Declaration of loss" means a written statement, made under penalty of perjury, to the effect that (i) the declarer lost possession of a check, (ii) the declarer is the drawer or payee of the check, in the case of a certified check, or the remitter or payee of the check, in the case of a cashier's check or teller's check, (iii) the loss of possession was not the result of a transfer by the declarer or a lawful seizure, and (iv) the declarer cannot reasonably obtain possession of the check because the check was destroyed, its whereabouts cannot be determined, or it is in the wrongful possession of an unknown person or a person that cannot be found or is not amenable to service of process.

(4) "Obligated bank" means the issuer of a cashier's check or teller's check or the acceptor of a certified check.

(b) A claimant may assert a claim to the amount of a check by a communication to the obligated bank describing the check with reasonable certainty and requesting payment of the amount of the check, if (i) the claimant is the drawer or payee of a certified check or the remitter or payee of a cashier's check or teller's check, (ii) the communication contains or is accompanied by a declaration of loss of the claimant with respect to the check, (iii) the communication is received at a time and in a manner affording the bank a reasonable time to act on it before the check is paid, and (iv) the claimant provides reasonable identification if requested by the obligated bank. Delivery of a declaration of loss is a warranty of the truth of the statements made in the declaration. If a claim is asserted in compliance with this subsection, the following rules apply:

(1) The claim becomes enforceable at the later of (i) the time the claim is asserted, or (ii) the 90th day following the date of the check, in the case of a cashier's check or teller's check, or the 90th day following the date of the acceptance, in the case of a certified check.

(2) Until the claim becomes enforceable, it has no legal effect and the obligated bank may pay the check or, in the case of a teller's check, may permit the drawee to pay the check. Payment to a person entitled to enforce the check discharges all liability of the obligated bank with respect to the check.

(3) If the claim becomes enforceable before the check is presented for payment, the obligated bank is not obliged to pay the check.

(4) When the claim becomes enforceable, the obligated bank becomes obliged to pay the amount of the check to the claimant if payment of the check has not been made to a person entitled to enforce the check. Subject to Section 4–302(a)(1), payment to the claimant discharges all liability of the obligated bank with respect to the check.

(c) If the obligated bank pays the amount of a check to a claimant under subsection (b)(4) and the check is presented for payment by a person having rights of a holder in due course, the claimant is obliged to (i) refund the payment to the obligated bank if the check is paid, or (ii) pay the amount of the check to the person having rights of a holder in due course if the check is dishonored.

(d) If a claimant has the right to assert a claim under subsection (b) and is also a person entitled to enforce a cashier's check, teller's check, or certified check which is lost, destroyed, or stolen, the claimant may assert rights with respect to the check either under this section or Section 3–309.
Added in 1991.

## Part 4—Liability of Parties

### § 3–401. Signature.

(a) A person is not liable on an instrument unless (i) the person signed the instrument, or (ii) the person is represented by an agent or representative who signed the instrument and the signature is binding on the represented person under Section 3–402.

---

*[Section 3–312 was not adopted as part of the 1990 Official Text of Revised Article 3. It was officially approved and recommended for enactment in all states in August 1991 by the National Conference of Commissioners on Uniform State Laws.]

**(b)** A signature may be made (i) manually or by means of a device or machine, and (ii) by the use of any name, including a trade or assumed name, or by a word, mark, or symbol executed or adopted by a person with present intention to authenticate a writing.

### § 3–402. Signature by Representative.

**(a)** If a person acting, or purporting to act, as a representative signs an instrument by signing either the name of the represented person or the name of the signer, the represented person is bound by the signature to the same extent the represented person would be bound if the signature were on a simple contract. If the represented person is bound, the signature of the representative is the "authorized signature of the represented person" and the represented person is liable on the instrument, whether or not identified in the instrument.

**(b)** If a representative signs the name of the representative to an instrument and the signature is an authorized signature of the represented person, the following rules apply:

**(1)** If the form of the signature shows unambiguously that the signature is made on behalf of the represented person who is identified in the instrument, the representative is not liable on the instrument.

**(2)** Subject to subsection (c), if (i) the form of the signature does not show unambiguously that the signature is made in a representative capacity or (ii) the represented person is not identified in the instrument, the representative is liable on the instrument to a holder in due course that took the instrument without notice that the representative was not intended to be liable on the instrument. With respect to any other person, the representative is liable on the instrument unless the representative proves that the original parties did not intend the representative to be liable on the instrument.

**(c)** If a representative signs the name of the representative as drawer of a check without indication of the representative status and the check is payable from an account of the represented person who is identified on the check, the signer is not liable on the check if the signature is an authorized signature of the represented person.

### § 3–403. Unauthorized Signature.

**(a)** Unless otherwise provided in this Article or Article 4, an unauthorized signature is ineffective except as the signature of the unauthorized signer in favor of a person who in good faith pays the instrument or takes it for value. An unauthorized signature may be ratified for all purposes of this Article.

**(b)** If the signature of more than one person is required to constitute the authorized signature of an organization, the signature of the organization is unauthorized if one of the required signatures is lacking.

**(c)** The civil or criminal liability of a person who makes an unauthorized signature is not affected by any provision of this Article which makes the unauthorized signature effective for the purposes of this Article.

### § 3–404. Impostors; Fictitious Payees.

**(a)** If an impostor, by use of the mails or otherwise, induces the issuer of an instrument to issue the instrument to the impostor, or to a person acting in concert with the impostor, by impersonating the payee of the instrument or a person authorized to act for the payee, an indorsement of the instrument by any person in the name of the payee is effective as the indorsement of the payee in favor of a person who, in good faith, pays the instrument or takes it for value or for collection.

**(b)** If (i) a person whose intent determines to whom an instrument is payable (Section 3–110(a) or (b)) does not intend the person identified as payee to have any interest in the instrument, or (ii) the person identified as payee of an instrument is a fictitious person, the following rules apply until the instrument is negotiated by special indorsement:

**(1)** Any person in possession of the instrument is its holder.

**(2)** An indorsement by any person in the name of the payee stated in the instrument is effective as the indorsement of the payee in favor of a person who, in good faith, pays the instrument or takes it for value or for collection.

**(c)** Under subsection (a) or (b), an indorsement is made in the name of a payee if (i) it is made in a name substantially similar to that of the payee or (ii) the instrument, whether or not indorsed, is deposited in a depository bank to an account in a name substantially similar to that of the payee.

**(d)** With respect to an instrument to which subsection (a) or (b) applies, if a person paying the instrument or taking it for value or for collection fails to exercise ordinary care in paying or taking the instrument and that failure substantially contributes to loss resulting from payment of the instrument, the person bearing the loss may recover from the person failing to exercise ordinary care to the extent the failure to exercise ordinary care contributed to the loss.

### § 3–405. Employer's Responsibility for Fraudulent Indorsement by Employee.

**(a)** In this section:

**(1)** "Employee" includes an independent contractor and employee of an independent contractor retained by the employer.

**(2)** "Fraudulent indorsement" means (i) in the case of an instrument payable to the employer, a forged indorsement purporting to be that of the employer, or (ii) in the case of an instrument with respect to which the employer is the issuer, a forged indorsement purporting to be that of the person identified as payee.

**(3)** "Responsibility" with respect to instruments means authority (i) to sign or indorse instruments on behalf of the employer, (ii) to process instruments received by the employer for bookkeeping purposes, for deposit to an account, or for other disposition, (iii) to prepare or process instruments for issue in the name of the employer, (iv) to supply information determining the names or addresses of payees of instruments to be issued in the name of the employer, (v) to control the disposition of instruments to be issued in the name of the employer, or (vi) to act otherwise with respect to instruments in a responsible capacity. "Responsibility" does not include authority that merely allows an employee to have access to instruments or blank or incomplete instrument forms that are being stored or transported or are part of incoming or outgoing mail, or similar access.

**(b)** For the purpose of determining the rights and liabilities of a person who, in good faith, pays an instrument or takes it for value or for collection, if an employer entrusted an employee with responsibility with respect to the instrument and the employee or a person acting in concert with the employee makes a fraudulent indorsement of the instrument, the indorsement is effective as the indorsement of the person to whom the instrument is payable if it is made in the name of that person. If the person paying the instrument or taking it for value or for collection fails to exercise ordinary care in paying or taking the instrument and that failure substantially contributes to loss resulting from the fraud, the person bearing the loss may recover from the person failing to exercise ordinary care to the extent the failure to exercise ordinary care contributed to the loss.

(c) Under subsection (b), an indorsement is made in the name of the person to whom an instrument is payable if (i) it is made in a name substantially similar to the name of that person or (ii) the instrument, whether or not indorsed, is deposited in a depositary bank to an account in a name substantially similar to the name of that person.

### § 3–406. Negligence Contributing to Forged Signature or Alteration of Instrument.

(a) A person whose failure to exercise ordinary care substantially contributes to an alteration of an instrument or to the making of a forged signature on an instrument is precluded from asserting the alteration or the forgery against a person who, in good faith, pays the instrument or takes it for value or for collection.

(b) Under subsection (a), if the person asserting the preclusion fails to exercise ordinary care in paying or taking the instrument and that failure substantially contributes to loss, the loss is allocated between the person precluded and the person asserting the preclusion according to the extent to which the failure of each to exercise ordinary care contributed to the loss.

(c) Under subsection (a), the burden of proving failure to exercise ordinary care is on the person asserting the preclusion. Under subsection (b), the burden of proving failure to exercise ordinary care is on the person precluded.

### § 3–407. Alteration.

(a) "Alteration" means (i) an unauthorized change in an instrument that purports to modify in any respect the obligation of a party, or (ii) an unauthorized addition of words or numbers or other change to an incomplete instrument relating to the obligation of a party.

(b) Except as provided in subsection (c), an alteration fraudulently made discharges a party whose obligation is affected by the alteration unless that party assents or is precluded from asserting the alteration. No other alteration discharges a party, and the instrument may be enforced according to its original terms.

(c) A payor bank or drawee paying a fraudulently altered instrument or a person taking it for value, in good faith and without notice of the alteration, may enforce rights with respect to the instrument (i) according to its original terms, or (ii) in the case of an incomplete instrument altered by unauthorized completion, according to its terms as completed.

### § 3–408. Drawee Not Liable on Unaccepted Draft.

A check or other draft does not of itself operate as an assignment of funds in the hands of the drawee available for its payment, and the drawee is not liable on the instrument until the drawee accepts it.

### § 3–409. Acceptance of Draft; Certified Check.

(a) "Acceptance" means the drawee's signed agreement to pay a draft as presented. It must be written on the draft and may consist of the drawee's signature alone. Acceptance may be made at any time and becomes effective when notification pursuant to instructions is given or the accepted draft is delivered for the purpose of giving rights on the acceptance to any person.

(b) A draft may be accepted although it has not been signed by the drawer, is otherwise incomplete, is overdue, or has been dishonored.

(c) If a draft is payable at a fixed period after sight and the acceptor fails to date the acceptance, the holder may complete the acceptance by supplying a date in good faith.

(d) "Certified check" means a check accepted by the bank on which it is drawn. Acceptance may be made as stated in subsection (a) or by a writing on the check which indicates that the check is certified. The drawee of a check has no obligation to certify the check, and refusal to certify is not dishonor of the check.

### § 3–410. Acceptance Varying Draft.

(a) If the terms of a drawee's acceptance vary from the terms of the draft as presented, the holder may refuse the acceptance and treat the draft as dishonored. In that case, the drawee may cancel the acceptance.

(b) The terms of a draft are not varied by an acceptance to pay at a particular bank or place in the United States, unless the acceptance states that the draft is to be paid only at that bank or place.

(c) If the holder assents to an acceptance varying the terms of a draft, the obligation of each drawer and indorser that does not expressly assent to the acceptance is discharged.

### § 3–411. Refusal to Pay Cashier's Checks, Teller's Checks, and Certified Checks.

(a) In this section, "obligated bank" means the acceptor of a certified check or the issuer of a cashier's check or teller's check bought from the issuer.

(b) If the obligated bank wrongfully (i) refuses to pay a cashier's check or certified check, (ii) stops payment of a teller's check, or (iii) refuses to pay a dishonored teller's check, the person asserting the right to enforce the check is entitled to compensation for expenses and loss of interest resulting from the nonpayment and may recover consequential damages if the obligated bank refuses to pay after receiving notice of particular circumstances giving rise to the damages.

(c) Expenses or consequential damages under subsection (b) are not recoverable if the refusal of the obligated bank to pay occurs because (i) the bank suspends payments, (ii) the obligated bank asserts a claim or defense of the bank that it has reasonable grounds to believe is available against the person entitled to enforce the instrument, (iii) the obligated bank has a reasonable doubt whether the person demanding payment is the person entitled to enforce the instrument, or (iv) payment is prohibited by law.

### § 3–412. Obligation of Issuer of Note or Cashier's Check.

The issuer of a note or cashier's check or other draft drawn on the drawer is obliged to pay the instrument (i) according to its terms at the time it was issued or, if not issued, at the time it first came into possession of a holder, or (ii) if the issuer signed an incomplete instrument, according to its terms when completed, to the extent stated in Sections 3–115 and 3–407. The obligation is owed to a person entitled to enforce the instrument or to an indorser who paid the instrument under Section 3–415.

### § 3–413. Obligation of Acceptor.

**(a)** The acceptor of a draft is obliged to pay the draft (i) according to its terms at the time it was accepted, even though the acceptance states that the draft is payable "as originally drawn" or equivalent terms, (ii) if the acceptance varies the terms of the draft, according to the terms of the draft as varied, or (iii) if the acceptance is of a draft that is an incomplete instrument, according to its terms when completed, to the extent stated in Sections 3–115 and 3–407. The obligation is owed to a person entitled to enforce the draft or to the drawer or an indorser who paid the draft under Section 3–414 or 3–415.

**(b)** If the certification of a check or other acceptance of a draft states the amount certified or accepted, the obligation of the acceptor is that amount. If (i) the certification or acceptance does not state an amount, (ii) the amount of the instrument is subsequently raised, and (iii) the instrument is then negotiated to a holder in due course, the obligation of the acceptor is the amount of the instrument at the time it was taken by the holder in due course.

### § 3–414. Obligation of Drawer.

**(a)** This section does not apply to cashier's checks or other drafts drawn on the drawer.

**(b)** If an unaccepted draft is dishonored, the drawer is obliged to pay the draft (i) according to its terms at the time it was issued or, if not issued, at the time it first came into possession of a holder, or (ii) if the drawer signed an incomplete instrument, according to its terms when completed, to the extent stated in Sections 3–115 and 3–407. The obligation is owed to a person entitled to enforce the draft or to an indorser who paid the draft under Section 3–415.

**(c)** If a draft is accepted by a bank, the drawer is discharged, regardless of when or by whom acceptance was obtained.

**(d)** If a draft is accepted and the acceptor is not a bank, the obligation of the drawer to pay the draft if the draft is dishonored by the acceptor is the same as the obligation of an indorser under Section 3–415(a) and (c).

**(e)** If a draft states that it is drawn "without recourse" or otherwise disclaims liability of the drawer to pay the draft, the drawer is not liable under subsection (b) to pay the draft if the draft is not a check. A disclaimer of the liability stated in subsection (b) is not effective if the draft is a check.

**(f)** If (i) a check is not presented for payment or given to a depositary bank for collection within 30 days after its date, (ii) the drawee suspends payments after expiration of the 30-day period without paying the check, and (iii) because of the suspension of payments, the drawer is deprived of funds maintained with the drawee to cover payment of the check, the drawer to the extent deprived of funds may discharge its obligation to pay the check by assigning to the person entitled to enforce the check the rights of the drawer against the drawee with respect to the funds.

### § 3–415. Obligation of Indorser.

**(a)** Subject to subsections (b), (c), and (d) and to Section 3–419(d), if an instrument is dishonored, an indorser is obliged to pay the amount due on the instrument (i) according to the terms of the instrument at the time it was indorsed, or (ii) if the indorser indorsed an incomplete instrument, according to its terms when completed, to the extent stated in Sections 3–115 and 3–407. The obligation of the indorser is owed to a person entitled to enforce the instrument or to a subsequent indorser who paid the instrument under this section.

**(b)** If an indorsement states that it is made "without recourse" or otherwise disclaims liability of the indorser, the indorser is not liable under subsection (a) to pay the instrument.

**(c)** If notice of dishonor of an instrument is required by Section 3–503 and notice of dishonor complying with that section is not given to an indorser, the liability of the indorser under subsection (a) is discharged.

**(d)** If a draft is accepted by a bank after an indorsement is made, the liability of the indorser under subsection (a) is discharged.

**(e)** If an indorser of a check is liable under subsection (a) and the check is not presented for payment, or given to a depositary bank for collection, within 30 days after the day the indorsement was made, the liability of the indorser under subsection (a) is discharged.

As amended in 1993.

### § 3–416. Transfer Warranties.

**(a)** A person who transfers an instrument for consideration warrants to the transferee and, if the transfer is by indorsement, to any subsequent transferee that:

> **(1)** the warrantor is a person entitled to enforce the instrument;
>
> **(2)** all signatures on the instrument are authentic and authorized;
>
> **(3)** the instrument has not been altered;
>
> **(4)** the instrument is not subject to a defense or claim in recoupment of any party which can be asserted against the warrantor; and
>
> **(5)** the warrantor has no knowledge of any insolvency proceeding commenced with respect to the maker or acceptor or, in the case of an unaccepted draft, the drawer.

**(b)** A person to whom the warranties under subsection (a) are made and who took the instrument in good faith may recover from the warrantor as damages for breach of warranty an amount equal to the loss suffered as a result of the breach, but not more than the amount of the instrument plus expenses and loss of interest incurred as a result of the breach.

**(c)** The warranties stated in subsection (a) cannot be disclaimed with respect to checks. Unless notice of a claim for breach of warranty is given to the warrantor within 30 days after the claimant has reason to know of the breach and the identity of the warrantor, the liability of the warrantor under subsection (b) is discharged to the extent of any loss caused by the delay in giving notice of the claim.

**(d)** A [cause of action] for breach of warranty under this section accrues when the claimant has reason to know of the breach.

## § 3–417. Presentment Warranties.

(a) If an unaccepted draft is presented to the drawee for payment or acceptance and the drawee pays or accepts the draft, (i) the person obtaining payment or acceptance, at the time of presentment, and (ii) a previous transferor of the draft, at the time of transfer, warrant to the drawee making payment or accepting the draft in good faith that:

(1) the warrantor is, or was, at the time the warrantor transferred the draft, a person entitled to enforce the draft or authorized to obtain payment or acceptance of the draft on behalf of a person entitled to enforce the draft;

(2) the draft has not been altered; and

(3) the warrantor has no knowledge that the signature of the drawer of the draft is unauthorized.

(b) A drawee making payment may recover from any warrantor damages for breach of warranty equal to the amount paid by the drawee less the amount the drawee received or is entitled to receive from the drawer because of the payment. In addition, the drawee is entitled to compensation for expenses and loss of interest resulting from the breach. The right of the drawee to recover damages under this subsection is not affected by any failure of the drawee to exercise ordinary care in making payment. If the drawee accepts the draft, breach of warranty is a defense to the obligation of the acceptor. If the acceptor makes payment with respect to the draft, the acceptor is entitled to recover from any warrantor for breach of warranty the amounts stated in this subsection.

(c) If a drawee asserts a claim for breach of warranty under subsection (a) based on an unauthorized indorsement of the draft or an alteration of the draft, the warrantor may defend by proving that the indorsement is effective under Section 3–404 or 3–405 or the drawer is precluded under Section 3–406 or 4–406 from asserting against the drawee the unauthorized indorsement or alteration.

(d) If (i) a dishonored draft is presented for payment to the drawer or an indorser or (ii) any other instrument is presented for payment to a party obliged to pay the instrument, and (iii) payment is received, the following rules apply:

(1) The person obtaining payment and a prior transferor of the instrument warrant to the person making payment in good faith that the warrantor is, or was, at the time the warrantor transferred the instrument, a person entitled to enforce the instrument or authorized to obtain payment on behalf of a person entitled to enforce the instrument.

(2) The person making payment may recover from any warrantor for breach of warranty an amount equal to the amount paid plus expenses and loss of interest resulting from the breach.

(e) The warranties stated in subsections (a) and (d) cannot be disclaimed with respect to checks. Unless notice of a claim for breach of warranty is given to the warrantor within 30 days after the claimant has reason to know of the breach and the identity of the warrantor, the liability of the warrantor under subsection (b) or (d) is discharged to the extent of any loss caused by the delay in giving notice of the claim.

(f) A [cause of action] for breach of warranty under this section accrues when the claimant has reason to know of the breach.

## § 3–418. Payment or Acceptance by Mistake.

(a) Except as provided in subsection (c), if the drawee of a draft pays or accepts the draft and the drawee acted on the mistaken belief that (i) payment of the draft had not been stopped pursuant to Section 4–403 or (ii) the signature of the drawer of the draft was authorized, the drawee may recover the amount of the draft from the person to whom or for whose benefit payment was made or, in the case of acceptance, may revoke the acceptance. Rights of the drawee under this subsection are not affected by failure of the drawee to exercise ordinary care in paying or accepting the draft.

(b) Except as provided in subsection (c), if an instrument has been paid or accepted by mistake and the case is not covered by subsection (a), the person paying or accepting may, to the extent permitted by the law governing mistake and restitution, (i) recover the payment from the person to whom or for whose benefit payment was made or (ii) in the case of acceptance, may revoke the acceptance.

(c) The remedies provided by subsection (a) or (b) may not be asserted against a person who took the instrument in good faith and for value or who in good faith changed position in reliance on the payment or acceptance. This subsection does not limit remedies provided by Section 3–417 or 4–407.

(d) Notwithstanding Section 4–215, if an instrument is paid or accepted by mistake and the payor or acceptor recovers payment or revokes acceptance under subsection (a) or (b), the instrument is deemed not to have been paid or accepted and is treated as dishonored, and the person from whom payment is recovered has rights as a person entitled to enforce the dishonored instrument.

## § 3–419. Instruments Signed for Accommodation.

(a) If an instrument is issued for value given for the benefit of a party to the instrument ("accommodated party") and another party to the instrument ("accommodation party") signs the instrument for the purpose of incurring liability on the instrument without being a direct beneficiary of the value given for the instrument, the instrument is signed by the accommodation party "for accommodation."

(b) An accommodation party may sign the instrument as maker, drawer, acceptor, or indorser and, subject to subsection (d), is obliged to pay the instrument in the capacity in which the accommodation party signs. The obligation of an accommodation party may be enforced notwithstanding any statute of frauds and whether or not the accommodation party receives consideration for the accommodation.

(c) A person signing an instrument is presumed to be an accommodation party and there is notice that the instrument is signed for accommodation if the signature is an anomalous indorsement or is accompanied by words indicating that the signer is acting as surety or guarantor with respect to the obligation of another party to the instrument. Except as provided in Section 3–605, the obligation of an accommodation party to pay the instrument is not affected by the fact that the person enforcing the obligation had notice when the instrument was taken by that person that the accommodation party signed the instrument for accommodation.

**(d)** If the signature of a party to an instrument is accompanied by words indicating unambiguously that the party is guaranteeing collection rather than payment of the obligation of another party to the instrument, the signer is obliged to pay the amount due on the instrument to a person entitled to enforce the instrument only if (i) execution of judgment against the other party has been returned unsatisfied, (ii) the other party is insolvent or in an insolvency proceeding, (iii) the other party cannot be served with process, or (iv) it is otherwise apparent that payment cannot be obtained from the other party.

**(e)** An accommodation party who pays the instrument is entitled to reimbursement from the accommodated party and is entitled to enforce the instrument against the accommodated party. An accommodated party who pays the instrument has no right of recourse against, and is not entitled to contribution from, an accommodation party.

### § 3–420. Conversion of Instrument.

**(a)** The law applicable to conversion of personal property applies to instruments. An instrument is also converted if it is taken by transfer, other than a negotiation, from a person not entitled to enforce the instrument or a bank makes or obtains payment with respect to the instrument for a person not entitled to enforce the instrument or receive payment. An action for conversion of an instrument may not be brought by (i) the issuer or acceptor of the instrument or (ii) a payee or indorsee who did not receive delivery of the instrument either directly or through delivery to an agent or a co-payee.

**(b)** In an action under subsection (a), the measure of liability is presumed to be the amount payable on the instrument, but recovery may not exceed the amount of the plaintiff's interest in the instrument.

**(c)** A representative, other than a depositary bank, who has in good faith dealt with an instrument or its proceeds on behalf of one who was not the person entitled to enforce the instrument is not liable in conversion to that person beyond the amount of any proceeds that it has not paid out.

### Part 5—Dishonor

### § 3–501. Presentment.

**(a)** "Presentment" means a demand made by or on behalf of a person entitled to enforce an instrument (i) to pay the instrument made to the drawee or a party obliged to pay the instrument or, in the case of a note or accepted draft payable at a bank, to the bank, or (ii) to accept a draft made to the drawee.

**(b)** The following rules are subject to Article 4, agreement of the parties, and clearing-house rules and the like:

(1) Presentment may be made at the place of payment of the instrument and must be made at the place of payment if the instrument is payable at a bank in the United States; may be made by any commercially reasonable means, including an oral, written, or electronic communication; is effective when the demand for payment or acceptance is received by the person to whom presentment is made; and is effective if made to any one of two or more makers, acceptors, drawees, or other payors.

(2) Upon demand of the person to whom presentment is made, the person making presentment must (i) exhibit the instrument, (ii) give reasonable identification and, if pre-

sentment is made on behalf of another person, reasonable evidence of authority to do so, and ( . . . ) sign a receipt on the instrument for any payment made or surrender the instrument if full payment is made.

(3) Without dishonoring the instrument, the party to whom presentment is made may (i) return the instrument for lack of a necessary indorsement, or (ii) refuse payment or acceptance for failure of the presentment to comply with the terms of the instrument, an agreement of the parties, or other applicable law or rule.

(4) The party to whom presentment is made may treat presentment as occurring on the next business day after the day of presentment if the party to whom presentment is made has established a cut-off hour not earlier than 2 p.m. for the receipt and processing of instruments presented for payment or acceptance and presentment is made after the cut-off hour.

### § 3–502. Dishonor.

**(a)** Dishonor of a note is governed by the following rules:

(1) If the note is payable on demand, the note is dishonored if presentment is duly made to the maker and the note is not paid on the day of presentment.

(2) If the note is not payable on demand and is payable at or through a bank or the terms of the note require presentment, the note is dishonored if presentment is duly made and the note is not paid on the day it becomes payable or the day of presentment, whichever is later.

(3) If the note is not payable on demand and paragraph (2) does not apply, the note is dishonored if it is not paid on the day it becomes payable.

**(b)** Dishonor of an unaccepted draft other than a documentary draft is governed by the following rules:

(1) If a check is duly presented for payment to the payor bank otherwise than for immediate payment over the counter, the check is dishonored if the payor bank makes timely return of the check or sends timely notice of dishonor or nonpayment under Section 4–301 or 4–302, or becomes accountable for the amount of the check under Section 4–302.

(2) If a draft is payable on demand and paragraph (1) does not apply, the draft is dishonored if presentment for payment is duly made to the drawee and the draft is not paid on the day of presentment.

(3) If a draft is payable on a date stated in the draft, the draft is dishonored if (i) presentment for payment is duly made to the drawee and payment is not made on the day the draft becomes payable or the day of presentment, whichever is later, or (ii) presentment for acceptance is duly made before the day the draft becomes payable and the draft is not accepted on the day of presentment.

(4) If a draft is payable on elapse of a period of time after sight or acceptance, the draft is dishonored if presentment for acceptance is duly made and the draft is not accepted on the day of presentment.

**(c)** Dishonor of an unaccepted documentary draft occurs according to the rules stated in subsection (b)(2), (3), and (4), except that payment or acceptance may be delayed without dishonor until no later than the close of the third business day of the drawee following the day on which payment or acceptance is required by those paragraphs.

(d) Dishonor of an accepted draft is governed by the following rules:

(1) If the draft is payable on demand, the draft is dishonored if presentment for payment is duly made to the acceptor and the draft is not paid on the day of presentment.

(2) If the draft is not payable on demand, the draft is dishonored if presentment for payment is duly made to the acceptor and payment is not made on the day it becomes payable or the day of presentment, whichever is later.

(e) In any case in which presentment is otherwise required for dishonor under this section and presentment is excused under Section 3–504, dishonor occurs without presentment if the instrument is not duly accepted or paid.

(f) If a draft is dishonored because timely acceptance of the draft was not made and the person entitled to demand acceptance consents to a late acceptance, from the time of acceptance the draft is treated as never having been dishonored.

### § 3–503. Notice of Dishonor.

(a) The obligation of an indorser stated in Section 3–415(a) and the obligation of a drawer stated in Section 3–414(d) may not be enforced unless (i) the indorser or drawer is given notice of dishonor of the instrument complying with this section or (ii) notice of dishonor is excused under Section 3–504(b).

(b) Notice of dishonor may be given by any person; may be given by any commercially reasonable means, including an oral, written, or electronic communication; and is sufficient if it reasonably identifies the instrument and indicates that the instrument has been dishonored or has not been paid or accepted. Return of an instrument given to a bank for collection is sufficient notice of dishonor.

(c) Subject to Section 3–504(c), with respect to an instrument taken for collection by a collecting bank, notice of dishonor must be given (i) by the bank before midnight of the next banking day following the banking day on which the bank receives notice of dishonor of the instrument, or (ii) by any other person within 30 days following the day on which the person receives notice of dishonor. With respect to any other instrument, notice of dishonor must be given within 30 days following the day on which dishonor occurs.

### § 3–504. Excused Presentment and Notice of Dishonor.

(a) Presentment for payment or acceptance of an instrument is excused if (i) the person entitled to present the instrument cannot with reasonable diligence make presentment, (ii) the maker or acceptor has repudiated an obligation to pay the instrument or is dead or in insolvency proceedings, (iii) by the terms of the instrument presentment is not necessary to enforce the obligation of indorsers or the drawer, (iv) the drawer or indorser whose obligation is being enforced has waived presentment or otherwise has no reason to expect or right to require that the instrument be paid or accepted, or (v) the drawer instructed the drawee not to pay or accept the draft or the drawee was not obligated to the drawer to pay the draft.

(b) Notice of dishonor is excused if (i) by the terms of the instrument notice of dishonor is not necessary to enforce the obligation of a party to pay the instrument, or (ii) the party whose obligation is being enforced waived notice of dishonor. A waiver of presentment is also a waiver of notice of dishonor.

(c) Delay in giving notice of dishonor is excused if the delay was caused by circumstances beyond the control of the person giving the notice and the person giving the notice exercised reasonable diligence after the cause of the delay ceased to operate.

### § 3–505. Evidence of Dishonor.

(a) The following are admissible as evidence and create a presumption of dishonor and of any notice of dishonor stated:

(1) a document regular in form as provided in subsection (b) which purports to be a protest;

(2) a purported stamp or writing of the drawee, payor bank, or presenting bank on or accompanying the instrument stating that acceptance or payment has been refused unless reasons for the refusal are stated and the reasons are not consistent with dishonor;

(3) a book or record of the drawee, payor bank, or collecting bank, kept in the usual course of business which shows dishonor, even if there is no evidence of who made the entry.

(b) A protest is a certificate of dishonor made by a United States consul or vice consul, or a notary public or other person authorized to administer oaths by the law of the place where dishonor occurs. It may be made upon information satisfactory to that person. The protest must identify the instrument and certify either that presentment has been made or, if not made, the reason why it was not made, and that the instrument has been dishonored by nonacceptance or nonpayment. The protest may also certify that notice of dishonor has been given to some or all parties.

### Part 6—Discharge and Payment

### § 3–601. Discharge and Effect of Discharge.

(a) The obligation of a party to pay the instrument is discharged as stated in this Article or by an act or agreement with the party which would discharge an obligation to pay money under a simple contract.

(b) Discharge of the obligation of a party is not effective against a person acquiring rights of a holder in due course of the instrument without notice of the discharge.

### § 3–602. Payment.

(a) Subject to subsection (b), an instrument is paid to the extent payment is made (i) by or on behalf of a party obliged to pay the instrument, and (ii) to a person entitled to enforce the instrument. To the extent of the payment, the obligation of the party obliged to pay the instrument is discharged even though payment is made with knowledge of a claim to the instrument under Section 3–306 by another person.

(b) The obligation of a party to pay the instrument is not discharged under subsection (a) if:

(1) a claim to the instrument under Section 3–306 is enforceable against the party receiving payment and (i) payment is made with knowledge by the payor that payment is prohibited by injunction or similar process of a court of competent jurisdiction, or (ii) in the case of an

instrument other than a cashier's check, teller's check, or certified check, the party making payment accepted, from the person having a claim to the instrument, indemnity against loss resulting from refusal to pay the person entitled to enforce the instrument; or

**(2)** the person making payment knows that the instrument is a stolen instrument and pays a person it knows is in wrongful possession of the instrument.

### § 3–603. Tender of Payment.

**(a)** If tender of payment of an obligation to pay an instrument is made to a person entitled to enforce the instrument, the effect of tender is governed by principles of law applicable to tender of payment under a simple contract.

**(b)** If tender of payment of an obligation to pay an instrument is made to a person entitled to enforce the instrument and the tender is refused, there is discharge, to the extent of the amount of the tender, of the obligation of an indorser or accommodation party having a right of recourse with respect to the obligation to which the tender relates.

**(c)** If tender of payment of an amount due on an instrument is made to a person entitled to enforce the instrument, the obligation of the obligor to pay interest after the due date on the amount tendered is discharged. If presentment is required with respect to an instrument and the obligor is able and ready to pay on the due date at every place of payment stated in the instrument, the obligor is deemed to have made tender of payment on the due date to the person entitled to enforce the instrument.

### § 3–604. Discharge by Cancellation or Renunciation.

**(a)** A person entitled to enforce an instrument, with or without consideration, may discharge the obligation of a party to pay the instrument (i) by an intentional voluntary act, such as surrender of the instrument to the party, destruction, mutilation, or cancellation of the instrument, cancellation or striking out of the party's signature, or the addition of words to the instrument indicating discharge, or (ii) by agreeing not to sue or otherwise renouncing rights against the party by a signed writing.

**(b)** Cancellation or striking out of an indorsement pursuant to subsection (a) does not affect the status and rights of a party derived from the indorsement.

### § 3–605. Discharge of Indorsers and Accommodation Parties.

**(a)** In this section, the term "indorser" includes a drawer having the obligation described in Section 3–414(d).

**(b)** Discharge, under Section 3–604, of the obligation of a party to pay an instrument does not discharge the obligation of an indorser or accommodation party having a right of recourse against the discharged party.

**(c)** If a person entitled to enforce an instrument agrees, with or without consideration, to an extension of the due date of the obligation of a party to pay the instrument, the extension discharges an indorser or accommodation party having a right of recourse against the party whose obligation is extended to the extent the indorser or accommodation party proves that the extension caused loss to the indorser or accommodation party with respect to the right of recourse.

**(d)** If a person entitled to enforce an instrument agrees, with or without consideration, to a material modification of the obligation of a party other than an extension of the due date, the modification discharges the obligation of an indorser or accommodation party having a right of recourse against the person whose obligation is modified to the extent the modification causes loss to the indorser or accommodation party with respect to the right of recourse. The loss suffered by the indorser or accommodation party as a result of the modification is equal to the amount of the right of recourse unless the person enforcing the instrument proves that no loss was caused by the modification or that the loss caused by the modification was an amount less than the amount of the right of recourse.

**(e)** If the obligation of a party to pay an instrument is secured by an interest in collateral and a person entitled to enforce the instrument impairs the value of the interest in collateral, the obligation of an indorser or accommodation party having a right of recourse against the obligor is discharged to the extent of the impairment. The value of an interest in collateral is impaired to the extent (i) the value of the interest is reduced to an amount less than the amount of the right of recourse of the party asserting discharge, or (ii) the reduction in value of the interest causes an increase in the amount by which the amount of the right of recourse exceeds the value of the interest. The burden of proving impairment is on the party asserting discharge.

**(f)** If the obligation of a party is secured by an interest in collateral not provided by an accommodation party and a person entitled to enforce the instrument impairs the value of the interest in collateral, the obligation of any party who is jointly and severally liable with respect to the secured obligation is discharged to the extent the impairment causes the party asserting discharge to pay more than that party would have been obliged to pay, taking into account rights of contribution, if impairment had not occurred. If the party asserting discharge is an accommodation party not entitled to discharge under subsection (e), the party is deemed to have a right to contribution based on joint and several liability rather than a right to reimbursement. The burden of proving impairment is on the party asserting discharge.

**(g)** Under subsection (e) or (f), impairing value of an interest in collateral includes (i) failure to obtain or maintain perfection or recordation of the interest in collateral, (ii) release of collateral without substitution of collateral of equal value, (iii) failure to perform a duty to preserve the value of collateral owed, under Article 9 or other law, to a debtor or surety or other person secondarily liable, or (iv) failure to comply with applicable law in disposing of collateral.

**(h)** An accommodation party is not discharged under subsection (c), (d), or (e) unless the person entitled to enforce the instrument knows of the accommodation or has notice under Section 3–419(c) that the instrument was signed for accommodation.

**(i)** A party is not discharged under this section if (i) the party asserting discharge consents to the event or conduct that is the basis of the discharge, or (ii) the instrument or a separate agreement of the party provides for waiver of discharge under this section either specifically or by general language indicating that parties waive defenses based on suretyship or impairment of collateral.

## ADDENDUM TO REVISED ARTICLE 3
### Notes to Legislative Counsel

**1.** If revised Article 3 is adopted in your state, the reference in Section 2–511 to Section 3–802 should be changed to Section 3–310.

**2.** If revised Article 3 is adopted in your state and the Uniform Fiduciaries Act is also in effect in your state, you may want to consider amending Uniform Fiduciaries Act § 9 to conform to Section 3–307(b)(2)(iii) and (4)(iii). See Official Comment 3 to Section 3–307.

## REVISED ARTICLE 4: BANK DEPOSITS AND COLLECTIONS

### Part 1—General Provisions and Definitions

#### § 4–101. Short Title.

This Article may be cited as Uniform Commercial Code—Bank Deposits and Collections.
As amended in 1990.

#### § 4–102. Applicability.

**(a)** To the extent that items within this Article are also within Articles 3 and 8, they are subject to those Articles. If there is conflict, this Article governs Article 3, but Article 8 governs this Article.

**(b)** The liability of a bank for action or non-action with respect to an item handled by it for purposes of presentment, payment, or collection is governed by the law of the place where the bank is located. In the case of action or non-action by or at a branch or separate office of a bank, its liability is governed by the law of the place where the branch or separate office is located.

#### § 4–103. Variation by Agreement; Measure of Damages; Action Constituting Ordinary Care.

**(a)** The effect of the provisions of this Article may be varied by agreement, but the parties to the agreement cannot disclaim a bank's responsibility for its lack of good faith or failure to exercise ordinary care or limit the measure of damages for the lack or failure. However, the parties may determine by agreement the standards by which the bank's responsibility is to be measured if those standards are not manifestly unreasonable.

**(b)** Federal Reserve regulations and operating circulars, clearing-house rules, and the like have the effect of agreements under subsection (a), whether or not specifically assented to by all parties interested in items handled.

**(c)** Action or non-action approved by this Article or pursuant to Federal Reserve regulations or operating circulars is the exercise of ordinary care and, in the absence of special instructions, action or non-action consistent with clearing-house rules and the like or with a general banking usage not disapproved by this Article, is *prima facie* the exercise of ordinary care.

**(d)** The specification or approval of certain procedures by this Article is not disapproval of other procedures that may be reasonable under the circumstances.

**(e)** The measure of damages for failure to exercise ordinary care in handling an item is the amount of the item reduced by an amount that could not have been realized by the exercise of ordinary care. If there is also bad faith it includes any other damages the party suffered as a proximate consequence.

As amended in 1990.

#### § 4–104. Definitions and Index of Definitions.

**(a)** In this Article, unless the context otherwise requires:

(1) "Account" means any deposit or credit account with a bank, including a demand, time, savings, passbook, share draft, or like account, other than an account evidenced by a certificate of deposit;

(2) "Afternoon" means the period of a day between noon and midnight;

(3) "Banking day" means the part of a day on which a bank is open to the public for carrying on substantially all of its banking functions;

(4) "Clearing house" means an association of banks or other payors regularly clearing items;

(5) "Customer" means a person having an account with a bank or for whom a bank has agreed to collect items, including a bank that maintains an account at another bank;

(6) "Documentary draft" means a draft to be presented for acceptance or payment if specified documents, certificated securities (Section 8–102) or instructions for uncertificated securities (Section 8–102), or other certificates, statements, or the like are to be received by the drawee or other payor before acceptance or payment of the draft;

(7) "Draft" means a draft as defined in Section 3–104 or an item, other than an instrument, that is an order;

(8) "Drawee" means a person ordered in a draft to make payment;

(9) "Item" means an instrument or a promise or order to pay money handled by a bank for collection or payment. The term does not include a payment order governed by Article 4A or a credit or debit card slip;

(10) "Midnight deadline" with respect to a bank is midnight on its next banking day following the banking day on which it receives the relevant item or notice or from which the time for taking action commences to run, whichever is later;

(11) "Settle" means to pay in cash, by clearing-house settlement, in a charge or credit or by remittance, or otherwise as agreed. A settlement may be either provisional or final;

(12) "Suspends payments" with respect to a bank means that it has been closed by order of the supervisory authorities, that a public officer has been appointed to take it over, or that it ceases or refuses to make payments in the ordinary course of business.

**(b)** [Other definitions' section references deleted.]

**(c)** [Other definitions' section references deleted.]

**(d)** In addition, Article 1 contains general definitions and principles of construction and interpretation applicable throughout this Article.

#### § 4–105. "Bank"; "Depositary Bank"; "Payor Bank"; "Intermediary Bank"; "Collecting Bank"; "Presenting Bank".

In this Article:

(1) "Bank" means a person engaged in the business of banking, including a savings bank, savings and loan association, credit union, or trust company;

(2) "Depositary bank" means the first bank to take an item even though it is also the payor bank, unless the item is presented for immediate payment over the counter;

(3) "Payor bank" means a bank that is the drawee of a draft;

(4) "Intermediary bank" means a bank to which an item is transferred in course of collection except the depositary or payor bank;

(5) "Collecting bank" means a bank handling an item for collection except the payor bank;

(6) "Presenting bank" means a bank presenting an item except a payor bank.

### § 4–106. Payable Through or Payable at Bank: Collecting Bank.

(a) If an item states that it is "payable through" a bank identified in the item, (i) the item designates the bank as a collecting bank and does not by itself authorize the bank to pay the item, and (ii) the item may be presented for payment only by or through the bank.

### Alternative A

(b) If an item states that it is "payable at" a bank identified in the item, the item is equivalent to a draft drawn on the bank.

### Alternative B

(b) If an item states that it is "payable at" a bank identified in the item, (i) the item designates the bank as a collecting bank and does not by itself authorize the bank to pay the item, and (ii) the item may be presented for payment only by or through the bank.

(c) If a draft names a nonbank drawee and it is unclear whether a bank named in the draft is a co-drawee or a collecting bank, the bank is a collecting bank.

As added in 1990.

### § 4–107. Separate Office of Bank.

A branch or separate office of a bank is a separate bank for the purpose of computing the time within which and determining the place at or to which action may be taken or notices or orders shall be given under this Article and under Article 3.

As amended in 1962 and 1990.

### § 4–108. Time of Receipt of Items.

(a) For the purpose of allowing time to process items, prove balances, and make the necessary entries on its books to determine its position for the day, a bank may fix an afternoon hour of 2 P.M. or later as a cutoff hour for the handling of money and items and the making of entries on its books.

(b) An item or deposit of money received on any day after a cutoff hour so fixed or after the close of the banking day may be treated as being received at the opening of the next banking day.

As amended in 1990.

### § 4–109. Delays.

(a) Unless otherwise instructed, a collecting bank in a good faith effort to secure payment of a specific item drawn on a payor other than a bank, and with or without the approval of any person involved, may waive, modify, or extend time limits imposed or permitted by this [act] for a period not exceeding two additional banking days without discharge of drawers or indorsers or liability to its transferor or a prior party.

(b) Delay by a collecting bank or payor bank beyond time limits prescribed or permitted by this [act] or by instructions is excused if (i) the delay is caused by interruption of communication or computer facilities, suspension of payments by another bank, war, emergency conditions, failure of equipment, or other circumstances beyond the control of the bank, and (ii) the bank exercises such diligence as the circumstances require.

### § 4–110. Electronic Presentment.

(a) "Agreement for electronic presentment" means an agreement, clearing-house rule, or Federal Reserve regulation or operating circular, providing that presentment of an item may be made by transmission of an image of an item or information describing the item ("presentment notice") rather than delivery of the item itself. The agreement may provide for procedures governing retention, presentment, payment, dishonor, and other matters concerning items subject to the agreement.

(b) Presentment of an item pursuant to an agreement for presentment is made when the presentment notice is received.

(c) If presentment is made by presentment notice, a reference to "item" or "check" in this Article means the presentment notice unless the context otherwise indicates.

As added in 1990.

### § 4–111. Statute of Limitations.

An action to enforce an obligation, duty, or right arising under this Article must be commenced within three years after the [cause of action] accrues.

As added in 1990.

### Part 2—Collection of Items: Depositary and Collecting Banks

### § 4–201. Status of Collecting Bank as Agent and Provisional Status of Credits; Applicability of Article; Item Indorsed "Pay Any Bank".

(a) Unless a contrary intent clearly appears and before the time that a settlement given by a collecting bank for an item is or becomes final, the bank, with respect to an item, is an agent or sub-agent of the owner of the item and any settlement given for the item is provisional. This provision applies regardless of the form of indorsement or lack of indorsement and even though credit given for the item is subject to immediate withdrawal as of right or is in fact withdrawn; but the continuance of ownership of an item by its owner and any rights of the owner to proceeds of the item are subject to rights of a collecting bank, such as those resulting from outstanding advances on the item and rights of recoupment or setoff. If an item is handled by banks for purposes of presentment, payment, collection, or return, the relevant provisions of this Article apply even though action of the parties clearly establishes that a particular bank has purchased the item and is the owner of it.

(b) After an item has been indorsed with the words "pay any bank" or the like, only a bank may acquire the rights of a holder until the item has been:

(1) returned to the customer initiating collection; or

(2) specially indorsed by a bank to a person who is not a bank.

As amended in 1990.

## § 4–202. Responsibility for Collection or Return; When Action Timely.

(a) A collecting bank must exercise ordinary care in:

(1) presenting an item or sending it for presentment;

(2) sending notice of dishonor or nonpayment or returning an item other than a documentary draft to the bank's transferor after learning that the item has not been paid or accepted, as the case may be;

(3) settling for an item when the bank receives final settlement; and

(4) notifying its transferor of any loss or delay in transit within a reasonable time after discovery thereof.

(b) A collecting bank exercises ordinary care under subsection (a) by taking proper action before its midnight deadline following receipt of an item, notice, or settlement. Taking proper action within a reasonably longer time may constitute the exercise of ordinary care, but the bank has the burden of establishing timeliness.

(c) Subject to subsection (a)(1), a bank is not liable for the insolvency, neglect, misconduct, mistake, or default of another bank or person or for loss or destruction of an item in the possession of others or in transit.

As amended in 1990.

## § 4–203. Effect of Instructions.

Subject to Article 3 concerning conversion of instruments (Section 3–420) and restrictive indorsements (Section 3–206), only a collecting bank's transferor can give instructions that affect the bank or constitute notice to it, and a collecting bank is not liable to prior parties for any action taken pursuant to the instructions or in accordance with any agreement with its transferor.

## § 4–204. Methods of Sending and Presenting; Sending Directly to Payor Bank.

(a) A collecting bank shall send items by a reasonably prompt method, taking into consideration relevant instructions, the nature of the item, the number of those items on hand, the cost of collection involved, and the method generally used by it or others to present those items.

(b) A collecting bank may send:

(1) an item directly to the payor bank;

(2) an item to a nonbank payor if authorized by its transferor; and

(3) an item other than documentary drafts to a nonbank payor, if authorized by Federal Reserve regulation or operating circular, clearing-house rule, or the like.

(c) Presentment may be made by a presenting bank at a place where the payor bank or other payor has requested that presentment be made.

As amended in 1990.

## § 4–205. Depositary Bank Holder of Unindorsed Item.

If a customer delivers an item to a depositary bank for collection:

(1) the depositary bank becomes a holder of the item at the time it receives the item for collection if the customer at the time of delivery was a holder of the item, whether or not the customer indorses the item, and, if the bank satisfies the other requirements of Section 3–302, it is a holder in due course; and

(2) the depositary bank warrants to collecting banks, the payor bank or other payor, and the drawer that the amount of the item was paid to the customer or deposited to the customer's account.

As amended in 1990.

## § 4–206. Transfer Between Banks.

Any agreed method that identifies the transferor bank is sufficient for the item's further transfer to another bank.

As amended in 1990.

## § 4–207. Transfer Warranties.

(a) A customer or collecting bank that transfers an item and receives a settlement or other consideration warrants to the transferee and to any subsequent collecting bank that:

(1) the warrantor is a person entitled to enforce the item;

(2) all signatures on the item are authentic and authorized;

(3) the item has not been altered;

(4) the item is not subject to a defense or claim in recoupment (Section 3–305(a)) of any party that can be asserted against the warrantor; and

(5) the warrantor has no knowledge of any insolvency proceeding commenced with respect to the maker or acceptor or, in the case of an unaccepted draft, the drawer.

(b) If an item is dishonored, a customer or collecting bank transferring the item and receiving settlement or other consideration is obliged to pay the amount due on the item (i) according to the terms of the item at the time it was transferred, or (ii) if the transfer was of an incomplete item, according to its terms when completed as stated in Sections 3–115 and 3–407. The obligation of a transferor is owed to the transferee and to any subsequent collecting bank that takes the item in good faith. A transferor cannot disclaim its obligation under this subsection by an indorsement stating that it is made "without recourse" or otherwise disclaiming liability.

(c) A person to whom the warranties under subsection (a) are made and who took the item in good faith may recover from the warrantor as damages for breach of warranty an amount equal to the loss suffered as a result of the breach, but not more than the amount of the item plus expenses and loss of interest incurred as a result of the breach.

(d) The warranties stated in subsection (a) cannot be disclaimed with respect to checks. Unless notice of a claim for breach of warranty is given to the warrantor within 30 days after the claimant has reason to know of the breach and the identity of the warrantor, the warrantor is discharged to the extent of any loss caused by the delay in giving notice of the claim.

(e) A cause of action for breach of warranty under this section accrues when the claimant has reason to know of the breach.

As amended in 1990.

## § 4–208. Presentment Warranties.

(a) If an unaccepted draft is presented to the drawee for payment or acceptance and the drawee pays or accepts the draft, (i) the person obtaining payment or acceptance, at the time of presentment, and (ii) a previous transferor of the draft, at the time of transfer, warrant to the drawee that pays or accepts the draft in good faith that:

**(1)** the warrantor is, or was, at the time the warrantor transferred the draft, a person entitled to enforce the draft or authorized to obtain payment or acceptance of the draft on behalf of a person entitled to enforce the draft;

**(2)** the draft has not been altered; and

**(3)** the warrantor has no knowledge that the signature of the purported drawer of the draft is unauthorized.

**(b)** A drawee making payment may recover from a warrantor damages for breach of warranty equal to the amount paid by the drawee less the amount the drawee received or is entitled to receive from the drawer because of the payment. In addition, the drawee is entitled to compensation for expenses and loss of interest resulting from the breach. The right of the drawee to recover damages under this subsection is not affected by any failure of the drawee to exercise ordinary care in making payment. If the drawee accepts the draft (i) breach of warranty is a defense to the obligation of the acceptor, and (ii) if the acceptor makes payment with respect to the draft, the acceptor is entitled to recover from a warrantor for breach of warranty the amounts stated in this subsection.

**(c)** If a drawee asserts a claim for breach of warranty under subsection (a) based on an unauthorized indorsement of the draft or an alteration of the draft, the warrantor may defend by proving that the indorsement is effective under Section 3–404 or 3–405 or the drawer is precluded under Section 3–406 or 4–406 from asserting against the drawee the unauthorized indorsement or alteration.

**(d)** If (i) a dishonored draft is presented for payment to the drawer or an indorser or (ii) any other item is presented for payment to a party obliged to pay the item, and the item is paid, the person obtaining payment and a prior transferor of the item warrant to the person making payment in good faith that the warrantor is, or was, at the time the warrantor transferred the item, a person entitled to enforce the item or authorized to obtain payment on behalf of a person entitled to enforce the item. The person making payment may recover from any warrantor for breach of warranty an amount equal to the amount paid plus expenses and loss of interest resulting from the breach.

**(e)** The warranties stated in subsections (a) and (d) cannot be disclaimed with respect to checks. Unless notice of a claim for breach of warranty is given to the warrantor within 30 days after the claimant has reason to know of the breach and the identity of the warrantor, the warrantor is discharged to the extent of any loss caused by the delay in giving notice of the claim.

**(f)** A cause of action for breach of warranty under this section accrues when the claimant has reason to know of the breach.
As amended in 1990.

### § 4–209. Encoding and Retention Warranties.

**(a)** A person who encodes information on or with respect to an item after issue warrants to any subsequent collecting bank and to the payor bank or other payor that the information is correctly encoded. If the customer of a depositary bank encodes, that bank also makes the warranty.

**(b)** A person who undertakes to retain an item pursuant to an agreement for electronic presentment warrants to any subsequent collecting bank and to the payor bank or other payor

that retention and presentment of the item comply with the agreement. If a customer of a depositary bank undertakes to retain an item, that bank also makes this warranty.

**(c)** A person to whom warranties are made under this section and who took the item in good faith may recover from the warrantor as damages for breach of warranty an amount equal to the loss suffered as a result of the breach, plus expenses and loss of interest incurred as a result of the breach.
As added in 1990.

### § 4–210. Security Interest of Collecting Bank in Items, Accompanying Documents and Proceeds.

**(a)** A collecting bank has a security interest in an item and any accompanying documents or the proceeds of either:

**(1)** in case of an item deposited in an account, to the extent to which credit given for the item has been withdrawn or applied;

**(2)** in case of an item for which it has given credit available for withdrawal as of right, to the extent of the credit given, whether or not the credit is drawn upon or there is a right of charge-back; or

**(3)** if it makes an advance on or against the item.

**(b)** If credit given for several items received at one time or pursuant to a single agreement is withdrawn or applied in part, the security interest remains upon all the items, any accompanying documents or the proceeds of either. For the purpose of this section, credits first given are first withdrawn.

**(c)** Receipt by a collecting bank of a final settlement for an item is a realization on its security interest in the item, accompanying documents, and proceeds. So long as the bank does not receive final settlement for the item or give up possession of the item or accompanying documents for purposes other than collection, the security interest continues to that extent and is subject to Article 9, but:

**(1)** no security agreement is necessary to make the security interest enforceable (Section 9–203(1)(a));

**(2)** no filing is required to perfect the security interest; and

**(3)** the security interest has priority over conflicting perfected security interests in the item, accompanying documents, or proceeds.
As amended in 1990 and 1999.

### § 4–211. When Bank Gives Value for Purposes of Holder in Due Course.

For purposes of determining its status as a holder in due course, a bank has given value to the extent it has a security interest in an item, if the bank otherwise complies with the requirements of Section 3–302 on what constitutes a holder in due course.
As amended in 1990.

### § 4–212. Presentment by Notice of Item Not Payable by, Through, or at Bank; Liability of Drawer or Indorser.

**(a)** Unless otherwise instructed, a collecting bank may present an item not payable by, through, or at a bank by sending to the party to accept or pay a written notice that the bank holds the item for acceptance or payment. The notice must be sent in time to be received on or before the day when presentment is due and the bank must meet any requirement of the party to accept or pay under Section 3–501 by the close of the bank's next banking day after it knows of the requirement.

(b) If presentment is made by notice and payment, acceptance, or request for compliance with a requirement under Section 3–501 is not received by the close of business on the day after maturity or, in the case of demand items, by the close of business on the third banking day after notice was sent, the presenting bank may treat the item as dishonored and charge any drawer or indorser by sending it notice of the facts.

As amended in 1990.

### § 4–213.  Medium and Time of Settlement by Bank.

(a) With respect to settlement by a bank, the medium and time of settlement may be prescribed by Federal Reserve regulations or circulars, clearing-house rules, and the like, or agreement. In the absence of such prescription:

> (1) the medium of settlement is cash or credit to an account in a Federal Reserve bank of or specified by the person to receive settlement; and
>
> (2) the time of settlement is:
>
>> (i) with respect to tender of settlement by cash, a cashier's check, or teller's check, when the cash or check is sent or delivered;
>>
>> (ii) with respect to tender of settlement by credit in an account in a Federal Reserve Bank, when the credit is made;
>>
>> (iii) with respect to tender of settlement by a credit or debit to an account in a bank, when the credit or debit is made or, in the case of tender of settlement by authority to charge an account, when the authority is sent or delivered; or
>>
>> (iv) with respect to tender of settlement by a funds transfer, when payment is made pursuant to Section 4A–406(a) to the person receiving settlement.

(b) If the tender of settlement is not by a medium authorized by subsection (a) or the time of settlement is not fixed by subsection (a), no settlement occurs until the tender of settlement is accepted by the person receiving settlement.

(c) If settlement for an item is made by cashier's check or teller's check and the person receiving settlement, before its midnight deadline:

> (1) presents or forwards the check for collection, settlement is final when the check is finally paid; or
>
> (2) fails to present or forward the check for collection, settlement is final at the midnight deadline of the person receiving settlement.

(d) If settlement for an item is made by giving authority to charge the account of the bank giving settlement in the bank receiving settlement, settlement is final when the charge is made by the bank receiving settlement if there are funds available in the account for the amount of the item.

As amended in 1990.

### § 4–214.  Right of Charge-Back or Refund;
### Liability of Collecting Bank: Return of Item.

(a) If a collecting bank has made provisional settlement with its customer for an item and fails by reason of dishonor, suspension of payments by a bank, or otherwise to receive settlement for the item which is or becomes final, the bank may revoke the settlement given by it, charge back the amount of any credit given for the item to its customer's account, or obtain refund from its customer, whether or not it is able to return the item, if by its midnight deadline or within a longer reasonable time after it learns the facts it returns the item or sends notification of the facts. If the return or notice is delayed beyond the bank's midnight deadline or a longer reasonable time after it learns the facts, the bank may revoke the settlement, charge back the credit, or obtain refund from its customer, but it is liable for any loss resulting from the delay. These rights to revoke, charge back, and obtain refund terminate if and when a settlement for the item received by the bank is or becomes final.

(b) A collecting bank returns an item when it is sent or delivered to the bank's customer or transferor or pursuant to its instructions.

(c) A depositary bank that is also the payor may charge back the amount of an item to its customer's account or obtain refund in accordance with the section governing return of an item received by a payor bank for credit on its books (Section 4–301).

(d) The right to charge back is not affected by:

> (1) previous use of a credit given for the item; or
>
> (2) failure by any bank to exercise ordinary care with respect to the item, but a bank so failing remains liable.

(e) A failure to charge back or claim refund does not affect other rights of the bank against the customer or any other party.

(f) If credit is given in dollars as the equivalent of the value of an item payable in foreign money, the dollar amount of any charge-back or refund must be calculated on the basis of the bank-offered spot rate for the foreign money prevailing on the day when the person entitled to the charge-back or refund learns that it will not receive payment in ordinary course.

As amended in 1990.

### § 4–215.  Final Payment of Item by Payor Bank; When Provisional Debits and Credits Become Final; When Certain Credits Become Available for Withdrawal.

(a) An item is finally paid by a payor bank when the bank has first done any of the following:

> (1) paid the item in cash;
>
> (2) settled for the item without having a right to revoke the settlement under statute, clearing-house rule, or agreement; or
>
> (3) made a provisional settlement for the item and failed to revoke the settlement in the time and manner permitted by statute, clearing-house rule, or agreement.

(b) If provisional settlement for an item does not become final, the item is not finally paid.

(c) If provisional settlement for an item between the presenting and payor banks is made through a clearing house or by debits or credits in an account between them, then to the extent that provisional debits or credits for the item are entered in accounts between the presenting and payor banks or between the presenting and successive prior collecting banks seriatim, they become final upon final payment of the item by the payor bank.

(d) If a collecting bank receives a settlement for an item which is or becomes final, the bank is accountable to its customer for the amount of the item and any provisional credit given for the item in an account with its customer becomes final.

(e) Subject to (i) applicable law stating a time for availability of funds and (ii) any right of the bank to apply the credit to an obligation of the customer, credit given by a bank for an item in a customer's account becomes available for withdrawal as of right:

(1) if the bank has received a provisional settlement for the item, when the settlement becomes final and the bank has had a reasonable time to receive return of the item and the item has not been received within that time;

(2) if the bank is both the depositary bank and the payor bank, and the item is finally paid, at the opening of the bank's second banking day following receipt of the item.

(f) Subject to applicable law stating a time for availability of funds and any right of a bank to apply a deposit to an obligation of the depositor, a deposit of money becomes available for withdrawal as of right at the opening of the bank's next banking day after receipt of the deposit.

As amended in 1990.

### § 4– 216. Insolvency and Preference.

(a) If an item is in or comes into the possession of a payor or collecting bank that suspends payment and the item has not been finally paid, the item must be returned by the receiver, trustee, or agent in charge of the closed bank to the presenting bank or the closed bank's customer.

(b) If a payor bank finally pays an item and suspends payments without making a settlement for the item with its customer or the presenting bank which settlement is or becomes final, the owner of the item has a preferred claim against the payor bank.

(c) If a payor bank gives or a collecting bank gives or receives a provisional settlement for an item and thereafter suspends payments, the suspension does not prevent or interfere with the settlement's becoming final if the finality occurs automatically upon the lapse of certain time or the happening of certain events.

(d) If a collecting bank receives from subsequent parties settlement for an item, which settlement is or becomes final and the bank suspends payments without making a settlement for the item with its customer which settlement is or becomes final, the owner of the item has a preferred claim against the collecting bank.

As amended in 1990.

### Part 3—Collection of Items: Payor Banks

### § 4–301. Deferred Posting; Recovery of Payment by Return of Items; Time of Dishonor; Return of Items by Payor Bank.

(a) If a payor bank settles for a demand item other than a documentary draft presented otherwise than for immediate payment over the counter before midnight of the banking day of receipt, the payor bank may revoke the settlement and recover the settlement if, before it has made final payment and before its midnight deadline, it

(1) returns the item; or

(2) sends written notice of dishonor or non-payment if the item is unavailable for return.

(b) If a demand item is received by a payor bank for credit on its books, it may return the item or send notice of dishonor and may revoke any credit given or recover the amount thereof

withdrawn by its customer, if it acts within the time limit and in the manner specified in subsection (a).

(c) Unless previous notice of dishonor has been sent, an item is dishonored at the time when for purposes of dishonor it is returned or notice sent in accordance with this section.

(d) An item is returned:

(1) as to an item presented through a clearing house, when it is delivered to the presenting or last collecting bank or to the clearing house or is sent or delivered in accordance with clearing-house rules; or (2) in all other cases, when it is sent or delivered to the bank's customer or transferor or pursuant to instructions.

As amended in 1990.

### § 4–302. Payor Bank's Responsibility for Late Return of Item.

(a) If an item is presented to and received by a payor bank, the bank is accountable for the amount of:

(1) a demand item, other than a documentary draft, whether properly payable or not, if the bank, in any case in which it is not also the depositary bank, retains the item beyond midnight of the banking day of receipt without settling for it or, whether or not it is also the depositary bank, does not pay or return the item or send notice of dishonor until after its midnight deadline; or

(2) any other properly payable item unless, within the time allowed for acceptance or payment of that item, the bank either accepts or pays the item or returns it and accompanying documents.

(b) The liability of a payor bank to pay an item pursuant to subsection (a) is subject to defenses based on breach of a presentment warranty (Section 4–208) or proof that the person seeking enforcement of the liability presented or transferred the item for the purpose of defrauding the payor bank.

As amended in 1990.

### § 4–303. When Items Subject to Notice, Stop-Payment Order, Legal Process, or Setoff; Order in Which Items May Be Charged or Certified.

(a) Any knowledge, notice, or stop-payment order received by, legal process served upon, or setoff exercised by a payor bank comes too late to terminate, suspend, or modify the bank's right or duty to pay an item or to charge its customer's account for the item if the knowledge, notice, stop-payment order, or legal process is received or served and a reasonable time for the bank to act thereon expires or the setoff is exercised after the earliest of the following:

(1) the bank accepts or certifies the item;

(2) the bank pays the item in cash;

(3) the bank settles for the item without having a right to revoke the settlement under statute, clearing-house rule, or agreement;

(4) the bank becomes accountable for the amount of the item under Section 4–302 dealing with the payor bank's responsibility for late return of items; or

(5) with respect to checks, a cutoff hour no earlier than one hour after the opening of the next banking day after the banking day on which the bank received the check and no later than the close of that next banking day or, if no cutoff

hour is fixed, the close of the next banking day after the banking day on which the bank received the check.

**(b)** Subject to subsection (a), items may be accepted, paid, certified, or charged to the indicated account of its customer in any order.

As amended in 1990.

### Part 4—Relationship Between Payor Bank and Its Customer

#### § 4–401. When Bank May Charge Customer's Account.

**(a)** A bank may charge against the account of a customer an item that is properly payable from the account even though the charge creates an overdraft. An item is properly payable if it is authorized by the customer and is in accordance with any agreement between the customer and bank.

**(b)** A customer is not liable for the amount of an overdraft if the customer neither signed the item nor benefited from the proceeds of the item.

**(c)** A bank may charge against the account of a customer a check that is otherwise properly payable from the account, even though payment was made before the date of the check, unless the customer has given notice to the bank of the postdating describing the check with reasonable certainty. The notice is effective for the period stated in Section 4–403(b) for stop-payment orders, and must be received at such time and in such manner as to afford the bank a reasonable opportunity to act on it before the bank takes any action with respect to the check described in Section 4–303. If a bank charges against the account of a customer a check before the date stated in the notice of postdating, the bank is liable for damages for the loss resulting from its act. The loss may include damages for dishonor of subsequent items under Section 4–402.

**(d)** A bank that in good faith makes payment to a holder may charge the indicated account of its customer according to:

**(1)** the original terms of the altered item; or

**(2)** the terms of the completed item, even though the bank knows the item has been completed unless the bank has notice that the completion was improper.

As amended in 1990.

#### § 4–402. Bank's Liability to Customer for Wrongful Dishonor; Time of Determining Insufficiency of Account.

**(a)** Except as otherwise provided in this Article, a payor bank wrongfully dishonors an item if it dishonors an item that is properly payable, but a bank may dishonor an item that would create an overdraft unless it has agreed to pay the overdraft.

**(b)** A payor bank is liable to its customer for damages proximately caused by the wrongful dishonor of an item. Liability is limited to actual damages proved and may include damages for an arrest or prosecution of the customer or other consequential damages. Whether any consequential damages are proximately caused by the wrongful dishonor is a question of fact to be determined in each case.

**(c)** A payor bank's determination of the customer's account balance on which a decision to dishonor for insufficiency of available funds is based may be made at any time between the time the item is received by the payor bank and the time that the payor bank returns the item or gives notice in lieu of return, and no more than one determination need be made. If, at the election of the payor bank, a subsequent balance determination is made for the purpose of reevaluating the bank's decision to dishonor the item, the account balance at that time is determinative of whether a dishonor for insufficiency of available funds is wrongful.

As amended in 1990.

#### § 4–403. Customer's Right to Stop Payment; Burden of Proof of Loss.

**(a)** A customer or any person authorized to draw on the account if there is more than one person may stop payment of any item drawn on the customer's account or close the account by an order to the bank describing the item or account with reasonable certainty received at a time and in a manner that affords the bank a reasonable opportunity to act on it before any action by the bank with respect to the item described in Section 4–303. If the signature of more than one person is required to draw on an account, any of these persons may stop payment or close the account.

**(b)** A stop-payment order is effective for six months, but it lapses after 14 calendar days if the original order was oral and was not confirmed in writing within that period. A stop-payment order may be renewed for additional six-month periods by a writing given to the bank within a period during which the stop-payment order is effective.

**(c)** The burden of establishing the fact and amount of loss resulting from the payment of an item contrary to a stop-payment order or order to close an account is on the customer. The loss from payment of an item contrary to a stop-payment order may include damages for dishonor of subsequent items under Section 4–402.

As amended in 1990.

#### § 4–404. Bank Not Obliged to Pay Check More Than Six Months Old.

A bank is under no obligation to a customer having a checking account to pay a check, other than a certified check, which is presented more than six months after its date, but it may charge its customer's account for a payment made thereafter in good faith.

#### § 4–405. Death or Incompetence of Customer.

**(a)** A payor or collecting bank's authority to accept, pay, or collect an item or to account for proceeds of its collection, if otherwise effective, is not rendered ineffective by incompetence of a customer of either bank existing at the time the item is issued or its collection is undertaken if the bank does not know of an adjudication of incompetence. Neither death nor incompetence of a customer revokes the authority to accept, pay, collect, or account until the bank knows of the fact of death or of an adjudication of incompetence and has reasonable opportunity to act on it.

**(b)** Even with knowledge, a bank may for 10 days after the date of death pay or certify checks drawn on or before the date unless ordered to stop payment by a person claiming an interest in the account.

As amended in 1990.

## § 4–406. Customer's Duty to Discover and Report Unauthorized Signature or Alteration.

**(a)** A bank that sends or makes available to a customer a statement of account showing payment of items for the account shall either return or make available to the customer the items paid or provide information in the statement of account sufficient to allow the customer reasonably to identify the items paid. The statement of account provides sufficient information if the item is described by item number, amount, and date of payment.

**(b)** If the items are not returned to the customer, the person retaining the items shall either retain the items or, if the items are destroyed, maintain the capacity to furnish legible copies of the items until the expiration of seven years after receipt of the items. A customer may request an item from the bank that paid the item, and that bank must provide in a reasonable time either the item or, if the item has been destroyed or is not otherwise obtainable, a legible copy of the item.

**(c)** If a bank sends or makes available a statement of account or items pursuant to subsection (a), the customer must exercise reasonable promptness in examining the statement or the items to determine whether any payment was not authorized because of an alteration of an item or because a purported signature by or on behalf of the customer was not authorized. If, based on the statement or items provided, the customer should reasonably have discovered the unauthorized payment, the customer must promptly notify the bank of the relevant facts.

**(d)** If the bank proves that the customer failed, with respect to an item, to comply with the duties imposed on the customer by subsection (c), the customer is precluded from asserting against the bank:

**(1)** the customer's unauthorized signature or any alteration on the item, if the bank also proves that it suffered a loss by reason of the failure; and

**(2)** the customer's unauthorized signature or alteration by the same wrongdoer on any other item paid in good faith by the bank if the payment was made before the bank received notice from the customer of the unauthorized signature or alteration and after the customer had been afforded a reasonable period of time, not exceeding 30 days, in which to examine the item or statement of account and notify the bank.

**(e)** If subsection (d) applies and the customer proves that the bank failed to exercise ordinary care in paying the item and that the failure substantially contributed to loss, the loss is allocated between the customer precluded and the bank asserting the preclusion according to the extent to which the failure of the customer to comply with subsection (c) and the failure of the bank to exercise ordinary care contributed to the loss. If the customer proves that the bank did not pay the item in good faith, the preclusion under subsection (d) does not apply.

**(f)** Without regard to care or lack of care of either the customer or the bank, a customer who does not within one year after the statement or items are made available to the customer (subsection (a)) discover and report the customer's unauthorized signature on or any alteration on the item is precluded from asserting against the bank the unauthorized signature or alteration. If there is a preclusion under this subsection, the payor bank may not recover for breach or warranty under Section 4–208 with respect to the unauthorized signature or alteration to which the preclusion applies. As amended in 1990.

## § 4–407. Payor Bank's Right to Subrogation on Improper Payment.

If a payor has paid an item over the order of the drawer or maker to stop payment, or after an account has been closed, or otherwise under circumstances giving a basis for objection by the drawer or maker, to prevent unjust enrichment and only to the extent necessary to prevent loss to the bank by reason of its payment of the item, the payor bank is subrogated to the rights

**(1)** of any holder in due course on the item against the drawer or maker;

**(2)** of the payee or any other holder of the item against the drawer or maker either on the item or under the transaction out of which the item arose; and

**(3)** of the drawer or maker against the payee or any other holder of the item with respect to the transaction out of which the item arose.

As amended in 1990.

### Part 5—Collection of Documentary Drafts

## § 4–501. Handling of Documentary Drafts; Duty to Send for Presentment and to Notify Customer of Dishonor.

A bank that takes a documentary draft for collection shall present or send the draft and accompanying documents for presentment and, upon learning that the draft has not been paid or accepted in due course, shall seasonably notify its customer of the fact even though it may have discounted or bought the draft or extended credit available for withdrawal as of right. As amended in 1990.

## § 4–502. Presentment of "On Arrival" Drafts.

If a draft or the relevant instructions require presentment "on arrival", "when goods arrive" or the like, the collecting bank need not present until in its judgment a reasonable time for arrival of the goods has expired. Refusal to pay or accept because the goods have not arrived is not dishonor; the bank must notify its transferor of the refusal but need not present the draft again until it is instructed to do so or learns of the arrival of the goods.

## § 4–503. Responsibility of Presenting Bank for Documents and Goods; Report of Reasons for Dishonor; Referee in Case of Need.

Unless otherwise instructed and except as provided in Article 5, a bank presenting a documentary draft:

**(1)** must deliver the documents to the drawee on acceptance of the draft if it is payable more than three days after presentment, otherwise, only on payment; and

**(2)** upon dishonor, either in the case of presentment for acceptance or presentment for payment, may seek and follow instructions from any referee in case of need designated in the draft or, if the presenting bank does not choose to utilize the referee's services, it must use diligence and good faith to ascertain the reason for dishonor, must notify its transferor of the dishonor and of the results of its effort to ascertain the reasons therefor, and must request instructions.

However, the presenting bank is under no obligation with respect to goods represented by the documents except to follow any reasonable instructions seasonably received; it has a right to reimbursement for any expense incurred in following instructions and to prepayment of or indemnity for those expenses.
As amended in 1990.

### § 4–504. Privilege of Presenting Bank to Deal With Goods; Security Interest for Expenses.

(a) A presenting bank that, following the dishonor of a documentary draft, has seasonably requested instructions but does not receive them within a reasonable time may store, sell, or otherwise deal with the goods in any reasonable manner.

(b) For its reasonable expenses incurred by action under subsection (a) the presenting bank has a lien upon the goods or their proceeds, which may be foreclosed in the same manner as an unpaid seller's lien.
As amended in 1990.

## ARTICLE 4A: FUNDS TRANSFERS

### Part 1—Subject Matter and Definitions

### § 4A–101. Short Title.
This Article may be cited as Uniform Commercial Code—Funds Transfers.

### § 4A–102. Subject Matter.
Except as otherwise provided in Section 4A–108, this Article applies to funds transfers defined in Section 4A–104.

### § 4A–103. Payment Order–Definitions.
(a) In this Article:

(1) "Payment order" means an instruction of a sender to a receiving bank, transmitted orally, electronically, or in writing, to pay, or to cause another bank to pay, a fixed or determinable amount of money to a beneficiary if:

   (i) the instruction does not state a condition to payment to the beneficiary other than time of payment,

   (ii) the receiving bank is to be reimbursed by debiting an account of, or otherwise receiving payment from, the sender, and

   (iii) the instruction is transmitted by the sender directly to the receiving bank or to an agent, funds-transfer system, or communication system for transmittal to the receiving bank.

(2) "Beneficiary" means the person to be paid by the beneficiary's bank.

(3) "Beneficiary's bank" means the bank identified in a payment order in which an account of the beneficiary is to be credited pursuant to the order or which otherwise is to make payment to the beneficiary if the order does not provide for payment to an account.

(4) "Receiving bank" means the bank to which the sender's instruction is addressed.

(5) "Sender" means the person giving the instruction to the receiving bank.

(b) If an instruction complying with subsection (a)(1) is to make more than one payment to a beneficiary, the instruction is a separate payment order with respect to each payment.

(c) A payment order is issued when it is sent to the receiving bank.

### § 4A–104. Funds Transfer–Definitions.
In this Article:

(a) "Funds transfer" means the series of transactions, beginning with the originator's payment order, made for the purpose of making payment to the beneficiary of the order. The term includes any payment order issued by the originator's bank or an intermediary bank intended to carry out the originator's payment order. A funds transfer is completed by acceptance by the beneficiary's bank of a payment order for the benefit of the beneficiary of the originator's payment order.

(b) "Intermediary bank" means a receiving bank other than the originator's bank or the beneficiary's bank.

(c) "Originator" means the sender of the first payment order in a funds transfer.

(d) "Originator's bank" means (i) the receiving bank to which the payment order of the originator is issued if the originator is not a bank, or (ii) the originator if the originator is a bank.

### § 4A–105. Other Definitions.
(a) In this Article:

(1) "Authorized account" means a deposit account of a customer in a bank designated by the customer as a source of payment of payment orders issued by the customer to the bank. If a customer does not so designate an account, any account of the customer is an authorized account if payment of a payment order from that account is not inconsistent with a restriction on the use of that account.

(2) "Bank" means a person engaged in the business of banking and includes a savings bank, savings and loan association, credit union, and trust company. A branch or separate office of a bank is a separate bank for purposes of this Article.

(3) "Customer" means a person, including a bank, having an account with a bank or from whom a bank has agreed to receive payment orders.

(4) "Funds-transfer business day" of a receiving bank means the part of a day during which the receiving bank is open for the receipt, processing, and transmittal of payment orders and cancellations and amendments of payment orders.

(5) "Funds-transfer system" means a wire transfer network, automated clearing house, or other communication system of a clearing house or other association of banks through which a payment order by a bank may be transmitted to the bank to which the order is addressed.

(6) "Good faith" means honesty in fact and the observance of reasonable commercial standards of fair dealing.

(7) "Prove" with respect to a fact means to meet the burden of establishing the fact (Section 1–201(8)).

(b) Other definitions applying to this Article and the sections in which they appear are:

| | |
|---|---|
| "Acceptance" | Section 4A–209 |
| "Beneficiary" | Section 4A–103 |
| "Beneficiary's bank" | Section 4A–103 |
| "Executed" | Section 4A–301 |

| "Execution date" | Section 4A–301 |
| "Funds transfer" | Section 4A–104 |
| "Funds-transfer system rule" | Section 4A–501 |
| "Intermediary bank" | Section 4A–104 |
| "Originator" | Section 4A–104 |
| "Originator's bank" | Section 4A–104 |
| "Payment by beneficiary's bank to beneficiary" | Section 4A–405 |
| "Payment by originator to beneficiary" | Section 4A–406 |
| "Payment by sender to receiving bank" | Section 4A–403 |
| "Payment date" | Section 4A–401 |
| "Payment order" | Section 4A–103 |
| "Receiving bank" | Section 4A–103 |
| "Security procedure" | Section 4A–201 |
| "Sender" | Section 4A–103 |

(c) The following definitions in Article 4 apply to this Article:

| "Clearing house" | Section 4–104 |
| "Item" | Section 4–104 |
| "Suspends payments" | Section 4–104 |

(d) In addition, Article 1 contains general definitions and principles of construction and interpretation applicable throughout this Article.

### § 4A–106. Time Payment Order Is Received.

(a) The time of receipt of a payment order or communication cancelling or amending a payment order is determined by the rules applicable to receipt of a notice stated in Section 1–201(27). A receiving bank may fix a cut-off time or times on a funds-transfer business day for the receipt and processing of payment orders and communications cancelling or amending payment orders. Different cut-off times may apply to payment orders, cancellations, or amendments, or to different categories of payment orders, cancellations, or amendments. A cut-off time may apply to senders generally or different cut-off times may apply to different senders or categories of payment orders. If a payment order or communication cancelling or amending a payment order is received after the close of a funds-transfer business day or after the appropriate cut-off time on a funds-transfer business day, the receiving bank may treat the payment order or communication as received at the opening of the next funds-transfer business day.

(b) If this Article refers to an execution date or payment date or states a day on which a receiving bank is required to take action, and the date or day does not fall on a funds-transfer business day, the next day that is a funds-transfer business day is treated as the date or day stated, unless the contrary is stated in this Article.

### § 4A–107. Federal Reserve Regulations and Operating Circulars.

Regulations of the Board of Governors of the Federal Reserve System and operating circulars of the Federal Reserve Banks supersede any inconsistent provision of this Article to the extent of the inconsistency.

### § 4A–108. Exclusion of Consumer Transactions Governed by Federal Law.

This Article does not apply to a funds transfer any part of which is governed by the Electronic Fund Transfer Act of 1978 (Title XX, Public Law 95–630, 92 Stat. 3728, 15 U.S.C. § 1693 *et seq.)* as amended from time to time.

## Part 2—Issue and Acceptance of Payment Order

### § 4A–201. Security Procedure.

"Security procedure" means a procedure established by agreement of a customer and a receiving bank for the purpose of (i) verifying that a payment order or communication amending or cancelling a payment order is that of the customer, or (ii) detecting error in the transmission or the content of the payment order or communication. A security procedure may require the use of algorithms or other codes, identifying words or numbers, encryption, callback procedures, or similar security devices. Comparison of a signature on a payment order or communication with an authorized specimen signature of the customer is not by itself a security procedure.

### § 4A–202. Authorized and Verified Payment Orders.

(a) A payment order received by the receiving bank is the authorized order of the person identified as sender if that person authorized the order or is otherwise bound by it under the law of agency.

(b) If a bank and its customer have agreed that the authenticity of payment orders issued to the bank in the name of the customer as sender will be verified pursuant to a security procedure, a payment order received by the receiving bank is effective as the order of the customer, whether or not authorized, if (i) the security procedure is a commercially reasonable method of providing security against unauthorized payment orders, and (ii) the bank proves that it accepted the payment order in good faith and in compliance with the security procedure and any written agreement or instruction of the customer restricting acceptance of payment orders issued in the name of the customer. The bank is not required to follow an instruction that violates a written agreement with the customer or notice of which is not received at a time and in a manner affording the bank a reasonable opportunity to act on it before the payment order is accepted.

(c) Commercial reasonableness of a security procedure is a question of law to be determined by considering the wishes of the customer expressed to the bank, the circumstances of the customer known to the bank, including the size, type, and frequency of payment orders normally issued by the customer to the bank, alternative security procedures offered to the customer, and security procedures in general use by customers and receiving banks similarly situated. A security procedure is deemed to be commercially reasonable if (i) the security procedure was chosen by the customer after the bank offered, and the customer refused, a security procedure that was commercially reasonable for that customer, and (ii) the customer expressly agreed in writing to be bound by any payment order, whether or not authorized, issued in its name and accepted by the bank in compliance with the security procedure chosen by the customer.

(d) The term "sender" in this Article includes the customer in whose name a payment order is issued if the order is the authorized order of the customer under subsection (a), or it is effective as the order of the customer under subsection (b).

(e) This section applies to amendments and cancellations of payment orders to the same extent it applies to payment orders.

(f) Except as provided in this section and in Section 4A–203(a)(1), rights and obligations arising under this section or Section 4A–203 may not be varied by agreement.

### § 4A–203. Unenforceability of Certain Verified Payment Orders.

(a) If an accepted payment order is not, under Section 4A–202(a), an authorized order of a customer identified as sender, but is effective as an order of the customer pursuant to Section 4A–202(b), the following rules apply:

(1) By express written agreement, the receiving bank may limit the extent to which it is entitled to enforce or retain payment of the payment order.

(2) The receiving bank is not entitled to enforce or retain payment of the payment order if the customer proves that the order was not caused, directly or indirectly, by a person (i) entrusted at any time with duties to act for the customer with respect to payment orders or the security procedure, or (ii) who obtained access to transmitting facilities of the customer or who obtained, from a source controlled by the customer and without authority of the receiving bank, information facilitating breach of the security procedure, regardless of how the information was obtained or whether the customer was at fault. Information includes any access device, computer software, or the like.

(b) This section applies to amendments of payment orders to the same extent it applies to payment orders.

### § 4A–204. Refund of Payment and Duty of Customer to Report with Respect to Unauthorized Payment Order.

(a) If a receiving bank accepts a payment order issued in the name of its customer as sender which is (i) not authorized and not effective as the order of the customer under Section 4A–202, or (ii) not enforceable, in whole or in part, against the customer under Section 4A–203, the bank shall refund any payment of the payment order received from the customer to the extent the bank is not entitled to enforce payment and shall pay interest on the refundable amount calculated from the date the bank received payment to the date of the refund. However, the customer is not entitled to interest from the bank on the amount to be refunded if the customer fails to exercise ordinary care to determine that the order was not authorized by the customer and to notify the bank of the relevant facts within a reasonable time not exceeding 90 days after the date the customer received notification from the bank that the order was accepted or that the customer's account was debited with respect to the order. The bank is not entitled to any recovery from the customer on account of a failure by the customer to give notification as stated in this section.

(b) Reasonable time under subsection (a) may be fixed by agreement as stated in Section 1–204(1), but the obligation of a receiving bank to refund payment as stated in subsection (a) may not otherwise be varied by agreement.

### § 4A–205. Erroneous Payment Orders.

(a) If an accepted payment order was transmitted pursuant to a security procedure for the detection of error and the payment order (i) erroneously instructed payment to a beneficiary not intended by the sender, (ii) erroneously instructed payment in an amount greater than the amount intended by the sender, or (iii) was an erroneously transmitted duplicate of a payment order previously sent by the sender, the following rules apply:

(1) If the sender proves that the sender or a person acting on behalf of the sender pursuant to Section 4A–206 complied with the security procedure and that the error would have been detected if the receiving bank had also complied, the sender is not obliged to pay the order to the extent stated in paragraphs (2) and (3).

(2) If the funds transfer is completed on the basis of an erroneous payment order described in clause (i) or (iii) of subsection (a), the sender is not obliged to pay the order and the receiving bank is entitled to recover from the beneficiary any amount paid to the beneficiary to the extent allowed by the law governing mistake and restitution.

(3) If the funds transfer is completed on the basis of a payment order described in clause (ii) of subsection (a), the sender is not obliged to pay the order to the extent the amount received by the beneficiary is greater than the amount intended by the sender. In that case, the receiving bank is entitled to recover from the beneficiary the excess amount received to the extent allowed by the law governing mistake and restitution.

(b) If (i) the sender of an erroneous payment order described in subsection (a) is not obliged to pay all or part of the order, and (ii) the sender receives notification from the receiving bank that the order was accepted by the bank or that the sender's account was debited with respect to the order, the sender has a duty to exercise ordinary care, on the basis of information available to the sender, to discover the error with respect to the order and to advise the bank of the relevant facts within a reasonable time, not exceeding 90 days, after the bank's notification was received by the sender. If the bank proves that the sender failed to perform that duty, the sender is liable to the bank for the loss the bank proves it incurred as a result of the failure, but the liability of the sender may not exceed the amount of the sender's order.

(c) This section applies to amendments to payment orders to the same extent it applies to payment orders.

### § 4A–206. Transmission of Payment Order through Funds-Transfer or Other Communication System.

(a) If a payment order addressed to a receiving bank is transmitted to a funds-transfer system or other third party communication system for transmittal to the bank, the system is deemed to be an agent of the sender for the purpose of transmitting the payment order to the bank. If there is a discrepancy between the terms of the payment order transmitted to the system and the terms of the payment order transmitted by the system to the bank, the terms of the payment order of the sender are those transmitted by the system. This section does not apply to a funds-transfer system of the Federal Reserve Banks.

(b) This section applies to cancellations and amendments to payment orders to the same extent it applies to payment orders.

### § 4A–207. Misdescription of Beneficiary.

(a) Subject to subsection (b), if, in a payment order received by the beneficiary's bank, the name, bank account number, or other identification of the beneficiary refers to a nonexistent or unidentifiable person or account, no person has rights as a beneficiary of the order and acceptance of the order cannot occur.

**(b)** If a payment order received by the beneficiary's bank identifies the beneficiary both by name and by an identifying or bank account number and the name and number identify different persons, the following rules apply:

**(1)** Except as otherwise provided in subsection (c), if the beneficiary's bank does not know that the name and number refer to different persons, it may rely on the number as the proper identification of the beneficiary of the order. The beneficiary's bank need not determine whether the name and number refer to the same person.

**(2)** If the beneficiary's bank pays the person identified by name or knows that the name and number identify different persons, no person has rights as beneficiary except the person paid by the beneficiary's bank if that person was entitled to receive payment from the originator of the funds transfer. If no person has rights as beneficiary, acceptance of the order cannot occur.

**(c)** If (i) a payment order described in subsection (b) is accepted, (ii) the originator's payment order described the beneficiary inconsistently by name and number, and (iii) the beneficiary's bank pays the person identified by number as permitted by subsection (b)(1), the following rules apply:

**(1)** If the originator is a bank, the originator is obliged to pay its order.

**(2)** If the originator is not a bank and proves that the person identified by number was not entitled to receive payment from the originator, the originator is not obliged to pay its order unless the originator's bank proves that the originator, before acceptance of the originator's order, had notice that payment of a payment order issued by the originator might be made by the beneficiary's bank on the basis of an identifying or bank account number even if it identifies a person different from the named beneficiary. Proof of notice may be made by any admissible evidence. The originator's bank satisfies the burden of proof if it proves that the originator, before the payment order was accepted, signed a writing stating the information to which the notice relates.

**(d)** In a case governed by subsection (b)(1), if the beneficiary's bank rightfully pays the person identified by number and that person was not entitled to receive payment from the originator, the amount paid may be recovered from that person to the extent allowed by the law governing mistake and restitution as follows:

**(1)** If the originator is obliged to pay its payment order as stated in subsection (c), the originator has the right to recover.

**(2)** If the originator is not a bank and is not obliged to pay its payment order, the originator's bank has the right to recover.

### § 4A–208. Misdescription of Intermediary Bank or Beneficiary's Bank.

**(a)** This subsection applies to a payment order identifying an intermediary bank or the beneficiary's bank only by an identifying number.

**(1)** The receiving bank may rely on the number as the proper identification of the intermediary or beneficiary's bank and need not determine whether the number identifies a bank.

**(2)** The sender is obliged to compensate the receiving bank for any loss and expenses incurred by the receiving bank as a result of its reliance on the number in executing or attempting to execute the order.

**(b)** This subsection applies to a payment order identifying an intermediary bank or the beneficiary's bank both by name and an identifying number if the name and number identify different persons.

**(1)** If the sender is a bank, the receiving bank may rely on the number as the proper identification of the intermediary or beneficiary's bank if the receiving bank, when it executes the sender's order, does not know that the name and number identify different persons. The receiving bank need not determine whether the name and number refer to the same person or whether the number refers to a bank. The sender is obliged to compensate the receiving bank for any loss and expenses incurred by the receiving bank as a result of its reliance on the number in executing or attempting to execute the order.

**(2)** If the sender is not a bank and the receiving bank proves that the sender, before the payment order was accepted, had notice that the receiving bank might rely on the number as the proper identification of the intermediary or beneficiary's bank even if it identifies a person different from the bank identified by name, the rights and obligations of the sender and the receiving bank are governed by subsection (b)(1), as though the sender were a bank. Proof of notice may be made by any admissible evidence. The receiving bank satisfies the burden of proof if it proves that the sender, before the payment order was accepted, signed a writing stating the information to which the notice relates.

**(3)** Regardless of whether the sender is a bank, the receiving bank may rely on the name as the proper identification of the intermediary or beneficiary's bank if the receiving bank, at the time it executes the sender's order, does not know that the name and number identify different persons. The receiving bank need not determine whether the name and number refer to the same person.

**(4)** If the receiving bank knows that the name and number identify different persons, reliance on either the name or the number in executing the sender's payment order is a breach of the obligation stated in Section 4A–302(a)(1).

### § 4A–209. Acceptance of Payment Order.

**(a)** Subject to subsection (d), a receiving bank other than the beneficiary's bank accepts a payment order when it executes the order.

**(b)** Subject to subsections (c) and (d), a beneficiary's bank accepts a payment order at the earliest of the following times:

**(1)** When the bank (i) pays the beneficiary as stated in Section 4A–405(a) or 4A–405(b), or (ii) notifies the beneficiary of receipt of the order or that the account of the beneficiary has been credited with respect to the order unless the notice indicates that the bank is rejecting the order or that funds with respect to the order may not be withdrawn or used until receipt of payment from the sender of the order;

**(2)** When the bank receives payment of the entire amount of the sender's order pursuant to Section 4A–403(a)(1) or 4A–403(a)(2); or

**(3)** The opening of the next funds-transfer business day of the bank following the payment date of the order if, at that time, the amount of the sender's order is fully covered by a withdrawable credit balance in an authorized account of the sender or the bank has otherwise received full payment from the sender, unless the order was rejected before that time or is rejected within (i) one hour after that time, or (ii) one hour after the opening of the next business day of the sender following the payment date if that time is later. If notice of rejection is received by the sender after the payment date and the authorized account of the sender does not bear interest, the bank is obliged to pay interest to the sender on the amount of the order for the number of days elapsing after the payment date to the day the sender receives notice or learns that the order was not accepted, counting that day as an elapsed day. If the withdrawable credit balance during that period falls below the amount of the order, the amount of interest payable is reduced accordingly.

**(c)** Acceptance of a payment order cannot occur before the order is received by the receiving bank. Acceptance does not occur under subsection (b)(2) or (b)(3) if the beneficiary of the payment order does not have an account with the receiving bank, the account has been closed, or the receiving bank is not permitted by law to receive credits for the beneficiary's account.

**(d)** A payment order issued to the originator's bank cannot be accepted until the payment date if the bank is the beneficiary's bank, or the execution date if the bank is not the beneficiary's bank. If the originator's bank executes the originator's payment order before the execution date or pays the beneficiary of the originator's payment order before the payment date and the payment order is subsequently cancelled pursuant to Section 4A–211(b), the bank may recover from the beneficiary any payment received to the extent allowed by the law governing mistake and restitution.

### § 4A–210. Rejection of Payment Order.

**(a)** A payment order is rejected by the receiving bank by a notice of rejection transmitted to the sender orally, electronically, or in writing. A notice of rejection need not use any particular words and is sufficient if it indicates that the receiving bank is rejecting the order or will not execute or pay the order. Rejection is effective when the notice is given if transmission is by a means that is reasonable in the circumstances. If notice of rejection is given by a means that is not reasonable, rejection is effective when the notice is received. If an agreement of the sender and receiving bank establishes the means to be used to reject a payment order, (i) any means complying with the agreement is reasonable and (ii) any means not complying is not reasonable unless no significant delay in receipt of the notice resulted from the use of the noncomplying means.

**(b)** This subsection applies if a receiving bank other than the beneficiary's bank fails to execute a payment order despite the existence on the execution date of a withdrawable credit balance in an authorized account of the sender sufficient to cover the order. If the sender does not receive notice of rejection of the order on the execution date and the authorized account of the sender does not bear interest, the bank is obliged to pay interest to the sender on the amount of the order for the number of days elapsing after the execution date to the earlier of the day the order is cancelled pursuant to Section 4A–211(d) or the day the sender receives notice or learns that the order was not executed, counting the final day of the period as an elapsed day. If the withdrawable credit balance during that period falls below the amount of the order, the amount of interest is reduced accordingly.

**(c)** If a receiving bank suspends payments, all unaccepted payment orders issued to it are are deemed rejected at the time the bank suspends payments.

**(d)** Acceptance of a payment order precludes a later rejection of the order. Rejection of a payment order precludes a later acceptance of the order.

### § 4A–211. Cancellation and Amendment of Payment Order.

**(a)** A communication of the sender of a payment order cancelling or amending the order may be transmitted to the receiving bank orally, electronically, or in writing. If a security procedure is in effect between the sender and the receiving bank, the communication is not effective to cancel or amend the order unless the communication is verified pursuant to the security procedure or the bank agrees to the cancellation or amendment.

**(b)** Subject to subsection (a), a communication by the sender cancelling or amending a payment order is effective to cancel or amend the order if notice of the communication is received at a time and in a manner affording the receiving bank a reasonable opportunity to act on the communication before the bank accepts the payment order.

**(c)** After a payment order has been accepted, cancellation or amendment of the order is not effective unless the receiving bank agrees or a funds-transfer system rule allows cancellation or amendment without agreement of the bank.

**(1)** With respect to a payment order accepted by a receiving bank other than the beneficiary's bank, cancellation or amendment is not effective unless a conforming cancellation or amendment of the payment order issued by the receiving bank is also made.

**(2)** With respect to a payment order accepted by the beneficiary's bank, cancellation or amendment is not effective unless the order was issued in execution of an unauthorized payment order, or because of a mistake by a sender in the funds transfer which resulted in the issuance of a payment order (i) that is a duplicate of a payment order previously issued by the sender, (ii) that orders payment to a beneficiary not entitled to receive payment from the originator, or (iii) that orders payment in an amount greater than the amount the beneficiary was entitled to receive from the originator. If the payment order is cancelled or amended, the beneficiary's bank is entitled to recover from the beneficiary any amount paid to the beneficiary to the extent allowed by the law governing mistake and restitution.

**(d)** An unaccepted payment order is cancelled by operation of law at the close of the fifth funds-transfer business day of the receiving bank after the execution date or payment date of the order.

**(e)** A cancelled payment order cannot be accepted. If an accepted payment order is cancelled, the acceptance is nullified and no person has any right or obligation based on the acceptance. Amendment of a payment order is deemed to be cancellation of the original order at the time of amendment and issue of a new payment order in the amended form at the same time.

**(f)** Unless otherwise provided in an agreement of the parties or in a funds-transfer system rule, if the receiving bank, after accepting a payment order, agrees to cancellation or amendment of the order by the sender or is bound by a funds-transfer system rule allowing cancellation or amendment without the bank's agreement, the sender, whether or not cancellation or amendment is effective, is liable to the bank for any loss and expenses, including reasonable attorney's fees, incurred by the bank as a result of the cancellation or amendment or attempted cancellation or amendment.

**(g)** A payment order is not revoked by the death or legal incapacity of the sender unless the receiving bank knows of the death or of an adjudication of incapacity by a court of competent jurisdiction and has reasonable opportunity to act before acceptance of the order.

**(h)** A funds-transfer system rule is not effective to the extent it conflicts with subsection (c)(2).

### § 4A–212. Liability and Duty of Receiving Bank Regarding Unaccepted Payment Order.

If a receiving bank fails to accept a payment order that it is obliged by express agreement to accept, the bank is liable for breach of the agreement to the extent provided in the agreement or in this Article, but does not otherwise have any duty to accept a payment order or, before acceptance, to take any action, or refrain from taking action, with respect to the order except as provided in this Article or by express agreement. Liability based on acceptance arises only when acceptance occurs as stated in Section 4A–209, and liability is limited to that provided in this Article. A receiving bank is not the agent of the sender or beneficiary of the payment order it accepts, or of any other party to the funds transfer, and the bank owes no duty to any party to the funds transfer except as provided in this Article or by express agreement.

### Part 3—Execution of Sender's Payment Order by Receiving Bank

### § 4A–301. Execution and Execution Date.

**(a)** A payment order is "executed" by the receiving bank when it issues a payment order intended to carry out the payment order received by the bank. A payment order received by the beneficiary's bank can be accepted but cannot be executed.

**(b)** "Execution date" of a payment order means the day on which the receiving bank may properly issue a payment order in execution of the sender's order. The execution date may be determined by instruction of the sender but cannot be ear-

lier than the day the order is received and, unless otherwise determined, is the day the order is received. If the sender's instruction states a payment date, the execution date is the payment date or an earlier date on which execution is reasonably necessary to allow payment to the beneficiary on the payment date.

### § 4A–302. Obligations of Receiving Bank in Execution of Payment Order.

**(a)** Except as provided in subsections (b) through (d), if the receiving bank accepts a payment order pursuant to Section 4A–209(a), the bank has the following obligations in executing the order:

> **(1)** The receiving bank is obliged to issue, on the execution date, a payment order complying with the sender's order and to follow the sender's instructions concerning (i) any intermediary bank or funds-transfer system to be used in carrying out the funds transfer, or (ii) the means by which payment orders are to be transmitted in the funds transfer. If the originator's bank issues a payment order to an intermediary bank, the originator's bank is obliged to instruct the intermediary bank according to the instruction of the originator. An intermediary bank in the funds transfer is similarly bound by an instruction given to it by the sender of the payment order it accepts.
>
> **(2)** If the sender's instruction states that the funds transfer is to be carried out telephonically or by wire transfer or otherwise indicates that the funds transfer is to be carried out by the most expeditious means, the receiving bank is obliged to transmit its payment order by the most expeditious available means, and to instruct any intermediary bank accordingly. If a sender's instruction states a payment date, the receiving bank is obliged to transmit its payment order at a time and by means reasonably necessary to allow payment to the beneficiary on the payment date or as soon thereafter as is feasible.

**(b)** Unless otherwise instructed, a receiving bank executing a payment order may (i) use any funds-transfer system if use of that system is reasonable in the circumstances, and (ii) issue a payment order to the beneficiary's bank or to an intermediary bank through which a payment order conforming to the sender's order can expeditiously be issued to the beneficiary's bank if the receiving bank exercises ordinary care in the selection of the intermediary bank. A receiving bank is not required to follow an instruction of the sender designating a funds-transfer system to be used in carrying out the funds transfer if the receiving bank, in good faith, determines that it is not feasible to follow the instruction or that following the instruction would unduly delay completion of the funds transfer.

**(c)** Unless subsection (a)(2) applies or the receiving bank is otherwise instructed, the bank may execute a payment order by transmitting its payment order by first class mail or by any means reasonable in the circumstances. If the receiving bank is instructed to execute the sender's order by transmitting its payment order by a particular means, the receiving bank may issue its payment order by the means stated or by any means as expeditious as the means stated.

**(d)** Unless instructed by the sender, (i) the receiving bank may not obtain payment of its charges for services and expenses in connection with the execution of the sender's order by issuing a payment order in an amount equal to the amount of the sender's order less the amount of the charges, and (ii) may not instruct a subsequent receiving bank to obtain payment of its charges in the same manner.

### § 4A–303. Erroneous Execution of Payment Order.

(a) A receiving bank that (i) executes the payment order of the sender by issuing a payment order in an amount greater than the amount of the sender's order, or (ii) issues a payment order in execution of the sender's order and then issues a duplicate order, is entitled to payment of the amount of the sender's order under Section 4A–402(c) if that subsection is otherwise satisfied. The bank is entitled to recover from the beneficiary of the erroneous order the excess payment received to the extent allowed by the law governing mistake and restitution.

(b) A receiving bank that executes the payment order of the sender by issuing a payment order in an amount less than the amount of the sender's order is entitled to payment of the amount of the sender's order under Section 4A–402(c) if (i) that subsection is otherwise satisfied and (ii) the bank corrects its mistake by issuing an additional payment order for the benefit of the beneficiary of the sender's order. If the error is not corrected, the issuer of the erroneous order is entitled to receive or retain payment from the sender of the order it accepted only to the extent of the amount of the erroneous order. This subsection does not apply if the receiving bank executes the sender's payment order by issuing a payment order in an amount less than the amount of the sender's order for the purpose of obtaining payment of its charges for services and expenses pursuant to instruction of the sender.

(c) If a receiving bank executes the payment order of the sender by issuing a payment order to a beneficiary different from the beneficiary of the sender's order and the funds transfer is completed on the basis of that error, the sender of the payment order that was erroneously executed and all previous senders in the funds transfer are not obliged to pay the payment orders they issued. The issuer of the erroneous order is entitled to recover from the beneficiary of the order the payment received to the extent allowed by the law governing mistake and restitution.

### § 4A–304. Duty of Sender to Report Erroneously Executed Payment Order.

If the sender of a payment order that is erroneously executed as stated in Section 4A–303 receives notification from the receiving bank that the order was executed or that the sender's account was debited with respect to the order, the sender has a duty to exercise ordinary care to determine, on the basis of information available to the sender, that the order was erroneously executed and to notify the bank of the relevant facts within a reasonable time not exceeding 90 days after the notification from the bank was received by the sender. If the sender fails to perform that duty, the bank is not obliged to pay interest on any amount refundable to the sender under Section 4A–402(d) for the period before the bank learns of the execution error. The bank is not entitled to any recovery from the sender on account of a failure by the sender to perform the duty stated in this section.

### § 4A–305. Liability for Late or Improper Execution or Failure to Execute Payment Order.

(a) If a funds transfer is completed but execution of a payment order by the receiving bank in breach of Section 4A–302 results in delay in payment to the beneficiary, the bank is obliged to pay interest to either the originator or the beneficiary of the funds transfer for the period of delay caused by the improper execution. Except as provided in subsection (c), additional damages are not recoverable.

(b) If execution of a payment order by a receiving bank in breach of Section 4A–302 results in (i) noncompletion of the funds transfer, (ii) failure to use an intermediary bank designated by the originator, or (iii) issuance of a payment order that does not comply with the terms of the payment order of the originator, the bank is liable to the originator for its expenses in the funds transfer and for incidental expenses and interest losses, to the extent not covered by subsection (a), resulting from the improper execution. Except as provided in subsection (c), additional damages are not recoverable.

(c) In addition to the amounts payable under subsections (a) and (b), damages, including consequential damages, are recoverable to the extent provided in an express written agreement of the receiving bank.

(d) If a receiving bank fails to execute a payment order it was obliged by express agreement to execute, the receiving bank is liable to the sender for its expenses in the transaction and for incidental expenses and interest losses resulting from the failure to execute. Additional damages, including consequential damages, are recoverable to the extent provided in an express written agreement of the receiving bank, but are not otherwise recoverable.

(e) Reasonable attorney's fees are recoverable if demand for compensation under subsection (a) or (b) is made and refused before an action is brought on the claim. If a claim is made for breach of an agreement under subsection (d) and the agreement does not provide for damages, reasonable attorney's fees are recoverable if demand for compensation under subsection (d) is made and refused before an action is brought on the claim.

(f) Except as stated in this section, the liability of a receiving bank under subsections (a) and (b) may not be varied by agreement.

### Part 4—Payment

### § 4A–401. Payment Date.

"Payment date" of a payment order means the day on which the amount of the order is payable to the beneficiary by the beneficiary's bank. The payment date may be determined by instruction of the sender but cannot be earlier than the day the order is received by the beneficiary's bank and, unless otherwise determined, is the day the order is received by the beneficiary's bank.

### § 4A–402. Obligation of Sender to Pay Receiving Bank.

(a) This section is subject to Sections 4A–205 and 4A–207.

(b) With respect to a payment order issued to the beneficiary's bank, acceptance of the order by the bank obliges the sender to pay the bank the amount of the order, but payment is not due until the payment date of the order.

(c) This subsection is subject to subsection (e) and to Section 4A–303. With respect to a payment order issued to a receiving bank other than the beneficiary's bank, acceptance of the order by the receiving bank obliges the sender to pay the bank the amount of the sender's order. Payment by the sender is not due until the execution date of the sender's order. The obligation of that sender to pay its payment order is excused if the funds transfer is not completed by acceptance by the beneficiary's bank of a payment order instructing payment to the beneficiary of that sender's payment order.

(d) If the sender of a payment order pays the order and was not obliged to pay all or part of the amount paid, the bank receiving payment is obliged to refund payment to the extent the sender was not obliged to pay. Except as provided in Sections 4A–204 and 4A–304, interest is payable on the refundable amount from the date of payment.

(e) If a funds transfer is not completed as stated in subsection (c) and an intermediary bank is obliged to refund payment as stated in subsection (d) but is unable to do so because not permitted by applicable law or because the bank suspends payments, a sender in the funds transfer that executed a payment order in compliance with an instruction, as stated in Section 4A–302(a)(1), to route the funds transfer through that intermediary bank is entitled to receive or retain payment from the sender of the payment order that it accepted. The first sender in the funds transfer that issued an instruction requiring routing through that intermediary bank is subrogated to the right of the bank that paid the intermediary bank to refund as stated in subsection (d).

(f) The right of the sender of a payment order to be excused from the obligation to pay the order as stated in subsection (c) or to receive refund under subsection (d) may not be varied by agreement.

### § 4A–403. Payment by Sender to Receiving Bank.

(a) Payment of the sender's obligation under Section 4A–402 to pay the receiving bank occurs as follows:

(1) If the sender is a bank, payment occurs when the receiving bank receives final settlement of the obligation through a Federal Reserve Bank or through a funds-transfer system.

(2) If the sender is a bank and the sender (i) credited an account of the receiving bank with the sender, or (ii) caused an account of the receiving bank in another bank to be credited, payment occurs when the credit is withdrawn or, if not withdrawn, at midnight of the day on which the credit is withdrawable and the receiving bank learns of that fact.

(3) If the receiving bank debits an account of the sender with the receiving bank, payment occurs when the debit is made to the extent the debit is covered by a withdrawable credit balance in the account.

(b) If the sender and receiving bank are members of a funds-transfer system that nets obligations multilaterally among participants, the receiving bank receives final settlement when settlement is complete in accordance with the rules of the system. The obligation of the sender to pay the amount of a payment order transmitted through the funds-transfer system may be satisfied, to the extent permitted by the rules of the system, by setting off and applying against the sender's obligation the right of the sender to receive payment from the receiving bank of the amount of any other payment order transmitted to the sender by the receiving bank through the funds-transfer system. The aggregate balance of obligations owed by each sender to each receiving bank in the funds-transfer system may be satisfied, to the extent permitted by the rules of the system, by setting off and applying against that balance the aggregate balance of obligations owed to the sender by other members of the system. The aggregate balance is determined after the right of setoff stated in the second sentence of this subsection has been exercised.

(c) If two banks transmit payment orders to each other under an agreement that settlement of the obligations of each bank to the other under Section 4A–402 will be made at the end of the day or other period, the total amount owed with respect to all orders transmitted by one bank shall be set off against the total amount owed with respect to all orders transmitted by the other bank. To the extent of the setoff, each bank has made payment to the other.

(d) In a case not covered by subsection (a), the time when payment of the sender's obligation under Section 4A–402(b) or 4A–402(c) occurs is governed by applicable principles of law that determine when an obligation is satisfied.

### § 4A–404. Obligation of Beneficiary's Bank to Pay and Give Notice to Beneficiary.

(a) Subject to Sections 4A–211(e), 4A–405(d), and 4A–405(e), if a beneficiary's bank accepts a payment order, the bank is obliged to pay the amount of the order to the beneficiary of the order. Payment is due on the payment date of the order, but if acceptance occurs on the payment date after the close of the funds-transfer business day of the bank, payment is due on the next funds-transfer business day. If the bank refuses to pay after demand by the beneficiary and receipt of notice of particular circumstances that will give rise to consequential damages as a result of nonpayment, the beneficiary may recover damages resulting from the refusal to pay to the extent the bank had notice of the damages, unless the bank proves that it did not pay because of a reasonable doubt concerning the right of the beneficiary to payment.

(b) If a payment order accepted by the beneficiary's bank instructs payment to an account of the beneficiary, the bank is obliged to notify the beneficiary of receipt of the order before midnight of the next funds-transfer business day following the payment date. If the payment order does not instruct payment to an account of the beneficiary, the bank is required to notify the beneficiary only if notice is required by the order. Notice may be given by first class mail or any other means reasonable in the circumstances. If the bank fails to give the required notice, the bank is obliged to pay interest to the beneficiary on the amount of the payment order from the day notice should have been given until the day the beneficiary learned of receipt of the payment order by the bank. No other damages are recoverable. Reasonable attorney's fees are also recoverable if demand for interest is made and refused before an action is brought on the claim.

(c) The right of a beneficiary to receive payment and damages as stated in subsection (a) may not be varied by agreement or a funds-transfer system rule. The right of a beneficiary to be notified as stated in subsection (b) may be varied by agreement of the beneficiary or by a funds-transfer system rule if the beneficiary is notified of the rule before initiation of the funds transfer.

### § 4A–405. Payment by Beneficiary's Bank to Beneficiary.

(a) If the beneficiary's bank credits an account of the beneficiary of a payment order, payment of the bank's obligation under Section 4A–404(a) occurs when and to the extent (i) the beneficiary is notified of the right to withdraw the credit, (ii) the bank lawfully applies the credit to a debt of the beneficiary, or (iii) funds with respect to the order are otherwise made available to the beneficiary by the bank.

(b) If the beneficiary's bank does not credit an account of the beneficiary of a payment order, the time when payment of the bank's obligation under Section 4A–404(a) occurs is governed by principles of law that determine when an obligation is satisfied.

(c) Except as stated in subsections (d) and (e), if the beneficiary's bank pays the beneficiary of a payment order under a condition to payment or agreement of the beneficiary giving the bank the right to recover payment from the beneficiary if the bank does not receive payment of the order, the condition to payment or agreement is not enforceable.

(d) A funds-transfer system rule may provide that payments made to beneficiaries of funds transfers made through the system are provisional until receipt of payment by the beneficiary's bank of the payment order it accepted. A beneficiary's bank that makes a payment that is provisional under the rule is entitled to refund from the beneficiary if (i) the rule requires that both the beneficiary and the originator be given notice of the provisional nature of the payment before the funds transfer is initiated, (ii) the beneficiary, the beneficiary's bank, and the originator's bank agreed to be bound by the rule, and (iii) the beneficiary's bank did not receive payment of the payment order that it accepted. If the beneficiary is obliged to refund payment to the beneficiary's bank, acceptance of the payment order by the beneficiary's bank is nullified and no payment by the originator of the funds transfer to the beneficiary occurs under Section 4A–406.

(e) This subsection applies to a funds transfer that includes a payment order transmitted over a funds-transfer system that (i) nets obligations multilaterally among participants, and (ii) has in effect a loss-sharing agreement among participants for the purpose of providing funds necessary to complete settlement of the obligations of one or more participants that do not meet their settlement obligations. If the beneficiary's bank in the funds transfer accepts a payment order and the system fails to complete settlement pursuant to its rules with respect to any payment order in the funds transfer, (i) the acceptance by the beneficiary's bank is nullified and no person has any right or obligation based on the acceptance, (ii) the beneficiary's bank is entitled to recover payment from the beneficiary, (iii) no payment by the originator to the beneficiary occurs under Section 4A–406, and (iv) subject to Section 4A–402(e), each sender in

the funds transfer is excused from its obligation to pay its payment order under Section 4A–402(c) because the funds transfer has not been completed.

### § 4A–406. Payment by Originator to Beneficiary; Discharge of Underlying Obligation.

(a) Subject to Sections 4A–211(e), 4A–405(d), and 4A–405(e), the originator of a funds transfer pays the beneficiary of the originator's payment order (i) at the time a payment order for the benefit of the beneficiary is accepted by the beneficiary's bank in the funds transfer and (ii) in an amount equal to the amount of the order accepted by the beneficiary's bank, but not more than the amount of the originator's order.

(b) If payment under subsection (a) is made to satisfy an obligation, the obligation is discharged to the same extent discharge would result from payment to the beneficiary of the same amount in money, unless (i) the payment under subsection (a) was made by a means prohibited by the contract of the beneficiary with respect to the obligation, (ii) the beneficiary, within a reasonable time after receiving notice of receipt of the order by the beneficiary's bank, notified the originator of the beneficiary's refusal of the payment, (iii) funds with respect to the order were not withdrawn by the beneficiary or applied to a debt of the beneficiary, and (iv) the beneficiary would suffer a loss that could reasonably have been avoided if payment had been made by a means complying with the contract. If payment by the originator does not result in discharge under this section, the originator is subrogated to the rights of the beneficiary to receive payment from the beneficiary's bank under Section 4A–404(a).

(c) For the purpose of determining whether discharge of an obligation occurs under subsection (b), if the beneficiary's bank accepts a payment order in an amount equal to the amount of the originator's payment order less charges of one or more receiving banks in the funds transfer, payment to the beneficiary is deemed to be in the amount of the originator's order unless upon demand by the beneficiary the originator does not pay the beneficiary the amount of the deducted charges.

(d) Rights of the originator or of the beneficiary of a funds transfer under this section may be varied only by agreement of the originator and the beneficiary.

### Part 5—Miscellaneous Provisions

### § 4A–501. Variation by Agreement and Effect of Funds-Transfer System Rule.

(a) Except as otherwise provided in this Article, the rights and obligations of a party to a funds transfer may be varied by agreement of the affected party.

(b) "Funds-transfer system rule" means a rule of an association of banks (i) governing transmission of payment orders by means of a funds-transfer system of the association or rights and obligations with respect to those orders, or (ii) to the extent the rule governs rights and obligations between banks that are parties to a funds transfer in which a Federal Reserve Bank, acting as an intermediary bank, sends a payment order to the beneficiary's bank. Except as otherwise provided in this Article, a funds-transfer system rule governing rights and obligations between participating banks using the system may be effective even if the rule conflicts with this Article and indirectly affects another party to the funds transfer who does not consent to the rule. A funds-transfer system rule may also govern rights and obligations of parties other than participating banks using the system to the extent stated in Sections 4A–404(c), 4A–405(d), and 4A–507(c).

### § 4A–502. Creditor Process Served on Receiving Bank; Setoff by Beneficiary's Bank.

(a) As used in this section, "creditor process" means levy, attachment, garnishment, notice of lien, sequestration, or similar process issued by or on behalf of a creditor or other claimant with respect to an account.

(b) This subsection applies to creditor process with respect to an authorized account of the sender of a payment order if the creditor process is served on the receiving bank. For the purpose of determining rights with respect to the creditor process, if the receiving bank accepts the payment order the balance in the authorized account is deemed to be reduced by the amount of the payment order to the extent the bank did not otherwise receive payment of the order, unless the creditor process is served at a time and in a manner affording the bank a reasonable opportunity to act on it before the bank accepts the payment order.

(c) If a beneficiary's bank has received a payment order for payment to the beneficiary's account in the bank, the following rules apply:

(1) The bank may credit the beneficiary's account. The amount credited may be set off against an obligation owed by the beneficiary to the bank or may be applied to satisfy creditor process served on the bank with respect to the account.

(2) The bank may credit the beneficiary's account and allow withdrawal of the amount credited unless creditor process with respect to the account is served at a time and in a manner affording the bank a reasonable opportunity to act to prevent withdrawal.

(3) If creditor process with respect to the beneficiary's account has been served and the bank has had a reasonable opportunity to act on it, the bank may not reject the payment order except for a reason unrelated to the service of process.

(d) Creditor process with respect to a payment by the originator to the beneficiary pursuant to a funds transfer may be served only on the beneficiary's bank with respect to the debt owed by that bank to the beneficiary. Any other bank served with the creditor process is not obliged to act with respect to the process.

### § 4A–503. Injunction or Restraining Order with Respect to Funds Transfer.

For proper cause and in compliance with applicable law, a court may restrain (i) a person from issuing a payment order to initiate a funds transfer, (ii) an originator's bank from executing the payment order of the originator, or (iii) the beneficiary's bank from releasing funds to the beneficiary or the beneficiary from withdrawing the funds. A court may not otherwise restrain a person from issuing a payment order, paying or receiving payment of a payment order, or otherwise acting with respect to a funds transfer.

### § 4A–504. Order in Which Items and Payment Orders May Be Charged to Account; Order of Withdrawals from Account.

(a) If a receiving bank has received more than one payment order of the sender or one or more payment orders and other items that are payable from the sender's account, the bank may charge the sender's account with respect to the various orders and items in any sequence.

(b) In determining whether a credit to an account has been withdrawn by the holder of the account or applied to a debt of the holder of the account, credits first made to the account are first withdrawn or applied.

### § 4A–505. Preclusion of Objection to Debit of Customer's Account.

If a receiving bank has received payment from its customer with respect to a payment order issued in the name of the customer as sender and accepted by the bank, and the customer received notification reasonably identifying the order, the customer is precluded from asserting that the bank is not entitled to retain the payment unless the customer notifies the bank of the customer's objection to the payment within one year after the notification was received by the customer.

### § 4A–506. Rate of Interest.

(a) If, under this Article, a receiving bank is obliged to pay interest with respect to a payment order issued to the bank, the amount payable may be determined (i) by agreement of the sender and receiving bank, or (ii) by a funds-transfer system rule if the payment order is transmitted through a funds-transfer system.

(b) If the amount of interest is not determined by an agreement or rule as stated in subsection (a), the amount is calculated by multiplying the applicable Federal Funds rate by the amount on which interest is payable, and then multiplying the product by the number of days for which interest is payable. The applicable Federal Funds rate is the average of the Federal Funds rates published by the Federal Reserve Bank of New York for each of the days for which interest is payable divided by 360. The Federal Funds rate for any day on which a published rate is not available is the same as the published rate for the next preceding day for which there is a published rate. If a receiving bank that accepted a payment order is required to refund payment to the sender of the order because the funds transfer was not completed, but the failure to complete was not due to any fault by the bank, the interest payable is reduced by a percentage equal to the reserve requirement on deposits of the receiving bank.

### § 4A–507. Choice of Law.

(a) The following rules apply unless the affected parties otherwise agree or subsection (c) applies:

(1) The rights and obligations between the sender of a payment order and the receiving bank are governed by the law of the jurisdiction in which the receiving bank is located.

(2) The rights and obligations between the beneficiary's bank and the beneficiary are governed by the law of the jurisdiction in which the beneficiary's bank is located.

(3) The issue of when payment is made pursuant to a funds transfer by the originator to the beneficiary is governed by

the law of the jurisdiction in which the beneficiary's bank is located.

**(b)** If the parties described in each paragraph of subsection (a) have made an agreement selecting the law of a particular jurisdiction to govern rights and obligations between each other, the law of that jurisdiction governs those rights and obligations, whether or not the payment order or the funds transfer bears a reasonable relation to that jurisdiction.

**(c)** A funds-transfer system rule may select the law of a particular jurisdiction to govern (i) rights and obligations between participating banks with respect to payment orders transmitted or processed through the system, or (ii) the rights and obligations of some or all parties to a funds transfer any part of which is carried out by means of the system. A choice of law made pursuant to clause (i) is binding on participating banks. A choice of law made pursuant to clause (ii) is binding on the originator, other sender, or a receiving bank having notice that the funds-transfer system might be used in the funds transfer and of the choice of law by the system when the originator, other sender, or receiving bank issued or accepted a payment order. The beneficiary of a funds transfer is bound by the choice of law if, when the funds transfer is initiated, the beneficiary has notice that the funds-transfer system might be used in the funds transfer and of the choice of law by the system. The law of a jurisdiction selected pursuant to this subsection may govern, whether or not that law bears a reasonable relation to the matter in issue.

**(d)** In the event of inconsistency between an agreement under subsection (b) and a choice-of-law rule under subsection (c), the agreement under subsection (b) prevails.

**(e)** If a funds transfer is made by use of more than one funds-transfer system and there is inconsistency between choice-of-law rules of the systems, the matter in issue is governed by the law of the selected jurisdiction that has the most significant relationship to the matter in issue.

## REVISED ARTICLE 5: LETTERS OF CREDIT

### § 5–101 Short Title.
This article may be cited as Uniform Commercial Code—Letters of Credit.

### § 5–102. Definitions.
**(a)** In this article:

(1) "Adviser" means a person who, at the request of the issuer, a confirmer, or another adviser, notifies or requests another adviser to notify the beneficiary that a letter of credit has been issued, confirmed, or amended.

(2) "Applicant" means a person at whose request or for whose account a letter of credit is issued. The term includes a person who requests an issuer to issue a letter of credit on behalf of another if the person making the request undertakes an obligation to reimburse the issuer.

(3) "Beneficiary" means a person who under the terms of a letter of credit is entitled to have its complying presentation honored. The term includes a person to whom drawing rights have been transferred under a transferable letter of credit.

(4) "Confirmer" means a nominated person who undertakes, at the request or with the consent of the issuer, to honor a presentation under a letter of credit issued by another.

(5) "Dishonor" of a letter of credit means failure timely to honor or to take an interim action, such as acceptance of a draft, that may be required by the letter of credit.

(6) "Document" means a draft or other demand, document of title, investment security, certificate, invoice, or other record, statement, or representation of fact, law, right, or opinion (i) which is presented in a written or other medium permitted by the letter of credit or, unless prohibited by the letter of credit, by the standard practice referred to in Section 5–108(e) and (ii) which is capable of being examined for compliance with the terms and conditions of the letter of credit. A document may not be oral.

(7) "Good faith" means honesty in fact in the conduct or transaction concerned.

(8) "Honor" of a letter of credit means performance of the issuer's undertaking in the letter of credit to pay or deliver an item of value. Unless the letter of credit otherwise provides, "honor" occurs

(i) upon payment,

(ii) if the letter of credit provides for acceptance, upon acceptance of a draft and, at maturity, its payment, or

(iii) if the letter of credit provides for incurring a deferred obligation, upon incurring the obligation and, at maturity, its performance.

(9) "Issuer" means a bank or other person that issues a letter of credit, but does not include an individual who makes an engagement for personal, family, or household purposes.

(10) "Letter of credit" means a definite undertaking that satisfies the requirements of Section 5–104 by an issuer to a beneficiary at the request or for the account of an applicant or, in the case of a financial institution, to itself or for its own account, to honor a documentary presentation by payment or delivery of an item of value.

(11) "Nominated person" means a person whom the issuer (i) designates or authorizes to pay, accept, negotiate, or otherwise give value under a letter of credit and (ii) undertakes by agreement or custom and practice to reimburse.

(12) "Presentation" means delivery of a document to an issuer or nominated person for honor or giving of value under a letter of credit.

(13) "Presenter" means a person making a presentation as or on behalf of a beneficiary or nominated person.

(14) "Record" means information that is inscribed on a tangible medium, or that is stored in an electronic or other medium and is retrievable in perceivable form.

(15) "Successor of a beneficiary" means a person who succeeds to substantially all of the rights of a beneficiary by operation of law, including a corporation with or into which the beneficiary has been merged or consolidated, an administrator, executor, personal representative, trustee in bankruptcy, debtor in possession, liquidator, and receiver.

**(b)** Definitions in other Articles applying to this article and the sections in which they appear are:

"Accept" or "Acceptance" Section 3–409

"Value" Sections 3–303, 4–211

**(c)** Article 1 contains certain additional general definitions and principles of construction and interpretation applicable throughout this article.

### § 5–103. Scope.
**(a)** This article applies to letters of credit and to certain rights and obligations arising out of transactions involving letters of credit.

**(b)** The statement of a rule in this article does not by itself require, imply, or negate application of the same or a different rule to a situation not provided for, or to a person not specified, in this article.

**(c)** With the exception of this subsection, subsections (a) and (d), Sections 5–102(a)(9) and (10), 5–106(d), and 5–114(d), and except to the extent prohibited in Sections 1–102(3) and 5–117(d), the effect of this article may be varied by agreement or by a provision stated or incorporated by reference in an undertaking. A term in an agreement or undertaking generally excusing liability or generally limiting remedies for failure to perform obligations is not sufficient to vary obligations prescribed by this article.

**(d)** Rights and obligations of an issuer to a beneficiary or a nominated person under a letter of credit are independent of the existence, performance, or nonperformance of a contract or arrangement out of which the letter of credit arises or which underlies it, including contracts or arrangements between the issuer and the applicant and between the applicant and the beneficiary.

### § 5–104. Formal Requirements.
A letter of credit, confirmation, advice, transfer, amendment, or cancellation may be issued in any form that is a record and is authenticated (i) by a signature or (ii) in accordance with the agreement of the parties or the standard practice referred to in Section 5–108(e).

### § 5–105. Consideration.
Consideration is not required to issue, amend, transfer, or cancel a letter of credit, advice, or confirmation.

### § 5–106. Issuance, Amendment, Cancellation, and Duration.
**(a)** A letter of credit is issued and becomes enforceable according to its terms against the issuer when the issuer sends or otherwise transmits it to the person requested to advise or to the beneficiary. A letter of credit is revocable only if it so provides.

**(b)** After a letter of credit is issued, rights and obligations of a beneficiary, applicant, confirmer, and issuer are not affected by an amendment or cancellation to which that person has not consented except to the extent the letter of credit provides that it is revocable or that the issuer may amend or cancel the letter of credit without that consent.

**(c)** If there is no stated expiration date or other provision that determines its duration, a letter of credit expires one year after its stated date of issuance or, if none is stated, after the date on which it is issued.

**(d)** A letter of credit that states that it is perpetual expires five years after its stated date of issuance, or if none is stated, after the date on which it is issued.

### § 5–107. Confirmer, Nominated Person, and Adviser.
**(a)** A confirmer is directly obligated on a letter of credit and has the rights and obligations of an issuer to the extent of its confirmation. The confirmer also has rights against and obligations to the issuer as if the issuer were an applicant and the confirmer had issued the letter of credit at the request and for the account of the issuer.

**(b)** A nominated person who is not a confirmer is not obligated to honor or otherwise give value for a presentation.

**(c)** A person requested to advise may decline to act as an adviser. An adviser that is not a confirmer is not obligated to honor or give value for a presentation. An adviser undertakes to the issuer and to the beneficiary accurately to advise the terms of the letter of credit, confirmation, amendment, or advice received by that person and undertakes to the beneficiary to check the apparent authenticity of the request to advise. Even if the advice is inaccurate, the letter of credit, confirmation, or amendment is enforceable as issued.

**(d)** A person who notifies a transferee beneficiary of the terms of a letter of credit, confirmation, amendment, or advice has the rights and obligations of an adviser under subsection (c). The terms in the notice to the transferee beneficiary may differ from the terms in any notice to the transferor beneficiary to the extent permitted by the letter of credit, confirmation, amendment, or advice received by the person who so notifies.

### § 5–108. Issuer's Rights and Obligations.
**(a)** Except as otherwise provided in Section 5–109, an issuer shall honor a presentation that, as determined by the standard practice referred to in subsection (e), appears on its face strictly to comply with the terms and conditions of the letter of credit. Except as otherwise provided in Section 5–113 and unless otherwise agreed with the applicant, an issuer shall dishonor a presentation that does not appear so to comply.

**(b)** An issuer has a reasonable time after presentation, but not beyond the end of the seventh business day of the issuer after the day of its receipt of documents:
>**(1)** to honor,
>**(2)** if the letter of credit provides for honor to be completed more than seven business days after presentation, to accept a draft or incur a deferred obligation, or
>**(3)** to give notice to the presenter of discrepancies in the presentation.

**(c)** Except as otherwise provided in subsection (d), an issuer is precluded from asserting as a basis for dishonor any discrepancy if timely notice is not given, or any discrepancy not stated in the notice if timely notice is given.

**(d)** Failure to give the notice specified in subsection (b) or to mention fraud, forgery, or expiration in the notice does not preclude the issuer from asserting as a basis for dishonor fraud or forgery as described in Section 5–109(a) or expiration of the letter of credit before presentation.

**(e)** An issuer shall observe standard practice of financial institutions that regularly issue letters of credit. Determination of the issuer's observance of the standard practice is a matter of interpretation for the court. The court shall offer the parties a reasonable opportunity to present evidence of the standard practice.

**(f)** An issuer is not responsible for:

**(1)** the performance or nonperformance of the underlying contract, arrangement, or transaction,

**(2)** an act or omission of others, or

**(3)** observance or knowledge of the usage of a particular trade other than the standard practice referred to in subsection (e).

**(g)** If an undertaking constituting a letter of credit under Section 5–102(a)(10) contains nondocumentary conditions, an issuer shall disregard the nondocumentary conditions and treat them as if they were not stated.

**(h)** An issuer that has dishonored a presentation shall return the documents or hold them at the disposal of, and send advice to that effect to, the presenter.

**(i)** An issuer that has honored a presentation as permitted or required by this article:

**(1)** is entitled to be reimbursed by the applicant in immediately available funds not later than the date of its payment of funds;

**(2)** takes the documents free of claims of the beneficiary or presenter;

**(3)** is precluded from asserting a right of recourse on a draft under Sections 3–414 and 3–415;

**(4)** except as otherwise provided in Sections 5–110 and 5–117, is precluded from restitution of money paid or other value given by mistake to the extent the mistake concerns discrepancies in the documents or tender which are apparent on the face of the presentation; and

**(5)** is discharged to the extent of its performance under the letter of credit unless the issuer honored a presentation in which a required signature of a beneficiary was forged.

### § 5–109. Fraud and Forgery.

**(a)** If a presentation is made that appears on its face strictly to comply with the terms and conditions of the letter of credit, but a required document is forged or materially fraudulent, or honor of the presentation would facilitate a material fraud by the beneficiary on the issuer or applicant:

**(1)** the issuer shall honor the presentation, if honor is demanded by (i) a nominated person who has given value in good faith and without notice of forgery or material fraud, (ii) a confirmer who has honored its confirmation in good faith, (iii) a holder in due course of a draft drawn under the letter of credit which was taken after acceptance by the issuer or nominated person, or (iv) an assignee of the issuer's or nominated person's deferred obligation that was taken for value and without notice of forgery or material fraud after the obligation was incurred by the issuer or nominated person; and

**(2)** the issuer, acting in good faith, may honor or dishonor the presentation in any other case.

**(b)** If an applicant claims that a required document is forged or materially fraudulent or that honor of the presentation would facilitate a material fraud by the beneficiary on the issuer or applicant, a court of competent jurisdiction may temporarily or permanently enjoin the issuer from honoring a presentation or grant similar relief against the issuer or other persons only if the court finds that:

**(1)** the relief is not prohibited under the law applicable to an accepted draft or deferred obligation incurred by the issuer;

**(2)** a beneficiary, issuer, or nominated person who may be adversely affected is adequately protected against loss that it may suffer because the relief is granted;

**(3)** all of the conditions to entitle a person to the relief under the law of this State have been met; and

**(4)** on the basis of the information submitted to the court, the applicant is more likely than not to succeed under its claim of forgery or material fraud and the person demanding honor does not qualify for protection under subsection (a)(1).

### § 5–110. Warranties.

**(a)** If its presentation is honored, the beneficiary warrants:

**(1)** to the issuer, any other person to whom presentation is made, and the applicant that there is no fraud or forgery of the kind described in Section 5–109(a); and

**(2)** to the applicant that the drawing does not violate any agreement between the applicant and beneficiary or any other agreement intended by them to be augmented by the letter of credit.

**(b)** The warranties in subsection (a) are in addition to warranties arising under Article 3, 4, 7, and 8 because of the presentation or transfer of documents covered by any of those articles.

### § 5–111. Remedies.

**(a)** If an issuer wrongfully dishonors or repudiates its obligation to pay money under a letter of credit before presentation, the beneficiary, successor, or nominated person presenting on its own behalf may recover from the issuer the amount that is the subject of the dishonor or repudiation. If the issuer's obligation under the letter of credit is not for the payment of money, the claimant may obtain specific performance or, at the claimant's election, recover an amount equal to the value of performance from the issuer. In either case, the claimant may also recover incidental but not consequential damages. The claimant is not obligated to take action to avoid damages that might be due from the issuer under this subsection. If, although not obligated to do so, the claimant avoids damages, the claimant's recovery from the issuer must be reduced by the amount of damages avoided. The issuer has the burden of proving the amount of damages avoided. In the case of repudiation the claimant need not present any document.

**(b)** If an issuer wrongfully dishonors a draft or demand presented under a letter of credit or honors a draft or demand in breach of its obligation to the applicant, the applicant may recover damages resulting from the breach, including incidental but not consequential damages, less any amount saved as a result of the breach.

**(c)** If an adviser or nominated person other than a confirmer breaches an obligation under this article or an issuer breaches an obligation not covered in subsection (a) or (b), a person to whom the obligation is owed may recover damages resulting from the breach, including incidental but not consequential damages, less any amount saved as a result of the breach. To the extent of the confirmation, a confirmer has the liability of an issuer specified in this subsection and subsections (a) and (b).

**(d)** An issuer, nominated person, or adviser who is found liable under subsection (a), (b), or (c) shall pay interest on the amount owed thereunder from the date of wrongful dishonor or other appropriate date.

**(e)** Reasonable attorney's fees and other expenses of litigation must be awarded to the prevailing party in an action in which a remedy is sought under this article.

**(f)** Damages that would otherwise be payable by a party for breach of an obligation under this article may be liquidated by agreement or undertaking, but only in an amount or by a formula that is reasonable in light of the harm anticipated.

## § 5–112. Transfer of Letter of Credit.

**(a)** Except as otherwise provided in Section 5–113, unless a letter of credit provides that it is transferable, the right of a beneficiary to draw or otherwise demand performance under a letter of credit may not be transferred.

**(b)** Even if a letter of credit provides that it is transferable, the issuer may refuse to recognize or carry out a transfer if:

  **(1)** the transfer would violate applicable law; or

  **(2)** the transferor or transferee has failed to comply with any requirement stated in the letter of credit or any other requirement relating to transfer imposed by the issuer which is within the standard practice referred to in Section 5–108(e) or is otherwise reasonable under the circumstances.

## § 5–113. Transfer by Operation of Law.

**(a)** A successor of a beneficiary may consent to amendments, sign and present documents, and receive payment or other items of value in the name of the beneficiary without disclosing its status as a successor.

**(b)** A successor of a beneficiary may consent to amendments, sign and present documents, and receive payment or other items of value in its own name as the disclosed successor of the beneficiary. Except as otherwise provided in subsection (e), an issuer shall recognize a disclosed successor of a beneficiary as beneficiary in full substitution for its predecessor upon compliance with the requirements for recognition by the issuer of a transfer of drawing rights by operation of law under the standard practice referred to in Section 5–108(e) or, in the absence of such a practice, compliance with other reasonable procedures sufficient to protect the issuer.

**(c)** An issuer is not obliged to determine whether a purported successor is a successor of a beneficiary or whether the signature of a purported successor is genuine or authorized.

**(d)** Honor of a purported successor's apparently complying presentation under subsection (a) or (b) has the consequences specified in Section 5–108(i) even if the purported successor is not the successor of a beneficiary. Documents signed in the name of the beneficiary or of a disclosed successor by a person who is neither the beneficiary nor the successor of the beneficiary are forged documents for the purposes of Section 5–109.

**(e)** An issuer whose rights of reimbursement are not covered by subsection (d) or substantially similar law and any confirmer or nominated person may decline to recognize a presentation under subsection (b).

**(f)** A beneficiary whose name is changed after the issuance of a letter of credit has the same rights and obligations as a successor of a beneficiary under this section.

## § 5–114. Assignment of Proceeds.

**(a)** In this section, "proceeds of a letter of credit" means the cash, check, accepted draft, or other item of value paid or delivered upon honor or giving of value by the issuer or any nominated person under the letter of credit. The term does not include a beneficiary's drawing rights or documents presented by the beneficiary.

**(b)** A beneficiary may assign its right to part or all of the proceeds of a letter of credit. The beneficiary may do so before presentation as a present assignment of its right to receive proceeds contingent upon its compliance with the terms and conditions of the letter of credit.

**(c)** An issuer or nominated person need not recognize an assignment of proceeds of a letter of credit until it consents to the assignment.

**(d)** An issuer or nominated person has no obligation to give or withhold its consent to an assignment of proceeds of a letter of credit, but consent may not be unreasonably withheld if the assignee possesses and exhibits the letter of credit and presentation of the letter of credit is a condition to honor.

**(e)** Rights of a transferee beneficiary or nominated person are independent of the beneficiary's assignment of the proceeds of a letter of credit and are superior to the assignee's right to the proceeds.

**(f)** Neither the rights recognized by this section between an assignee and an issuer, transferee beneficiary, or nominated person nor the issuer's or nominated person's payment of proceeds to an assignee or a third person affect the rights between the assignee and any person other than the issuer, transferee beneficiary, or nominated person. The mode of creating and perfecting a security interest in or granting an assignment of a beneficiary's rights to proceeds is governed by Article 9 or other law. Against persons other than the issuer, transferee beneficiary, or nominated person, the rights and obligations arising upon the creation of a security interest or other assignment of a beneficiary's right to proceeds and its perfection are governed by Article 9 or other law.

## § 5–115. Statute of Limitations.

An action to enforce a right or obligation arising under this article must be commenced within one year after the expiration date of the relevant letter of credit or one year after the [claim for relief] [cause of action] accrues, whichever occurs later. A [claim for relief] [cause of action] accrues when the breach occurs, regardless of the aggrieved party's lack of knowledge of the breach.

## § 5–116. Choice of Law and Forum.

**(a)** The liability of an issuer, nominated person, or adviser for action or omission is governed by the law of the jurisdiction chosen by an agreement in the form of a record signed or otherwise authenticated by the affected parties in the manner provided in Section 5–104 or by a provision in the person's letter of credit, confirmation, or other undertaking. The jurisdiction whose law is chosen need not bear any relation to the transaction.

**(b)** Unless subsection (a) applies, the liability of an issuer, nominated person, or adviser for action or omission is governed by the law of the jurisdiction in which the person is located. The person is considered to be located at the address indicated in the person's undertaking. If more than one address is indicated, the person is considered to be located at the address from which the person's undertaking was issued. For the purpose of jurisdiction, choice of law, and recognition of interbranch letters of credit, but not enforcement of a judgment, all branches of a bank are considered separate juridical entities and a bank is considered to be located at the place where its relevant branch is considered to be located under this subsection.

**(c)** Except as otherwise provided in this subsection, the liability of an issuer, nominated person, or adviser is governed by any rules of custom or practice, such as the Uniform Customs and Practice for Documentary Credits, to which the letter of credit, confirmation, or other undertaking is expressly made subject. If (i) this article would govern the liability of an issuer, nominated person, or adviser under subsection (a) or (b), (ii) the relevant undertaking incorporates rules of custom or practice, and (iii) there is conflict between this article and those rules as applied to that undertaking, those rules govern except to the extent of any conflict with the nonvariable provisions specified in Section 5–103(c).

**(d)** If there is conflict between this article and Article 3, 4, 4A, or 9, this article governs.

**(e)** The forum for settling disputes arising out of an undertaking within this article may be chosen in the manner and with the binding effect that governing law may be chosen in accordance with subsection (a).

## § 5–117. Subrogation of Issuer, Applicant, and Nominated Person.

**(a)** An issuer that honors a beneficiary's presentation is subrogated to the rights of the beneficiary to the same extent as if the issuer were a secondary obligor of the underlying obligation owed to the beneficiary and of the applicant to the same extent as if the issuer were the secondary obligor of the underlying obligation owed to the applicant.

**(b)** An applicant that reimburses an issuer is subrogated to the rights of the issuer against any beneficiary, presenter, or nominated person to the same extent as if the applicant were the secondary obligor of the obligations owed to the issuer and has the rights of subrogation of the issuer to the rights of the beneficiary stated in subsection (a).

**(c)** A nominated person who pays or gives value against a draft or demand presented under a letter of credit is subrogated to the rights of:

(1) the issuer against the applicant to the same extent as if the nominated person were a secondary obligor of the obligation owed to the issuer by the applicant;

(2) the beneficiary to the same extent as if the nominated person were a secondary obligor of the underlying obligation owed to the beneficiary; and

(3) the applicant to same extent as if the nominated person were a secondary obligor of the underlying obligation owed to the applicant.

**(d)** Notwithstanding any agreement or term to the contrary, the rights of subrogation stated in subsections (a) and (b) do not arise until the issuer honors the letter of credit or otherwise pays and the rights in subsection (c) do not arise until the nominated person pays or otherwise gives value. Until then, the issuer, nominated person, and the applicant do not derive under this section present or prospective rights forming the basis of a claim, defense, or excuse.

## § 5–118. Security Interest of Issuer or Nominated Person.

**(a)** An issuer or nominated person has a security interest in a document presented under a letter of credit to the extent that the issuer or nominated person honors or gives value for the presentation.

**(b)** So long as and to the extent that an issuer or nominated person has not been reimbursed or has not otherwise recovered the value given with respect to a security interest in a document under subsection (a), the security interest continues and is subject to Article 9, but:

(1) a security agreement is not necessary to make the security interest enforceable under Section 9–203(b)(3);

(2) if the document is presented in a medium other than a written or other tangible medium, the security interest is perfected; and

(3) if the document is presented in a written or other tangible medium and is not a certificated security, chattel paper, a document of title, an instrument, or a letter of credit, the security interest is perfected and has priority over a conflicting security interest in the document so long as the debtor does not have possession of the document.

As added in 1999.

### Transition Provisions

### § [  ]. Effective Date.
This [Act] shall become effective on _____, 20__.

### § [  ]. Repeal.
This [Act] [repeals] [amends] [insert citation to existing Article 5].

### § [  ]. Applicability.
This [Act] applies to a letter of credit that is issued on or after the effective date of this [Act]. This [Act] does not apply to a transaction, event, obligation, or duty arising out of or associated with a letter of credit that was issued before the effective date of this [Act].

### § [  ]. Savings Clause.
A transaction arising out of or associated with a letter of credit that was issued before the effective date of this [Act] and the rights, obligations, and interests flowing from that transaction are governed by any statute or other law amended or repealed by this [Act] as if repeal or amendment had not occurred and may be terminated, completed, consummated, or enforced under that statute or other law.

## REPEALER OF ARTICLE 6

**BULK TRANSFERS and [Revised] ARTICLE 6 BULK SALES (States to Select One Alternative)**

**Alternative A**

### § 1. Repeal
Article 6 and Section 9–111 of the Uniform Commercial Code are hereby repealed, effective _____.

## § 2. Amendment

Section 1–105(2) of the Uniform Commercial Code is hereby amended to read as follows:

**(2)** Where one of the following provisions of this Act specifies the applicable law, that provision governs and a contrary agreement is effective only to the extent permitted by the law (including the conflict of laws rules) so specified:

Rights of creditors against sold goods. Section 2–402.

Applicability of the Article on Leases. Section 2A–105 and 2A-106.

Applicability of the Article on Bank Deposits and Collections. Section 4–102.

Applicability of the Article on Investment Securities. Section 8–106.

Perfection provisions of the Article on Secured Transactions. Section 9–103.

## § 3. Amendment.

Section 2–403(4) of the Uniform Commercial Code is hereby amended to read as follows:

**(4)** The rights of other purchasers of goods and of lien creditors are governed by the Articles on Secured Transactions (Article 9) and Documents of Title (Article 7).

## § 4. Savings Clause.

Rights and obligations that arose under Article 6 and Section 9–111 of the Uniform Commercial Code before their repeal remain valid and may be enforced as though those statutes had not been repealed.]

## § 6–101. Short Title.

This Article shall be known and may be cited as Uniform Commercial Code—Bulk Sales.

## § 6–102. Definitions and Index of Definitions.

**(1)** In this Article, unless the context otherwise requires:

**(a)** "Assets" means the inventory that is the subject of a bulk sale and any tangible and intangible personal property used or held for use primarily in, or arising from, the seller's business and sold in connection with that inventory, but the term does not include:

  **(i)** fixtures (Section 9–102(a)(41)) other than readily removable factory and office machines;

  **(ii)** the lessee's interest in a lease of real property; or

  **(iii)** property to the extent it is generally exempt from creditor process under nonbankruptcy law.

**(b)** "Auctioneer" means a person whom the seller engages to direct, conduct, control, or be responsible for a sale by auction.

**(c)** "Bulk sale" means:

  **(i)** in the case of a sale by auction or a sale or series of sales conducted by a liquidator on the seller's behalf, a sale or series of sales not in the ordinary course of the seller's business of more than half of the seller's inventory, as measured by value on the date of the bulk-sale agreement, if on that date the auctioneer or liquidator has notice, or after reasonable inquiry would have had notice, that the seller will not continue to operate the same or a similar kind of business after the sale or series of sales; and

  **(ii)** in all other cases, a sale not in the ordinary course of the seller's business of more than half the seller's inventory, as measured by value on the date of the bulk-sale agreement, if on that date the buyer has notice, or after reasonable inquiry would have had notice, that the seller will not continue to operate the same or a similar kind of business after the sale.

**(d)** "Claim" means a right to payment from the seller, whether or not the right is reduced to judgment, liquidated, fixed, matured, disputed, secured, legal, or equitable. The term includes costs of collection and attorney's fees only to the extent that the laws of this state permit the holder of the claim to recover them in an action against the obligor.

**(e)** "Claimant" means a person holding a claim incurred in the seller's business other than:

  **(i)** an unsecured and unmatured claim for employment compensation and benefits, including commissions and vacation, severance, and sick-leave pay;

  **(ii)** a claim for injury to an individual or to property, or for breach of warranty, unless:

    **(A)** a right of action for the claim has accrued;

    **(B)** the claim has been asserted against the seller; and

    **(C)** the seller knows the identity of the person asserting the claim and the basis upon which the person has asserted it; and

(States to Select One Alternative)

*Alternative A*

[**(iii)** a claim for taxes owing to a governmental unit.]

*Alternative B*

[**(iii)** a claim for taxes owing to a governmental unit, if:

    **(A)** a statute governing the enforcement of the claim permits or requires notice of the bulk sale to be given to the governmental unit in a manner other than by compliance with the requirements of this Article; and

    **(B)** notice is given in accordance with the statute.]

**(f)** "Creditor" means a claimant or other person holding a claim.

**(g)(i)** "Date of the bulk sale" means:

    **(A)** if the sale is by auction or is conducted by a liquidator on the seller's behalf, the date on which more than ten percent of the net proceeds is paid to or for the benefit of the seller; and

    **(B)** in all other cases, the later of the date on which:

      **(I)** more than ten percent of the net contract price is paid to or for the benefit of the seller; or

      **(II)** more than ten percent of the assets, as measured by value, are transferred to the buyer.

  **(ii)** For purposes of this subsection:

    **(A)** delivery of a negotiable instrument (Section 3–104(1)) to or for the benefit of the seller in exchange for assets constitutes payment of the contract price pro tanto;

    **(B)** to the extent that the contract price is deposited in an escrow, the contract price is paid to or for the benefit of the seller when the seller acquires the unconditional right to receive the deposit or when the deposit is delivered to the seller or for the benefit of the seller, whichever is earlier; and

**(C)** an asset is transferred when a person holding an unsecured claim can no longer obtain through judicial proceedings rights to the asset that are superior to those of the buyer arising as a result of the bulk sale. A person holding an unsecured claim can obtain those superior rights to a tangible asset at least until the buyer has an unconditional right, under the bulk-sale agreement, to possess the asset, and a person holding an unsecured claim can obtain those superior rights to an intangible asset at least until the buyer has an unconditional right, under the bulk-sale agreement, to use the asset.

**(h)** "Date of the bulk-sale agreement" means:

**(i)** in the case of a sale by auction or conducted by a liquidator (subsection (c)(i)), the date on which the seller engages the auctioneer or liquidator; and

**(ii)** in all other cases, the date on which a bulk-sale agreement becomes enforceable between the buyer and the seller.

**(i)** "Debt" means liability on a claim.

**(j)** "Liquidator" means a person who is regularly engaged in the business of disposing of assets for businesses contemplating liquidation or dissolution.

**(k)** "Net contract price" means the new consideration the buyer is obligated to pay for the assets less:

**(i)** the amount of any proceeds of the sale of an asset, to the extent the proceeds are applied in partial or total satisfaction of a debt secured by the asset; and

**(ii)** the amount of any debt to the extent it is secured by a security interest or lien that is enforceable against the asset before and after it has been sold to a buyer. If a debt is secured by an asset and other property of the seller, the amount of the debt secured by a security interest or lien that is enforceable against the asset is determined by multiplying the debt by a fraction, the numerator of which is the value of the new consideration for the asset on the date of the bulk sale and the denominator of which is the value of all property securing the debt on the date of the bulk sale.

**(l)** "Net proceeds" means the new consideration received for assets sold at a sale by auction or a sale conducted by a liquidator on the seller's behalf less:

**(i)** commissions and reasonable expenses of the sale;

**(ii)** the amount of any proceeds of the sale of an asset, to the extent the proceeds are applied in partial or total satisfaction of a debt secured by the asset; and

**(iii)** the amount of any debt to the extent it is secured by a security interest or lien that is enforceable against the asset before and after it has been sold to a buyer. If a debt is secured by an asset and other property of the seller, the amount of the debt secured by a security interest or lien that is enforceable against the asset is determined by multiplying the debt by a fraction, the numerator of which is the value of the new consideration for the asset on the date of the bulk sale and the denominator of which is the value of all property securing the debt on the date of the bulk sale.

**(m)** A sale is "in the ordinary course of the seller's business" if the sale comports with usual or customary practices in the kind of business in which the seller is engaged or with the seller's own usual or customary practices.

**(n)** "United States" includes its territories and possessions and the Commonwealth of Puerto Rico.

**(o)** "Value" means fair market value.

**(p)** "Verified" means signed and sworn to or affirmed.

**(2)** The following definitions in other Articles apply to this Article:

| | | |
|---|---|---|
| **(a)** | "Buyer." | Section 2–103(1)(a). |
| **(b)** | "Equipment." | Section 9–102(a)(33). |
| **(c)** | "Inventory." | Section 9–102(a)(48). |
| **(d)** | "Sale." | Section 2–106(1). |
| **(e)** | "Seller." | Section 2–103(1)(d). |

**(3)** In addition, Article 1 contains general definitions and principles of construction and interpretation applicable throughout this Article.

As amended in 1999.

### § 6–103. Applicability of Article.

**(1)** Except as otherwise provided in subsection (3), this Article applies to a bulk sale if:

**(a)** the seller's principal business is the sale of inventory from stock; and

**(b)** on the date of the bulk-sale agreement the seller is located in this state or, if the seller is located in a jurisdiction that is not a part of the United States, the seller's major executive office in the United States is in this state.

**(2)** A seller is deemed to be located at his [or her] place of business. If a seller has more than one place of business, the seller is deemed located at his [or her] chief executive office.

**(3)** This Article does not apply to:

**(a)** a transfer made to secure payment or performance of an obligation;

**(b)** a transfer of collateral to a secured party pursuant to Section 9–503;

**(c)** a disposition of collateral pursuant to Section 9–610;

**(d)** retention of collateral pursuant to Section 9–620;

**(e)** a sale of an asset encumbered by a security interest or lien if (i) all the proceeds of the sale are applied in partial or total satisfaction of the debt secured by the security interest or lien or (ii) the security interest or lien is enforceable against the asset after it has been sold to the buyer and the net contract price is zero;

**(f)** a general assignment for the benefit of creditors or to a subsequent transfer by the assignee;

**(g)** a sale by an executor, administrator, receiver, trustee in bankruptcy, or any public officer under judicial process;

**(h)** a sale made in the course of judicial or administrative proceedings for the dissolution or reorganization of an organization;

**(i)** a sale to a buyer whose principal place of business is in the United States and who:

**(i)** not earlier than 21 days before the date of the bulk sale, (A) obtains from the seller a verified and dated list of claimants of whom the seller has notice three days before the seller sends or delivers the list to the buyer or (B) conducts a reasonable inquiry to discover the claimants;

**(ii)** assumes in full the debts owed to claimants of whom the buyer has knowledge on the date the buyer receives the list of claimants from the seller or on the date the buyer completes the reasonable inquiry, as the case may be;

**(iii)** is not insolvent after the assumption; and

**(iv)** gives written notice of the assumption not later than 30 days after the date of the bulk sale by sending or delivering a notice to the claimants identified in subparagraph (ii) or by filing a notice in the office of the [Secretary of State];

**(j)** a sale to a buyer whose principal place of business is in the United States and who:

**(i)** assumes in full the debts that were incurred in the seller's business before the date of the bulk sale;

**(ii)** is not insolvent after the assumption; and

**(iii)** gives written notice of the assumption not later than 30 days after the date of the bulk sale by sending or delivering a notice to each creditor whose debt is assumed or by filing a notice in the office of the [Secretary of State];

**(k)** a sale to a new organization that is organized to take over and continue the business of the seller and that has its principal place of business in the United States if:

**(i)** the buyer assumes in full the debts that were incurred in the seller's business before the date of the bulk sale;

**(ii)** the seller receives nothing from the sale except an interest in the new organization that is subordinate to the claims against the organization arising from the assumption; and

**(iii)** the buyer gives written notice of the assumption not later than 30 days after the date of the bulk sale by sending or delivering a notice to each creditor whose debt is assumed or by filing a notice in the office of the [Secretary of State];

**(l)** a sale of assets having:

**(i)** a value, net of liens and security interests, of less than $10,000. If a debt is secured by assets and other property of the seller, the net value of the assets is determined by subtracting from their value an amount equal to the product of the debt multiplied by a fraction, the numerator of which is the value of the assets on the date of the bulk sale and the denominator of which is the value of all property securing the debt on the date of the bulk sale; or

**(ii)** a value of more than $25,000,000 on the date of the bulk-sale agreement; or

**(m)** a sale required by, and made pursuant to, statute.

**(4)** The notice under subsection (3)(i)(iv) must state:(i) that a sale that may constitute a bulk sale has been or will be made; (ii) the date or prospective date of the bulk sale; (iii) the individual, partnership, or corporate names and the addresses of the seller and buyer; (iv) the address to which inquiries about the sale may be made, if different from the seller's address; and (v) that the buyer has assumed or will assume in full the debts

owed to claimants of whom the buyer has knowledge on the date the buyer receives the list of claimants from the seller or completes a reasonable inquiry to discover the claimants.

**(5)** The notice under subsections (3)(j)(iii) and (3)(k)(iii) must state: (i) that a sale that may constitute a bulk sale has been or will be made; (ii) the date or prospective date of the bulk sale; (iii) the individual, partnership, or corporate names and the addresses of the seller and buyer; (iv) the address to which inquiries about the sale may be made, if different from the seller's address; and (v) that the buyer has assumed or will assume the debts that were incurred in the seller's business before the date of the bulk sale.

**(6)** For purposes of subsection (3)(l), the value of assets is presumed to be equal to the price the buyer agrees to pay for the assets. However, in a sale by auction or a sale conducted by a liquidator on the seller's behalf, the value of assets is presumed to be the amount the auctioneer or liquidator reasonably estimates the assets will bring at auction or upon liquidation.
As amended in 1999.

### § 6–104. Obligations of Buyer.

**(1)** In a bulk sale as defined in Section 6–102(1)(c)(ii) the buyer shall:

**(a)** obtain from the seller a list of all business names and addresses used by the seller within three years before the date the list is sent or delivered to the buyer;

**(b)** unless excused under subsection (2), obtain from the seller a verified and dated list of claimants of whom the seller has notice three days before the seller sends or delivers the list to the buyer and including, to the extent known by the seller, the address of and the amount claimed by each claimant;

**(c)** obtain from the seller or prepare a schedule of distribution (Section 6–106(1));

**(d)** give notice of the bulk sale in accordance with Section 6–105;

**(e)** unless excused under Section 6–106(4), distribute the net contract price in accordance with the undertakings of the buyer in the schedule of distribution; and

**(f)** unless excused under subsection (2), make available the list of claimants (subsection (1)(b)) by:

**(i)** promptly sending or delivering a copy of the list without charge to any claimant whose written request is received b]y the buyer no later than six months after the date of the bulk sale;

**(ii)** permitting any claimant to inspect and copy the list at any reasonable hour upon request received by the buyer no later than six months after the date of the bulk sale; or

**(iii)** filing a copy of the list in the office of the [Secretary of State] no later than the time for giving a notice of the bulk sale (Section 6–105(5)). A list filed in accordance with this subparagraph must state the individual, partnership, or corporate name and a mailing address of the seller.

**(2)** A buyer who gives notice in accordance with Section 6–105(2) is excused from complying with the requirements of subsections (1)(b) and (1)(f).

## § 6–105. **Notice to Claimants.**

**(1)** Except as otherwise provided in subsection (2), to comply with Section 6–104(1)(d) the buyer shall send or deliver a written notice of the bulk sale to each claimant on the list of claimants (Section 6–104(1)(b)) and to any other claimant of which the buyer has knowledge at the time the notice of the bulk sale is sent or delivered.

**(2)** A buyer may comply with Section 6–104(1)(d) by filing a written notice of the bulk sale in the office of the [Secretary of State] if:

> **(a)** on the date of the bulk-sale agreement the seller has 200 or more claimants, exclusive of claimants holding secured or matured claims for employment compensation and benefits, including commissions and vacation, severance, and sick-leave pay; or
>
> **(b)** the buyer has received a verified statement from the seller stating that, as of the date of the bulk-sale agreement, the number of claimants, exclusive of claimants holding secured or matured claims for employment compensation and benefits, including commissions and vacation, severance, and sick-leave pay, is 200 or more.

**(3)** The written notice of the bulk sale must be accompanied by a copy of the schedule of distribution (Section 6–106(1)) and state at least:

> **(a)** that the seller and buyer have entered into an agreement for a sale that may constitute a bulk sale under the laws of the State of _____ ;
>
> **(b)** the date of the agreement;
>
> **(c)** the date on or after which more than ten percent of the assets were or will be transferred;
>
> **(d)** the date on or after which more than ten percent of the net contract price was or will be paid, if the date is not stated in the schedule of distribution;
>
> **(e)** the name and a mailing address of the seller;
>
> **(f)** any other business name and address listed by the seller pursuant to Section 6–104(1)(a);
>
> **(g)** the name of the buyer and an address of the buyer from which information concerning the sale can be obtained;
>
> **(h)** a statement indicating the type of assets or describing the assets item by item;
>
> **(i)** the manner in which the buyer will make available the list of claimants (Section 6–104(1)(f)), if applicable; and
>
> **(j)** if the sale is in total or partial satisfaction of an antecedent debt owed by the seller, the amount of the debt to be satisfied and the name of the person to whom it is owed.

**(4)** For purposes of subsections (3)(e) and (3)(g), the name of a person is the person's individual, partnership, or corporate name.

**(5)** The buyer shall give notice of the bulk sale not less than 45 days before the date of the bulk sale and, if the buyer gives notice in accordance with subsection (1), not more than 30 days after obtaining the list of claimants.

**(6)** A written notice substantially complying with the requirements of subsection (3) is effective even though it contains minor errors that are not seriously misleading.

**(7)** A form substantially as follows is sufficient to comply with subsection (3):

*Notice of Sale*

**(1)** _____, whose address is _____, is described in this notice as the "seller."

**(2)** _____, whose address is _____, is described in this notice as the "buyer."

**(3)** The seller has disclosed to the buyer that within the past three years the seller has used other business names, operated at other addresses, or both, as follows: _____

_____ .

**(4)** The seller and the buyer have entered into an agreement dated _____, for a sale that may constitute a bulk sale under the laws of the state of _____.

**(5)** The date on or after which more than ten percent of the assets that are the subject of the sale were or will be transferred is _____, and [if not stated in the schedule of distribution] the date on or after which more than ten percent of the net contract price was or will be paid is _____ .

**(6)** The following assets are the subject of the sale: _____ .

**(7)** [If applicable] The buyer will make available to claimants of the seller a list of the seller's claimants in the following manner: _____ .

**(8)** [If applicable] The sale is to satisfy $ _____ of an antecedent debt owed by the seller to _____ .

**(9)** A copy of the schedule of distribution of the net contract price accompanies this notice.

*[End of Notice]*

## § 6–106. **Schedule of Distribution.**

**(1)** The seller and buyer shall agree on how the net contract price is to be distributed and set forth their agreement in a written schedule of distribution.

**(2)** The schedule of distribution may provide for distribution to any person at any time, including distribution of the entire net contract price to the seller.

**(3)** The buyer's undertakings in the schedule of distribution run only to the seller. However, a buyer who fails to distribute the net contract price in accordance with the buyer's undertakings in the schedule of distribution is liable to a creditor only as provided in Section 6–107(1).

**(4)** If the buyer undertakes in the schedule of distribution to distribute any part of the net contract price to a person other than the seller, and, after the buyer has given notice in accordance with Section 6–105, some or all of the anticipated net contract price is or becomes unavailable for distribution as a consequence of the buyer's or seller's having complied with an order of court, legal process, statute, or rule of law, the buyer is excused from any obligation arising under this Article or under any contract with the seller to distribute the net contract price in accordance with the buyer's undertakings in the schedule if the buyer:

> **(a)** distributes the net contract price remaining available in accordance with any priorities for payment stated in the schedule of distribution and, to the extent that the price is insufficient to pay all the debts having a given priority, distributes the price pro rata among those debts shown in the schedule as having the same priority;

(b) distributes the net contract price remaining available in accordance with an order of court;

(c) commences a proceeding for interpleader in a court of competent jurisdiction and is discharged from the proceeding; or

(d) reaches a new agreement with the seller for the distribution of the net contract price remaining available, sets forth the new agreement in an amended schedule of distribution, gives notice of the amended schedule, and distributes the net contract price remaining available in accordance with the buyer's undertakings in the amended schedule.

(5) The notice under subsection (4)(d) must identify the buyer and the seller, state the filing number, if any, of the original notice, set forth the amended schedule, and be given in accordance with subsection (1) or (2) of Section 6–105, whichever is applicable, at least 14 days before the buyer distributes any part of the net contract price remaining available.

(6) If the seller undertakes in the schedule of distribution to distribute any part of the net contract price, and, after the buyer has given notice in accordance with Section 6–105, some or all of the anticipated net contract price is or becomes unavailable for distribution as a consequence of the buyer's or seller's having complied with an order of court, legal process, statute, or rule of law, the seller and any person in control of the seller are excused from any obligation arising under this Article or under any agreement with the buyer to distribute the net contract price in accordance with the seller's undertakings in the schedule if the seller:

(a) distributes the net contract price remaining available in accordance with any priorities for payment stated in the schedule of distribution and, to the extent that the price is insufficient to pay all the debts having a given priority, distributes the price pro rata among those debts shown in the schedule as having the same priority;

(b) distributes the net contract price remaining available in accordance with an order of court;

(c) commences a proceeding for interpleader in a court of competent jurisdiction and is discharged from the proceeding; or

(d) prepares a written amended schedule of distribution of the net contract price remaining available for distribution, gives notice of the amended schedule, and distributes the net contract price remaining available in accordance with the amended schedule.

(7) The notice under subsection (6)(d) must identify the buyer and the seller, state the filing number, if any, of the original notice, set forth the amended schedule, and be given in accordance with subsection (1) or (2) of Section 6–105, whichever is applicable, at least 14 days before the seller distributes any part of the net contract price remaining available.

## § 6–107. Liability for Noncompliance.

(1) Except as provided in subsection (3), and subject to the limitation in subsection (4):

(a) a buyer who fails to comply with the requirements of Section 6–104(1)(e) with respect to a creditor is liable to the creditor for damages in the amount of the claim,

reduced by any amount that the creditor would not have realized if the buyer had complied; and

(b) a buyer who fails to comply with the requirements of any other subsection of Section 6–104 with respect to a claimant is liable to the claimant for damages in the amount of the claim, reduced by any amount that the claimant would not have realized if the buyer had complied.

(2) In an action under subsection (1), the creditor has the burden of establishing the validity and amount of the claim, and the buyer has the burden of establishing the amount that the creditor would not have realized if the buyer had complied.

(3) A buyer who:

(a) made a good faith and commercially reasonable effort to comply with the requirements of Section 6–104(1) or to exclude the sale from the application of this Article under Section 6–103(3); or

(b) on or after the date of the bulk-sale agreement, but before the date of the bulk sale, held a good faith and commercially reasonable belief that this Article does not apply to the particular sale is not liable to creditors for failure to comply with the requirements of Section 6–104. The buyer has the burden of establishing the good faith and commercial reasonableness of the effort or belief.

(4) In a single bulk sale the cumulative liability of the buyer for failure to comply with the requirements of Section 6–104(1) may not exceed an amount equal to:

(a) if the assets consist only of inventory and equipment, twice the net contract price, less the amount of any part of the net contract price paid to or applied for the benefit of the seller or a creditor; or

(b) if the assets include property other than inventory and equipment, twice the net value of the inventory and equipment less the amount of the portion of any part of the net contract price paid to or applied for the benefit of the seller or a creditor which is allocable to the inventory and equipment.

(5) For the purposes of subsection (4)(b), the "net value" of an asset is the value of the asset less (i) the amount of any proceeds of the sale of an asset, to the extent the proceeds are applied in partial or total satisfaction of a debt secured by the asset and (ii) the amount of any debt to the extent it is secured by a security interest or lien that is enforceable against the asset before and after it has been sold to a buyer. If a debt is secured by an asset and other property of the seller, the amount of the debt secured by a security interest or lien that is enforceable against the asset is determined by multiplying the debt by a fraction, the numerator of which is the value of the asset on the date of the bulk sale and the denominator of which is the value of all property securing the debt on the date of the bulk sale. The portion of a part of the net contract price paid to or applied for the benefit of the seller or a creditor that is "allocable to the inventory and equipment" is the portion that bears the same ratio to that part of the net contract price as the net value of the inventory and equipment bears to the net value of all of the assets.

(6) A payment made by the buyer to a person to whom the buyer is, or believes he [or she] is, liable under subsection (1) reduces pro tanto the buyer's cumulative liability under subsection (4).

**(7)** No action may be brought under subsection (1)(b) by or on behalf of a claimant whose claim is unliquidated or contingent.

**(8)** A buyer's failure to comply with the requirements of Section 6–104(1) does not (i) impair the buyer's rights in or title to the assets, (ii) render the sale ineffective, void, or voidable, (iii) entitle a creditor to more than a single satisfaction of his [or her] claim, or (iv) create liability other than as provided in this Article.

**(9)** Payment of the buyer's liability under subsection (1) discharges pro tanto the seller's debt to the creditor.

**(10)** Unless otherwise agreed, a buyer has an immediate right of reimbursement from the seller for any amount paid to a creditor in partial or total satisfaction of the buyer's liability under subsection (1).

**(11)** If the seller is an organization, a person who is in direct or indirect control of the seller, and who knowingly, intentionally, and without legal justification fails, or causes the seller to fail, to distribute the net contract price in accordance with the schedule of distribution is liable to any creditor to whom the seller undertook to make payment under the schedule for damages caused by the failure.

### § 6–108. Bulk Sales by Auction; Bulk Sales Conducted by Liquidator.

**(1)** Sections 6–104, 6–105, 6–106, and 6–107 apply to a bulk sale by auction and a bulk sale conducted by a liquidator on the seller's behalf with the following modifications:

    **(a)** "buyer" refers to auctioneer or liquidator, as the case may be;

    **(b)** "net contract price" refers to net proceeds of the auction or net proceeds of the sale, as the case may be;

    **(c)** the written notice required under Section 6–105(3) must be accompanied by a copy of the schedule of distribution (Section 6–106(1)) and state at least:

        **(i)** that the seller and the auctioneer or liquidator have entered into an agreement for auction or liquidation services that may constitute an agreement to make a bulk sale under the laws of the State of _____ ;

        **(ii)** the date of the agreement;

        **(iii)** the date on or after which the auction began or will begin or the date on or after which the liquidator began or will begin to sell assets on the seller's behalf;

        **(iv)** the date on or after which more than ten percent of the net proceeds of the sale were or will be paid, if the date is not stated in the schedule of distribution;

        **(v)** the name and a mailing address of the seller;

        **(vi)** any other business name and address listed by the seller pursuant to Section 6–104(1)(a);

        **(vii)** the name of the auctioneer or liquidator and an address of the auctioneer or liquidator from which information concerning the sale can be obtained;

        **(viii)** a statement indicating the type of assets or describing the assets item by item;

        **(ix)** the manner in which the auctioneer or liquidator will make available the list of claimants (Section 6–104(1)(f)), if applicable; and

        **(x)** if the sale is in total or partial satisfaction of an antecedent debt owed by the seller, the amount of the debt to be satisfied and the name of the person to whom it is owed; and

    **(d)** in a single bulk sale the cumulative liability of the auctioneer or liquidator for failure to comply with the requirements of this section may not exceed the amount of the net proceeds of the sale allocable to inventory and equipment sold less the amount of the portion of any part of the net proceeds paid to or applied for the benefit of a creditor which is allocable to the inventory and equipment.

**(2)** A payment made by the auctioneer or liquidator to a person to whom the auctioneer or liquidator is, or believes he [or she] is, liable under this section reduces pro tanto the auctioneer's or liquidator's cumulative liability under subsection (1)(d).

**(3)** A form substantially as follows is sufficient to comply with subsection (1)(c):

*Notice of Sale*

**(1)** _____, whose address is _____, is described in this notice as the "seller."

**(2)** _____, whose address is _____ , is described in this notice as the "auctioneer" or "liquidator."

**(3)** The seller has disclosed to the auctioneer or liquidator that within the past three years the seller has used other business names, operated at other addresses, or both, as follows: _____ .

**(4)** The seller and the auctioneer or liquidator have entered into an agreement dated _____ for auction or liquidation services that may constitute an agreement to make a bulk sale under the laws of the State of _____ .

**(5)** The date on or after which the auction began or will begin or the date on or after which the liquidator began or will begin to sell assets on the seller's behalf is _____, and [if not stated in the schedule of distribution] the date on or after which more than ten percent of the net proceeds of the sale were or will be paid is _____ .

**(6)** The following assets are the subject of the sale:

_____ .

**(7)** [If applicable] The auctioneer or liquidator will make available to claimants of the seller a list of the seller's claimants in the following manner: _____ .

**(8)** [If applicable] The sale is to satisfy $ _____ of an antecedent debt owed by the seller to _____ .

**(9)** A copy of the schedule of distribution of the net proceeds accompanies this notice.

*[End of Notice]*

**(4)** A person who buys at a bulk sale by auction or conducted by a liquidator need not comply with the requirements of Section 6–104(1) and is not liable for the failure of an auctioneer or liquidator to comply with the requirements of this section.

### § 6–109. What Constitutes Filing; Duties of Filing Officer; Information from Filing Officer.

**(1)** Presentation of a notice or list of claimants for filing and tender of the filing fee or acceptance of the notice or list by the filing officer constitutes filing under this Article.

**(2)** The filing officer shall:

    **(a)** mark each notice or list with a file number and with the date and hour of filing;

    **(b)** hold the notice or list or a copy for public inspection;

    **(c)** index the notice or list according to each name given for the seller and for the buyer; and

**(d)** note in the index the file number and the addresses of the seller and buyer given in the notice or list.

**(3)** If the person filing a notice or list furnishes the filing officer with a copy, the filing officer upon request shall note upon the copy the file number and date and hour of the filing of the original and send or deliver the copy to the person.

**(4)** The fee for filing and indexing and for stamping a copy furnished by the person filing to show the date and place of filing is $ _____ for the first page and $ _____ for each additional page. The fee for indexing each name beyond the first two is $ _____ .

**(5)** Upon request of any person, the filing officer shall issue a certificate showing whether any notice or list with respect to a particular seller or buyer is on file on the date and hour stated in the certificate. If a notice or list is on file, the certificate must give the date and hour of filing of each notice or list and the name and address of each seller, buyer, auctioneer, or liquidator. The fee for the certificate is $ _____ if the request for the certificate is in the standard form prescribed by the [Secretary of State] and otherwise is $ _____ . Upon request of any person, the filing officer shall furnish a copy of any filed notice or list for a fee of $ _____ .

**(6)** The filing officer shall keep each notice or list for two years after it is filed.

### § 6–110. Limitation of Actions.

**(1)** Except as provided in subsection (2), an action under this Article against a buyer, auctioneer, or liquidator must be commenced within one year after the date of the bulk sale.

**(2)** If the buyer, auctioneer, or liquidator conceals the fact that the sale has occurred, the limitation is tolled and an action under this Article may be commenced within the earlier of (i) one year after the person bringing the action discovers that the sale has occurred or (ii) one year after the person bringing the action should have discovered that the sale has occurred, but no later than two years after the date of the bulk sale. Complete noncompliance with the requirements of this Article does not of itself constitute concealment.

**(3)** An action under Section 6–107(11) must be commenced within one year after the alleged violation occurs.

### Conforming Amendment to Section 2–403

States adopting Alternative B should amend Section 2–403(4) of the Uniform Commercial Code to read as follows:

**(4)** The rights of other purchasers of goods and of lien creditors are governed by the Articles on Secured Transactions (Article 9), Bulk Sales (Article 6) and Documents of Title (Article 7).

### ARTICLE 7: WAREHOUSE RECEIPTS, BILLS OF LADING AND OTHER DOCUMENTS OF TITLE

#### Part 1—General

### § 7–101. Short Title.

This Article shall be known and may be cited as Uniform Commercial Code–Documents of Title.

### § 7–102. Definitions and Index of Definitions.

**(1)** In this Article, unless the context otherwise requires:

**(a)** "Bailee" means the person who by a warehouse receipt, bill of lading or other document of title acknowledges possession of goods and contracts to deliver them.

**(b)** "Consignee" means the person named in a bill to whom or to whose order the bill promises delivery.

**(c)** "Consignor" means the person named in a bill as the person from whom the goods have been received for shipment.

**(d)** "Delivery order" means a written order to deliver goods directed to a warehouseman, carrier or other person who in the ordinary course of business issues warehouse receipts or bills of lading.

**(e)** "Document" means document of title as defined in the general definitions in Article 1 (Section 1–201).

**(f)** "Goods" means all things which are treated as movable for the purposes of a contract of storage or transportation.

**(g)** "Issuer" means a bailee who issues a document except that in relation to an unaccepted delivery order it means the person who orders the possessor of goods to deliver. Issuer includes any person for whom an agent or employee purports to act in issuing a document if the agent or employee has real or apparent authority to issue documents, notwithstanding that the issuer received no goods or that the goods were misdescribed or that in any other respect the agent or employee violated his instructions.

**(h)** "Warehouseman" is a person engaged in the business of storing goods for hire.

**(2)** Other definitions applying to this Article or to specified Parts thereof, and the sections in which they appear are:

"Duly negotiate". Section 7–501.

"Person entitled under the document". Section 7–403(4).

**(3)** Definitions in other Articles applying to this Article and the sections in which they appear are:

"Contract for sale". Section 2–106.

"Overseas". Section 2–323.

"Receipt" of goods. Section 2–103.

**(4)** In addition Article 1 contains general definitions and principles of construction and interpretation applicable throughout this Article.

### § 7–103. Relation of Article to Treaty, Statute, Tariff, Classification or Regulation.

To the extent that any treaty or statute of the United States, regulatory statute of this State or tariff, classification or regulation filed or issued pursuant thereto is applicable, the provisions of this Article are subject thereto.

### § 7–104. Negotiable and Non-Negotiable Warehouse Receipt, Bill of Lading or Other Document of Title.

**(1)** A warehouse receipt, bill of lading or other document of title is negotiable

**(a)** if by its terms the goods are to be delivered to bearer or to the order of a named person; or

**(b)** where recognized in overseas trade, if it runs to a named person or assigns.

**(2)** Any other document is nonnegotiable. A bill of lading in which it is stated that the goods are consigned to a named person is not made negotiable by a provision that the goods are to be delivered only against a written order signed by the same or another named person.

### § 7–105. Construction Against Negative Implication.

The omission from either Part 2 or Part 3 of this Article of a provision corresponding to a provision made in the other Part does not imply that a corresponding rule of law is not applicable.

**Part 2—Warehouse Receipts: Special Provisions**

### § 7–201. Who May Issue a Warehouse Receipt; Storage Under Government Bond.

(1) A warehouse receipt may be issued by any warehouseman.

(2) Where goods including distilled spirits and agricultural commodities are stored under a statute requiring a bond against withdrawal or a license for the issuance of receipts in the nature of warehouse receipts, a receipt issued for the goods has like effect as a warehouse receipt even though issued by a person who is the owner of the goods and is not a warehouseman.

### § 7–202. Form of Warehouse Receipt; Essential Terms; Optional Terms.

(1) A warehouse receipt need not be in any particular form.

(2) Unless a warehouse receipt embodies within its written or printed terms each of the following, the warehouseman is liable for damages caused by the omission to a person injured thereby:

    (a) the location of the warehouse where the goods are stored;

    (b) the date of issue of the receipt;

    (c) the consecutive number of the receipt;

    (d) a statement whether the goods received will be delivered to the bearer, to a specified person, or to a specified person or his order;

    (e) the rate of storage and handling charges, except that where goods are stored under a field warehousing arrangement a statement of that fact is sufficient on a non-negotiable receipt;

    (f) a description of the goods or of the packages containing them;

    (g) the signature of the warehouseman, which may be made by his authorized agent;

    (h) if the receipt is issued for goods of which the warehouseman is owner, either solely or jointly or in common with others, the fact of such ownership; and

    (i) a statement of the amount of advances made and of liabilities incurred for which the warehouseman claims a lien or security interest (Section 7–209). If the precise amount of such advances made or of such liabilities incurred is, at the time of the issue of the receipt, unknown to the warehouseman or to his agent who issues it, a statement of the fact that advances have been made or liabilities incurred and the purpose thereof is sufficient.

(3) A warehouseman may insert in his receipt any other terms which are not contrary to the provisions of this Act and do not impair his obligation of delivery (Section 7–403) or his duty of care (Section 7–204). Any contrary provisions shall be ineffective.

### § 7–203. Liability for Non-Receipt or Misdescription.

A party to or purchaser for value in good faith of a document of title other than a bill of lading relying in either case upon the description therein of the goods may recover from the issuer damages caused by the nonreceipt or misdescription of the goods, except to the extent that the document conspicuously indicates that the issuer does not know whether any part or all of the goods in fact were received or conform to the description, as where the description is in terms of marks or labels or kind, quantity or condition, or the receipt or description is qualified by "contents, condition and quality unknown", "said to contain" or the like, if such indication be true, or the party or purchaser otherwise has notice.

### § 7–204. Duty of Care; Contractual Limitation of Warehouseman's Liability.

(1) A warehouseman is liable for damages for loss of or injury to the goods caused by his failure to exercise such care in regard to them as a reasonably careful man would exercise under like circumstances but unless otherwise agreed he is not liable for damages which could not have been avoided by the exercise of such care.

(2) Damages may be limited by a term in the warehouse receipt or storage agreement limiting the amount of liability in case of loss or damage, and setting forth a specific liability per article or item, or value per unit of weight, beyond which the warehouseman shall not be liable; provided, however, that such liability may on written request of the bailor at the time of signing such storage agreement or within a reasonable time after receipt of the warehouse receipt be increased on part or all of the goods thereunder, in which event increased rates may be charged based on such increased valuation, but that no such increase shall be permitted contrary to a lawful limitation of liability contained in the warehouseman's tariff, if any. No such limitation is effective with respect to the warehouseman's liability for conversion to his own use.

(3) Reasonable provisions as to the time and manner of presenting claims and instituting actions based on the bailment may be included in the warehouse receipt or tariff.

(4) This section does not impair or repeal . . .

Note: *Insert in subsection (4) a reference to any statute which imposes a higher responsibility upon the warehouseman or invalidates contractual limitations which would be permissible under this Article.*

### § 7–205. Title Under Warehouse Receipt Defeated in Certain Cases.

A buyer in the ordinary course of business of fungible goods sold and delivered by a warehouseman who is also in the business of buying and selling such goods takes free of any claim under a warehouse receipt even though it has been duly negotiated.

### § 7–206. Termination of Storage at Warehouseman's Option.

(1) A warehouseman may on notifying the person on whose account the goods are held and any other person known to claim an interest in the goods require payment of any charges and removal of the goods from the warehouse at the termination of the period of storage fixed by the document, or, if no period is fixed, within a stated period not less than thirty days after the notification. If the goods are not removed before the date specified in the notification, the warehouseman may sell them in accordance with the provisions of the section on enforcement of a warehouseman's lien (Section 7–210).

**(2)** If a warehouseman in good faith believes that the goods are about to deteriorate or decline in value to less than the amount of his lien within the time prescribed in subsection (1) for notification, advertisement and sale, the warehouseman may specify in the notification any reasonable shorter time for removal of the goods and in case the goods are not removed, may sell them at public sale held not less than one week after a single advertisement or posting.

**(3)** If as a result of a quality or condition of the goods of which the warehouseman had no notice at the time of deposit the goods are a hazard to other property or to the warehouse or to persons, the warehouseman may sell the goods at public or private sale without advertisement on reasonable notification to all persons known to claim an interest in the goods. If the warehouseman after a reasonable effort is unable to sell the goods he may dispose of them in any lawful manner and shall incur no liability by reason of such disposition.

**(4)** The warehouseman must deliver the goods to any person entitled to them under this Article upon due demand made at any time prior to sale or other disposition under this section.

**(5)** The warehouseman may satisfy his lien from the proceeds of any sale or disposition under this section but must hold the balance for delivery on the demand of any person to whom he would have been bound to deliver the goods.

### § 7–207. Goods Must Be Kept Separate; Fungible Goods.

**(1)** Unless the warehouse receipt otherwise provides, a warehouseman must keep separate the goods covered by each receipt so as to permit at all times identification and delivery of those goods except that different lots of fungible goods may be commingled.

**(2)** Fungible goods so commingled are owned in common by the persons entitled thereto and the warehouseman is severally liable to each owner for that owner's share. Where because of overissue a mass of fungible goods is insufficient to meet all the receipts which the warehouseman has issued against it, the persons entitled include all holders to whom overissued receipts have been duly negotiated.

### § 7–208. Altered Warehouse Receipts.

Where a blank in a negotiable warehouse receipt has been filled in without authority, a purchaser for value and without notice of the want of authority may treat the insertion as authorized. Any other unauthorized alteration leaves any receipt enforceable against the issuer according to its original tenor.

### § 7–209. Lien of Warehouseman.

**(1)** A warehouseman has a lien against the bailor on the goods covered by a warehouse receipt or on the proceeds thereof in his possession for charges for storage or transportation (including demurrage and terminal charges), insurance, labor, or charges present or future in relation to the goods, and for expenses necessary for preservation of the goods or reasonably incurred in their sale pursuant to law. If the person on whose account the goods are held is liable for like charges or expenses in relation to other goods whenever deposited and it is stated in the receipt that a lien is claimed for charges and expenses in relation to other goods, the warehouseman also has a lien against him for such charges and expenses whether or not the other goods have been delivered by the warehouseman. But against a person to whom a negotiable warehouse receipt is duly negotiated a warehouseman's lien is limited to charges in an amount or at a rate specified on the receipt or if no charges are so specified then to a reasonable charge for storage of the goods covered by the receipt subsequent to the date of the receipt.

**(2)** The warehouseman may also reserve a security interest against the bailor for a maximum amount specified on the receipt for charges other than those specified in subsection (1), such as for money advanced and interest. Such a security interest is governed by the Article on Secured Transactions (Article 9).

**(3)(a)** A warehouseman's lien for charges and expenses under subsection (1) or a security interest under subsection (2) is also effective against any person who so entrusted the bailor with possession of the goods that a pledge of them by him to a good faith purchaser for value would have been valid but is not effective against a person as to whom the document confers no right in the goods covered by it under Section 7–503.

   **(b)** A warehouseman's lien on household goods for charges and expenses in relation to the goods under subsection (1) is also effective against all persons if the depositor was the legal possessor of the goods at the time of deposit. "Household goods" means furniture, furnishings and personal effects used by the depositor in a dwelling.

**(4)** A warehouseman loses his lien on any goods which he voluntarily delivers or which he unjustifiably refuses to deliver.

### § 7–210. Enforcement of Warehouseman's Lien.

**(1)** Except as provided in subsection (2), a warehouseman's lien may be enforced by public or private sale of the goods in bloc or in parcels, at any time or place and on any terms which are commercially reasonable, after notifying all persons known to claim an interest in the goods. Such notification must include a statement of the amount due, the nature of the proposed sale and the time and place of any public sale. The fact that a better price could have been obtained by a sale at a different time or in a different method from that selected by the warehouseman is not of itself sufficient to establish that the sale was not made in a commercially reasonable manner. If the warehouseman either sells the goods in the usual manner in any recognized market therefor, or if he sells at the price current in such market at the time of his sale, or if he has otherwise sold in conformity with commercially reasonable practices among dealers in the type of goods sold, he has sold in a commercially reasonable manner. A sale of more goods than apparently necessary to be offered to ensure satisfaction of the obligation is not commercially reasonable except in cases covered by the preceding sentence.

**(2)** A warehouseman's lien on goods other than goods stored by a merchant in the course of his business may be enforced only as follows:

   **(a)** All persons known to claim an interest in the goods must be notified.

   **(b)** The notification must be delivered in person or sent by registered or certified letter to the last known address of any person to be notified.

(c) The notification must include an itemized statement of the claim, a description of the goods subject to the lien, a demand for payment within a specified time not less than ten days after receipt of the notification, and a conspicuous statement that unless the claim is paid within the time the goods will be advertised for sale and sold by auction at a specified time and place.

(d) The sale must conform to the terms of the notification.

(e) The sale must be held at the nearest suitable place to that where the goods are held or stored.

(f) After the expiration of the time given in the notification, an advertisement of the sale must be published once a week for two weeks consecutively in a newspaper of general circulation where the sale is to be held. The advertisement must include a description of the goods, the name of the person on whose account they are being held, and the time and place of the sale. The sale must take place at least fifteen days after the first publication. If there is no newspaper of general circulation where the sale is to be held, the advertisement must be posted at least ten days before the sale in not less than six conspicuous places in the neighborhood of the proposed sale.

(3) Before any sale pursuant to this section any person claiming a right in the goods may pay the amount necessary to satisfy the lien and the reasonable expenses incurred under this section. In that event the goods must not be sold, but must be retained by the warehouseman subject to the terms of the receipt and this Article.

(4) The warehouseman may buy at any public sale pursuant to this section.

(5) A purchaser in good faith of goods sold to enforce a warehouseman's lien takes the goods free of any rights of persons against whom the lien was valid, despite noncompliance by the warehouseman with the requirements of this section.

(6) The warehouseman may satisfy his lien from the proceeds of any sale pursuant to this section but must hold the balance, if any, for delivery on demand to any person to whom he would have been bound to deliver the goods.

(7) The rights provided by this section shall be in addition to all other rights allowed by law to a creditor against his debtor.

(8) Where a lien is on goods stored by a merchant in the course of his business the lien may be enforced in accordance with either subsection (1) or (2).

(9) The warehouseman is liable for damages caused by failure to comply with the requirements for sale under this section and in case of willful violation is liable for conversion.

As amended in 1962.

### Part 3—Bills of Lading: Special Provisions

### § 7–301. Liability for Non-Receipt or Misdescription; "Said to Contain"; "Shipper's Load and Count"; Improper Handling.

(1) A consignee of a non-negotiable bill who has given value in good faith or a holder to whom a negotiable bill has been duly negotiated relying in either case upon the description therein of the goods, or upon the date therein shown, may recover from the issuer damages caused by the misdating of the bill or the nonreceipt or misdescription of the goods, except to the extent that the document indicates that the issuer does not know whether any part of all of the goods in fact were received or conform to the description, as where the description is in terms of marks or labels or kind, quantity, or condition or the receipt or description is qualified by "contents or condition of contents of packages unknown", "said to contain", "shipper's weight, load and count" or the like, if such indication be true.

(2) When goods are loaded by an issuer who is a common carrier, the issuer must count the packages of goods if package freight and ascertain the kind and quantity if bulk freight. In such cases "shipper's weight, load and count" or other words indicating that the description was made by the shipper are ineffective except as to freight concealed by packages.

(3) When bulk freight is loaded by a shipper who makes available to the issuer adequate facilities for weighing such freight, an issuer who is a common carrier must ascertain the kind and quantity within a reasonable time after receiving the written request of the shipper to do so. In such cases "shipper's weight" or other words of like purport are ineffective.

(4) The issuer may by inserting in the bill the words "shipper's weight, load and count" or other words of like purport indicate that the goods were loaded by the shipper; and if such statement be true the issuer shall not be liable for damages caused by the improper loading. But their omission does not imply liability for such damages.

(5) The shipper shall be deemed to have guaranteed to the issuer the accuracy at the time of shipment of the description, marks, labels, number, kind, quantity, condition and weight, as furnished by him; and the shipper shall indemnify the issuer against damage caused by inaccuracies in such particulars. The right of the issuer to such indemnity shall in no way limit his responsibility and liability under the contract of carriage to any person other than the shipper.

### § 7–302. Through Bills of Lading and Similar Documents.

(1) The issuer of a through bill of lading or other document embodying an undertaking to be performed in part by persons acting as its agents or by connecting carriers is liable to anyone entitled to recover on the document for any breach by such other persons or by a connecting carrier of its obligation under the document but to the extent that the bill covers an undertaking to be performed overseas or in territory not contiguous to the continental United States or an undertaking including matters other than transportation this liability may be varied by agreement of the parties.

(2) Where goods covered by a through bill of lading or other document embodying an undertaking to be performed in part by persons other than the issuer are received by any such person, he is subject with respect to his own performance while the goods are in his possession to the obligation of the issuer. His obligation is discharged by delivery of the goods to another such person pursuant to the document, and does not include liability for breach by any other such persons or by the issuer.

(3) The issuer of such through bill of lading or other document shall be entitled to recover from the connecting carrier or such other person in possession of the goods when the breach of the obligation under the document occurred, the amount it may be required to pay to anyone entitled to recover on the

document therefor, as may be evidenced by any receipt, judgment, or transcript thereof, and the amount of any expense reasonably incurred by it in defending any action brought by anyone entitled to recover on the document therefor.

### § 7–303. Diversion; Reconsignment; Change of Instructions.

(1) Unless the bill of lading otherwise provides, the carrier may deliver the goods to a person or destination other than that stated in the bill or may otherwise dispose of the goods on instructions from

(a) the holder of a negotiable bill; or

(b) the consignor on a non-negotiable bill not-withstanding contrary instructions from the consignee; or

(c) the consignee on a non-negotiable bill in the absence of contrary instructions from the consignor, if the goods have arrived at the billed destination or if the consignee is in possession of the bill; or

(d) the consignee on a non-negotiable bill if he is entitled as against the consignor to dispose of them.

(2) Unless such instructions are noted on a negotiable bill of lading, a person to whom the bill is duly negotiated can hold the bailee according to the original terms.

### § 7–304. Bills of Lading in a Set.

(1) Except where customary in overseas transportation, a bill of lading must not be issued in a set of parts. The issuer is liable for damages caused by violation of this subsection.

(2) Where a bill of lading is lawfully drawn in a set of parts, each of which is numbered and expressed to be valid only if the goods have not been delivered against any other part, the whole of the parts constitute one bill.

(3) Where a bill of lading is lawfully issued in a set of parts and different parts are negotiated to different persons, the title of the holder to whom the first due negotiation is made prevails as to both the document and the goods even though any later holder may have received the goods from the carrier in good faith and discharged the carrier's obligation by surrender of his part.

(4) Any person who negotiates or transfers a single part of a bill of lading drawn in a set is liable to holders of that part as if it were the whole set.

(5) The bailee is obliged to deliver in accordance with Part 4 of this Article against the first presented part of a bill of lading lawfully drawn in a set. Such delivery discharges the bailee's obligation on the whole bill.

### § 7–305. Destination Bills.

(1) Instead of issuing a bill of lading to the consignor at the place of shipment a carrier may at the request of the consignor procure the bill to be issued at destination or at any other place designated in the request.

(2) Upon request of anyone entitled as against the carrier to control the goods while in transit and on surrender of any outstanding bill of lading or other receipt covering such goods, the issuer may procure a substitute bill to be issued at any place designated in the request.

### § 7–306. Altered Bills of Lading.

An unauthorized alteration or filling in of a blank in a bill of lading leaves the bill enforceable according to its original tenor.

### § 7–307. Lien of Carrier.

(1) A carrier has a lien on the goods covered by a bill of lading for charges subsequent to the date of its receipt of the goods for storage or transportation (including demurrage and terminal charges) and for expenses necessary for preservation of the goods incident to their transportation or reasonably incurred in their sale pursuant to law. But against a purchaser for value of a negotiable bill of lading a carrier's lien is limited to charges stated in the bill or the applicable tariffs, or if no charges are stated then to a reasonable charge.

(2) A lien for charges and expenses under subsection (1) on goods which the carrier was required by law to receive for transportation is effective against the consignor or any person entitled to the goods unless the carrier had notice that the consignor lacked authority to subject the goods to such charges and expenses. Any other lien under subsection (1) is effective against the consignor and any person who permitted the bailor to have control or possession of the goods unless the carrier had notice that the bailor lacked such authority.

(3) A carrier loses his lien on any goods which he voluntarily delivers or which he unjustifiably refuses to deliver.

### § 7–308. Enforcement of Carrier's Lien.

(1) A carrier's lien may be enforced by public or private sale of the goods, in bloc or in parcels, at any time or place and on any terms which are commercially reasonable, after notifying all persons known to claim an interest in the goods. Such notification must include a statement of the amount due, the nature of the proposed sale and the time and place of any public sale. The fact that a better price could have been obtained by a sale at a different time or in a different method from that selected by the carrier is not of itself sufficient to establish that the sale was not made in a commercially reasonable manner. If the carrier either sells the goods in the usual manner in any recognized market therefor or if he sells at the price current in such market at the time of his sale or if he has otherwise sold in conformity with commercially reasonable practices among dealers in the type of goods sold he has sold in a commercially reasonable manner. A sale of more goods than apparently necessary to be offered to ensure satisfaction of the obligation is not commercially reasonable except in cases covered by the preceding sentence.

(2) Before any sale pursuant to this section any person claiming a right in the goods may pay the amount necessary to satisfy the lien and the reasonable expenses incurred under this section. In that event the goods must not be sold, but must be retained by the carrier subject to the terms of the bill and this Article.

(3) The carrier may buy at any public sale pursuant to this section.

(4) A purchaser in good faith of goods sold to enforce a carrier's lien takes the goods free of any rights of persons against whom the lien was valid, despite noncompliance by the carrier with the requirements of this section.

(5) The carrier may satisfy his lien from the proceeds of any sale pursuant to this section but must hold the balance, if any, for delivery on demand to any person to whom he would have been bound to deliver the goods.

(6) The rights provided by this section shall be in addition to all other rights allowed by law to a creditor against his debtor.

**(7)** A carrier's lien may be enforced in accordance with either subsection (1) or the procedure set forth in subsection (2) of Section 7–210.

**(8)** The carrier is liable for damages caused by failure to comply with the requirements for sale under this section and in case of willful violation is liable for conversion.

### § 7–309.  Duty of Care; Contractual Limitation of Carrier's Liability.

**(1)** A carrier who issues a bill of lading whether negotiable or nonnegotiable must exercise the degree of care in relation to the goods which a reasonably careful man would exercise under like circumstances. This subsection does not repeal or change any law or rule of law which imposes liability upon a common carrier for damages not caused by its negligence.

**(2)** Damages may be limited by a provision that the carrier's liability shall not exceed a value stated in the document if the carrier's rates are dependent upon value and the consignor by the carrier's tariff is afforded an opportunity to declare a higher value or a value as lawfully provided in the tariff, or where no tariff is filed he is otherwise advised of such opportunity; but no such limitation is effective with respect to the carrier's liability for conversion to its own use.

**(3)** Reasonable provisions as to the time and manner of presenting claims and instituting actions based on the shipment may be included in a bill of lading or tariff.

### Part 4—Warehouse Receipts and Bills of Lading: General Obligations

### § 7–401.  Irregularities in Issue of Receipt or Bill or Conduct of Issuer.

The obligations imposed by this Article on an issuer apply to a document of title regardless of the fact that

**(a)** the document may not comply with the requirements of this Article or of any other law or regulation regarding its issue, form or content; or

**(b)** the issuer may have violated laws regulating the conduct of his business; or

**(c)** the goods covered by the document were owned by the bailee at the time the document was issued; or

**(d)** the person issuing the document does not come within the definition of warehouseman if it purports to be a warehouse receipt.

### § 7–402.  Duplicate Receipt or Bill; Overissue.

Neither a duplicate nor any other document of title purporting to cover goods already represented by an outstanding document of the same issuer confers any right in the goods, except as provided in the case of bills in a set, overissue of documents for fungible goods and substitutes for lost, stolen or destroyed documents. But the issuer is liable for damages caused by his overissue or failure to identify a duplicate document as such by conspicuous notation on its face.

### § 7–403.  Obligation of Warehouseman or Carrier to Deliver; Excuse.

**(1)** The bailee must deliver the goods to a person entitled under the document who complies with subsections (2) and (3), unless and to the extent that the bailee establishes any of the following:

**(a)** delivery of the goods to a person whose receipt was rightful as against the claimant;

**(b)** damage to or delay, loss or destruction of the goods for which the bailee is not liable [, but the burden of establishing negligence in such cases is on the person entitled under the document];

Note: *The brackets in (1)(b) indicate that State enactments may differ on this point without serious damage to the principle of uniformity.*

**(c)** previous sale or other disposition of the goods in lawful enforcement of a lien or on warehouseman's lawful termination of storage;

**(d)** the exercise by a seller of his right to stop delivery pursuant to the provisions of the Article on Sales (Section 2–705);

**(e)** a diversion, reconsignment or other disposition pursuant to the provisions of this Article (Section 7–303) or tariff regulating such right;

**(f)** release, satisfaction or any other fact affording a personal defense against the claimant;

**(g)** any other lawful excuse.

**(2)** A person claiming goods covered by a document of title must satisfy the bailee's lien where the bailee so requests or where the bailee is prohibited by law from delivering the goods until the charges are paid.

**(3)** Unless the person claiming is one against whom the document confers no right under Sec. 7–503(1), he must surrender for cancellation or notation of partial deliveries any outstanding negotiable document covering the goods, and the bailee must cancel the document or conspicuously note the partial delivery thereon or be liable to any person to whom the document is duly negotiated.

**(4)** "Person entitled under the document" means holder in the case of a negotiable document, or the person to whom delivery is to be made by the terms of or pursuant to written instructions under a non-negotiable document.

### § 7–404.  No Liability for Good Faith Delivery Pursuant to Receipt or Bill.

A bailee who in good faith including observance of reasonable commercial standards has received goods and delivered or otherwise disposed of them according to the terms of the document of title or pursuant to this Article is not liable therefor. This rule applies even though the person from whom he received the goods had no authority to procure the document or to dispose of the goods and even though the person to whom he delivered the goods had no authority to receive them.

### Part 5—Warehouse Receipts and Bills of Lading: Negotiation and Transfer

### § 7–501.  Form of Negotiation and Requirements of "Due Negotiation".

**(1)** A negotiable document of title running to the order of a named person is negotiated by his indorsement and delivery. After his indorsement in blank or to bearer any person can negotiate it by delivery alone.

**(2)(a)** A negotiable document of title is also negotiated by delivery alone when by its original terms it runs to bearer.

**(b)** When a document running to the order of a named person is delivered to him the effect is the same as if the document had been negotiated.

**(3)** Negotiation of a negotiable document of title after it has been indorsed to a specified person requires indorsement by the special indorsee as well as delivery.

**(4)** A negotiable document of title is "duly negotiated" when it is negotiated in the manner stated in this section to a holder who purchases it in good faith without notice of any defense against or claim to it on the part of any person and for value, unless it is established that the negotiation is not in the regular course of business or financing or involves receiving the document in settlement or payment of a money obligation.

**(5)** Indorsement of a nonnegotiable document neither makes it negotiable nor adds to the transferee's rights.

**(6)** The naming in a negotiable bill of a person to be notified of the arrival of the goods does not limit the negotiability of the bill nor constitute notice to a purchaser thereof of any interest of such person in the goods.

### § 7–502. Rights Acquired by Due Negotiation.

**(1)** Subject to the following section and to the provisions of Section 7–205 on fungible goods, a holder to whom a negotiable document of title has been duly negotiated acquires thereby:

  **(a)** title to the document;

  **(b)** title to the goods;

  **(c)** all rights accruing under the law of agency or estoppel, including rights to goods delivered to the bailee after the document was issued; and

  **(d)** the direct obligation of the issuer to hold or deliver the goods according to the terms of the document free of any defense or claim by him except those arising under the terms of the document or under this Article. In the case of a delivery order the bailee's obligation accrues only upon acceptance and the obligation acquired by the holder is that the issuer and any indorser will procure the acceptance of the bailee.

**(2)** Subject to the following section, title and rights so acquired are not defeated by any stoppage of the goods represented by the document or by surrender of such goods by the bailee, and are not impaired even though the negotiation or any prior negotiation constituted a breach of duty or even though any person has been deprived of possession of the document by misrepresentation, fraud, accident, mistake, duress, loss, theft or conversion, or even though a previous sale or other transfer of the goods or document has been made to a third person.

### § 7–503. Document of Title to Goods Defeated in Certain Cases.

**(1)** A document of title confers no right in goods against a person who before issuance of the document had a legal interest or a perfected security interest in them and who neither

  **(a)** delivered or entrusted them or any document of title covering them to the bailor or his nominee with actual or apparent authority to ship, store or sell or with power to obtain delivery under this Article (Section 7–403) or with power of disposition under this Act (Sections 2–403 and 9–307) or other statute or rule of law; nor

  **(b)** acquiesced in the procurement by the bailor or his nominee of any document of title.

**(2)** Title to goods based upon an unaccepted delivery order is subject to the rights of anyone to whom a negotiable warehouse receipt or bill of lading covering the goods has been duly negotiated. Such a title may be defeated under the next section to the same extent as the rights of the issuer or a transferee from the issuer.

**(3)** Title to goods based upon a bill of lading issued to a freight forwarder is subject to the rights of anyone to whom a bill issued by the freight forwarder is duly negotiated; but delivery by the carrier in accordance with Part 4 of this Article pursuant to its own bill of lading discharges the carrier's obligation to deliver. As amended in 1999.

### § 7–504. Rights Acquired in the Absence of Due Negotiation; Effect of Diversion; Seller's Stoppage of Delivery.

**(1)** A transferee of a document, whether negotiable or nonnegotiable, to whom the document has been delivered but not duly negotiated, acquires the title and rights which his transferor had or had actual authority to convey.

**(2)** In the case of a nonnegotiable document, until but not after the bailee receives notification of the transfer, the rights of the transferee may be defeated

  **(a)** by those creditors of the transferor who could treat the sale as void under Section 2–402; or

  **(b)** by a buyer from the transferor in ordinary course of business if the bailee has delivered the goods to the buyer or received notification of his rights; or

  **(c)** as against the bailee by good faith dealings of the bailee with the transferor.

**(3)** A diversion or other change of shipping instructions by the consignor in a nonnegotiable bill of lading which causes the bailee not to deliver to the consignee defeats the consignee's title to the goods if they have been delivered to a buyer in ordinary course of business and in any event defeats the consignee's rights against the bailee.

**(4)** Delivery pursuant to a nonnegotiable document may be stopped by a seller under Section 2–705, and subject to the requirement of due notification there provided. A bailee honoring the seller's instructions is entitled to be indemnified by the seller against any resulting loss or expense.

### § 7–505. Indorser Not a Guarantor for Other Parties.
The indorsement of a document of title issued by a bailee does not make the indorser liable for any default by the bailee or by previous indorsers.

### § 7–506. Delivery Without Indorsement: Right to Compel Indorsement.
The transferee of a negotiable document of title has a specifically enforceable right to have his transferor supply any necessary indorsement but the transfer becomes a negotiation only as of the time the indorsement is supplied.

### § 7–507. Warranties on Negotiation or Transfer of Receipt or Bill.
Where a person negotiates or transfers a document of title for value otherwise than as a mere intermediary under the next

following section, then unless otherwise agreed he warrants to his immediate purchaser only in addition to any warranty made in selling the goods

(a) that the document is genuine; and

(b) that he has no knowledge of any fact which would impair its validity or worth; and

(c) that his negotiation or transfer is rightful and fully effective with respect to the title to the document and the goods it represents.

### § 7–508. Warranties of Collecting Bank as to Documents.

A collecting bank or other intermediary known to be entrusted with documents on behalf of another or with collection of a draft or other claim against delivery of documents warrants by such delivery of the documents only its own good faith and authority. This rule applies even though the intermediary has purchased or made advances against the claim or draft to be collected.

### § 7–509. Receipt or Bill: When Adequate Compliance With Commercial Contract.

The question whether a document is adequate to fulfill the obligations of a contract for sale or the conditions of a credit is governed by the Articles on Sales (Article 2) and on Letters of Credit (Article 5).

### Part 6—Warehouse Receipts and Bills of Lading: Miscellaneous Provisions

### § 7–601. Lost and Missing Documents.

(1) If a document has been lost, stolen or destroyed, a court may order delivery of the goods or issuance of a substitute document and the bailee may without liability to any person comply with such order. If the document was negotiable the claimant must post security approved by the court to indemnify any person who may suffer loss as a result of non-surrender of the document. If the document was not negotiable, such security may be required at the discretion of the court. The court may also in its discretion order payment of the bailee's reasonable costs and counsel fees.

(2) A bailee who without court order delivers goods to a person claiming under a missing negotiable document is liable to any person injured thereby, and if the delivery is not in good faith becomes liable for conversion. Delivery in good faith is not conversion if made in accordance with a filed classification or tariff or, where no classification or tariff is filed, if the claimant posts security with the bailee in an amount at least double the value of the goods at the time of posting to indemnify any person injured by the delivery who files a notice of claim within one year after the delivery.

### § 7–602. Attachment of Goods Covered by a Negotiable Document.

Except where the document was originally issued upon delivery of the goods by a person who had no power to dispose of them, no lien attaches by virtue of any judicial process to goods in the possession of a bailee for which a negotiable document of title is outstanding unless the document be first surrendered to the bailee or its negotiation enjoined, and the bailee shall not be compelled to deliver the goods pursuant to process until the document is surrendered to him or impounded by the court. One who purchases the document for value without notice of the process or injunction takes free of the lien imposed by judicial process.

### § 7–603. Conflicting Claims; Interpleader.

If more than one person claims title or possession of the goods, the bailee is excused from delivery until he has had a reasonable time to ascertain the validity of the adverse claims or to bring an action to compel all claimants to interplead and may compel such interpleader, either in defending an action for nondelivery of the goods, or by original action, whichever is appropriate.

## REVISED (1994) ARTICLE 8: INVESTMENT SECURITIES

### Part 1—Short Title and General Matters

### § 8–101. Short Title.

This Article may be cited as Uniform Commercial Code— Investment Securities.

### § 8–102. Definitions.

(a) In this Article:

(1) "Adverse claim" means a claim that a claimant has a property interest in a financial asset and that it is a violation of the rights of the claimant for another person to hold, transfer, or deal with the financial asset.

(2) "Bearer form," as applied to a certificated security, means a form in which the security is payable to the bearer of the security certificate according to its terms but not by reason of an indorsement.

(3) "Broker" means a person defined as a broker or dealer under the federal securities laws, but without excluding a bank acting in that capacity.

(4) "Certificated security" means a security that is represented by a certificate.

(5) "Clearing corporation" means:

(i) a person that is registered as a "clearing agency" under the federal securities laws;

(ii) a federal reserve bank; or

(iii) any other person that provides clearance or settlement services with respect to financial assets that would require it to register as a clearing agency under the federal securities laws but for an exclusion or exemption from the registration requirement, if its activities as a clearing corporation, including promulgation of rules, are subject to regulation by a federal or state governmental authority.

(6) "Communicate" means to:

(i) send a signed writing; or

(ii) transmit information by any mechanism agreed upon by the persons transmitting and receiving the information.

(7) "Entitlement holder" means a person identified in the records of a securities intermediary as the person having a security entitlement against the securities intermediary. If a person acquires a security entitlement by virtue of Section 8–501(b)(2) or (3), that person is the entitlement holder.

(8) "Entitlement order" means a notification communicated to a securities intermediary directing transfer or

redemption of a financial asset to which the entitlement holder has a security entitlement.

**(9)** "Financial asset," except as otherwise provided in Section 8–103, means:

**(i)** a security;

**(ii)** an obligation of a person or a share, participation, or other interest in a person or in property or an enterprise of a person, which is, or is of a type, dealt in or traded on financial markets, or which is recognized in any area in which it is issued or dealt in as a medium for investment; or

**(iii)** any property that is held by a securities intermediary for another person in a securities account if the securities intermediary has expressly agreed with the other person that the property is to be treated as a financial asset under this Article.

As context requires, the term means either the interest itself or the means by which a person's claim to it is evidenced, including a certificated or uncertificated security, a security certificate, or a security entitlement.

**(10)** "Good faith," for purposes of the obligation of good faith in the performance or enforcement of contracts or duties within this Article, means honesty in fact and the observance of reasonable commercial standards of fair dealing.

**(11)** "Indorsement" means a signature that alone or accompanied by other words is made on a security certificate in registered form or on a separate document for the purpose of assigning, transferring, or redeeming the security or granting a power to assign, transfer, or redeem it.

**(12)** "Instruction" means a notification communi-cated to the issuer of an uncertificated security which directs that the transfer of the security be registered or that the security be redeemed.

**(13)** "Registered form," as applied to a certificated security, means a form in which:

**(i)** the security certificate specifies a person entitled to the security; and

**(ii)** a transfer of the security may be registered upon books maintained for that purpose by or on behalf of the issuer, or the security certificate so states.

**(14)** "Securities intermediary" means:

**(i)** a clearing corporation; or

**(ii)** a person, including a bank or broker, that in the ordinary course of its business maintains securities accounts for others and is acting in that capacity.

**(15)** "Security," except as otherwise provided in Section 8–103, means an obligation of an issuer or a share, participation, or other interest in an issuer or in property or an enterprise of an issuer:

**(i)** which is represented by a security certificate in bearer or registered form, or the transfer of which may be registered upon books maintained for that purpose by or on behalf of the issuer;

**(ii)** which is one of a class or series or by its terms is divisible into a class or series of shares, participations, interests, or obligations; and

**(iii)** which:

**(A)** is, or is of a type, dealt in or traded on securities exchanges or securities markets; or

**(B)** is a medium for investment and by its terms expressly provides that it is a security governed by this Article.

**(16)** "Security certificate" means a certificate representing a security.

**(17)** "Security entitlement" means the rights and property interest of an entitlement holder with respect to a financial asset specified in Part 5.

**(18)** "Uncertificated security" means a security that is not represented by a certificate.

**(b)** Other definitions applying to this Article and the sections in which they appear are:

| | |
|---|---|
| Appropriate person | Section 8–107 |
| Control | Section 8–106 |
| Delivery | Section 8–301 |
| Investment company security | Section 8–103 |
| Issuer | Section 8–201 |
| Overissue | Section 8–210 |
| Protected purchaser | Section 8–303 |
| Securities account | Section 8–501 |

**(c)** In addition, Article 1 contains general definitions and principles of construction and interpretation applicable throughout this Article.

**(d)** The characterization of a person, business, or transaction for purposes of this Article does not determine the characterization of the person, business, or transaction for purposes of any other law, regulation, or rule.

## § 8–103. Rules for Determining Whether Certain Obligations and Interests Are Securities or Financial Assets.

**(a)** A share or similar equity interest issued by a corporation, business trust, joint stock company, or similar entity is a security.

**(b)** An "investment company security" is a security. "Investment company security" means a share or similar equity interest issued by an entity that is registered as an investment company under the federal investment company laws, an interest in a unit investment trust that is so registered, or a face-amount certificate issued by a face-amount certificate company that is so registered. Investment company security does not include an insurance policy or endowment policy or annuity contract issued by an insurance company.

**(c)** An interest in a partnership or limited liability company is not a security unless it is dealt in or traded on securities exchanges or in securities markets, its terms expressly provide that it is a security governed by this Article, or it is an investment company security. However, an interest in a partnership or limited liability company is a financial asset if it is held in a securities account.

**(d)** A writing that is a security certificate is governed by this Article and not by Article 3, even though it also meets the requirements of that Article. However, a negotiable instrument governed by Article 3 is a financial asset if it is held in a securities account.

**(e)** An option or similar obligation issued by a clearing corporation to its participants is not a security, but is a financial asset.

**(f)** A commodity contract, as defined in Section 9–102(a)(15), is not a security or a financial asset.
As amended in 1999.

### § 8–104. Acquisition of Security or Financial Asset or Interest Therein.

**(a)** A person acquires a security or an interest therein, under this Article, if:

**(1)** the person is a purchaser to whom a security is delivered pursuant to Section 8–301; or

**(2)** the person acquires a security entitlement to the security pursuant to Section 8–501.

**(b)** A person acquires a financial asset, other than a security, or an interest therein, under this Article, if the person acquires a security entitlement to the financial asset.

**(c)** A person who acquires a security entitlement to a security or other financial asset has the rights specified in Part 5, but is a purchaser of any security, security entitlement, or other financial asset held by the securities intermediary only to the extent provided in Section 8–503.

**(d)** Unless the context shows that a different meaning is intended, a person who is required by other law, regulation, rule, or agreement to transfer, deliver, present, surrender, exchange, or otherwise put in the possession of another person a security or financial asset satisfies that requirement by causing the other person to acquire an interest in the security or financial asset pursuant to subsection (a) or (b).

### § 8–105. Notice of Adverse Claim.

**(a)** A person has notice of an adverse claim if:

**(1)** the person knows of the adverse claim;

**(2)** the person is aware of facts sufficient to indicate that there is a significant probability that the adverse claim exists and deliberately avoids information that would establish the existence of the adverse claim; or

**(3)** the person has a duty, imposed by statute or regulation, to investigate whether an adverse claim exists, and the investigation so required would establish the existence of the adverse claim.

**(b)** Having knowledge that a financial asset or interest therein is or has been transferred by a representative imposes no duty of inquiry into the rightfulness of a transaction and is not notice of an adverse claim. However, a person who knows that a representative has transferred a financial asset or interest therein in a transaction that is, or whose proceeds are being used, for the individual benefit of the representative or otherwise in breach of duty has notice of an adverse claim.

**(c)** An act or event that creates a right to immediate performance of the principal obligation represented by a security certificate or sets a date on or after which the certificate is to be presented or surrendered for redemption or exchange does not itself constitute notice of an adverse claim except in the case of a transfer more than:

**(1)** one year after a date set for presentment or surrender for redemption or exchange; or

**(2)** six months after a date set for payment of money against presentation or surrender of the certificate, if money was available for payment on that date.

**(d)** A purchaser of a certificated security has notice of an adverse claim if the security certificate:

**(1)** whether in bearer or registered form, has been indorsed "for collection" or "for surrender" or for some other purpose not involving transfer; or

**(2)** is in bearer form and has on it an unambiguous statement that it is the property of a person other than the transferor, but the mere writing of a name on the certificate is not such a statement.

**(e)** Filing of a financing statement under Article 9 is not notice of an adverse claim to a financial asset.

### § 8–106. Control.

**(a)** A purchaser has "control" of a certificated security in bearer form if the certificated security is delivered to the purchaser.

**(b)** A purchaser has "control" of a certificated security in registered form if the certificated security is delivered to the purchaser, and:

**(1)** the certificate is indorsed to the purchaser or in blank by an effective indorsement; or

**(2)** the certificate is registered in the name of the purchaser, upon original issue or registration of transfer by the issuer.

**(c)** A purchaser has "control" of an uncertificated secu-rity if:

**(1)** the uncertificated security is delivered to the purchaser; or

**(2)** the issuer has agreed that it will comply with instructions originated by the purchaser without further consent by the registered owner.

**(d)** A purchaser has "control" of a security entitlement if:

**(1)** the purchaser becomes the entitlement holder;

**(2)** the securities intermediary has agreed that it will comply with entitlement orders originated by the purchaser without further consent by the entitlement holder; or

**(3)** another person has control of the security entitlement on behalf of the purchaser or, having previously acquired control of the security entitlement, acknowledges that it has control on behalf of the purchaser.

**(e)** If an interest in a security entitlement is granted by the entitlement holder to the entitlement holder's own securities intermediary, the securities intermediary has control.

**(f)** A purchaser who has satisfied the requirements of subsection (c) or (d) has control, even if the registered owner in the case of subsection (c) or the entitlement holder in the case of subsection (d) retains the right to make substitutions for the uncertificated security or security entitlement, to originate instructions or entitlement orders to the issuer or securities intermediary, or otherwise to deal with the uncertificated security or security entitlement.

**(g)** An issuer or a securities intermediary may not enter into an agreement of the kind described in subsection (c)(2) or (d)(2) without the consent of the registered owner or entitlement holder, but an issuer or a securities intermediary is not required to enter into such an agreement even though the registered owner or entitlement holder so directs. An issuer or securities intermediary that has entered into such an agreement is not required to confirm the existence of the agreement to another party unless requested to do so by the registered owner or entitlement holder.
As amended in 1999.

### § 8–107. Whether Indorsement, Instruction, or Entitlement Order Is Effective.

**(a)** "Appropriate person" means:

**(1)** with respect to an indorsement, the person specified by a security certificate or by an effective special indorsement to be entitled to the security;

**(2)** with respect to an instruction, the registered owner of an uncertificated security;

**(3)** with respect to an entitlement order, the entitlement holder;

**(4)** if the person designated in paragraph (1), (2), or (3) is deceased, the designated person's successor taking under other law or the designated person's personal representative acting for the estate of the decedent; or

**(5)** if the person designated in paragraph (1), (2), or (3) lacks capacity, the designated person's guardian, conservator, or other similar representative who has power under other law to transfer the security or financial asset.

**(b)** An indorsement, instruction, or entitlement order is effective if:

**(1)** it is made by the appropriate person;

**(2)** it is made by a person who has power under the law of agency to transfer the security or financial asset on behalf of the appropriate person, including, in the case of an instruction or entitlement order, a person who has control under Section 8–106(c)(2) or (d)(2); or

**(3)** the appropriate person has ratified it or is otherwise precluded from asserting its ineffectiveness.

**(c)** An indorsement, instruction, or entitlement order made by a representative is effective even if:

**(1)** the representative has failed to comply with a controlling instrument or with the law of the State having jurisdiction of the representative relationship, including any law requiring the representative to obtain court approval of the transaction; or

**(2)** the representative's action in making the indorsement, instruction, or entitlement order or using the proceeds of the transaction is otherwise a breach of duty.

**(d)** If a security is registered in the name of or specially indorsed to a person described as a representative, or if a securities account is maintained in the name of a person described as a representative, an indorsement, instruction, or entitlement order made by the person is effective even though the person is no longer serving in the described capacity.

**(e)** Effectiveness of an indorsement, instruction, or entitlement order is determined as of the date the indorsement, instruction, or entitlement order is made, and an indorsement, instruction, or entitlement order does not become ineffective by reason of any later change of circumstances.

### § 8–108. Warranties in Direct Holding.

**(a)** A person who transfers a certificated security to a purchaser for value warrants to the purchaser, and an indorser, if the transfer is by indorsement, warrants to any subsequent purchaser, that:

**(1)** the certificate is genuine and has not been materially altered;

**(2)** the transferor or indorser does not know of any fact that might impair the validity of the security;

**(3)** there is no adverse claim to the security;

**(4)** the transfer does not violate any restriction on transfer;

**(5)** if the transfer is by indorsement, the indorsement is made by an appropriate person, or if the indorsement is by an agent, the agent has actual authority to act on behalf of the appropriate person; and

**(6)** the transfer is otherwise effective and rightful.

**(b)** A person who originates an instruction for registration of transfer of an uncertificated security to a purchaser for value warrants to the purchaser that:

**(1)** the instruction is made by an appropriate person, or if the instruction is by an agent, the agent has actual authority to act on behalf of the appropriate person;

**(2)** the security is valid;

**(3)** there is no adverse claim to the security; and

**(4)** at the time the instruction is presented to the issuer:

**(i)** the purchaser will be entitled to the registration of transfer;

**(ii)** the transfer will be registered by the issuer free from all liens, security interests, restrictions, and claims other than those specified in the instruction;

**(iii)** the transfer will not violate any restriction on transfer; and

**(iv)** the requested transfer will otherwise be effective and rightful.

**(c)** A person who transfers an uncertificated security to a purchaser for value and does not originate an instruction in connection with the transfer warrants that:

**(1)** the uncertificated security is valid;

**(2)** there is no adverse claim to the security;

**(3)** the transfer does not violate any restriction on transfer; and

**(4)** the transfer is otherwise effective and rightful.

**(d)** A person who indorses a security certificate warrants to the issuer that:

**(1)** there is no adverse claim to the security; and

**(2)** the indorsement is effective.

**(e)** A person who originates an instruction for registration of transfer of an uncertificated security warrants to the issuer that:

**(1)** the instruction is effective; and

**(2)** at the time the instruction is presented to the issuer the purchaser will be entitled to the registration of transfer.

**(f)** A person who presents a certificated security for registration of transfer or for payment or exchange warrants to the issuer that the person is entitled to the registration, payment, or exchange, but a purchaser for value and without notice of adverse claims to whom transfer is registered warrants only that the person has no knowledge of any unauthorized signature in a necessary indorsement.

**(g)** If a person acts as agent of another in delivering a certificated security to a purchaser, the identity of the principal was known to the person to whom the certificate was delivered, and the certificate delivered by the agent was received by the agent from the principal or received by the agent from another person at the direction of the principal, the person delivering the security certificate warrants only that the delivering person has authority to act for the principal and does not know of any adverse claim to the certificated security.

**(h)** A secured party who redelivers a security certificate received, or after payment and on order of the debtor delivers the security certificate to another person, makes only the warranties of an agent under subsection (g).

**(i)** Except as otherwise provided in subsection (g), a broker acting for a customer makes to the issuer and a purchaser the warranties provided in subsections (a) through (f). A broker that delivers a security certificate to its customer, or causes its customer to be registered as the owner of an uncertificated security, makes to the customer the warranties provided in subsection (a) or (b), and has the rights and privileges of a purchaser under this section. The warranties of and in favor of the broker acting as an agent are in addition to applicable warranties given by and in favor of the customer.

### § 8–109. Warranties in Indirect Holding.

**(a)** A person who originates an entitlement order to a securities intermediary warrants to the securities intermediary that:

   **(1)** the entitlement order is made by an appropriate person, or if the entitlement order is by an agent, the agent has actual authority to act on behalf of the appropriate person; and

   **(2)** there is no adverse claim to the security entitlement.

**(b)** A person who delivers a security certificate to a securities intermediary for credit to a securities account or originates an instruction with respect to an uncertificated security directing that the uncertificated security be credited to a securities account makes to the securities intermediary the warranties specified in Section 8–108(a) or (b).

**(c)** If a securities intermediary delivers a security certificate to its entitlement holder or causes its entitlement holder to be registered as the owner of an uncertificated security, the securities intermediary makes to the entitlement holder the warranties specified in Section 8–108(a) or (b).

### § 8–110. Applicability; Choice of Law.

**(a)** The local law of the issuer's jurisdiction, as specified in subsection (d), governs:

   **(1)** the validity of a security;

   **(2)** the rights and duties of the issuer with respect to registration of transfer;

   **(3)** the effectiveness of registration of transfer by the issuer;

   **(4)** whether the issuer owes any duties to an adverse claimant to a security; and

   **(5)** whether an adverse claim can be asserted against a person to whom transfer of a certificated or uncertificated security is registered or a person who obtains control of an uncertificated security.

**(b)** The local law of the securities intermediary's jurisdiction, as specified in subsection (e), governs:

   **(1)** acquisition of a security entitlement from the securities intermediary;

   **(2)** the rights and duties of the securities intermediary and entitlement holder arising out of a security entitlement;

   **(3)** whether the securities intermediary owes any duties to an adverse claimant to a security entitlement; and

   **(4)** whether an adverse claim can be asserted against a person who acquires a security entitlement from the securities intermediary or a person who purchases a security entitlement or interest therein from an entitlement holder.

**(c)** The local law of the jurisdiction in which a security certificate is located at the time of delivery governs whether an adverse claim can be asserted against a person to whom the security certificate is delivered.

**(d)** "Issuer's jurisdiction" means the jurisdiction under which the issuer of the security is organized or, if permitted by the law of that jurisdiction, the law of another jurisdiction specified by the issuer. An issuer organized under the law of this State may specify the law of another jurisdiction as the law governing the matters specified in subsection (a)(2) through (5).

**(e)** The following rules determine a "securities intermediary's jurisdiction" for purposes of this section:

   **(1)** If an agreement between the securities intermediary and its entitlement holder specifies that it is governed by the law of a particular jurisdiction, that jurisdiction is the securities intermediary's jurisdiction.

   **(2)** If an agreement between the securities intermediary and its entitlement holder does not specify the governing law as provided in paragraph (1), but expressly specifies that the securities account is maintained at an office in a particular jurisdiction, that jurisdiction is the securities intermediary's jurisdiction.

   **(3)** If neither paragraph (1) nor paragraph (2) applies and an agreement between the securities intermediary and its entitlement holder governing the securities account expressly provides that the securities account is maintained at an office in a particular jurisdiction, that jurisdiction is the securities intermediary's jurisdiction.

   **(4)** If none of the preceding paragraph applies, the securities intermediary's jurisdiction is the jurisdiction in which the office identified in an account statement as the office serving the entitlement holder's account is located.

   **(5)** If none of the preceding paragraphs applies, the securities intermediary's jurisdiction is the jurisdiction in which the chief executive office of the securities intermediary is located.

**(f)** A securities intermediary's jurisdiction is not determined by the physical location of certificates representing financial assets, or by the jurisdiction in which is organized the issuer of the financial asset with respect to which an entitlement holder has a security entitlement, or by the location of facilities for data processing or other record keeping concerning the account. As amended in 1999.

### § 8–111. Clearing Corporation Rules.

A rule adopted by a clearing corporation governing rights and obligations among the clearing corporation and its participants in the clearing corporation is effective even if the rule conflicts with this [Act] and affects another party who does not consent to the rule.

### § 8–112. Creditor's Legal Process.

**(a)** The interest of a debtor in a certificated security may be reached by a creditor only by actual seizure of the security certificate by the officer making the attachment or levy, except as otherwise provided in subsection (d). However, a certificated security for which the certificate has been surrendered to the issuer may be reached by a creditor by legal process upon the issuer.

**(b)** The interest of a debtor in an uncertificated security may be reached by a creditor only by legal process upon the issuer at its chief executive office in the United States, except as otherwise provided in subsection (d).

**(c)** The interest of a debtor in a security entitlement may be reached by a creditor only by legal process upon the securities intermediary with whom the debtor's securities account is maintained, except as otherwise provided in subsection (d).

**(d)** The interest of a debtor in a certificated security for which the certificate is in the possession of a secured party, or in an uncertificated security registered in the name of a secured party, or a security entitlement maintained in the name of a secured party, may be reached by a creditor by legal process upon the secured party.

**(e)** A creditor whose debtor is the owner of a certificated security, uncertificated security, or security entitlement is entitled to aid from a court of competent jurisdiction, by injunction or otherwise, in reaching the certificated security, uncertificated security, or security entitlement or in satisfying the claim by means allowed at law or in equity in regard to property that cannot readily be reached by other legal process.

### § 8–113. Statute of Frauds Inapplicable.

A contract or modification of a contract for the sale or purchase of a security is enforceable whether or not there is a writing signed or record authenticated by a party against whom enforcement is sought, even if the contract or modification is not capable of performance within one year of its making.

### § 8–114. Evidentiary Rules Concerning Certificated Securities.

The following rules apply in an action on a certificated security against the issuer:

(1) Unless specifically denied in the pleadings, each signature on a security certificate or in a necessary indorsement is admitted.

(2) If the effectiveness of a signature is put in issue, the burden of establishing effectiveness is on the party claiming under the signature, but the signature is presumed to be genuine or authorized.

(3) If signatures on a security certificate are admitted or established, production of the certificate entitles a holder to recover on it unless the defendant establishes a defense or a defect going to the validity of the security.

(4) If it is shown that a defense or defect exists, the plaintiff has the burden of establishing that the plaintiff or some person under whom the plaintiff claims is a person against whom the defense or defect cannot be asserted.

### § 8–115. Securities Intermediary and Others Not Liable to Adverse Claimant.

A securities intermediary that has transferred a financial asset pursuant to an effective entitlement order, or a broker or other agent or bailee that has dealt with a financial asset at the direction of its customer or principal, is not liable to a person having an adverse claim to the financial asset, unless the securities intermediary, or broker or other agent or bailee:

(1) took the action after it had been served with an injunction, restraining order, or other legal process enjoining it from doing so, issued by a court of competent jurisdiction,

and had a reasonable opportunity to act on the injunction, restraining order, or other legal process; or

(2) acted in collusion with the wrongdoer in violating the rights of the adverse claimant; or

(3) in the case of a security certificate that has been stolen, acted with notice of the adverse claim.

### § 8–116. Securities Intermediary as Purchaser for Value.

A securities intermediary that receives a financial asset and establishes a security entitlement to the financial asset in favor of an entitlement holder is a purchaser for value of the financial asset. A securities intermediary that acquires a security entitlement to a financial asset from another securities intermediary acquires the security entitlement for value if the securities intermediary acquiring the security entitlement establishes a security entitlement to the financial asset in favor of an entitlement holder.

**Part 2—Issue and Issuer**

### § 8–201. Issuer.

**(a)** With respect to an obligation on or a defense to a security, an "issuer" includes a person that:

(1) places or authorizes the placing of its name on a security certificate, other than as authenticating trustee, registrar, transfer agent, or the like, to evidence a share, participation, or other interest in its property or in an enterprise, or to evidence its duty to perform an obligation represented by the certificate;

(2) creates a share, participation, or other interest in its property or in an enterprise, or undertakes an obligation, that is an uncertificated security;

(3) directly or indirectly creates a fractional interest in its rights or property, if the fractional interest is represented by a security certificate; or

(4) becomes responsible for, or in place of, another person described as an issuer in this section.

**(b)** With respect to an obligation on or defense to a security, a guarantor is an issuer to the extent of its guaranty, whether or not its obligation is noted on a security certificate.

**(c)** With respect to a registration of a transfer, issuer means a person on whose behalf transfer books are maintained.

### § 8–202. Issuer's Responsibility and Defenses; Notice of Defect or Defense.

**(a)** Even against a purchaser for value and without notice, the terms of a certificated security include terms stated on the certificate and terms made part of the security by reference on the certificate to another instrument, indenture, or document or to a constitution, statute, ordinance, rule, regulation, order, or the like, to the extent the terms referred to do not conflict with terms stated on the certificate. A reference under this subsection does not of itself charge a purchaser for value with notice of a defect going to the validity of the security, even if the certificate expressly states that a person accepting it admits notice. The terms of an uncertificated security include those stated in any instrument, indenture, or document or in a constitution, statute, ordinance, rule, regulation, order, or the like, pursuant to which the security is issued.

**(b)** The following rules apply if an issuer asserts that a security is not valid:

> **(1)** A security other than one issued by a government or governmental subdivision, agency, or instrumentality, even though issued with a defect going to its validity, is valid in the hands of a purchaser for value and without notice of the particular defect unless the defect involves a violation of a constitutional provision. In that case, the security is valid in the hands of a purchaser for value and without notice of the defect, other than one who takes by original issue.
>
> **(2)** Paragraph (1) applies to an issuer that is a government or governmental subdivision, agency, or instrumentality only if there has been substantial compliance with the legal requirements governing the issue or the issuer has received a substantial consideration for the issue as a whole or for the particular security and a stated purpose of the issue is one for which the issuer has power to borrow money or issue the security.

**(c)** Except as otherwise provided in Section 8–205, lack of genuineness of a certificated security is a complete defense, even against a purchaser for value and without notice.

**(d)** All other defenses of the issuer of a security, including non-delivery and conditional delivery of a certificated security, are ineffective against a purchaser for value who has taken the certificated security without notice of the particular defense.

**(e)** This section does not affect the right of a party to cancel a contract for a security "when, as and if issued" or "when distributed" in the event of a material change in the character of the security that is the subject of the contract or in the plan or arrangement pursuant to which the security is to be issued or distributed.

**(f)** If a security is held by a securities intermediary against whom an entitlement holder has a security entitlement with respect to the security, the issuer may not assert any defense that the issuer could not assert if the entitlement holder held the security directly.

### § 8–203. Staleness as Notice of Defect or Defense.

After an act or event, other than a call that has been revoked, creating a right to immediate performance of the principal obligation represented by a certificated security or setting a date on or after which the security is to be presented or surrendered for redemption or exchange, a purchaser is charged with notice of any defect in its issue or defense of the issuer, if the act or event:

> **(1)** requires the payment of money, the delivery of a certificated security, the registration of transfer of an uncertificated security, or any of them on presentation or surrender of the security certificate, the money or security is available on the date set for payment or exchange, and the purchaser takes the security more than one year after that date; or
>
> **(2)** is not covered by paragraph (1) and the purchaser takes the security more than two years after the date set for surrender or presentation or the date on which performance became due.

### § 8–204. Effect of Issuer's Restriction on Transfer.

A restriction on transfer of a security imposed by the issuer, even if otherwise lawful, is ineffective against a person without knowledge of the restriction unless:

> **(1)** the security is certificated and the restriction is noted conspicuously on the security certificate; or
>
> **(2)** the security is uncertificated and the registered owner has been notified of the restriction.

### § 8–205. Effect of Unauthorized Signature on Security Certificate.

An unauthorized signature placed on a security certificate before or in the course of issue is ineffective, but the signature is effective in favor of a purchaser for value of the certificated security if the purchaser is without notice of the lack of authority and the signing has been done by:

> **(1)** an authenticating trustee, registrar, transfer agent, or other person entrusted by the issuer with the signing of the security certificate or of similar security certificates, or the immediate preparation for signing of any of them; or
>
> **(2)** an employee of the issuer, or of any of the persons listed in paragraph (1), entrusted with responsible handling of the security certificate.

### § 8–206. Completion of Alteration of Security Certificate.

**(a)** If a security certificate contains the signatures necessary to its issue or transfer but is incomplete in any other respect:

> **(1)** any person may complete it by filling in the blanks as authorized; and
>
> **(2)** even if the blanks are incorrectly filled in, the security certificate as completed is enforceable by a purchaser who took it for value and without notice of the incorrectness.

**(b)** A complete security certificate that has been improperly altered, even if fraudulently, remains enforceable, but only according to its original terms.

### § 8–207. Rights and Duties of Issuer with Respect to Registered Owners.

**(a)** Before due presentment for registration of transfer of a certificated security in registered form or of an instruction requesting registration of transfer of an uncertificated security, the issuer or indenture trustee may treat the registered owner as the person exclusively entitled to vote, receive notifications, and otherwise exercise all the rights and powers of an owner.

**(b)** This Article does not affect the liability of the registered owner of a security for a call, assessment, or the like.

### § 8–208. Effect of Signature of Authenticating Trustee, Registrar, or Transfer Agent.

**(a)** A person signing a security certificate as authenticating trustee, registrar, transfer agent, or the like, warrants to a purchaser for value of the certificated security, if the purchaser is without notice of a particular defect, that:

> **(1)** the certificate is genuine;
>
> **(2)** the person's own participation in the issue of the security is within the person's capacity and within the scope of the authority received by the person from the issuer; and
>
> **(3)** the person has reasonable grounds to believe that the certificated security is in the form and within the amount the issuer is authorized to issue.

**(b)** Unless otherwise agreed, a person signing under subsection (a) does not assume responsibility for the validity of the security in other respects.

### § 8–209. Issuer's Lien.

A lien in favor of an issuer upon a certificated security is valid against a purchaser only if the right of the issuer to the lien is noted conspicuously on the security certificate.

### § 8–210. Overissue.

**(a)** In this section, "overissue" means the issue of securities in excess of the amount the issuer has corporate power to issue, but an overissue does not occur if appropriate action has cured the overissue.

**(b)** Except as otherwise provided in subsections (c) and (d), the provisions of this Article which validate a security or compel its issue or reissue do not apply to the extent that validation, issue, or reissue would result in overissue.

**(c)** If an identical security not constituting an overissue is reasonably available for purchase, a person entitled to issue or validation may compel the issuer to purchase the security and deliver it if certificated or register its transfer if uncertificated, against surrender of any security certificate the person holds.

**(d)** If a security is not reasonably available for purchase, a person entitled to issue or validation may recover from the issuer the price the person or the last purchaser for value paid for it with interest from the date of the person's demand.

### Part 3—Transfer of Certificated and Uncertificated Securities

### § 8–301. Delivery.

**(a)** Delivery of a certificated security to a purchaser occurs when:

> **(1)** the purchaser acquires possession of the security certificate;
>
> **(2)** another person, other than a securities intermediary, either acquires possession of the security certificate on behalf of the purchaser or, having previously acquired possession of the certificate, acknowledges that it holds for the purchaser; or
>
> **(3)** a securities intermediary acting on behalf of the purchaser acquires possession of the security certificate, only if the certificate is in registered form and is (i) registered in the name of the purchaser, (ii) payable to the order of the purchaser, or (iii) specially indorsed to the purchaser by an effective indorsement and has not been indorsed to the securities intermediary or in blank.

**(b)** Delivery of an uncertificated security to a purchaser occurs when:

> **(1)** the issuer registers the purchaser as the registered owner, upon original issue or registration of transfer; or
>
> **(2)** another person, other than a securities intermediary, either becomes the registered owner of the uncertificated security on behalf of the purchaser or, having previously become the registered owner, acknowledges that it holds for the purchaser.

As amended in 1999.

### § 8–302. Rights of Purchaser.

**(a)** Except as otherwise provided in subsections (b) and (c), upon delivery of a certificated or uncertificated security to a purchaser, the purchaser acquires all rights in the security that the transferor had or had power to transfer.

**(b)** A purchaser of a limited interest acquires rights only to the extent of the interest purchased.

**(c)** A purchaser of a certificated security who as a previous holder had notice of an adverse claim does not improve its position by taking from a protected purchaser.

As amended in 1999.

### § 8–303. Protected Purchaser.

**(a)** "Protected purchaser" means a purchaser of a certificated or uncertificated security, or of an interest therein, who:

> **(1)** gives value;
>
> **(2)** does not have notice of any adverse claim to the security; and
>
> **(3)** obtains control of the certificated or uncertificated security.

**(b)** In addition to acquiring the rights of a purchaser, a protected purchaser also acquires its interest in the security free of any adverse claim.

### § 8–304. Indorsement.

**(a)** An indorsement may be in blank or special. An indorsement in blank includes an indorsement to bearer. A special indorsement specifies to whom a security is to be transferred or who has power to transfer it. A holder may convert a blank indorsement to a special indorsement.

**(b)** An indorsement purporting to be only of part of a security certificate representing units intended by the issuer to be separately transferable is effective to the extent of the indorsement.

**(c)** An indorsement, whether special or in blank, does not constitute a transfer until delivery of the certificate on which it appears or, if the indorsement is on a separate document, until delivery of both the document and the certificate.

**(d)** If a security certificate in registered form has been delivered to a purchaser without a necessary indorsement, the purchaser may become a protected purchaser only when the indorsement is supplied. However, against a transferor, a transfer is complete upon delivery and the purchaser has a specifically enforceable right to have any necessary indorsement supplied.

**(e)** An indorsement of a security certificate in bearer form may give notice of an adverse claim to the certificate, but it does not otherwise affect a right to registration that the holder possesses.

**(f)** Unless otherwise agreed, a person making an indorsement assumes only the obligations provided in Section 8–108 and not an obligation that the security will be honored by the issuer.

### § 8–305. Instruction.

**(a)** If an instruction has been originated by an appropriate person but is incomplete in any other respect, any person may complete it as authorized and the issuer may rely on it as completed, even though it has been completed incorrectly.

**(b)** Unless otherwise agreed, a person initiating an instruction assumes only the obligations imposed by Section 8–108 and not an obligation that the security will be honored by the issuer.

## § 8–306. Effect of Guaranteeing Signature, Indorsement, or Instruction.

(a) A person who guarantees a signature of an indorser of a security certificate warrants that at the time of signing:

(1) the signature was genuine;

(2) the signer was an appropriate person to indorse, or if the signature is by an agent, the agent had actual authority to act on behalf of the appropriate person; and

(3) the signer had legal capacity to sign.

(b) A person who guarantees a signature of the originator of an instruction warrants that at the time of signing:

(1) the signature was genuine;

(2) the signer was an appropriate person to originate the instruction, or if the signature is by an agent, the agent had actual authority to act on behalf of the appropriate person, if the person specified in the instruction as the registered owner was, in fact, the registered owner, as to which fact the signature guarantor does not make a warranty; and

(3) the signer had legal capacity to sign.

(c) A person who specially guarantees the signature of an originator of an instruction makes the warranties of a signature guarantor under subsection (b) and also warrants that at the time the instruction is presented to the issuer:

(1) the person specified in the instruction as the registered owner of the uncertificated security will be the registered owner; and

(2) the transfer of the uncertificated security requested in the instruction will be registered by the issuer free from all liens, security interests, restrictions, and claims other than those specified in the instruction.

(d) A guarantor under subsections (a) and (b) or a special guarantor under subsection (c) does not otherwise warrant the rightfulness of the transfer.

(e) A person who guarantees an indorsement of a security certificate makes the warranties of a signature guarantor under subsection (a) and also warrants the rightfulness of the transfer in all respects.

(f) A person who guarantees an instruction requesting the transfer of an uncertificated security makes the warranties of a special signature guarantor under subsection (c) and also warrants the rightfulness of the transfer in all respects.

(g) An issuer may not require a special guaranty of signature, a guaranty of indorsement, or a guaranty of instruction as a condition to registration of transfer.

(h) The warranties under this section are made to a person taking or dealing with the security in reliance on the guaranty, and the guarantor is liable to the person for loss resulting from their breach. An indorser or originator of an instruction whose signature, indorsement, or instruction has been guaranteed is liable to a guarantor for any loss suffered by the guarantor as a result of breach of the warranties of the guarantor.

## § 8–307. Purchaser's Right to Requisites for Registration of Transfer.

Unless otherwise agreed, the transferor of a security on due demand shall supply the purchaser with proof of authority to transfer or with any other requisite necessary to obtain registration of the transfer of the security, but if the transfer is not for value, a transferor need not comply unless the purchaser pays the necessary expenses. If the transferor fails within a reasonable time to comply with the demand, the purchaser may reject or rescind the transfer.

## Part 4—Registration

### § 8–401. Duty of Issuer to Register Transfer.

(a) If a certificated security in registered form is presented to an issuer with a request to register transfer or an instruction is presented to an issuer with a request to register transfer of an uncertificated security, the issuer shall register the transfer as requested if:

(1) under the terms of the security the person seeking registration of transfer is eligible to have the security registered in its name;

(2) the indorsement or instruction is made by the appropriate person or by an agent who has actual authority to act on behalf of the appropriate person;

(3) reasonable assurance is given that the indorsement or instruction is genuine and authorized (Section 8–402);

(4) any applicable law relating to the collection of taxes has been complied with;

(5) the transfer does not violate any restriction on transfer imposed by the issuer in accordance with Section 8–204;

(6) a demand that the issuer not register transfer has not become effective under Section 8–403, or the issuer has complied with Section 8–403(b) but no legal process or indemnity bond is obtained as provided in Section 8–403(d); and

(7) the transfer is in fact rightful or is to a protected purchaser.

(b) If an issuer is under a duty to register a transfer of a security, the issuer is liable to a person presenting a certificated security or an instruction for registration or to the person's principal for loss resulting from unreasonable delay in registration or failure or refusal to register the transfer.

### § 8–402. Assurance That Indorsement or Instruction Is Effective.

(a) An issuer may require the following assurance that each necessary indorsement or each instruction is genuine and authorized:

(1) in all cases, a guaranty of the signature of the person making an indorsement or originating an instruction including, in the case of an instruction, reasonable assurance of identity;

(2) if the indorsement is made or the instruction is originated by an agent, appropriate assurance of actual authority to sign;

(3) if the indorsement is made or the instruction is originated by a fiduciary pursuant to Section 8–107(a)(4) or (a)(5), appropriate evidence of appointment or incumbency;

(4) if there is more than one fiduciary, reasonable assurance that all who are required to sign have done so; and

(5) if the indorsement is made or the instruction is originated by a person not covered by another provision of this subsection, assurance appropriate to the case corresponding as nearly as may be to the provisions of this subsection.

**(b)** An issuer may elect to require reasonable assurance beyond that specified in this section.

**(c)** In this section:

(1) "Guaranty of the signature" means a guaranty signed by or on behalf of a person reasonably believed by the issuer to be responsible. An issuer may adopt standards with respect to responsibility if they are not manifestly unreasonable.

(2) "Appropriate evidence of appointment or incumbency" means:

(i) in the case of a fiduciary appointed or qualified by a court, a certificate issued by or under the direction or supervision of the court or an officer thereof and dated within 60 days before the date of presentation for transfer; or

(ii) in any other case, a copy of a document showing the appointment or a certificate issued by or on behalf of a person reasonably believed by an issuer to be responsible or, in the absence of that document or certificate, other evidence the issuer reasonably considers appropriate.

## § 8–403. Demand That Issuer Not Register Transfer.

**(a)** A person who is an appropriate person to make an indorsement or originate an instruction may demand that the issuer not register transfer of a security by communicating to the issuer a notification that identifies the registered owner and the issue of which the security is a part and provides an address for communications directed to the person making the demand. The demand is effective only if it is received by the issuer at a time and in a manner affording the issuer reasonable opportunity to act on it.

**(b)** If a certificated security in registered form is presented to an issuer with a request to register transfer or an instruction is presented to an issuer with a request to register transfer of an uncertificated security after a demand that the issuer not register transfer has become effective, the issuer shall promptly communicate to (i) the person who initiated the demand at the address provided in the demand and (ii) the person who presented the security for registration of transfer or initiated the instruction requesting registration of transfer a notification stating that:

(1) the certificated security has been presented for registration of transfer or the instruction for registration of transfer of the uncertificated security has been received;

(2) a demand that the issuer not register transfer had previously been received; and

(3) the issuer will withhold registration of transfer for a period of time stated in the notification in order to provide the person who initiated the demand an opportunity to obtain legal process or an indemnity bond.

**(c)** The period described in subsection (b)(3) may not exceed 30 days after the date of communication of the notification. A shorter period may be specified by the issuer if it is not manifestly unreasonable.

**(d)** An issuer is not liable to a person who initiated a demand that the issuer not register transfer for any loss the person suffers as a result of registration of a transfer pursuant to an effective indorsement or instruction if the person who initiated the demand does not, within the time stated in the issuer's communication, either:

(1) obtain an appropriate restraining order, injunction, or other process from a court of competent jurisdiction enjoining the issuer from registering the transfer; or

(2) file with the issuer an indemnity bond, sufficient in the issuer's judgment to protect the issuer and any transfer agent, registrar, or other agent of the issuer involved from any loss it or they may suffer by refusing to register the transfer.

**(e)** This section does not relieve an issuer from liability for registering transfer pursuant to an indorsement or instruction that was not effective.

## § 8–404. Wrongful Registration.

**(a)** Except as otherwise provided in Section 8–406, an issuer is liable for wrongful registration of transfer if the issuer has registered a transfer of a security to a person not entitled to it, and the transfer was registered:

(1) pursuant to an ineffective indorsement or instruction;

(2) after a demand that the issuer not register transfer became effective under Section 8–403(a) and the issuer did not comply with Section 8–403(b);

(3) after the issuer had been served with an injunction, restraining order, or other legal process enjoining it from registering the transfer, issued by a court of competent jurisdiction, and the issuer had a reasonable opportunity to act on the injunction, restraining order, or other legal process; or

(4) by an issuer acting in collusion with the wrongdoer.

**(b)** An issuer that is liable for wrongful registration of transfer under subsection (a) on demand shall provide the person entitled to the security with a like certificated or uncertificated security, and any payments or distributions that the person did not receive as a result of the wrongful registration. If an overissue would result, the issuer's liability to provide the person with a like security is governed by Section 8–210.

**(c)** Except as otherwise provided in subsection (a) or in a law relating to the collection of taxes, an issuer is not liable to an owner or other person suffering loss as a result of the registration of a transfer of a security if registration was made pursuant to an effective indorsement or instruction.

## § 8–405. Replacement of Lost, Destroyed, or Wrongfully Taken Security Certificate.

**(a)** If an owner of a certificated security, whether in registered or bearer form, claims that the certificate has been lost, destroyed, or wrongfully taken, the issuer shall issue a new certificate if the owner:

(1) so requests before the issuer has notice that the certificate has been acquired by a protected purchaser;

(2) files with the issuer a sufficient indemnity bond; and

(3) satisfies other reasonable requirements imposed by the issuer.

**(b)** If, after the issue of a new security certificate, a protected purchaser of the original certificate presents it for registration of transfer, the issuer shall register the transfer unless an overissue would result. In that case, the issuer's liability is governed by Section 8–210. In addition to any rights on the indemnity bond, an issuer may recover the new certificate from a person to whom it was issued or any person taking under that person, except a protected purchaser.

### § 8–406. Obligation to Notify Issuer of Lost, Destroyed, or Wrongfully Taken Security Certificate.

If a security certificate has been lost, apparently destroyed, or wrongfully taken, and the owner fails to notify the issuer of that fact within a reasonable time after the owner has notice of it and the issuer registers a transfer of the security before receiving notification, the owner may not assert against the issuer a claim for registering the transfer under Section 8–404 or a claim to a new security certificate under Section 8–405.

### § 8–407. Authenticating Trustee, Transfer Agent, and Registrar.

A person acting as authenticating trustee, transfer agent, registrar, or other agent for an issuer in the registration of a transfer of its securities, in the issue of new security certificates or uncertificated securities, or in the cancellation of surrendered security certificates has the same obligation to the holder or owner of a certificated or uncertificated security with regard to the particular functions performed as the issuer has in regard to those functions.

### Part 5  Security Entitlements

### § 8–501. Securities Account; Acquisition of Security Entitlement from Securities Intermediary.

(a) "Securities account" means an account to which a financial asset is or may be credited in accordance with an agreement under which the person maintaining the account undertakes to treat the person for whom the account is maintained as entitled to exercise the rights that comprise the financial asset.

(b) Except as otherwise provided in subsections (d) and (e), a person acquires a security entitlement if a securities intermediary:

    (1) indicates by book entry that a financial asset has been credited to the person's securities account;

    (2) receives a financial asset from the person or acquires a financial asset for the person and, in either case, accepts it for credit to the person's securities account; or

    (3) becomes obligated under other law, regulation, or rule to credit a financial asset to the person's securities account.

(c) If a condition of subsection (b) has been met, a person has a security entitlement even though the securities intermediary does not itself hold the financial asset.

(d) If a securities intermediary holds a financial asset for another person, and the financial asset is registered in the name of, payable to the order of, or specially indorsed to the other person, and has not been indorsed to the securities intermediary or in blank, the other person is treated as holding the financial asset directly rather than as having a security entitlement with respect to the financial asset.

(e) Issuance of a security is not establishment of a security entitlement.

### § 8–502. Assertion of Adverse Claim against Entitlement Holder.

An action based on an adverse claim to a financial asset, whether framed in conversion, replevin, constructive trust,

equitable lien, or other theory, may not be asserted against a person who acquires a security entitlement under Section 8–501 for value and without notice of the adverse claim.

### § 8–503. Property Interest of Entitlement Holder in Financial Asset Held by Securities Intermediary.

(a) To the extent necessary for a securities intermediary to satisfy all security entitlements with respect to a particular financial asset, all interests in that financial asset held by the securities intermediary are held by the securities intermediary for the entitlement holders, are not property of the securities intermediary, and are not subject to claims of creditors of the securities intermediary, except as otherwise provided in Section 8–511.

(b) An entitlement holder's property interest with respect to a particular financial asset under subsection (a) is a pro rata property interest in all interests in that financial asset held by the securities intermediary, without regard to the time the entitlement holder acquired the security entitlement or the time the securities intermediary acquired the interest in that financial asset.

(c) An entitlement holder's property interest with respect to a particular financial asset under subsection (a) may be enforced against the securities intermediary only by exercise of the entitlement holder's rights under Sections 8–505 through 8–508.

(d) An entitlement holder's property interest with respect to a particular financial asset under subsection (a) may be enforced against a purchaser of the financial asset or interest therein only if:

    (1) insolvency proceedings have been initiated by or against the securities intermediary;

    (2) the securities intermediary does not have sufficient interests in the financial asset to satisfy the security entitlements of all of its entitlement holders to that financial asset;

    (3) the securities intermediary violated its obligations under Section 8–504 by transferring the financial asset or interest therein to the purchaser; and

    (4) the purchaser is not protected under sub-section (e).

The trustee or other liquidator, acting on behalf of all entitlement holders having security entitlements with respect to a particular financial asset, may recover the financial asset, or interest therein, from the purchaser. If the trustee or other liquidator elects not to pursue that right, an entitlement holder whose security entitlement remains unsatisfied has the right to recover its interest in the financial asset from the purchaser.

(e) An action based on the entitlement holder's property interest with respect to a particular financial asset under subsection (a), whether framed in conversion, replevin, constructive trust, equitable lien, or other theory, may not be asserted against any purchaser of a financial asset or interest therein who gives value, obtains control, and does not act in collusion with the securities intermediary in violating the securities intermediary's obligations under Section 8–504.

### § 8–504. Duty of Securities Intermediary to Maintain Financial Asset.

(a) A securities intermediary shall promptly obtain and thereafter maintain a financial asset in a quantity corresponding to the aggregate of all security entitlements it has established in favor of its entitlement holders with respect to that financial asset. The securities intermediary may maintain those financial assets directly or through one or more other securities intermediaries.

**(b)** Except to the extent otherwise agreed by its entitlement holder, a securities intermediary may not grant any security interests in a financial asset it is obligated to maintain pursuant to subsection (a).

**(c)** A securities intermediary satisfies the duty in subsection (a) if:

    **(1)** the securities intermediary acts with respect to the duty as agreed upon by the entitlement holder and the securities intermediary; or

    **(2)** in the absence of agreement, the securities intermediary exercises due care in accordance with reasonable commercial standards to obtain and maintain the financial asset.

**(d)** This section does not apply to a clearing corporation that is itself the obligor of an option or similar obligation to which its entitlement holders have security entitlements.

### § 8–505. Duty of Securities Intermediary with Respect to Payments and Distributions.

**(a)** A securities intermediary shall take action to obtain a payment or distribution made by the issuer of a financial asset. A securities intermediary satisfies the duty if:

    **(1)** the securities intermediary acts with respect to the duty as agreed upon by the entitlement holder and the securities intermediary; or

    **(2)** in the absence of agreement, the securities intermediary exercises due care in accordance with reasonable commercial standards to attempt to obtain the payment or distribution.

**(b)** A securities intermediary is obligated to its entitlement holder for a payment or distribution made by the issuer of a financial asset if the payment or distribution is received by the securities intermediary.

### § 8–506. Duty of Securities Intermediary to Exercise Rights as Directed by Entitlement Holder.

A securities intermediary shall exercise rights with respect to a financial asset if directed to do so by an entitlement holder. A securities intermediary satisfies the duty if:

    **(1)** the securities intermediary acts with respect to the duty as agreed upon by the entitlement holder and the securities intermediary; or

    **(2)** in the absence of agreement, the securities intermediary either places the entitlement holder in a position to exercise the rights directly or exercises due care in accordance with reasonable commercial standards to follow the direction of the entitlement holder.

### § 8–507. Duty of Securities Intermediary to Comply with Entitlement Order.

**(a)** A securities intermediary shall comply with an entitlement order if the entitlement order is originated by the appropriate person, the securities intermediary has had reasonable opportunity to assure itself that the entitlement order is genuine and authorized, and the securities intermediary has had reasonable opportunity to comply with the entitlement order. A securities intermediary satisfies the duty if:

    **(1)** the securities intermediary acts with respect to the duty as agreed upon by the entitlement holder and the securities intermediary; or

    **(2)** in the absence of agreement, the securities intermediary exercises due care in accordance with reasonable commercial standards to comply with the entitlement order.

**(b)** If a securities intermediary transfers a financial asset pursuant to an ineffective entitlement order, the securities intermediary shall reestablish a security entitlement in favor of the person entitled to it, and pay or credit any payments or distributions that the person did not receive as a result of the wrongful transfer. If the securities intermediary does not reestablish a security entitlement, the securities intermediary is liable to the entitlement holder for damages.

### § 8–508. Duty of Securities Intermediary to Change Entitlement Holder's Position to Other Form of Security Holding.

A securities intermediary shall act at the direction of an entitlement holder to change a security entitlement into another available form of holding for which the entitlement holder is eligible, or to cause the financial asset to be transferred to a securities account of the entitlement holder with another securities intermediary. A securities intermediary satisfies the duty if:

    **(1)** the securities intermediary acts as agreed upon by the entitlement holder and the securities intermediary; or

    **(2)** in the absence of agreement, the securities intermediary exercises due care in accordance with reasonable commercial standards to follow the direction of the entitlement holder.

### § 8–509. Specification of Duties of Securities Intermediary by Other Statute or Regulation; Manner of Performance of Duties of Securities Intermediary and Exercise of Rights of Entitlement Holder.

**(a)** If the substance of a duty imposed upon a securities intermediary by Sections 8–504 through 8–508 is the subject of other statute, regulation, or rule, compliance with that statute, regulation, or rule satisfies the duty.

**(b)** To the extent that specific standards for the performance of the duties of a securities intermediary or the exercise of the rights of an entitlement holder are not specified by other statute, regulation, or rule or by agreement between the securities intermediary and entitlement holder, the securities intermediary shall perform its duties and the entitlement holder shall exercise its rights in a commercially reasonable manner.

**(c)** The obligation of a securities intermediary to perform the duties imposed by Sections 8–504 through 8–508 is subject to:

    **(1)** rights of the securities intermediary arising out of a security interest under a security agreement with the entitlement holder or otherwise; and

    **(2)** rights of the securities intermediary under other law, regulation, rule, or agreement to withhold performance of its duties as a result of unfulfilled obligations of the entitlement holder to the securities intermediary.

**(d)** Sections 8–504 through 8–508 do not require a securities intermediary to take any action that is prohibited by other statute, regulation, or rule.

### § 8–510. Rights of Purchaser of Security Entitlement from Entitlement Holder.

**(a)** An action based on an adverse claim to a financial asset or security entitlement, whether framed in conversion, replevin, constructive trust, equitable lien, or other theory, may not be asserted against a person who purchases a security entitlement, or an interest therein, from an entitlement holder if the purchaser gives value, does not have notice of the adverse claim, and obtains control.

**(b)** If an adverse claim could not have been asserted against an entitlement holder under Section 8–502, the adverse claim cannot be asserted against a person who purchases a security entitlement, or an interest therein, from the entitlement holder.

**(c)** In a case not covered by the priority rules in Article 9, a purchaser for value of a security entitlement, or an interest therein, who obtains control has priority over a purchaser of a security entitlement, or an interest therein, who does not obtain control. Except as otherwise provided in subsection (d), purchasers who have control rank according to priority in time of:

> **(1)** the purchaser's becoming the person for whom the securities account, in which the security entitlement is carried, is maintained, if the purchaser obtained control under Section 8–106(d)(1);

> **(2)** the securities intermediary's agreement to comply with the purchaser's entitlement orders with respect to security entitlements carried or to be carried in the securities account in which the security entitlement is carried, if the purchaser obtained control under Section 8–106(d)(2); or

> **(3)** if the purchaser obtained control through another person under Section 8–106(d)(3), the time on which priority would be based under this subsection if the other person were the secured party.

**(d)** A securities intermediary as purchaser has priority over a conflicting purchaser who has control unless otherwise agreed by the securities intermediary.
As amended in 1999.

### § 8–511. Priority among Security Interests and Entitlement Holders.

**(a)** Except as otherwise provided in subsections (b) and (c), if a securities intermediary does not have sufficient interests in a particular financial asset to satisfy both its obligations to entitlement holders who have security entitlements to that financial asset and its obligation to a creditor of the securities intermediary who has a security interest in that financial asset, the claims of entitlement holders, other than the creditor, have priority over the claim of the creditor.

**(b)** A claim of a creditor of a securities intermediary who has a security interest in a financial asset held by a securities intermediary has priority over claims of the securities intermediary's entitlement holders who have security entitlements with respect to that financial asset if the creditor has control over the financial asset.

**(c)** If a clearing corporation does not have sufficient financial assets to satisfy both its obligations to entitlement holders who have security entitlements with respect to a financial asset and its obligation to a creditor of the clearing corporation who has a security interest in that financial asset, the claim of the creditor has priority over the claims of entitlement holders.

### Part 6—Transition Provisions for Revised Article 8

### § 8–601. Effective Date.
This [Act] takes effect . . . .

### § 8–602. Repeals.
This [Act] repeals . . . .

### § 8–603. Savings Clause.

**(a)** This [Act] does not affect an action or proceeding commenced before this [Act] takes effect.

**(b)** If a security interest in a security is perfected at the date this [Act] takes effect, and the action by which the security interest was perfected would suffice to perfect a security interest under this [Act], no further action is required to continue perfection. If a security interest in a security is perfected at the date this [Act] takes effect but the action by which the security interest was perfected would not suffice to perfect a security interest under this [Act], the security interest remains perfected for a period of four months after the effective date and continues perfected thereafter if appropriate action to perfect under this [Act] is taken within that period. If a security interest is perfected at the date this [Act] takes effect and the security interest can be perfected by filing under this [Act], a financing statement signed by the secured party instead of the debtor may be filed within that period to continue perfection or thereafter to perfect.

## REVISED ARTICLE 9: SECURED TRANSACTIONS

### Part 1—General Provisions

### [Subpart 1. Short Title, Definitions, and General Concepts]

### § 9–101. Short Title.
This article may be cited as Uniform Commercial Code—Secured Transactions.

### § 9–102. Definitions and Index of Definitions.

**(a)** In this article:

> **(1)** "Accession" means goods that are physically united with other goods in such a manner that the identity of the original goods is not lost.

> **(2)** "Account", except as used in "account for", means a right to payment of a monetary obligation, whether or not earned by performance, (i) for property that has been or is to be sold, leased, licensed, assigned, or otherwise disposed of, (ii) for services rendered or to be rendered, (iii) for a policy of insurance issued or to be issued, (iv) for a secondary obligation incurred or to be incurred, (v) for energy provided or to be pro-vided, (vi) for the use or hire of a vessel under a charter or other contract, (vii) arising out of the use of a credit or charge card or information contained on or for use with the card, or (viii) as winnings in a lottery or other game of chance operated or sponsored by a State, governmental unit of a State, or person licensed or authorized to operate the game by a State or governmental unit

of a State. The term includes health-care insurance receivables. The term does not include (i) rights to payment evidenced by chattel paper or an instrument, (ii) commercial tort claims, (iii) deposit accounts, (iv) investment property, (v) letter-of-credit rights or letters of credit, or (vi) rights to payment for money or funds advanced or sold, other than rights arising out of the use of a credit or charge card or information contained on or for use with the card.

**(3)** "Account debtor" means a person obligated on an account, chattel paper, or general intangible. The term does not include persons obligated to pay a negotiable instrument, even if the instrument constitutes part of chattel paper.

**(4)** "Accounting", except as used in "accounting for", means a record:

(A) authenticated by a secured party;

(B) indicating the aggregate unpaid secured obligations as of a date not more than 35 days earlier or 35 days later than the date of the record; and

(C) identifying the components of the obligations in reasonable detail.

**(5)** "Agricultural lien" means an interest, other than a security interest, in farm products:

(A) which secures payment or performance of an obligation for:

(i) goods or services furnished in connection with a debtor's farming operation; or

(ii) rent on real property leased by a debtor in connection with its farming operation;

(B) which is created by statute in favor of a person that:

(i) in the ordinary course of its business furnished goods or services to a debtor in connection with a debtor's farming operation; or

(ii) leased real property to a debtor in connection with the debtor's farming operation; and

(C) whose effectiveness does not depend on the person's possession of the personal property.

**(6)** "As-extracted collateral" means:

(A) oil, gas, or other minerals that are subject to a security interest that:

(i) is created by a debtor having an interest in the minerals before extraction; and

(ii) attaches to the minerals as extracted; or

(B) accounts arising out of the sale at the wellhead or minehead of oil, gas, or other minerals in which the debtor had an interest before extraction.

**(7)** "Authenticate" means:

(A) to sign; or

(B) to execute or otherwise adopt a symbol, or encrypt or similarly process a record in whole or in part, with the present intent of the authenticating person to identify the person and adopt or accept a record.

**(8)** "Bank" means an organization that is engaged in the business of banking. The term includes savings banks, savings and loan associations, credit unions, and trust companies.

**(9)** "Cash proceeds" means proceeds that are money, checks, deposit accounts, or the like.

**(10)** "Certificate of title" means a certificate of title with respect to which a statute provides for the security interest in question to be indicated on the certificate as a condition or result of the security interest's obtaining priority over the rights of a lien creditor with respect to the collateral.

**(11)** "Chattel paper" means a record or records that evidence both a monetary obligation and a security interest in specific goods, a security interest in specific goods and software used in the goods, a security interest in specific goods and license of software used in the goods, a lease of specific goods, or a lease of specific goods and license of software used in the goods. In this paragraph, "monetary obligation" means a monetary obligation secured by the goods or owed under a lease of the goods and includes a monetary obligation with respect to software used in the goods. The term does not include (i) charters or other contracts involving the use or hire of a vessel or (ii) records that evidence a right to payment arising out of the use of a credit or charge card or information contained on or for use with the card. If a transaction is evidenced by records that include an instrument or series of instruments, the group of records taken together constitutes chattel paper.

**(12)** "Collateral" means the property subject to a security interest or agricultural lien. The term includes:

(A) proceeds to which a security interest attaches;

(B) accounts, chattel paper, payment intangibles, and promissory notes that have been sold; and

(C) goods that are the subject of a consignment.

**(13)** "Commercial tort claim" means a claim arising in tort with respect to which:

(A) the claimant is an organization; or

(B) the claimant is an individual and the claim:

(i) arose in the course of the claimant's business or profession; and

(ii) does not include damages arising out of personal injury to or the death of an individual.

**(14)** "Commodity account" means an account maintained by a commodity intermediary in which a commodity contract is carried for a commodity customer.

**(15)** "Commodity contract" means a commodity futures contract, an option on a commodity futures contract, a commodity option, or another contract if the contract or option is:

(A) traded on or subject to the rules of a board of trade that has been designated as a contract market for such a contract pursuant to federal commodities laws; or

(B) traded on a foreign commodity board of trade, exchange, or market, and is carried on the books of a commodity intermediary for a commodity customer.

**(16)** "Commodity customer" means a person for which a commodity intermediary carries a commodity contract on its books.

**(17)** "Commodity intermediary" means a person that:

(A) is registered as a futures commission merchant under federal commodities law; or

(B) in the ordinary course of its business provides clearance or settlement services for a board of trade that has been designated as a contract market pursuant to federal commodities law.

**(18)** "Communicate" means:

**(A)** to send a written or other tangible record;

**(B)** to transmit a record by any means agreed upon by the persons sending and receiving the record; or

**(C)** in the case of transmission of a record to or by a filing office, to transmit a record by any means prescribed by filing-office rule.

**(19)** "Consignee" means a merchant to which goods are delivered in a consignment.

**(20)** "Consignment" means a transaction, regardless of its form, in which a person delivers goods to a merchant for the purpose of sale and:

**(A)** the merchant:

**(i)** deals in goods of that kind under a name other than the name of the person making delivery;

**(ii)** is not an auctioneer; and

**(iii)** is not generally known by its creditors to be substantially engaged in selling the goods of others;

**(B)** with respect to each delivery, the aggregate value of the goods is $1,000 or more at the time of delivery;

**(C)** the goods are not consumer goods immediately before delivery; and

**(D)** the transaction does not create a security interest that secures an obligation.

**(21)** "Consignor" means a person that delivers goods to a consignee in a consignment.

**(22)** "Consumer debtor" means a debtor in a consumer transaction.

**(23)** "Consumer goods" means goods that are used or bought for use primarily for personal, family, or household purposes.

**(24)** "Consumer-goods transaction" means a consumer transaction in which:

**(A)** an individual incurs an obligation primarily for personal, family, or household purposes; and

**(B)** a security interest in consumer goods secures the obligation.

**(25)** "Consumer obligor" means an obligor who is an individual and who incurred the obligation as part of a transaction entered into primarily for personal, family, or household purposes.

**(26)** "Consumer transaction" means a transaction in which (i) an individual incurs an obligation primarily for personal, family, or household purposes, (ii) a security interest secures the obligation, and (iii) the collateral is held or acquired primarily for personal, family, or household purposes. The term includes consumer-goods transactions.

**(27)** "Continuation statement" means an amendment of a financing statement which:

**(A)** identifies, by its file number, the initial financing statement to which it relates; and

**(B)** indicates that it is a continuation statement for, or that it is filed to continue the effectiveness of, the identified financing statement.

**(28)** "Debtor" means:

**(A)** a person having an interest, other than a security interest or other lien, in the collateral, whether or not the person is an obligor;

**(B)** a seller of accounts, chattel paper, payment intangibles, or promissory notes; or

**(C)** a consignee.

**(29)** "Deposit account" means a demand, time, savings, passbook, or similar account maintained with a bank. The term does not include investment property or accounts evidenced by an instrument.

**(30)** "Document" means a document of title or a receipt of the type described in Section 7–201(2).

**(31)** "Electronic chattel paper" means chattel paper evidenced by a record or records consisting of information stored in an electronic medium.

**(32)** "Encumbrance" means a right, other than an ownership interest, in real property. The term includes mortgages and other liens on real property.

**(33)** "Equipment" means goods other than inventory, farm products, or consumer goods.

**(34)** "Farm products" means goods, other than standing timber, with respect to which the debtor is engaged in a farming operation and which are:

**(A)** crops grown, growing, or to be grown, including:

**(i)** crops produced on trees, vines, and bushes; and

**(ii)** aquatic goods produced in aquacultural operations;

**(B)** livestock, born or unborn, including aquatic goods produced in aquacultural operations;

**(C)** supplies used or produced in a farming operation; or

**(D)** products of crops or livestock in their unmanufactured states.

**(35)** "Farming operation" means raising, cultivating, propagating, fattening, grazing, or any other farming, livestock, or aquacultural operation.

**(36)** "File number" means the number assigned to an initial financing statement pursuant to Section 9–519(a).

**(37)** "Filing office" means an office designated in Section 9–501 as the place to file a financing statement.

**(38)** "Filing-office rule" means a rule adopted pursuant to Section 9–526.

**(39)** "Financing statement" means a record or records composed of an initial financing statement and any filed record relating to the initial financing statement.

**(40)** "Fixture filing" means the filing of a financing statement covering goods that are or are to become fixtures and satisfying Section 9–502(a) and (b). The term includes the filing of a financing statement covering goods of a transmitting utility which are or are to become fixtures.

**(41)** "Fixtures" means goods that have become so related to particular real property that an interest in them arises under real property law.

**(42)** "General intangible" means any personal property, including things in action, other than accounts, chattel paper, commercial tort claims, deposit accounts, documents, goods, instruments, investment property, letter-of-credit rights, letters of credit, money, and oil, gas, or other minerals before extraction. The term includes payment intangibles and software.

**(43)** "Good faith" means honesty in fact and the observance of reasonable commercial standards of fair dealing.

**(44)** "Goods" means all things that are movable when a security interest attaches. The term includes (i) fixtures, (ii) standing timber that is to be cut and removed under a conveyance or contract for sale, (iii) the unborn young of animals, (iv) crops grown, growing, or to be grown, even if the crops are produced on trees, vines, or bushes, and (v) manufactured homes. The term also includes a computer program embedded in goods and any supporting information provided in connection with a transaction relating to the program if (i) the program is associated with the goods in such a manner that it customarily is considered part of the goods, or (ii) by becoming the owner of the goods, a person acquires a right to use the program in connection with the goods. The term does not include a computer program embedded in goods that consist solely of the medium in which the program is embedded. The term also does not include accounts, chattel paper, commercial tort claims, deposit accounts, documents, general intangibles, instruments, investment property, letter-of-credit rights, letters of credit, money, or oil, gas, or other minerals before extraction.

**(45)** "Governmental unit" means a subdivision, agency, department, county, parish, municipality, or other unit of the government of the United States, a State, or a foreign country. The term includes an organization having a separate corporate existence if the organization is eligible to issue debt on which interest is exempt from income taxation under the laws of the United States.

**(46)** "Health-care-insurance receivable" means an interest in or claim under a policy of insurance which is a right to payment of a monetary obligation for health-care goods or services provided.

**(47)** "Instrument" means a negotiable instrument or any other writing that evidences a right to the payment of a monetary obligation, is not itself a security agreement or lease, and is of a type that in ordinary course of business is transferred by delivery with any necessary indorsement or assignment. The term does not include (i) investment property, (ii) letters of credit, or (iii) writings that evidence a right to payment arising out of the use of a credit or charge card or information contained on or for use with the card.

**(48)** "Inventory" means goods, other than farm products, which:

    **(A)** are leased by a person as lessor;

    **(B)** are held by a person for sale or lease or to be furnished under a contract of service;

    **(C)** are furnished by a person under a contract of service; or

    **(D)** consist of raw materials, work in process, or materials used or consumed in a business.

**(49)** "Investment property" means a security, whether certificated or uncertificated, security entitlement, securities account, commodity contract, or commodity account.

**(50)** "Jurisdiction of organization", with respect to a registered organization, means the jurisdiction under whose law the organization is organized.

**(51)** "Letter-of-credit right" means a right to payment or performance under a letter of credit, whether or not the beneficiary has demanded or is at the time entitled to demand payment or performance. The term does not include the right of a beneficiary to demand payment or performance under a letter of credit.

**(52)** "Lien creditor" means:

    **(A)** a creditor that has acquired a lien on the property involved by attachment, levy, or the like;

    **(B)** an assignee for benefit of creditors from the time of assignment;

    **(C)** a trustee in bankruptcy from the date of the filing of the petition; or

    **(D)** a receiver in equity from the time of appointment.

**(53)** "Manufactured home" means a structure, transportable in one or more sections, which, in the traveling mode, is eight body feet or more in width or 40 body feet or more in length, or, when erected on site, is 320 or more square feet, and which is built on a permanent chassis and designed to be used as a dwelling with or without a permanent foundation when connected to the required utilities, and includes the plumbing, heating, air-conditioning, and electrical systems contained therein. The term includes any structure that meets all of the requirements of this paragraph except the size requirements and with respect to which the manufacturer voluntarily files a certification required by the United States Secretary of Housing and Urban Development and complies with the standards established under Title 42 of the United States Code.

**(54)** "Manufactured-home transaction" means a secured transaction:

    **(A)** that creates a purchase-money security interest in a manufactured home, other than a manufactured home held as inventory; or

    **(B)** in which a manufactured home, other than a manufactured home held as inventory, is the primary collateral.

**(55)** "Mortgage" means a consensual interest in real property, including fixtures, which secures payment or performance of an obligation.

**(56)** "New debtor" means a person that becomes bound as debtor under Section 9–203(d) by a security agreement previously entered into by another person.

**(57)** "New value" means (i) money, (ii) money's worth in property, services, or new credit, or (iii) release by a transferee of an interest in property previously transferred to the transferee. The term does not include an obligation substituted for another obligation.

**(58)** "Noncash proceeds" means proceeds other than cash proceeds.

**(59)** "Obligor" means a person that, with respect to an obligation secured by a security interest in or an agricultural lien on the collateral, (i) owes payment or other performance of the obligation, (ii) has provided property other than the collateral to secure payment or other performance of the obligation, or (iii) is otherwise accountable in whole or in part for payment or other performance of the obligation. The term does not include issuers or nominated persons under a letter of credit.

**(60)** "Original debtor", except as used in Section 9–310(c), means a person that, as debtor, entered into a security agreement to which a new debtor has become bound under Section 9–203(d).

**(61)** "Payment intangible" means a general intangible under which the account debtor's principal obligation is a monetary obligation.

**(62)** "Person related to", with respect to an individual, means:

**(A)** the spouse of the individual;

**(B)** a brother, brother-in-law, sister, or sister-in-law of the individual;

**(C)** an ancestor or lineal descendant of the individual or the individual's spouse; or

**(D)** any other relative, by blood or marriage, of the individual or the individual's spouse who shares the same home with the individual.

**(63)** "Person related to", with respect to an organization, means:

**(A)** a person directly or indirectly controlling, controlled by, or under common control with the organization;

**(B)** an officer or director of, or a person performing similar functions with respect to, the organization;

**(C)** an officer or director of, or a person performing similar functions with respect to, a person described in subparagraph (A);

**(D)** the spouse of an individual described in subparagraph (A), (B), or (C); or

**(E)** an individual who is related by blood or marriage to an individual described in subparagraph (A), (B), (C), or (D) and shares the same home with the individual.

**(64)** "Proceeds", except as used in Section 9–609(b), means the following property:

**(A)** whatever is acquired upon the sale, lease, license, exchange, or other disposition of collateral;

**(B)** whatever is collected on, or distributed on account of, collateral;

**(C)** rights arising out of collateral;

**(D)** to the extent of the value of collateral, claims arising out of the loss, nonconformity, or interference with the use of, defects or infringement of rights in, or damage to, the collateral; or

**(E)** to the extent of the value of collateral and to the extent payable to the debtor or the secured party, insurance payable by reason of the loss or nonconformity of, defects or infringement of rights in, or damage to, the collateral.

**(65)** "Promissory note" means an instrument that evidences a promise to pay a monetary obligation, does not evidence an order to pay, and does not contain an acknowledgment by a bank that the bank has received for deposit a sum of money or funds.

**(66)** "Proposal" means a record authenticated by a secured party which includes the terms on which the secured party is willing to accept collateral in full or partial satisfaction of the obligation it secures pursuant to Sections 9–620, 9–621, and 9–622.

**(67)** "Public-finance transaction" means a secured transaction in connection with which:

**(A)** debt securities are issued;

**(B)** all or a portion of the securities issued have an initial stated maturity of at least 20 years; and

**(C)** the debtor, obligor, secured party, account debtor or other person obligated on collateral, assignor or assignee of a secured obligation, or assignor or assignee of a security interest is a State or a governmental unit of a State.

**(68)** "Pursuant to commitment", with respect to an advance made or other value given by a secured party, means pursuant to the secured party's obligation, whether or not a subsequent event of default or other event not within the secured party's control has relieved or may relieve the secured party from its obligation.

**(69)** "Record", except as used in "for record", "of record", "record or legal title", and "record owner", means information that is inscribed on a tangible medium or which is stored in an electronic or other medium and is retrievable in perceivable form.

**(70)** "Registered organization" means an organization organized solely under the law of a single State or the United States and as to which the State or the United States must maintain a public record showing the organization to have been organized.

**(71)** "Secondary obligor" means an obligor to the extent that:

**(A)** the obligor's obligation is secondary; or

**(B)** the obligor has a right of recourse with respect to an obligation secured by collateral against the debtor, another obligor, or property of either.

**(72)** "Secured party" means:

**(A)** a person in whose favor a security interest is created or provided for under a security agreement, whether or not any obligation to be secured is outstanding;

**(B)** a person that holds an agricultural lien;

**(C)** a consignor;

**(D)** a person to which accounts, chattel paper, payment intangibles, or promissory notes have been sold;

**(E)** a trustee, indenture trustee, agent, collateral agent, or other representative in whose favor a security interest or agricultural lien is created or provided for; or

**(F)** a person that holds a security interest arising under Section 2–401, 2–505, 2–711(3), 2A–508(5), 4–210, or 5–118.

**(73)** "Security agreement" means an agreement that creates or provides for a security interest.

**(74)** "Send", in connection with a record or notification, means:

**(A)** to deposit in the mail, deliver for transmission, or transmit by any other usual means of communication, with postage or cost of transmission provided for, addressed to any address reasonable under the circumstances; or

**(B)** to cause the record or notification to be received within the time that it would have been received if properly sent under subparagraph (A).

**(75)** "Software" means a computer program and any supporting information provided in connection with a transaction relating to the program. The term does not include a computer program that is included in the definition of goods.

**(76)** "State" means a State of the United States, the District of Columbia, Puerto Rico, the United States Virgin Islands, or any territory or insular possession subject to the jurisdiction of the United States.

**(77)** "Supporting obligation" means a letter-of-credit right or secondary obligation that supports the payment or performance of an account, chattel paper, a document, a general intangible, an instrument, or investment property.

**(78)** "Tangible chattel paper" means chattel paper evidenced by a record or records consisting of information that is inscribed on a tangible medium.

**(79)** "Termination statement" means an amendment of a financing statement which:

**(A)** identifies, by its file number, the initial financing statement to which it relates; and

**(B)** indicates either that it is a termination statement or that the identified financing statement is no longer effective.

**(80)** "Transmitting utility" means a person primarily engaged in the business of:

**(A)** operating a railroad, subway, street railway, or trolley bus;

**(B)** transmitting communications electrically, electromagnetically, or by light;

**(C)** transmitting goods by pipeline or sewer; or

**(D)** transmitting or producing and transmitting electricity, steam, gas, or water.

**(b)** The following definitions in other articles apply to this article:

| | |
|---|---|
| "Applicant." | Section 5–102 |
| "Beneficiary." | Section 5–102 |
| "Broker." | Section 8–102 |
| "Certificated security." | Section 8–102 |
| "Check." | Section 3–104 |
| "Clearing corporation." | Section 8–102 |
| "Contract for sale." | Section 2–106 |
| "Customer." | Section 4–104 |
| "Entitlement holder." | Section 8–102 |
| "Financial asset." | Section 8–102 |
| "Holder in due course." | Section 3–302 |
| "Issuer" (with respect to a letter of credit or letter-of-credit right). | Section 5–102 |
| "Issuer" (with respect to a security). | Section 8–201 |
| "Lease." | Section 2A–103 |
| "Lease agreement." | Section 2A–103 |
| "Lease contract." | Section 2A–103 |
| "Leasehold interest." | Section 2A–103 |
| "Lessee." | Section 2A–103 |
| "Lessee in ordinary course of business." | Section 2A–103 |
| "Lessor." | Section 2A–103 |
| "Lessor's residual interest." | Section 2A–103 |
| "Letter of credit." | Section 5–102 |
| "Merchant." | Section 2–104 |
| "Negotiable instrument." | Section 3–104 |
| "Nominated person." | Section 5–102 |
| "Note." | Section 3–104 |
| "Proceeds of a letter of credit." | Section 5–114 |
| "Prove." | Section 3–103 |
| "Sale." | Section 2–106 |
| "Securities account." | Section 8–501 |
| "Securities intermediary." | Section 8–102 |
| "Security." | Section 8–102 |
| "Security certificate." | Section 8–102 |
| "Security entitlement." | Section 8–102 |
| "Uncertificated security." | Section 8–102 |

**(c)** Article 1 contains general definitions and principles of construction and interpretation applicable throughout this article. Amended in 1999 and 2000.

### § 9–103. Purchase-Money Security Interest; Application of Payments; Burden of Establishing.

**(a)** In this section:

**(1)** "purchase-money collateral" means goods or software that secures a purchase-money obligation incurred with respect to that collateral; and

**(2)** "purchase-money obligation" means an obligation of an obligor incurred as all or part of the price of the collateral or for value given to enable the debtor to acquire rights in or the use of the collateral if the value is in fact so used.

**(b)** A security interest in goods is a purchase-money security interest:

**(1)** to the extent that the goods are purchase-money collateral with respect to that security interest;

**(2)** if the security interest is in inventory that is or was purchase-money collateral, also to the extent that the security interest secures a purchase-money obligation incurred with respect to other inventory in which the secured party holds or held a purchase-money security interest; and

**(3)** also to the extent that the security interest secures a purchase-money obligation incurred with respect to software in which the secured party holds or held a purchase-money security interest.

**(c)** A security interest in software is a purchase-money security interest to the extent that the security interest also secures a purchase-money obligation incurred with respect to goods in which the secured party holds or held a purchase-money security interest if:

**(1)** the debtor acquired its interest in the software in an integrated transaction in which it acquired an interest in the goods; and

**(2)** the debtor acquired its interest in the software for the principal purpose of using the software in the goods.

**(d)** The security interest of a consignor in goods that are the subject of a consignment is a purchase-money security interest in inventory.

**(e)** In a transaction other than a consumer-goods transaction, if the extent to which a security interest is a purchase-money security interest depends on the application of a payment to a particular obligation, the payment must be applied:

    **(1)** in accordance with any reasonable method of application to which the parties agree;

    **(2)** in the absence of the parties' agreement to a reasonable method, in accordance with any intention of the obligor manifested at or before the time of payment; or

    **(3)** in the absence of an agreement to a reasonable method and a timely manifestation of the obligor's intention, in the following order:

        **(A)** to obligations that are not secured; and

        **(B)** if more than one obligation is secured, to obligations secured by purchase-money security interests in the order in which those obligations were incurred.

**(f)** In a transaction other than a consumer-goods transaction, a purchase-money security interest does not lose its status as such, even if:

    **(1)** the purchase-money collateral also secures an obligation that is not a purchase-money obligation;

    **(2)** collateral that is not purchase-money collateral also secures the purchase-money obligation; or

    **(3)** the purchase-money obligation has been renewed, refinanced, consolidated, or restructured.

**(g)** In a transaction other than a consumer-goods transaction, a secured party claiming a purchase-money security interest has the burden of establishing the extent to which the security interest is a purchase-money security interest.

**(h)** The limitation of the rules in subsections (e), (f), and (g) to transactions other than consumer-goods transactions is intended to leave to the court the determination of the proper rules in consumer-goods transactions. The court may not infer from that limitation the nature of the proper rule in consumer-goods transactions and may continue to apply established approaches.

### § 9–104. Control of Deposit Account.

**(a)** A secured party has control of a deposit account if:

    **(1)** the secured party is the bank with which the deposit account is maintained;

    **(2)** the debtor, secured party, and bank have agreed in an authenticated record that the bank will comply with instructions originated by the secured party directing disposition of the funds in the deposit account without further consent by the debtor; or

    **(3)** the secured party becomes the bank's customer with respect to the deposit account.

**(b)** A secured party that has satisfied subsection (a) has control, even if the debtor retains the right to direct the disposition of funds from the deposit account.

### § 9–105. Control of Electronic Chattel Paper.

A secured party has control of electronic chattel paper if the record or records comprising the chattel paper are created, stored, and assigned in such a manner that:

    **(1)** a single authoritative copy of the record or records exists which is unique, identifiable and, except as otherwise provided in paragraphs (4), (5), and (6), unalterable;

    **(2)** the authoritative copy identifies the secured party as the assignee of the record or records;

    **(3)** the authoritative copy is communicated to and maintained by the secured party or its designated custodian;

    **(4)** copies or revisions that add or change an identified assignee of the authoritative copy can be made only with the participation of the secured party;

    **(5)** each copy of the authoritative copy and any copy of a copy is readily identifiable as a copy that is not the authoritative copy; and

    **(6)** any revision of the authoritative copy is readily identifiable as an authorized or unauthorized revision.

### § 9–106. Control of Investment Property.

**(a)** A person has control of a certificated security, uncertificated security, or security entitlement as provided in Section 8–106.

**(b)** A secured party has control of a commodity contract if:

    **(1)** the secured party is the commodity intermediary with which the commodity contract is carried; or

    **(2)** the commodity customer, secured party, and commodity intermediary have agreed that the commodity intermediary will apply any value distributed on account of the commodity contract as directed by the secured party without further consent by the commodity customer.

**(c)** A secured party having control of all security entitlements or commodity contracts carried in a securities account or commodity account has control over the securities account or commodity account.

### § 9–107. Control of Letter-of-Credit Right.

A secured party has control of a letter-of-credit right to the extent of any right to payment or performance by the issuer or any nominated person if the issuer or nominated person has consented to an assignment of proceeds of the letter of credit under Section 5–114(c) or otherwise applicable law or practice.

### § 9–108. Sufficiency of Description.

**(a)** Except as otherwise provided in subsections (c), (d), and (e), a description of personal or real property is sufficient, whether or not it is specific, if it reasonably identifies what is described.

**(b)** Except as otherwise provided in subsection (d), a description of collateral reasonably identifies the collateral if it identifies the collateral by:

    **(1)** specific listing;

    **(2)** category;

    **(3)** except as otherwise provided in subsection (e), a type of collateral defined in [the Uniform Commercial Code];

    **(4)** quantity;

    **(5)** computational or allocational formula or procedure; or

    **(6)** except as otherwise provided in subsection (c), any other method, if the identity of the collateral is objectively determinable.

**(c)** A description of collateral as "all the debtor's assets" or "all the debtor's personal property" or using words of similar import does not reasonably identify the collateral.

**(d)** Except as otherwise provided in subsection (e), a description of a security entitlement, securities account, or commodity account is sufficient if it describes:

    **(1)** the collateral by those terms or as investment property; or

**(2)** the underlying financial asset or commodity contract.

**(e)** A description only by type of collateral defined in [the Uniform Commercial Code] is an insufficient description of:

**(1)** a commercial tort claim; or

**(2)** in a consumer transaction, consumer goods, a security entitlement, a securities account, or a commodity account.

### [Subpart 2. Applicability of Article]

### § 9–109. Scope.

**(a)** Except as otherwise provided in subsections (c) and (d), this article applies to:

**(1)** a transaction, regardless of its form, that creates a security interest in personal property or fixtures by contract;

**(2)** an agricultural lien;

**(3)** a sale of accounts, chattel paper, payment intangibles, or promissory notes;

**(4)** a consignment;

**(5)** a security interest arising under Section 2–401, 2–505, 2–711(3), or 2A–508(5), as provided in Section 9–110; and

**(6)** a security interest arising under Section 4–210 or 5–118.

**(b)** The application of this article to a security interest in a secured obligation is not affected by the fact that the obligation is itself secured by a transaction or interest to which this article does not apply.

**(c)** This article does not apply to the extent that:

**(1)** a statute, regulation, or treaty of the United States preempts this article;

**(2)** another statute of this State expressly governs the creation, perfection, priority, or enforcement of a security interest created by this State or a governmental unit of this State;

**(3)** a statute of another State, a foreign country, or a governmental unit of another State or a foreign country, other than a statute generally applicable to security interests, expressly governs creation, perfection, priority, or enforcement of a security interest created by the State, country, or governmental unit; or

**(4)** the rights of a transferee beneficiary or nominated person under a letter of credit are independent and superior under Section 5–114.

**(d)** This article does not apply to:

**(1)** a landlord's lien, other than an agricultural lien;

**(2)** a lien, other than an agricultural lien, given by statute or other rule of law for services or materials, but Section 9–333 applies with respect to priority of the lien;

**(3)** an assignment of a claim for wages, salary, or other compensation of an employee;

**(4)** a sale of accounts, chattel paper, payment intangibles, or promissory notes as part of a sale of the business out of which they arose;

**(5)** an assignment of accounts, chattel paper, payment intangibles, or promissory notes which is for the purpose of collection only;

**(6)** an assignment of a right to payment under a contract to an assignee that is also obligated to perform under the contract;

**(7)** an assignment of a single account, payment intangible, or promissory note to an assignee in full or partial satisfaction of a preexisting indebtedness;

**(8)** a transfer of an interest in or an assignment of a claim under a policy of insurance, other than an assignment by or to a health-care provider of a health-care-insurance receivable and any subsequent assignment of the right to payment, but Sections 9–315 and 9–322 apply with respect to proceeds and priorities in proceeds;

**(9)** an assignment of a right represented by a judgment, other than a judgment taken on a right to payment that was collateral;

**(10)** a right of recoupment or set-off, but:

**(A)** Section 9–340 applies with respect to the effectiveness of rights of recoupment or set-off against deposit accounts; and

**(B)** Section 9–404 applies with respect to defenses or claims of an account debtor;

**(11)** the creation or transfer of an interest in or lien on real property, including a lease or rents thereunder, except to the extent that provision is made for:

**(A)** liens on real property in Sections 9–203 and 9–308;

**(B)** fixtures in Section 9–334;

**(C)** fixture filings in Sections 9–501, 9–502, 9–512, 9–516, and 9–519; and

**(D)** security agreements covering personal and real property in Section 9–604;

**(12)** an assignment of a claim arising in tort, other than a commercial tort claim, but Sections 9–315 and 9–322 apply with respect to proceeds and priorities in proceeds; or

**(13)** an assignment of a deposit account in a consumer transaction, but Sections 9–315 and 9–322 apply with respect to proceeds and priorities in proceeds.

### § 9–110. Security Interests Arising under Article 2 or 2A.

A security interest arising under Section 2–401, 2–505, 2–711(3), or 2A–508(5) is subject to this article. However, until the debtor obtains possession of the goods:

**(1)** the security interest is enforceable, even if Section 9–203(b)(3) has not been satisfied;

**(2)** filing is not required to perfect the security interest;

**(3)** the rights of the secured party after default by the debtor are governed by Article 2 or 2A; and

**(4)** the security interest has priority over a conflicting security interest created by the debtor.

### Part 2—Effectiveness of Security Agreement; Attachment of Security Interest; Rights of Parties to Security Agreement

### [Subpart 1. Effectiveness and Attachment]

### § 9–201. General Effectiveness of Security Agreement.

**(a)** Except as otherwise provided in [the Uniform Commercial Code], a security agreement is effective according to its terms between the parties, against purchasers of the collateral, and against creditors.

**(b)** A transaction subject to this article is subject to any applicable rule of law which establishes a different rule for consumers and [insert reference to (i) any other statute or regulation that regulates the rates, charges, agreements, and practices for loans, credit sales, or other extensions of credit and (ii) any consumer-protection statute or regulation].

**(c)** In case of conflict between this article and a rule of law, statute, or regulation described in subsection (b), the rule of law, statute, or regulation controls. Failure to comply with a statute or regulation described in subsection (b) has only the effect the statute or regulation specifies.

**(d)** This article does not:

    **(1)** validate any rate, charge, agreement, or practice that violates a rule of law, statute, or regulation described in subsection (b); or

    **(2)** extend the application of the rule of law, statute, or regulation to a transaction not otherwise subject to it.

### § 9–202. Title to Collateral Immaterial.

Except as otherwise provided with respect to consignments or sales of accounts, chattel paper, payment intangibles, or promissory notes, the provisions of this article with regard to rights and obligations apply whether title to collateral is in the secured party or the debtor.

### § 9–203. Attachment and Enforceability of Security Interest; Proceeds; Supporting Obligations; Formal Requisites.

**(a)** A security interest attaches to collateral when it becomes enforceable against the debtor with respect to the collateral, unless an agreement expressly postpones the time of attachment.

**(b)** Except as otherwise provided in subsections (c) through (i), a security interest is enforceable against the debtor and third parties with respect to the collateral only if:

    **(1)** value has been given;

    **(2)** the debtor has rights in the collateral or the power to transfer rights in the collateral to a secured party; and

    **(3)** one of the following conditions is met:

        **(A)** the debtor has authenticated a security agreement that provides a description of the collateral and, if the security interest covers timber to be cut, a description of the land concerned;

        **(B)** the collateral is not a certificated security and is in the possession of the secured party under Section 9–313 pursuant to the debtor's security agreement;

        **(C)** the collateral is a certificated security in registered form and the security certificate has been delivered to the secured party under Section 8–301 pursuant to the debtor's security agreement; or

        **(D)** the collateral is deposit accounts, electronic chattel paper, investment property, or letter-of-credit rights, and the secured party has control under Section 9–104, 9–105, 9–106, or 9–107 pursuant to the debtor's security agreement.

**(c)** Subsection (b) is subject to Section 4–210 on the security interest of a collecting bank, Section 5–118 on the security interest of a letter-of-credit issuer or nominated person, Section 9–110 on a security interest arising under Article 2 or 2A, and Section 9–206 on security interests in investment property.

**(d)** A person becomes bound as debtor by a security agreement entered into by another person if, by operation of law other than this article or by contract:

    **(1)** the security agreement becomes effective to create a security interest in the person's property; or

    **(2)** the person becomes generally obligated for the obligations of the other person, including the obligation secured under the security agreement, and acquires or succeeds to all or substantially all of the assets of the other person.

**(e)** If a new debtor becomes bound as debtor by a security agreement entered into by another person:

    **(1)** the agreement satisfies subsection (b)(3) with respect to existing or after-acquired property of the new debtor to the extent the property is described in the agreement; and

    **(2)** another agreement is not necessary to make a security interest in the property enforceable.

**(f)** The attachment of a security interest in collateral gives the secured party the rights to proceeds provided by Section 9–315 and is also attachment of a security interest in a supporting obligation for the collateral.

**(g)** The attachment of a security interest in a right to payment or performance secured by a security interest or other lien on personal or real property is also attachment of a security interest in the security interest, mortgage, or other lien.

**(h)** The attachment of a security interest in a securities account is also attachment of a security interest in the security entitlements carried in the securities account.

**(i)** The attachment of a security interest in a commodity account is also attachment of a security interest in the commodity contracts carried in the commodity account.

### § 9–204. After-Acquired Property; Future Advances.

**(a)** Except as otherwise provided in subsection (b), a security agreement may create or provide for a security interest in after-acquired collateral.

**(b)** A security interest does not attach under a term constituting an after-acquired property clause to:

    **(1)** consumer goods, other than an accession when given as additional security, unless the debtor acquires rights in them within 10 days after the secured party gives value; or

    **(2)** a commercial tort claim.

**(c)** A security agreement may provide that collateral secures, or that accounts, chattel paper, payment intangibles, or promissory notes are sold in connection with, future advances or other value, whether or not the advances or value are given pursuant to commitment.

### § 9–205. Use or Disposition of Collateral Permissible.

**(a)** A security interest is not invalid or fraudulent against creditors solely because:

    **(1)** the debtor has the right or ability to:

        **(A)** use, commingle, or dispose of all or part of the collateral, including returned or repossessed goods;

        **(B)** collect, compromise, enforce, or otherwise deal with collateral;

        **(C)** accept the return of collateral or make repossessions; or

        **(D)** use, commingle, or dispose of proceeds; or

**(2)** the secured party fails to require the debtor to account for proceeds or replace collateral.

**(b)** This section does not relax the requirements of possession if attachment, perfection, or enforcement of a security interest depends upon possession of the collateral by the secured party.

## § 9–206. Security Interest Arising in Purchase or Delivery of Financial Asset.

**(a)** A security interest in favor of a securities intermediary attaches to a person's security entitlement if:

    **(1)** the person buys a financial asset through the securities intermediary in a transaction in which the person is obligated to pay the purchase price to the securities intermediary at the time of the purchase; and

    **(2)** the securities intermediary credits the financial asset to the buyer's securities account before the buyer pays the securities intermediary.

**(b)** The security interest described in subsection (a) secures the person's obligation to pay for the financial asset.

**(c)** A security interest in favor of a person that delivers a certificated security or other financial asset represented by a writing attaches to the security or other financial asset if:

    **(1)** the security or other financial asset:

        **(A)** in the ordinary course of business is transferred by delivery with any necessary indorsement or assignment; and

        **(B)** is delivered under an agreement between persons in the business of dealing with such securities or financial assets; and

    **(2)** the agreement calls for delivery against payment.

**(d)** The security interest described in subsection (c) secures the obligation to make payment for the delivery.

## [Subpart 2. Rights and Duties]

## § 9–207. Rights and Duties of Secured Party Having Possession or Control of Collateral.

**(a)** Except as otherwise provided in subsection (d), a secured party shall use reasonable care in the custody and preservation of collateral in the secured party's possession. In the case of chattel paper or an instrument, reasonable care includes taking necessary steps to preserve rights against prior parties unless otherwise agreed.

**(b)** Except as otherwise provided in subsection (d), if a secured party has possession of collateral:

    **(1)** reasonable expenses, including the cost of insurance and payment of taxes or other charges, incurred in the custody, preservation, use, or operation of the collateral are chargeable to the debtor and are secured by the collateral;

    **(2)** the risk of accidental loss or damage is on the debtor to the extent of a deficiency in any effective insurance coverage;

    **(3)** the secured party shall keep the collateral identifiable, but fungible collateral may be commingled; and

    **(4)** the secured party may use or operate the collateral:

        **(A)** for the purpose of preserving the collateral or its value;

        **(B)** as permitted by an order of a court having competent jurisdiction; or

        **(C)** except in the case of consumer goods, in the manner and to the extent agreed by the debtor.

**(c)** Except as otherwise provided in subsection (d), a secured party having possession of collateral or control of collateral under Section 9–104, 9–105, 9–106, or 9–107:

    **(1)** may hold as additional security any proceeds, except money or funds, received from the collateral;

    **(2)** shall apply money or funds received from the collateral to reduce the secured obligation, unless remitted to the debtor; and

    **(3)** may create a security interest in the collateral.

**(d)** If the secured party is a buyer of accounts, chattel paper, payment intangibles, or promissory notes or a consignor:

    **(1)** subsection (a) does not apply unless the secured party is entitled under an agreement:

        **(A)** to charge back uncollected collateral; or

        **(B)** otherwise to full or limited recourse against the debtor or a secondary obligor based on the nonpayment or other default of an account debtor or other obligor on the collateral; and

    **(2)** subsections (b) and (c) do not apply.

## § 9–208. Additional Duties of Secured Party Having Control of Collateral.

**(a)** This section applies to cases in which there is no outstanding secured obligation and the secured party is not committed to make advances, incur obligations, or otherwise give value.

**(b)** Within 10 days after receiving an authenticated demand by the debtor:

    **(1)** a secured party having control of a deposit account under Section 9–104(a)(2) shall send to the bank with which the deposit account is maintained an authenticated statement that releases the bank from any further obligation to comply with instructions originated by the secured party;

    **(2)** a secured party having control of a deposit account under Section 9–104(a)(3) shall:

        **(A)** pay the debtor the balance on deposit in the deposit account; or

        **(B)** transfer the balance on deposit into a deposit account in the debtor's name;

    **(3)** a secured party, other than a buyer, having control of electronic chattel paper under Section 9–105 shall:

        **(A)** communicate the authoritative copy of the electronic chattel paper to the debtor or its designated custodian;

        **(B)** if the debtor designates a custodian that is the designated custodian with which the authoritative copy of the electronic chattel paper is maintained for the secured party, communicate to the custodian an authenticated record releasing the designated custodian from any further obligation to comply with instructions originated by the secured party and instructing the custodian to comply with instructions originated by the debtor; and

        **(C)** take appropriate action to enable the debtor or its designated custodian to make copies of or revisions to the authoritative copy which add or change an identified assignee of the authoritative copy without the consent of the secured party;

**(4)** a secured party having control of investment property under Section 8–106(d)(2) or 9–106(b) shall send to the securities intermediary or commodity intermediary with which the security entitlement or commodity contract is maintained an authenticated record that releases the securities intermediary or commodity intermediary from any further obligation to comply with entitlement orders or directions originated by the secured party; and

**(5)** a secured party having control of a letter-of-credit right under Section 9–107 shall send to each person having an unfulfilled obligation to pay or deliver proceeds of the letter of credit to the secured party an authenticated release from any further obligation to pay or deliver proceeds of the letter of credit to the secured party.

### § 9–209. Duties of Secured Party If Account Debtor Has Been Notified of Assignment.

**(a)** Except as otherwise provided in subsection (c), this section applies if:

**(1)** there is no outstanding secured obligation; and

**(2)** the secured party is not committed to make advances, incur obligations, or otherwise give value.

**(b)** Within 10 days after receiving an authenticated demand by the debtor, a secured party shall send to an account debtor that has received notification of an assignment to the secured party as assignee under Section 9–406(a) an authenticated record that releases the account debtor from any further obligation to the secured party.

**(c)** This section does not apply to an assignment constituting the sale of an account, chattel paper, or payment intangible.

### § 9–210. Request for Accounting; Request Regarding List of Collateral or Statement of Account.

**(a)** In this section:

**(1)** "Request" means a record of a type described in paragraph (2), (3), or (4).

**(2)** "Request for an accounting" means a record authenticated by a debtor requesting that the recipient provide an accounting of the unpaid obligations secured by collateral and reasonably identifying the transaction or relationship that is the subject of the request.

**(3)** "Request regarding a list of collateral" means a record authenticated by a debtor requesting that the recipient approve or correct a list of what the debtor believes to be the collateral securing an obligation and reasonably identifying the transaction or relationship that is the subject of the request.

**(4)** "Request regarding a statement of account" means a record authenticated by a debtor requesting that the recipient approve or correct a statement indicating what the debtor believes to be the aggregate amount of unpaid obligations secured by collateral as of a specified date and reasonably identifying the transaction or relationship that is the subject of the request.

**(b)** Subject to subsections (c), (d), (e), and (f), a secured party, other than a buyer of accounts, chattel paper, payment intangibles, or promissory notes or a consignor, shall comply with a request within 14 days after receipt:

**(1)** in the case of a request for an accounting, by authenticating and sending to the debtor an accounting; and

**(2)** in the case of a request regarding a list of collateral or a request regarding a statement of account, by authenticating and sending to the debtor an approval or correction.

**(c)** A secured party that claims a security interest in all of a particular type of collateral owned by the debtor may comply with a request regarding a list of collateral by sending to the debtor an authenticated record including a statement to that effect within 14 days after receipt.

**(d)** A person that receives a request regarding a list of collateral, claims no interest in the collateral when it receives the request, and claimed an interest in the collateral at an earlier time shall comply with the request within 14 days after receipt by sending to the debtor an authenticated record:

**(1)** disclaiming any interest in the collateral; and

**(2)** if known to the recipient, providing the name and mailing address of any assignee of or successor to the recipient's interest in the collateral.

**(e)** A person that receives a request for an accounting or a request regarding a statement of account, claims no interest in the obligations when it receives the request, and claimed an interest in the obligations at an earlier time shall comply with the request within 14 days after receipt by sending to the debtor an authenticated record:

**(1)** disclaiming any interest in the obligations; and

**(2)** if known to the recipient, providing the name and mailing address of any assignee of or successor to the recipient's interest in the obligations.

**(f)** A debtor is entitled without charge to one response to a request under this section during any six-month period. The secured party may require payment of a charge not exceeding $25 for each additional response.

As amended in 1999.

### Part 3—Perfection and Priority

### [Subpart 1. Law Governing Perfection and Priority]

### § 9–301. Law Governing Perfection and Priority of Security Interests.

Except as otherwise provided in Sections 9–303 through 9–306, the following rules determine the law governing perfection, the effect of perfection or nonperfection, and the priority of a security interest in collateral:

**(1)** Except as otherwise provided in this section, while a debtor is located in a jurisdiction, the local law of that jurisdiction governs perfection, the effect of perfection or nonperfection, and the priority of a security interest in collateral.

**(2)** While collateral is located in a jurisdiction, the local law of that jurisdiction governs perfection, the effect of perfection or nonperfection, and the priority of a possessory security interest in that collateral.

**(3)** Except as otherwise provided in paragraph (4), while negotiable documents, goods, instruments, money, or tangible chattel paper is located in a jurisdiction, the local law of that jurisdiction governs:

**(A)** perfection of a security interest in the goods by filing a fixture filing;

**(B)** perfection of a security interest in timber to be cut; and

**(C)** the effect of perfection or nonperfection and the priority of a nonpossessory security interest in the collateral.

**(4)** The local law of the jurisdiction in which the wellhead or minehead is located governs perfection, the effect of perfection or nonperfection, and the priority of a security interest in as-extracted collateral.

### § 9–302. Law Governing Perfection and Priority of Agricultural Liens.

While farm products are located in a jurisdiction, the local law of that jurisdiction governs perfection, the effect of perfection or nonperfection, and the priority of an agricultural lien on the farm products.

### § 9–303. Law Governing Perfection and Priority of Security Interests in Goods Covered by a Certificate of Title.

**(a)** This section applies to goods covered by a certificate of title, even if there is no other relationship between the jurisdiction under whose certificate of title the goods are covered and the goods or the debtor.

**(b)** Goods become covered by a certificate of title when a valid application for the certificate of title and the applicable fee are delivered to the appropriate authority. Goods cease to be covered by a certificate of title at the earlier of the time the certificate of title ceases to be effective under the law of the issuing jurisdiction or the time the goods become covered subsequently by a certificate of title issued by another jurisdiction.

**(c)** The local law of the jurisdiction under whose certificate of title the goods are covered governs perfection, the effect of perfection or nonperfection, and the priority of a security interest in goods covered by a certificate of title from the time the goods become covered by the certificate of title until the goods cease to be covered by the certificate of title.

### § 9–304. Law Governing Perfection and Priority of Security Interests in Deposit Accounts.

**(a)** The local law of a bank's jurisdiction governs perfection, the effect of perfection or nonperfection, and the priority of a security interest in a deposit account maintained with that bank.

**(b)** The following rules determine a bank's jurisdiction for purposes of this part:

**(1)** If an agreement between the bank and the debtor governing the deposit account expressly provides that a particular jurisdiction is the bank's jurisdiction for purposes of this part, this article, or [the Uniform Commercial Code], that jurisdiction is the bank's jurisdiction.

**(2)** If paragraph (1) does not apply and an agreement between the bank and its customer governing the deposit account expressly provides that the agreement is governed by the law of a particular jurisdiction, that jurisdiction is the bank's jurisdiction.

**(3)** If neither paragraph (1) nor paragraph (2) applies and an agreement between the bank and its customer governing the deposit account expressly provides that the deposit account is maintained at an office in a particular jurisdiction, that jurisdiction is the bank's jurisdiction.

**(4)** If none of the preceding paragraphs applies, the bank's jurisdiction is the jurisdiction in which the office identified in an account statement as the office serving the customer's account is located.

**(5)** If none of the preceding paragraphs applies, the bank's jurisdiction is the jurisdiction in which the chief executive office of the bank is located.

### § 9–305. Law Governing Perfection and Priority of Security Interests in Investment Property.

**(a)** Except as otherwise provided in subsection (c), the following rules apply:

**(1)** While a security certificate is located in a jurisdiction, the local law of that jurisdiction governs perfection, the effect of perfection or nonperfection, and the priority of a security interest in the certificated security represented thereby.

**(2)** The local law of the issuer's jurisdiction as specified in Section 8–110(d) governs perfection, the effect of perfection or nonperfection, and the priority of a security interest in an uncertificated security.

**(3)** The local law of the securities intermediary's jurisdiction as specified in Section 8–110(e) governs perfection, the effect of perfection or nonperfection, and the priority of a security interest in a security entitlement or securities account.

**(4)** The local law of the commodity intermediary's jurisdiction governs perfection, the effect of perfection or nonperfection, and the priority of a security interest in a commodity contract or commodity account.

**(b)** The following rules determine a commodity intermediary's jurisdiction for purposes of this part:

**(1)** If an agreement between the commodity intermediary and commodity customer governing the commodity account expressly provides that a particular jurisdiction is the commodity intermediary's jurisdiction for purposes of this part, this article, or [the Uniform Commercial Code], that jurisdiction is the commodity intermediary's jurisdiction.

**(2)** If paragraph (1) does not apply and an agreement between the commodity intermediary and commodity customer governing the commodity account expressly provides that the agreement is governed by the law of a particular jurisdiction, that jurisdiction is the commodity intermediary's jurisdiction.

**(3)** If neither paragraph (1) nor paragraph (2) applies and an agreement between the commodity intermediary and commodity customer governing the commodity account expressly provides that the commodity account is maintained at an office in a particular jurisdiction, that jurisdiction is the commodity intermediary's jurisdiction.

**(4)** If none of the preceding paragraphs applies, the commodity intermediary's jurisdiction is the jurisdiction in which the office identified in an account statement as the office serving the commodity customer's account is located.

**(5)** If none of the preceding paragraphs applies, the commodity intermediary's jurisdiction is the jurisdiction in which the chief executive office of the commodity intermediary is located.

(c) The local law of the jurisdiction in which the debtor is located governs:

(1) perfection of a security interest in investment property by filing;

(2) automatic perfection of a security interest in investment property created by a broker or securities intermediary; and

(3) automatic perfection of a security interest in a commodity contract or commodity account created by a commodity intermediary.

### § 9–306. Law Governing Perfection and Priority of Security Interests in Letter-of-Credit Rights.

(a) Subject to subsection (c), the local law of the issuer's jurisdiction or a nominated person's jurisdiction governs perfection, the effect of perfection or nonperfection, and the priority of a security interest in a letter-of-credit right if the issuer's jurisdiction or nominated person's jurisdiction is a State.

(b) For purposes of this part, an issuer's jurisdiction or nominated person's jurisdiction is the jurisdiction whose law governs the liability of the issuer or nominated person with respect to the letter-of-credit right as provided in Section 5–116.

(c) This section does not apply to a security interest that is perfected only under Section 9–308(d).

### § 9–307. Location of Debtor.

(a) In this section, "place of business" means a place where a debtor conducts its affairs.

(b) Except as otherwise provided in this section, the following rules determine a debtor's location:

(1) A debtor who is an individual is located at the individual's principal residence.

(2) A debtor that is an organization and has only one place of business is located at its place of business.

(3) A debtor that is an organization and has more than one place of business is located at its chief executive office.

(c) Subsection (b) applies only if a debtor's residence, place of business, or chief executive office, as applicable, is located in a jurisdiction whose law generally requires information concerning the existence of a nonpossessory security interest to be made generally available in a filing, recording, or registration system as a condition or result of the security interest's obtaining priority over the rights of a lien creditor with respect to the collateral. If subsection (b) does not apply, the debtor is located in the District of Columbia.

(d) A person that ceases to exist, have a residence, or have a place of business continues to be located in the jurisdiction specified by subsections (b) and (c).

(e) A registered organization that is organized under the law of a State is located in that State.

(f) Except as otherwise provided in subsection (i), a registered organization that is organized under the law of the United States and a branch or agency of a bank that is not organized under the law of the United States or a State are located:

(1) in the State that the law of the United States designates, if the law designates a State of location;

(2) in the State that the registered organization, branch, or agency designates, if the law of the United States authorizes the registered organization, branch, or agency to designate its State of location; or

(3) in the District of Columbia, if neither paragraph (1) nor paragraph (2) applies.

(g) A registered organization continues to be located in the jurisdiction specified by subsection (e) or (f) notwithstanding:

(1) the suspension, revocation, forfeiture, or lapse of the registered organization's status as such in its jurisdiction of organization; or

(2) the dissolution, winding up, or cancellation of the existence of the registered organization.

(h) The United States is located in the District of Columbia.

(i) A branch or agency of a bank that is not organized under the law of the United States or a State is located in the State in which the branch or agency is licensed, if all branches and agencies of the bank are licensed in only one State.

(j) A foreign air carrier under the Federal Aviation Act of 1958, as amended, is located at the designated office of the agent upon which service of process may be made on behalf of the carrier.

(k) This section applies only for purposes of this part.

### [Subpart 2. Perfection]

### § 9–308. When Security Interest or Agricultural Lien Is Perfected; Continuity of Perfection.

(a) Except as otherwise provided in this section and Section 9–309, a security interest is perfected if it has attached and all of the applicable requirements for perfection in Sections 9–310 through 9–316 have been satisfied. A security interest is perfected when it attaches if the applicable requirements are satisfied before the security interest attaches.

(b) An agricultural lien is perfected if it has become effective and all of the applicable requirements for perfection in Section 9–310 have been satisfied. An agricultural lien is perfected when it becomes effective if the applicable requirements are satisfied before the agricultural lien becomes effective.

(c) A security interest or agricultural lien is perfected continuously if it is originally perfected by one method under this article and is later perfected by another method under this article, without an intermediate period when it was unperfected.

(d) Perfection of a security interest in collateral also perfects a security interest in a supporting obligation for the collateral.

(e) Perfection of a security interest in a right to payment or performance also perfects a security interest in a security interest, mortgage, or other lien on personal or real property securing the right.

(f) Perfection of a security interest in a securities account also perfects a security interest in the security entitlements carried in the securities account.

(g) Perfection of a security interest in a commodity account also perfects a security interest in the commodity contracts carried in the commodity account.

Legislative Note: *Any statute conflicting with subsection (e) must be made expressly subject to that subsection.*

### § 9–309. Security Interest Perfected upon Attachment.

The following security interests are perfected when they attach:

(1) a purchase-money security interest in consumer goods, except as otherwise provided in Section 9–311(b)

with respect to consumer goods that are subject to a statute or treaty described in Section 9–311(a);

**(2)** an assignment of accounts or payment intangibles which does not by itself or in conjunction with other assignments to the same assignee transfer a significant part of the assignor's outstanding accounts or payment intangibles;

**(3)** a sale of a payment intangible;

**(4)** a sale of a promissory note;

**(5)** a security interest created by the assignment of a health-care-insurance receivable to the provider of the health-care goods or services;

**(6)** a security interest arising under Section 2–401, 2–505, 2–711(3), or 2A–508(5), until the debtor obtains possession of the collateral;

**(7)** a security interest of a collecting bank arising under Section 4–210;

**(8)** a security interest of an issuer or nominated person arising under Section 5–118;

**(9)** a security interest arising in the delivery of a financial asset under Section 9–206(c);

**(10)** a security interest in investment property created by a broker or securities intermediary;

**(11)** a security interest in a commodity contract or a commodity account created by a commodity intermediary;

**(12)** an assignment for the benefit of all creditors of the transferor and subsequent transfers by the assignee thereunder; and

**(13)** a security interest created by an assignment of a beneficial interest in a decedent's estate; and

**(14)** a sale by an individual of an account that is a right to payment of winnings in a lottery or other game of chance.

## § 9–310. When Filing Required to Perfect Security Interest or Agricultural Lien; Security Interests and Agricultural Liens to Which Filing Provisions Do Not Apply.

**(a)** Except as otherwise provided in subsection (b) and Section 9–312(b), a financing statement must be filed to perfect all security interests and agricultural liens.

**(b)** The filing of a financing statement is not necessary to perfect a security interest:

**(1)** that is perfected under Section 9–308(d), (e), (f), or (g);

**(2)** that is perfected under Section 9–309 when it attaches;

**(3)** in property subject to a statute, regulation, or treaty described in Section 9–311(a);

**(4)** in goods in possession of a bailee which is perfected under Section 9–312(d)(1) or (2);

**(5)** in certificated securities, documents, goods, or instruments which is perfected without filing or possession under Section 9–312(e), (f), or (g);

**(6)** in collateral in the secured party's possession under Section 9–313;

**(7)** in a certificated security which is perfected by delivery of the security certificate to the secured party under Section 9–313;

**(8)** in deposit accounts, electronic chattel paper, investment property, or letter-of-credit rights which is perfected by control under Section 9–314;

**(9)** in proceeds which is perfected under Section 9–315; or

**(10)** that is perfected under Section 9–316.

**(c)** If a secured party assigns a perfected security interest or agricultural lien, a filing under this article is not required to continue the perfected status of the security interest against creditors of and transferees from the original debtor.

## § 9–311. Perfection of Security Interests in Property Subject to Certain Statutes, Regulations, and Treaties.

**(a)** Except as otherwise provided in subsection (d), the filing of a financing statement is not necessary or effective to perfect a security interest in property subject to:

**(1)** a statute, regulation, or treaty of the United States whose requirements for a security interest's obtaining priority over the rights of a lien creditor with respect to the property pre-empt Section 9–310(a);

**(2)** [list any certificate-of-title statute covering automobiles, trailers, mobile homes, boats, farm tractors, or the like, which provides for a security interest to be indicated on the certificate as a condition or result of perfection, and any non-Uniform Commercial Code central filing statute]; or

**(3)** a certificate-of-title statute of another jurisdiction which provides for a security interest to be indicated on the certificate as a condition or result of the security interest's obtaining priority over the rights of a lien creditor with respect to the property.

**(b)** Compliance with the requirements of a statute, regulation, or treaty described in subsection (a) for obtaining priority over the rights of a lien creditor is equivalent to the filing of a financing statement under this article. Except as otherwise provided in subsection (d) and Sections 9–313 and 9–316(d) and (e) for goods covered by a certificate of title, a security interest in property subject to a statute, regulation, or treaty described in subsection (a) may be perfected only by compliance with those requirements, and a security interest so perfected remains perfected notwithstanding a change in the use or transfer of possession of the collateral.

**(c)** Except as otherwise provided in subsection (d) and Section 9–316(d) and (e), duration and renewal of perfection of a security interest perfected by compliance with the requirements prescribed by a statute, regulation, or treaty described in subsection (a) are governed by the statute, regulation, or treaty. In other respects, the security interest is subject to this article.

**(d)** During any period in which collateral subject to a statute specified in subsection (a)(2) is inventory held for sale or lease by a person or leased by that person as lessor and that person is in the business of selling goods of that kind, this section does not apply to a security interest in that collateral created by that person.

Legislative Note: *This Article contemplates that perfection of a security interest in goods covered by a certificate of title occurs upon receipt by appropriate State officials of a properly tendered application for a certificate of title on which the security interest is to be indicated, without a relation back to an earlier time. States whose certificate-of-title statutes provide for perfection at a different time or contain a relation-back provision should amend the statutes accordingly.*

## § 9–312. Perfection of Security Interests in Chattel Paper, Deposit Accounts, Documents, Goods Covered by Documents, Instruments, Investment Property, Letter-of-Credit Rights, and Money; Perfection by Permissive Filing; Temporary Perfection without Filing or Transfer of Possession.

(a) A security interest in chattel paper, negotiable documents, instruments, or investment property may be perfected by filing.

(b) Except as otherwise provided in Section 9–315(c) and (d) for proceeds:

(1) a security interest in a deposit account may be perfected only by control under Section 9–314;

(2) and except as otherwise provided in Section 9–308(d), a security interest in a letter-of-credit right may be perfected only by control under Section 9–314; and

(3) a security interest in money may be perfected only by the secured party's taking possession under Section 9–313.

(c) While goods are in the possession of a bailee that has issued a negotiable document covering the goods:

(1) a security interest in the goods may be perfected by perfecting a security interest in the document; and

(2) a security interest perfected in the document has priority over any security interest that becomes perfected in the goods by another method during that time.

(d) While goods are in the possession of a bailee that has issued a nonnegotiable document covering the goods, a security interest in the goods may be perfected by:

(1) issuance of a document in the name of the secured party;

(2) the bailee's receipt of notification of the secured party's interest; or

(3) filing as to the goods.

(e) A security interest in certificated securities, negotiable documents, or instruments is perfected without filing or the taking of possession for a period of 20 days from the time it attaches to the extent that it arises for new value given under an authenticated security agreement.

(f) A perfected security interest in a negotiable document or goods in possession of a bailee, other than one that has issued a negotiable document for the goods, remains perfected for 20 days without filing if the secured party makes available to the debtor the goods or documents representing the goods for the purpose of:

(1) ultimate sale or exchange; or

(2) loading, unloading, storing, shipping, transshipping, manufacturing, processing, or otherwise dealing with them in a manner preliminary to their sale or exchange.

(g) A perfected security interest in a certificated security or instrument remains perfected for 20 days without filing if the secured party delivers the security certificate or instrument to the debtor for the purpose of:

(1) ultimate sale or exchange; or

(2) presentation, collection, enforcement, renewal, or registration of transfer.

(h) After the 20-day period specified in subsection (e), (f), or (g) expires, perfection depends upon compliance with this article.

## § 9–313. When Possession by or Delivery to Secured Party Perfects Security Interest without Filing.

(a) Except as otherwise provided in subsection (b), a secured party may perfect a security interest in negotiable documents, goods, instruments, money, or tangible chattel paper by taking possession of the collateral. A secured party may perfect a security interest in certificated securities by taking delivery of the certificated securities under Section 8–301.

(b) With respect to goods covered by a certificate of title issued by this State, a secured party may perfect a security interest in the goods by taking possession of the goods only in the circumstances described in Section 9–316(d).

(c) With respect to collateral other than certificated securities and goods covered by a document, a secured party takes possession of collateral in the possession of a person other than the debtor, the secured party, or a lessee of the collateral from the debtor in the ordinary course of the debtor's business, when:

(1) the person in possession authenticates a record acknowledging that it holds possession of the collateral for the secured party's benefit; or

(2) the person takes possession of the collateral after having authenticated a record acknowledging that it will hold possession of collateral for the secured party's benefit.

(d) If perfection of a security interest depends upon possession of the collateral by a secured party, perfection occurs no earlier than the time the secured party takes possession and continues only while the secured party retains possession.

(e) A security interest in a certificated security in registered form is perfected by delivery when delivery of the certificated security occurs under Section 8–301 and remains perfected by delivery until the debtor obtains possession of the security certificate.

(f) A person in possession of collateral is not required to acknowledge that it holds possession for a secured party's benefit.

(g) If a person acknowledges that it holds possession for the secured party's benefit:

(1) the acknowledgment is effective under subsection (c) or Section 8–301(a), even if the acknowledgment violates the rights of a debtor; and

(2) unless the person otherwise agrees or law other than this article otherwise provides, the person does not owe any duty to the secured party and is not required to confirm the acknowledgment to another person.

(h) A secured party having possession of collateral does not relinquish possession by delivering the collateral to a person other than the debtor or a lessee of the collateral from the debtor in the ordinary course of the debtor's business if the person was instructed before the delivery or is instructed contemporaneously with the delivery:

(1) to hold possession of the collateral for the secured party's benefit; or

(2) to redeliver the collateral to the secured party.

(i) A secured party does not relinquish possession, even if a delivery under subsection (h) violates the rights of a debtor. A person to which collateral is delivered under subsection (h) does not owe any duty to the secured party and is not required to confirm the delivery to another person unless the person otherwise agrees or law other than this article otherwise provides.

### § 9–314. Perfection by Control.

**(a)** A security interest in investment property, deposit accounts, letter-of-credit rights, or electronic chattel paper may be perfected by control of the collateral under Section 9–104, 9–105, 9–106, or 9–107.

**(b)** A security interest in deposit accounts, electronic chattel paper, or letter-of-credit rights is perfected by control under Section 9–104, 9–105, or 9–107 when the secured party obtains control and remains perfected by control only while the secured party retains control.

**(c)** A security interest in investment property is perfected by control under Section 9–106 from the time the secured party obtains control and remains perfected by control until:

   **(1)** the secured party does not have control; and

   **(2)** one of the following occurs:

      **(A)** if the collateral is a certificated security, the debtor has or acquires possession of the security certificate;

      **(B)** if the collateral is an uncertificated security, the issuer has registered or registers the debtor as the registered owner; or

      **(C)** if the collateral is a security entitlement, the debtor is or becomes the entitlement holder.

### § 9–315. Secured Party's Rights on Disposition of Collateral and in Proceeds.

**(a)** Except as otherwise provided in this article and in Section 2–403(2):

   **(1)** a security interest or agricultural lien continues in collateral notwithstanding sale, lease, license, exchange, or other disposition thereof unless the secured party authorized the disposition free of the security interest or agricultural lien; and

   **(2)** a security interest attaches to any identifiable proceeds of collateral.

**(b)** Proceeds that are commingled with other property are identifiable proceeds:

   **(1)** if the proceeds are goods, to the extent provided by Section 9–336; and

   **(2)** if the proceeds are not goods, to the extent that the secured party identifies the proceeds by a method of tracing, including application of equitable principles, that is permitted under law other than this article with respect to commingled property of the type involved.

**(c)** A security interest in proceeds is a perfected security interest if the security interest in the original collateral was perfected.

**(d)** A perfected security interest in proceeds becomes unperfected on the 21st day after the security interest attaches to the proceeds unless:

   **(1)** the following conditions are satisfied:

      **(A)** a filed financing statement covers the original collateral;

      **(B)** the proceeds are collateral in which a security interest may be perfected by filing in the office in which the financing statement has been filed; and

      **(C)** the proceeds are not acquired with cash proceeds;

   **(2)** the proceeds are identifiable cash proceeds; or

   **(3)** the security interest in the proceeds is perfected other than under subsection (c) when the security interest attaches to the proceeds or within 20 days thereafter.

**(e)** If a filed financing statement covers the original collateral, a security interest in proceeds which remains perfected under subsection (d)(1) becomes unperfected at the later of:

   **(1)** when the effectiveness of the filed financing statement lapses under Section 9–515 or is terminated under Section 9–513; or

   **(2)** the 21st day after the security interest attaches to the proceeds.

### § 9–316. Continued Perfection of Security Interest Following Change in Governing Law.

**(a)** A security interest perfected pursuant to the law of the jurisdiction designated in Section 9–301(1) or 9–305(c) remains perfected until the earliest of:

   **(1)** the time perfection would have ceased under the law of that jurisdiction;

   **(2)** the expiration of four months after a change of the debtor's location to another jurisdiction; or

   **(3)** the expiration of one year after a transfer of collateral to a person that thereby becomes a debtor and is located in another jurisdiction.

**(b)** If a security interest described in subsection (a) becomes perfected under the law of the other jurisdiction before the earliest time or event described in that subsection, it remains perfected thereafter. If the security interest does not become perfected under the law of the other jurisdiction before the earliest time or event, it becomes unperfected and is deemed never to have been perfected as against a purchaser of the collateral for value.

**(c)** A possessory security interest in collateral, other than goods covered by a certificate of title and as-extracted collateral consisting of goods, remains continuously perfected if:

   **(1)** the collateral is located in one jurisdiction and subject to a security interest perfected under the law of that jurisdiction;

   **(2)** thereafter the collateral is brought into another jurisdiction; and

   **(3)** upon entry into the other jurisdiction, the security interest is perfected under the law of the other jurisdiction.

**(d)** Except as otherwise provided in subsection (e), a security interest in goods covered by a certificate of title which is perfected by any method under the law of another jurisdiction when the goods become covered by a certificate of title from this State remains perfected until the security interest would have become unperfected under the law of the other jurisdiction had the goods not become so covered.

**(e)** A security interest described in subsection (d) becomes unperfected as against a purchaser of the goods for value and is deemed never to have been perfected as against a purchaser of the goods for value if the applicable requirements for perfection under Section 9–311(b) or 9–313 are not satisfied before the earlier of:

   **(1)** the time the security interest would have become unperfected under the law of the other jurisdiction had the goods not become covered by a certificate of title from this State; or

**(2)** the expiration of four months after the goods had become so covered.

**(f)** A security interest in deposit accounts, letter-of-credit rights, or investment property which is perfected under the law of the bank's jurisdiction, the issuer's jurisdiction, a nominated person's jurisdiction, the securities intermediary's jurisdiction, or the commodity intermediary's jurisdiction, as applicable, remains perfected until the earlier of:

**(1)** the time the security interest would have become unperfected under the law of that jurisdiction; or

**(2)** the expiration of four months after a change of the applicable jurisdiction to another jurisdiction.

**(g)** If a security interest described in subsection (f) becomes perfected under the law of the other jurisdiction before the earlier of the time or the end of the period described in that subsection, it remains perfected thereafter. If the security interest does not become perfected under the law of the other jurisdiction before the earlier of that time or the end of that period, it becomes unperfected and is deemed never to have been perfected as against a purchaser of the collateral for value.

### [Subpart 3. Priority]

### § 9–317. Interests That Take Priority over or Take Free of Security Interest or Agricultural Lien.

**(a)** A security interest or agricultural lien is subordinate to the rights of:

**(1)** a person entitled to priority under Section 9–322; and

**(2)** except as otherwise provided in subsection (e), a person that becomes a lien creditor before the earlier of the time:

**(A)** the security interest or agricultural lien is perfected; or

**(B)** one of the conditions specified in Section 9–203(b)(3) is met and a financing statement covering the collateral is filed.

**(b)** Except as otherwise provided in subsection (e), a buyer, other than a secured party, of tangible chattel paper, documents, goods, instruments, or a security certificate takes free of a security interest or agricultural lien if the buyer gives value and receives delivery of the collateral without knowledge of the security interest or agricultural lien and before it is perfected.

**(c)** Except as otherwise provided in subsection (e), a lessee of goods takes free of a security interest or agricultural lien if the lessee gives value and receives delivery of the collateral without knowledge of the security interest or agricultural lien and before it is perfected.

**(d)** A licensee of a general intangible or a buyer, other than a secured party, of accounts, electronic chattel paper, general intangibles, or investment property other than a certificated security takes free of a security interest if the licensee or buyer gives value without knowledge of the security interest and before it is perfected.

**(e)** Except as otherwise provided in Sections 9–320 and 9–321, if a person files a financing statement with respect to a purchase-money security interest before or within 20 days after the debtor receives delivery of the collateral, the security interest takes priority over the rights of a buyer, lessee, or lien creditor which arise between the time the security interest attaches and the time of filing.

As amended in 2000.

### § 9–318. No Interest Retained in Right to Payment That Is Sold; Rights and Title of Seller of Account or Chattel Paper with Respect to Creditors and Purchasers.

**(a)** A debtor that has sold an account, chattel paper, payment intangible, or promissory note does not retain a legal or equitable interest in the collateral sold.

**(b)** For purposes of determining the rights of creditors of, and purchasers for value of an account or chattel paper from, a debtor that has sold an account or chattel paper, while the buyer's security interest is unperfected, the debtor is deemed to have rights and title to the account or chattel paper identical to those the debtor sold.

### § 9–319. Rights and Title of Consignee with Respect to Creditors and Purchasers.

**(a)** Except as otherwise provided in subsection (b), for purposes of determining the rights of creditors of, and purchasers for value of goods from, a consignee, while the goods are in the possession of the consignee, the consignee is deemed to have rights and title to the goods identical to those the consignor had or had power to transfer.

**(b)** For purposes of determining the rights of a creditor of a consignee, law other than this article determines the rights and title of a consignee while goods are in the consignee's possession if, under this part, a perfected security interest held by the consignor would have priority over the rights of the creditor.

### § 9–320. Buyer of Goods.

**(a)** Except as otherwise provided in subsection (e), a buyer in ordinary course of business, other than a person buying farm products from a person engaged in farming operations, takes free of a security interest created by the buyer's seller, even if the security interest is perfected and the buyer knows of its existence.

**(b)** Except as otherwise provided in subsection (e), a buyer of goods from a person who used or bought the goods for use primarily for personal, family, or household purposes takes free of a security interest, even if perfected, if the buyer buys:

**(1)** without knowledge of the security interest;

**(2)** for value;

**(3)** primarily for the buyer's personal, family, or household purposes; and

**(4)** before the filing of a financing statement covering the goods.

**(c)** To the extent that it affects the priority of a security interest over a buyer of goods under subsection (b), the period of effectiveness of a filing made in the jurisdiction in which the seller is located is governed by Section 9–316(a) and (b).

**(d)** A buyer in ordinary course of business buying oil, gas, or other minerals at the wellhead or minehead or after extraction takes free of an interest arising out of an encumbrance.

**(e)** Subsections (a) and (b) do not affect a security interest in goods in the possession of the secured party under Section 9–313.

## § 9–321. Licensee of General Intangible and Lessee of Goods in Ordinary Course of Business.

(a) In this section, "licensee in ordinary course of business" means a person that becomes a licensee of a general intangible in good faith, without knowledge that the license violates the rights of another person in the general intangible, and in the ordinary course from a person in the business of licensing general intangibles of that kind. A person becomes a licensee in the ordinary course if the license to the person comports with the usual or customary practices in the kind of business in which the licensor is engaged or with the licensor's own usual or customary practices.

(b) A licensee in ordinary course of business takes its rights under a nonexclusive license free of a security interest in the general intangible created by the licensor, even if the security interest is perfected and the licensee knows of its existence.

(c) A lessee in ordinary course of business takes its leasehold interest free of a security interest in the goods created by the lessor, even if the security interest is perfected and the lessee knows of its existence.

## § 9–322. Priorities among Conflicting Security Interests in and Agricultural Liens on Same Collateral.

(a) Except as otherwise provided in this section, priority among conflicting security interests and agricultural liens in the same collateral is determined according to the following rules:

(1) Conflicting perfected security interests and agricultural liens rank according to priority in time of filing or perfection. Priority dates from the earlier of the time a filing covering the collateral is first made or the security interest or agricultural lien is first perfected, if there is no period thereafter when there is neither filing nor perfection.

(2) A perfected security interest or agricultural lien has priority over a conflicting unperfected security interest or agricultural lien.

(3) The first security interest or agricultural lien to attach or become effective has priority if conflicting security interests and agricultural liens are unperfected.

(b) For the purposes of subsection (a)(1):

(1) the time of filing or perfection as to a security interest in collateral is also the time of filing or perfection as to a security interest in proceeds; and

(2) the time of filing or perfection as to a security interest in collateral supported by a supporting obligation is also the time of filing or perfection as to a security interest in the supporting obligation.

(c) Except as otherwise provided in subsection (f), a security interest in collateral which qualifies for priority over a conflicting security interest under Section 9–327, 9–328, 9–329, 9–330, or 9–331 also has priority over a conflicting security interest in:

(1) any supporting obligation for the collateral; and

(2) proceeds of the collateral if:

(A) the security interest in proceeds is perfected;

(B) the proceeds are cash proceeds or of the same type as the collateral; and

(C) in the case of proceeds that are proceeds of proceeds, all intervening proceeds are cash proceeds, proceeds of the same type as the collateral, or an account relating to the collateral.

(d) Subject to subsection (e) and except as otherwise provided in subsection (f), if a security interest in chattel paper, deposit accounts, negotiable documents, instruments, investment property, or letter-of-credit rights is perfected by a method other than filing, conflicting perfected security interests in proceeds of the collateral rank according to priority in time of filing.

(e) Subsection (d) applies only if the proceeds of the collateral are not cash proceeds, chattel paper, negotiable documents, instruments, investment property, or letter-of-credit rights.

(f) Subsections (a) through (e) are subject to:

(1) subsection (g) and the other provisions of this part;

(2) Section 4–210 with respect to a security interest of a collecting bank;

(3) Section 5–118 with respect to a security interest of an issuer or nominated person; and

(4) Section 9–110 with respect to a security interest arising under Article 2 or 2A.

(g) A perfected agricultural lien on collateral has priority over a conflicting security interest in or agricultural lien on the same collateral if the statute creating the agricultural lien so provides.

## § 9–323. Future Advances.

(a) Except as otherwise provided in subsection (c), for purposes of determining the priority of a perfected security interest under Section 9–322(a)(1), perfection of the security interest dates from the time an advance is made to the extent that the security interest secures an advance that:

(1) is made while the security interest is perfected only:

(A) under Section 9–309 when it attaches; or

(B) temporarily under Section 9–312(e), (f), or (g); and

(2) is not made pursuant to a commitment entered into before or while the security interest is perfected by a method other than under Section 9–309 or 9–312(e), (f), or (g).

(b) Except as otherwise provided in subsection (c), a security interest is subordinate to the rights of a person that becomes a lien creditor to the extent that the security interest secures an advance made more than 45 days after the person becomes a lien creditor unless the advance is made:

(1) without knowledge of the lien; or

(2) pursuant to a commitment entered into without knowledge of the lien.

(c) Subsections (a) and (b) do not apply to a security interest held by a secured party that is a buyer of accounts, chattel paper, payment intangibles, or promissory notes or a consignor.

(d) Except as otherwise provided in subsection (e), a buyer of goods other than a buyer in ordinary course of business takes free of a security interest to the extent that it secures advances made after the earlier of:

(1) the time the secured party acquires knowledge of the buyer's purchase; or

(2) 45 days after the purchase.

(e) Subsection (d) does not apply if the advance is made pursuant to a commitment entered into without knowledge of the buyer's purchase and before the expiration of the 45-day period.

(f) Except as otherwise provided in subsection (g), a lessee of goods, other than a lessee in ordinary course of business, takes the leasehold interest free of a security interest to the extent that it secures advances made after the earlier of:

(1) the time the secured party acquires knowledge of the lease; or

(2) 45 days after the lease contract becomes enforceable.

(g) Subsection (f) does not apply if the advance is made pursuant to a commitment entered into without knowledge of the lease and before the expiration of the 45-day period.

As amended in 1999.

### § 9–324. Priority of Purchase-Money Security Interests.

(a) Except as otherwise provided in subsection (g), a perfected purchase-money security interest in goods other than inventory or livestock has priority over a conflicting security interest in the same goods, and, except as otherwise provided in Section 9–327, a perfected security interest in its identifiable proceeds also has priority, if the purchase-money security interest is perfected when the debtor receives possession of the collateral or within 20 days thereafter.

(b) Subject to subsection (c) and except as otherwise provided in subsection (g), a perfected purchase-money security interest in inventory has priority over a conflicting security interest in the same inventory, has priority over a conflicting security interest in chattel paper or an instrument constituting proceeds of the inventory and in proceeds of the chattel paper, if so provided in Section 9–330, and, except as otherwise provided in Section 9–327, also has priority in identifiable cash proceeds of the inventory to the extent the identifiable cash proceeds are received on or before the delivery of the inventory to a buyer, if:

(1) the purchase-money security interest is perfected when the debtor receives possession of the inventory;

(2) the purchase-money secured party sends an authenticated notification to the holder of the conflicting security interest;

(3) the holder of the conflicting security interest receives the notification within five years before the debtor receives possession of the inventory; and

(4) the notification states that the person sending the notification has or expects to acquire a purchase-money security interest in inventory of the debtor and describes the inventory.

(c) Subsections (b)(2) through (4) apply only if the holder of the conflicting security interest had filed a financing statement covering the same types of inventory:

(1) if the purchase-money security interest is perfected by filing, before the date of the filing; or

(2) if the purchase-money security interest is temporarily perfected without filing or possession under Section 9–312(f), before the beginning of the 20-day period thereunder.

(d) Subject to subsection (e) and except as otherwise provided in subsection (g), a perfected purchase-money security interest in livestock that are farm products has priority over a conflicting security interest in the same livestock, and, except as otherwise provided in Section 9–327, a perfected security interest in their identifiable proceeds and identifiable products in their unmanufactured states also has priority, if:

(1) the purchase-money security interest is perfected when the debtor receives possession of the livestock;

(2) the purchase-money secured party sends an authenticated notification to the holder of the conflicting security interest;

(3) the holder of the conflicting security interest receives the notification within six months before the debtor receives possession of the livestock; and

(4) the notification states that the person sending the notification has or expects to acquire a purchase-money security interest in livestock of the debtor and describes the livestock.

(e) Subsections (d)(2) through (4) apply only if the holder of the conflicting security interest had filed a financing statement covering the same types of livestock:

(1) if the purchase-money security interest is perfected by filing, before the date of the filing; or

(2) if the purchase-money security interest is temporarily perfected without filing or possession under Section 9–312(f), before the beginning of the 20-day period thereunder.

(f) Except as otherwise provided in subsection (g), a perfected purchase-money security interest in software has priority over a conflicting security interest in the same collateral, and, except as otherwise provided in Section 9–327, a perfected security interest in its identifiable proceeds also has priority, to the extent that the purchase-money security interest in the goods in which the software was acquired for use has priority in the goods and proceeds of the goods under this section.

(g) If more than one security interest qualifies for priority in the same collateral under subsection (a), (b), (d), or (f):

(1) a security interest securing an obligation incurred as all or part of the price of the collateral has priority over a security interest securing an obligation incurred for value given to enable the debtor to acquire rights in or the use of collateral; and

(2) in all other cases, Section 9–322(a) applies to the qualifying security interests.

### § 9–325. Priority of Security Interests in Transferred Collateral.

(a) Except as otherwise provided in subsection (b), a security interest created by a debtor is subordinate to a security interest in the same collateral created by another person if:

(1) the debtor acquired the collateral subject to the security interest created by the other person;

(2) the security interest created by the other person was perfected when the debtor acquired the collateral; and

(3) there is no period thereafter when the security interest is unperfected.

(b) Subsection (a) subordinates a security interest only if the security interest:

(1) otherwise would have priority solely under Section 9–322(a) or 9–324; or

(2) arose solely under Section 2–711(3) or 2A–508(5).

### § 9–326. Priority of Security Interests Created by New Debtor.

(a) Subject to subsection (b), a security interest created by a new debtor which is perfected by a filed financing statement that is effective solely under Section 9–508 in collateral in which a new debtor has or acquires rights is subordinate to a security interest in the same collateral which is perfected other than by a filed financing statement that is effective solely under Section 9–508.

**(b)** The other provisions of this part determine the priority among conflicting security interests in the same collateral perfected by filed financing statements that are effective solely under Section 9–508. However, if the security agreements to which a new debtor became bound as debtor were not entered into by the same original debtor, the conflicting security interests rank according to priority in time of the new debtor's having become bound.

### § 9–327. Priority of Security Interests in Deposit Account.

The following rules govern priority among conflicting security interests in the same deposit account:

**(1)** A security interest held by a secured party having control of the deposit account under Section 9–104 has priority over a conflicting security interest held by a secured party that does not have control.

**(2)** Except as otherwise provided in paragraphs (3) and (4), security interests perfected by control under Section 9–314 rank according to priority in time of obtaining control.

**(3)** Except as otherwise provided in paragraph (4), a security interest held by the bank with which the deposit account is maintained has priority over a conflicting security interest held by another secured party.

**(4)** A security interest perfected by control under Section 9–104(a)(3) has priority over a security interest held by the bank with which the deposit account is maintained.

### § 9–328. Priority of Security Interests in Investment Property.

The following rules govern priority among conflicting security interests in the same investment property:

**(1)** A security interest held by a secured party having control of investment property under Section 9–106 has priority over a security interest held by a secured party that does not have control of the investment property.

**(2)** Except as otherwise provided in paragraphs (3) and (4), conflicting security interests held by secured parties each of which has control under Section 9–106 rank according to priority in time of:

  **(A)** if the collateral is a security, obtaining control;

  **(B)** if the collateral is a security entitlement carried in a securities account and:

    **(i)** if the secured party obtained control under Section 8–106(d)(1), the secured party's becoming the person for which the securities account is maintained;

    **(ii)** if the secured party obtained control under Section 8–106(d)(2), the securities intermediary's agreement to comply with the secured party's entitlement orders with respect to security entitlements carried or to be carried in the securities account; or

    **(iii)** if the secured party obtained control through another person under Section 8–106(d)(3), the time on which priority would be based under this paragraph if the other person were the secured party; or

  **(C)** if the collateral is a commodity contract carried with a commodity intermediary, the satisfaction of the requirement for control specified in Section 9–106(b)(2) with respect to commodity contracts carried or to be carried with the commodity intermediary.

**(3)** A security interest held by a securities intermediary in a security entitlement or a securities account maintained with the securities intermediary has priority over a conflicting security interest held by another secured party.

**(4)** A security interest held by a commodity intermediary in a commodity contract or a commodity account maintained with the commodity intermediary has priority over a conflicting security interest held by another secured party.

**(5)** A security interest in a certificated security in registered form which is perfected by taking delivery under Section 9–313(a) and not by control under Section 9–314 has priority over a conflicting security interest perfected by a method other than control.

**(6)** Conflicting security interests created by a broker, securities intermediary, or commodity intermediary which are perfected without control under Section 9–106 rank equally.

**(7)** In all other cases, priority among conflicting security interests in investment property is governed by Sections 9–322 and 9–323.

### § 9–329. Priority of Security Interests in Letter-of-Credit Right.

The following rules govern priority among conflicting security interests in the same letter-of-credit right:

**(1)** A security interest held by a secured party having control of the letter-of-credit right under Section 9–107 has priority to the extent of its control over a conflicting security interest held by a secured party that does not have control.

**(2)** Security interests perfected by control under Section 9–314 rank according to priority in time of obtaining control.

### § 9–330. Priority of Purchaser of Chattel Paper or Instrument.

**(a)** A purchaser of chattel paper has priority over a security interest in the chattel paper which is claimed merely as proceeds of inventory subject to a security interest if:

**(1)** in good faith and in the ordinary course of the purchaser's business, the purchaser gives new value and takes possession of the chattel paper or obtains control of the chattel paper under Section 9–105; and

**(2)** the chattel paper does not indicate that it has been assigned to an identified assignee other than the purchaser.

**(b)** A purchaser of chattel paper has priority over a security interest in the chattel paper which is claimed other than merely as proceeds of inventory subject to a security interest if the purchaser gives new value and takes possession of the chattel paper or obtains control of the chattel paper under Section 9–105 in good faith, in the ordinary course of the purchaser's business, and without knowledge that the purchase violates the rights of the secured party.

(c) Except as otherwise provided in Section 9–327, a purchaser having priority in chattel paper under subsection (a) or (b) also has priority in proceeds of the chattel paper to the extent that:

(1) Section 9–322 provides for priority in the proceeds; or

(2) the proceeds consist of the specific goods covered by the chattel paper or cash proceeds of the specific goods, even if the purchaser's security interest in the proceeds is unperfected.

(d) Except as otherwise provided in Section 9–331(a), a purchaser of an instrument has priority over a security interest in the instrument perfected by a method other than possession if the purchaser gives value and takes possession of the instrument in good faith and without knowledge that the purchase violates the rights of the secured party.

(e) For purposes of subsections (a) and (b), the holder of a purchase-money security interest in inventory gives new value for chattel paper constituting proceeds of the inventory.

(f) For purposes of subsections (b) and (d), if chattel paper or an instrument indicates that it has been assigned to an identified secured party other than the purchaser, a purchaser of the chattel paper or instrument has knowledge that the purchase violates the rights of the secured party.

### § 9–331. Priority of Rights of Purchasers of Instruments, Documents, and Securities under Other Articles; Priority of Interests in Financial Assets and Security Entitlements under Article 8.

(a) This article does not limit the rights of a holder in due course of a negotiable instrument, a holder to which a negotiable document of title has been duly negotiated, or a protected purchaser of a security. These holders or purchasers take priority over an earlier security interest, even if perfected, to the extent provided in Articles 3, 7, and 8.

(b) This article does not limit the rights of or impose liability on a person to the extent that the person is protected against the assertion of a claim under Article 8.

(c) Filing under this article does not constitute notice of a claim or defense to the holders, or purchasers, or persons described in subsections (a) and (b).

### § 9–332. Transfer of Money; Transfer of Funds from Deposit Account.

(a) A transferee of money takes the money free of a security interest unless the transferee acts in collusion with the debtor in violating the rights of the secured party.

(b) A transferee of funds from a deposit account takes the funds free of a security interest in the deposit account unless the transferee acts in collusion with the debtor in violating the rights of the secured party.

### § 9–333. Priority of Certain Liens Arising by Operation of Law.

(a) In this section, "possessory lien" means an interest, other than a security interest or an agricultural lien:

(1) which secures payment or performance of an obligation for services or materials furnished with respect to goods by a person in the ordinary course of the person's business;

(2) which is created by statute or rule of law in favor of the person; and

(3) whose effectiveness depends on the person's possession of the goods.

(b) A possessory lien on goods has priority over a security interest in the goods unless the lien is created by a statute that expressly provides otherwise.

### § 9–334. Priority of Security Interests in Fixtures and Crops.

(a) A security interest under this article may be created in goods that are fixtures or may continue in goods that become fixtures. A security interest does not exist under this article in ordinary building materials incorporated into an improvement on land.

(b) This article does not prevent creation of an encumbrance upon fixtures under real property law.

(c) In cases not governed by subsections (d) through (h), a security interest in fixtures is subordinate to a conflicting interest of an encumbrancer or owner of the related real property other than the debtor.

(d) Except as otherwise provided in subsection (h), a perfected security interest in fixtures has priority over a conflicting interest of an encumbrancer or owner of the real property if the debtor has an interest of record in or is in possession of the real property and:

(1) the security interest is a purchase-money security interest;

(2) the interest of the encumbrancer or owner arises before the goods become fixtures; and

(3) the security interest is perfected by a fixture filing before the goods become fixtures or within 20 days thereafter.

(e) A perfected security interest in fixtures has priority over a conflicting interest of an encumbrancer or owner of the real property if:

(1) the debtor has an interest of record in the real property or is in possession of the real property and the security interest:

(A) is perfected by a fixture filing before the interest of the encumbrancer or owner is of record; and

(B) has priority over any conflicting interest of a predecessor in title of the encumbrancer or owner;

(2) before the goods become fixtures, the security interest is perfected by any method permitted by this article and the fixtures are readily removable:

(A) factory or office machines;

(B) equipment that is not primarily used or leased for use in the operation of the real property; or

(C) replacements of domestic appliances that are consumer goods;

(3) the conflicting interest is a lien on the real property obtained by legal or equitable proceedings after the security interest was perfected by any method permitted by this article; or

(4) the security interest is:

**(A)** created in a manufactured home in a manufactured-home transaction; and

**(B)** perfected pursuant to a statute described in Section 9–311(a)(2).

**(f)** A security interest in fixtures, whether or not perfected, has priority over a conflicting interest of an encumbrancer or owner of the real property if:

**(1)** the encumbrancer or owner has, in an authenticated record, consented to the security interest or disclaimed an interest in the goods as fixtures; or

**(2)** the debtor has a right to remove the goods as against the encumbrancer or owner.

**(g)** The priority of the security interest under paragraph (f)(2) continues for a reasonable time if the debtor's right to remove the goods as against the encumbrancer or owner terminates.

**(h)** A mortgage is a construction mortgage to the extent that it secures an obligation incurred for the construction of an improvement on land, including the acquisition cost of the land, if a recorded record of the mortgage so indicates. Except as otherwise provided in subsections (e) and (f), a security interest in fixtures is subordinate to a construction mortgage if a record of the mortgage is recorded before the goods become fixtures and the goods become fixtures before the completion of the construction. A mortgage has this priority to the same extent as a construction mortgage to the extent that it is given to refinance a construction mortgage.

**(i)** A perfected security interest in crops growing on real property has priority over a conflicting interest of an encumbrancer or owner of the real property if the debtor has an interest of record in or is in possession of the real property.

**(j)** Subsection (i) prevails over any inconsistent provisions of the following statutes:

[List here any statutes containing provisions inconsistent with subsection (i).]

Legislative Note: *States that amend statutes to remove provisions inconsistent with subsection (i) need not enact subsection (j).*

### § 9–335. Accessions.

**(a)** A security interest may be created in an accession and continues in collateral that becomes an accession.

**(b)** If a security interest is perfected when the collateral becomes an accession, the security interest remains perfected in the collateral.

**(c)** Except as otherwise provided in subsection (d), the other provisions of this part determine the priority of a security interest in an accession.

**(d)** A security interest in an accession is subordinate to a security interest in the whole which is perfected by compliance with the requirements of a certificate-of-title statute under Section 9–311(b).

**(e)** After default, subject to Part 6, a secured party may remove an accession from other goods if the security interest in the accession has priority over the claims of every person having an interest in the whole.

**(f)** A secured party that removes an accession from other goods under subsection (e) shall promptly reimburse any holder of a security interest or other lien on, or owner of, the whole or of the other goods, other than the debtor, for the cost of repair of any physical injury to the whole or the other goods. The secured party need not reimburse the holder or owner for any diminution in value of the whole or the other goods caused by the absence of the accession removed or by any necessity for replacing it. A person entitled to reimbursement may refuse permission to remove until the secured party gives adequate assurance for the performance of the obligation to reimburse.

### § 9–336. Commingled Goods.

**(a)** In this section, "commingled goods" means goods that are physically united with other goods in such a manner that their identity is lost in a product or mass.

**(b)** A security interest does not exist in commingled goods as such. However, a security interest may attach to a product or mass that results when goods become commingled goods.

**(c)** If collateral becomes commingled goods, a security interest attaches to the product or mass.

**(d)** If a security interest in collateral is perfected before the collateral becomes commingled goods, the security interest that attaches to the product or mass under subsection (c) is perfected.

**(e)** Except as otherwise provided in subsection (f), the other provisions of this part determine the priority of a security interest that attaches to the product or mass under subsection (c).

**(f)** If more than one security interest attaches to the product or mass under subsection (c), the following rules determine priority:

**(1)** A security interest that is perfected under subsection (d) has priority over a security interest that is unperfected at the time the collateral becomes commingled goods.

**(2)** If more than one security interest is perfected under subsection (d), the security interests rank equally in proportion to the value of the collateral at the time it became commingled goods.

### § 9–337. Priority of Security Interests in Goods Covered by Certificate of Title.

If, while a security interest in goods is perfected by any method under the law of another jurisdiction, this State issues a certificate of title that does not show that the goods are subject to the security interest or contain a statement that they may be subject to security interests not shown on the certificate:

**(1)** a buyer of the goods, other than a person in the business of selling goods of that kind, takes free of the security interest if the buyer gives value and receives delivery of the goods after issuance of the certificate and without knowledge of the security interest; and

**(2)** the security interest is subordinate to a conflicting security interest in the goods that attaches, and is perfected under Section 9–311(b), after issuance of the certificate and without the conflicting secured party's knowledge of the security interest.

### § 9–338. Priority of Security Interest or Agricultural Lien Perfected by Filed Financing Statement Providing Certain Incorrect Information.

If a security interest or agricultural lien is perfected by a filed financing statement providing information described in Section 9–516(b)(5) which is incorrect at the time the financing statement is filed:

**(1)** the security interest or agricultural lien is subordinate to a conflicting perfected security interest in the collateral to the extent that the holder of the conflicting security interest gives value in reasonable reliance upon the incorrect information; and

**(2)** a purchaser, other than a secured party, of the collateral takes free of the security interest or agricultural lien to the extent that, in reasonable reliance upon the incorrect information, the purchaser gives value and, in the case of chattel paper, documents, goods, instruments, or a security certificate, receives delivery of the collateral.

### § 9–339. Priority Subject to Subordination.
This article does not preclude subordination by agreement by a person entitled to priority.

### [Subpart 4. Rights of Bank]

### § 9–340. Effectiveness of Right of Recoupment or Set-Off against Deposit Account.
**(a)** Except as otherwise provided in subsection (c), a bank with which a deposit account is maintained may exercise any right of recoupment or set-off against a secured party that holds a security interest in the deposit account.

**(b)** Except as otherwise provided in subsection (c), the application of this article to a security interest in a deposit account does not affect a right of recoupment or set-off of the secured party as to a deposit account maintained with the secured party.

**(c)** The exercise by a bank of a set-off against a deposit account is ineffective against a secured party that holds a security interest in the deposit account which is perfected by control under Section 9–104(a)(3), if the set-off is based on a claim against the debtor.

### § 9–341. Bank's Rights and Duties with Respect to Deposit Account.
Except as otherwise provided in Section 9–340(c), and unless the bank otherwise agrees in an authenticated record, a bank's rights and duties with respect to a deposit account maintained with the bank are not terminated, suspended, or modified by:

**(1)** the creation, attachment, or perfection of a security interest in the deposit account;

**(2)** the bank's knowledge of the security interest; or

**(3)** the bank's receipt of instructions from the secured party.

### § 9–342. Bank's Right to Refuse to Enter into or Disclose Existence of Control Agreement.
This article does not require a bank to enter into an agreement of the kind described in Section 9–104(a)(2), even if its customer so requests or directs. A bank that has entered into such an agreement is not required to confirm the existence of the agreement to another person unless requested to do so by its customer.

### Part 4—Rights of Third Parties

### § 9–401. Alienability of Debtor's Rights.
**(a)** Except as otherwise provided in subsection (b) and Sections 9–406, 9–407, 9–408, and 9–409, whether a debtor's rights in collateral may be voluntarily or involuntarily transferred is governed by law other than this article.

**(b)** An agreement between the debtor and secured party which prohibits a transfer of the debtor's rights in collateral or makes the transfer a default does not prevent the transfer from taking effect.

### § 9–402. Secured Party Not Obligated on Contract of Debtor or in Tort.
The existence of a security interest, agricultural lien, or authority given to a debtor to dispose of or use collateral, without more, does not subject a secured party to liability in contract or tort for the debtor's acts or omissions.

### § 9–403. Agreement Not to Assert Defenses against Assignee.
**(a)** In this section, "value" has the meaning provided in Section 3–303(a).

**(b)** Except as otherwise provided in this section, an agreement between an account debtor and an assignor not to assert against an assignee any claim or defense that the account debtor may have against the assignor is enforceable by an assignee that takes an assignment:

**(1)** for value;

**(2)** in good faith;

**(3)** without notice of a claim of a property or possessory right to the property assigned; and

**(4)** without notice of a defense or claim in recoupment of the type that may be asserted against a person entitled to enforce a negotiable instrument under Section 3–305(a).

**(c)** Subsection (b) does not apply to defenses of a type that may be asserted against a holder in due course of a negotiable instrument under Section 3–305(b).

**(d)** In a consumer transaction, if a record evidences the account debtor's obligation, law other than this article requires that the record include a statement to the effect that the rights of an assignee are subject to claims or defenses that the account debtor could assert against the original obligee, and the record does not include such a statement:

**(1)** the record has the same effect as if the record included such a statement; and

**(2)** the account debtor may assert against an assignee those claims and defenses that would have been available if the record included such a statement.

**(e)** This section is subject to law other than this article which establishes a different rule for an account debtor who is an individual and who incurred the obligation primarily for personal, family, or household purposes.

**(f)** Except as otherwise provided in subsection (d), this section does not displace law other than this article which gives effect to an agreement by an account debtor not to assert a claim or defense against an assignee.

### § 9–404. Rights Acquired by Assignee; Claims and Defenses against Assignee.
**(a)** Unless an account debtor has made an enforceable agreement not to assert defenses or claims, and subject to subsections (b) through (e), the rights of an assignee are subject to:

**(1)** all terms of the agreement between the account debtor and assignor and any defense or claim in recoupment arising from the transaction that gave rise to the contract; and

**(2)** any other defense or claim of the account debtor against the assignor which accrues before the account debtor receives a notification of the assignment authenticated by the assignor or the assignee.

**(b)** Subject to subsection (c) and except as otherwise provided in subsection (d), the claim of an account debtor against an assignor may be asserted against an assignee under subsection (a) only to reduce the amount the account debtor owes.

**(c)** This section is subject to law other than this article which establishes a different rule for an account debtor who is an individual and who incurred the obligation primarily for personal, family, or household purposes.

**(d)** In a consumer transaction, if a record evidences the account debtor's obligation, law other than this article requires that the record include a statement to the effect that the account debtor's recovery against an assignee with respect to claims and defenses against the assignor may not exceed amounts paid by the account debtor under the record, and the record does not include such a statement, the extent to which a claim of an account debtor against the assignor may be asserted against an assignee is determined as if the record included such a statement.

**(e)** This section does not apply to an assignment of a health-care-insurance receivable.

### § 9–405. Modification of Assigned Contract.

**(a)** A modification of or substitution for an assigned contract is effective against an assignee if made in good faith. The assignee acquires corresponding rights under the modified or substituted contract. The assignment may provide that the modification or substitution is a breach of contract by the assignor. This subsection is subject to subsections (b) through (d).

**(b)** Subsection (a) applies to the extent that:

**(1)** the right to payment or a part thereof under an assigned contract has not been fully earned by performance; or

**(2)** the right to payment or a part thereof has been fully earned by performance and the account debtor has not received notification of the assignment under Section 9–406(a).

**(c)** This section is subject to law other than this article which establishes a different rule for an account debtor who is an individual and who incurred the obligation primarily for personal, family, or household purposes.

**(d)** This section does not apply to an assignment of a health-care-insurance receivable.

### § 9–406. Discharge of Account Debtor; Notification of Assignment; Identification and Proof of Assignment; Restrictions on Assignment of Accounts, Chattel Paper, Payment Intangibles, and Promissory Notes Ineffective.

**(a)** Subject to subsections (b) through (i), an account debtor on an account, chattel paper, or a payment intangible may discharge its obligation by paying the assignor until, but not after, the account debtor receives a notification, authenticated by the assignor or the assignee, that the amount due or to become due has been assigned and that payment is to be made to the assignee. After receipt of the notification, the account debtor may discharge its obligation by paying the assignee and may not discharge the obligation by paying the assignor.

**(b)** Subject to subsection (h), notification is ineffective under subsection (a):

**(1)** if it does not reasonably identify the rights assigned;

**(2)** to the extent that an agreement between an account debtor and a seller of a payment intangible limits the account debtor's duty to pay a person other than the seller and the limitation is effective under law other than this article; or

**(3)** at the option of an account debtor, if the notification notifies the account debtor to make less than the full amount of any installment or other periodic payment to the assignee, even if:

**(A)** only a portion of the account, chattel paper, or payment intangible has been assigned to that assignee;

**(B)** a portion has been assigned to another assignee; or

**(C)** the account debtor knows that the assignment to that assignee is limited.

**(c)** Subject to subsection (h), if requested by the account debtor, an assignee shall seasonably furnish reasonable proof that the assignment has been made. Unless the assignee complies, the account debtor may discharge its obligation by paying the assignor, even if the account debtor has received a notification under subsection (a).

**(d)** Except as otherwise provided in subsection (e) and Sections 2A–303 and 9–407, and subject to subsection (h), a term in an agreement between an account debtor and an assignor or in a promissory note is ineffective to the extent that it:

**(1)** prohibits, restricts, or requires the consent of the account debtor or person obligated on the promissory note to the assignment or transfer of, or the creation, attachment, perfection, or enforcement of a security interest in, the account, chattel paper, payment intangible, or promissory note; or

**(2)** provides that the assignment or transfer or the creation, attachment, perfection, or enforcement of the security interest may give rise to a default, breach, right of recoupment, claim, defense, termination, right of termination, or remedy under the account, chattel paper, payment intangible, or promissory note.

**(e)** Subsection (d) does not apply to the sale of a payment intangible or promissory note.

**(f)** Except as otherwise provided in Sections 2A–303 and 9–407 and subject to subsections (h) and (i), a rule of law, statute, or regulation that prohibits, restricts, or requires the consent of a government, governmental body or official, or account debtor to the assignment or transfer of, or creation of a security interest in, an account or chattel paper is ineffective to the extent that the rule of law, statute, or regulation:

**(1)** prohibits, restricts, or requires the consent of the government, governmental body or official, or account debtor to the assignment or transfer of, or the creation, attachment, perfection, or enforcement of a security interest in the account or chattel paper; or

**(2)** provides that the assignment or transfer or the creation, attachment, perfection, or enforcement of the security interest may give rise to a default, breach, right of recoupment, claim, defense, termination, right of termination, or remedy under the account or chattel paper.

**(g)** Subject to subsection (h), an account debtor may not waive or vary its option under subsection (b)(3).

**(h)** This section is subject to law other than this article which establishes a different rule for an account debtor who is an individual and who incurred the obligation primarily for personal, family, or household purposes.

**(i)** This section does not apply to an assignment of a health-care-insurance receivable.

**(j)** This section prevails over any inconsistent provisions of the following statutes, rules, and regulations:

[List here any statutes, rules, and regulations containing provisions inconsistent with this section.]

Legislative Note: *States that amend statutes, rules, and regulations to remove provisions inconsistent with this section need not enact subsection (j).*

As amended in 1999 and 2000.

### § 9–407. Restrictions on Creation or Enforcement of Security Interest in Leasehold Interest or in Lessor's Residual Interest.

**(a)** Except as otherwise provided in subsection (b), a term in a lease agreement is ineffective to the extent that it:

　**(1)** prohibits, restricts, or requires the consent of a party to the lease to the assignment or transfer of, or the creation, attachment, perfection, or enforcement of a security interest in an interest of a party under the lease contract or in the lessor's residual interest in the goods; or

　**(2)** provides that the assignment or transfer or the creation, attachment, perfection, or enforcement of the security interest may give rise to a default, breach, right of recoupment, claim, defense, termination, right of termination, or remedy under the lease.

**(b)** Except as otherwise provided in Section 2A–303(7), a term described in subsection (a)(2) is effective to the extent that there is:

　**(1)** a transfer by the lessee of the lessee's right of possession or use of the goods in violation of the term; or

　**(2)** a delegation of a material performance of either party to the lease contract in violation of the term.

**(c)** The creation, attachment, perfection, or enforcement of a security interest in the lessor's interest under the lease contract or the lessor's residual interest in the goods is not a transfer that materially impairs the lessee's prospect of obtaining return performance or materially changes the duty of or materially increases the burden or risk imposed on the lessee within the purview of Section 2A–303(4) unless, and then only to the extent that, enforcement actually results in a delegation of material performance of the lessor.

As amended in 1999.

### § 9–408. Restrictions on Assignment of Promissory Notes, Health-Care-Insurance Receivables, and Certain General Intangibles Ineffective.

**(a)** Except as otherwise provided in subsection (b), a term in a promissory note or in an agreement between an account debtor and a debtor which relates to a health-care-insurance receivable or a general intangible, including a contract, permit, license, or franchise, and which term prohibits, restricts, or requires the consent of the person obligated on the promissory note or the account debtor to, the assignment or transfer of, or creation, attachment, or perfection of a security interest in, the promissory note, health-care-insurance receivable, or general intangible, is ineffective to the extent that the term:

　**(1)** would impair the creation, attachment, or perfection of a security interest; or

　**(2)** provides that the assignment or transfer or the creation, attachment, or perfection of the security interest may give rise to a default, breach, right of recoupment, claim, defense, termination, right of termination, or remedy under the promissory note, health-care-insurance receivable, or general intangible.

**(b)** Subsection (a) applies to a security interest in a payment intangible or promissory note only if the security interest arises out of a sale of the payment intangible or promissory note.

**(c)** A rule of law, statute, or regulation that prohibits, restricts, or requires the consent of a government, governmental body or official, person obligated on a promissory note, or account debtor to the assignment or transfer of, or creation of a security interest in, a promissory note, health-care-insurance receivable, or general intangible, including a contract, permit, license, or franchise between an account debtor and a debtor, is ineffective to the extent that the rule of law, statute, or regulation:

　**(1)** would impair the creation, attachment, or perfection of a security interest; or

　**(2)** provides that the assignment or transfer or the creation, attachment, or perfection of the security interest may give rise to a default, breach, right of recoupment, claim, defense, termination, right of termination, or remedy under the promissory note, health-care-insurance receivable, or general intangible.

**(d)** To the extent that a term in a promissory note or in an agreement between an account debtor and a debtor which relates to a health-care-insurance receivable or general intangible or a rule of law, statute, or regulation described in subsection (c) would be effective under law other than this article but is ineffective under subsection (a) or (c), the creation, attachment, or perfection of a security interest in the promissory note, health-care-insurance receivable, or general intangible:

　**(1)** is not enforceable against the person obligated on the promissory note or the account debtor;

　**(2)** does not impose a duty or obligation on the person obligated on the promissory note or the account debtor;

　**(3)** does not require the person obligated on the promissory note or the account debtor to recognize the security interest, pay or render performance to the secured party, or accept payment or performance from the secured party;

　**(4)** does not entitle the secured party to use or assign the debtor's rights under the promissory note, health-care-insurance receivable, or general intangible, including any related information or materials furnished to the debtor in the transaction giving rise to the promissory note, health-care-insurance receivable, or general intangible;

　**(5)** does not entitle the secured party to use, assign, possess, or have access to any trade secrets or confidential information of the person obligated on the promissory note or the account debtor; and

　**(6)** does not entitle the secured party to enforce the security interest in the promissory note, health-care-insurance receivable, or general intangible.

**(e)** This section prevails over any inconsistent provisions of the following statutes, rules, and regulations:

[List here any statutes, rules, and regulations containing provisions inconsistent with this section.]

Legislative Note: *States that amend statutes, rules, and regulations to remove provisions inconsistent with this section need not enact subsection (e).*

As amended in 1999.

### § 9–409. Restrictions on Assignment of Letter-of-Credit Rights Ineffective.

**(a)** A term in a letter of credit or a rule of law, statute, regulation, custom, or practice applicable to the letter of credit which prohibits, restricts, or requires the consent of an applicant, issuer, or nominated person to a beneficiary's assignment of or creation of a security interest in a letter-of-credit right is ineffective to the extent that the term or rule of law, statute, regulation, custom, or practice:

    **(1)** would impair the creation, attachment, or perfection of a security interest in the letter-of-credit right; or

    **(2)** provides that the assignment or the creation, attachment, or perfection of the security interest may give rise to a default, breach, right of recoupment, claim, defense, termination, right of termination, or remedy under the letter-of-credit right.

**(b)** To the extent that a term in a letter of credit is ineffective under subsection (a) but would be effective under law other than this article or a custom or practice applicable to the letter of credit, to the transfer of a right to draw or otherwise demand performance under the letter of credit, or to the assignment of a right to proceeds of the letter of credit, the creation, attachment, or perfection of a security interest in the letter-of-credit right:

    **(1)** is not enforceable against the applicant, issuer, nominated person, or transferee beneficiary;

    **(2)** imposes no duties or obligations on the applicant, issuer, nominated person, or transferee beneficiary; and

    **(3)** does not require the applicant, issuer, nominated person, or transferee beneficiary to recognize the security interest, pay or render performance to the secured party, or accept payment or other performance from the secured party.

As amended in 1999.

### Part 5—Filing

### [Subpart 1. Filing Office; Contents and Effectiveness of Financing Statement]

### § 9–501. Filing Office.

**(a)** Except as otherwise provided in subsection (b), if the local law of this State governs perfection of a security interest or agricultural lien, the office in which to file a financing statement to perfect the security interest or agricultural lien is:

    **(1)** the office designated for the filing or recording of a record of a mortgage on the related real property, if:

        **(A)** the collateral is as-extracted collateral or timber to be cut; or

        **(B)** the financing statement is filed as a fixture filing and the collateral is goods that are or are to become fixtures; or

    **(2)** the office of [ ] [or any office duly authorized by [ ]], in all other cases, including a case in which the collateral is goods that are or are to become fixtures and the financing statement is not filed as a fixture filing.

**(b)** The office in which to file a financing statement to perfect a security interest in collateral, including fixtures, of a transmitting utility is the office of [ ]. The financing statement also constitutes a fixture filing as to the collateral indicated in the financing statement which is or is to become fixtures.

Legislative Note: *The State should designate the filing office where the brackets appear. The filing office may be that of a governmental official (e.g., the Secretary of State) or a private party that maintains the State's filing system.*

### § 9–502. Contents of Financing Statement; Record of Mortgage as Financing Statement; Time of Filing Financing Statement.

**(a)** Subject to subsection (b), a financing statement is sufficient only if it:

**(1)** provides the name of the debtor;

**(2)** provides the name of the secured party or a representative of the secured party; and

**(3)** indicates the collateral covered by the financing statement.

**(b)** Except as otherwise provided in Section 9–501(b), to be sufficient, a financing statement that covers as-extracted collateral or timber to be cut, or which is filed as a fixture filing and covers goods that are or are to become fixtures, must satisfy subsection (a) and also:

    **(1)** indicate that it covers this type of collateral;

    **(2)** indicate that it is to be filed [for record] in the real property records;

    **(3)** provide a description of the real property to which the collateral is related [sufficient to give constructive notice of a mortgage under the law of this State if the description were contained in a record of the mortgage of the real property]; and

    **(4)** if the debtor does not have an interest of record in the real property, provide the name of a record owner.

**(c)** A record of a mortgage is effective, from the date of recording, as a financing statement filed as a fixture filing or as a financing statement covering as-extracted collateral or timber to be cut only if:

    **(1)** the record indicates the goods or accounts that it covers;

    **(2)** the goods are or are to become fixtures related to the real property described in the record or the collateral is related to the real property described in the record and is as-extracted collateral or timber to be cut;

    **(3)** the record satisfies the requirements for a financing statement in this section other than an indication that it is to be filed in the real property records; and

    **(4)** the record is [duly] recorded.

**(d)** A financing statement may be filed before a security agreement is made or a security interest otherwise attaches.

Legislative Note: Language in brackets is optional. Where the State has any *special recording system for real property other than the usual grantor-grantee index (as, for instance, a tract system or a title registration or Torrens system) local adaptations of subsection (b) and Section 9–519(d) and (e) may be necessary. See, e.g., Mass. Gen. Laws Chapter 106, Section 9–410.*

## § 9–503. **Name of Debtor and Secured Party.**

(a) A financing statement sufficiently provides the name of the debtor:

> (1) if the debtor is a registered organization, only if the financing statement provides the name of the debtor indicated on the public record of the debtor's jurisdiction of organization which shows the debtor to have been organized;
>
> (2) if the debtor is a decedent's estate, only if the financing statement provides the name of the decedent and indicates that the debtor is an estate;
>
> (3) if the debtor is a trust or a trustee acting with respect to property held in trust, only if the financing statement:
>
>> (A) provides the name specified for the trust in its organic documents or, if no name is specified, provides the name of the settlor and additional information sufficient to distinguish the debtor from other trusts having one or more of the same settlors; and
>>
>> (B) indicates, in the debtor's name or otherwise, that the debtor is a trust or is a trustee acting with respect to property held in trust; and
>
> (4) in other cases:
>
>> (A) if the debtor has a name, only if it provides the individual or organizational name of the debtor; and
>>
>> (B) if the debtor does not have a name, only if it provides the names of the partners, members, associates, or other persons comprising the debtor.
>
> (b) A financing statement that provides the name of the debtor in accordance with subsection (a) is not rendered ineffective by the absence of:
>
> (1) a trade name or other name of the debtor; or
>
> (2) unless required under subsection (a)(4)(B), names of partners, members, associates, or other persons comprising the debtor.

(c) A financing statement that provides only the debtor's trade name does not sufficiently provide the name of the debtor.

(d) Failure to indicate the representative capacity of a secured party or representative of a secured party does not affect the sufficiency of a financing statement.

(e) A financing statement may provide the name of more than one debtor and the name of more than one secured party.

## § 9–504. **Indication of Collateral.**

A financing statement sufficiently indicates the collateral that it covers if the financing statement provides:

> (1) a description of the collateral pursuant to Section 9–108; or
>
> (2) an indication that the financing statement covers all assets or all personal property.

As amended in 1999.

## § 9–505. **Filing and Compliance with Other Statutes and Treaties for Consignments, Leases, Other Bailments, and Other Transactions.**

(a) A consignor, lessor, or other bailor of goods, a licensor, or a buyer of a payment intangible or promissory note may file a financing statement, or may comply with a statute or treaty described in Section 9–311(a), using the terms "consignor", "consignee", "lessor", "lessee", "bailor", "bailee", "licensor", "licensee", "owner", "registered owner", "buyer", "seller", or words of similar import, instead of the terms "secured party" and "debtor".

(b) This part applies to the filing of a financing statement under subsection (a) and, as appropriate, to compliance that is equivalent to filing a financing statement under Section 9–311(b), but the filing or compliance is not of itself a factor in determining whether the collateral secures an obligation. If it is determined for another reason that the collateral secures an obligation, a security interest held by the consignor, lessor, bailor, licensor, owner, or buyer which attaches to the collateral is perfected by the filing or compliance.

## § 9–506. **Effect of Errors or Omissions.**

(a) A financing statement substantially satisfying the requirements of this part is effective, even if it has minor errors or omissions, unless the errors or omissions make the financing statement seriously misleading.

(b) Except as otherwise provided in subsection (c), a financing statement that fails sufficiently to provide the name of the debtor in accordance with Section 9–503(a) is seriously misleading.

(c) If a search of the records of the filing office under the debtor's correct name, using the filing office's standard search logic, if any, would disclose a financing statement that fails sufficiently to provide the name of the debtor in accordance with Section 9–503(a), the name provided does not make the financing statement seriously misleading.

(d) For purposes of Section 9–508(b), the "debtor's correct name" in subsection (c) means the correct name of the new debtor.

## § 9–507. **Effect of Certain Events on Effectiveness of Financing Statement.**

(a) A filed financing statement remains effective with respect to collateral that is sold, exchanged, leased, licensed, or otherwise disposed of and in which a security interest or agricultural lien continues, even if the secured party knows of or consents to the disposition.

(b) Except as otherwise provided in subsection (c) and Section 9–508, a financing statement is not rendered ineffective if, after the financing statement is filed, the information provided in the financing statement becomes seriously misleading under Section 9–506.

(c) If a debtor so changes its name that a filed financing statement becomes seriously misleading under Section 9–506:

> (1) the financing statement is effective to perfect a security interest in collateral acquired by the debtor before, or within four months after, the change; and
>
> (2) the financing statement is not effective to perfect a security interest in collateral acquired by the debtor more than four months after the change, unless an amendment to the financing statement which renders the financing statement not seriously misleading is filed within four months after the change.

## § 9–508. **Effectiveness of Financing Statement If New Debtor Becomes Bound by Security Agreement.**

(a) Except as otherwise provided in this section, a filed financing statement naming an original debtor is effective to perfect a security interest in collateral in which a new debtor has or acquires rights to the extent that the financing statement would have been effective had the original debtor acquired rights in the collateral.

**(b)** If the difference between the name of the original debtor and that of the new debtor causes a filed financing statement that is effective under subsection (a) to be seriously misleading under Section 9–506:

> **(1)** the financing statement is effective to perfect a security interest in collateral acquired by the new debtor before, and within four months after, the new debtor becomes bound under Section 9B–203(d); and

> **(2)** the financing statement is not effective to perfect a security interest in collateral acquired by the new debtor more than four months after the new debtor becomes bound under Section 9–203(d) unless an initial financing statement providing the name of the new debtor is filed before the expiration of that time.

**(c)** This section does not apply to collateral as to which a filed financing statement remains effective against the new debtor under Section 9–507(a).

### § 9–509. Persons Entitled to File a Record.

**(a)** A person may file an initial financing statement, amendment that adds collateral covered by a financing statement, or amendment that adds a debtor to a financing statement only if:

> **(1)** the debtor authorizes the filing in an authenticated record or pursuant to subsection (b) or (c); or

> **(2)** the person holds an agricultural lien that has become effective at the time of filing and the financing statement covers only collateral in which the person holds an agricultural lien.

**(b)** By authenticating or becoming bound as debtor by a security agreement, a debtor or new debtor authorizes the filing of an initial financing statement, and an amendment, covering:

> **(1)** the collateral described in the security agreement; and

> **(2)** property that becomes collateral under Section 9–315(a)(2), whether or not the security agreement expressly covers proceeds.

**(c)** By acquiring collateral in which a security interest or agricultural lien continues under Section 9–315(a)(1), a debtor authorizes the filing of an initial financing statement, and an amendment, covering the collateral and property that becomes collateral under Section 9–315(a)(2).

**(d)** A person may file an amendment other than an amendment that adds collateral covered by a financing statement or an amendment that adds a debtor to a financing statement only if:

> **(1)** the secured party of record authorizes the filing; or

> **(2)** the amendment is a termination statement for a financing statement as to which the secured party of record has failed to file or send a termination statement as required by Section 9–513(a) or (c), the debtor authorizes the filing, and the termination statement indicates that the debtor authorized it to be filed.

**(e)** If there is more than one secured party of record for a financing statement, each secured party of record may authorize the filing of an amendment under subsection (d).
As amended in 2000.

### § 9–510. Effectiveness of Filed Record.

**(a)** A filed record is effective only to the extent that it was filed by a person that may file it under Section 9–509.

**(b)** A record authorized by one secured party of record does not affect the financing statement with respect to another secured party of record.

**(c)** A continuation statement that is not filed within the six-month period prescribed by Section 9–515(d) is ineffective.

### § 9–511. Secured Party of Record.

**(a)** A secured party of record with respect to a financing statement is a person whose name is provided as the name of the secured party or a representative of the secured party in an initial financing statement that has been filed. If an initial financing statement is filed under Section 9–514(a), the assignee named in the initial financing statement is the secured party of record with respect to the financing statement.

**(b)** If an amendment of a financing statement which provides the name of a person as a secured party or a representative of a secured party is filed, the person named in the amendment is a secured party of record. If an amendment is filed under Section 9–514(b), the assignee named in the amendment is a secured party of record.

**(c)** A person remains a secured party of record until the filing of an amendment of the financing statement which deletes the person.

### § 9–512. Amendment of Financing Statement.

**[Alternative A]**
**(a)** Subject to Section 9–509, a person may add or delete collateral covered by, continue or terminate the effectiveness of, or, subject to subsection (e), otherwise amend the information provided in, a financing statement by filing an amendment that:

> **(1)** identifies, by its file number, the initial financing statement to which the amendment relates; and

> **(2)** if the amendment relates to an initial financing statement filed [or recorded] in a filing office described in Section 9–501(a)(1), provides the information specified in Section 9–502(b).

**[Alternative B]**
**(a)** Subject to Section 9–509, a person may add or delete collateral covered by, continue or terminate the effectiveness of, or, subject to subsection (e), otherwise amend the information provided in, a financing statement by filing an amendment that:

> **(1)** identifies, by its file number, the initial financing statement to which the amendment relates; and

> **(2)** if the amendment relates to an initial financing statement filed [or recorded] in a filing office described in Section 9–501(a)(1), provides the date [and time] that the initial financing statement was filed [or recorded] and the information specified in Section 9–502(b).

**[End of Alternatives]**

**(b)** Except as otherwise provided in Section 9–515, the filing of an amendment does not extend the period of effectiveness of the financing statement.

**(c)** A financing statement that is amended by an amendment that adds collateral is effective as to the added collateral only from the date of the filing of the amendment.

**(d)** A financing statement that is amended by an amendment that adds a debtor is effective as to the added debtor only from the date of the filing of the amendment.

**(e)** An amendment is ineffective to the extent it:

   **(1)** purports to delete all debtors and fails to provide the name of a debtor to be covered by the financing statement; or

   **(2)** purports to delete all secured parties of record and fails to provide the name of a new secured party of record.

Legislative Note: *States whose real-estate filing offices require additional information in amendments and cannot search their records by both the name of the debtor and the file number should enact Alternative B to Sections 9–512(a), 9–518(b), 9–519(f), and 9–522(a).*

### § 9–513. Termination Statement.

**(a)** A secured party shall cause the secured party of record for a financing statement to file a termination statement for the financing statement if the financing statement covers consumer goods and:

   **(1)** there is no obligation secured by the collateral covered by the financing statement and no commitment to make an advance, incur an obligation, or otherwise give value; or

   **(2)** the debtor did not authorize the filing of the initial financing statement.

**(b)** To comply with subsection (a), a secured party shall cause the secured party of record to file the termination statement:

   **(1)** within one month after there is no obligation secured by the collateral covered by the financing statement and no commitment to make an advance, incur an obligation, or otherwise give value; or

   **(2)** if earlier, within 20 days after the secured party receives an authenticated demand from a debtor.

**(c)** In cases not governed by subsection (a), within 20 days after a secured party receives an authenticated demand from a debtor, the secured party shall cause the secured party of record for a financing statement to send to the debtor a termination statement for the financing statement or file the termination statement in the filing office if:

   **(1)** except in the case of a financing statement covering accounts or chattel paper that has been sold or goods that are the subject of a consignment, there is no obligation secured by the collateral covered by the financing statement and no commitment to make an advance, incur an obligation, or otherwise give value;

   **(2)** the financing statement covers accounts or chattel paper that has been sold but as to which the account debtor or other person obligated has discharged its obligation;

   **(3)** the financing statement covers goods that were the subject of a consignment to the debtor but are not in the debtor's possession; or

   **(4)** the debtor did not authorize the filing of the initial financing statement.

**(d)** Except as otherwise provided in Section 9–510, upon the filing of a termination statement with the filing office, the financing statement to which the termination statement relates ceases to be effective. Except as otherwise provided in Section 9–510, for purposes of Sections 9–519(g), 9–522(a), and 9–523(c), the filing with the filing office of a termination statement relating to a financing statement that indicates that the debtor is a transmitting utility also causes the effectiveness of the financing statement to lapse.

As amended in 2000.

### § 9–514. Assignment of Powers of Secured Party of Record.

**(a)** Except as otherwise provided in subsection (c), an initial financing statement may reflect an assignment of all of the secured party's power to authorize an amendment to the financing statement by providing the name and mailing address of the assignee as the name and address of the secured party.

**(b)** Except as otherwise provided in subsection (c), a secured party of record may assign of record all or part of its power to authorize an amendment to a financing statement by filing in the filing office an amendment of the financing statement which:

   **(1)** identifies, by its file number, the initial financing statement to which it relates;

   **(2)** provides the name of the assignor; and

   **(3)** provides the name and mailing address of the assignee.

**(c)** An assignment of record of a security interest in a fixture covered by a record of a mortgage which is effective as a financing statement filed as a fixture filing under Section 9–502(c) may be made only by an assignment of record of the mortgage in the manner provided by law of this State other than [the Uniform Commercial Code].

### § 9–515. Duration and Effectiveness of Financing Statement; Effect of Lapsed Financing Statement.

**(a)** Except as otherwise provided in subsections (b), (e), (f), and (g), a filed financing statement is effective for a period of five years after the date of filing.

**(b)** Except as otherwise provided in subsections (e), (f), and (g), an initial financing statement filed in connection with a public-finance transaction or manufactured-home transaction is effective for a period of 30 years after the date of filing if it indicates that it is filed in connection with a public-finance transaction or manufactured-home transaction.

**(c)** The effectiveness of a filed financing statement lapses on the expiration of the period of its effectiveness unless before the lapse a continuation statement is filed pursuant to subsection (d). Upon lapse, a financing statement ceases to be effective and any security interest or agricultural lien that was perfected by the financing statement becomes unperfected, unless the security interest is perfected otherwise. If the security interest or agricultural lien becomes unperfected upon lapse, it is deemed never to have been perfected as against a purchaser of the collateral for value.

**(d)** A continuation statement may be filed only within six months before the expiration of the five-year period specified in subsection (a) or the 30-year period specified in subsection (b), whichever is applicable.

**(e)** Except as otherwise provided in Section 9–510, upon timely filing of a continuation statement, the effectiveness of the initial financing statement continues for a period of five years commencing on the day on which the financing statement would have become ineffective in the absence of the filing. Upon the expiration of the five-year period, the financing statement lapses in the same manner as provided in subsection (c), unless, before the lapse, another continuation statement is filed pursuant to subsection (d). Succeeding continuation statements may be filed in the same manner to continue the effectiveness of the initial financing statement.

**(f)** If a debtor is a transmitting utility and a filed financing statement so indicates, the financing statement is effective until a termination statement is filed.

**(g)** A record of a mortgage that is effective as a financing statement filed as a fixture filing under Section 9–502(c) remains effective as a financing statement filed as a fixture filing until the mortgage is released or satisfied of record or its effectiveness otherwise terminates as to the real property.

## § 9–516. What Constitutes Filing; Effectiveness of Filing.

**(a)** Except as otherwise provided in subsection (b), communication of a record to a filing office and tender of the filing fee or acceptance of the record by the filing office constitutes filing.

**(b)** Filing does not occur with respect to a record that a filing office refuses to accept because:

> **(1)** the record is not communicated by a method or medium of communication authorized by the filing office;
> **(2)** an amount equal to or greater than the applicable filing fee is not tendered;
> **(3)** the filing office is unable to index the record because:
>> **(A)** in the case of an initial financing statement, the record does not provide a name for the debtor;
>> **(B)** in the case of an amendment or correction statement, the record:
>>> **(i)** does not identify the initial financing statement as required by Section 9–512 or 9–518, as applicable; or
>>> **(ii)** identifies an initial financing statement whose effectiveness has lapsed under Section 9–515;
>> **(C)** in the case of an initial financing statement that provides the name of a debtor identified as an individual or an amendment that provides a name of a debtor identified as an individual which was not previously provided in the financing statement to which the record relates, the record does not identify the debtor's last name; or
>> **(D)** in the case of a record filed [or recorded] in the filing office described in Section 9–501(a)(1), the record does not provide a sufficient description of the real property to which it relates;
> **(4)** in the case of an initial financing statement or an amendment that adds a secured party of record, the record does not provide a name and mailing address for the secured party of record;
> **(5)** in the case of an initial financing statement or an amendment that provides a name of a debtor which was not previously provided in the financing statement to which the amendment relates, the record does not:
>> **(A)** provide a mailing address for the debtor;

>> **(B)** indicate whether the debtor is an individual or an organization; or
>> **(C)** if the financing statement indicates that the debtor is an organization, provide:
>>> **(i)** a type of organization for the debtor;
>>> **(ii)** a jurisdiction of organization for the debtor; or
>>> **(iii)** an organizational identification number for the debtor or indicate that the debtor has none;
> **(6)** in the case of an assignment reflected in an initial financing statement under Section 9–514(a) or an amendment filed under Section 9–514(b), the record does not provide a name and mailing address for the assignee; or
> **(7)** in the case of a continuation statement, the record is not filed within the six-month period prescribed by Section 9–515(d).

**(c)** For purposes of subsection (b):

> **(1)** a record does not provide information if the filing office is unable to read or decipher the information; and
> **(2)** a record that does not indicate that it is an amendment or identify an initial financing statement to which it relates, as required by Section 9–512, 9–514, or 9–518, is an initial financing statement.

**(d)** A record that is communicated to the filing office with tender of the filing fee, but which the filing office refuses to accept for a reason other than one set forth in subsection (b), is effective as a filed record except as against a purchaser of the collateral which gives value in reasonable reliance upon the absence of the record from the files.

## § 9–517. Effect of Indexing Errors.

The failure of the filing office to index a record correctly does not affect the effectiveness of the filed record.

## § 9–518. Claim Concerning Inaccurate or Wrongfully Filed Record.

**(a)** A person may file in the filing office a correction statement with respect to a record indexed there under the person's name if the person believes that the record is inaccurate or was wrongfully filed.

**[Alternative A]**

**(b)** A correction statement must:

> **(1)** identify the record to which it relates by the file number assigned to the initial financing statement to which the record relates;
> **(2)** indicate that it is a correction statement; and
> **(3)** provide the basis for the person's belief that the record is inaccurate and indicate the manner in which the person believes the record should be amended to cure any inaccuracy or provide the basis for the person's belief that the record was wrongfully filed.

**[Alternative B]**

**(b)** A correction statement must:

> **(1)** identify the record to which it relates by:
>> **(A)** the file number assigned to the initial financing statement to which the record relates; and
>> **(B)** if the correction statement relates to a record filed [or recorded] in a filing office described in Section 9–501(a)(1), the date [and time] that the initial financ-

ing statement was filed [or recorded] and the information specified in Section 9–502(b);

**(2)** indicate that it is a correction statement; and

**(3)** provide the basis for the person's belief that the record is inaccurate and indicate the manner in which the person believes the record should be amended to cure any inaccuracy or provide the basis for the person's belief that the record was wrongfully filed.

**[End of Alternatives]**

**(c)** The filing of a correction statement does not affect the effectiveness of an initial financing statement or other filed record.

Legislative Note: *States whose real-estate filing offices require additional information in amendments and cannot search their records by both the name of the debtor and the file number should enact Alternative B to Sections 9–512(a), 9–518(b), 9–519(f), and 9–522(a).*

**[Subpart 2. Duties and Operation of Filing Office]**

### § 9–519. Numbering, Maintaining, and Indexing Records; Communicating Information Provided in Records.

**(a)** For each record filed in a filing office, the filing office shall:

**(1)** assign a unique number to the filed record;

**(2)** create a record that bears the number assigned to the filed record and the date and time of filing;

**(3)** maintain the filed record for public inspection; and

**(4)** index the filed record in accordance with subsections (c), (d), and (e).

**(b)** A file number [assigned after January 1, 2002,] must include a digit that:

**(1)** is mathematically derived from or related to the other digits of the file number; and

**(2)** aids the filing office in determining whether a number communicated as the file number includes a single-digit or transpositional error.

**(c)** Except as otherwise provided in subsections (d) and (e), the filing office shall:

**(1)** index an initial financing statement according to the name of the debtor and index all filed records relating to the initial financing statement in a manner that associates with one another an initial financing statement and all filed records relating to the initial financing statement; and

**(2)** index a record that provides a name of a debtor which was not previously provided in the financing statement to which the record relates also according to the name that was not previously provided.

**(d)** If a financing statement is filed as a fixture filing or covers as-extracted collateral or timber to be cut, [it must be filed for record and] the filing office shall index it:

**(1)** under the names of the debtor and of each owner of record shown on the financing statement as if they were the mortgagors under a mortgage of the real property described; and

**(2)** to the extent that the law of this State provides for indexing of records of mortgages under the name of the mortgagee, under the name of the secured party as if the secured party were the mortgagee thereunder, or, if index-

ing is by description, as if the financing statement were a record of a mortgage of the real property described.

**(e)** If a financing statement is filed as a fixture filing or covers as-extracted collateral or timber to be cut, the filing office shall index an assignment filed under Section 9–514(a) or an amendment filed under Section 9–514(b):

**(1)** under the name of the assignor as grantor; and

**(2)** to the extent that the law of this State provides for indexing a record of the assignment of a mortgage under the name of the assignee, under the name of the assignee.

**[Alternative A]**

**(f)** The filing office shall maintain a capability:

**(1)** to retrieve a record by the name of the debtor and by the file number assigned to the initial financing statement to which the record relates; and

**(2)** to associate and retrieve with one another an initial financing statement and each filed record relating to the initial financing statement.

**[Alternative B]**

**(f)** The filing office shall maintain a capability:

**(1)** to retrieve a record by the name of the debtor and:

    **(A)** if the filing office is described in Section 9–501(a)(1), by the file number assigned to the initial financing statement to which the record relates and the date [and time] that the record was filed [or recorded]; or

    **(B)** if the filing office is described in Section 9–501(a)(2), by the file number assigned to the initial financing statement to which the record relates; and

**(2)** to associate and retrieve with one another an initial financing statement and each filed record relating to the initial financing statement.

**[End of Alternatives]**

**(g)** The filing office may not remove a debtor's name from the index until one year after the effectiveness of a financing statement naming the debtor lapses under Section 9–515 with respect to all secured parties of record.

**(h)** The filing office shall perform the acts required by subsections (a) through (e) at the time and in the manner prescribed by filing-office rule, but not later than two business days after the filing office receives the record in question.

[(i) Subsection[s] [(b)] [and] [(h)] do[es] not apply to a filing office described in Section 9–501(a)(1).]

*Legislative Notes:*

*1. States whose filing offices currently assign file numbers that include a verification number, commonly known as a "check digit," or can implement this requirement before the effective date of this Article should omit the bracketed language in subsection (b).*

*2. In States in which writings will not appear in the real property records and indices unless actually recorded the bracketed language in subsection (d) should be used.*

*3. States whose real-estate filing offices require additional information in amendments and cannot search their records by both the name of the debtor and the file number should enact Alternative B to Sections 9–512(a), 9–518(b), 9–519(f), and 9–522(a).*

*4. A State that elects not to require real-estate filing offices to comply with either or both of subsections (b) and (h) may adopt an applicable variation of subsection (i) and add "Except as otherwise provided in subsection (i)," to the appropriate subsection or subsections.*

### § 9–520. Acceptance and Refusal to Accept Record.

**(a)** A filing office shall refuse to accept a record for filing for a reason set forth in Section 9–516(b) and may refuse to accept a record for filing only for a reason set forth in Section 9–516(b).
**(b)** If a filing office refuses to accept a record for filing, it shall communicate to the person that presented the record the fact of and reason for the refusal and the date and time the record would have been filed had the filing office accepted it. The communication must be made at the time and in the manner prescribed by filing-office rule but [, in the case of a filing office described in Section 9–501(a)(2),] in no event more than two business days after the filing office receives the record.
**(c)** A filed financing statement satisfying Section 9–502(a) and (b) is effective, even if the filing office is required to refuse to accept it for filing under subsection (a). However, Section 9–338 applies to a filed financing statement providing information described in Section 9–516(b)(5) which is incorrect at the time the financing statement is filed.
**(d)** If a record communicated to a filing office provides information that relates to more than one debtor, this part applies as to each debtor separately.

Legislative Note: *A State that elects not to require real-property filing offices to comply with subsection (b) should include the bracketed language.*

### § 9–521. Uniform Form of Written Financing Statement and Amendment.

**(a)** A filing office that accepts written records may not refuse to accept a written initial financing statement in the following form and format except for a reason set forth in Section 9–516(b):

[NATIONAL UCC FINANCING STATEMENT (FORM UCC1) (REV. 7/29/98)]

[NATIONAL UCC FINANCING STATEMENT ADDENDUM (FORM UCC1Ad)(REV. 07/29/98)]

**(b)** A filing office that accepts written records may not refuse to accept a written record in the following form and format except for a reason set forth in Section 9–516(b):

[NATIONAL UCC FINANCING STATEMENT AMENDMENT (FORM UCC3)(REV. 07/29/98)]

[NATIONAL UCC FINANCING STATEMENT AMENDMENT ADDENDUM (FORM UCC3Ad)(REV. 07/29/98)]

### § 9–522. Maintenance and Destruction of Records.

**[Alternative A]**
**(a)** The filing office shall maintain a record of the information provided in a filed financing statement for at least one year after the effectiveness of the financing statement has lapsed under Section 9–515 with respect to all secured parties of record. The record must be retrievable by using the name of the debtor and by using the file number assigned to the initial financing statement to which the record relates.

**[Alternative B]**
**(a)** The filing office shall maintain a record of the information provided in a filed financing statement for at least one year after

the effectiveness of the financing statement has lapsed under Section 9–515 with respect to all secured parties of record. The record must be retrievable by using the name of the debtor and:

**(1)** if the record was filed [or recorded] in the filing office described in Section 9–501(a)(1), by using the file number assigned to the initial financing statement to which the record relates and the date [and time] that the record was filed [or recorded]; or

**(2)** if the record was filed in the filing office described in Section 9–501(a)(2), by using the file number assigned to the initial financing statement to which the record relates.

**[End of Alternatives]**

**(b)** Except to the extent that a statute governing disposition of public records provides otherwise, the filing office immediately may destroy any written record evidencing a financing statement. However, if the filing office destroys a written record, it shall maintain another record of the financing statement which complies with subsection (a).

Legislative Note: *States whose real-estate filing offices require additional information in amendments and cannot search their records by both the name of the debtor and the file number should enact Alternative B to Sections 9–512(a), 9–518(b), 9–519(f), and 9–522(a).*

### § 9–523. Information from Filing Office; Sale or License of Records.

**(a)** If a person that files a written record requests an acknowledgment of the filing, the filing office shall send to the person an image of the record showing the number assigned to the record pursuant to Section 9–519(a)(1) and the date and time of the filing of the record. However, if the person furnishes a copy of the record to the filing office, the filing office may instead:

**(1)** note upon the copy the number assigned to the record pursuant to Section 9–519(a)(1) and the date and time of the filing of the record; and

**(2)** send the copy to the person.

**(b)** If a person files a record other than a written record, the filing office shall communicate to the person an acknowledgment that provides:

**(1)** the information in the record;

**(2)** the number assigned to the record pursuant to Section 9–519(a)(1); and

**(3)** the date and time of the filing of the record.

**(c)** The filing office shall communicate or otherwise make available in a record the following information to any person that requests it:

**(1)** whether there is on file on a date and time specified by the filing office, but not a date earlier than three business days before the filing office receives the request, any financing statement that:

**(A)** designates a particular debtor [or, if the request so states, designates a particular debtor at the address specified in the request];

**(B)** has not lapsed under Section 9–515 with respect to all secured parties of record; and

**(C)** if the request so states, has lapsed under Section 9–515 and a record of which is maintained by the filing office under Section 9–522(a);

**(2)** the date and time of filing of each financing statement; and

**(3)** the information provided in each financing statement.

**(d)** In complying with its duty under subsection (c), the filing office may communicate information in any medium. However, if requested, the filing office shall communicate information by issuing [its written certificate] [a record that can be admitted into evidence in the courts of this State without extrinsic evidence of its authenticity].

**(e)** The filing office shall perform the acts required by subsections (a) through (d) at the time and in the manner prescribed by filing-office rule, but not later than two business days after the filing office receives the request.

**(f)** At least weekly, the [insert appropriate official or governmental agency] [filing office] shall offer to sell or license to the public on a nonexclusive basis, in bulk, copies of all records filed in it under this part, in every medium from time to time available to the filing office.

*Legislative Notes:*

*1. States whose filing office does not offer the additional service of responding to search requests limited to a particular address should omit the bracketed language in subsection (c)(1)(A).*

*2. A State that elects not to require real-estate filing offices to comply with either or both of subsections (e) and (f) should specify in the appropriate subsection(s) only the filing office described in Section 9–501(a)(2).*

## § 9–524. Delay by Filing Office.

Delay by the filing office beyond a time limit prescribed by this part is excused if:

**(1)** the delay is caused by interruption of communication or computer facilities, war, emergency conditions, failure of equipment, or other circumstances beyond control of the filing office; and

**(2)** the filing office exercises reasonable diligence under the circumstances.

## § 9–525. Fees.

**(a)** Except as otherwise provided in subsection (e), the fee for filing and indexing a record under this part, other than an initial financing statement of the kind described in subsection (b), is [the amount specified in subsection (c), if applicable, plus]:

**(1)** $[X] if the record is communicated in writing and consists of one or two pages;

**(2)** $[2X] if the record is communicated in writing and consists of more than two pages; and

**(3)** $[1/2X] if the record is communicated by another medium authorized by filing-office rule.

**(b)** Except as otherwise provided in subsection (e), the fee for filing and indexing an initial financing statement of the following kind is [the amount specified in subsection (c), if applicable, plus]:

**(1)** $_____ if the financing statement indicates that it is filed in connection with a public-finance transaction;

**(2)** $_____ if the financing statement indicates that it is filed in connection with a manufactured-home transaction.

**[Alternative A]**

**(c)** The number of names required to be indexed does not affect the amount of the fee in subsections (a) and (b).

**[Alternative B]**

**(c)** Except as otherwise provided in subsection (e), if a record is communicated in writing, the fee for each name more than two required to be indexed is $_____.

**[End of Alternatives]**

**(d)** The fee for responding to a request for information from the filing office, including for [issuing a certificate showing] [communicating] whether there is on file any financing statement naming a particular debtor, is:

**(1)** $_____ if the request is communicated in writing; and

**(2)** $_____ if the request is communicated by another medium authorized by filing-office rule.

**(e)** This section does not require a fee with respect to a record of a mortgage which is effective as a financing statement filed as a fixture filing or as a financing statement covering as-extracted collateral or timber to be cut under Section 9–502(c). However, the recording and satisfaction fees that otherwise would be applicable to the record of the mortgage apply.

*Legislative Notes:*

*1. To preserve uniformity, a State that places the provisions of this section together with statutes setting fees for other services should do so without modification.*

*2. A State should enact subsection (c), Alternative A, and omit the bracketed language in subsections (a) and (b) unless its indexing system entails a substantial additional cost when indexing additional names.*

As amended in 2000.

## § 9–526. Filing-Office Rules.

**(a)** The [insert appropriate governmental official or agency] shall adopt and publish rules to implement this article. The filing-office rules must be[:

**(1)**] consistent with this article[; and

**(2)** adopted and published in accordance with the [insert any applicable state administrative procedure act]].

**(b)** To keep the filing-office rules and practices of the filing office in harmony with the rules and practices of filing offices in other jurisdictions that enact substantially this part, and to keep the technology used by the filing office compatible with the technology used by filing offices in other jurisdictions that enact substantially this part, the [insert appropriate governmental official or agency], so far as is consistent with the purposes, policies, and provisions of this article, in adopting, amending, and repealing filing-office rules, shall:

**(1)** consult with filing offices in other jurisdictions that enact substantially this part; and

**(2)** consult the most recent version of the Model Rules promulgated by the International Association of Corporate Administrators or any successor organization; and

**(3)** take into consideration the rules and practices of, and the technology used by, filing offices in other jurisdictions that enact substantially this part.

## § 9–527. Duty to Report.

The [insert appropriate governmental official or agency] shall report [annually on or before _____] to the [Governor and Legislature] on the operation of the filing office. The report must contain a statement of the extent to which:

**(1)** the filing-office rules are not in harmony with the rules of filing offices in other jurisdictions that enact substantially this part and the reasons for these variations; and

**(2)** the filing-office rules are not in harmony with the most recent version of the Model Rules promulgated by the International Association of Corporate Administrators, or any successor organization, and the reasons for these variations.

## Part 6—Default

### [Subpart 1. Default and Enforcement of Security Interest]

### § 9–601. Rights after Default; Judicial Enforcement; Consignor or Buyer of Accounts, Chattel Paper, Payment Intangibles, or Promissory Notes.

**(a)** After default, a secured party has the rights provided in this part and, except as otherwise provided in Section 9–602, those provided by agreement of the parties. A secured party

    **(1)** may reduce a claim to judgment, foreclose, or otherwise enforce the claim, security interest, or agricultural lien by any available judicial procedure; and

    **(2)** if the collateral is documents, may proceed either as to the documents or as to the goods they cover.

**(b)** A secured party in possession of collateral or control of collateral under Section 9–104, 9–105, 9–106, or 9–107 has the rights and duties provided in Section 9–207.

**(c)** The rights under subsections (a) and (b) are cumulative and may be exercised simultaneously.

**(d)** Except as otherwise provided in subsection (g) and Section 9–605, after default, a debtor and an obligor have the rights provided in this part and by agreement of the parties.

**(e)** If a secured party has reduced its claim to judgment, the lien of any levy that may be made upon the collateral by virtue of an execution based upon the judgment relates back to the earliest of:

    **(1)** the date of perfection of the security interest or agricultural lien in the collateral;

    **(2)** the date of filing a financing statement covering the collateral; or

    **(3)** any date specified in a statute under which the agricultural lien was created.

**(f)** A sale pursuant to an execution is a foreclosure of the security interest or agricultural lien by judicial procedure within the meaning of this section. A secured party may purchase at the sale and thereafter hold the collateral free of any other requirements of this article.

**(g)** Except as otherwise provided in Section 9–607(c), this part imposes no duties upon a secured party that is a consignor or is a buyer of accounts, chattel paper, payment intangibles, or promissory notes.

### § 9–602. Waiver and Variance of Rights and Duties.

Except as otherwise provided in Section 9–624, to the extent that they give rights to a debtor or obligor and impose duties on a secured party, the debtor or obligor may not waive or vary the rules stated in the following listed sections:

    **(1)** Section 9–207(b)(4)(C), which deals with use and operation of the collateral by the secured party;

    **(2)** Section 9–210, which deals with requests for an accounting and requests concerning a list of collateral and statement of account;

    **(3)** Section 9–607(c), which deals with collection and enforcement of collateral;

    **(4)** Sections 9–608(a) and 9–615(c) to the extent that they deal with application or payment of noncash proceeds of collection, enforcement, or disposition;

    **(5)** Sections 9–608(a) and 9–615(d) to the extent that they require accounting for or payment of surplus proceeds of collateral;

    **(6)** Section 9–609 to the extent that it imposes upon a secured party that takes possession of collateral without judicial process the duty to do so without breach of the peace;

    **(7)** Sections 9–610(b), 9–611, 9–613, and 9–614, which deal with disposition of collateral;

    **(8)** Section 9–615(f), which deals with calculation of a deficiency or surplus when a disposition is made to the secured party, a person related to the secured party, or a secondary obligor;

    **(9)** Section 9–616, which deals with explanation of the calculation of a surplus or deficiency;

    **(10)** Sections 9–620, 9–621, and 9–622, which deal with acceptance of collateral in satisfaction of obligation;

    **(11)** Section 9–623, which deals with redemption of collateral;

    **(12)** Section 9–624, which deals with permissible waivers; and

    **(13)** Sections 9–625 and 9–626, which deal with the secured party's liability for failure to comply with this article.

### § 9–603. Agreement on Standards Concerning Rights and Duties.

**(a)** The parties may determine by agreement the standards measuring the fulfillment of the rights of a debtor or obligor and the duties of a secured party under a rule stated in Section 9–602 if the standards are not manifestly unreasonable.

**(b)** Subsection (a) does not apply to the duty under Section 9–609 to refrain from breaching the peace.

### § 9–604. Procedure If Security Agreement Covers Real Property or Fixtures.

**(a)** If a security agreement covers both personal and real property, a secured party may proceed:

    **(1)** under this part as to the personal property without prejudicing any rights with respect to the real property; or

    **(2)** as to both the personal property and the real property in accordance with the rights with respect to the real property, in which case the other provisions of this part do not apply.

**(b)** Subject to subsection (c), if a security agreement covers goods that are or become fixtures, a secured party may proceed:

    **(1)** under this part; or

    **(2)** in accordance with the rights with respect to real property, in which case the other provisions of this part do not apply.

**(c)** Subject to the other provisions of this part, if a secured party holding a security interest in fixtures has priority over all owners and encumbrancers of the real property, the secured party, after default, may remove the collateral from the real property.

**(d)** A secured party that removes collateral shall promptly reimburse any encumbrancer or owner of the real property, other than the debtor, for the cost of repair of any physical injury caused by the removal. The secured party need not reimburse the encumbrancer or owner for any diminution in value of the real property caused by the absence of the goods removed or by any necessity of replacing them. A person entitled to reimbursement may refuse permission to remove until the secured party gives adequate assurance for the performance of the obligation to reimburse.

### § 9–605. Unknown Debtor or Secondary Obligor.

A secured party does not owe a duty based on its status as secured party:

(1) to a person that is a debtor or obligor, unless the secured party knows:

(A) that the person is a debtor or obligor;

(B) the identity of the person; and

(C) how to communicate with the person; or

(2) to a secured party or lienholder that has filed a financing statement against a person, unless the secured party knows:

(A) that the person is a debtor; and

(B) the identity of the person.

### § 9–606. Time of Default for Agricultural Lien.

For purposes of this part, a default occurs in connection with an agricultural lien at the time the secured party becomes entitled to enforce the lien in accordance with the statute under which it was created.

### § 9–607. Collection and Enforcement by Secured Party.

**(a)** If so agreed, and in any event after default, a secured party:

(1) may notify an account debtor or other person obligated on collateral to make payment or otherwise render performance to or for the benefit of the secured party;

(2) may take any proceeds to which the secured party is entitled under Section 9–315;

(3) may enforce the obligations of an account debtor or other person obligated on collateral and exercise the rights of the debtor with respect to the obligation of the account debtor or other person obligated on collateral to make payment or otherwise render performance to the debtor, and with respect to any property that secures the obligations of the account debtor or other person obligated on the collateral;

(4) if it holds a security interest in a deposit account perfected by control under Section 9–104(a)(1), may apply the balance of the deposit account to the obligation secured by the deposit account; and

(5) if it holds a security interest in a deposit account perfected by control under Section 9–104(a)(2) or (3), may instruct the bank to pay the balance of the deposit account to or for the benefit of the secured party.

**(b)** If necessary to enable a secured party to exercise under subsection (a)(3) the right of a debtor to enforce a mortgage non-

judicially, the secured party may record in the office in which a record of the mortgage is recorded:

(1) a copy of the security agreement that creates or provides for a security interest in the obligation secured by the mortgage; and

(2) the secured party's sworn affidavit in recordable form stating that:

(A) a default has occurred; and

(B) the secured party is entitled to enforce the mortgage nonjudicially.

**(c)** A secured party shall proceed in a commercially reasonable manner if the secured party:

(1) undertakes to collect from or enforce an obligation of an account debtor or other person obligated on collateral; and

(2) is entitled to charge back uncollected collateral or otherwise to full or limited recourse against the debtor or a secondary obligor.

**(d)** A secured party may deduct from the collections made pursuant to subsection (c) reasonable expenses of collection and enforcement, including reasonable attorney's fees and legal expenses incurred by the secured party.

**(e)** This section does not determine whether an account debtor, bank, or other person obligated on collateral owes a duty to a secured party.

As amended in 2000.

### § 9–608. Application of Proceeds of Collection or Enforcement; Liability for Deficiency and Right to Surplus.

**(a)** If a security interest or agricultural lien secures payment or performance of an obligation, the following rules apply:

(1) A secured party shall apply or pay over for application the cash proceeds of collection or enforcement under Section 9–607 in the following order to:

(A) the reasonable expenses of collection and enforcement and, to the extent provided for by agreement and not prohibited by law, reasonable attorney's fees and legal expenses incurred by the secured party;

(B) the satisfaction of obligations secured by the security interest or agricultural lien under which the collection or enforcement is made; and

(C) the satisfaction of obligations secured by any subordinate security interest in or other lien on the collateral subject to the security interest or agricultural lien under which the collection or enforcement is made if the secured party receives an authenticated demand for proceeds before distribution of the proceeds is completed.

(2) If requested by a secured party, a holder of a subordinate security interest or other lien shall furnish reasonable proof of the interest or lien within a reasonable time. Unless the holder complies, the secured party need not comply with the holder's demand under paragraph (1)(C).

(3) A secured party need not apply or pay over for application noncash proceeds of collection and enforcement under Section 9–607 unless the failure to do so would be commercially unreasonable. A secured party that applies or pays over for application noncash proceeds shall do so in a commercially reasonable manner.

**(4)** A secured party shall account to and pay a debtor for any surplus, and the obligor is liable for any deficiency.

**(b)** If the underlying transaction is a sale of accounts, chattel paper, payment intangibles, or promissory notes, the debtor is not entitled to any surplus, and the obligor is not liable for any deficiency.

As amended in 2000.

### § 9–609. Secured Party's Right to Take Possession after Default.

**(a)** After default, a secured party:

**(1)** may take possession of the collateral; and

**(2)** without removal, may render equipment unusable and dispose of collateral on a debtor's premises under Section 9–610.

**(b)** A secured party may proceed under subsection (a):

**(1)** pursuant to judicial process; or

**(2)** without judicial process, if it proceeds without breach of the peace.

**(c)** If so agreed, and in any event after default, a secured party may require the debtor to assemble the collateral and make it available to the secured party at a place to be designated by the secured party which is reasonably convenient to both parties.

### § 9–610. Disposition of Collateral after Default.

**(a)** After default, a secured party may sell, lease, license, or otherwise dispose of any or all of the collateral in its present condition or following any commercially reasonable preparation or processing.

**(b)** Every aspect of a disposition of collateral, including the method, manner, time, place, and other terms, must be commercially reasonable. If commercially reasonable, a secured party may dispose of collateral by public or private proceedings, by one or more contracts, as a unit or in parcels, and at any time and place and on any terms.

**(c)** A secured party may purchase collateral:

**(1)** at a public disposition; or

**(2)** at a private disposition only if the collateral is of a kind that is customarily sold on a recognized market or the subject of widely distributed standard price quotations.

**(d)** A contract for sale, lease, license, or other disposition includes the warranties relating to title, possession, quiet enjoyment, and the like which by operation of law accompany a voluntary disposition of property of the kind subject to the contract.

**(e)** A secured party may disclaim or modify warranties under subsection (d):

**(1)** in a manner that would be effective to disclaim or modify the warranties in a voluntary disposition of property of the kind subject to the contract of disposition; or

**(2)** by communicating to the purchaser a record evidencing the contract for disposition and including an express disclaimer or modification of the warranties.

**(f)** A record is sufficient to disclaim warranties under subsection (e) if it indicates "There is no warranty relating to title, possession, quiet enjoyment, or the like in this disposition" or uses words of similar import.

### § 9–611. Notification before Disposition of Collateral.

**(a)** In this section, "notification date" means the earlier of the date on which:

**(1)** a secured party sends to the debtor and any secondary obligor an authenticated notification of disposition; or

**(2)** the debtor and any secondary obligor waive the right to notification.

**(b)** Except as otherwise provided in subsection (d), a secured party that disposes of collateral under Section 9–610 shall send to the persons specified in subsection (c) a reasonable authenticated notification of disposition.

**(c)** To comply with subsection (b), the secured party shall send an authenticated notification of disposition to:

**(1)** the debtor;

**(2)** any secondary obligor; and

**(3)** if the collateral is other than consumer goods:

**(A)** any other person from which the secured party has received, before the notification date, an authenticated notification of a claim of an interest in the collateral;

**(B)** any other secured party or lienholder that, 10 days before the notification date, held a security interest in or other lien on the collateral perfected by the filing of a financing statement that:

**(i)** identified the collateral;

**(ii)** was indexed under the debtor's name as of that date; and

**(iii)** was filed in the office in which to file a financing statement against the debtor covering the collateral as of that date; and

**(C)** any other secured party that, 10 days before the notification date, held a security interest in the collateral perfected by compliance with a statute, regulation, or treaty described in Section 9–311(a).

**(d)** Subsection (b) does not apply if the collateral is perishable or threatens to decline speedily in value or is of a type customarily sold on a recognized market.

**(e)** A secured party complies with the requirement for notification prescribed by subsection (c)(3)(B) if:

**(1)** not later than 20 days or earlier than 30 days before the notification date, the secured party requests, in a commercially reasonable manner, information concerning financing statements indexed under the debtor's name in the office indicated in subsection (c)(3)(B); and

**(2)** before the notification date, the secured party:

**(A)** did not receive a response to the request for information; or

**(B)** received a response to the request for information and sent an authenticated notification of disposition to each secured party or other lienholder named in that response whose financing statement covered the collateral.

### § 9–612. Timeliness of Notification before Disposition of Collateral.

**(a)** Except as otherwise provided in subsection (b), whether a notification is sent within a reasonable time is a question of fact.

**(b)** In a transaction other than a consumer transaction, a notification of disposition sent after default and 10 days or more before the earliest time of disposition set forth in the notification is sent within a reasonable time before the disposition.

## § 9–613. Contents and Form of Notification before Disposition of Collateral:  General.

Except in a consumer-goods transaction, the following rules apply:

**(1)** The contents of a notification of disposition are sufficient if the notification:

**(A)** describes the debtor and the secured party;

**(B)** describes the collateral that is the subject of the intended disposition;

**(C)** states the method of intended disposition;

**(D)** states that the debtor is entitled to an accounting of the unpaid indebtedness and states the charge, if any, for an accounting; and

**(E)** states the time and place of a public disposition or the time after which any other disposition is to be made.

**(2)** Whether the contents of a notification that lacks any of the information specified in paragraph (1) are nevertheless sufficient is a question of fact.

**(3)** The contents of a notification providing substantially the information specified in paragraph (1) are sufficient, even if the notification includes:

**(A)** information not specified by that paragraph; or

**(B)** minor errors that are not seriously misleading.

**(4)** A particular phrasing of the notification is not required.

**(5)** The following form of notification and the form appearing in Section 9–614(3), when completed, each provides sufficient information:

### NOTIFICATION OF DISPOSITION OF COLLATERAL

To: *[Name of debtor, obligor, or other person to which the notification is sent]*

From: *[Name, address, and telephone number of secured party]*

Name of Debtor(s): *[Include only if debtor(s) are not an addressee]*

[For a public disposition:]

We will sell [or lease or license, as applicable] the [describe collateral] [to the highest qualified bidder] in public as follows:

Day and Date: _____

Time: _____

Place: _____

*[For a private disposition:]*

We will sell [or lease or license, as *applicable*] the [*describe collateral*] privately sometime after [*day and date*].

You are entitled to an accounting of the unpaid indebtedness secured by the property that we intend to sell [or lease or license, as applicable] [for a charge of $_____]. You may request an accounting by calling us at [telephone number].

**[End of Form]**

As amended in 2000.

## § 9–614. Contents and Form of Notification before Disposition of Collateral: Consumer-Goods Transaction.

In a consumer-goods transaction, the following rules apply:

**(1)** A notification of disposition must provide the following information:

**(A)** the information specified in Section 9–613(1);

**(B)** a description of any liability for a deficiency of the person to which the notification is sent;

**(C)** a telephone number from which the amount that must be paid to the secured party to redeem the collateral under Section 9–623 is available; and

**(D)** a telephone number or mailing address from which additional information concerning the disposition and the obligation secured is available.

**(2)** A particular phrasing of the notification is not required.

**(3)** The following form of notification, when completed, provides sufficient information:

*[Name and address of secured party]*

*[Date]*

### NOTICE OF OUR PLAN TO SELL PROPERTY

*[Name and address of any obligor who is also a debtor]*

Subject: *[Identification of Transaction]*

We have your [describe collateral], because you broke promises in our agreement.

*[For a public disposition:]*

We will sell [describe collateral] at public sale. A sale could include a lease or license. The sale will be held as follows:

Date: _____

Time: _____

Place: _____

If you need more information about the sale call us at [*telephone number*] [or write us at [*secured party's address*]].

We are sending this notice to the following other people who have an interest in [describe collateral] or who owe money under your agreement:

*[Names of all other debtors and obligors, if any]*

**[End of Form]**

**(4)** A notification in the form of paragraph (3) is sufficient, even if additional information appears at the end of the form.

**(5)** A notification in the form of paragraph (3) is sufficient, even if it includes errors in information not required by paragraph (1), unless the error is misleading with respect to rights arising under this article.

**(6)** If a notification under this section is not in the form of paragraph (3), law other than this article determines the effect of including information not required by paragraph (1).

## § 9–615. Application of Proceeds of Disposition; Liability for Deficiency and Right to Surplus.

**(a)** A secured party shall apply or pay over for application the cash proceeds of disposition under Section 9–610 in the following order to:

**(1)** the reasonable expenses of retaking, holding, preparing for disposition, processing, and disposing, and, to the extent provided for by agreement and not prohibited by law, reasonable attorney's fees and legal expenses incurred by the secured party;

**(2)** the satisfaction of obligations secured by the security interest or agricultural lien under which the disposition is made;

**(3)** the satisfaction of obligations secured by any subordinate security interest in or other subordinate lien on the collateral if:

**(A)** the secured party receives from the holder of the subordinate security interest or other lien an authenticated demand for proceeds before distribution of the proceeds is completed; and

**(B)** in a case in which a consignor has an interest in the collateral, the subordinate security interest or other lien is senior to the interest of the consignor; and

**(4)** a secured party that is a consignor of the collateral if the secured party receives from the consignor an authenticated demand for proceeds before distribution of the proceeds is completed.

**(b)** If requested by a secured party, a holder of a subordinate security interest or other lien shall furnish reasonable proof of the interest or lien within a reasonable time. Unless the holder does so, the secured party need not comply with the holder's demand under subsection (a)(3).

**(c)** A secured party need not apply or pay over for application noncash proceeds of disposition under Section 9–610 unless the failure to do so would be commercially unreasonable. A secured party that applies or pays over for application noncash proceeds shall do so in a commercially reasonable manner.

**(d)** If the security interest under which a disposition is made secures payment or performance of an obligation, after making the payments and applications required by subsection (a) and permitted by subsection (c):

**(1)** unless subsection (a)(4) requires the secured party to apply or pay over cash proceeds to a consignor, the secured party shall account to and pay a debtor for any surplus; and

**(2)** the obligor is liable for any deficiency.

**(e)** If the underlying transaction is a sale of accounts, chattel paper, payment intangibles, or promissory notes:

**(1)** the debtor is not entitled to any surplus; and

**(2)** the obligor is not liable for any deficiency.

**(f)** The surplus or deficiency following a disposition is calculated based on the amount of proceeds that would have been realized in a disposition complying with this part to a transferee other than the secured party, a person related to the secured party, or a secondary obligor if:

**(1)** the transferee in the disposition is the secured party, a person related to the secured party, or a secondary obligor; and

**(2)** the amount of proceeds of the disposition is significantly below the range of proceeds that a complying disposition to a person other than the secured party, a person related to the secured party, or a secondary obligor would have brought.

**(g)** A secured party that receives cash proceeds of a disposition in good faith and without knowledge that the receipt violates the rights of the holder of a security interest or other lien that is not subordinate to the security interest or agricultural lien under which the disposition is made:

**(1)** takes the cash proceeds free of the security interest or other lien;

**(2)** is not obligated to apply the proceeds of the disposition to the satisfaction of obligations secured by the security interest or other lien; and

**(3)** is not obligated to account to or pay the holder of the security interest or other lien for any surplus.

As amended in 2000.

## § 9–616. Explanation of Calculation of Surplus or Deficiency.

**(a)** In this section:

**(1)** "Explanation" means a writing that:

**(A)** states the amount of the surplus or deficiency;

**(B)** provides an explanation in accordance with subsection (c) of how the secured party calculated the surplus or deficiency;

**(C)** states, if applicable, that future debits, credits, charges, including additional credit service charges or interest, rebates, and expenses may affect the amount of the surplus or deficiency; and

**(D)** provides a telephone number or mailing address from which additional information concerning the transaction is available.

**(2)** "Request" means a record:

**(A)** authenticated by a debtor or consumer obligor;

**(B)** requesting that the recipient provide an explanation; and

**(C)** sent after disposition of the collateral under Section 9–610.

**(b)** In a consumer-goods transaction in which the debtor is entitled to a surplus or a consumer obligor is liable for a deficiency under Section 9–615, the secured party shall:

**(1)** send an explanation to the debtor or consumer obligor, as applicable, after the disposition and:

**(A)** before or when the secured party accounts to the debtor and pays any surplus or first makes written demand on the consumer obligor after the disposition for payment of the deficiency; and

**(B)** within 14 days after receipt of a request; or

**(2)** in the case of a consumer obligor who is liable for a deficiency, within 14 days after receipt of a request, send to the consumer obligor a record waiving the secured party's right to a deficiency.

**(c)** To comply with subsection (a)(1)(B), a writing must provide the following information in the following order:

**(1)** the aggregate amount of obligations secured by the security interest under which the disposition was made, and, if the amount reflects a rebate of unearned interest or credit service charge, an indication of that fact, calculated as of a specified date:

**(A)** if the secured party takes or receives possession of the collateral after default, not more than 35 days before the secured party takes or receives possession; or

**(B)** if the secured party takes or receives possession of the collateral before default or does not take possession of the collateral, not more than 35 days before the disposition;

**(2)** the amount of proceeds of the disposition;

**(3)** the aggregate amount of the obligations after deducting the amount of proceeds;

**(4)** the amount, in the aggregate or by type, and types of expenses, including expenses of retaking, holding, preparing for disposition, processing, and disposing of the collateral, and attorney's fees secured by the collateral which are known to the secured party and relate to the current disposition;

**(5)** the amount, in the aggregate or by type, and types of credits, including rebates of interest or credit service charges, to which the obligor is known to be entitled and which are not reflected in the amount in paragraph (1); and

**(6)** the amount of the surplus or deficiency.

**(d)** A particular phrasing of the explanation is not required. An explanation complying substantially with the requirements of subsection (a) is sufficient, even if it includes minor errors that are not seriously misleading.

**(e)** A debtor or consumer obligor is entitled without charge to one response to a request under this section during any six-month period in which the secured party did not send to the debtor or consumer obligor an explanation pursuant to subsection (b)(1). The secured party may require payment of a charge not exceeding $25 for each additional response.

### § 9–617. Rights of Transferee of Collateral.

**(a)** A secured party's disposition of collateral after default:

**(1)** transfers to a transferee for value all of the debtor's rights in the collateral;

**(2)** discharges the security interest under which the disposition is made; and

**(3)** discharges any subordinate security interest or other subordinate lien [other than liens created under [cite acts or statutes providing for liens, if any, that are not to be discharged]].

**(b)** A transferee that acts in good faith takes free of the rights and interests described in subsection (a), even if the secured party fails to comply with this article or the requirements of any judicial proceeding.

**(c)** If a transferee does not take free of the rights and interests described in subsection (a), the transferee takes the collateral subject to:

**(1)** the debtor's rights in the collateral;

**(2)** the security interest or agricultural lien under which the disposition is made; and

**(3)** any other security interest or other lien.

### § 9–618. Rights and Duties of Certain Secondary Obligors.

**(a)** A secondary obligor acquires the rights and becomes obligated to perform the duties of the secured party after the secondary obligor:

**(1)** receives an assignment of a secured obligation from the secured party;

**(2)** receives a transfer of collateral from the secured party and agrees to accept the rights and assume the duties of the secured party; or

**(3)** is subrogated to the rights of a secured party with respect to collateral.

**(b)** An assignment, transfer, or subrogation described in subsection (a):

**(1)** is not a disposition of collateral under Section 9–610; and

**(2)** relieves the secured party of further duties under this article.

### § 9–619. Transfer of Record or Legal Title.

**(a)** In this section, "transfer statement" means a record authenticated by a secured party stating:

**(1)** that the debtor has defaulted in connection with an obligation secured by specified collateral;

**(2)** that the secured party has exercised its post-default remedies with respect to the collateral;

**(3)** that, by reason of the exercise, a transferee has acquired the rights of the debtor in the collateral; and

**(4)** the name and mailing address of the secured party, debtor, and transferee.

**(b)** A transfer statement entitles the transferee to the transfer of record of all rights of the debtor in the collateral specified in the statement in any official filing, recording, registration, or certificate-of-title system covering the collateral. If a transfer statement is presented with the applicable fee and request form to the official or office responsible for maintaining the system, the official or office shall:

**(1)** accept the transfer statement;

**(2)** promptly amend its records to reflect the transfer; and

**(3)** if applicable, issue a new appropriate certificate of title in the name of the transferee.

**(c)** A transfer of the record or legal title to collateral to a secured party under subsection (b) or otherwise is not of itself a disposition of collateral under this article and does not of itself relieve the secured party of its duties under this article.

### § 9–620. Acceptance of Collateral in Full or Partial Satisfaction of Obligation; Compulsory Disposition of Collateral.

**(a)** Except as otherwise provided in subsection (g), a secured party may accept collateral in full or partial satisfaction of the obligation it secures only if:

**(1)** the debtor consents to the acceptance under subsection (c);

**(2)** the secured party does not receive, within the time set forth in subsection (d), a notification of objection to the proposal authenticated by:

**(A)** a person to which the secured party was required to send a proposal under Section 9–621; or

**(B)** any other person, other than the debtor, holding an interest in the collateral subordinate to the security interest that is the subject of the proposal;

**(3)** if the collateral is consumer goods, the collateral is not in the possession of the debtor when the debtor consents to the acceptance; and

**(4)** subsection (e) does not require the secured party to dispose of the collateral or the debtor waives the requirement pursuant to Section 9–624.

**(b)** A purported or apparent acceptance of collateral under this section is ineffective unless:

**(1)** the secured party consents to the acceptance in an authenticated record or sends a proposal to the debtor; and

**(2)** the conditions of subsection (a) are met.

**(c)** For purposes of this section:

**(1)** a debtor consents to an acceptance of collateral in partial satisfaction of the obligation it secures only if the debtor agrees to the terms of the acceptance in a record authenticated after default; and

**(2)** a debtor consents to an acceptance of collateral in full satisfaction of the obligation it secures only if the debtor agrees to the terms of the acceptance in a record authenticated after default or the secured party:

**(A)** sends to the debtor after default a proposal that is unconditional or subject only to a condition that collateral not in the possession of the secured party be preserved or maintained;

**(B)** in the proposal, proposes to accept collateral in full satisfaction of the obligation it secures; and

**(C)** does not receive a notification of objection authenticated by the debtor within 20 days after the proposal is sent.

**(d)** To be effective under subsection (a)(2), a notification of objection must be received by the secured party:

**(1)** in the case of a person to which the proposal was sent pursuant to Section 9–621, within 20 days after notification was sent to that person; and

**(2)** in other cases:

**(A)** within 20 days after the last notification was sent pursuant to Section 9–621; or

**(B)** if a notification was not sent, before the debtor consents to the acceptance under subsection (c).

**(e)** A secured party that has taken possession of collateral shall dispose of the collateral pursuant to Section 9–610 within the time specified in subsection (f) if:

**(1)** 60 percent of the cash price has been paid in the case of a purchase-money security interest in consumer goods; or

**(2)** 60 percent of the principal amount of the obligation secured has been paid in the case of a non-purchase-money security interest in consumer goods.

**(f)** To comply with subsection (e), the secured party shall dispose of the collateral:

**(1)** within 90 days after taking possession; or

**(2)** within any longer period to which the debtor and all secondary obligors have agreed in an agreement to that effect entered into and authenticated after default.

**(g)** In a consumer transaction, a secured party may not accept collateral in partial satisfaction of the obligation it secures.

### § 9–621. Notification of Proposal to Accept Collateral.

**(a)** A secured party that desires to accept collateral in full or partial satisfaction of the obligation it secures shall send its proposal to:

**(1)** any person from which the secured party has received, before the debtor consented to the acceptance, an authenticated notification of a claim of an interest in the collateral;

**(2)** any other secured party or lienholder that, 10 days before the debtor consented to the acceptance, held a security interest in or other lien on the collateral perfected by the filing of a financing statement that:

**(A)** identified the collateral;

**(B)** was indexed under the debtor's name as of that date; and

**(C)** was filed in the office or offices in which to file a financing statement against the debtor covering the collateral as of that date; and

**(3)** any other secured party that, 10 days before the debtor consented to the acceptance, held a security interest in the collateral perfected by compliance with a statute, regulation, or treaty described in Section 9–311(a).

**(b)** A secured party that desires to accept collateral in partial satisfaction of the obligation it secures shall send its proposal to any secondary obligor in addition to the persons described in subsection (a).

### § 9–622. Effect of Acceptance of Collateral.

**(a)** A secured party's acceptance of collateral in full or partial satisfaction of the obligation it secures:

**(1)** discharges the obligation to the extent consented to by the debtor;

**(2)** transfers to the secured party all of a debtor's rights in the collateral;

**(3)** discharges the security interest or agricultural lien that is the subject of the debtor's consent and any subordinate security interest or other subordinate lien; and

**(4)** terminates any other subordinate interest.

**(b)** A subordinate interest is discharged or terminated under subsection (a), even if the secured party fails to comply with this article.

### § 9–623. Right to Redeem Collateral.

**(a)** A debtor, any secondary obligor, or any other secured party or lienholder may redeem collateral.

**(b)** To redeem collateral, a person shall tender:

**(1)** fulfillment of all obligations secured by the collateral; and

**(2)** the reasonable expenses and attorney's fees described in Section 9–615(a)(1).

**(c)** A redemption may occur at any time before a secured party:

**(1)** has collected collateral under Section 9–607;

**(2)** has disposed of collateral or entered into a contract for its disposition under Section 9–610; or

**(3)** has accepted collateral in full or partial satisfaction of the obligation it secures under Section 9–622.

### § 9–624. Waiver.

**(a)** A debtor or secondary obligor may waive the right to notification of disposition of collateral under Section 9–611 only by an agreement to that effect entered into and authenticated after default.

**(b)** A debtor may waive the right to require disposition of collateral under Section 9–620(e) only by an agreement to that effect entered into and authenticated after default.

**(c)** Except in a consumer-goods transaction, a debtor or secondary obligor may waive the right to redeem collateral under Section 9–623 only by an agreement to that effect entered into and authenticated after default.

### [Subpart 2. Noncompliance with Article]

### § 9–625. Remedies for Secured Party's Failure to Comply with Article.

**(a)** If it is established that a secured party is not proceeding in accordance with this article, a court may order or restrain collection, enforcement, or disposition of collateral on appropriate terms and conditions.

**(b)** Subject to subsections (c), (d), and (f), a person is liable for damages in the amount of any loss caused by a failure to comply with this article. Loss caused by a failure to comply may include loss resulting from the debtor's inability to obtain, or increased costs of, alternative financing.

**(c)** Except as otherwise provided in Section 9–628:

**(1)** a person that, at the time of the failure, was a debtor, was an obligor, or held a security interest in or other lien on the collateral may recover damages under subsection (b) for its loss; and

**(2)** if the collateral is consumer goods, a person that was a debtor or a secondary obligor at the time a secured party failed to comply with this part may recover for that failure in any event an amount not less than the credit service charge plus 10 percent of the principal amount of the obligation or the time-price differential plus 10 percent of the cash price.

**(d)** A debtor whose deficiency is eliminated under Section 9–626 may recover damages for the loss of any surplus. However, a debtor or secondary obligor whose deficiency is eliminated or reduced under Section 9–626 may not otherwise recover under subsection (b) for noncompliance with the provisions of this part relating to collection, enforcement, disposition, or acceptance.

**(e)** In addition to any damages recoverable under subsection (b), the debtor, consumer obligor, or person named as a debtor in a filed record, as applicable, may recover $500 in each case from a person that:

**(1)** fails to comply with Section 9–208;

**(2)** fails to comply with Section 9–209;

**(3)** files a record that the person is not entitled to file under Section 9–509(a);

**(4)** fails to cause the secured party of record to file or send a termination statement as required by Section 9–513(a) or (c);

**(5)** fails to comply with Section 9–616(b)(1) and whose failure is part of a pattern, or consistent with a practice, of noncompliance; or

**(6)** fails to comply with Section 9–616(b)(2).

**(f)** A debtor or consumer obligor may recover damages under subsection (b) and, in addition, $500 in each case from a person that, without reasonable cause, fails to comply with a request under Section 9–210. A recipient of a request under Section 9–210 which never claimed an interest in the collateral or obligations that are the subject of a request under that section has a reasonable excuse for failure to comply with the request within the meaning of this subsection.

**(g)** If a secured party fails to comply with a request regarding a list of collateral or a statement of account under Section 9–210, the secured party may claim a security interest only as shown in the list or statement included in the request as against a person that is reasonably misled by the failure.

As amended in 2000.

### § 9–626. Action in Which Deficiency or Surplus Is in Issue.

**(a)** In an action arising from a transaction, other than a consumer transaction, in which the amount of a deficiency or surplus is in issue, the following rules apply:

**(1)** A secured party need not prove compliance with the provisions of this part relating to collection, enforcement, disposition, or acceptance unless the debtor or a secondary obligor places the secured party's compliance in issue.

**(2)** If the secured party's compliance is placed in issue, the secured party has the burden of establishing that the collection, enforcement, disposition, or acceptance was conducted in accordance with this part.

**(3)** Except as otherwise provided in Section 9–628, if a secured party fails to prove that the collection, enforcement, disposition, or acceptance was conducted in accordance with the provisions of this part relating to collection, enforcement, disposition, or acceptance, the liability of a debtor or a secondary obligor for a deficiency is limited to an amount by which the sum of the secured obligation, expenses, and attorney's fees exceeds the greater of:

**(A)** the proceeds of the collection, enforcement, disposition, or acceptance; or

**(B)** the amount of proceeds that would have been realized had the noncomplying secured party proceeded in accordance with the provisions of this part relating to collection, enforcement, disposition, or acceptance.

**(4)** For purposes of paragraph (3)(B), the amount of proceeds that would have been realized is equal to the sum of the secured obligation, expenses, and attorney's fees unless the secured party proves that the amount is less than that sum.

**(5)** If a deficiency or surplus is calculated under Section 9–615(f), the debtor or obligor has the burden of establishing that the amount of proceeds of the disposition is significantly below the range of prices that a complying disposition to a person other than the secured party, a person related to the secured party, or a secondary obligor would have brought.

**(b)** The limitation of the rules in subsection (a) to transactions other than consumer transactions is intended to leave to the court the determination of the proper rules in consumer transactions. The court may not infer from that limitation the nature of the proper rule in consumer transactions and may continue to apply established approaches.

### § 9–627. Determination of Whether Conduct Was Commercially Reasonable.

**(a)** The fact that a greater amount could have been obtained by a collection, enforcement, disposition, or acceptance at a different time or in a different method from that selected by the secured party is not of itself sufficient to preclude the secured party from establishing that the collection, enforcement, disposition, or acceptance was made in a commercially reasonable manner.

**(b)** A disposition of collateral is made in a commercially reasonable manner if the disposition is made:

**(1)** in the usual manner on any recognized market;

**(2)** at the price current in any recognized market at the time of the disposition; or

**(3)** otherwise in conformity with reasonable commercial practices among dealers in the type of property that was the subject of the disposition.

(c) A collection, enforcement, disposition, or acceptance is commercially reasonable if it has been approved:

    (1) in a judicial proceeding;

    (2) by a bona fide creditors' committee;

    (3) by a representative of creditors; or

    (4) by an assignee for the benefit of creditors.

(d) Approval under subsection (c) need not be obtained, and lack of approval does not mean that the collection, enforcement, disposition, or acceptance is not commercially reasonable.

### § 9–628. Nonliability and Limitation on Liability of Secured Party; Liability of Secondary Obligor.

(a) Unless a secured party knows that a person is a debtor or obligor, knows the identity of the person, and knows how to communicate with the person:

    (1) the secured party is not liable to the person, or to a secured party or lienholder that has filed a financing statement against the person, for failure to comply with this article; and

    (2) the secured party's failure to comply with this article does not affect the liability of the person for a deficiency.

(b) A secured party is not liable because of its status as secured party:

    (1) to a person that is a debtor or obligor, unless the secured party knows:

        (A) that the person is a debtor or obligor;

        (B) the identity of the person; and

        (C) how to communicate with the person; or

    (2) to a secured party or lienholder that has filed a financing statement against a person, unless the secured party knows:

        (A) that the person is a debtor; and

        (B) the identity of the person.

(c) A secured party is not liable to any person, and a person's liability for a deficiency is not affected, because of any act or omission arising out of the secured party's reasonable belief that a transaction is not a consumer-goods transaction or a consumer transaction or that goods are not consumer goods, if the secured party's belief is based on its reasonable reliance on:

    (1) a debtor's representation concerning the purpose for which collateral was to be used, acquired, or held; or

    (2) an obligor's representation concerning the purpose for which a secured obligation was incurred.

(d) A secured party is not liable to any person under Section 9–625(c)(2) for its failure to comply with Section 9–616.

(e) A secured party is not liable under Section 9–625(c)(2) more than once with respect to any one secured obligation.

### Part 7—Transition

### § 9–701. Effective Date.

This [Act] takes effect on July 1, 2001.

### § 9–702. Savings Clause.

(a) Except as otherwise provided in this part, this [Act] applies to a transaction or lien within its scope, even if the transaction or lien was entered into or created before this [Act] takes effect.

(b) Except as otherwise provided in subsection (c) and Sections 9–703 through 9–709:

    (1) transactions and liens that were not governed by [former Article 9], were validly entered into or created before this [Act] takes effect, and would be subject to this [Act] if they had been entered into or created after this [Act] takes effect, and the rights, duties, and interests flowing from those transactions and liens remain valid after this [Act] takes effect; and

    (2) the transactions and liens may be terminated, completed, consummated, and enforced as required or permitted by this [Act] or by the law that otherwise would apply if this [Act] had not taken effect.

(c) This [Act] does not affect an action, case, or proceeding commenced before this [Act] takes effect.

As amended in 2000.

### § 9–703. Security Interest Perfected before Effective Date.

(a) A security interest that is enforceable immediately before this [Act] takes effect and would have priority over the rights of a person that becomes a lien creditor at that time is a perfected security interest under this [Act] if, when this [Act] takes effect, the applicable requirements for enforceability and perfection under this [Act] are satisfied without further action.

(b) Except as otherwise provided in Section 9–705, if, immediately before this [Act] takes effect, a security interest is enforceable and would have priority over the rights of a person that becomes a lien creditor at that time, but the applicable requirements for enforceability or perfection under this [Act] are not satisfied when this [Act] takes effect, the security interest:

    (1) is a perfected security interest for one year after this [Act] takes effect;

    (2) remains enforceable thereafter only if the security interest becomes enforceable under Section 9–203 before the year expires; and

    (3) remains perfected thereafter only if the applicable requirements for perfection under this [Act] are satisfied before the year expires.

### § 9–704. Security Interest Unperfected before Effective Date.

A security interest that is enforceable immediately before this [Act] takes effect but which would be subordinate to the rights of a person that becomes a lien creditor at that time:

    (1) remains an enforceable security interest for one year after this [Act] takes effect;

    (2) remains enforceable thereafter if the security interest becomes enforceable under Section 9–203 when this [Act] takes effect or within one year thereafter; and

    (3) becomes perfected:

        (A) without further action, when this [Act] takes effect if the applicable requirements for perfection under this [Act] are satisfied before or at that time; or

        (B) when the applicable requirements for perfection are satisfied if the requirements are satisfied after that time.

### § 9–705. Effectiveness of Action Taken before Effective Date.

(a) If action, other than the filing of a financing statement, is taken before this [Act] takes effect and the action would have resulted in priority of a security interest over the rights of a person that becomes a lien creditor had the security interest become enforceable before this [Act] takes effect, the action is effective to perfect a security interest that attaches under this [Act] within one year after this [Act] takes effect. An attached security interest becomes unperfected one year after this [Act] takes effect unless the security interest becomes a perfected security interest under this [Act] before the expiration of that period.

(b) The filing of a financing statement before this [Act] takes effect is effective to perfect a security interest to the extent the filing would satisfy the applicable requirements for perfection under this [Act].

(c) This [Act] does not render ineffective an effective financing statement that, before this [Act] takes effect, is filed and satisfies the applicable requirements for perfection under the law of the jurisdiction governing perfection as provided in [former Section 9–103]. However, except as otherwise provided in subsections (d) and (e) and Section 9–706, the financing statement ceases to be effective at the earlier of:

(1) the time the financing statement would have ceased to be effective under the law of the jurisdiction in which it is filed; or

(2) June 30, 2006.

(d) The filing of a continuation statement after this [Act] takes effect does not continue the effectiveness of the financing statement filed before this [Act] takes effect. However, upon the timely filing of a continuation statement after this [Act] takes effect and in accordance with the law of the jurisdiction governing perfection as provided in Part 3, the effectiveness of a financing statement filed in the same office in that jurisdiction before this [Act] takes effect continues for the period provided by the law of that jurisdiction.

(e) Subsection (c)(2) applies to a financing statement that, before this [Act] takes effect, is filed against a transmitting utility and satisfies the applicable requirements for perfection under the law of the jurisdiction governing perfection as provided in [former Section 9–103] only to the extent that Part 3 provides that the law of a jurisdiction other than the jurisdiction in which the financing statement is filed governs perfection of a security interest in collateral covered by the financing statement.

(f) A financing statement that includes a financing statement filed before this [Act] takes effect and a continuation statement filed after this [Act] takes effect is effective only to the extent that it satisfies the requirements of Part 5 for an initial financing statement.

### § 9–706. When Initial Financing Statement Suffices to Continue Effectiveness of Financing Statement.

(a) The filing of an initial financing statement in the office specified in Section 9–501 continues the effectiveness of a financing statement filed before this [Act] takes effect if:

(1) the filing of an initial financing statement in that office would be effective to perfect a security interest under this [Act];

(2) the pre-effective-date financing statement was filed in an office in another State or another office in this State; and

(3) the initial financing statement satisfies subsection (c).

(b) The filing of an initial financing statement under subsection (a) continues the effectiveness of the pre-effective-date financing statement:

(1) if the initial financing statement is filed before this [Act] takes effect, for the period provided in [former Section 9–403] with respect to a financing statement; and

(2) if the initial financing statement is filed after this [Act] takes effect, for the period provided in Section 9–515 with respect to an initial financing statement.

(c) To be effective for purposes of subsection (a), an initial financing statement must:

(1) satisfy the requirements of Part 5 for an initial financing statement;

(2) identify the pre-effective-date financing statement by indicating the office in which the financing statement was filed and providing the dates of filing and file numbers, if any, of the financing statement and of the most recent continuation statement filed with respect to the financing statement; and

(3) indicate that the pre-effective-date financing statement remains effective.

### § 9–707. Amendment of Pre-Effective-Date Financing Statement.

(a) In this section, "Pre-effective-date financing statement" means a financing statement filed before this [Act] takes effect.

(b) After this [Act] takes effect, a person may add or delete collateral covered by, continue or terminate the effectiveness of, or otherwise amend the information provided in, a pre-effective-date financing statement only in accordance with the law of the jurisdiction governing perfection as provided in Part 3. However, the effectiveness of a pre-effective-date financing statement also may be terminated in accordance with the law of the jurisdiction in which the financing statement is filed.

(c) Except as otherwise provided in subsection (d), if the law of this State governs perfection of a security interest, the information in a pre-effective-date financing statement may be amended after this [Act] takes effect only if:

(1) the pre-effective-date financing statement and an amendment are filed in the office specified in Section 9–501;

(2) an amendment is filed in the office specified in Section 9–501 concurrently with, or after the filing in that office of, an initial financing statement that satisfies Section 9–706(c); or

(3) an initial financing statement that provides the information as amended and satisfies Section 9–706(c) is filed in the office specified in Section 9–501.

(d) If the law of this State governs perfection of a security interest, the effectiveness of a pre-effective-date financing statement may be continued only under Section 9–705(d) and (f) or 9–706.

(e) Whether or not the law of this State governs perfection of a security interest, the effectiveness of a pre-effective-date financing statement filed in this State may be terminated after this [Act] takes effect by filing a termination statement in the office in which the pre-effective-date financing statement is filed, unless an initial financing statement that satisfies Section 9–706(c) has been filed in the office specified by the law of the jurisdiction governing perfection as provided in Part 3 as the office in which to file a financing statement.

As amended in 2000.

### § 9–708. Persons Entitled to File Initial Financing Statement or Continuation Statement.

A person may file an initial financing statement or a continuation statement under this part if:

(1) the secured party of record authorizes the filing; and

(2) the filing is necessary under this part:

(A) to continue the effectiveness of a financing statement filed before this [Act] takes effect; or

(B) to perfect or continue the perfection of a security interest.

As amended in 2000.

### § 9–709. Priority.

(a) This [Act] determines the priority of conflicting claims to collateral. However, if the relative priorities of the claims were established before this [Act] takes effect, [former Article 9] determines priority.

(b) For purposes of Section 9–322(a), the priority of a security interest that becomes enforceable under Section 9–203 of this [Act] dates from the time this [Act] takes effect if the security interest is perfected under this [Act] by the filing of a financing statement before this [Act] takes effect which would not have been effective to perfect the security interest under [former Article 9]. This subsection does not apply to conflicting security interests each of which is perfected by the filing of such a financing statement.

As amended in 2000.

**Note: The author's explanatory comments appear in italics following the excerpt from each section.**

## SECTION 302
### Corporate responsibility for financial reports[1]

**(a)** Regulations required

The Commission shall, by rule, require, for each company filing periodic reports under section 13(a) or 15(d) of the Securities Exchange Act of 1934 (15 U.S.C. 78m, 78o(d)), that the principal executive officer or officers and the principal financial officer or officers, or persons performing similar functions, certify in each annual or quarterly report filed or submitted under either such section of such Act that—

**(1)** the signing officer has reviewed the report;

**(2)** based on the officer's knowledge, the report does not contain any untrue statement of a material fact or omit to state a material fact necessary in order to make the statements made, in light of the circumstances under which such statements were made, not misleading;

**(3)** based on such officer's knowledge, the financial statements, and other financial information included in the report, fairly present in all material respects the financial condition and results of operations of the issuer as of, and for, the periods presented in the report;

**(4)** the signing officers—

**(A)** are responsible for establishing and maintaining internal controls;

**(B)** have designed such internal controls to ensure that material information relating to the issuer and its consolidated subsidiaries is made known to such officers by others within those entities, particularly during the period in which the periodic reports are being prepared;

**(C)** have evaluated the effectiveness of the issuer's internal controls as of a date within 90 days prior to the report; and

**(D)** have presented in the report their conclusions about the effectiveness of their internal controls based on their evaluation as of that date;

**(5)** the signing officers have disclosed to the issuer's auditors and the audit committee of the board of directors (or persons fulfilling the equivalent function)—

**(A)** all significant deficiencies in the design or operation of internal controls which could adversely affect the issuer's ability to record, process, summarize, and report financial data and have identified for the issuer's auditors any material weaknesses in internal controls; and

**(B)** any fraud, whether or not material, that involves management or other employees who have a significant role in the issuer's internal controls; and

**(6)** the signing officers have indicated in the report whether or not there were significant changes in internal controls or in other factors that could significantly affect internal controls subsequent to the date of their evaluation, including any corrective actions with regard to significant deficiencies and material weaknesses.

**(b)** Foreign reincorporations have no effect

Nothing in this section shall be interpreted or applied in any way to allow any issuer to lessen the legal force of the statement required under this section, by an issuer having reincorporated or having engaged in any other transaction that resulted in the transfer of the corporate domicile or offices of the issuer from inside the United States to outside of the United States.

**(c)** Deadline

The rules required by subsection (a) of this section shall be effective not later than 30 days after July 30, 2002.

* * * *

**Explanatory Comments:**

*Section 302 requires the chief executive officer (CEO) and chief financial officer (CFO) of each public company to certify that they have reviewed the company's quarterly and annual reports to be filed with the Securities and Exchange Commission (SEC). The CEO and CFO must certify that, based on their knowledge, the reports do not contain any untrue statement of a material fact or any half-truth that would make the report misleading, and that the information contained in the reports fairly presents the company's financial condition.*

*In addition, this section also requires the CEO and CFO to certify that they have created and designed an internal control system for their company and have recently evaluated that system to ensure that it is effectively providing them with relevant and accurate financial information. If the signing officers have found any significant deficiencies or weaknesses in the company's system or have discovered any evidence of fraud, they must have reported the situation, and any corrective actions they have taken, to the auditors and the audit committee.*

## SECTION 306
### Insider trades during pension fund blackout periods[2]

**(a)** Prohibition of insider trading during pension fund blackout periods

**(1)** In general

Except to the extent otherwise provided by rule of the Commission pursuant to paragraph (3), it shall be unlawful for any director or executive officer of an issuer of any

---

**1.** This section of the Sarbanes-Oxley Act is codified at 15 U.S.C. Section 7241.

**2.** Codified at 15 U.S.C. Section 7244.

equity security (other than an exempted security), directly or indirectly, to purchase, sell, or otherwise acquire or transfer any equity security of the issuer (other than an exempted security) during any blackout period with respect to such equity security if such director or officer acquires such equity security in connection with his or her service or employment as a director or executive officer.

**(2)** Remedy

**(A)** In general

Any profit realized by a director or executive officer referred to in paragraph (1) from any purchase, sale, or other acquisition or transfer in violation of this subsection shall inure to and be recoverable by the issuer, irrespective of any intention on the part of such director or executive officer in entering into the transaction.

**(B)** Actions to recover profits

An action to recover profits in accordance with this subsection may be instituted at law or in equity in any court of competent jurisdiction by the issuer, or by the owner of any security of the issuer in the name and in behalf of the issuer if the issuer fails or refuses to bring such action within 60 days after the date of request, or fails diligently to prosecute the action thereafter, except that no such suit shall be brought more than 2 years after the date on which such profit was realized.

**(3)** Rulemaking authorized

The Commission shall, in consultation with the Secretary of Labor, issue rules to clarify the application of this subsection and to prevent evasion thereof. Such rules shall provide for the application of the requirements of paragraph (1) with respect to entities treated as a single employer with respect to an issuer under section 414(b), (c), (m), or (o) of Title 26 to the extent necessary to clarify the application of such requirements and to prevent evasion thereof. Such rules may also provide for appropriate exceptions from the requirements of this subsection, including exceptions for purchases pursuant to an automatic dividend reinvestment program or purchases or sales made pursuant to an advance election.

**(4)** Blackout period

For purposes of this subsection, the term "blackout period", with respect to the equity securities of any issuer—

**(A)** means any period of more than 3 consecutive business days during which the ability of not fewer than 50 percent of the participants or beneficiaries under all individual account plans maintained by the issuer to purchase, sell, or otherwise acquire or transfer an interest in any equity of such issuer held in such an individual account plan is temporarily suspended by the issuer or by a fiduciary of the plan; and

**(B)** does not include, under regulations which shall be prescribed by the Commission—

**(i)** a regularly scheduled period in which the participants and beneficiaries may not purchase, sell, or otherwise acquire or transfer an interest in any equity of such issuer, if such period is—

**(I)** incorporated into the individual account plan; and

**(II)** timely disclosed to employees before becoming participants under the individual account plan or as a subsequent amendment to the plan; or

**(ii)** any suspension described in subparagraph (A) that is imposed solely in connection with persons becoming participants or beneficiaries, or ceasing to be participants or beneficiaries, in an individual account plan by reason of a corporate merger, acquisition, divestiture, or similar transaction involving the plan or plan sponsor.

**(5)** Individual account plan

For purposes of this subsection, the term "individual account plan" has the meaning provided in section 1002(34) of Title 29, except that such term shall not include a one-participant retirement plan (within the meaning of section 1021(i)(8)(B) of Title 29).

**(6)** Notice to directors, executive officers, and the Commission

In any case in which a director or executive officer is subject to the requirements of this subsection in connection with a blackout period (as defined in paragraph (4)) with respect to any equity securities, the issuer of such equity securities shall timely notify such director or officer and the Securities and Exchange Commission of such blackout period.

\* \* \* \*

**Explanatory Comments:**

*Corporate pension funds typically prohibit employees from trading shares of the corporation during periods when the pension fund is undergoing significant change. Before 2002, however, these blackout periods did not affect the corporation's executives, who frequently received shares of the corporate stock as part of their compensation. Section 306 was Congress's solution to the basic unfairness of this situation. This section of the act required the SEC to issue rules that prohibit any director or executive officer from trading during pension fund blackout periods. (The SEC later issued these rules, entitled Regulation Blackout Trading Restriction, or Reg BTR.)*

*Section 306 also provided shareholders with a right to file a shareholder's derivative suit against officers and directors who have profited from trading during these blackout periods (provided that the corporation has failed to bring a suit). The officer or director can be forced to return to the corporation any profits received, regardless of whether the director or officer acted with bad intent.*

### SECTION 402
**Periodical and other reports[3]**

\* \* \* \*

**(i)** Accuracy of financial reports

Each financial report that contains financial statements, and that is required to be prepared in accordance with (or reconciled to) generally accepted accounting principles under this chapter and filed with the Commission shall reflect all material correcting adjustments that have been identified by a registered

---

**3.** This section of the Sarbanes-Oxley Act amended some of the provisions of the 1934 Securities Exchange Act and added the paragraphs reproduced here at 15 U.S.C. Section 78m.

public accounting firm in accordance with generally accepted accounting principles and the rules and regulations of the Commission.

**(j)** Off-balance sheet transactions

Not later than 180 days after July 30, 2002, the Commission shall issue final rules providing that each annual and quarterly financial report required to be filed with the Commission shall disclose all material off-balance sheet transactions, arrangements, obligations (including contingent obligations), and other relationships of the issuer with unconsolidated entities or other persons, that may have a material current or future effect on financial condition, changes in financial condition, results of operations, liquidity, capital expenditures, capital resources, or significant components of revenues or expenses.

**(k)** Prohibition on personal loans to executives

**(1)** In general

It shall be unlawful for any issuer (as defined in section 7201 of this title), directly or indirectly, including through any subsidiary, to extend or maintain credit, to arrange for the extension of credit, or to renew an extension of credit, in the form of a personal loan to or for any director or executive officer (or equivalent thereof) of that issuer. An extension of credit maintained by the issuer on July 30, 2002, shall not be subject to the provisions of this subsection, provided that there is no material modification to any term of any such extension of credit or any renewal of any such extension of credit on or after July 30, 2002.

**(2)** Limitation

Paragraph (1) does not preclude any home improvement and manufactured home loans (as that term is defined in section 1464 of Title 12), consumer credit (as defined in section 1602 of this title), or any extension of credit under an open end credit plan (as defined in section 1602 of this title), or a charge card (as defined in section 1637(c)(4)(e) of this title), or any extension of credit by a broker or dealer registered under section 78o of this title to an employee of that broker or dealer to buy, trade, or carry securities, that is permitted under rules or regulations of the Board of Governors of the Federal Reserve System pursuant to section 78g of this title (other than an extension of credit that would be used to purchase the stock of that issuer), that is—

    **(A)** made or provided in the ordinary course of the consumer credit business of such issuer;

    **(B)** of a type that is generally made available by such issuer to the public; and

    **(C)** made by such issuer on market terms, or terms that are no more favorable than those offered by the issuer to the general public for such extensions of credit.

**(3)** Rule of construction for certain loans

Paragraph (1) does not apply to any loan made or maintained by an insured depository institution (as defined in section 1813 of Title 12), if the loan is subject to the insider lending restrictions of section 375b of Title 12.

**(l)** Real time issuer disclosures

Each issuer reporting under subsection (a) of this section or section 78o(d) of this title shall disclose to the public on a rapid and current basis such additional information concerning material changes in the financial condition or operations of the issuer, in plain English, which may include trend and qualitative information and graphic presentations, as the Commission determines, by rule, is necessary or useful for the protection of investors and in the public interest.

**Explanatory Comments:**

*Before this act, many corporate executives typically received extremely large salaries, significant bonuses, and abundant stock options, even when the companies for which they worked were suffering. Executives were also routinely given personal loans from corporate funds, many of which were never paid back. The average large company during that period loaned almost $1 million a year to top executives, and some companies loaned hundreds of millions of dollars to their executives every year. Section 402 amended the 1934 Securities Exchange Act to prohibit public companies from making personal loans to executive officers and directors.*

*There are a few exceptions to this prohibition, such as home-improvement loans made in the ordinary course of business. Note also that while loans are forbidden, outright gifts are not. A corporation is free to give gifts to its executives, including cash, provided that these gifts are disclosed on its financial reports. The idea is that corporate directors will be deterred from making substantial gifts to their executives by the disclosure requirement—particularly if the corporation's financial condition is questionable—because making such gifts could be perceived as abusing their authority.*

## SECTION 403
### Directors, officers, and principal stockholders[4]

**(a)** Disclosures required

    **(1)** Directors, officers, and principal stockholders required to file

Every person who is directly or indirectly the beneficial owner of more than 10 percent of any class of any equity security (other than an exempted security) which is registered pursuant to section 78l of this title, or who is a director or an officer of the issuer of such security, shall file the statements required by this subsection with the Commission (and, if such security is registered on a national securities exchange, also with the exchange).

    **(2)** Time of filing

The statements required by this subsection shall be filed—

        **(A)** at the time of the registration of such security on a national securities exchange or by the effective date of a registration statement filed pursuant to section 78l(g) of this title;

        **(B)** within 10 days after he or she becomes such beneficial owner, director, or officer;

        **(C)** if there has been a change in such ownership, or if such person shall have purchased or sold a security-based swap agreement (as defined in section 206(b) of the Gramm-Leach-Bliley Act (15 U.S.C. 78c note)) involving such equity security, before the end of the second business day following the day on which the subject transaction has been executed, or at such other

---

**4.** This section of the Sarbanes-Oxley Act amended the disclosure provisions of the 1934 Securities Exchange Act, at 15 U.S.C. Section 78p.

time as the Commission shall establish, by rule, in any case in which the Commission determines that such 2-day period is not feasible.

**(3)** Contents of statements

A statement filed—

**(A)** under subparagraph (A) or (B) of paragraph (2) shall contain a statement of the amount of all equity securities of such issuer of which the filing person is the beneficial owner; and

**(B)** under subparagraph (C) of such paragraph shall indicate ownership by the filing person at the date of filing, any such changes in such ownership, and such purchases and sales of the security-based swap agreements as have occurred since the most recent such filing under such subparagraph.

**(4)** Electronic filing and availability

Beginning not later than 1 year after July 30, 2002—

**(A)** a statement filed under subparagraph (C) of paragraph (2) shall be filed electronically;

**(B)** the Commission shall provide each such statement on a publicly accessible Internet site not later than the end of the business day following that filing; and

**(C)** the issuer (if the issuer maintains a corporate website) shall provide that statement on that corporate website, not later than the end of the business day following that filing.

\* \* \* \*

### Explanatory Comments:

*This section dramatically shortens the time period provided in the Securities Exchange Act of 1934 for disclosing transactions by insiders. The prior law stated that most transactions had to be reported within ten days of the beginning of the following month, although certain transactions did not have to be reported until the following fiscal year (within the first forty-five days).*

*In several instances, some insider trading was not disclosed (and was therefore not discovered) until long after the transactions. So Congress added this section to reduce the time period for making disclosures. Under Section 403, most transactions by insiders must be electronically filed with the SEC within two business days.*

*Also, any company that maintains a Web site must post these SEC filings on its site by the end of the next business day. Congress enacted this section in the belief that if insiders are required to file reports of their transactions promptly with the SEC, companies will do more to police themselves and prevent insider trading.*

## SECTION 404
### Management assessment of internal controls[5]

**(a)** Rules required

The Commission shall prescribe rules requiring each annual report required by section 78m(a) or 78o(d) of this title to contain an internal control report, which shall—

**(1)** state the responsibility of management for establishing and maintaining an adequate internal control structure and procedures for financial reporting; and

**(2)** contain an assessment, as of the end of the most recent fiscal year of the issuer, of the effectiveness of the internal

control structure and procedures of the issuer for financial reporting.

**(b)** Internal control evaluation and reporting

With respect to the internal control assessment required by subsection (a) of this section, each registered public accounting firm that prepares or issues the audit report for the issuer shall attest to, and report on, the assessment made by the management of the issuer. An attestation made under this subsection shall be made in accordance with standards for attestation engagements issued or adopted by the Board. Any such attestation shall not be the subject of a separate engagement.

\* \* \* \*

### Explanatory Comments:

*This section was enacted to prevent corporate executives from claiming they were ignorant of significant errors in their companies' financial reports. For instance, several CEOs testified before Congress that they simply had no idea that the corporations' financial statements were off by billions of dollars. Congress therefore passed Section 404, which requires each annual report to contain a description and assessment of the company's internal control structure and financial reporting procedures. The section also requires that an audit be conducted of the internal control assessment, as well as the financial statements contained in the report. This section goes hand in hand with Section 302 (which, as discussed previously, requires various certifications attesting to the accuracy of the information in financial reports).*

*Section 404 has been one of the more controversial and expensive provisions in the Sarbanes-Oxley Act because it requires companies to assess their own internal financial controls to make sure that their financial statements are reliable and accurate. A corporation might need to set up a disclosure committee and a coordinator, establish codes of conduct for accounting and financial personnel, create documentation procedures, provide training, and outline the individuals who are responsible for performing each of the procedures. Companies that were already well managed have not experienced substantial difficulty complying with this section. Other companies, however, have spent millions of dollars setting up, documenting, and evaluating their internal financial control systems. Although initially creating the internal financial control system is a one-time-only expense, the costs of maintaining and evaluating it are ongoing. Some corporations that spent considerable sums complying with Section 404 have been able to offset these costs by discovering and correcting inefficiencies or frauds within their systems. Nevertheless, it is unlikely that any corporation will find compliance with this section to be inexpensive.*

## SECTION 802(A)
### Destruction, alteration, or falsification of records in Federal investigations and bankruptcy[6]

Whoever knowingly alters, destroys, mutilates, conceals, covers up, falsifies, or makes a false entry in any record, document, or tangible object with the intent to impede, obstruct, or influence the investigation or proper administration of any matter within the jurisdiction of any department or agency of the United States or any case filed under title 11, or in relation to or

---

**5.** Codified at 15 U.S.C. Section 7262.

**6.** Codified at 15 U.S.C. Section 1519.

contemplation of any such matter or case, shall be fined under this title, imprisoned not more than 20 years, or both.

### Destruction of corporate audit records[7]

**(a)** **(1)** Any accountant who conducts an audit of an issuer of securities to which section 10A(a) of the Securities Exchange Act of 1934 (15 U.S.C. 78j-1(a)) applies, shall maintain all audit or review workpapers for a period of 5 years from the end of the fiscal period in which the audit or review was concluded.

**(2)** The Securities and Exchange Commission shall promulgate, within 180 days, after adequate notice and an opportunity for comment, such rules and regulations, as are reasonably necessary, relating to the retention of relevant records such as workpapers, documents that form the basis of an audit or review, memoranda, correspondence, communications, other documents, and records (including electronic records) which are created, sent, or received in connection with an audit or review and contain conclusions, opinions, analyses, or financial data relating to such an audit or review, which is conducted by any accountant who conducts an audit of an issuer of securities to which section 10A(a) of the Securities Exchange Act of 1934 (15 U.S.C. 78j-1(a)) applies. The Commission may, from time to time, amend or supplement the rules and regulations that it is required to promulgate under this section, after adequate notice and an opportunity for comment, in order to ensure that such rules and regulations adequately comport with the purposes of this section.

**(b)** Whoever knowingly and willfully violates subsection (a)(1), or any rule or regulation promulgated by the Securities and Exchange Commission under subsection (a)(2), shall be fined under this title, imprisoned not more than 10 years, or both.

**(c)** Nothing in this section shall be deemed to diminish or relieve any person of any other duty or obligation imposed by Federal or State law or regulation to maintain, or refrain from destroying, any document.
\* \* \* \*

### Explanatory Comments:
*Section 802(a) enacted two new statutes that punish those who alter or destroy documents. The first statute is not specifically limited to securities fraud cases. It provides that anyone who alters, destroys, or falsifies records in federal investigations or bankruptcy may be criminally prosecuted and sentenced to a fine or to up to twenty years in prison, or both. The second statute requires auditors of public companies to keep all audit or review working papers for five years but expressly allows the SEC to amend or supplement these requirements as it sees fit. The SEC has, in fact, amended this section by issuing a rule that requires auditors who audit reporting companies to retain working papers for seven years from the conclusion of the review. Section 802(a) further provides that anyone who knowingly and willfully violates this statute is subject to criminal prosecution and can be sentenced to a fine, imprisoned for up to ten years, or both if convicted.*

*This portion of the Sarbanes-Oxley Act implicitly recognizes that persons who are under investigation often are tempted to respond by destroying or falsifying documents that might prove their complicity in wrongdoing. The severity of the punishment should provide a strong incentive for these individuals to resist the temptation.*

### SECTION 804
### Time limitations on the commencement of civil actions arising under Acts of Congress[8]

**(a)** Except as otherwise provided by law, a civil action arising under an Act of Congress enacted after the date of the enactment of this section may not be commenced later than 4 years after the cause of action accrues.

**(b)** Notwithstanding subsection (a), a private right of action that involves a claim of fraud, deceit, manipulation, or contrivance in contravention of a regulatory requirement concerning the securities laws, as defined in section 3(a)(47) of the Securities Exchange Act of 1934 (15 U.S.C. 78c(a)(47)), may be brought not later than the earlier of—

    **(1)** 2 years after the discovery of the facts constituting the violation; or

    **(2)** 5 years after such violation.
\* \* \* \*

### Explanatory Comments:
*Before the enactment of this section, Section 10(b) of the Securities Exchange Act of 1934 had no express statute of limitations. The courts generally required plaintiffs to have filed suit within one year from the date that they should (using due diligence) have discovered that a fraud had been committed but no later than three years after the fraud occurred. Section 804 extends this period by specifying that plaintiffs must file a lawsuit within two years after they discover (or should have discovered) a fraud but no later than five years after the fraud's occurrence. This provision has prevented the courts from dismissing numerous securities fraud lawsuits.*

### SECTION 806
### Civil action to protect against retaliation in fraud cases[9]

**(a)** Whistleblower protection for employees of publicly traded companies.—

No company with a class of securities registered under section 12 of the Securities Exchange Act of 1934 (15 U.S.C. 78l), or that is required to file reports under section 15(d) of the Securities Exchange Act of 1934 (15 U.S.C. 78o(d)), or any officer, employee, contractor, subcontractor, or agent of such company, may discharge, demote, suspend, threaten, harass, or in any other manner discriminate against an employee in the terms and conditions of employment because of any lawful act done by the employee—

    **(1)** to provide information, cause information to be provided, or otherwise assist in an investigation regarding any conduct which the employee reasonably believes constitutes a violation of section 1341, 1343, 1344, or 1348, any rule or regulation of the Securities and Exchange Commission, or any provision of Federal law relating to fraud against shareholders, when the information or assistance is provided to or the investigation is conducted by—

---

**7.** Codified at 15 U.S.C. Section 1520.

**8.** Codified at 28 U.S.C. Section 1658.

**9.** Codified at 18 U.S.C. Section 1514A.

**(A)** a Federal regulatory or law enforcement agency;

**(B)** any Member of Congress or any committee of Congress; or

**(C)** a person with supervisory authority over the employee (or such other person working for the employer who has the authority to investigate, discover, or terminate misconduct); or

**(2)** to file, cause to be filed, testify, participate in, or otherwise assist in a proceeding filed or about to be filed (with any knowledge of the employer) relating to an alleged violation of section 1341, 1343, 1344, or 1348, any rule or regulation of the Securities and Exchange Commission, or any provision of Federal law relating to fraud against shareholders.

**(b)** Enforcement action.—

**(1)** In general.—A person who alleges discharge or other discrimination by any person in violation of subsection (a) may seek relief under subsection (c), by—

**(A)** filing a complaint with the Secretary of Labor; or

**(B)** if the Secretary has not issued a final decision within 180 days of the filing of the complaint and there is no showing that such delay is due to the bad faith of the claimant, bringing an action at law or equity for de novo review in the appropriate district court of the United States, which shall have jurisdiction over such an action without regard to the amount in controversy.

**(2)** Procedure.—

**(A)** In general.—An action under paragraph (1)(A) shall be governed under the rules and procedures set forth in section 42121(b) of title 49, United States Code.

**(B)** Exception.—Notification made under section 42121(b)(1) of title 49, United States Code, shall be made to the person named in the complaint and to the employer.

**(C)** Burdens of proof.—An action brought under paragraph (1)(B) shall be governed by the legal burdens of proof set forth in section 42121(b) of title 49, United States Code.

**(D)** Statute of limitations.—An action under paragraph (1) shall be commenced not later than 90 days after the date on which the violation occurs.

**(c)** Remedies.—

**(1)** In general.—An employee prevailing in any action under subsection (b)(1) shall be entitled to all relief necessary to make the employee whole.

**(2)** Compensatory damages.—Relief for any action under paragraph (1) shall include—

**(A)** reinstatement with the same seniority status that the employee would have had, but for the discrimination;

**(B)** the amount of back pay, with interest; and

**(C)** compensation for any special damages sustained as a result of the discrimination, including litigation costs, expert witness fees, and reasonable attorney fees.

**(d)** Rights retained by employee.—Nothing in this section shall be deemed to diminish the rights, privileges, or remedies of any employee under any Federal or State law, or under any collective bargaining agreement.

**Explanatory Comments:**

*Section 806 is one of several provisions that were included in the Sarbanes-Oxley Act to encourage and protect whistleblowers—that is, employees who report their employer's alleged violations of securities law to the authorities. This section applies to employees, agents, and independent contractors who work for publicly traded companies or testify about such a company during an investigation. It sets up an administrative procedure at the U.S. Department of Labor for individuals who claim that their employer retaliated against them (fired or demoted them, for example) for blowing the whistle on the employer's wrongful conduct. It also allows the award of civil damages—including back pay, reinstatement, special damages, attorneys' fees, and court costs—to employees who prove that they suffered retaliation. Since this provision was enacted, whistleblowers have filed numerous complaints with the U.S. Department of Labor under this section.*

## SECTION 807
### Securities fraud[10]

Whoever knowingly executes, or attempts to execute, a scheme or artifice—

**(1)** to defraud any person in connection with any security of an issuer with a class of securities registered under section 12 of the Securities Exchange Act of 1934 (15 U.S.C. 78l) or that is required to file reports under section 15(d) of the Securities Exchange Act of 1934 (15 U.S.C. 78o(d)); or

**(2)** to obtain, by means of false or fraudulent pretenses, representations, or promises, any money or property in connection with the purchase or sale of any security of an issuer with a class of securities registered under section 12 of the Securities Exchange Act of 1934 (15 U.S.C. 78l) or that is required to file reports under section 15(d) of the Securities Exchange Act of 1934 (15 U.S.C. 78o(d)); shall be fined under this title, or imprisoned not more than 25 years, or both.

\* \* \* \*

**Explanatory Comments:**

*Section 807 adds a new provision to the federal criminal code that addresses securities fraud. Before 2002, federal securities law had already made it a crime—under Section 10(b) of the Securities Exchange Act of 1934 and SEC Rule 10b-5—to intentionally defraud someone in connection with a purchase or sale of securities, but the offense was not listed in the federal criminal code.*

*Also, paragraph 2 of Section 807 goes beyond what is prohibited under securities law by making it a crime to obtain by means of false or fraudulent pretenses any money or property from the purchase or sale of securities. This new provision allows violators to be punished by up to twenty-five years in prison, a fine, or both.*

## SECTION 906
### Failure of corporate officers to certify financial reports[11]

**(a)** Certification of periodic financial reports.—Each periodic report containing financial statements filed by an issuer with the Securities Exchange Commission pursuant to section 13(a)

---

**10.** Codified at 18 U.S.C. Section 1348.

**11.** Codified at 18 U.S.C. Section 1350.

or 15(d) of the Securities Exchange Act of 1934 (15 U.S.C. 78m(a) or 78o(d)) shall be accompanied by a written statement by the chief executive officer and chief financial officer (or equivalent thereof) of the issuer.

(b) Content.—The statement required under subsection (a) shall certify that the periodic report containing the financial statements fully complies with the requirements of section 13(a) or 15(d) of the Securities Exchange Act of 1934 (15 U.S.C. 78m or 78o(d)) and that information contained in the periodic report fairly presents, in all material respects, the financial condition and results of operations of the issuer.

(c) Criminal penalties.—Whoever—

(1) certifies any statement as set forth in subsections (a) and (b) of this section knowing that the periodic report accompanying the statement does not comport with all the requirements set forth in this section shall be fined not more than $1,000,000 or imprisoned not more than 10 years, or both; or

(2) willfully certifies any statement as set forth in subsections (a) and (b) of this section knowing that the periodic report accompanying the statement does not comport with all the requirements set forth in this section shall be fined not more than $5,000,000, or imprisoned not more than 20 years, or both.

## Explanatory Comments:

*As previously discussed, under Section 302 a corporation's CEO and CFO are required to certify that they believe the quarterly and annual reports their company files with the SEC are accurate and fairly present the company's financial condition. Section 906 adds "teeth" to these requirements by authorizing criminal penalties for those officers who intentionally certify inaccurate SEC filings.*

*Knowing violations of the requirements are punishable by a fine of up to $1 million, ten years' imprisonment, or both. Willful violators may be fined up to $5 million, sentenced to up to twenty years' imprisonment, or both. Although the difference between a knowing and a willful violation is not entirely clear, the section is obviously intended to remind corporate officers of the serious consequences of certifying inaccurate reports to the SEC.*

## CHAPTER 1

**1. *Under what circumstances might a judge rely on case law to determine the intent and purpose of a statute?*** Case law includes courts' interpretations of statutes, as well as constitutional provisions and administrative rules. Statutes often codify common law rules. For these reasons, a judge might rely on the common law as a guide to the intent and purpose of a statute.

**2. *Assuming that these convicted war criminals had not disobeyed any law of their country and had merely been following their government's orders, what law had they violated? Explain.*** At the time of the Nuremberg trials, "crimes against humanity" were new international crimes. The laws criminalized such acts as murder, extermination, enslavement, deportation, and other inhumane acts committed against any civilian population. These international laws derived their legitimacy from "natural law."

Natural law, which is the oldest and one of the most significant schools of jurisprudence, holds that governments and legal systems should reflect the moral and ethical ideals that are inherent in human nature. Because natural law is universal and discoverable by reason, its adherents believe that all other law is derived from natural law. Natural law therefore supersedes laws created by humans (national, or "positive," law), and in a conflict between the two, national or positive law loses its legitimacy.

The Nuremberg defendants asserted that they had been acting in accordance with German law. The judges dismissed these claims, reasoning that the defendants' acts were commonly regarded as crimes and that the accused must have known that the acts would be considered criminal. The judges clearly believed the tenets of natural law and expected that the defendants, too, should have been able to realize that their acts ran afoul of it. The fact that the "positivist law" of Germany at the time required them to commit these acts is irrelevant. Under natural law theory, the international court was justified in finding the defendants guilty of crimes against humanity.

## CHAPTER 2

**1. *Does the court in Sue's state have jurisdiction over Tipton? What factors will the court consider?*** A corporation normally is subject to personal jurisdiction in the state in which it is incorporated, has its principal office, and/or is doing business. Under the authority of a state long arm statute, a court can exercise personal jurisdiction over certain out-of-state defendants based on activities that took place within the state. Before a court can exercise jurisdiction, though, it must be demonstrated that the defendant had minimum contacts with the state to justify the jurisdiction.

The minimum-contacts requirement is usually met if the corporation advertises or sells its products within the state, or places its goods into the "stream of commerce" with the intent that the goods be sold in the state. Therefore, a court will consider whether Tipton advertised or sold its product within Sue's state. The court may also look at whether the contract between Sue and Tipton was negotiated or signed within the state.

**2. *If the dispute is not resolved, or if either party disagrees with the decision of the mediator or arbitrator, will a court hear the case? Explain.*** Yes. Submission of the dispute to mediation or nonbinding arbitration is mandatory, but compliance with a decision of the mediator or arbitrator is voluntary.

## CHAPTER 3

**1. *Tom can call his first witness. What else might he do?*** Tom could file a motion for a directed verdict. This motion asks the judge to direct a verdict for Tom on the ground that Sue presented no evidence that would justify granting Jan relief. The judge grants the motion if there is insufficient evidence to raise an issue of fact.

**2. *Who can appeal to a higher court?*** Either a plaintiff or a defendant, or both, can appeal a judgment to a higher court. An appellate court can affirm, reverse, or remand a case, or take any of these actions in combination. To appeal successfully, it is best to appeal on the basis of an error of law, because appellate courts do not usually reverse on findings of fact.

## CHAPTER 4

**1. *Can a state, in the interest of energy conservation, ban all advertising by power utilities if conservation could be accomplished by less restrictive means? Why or why not?*** No. Even if commercial speech is not related to illegal activities nor misleading, it may be restricted if a state has a substantial interest that cannot be achieved by less restrictive means. In this case, the interest in energy conservation is substantial, but it could be achieved by less restrictive means. That would be the utilities' defense against the enforcement of this state law.

**2. *Is this a violation of equal protection if the only reason for the tax is to protect the local firms from out-of-state competition? Explain.*** Yes. The tax would limit the liberty of some persons (out of state businesses), so it is subject to a review under the equal protection clause. Protecting local businesses from out-of-state competition is not a legitimate government objective. Thus, such a tax would violate the equal protection clause.

## CHAPTER 5

**1. *Are there ethical concerns about putting trauma-tized children on the news immediately after an event like this? Why or why not?*** In determining whether it is ethical to interview these children soon after a tragic event, it is important to analyze the competing interests and reasons behind the interviews. The interviews may generate more view-ers, which may lead to higher ratings and more advertising rev-enue for the company and its shareholders. Alternatively, the value of the interview to the public or to any investigation may be minimal. The children may not have accurate information and may be further traumatized by the interview process.

**2. *Is it ethical for Johnny to take a performance-enhancing drug that has not been banned? Why or why not?*** Maybe. Individuals and businesses often face ethical dilemmas when the letter of the law seems clear but alternatives exist that may violate what is known as the spirit of the law or the purpose for the law. In this case, the restrictions exist to stop athletes from performing better than they would naturally because of a foreign substance. The list of banned substances may not be able to keep up with the advances in technology and science in developing performance enhancing drugs.

Some might argue that it is ethical for him to take any-thing that is not formally banned and that all competitors have the same ability to access and take those substances and therefore any advantage is eliminated. Because there seems to be no unfair advantage, the purpose of the restriction is not frustrated. There is an implicit assumption, however, that all performers have the connections and the resources to obtain the non-banned substance. Because this assumption is not nec-essarily true, it is more likely an ethical violation to take the non-banned performance enhancing drugs, even if it is not technically against the rules.

## CHAPTER 6

**1. *Can Lou recover from Jana? Why or why not?*** Probably. To recover on the basis of negligence, the injured party as a plaintiff must show that the truck's owner owed the plaintiff a duty of care, that the owner breached that duty, that the plain-tiff was injured, and that the breach caused the injury.

In this situation, the owner's actions breached the duty of reasonable care. The billboard falling on the plaintiff was the direct cause of the injury, not the plaintiff's own negligence. Thus, liability turns on whether the plaintiff can connect the breach of duty to the injury. This involves the test of proximate cause—the question of foreseeability. The consequences to the injured party must have been a foreseeable result of the owner's carelessness.

**2. *What might the firm successfully claim in defense?*** The company might defend against this electrician's claim by asserting that the electrician should have known of the risk and, therefore, the company had no duty to warn. According to the problem, the danger is common knowledge in the electri-cian's field and should have been apparent to this electrician, given his years of training and experience. In other words, the

company most likely had no need to warn the electrician of the risk.

The firm could also raise comparative negligence. Both parties' negligence, if any, could be weighed and the liability distributed proportionately. The defendant could also assert assumption of risk, claiming that the electrician voluntarily entered into a dangerous situation, knowing the risk involved.

## CHAPTER 7

**1. *Is Superior Vehicles liable? Explain your answer.*** Yes. The manufacturer is liable for the injuries to the user of the product. A manufacturer is liable for its failure to exercise due care to any person who sustains an injury proximately caused by a negligently made (defective) product.

**2. *If Real, Sweet, and Tasty were not negligent, can they be liable for the injury? Why or why not?*** Yes. Under the doctrine of strict liability, persons may be liable for the results of their acts regardless of their intentions or their exercise of reasonable care (that is, regardless of fault).

## CHAPTER 8

**1. *Has Roslyn violated any of the intellectual property rights discussed in this chapter? Explain.*** Yes, Roslyn has committed theft of trade secrets. Lists of suppliers and custom-ers cannot be patented, copyrighted, or trademarked, but the information they contain is protected against appropriation by others as trade secrets. And most likely, Roslyn signed a con-tract, agreeing not to use this information outside her employ-ment by Organic. But even without this contract, Organic could have made a convincing case against its ex-employee for a theft of trade secrets.

**2. *Is this patent infringement? If so, how might Global save the cost of suing World for infringement and at the same time profit from World's sales?*** This is patent infringement. A software maker in this situation might best protect its product, save litigation costs, and profit from its patent by the use of a license. In the context of this problem, a license would grant permission to sell a patented item. (A license can be limited to certain purposes and to the licensee only.)

## CHAPTER 9

**1. *Has Karl done anything wrong? Explain.*** Karl may have committed trademark infringement. Search engines compile their results by looking through Web sites' key-word fields. Key words, or meta tags, increase the likelihood that a site will be included in search engine results, even if the words have no connection to the site.

A site that appropriates the key words of other sites with more frequent hits will appear in the same search engine results as the more popular sites. But using another's trademark as a key word without the owner's permission normally constitutes trademark infringement. Of course, some uses of another's trade-mark as a meta tag may be permissible if the use is reasonably necessary and does not suggest that the owner authorized or sponsored the use.

**2. Can Eagle Corporation stop this use of eagle? If so, what must the company show? Explain.** Yes. This may be an instance of trademark dilution. Dilution occurs when a trademark is used, without permission, in a way that diminishes the distinctive quality of the mark. Dilution does not require proof that consumers are likely to be confused by the use of the unauthorized mark. The products involved do not have to be similar. Dilution does require, however, that a mark be famous when the dilution occurs.

## CHAPTER 10

**1. With respect to the gas station, has she committed a crime? If so, what is it?** Yes. With respect to the gas station, she has obtained goods by false pretenses. She might also be charged with larceny and forgery, and most states have special statutes covering illegal use of credit cards.

**2. Has Ben committed a crime? If so, what is it?** Yes. The Counterfeit Access Device and Computer Fraud and Abuse Act provides that a person who accesses a computer online, without permission, to obtain classified data—such as consumer credit files in a credit agency's database—is subject to criminal prosecution. The crime has two elements: accessing the computer without permission and taking data. It is a felony if done for private financial gain. Penalties include fines and imprisonment for up to twenty years. The victim of the theft can also bring a civil suit against the criminal to obtain damages and other relief.

## CHAPTER 11

**1. What standard determines whether these parties have a contract?** Under the objective theory of contracts, if a reasonable person would have thought that Joli had accepted Kerin's offer when she signed and returned the letter, then a contract was made, and Joli is obligated to buy the book. This depends, in part, on what was said in the letter and what was said in response. For instance, did the letter contain a valid offer, and did the response constitute a valid acceptance? Under any circumstances, the issue is not whether either party subjectively believed that they did, or did not, have a contract.

**2. Can Ed recover? Why or why not?** No. This contract, although not fully executed, is for an illegal purpose and therefore is void. A void contract gives rise to no legal obligation on the part of any party. A contract that is void is no contract. There is nothing to enforce.

## CHAPTER 12

**1. Do Fidelity and Ron have a contract? Why or why not?** No. Revocation of an offer may be implied by conduct inconsistent with the offer. When the corporation hired someone else, and the offeree learned of the hiring, the offer was revoked. The acceptance was too late.

**2. Under the Uniform Electronic Transactions Act, what determines the effect of the electronic documents evi-** *dencing the parties' deal? Is a party's "signature" necessary? Explain.* First, it might be noted that the UETA does not apply unless the parties to a contract agree to use e-commerce in their transaction. In this deal, of course, the parties used e-commerce. The UETA removes barriers to e-commerce by giving the same legal effect to e-records and e-signatures as to paper documents and signatures. The UETA it does not include rules for those transactions, however.

## CHAPTER 13

**1. Is the new contract binding? Explain.** Yes. The original contract was executory. The parties rescinded it and agreed to a new contract. If Sharyn had broken the contract to accept a contract with another employer, she might have been held liable for damages for the breach.

**2. Is Fred's promise binding? Explain.** Yes. Under the doctrine of detrimental reliance, or promissory estoppel, the promisee is entitled to payment of $5,000 from the promisor on graduation. There was a promise, on which the promisee relied, the reliance was substantial and definite (the promisee went to college for the full term, incurring considerable expenses, and will likely graduate), and it would only be fair to enforce the promise.

## CHAPTER 14

**1. Can Kenwood enforce the lease against Joan? Why or why not?** No. Joan is a minor and may disaffirm this contract. Because the apartment was a necessary, however, she remains liable for the reasonable value of her occupancy of the apartment.

**2. If the cause of an accident is found to be the airline's negligence, can it use the clause as a defense to liability? Why or why not?** No. Generally, an exculpatory clause (a clause attempting to absolve parties of negligence or other wrongs) is not enforced if the party seeking its enforcement is involved in a business that is important to the public as a matter of practical necessity, such as an airline. Because of the essential nature of such services, the parties have an advantage in bargaining strength and could insist that anyone contracting for its services agree not to hold it liable.

## CHAPTER 15

**1. Can she rescind the deal? Why or why not?** Yes. Rescission may be granted on the basis of fraudulent misrepresentation. The elements of fraudulent misrepresentation include intent to deceive, or *scienter*. *Scienter* exists if a party makes a statement recklessly, without regard to whether it is true or false, or if a party says or implies that a statement is made on some basis such as personal knowledge or personal investigation when it is not.

**2. Can Elle be held liable to GCC? Why or why not?** Yes. The accountant may be liable on the ground of negligent misrepresentation. A misrepresentation is negligent if a person fails to exercise reasonable care in disclosing material facts or does not use the skill and competence required by his or her business or profession.

## CHAPTER 16

**1. Can Midstate enforce a deal for $350 more? Explain your answer.** No. Under the UCC, a contract for a sale of goods priced at $500 or more must be in writing to be enforceable. In this case, the contract is not enforceable beyond the quantity already delivered and paid for.

**2. Next Corporation argues that there is no written contract between them. What will the court say?** The court might conclude that under the doctrine of promissory estoppel, the employer is estopped from claiming the lack of a written contract as a defense. The oral contract may be enforced because the employer made a promise on which the employee justifiably relied in moving to New York, the reliance was foreseeable, and injustice can be avoided only by enforcing the promise. If the court strictly enforces the Statute of Frauds, however, the employee may be without a remedy.

## CHAPTER 17

**1. Can Jeff successfully sue Ed for the $100?** Yes. When one person makes a promise with the intention of benefiting a third person, the third person can sue to enforce it. This is a third party beneficiary contract. The third party in this problem is an intended beneficiary.

**2. Can Good Credit enforce the contract against Frank? Why or why not?** Yes. Generally, if a contract clearly states that a right is not assignable, no assignment will be effective, but there are exceptions. Assignment of the right to receive monetary payment cannot be prohibited.

## CHAPTER 18

**1. Before Ready or Stealth starts performing, can the parties call off the deal? What if Stealth has already shipped the pizzas? Explain your answers.** Contracts that are executory on both sides—contracts on which neither party has performed—can be rescinded solely by agreement. Contracts that are executed on one side—contracts on which one party has performed—can be rescinded only if the party who has performed receives consideration for the promise to call off the deal.

**2. What type of agreement is this? Are Ace's obligations discharged? Why or why not?** This is a novation because it substitutes a new party for an original party, by agreement of all the parties. The requirements are a previous valid obligation, an agreement of all the parties to a new contract, extinguishment of the old obligation, and a new, valid contract. Ace's obligations are discharged.

## CHAPTER 19

**1. If Haney sues Greg, what would be the measure of recovery?** A nonbreaching party is entitled to his or her benefit of the bargain under the contract. Here, the innocent party is entitled to be put in the position she would have been in if the

contract had been fully performed. The measure of the benefit is the cost to complete the work ($500). These are compensatory damages.

**2. Is Lyle liable for Marley's expenses in providing for the cattle? Why or why not?** No. To recover damages that flow from the consequences of a breach but that are caused by circumstances beyond the contract (consequential damages), the breaching party must know, or have reason to know, that special circumstances will cause the nonbreaching party to suffer the additional loss. That was not the circumstance in this problem.

## CHAPTER 20

**1. Is this an acceptance of the offer or a counteroffer? If it is an acceptance, is it a breach of the contract? What if Fav-O-Rite told E-Design it was sending the printer stands as "an accommodation"?** A shipment of nonconforming goods constitutes an acceptance of the offer and a breach, unless the seller seasonably notifies the buyer that the nonconforming shipment does not constitute an acceptance and is offered only as an accommodation. Thus, since there was no notification here, the shipment was both an acceptance and a breach. If, however, Fav-O-Rite had notified E-Design that it was sending the printer stands as an accommodation, the shipment would not constitute an acceptance and Fav-O-Rite would not be in breach.

**2. Is there an enforceable contract between them? Why or why not?** Yes. In a transaction between merchants, the requirement of a writing is satisfied if one of them sends to the other a signed written confirmation that indicates the terms of the agreement, and the merchant receiving it has reason to know of its contents. If the merchant who receives the confirmation does not object in writing within ten days after receipt, the writing will be enforceable against him or her even though he or she has not signed anything.

## CHAPTER 21

**1. What are the consequences if Silk bore the risk? If Adams bore the risk?** Buyers and sellers can have an insurable interest in identical goods at the same time. If the buyer (Silk & Satin) bore the risk, it must pay and seek reimbursement from its insurance company. If the seller (Adams Textiles) bore the risk, it must seek reimbursement from its insurance company and may still have an obligation to deliver the identified goods (the fabric) to Silk & Satin.

**2. If Karlin files a lawsuit, will she prevail? Why or why not?** When a person "entrusts" goods to a merchant (a person who deals in goods of that kind), the merchant has the power to transfer a good title to any purchaser who acquires the goods in the *ordinary course of business*. Karlin entrusted her set to merchant Orken. Orken deals in goods of that kind. Therefore, Orken could pass good title to the set sold to a customer (Grady) because Grady purchased the goods in the ordinary course of business. Consequently, Karlin cannot get the set back from Grady. (But the merchant is liable to the true owner, Karlin, for the equivalent value of the set).

## CHAPTER 22

**1. *Does Country have the right to reject the shipment? Explain.*** Yes. A seller is obligated to deliver goods in conformity with a contract in every detail. This is the perfect tender rule. The exception of the seller's right to cure does not apply here, because the seller delivered too little too late to take advantage of this exception.

**2. *Can Poster Planet sue Brite without waiting until May 1? Why or why not?*** Yes. When anticipatory repudiation occurs, a buyer (or lessee) can resort to any remedy for breach even if the buyer tells the seller (the repudiating party in this problem) that the buyer will wait for the seller's performance.

## CHAPTER 23

**1. *When it does not perform to GCC's specifications, GCC sues Industrial, which claims, "We didn't expressly promise anything." What should GCC argue?*** The buyer should argue that the seller breached an implied warranty of fitness for a particular purpose. An implied warranty of fitness for a particular purpose arises when a seller knows a particular purpose for which a buyer will use goods and that the buyer is relying on the seller's skill and judgment to select suitable goods.

**2. *Can Stella recover for breach of the implied warranty of merchantability? Why or why not?*** Yes, Stella can recover from Roasted Bean for breach of the implied warranty of merchantability. An implied warranty of merchantability arises in every sale of goods sold by a merchant who deals in goods of the kind. Goods that are merchantable are fit for the ordinary purposes for which such goods are used. A sale of food or drink is a sale of goods. Merchantable food is food that is fit to eat or drink on the basis of consumer expectations. A consumer should reasonably expect hot coffee to be hot, but not to be so scalding that it causes third-degree burns.

## CHAPTER 24

**1. *Under what circumstances would a U.S. court enforce the judgment of the Ecuadoran court?*** Under the principle of comity, a U.S court would defer and give effect to foreign laws and judicial decrees that are consistent with U.S. law and public policy.

**2. *How can this attempt to undersell U.S. businesses be defeated?*** The practice described in this problem is known as dumping, which is regarded as an unfair international trade practice. Dumping is the sale of imported goods at "less than fair value." Based on the price of those goods in the exporting country, an extra tariff—known as an antidumping duty—can be imposed on the imports.

## CHAPTER 25

**1. *Was Winona an independent contractor?*** Yes. An independent contractor is a person who contracts with another—the principal—to do something but who is neither controlled by the other nor subject to the other's right to control with respect to the performance. Independent contractors are not employees, because those who hire them have no control over the details of their performance.

**2. *When Nadine learns the difference between the price that Dimka is willing to pay and the price at which the owner is willing to sell, she wants to buy the land and sell it to Dimka herself. Can she do this? Discuss.*** No. Nadine, as an agent, is prohibited from taking advantage of the agency relationship to obtain property that the principal (Dimka Corporation) wants to purchase. This is the duty of loyalty that arises with every agency relationship.

## CHAPTER 26

**1. *Can Davis hold Estee liable for whatever damages he has to pay? Why or why not?*** Yes. A principal has a duty to indemnify an agent for liabilities incurred because of authorized and lawful acts and transactions and for losses suffered because of the principal's failure to perform his or her duties.

**2. *In what circumstance is Vivian liable on the note?*** When a person enters into a contract on another's behalf without the authority to do so, the other may be liable on the contract if he or she approves or affirms that contract. In other words, the employer-principal would be liable for the note in this problem on ratifying it. Whether the employer-principal ratifies the note or not, the unauthorized agent is most likely also liable for it.

## CHAPTER 27

**1. *For Erin to obtain workers' compensation, does her injury have to have been caused by Fine Print's negligence? Does it matter whether the action causing the injury was intentional? Explain.*** Workers' compensation laws establish a procedure for compensating workers who are injured on the job. Instead of suing to collect benefits, an injured worker notifies the employer of an injury and files a claim with the appropriate state agency.

The right to recover is normally determined without regard to negligence or fault, but intentionally inflicted injuries are not covered. Unlike the potential for recovery in a lawsuit based on negligence or fault, recovery under a workers' compensation statute is limited to the specific amount designated in the statute for the employee's injury.

**2. *Are these conditions legal? Why or why not?*** No. A closed shop (a company that requires union membership as a condition of employment) is illegal. A union shop (a company that does not require union membership as a condition of employment but requires workers to join the union after a certain time on the job) is illegal in a state with a right-to-work law, which makes it illegal to require union membership for continued employment.

## CHAPTER 28

**1. *Is this sexual harassment? Why or why not?*** Yes. One type of sexual harassment occurs when a request for sexual favors is a condition of employment, and the person making the request is a supervisor or acts with the authority of the employer.

A tangible employment action, such as continued employment, may also lead to the employer's liability for the supervisor's conduct. That the injured employee is a male and the supervisor a female, instead of the other way around, would not affect the outcome. Same-gender harassment is also actionable.

**2. *Could Koko succeed in a suit against Lively for discrimination? Explain.*** Yes, if she can show that she was not hired solely because of her disability. The other elements for a discrimination suit based on a disability are that the plaintiff (1) has a disability and (2) is otherwise qualified for the job. Both of these elements appear to be satisfied in this problem.

## CHAPTER 29

**1. *Would a sole proprietorship be an appropriate form for Frank's business? Why or why not?*** Yes. When a business is relatively small and is not diversified, employs relatively few people, has modest profits, and is not likely to expand significantly or require extensive financing in the immediate future, the most appropriate form for doing business may be a sole proprietorship.

**2. *Does this constitute "cause" for termination? Why or why not?*** Yes. Failing to meet a specified sales quota can constitute a breach of a franchise agreement. If the franchisor is acting in good faith, "cause" may also include the death or disability of the franchisee, the insolvency of the franchisee, and a breach of another term of the franchise agreement.

## CHAPTER 30

**1. *When Darnell dies, his widow claims that as Darnell's heir, she is entitled to take his place as Eliana's partner or to receive a share of the firm's assets. Is she right? Why or why not?*** No. A widow (or widower) has no right to take a dead partner's place. A partner's death causes dissociation after which the partnership must purchase the dissociated partner's partnership interest. Therefore, the surviving partners must pay the decedent's estate (for his widow) the value of the deceased partner's interest in the partnership.

**2. *Because the vehicles would otherwise be sitting idle in a parking lot, can Finian keep the income that results from leasing the delivery vehicles? Explain your answer.*** No. Under the partners' fiduciary duty, a partner must account to the partnership for any personal profits or benefits derived without the consent of all the partners in connection with the use of any partnership property. Here, the leasing partner may not keep the money.

## CHAPTER 31

**1. *What are their options with respect to the management of their firm?*** The members of a limited liability company (LLC) may designate a group to run their firm, in which situation the firm would be considered a manager-managed LLC. The group may include only members, only nonmembers, or members and nonmembers. If instead, all members participate in management, the firm would be a member-managed LLC. In fact, unless the members agree otherwise, all members are considered to participate in the management of the firm.

**2. *What do these forms of business organization have in common?*** Although there are differences, all of these forms of business organizations resemble corporations. A joint stock company, for example, features ownership by shares of stock, it is managed by directors and officers, and it has perpetual existence. A business trust, like a corporation, distributes profits to persons who are not personally responsible for the debts of the organization. Management of a business trust is in the hands of trustees, just as the management of a corporation is in the hands of directors and officers. An incorporated cooperative, which is subject to state laws covering nonprofit corporations, distributes profits to its owners.

## CHAPTER 32

**1. *Is there a way for Northwest Brands to avoid this double taxation? Explain your answer.*** Yes. Small businesses that meet certain requirements can qualify as S corporations, created specifically to permit small businesses to avoid double taxation. The six requirements of an S corporation are (1) the firm must be a domestic corporation, (2) the firm must not be a member of an affiliated group of corporations, (3) the firm must have less than a certain number of shareholders, (4) the shareholders must be individuals, estates, or qualified trusts (or corporations in some cases), (5) there can be only one class of stock, and (6) no shareholder can be a nonresident alien.

**2. *Can they grant this authority to their firm? If so, how? If not, why not?*** Broad authority to conduct business can be granted in a corporation's articles of incorporation. For example, the term "any lawful purpose" is often used. This can be important because acts of a corporation that are beyond the authority given to it in its articles or charter (or state statutes) are considered illegal, *ultra vires* acts.

**PROBLEM 1–6.** *Reading Citations.* The court's opinion in this case—*United States v. Yi,* 704 F.3d 800 (9th Cir. 2013)—can be found in volume 704 of West's *Federal Reporter,* Third Series, on page 800. The United States Court of Appeals for the Ninth Circuit issued this opinion in 2013.

**PROBLEM 2–3.** *Arbitration Clause.* Based on a recent holding by the Washington state supreme court, the federal appeals court held that the arbitration provision was unconscionable and therefore invalid. Because it was invalid, the restriction on class-action suits was also invalid.

The state court held that placing class action restrictions in arbitrations agreements with consumers improperly stripped consumers of rights they would normally have to attack certain industry practices. Class-action suits are often brought in cases alleging deceptive or unfair industry practices when the losses suffered by the individual consumer are too small to warrant the consumer bringing suit. In other words, the supposed added cell phone fees were so small that no individual consumer would be likely to litigate or arbitrate the matter due to the expenses involved. Therefore, the clause in the arbitration agreement preventing consumers from joining together in a class-action suit violates public policy and is void and unenforceable.

**PROBLEM 3–8.** *Discovery.* Yes, the items that were deleted from a Facebook page can be recovered. Normally, a party must hire an expert to recover material in an electronic format, and this can be time consuming and expensive.

Electronic evidence, or e-evidence, consists of all computer-generated or electronically recorded information, such as posts on Facebook and other social media sites. The effect that e-evidence can have in a case depends on its relevance and what it reveals. In the facts presented in this problem, Isaiah should be sanctioned—he should be required to cover Allied's cost of hiring the recovery expert and attorneys' fees for confronting the misconduct. In a jury trial, the court might also instruct the jury to presume that any missing items are harmful to Isaiah's case. If all of the material is retrieved and presented at the trial, any prejudice to Allied's case might thereby be mitigated. If not, the court might go so far as to order a new trial.

In the actual case on which this problem is based, Allied hired an expert, who determined that Isaiah had in fact removed some photos and other items from his Facebook page. After the expert testified about the missing material, Isaiah provided Allied with all of it, including the photos that he had deleted. Allied requested a retrial, but the court instead reduced the amount of Isaiah's damages by the amount that it cost Allied to address his "misconduct."

**PROBLEM 4–6.** *Establishment Clause.* The establishment clause prohibits the government from passing laws or taking actions that promote religion or show a preference for one religion over another. In assessing a government action, the courts look at the predominant purpose of the action and ask whether the action has the effect of endorsing religion.

Although here DeWeese claimed to have a nonreligious purpose for displaying the poster of the Ten Commandments in a courtroom, his own statements showed a religious purpose. These statements reflected his views about "warring" legal philosophies and his belief that "our legal system is based on moral absolutes from divine law handed down by God through the Ten Commandments." This plainly constitutes a religious purpose that violates the establishment clause because it has the effect of endorsing Judaism or Christianity over other religions. In the case on which this problem is based, the court ruled in favor of the American Civil Liberties Union.

**PROBLEM 5–5.** *Online Privacy.* Facebook created a program that makes decisions for users. Many believe that privacy is an extremely important right that should be fiercely protected. Thus, using duty-based ethics, any program that has a default setting of giving out information is unethical. Facebook should create the program as an opt-in program.

In addition, under the Kantian categorical imperative, if every company used opt-out programs that allowed the disclosure of potentially personal information, privacy might become merely theoretical. If privacy were reduced or eliminated, the world might not be a better place. From a utilitarian or outcome-based approach, an opt-out program might offer the benefits of being easy to created and start, as well as making it easy to recruit partner programs. On the negative side, the program would eliminate users' ability to chose whether to disclose information about themselves. An opt-in program would maintain that user control but might entail higher start-up costs because it would require more marketing to users up front to persuade them to opt in.

**PROBLEM 6–8.** *Negligence.* Negligence requires proof that (a) the defendant owed a duty of care to the plaintiff, (b) the defendant breached that duty, (c) the defendant's breach caused the plaintiff's injury, and (d) the plaintiff suffered a legally recognizable injury. With respect to the duty of care, a business owner has a duty to use reasonable care to protect business invitees. This duty includes an obligation to discover and correct or warn of unreasonably dangerous conditions that the owner of the premises should reasonably foresee might endanger an invitee. Some risks are so obvious that an owner need not warn of them. But even if a risk is obvious, a business owner may not be excused from the duty to protect its customers from foreseeable harm.

Because Lucario was the Weatherford's business invitee, the hotel owed her a duty of reasonable care to make its premises safe for her use. The balcony ran nearly the entire width of the window in Lucario's room. She could have reasonably believed that the window was a means of access to the balcony. The window/ balcony configuration was dangerous, however, because the window opened wide enough for an adult to climb out, but the twelve-inch gap between one side of the window and the balcony was unprotected. This unprotected gap opened to a drop of more than three stories to a concrete surface below.

Should the hotel have anticipated the potential harm to a guest opening the window in Room 59 and attempting to access the balcony? The hotel encouraged guests to "step out onto the balcony" to smoke. The dangerous window/balcony configuration could have been remedied at a minimal cost. These circumstances could be perceived as creating an "unreasonably dangerous" condition. And it could be concluded that the hotel created or knew of the condition and failed to take reasonable steps to warn of it or correct it. Of course, the Weatherford might argue that the window/ balcony configuration was so obvious that the hotel was not liable for Lucario's fall.

In the actual case on which this problem is based, the court concluded that the Weatherford did not breach its duty of care to Lucario. On McMurtry's appeal, a state intermediate appellate court held that this conclusion was in error, vacated the lower court's judgment in favor of the hotel on this issue, and remanded the case.

**PROBLEM 7–8.  *Product Liability.*** Here, the accident was caused by Jett's inattention, not by the texting device in the cab of his truck. In a product liability case based on a design defect, the plaintiff has to prove that the product was defective at the time it left the hands of the seller or lessor. The plaintiff must also show that this defective condition made the product "unreasonably dangerous" to the user or consumer. If the product was delivered in a safe condition and subsequent mishandling made it harmful to the user, the seller or lessor normally is not liable. To successfully assert a design defect, a plaintiff has to show that a reasonable alternative design was available and that the defendant failed to use it.

The plaintiffs could contend that the defendant manufacturer of the texting device owed them a duty of care because injuries to vehicle drivers and passengers, and others on the roads, were reasonably foreseeable due to the product's design that (a) required the driver to divert his eyes from the road to view an incoming text from the dispatcher and (b) permitted the receipt of texts while the vehicle was moving. But manufacturers are not required to design a product incapable of distracting a driver. The duty owed by a manufacturer to the user or consumer of a product does not require guarding against hazards that are commonly known or obvious or protecting against injuries that result from a user's careless conduct. That is what happened here.

In the actual case on which this problem is based, the court reached the same conclusion, based on the reasoning stated above, and an intermediate appellate court affirmed the judgment.

**PROBLEM 8–5.  *Trade Secrets.*** Some business information that cannot be protected by trademark, patent, or copyright law is protected against appropriation by competitors as trade secrets. Trade secrets consist of anything that makes a company unique and that would have value to a competitor—customer lists, plans, research and development, pricing information, marketing techniques, and production techniques, for example. Theft of trade secrets is a federal crime.

In this problem, the documents in the boxes in the car could constitute trade secrets. But a number of factors suggest that a finding of theft and imposition of liability would not be appropriate. The boxes were not marked in any way that would indicate they contained confidential information. The boxes were stored in an employee's car. The alleged thief was the employee's spouse, not a CPR competitor, and she apparently had no idea what was in the boxes. Leaving trade secrets so accessible does not show an effort to protect the information.

In the case on which this problem is based, the court dismissed Jones's claim, in part on the reasoning stated above.

**PROBLEM 9–6.  *Privacy.*** No, Rolfe did not have a privacy interest in the information obtained by the subpoenas issued to Midcontinent Communications. The courts have held that the right to privacy is guaranteed by the U.S. Constitution's Bill of Rights, and some state constitutions contain an explicit guarantee of the right. A person must have a reasonable expectation of privacy, though, to maintain a suit or to assert a successful defense for an invasion of privacy.

People clearly have a reasonable expectation of privacy when they enter their personal banking or credit-card information online. They also have a reasonable expectation that online companies will follow their own privacy policies. But people do not a reasonable expectation of privacy in statements made on Twitter and other data that they publicly disseminate. In other words, there is no violation of a subscriber's right to privacy when a third party Internet service provider receives a subpoena and discloses the subscriber's information.

Here, Rolfe supplied his e-mail address and other personal information, including his Internet protocol address, to Midcontinent. In other words, Rolfe publicly disseminated this information. Law enforcement officers obtained this information from Midcontinent through the subpoenas issued by the South Dakota state court. Rolfe provided his information to Midcontinent—he has no legitimate expectation of privacy in that information.

In the actual case on which this problem is based, Rolfe was charged with, and convicted of, possessing, manufacturing, and distributing child pornography, as well as other crimes. As part of the proceedings, the court found that Rolfe had no expectation of privacy in the information that he made available to Midcontinent. On appeal, the South Dakota Supreme Court upheld the conviction.

**PROBLEM 10–8.  *Criminal Liability.*** Yes, Green exhibited the required mental state to establish criminal liability. A wrongful mental state *(mens rea)* is one of the elements typically required to establish criminal liability. The required mental state, or intent, is indicated in an applicable statute or law. For example, for murder, the required mental state is the intent to take another's life. A court can also find that the required mental state is present when a defendant's acts are reckless or criminally negligent. A defendant is criminally reckless if he or she consciously disregards a substantial and unjustifiable risk.

In this problem, Green was clearly aware of the danger to which he was exposing people on the street below, but he did not indicate that he specifically intended to harm anyone. The risk of death created by his conduct, however, was obvious. He must have known what was likely to happen if a bottle or plate thrown from the height of twenty-six stories hit a pedestrian or the windshield of an occupied motor vehicle on the street below. Despite his claim that he was intoxicated, he was sufficiently aware to stop throwing things from the balcony when he saw police in the area, and he later recalled what he had done and what had happened.

In the actual case on which this problem is based, after a jury trial, Green was convicted of reckless endangerment. On appeal, a state intermediate appellate court affirmed the conviction, based in part on the reasoning stated above.

**PROBLEM 11–7. *Quasi Contract.*** Gutkowski does not have a valid claim for payment, nor should he recover on the basis of a quasi contract. Courts impose quasi contracts on parties in the interest of fairness and justice.

Usually, a quasi contract is imposed to avoid the unjust enrichment of one party at the expense of another. Here, Gutkowski was compensated as a consultant. To establish a claim that he is due more compensation based on unjust enrichment, he must have proof. As it is, he has only his claim that there were discussions about him being a part owner of YES. Discussions and negotiations are not a basis for recovery on a quasi contract.

In the actual case on which this problem is based, the court dismissed Gutkowski's claim for payment.

**PROBLEM 12–5. *Offer and Acceptance.*** No, a contract was not formed in this case. As the Iowa Supreme Court pointed out, the parties must voluntarily agree to enter into a contract. Courts determine whether an offer has been made objectively—not subjectively.

Under the *Restatement of Contracts (Second)*, "the test for an offer is whether it induces a reasonable belief in the recipient that [the recipient] can, by accepting, bind the sender." The offeror may decide to whom to extend the offer. According to the *Restatement*, an offer may create a power of acceptance in a specified person or in one or more of a specified group or class of persons, acting separately or together.

The court hearing this case explained: "In this situation, Prairie Meadows is the offeror. It makes an offer to its patrons that, if accepted by wagering an amount and the patron wins, it will pay off the wager. Simply stated, the issue is whether Prairie Meadows made an offer to Blackford. Because Prairie Meadows has the ability to determine the class of individuals to whom the offer is made, it may also exclude certain individuals. Blackford had been banned for life from the casino. . . . Under an objective test, unless the ban had been lifted, Blackford could not have reasonably believed he was among the class of individuals invited to accept Prairie Meadows's offer."

In the actual case on which this problem is based, the jury found that the ban against Blackford had not been lifted and, therefore, Prairie Meadows had not extended him an offer to wager. Because there was no offer to him, no contract could result. The state supreme court therefore reversed the decision of the state appellate court and affirmed the trial court's judgment.

**PROBLEM 13–6. *Rescission.*** As the reviewing court noted, "rescission is intended to restore the parties as nearly as possible to their former positions and 'to bring about substantial justice by adjusting the equities between the parties.'" Rescission does not occur if a contract is affirmed—it means the contract is repudiated.

Here, rescission is appropriate because the contracting parties were mutually mistaken as to the condition of the property. The environmental contamination substantially reduced the property's value. When an agreement to purchase property is subject to rescission, "the seller must refund all payments received in connection with the sale." Hence, the award of damages to the Berensteins was reversed, and the Sharabianlous' deposit was refunded.

**PROBLEM 14–5. *Unconscionable Contracts or Clauses.*** In this case, the agreement restricted the buyer's options for resolution of a dispute to arbitration and limited the amount of damages. This agreement was both procedurally and substantively unconscionable. Procedural unconscionability concerns the manner in which the parties enter into a contract. Substantive unconscionability can occur when a contract leaves one party to the agreement without a remedy for the nonperformance of the other.

Here, GeoEx told customers that the arbitration terms in its release form were nonnegotiable and that climbers would encounter the same requirements with any other travel company. This amounted to procedural unconscionability, underscoring the customers' lack of bargaining power. The imbalance resulted in oppressive terms, with no real negotiation and an absence of meaningful choice. Furthermore, the restriction on forum (San Francisco) and the limitation on damages (the cost of the trip)—with no limitation on GeoEx's damages—amounted to substantive unconscionability. In the actual case on which this problem is based, the court ruled that the agreement was unconscionable.

**PROBLEM 15–5. *Fraudulent Misrepresentation.*** Esprit's argument is not credible because the fact that the house was later sold for a good price had nothing to do with the extra costs incurred by the Wilcoxes. The Wilcoxes had borrowed about a million dollars to finance the project, and Esprit knew that. The court determined that "a promise made without a present intent to perform is a misrepresentation of a material fact and is sufficient to support a cause of action for fraud."

Esprit had promised to deliver precut and predrilled logs that could be assembled quickly. It knew the delivery of unfinished logs would cause problems. "After the logs arrived at the home, Esprit further misrepresented that there would be only a two- or three-day delay while the logs where cut and drilled on site. The jury could conclude that Esprit's actions amounted to fraud or such indifference to negative consequences for the buyers as to support an award for punitive damages." The judgment of the lower court was affirmed.

**PROBLEM 16–5.** *The Parol Evidence Rule.* Vaks and Mangano may not recover for breach of an oral contract. Under the parol evidence rule, if there is a written contract representing the complete and final statement of the parties' agreement, a party may not introduce any evidence of past agreements. Here, the written agreement was an integrated contract because the parties intended it to be a complete and final statement of the terms of their agreement. Vaks and Mangano therefore may not introduce evidence of any inconsistent oral representations made before the contract was executed.

**PROBLEM 17–5.** *Duties That Cannot Be Delegated.* No. As a general rule, any duty can be delegated. Delegation is prohibited, however, when the contract expressly prohibits delegation. An attempted delegation will render the contract void. But the other party to the contract can consent to the delegation by accepting the delegatee's performance, and the contract will remain valid. If so, that party cannot later object that the delegation breached the contract.

An antidelegation clause, as in the contract in this problem, must be enforced when the delegation is attempted, not after the delegatee's performance is accepted. Because Albea consented to the delegation of APAC's duties under the subcontract to Matthews, Albea is liable to APAC for the labor and materials expended before that delegation.

In the actual case on which this problem is based, the court granted a judgment to APAC.

**PROBLEM 18–6.** *Conditions of Performance.* Maciel was not correct. In this problem, the performance of a legal obligation under the parties' contract was contingent on a condition—the occurrence of a certain event. If the condition was not satisfied, the obligations of the parties were discharged. Here, Regent University promised to provide an apartment in its housing facility to Maciel as long as he maintained his status as a Regent student. Maintaining student status was the condition for the university's provision of an apartment. On the termination of that status, Regent was entitled to require Maciel to vacate the apartment.

Maciel chose to withdraw from the university at the end of the spring semester, which rendered him ineligible to remain in the apartment. In other words, this decision resulted in noncompliance with the condition for the university's provision of an apartment, and the university was thus no longer bound to perform. Contrary to Maciel's argument in court, he did not have the "legal authority" to continue to occupy the apartment.

In the actual case on which this problem is based, the court convicted Maciel of trespassing. In response to Maciel's argument, a state intermediate appellate court applied the reasoning set out above to affirm the conviction.

**PROBLEM 19–6.** *Consequential Damages.* Simard is liable only for the losses and expenses related to the first resale. Simard could reasonably anticipate that his breach would require another sale and that the sales price might be less than what he agreed to pay. Therefore, he should be liable for the difference between his sales price and the first resale price ($29,000), plus any expenses arising from the first resale. Simard is not liable, however, for any expenses and losses related to the second resale. After all, Simard did not cause the second purchaser's default, and he could not reasonably foresee that default as a probable result of his breach.

**PROBLEM 20–4.** *Additional Terms.* No. The Uniform Commercial Code (UCC) dispenses with the common law mirror image rule, which requires that the terms of an acceptance exactly mirror the terms of the offer. Under the UCC, a contract is formed if the offeree makes a definite expression of acceptance even though the terms of the acceptance modify or add to the terms of the offer.

When both parties to the contract are merchants, the additional terms become part of their contract *unless* (a) the original offer expressly required acceptance of its terms, (b) the new or changed terms materially alter the contract, or (c) the offeror rejects the new or changed terms within a reasonable time.

In this problem, the UCC applies because the transactions involve sales of goods. The original offer stated, "By signing below, you agree to the terms." This statement could be construed to expressly require acceptance of the terms to make the offer a binding contract (exception a above).

The contract stated that JMAM was to receive credit for any rejected merchandise. Nothing indicated that the merchandise would be returned to BSI. Baracsi, BSI's owner (the offeree), signed JMAM's (the offeror's) letter in the appropriate location, thereby indicating BSI's agreement to the terms. Thus, BSI made a definite expression of acceptance. The practice of the parties—for six years rejected items were not returned—further supports the conclusion that their contract did not contemplate the return of those items. The "PS" could be interpreted as materially altering the contract (exception b above).

In the actual case on which this problem is based, the court dismissed BSI's complaint.

**PROBLEM 21–6.** *Passage of Title.* Altieri held title to the car that she was driving at the time of the accident in which Godfrey was injured. Once goods exist and are identified, title can be determined. Under the Uniform Commercial Code (UCC), any explicit understanding between the buyer and the seller determines when title passes. If there is no such agreement, title passes to the buyer at the time and place that the seller physically delivers the goods. In lease contracts, title to the goods is retained by the lessor-owner of the goods. The UCC's provisions relating to passage to title do not apply to leased goods.

Here, Altieri originally leased the car from G.E. Capital Auto Lease, Inc., but by the time of the accident, she had bought it. Even though she had not fully paid for the car or completed the transfer-of-title paperwork, she owned it. Title to the car passed to Altieri when she bought it and took delivery of it. Thus, Altieri, not G.E., was the owner of the car at the time of the accident. In the actual case on which this problem is based, the court concluded that G.E. was not the owner of the vehicle when Godfrey was injured.

**PROBLEM 22–8.** *Nonconforming Goods.* Padma Paper Mills notified Universal Exports about its breach, so Padma has two ways to recover even though it accepted the goods.

Padma's first option is to argue that it revoked its acceptance, giving it the right to reject the goods. To revoke acceptance, Padma would have to show that (a) the nonconformity substantially impaired the value of the shipment, (b) it predicated its acceptance on a reasonable assumption that Universal Exports would cure the nonconformity, and (c) Universal Exports did not cure the nonconformity within a reasonable time.

Padma's second option is to keep the goods and recover for the damages caused by Universal Exports' breach. Under this option, Padma could recover at least the difference between the value of the goods as promised and their value as accepted.

**PROBLEM 23–3.** *Express Warranties.* The statements that the tapes would last a lifetime were statements of opinion (puffery) and did not constitute an express warranty. Puffery is not actionable. Therefore, the court should rule in favor of the defendants.

As the court hearing this case explained, calling something the "Gold Collection" or "Masterpiece Collection" is not an affirmation of fact or a promise that the tapes will last for generations or otherwise have an extraordinary life span. A "collection" is "a number of objects or persons or a quantity of a substance that has been collected or has collected often according to some unifying principle or orderly arrangement." Thus, use of the word *collection* did not convey a promise of a lengthy life span.

Also, the use of statements such as "Give Your Children the Memories of a Lifetime—Collect Each Timeless Masterpiece!" or "Available for a Limited Time Only!" did not constitute an express warranty. The court reasoned that even if ads had stated that the tapes would last a lifetime, this would have been an expression of opinion or puffery. The court dismissed the plaintiffs' complaint, and on the plaintiffs' appeal, a state intermediate appellate court affirmed the dismissal.

**PROBLEM 24–6.** *Sovereign Immunity.* The doctrine of sovereign immunity exempts foreign nations from the jurisdiction of U.S. courts, subject to certain conditions. The Foreign Sovereign Immunities Act (FSIA) of 1976 codifies this doctrine and exclusively governs the circumstances in which an action may be brought in a U.S. court against a foreign nation.

A foreign state is not immune from the jurisdiction of U.S. courts when the state (a) waives immunity, (b) engages in commercial activity, or (c) commits a tort in the United States or violates certain international laws. Under the FSIA, a foreign state includes its political subdivisions and "instrumentalities"—departments and agencies. A commercial activity is a regular course of commercial conduct, transaction, or act that is carried out by the foreign state within the United States or has a direct effect in the United States.

The details of what constitutes a commercial activity are left to the courts. But it seems clear that a foreign government can be considered to engage in commercial activity when, instead of regulating a market, the government participates in it. In other words, when a foreign state, or its political subdivisions or instrumentalities, performs the type of actions in which a private party engages in commerce, the state's actions are likewise commercial.

In the facts of this problem, Iran engaged in commercial activity outside the United States by making and marketing its counterfeit versions of Bell's Model 206 Series helicopters. This activity caused a direct effect in the United States by the consumer confusion that will likely result from Iran's unauthorized use of Bell's trade dress. Thus, the court can exercise jurisdiction in these circumstances, and Iran may be as liable as a private party would be for the same acts.

In the actual case on which this problem is based, Iran did not respond to Bell's complaint. The court held that it had jurisdiction under the FSIA's commercial activity exception, as explained above. The court entered a default judgment against Iran and awarded damages and an injunction to Bell.

**PROBLEM 25–7.** *Employment Relationships.* The facts support a conclusion that Jonathan was an independent contractor and not an employee. In deciding whether a worker is categorized as an employee or an independent contractor, the courts generally consider the amount of control that the employer exercises over the details of the work. Is the work done under the employer's direction or by a specialist without supervision? Control indicates employee status.

In this problem, Jonathan could argue that he was under William's direction and control. It was his first day on the new job. There was no way for him to know what to do without William's direction. He might assert that William told him to load certain tires on a trailer and that thus he was an employee. But this instruction is minimal. The relationship between the parties before the accident was independent contractor and employer. For a decade, Jonathan operated his own business. His accumulated skill, experience, and judgment in the business established that he controlled his work without oversight.

In the actual case on which this problem is based, the court held that Jonathan was an independent contractor.

**PROBLEM 26–7.** *Liability for Contracts.* Hall may be held personally liable. Hall could not be an agent for House Medic because it was a fictitious name and not a real entity. Moreover, when the contract was formed, Hall did not disclose his true principal, which was Hall Hauling, Ltd. Thus, Hall may be held personally liable as a party to the contract.

**PROBLEM 27–6.** *Workers' Compensation.* Fairbanks's claim qualifies for workers' compensation benefits. To recover benefits under state workers' compensation laws, the requirements are that the injury (a) was accidental and (b) occurred on the job or in the course of employment. Fault is not an issue. The employee must file a claim with the appropriate state agency or board that administers local workers' compensation claims.

In this problem, Fairbanks's claim for workers' compensation benefits appears to have been timely filed with the appropriate state agency. The focus of the dispute is on the second requirement listed above—an accidental injury that occurred on the job or in the course of employment. Dynea required its employees to wear certain boots as a safety measure. One of the boots caused a sore on Fairbanks's leg. The sore developed into a pustule and broke into a lesion. Within a week, Fairbanks was hospitalized with an MRSA infection.

Dynea argued that the bacteria were on Fairbanks's skin before he came to work. Even if this were true, however, it was the rubbing of the boot that caused the sore through which the bacteria entered his body. This fact fulfills the second requirement for the recovery of workers' compensation benefits.

In the actual case on which this problem is based, the court issued a decision in favor of Fairbanks's claim for benefits.

**PROBLEM 28–5.** *Retaliation by Employers.* Yes. Dawson could establish a claim for retaliation. Title VII prohibits retaliation. In a retaliation claim, an individual asserts that she or he suffered harm as a result of making a charge, testifying, or participating in a Title VII investigation or proceeding. To prove retaliation, a plaintiff must show that the challenged action was one that would likely have dissuaded a reasonable worker from making or supporting a charge of discrimination.

In this problem, under applicable state law, it was unlawful for an employer to discriminate against an individual based on sexual orientation. Dawson was subjected to derision on the part of co-workers, including his supervisor, based on his sexual orientation. He filed a complaint with his employer's human resources department. Two days later, he was fired. The proximity in time and the other circumstances, especially the supervisor's conduct, would support a retaliation claim. Also, the discharge would likely have dissuaded Dawson, or any reasonable worker, from making a claim of discrimination. In the actual case on which this problem is based, the court held that Dawson offered enough evidence that "a reasonable trier of fact could find in favor of Dawson on his retaliation claim."

**PROBLEM 29–6.** *Franchise Termination.* Oshana and GTO have stated a claim for wrongful termination of their franchise. A franchisor must act in good faith when terminating a franchise agreement. If the termination is arbitrary or unfair, a franchisee may have a claim for wrongful termination. In this case, Oshana and GTO have alleged that Buchanan acted in bad faith. Their failure to pay rent would ordinarily be a valid basis for termination, but not if the failure was entirely precipitated by Buchanan. Thus, Oshana and GTO may recover if they can prove that their allegations are true.

**PROBLEM 30–7.** *Partnership Formation.* Garcia and Lucero probably satisfied all three requirements for forming a partnership. They owned the two properties equally, agreed to share both profits and losses, and enjoyed equal management rights. Moreover, it is immaterial that they lacked a written partnership agreement. The writing requirement (Statute of Frauds) does not apply to these facts, and a partnership agreement can be oral or implied by the parties' conduct.

**PROBLEM 31–6.** *LLC Operation.* No. One Bluewater member could not unilaterally "fire" another member without providing a reason. Part of the attractiveness of the limited liability company (LLC) as a form of business enterprise is its flexibility. The members can decide how to operate the business through an operating agreement. For example, the agreement can set forth procedures for choosing or removing members or managers.

Here, the Bluewater operating agreement provided for a "super majority" vote to remove a member under circumstances that would jeopardize the firm's contractor status. Thus, one Bluewater member could not unilaterally "fire" another member without providing a reason. In fact, a majority of the members could not terminate the other's interest in the firm without providing a reason. Moreover, the only acceptable reason would be a circumstance that undercut the firm's status as a contractor.

The flexibility of the LLC business form relates to its framework, not to its members' capacity to violate its operating agreement. In the actual case on which this problem is based, Smith attempted to "fire" Williford without providing a reason. In Williford's suit, the court issued a judgment in his favor.

**PROBLEM 32–7.** *Close Corporations.* Yes, Pourgol's acts may likely have constituted misconduct. In this problem, Burnett charged Pourgol with the submission of incorrect plans to obtain the building permit, misrepresentation of the extent of the renovations, and failure to fix the house. The submission of incorrect plans might arguably have been a mistake, and the misrepresentation might have been a misstatement in good faith. But these acts may instead have been intentional and fraudulent. Assuming the charges are true and all of the acts were wrongful, including the misrepresentation and failure to fix the house, they certainly form the basis for a finding of misconduct.

A close corporation is a private corporation with a small number of shareholders. Close corporations are often managed by their shareholders. To prevent such situations as the one that arose in this problem, shareholders must take an active role in the governance of a corporation. The corporate articles or bylaws might be amended to, for example, require more than a single shareholder or a simple majority to approve an action. A minority shareholder, or a dominated shareholder, or a formerly disinterested shareholder may also pursue a remedy through a direct or derivative (on behalf of the corporation) suit.

Here, the facts do not state which shareholder, if either, held a majority of the shares. But Burnett might have taken any of the steps mentioned above to prevent misconduct. In the problem, Burnett has taken the step of filing a suit against Pourgol. In the actual case on which this problem is based, the court denied Pourgol's motion to dismiss Burnett's complaint.

# GLOSSARY

## A

**Accord and satisfaction** An agreement for payment (or other performance) between two parties, one of whom has a right of action against the other. After the payment has been accepted or other performance has been made, the "accord and satisfaction" is complete and the obligation is discharged.

**Acquittal** A certification or declaration following a trial that the individual accused of a crime is innocent, or free from guilt, and is thus absolved of the charges.

**Act of state doctrine** A doctrine that provides that the judicial branch of one country will not examine the validity of public acts committed by a recognized foreign government within its own territory.

**Actionable** Capable of serving as the basis of a lawsuit.

**Actual authority** Authority of an agent that is express or implied.

**Actual malice** A condition that exists when a person makes a statement with either knowledge of its falsity or a reckless disregard for the truth. In a defamation suit, a statement made about a public figure normally must be made with actual malice for liability to be incurred.

**Actus reus** (pronounced *ak*-tus *ray*-uhs) A guilty (prohibited) act. The commission of a prohibited act is one of the two essential elements required for criminal liability, the other element being the intent to commit a crime.

**Adhesion contract** A "standard-form" contract, such as that between a large retailer and a consumer, in which the stronger party dictates the terms.

**Administrative agency** A federal, state, or local government agency established to perform a specific function. Administrative agencies are authorized by legislative acts to make and enforce rules to administer and enforce the acts.

**Administrative law** The body of law created by administrative agencies (in the form of rules, regulations, orders, and decisions) in order to carry out their duties and responsibilities.

**Administrative law judge (ALJ)** One who presides over an administrative agency hearing and who has the power to administer oaths, take testimony, rule on questions of evidence, and make determinations of fact.

**Affidavit** A written or printed voluntary statement of facts, confirmed by the oath or affirmation of the party making it and made before a person having the authority to administer the oath or affirmation.

**Affirm** To validate; to give legal force to. *See also* Ratification

**Affirmative action** Job-hiring policies that give special consideration to members of protected classes in an effort to overcome present effects of past discrimination.

**Affirmative defense** A response to a plaintiff's claim that does not deny the plaintiff's facts but attacks the plaintiff's legal right to bring an action. An example is the running of the statute of limitations.

**After-acquired evidence** A type of evidence submitted in support of an affirmative defense in employment discrimination cases. Evidence that, prior to the employer's discriminatory act, the employee engaged in misconduct sufficient to warrant dismissal had the employer known of it earlier.

**Age of majority** The age at which an individual is considered legally capable of conducting himself or herself responsibly. A person of this age is entitled to the full rights of citizenship, including the right to vote. In contract law, the age at which one is no longer an infant and can no longer disaffirm a contract.

**Agency** A relationship between two parties in which one party (the agent) agrees to represent or act for the other (the principal).

**Agreement** A meeting of two or more minds in regard to the terms of a contract; usually broken down into two events—an offer by one party to form a contract, and an acceptance of the offer by the person to whom the offer is made.

**Alien corporation** A designation in the United States for a corporation formed in another country but doing business in the United States.

**Alternative dispute resolution (ADR)** The resolution of disputes in ways other than those involved in the traditional judicial process. Negotiation, mediation, and arbitration are forms of ADR.

**American Arbitration Association (AAA)** The major organization offering arbitration services in the United States.

**Analogy** In logical reasoning, an assumption that if two things are similar in some respects, they will be similar in other respects also. Often used in legal reasoning to infer the appropriate application of legal principles in a case being decided by referring to previous cases involving different facts but considered to come within the policy underlying the rule.

**Annul** To cancel or to make void.

**Answer** Procedurally, a defendant's response to the plaintiff's complaint.

**Anticipatory repudiation** An assertion or action by a party indicating that he or she will not perform an obligation that the party is contractually obligated to perform at a future time.

**Apparent authority** Authority that is only apparent, not real. In agency law, a person may be deemed to have had the power to act as an agent for another party if the other party's manifestations to a third party led the third party to believe that an agency existed when, in fact, it did not.

**Appeal** Resort to a superior court, such as an appellate court, to review the decision of an inferior court, such as a trial court or an administrative agency.

**Appellant** The party who takes an appeal from one court to another.

**Appellate court** A court having appellate jurisdiction.

**Appellate jurisdiction** Courts having appellate jurisdiction act as reviewing courts, or appellate courts. Generally, cases can be brought before appellate courts only on appeal from an order or a judgment of a trial court or other lower court.

**Appellee** The party against whom an appeal is taken—that is, the party who opposes setting aside or reversing the judgment.

**Appropriation** In tort law, the use by one person of another person's name, likeness, or other identifying characteristic without permission and for the benefit of the user.

**Arbitration** The settling of a dispute by submitting it to a disinterested third party (other than a court), who renders a decision. The decision may or may not be legally binding.

**Arbitration clause** A clause in a contract that provides that, in the event of a dispute, the parties will submit the dispute to arbitration rather than litigate the dispute in court.

**Arraignment** A procedure in which an accused person is brought before the court to answer criminal charges. The charge is read to the person, and he or she is asked to enter a plea—such as "guilty" or "not guilty."

**Arson** The malicious burning of another's dwelling. Some statutes have expanded this to include any real property regardless of ownership and the destruction of property by other means—for example, by explosion.

**Articles of incorporation** The document filed with the appropriate governmental agency, usually the secretary of state, when a business is incorporated; state statutes usually prescribe what kind of information must be contained in the articles of incorporation.

**Articles of organization** The document filed with a designated state official by which a limited liability company is formed.

**Articles of partnership** A written agreement that sets forth each partner's rights and obligations with respect to the partnership.

**Assault** Any word or action intended to make another person fearful of immediate physical harm; a reasonably believable threat.

**Assignee** The person to whom contract rights are assigned.

**Assignment** The act of transferring to another all or part of one's rights arising under a contract.

**Assignor** The person who assigns contract rights.

**Assumption of risk** A defense against negligence that can be used when the plaintiff was aware of a danger and voluntarily assumed the risk of injury from that danger.

**Award** In the context of litigation, the amount of money awarded to a plaintiff in a civil lawsuit as damages. In the context of arbitration, the arbitrator's decision.

# B

**Bankruptcy court** A federal court of limited jurisdiction that handles only bankruptcy proceedings. Bankruptcy proceedings are governed by federal bankruptcy law.

**Bargain** A mutual undertaking, contract, or agreement between two parties; to negotiate over the terms of a purchase or contract.

**Basis of the bargain** In contract law, the affirmation of fact or promise on which the sale of goods is predicated, creating an express warranty.

**Battery** The unprivileged, intentional touching of another.

**Benefit corporation** A for-profit corporation that seeks to have a material positive impact on society and the environment. This new business form is available by statute in a growing number of states.

**Beyond a reasonable doubt** The standard used to determine the guilt or innocence of a person criminally charged. To be guilty of a crime, one must be proved guilty "beyond and to the exclusion of every reasonable doubt." A reasonable doubt is one that would cause a prudent person to hesitate before acting in matters important to him or her.

**Bilateral contract** A type of contract that arises when a promise is given in exchange for a return promise.

**Bill of Rights** The first ten amendments to the U.S. Constitution.

**Binding authority** Any source of law that a court must follow when deciding a case. Binding authorities include constitutions, statutes, and regulations that govern the issue being decided, as well as court decisions that are controlling precedents within the jurisdiction.

**Bond** A certificate that evidences a corporate (or government) debt. It is a security that involves no ownership interest in the issuing entity.

**Breach** To violate a law, by an act or an omission, or to break a legal obligation that one owes to another person or to society.

**Breach of contract** The failure, without legal excuse, of a promisor to perform the obligations of a contract.

**Bribery** The offering, giving, receiving, or soliciting of anything of value with the aim of influencing an official action or an official's discharge of a legal or public duty or (with respect to commercial bribery) a business decision.

**Brief** A formal legal document submitted by the attorney for the appellant—or the appellee (in answer to the appellant's brief)—to an appellate court when a case is appealed. The appellant's brief outlines the facts and issues of the case, the judge's rulings or jury's findings that should be reversed or modified, the applicable law, and the arguments on the client's behalf.

**Browse-wrap terms** Terms and conditions of use that are presented to an Internet user at the time certain products, such as software, are being downloaded but that need not be agreed to (by clicking "I agree," for example) before being able to install or use the product.

**Burglary** The unlawful entry into a building with the intent to commit a felony. (Some state statutes expand this to include the intent to commit any crime.)

**Business ethics** Ethics in a business context; a consensus of what constitutes right or wrong behavior in the world of business and the application of moral principles to situations that arise in a business setting.

**Business invitees** Those people, such as customers or clients, who are invited onto business premises by the owner of those premises for business purposes.

**Business necessity** A defense to allegations of employment discrimination in which the employer demonstrates that an employment practice that discriminates against members of a protected class is related to job performance.

**Business plan** A document describing a company, its products, and its anticipated future performance. Creating a business plan is normally the first step in obtaining loans or venture-capital funds for a new business enterprise.

**Business tort** Wrongful interference with the business rights of another.

**Business trust** A voluntary form of business organization in which investors (trust beneficiaries) transfer cash or property to trustees in exchange for trust certificates that represent their investment shares. Management of the business and trust property is handled by the trustees for the use and benefit of the investors. The certificate holders have limited liability (are not responsible for the debts and obligations incurred by the trust) and share in the trust's profits.

**Buyer in the ordinary course of business** A buyer who, in good faith and without knowledge that the sale violates the ownership rights or security interest of a third party in the goods, purchases goods in the ordinary course of business from a person in the business of selling goods of that kind.

**Buyout price** The amount payable to a partner on his or her dissociation from a partnership, based on the amount distributable to that partner if the firm were wound up on that date, and offset by any damages for wrongful dissociation.

**Buy-sell agreement** In the context of partnerships, an express agreement made at the time of partnership formation for one or more of the partners to buy out the other or others should the situation warrant—and thus provide for the smooth dissolution of the partnership.

**Bylaws** A set of governing rules adopted by a corporation or other association.

# C

**C.I.F. or C.&F.** Cost, insurance, and freight—or just cost and freight. A pricing term in a contract for the sale of goods requiring, among other things, that the seller place the goods in the possession of a carrier before risk passes to the buyer.

**C.O.D.** Cash on delivery. In sales transactions, a term meaning that the buyer will pay for the goods on delivery and before inspecting the goods.

**Cancellation** The act of nullifying, or making void. *See also* Rescission

**Capital** Accumulated goods, possessions, and assets used for the production of profits and wealth; the equity of owners in a business.

**Case law** The rules of law announced in court decisions. Case law includes the aggregate of reported cases that interpret judicial precedents, statutes, regulations, and constitutional provisions.

**Case on point** A previous case involving factual circumstances and issues that are similar to those in the case before the court.

**Categorical imperative** A concept developed by the philosopher Immanuel Kant as an ethical guideline for behavior. In deciding whether an action is right or wrong, or desirable or undesirable, a person should evaluate the action in terms of what would happen if everybody else in the same situation, or category, acted the same way.

**Causation in fact** An act or omission without ("but for") which an event would not have occurred.

**Cause of action** A situation or set of facts sufficient to justify a right to sue.

**Certificate of limited partnership** The basic document filed with a designated state official by which a limited partnership is formed.

**Certification mark** A mark used by one or more persons, other than the owner, to certify the region, materials, mode of manufacture, quality, or accuracy of the owner's goods or services. When used by members of a cooperative, association, or other organization, such a mark is referred to as a collective mark. Examples of certification marks include the "Good Housekeeping Seal of Approval" and "UL Tested."

**Certiorari** *See* Writ of *certiorari*

**Chain-style business franchise** A franchise that operates under a franchisor's trade name and that is identified as a member of a select group of dealers that engage in the franchisor's business. The franchisee is generally required to follow standardized or prescribed methods of operation. Examples of this type of franchise are McDonald's and most other fast-food chains.

**Chancellor** An adviser to the king at the time of the early king's courts of England. Individuals petitioned the king for relief when they could not obtain an adequate remedy in a court of law, and these petitions were decided by the chancellor.

**Charging order** In partnership law, an order granted by a court to a judgment creditor that entitles the creditor to attach profits or assets of a partner on dissolution of the partnership.

**Chattel paper** Any writing or writings that show both a debt and the fact that the debt is secured by personal property. In many instances, chattel paper consists of a negotiable instrument coupled with a security agreement.

**Checks and balances** The system by which each of the three branches of the national government (executive, legislative, and judicial) exercises checks on the powers of the other branches.

**Choice-of-language clause** A clause in a contract designating the official language by which the contract will be interpreted in the event of a future disagreement over the contract's terms.

**Choice-of-law clause** A clause in a contract designating the law (such as the law of a particular state or nation) that will govern the contract.

**Citation** A reference to a publication in which a legal authority—such as a statute or a court decision—or other source can be found.

**Civil law** The branch of law dealing with the definition and enforcement of all private or public rights, as opposed to criminal matters.

**Civil law system** A system of law derived from that of the Roman Empire and based on a code rather than case law; the predominant system of law in the nations of continental Europe and the nations that were once their colonies. In the United States, Louisiana is the only state that has a civil law system.

**Claim** As a verb, to assert or demand. As a noun, a right to payment.

**Click-on agreement** An agreement that arises when a buyer, engaging in a transaction on a computer, indicates his or her assent to be bound by the terms of an offer by clicking on a button that says, for example, "I agree"; sometimes referred to as a click-on license or a click-wrap agreement.

**Close corporation** A corporation whose shareholders are limited to a small group of persons, often only family members. The rights of shareholders of a close corporation usually are restricted regarding the transfer of shares to others.

**Closed shop** A firm that requires union membership by its workers as a condition of employment. The closed shop was made illegal by the Labor-Management Relations Act of 1947.

**Closing argument** An argument made after the plaintiff and defendant have rested their cases. Closing arguments are made prior to the jury charges.

**Cloud computing** The delivery to users of on-demand services from third-party servers over a network. Cloud computing is a delivery model. The most widely used cloud computing services are Software as a Service (SaaS), which offers companies a cheaper way to buy and use packaged applications that are no longer run on servers in house.

**Collateral promise** A secondary promise that is ancillary (subsidiary) to a principal transaction or primary contractual relationship, such as a promise made by one person to pay the debts of another if the latter fails to perform. A collateral promise normally must be in writing to be enforceable.

**Collective bargaining** The process by which labor and management negotiate the terms and conditions of employment, including working hours and workplace conditions.

**Collective mark** A mark used by members of a cooperative, association, or other organization to certify the region, materials, mode of manufacture, quality, or accuracy of the specific goods or services. Examples of collective marks include the labor union marks found on tags of certain products and the credits of movies, which indicate the various associations and organizations that participated in the making of the movies.

**Comity** A deference by which one nation gives effect to the laws and judicial decrees of another nation. This recognition is based primarily on respect.

**Commerce clause** The provision in Article I, Section 8, of the U.S. Constitution that gives Congress the power to regulate interstate commerce.

**Commercial impracticability** A doctrine under which a seller may be excused from performing a contract when (1) a contingency occurs, (2) the contingency's occurrence makes performance impracticable, and (3) the nonoccurrence of the contingency was a basic assumption on which the contract was made. Despite the fact that UCC 2–615 expressly frees only sellers under this doctrine, courts have not distinguished between buyers and sellers in applying it.

**Commingle** To put funds or goods together into one mass so that the funds or goods are so mixed that they no longer have separate identities. In corporate law, if personal and corporate interests are commingled to the extent that the corporation has no separate identity, a court may "pierce the corporate veil" and expose the shareholders to personal liability.

**Common carrier** A carrier that transfers people or goods for hire to the general public.

**Common law** That body of law developed from custom or judicial decisions in English and U.S. courts, not attributable to a legislature.

**Common stock** Shares of ownership in a corporation that give the owner of the stock a proportionate interest in the corporation with regard to control, earnings, and net assets; shares of common stock are lowest in priority with respect to payment of dividends and distribution of the corporation's assets on dissolution.

**Comparative negligence** A theory in tort law under which the liability for injuries resulting from negligent acts is shared by all parties who were negligent (including the injured party), on the basis of each person's proportionate negligence.

**Compelling government interest** A test of constitutionality that requires the government to have compelling reasons for passing any law that restricts fundamental rights, such as free speech, or distinguishes between people based on a suspect trait.

**Compensatory damages** A money award equivalent to the actual value of injuries or damages sustained by the aggrieved party.

**Complaint** The pleading made by a plaintiff alleging wrongdoing on the part of the defendant; the document that, when filed with a court, initiates a lawsuit.

**Complete performance** Performance of a contract strictly in accordance with the contract's terms.

**Composition agreement** *See* Creditors' composition agreement

**Computer crime** Any violation of criminal law that involves knowledge of computer technology for its perpetration, investigation, or prosecution.

**Concurrent conditions** Conditions in a contract that must occur or be performed at the same time; they are mutually dependent. No obligations arise until these conditions are simultaneously performed.

**Concurrent jurisdiction** Jurisdiction that exists when two different courts have the power to hear a case. For example, some cases can be heard in either a federal or a state court.

**Concurring opinion** A written opinion outlining the views of a judge or justice to make or emphasize a point that was not made or emphasized in the majority opinion.

**Condition** A possible future event, the occurrence or nonoccurrence of which will trigger the performance of a legal obligation or terminate an existing obligation under a contract.

**Condition precedent** A condition in a contract that must be met before a party's promise becomes absolute.

**Condition subsequent** A condition in a contract that operates to terminate a party's absolute promise to perform.

**Confiscation** A government's taking of privately owned business or personal property without a proper public purpose or an award of just compensation.

**Conforming goods** Goods that conform to contract specifications.

**Conglomerate merger** A merger between firms that do not compete with each other because they are in different markets (as opposed to horizontal and vertical mergers).

**Consequential damages** Special damages that compensate for a loss that is not direct or immediate (for example, lost profits). The special damages must have been reasonably foreseeable at the time the breach or injury occurred in order for the plaintiff to collect them.

**Consideration** Generally, the value given in return for a promise or a performance. The consideration, which must be present to make the contract legally binding, must be something of legally sufficient value and bargained for.

**Constitutional law** Law that is based on the U.S. Constitution and the constitutions of the various states.

**Constructive condition** A condition in a contract that is neither expressed nor implied by the contract but rather is imposed by law for reasons of justice.

**Constructive discharge** A termination of employment brought about by making an employee's working conditions so intolerable that the employee reasonably feels compelled to leave.

**Consumer goods** Goods that are primarily for personal or household use.

**Contingency fee** An attorney's fee that is based on a percentage of the final award received by his or her client as a result of litigation.

**Contract** An agreement that can be enforced in court; formed by two or more parties, each of whom agrees to perform or to refrain from performing some act now or in the future.

**Contractual capacity** The legal ability to enter into contracts. The threshold mental capacity required by law for a party who enters into a contract to be bound by that contract.

**Contribution** *See* Right of contribution

**Contributory negligence** A theory in tort law under which a complaining party's own negligence contributed to or caused his or her injuries. Contributory negligence is an absolute bar to recovery in a minority of jurisdictions.

**Conversion** The wrongful taking, using, or retaining possession of personal property that belongs to another.

**Convertible bond** A bond that can be exchanged for a specified number of shares of common stock under certain conditions.

**Conviction** The outcome of a criminal trial in which the defendant has been found guilty of the crime.

**Cooperative** An association that is organized to provide an economic service to its members (or shareholders). An incorporated cooperative is a nonprofit corporation. It will make distributions of dividends, or profits, to its owners on the basis of their transactions with the cooperative rather than on the basis of the amount of capital they contributed. Examples of cooperatives are consumer purchasing cooperatives, credit cooperatives, and farmers' cooperatives.

**Co-ownership** Joint ownership.

**Copyright** The exclusive right of authors to publish, print, or sell an intellectual production for a statutory period of time. A copyright has the same monopolistic nature as a patent or trademark, but it differs in that it applies exclusively to works of art, literature, and other works of authorship, including computer programs.

**Corporate social responsibility** The concept that corporations can and should act ethically and be accountable to society for their actions.

**Corporation** A legal entity formed in compliance with statutory requirements. The entity is distinct from its shareholders-owners.

**Cost-benefit analysis** A decision-making technique that involves weighing the costs of a given action against the benefits of the action.

**Counterclaim** A claim made by a defendant in a civil lawsuit that in effect sues the plaintiff.

**Counteroffer** An offeree's response to an offer in which the offeree rejects the original offer and at the same time makes a new offer.

**Course of dealing** Prior conduct between parties to a contract that establishes a common basis for their understanding.

**Course of performance** The conduct that occurs under the terms of a particular agreement; such conduct indicates what the parties to an agreement intended it to mean.

**Court of equity** A court that decides controversies and administers justice according to the rules, principles, and precedents of equity.

**Court of law** A court in which the only remedies that could be granted were things of value, such as money damages. In the early English king's courts, courts of law were distinct from courts of equity.

**Covenant against encumbrances** A grantor's assurance that there are no encumbrances on land conveyed—that is, that no third parties have rights to or interests in the land that would diminish its value to the grantee.

**Covenant not to compete** A contractual promise to refrain from competing with another party for a certain period of time and within a certain geographic area. Although covenants not to compete restrain trade, they are commonly found in partnership agreements, business sale agreements, and employment contracts. If they are ancillary to such agreements, covenants not to compete will normally be enforced by the courts unless the time period or geographic area is deemed unreasonable.

**Covenant not to sue** An agreement to substitute a contractual obligation for some other type of legal action based on a valid claim.

**Cover** A buyer or lessee's purchase on the open market of goods to substitute for those promised but never delivered by the seller. Under the Uniform Commercial Code, if the cost of cover exceeds the cost of the contract goods, the buyer or lessee can recover the difference, plus incidental and consequential damages.

**Creditor** A person to whom a debt is owed by another person (the debtor).

**Creditor beneficiary** A third party beneficiary who has rights in a contract made by the debtor and a third person. The terms of the contract obligate the third person to pay the debt owed to the creditor. The creditor beneficiary can enforce the debt against either party.

**Crime** A wrong against society proclaimed in a statute and punishable by society through fines and/or imprisonment—or, in some cases, death.

**Criminal act** *See Actus reus*

**Criminal intent** *See Mens rea*

**Criminal law** Law that defines and governs actions that constitute crimes. Generally, criminal law has to do with wrongful actions committed against society for which society demands redress.

**Cross-examination** The questioning of an opposing witness during a trial.

**Crowdfunding** A cooperative activity in which people network and pool funds and other resources via the Internet to assist a cause (such as disaster relief) or invest in a venture (business).

**Cumulative voting** A method of shareholder voting designed to allow minority shareholders to be represented on the board of directors. With cumulative voting, the number of members of the board to be elected is multiplied by the total number of voting shares held. The result equals the number of votes a shareholder has, and this total can be cast for one or more nominees for director.

**Cure** Under the Uniform Commercial Code, the right of a party who tenders nonconforming performance to correct his or her performance within the contract period.

**Cyber crime** A crime that occurs online, in the virtual community of the Internet, as opposed to the physical world.

**Cyber fraud** Fraud that involves the online theft of credit card information, banking details, and other information for criminal use.

**Cyber mark** A trademark in cyberspace.

**Cyber tort** A tort committed via the Internet.

**Cyberlaw** An informal term used to refer to all laws governing electronic communications and transactions, particularly those conducted via the Internet.

**Cybersquatting** The act of registering a domain name that is the same as, or confusingly similar to, the trademark of another and then offering to sell that domain name back to the trademark owner.

**Cyberterrorist** A hacker whose purpose is to exploit a target computer for a serious impact, such as the corruption of a program to sabotage a business.

# D

**Damages** Money sought as a remedy for a breach of contract or for a tortious act.

**Debenture bond** A bond backed only by the general credit rating of the corporation, plus any assets that can be seized if the corporation allows the debentures to go into default.

**Declaratory judgment** A court's judgment on a justiciable controversy when the plaintiff is in doubt as to his or her legal rights; a binding adjudication of the rights and status of litigants even though no consequential relief is awarded.

**Decree** The judgment of a court of equity.

**Defamation** Any published or publicly spoken false statement that causes injury to another's good name, reputation, or character.

**Default judgment** A judgment entered by a court against a defendant who has failed to appear in court to answer or defend against the plaintiff's claim.

**Defendant** One against whom a lawsuit is brought; the accused person in a criminal proceeding.

**Deficiency judgment** A judgment against a debtor for the amount of a debt remaining unpaid after collateral has been repossessed and sold.

**Delegatee** One to whom contract duties are delegated by another, called the delegator.

**Delegation** The transfer of a contractual duty to a third party. The party delegating the duty (the delegator) to the third party (the delegatee) is still obliged to perform on the contract should the delegatee fail to perform.

**Delegator** One who delegates his or her duties under a contract to another, called the delegatee.

**Delivery** In contract law, one party's act of placing the subject matter of the contract within the other party's possession or control.

**Delivery order** A written order to deliver goods directed to a warehouser, carrier, or other person who, in the ordinary course of business, issues warehouse receipts or bills of lading [UCC 7–102(1)(d)].

*De novo* Anew; afresh; a second time. In a hearing *de novo*, an appellate court hears the case as a court of original jurisdiction—that is, as if the case had not previously been tried and a decision rendered.

**Deposition** The testimony of a party to a lawsuit or a witness taken under oath before a trial.

**Destination contract** A contract in which the seller is required to ship the goods by carrier and deliver them at a particular destination. The seller assumes liability for any losses or damage to the goods until they are tendered at the destination specified in the contract.

**Dilution** With respect to trademarks, a doctrine under which distinctive or famous trademarks are protected from certain unauthorized uses of the marks regardless of a showing of competition or a likelihood of confusion. Congress created a federal cause of action for dilution in 1995 with the passage of the Federal Trademark Dilution Act.

**Direct examination** The examination of a witness by the attorney who calls the witness to the stand to testify on behalf of the attorney's client.

**Directed verdict** *See* Motion for a directed verdict

**Disaffirmance** The legal avoidance, or setting aside, of a contractual obligation.

**Discharge** The termination of an obligation. (1) In contract law, discharge occurs when the parties have fully performed their contractual obligations or when events, conduct of the parties, or operation of the law releases the parties from performance. (2) In bankruptcy proceedings, the extinction of the debtor's dischargeable debts.

**Disclosed principal** A principal whose identity is known to a third party at the time the agent makes a contract with the third party.

**Discovery** A phase in the litigation process during which the opposing parties may obtain information from each other and from third parties prior to trial.

**Disparagement of property** An economically injurious false statement made about another's product or property. A general term for torts that are more specifically referred to as slander of quality or slander of title.

**Disparate-impact discrimination** A form of employment discrimination that results from certain employer practices or procedures that, although not discriminatory on their face, have a discriminatory effect.

**Disparate-treatment discrimination** A form of employment discrimination that results when an employer intentionally discriminates against employees who are members of protected classes.

**Dissenting opinion** A written opinion by a judge or justice who disagrees with the majority opinion.

**Dissolution** The formal disbanding of a partnership or a corporation. It can take place by (1) acts of the partners or, in a corporation, of the shareholders and board of directors; (2) the death of a partner; (3) the expiration of a time period stated in a partnership agreement or a certificate of incorporation; or (4) judicial decree.

**Distributed network** A network that can be used by persons located (distributed) around the country or the globe to share computer files.

**Distribution agreement** A contract between a seller and a distributor of the seller's products setting out the terms and conditions of the distributorship.

**Distributorship** A business arrangement that is established when a manufacturer licenses a dealer to sell its product. An example of a distributorship is an automobile dealership.

**Diversity of citizenship** Under Article III, Section 2, of the Constitution, a basis for federal court jurisdiction over a lawsuit between (1) citizens of different states, (2) a foreign country and citizens of a state or of different states, or (3) citizens of a state and citizens or subjects of a foreign country. The amount in controversy must be more than $75,000 before a federal court can take jurisdiction in such cases.

**Docket** The list of cases entered on a court's calendar and thus scheduled to be heard by the court.

**Document of title** Paper exchanged in the regular course of business that evidences the right to possession of goods (for example, a bill of lading or a warehouse receipt).

**Domain name** The series of letters and symbols used to identify site operators on the Internet; Internet "addresses."

**Domestic corporation** In a given state, a corporation that does business in, and is organized under the laws of, that state.

**Donee beneficiary** A third party beneficiary who has rights under a contract as a direct result of the intention of the contract parties to make a gift to the third party.

**Double jeopardy** A situation occurring when a person is tried twice for the same criminal offense; prohibited by the Fifth Amendment to the Constitution.

**Double taxation** A feature (and disadvantage) of the corporate form of business. Because a corporation is a separate legal entity, corporate profits are taxed by state and federal governments. Dividends are again taxable as ordinary income to the shareholders receiving them.

**Dram shop act** A state statute that imposes liability on the owners of bars and taverns, as well as those who serve alcoholic drinks to the public, for injuries resulting from accidents caused by intoxicated persons when the sellers or servers of alcoholic drinks contributed to the intoxication.

**Due process clause** The provisions of the Fifth and Fourteenth Amendments to the Constitution that guarantee that no person shall be deprived of life, liberty, or property without due process of law. Similar clauses are found in most state constitutions.

**Dumping** The selling of goods in a foreign country at a price below the price charged for the same goods in the domestic market.

**Duress** Unlawful pressure brought to bear on a person, causing the person to perform an act that he or she would not otherwise perform.

**Duty-based ethics** An ethical philosophy rooted in the idea that every person has certain duties to others, including both humans and the planet. Those duties may be derived from religious principles or from other philosophical reasoning.

**Duty of care** The duty of all persons, as established by tort law, to exercise a reasonable amount of care in their dealings with others. Failure to exercise due care, which is normally determined by the "reasonable person standard," constitutes the tort of negligence.

# E

**E-agent** A semiautonomous computer program that is capable of executing specific tasks.

**E-commerce** Business transacted in cyberspace.

**E-contract** A contract that is entered into in cyberspace and is evidenced only by electronic impulses (such as those that make up a computer's memory), rather than, for example, a typewritten form.

**E-evidence** A type of evidence that consists of computer-generated or electronically recorded information, including e-mail, voice mail, spreadsheets, word-processing documents, and other data.

**E-signature** As defined by the Uniform Electronic Transactions Act, "an electronic sound, symbol, or process attached to or logically associated with a record and executed or adopted by a person with the intent to sign the record."

**Early neutral case evaluation** A form of alternative dispute resolution in which a neutral third party evaluates the strengths and weakness of the disputing parties' positions; the evaluator's opinion forms the basis for negotiating a settlement.

**Emancipation** In regard to minors, the act of being freed from parental control; occurs when a child's parent or legal guardian relinquishes the legal right to exercise control over the child. Normally, a minor who leaves home to support himself or herself is considered emancipated.

**Embezzlement** The fraudulent appropriation of money or other property by a person to whom the money or property has been entrusted.

**Employee** A person who works for an employer for a salary or for wages.

**Employer** An individual or business entity that hires employees, pays them salaries or wages, and exercises control over their work.

**Employment at will** A common law doctrine under which either party may terminate an employment relationship at any time for any reason, unless a contract specifies otherwise.

**Employment discrimination** Treating employees or job applicants unequally on the basis of race, color, national origin, religion, gender, age, or disability; prohibited by federal statutes.

**Entrapment** In criminal law, a defense in which the defendant claims that he or she was induced by a public official—usually an undercover agent or police officer—to commit a crime that he or she would otherwise not have committed.

**Entrepreneur** One who initiates and assumes the financial risks of a new enterprise and who undertakes to provide or control its management.

**Entrustment** The transfer of goods to a merchant who deals in goods of that kind and who may transfer those goods and all rights to them to a buyer in the ordinary course of business [UCC 2–403(2)].

**Equal dignity rule** In most states, a rule stating that express authority given to an agent must be in writing if the contract to be made on behalf of the principal is required to be in writing.

**Equal protection clause** The provision in the Fourteenth Amendment to the Constitution that guarantees that no state will "deny to any person within its jurisdiction the equal protection of the laws." This clause mandates that state governments treat similarly situated individuals in a similar manner.

**Equitable maxim** A general proposition or principle of law having to do with fairness (equity) that influences judicial decisions.

**Establishment clause** The provision in the First Amendment to the U.S. Constitution that prohibits Congress from creating any law "respecting an establishment of religion."

**Estop** To bar, impede, or preclude.

**Estoppel** The principle that a party's own acts prevent him or her from claiming a right to the detriment of another who was entitled to and did rely on those acts. *See also* Agency by estoppel; Promissory estoppel

**Ethical reasoning** A reasoning process in which an individual links his or her moral convictions or ethical standards to the particular situation at hand.

**Ethics** Moral principles and values applied to social behavior.

**Evidence** Proof offered at trial—in the form of testimony, documents, records, exhibits, objects, and so on—for the purpose of convincing the court or jury of the truth of a contention.

**Exclusionary rule** In criminal procedure, a rule under which any evidence that is obtained in violation of the accused's constitutional rights guaranteed by the Fourth, Fifth, and Sixth Amendments, as well as any evidence derived from illegally obtained evidence, will not be admissible in court.

**Exclusive agency** An agency in which a principal grants an agent an exclusive territory and does not allow another agent to compete in that territory.

**Exclusive distributorship** A distributorship in which the seller and the distributor of the seller's products agree that the distributor has the exclusive right to distribute the seller's products in a certain geographic area.

**Exclusive jurisdiction** Jurisdiction that exists when a case can be heard only in a particular court or type of court, such as a federal court or a state court.

**Exculpatory clause** A clause that releases a contractual party from liability in the event of monetary or physical injury, no matter who is at fault.

**Executed contract** A contract that has been completely performed by both parties.

**Executive agency** An administrative agency within the executive branch of government. At the federal level, executive agencies are those within the cabinet departments.

**Executory contract** A contract that has not as yet been fully performed.

**Export** To sell products to buyers located in other countries.

**Express authority** Authority expressly given by one party to another. In agency law, an agent has express authority to act for a principal if both parties agree, orally or in writing, that an agency relationship exists in which the agent had the power (authority) to act in the place of, and on behalf of, the principal.

**Express contract** A contract in which the terms of the agreement are fully and explicitly stated in words, oral or written.

**Express warranty** A seller's or lessor's oral or written promise, ancillary to an underlying sales or lease agreement, as to the quality, description, or performance of the goods being sold or leased.

**Extrinsic evidence** Evidence that relates to a contract but is not contained within the document itself, such as the testimony of parties and witnesses, or additional agreements or communi-

cations. A court may consider extrinsic evidence only when a contract term is ambiguous and the evidence does not contradict the express terms of the contract.

# F

**F.A.S.** Free alongside. A contract term that requires the seller, at his or her own expense and risk, to deliver the goods alongside the ship before risk passes to the buyer.

**F.O.B.** Free on board. A contract term that indicates that the selling price of the goods includes transportation costs (and that the seller carries the risk of loss) to the specific F.O.B. place named in the contract. The place can be either the place of initial shipment (for example, the seller's city or place of business) or the place of destination (for example, the buyer's city or place of business).

**Family limited liability partnership (FLLP)** A limited liability partnership (LLP) in which the majority of the partners are persons related to each other, essentially as spouses, parents, grandparents, siblings, cousins, nephews, or nieces. A person acting in a fiduciary capacity for persons so related could also be a partner. All of the partners must be natural persons or persons acting in a fiduciary capacity for the benefit of natural persons.

**Federal form of government** A system of government in which the states form a union and the sovereign power is divided between a central government and the member states.

**Federal question** A question that pertains to the U.S. Constitution, acts of Congress, or treaties. A federal question provides a basis for federal jurisdiction.

**Federal Rules of Civil Procedure (FRCP)** The rules controlling procedural matters in civil trials brought before the federal district courts.

**Felony** A crime—such as arson, murder, rape, or robbery—that carries the most severe sanctions, usually ranging from one year in a state or federal prison to the forfeiture of one's life.

**Fiduciary** As a noun, a person having a duty created by his or her undertaking to act primarily for another's benefit in matters connected with the undertaking. As an adjective, a relationship founded on trust and confidence.

**Fiduciary duty** The duty, imposed on a fiduciary by virtue of his or her position, to act primarily for another's benefit.

**Filtering software** A computer program that includes a pattern through which data are passed. When designed to block access to certain Web sites, the pattern blocks the retrieval of a site whose URL or key words are on a list within the program.

**Financial institution** An organization authorized to do business under state or federal laws relating to financial institutions, such as banks, savings and loan associations, and credit unions.

**Firm offer** An offer (by a merchant) that is irrevocable without consideration for a period of time (not longer than three months). A firm offer by a merchant must be in writing and must be signed by the offeror.

**Fitness for a particular purpose** *See* Implied warranty of fitness for a particular purpose

***Force majeure*** (pronounced mah-*zhure*) **clause** A provision in a contract stipulating that certain unforeseen events—such as war, political upheavals, acts of God, or other events—will excuse a party from liability for nonperformance of contractual obligations.

**Foreign corporation** In a given state, a corporation that does business in the state without being incorporated therein.

**Foreseeable risk** In negligence law, the risk of harm or injury to another that a person of ordinary intelligence and prudence should have reasonably anticipated or foreseen when undertaking an action or refraining from undertaking an action.

**Forgery** The fraudulent making or altering of any writing in a way that changes the legal rights and liabilities of another.

**Formal contract** A contract that by law requires a specific form, such as being executed under seal, to be valid.

**Forum** A jurisdiction, court, or place in which disputes are litigated and legal remedies are sought.

**Forum-selection clause** A provision in a contract designating the court, jurisdiction, or tribunal that will decide any disputes arising under the contract.

**Franchise** Any arrangement in which the owner of a trademark, trade name, or copyright licenses another to use that trademark, trade name, or copyright, under specified conditions or limitations, in the selling of goods and services.

**Franchise tax** A state or local government tax on the right and privilege of carrying on a business in the form of a corporation.

**Franchisee** One receiving a license to use another's (the franchisor's) trademark, trade name, or copyright in the sale of goods and services.

**Franchisor** One licensing another (the franchisee) to use his or her trademark, trade name, or copyright in the sale of goods or services.

**Fraud** Any misrepresentation, either by misstatement or omission of a material fact, knowingly made with the intention of deceiving another and on which a reasonable person would and does rely to his or her detriment.

**Fraud in the execution** In the law of negotiable instruments, a type of fraud that occurs when a person is deceived into signing a negotiable instrument, believing that he or she is signing something else (such as a receipt); also called fraud in the inception. Fraud in the execution is a universal defense to payment on a negotiable instrument.

**Fraudulent misrepresentation (fraud)** Any misrepresentation, either by misstatement or omission of a material fact, knowingly made with the intention of deceiving another and on which a reasonable person would and does rely to his or her detriment.

**Free exercise clause** The provision in the First Amendment to the U.S. Constitution that prohibits Congress from making any law "prohibiting the free exercise" of religion.

**Frustration of purpose** A court-created doctrine under which a party to a contract will be relieved of his or her duty to perform when the objective purpose for performance no longer exists (due to reasons beyond that party's control).

**Full faith and credit clause** A clause in Article IV, Section 1, of the Constitution that provides that "Full Faith and Credit shall be given in each State to the public Acts, Records, and Judicial Proceedings of every other State." The clause ensures that rights established under deeds, wills, contracts, and the like in one state will be honored by the other states and that any judicial decision with respect to such property rights will be honored and enforced in all states.

**Full warranty** A warranty as to full performance covering generally both labor and materials.

## G

**General jurisdiction** Exists when a court's subject-matter jurisdiction is not restricted. A court of general jurisdiction normally can hear any type of case.

**General partner** In a limited partnership, a partner who assumes responsibility for the management of the partnership and liability for all partnership debts.

**General partnership** *See* Partnership

**Good faith** Under the Uniform Commercial Code, good faith means honesty in fact; with regard to merchants, good faith means honesty in fact *and* the observance of reasonable commercial standards of fair dealing in the trade.

**Good faith purchaser** A purchaser who buys without notice of any circumstance that would put a person of ordinary prudence on inquiry as to whether the seller has valid title to the goods being sold.

**Good Samaritan statute** A state statute that provides that persons who rescue or provide emergency services to others in peril—unless they do so recklessly, thus causing further harm—cannot be sued for negligence.

**Goodwill** In the business context, the valuable reputation of a business viewed as an intangible asset.

**Grand jury** A group of citizens called to decide, after hearing the state's evidence, whether a reasonable basis (probable cause) exists for believing that a crime has been committed and whether a trial ought to be held.

**Grantee** One to whom a grant (of land or property, for example) is made.

**Grantor** A person who makes a grant, such as a transferor of property or the creator of a trust.

## H

**Habitability** *See* Implied warranty of habitability

**Hacker** A person who uses one computer to break into another. Professional computer programmers refer to such persons as "crackers."

**Hearsay** An oral or written statement made out of court that is later offered in court by a witness (not the person who made the statement) to prove the truth of the matter asserted in the statement. Hearsay is generally inadmissible as evidence.

**Historical school** A school of legal thought that emphasizes the evolutionary process of law and that looks to the past to discover what the principles of contemporary law should be.

**Holding company** A company whose business activity is holding shares in another company.

**Home equity loan** A loan in which the lender accepts a person's home equity (the portion of the home's value that is paid off) as collateral, which can be seized if the loan is not repaid on time. Borrowers often take out home equity loans to finance the renovation of the property or to pay off debt that carries a higher interest rate, such as credit-card debt.

**Homeowners' insurance** Insurance that protects a homeowner's property against damage from storms, fire, and other hazards. Lenders may require that a borrower carry homeowners' insurance on mortgaged property.

**Hot-cargo agreement** An agreement in which employers voluntarily agree with unions not to handle, use, or deal in nonunion-produced goods of other employers; a type of secondary boycott explicitly prohibited by the Labor-Management Reporting and Disclosure Act of 1959.

## I

**I-551 Alien Registration Receipt** Proof that a noncitizen has obtained permanent residency in the United States; the so-called green card.

**I-9 verification** A form from the Department of Homeland Security, U.S. Citizenship and Immigration Services, used for employment eligibility verification; a form that documents that each new employee is authorized to work in the United States

**Identification** In a sale of goods, the express designation of the specific goods provided for in the contract.

**Identity theft** The act of stealing another's identifying information—such as a name, date of birth, or Social Security number—and using that information to access the victim's financial resources.

**Illusory promise** A promise made without consideration, which renders the promise unenforceable.

**Immunity** A status of being exempt, or free, from certain duties or requirements. In criminal law, the state may grant an accused person immunity from prosecution—or agree to prosecute for a lesser offense—if the accused person agrees to give the state information that would assist the state in prosecuting other individuals for crimes. In tort law, freedom from liability for defamatory speech. *See also* Privilege

**Impeach** To challenge the credibility of a person's testimony or attempt to discredit a party or witness.

**Implied authority** Authority that is created not by an explicit oral or written agreement but by implication. In agency law, implied authority (of the agent) can be conferred by custom, inferred from the position the agent occupies, or implied by virtue of being reasonably necessary to carry out express authority.

**Implied warranty** A warranty that the law derives by implication or inference from the nature of the transaction or the relative situation or circumstances of the parties.

**Implied warranty of fitness for a particular purpose** A warranty that goods sold or leased are fit for a particular purpose. The warranty arises when any seller or lessor knows the particular purpose for which a buyer or lessee will use the goods and knows that the buyer or lessee is relying on the skill and judgment of the seller or lessor to select suitable goods.

**Implied warranty of merchantability** A warranty that goods being sold or leased are reasonably fit for the ordinary purpose for which they are sold or leased, are properly packaged and labeled, and are of fair quality. The warranty automatically arises in every sale or lease of goods made by a merchant who deals in goods of the kind sold or leased.

**Implied contract** A contract formed in whole or in part from the conduct of the parties (as opposed to an express contract). Also known as implied-in-fact contract.

**Impossibility of performance** A doctrine under which a party to a contract is relieved of his or her duty to perform when performance becomes impossible or totally impracticable (through no fault of either party).

**In personam jurisdiction** Court jurisdiction over the "person" involved in a legal action; personal jurisdiction.

**In rem jurisdiction** Court jurisdiction over a defendant's property.

**Incidental beneficiary** A third party who incidentally benefits from a contract but whose benefit was not the reason the contract was formed; an incidental beneficiary has no rights in a contract and cannot sue to have the contract enforced.

**Indemnify** To compensate or reimburse another for losses or expenses incurred.

**Independent contractor** One who works for, and receives payment from, an employer but whose working conditions and methods are not controlled by the employer. An independent contractor is not an employee but may be an agent.

**Independent regulatory agency** An administrative agency that is not considered part of the government's executive branch and is not subject to the authority of the president. Independent agency officials cannot be removed without cause.

**Indictment** (pronounced in-*dyte*-ment) A charge by a grand jury that a reasonable basis (probable cause) exists for believing that a crime has been committed and that a trial should be held.

**Informal contract** A contract that does not require a specified form or formality in order to be valid.

**Information** A formal accusation or complaint (without an indictment) issued in certain types of actions (usually criminal actions involving lesser crimes) by a law officer, such as a magistrate.

**Information return** A tax return submitted by a partnership that reports the income earned by the business. The partnership as an entity does not pay taxes on the income received by the partnership. A partner's profit from the partnership (whether distributed or not) is taxed as individual income to the individual partner.

**Infringement** A violation of another's legally recognized right. The term is commonly used with reference to the invasion by one party of another party's rights in a patent, trademark, or copyright.

**Injunction** A court decree ordering a person to do or refrain from doing a certain act or activity.

**Innocent misrepresentation** A false statement of fact or an act made in good faith that deceives and causes harm or injury to another.

**Insolvent** Under the Uniform Commercial Code, a term describing a person who ceases to pay "his debts in the ordinary course of business or cannot pay his debts as they become due or is insolvent within the meaning of federal bankruptcy law" [UCC 1–201(23)].

**Installment contract** Under the Uniform Commercial Code, a contract that requires or authorizes delivery in two or more separate lots to be accepted and paid for separately.

**Intangible property** Property that is incapable of being apprehended by the senses (such as by sight or touch); intellectual property is an example of intangible property.

**Integrated contract** A written contract that constitutes the final expression of the parties' agreement. If a contract is integrated, evidence extraneous to the contract that contradicts or alters the meaning of the contract in any way is inadmissible.

**Intellectual property** Property resulting from intellectual, creative processes. Patents, trademarks, and copyrights are examples of intellectual property.

**Intended beneficiary** A third party for whose benefit a contract is formed; an intended beneficiary can sue the promisor if such a contract is breached.

**Intentional tort** A wrongful act knowingly committed.

**International law** The law that governs relations among nations. International customs and treaties are generally considered to be two of the most important sources of international law.

**International organization** In international law, a term that generally refers to an organization composed mainly of nations and usually established by treaty. The United States is a member of more than one hundred multilateral and bilateral orga-

nizations, including at least twenty through the United Nations.

**Internet service provider (ISP)** A business or organization that offers users access to the Internet and related services.

**Interrogatories** A series of written questions for which written answers are prepared and then signed under oath by a party to a lawsuit, usually with the assistance of the party's attorney.

**Invitee** A person who, either expressly or impliedly, is privileged to enter onto another's land. The inviter owes the invitee (for example, a customer in a store) the duty to exercise reasonable care to protect the invitee from harm.

**Irrevocable offer** An offer that cannot be revoked or recalled by the offeror without liability. A merchant's firm offer is an example of an irrevocable offer.

# J

**Joint and several liability** In partnership law, a doctrine under which a plaintiff may sue, and collect a judgment from, one or more of the partners separately (severally, or individually) or all of the partners together (jointly). This is true even if one of the partners sued did not participate in, ratify, or know about whatever gave rise to the cause of action.

**Joint liability** Shared liability. In partnership law, partners incur joint liability for partnership obligations and debts. For example, if a third party sues a partner on a partnership debt, the partner has the right to insist that the other partners be sued with him or her.

**Joint stock company** A hybrid form of business organization that combines characteristics of a corporation (shareholder-owners, management by directors and officers of the company, and perpetual existence) and a partnership (it is formed by agreement, not statute; property is usually held in the names of the members; and the shareholders have personal liability for business debts). Usually, the joint stock company is regarded as a partnership for tax and other legally related purposes.

**Joint venture** A joint undertaking of a specific commercial enterprise by an association of persons.

A joint venture is normally not a legal entity and is treated like a partnership for federal income tax purposes.

**Judgment** The final order or decision resulting from a legal action.

**Judgment rate of interest** A rate of interest fixed by statute that is applied to a monetary judgment from the moment the judgment is awarded by a court until the judgment is paid or terminated.

**Judicial process** The procedures relating to, or connected with, the administration of justice through the judicial system.

**Judicial review** The process by which courts decide on the constitutionality of legislative enactments and actions of the executive branch.

**Jurisdiction** The authority of a court to hear and decide a specific action.

**Jurisprudence** The science or philosophy of law.

**Justiciable controversy** A controversy that is not hypothetical or academic but real and substantial. A requirement that must be satisfied before a court will hear a case.

# K

**King's court** A medieval English court. The king's courts, or *curiae regis,* were established by the Norman conquerors of England. The body of law that developed in these courts was common to the entire English realm and thus became known as the common law.

# L

**Laches** The equitable doctrine that bars a party's right to legal action if the party has neglected for an unreasonable length of time to act on his or her rights.

**Larceny** The wrongful taking and carrying away of another person's personal property with the intent to permanently deprive the owner of the property. Some states classify larceny as either grand or petit, depending on the property's value.

**Latent defects** A defect that is not obvious or cannot readily be ascertained.

**Law** A body of enforceable rules governing relationships among individuals and between individuals and their society.

**Lawsuit** The litigation process.

**Lease agreement** In regard to the lease of goods, an agreement in which one person (the lessor) agrees to transfer the right to the possession and use of property to another person (the lessee) in exchange for rental payments.

**Legal positivism** A school of legal thought centered on the assumption that there is no law higher than the laws created by a national government. Laws must be obeyed, even if they are unjust, to prevent anarchy.

**Legal positivists** Adherents to the positivist school of legal thought who believe that there can be no higher law than a nation's positive law—law created by a particular society at a particular point in time. In contrast to the natural law school, the positivist school maintains that there are no "natural" rights. Rights come into existence only when there is a sovereign power (government) to confer and enforce those rights.

**Legal rate of interest** A rate of interest fixed by statute as either the maximum rate of interest allowed by law or a rate of interest applied when the parties to a contract intend, but do not fix, an interest rate in the contract. In the latter case, the rate is frequently the same as the statutory maximum rate permitted.

**Legal realism** A school of legal thought that was popular in the 1920s and 1930s and that challenged many existing jurisprudential assumptions, particularly the assumption that subjective elements play no part in judicial reasoning. Legal realists generally advocated a less abstract and more pragmatic approach to the law, an approach that would take into account customary practices and the circumstances in which transactions take place. The school left a lasting imprint on American jurisprudence.

**Legal reasoning** The process of reasoning by which a judge harmonizes his or her decision with the judicial decisions of previous cases.

**Letter of credit** A written instrument, usually issued by a bank on behalf of a customer or other person, in which the issuer promises to honor drafts or other demands for payment by third persons in accordance with the terms of the instrument.

**Liability** Any actual or potential legal obligation, duty, debt, or responsibility.

**Libel** Defamation in writing or other form (such as in a digital recording) having the quality of permanence.

**License** In the context of intellectual property, a contract permitting the use of a trademark, copyright, patent, or trade secret for certain purposes. In the context of real property, a revocable right or privilege of a person to come on another person's land.

**Licensee** One who receives a license to use, or enter onto, another's property.

**Limited jurisdiction** Exists when a court's subject-matter jurisdiction is limited. Bankruptcy courts and probate courts are examples of courts with limited jurisdiction.

**Limited liability** Exists when the liability of the owners of a business is limited to the amount of their investments in the firm.

**Limited liability company (LLC)** A hybrid form of business enterprise that offers the limited liability of the corporation but the tax advantages of a partnership.

**Limited liability limited partnership (LLLP)** A type of limited partnership. The difference between a limited partnership and an LLLP is that the liability of the general partner in an LLLP is the same as the liability of the limited partner. That is, the liability of all partners is limited to the amount of their investments in the firm.

**Limited liability partnership (LLP)** A form of partnership that allows professionals to enjoy the tax benefits of a partnership while limiting their personal liability for the malpractice of other partners.

**Limited partner** In a limited partnership, a partner who contributes capital to the partnership but has no right to participate in the management and operation of the business. The limited partner assumes no liability for partnership debts beyond the capital contributed.

**Limited partnership (LP)** A partnership consisting of one or more general partners (who manage the business and are liable to the full extent of their personal assets for debts of the partnership) and one or more limited partners (who contribute only assets and are liable only to the extent of their contributions).

**Limited warranty** A written warranty that fails to meet one or more of the minimum standards for a full warranty.

**Liquidated damages** An amount, stipulated in the contract, that the parties to a contract believe to be a reasonable estimation of the damages that will occur in the event of a breach.

**Liquidated debt** A debt that is due and certain in amount.

**Litigant** A party to a lawsuit.

**Litigation** The process of resolving a dispute through the court system.

**Lockout** Occurs when an employer shuts down to prevent employees from working typically because it cannot reach a collective bargaining agreement with the union.

**Long arm statute** A state statute that permits a state to obtain personal jurisdiction over nonresident defendants. A defendant must have "minimum contacts" with that state for the statute to apply.

# M

**Mailbox rule** A rule providing that an acceptance of an offer becomes effective on dispatch. Acceptance takes effect, thus completing formation of the contract, at the time the offeree sends or delivers the communication via the mode expressly or impliedly authorized by the offeror.

**Main purpose rule** A rule of contract law under which an exception to the Statute of Frauds is made if the main purpose in accepting secondary liability under a contract is to secure a personal benefit. If this situation exists, the contract need not be in writing to be enforceable.

**Majority** *See* Age of majority

**Majority opinion** A court's written opinion, outlining the views of the majority of the judges or justices deciding the case.

**Malpractice** Professional misconduct or the failure to exercise the requisite degree of skill as a professional. Negligence—the failure to exercise due care—on the part of a professional, such as a physician or an attorney, is commonly referred to as malpractice.

**Malware** Malicious software programs designed to disrupt or harm a computer, network, smartphone, or other device.

**Manufacturing or processing-plant franchise** A franchise that is created when the franchisor transmits to the franchisee the essential ingredients or formula to make a particular product. The franchisee then markets the product either at wholesale or at retail in accordance with the franchisor's standards. Examples of this type of franchise are Coca-Cola and other soft-drink bottling companies.

**Market-share test** The primary measure of monopoly power. A firm's market share is the percentage of a market that the firm controls.

**Material alteration** An alteration to a negotiable instrument that changes the contract terms between two parties in any way.

**Material fact** A fact to which a reasonable person would attach importance in determining his or her course of action. In regard to tender offers, for example, a fact is material if there is a substantial likelihood that a reasonable shareholder would consider it important in deciding how to vote.

**Mechanic's lien** A statutory lien on the real property of another, created to ensure payment for work performed and materials furnished in the repair or improvement of real property, such as a building.

**Mediation** A method of settling disputes outside of court by using the services of a neutral third party, called a mediator. The mediator acts as a communicating agent between the parties and suggests ways in which the parties can resolve their dispute.

**Member** The term used to designate a person who has an ownership interest in a limited liability company.

**Mens rea** (pronounced *mehns ray*-uh) Criminal intent. A wrongful mental state, which is as necessary as a wrongful act, to establish criminal liability. What constitutes a guilty mental state varies according to the wrongful action. Thus, for murder, the *mens rea* is the intent to take a life. For theft, the *mens rea* must involve both the knowledge that the property belongs to another and the intent to deprive the owner of it.

**Merchant** A person who is engaged in the purchase and sale of goods. Under the Uniform Commercial Code, a person who deals in goods of the kind involved in the sales contract; for further definitions, see UCC 2–104.

**Meta tags** Words inserted into a Web site's keywords field to increase the site's appearance in search engine results.

**Metadata** Data that are automatically recorded by electronic devices and provide information about who created a file and when, and who accessed, modified, or transmitted it on their hard drives. Can be described as data about data.

**Minimum-contacts requirement** The requirement that before a state court can exercise jurisdiction over a foreign corporation, the foreign corporation must have sufficient contacts with the state. A foreign corporation that has its home office in the state or that has manufacturing plants in the state meets this requirement.

**Minimum wage** The lowest wage, either by government regulation or union contract, that an employer may pay an hourly worker.

**Mini-trial** A private proceeding in which each party to a dispute argues its position before the other side and vice versa. A neutral third party may be present and act as an adviser if the parties fail to reach an agreement.

**Mirror image rule** A common law rule that requires, for a valid contractual agreement, that the terms of the offeree's acceptance adhere exactly to the terms of the offeror's offer.

**Misdemeanor** A lesser crime than a felony, punishable by a fine or imprisonment for up to one year in other than a state or federal penitentiary.

**Misrepresentation** A false statement of fact or an action that deceives and causes harm or injury to another. *See also* Fraudulent misrepresentation (fraud); Innocent misrepresentation

**Mitigation of damages** A rule requiring a plaintiff to have done whatever was reasonable to minimize the damages caused by the defendant.

**Money laundering** Falsely reporting income that has been obtained through criminal activity as income obtained through a legitimate business enterprise—in effect, "laundering" the "dirty money."

**Moral minimum** The minimum degree of ethical behavior expected of a business firm, which is usually defined as compliance with the law.

**Motion** A procedural request or application presented by an attorney to the court on behalf of a client.

**Motion for a directed verdict** In a state court, a party's request that the judge enter a judgment in her or his favor before the case is submitted to a jury because the other party has not presented sufficient evidence to support the claim. The federal courts refer to this request as a *motion for judgment as a matter of law.*

**Motion for a new trial** A motion asserting that the trial was so fundamentally flawed (because of error, newly discovered evidence, prejudice, or other reason) that a new trial is necessary to prevent a miscarriage of justice.

**Motion for judgment as a matter of law** In a federal court, a party's request that the judge enter a judgment in her or his favor before the case is submitted to a jury because the other party has not presented sufficient evidence to support the claim. The state courts refer to this request as a *motion for a directed verdict.*

**Motion for judgment *n.o.v.*** A motion requesting the court to grant judgment in favor of the party making the motion on the ground that the jury verdict against him or her was unreasonable and erroneous.

**Motion for judgment on the pleadings** A motion by either party to a lawsuit at the close of the pleadings requesting the court to decide the issue solely on the pleadings without proceeding to trial. The motion will be granted only if no facts are in dispute.

**Motion for summary judgment** A motion requesting the court to enter a judgment without proceeding to trial. The motion can be based on evidence outside the pleadings and will be granted only if no facts are in dispute.

**Motion to dismiss** A pleading in which a defendant asserts that the plaintiff's claim fails to state a cause of action (that is, has no basis in law) or that there are other grounds on which a suit should be dismissed.

**Municipal court** A city or community court with criminal jurisdiction over traffic violations and, less frequently, with civil jurisdiction over other minor matters.

**Mutual rescission** An agreement between the parties to cancel their contract, releasing the parties from further obligations under the contract. The object of the agreement is to restore the parties to the positions they would have occupied had no contract ever been formed. *See also* Rescission

# N

**National law** Law that pertains to a particular nation (as opposed to international law).

**Natural law** The belief that government and the legal system should reflect universal moral and ethical principles that are inherent in human nature. The natural law school is the oldest and one of the most significant schools of legal thought.

**Necessaries** Necessities required for life, such as food, shelter, clothing, and medical attention; may include whatever is believed to be necessary to maintain a person's standard of living or financial and social status.

**Negative amortization** Occurs when the payment made by the borrower is less than the interest due on the loan and the difference is added to the principal. The result of negative amortization is that the balance owed on the loan increases rather than decreases over time.

**Negligence** The failure to exercise the standard of care that a reasonable person would exercise in similar circumstances.

**Negligence *per se*** An act (or failure to act) in violation of a statutory requirement.

**Negligent misrepresentation** Any manifestation through words or conduct that amounts to an untrue statement of fact made in circumstances in which a reasonable and prudent person would not have done (or failed to do) that which led to the misrepresentation. A representation made with an honest belief in its truth may still be negligent due to (1) a lack of reasonable care in ascertaining the facts, (2) the manner of expression, or (3) the absence of the skill or competence required by a particular business or profession.

**Nominal damages** A small monetary award (often one dollar) granted to a plaintiff when no actual damage was suffered or when the plaintiff is unable to show such loss with sufficient certainty.

**Nonconforming goods** Goods that do not conform to contract specifications.

**No-par shares** Corporate shares that have no face value—that is, no specific dollar amount is printed on their face.

**Normal trade relations (NTR) status** A status granted through an international treaty by which each member nation must treat other members at least as well as it treats the country that receives its most favorable treatment. This status was formerly known as most-favored-nation status.

**Notary public** A public official authorized to attest to the authenticity of signatures.

**Novation** The substitution, by agreement, of a new contract for an old one, with the rights under the old one being terminated. Typically, there is a substitution of a new person who is responsible for the contract and the removal of an original party's rights and duties under the contract.

# O

**Objective theory of contracts** A theory under which the intent to form a contract will be judged by outward, objective facts (what the party said when entering into the contract, how the party acted or appeared, and the circumstances surrounding the transaction) as interpreted by a reasonable person, rather than by the party's own secret, subjective intentions.

**Obligee** One to whom an obligation is owed.

**Obligor** One who owes an obligation to another.

**Offer** A promise or commitment to perform or refrain from performing some specified act in the future.

**Offeree** A person to whom an offer is made.

**Offeror** A person who makes an offer.

**Online dispute resolution (ODR)** The resolution of disputes with the assistance of organizations that offer dispute-resolution services via the Internet.

**Opening statement** A statement made to the jury at the beginning of a trial by a party's attorney, prior to the presentation of evidence. The attorney briefly outlines the evidence that will be offered and the legal theory that will be pursued.

**Operating agreement** In a limited liability company, an agreement in which the members set forth the details of how the business will be managed and operated.

**Opinion** A statement by the court expressing the reasons for its decision in a case.

**Option contract** A contract under which the offeror cannot revoke his or her offer for a stipulated time period and the offeree can accept or reject the offer during this period without fear that the offer will be made to another person. The offeree must give consideration for the option (the irrevocable offer) to be enforceable.

**Ordinance** A law passed by a local governing unit, such as a municipality or a county.

**Original jurisdiction** Courts having original jurisdiction are courts of the first instance, or trial courts—that is, courts in which lawsuits begin, trials take place, and evidence is presented.

**Outcome-based ethics** An ethical philosophy that focuses on the impacts of a decision on society or on key stakeholders.

**Output contract** An agreement in which a seller agrees to sell and a buyer agrees to buy all or up to a stated amount of what the seller produces.

# P

**Parol evidence** A term that originally meant "oral evidence," but that has come to refer to any negotiations or agreements made prior to a contract or any contemporaneous oral agreements made by the parties.

**Parol evidence rule** A substantive rule of contracts under which a court will not receive into evidence the parties' prior negotiations, prior agreements, or contemporaneous oral agreements if that evidence contradicts or varies the terms of the parties' written contract.

**Partially disclosed principal** A principal whose identity is unknown by a third person, but the third person knows that the agent is or may be acting for a principal at the time the agent and the third person form a contract.

**Partner** A co-owner of a partnership.

**Partnering agreement** An agreement between a seller and a buyer who frequently do business with each other on the terms and conditions that will apply to all subsequently formed electronic contracts.

**Partnership** An agreement by two or more persons to carry on, as co-owners, a business for profit.

**Partnership by estoppel** A judicially created partnership that may, at the court's discretion, be imposed for purposes of fairness. The court can prevent those who present themselves as partners (but who are not) from escaping liability if a third person relies on an alleged partnership in good faith and is harmed as a result.

**Par-value shares** Corporate shares that have a specific face value, or formal cash-in value, written on them, such as one dollar.

**Pass-through entity** Any entity that does not have its income taxed at the level of that entity; examples are partnerships, S corporations, and limited liability companies.

**Past consideration** Something given or some act done in the past, which cannot ordinarily be consideration for a later bargain.

**Patent** A government grant that gives an inventor the exclusive right or privilege to make, use, or sell his or her invention for a limited time period. The word *patent* usually refers to some invention and designates either the instrument by which patent rights are evidenced or the patent itself.

**Peer-to-peer (P2P) networking** The sharing of resources (such as files, hard drives, and processing styles) among multiple computers without necessarily requiring a central network server.

**Penalty** A sum inserted into a contract, not as a measure of compensation for its breach but rather as punishment for a default. The agreement as to the amount will not be enforced, and recovery will be limited to actual damages.

**Per curiam** By the whole court; a court opinion written by the court as a whole instead of being authored by a judge or justice.

**Per se** A Latin term meaning "in itself" or "by itself."

**Perfect tender rule** A common law rule under which a seller was required to deliver to the buyer goods that conformed perfectly to the requirements stipulated in the sales contract. A tender of nonconforming goods would automatically constitute a breach of contract. Under the Uniform Commercial Code, the rule has been greatly modified.

**Performance** In contract law, the fulfillment of one's duties arising under a contract with another; the normal way of discharging one's contractual obligations.

**Personal jurisdiction** *See In personam* jurisdiction

**Personalty** Personal property.

**Persuasive authority** Any legal authority or source of law that a court may look to for guidance but need not follow when making its decision.

**Petitioner** In equity practice, a party that initiates a lawsuit.

**Petty offense** In criminal law, the least serious kind of criminal offense, such as a traffic or building-code violation.

**Phishing** Online fraud in which criminals pretend to be legitimate companies by using e-mails or malicious Web sites that trick individuals and companies into providing useful information, such as bank account numbers, Social Security numbers, and credit card numbers.

**Pierce the corporate veil** To disregard the corporate entity, which limits the liability of shareholders, and hold the shareholders personally liable for a corporate obligation.

**Plaintiff** One who initiates a lawsuit.

**Plea** In criminal law, a defendant's allegation, in response to the charges brought against him or her, of guilt or innocence.

**Plea bargaining** The process by which a criminal defendant and the prosecutor in a criminal case work out a mutually satisfactory disposition of the case, subject to court approval; usually involves the defendant's pleading guilty to a lesser offense in return for a lighter sentence.

**Pleadings** Statements made by the plaintiff and the defendant in a lawsuit that detail the facts, charges, and defenses involved in the litigation; the complaint and answer are part of the pleadings.

**Plurality opinion** A court opinion that is joined by the largest number of the judges or justices hearing the case, but less than half of the total number.

**Police powers** Powers possessed by states as part of their inherent sovereignty. These powers may be exercised to protect or promote the public order, health, safety, morals, and general welfare.

**Positive law** The body of conventional, or written, law of a particular society at a particular point in time.

**Positivist school** A school of legal thought whose adherents believe that there can be no higher law than a nation's positive law—the body of conventional, or written, law of a particular society at a particular time.

**Power of attorney** A written document, which is usually notarized, authorizing another to act as one's agent; can be special (permitting the agent to do specified acts only) or general (permitting the agent to transact all business for the principal).

**Preauthorized transfer** A transfer of funds authorized in advance to recur at substantially regular intervals. The terms and procedures for preauthorized electronic fund transfers through certain financial institutions are subject to the Electronic Fund Transfer Act.

**Precedent** A court decision that furnishes an example or authority for deciding subsequent cases involving identical or similar facts.

**Predominant-factor test** A test courts use to determine whether a contract is primarily for the sale of goods or for the sale of services.

**Preemption** A doctrine under which certain federal laws preempt, or take precedence over, conflicting state or local laws.

**Preferred stock** Classes of stock that have priority over common stock as to payment of dividends and distribution of assets on the corporation's dissolution.

**Prejudgment interest** Interest that accrues on the amount of a court judgment from the time of the filing of a lawsuit to the court's issuance of a judgment.

**Preliminary hearing** An initial hearing used in many felony cases to establish whether it is proper to detain the defendant. A magistrate reviews the evidence and decides if there is probable cause to believe that the defendant committed the crime with which he or she has been charged.

**Prenuptial agreement** An agreement made before marriage that defines each partner's ownership rights in the other partner's property. Prenuptial agreements must be in writing to be enforceable.

**Preponderance of the evidence** A standard in civil law cases under which the plaintiff must convince the court that, based on the evidence presented by both parties, it is more likely than not that the plaintiff's allegation is true.

**Pretrial conference** A conference, scheduled before the trial begins, between the judge and the attorneys litigating the suit. The parties may settle the dispute, clarify the issues, schedule discovery, and so on during the conference.

**Pretrial motion** A written or oral application to a court for a ruling or order, made before trial.

***Prima facie* case** A case in which the plaintiff has produced sufficient evidence of his or her conclusion that the case can go to a jury; a case in which the evidence compels the plaintiff's conclusion if the defendant produces no evidence to disprove it.

**Primary liability** In negotiable instruments law, absolute responsibility for paying a negotiable instrument. Makers and acceptors are primarily liable.

**Principle of rights** The principle that human beings have certain fundamental rights (to life, freedom, and the pursuit of happiness, for example). Those who adhere to this "rights theory" believe that a key factor in determining whether a business decision is ethical is how that decision affects the rights of others. These others include the firm's owners, its employees, the consumers of its products or services, its suppliers, the community in which it does business, and society as a whole.

**Private equity capital** Equity capital that is not quoted on a public exchange. Funds invested in a private company in exchange for an ownership interest in that company. Capital for private equity is raised from retail and institutional investors, and can be used to fund new technologies, expand working capital within an owned company, make acquisitions, or to strengthen a balance sheet.

**Privilege** In tort law, the ability to act contrary to another person's right without that person's having legal redress for such acts. Privilege may be raised as a defense to defamation.

**Privileges and immunities clause** Article IV, Section 2, of the Constitution requires states not to discriminate against one another's citizens. A resident of one state cannot be treated as an alien when in another state; he or she may not be denied such privileges and immunities as legal protection, access to courts, travel rights, and property rights.

**Privity of contract** The relationship that exists between the promisor and the promisee of a contract.

**Pro rata** Proportionately; in proportion.

**Probable cause** Reasonable grounds to believe the existence of facts warranting certain actions, such as the search or arrest of a person.

**Probate court** A state court of limited jurisdiction that conducts proceedings relating to the settlement of a deceased person's estate.

**Procedural due process** The requirement that any government decision to take life, liberty, or property must be made fairly. For example, fair procedures must be used in determining whether a person will be subjected to punishment or have some burden imposed on him or her.

**Procedural law** Rules that define the manner in which the rights and duties of individuals may be enforced.

**Procedural unconscionability** Occurs when one contractual party lacks knowledge or understanding of the contract terms, often due to inconspicuous print or the lack of an opportunity to read the contract or to ask questions about its meaning. Procedural unconscionability often involves an *adhesion contract,* which is a contract drafted by the dominant party and then presented to the other—the adhering party—on a take-it-or-leave-it basis.

**Product liability** The legal liability of manufacturers, sellers, and lessors of goods to consumers, users, and bystanders for injuries or damages that are caused by the goods.

**Product misuse** A defense against product liability that may be raised when the plaintiff used a product in a manner not intended by the manufacturer. If the misuse is reasonably foreseeable, the seller will not escape liability unless measures were taken to guard against the harm that could result from the misuse.

**Professional corporation** A corporation formed by professional persons, such as physicians, lawyers, dentists, or accountants, to gain tax benefits. Subject to certain exceptions (when a court may treat a professional corporation as a partnership for liability purposes), the shareholders of a professional corporation have the limited liability characteristic of the corporate form of business.

**Promise** A person's assurance that he or she will or will not do something.

**Promisee** A person to whom a promise is made.

**Promisor** A person who makes a promise.

**Promissory estoppel** A doctrine that applies when a promisor makes a clear and definite promise on which the promisee justifiably relies; such a promise is binding if justice will be better served by the enforcement of the promise. *See also* Estoppel

**Protected class** A class of persons with identifiable characteristics who historically have been victimized by discriminatory treatment for certain purposes. Depending on the context, these characteristics include age, color, gender, national origin, race, and religion.

**Proximate cause** Legal cause; exists when the connection between an act and an injury is strong enough to justify imposing liability.

**Public corporation** A corporation owned by a federal, state, or municipal government—not to be confused with a publicly held corporation.

**Public figures** Individuals who are thrust into the public limelight. Public figures include government officials and politicians, movie stars, well-known businesspersons, and generally anybody who becomes known to the public because of his or her position or activities.

**Public policy** A government policy based on widely held societal values and (usually) expressed or implied in laws or regulations.

**Public prosecutor** An individual, acting as a trial lawyer, who initiates and conducts criminal cases in the government's name and on behalf of the people.

**Publicly held corporation** A corporation for which shares of stock have been sold to the public.

**Puffery** A salesperson's exaggerated claims concerning the quality of goods offered for sale. Such claims involve opinions rather than facts and are not considered to be legally binding promises or warranties.

**Punitive damages** Money damages that may be awarded to a plaintiff to punish the defendant and deter future similar conduct.

# Q

**Quantum meruit** (pronounced *kwahn-*tuhm *mehr*-oo-wuht) Literally, "as much as he deserves"—an expression describing the extent of liability on a contract implied in law (quasi contract). An equitable doctrine based on the concept that one who benefits from another's labor and materials should not be unjustly enriched thereby but should be required to pay a reasonable amount for the benefits received, even absent a contract.

**Quasi contract** A fictional contract imposed on parties by a court in the interests of fairness and justice; usually, quasi contracts are imposed to avoid the unjust enrichment of one party at the expense of another.

**Question of fact** In a lawsuit, an issue involving a factual dispute that can only be decided by a judge (or, in a jury trial, a jury).

**Question of law** In a lawsuit, an issue involving the application or interpretation of a law; therefore, the judge, and not the jury, decides the issue.

**Quota** An assigned import limit on goods.

# R

**Ratification** The act of accepting and giving legal force to an obligation that previously was not enforceable.

**Reasonable care** The degree of care that a person of ordinary prudence would exercise in the same or similar circumstances.

**Reasonable doubt** *See* Beyond a reasonable doubt

**Reasonable person standard** The standard of behavior expected of a hypothetical "reasonable person." The standard against which negligence is measured and that must be observed to avoid liability for negligence.

**Rebuttal** The refutation of evidence introduced by an adverse party's attorney.

**Record** According to the Uniform Electronic Transactions Act, information that is either inscribed on a tangible medium or stored in an electronic or other medium and that is retrievable. The Uniform Computer Information Transactions Act uses the term *record* instead of *writing*.

**Reformation** A court-ordered correction of a written contract so that it reflects the true intentions of the parties.

**Rejection** In contract law, an offeree's express or implied manifestation not to accept an offer. In the law governing contracts for the sale of goods, a buyer's manifest refusal to accept goods on the ground that they do not conform to contract specifications.

**Rejoinder** The defendant's answer to the plaintiff's rebuttal.

**Release** A contract in which one party forfeits the right to pursue a legal claim against the other party.

**Relevant evidence** Evidence tending to make a fact at issue in the case more or less probable than it would be without the evidence. Only relevant evidence is admissible in court.

**Remanded** Sent back. If an appellate court disagrees with a lower court's judgment, the case may be remanded to the lower court for further proceedings in which the lower court's decision should be consistent with the appellate court's opinion on the matter.

**Remedy** The relief given to an innocent party to enforce a right or compensate for the violation of a right.

**Remedy at law** A remedy available in a court of law. Money damages are awarded as a remedy at law.

**Remedy in equity** A remedy allowed by courts in situations where remedies at law are not appropriate. Remedies in equity are based on settled rules of fairness, justice, and honesty, and include injunction, specific performance, rescission and restitution, and reformation.

**Replevin** (pronounced rih-*pleh*-vin) An action to recover specific goods in the hands of a party who is wrongfully withholding them from the other party.

**Reply** Procedurally, a plaintiff's response to a defendant's answer.

**Reporter** A publication in which court cases are published, or reported.

**Repudiation** The renunciation of a right or duty; the act of a buyer or seller in rejecting a contract either partially or totally. *See also* Anticipatory repudiation

**Requirements contract** An agreement in which a buyer agrees to purchase and the seller agrees to sell all or up to a stated amount of what the buyer needs or requires.

***Res ipsa loquitur*** (pronounced *rehs ehp*-suh *low*-quuh-tuhr) A doctrine under which negligence may be inferred simply because an event occurred, if it is the type of event that would not occur in the absence of negligence. Literally, the term means "the facts speak for themselves."

**Rescind** (pronounced rih-*sihnd*) To cancel. *See also* Rescission

**Rescission** (pronounced rih-*sih*-zhen) A remedy whereby a contract is canceled and the parties are returned to the positions they occupied before the contract was made; may be effected through the mutual consent of the parties, by their conduct, or by court decree.

**Residuary** The surplus of a testator's estate remaining after all of the debts and particular legacies have been discharged.

***Respondeat superior*** (pronounced ree-*spahn*-dee-uht soo-*peer*-ee-your) In Latin, "Let the master respond." A doctrine under which a principal or an employer is held liable for the wrongful acts committed by agents or employees while acting within the course and scope of their agency or employment.

**Respondent** In equity practice, the party who answers a bill or other proceeding.

**Restitution** An equitable remedy under which a person is restored to his or her original position prior to loss or injury, or placed in the position he or she would have been in had the breach not occurred.

**Retained earnings** The portion of a corporation's profits that has not been paid out as dividends to shareholders.

**Retainer** An advance payment made by a client to a law firm to cover part of the legal fees and/or costs that will be incurred on that client's behalf.

**Reverse** To reject or overrule a court's judgment. An appellate court, for example, might reverse a lower court's judgment on an issue if it feels that the lower court committed an error during the trial or that the jury was improperly instructed.

**Reverse discrimination** Discrimination against majority groups, such as white males, that results from affirmative action programs, in which preferences are given to minority members and women.

**Reversible error** An error by a lower court that is sufficiently substantial to justify an appellate court's reversal of the lower court's decision.

**Revocation** In contract law, the withdrawal of an offer by an offeror. Unless an offer is irrevocable, it can be revoked at any time prior to acceptance without liability.

**Right of first refusal** The right to purchase personal or real property—such as corporate shares or real estate—before the property is offered for sale to others.

**Right-to-work law** A state law providing that employees are not to be required to join a union as a condition of obtaining or retaining employment.

**Robbery** The act of forcefully and unlawfully taking personal property of any value from another; force or intimidation is usually necessary for an act of theft to be considered a robbery.

**Rule of four** A rule of the United States Supreme Court under which the Court will not issue a writ of *certiorari* unless at least four justices approve of the decision to issue the writ.

**Rule 10b-5** *See* SEC Rule 10b-5

**Rules of evidence** Rules governing the admissibility of evidence in trial courts.

# S

**S corporation** A close business corporation that has met certain requirements as set out by the Internal Revenue Code and thus qualifies for special income tax treatment. Essentially, an S corporation is taxed the same as a partnership, but its owners enjoy the privilege of limited liability.

**Sale** The passing of title (evidence of ownership rights) from the seller to the buyer for a price.

**Sale on approval** A type of conditional sale in which the buyer may take the goods on a trial basis. The sale becomes absolute only when the buyer approves of (or is satisfied with) the goods being sold.

**Sale or return** A type of conditional sale in which title and possession pass from the seller to the buyer; however, the buyer retains the option to return the goods during a specified period even though the goods conform to the contract.

**Sales contract** A contract for the sale of goods under which the ownership of goods is transferred from a seller to a buyer for a price.

**Scienter** (pronounced *sy-en*-ter) Knowledge by the misrepresenting party that material facts have been falsely represented or omitted with an intent to deceive.

**Search warrant** An order granted by a public authority, such as a judge, that authorizes law enforcement personnel to search particular premises or property.

**Seasonably** Within a specified time period. If no period is specified, within a reasonable time.

**Secondary boycott** A union's refusal to work for, purchase from, or handle the products of a secondary employer, with whom the union has no dispute, for the purpose of forcing that employer to stop doing business with the primary employer, with whom the union has a labor dispute.

**Self-defense** The legally recognized privilege to protect one's self or property against injury by another. The privilege of self-defense protects only acts that are reasonably necessary to protect one's self or property.

**Seniority system** In regard to employment relationships, a system in which those who have worked longest for the company are first in line for promotions, salary increases, and other benefits; they are also the last to be laid off if the workforce must be reduced.

**Service mark** A mark used in the sale or the advertising of services, such as to distinguish the services of one person from the services of others. Titles, character names, and other distinctive features of radio and television programs may be registered as service marks.

**Service of process** The delivery of the complaint and summons to a defendant.

**Settlor** One creating a trust; also called a *grantor*.

**Severance pay** A payment by an employer to an employee that exceeds the employee's wages due on termination.

**Sexual harassment** In the employment context, the granting of job promotions or other benefits in return for sexual favors or conduct that is so sexually offensive that it creates a hostile working environment.

**Share** A unit of stock. *See also* Stock

**Shareholder** One who purchases shares of a corporation's stock, thus acquiring an equity interest in the corporation.

**Sharia** Civil law principles of some Middle Eastern countries that are based on the Islamic directives that follow the teachings of the prophet Muhammad.

**Shipment contract** A contract in which the seller is required to ship the goods by carrier. The buyer assumes liability for any losses or damage to the goods after they are delivered to the carrier. Generally, all contracts are assumed to be shipment contracts if nothing to the contrary is stated in the contract.

**Short-swing profits** Profits made by officers, directors, and certain large stockholders resulting from the use of nonpublic (inside) information about their companies; prohibited by Section 12 of the 1934 Securities Exchange Act.

**Shrink-wrap agreement** An agreement whose terms are expressed in a document located inside a box in which goods (usually software) are packaged; sometimes called a *shrink-wrap license.*

**Slander** Defamation in oral form.

**Slander of quality** The publication of false information about another's product, alleging that it is not what its seller claims.

**Slander of title** The publication of a statement that denies or casts doubt on another's legal ownership of any property, causing financial loss to that property's owner. Also called trade libel.

**Small claims courts** Special courts in which parties may litigate small claims (usually, claims involving $2,500 or less). Attorneys are not required in small claims courts, and in many states attorneys are not allowed to represent the parties.

**Social media** The means by which people can create, share, and exchange ideas and comments via the Internet.

**Sociological school** A school of legal thought that views the law as a tool for promoting justice in society.

**Sole proprietorship** The simplest form of business, in which the owner is the business; the owner reports business income on his or her personal income tax return and is legally responsible for all debts and obligations incurred by the business.

**Sovereign immunity** A doctrine that immunizes foreign nations from the jurisdiction of U.S. courts when certain conditions are satisfied.

**Sovereignty** The quality of having independent authority over a geographic area. For instance, state governments have the authority to regulate affairs within their border.

**Spam** Bulk, unsolicited (junk) e-mail.

**Specific performance** An equitable remedy requiring the breaching party to perform as promised under the contract; usually granted only when money damages would be an inadequate remedy and the subject matter of the contract is unique (for example, real property).

**Stakeholders** Groups, other than the company's shareholders, that are affected by corporate decisions. Stakeholders include employees, customers, creditors, suppliers, and the community in which the corporation operates.

**Standing to sue** The requirement that an individual must have a sufficient stake in a controversy before he or she can bring a lawsuit. The plaintiff must demonstrate that he or she either has been injured or threatened with injury.

***Stare decisis*** (pronounced *ster*-ay dih-*si*-ses) A common law doctrine under which judges are obligated to follow the precedents established in prior decisions.

**Statute of Frauds** A state statute under which certain types of contracts must be in writing to be enforceable.

**Statute of limitations** A federal or state statute setting the maximum time period during which a certain action can be brought or certain rights enforced.

**Statute of repose** Basically, a statute of limitations that is not dependent on the happening of a cause of action. Statutes of repose generally begin to run at an earlier date and run for a longer period of time than statutes of limitations.

**Statutory law** The body of law enacted by legislative bodies (as opposed to constitutional law, administrative law, or case law).

**Statutory lien** A lien created by statute.

**Stock** An equity (ownership) interest in a corporation, measured in units of shares.

**Stockholder** *See* Shareholder

**Strict liability** Liability regardless of fault. In tort law, strict liability may be imposed on defendants in cases involving abnormally dangerous activities, dangerous animals, or defective products.

**Strike** An extreme action undertaken by unionized workers when collective bargaining fails; the workers leave their jobs, refuse to work, and (typically) picket the employer's workplace.

**Subject-matter jurisdiction** Jurisdiction over the subject matter of a lawsuit.

**Subpoena** A document commanding a person to appear at a certain time and place or give testimony concerning a certain matter.

**Subsidiary corporation** A corporation that wholly owned by another corporate entity (the parent corporation).

**Substantial performance** Performance that does not vary greatly from the performance promised in a contract; the performance must create substantially the same benefits as those promised in the contract.

**Substantive due process** A requirement that focuses on the content, or substance, of legislation. If a law or other governmental action limits a fundamental right, such as the right to travel or to vote, it will be held to violate substantive due process unless it promotes a compelling or overriding state interest.

**Substantive law** Law that defines the rights and duties of individuals with respect to each other, as opposed to procedural law, which defines the manner in which these rights and duties may be enforced.

**Substantive unconscionability** Occurs when contracts, or portions of contracts, are oppressive or overly harsh. Courts generally focus on provisions that deprive one party of the benefits of the agreement or leave that party without remedy for nonperformance by the other. An example of substantive unconscionability is the agreement by a welfare recipient with a fourth-grade education to purchase a refrigerator for $2,000 under an installment contract.

**Summary judgment** *See* Motion for summary judgment

**Summary jury trial (SJT)** A method of settling disputes in which a trial is held, but the jury's verdict is not binding. The verdict acts only as a guide to both sides in reaching an agreement during the mandatory negotiations that immediately follow the summary jury trial.

**Summons** A document informing a defendant that a legal action has been commenced against him or her and that the defendant must appear in court on a certain date to answer the plaintiff's complaint. The document is delivered by a sheriff or any other person so authorized.

**Superseding cause** An intervening force or event that breaks the connection between a wrongful act and an injury to another; in negligence law, a defense to liability.

**Supremacy clause** The provision in Article VI of the Constitution that provides that the Constitution, laws, and treaties of the United States are "the supreme Law of the Land." Under this clause, state and local laws that directly conflict with federal law will be rendered invalid.

**Syllogism** A form of deductive reasoning consisting of a major premise, a minor premise, and a conclusion.

**Symbolic speech** Nonverbal conduct that expresses opinions or thoughts about a subject. Symbolic speech is protected under the First Amendment's guarantee of freedom of speech.

**Syndicate** An investment group of persons or firms brought together for the purpose of financing a project that they would not or could not undertake independently.

# T

**Tangible employment action** A significant change in employment status, such as firing or failing to promote an employee, reassigning the employee to a position with significantly different responsibilities, or effecting a significant change in employment benefits.

**Tangible property** Property that has physical existence and can be distinguished by the senses of touch, sight, and so on. A car is tangible property; a patent right is intangible property.

**Tariff** A tax on imported goods.

**Tender** An unconditional offer to perform an obligation by a person who is ready, willing, and able to do so.

**Tender of delivery** Under the Uniform Commercial Code, a seller's or lessor's act of placing conforming goods at the disposal of the buyer or lessee and giving the buyer or lessee whatever notification is reasonably necessary to enable the buyer or lessee to take delivery.

**Third party beneficiary** One for whose benefit a promise is made in a contract but who is not a party to the contract.

**Tolling** Temporary suspension of the running of a prescribed period (such as a statute of limitations). For instance, a statute of limitations may be tolled until the party suffering an injury has discovered it or should have discovered it.

**Tort** A civil wrong not arising from a breach of contract. A breach of a legal duty that proximately causes harm or injury to another.

**Tortfeasor** One who commits a tort.

**Trade dress** The image and overall appearance of a product—for example, the distinctive decor, menu, layout, and style of service of a particular restaurant. Basically, trade dress is subject to the same protection as trademarks.

**Trade libel** The publication of false information about another's product, alleging it is not what its seller claims; also referred to as slander of quality.

**Trade name** A term that is used to indicate part or all of a business's name and that is directly related to the business's reputation and goodwill. Trade names are protected under the common law (and under trademark law, if the name is the same as the firm's trademark).

**Trade secret** Information or a process that gives a business an advantage over competitors who do not know the information or process.

**Trademark** A distinctive mark, motto, device, or implement that a manufacturer stamps, prints, or otherwise affixes to the goods it produces so that they may be identified on the market and their origins made known. Once a trademark is established (under the common law or through registration), the owner is entitled to its exclusive use.

**Treaty** An agreement formed between two or more independent nations.

**Trespass to land** The entry onto, above, or below the surface of land owned by another without the owner's permission or legal authorization.

**Trespass to personal property** The unlawful taking or harming of another's personal property; interference with another's right to the exclusive possession of his or her personal property.

**Trespasser** One who commits the tort of trespass in one of its forms.

**Trial court** A court in which trials are held and testimony taken.

**Typosquatting** A form of cybersquatting that relies on mistakes, such as typographical errors, made by Internet users when inputting information into a Web browser.

# U

**Ultra vires** (pronounced *uhl*-trah *vye*-reez) A Latin term meaning "beyond the powers"; in corporate law, acts of a corporation that are beyond its express and implied powers to undertake.

**Unanimous opinion** A court opinion in which all of the judges or justices of the court agree to the court's decision.

**Unconscionable** (pronounced un-*kon*-shun-uh-bul) **contract or clause** A contract or clause that is void on the basis of public policy because one party, as a result of his or her disproportionate bargaining power, is forced to accept terms that are unfairly burdensome and that unfairly benefit the dominating party. *See also* Procedural unconscionability; Substantive unconscionability

**Undisclosed principal** A principal whose identity is unknown by a third person, and the third person has no knowledge that the agent is acting for a principal at the time the agent and the third person form a contract.

**Unenforceable contract** A valid contract rendered unenforceable by some statute or law.

**Uniform law** A model law created by the National Conference of Commissioners on Uniform State Laws and/or the American Law Institute for the states to consider adopting. If the state adopts the law, it becomes statutory law in that state. Each state has the option of adopting or rejecting all or part of a uniform law.

**Unilateral contract** A contract that results when an offer can only be accepted by the offeree's performance.

**Union shop** A place of employment in which all workers, once employed, must become union members within a specified period of time as a condition of their continued employment.

**Unliquidated debt** A debt that is uncertain in amount.

**Unreasonably dangerous product** In product liability, a product that is defective to the point of threatening a consumer's health and safety. A product will be considered unreasonably dangerous if it is dangerous beyond the expectation of the ordinary consumer or if a less dangerous alternative was economically feasible for the manufacturer, but the manufacturer failed to produce it.

**Usage of trade** Any practice or method of dealing having such regularity of observance in a place, vocation, or trade as to justify an expectation that it will be observed with respect to the transaction in question.

**Utilitarianism** An approach to ethical reasoning in which ethically correct behavior is related to an evaluation of the consequences of a given action on those who will be affected by it. In utilitarian reasoning, a "good" decision is one that results in the greatest good for the greatest number of people affected by the decision.

# V

**Valid contract** A contract that results when elements necessary for contract formation (agreement, consideration, legal purpose, and contractual capacity) are present.

**Venture capital** Capital (funds and other assets) provided by professional, outside investors (*venture capitalists,* usually groups of wealthy investors and investment banks) to start new business ventures.

**Venture capitalist** A person or entity that seeks out promising entrepreneurial ventures and funds them in exchange for equity stakes.

**Venue** (pronounced *ven*-yoo) The geographical district in which an action is tried and from which the jury is selected.

**Verdict** A formal decision made by a jury.

**Vesting** Under the Employee Retirement Income Security Act of 1974, a pension plan becomes vested when an employee has a legal right to the benefits purchased with the employer's contributions, even if the employee is no longer working for this employer.

**Vicarious liability** Legal responsibility placed on one person for the acts of another.

**Virtual property** Property that exists in cyberspace and thus is conceptual, as opposed to physical. Intellectual property that exists on the Internet is virtual property.

**Virus** A type of malware that is transmitted between computers and attempts to do deliberate damage to systems and data.

**Vishing** The voice counterpart of phishing; vishers use an e-mail or a notice on a Web site that encourage persons to make a phone call which then triggers a voice response system that asks for valuable personal information such as credit card numbers.

**Void contract** A contract having no legal force or binding effect.

**Voidable contract** A contract that may be legally avoided (canceled, or annulled) at the option of one of the parties.

**Voir dire** (pronounced *vwahr deehr*) A French phrase meaning, literally, "to see, to speak." In jury trials, the phrase refers to the process in which the attorneys question prospective jurors to determine whether they are biased or have any connection with a party to the action or with a prospective witness.

**Voluntary consent** The element of agreement in the formation of a contract. The knowledge of, and assent to, the terms of a contract.

# W

**Waiver** An intentional, knowing relinquishment of a legal right.

**Warranty** A promise that certain facts are truly as they are represented to be.

**Warranty disclaimer** A seller's or lessor's negation or qualification of a warranty.

**Warranty of fitness** *See* Implied warranty of fitness for a particular purpose.

**Warranty of merchantability** *See* Implied warranty of merchantability.

**Warranty of title** An implied warranty made by a seller that the seller has good and valid title to the goods sold and that the transfer of the title is rightful.

**Whistleblowing** An employee's disclosure to government, the press, or upper-management authorities that the employer is engaged in unsafe or illegal activities.

**White-collar crime** Nonviolent crime committed by individuals or corporations to obtain a personal or business advantage.

**Winding up** The second of two stages involved in the termination of a partnership or corporation. Once the firm is dissolved, it continues to exist legally until the process of winding up all business affairs (collecting and distributing the firm's assets) is complete.

**Workers' compensation laws** State statutes establishing an administrative procedure for compensating workers' injuries that arise out of—or in the course of—their employment, regardless of fault.

**Writ of *certiorari*** (pronounced sur-shee-uh-*rah*-ree) A writ from a higher court asking the lower court for the record of a case.

**Wrongful discharge** An employer's termination of an employee's employment in violation of an employment contract or laws that protect employees.

# TABLE OF CASES

For your convenience and reference, here is a list of all the cases mentioned in this text, including those within the footnotes, features, and case problems. Any case that was presented as a summarized case in a chapter is given special emphasis by having its title **boldfaced**.

# INDEX